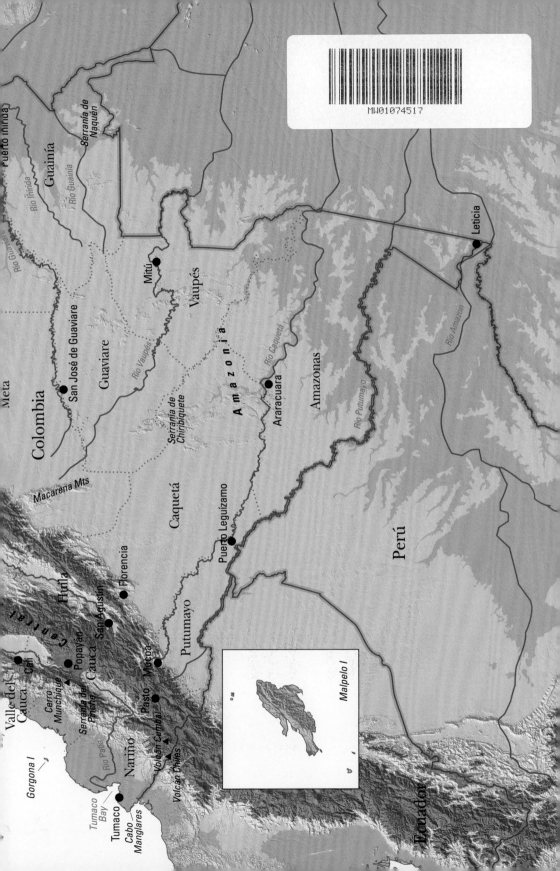

Birds of Colombia

Steven L. Hilty

Lynx and BirdLife International Field Guides

Birds of Colombia

Steven L. Hilty

Colour plates by

Richard Allen
Norman Arlott
Eustace Barnes
Hilary Burn
Clive Byers
John Cox
Martin Elliott
Al Gilbert
Alan Harris
Ren Hathway
Mark Hulme
Àngels Jutglar
Francesc Jutglar
Ian Lewington
Toni Llobet

Alex Mascarell
Dave Nurney
Douglas Pratt
David Quinn
Chris Rose
Lluís Sanz
Brian Small
Lluís Solé
Juan Varela
Ilian Velikov
Etel Vilaró
Lyn Wells
Jan Wilczur
Ian Willis
Tim Worfolk

For contributions by family, see CONTENTS:

Illustrations

RA	— Richard Allen	AM	— Alex Mascarell
NA	— Norman Arlott	DN	— Dave Nurney
EB	— Eustace Barnes	DP	— Douglas Pratt
HB	— Hilary Burn	DQ	— David Quinn
CB	— Clive Byers	CR	— Chris Rose
JC	— John Cox	LS	— Lluís Sanz
ME	— Martin Elliott	BS	— Brian Small
AG	— Al Gilbert	LSo	— Lluís Solé
AH	— Alan Harris	JV	— Juan Varela
RH	— Ren Hathway	IV	— Ilian Velikov
MH	— Mark Hulme	EV	— Etel Vilaró
ÀJ	— Àngels Jutglar	LW	— Lyn Wells
FJ	— Francesc Jutglar	JW	— Jan Wilczur
IL	— Ian Lewington	IW	— Ian Willis
TL	— Toni Llobet	TW	— Tim Worfolk

First Edition: March 2021

© Lynx Edicions – www.lynxeds.com
Lynx Edicions®: Alada Gestió Empresarial, S.L.

Recommended citation:
Hilty, S.L. (2021). *Birds of Colombia*. Lynx and BirdLife International Field Guides. Lynx Edicions, Barcelona.

Project co-ordinators: Arnau Bonan-Barfull, Amy Chernasky, Guy M. Kirwan
Map production: Anna Motis
Cover design: Susanna Silva
Interior book design: Xavier Ruiz
Layout: Daniel Roca

Cover illustration by Ilian Velikov
Reference photographs by Jaime Andrés Herrera-Villarreal
Blue-billed Curassow (*Crax alberti*)

Printed and bound in Barcelona by Índice Arts Gràfiques
Legal Deposit flexi bound: B 3971-2021
Legal Deposit hardcover: B 3970-2021
ISBN flexi bound: 978-84-16728-24-4
ISBN hardcover: 978-84-16728-23-7

CONTENTS

GENERAL INTRODUCTION

Historical background

Most books build on a foundation laid by earlier workers and this is nowhere more evident than with the present book. The foundation for books dealing with bird identification has traditionally been built on systematic collections of birds made by early collectors or scientists. These collections, often financed by museums and housed in such institutions around the world, represent a repository of data of inestimable value. Colombia's history of bird collecting dates to around 1825–30. But almost from the onset the story in Colombia differs, not so much because the earliest collections were made by native hunters, but because they were not destined for science but for the millinery trade in Europe and soon thereafter also in North America. As the seemingly insatiable demand for exotic birds and feathers in Victorian-era fashion expanded, Bogotá became the most important shipping point in South America for these specimens for more than half a century.

The demand for colourful feathers, plumes, aigrettes and stuffed or dried bodies of colourful small birds for fashion ornaments began well before the mid-1850s, but reached a frenetic peak from the 1870s to the end of the century. The number of birds shipped to London and Paris during this era was truly staggering, estimated in excess of five million per year, with hundreds of thousands, perhaps millions, shipped each year from 'Bogota'. Exotic species also arrived in Europe from localities in Asia and elsewhere, but what set Bogotá apart was the immense numbers of birds that passed through its port. Mercifully this carnage began to decline by the end of the 19th century, in part due to changing whims of fashion, but more importantly due to the efforts of numerous women's groups in North America and England. Alarmed by the immense losses being suffered by birds, their outcries resulted in the birth of several conservation movements.

A tiny fraction of these infamous 'Bogota' trade skins, as they came to be known, were intercepted at European ports and purchased by museums and private collectors for scientific work and illustration. However, with little information on their precise origin, the value of these specimens to science was diminished. Even with this handicap, a number of species new to science were found in these shipments, especially of hummingbirds, and were described by John Gould and others. The vast majority, however, mainly hummingbirds, tanagers, dacnises, cotingas and other colourful species, disappeared into the fickle void of fashion, providing amusing ornaments for fashionable ladies' hats, earrings, broaches and accessories, before eventually being cast aside and lost forever. Sadly, a few specimens, salvaged from these shipments, were so rare that they have never been found in the wild.

One of the earliest scientific collections of Colombian birds was made by Delattre, who worked in areas between Buenaventura and Pasto in 1849. Over the course of the next 130 years or more many collections, large and small, would be made, especially in western Colombia. Independent collectors, and others hired directly by museums, amassed collections, most of which found their way to institutions overseas. In the early part of the 20th century, several prominent Colombian ornithologists, among them A. Dugand, J. I. Borrero, M. Nicéforo, and the Mena brothers, made collections that largely stayed in Colombia. From the early 1950s to the mid-1970s Padre Antonio Olivares, based at the

National University in Bogotá, directed collecting expeditions to many parts of the country, including especially the Macarena and Vaupés regions.

The American Museum of Natural History sponsored eight expeditions in Colombia between 1910 and 1915, sampling birdlife along transects of all three Andean ranges from the lowlands to the *páramo*. These expeditions resulted in Chapman's 1917 *The Distribution of Bird Life in Colombia*, the first publication to attempt a zoogeographic analysis of the country's birds. Chapman's work was based almost entirely on the 1285 species of birds collected during these expeditions, and was limited to areas they visited, but it revealed, for the first time, insights into the elevations and distributions of Colombia's avifauna, something previously undocumented.

A few years later Todd and Carriker's *The Birds of the Santa Marta Region of Colombia: A Study in Altitudinal Distribution* (1922) provided further insight into the distribution of species along elevational transects in the Sierra Nevada de Santa Marta. Still, it would be another 25 years or more before the country's entire avifauna would be catalogued, and during that period two collectors stand out for their prolific efforts.

The first of these two was Kjell von Sneidern, a Swedish-born ornithologist and botanist who lived most of his life in Colombia and for many years was director of the Museo de Historia Natural del Cauca in Popayán. He collected extensively in western and southern Colombia from the 1940s to mid-1970s, and his collections are represented in numerous museums abroad as well as in Colombia. The other, Melvin Carriker, spent much of his life in the Santa Marta Mts and was perhaps the most prolific collector of all time. Although Carriker worked from Guatemala to Bolivia, his single largest collection of Colombian birds, numbering nearly 24,000 specimens, along with journal entries, was made between 1941 and 1953 for the Smithsonian Institution. Today, many of the sites where he worked are deforested and the only record of what was once there comes from his collections and journals.

Meyer de Schauensee, a taxonomist at the Academy of Natural Sciences in Philadelphia, was the first to summarize the entire Colombian avifauna in his multi-volume *The Birds of the Republic of Colombia* in the journal *Caldasia*. Published between 1948 and 1952 it listed all known sites where each species had been taken. This was followed by his *The Birds of Colombia and Adjacent Areas of South and Central America* (1964), the first book on Colombian birds to provide a brief written description and the distribution of each species. It was also the first book to illustrate a few of Colombia's birds in colour. Although rather modest by present-day standards, it was an important step forward, and remarkable also because it was based entirely upon museum specimens—Meyer de Schauensee never visited Colombia.

Five years later Padre Antonio Olivares published a regional work, *Aves de Cundinamarca* (1969). This book, and the Meyer de Schauensee volume, were the ones I carried when I arrived in Colombia in 1971. While helpful to varying degrees, neither was up to the task of critical field identification. Learning birds at that time still involved endless field notes, sketches, and innumerable trips to museums. In this regard, the regional bird collection at the Museo de Historia Natural in Cali, and the encouragement and help of F. Carlos Lehmann who was the museum's director, were indispensable.

In 1986 with the able collaboration of Bill Brown, a Canadian geologist, and the immense talent of artist Guy Tudor, we published *A Guide to the Birds of Colombia* (English edition), the first Colombian bird book to provide a broad synthesis of ecological, behavioural and biogeographical information. Later it became available in Spanish (2001) thanks to a magnificent translation by Umberto Álvarez-López, and was reprinted (2009) with updates, by the Asociación Colombiana de Ornitología (ACO). Both the English and Spanish editions provided much helpful information for birders and scientists and many excellent illustrations by Guy Tudor, but were heavy for field use and, in the interim, avian taxonomy has been revolutionized. These editions, however, provided a springboard for modern fieldwork by a generation or more of Colombian students, researchers and educators eager to explore their country, even in the face of the armed upheaval that lasted from the mid-1980s to c. 2000.

By the turn of the century several regional or focused works began to appear, among them *Aves de la Sabana de Bogotá* (2000) a multi-author work published by the Asociación Bogotana de Ornitología. It was small, portable, packed with useful information, and aimed squarely at the most populous region in the country. Shortly thereafter Luis Miguel Renjifo and others provided the first countrywide synthesis of the status of Colombia's birds with their invaluable *Libro Rojo de Aves de Colombia* (2002) and two subsequent updates. José Vicente Rodríguez-Mahecha's *Loros de Colombia* (2002) focused on conservation issues, and Thomas McNish's *Las Aves de los Llanos de la Orinoquía* (2007) showcased the spectacular avifauna of the Colombian *llanos*. Several photographic works treating Colombia birds have also appeared in the last two decades, beginning with the stunningly beautiful images of Luis A. Mazariegos' *Hummingbirds of Colombia* (2000), Murray Cooper's *Birds in Colombia* (2011), and Rodrigo Gaviria Obregón's *Aves Silvestres de Colombia* and *Las Aves Más Hermosas de Colombia*. More recently, a charming multi-author (2017) volume, *La Magia de las Aves de Chingaza*, introduced visitors to Chingaza National Park, a fairyland of dwarf forests, whimsical plants and scintillating hummingbirds barely two hours from Bogotá. In addition to these just-mentioned works, many smaller regional or focused materials have appeared.

The first truly portable guides covering all of Colombia's birds were two editions of a pocket-sized *Field Guide to the Birds of Colombia* (2010, 2014) authored by Miles McMullan and Thomas Donegan. During or following the same period various regional works focusing on hummingbirds, tanagers and mammals, especially from the department of Cauca, appeared by artist and author Fernando Ayerbe-Quiñones. These were followed by his excellent small, portable guide, *Guía Ilustrada de la Avifauna Colombiana* (2018) and an English translation (2019), both editions extremely compact and featuring superb illustrations and maps.

Over the past 20 years Colombia has seen an almost meteoric rise in interest in birds and environmental issues, especially among younger generations. And, over the past dozen years there has been an equally remarkable rise in birdwatching and ecotourism at both the national and international level. It is not surprising then that two intrepid birders, Jurgen Beckers and Pablo Flórez, teamed up to publish *Birdwatching in Colombia* (2013), a compilation of 127 birding sites throughout the country. Anyone, national resident or foreign visitor, will surely find numerous exciting Colombian 'hotspots' in this attractive book that features an abundance of maps and colour photos. Many resources focusing on birds, popular and scientific, have appeared during the past two decades. These range from informal online chat services to a fully online professional journal, *Ornitología Colombiana*, published by the Asociación Colombiana de Ornitología.

No published work, however, has played a more significant part in the advancement of knowledge of the planet's avifauna than the monumental 17-volume *Handbook of the Birds of the World*, by Lynx Edicions, and its companion online resource *HBW Alive*. Almost all of the illustrations for the present book are taken from these incredible resources. During the preparation of this book *HBW Alive* was incorporated into the Cornell Lab of Ornithology's already magnificent online website *Birds of the World*. These combined resources have provided indispensable references for photographs, sound-recordings, multimedia and taxonomy for this guide, as has the immense and ever-growing eBird database also hosted by the Cornell Lab. Additionally, Xeno-canto, a Netherlands-based online repository of avian sounds, houses a large number of recordings from Colombia and adjacent countries, and these also have been of immense value to this work.

Now, via the 'magic' of QR codes, anyone with a mobile phone can use the codes in this book to access additional information about Colombia's birds, including audio, video and photos presently hosted on the Cornell Lab's eBird website. Lastly, BirdLife International, a collaborator on this book, has been instrumental in assimilating vital information on the status of birds worldwide for decades. Keeping their fingers on the pulse of Colombia's magnificent avifauna, as well as many other countries worldwide, they provide an invaluable link between conservation planning and boots-on-the-ground conservation work.

Since the 1970s the role of museums in collecting physical bird specimens in Colombia has declined sharply, but a major effort was undertaken to assemble Colombia's existing but widely scattered bird collections into a single accessible database (www.biomap.net). And, while museum bird collections remain important, research today has broadened dramatically to include ecological, behavioural and molecular work, as well as detailed species-specific studies. The Alexander von Humboldt Institute in Bogotá, for example, now features extensive audio collections of Colombia's birds. With the dawn of the current decade, Colombia's ornithological history now spans nearly 200 years, and reflects the efforts of hundreds of collectors, as well as thousands of students, scientists and conservationists. It is upon the shoulders of all those who have gone before that modern-day bird guides like this one are built. They are the foundation.

GEOGRAPHICAL SCOPE

Topography

Colombia's political boundary could hardly have been better positioned to encompass greater biodiversity. Long acknowledged as one of the most biodiverse countries on the planet, and the caretaker of the longest bird list of any country, the reasons for such superlatives become apparent when reviewing Colombia's geographical position and physical topography.

Colombia is the only South American nation bordered extensively by two oceans, and it also administers far-flung island possessions in the Caribbean and the Pacific, and numerous coastal islands. At c. 09–12°N Colombia's northern latitudes are close enough to a vast reservoir of boreal migrants to host many of them as non-breeding residents or transients for parts of the year. Colombia also receives a small number of Central American species that move south post-breeding, and its southernmost latitudes (at about 04°S) receive austral-breeding migrants that move north. Less well documented is the presence of various intra-tropical migrants whose movements are still being documented.

Colombia's complex mainland topography, while creating innumerable challenges for modern economic development has, conversely, offered innumerable opportunities for speciation over the past 10–20 million years or more as the Andes have risen. Along Colombia's southern border with Ecuador the Andes form a great knot that continuing northward separates into three spectacular cordilleras, a western, central and eastern branch. These cordilleras are separated by two large river valleys, the Cauca between the West and Central Andes, and the Magdalena between the Central and East Andes.

In addition to the three Andean cordilleras, Colombia counts an amazing number of isolated sierras and smaller serranías within its boundaries. Each of these is isolated from the main Andes. These include the Serranía de Baudó (c. 1800 m) in northern Chocó, the eastern tip of the Serranía del Darién (Cerro Tacarcuna, c. 1910 m) along the Panama border, the Serranía de San Lucas (c. 1500 m) north of the Central Andes, the Sierra de San Jacinto (c. 800 m) in coastal Sucre and Magdalena, the magnificent Sierra Nevada de Santa Marta, with permanently snow-capped peaks soaring to c. 5775 m that are visible from the Caribbean coast, the Serranía de Macuira (c. 500 m) and some associated lower hills, with moist forest surrounded by the desert of eastern Guajira, and the vast Sierra de Perijá (c. 2250 m with peaks to 3700 m) and adjacent Serranía de Los Motilones, both shared with Venezuela.

East of the Andes, Colombia's terrain flattens dramatically, with rivers draining eastward toward the Ríos Orinoco, Negro and Amazon. Just east of the Andes, in southern Meta, the isolated Serranía de la Macarena (c. 2500 m) rises abruptly from the surrounding rainforest, and south-east in Caquetá the sprawling Serranía de Chiribiquete (c. 500–700 m) forms the last south-western extension of the ancient Guianan Shield. Elsewhere across much of Vaupés, Guaviare, Guainía and eastern Vichada, hundreds of picturesque but isolated sandstone-quartzite cerros, all of them remnants of the ancient Guianan Shield, and some rising almost 300 m, are sprinkled across the landscape. Among the best known of these are the striking and now easily accessible Cerros de Mavecure south-west of Puerto Inírida.

CLIMATE

Rainfall is Colombia's most important seasonal change. This is caused by the twice-annual passage of the sun overhead as its declination shifts between the north and south tropical-latitude boundaries. Each passage produces increased warming, rising air masses and a renewed expansion of low pressure zones—twice-annual passages that, at least in theory, result in two slightly wetter periods each year. These are followed by two drier periods when the sun is further away. Near the equator, especially in Amazonia, there is often little evident seasonality to rainfall. Further north (or south) from the equator the rainfall patterns become more obvious and predictable, resulting in a single long dry period (with the sun's declination far to the south) and a single long wet season as the sun's declination passes more quickly overhead twice. This simple pattern, however, is almost everywhere complicated by topographic relief and other local features in the landscape.

Day length varies only slightly over the year and average temperatures are apt to vary more during the course of a day than month to month. Mean temperatures do change with elevation, decreasing about 6°C with each 1000 m increase in elevation, and this produces striking changes in flora and fauna as one ascends tropical mountains. Air temperatures are highest on the Caribbean coast, averaging c. 29–32°C. Although three important cities, Cartagena, Barranquilla and Santa Marta are located on Colombia's north coast, the country's largest cities are in the Andes where temperatures are cooler. Medellín (at c. 1500 m), regarded as the city of eternal spring, has balmy temperatures year-round; Cali (c. 1000 m) is hotter during the day but enjoys lovely night-time temperatures; and Bogotá (c. 2600 m) is cooler with more variable temperatures but typically enjoys warmer mini-dry periods in December–March and July–September. During rainier periods temperatures can be chilly and damp.

TOPOGRAPHIC REGIONS

Colombia's physical topography from any approach is complex but divides roughly into seven distinct regions—the dry Caribbean, arid Guajira Peninsula, super-wet Chocó Pacific, mixed inter-Andean valleys and cordilleras, flat grasslands (*llanos*), white-sand soils of the Guianan Shield, and Amazonia. The total area of Colombia is c. 1,141,748 km², making it the fourth-largest country in South America.

The Caribbean region

This region is a mix of scrub and dry forest, with mangroves lining parts of the coast. The area generally experiences a long hot dry season from the end of November to early May, and while a wet season occurs from late May to October, annual rainfall is low, ranging from c. 500 mm at Santa Marta to 900 mm at Cartagena, but these values gradually increase inland, to c. 1500 mm near the base of the Andes. During the dry season coastal areas experience strong north-east trade winds, which create drying desert-like conditions for plant growth. In many areas large columnar cacti thrive and most trees drop their leaves. East of the city of Santa Marta, however, trade winds are forced upward against the massive north slope of the Sierra Nevada de Santa Marta, producing a band of higher precipitation and tall humid forest. By contrast, the western and south-eastern slopes are relatively dry. These mountains, isolated and triangular in shape, rise from sea level to c. 5775 m only 42 km inland—the highest in Colombia and the tallest coastal mountains anywhere on the planet. North-east away from these mountains precipitation declines sharply across the flat desert-like Guajira Peninsula.

Guajira Peninsula

Projecting north-east into the Caribbean, the Guajira Peninsula is unlike any other region of Colombia. It is low and mostly flat, covered by thorny desert scrub and low acacia-like trees, and experiences extremely low rainfall and hot daytime temperatures. During the long dry season the area experiences near-constant trade winds. There is little orographic relief except at its far north-eastern tip, where a small band of dry to moderately humid forest covers the hills of the Serranía de Macuira. Although rainfall across much of the peninsula averages only c. 300–550 mm annually, temperatures moderate somewhat during the wetter May–October period but humidity increases. Despite the harsh environmental conditions, a remarkable number of birds thrive in this desert and many occur nowhere else except here and in adjacent areas of similar desert in Venezuela.

The Chocó-Pacific

The dry seasonal climate of the Caribbean quickly diminishes in the vicinity of the Gulf of Urabá and the Panama border, and is replaced southward along the Pacific coast by a hot, humid, super-wet climate. Rainfall is c. 2000–3000 mm near the Panama and Ecuador borders, but soars in the central Chocó to c. 6000–8000 mm annually across much of the region, and is higher still in the Pacific-slope foothills. A few stations in the upper Atrato-San Juan watershed report long-term annual averages exceeding 10,000 mm (e.g. Tutuendo, c. 11,770 mm, although total subject to verification). This belt of high rainfall extends some 400 km or more from north of Quibdó to as far south as the department of Cauca and east into the western foothills. Here rain falls an average of 250–300 days per year (c. 305 days/year at Quibdó). No area of similar extent anywhere has such high mean rainfall. The climatic engine driving this high rainfall is a strong equatorial counter-current flowing west to east directly towards the Chocó coast. This current pulls moisture-laden clouds ashore year-round. Typically mornings are sunny and bright, with rainfall occurring in the afternoon and especially at night. Highest annual rainfall occurs in the lower foothills.

Despite soaring rainfall, the upper reaches of a few valleys on this same Pacific slope, most notably the Dagua and Patía, lie in rain-shadows where mountains block the prevailing moisture-laden clouds from reaching them. Consequently, these valleys receive relatively little rainfall and their upper reaches are essentially desert islands surrounded by 'cloud forests'. Unsurprisingly, the juxtaposition of these small arid upper valleys, isolated within a much larger super-wet belt, as well as the relative isolation of the entire Chocó-Pacific region, has resulted in numerous curious distributions, and extremely high endemism among birds and other organisms.

Inter-Andean valleys and cordilleras

Most of this region broadly experiences two wetter and two drier periods with higher rainfall in March–June and October–November, although there is much local variation. Annual averages range from 1500–4000 mm, with arid rain-shadow valleys receiving considerably less. In general, the floors of the Cauca and Magdalena Valleys, being partially blocked by high mountains to the east and west, receive less rainfall than the cooler and wetter slopes above them. Both rivers offer a variety of arid to humid habitats. Over much of its length, the Cauca Valley as it passes through the Andes is higher in elevation and narrower than the Magdalena Valley, but soils in the floors of both valleys are fertile and were heavily deforested and converted to agricultural purposes long ago.

The eastern slope of the East Andes near its northern end in Norte de Santander is drained by the Río Catatumbo, which empties north-east towards the vast Maracaibo Basin lowlands of Venezuela. Being partially blocked by high mountains to the west and south, rainfall in the Catatumbo watershed is low and temperatures high.

The West Andes are younger, narrower and lower in average height than the Central and East Andes, and only a few isolated peaks are higher than the treeline (c. 3300–3400 m) and none is volcanic. While the Pacific slope is extremely wet, the eastern slope of the West Andes receives considerably less rainfall and is now heavily deforested.

The Central Andes, flanked by the Cauca Valley to the west and Magdalena to the east is the highest of the three cordilleras and the only range with active volcanos. The northernmost volcano, Nevado del Ruiz, is near the city of Manizales. In 1985 Nevado del Ruiz erupted with devastating loss of life and property. Southward a dozen major active volcanos and several smaller ones are located in a line extending to the Ecuador border. The five northernmost, Nevados del Ruiz, Santa Isabel, Quindío, Tolima and Huila, all exceed 5000 m in height (Huila is the highest at c. 5400 m) and all are capped by extensive glaciers. Nevado del Tolima, younger than the others and with a near-perfect symmetrical shape, is the only one with a benevolent recent history. Continuing south, the remainder, including Volcán Puracé, Pan de Azúcar,

Sotará, Doña Juana, Galeras, Cumbal and Chiles, all exceed 4000 m and all have a history of intermittent threatening activity. Volcán Puracé, with its smoking fumaroles, and Doña Juana, are particularly active and restless.

The East Andes are the broadest and most massive of the three Andean ranges, higher than the West Andes but slightly lower than the Central Andes. The nation's capital, Bogotá (c. 2600 m) is located in the East Andes. Positioned at the eastern and southern end of a broad flat high-elevation wetland known as the Sabana de Bogotá, this vast area is now largely drained or canalized. Scattered remnants of this once vast wetland remain, however, including several within the city of Bogotá. These scattered remnant wetlands (*humedales*) still harbour small populations of formerly more widespread birds. Several national parks and reserves near Bogotá provide access to spectacular high wet montane forest, elfin woodland and *páramo*. The northern half of the East Andes is drier than the central and western ranges. The highest peaks in the East Andes, the Sierra Nevada del Cocuy (3000–4800 m) lie far to the north, near the Venezuelan border.

Grasslands (*llanos*)

Beginning along the eastern base of the East Andes from the city of Villavicencio north and east to Venezuela's borders, one enters a world unlike anything in the western half of the country. Here, the land runs almost ruler flat for 600 km east to the Río Orinoco, which forms a portion of the eastern boundary of the country. These are the plains or *llanos*, a vast grassland that extends far north into Venezuela. These grasslands are dissected by ribbon-like gallery forests clinging to borders of rivers that flow in long straight lines east to the Orinoco. Here, cattle, cowboys, *llanero* music and larger-than life ranches (*hatos*) conjure images of a romanticized old American west. The region boasts great wildlife spectacles. Leathery caiman, slow-moving capybara and vast numbers of waterfowl and waders gather at drying waterholes during the long dusty dry season between late November and early May. Additionally, a remarkable assortment of smaller species inhabits the gallery forests and grasslands. The *llanos* climate is monsoonal, with almost no rain falling for months. Then, abruptly the rains return, and 90% of the annual precipitation falls in a single April/May–early October wet season. During this period rivers overflow their banks and spread widely across the flat lowlands. Annual rainfall over much of the region is c. 2000–2500 mm, somewhat less in parts of Vichada, but increases to 3000 mm or more at the base of the Andes and near the Río Orinoco.

Amazonia

Southward from the *llanos* rainfall gradually increases and is spread more evenly throughout the year. Over most of Colombia's Amazonian region rain is likely to fall on 200–250 days of the year, although this can differ from year to year and place to place. Near Leticia annual rainfall (c. 3300 mm) is, on average, a little higher in January–April, although almost any month can record the highest or lowest monthly total during a year. Closer to the Andes, e.g. near the Macarena Mts, annual rainfall is higher (c. 3900 mm) with an April–July peak. In the warm equatorial climate of Colombia's Amazonian rainforests, where large relatively stationary air masses predominate, heat builds on most days, air masses rise, carrying moisture upward, which cools and falls as rain. It is a near-daily pattern—morning cloud build-up followed by local afternoon showers, clearing skies and stunning sunsets. It is estimated that up to three-quarters of all water that falls as rain in Amazonia is produced by this cyclical convectional system, driven in large part by evapotranspiration from the forest itself as water is recycled over and over. On a larger scale the ultimate source of moisture across much of Amazonia is derived from south-east trade winds. Over tropical latitudes generally (especially over oceans) the convergence of both north-east and south-east trade winds contribute to rainfall seasonality, as this converging zone of winds (the Intertropical Convergence Zone) shifts north then south with the sun's declination. However, over continents many regional factors obscure or disrupt this simplistic pattern.

Temperatures across Amazonia are consistently warm during the day (c. 30–31°C), declining only moderately at night (22°C) with daily fluctuations greater than seasonal averages. Humidity is high throughout the year, averaging c. 80%.

On the other hand, seasonal changes in the level of the Amazon River and its vast network of tributaries along Colombia's southern border are dramatic, varying as much as 10–12 m between December–May peaks and June–November lows. During peak levels almost all rivers overflow their banks and forests flood for miles inland. These river level changes, however, result not from local weather events but from wet and dry seasons far to the north or south. In the Amazon River's headwaters on the slopes of central and southern Peru, rainfall is highest in November–April (the southern climatic cycle) causing the Amazon to rise during the first half of the year as it passes Leticia. Conversely, higher river levels in Colombia's Caquetá and Putumayo region are derived from peak rainfall on Colombia's east Andean slopes during April–July (northern climatic cycle), at a time when it is dry far to the south, but the contributions of these rivers enter the Amazon far downstream of Colombia. These relatively predictable seasonal cycles of high and low water levels are vital for wildlife (e.g. terns, nightjars, skimmers, plovers) that depend on exposed sandbars during low water for breeding sites. Andean slope deforestation, however, has accelerated run-off in some areas, causing short-term spikes in river flooding that now interfere with traditional breeding cycles.

White-sand soils of the Guianan Shield

This broad area, which includes principally the departments of Guainía, Vaupés and Guaviare, is one of the most biogeographically distinct in Colombia. Wedged between the *llanos* to the north and Amazonia to the south, this white-sand soil zone extends west slightly beyond the Serranía de Chiribiquete and is the south-westernmost extension of the vast Guianan Shield. Rivers in northern Guainía flow north-east to the Orinoco while those in southern Guainía, as well as all those in Vaupés and Guaviare, flow south-east to the Ríos Negro or Caquetá and ultimately into the Amazon (Solimões) River in Brazil. The vegetation of this white-sand soil region is not quite like the lush grasslands of the *llanos*, nor the luxuriant and wetter Amazonian rainforest to the south, but frequently closer to a mix of the two, often tall forest is juxtaposed with scrubby, lower-stature woodland or a pin-cushion scattering of bushes and small isolated forests. In some areas there is extensive grassland, here maintained less by climate than by combinations of fire, drought, seasonal flooding, soil porosity and low fertility.

Over much of this region the soil is pure white sand, as white as a coralline beach and, in fact, it once was an ancient shallow sea that over time built up the vast sedimentary rock known as the Guianan Shield. In Venezuela these characteristic rock formations, known as tepuis, are mostly flat-topped. But in Colombia all that remains visible of this great massif are scattered outcrops, rock domes and the erosional remnants we see as white-sand soil. In some areas this white sand is mixed or alternates with iron-rich red lateritic soils typical of Amazonia. The massive domes that rise far above the forest, rounded and weathered black, impart an otherworldly aspect to this remarkable region. It is a difficult medium for plants, with few nutrients and water that quickly drains away. A few plant groups, however, thrive here, among them carnivorous sundews. Other plants struggle to survive and jealously guard their leaves by lacing them with noxious chemicals like tannins and phenols to ward off insects. And when leaves do fall they stain the water as black as strong tea. All the rivers here are black and clear and clean, devoid of the massive loads of sediment carried by Amazonian rivers. The diversity of birdlife also seems slightly lower than in Amazonia, but this endlessly fascinating region harbours many species that occur nowhere else except these sandy soil forests and scrub. It is also one of the least populated, least accessible, and surely the least-visited biogeographic regions in Colombia.

VEGETATION ZONES AND HABITAT DESCRIPTIONS

All natural plant communities respond to and are shaped by abiotic factors such as rainfall, temperature, evapotranspiration rates, soil moisture, flood regimes, and fire. They also are affected by the structure and composition of other plants in the environment and the change or succession of plants over time. These major vegetation zones, which may go by various names but are often called plant formations, loosely follow those of Leslie Holdridge (1967), and are used here as a starting point for describing the habitat of each bird occurring in Colombia.

Most birds are found in more restricted habitats within these broader vegetation zones. For example, within tropical humid forest (a vegetation zone or plant formation), a species may occur primarily in forest that does not flood (*terra firme*) or only periodically floods (transition forest), or predictably floods every year, often for months (*várzea*). And, within each of these subdivisions, a bird may live in an even more restricted stratum or microhabitat, such as only in the canopy or understorey of the forest, along the forest border, in a shrubby clearing, or a river edge. Consequently, habitat descriptions will usually be combinations of major vegetation zones (the broadest habitat classification) and various more restrictive habitats. Bear in mind that there is always some overlap between vegetation zones, and recognizing them is made easier by paying attention to the climatic factors (rainfall, temperature, soils, etc.) that shape them. Each major vegetation zone or habitat is described in the following paragraphs and these are followed by descriptions of a variety of more specific habitats, all of which are frequently used in combinations in the text to describe where species occur. In a few cases key points for major vegetation zones are repeated, for convenience, in the section listing specific habitats. Stated lower and upper elevations for vegetation zones are approximate (when given) and vary considerably depending upon slope and rainfall (e.g. usually lower on the wet Pacific slope, higher in drier regions).

VEGETATION ZONES

Desert scrub/arid scrub

Rainfall 300–800 mm. A variety of permanent vegetation stages that develop under low seasonal rainfall and long, severe dry seasons, sometimes also including strong prevailing north-east trade winds. Desert scrub is found mainly close to the Caribbean coast. It is characterized by thorny bushes, drought-resistant trees, e.g. *Acacia, Prosopis, Mimosa, Calotropis*, and various cacti including, locally, large picturesque multi-armed *Lemaireocereus*. Structurally similar vegetation also occurs in a few small isolated valleys on the wet Pacific-slope region where incoming moisture on prevailing westerly winds is blocked by high mountains, thus resulting in a classic rain-shadow effect. Examples include the upper Dagua and upper Patía Valleys. Similar areas also occur in the upper Magdalena Valley near Neiva.

Tropical dry forest (also deciduous forest)

Rainfall 750–1500 mm. Any of a variety of rather low- to medium-stature forests with marked to severe dry seasons in which a large proportion of trees loses their leaves for up to half of the year. In the text usually prefaced as tropical dry forest or (if in the mountains) montane dry forest. Occurs across northern Colombia north of the Andes, locally on the floor of the Cauca and Magdalena Valleys, and east of the Andes in parts of the *llanos*.

Tropical moist forest

Rainfall 1000–2000 mm. Forests that receive less rainfall than evergreen humid or wet forests, but more than dry or deciduous forests. In general this is a transition semi-evergreen forest that occurs (or formerly occurred) at low to moderate elevations, especially across parts of northern Colombia. It is often included within tropical dry forest by botanists. Much of Colombia's tropical dry and moist forests have been lost to deforestation, often having been converted to smaller-scale cattle-ranching and agricultural activities.

Tropical humid forest

Rainfall 2000–4000 mm; lowlands to c. 1600 m. This is tall, canopied evergreen forest, in popular vernacular called 'rainforest' with rainfall of c. 2000–4000 mm in the lowlands and decreasing somewhat with elevation. In Colombia, typically there is one longer dry and wet season, and a shorter dry and wet period, with this asymmetry more obvious further from the equator. Closer to the equator the wet-dry pattern is more evenly distributed. However, across much of Amazonia (e.g. Putumayo, Amazonas) there is little obvious seasonality to rainfall.

Tropical wet (pluvial) forest

Rainfall c. 4000–12,000 mm. A limited forest type, primarily of the Chocó-Pacific lowlands and foothills, characterized by extremely high rainfall. Forests are tall and canopied in the lowlands, the canopy more broken in the foothills, but even low in the foothills (200–800 m) forests may become extremely mossy and festooned with epiphytes. Rainfall is among the highest in the world but gradually decreases with elevation.

Premontane and montane dry forest

Rainfall c. 500–1500 mm; c. 500–3000 m elevation. These vegetation types are not especially widespread in the Colombian Andes. Much of the valley floor and lower slopes above the Cauca Valley is (or was) premontane dry to moist forest. A larger expanse of similar or even drier tropical and premontane forest and scrub is typical of much of the floor and lower slopes of the middle and upper Magdalena Valley. Rainfall is low in both regions. The most extensive montane dry to moist forest vegetation runs north at higher elevations (2000–3000 m) in a variable-width band from the Cundinamarca/Boyacá border almost to Venezuela. Montane dry forest and scrub also is found in central Nariño in the vicinity of Pasto and south to the Ecuador border.

Premontane humid and wet forest

(used interchangeably with humid and wet foothill forest)

Rainfall c. 1500–5000 mm; c. 500–1600 m elevation. These forests predominate at lower elevations in the Andes and on the northern face of the Santa Marta Mts. They differ somewhat in total annual rainfall but, to anyone other than a trained botanist, they may not appear much different physically. Trees in all areas can carry heavy loads of epiphytes. Avifaunas are exceptionally rich and include a mix of lowland and higher-elevation species.

Montane humid and wet forest

Rainfall c. 1000–4000 mm; c. 1600–3000 m elevation. Frequently foggy for much of the day. Forests in the lower half of this elevation zone are often quite tall, carry abundant epiphytes, and are popularly termed 'cloud forests'. Characteristic families of trees include Lauraceae, Moraceae and Myrtaceae. Locally oak (*Quercus humboldtii*) is numerous. Forest undergrowth is dense, cluttered and tree-ferns are characteristic, along with bamboo (*Chusquea*). With increasing elevation bamboo becomes even more common, the forest lower in stature, the canopy more broken, and trees somewhat gnarled and always with massive burdens of epiphytes. At these elevations (c. 2500–3000 m) Colombia's national tree, the Wax Palm (*Ceroxylon*), is locally common.

Savanna

Rainfall 1700–3000 mm (higher at the base of the Andes). This tropical grassland is best represented by the plains or *llanos* north-east of the Andes. Rainfall over most of the region is moderate but sharply seasonal, with a severe dry season from November or December to the end of April or early May, and a strong rainy season beginning in May and abating gradually by September or October. The *llanos* consists broadly of two areas, a higher zone closer to the Andes which is not subject to flooding, and a flatter lower zone further east that is subject to seasonal flooding. The high area may support dry forest that is not associated with rivers. One of the most characteristic trees of the higher zone is the large spreading *Pithecellobium* (Fabaceae), widely known as 'Saman'. The lower zone is more open, often with extensive grassland, and forests are usually close to riverbanks where they can reach water during the long dry season. Large areas of the lower *llanos* are subject to shallow seasonal flooding, often for several months. Almost everywhere, the *llanos* is a region of wildlife spectacles, with large numbers of raptors, waders and a surprising number of smaller birds, as well as many reptiles and mammals. The *llanos* of Colombia and Venezuela are the largest grasslands in northern South America, mirrored south of the Amazon Basin by the Pantanal of Brazil, Bolivia and Paraguay.

Savanna woodland and savanna scrub

Not unlike sandy-soil forests but variable in appearance and best visualized as vegetation intermediate between sandy-belt forest and grassland. In general savanna woodland is lower in stature and more open than sandy-belt forest, and may occur in isolated pockets surrounded by grassland pin-cushioned with shrubs. In some areas it resembles Brazilian *cerrado*, with short, well-spaced scrubby trees forming a partially closed canopy, or more open *campina* of Brazil's grasslands. In more open regions vulnerable to seasonal fires, scrubby fire-resistant *Byrsonima* and *Curatella* trees predominate.

Páramo

3200–4800 m (upper and lower limits vary). This is Colombia's most distinctive plant formation. *Páramo* is a moderately dry to very wet tropical high-elevation grassland (rainfall c. 1000–2000 mm) that is dominant at the limit of tree growth and continues upward to the limit of plant growth. *Páramo* develops under conditions that include low soil temperature, low daily temperatures, fog, wind, and frequently also acidic soils, all of which greatly retard plant growth. Dominant plants include tussock grasses (*Calamagrostris*), cushion plants (*Azorella, Distichia, Plantago*), and many species of rosette-shaped *Espeletia* shrubs (Asteraceae), known as *frailejones*, which afford the *páramo* its distinctive appearance. In general *páramos* are cold and wet, with overnight temperatures at or below freezing, but with intense solar radiation on sunny days. Snow is frequent at higher elevations and almost any day may experience rain, snow, fog and icy conditions. Mossy bogs, cold lagoons, and poorly drained soils predominate. Patches of *Polylepis* (Rosaceae) trees occur very locally in the *páramo* and are the only trees capable of growing well above the normal treeline. *Páramos* are drier in the Santa Marta Mts and the northern portion of Colombia's Andes, much wetter and more floristically diverse southward, especially in Cauca and Nariño. Most areas experience a spectacular bloom of flowers during July to September or October.

HABITATS

Terra firme forest

A widely used term for forests in Amazonia that are not subject to seasonal or periodic flooding. Tree species diversity is among the highest in Amazonia.

Transition forest

A term used to identify Amazonian forests that lie between *terra firme* and *várzea*, and are therefore subject to periodic but not annual flooding. Some of the tallest, most diverse and grandest tropical lowland forests occur in this zone.

Várzea forest

Denotes mainly Amazonian forests that are close enough to rivers and sufficiently low to flood annually to depths of c. 1–6 m, often for many months, or even twice annually. Tree species diversity is lower than in *terra firme* forest and the understorey more open. *Várzea* forest also occurs in sandy-soil regions of Guainía and Vaupés, especially where soils are heavier and less sandy.

Army ants

A mobile habitat. These are carnivorous ants and the best-known species, *Eciton burchellii*, is widely followed by obligate ant-following antbirds. Its swarms, often numbering hundreds of thousands of individuals, fan out in raids across the floor of humid lowland forest. These voracious, fast-moving ants flush many small prey items during daily raids and are followed by a select group of 'obligate' army-ant following birds that use the ants as 'beaters'. These birds capture prey attempting to escape the ants, but do not eat the ants, and are so dependent upon these ants that they do not feed independent of them. Consequently, they have evolved a fascinating array of social behaviours and breeding activities associated with following a mobile food source. Other birds also opportunistically follow these swarms for short periods. A second smaller species, *Labidus praedator*, occurs in both lowland and highland areas but its swarms are smaller, unpredictable in occurrence, and followed only opportunistically by a few birds.

River-edge forest

This is a mix of grass, shrubs and forest types bordering rivers. It is most distinctive in Amazonia where younger river-edge vegetation is quickly colonized by grasses, shrubs, tall cane (*Gynerium*), *Tessaria* and *Salix*. In places where the vegetation stabilizes, long lines of even-age stands of trees such as *Cecropia* mixed with rank herbaceous vegetation (especially *Heliconia*) soon develop along with *Ochroma* and vines. Older stages are more diverse with *Ficus*,

Erythrina and other fast-growing invading plants. As rivers sweep back and forth across floodplains they cut into tall old forest, often leaving immense piles of driftwood and debris on the adjacent banks, while sandbars develop on the opposite shore and are quickly colonized by pioneering vegetation.

Forest borders

The edge of a forest or woodland, e.g. along a road, clearing, treefall or river and stream borders. Older stages typically possess dense shrubby vegetation and numerous fast-growing plants, e.g. *Cecropia, Heliconia, Trema, Piper* and vines. This is a frequently visited habitat by naturalists, where a sampling of both forest and non-forest bird species may be encountered. Generally regarded as vertical in physical appearance, borders can also include horizontal interfaces such as the crown of lowland rainforest canopy, a zone utilized for varying periods of time by a surprising number of non-forest species for dispersal or other activities.

Amazonian river islands

These are ephemeral to semi-permanent islands that form in the Amazon River and its large tributaries, often reaching substantial size in a single river flood cycle. Pioneering grasses, *Tessaria* (Asteraceae), *Salix* (Salicaceae), cane (*Gynerium*) and a few other plants quickly colonize sandbars at the downstream ends of river islands, and this habitat is used by several rapid-breeding species with good dispersal ability. Most are seldom found elsewhere. Later vegetation stages, e.g. with *Heliconia, Cecropia* and *Ficus*, are colonized by additional species. If an island survives a few decades, tall second-growth forest develops. Island vegetation, especially younger stages, are relatively predator-free, and oropendolas, caciques, parakeets and passage boreal migrants often commute to islands for roosting, especially in tall cane (*Gynerium*).

Sandy-soil forest

Humid forest growing on a variety of white-sand soils. These soils, white as beach sand, are erosional remnants of the once vast Guianan Shield, an ancient uplifted shallow sea floor that extended from eastern Colombia across southern Venezuela and northern Brazil to the Guianas. Forests are usually less luxuriant than in Amazonia, and frequently characterized by a somewhat lower canopy height and fewer immense emergent trees. Notably, the leaves of many trees in these areas contain high concentrations of tannins, phenols and defensive chemicals that reduce insect damage. Rivers draining forests growing on these soils are always black water, the result of leaves containing tannin, and are more acidic than other rivers. Some sandy-soil forests are seasonally or more or less permanently inundated, quite low in stature, scrubby, and locally dominated by a nearly impenetrable undergrowth of spiny bromeliads, bamboo or low palms.

Savanna woodland

Resembles sandy-belt forest but lower-canopied (5–20 m), typically somewhat scrubby and with a more open understorey. May be subject to both fire and/or flooding. In its most extreme form it may possess only a semi-closed canopy and somewhat resembles Brazilian *cerrado*. Occurs locally through the white-sand soil region, especially around large rock outcrops with low-nutrient soils and minimal moisture, also in some lower areas subject to prolonged seasonal flooding.

Gallery forest and riparian woodland

Roughly synonymous terms referring to bands of tree growth confined to watercourses in regions too dry for permanent tree cover, or regions too exposed to seasonal fires to allow all but a few hardy fire-resistant species to thrive. Gallery forests line almost all rivers flowing east-northeast across the vast *llanos* or plains of the departments of Arauca, Casanare, Vichada and northern Meta.

Premontane forest

A term denoting forest present in an elevational zone of c. 500–1600 m. Also called foothill forest, especially at lower elevations. Depending on location, it varies from arid to wet.

Montane forest

Denotes forest between elevations of c. 1600 and 3000 m. Where rainfall is high, popularly called cloud forest. As with premontane forest, rainfall varies regionally but in Colombia most montane forests receive high rainfall.

Bamboo

At high elevations where rainfall is abundant, *Chusquea* bamboo is an important native component of montane forest. It grows in picturesque arching clumps and is used in various ways by many birds. Patches of *Chusquea* typically flower and seed only once after many years. Thereafter it dies and is usually replaced by a new generation. A few highly specialized nomadic birds seek these extremely localized bamboo seeding events and breed quickly, availing themselves of the temporarily super-abundant seed crops. Smaller, more dispersed, species of bamboo occur at lower elevations, a few of which are used by the Recurve-billed Bushbird, which splits the stems with its knife-like bill. Tall lowland bamboos west of the Andes are mostly introduced Asian varieties. In the lowlands east of the Andes tall native *Guadua* occurs very locally, but lacks the large numbers of bird species associated with it, unlike further south.

Elfin forest (dwarf or stunted forest), elfin woodland

These forests are usually found at elevations near the treeline (3200–3600 m), but may occur lower on wet ridgelines or exposed slopes. Trees are low in stature (3–10 m), gnarled, mossy, and twisted into fanciful shapes by constant exposure to wind, fog and cold temperatures that reduce growth rates. Elfin woodland is similar but trees and shrubs are more widely spaced.

Páramo

Described under plant formations. A high-elevation grass-and-shrub zone that occurs above the limit of tree growth. Easily recognized by distinctive rosette-shaped *Espeletia* (Asteraceae); spectacular during the annual blooming period.

Polylepis woodland

A genus *Polylepis* (Rosaceae) of low trees with loose reddish papery bark. Forms small low-stature woodlands well above the normal treeline (especially southward in Andes) but also present at the treeline. Occurs mostly as scattered trees at the treeline in Colombia.

Light woodland, plantations

Park-like areas partially cleared by human activity; includes plantations of coffee, citrus, cacao, papaya, borojó (*Alibertia*) and others, usually where the original forest canopy and much of the undergrowth has been removed.

Second-growth (or regrowth) woodland

Includes a wide variety of regrowth vegetation stages that differ from mature forest in plant species composition, lower canopy height, and trees that often appear more even-aged. Young stages, with much sunlight, are typically bushy and dense, but older stages are taller and somewhat more open.

Savanna or grassland

These tropical grasslands characterize the *llanos* or plains region of north-eastern Colombia, and extend from the base of the Andes to the Río Orinoco. Wildlife activity and movements are strongly influenced by rainfall, and much of the region is largely or completely inaccessible during the wettest months when vast areas flood.

Second growth

Any type of regenerating forest. Usually develops following wood-cutting and disturbance by humans; also at river bends and margins of old oxbows. Initial stages are dense, shrubby, and dominated by vines and a few fast-growing species, e.g. *Cecropia*, *Miconia*, *Ochroma*, *Trema* and *Piper*, which thrive in high sunlight environments, but left undisturbed and given time, will revert to mature forest. Also commonly colonizes landslides on steep Andean hillsides where *Alder*, *Clusia*, and *Miconia* and other melastomes may dominate.

Shrubby areas

Any regrowth vegetation (especially in humid areas), with or without scattered tall trees, which follows deforestation and precedes tall forest. Mostly grass, shrubs, vines, thickets and small trees.

Scrubby areas

A relatively permanent plant community of woody bushes and small trees, e.g. *Acacia*, especially in drier areas. Usually the result of human activity and environmental degradation (erosion, overgrazing, wood-cutting) so severe that forest regeneration is unlikely.

Desert scrub (arid scrub)

Interchangeable terms for a natural permanent scrub zone characterized by high temperatures and very low rainfall. Best developed close to the Caribbean coast and on the Guajira Peninsula. Also considered a major plant formation.

Swamp forest

Forest that grows in a more or less permanently flooded zone. Some swamps are dominated by palms (e.g. *Mauritia*). Swamp vegetation is widespread (at least formerly) in the lower Atrato and Magdalena Valleys, more locally in Amazonia on river islands, around oxbow lakes, or as extensions of *várzea* forest in low-lying areas.

Marshes

More or less permanent wetlands dominated by grasses or reeds, but not trees. Scattered shrubs may be present.

Morichal

An area dominated almost exclusively by Moriche palms (*Mauritia*). Can occur in forest or savanna but generally where the soil is wet or poorly drained.

Mangroves

A forest community with a few species of highly specialized evergreen trees that is capable of growing within the tidal zone. Thick shiny leaves; some have aerial or stilt (prop) roots. Bird diversity is low but mangroves are vital for stabilizing coastal areas.

Coastal, offshore and pelagic

Three marine terms that are, respectively, within sight of land, beyond sight of land but over a continental shelf, and open ocean beyond a continental shelf.

Ranchland, cultivated and settled areas, parks and gardens

These are all more or less self-descriptive terms used to denote a variety of environments modified by humans.

BIRD CONSERVATION IN COLOMBIA

Colombia occupies a unique location on our planet. Situated in the north-west corner of South America, its shores are washed by two oceans, it has vast lowlands ranging from deserts to rainforests, three Andean ranges whose feet are bathed in steamy tropical forests, and peaks permanently covered in glaciers. Spread over its coasts, islands, mountains, vast grasslands and Amazonian forests is a staggering array of biodiversity; the longest lists of birds and amphibians, the second highest list of plant species, the third longest list of reptiles, and even the fifth highest number of mammal species.

Ironically, the strongest incentives for the preservation of this biodiversity begin with two basic human needs: a reliable water supply and a sustainable source of energy. Decades ago Colombia recognized the value of protecting forested watersheds above cities for water. It also is essential to protect watersheds above hydropower plants from the destructive effects of erosion that inevitably follows deforestation. Colombia has water, which originates in its *páramos* and high cold montane forests, and it has the mountains for hydropower. For example, Bogotá, the nation's capital and largest city, derives its water from the high wet forests and *páramos* in Chingaza National Park, while cities such as Manizales have protected nearby watersheds for their municipal water supplies. But the story only begins here.

Colombia's first national protected area, Parque Nacional Natural Cueva de los Guácharos (Oilbird Cave National Park) was designated in 1960. Many others followed. Today, the Colombian park system (Parques Nacionales de Colombia) administers some 59 magnificent parks (see map inside back cover), protected areas, reserves, and archaeological and historical sites covering more than 14% of the country. Over the years two of these conservation areas were abandoned because of human-caused degradation. Maintenance and protection of reserves everywhere represent ongoing problems. Of critical importance is the integration of at least 40 indigenous peoples and Afro-Colombian communities that live near or inside protected areas and depend upon these areas for their livelihood and to maintain ancestral cultures. They are of great importance in the maintenance and stability of numerous protected areas.

In recent decades small landowners, as well as national and even international organizations, have become involved to varying degrees with land preservation, especially for areas critical to birds. The relatively small but lovely 140 ha Reserva Natural Los Tananeos is an example. Through the inspiration of the Ropero family, their property is now operated as a non-profit with an emphasis on birds, tropical dry forests, local education and ecotourism. The Hummingbird Conservancy (Fundación Colibrí), founded by renowned hummingbird photographer Luis Mazariegos, established the privately operated 7000 ha Mesenia-Paramillo

Nature Reserve in upper-elevation forests of Antioquia, Risaralda and Caldas. Foundations such as Colibríes de Altaquer (FELCA) have partnered with various organizations to purchase private reserves such as the pristine and bird-rich 1000 ha Reserva Natural Río Ñambí near Altaquer, Nariño. Still others, like Fundación Natura, work primarily in education, communication and advisory capacities to sustain biodiversity.

Over the past decade or more hundreds of private landholders across rural western Colombia, and more recently also east of the Andes, have converted properties to private reserves. Many now support themselves largely via ecotourism, offering not only day visits and guide services to birders but overnight accommodations. Whether small or large, private foundations and reserves contribute substantially to bird conservation in Colombia. According to the National System of Protected Areas (Sistema Nacional de Áreas Protegidas, SINAP) more than 28 million ha are currently protected in national, regional and private reserves—an astonishing 20% of the country. BirdLife International also has identified several Important Bird Areas (Áreas de Importancia para la Conservación de las Aves, AICA) that if formally protected could increase conserved land even more.

Large international organizations including the Wildlife Conservation Society (WCS), World Wildlife Fund (WWF) and Amazon Conservation Team (ACT) have ongoing projects in numerous areas in Colombia, and fund a wide array of scientific studies. WWF has for some time funded work on habitat utilization by boreal migrants, while ACT works with indigenous Amazonian groups. Rainforest Trust and The Nature Conservancy (TNC) also work to preserve sites thought critical for birds and biodiversity. While the emphasis among these organizations varies, there is a common commitment to preserving biodiversity and a healthy environment.

Fundación ProAves, a Colombian NGO funded largely from outside sources, has promoted conservation awareness since its establishment in 1998. Despite some difficulties they have purchased and established 17 reserves chosen primarily for bird and habitat protection. Via an umbrella organization, Conservation Alliance, several of these possess overnight facilities for visitors.

CALIDRIS

The NGO Asociación Calidris, the BirdLife International partner in Colombia, has been active in a broad array of bird-related projects. Founded in 1991 and based in Cali, their stated mission is the conservation of birds and ecosystems. Their focus includes research and working with local communities to foster sustainable use of natural resources. The wide-ranging goals of this partnership are reflected in their activities, which include monitoring wintering shorebird populations, often in association with the Western Hemisphere Shorebird Group (WHSG), working to protect vulnerable terrestrial species in the West Andes, and protection of marine species. They have collaborated with the Alexander von Humboldt Institute on Important Bird Areas (AICA), worked with National Audubon to establish birding trails and ecotourism corridors in Colombia's dry Caribbean forests, published regional bird identification guides, and collaborated on the creation of Wiki Aves de Colombia.

Despite efforts to increase public awareness much work remains to do. Recent data suggest that of the more than 1900 species of birds in Colombia, 133 are at some risk of extinction, 14 Critically Endangered, 35 Endangered and 84 Vulnerable. Furthermore, of approximately 93 endemic species, c. 54% are threatened, c. 12% Critically Endangered and one is considered Extinct. Subspecific populations of others also appear to be extinct (e.g. *niceforoi* Yellow-billed Pintail; *borreroi* Cinnamon Teal; and *bogotensis* Bearded Tachuri) and for a few (e.g. Turquoise-throated Puffleg) there are few or no modern records. On the positive side, more individuals and organizations than ever are now involved in conservation efforts. Knowledge of the country's biodiversity, especially birdlife, is improving, in no small part due to the fantastic success of the Cornell Lab of Ornithology's eBird platform, via which users submit and document their observations. Also encouraging, one species formerly believed extinct (Antioquia Brushfinch), has been rediscovered, and others formerly known from just one or a few sites (e.g. Gorgeted Wood-quail, Black Inca, Niceforo's Wren) have been found in additional locations.

While Colombia's immense biodiversity has attracted the attention of many national and international conservations groups, it also has drawn the interest of some of the country's most prominent politicians. Under the leadership of former president Juan Manuel Santos, national conserved areas in Colombia more than doubled, from c. 13 million ha to 28.4 million ha during his tenure between 2010 and 2018. This is a remarkable achievement, especially when viewed against Colombia's history of armed conflict, coca production and illegal wildlife trafficking. Complicating this drive to increase conserved areas is the need to recognize indigenous and Afro-Colombian cultures, and to improve economic opportunities for the broader population.

Is an expansion of conserved land as bold as this sustainable? It is a legitimate question, and longer term it may be both viable and necessary. If it is, this will doubtless be a legacy as important to President Santos as the peace process over which he also presided. A provision in Colombia's constitution states that protected areas cannot be rescinded by future administrations without constitutional change—a significant deterrent to undoing conserved areas. But the ability to provide protection to existing and newly designated areas is problematic. Some recently designated sites were former FARC strongholds. Ironically, when held by FARC, they remained off-limits to logging and development because they were dangerous. Under President Santos deforestation declined from c. 400,000 ha/year in 2010 to c. 144,000 ha/year by 2015, but as the peace process began to take shape, security improved and deforestation increased again, although it remains well below earlier levels. Increased security in these areas, however, now brings squatters, illegal mining, increased coca production, and pressure to exploit natural resources. Ambitious new roadbuilding projects bring benefits but also controversies. The ability to protect conservation units, and simultaneously address economic issues facing local communities, who may wish to exploit natural resources in these areas, is also a formidable challenge.

Importantly, Colombian society has become more enlightened and progressive in the last few decades. There is now awareness that environmental protection, climate change and biodiversity are interconnected. Colombia has shown a commitment to its environment, even resisting strong international pressure to use toxic and damaging fumigation to control coca production. Appreciation of environmental protection and biodiversity is now a priority, but comes with challenges that may require international financial investment, especially as global climate changes. Balancing conservation with development is a tug-of-war that brings the varied needs of birds, wildlife, indigenous communities and modern society into play.

Colombia is a strong nation with one of the most diverse economies in Latin America, placing it in an enviable position to be a global leader in sustainable biodiversity and development, as well as furthering social and economic progress. It also is one of the best birding destinations on the planet. Bird song can still be heard throughout its varied landscape—songs of hope that invite everyone to enjoy this marvellous country, and to dream of an even brighter future.

USING THE FIELD GUIDE

Systematic and taxonomic treatment

The systematics and taxonomy used in this field guide start with the two volumes of the *HBW and BirdLife International Illustrated Checklist of the Birds of the World* (del Hoyo & Collar 2014, 2016) with numerous more recent updates based on molecular and field research undertaken by researchers at academic institutions throughout North and South America. Where molecular data and field research are as yet unavailable, or are inconclusive, the taxonomy used here draws on the Tobias scoring system (del Hoyo & Collar 2014: 30–41), which makes taxonomic decisions based on a range of factors including plumage pattern, bare-part colours, morphometrics and, if known, vocalizations, and ecological and behavioural traits. However, with respect to hummingbirds, numerous antbirds, *Grallaria* antpittas, tapaculos, Onychorhynchidae flycatchers, Tityridae, *Myiopagis* flycatchers, manakins, various wrens, thrushes, Fringillidae, Passerellidae, tanagers, and other select genera, taxonomy herein follows recent molecular work now adopted by eBird/Clements and the American Ornithological Society's South American Checklist Committee.

Explanation of species accounts

Each family section starts with the name and a breakdown of the number of species that are recognized worldwide (mainly according to current HBW/BirdLife taxonomy), and those that have occurred in the region, with the number considered to be vagrants, introduced or extinct listed separately. Note that as a result of some taxonomic changes (see Systematic and taxonomic treatment) the total number of species in each family does not always match those in the Checklist. Furthermore, although English names principally follow the Checklist, many are based on Clements/eBird (and particularly well-used alternatives are frequently given in parentheses, rather than as Alternative names).

Family and generic introductions: brief overviews of every family, and many (but not all) genera, punctuate the species accounts. The family texts describe general behaviours and ecology, whilst the genus texts focus on shared (or unique) characters that are useful for identification.

Subspecies groups: this field guide is novel, compared to most others that readers will have used, in providing separate accounts and illustrations for each subspecies group recognized under current HBW/BirdLife (or in some cases eBird/Clements) taxonomy; particularly notable discrepancies between these two lists are also highlighted. Subspecies groups are informal taxonomic units used in several recent world checklists to highlight seemingly monophyletic groups of taxa (sometimes single subspecies) that at present appear to sit between the species and subspecies levels (although in some cases it is plausible that fuller scrutiny and better evidence will result in their being awarded species rank). Such groups are identified by their possession of one or several reasonably distinct characters and which therefore seem worthy of attention. In some cases they may already have been recognized as species in other lists or accorded a taxonomic status such as 'megasubspecies' or 'allospecies'.

Accordingly, where two or more such subspecies groups belonging to a single species occur in the region, this necessitates inclusion of more than one account. However, the focus is always on that subspecies group most widespread or likely to be encountered by birdwatchers in the region, with more comparative details alone being provided for other subspecies groups of the same species.

Because many subspecies groups comprise multiple races and the name of the group is always determined by the first of the relevant subspecies to have been named, readers should be aware that the subspecies group name and the race/s belonging to that group recorded in Colombia can be different. For example, a subspecies present in Colombia may form part of a subspecies group bearing the name of a subspecies that is not present in the country but whose name is older, which follows the principle of priority of the *International Code of Zoological Nomenclature* (ICZN) for naming the group. This may initially prove confusing to some users, but we decided that the benefits of giving separate coverage to reasonably well-defined groups of taxa, currently treated below species level, outweighed the disadvantages.

QR codes: link to online resources at the Cornell Lab of Ornithology where you can view photos and videos, and listen to sounds of the species in question. Often there are hundreds of audio-visual records for a single species and in many cases they illustrate distinctive behaviours and aspects of biology. To access this information directly from the book you may need to first download any one of the free smartphone apps that scans QR codes. Then open the QR code reader, and hold your device over the QR code that you wish to scan so that it is clearly visible within the phone's screen; depending on the type of phone, it will either automatically scan the code, or you may need to click or touch an on screen message, somewhat like taking a photo using your phone. Within a few seconds your phone should have navigated to the relevant page.

Each species account is given in the following format:

Name, conservation status and presence: common English names are followed by the scientific name in italics, along with the Spanish name used in Colombia on the line below. The global conservation status is denoted by two-letter codes summarizing the IUCN Red List category of extinction risk, as follows: LC (Least Concern), NT (Near Threatened), VU (Vulnerable), EN (Endangered), CR (Critically Endangered), CR (PE) (Critically Endangered [Possibly Extinct]), EX (Extinct), DD (Data Deficient) and NA (Not Assessed). Colombian conservation status (where available) appears in grey and is based on the *Libro Rojo de Aves de Colombia* (Renjifo *et al.* 2002) and subsequent updates. Immediately below this the reader will find a general statement of relative abundance and temporal status (whether resident, migrant or vagrant) in Colombia. Extinct, hypothetical and potential species are also specified here. The names of hypothetical species are placed in square brackets.

Size: 'L' denotes length in centimetres (metric), followed in parentheses by inches. For hummingbirds and certain other species 'B' denotes bill length, also given in centimetres and inches.

Subspecies: each account begins with a list of recognized subspecies that occur in the region; use of superscript letters is keyed to the relevant map, wherein the boundaries between different races of resident or breeding species are delimited as accurately as possible. If a species is monotypic, this is clearly stated.

Habitat and habits: a brief description is provided of the species' preferred habitat and elevational range in Colombia. Where relevant, notes are also provided on general habits, especially where these can assist identification. For vagrants, or for some especially rare and localized taxa, specific details are often provided concerning occurrence. Any species or subspecies group that is Endemic (E) or almost so (Near-endemic; NE) to the region is clearly indicated, and the appropriate codes are also used next to the maps. Those species deemed to be near-endemic are generally those whose ranges are concentrated within Colombia's borders (80% or greater), or have tiny ranges that straddle the borders with Panama and Venezuela, and to a lesser extent Ecuador.

Identification (ID): unless otherwise stated, the initial description involves the nominate race or, where relevant, the unique race occurring in Colombia. Adult plumages are generally listed before immature or juvenile plumages. Additional notes are provided on seasonal differences as appropriate.

Voice: vocalizations are typically based on a description of the song, followed by any regularly heard calls. For some non-breeding migrants that are very unlikely to be heard singing, only a call is given. For some species, such as seabirds, vocalizations are not transcribed as they are unlikely to aid field identification. Onomatopoeic transcriptions of songs, calls and mechanical sounds are presented (in quotes) when believed to be useful, but their interpretation is always subjective. Terms such as high, low, rising-falling, etc. apply to pitch, and the actual frequency (in kilohertz) also is sometimes given. Sounds of 1–2 kHz would be regarded as low-pitched, 3–4 kHz medium-pitched, 5–8 kHz moderately high-pitched, and 9–11 kHz extremely high-pitched (even inaudible). Vowels are sounded following English rules of pronunciation. For native Spanish speakers, translating Spanish vowel sounds into English vowel sounds may help interpret some vocal transcriptions.
Accent: an emphasized note or phrase, but not otherwise unusually loud.
Letters connected by apostrophes ("i'i'i'i'i'i"): a series of rapidly repeated notes.
Letters without spaces ("iiiiiiii"): a trill.
Capital letters: a loud sound.
Hyphen between notes: (ti-ti-ti): a steady series of notes without pause.
Exclamation mark at end of song or call (!): an abrupt, emphatic or explosive ending.
Series of periods at end of song: vocalization continues.
Series of periods of different lengths: progressively longer pauses between notes.
Letters "ii" or "ee": high-pitched sounds or with diphthongs as "ti'ti'ti" or "se'se'se".
Letters with w, c, o, oo and u: low-pitched sounds.
Short English phrases: intended to capture syncopation or 'beat' of a vocalization.

Similar species (SS): species that may cause confusion in identification are mentioned here.

Taxonomic notes (TN): these are focused on recent, species-level changes in taxonomy, with special reference to those arrangements introduced in either volume of the *HBW and BirdLife International Illustrated Checklist of the Birds of the World* or on recent changes reflected in eBird/Clements taxonomy where the two taxonomies differ.

Alternative names (AN): where other common English names are, or occasionally have been, in use, especially in other works likely to be consulted by visiting or resident birdwatchers, such alternative names are stated. However, we generally do not provide spelling variants or alternative names that differ only slightly from the name employed.

Plates

Subspecies and female plumages may be illustrated where they differ sufficiently to be recognized under field conditions. Small differences may not be illustrated but are usually mentioned in the text. In general, juvenile plumages are not shown. When a juvenile plumage (or older immature/first-year plumage) is retained for most of a year, as with raptors, some waders, and boreal migrants, these plumages are discussed and often illustrated.

TERMINOLOGY USED IN THE FIELD GUIDE

Abundance

The terms—common, fairly common, uncommon (or scarce) and rare—are subjective and will mean different things to different observers. In general, they are indicative of how likely a reasonably experienced observer is to encounter a species visually or vocally, but may also provide some indication of a bird's numerical abundance. An obvious caveat is that small birds will usually occur in greater numbers than large birds, so the terms are intended to reflect relative rather than absolute abundance. In addition, these terms are best used to compare various species within a family or in a similar habitat.

Common: expected almost daily, often in some numbers.
Fairly common: recorded on at least half of all days.
Uncommon: not encountered daily but likely on about a quarter of all field trips.
Rare: from less than a quarter of all trips to only a small number of country records.
Vagrant or accidental: recorded only about 1–3 times in the country.
Erratic: denotes a migrant or species with large fluctuations in numbers.
Hypothetical: a species that lacks documented evidence (e.g. photo, audio or specimen) of occurrence; denoted by square brackets.
Local: a function of locating appropriate habitat; also may be due to habitat fragmentation or disturbance, and in some cases a reflection of the fact that the bird's specific requirements may, as yet, simply not be well known to the author.
Status unknown: used when knowledge of a species is inadequate, but does not necessarily imply the species is rare; used especially for some seabirds whose presence or seasonal occurrence in Colombian waters is poorly documented.

Foraging behaviour

Behavioural information is brief and varies widely by family or even within a family. Common foraging terms include:

Aerial hawking: sallying to the air.
Perch-gleaning: glean while perched.
Sally: fly out to capture prey in air, on a physical substrate, or ground.
Sally-strike: sally to physical substrate, e.g. a leaf.
Hover-glean: momentary pause in air, hovering, to take fruit or other food item.
Glean (also perch-glean): capturing prey from a physical surface while perched.
Still-hunt: alternately perch and watch, then move; applied to raptors.
Stoop: dive from the air.

ABBREVIATIONS USED IN THE FIELD GUIDE

N	north
S	south
E	east
W	west
C	central
NE	north-east
NW	north-west
SE	south-east
SW	south-west
NC	north-central
SC	south-central
EC	east-central
WC	west-central
Ad/ad	adult
Subad	subadult
br	breeding plumage
non-br	non-breeding plumage
Juv/juv	juvenile
Imm/imm	immature
1st-y/1st-w	first-year/first-winter (plumages), etc.
km	kilometres
m	metres
cm	centimetres
"	inches
I	Island
Is	Islands

MAP KEY

Resident/present all-year round.

Breeding visitor; known to breed in Colombia but not present year-round.

Winter/Non-breeding visitor: indicates zones occupied by the species outside of the breeding season. Where it is possible to delimit the ranges occupied by subspecies that do not breed in Colombia, but only visit the country, this has been attempted.

Passage migrant: indicates areas used by a species only when moving between breeding and non-breeding ranges; but only when such regions are particularly well known are these mapped. Areas where the species might be seen or occasionally appears on migration are not mapped, but may be highlighted in the text.

Introduced: populations either wholly or partially the result of actions by humans, both deliberately introduced or the product of escapes from captivity.

Best-guess ranges of recently extinct (or probably extinct) species in the region; usually the last known areas, rather than the entire historical distribution. Note that mountain ranges are shown in a paler grey (see sample map below).

A B Resident or breeding subspecies; letters correspond to those in superscript in the relevant text.

A B Winter/non-breeding subspecies; letters correspond to those in superscript in the relevant text.

Boundaries between different resident or breeding subspecies.

Potential boundaries between different resident or breeding subspecies whose distributional limits are especially poorly known.

Indicates that a taxon is suspected to occupy a larger range than is presently known.

Highlighting presence within certain small, well-circumscribed areas. Keep in mind that very small pockets of distribution are often deliberately amplified on the maps, to enable readers to see them more easily.

? Highlighting historical collection but current status unknown, or species whose modern status is uncertain.

? Highlights that the subspecies present in the relevant region is uncertain or unknown.

E Endemic.

NE Near-endemic.

19

BIRD TOPOGRAPHY

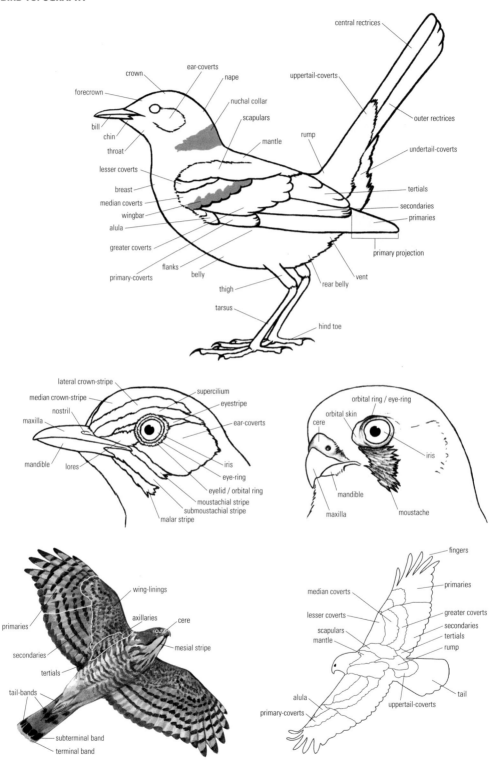

ABOUT THE AUTHOR

Steven L. Hilty

Steve received his Ph.D. in Zoology from the University of Arizona and is currently a Research Associate in Ornithology at the Biodiversity Institute & Natural History Museum of the University of Kansas. He has worked as a birding guide for Victor Emanuel Nature Tours (VENT) since 1983, leading tours throughout North and South America, and co-leading trips to India, the Orient and Australasia. Currently his tour schedule is filled with interesting trips to different areas of Colombia.

Steve is an ornithologist and senior author of *A Guide to the Birds of Colombia* and author of *Birds of Venezuela* and *Birds of Tropical America: A Watcher's Introduction to Behavior, Breeding, and Diversity*. He also wrote the tanager chapter for Vol. 16 of Lynx Edicions' *Handbook of the Birds of the World*. Steve has published many scientific papers and has described two bird species new to science in Venezuela, and another with a team of colleagues in Colombia.

ACKNOWLEDGEMENTS

A book of this scope cannot be written without the input of many people. Foremost is Josep del Hoyo, of Lynx Edicions, who gave me the opportunity to tackle this project and agreed to many departures from previous Lynx style, presentation and taxonomy. From the outset I have had superb support from everyone at Lynx, including project coordinators Amy Chernasky and Arnau Bonan-Barfull, and cartographer Anna Motis, all who have worked tirelessly to see this project to conclusion. I also thank Marc Olivé for critically cross-checking page proofs, and Guy Kirwan for skilful editing. Alex Mascarell and Francesc Jutglar prepared new illustrations, and attended to endless improvements of other illustrations; Alex Mascarell also produced the images of flying birds. The striking cover illustration was prepared by Ilian Velikov using reference photos by Jaime Andrés Herrera-Villarreal. I extend my appreciation to the many highly skilled persons in layout and production, especially Daniel Roca for stunning layout and arrangement of the material, and Gustavo A. Rodríguez, Nárgila Moura and Juan F. Freile for some initial text material and taxonomic comments. Christian Jofré expertly produced the base maps for the inside covers. Chris Sharpe sent material on Colombia's Caribbean islands. Guy Kirwan, in addition to editing, also provided information on these islands' birds, helped categorize the status of vagrants, hypotheticals, endemic and near-endemic species, and searched the literature that documented several new species for Colombia's bird list. I thank Luis Fernando Castillo of Asociación Calidris for valuable input and contributions to the Bird Conservation in Colombia section in the Introductory material.

Two resources have been extremely valuable in the production of this guide. The first is the Xeno-canto library of sound-recordings, which has been used frequently to check or verify vocalizations.

The second, Cornell's Lab of Ornithology, with its incomparable *Birds of the World* website, Macaulay Library for sound-recordings, photos and videos, and massive eBird database, has been of enormous value.

I also thank the many Colombian guides with whom I have had the privilege of working over the last ten years or more, several of whom now operate Colombian birding and natural history companies of their own. These guides include Luis Eduardo Urueña, Christian Daza, Hernán Arias, Alejandro Pinto, Diana Balcázar Niño, Diego Cueva, Gabriel Utría, Iván Lau, Yesennia Tapasco, Leopoldina Tapasco, José Albeiro Uribe Rodríguez, Gilberto Collazos, Juan Carlos Luna, José Luis Pushaina Epiayu, Balmes Mabel Mosquera Lima, Daniel Camilo Orjuela, Michael Antonio Molina-Cruz, Edilson Rosero Chates, Hernán Álvarez, Christian Flórez, Jonathan Sequeda, Dayber Hernández, Marcela Cabanzo, Vinicio E. Góngora Fuenmayor, William & Carlos Bran Castrillón, Eibar Algarra Sánchez, León Emilio Sanchez, and the late Carlos Rivas (Chu).

A large number of contributors have uploaded thousands of birding trip reports, photos, videos and sound-recordings to Cornell's eBird platform or to Xeno-canto. Their records, especially when accompanied by photos and sound-recordings, have been extremely helpful in map development, verifying the locations for specific and even the subspecific identity of birds, and for checking vocalizations. Especially valuable have been the records, photos and audio-recordings of Jorge Muñoz Garcia, Brayan Coral Jaramillo, Daniel Uribe-Restrepo, Edwin Múnera, Andrés Cuervo, Iván Lau, Vinicio E. Góngora Fuenmayor, Yanira Cifuentes-Sarmiento, Carlos Ruíz-Guerra, Gabriel Utría Ortega, Diego Calderón-Franco, J. L. Peña, Ottavio Janni, Nicole Desnoyers, Fábio Olmos, Jurgen Beckers, Daniel Orozco Montoya, Alejandro Pinto, Christian Daza, Luis Eduardo Urueña, Johana Zuluaga-Bonilla, Diego Carantón, Gleison Fernando Guarín Largo, Wilmer Andrés Ramírez Riaño, Diego Rocha López, Johnnier Arango-B., Sergio León, Shtid Tapasco, Gustavo Bravo, Elvis Felipe Quintero Quintero, Rodolfo Dodero, José Castaño, Orlando Acevedo-Charry, José Luna Solarte, Jorge Avendaño, Sergio Ocampo-Tobón, Pablo Flórez, Felipe Estela, Christian Trejos, Christian Flórez-Paí, Arnulfo Sanchez, Juan Carlos

Luna, Ronald Parra, Santiago Pérez, Ferney Salgado Coraves, Carlos Mario Wagner, Julio Delgado, Tatiana Botero J., Sebastian Pérez-Peña, Juan Pablo Arboleda, Roger Rodríguez Ardila, Juan Lopez Z., Luis Carlos Mora Medina, Alejandro Nagy, Luisa Fernanda Chávez Paz, Diana Patricia Deaza, Otto Valerio, Oswaldo Cortés, Luís Germán Naranjo, Rob Felix, Avery Bartels, Peter Boesman, Chris Bell, Glenn Seeholzer, Jerome Fisher, Niels Krabbe, Justyn Stahl, Chris Bell, Andrew Spenser, Trevor Ellery, Thomas Donegan, Miles McMullen, Nick Bayly, Fabrice Schmidt, Ben Freeman, and doubtless many more whose names I may have forgotten or omitted but whose contributions, no matter how large or small, are gratefully acknowledged.

I thank F. Gary Stiles for invitations to participate in two Colombian ornithological congresses, for answering numerous questions and for allowing me to work in the bird collection at the Universidad Nacional de Colombia. Loreta Rosselli provided information on various publications, Andrés Cuervo supplied photos and manuscript references, David Ricardo Rodríguez Villamil assisted with information regarding the Santa María area, and Luis Eduardo Urueña and Diana Balcázar Niño provided Spanish names for certain Colombian birds. Paul Sweet (American Museum of Natural History, New York), Nate Rice (Academy of Natural Sciences, Philadelphia) and Gary Graves (National Museum of Natural History, Washington, D.C.) answered taxonomic questions or checked specimens, and Thomas Donegan's annual updates and avifaunal publications were very helpful. I also acknowledge, during my earliest years working in Colombia, the generous help of the late F. Carlos Lehman, the assistance of the CVC (Corporación Autónoma del Valle del Cauca) in Cali, and encouragement from Jorge Orejuela, Peter Jennings, and the late José Ignacio Borrero.

Over the years many people have helped with support, logistics and related travel activities; in particular I thank Jovani Flórez, Andréa Borras, Diana Balcázar Niño, Angela Gómez, Tomás Dario, Juan F. Conde, Sergio Ocampo-Tobón and Katty Ropero. I also thank Carlos Mario Wagner for the opportunity to participate in the 2016 Colombia Birdfair de Cali.

I am especially grateful to Victor Emanuel of Victor Emanuel Nature Tours (VENT) who has, for nearly 40 years, provided me with an opportunity to travel and guide widely in Latin America and elsewhere worldwide. This included initially offering Colombia birding trips from 1982 to 1986 and later, with encouragement from Sergio Ocampo-Tobón and the logistical support of Manakin Nature Tours, the re-initiation of VENT trips starting in 2009 and continuing to the present.

My initial research in Colombia began in 1971 and continued until 1986, when internal events made travel in the field difficult. After an 18-year hiatus I returned in 2004 to attend Colombia's first ornithological congress and discovered an astonishing groundswell of interest among Colombians, especially younger generations, in the birds and environment of their country. Today it is particularly gratifying to see that this 'explosion' of interest has not only continued but accelerated.

With a well-established national parks system administered by Parques Nacionales Naturales de Colombia (PNN), and numerous private reserves, it is now possible to explore many sites once difficult or impossible to visit. And, from just one or two international companies offering a few limited birding adventures in Colombia years ago, I have witnessed a remarkable transformation that now involves numerous 'home-grown' Colombian birding and ecotourism companies offering access to sites once just a dream. And, with these companies, there has evolved a growing cadre of extremely capable and enthusiastic students, guides and professionals in various disciplines who are passionate about birds, wildlife and the incredible biological riches of their country. Whether they are aware of it or not, they have all played a role in the development of this book, and they provide a beacon of hope for the future.

Last, and most importantly, I thank my wife Beverly, for accompanying me during two initial years in Colombia, and for her steadfast support and encouragement through the years, raising our daughters, often alone, when I was travelling, and for help in ways far too numerous to mention. She has been a quiet but essential partner in helping me see this project to completion.

BIRDLIFE INTERNATIONAL

BirdLife International is a global partnership of conservation organizations (NGOs) that strives to conserve birds, their habitats and global biodiversity, working with people towards sustainability in the use of natural resources. Together we are over 100 BirdLife Partners worldwide—one per country or territory—and growing.

We are driven by our belief that local people, working for nature in their own places but connected nationally and internationally via our global Partnership, are the key to sustaining all life on this planet. This unique local-to-global approach delivers high-impact and long-term conservation for the benefit of nature and people.

BirdLife is widely recognized as the world leader in bird conservation. Rigorous science informed by practical feedback from projects on the ground in important sites and habitats enables us to implement successful conservation programmes for birds and all nature. Our actions are providing both practical and sustainable solutions significantly benefiting nature and people.

The Lynx and BirdLife International Field Guides project came to life after years of conversations motivated by a shared idea between Lynx and BirdLife that the existence of country field guides is a basic element for the 'emergence' and education of birdwatchers, ornithologists, bird guides and naturalists in any country, which, in turn, has important repercussions for the conservation of nature and biodiversity, both locally and globally.

In addition to the principal goal of the collection to produce modern, standardized field guides, especially for countries without any recent or country-level guide, we have a secondary goal of publishing a number of the titles in their local languages, to enhance the impacts of the work.

Apart from sharing and promoting the important vision of the collection, BirdLife also collaborates on the field guides via application of the systematics and taxonomy of the *HBW and BirdLife International Illustrated Checklist of the Birds of the World*. Of course, the global conservation status for each species in the collection reflects the current version of the IUCN Red List, for which BirdLife International acts as the authority for birds.

SPECIES ACCOUNTS

TINAMIDAE
Tinamous
48 extant species, 18 in region

Tinamous are terrestrial birds of Central and South America. They have plump bodies, small heads, rounded wings and short tails. Colombian species occur inside forest and are often heard but infrequently seen. Sex roles are reversed (polyandry); ♀♀ mate with several ♂♂, and the latter independently incubate the eggs and care for the precocial young. Nests are leafy depressions on the ground.

Genus *Nothocercus* Medium-sized terrestrial species of mossy Andean forests; seen even less often than lowland tinamous.

Tawny-breasted Tinamou *Nothocercus julius* `LC`
Tinamú Leonado
Uncommon resident.

 L 39 cm (15.5"). Monotypic. Floor of humid and wet montane forest. 2300–3100 m (rarely 1700–3500 m). Solitary or widely scattered pairs; occasionally emerges onto forest trails at dawn. **ID** Rich rufous-brown, head brighter, throat white, rear parts obscurely barred black (buff on wings). **Voice** Long series (to 30 seconds) of blurred trills "t'r'r'r'a, t'r'r'r'a...", faster than c. 1 phrase/second, fading at end; far-carrying; mostly at dawn. **SS** Highland Tinamou.

Highland Tinamou *Nothocercus bonapartei* `LC`
Tinamú Montañero
Uncommon resident.

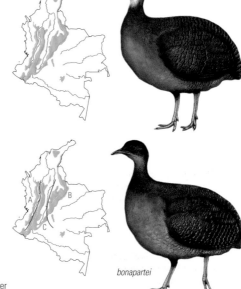 **L** 39 cm (15.5"). Races *intercedens*[A], *bonapartei*[B], *discrepans*[C]. 1500–2200 m (rarely 700 m). Floor of humid and wet montane forest. Solitary or scattered pairs. **ID** Mainly dark rufous-brown, crown and nape blackish, throat buff, rear parts obscurely barred black. **Voice** Infrequently heard loud nasal honking "tuy-onk" 3–4 times, sometimes steadily repeated c. 1/second for a minute or more. **SS** Tawny-breasted Tinamou mostly occurs higher; Little Tinamou lower.

bonapartei

Genus *Tinamus* Medium to large species of humid lowland to lower montane forest; rear toe rudimentary. Roost on low branches. Frequently heard; difficult to see.

Grey Tinamou *Tinamus tao* `VU`
Tinamú Gris
Scarce and local resident.

 L 46 cm (18"). Races *larensis*[A], *kleei*[B]. To 1900 m. Humid lowland, foothill and montane forest. Solitary; distribution spotty, poorly known. **ID** Large; freckled blackish band across cheeks and down sides of neck; otherwise above dark olive-grey, below greyish brown, obscurely vermiculated and barred throughout. **Voice** Infrequently at dawn, dusk or at night, single low (c. 1.6 kHz) whistle "wuuuuuu" at 5–8-second intervals, slightly tremulous, fading. **SS** Great Tinamou; Black Tinamou call even lower-pitched.

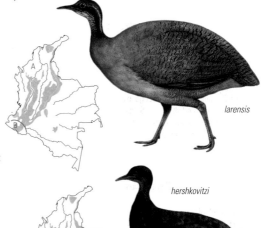

larensis

hershkovitzi

Black Tinamou *Tinamus osgoodi* `VU`
Tinamú Negro `EN`
Rare and local resident.

 **L** 41 cm (16"). Race *hershkovitzi*. 800–2100 m. Humid premontane and montane forest. Solitary, secretive; known from only a few verified sites. **ID** Bill dusky yellow, legs yellowish grey; plumage sooty black, thighs and vent tinged brownish. **Voice** Most vocal Mar–Apr, least Jul–Dec (S Colombia); call 1–3 or up to six very low (1.0 kHz) hollow melancholy notes, first drawn-out, a pause, rest slowly descending; recalls Great Tinamou but weaker, less melodic. ♀ longer tremulous higher notes. **SS** Great and Grey Tinamous.

Great Tinamou *Tinamus major*
Tinamú Grande
Fairly common resident.

 L 43 cm (17"). Races *saturatus*[A], *latifrons*[B], *zuliensis*[C], *peruvianus*[D]. To 1500 m. Humid lowland and lower montane forest, older second growth. Solitary; retiring; if surprised may flush with flurry of wing noise, or more often freezes or creeps away slowly. **ID** Large; brownish, rufescent head, few or no markings above. **Voice** Song, especially dusk, loud rich hauntingly beautiful, typically 1–2 brief tremulous whistles, then 6+ long, rich tremulous whistles, swelling in volume, notes typically in pairs; lower-pitched, more resonant than Little Tinamou. **SS** Other *Tinamus*.

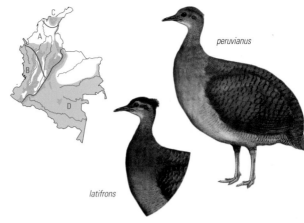

peruvianus

latifrons

White-throated Tinamou *Tinamus guttatus*
Tinamú Gorgiblanco
Fairly common and local resident.

 L 34 cm (13.5"). Monotypic. Humid *terra firme* forest, occasionally *várzea*. To 500 m. Behaviour like Great Tinamou; feeds on fallen fruit. **ID** Relatively large; white-spotted upperparts unique. **Voice** Low slow mournful "huuuuuuu … huuua", second note quavering, after 1–2-second pause, upslurred; mainly dawn and dusk. **SS** Great Tinamou.

Genus *Crypturellus* Small- to medium-sized tinamous of dry to humid lowlands and foothills; one (Brown Tinamou) in montane forest. Slaty to boldly barred; note leg and head colours, and voice.

Berlepsch's Tinamou *Crypturellus berlepschi*
Tinamú de Berlepsch
Uncommon and possibly local resident.

 L 28 cm (11"). Monotypic. Near-endemic (also far NW Ecuador). Humid and wet lowland forest, dense second growth. To 500 m; rarely 900 m. Singles; furtive. **ID** Fairly small; blackish plumage unique in Pacific range; eyes yellowish, mandible dull reddish orange, legs dark reddish. **Voice** Single thin high-pitched whistle (unlike other tinamous), at 10–30-second intervals. **SS** Little Tinamou; Choco Tinamou much paler below, legs brighter red.

Cinereous Tinamou *Crypturellus cinereus*
Tinamú Cenizo
Common resident.

 L 30 cm (12"). Monotypic. To 500 m. Dense undergrowth of young to old second growth, *várzea* forest and adjacent overgrown pastures, gallery forest. Unlike Undulated Tinamou seldom emerges from cover. **ID** Dark sooty brown, virtually unmarked; belly and vent rufescent; legs greyish. **Voice** Often quite vocal; single slightly tremulous whistle (recalls Sunbittern), easily imitated. **SS** No other medium-sized Amazonian tinamou is so dark.

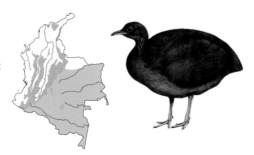

Little Tinamou *Crypturellus soui* `LC`
Tinamú Chico

Locally fairly common resident.

 L 23 cm (9"). Races *panamensis*[A], *harterti*[B], *caucae*[C], *mustelinus*[D], *soui*[E], *caquetae*[F]; *nigriceps* (R Putumayo?). To 2000 m. Thickets in young to old second growth, forest borders, plantations; dry to humid areas. **ID** Small; plumage variable, brighter in ♀, both sexes largely unmarked; crown sooty, sides of head greyish, throat pale, foreneck and chest rich rufous, paler more ochre on belly. **Voice** Dusk song, several quavering notes rising, accelerating a little; recalls Great Tinamou but less melodic, notes unpaired; frequent day song a single quavering rising note, abruptly dropping at end. **SS** Other *Crypturellus*.

soui ♀

♂

Brown Tinamou *Crypturellus obsoletus* `LC`
Tinamú Pardo

Rare resident (few records).

 L 28 cm (11"). Races *castaneus*[A], *knoxi*[B]. 1000–2200 m (to 2700 m?). Humid montane forest; E slope of E Andes (?). **ID** Sides of head and throat grey, crown darker, otherwise above dark brown, below rich rufous-brown, lower underparts narrowly barred blackish; eyes yellow to dark orange. **Voice** Infrequent slurred whistles "peeeeu..puu-pu", same pitch, slightly tremulous, last note brief, *castaneus* (Boyacá); or long series of tremulous whistles (like police whistle), hesitant, gradually accelerating, rising, frantic at end, *knoxi* (Mérida, Venezuela). **SS** Highland Tinamou.

castaneus

Undulated Tinamou *Crypturellus undulatus* `LC`
Tinamú Ondulado

Common resident.

 L 30 cm (12"). Race *yapura*. *Várzea* and gallery forest, large river islands, wet low-lying second growth. To 1400 m. Often emerges onto open trails at dawn. During high water departs flooded river islands, flying 1 km or more over water to higher ground. **ID** Above plain dull brown, throat whitish; below greyish, paler than allies; faintly barred flanks and vent; eyes pale brown. **Voice** Song, day and night during peak low-water breeding, resonant rhythmic "whuu, hu, huu-hu", last note sliding upward. **SS** Cinereous Tinamou.

yapura

Grey-legged Tinamou *Crypturellus duidae* `NT`
Tinamú Patigrís

Poorly known resident.

 L 30 cm (12"). Monotypic. White sandy soil forest; borders; bushy savanna woodland. To 400 m. **ID** Medium size; rufous head and foreparts, barred vent. **Voice** Single medium-pitched two-part whistle, c. 2 seconds, "wuuuuwooouuuu", melancholy, last half stronger. **SS** Little, Undulated, Rusty and Great Tinamous.

Red-legged Tinamou *Crypturellus erythropus* `LC`
Tinamú Patirrojo

Rare and declining resident (poorly known W of Andes).

 L 30 cm (12"). Races *columbianus*[A], *saltuarius*[B], *idoneus*[C], *cursitans*[D]. Dry to moist forest, scrub; lowlands and foothills W of Andes; gallery forest in *llanos* (easier to see). To 1000 m. Range now fragmented. **ID** Reddish legs; overall rufescent brown, contrasting grey wash on chest (varies with race); or paler, lower underparts buffy whitish (*saltuarius*). **Voice** In all areas, low-pitched, whistled "wuuuu-who-who", last two notes slightly higher. Vocal in dry months in *llanos* (Venezuela). **SS** Little Tinamou. **TN** Races *columbianus*, *saltuarius* and *idoneus* sometimes regarded as separate species, Magdalena, Colombian and Santa Marta Tinamous respectively, but songs apparently similar and plumages clinal.

Choco Tinamou *Crypturellus kerriae* `VU`
Tinamú del Chocó `VU`

Poorly known resident.

 L 30 cm (12"). Monotypic. Near-endemic (also extreme SE Panama). Humid and wet foothill forest. 100–800 m. **ID** Reddish legs. ♂ dark grey crown and foreneck, dull rufous-brown breast, buff lower underparts strongly barred. ♀ foreparts to mid-breast dark grey. **Voice** Low-pitched slow three-syllable whistle, last note sliding upward (recalls Red-legged Tinamou). **SS** Little Tinamou; Berlepsch's Tinamou (overlap?).

Variegated Tinamou *Crypturellus variegatus* `LC`
Tinamú Variegado

Fairly common resident.

 L 33 cm (13"). Monotypic. Humid *terra firme* forest. To 500 m. Solitary; apt to freeze or creep away slowly, rather than fly, if discovered. **ID** Above boldly barred rufous and black, head to below eyes contrasting slaty grey to blackish, neck and breast rufous, flanks and vent much paler buff to whitish barred dusky; legs yellowish. **Voice** Mostly vespertine song 1–2 melancholy tremulous drawn-out whistles, a 2–3-second pause, then up to 12 quicker ascending notes. **SS** Rusty, Barred and Bartlett's Tinamous.

Rusty Tinamou *Crypturellus brevirostris* `LC`
Tinamú Ferruginoso

Status unknown.

 L 28 cm (11"). Monotypic. One presumed sight record (Serranía de Naquén, Guainía); humid white sandy soil forest. To 200 m. **ID** Much like Variegated Tinamou but head rufescent brown (not blackish), legs duller. **Voice** Recalls Variegated Tinamou; song 1–3 well-spaced whistles, a pause, then long series of short gradually accelerating, then slowing whistles (30+ seconds). **SS** Barred Tinamou (greyish white below). **TN** Possibly a race of Bartlett's Tinamou.

columbianus

idoneus

saltuarius

[Bartlett's Tinamou *Crypturellus bartletti*] LC
Tinamú de Bartlett
Hypothetical.

 L 24 cm (9.5"). Monotypic. Likely in S Putumayo and Amazonas; lowland *terra firme* forest. **ID** Plumage variable, above brownish to tawny-rufous, head darker sooty brown, back and wing-coverts barred buff to rufous, throat whitish, foreneck and breast greyish brown to bright tawny, lower underparts paler, flanks and vent barred dusky; legs olive-yellow; base of mandible olive-yellow. **Voice** Several well-spaced rich whistles (5–8 seconds apart), then several gradually rising accelerating whistles; recalls Variegated Tinamou. **SS** Rusty Tinamou.

Barred Tinamou *Crypturellus casiquiare* LC
Tinamú Barrado
Poorly known resident.

 L 25 cm (10"). Monotypic. Near-endemic (also adjacent S Venezuela). Humid white sandy soil forest. To 350 m. **ID** Rufous head; above boldly barred rufous and black; underparts divided, throat white; foreneck and breast greyish white, belly whitish, slight flank barring. **Voice** Song, up to c. 40 seconds (Amazonas, Venezuela), steady series of pure whistles on same pitch or very slightly rising, then slowing, diminishing. **SS** No other overlapping tinamou is so pale below. Variegated and Rusty Tinamous.

Curve-billed Tinamou *Nothoprocta curvirostris* LC
Tinamú Piquicurvo
Local resident.

 L 28 cm (11"). Race *curvirostris*. High-elevation grassland, scrubby woodland, *páramo*, agricultural areas near treeline. 3000–4000 m. Flushes reluctantly; may forage along edges at dawn. **ID** Small; brownish crest; cryptically patterned above, rich buff lower underparts, yellowish legs, pointed slightly decurved bill, rufous on inner flight feathers visible as flushes. **Voice** Sharp metallic scraping "skEEEZ, ip-ip-ip, ip", c. 5.5 kHz. **SS** Only treeline tinamou in Colombia.

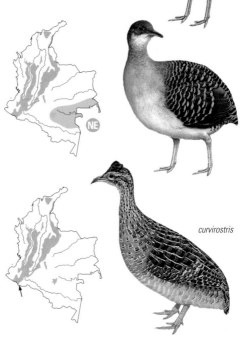

curvirostris

CRACIDAE
Guans, Chachalacas and Curassows
55 extant species, 25 in region

Cracids are an ancient group of Neotropical birds. Guans and chachalacas are primarily arboreal and feed heavily on fruit and flowers. Curassows are terrestrial but roost and seek safety in trees, and feed on fallen fruit, seeds and animal matter. Vocalizations differ dramatically; chachalacas give loud dawn choruses; guans whistle and have rattling wing displays; curassows produce humming sounds that are among the lowest among birds. In Colombia cracids have declined dramatically, in some areas having disappeared completely.

Sickle-winged Guan *Chamaepetes goudotii* LC
Pava Maraquera
Fairly common resident.

 L 51–64 cm (20–25"). Races *sanctaemarthae*[A], *goudotii*[B], *fagani*[C], *tschudii*[D]. Humid and wet montane forest, older second growth. 800–3000 m (500 m, Pacific slope). Pairs or 3–5; mid-levels to canopy, occasionally on ground. **ID** Blue facial skin, chestnut underparts, no dewlap; *tschudii* larger, more extensively rufous below; *fagani* darkest overall. **Voice** Short dawn wing-rattle display by gliding between tree branches; also thin high whistles; alarm, loud, harsh honking "KEE-uck". **SS** Andean, Band-tailed and Baudo Guans.

goudotii

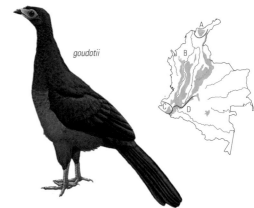

Genus *Penelope* Arboreal. Red dewlap, bare slaty-blue ocular area, and white-streaked foreparts. Curved outer primaries narrow at tips and enable loud wing-rattle displays within or between trees. Loud honking alarm.

argyrotis

Band-tailed Guan *Penelope argyrotis* `LC`
Pava Canosa
Fairly common resident.

 L 66 cm (26"). Races *albicauda*[A], *colombiana*[B], *argyrotis*[C]. Humid montane forest. 500–2800 m. Pairs or small groups; mid-levels to canopy. **ID** Whitish brow, rufescent rear parts, pale brown tail tips diagnostic but obscure. **Voice** Generally quiet but noisy when breeding (first half of year); in pre-dawn darkness 3–4 hollow squealing upslurred whistles "whoooe, woooee, woeeee"; single wing-rattles in short glide. **SS** Andean, Spix's and (larger) Crested Guans.

colombiana

Baudo Guan *Penelope ortoni* `EN`
Pava del Baudó `VU`
Uncommon and local resident.

 L 66 cm (26"). Monotypic. Near-endemic (also NW Ecuador). Wet mossy foothill and premontane forest. To 1500 m. Pairs or small groups. **ID** Small dark guan, lacks strong markings; head uniformly dark, small red dewlap, white-streaked underparts. **Voice** Two-part wing-rattle notably slow, second part short; call, guttural "waou"; loud honking alarm. **SS** Crested Guan much larger, rear parts rufescent; Sickle-winged Guan.

Andean Guan *Penelope montagnii* `LC`
Pava Andina
Locally common resident.

montagnii

 L 58 cm (24"). Races *montagnii*[A], *atrogularis*[B], *brooki*[C]. Humid and wet montane forest, second growth, patches of woodland to treeline. 2200–3700 m. Pairs or groups, occasionally up to 12; usually high in trees, occasionally low or on ground. **ID** Small and sturdy; red dewlap inconspicuous, prominent whitish (grizzled) eyebrows. **Voice** Soft wheezy squeals when disturbed; loud harsh alarm notes; single low "cluck" precedes slow single wing-rattle display during short glide. **SS** Smaller and at higher elevations than most allies.

Spix's Guan *Penelope jacquacu* `LC`
Pava Llanera

 Four subspecies in two subspecies groups; one in Colombia.

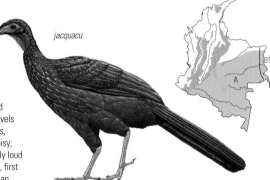
jacquacu

Spix's Guan *Penelope (jacquacu) jacquacu*
Fairly common resident.
L 81 cm (32"). Races *jacquacu*[A], *orienticola*[B] (E Vichada?). Humid lowland forest. To 500 m (higher?). Pairs or small groups; mid-levels to canopy, seldom on ground. **ID** Large; white-streaked foreparts, rufescent rump and vent, bronzy wings and tail. **Voice** Often noisy; at dawn and dusk powerful honking "Q'OOEEE"; alarm startlingly loud "CA-OOU!"; in short pre-dawn or dusk glide, double wing-rattle, first brief, slow and heavy, second longer, faster. **SS** Band-tailed Guan.

Crested Guan *Penelope purpurascens* LC
Pava Moñuda

Uncommon and local resident.

 L 89 cm (35"). Races *aequatorialis*[A], *brunnescens*[B]. Humid lowland and foothill forest. To 1000 m (rarely 1500 m). **ID** Quite large; rufescent rear parts, bushy crest, large red dewlap, white-streaked foreneck and breast. **Voice** Whistles, muffled barks, grunts when disturbed; loud honking alarm; at dawn powerful whistle and growling "kuLEEE-rrr"; slow two-part wing-rattle display in short pre-dawn glide. **SS** Much larger than other *Penelope*.

brunnescens

Cauca Guan *Penelope perspicax* EN
Pava Caucana EN

Common but very local resident.

 L 74 cm (29"). Monotypic. Endemic. Humid montane forest, borders, older second growth. 1200–2200 m. Now restricted mostly to isolated forest patches. Singles, pairs or several gather in canopy of fruiting trees, occasionally low or on ground. Unsuspicious where not persecuted. **ID** Large; conspicuous red dewlap, back, wings, rear parts and tail chestnut. **Voice** Loud honks and yelps; drawn-out "kōō'EEL"; rapid (3/second) rising-falling "keea…" if disturbed; single rumbling wing-rattle is protracted. **SS** Andean Guan.

Blue-throated Piping-guan *Pipile cumanensis* LC
Pava Rajadora

Fairly common but declining resident.

 L 71 cm (28"). Monotypic. Humid *terra firme* and *várzea* forest, now mostly in remote areas. To 500 m. Highly arboreal; pairs or up to 12 in canopy of fruiting trees. **ID** Bare white ocular area, shaggy white crown, large white wing patch; bill light blue tipped black, dewlap blue. **Voice** Vocal when breeding; slow ascending series of thin piping whistles (hence name) day and night; fast two-part wing-rattle display (like cards fanned forward, then back) in short pre-dawn glide. **SS** None.

Wattled Guan *Aburria aburri* NT
Pava Negra NT

Locally fairly common resident.

 L 76 cm (30"). Monotypic. Humid and wet foothill and montane forest. 1200–2500 m (rarely 400 m). Singles, pairs or families; wary, stay concealed by foliage, mid-level to canopy, seldom in open. **ID** Large black guan; bright yellow legs, dangling yellow wattle. **Voice** Sings incessantly day and night when breeding, buzzy whirring "baaaaarrREEEeeer", rising-falling. Infrequent pre-dawn flight display 1–2 wing-claps and two short wing-rattles that sound as if fanned forward, then back (like *Pipile*) during short glide. **SS** None.

Genus *Ortalis* Slender, dull and plain, with small bare red patch either side of throat. Brushy areas and forest borders, mostly at low elevations. Raucous dawn chorus often long-sustained.

Grey-headed Chachalaca *Ortalis cinereiceps* `LC`
Guacharaca del Chocó
Common resident.

L 46–51 cm (18–20"). Monotypic. Humid forest borders, overgrown clearings with thickets and taller trees. To 1700 m. Gregarious. Forages at various heights, infrequently on ground. **ID** Small dull chachalaca; grey head, chestnut primaries, white tail corners. **Voice** Song at dawn, incessant tinny "cha'cha'lock" chorus; like other *Ortalis* but higher-pitched, thinner, lacking clear syncopation and pattern. **SS** Only chachalaca in far NW.

Chestnut-winged Chachalaca *Ortalis garrula* `LC`
Guacharaca Caribeña
Local resident.

L 53 cm (21"). Monotypic. Endemic. Dry woodland, gallery forest, scrubby clearings with thickets and scattered trees, mangroves. Habitat fragmented. To 800 m (rarely 1600 m). Gregarious; noisy at dawn, groups calling in raucous choruses from tops of trees or thickets; quietly disperse during day. **ID** Contrasting chestnut head and primaries, white belly and tail tips. **Voice** Dawn chorus, loud coarse "what-cha-läk" with variations and distinct syncopation. **SS** No other chachalaca shares same range.

Rufous-vented Chachalaca *Ortalis ruficauda* `LC`
Guacharaca Guajira
Common resident.

L 56 cm (22"). Races *ruficrissa*[A], *ruficauda*[B]. Arid scrub, dry to moist woodland and thickets, gallery forest. To 1000 m. Gregarious; vocal in treetops at dawn; lower, quiet, stealthy and in cover by day. **ID** Greyish head, rufous vent, whitish (*ruficrissa*) or rufous tail tips (*ruficauda*). **Voice** Dawn choruses brief or last hours as groups yell; ♂ loud "OTRA MAS", ♀ higher "WATCH-a läk" in antiphonal duet with distinct rhythm. **SS** E of Andes meets Speckled Chachalaca.

ruficauda

ruficrissa

Rufous-headed Chachalaca *Ortalis erythroptera* `VU`
Guacharaca Cabecirrufa `NT`
Uncommon and local resident.

L 58 cm (23"). Monotypic. Dry deciduous woodland, moist forest, second growth. To 300 m (higher in Ecuador). Recent expansion into Colombia following deforestation. Small groups at various heights; persists even in settled areas if not persecuted. **ID** Plain; rufous head, rufous flight feathers and outer tail tips, lower underparts whitish. **Voice** Loud cacophonous groups at dawn or variously by day. Harsh rhythmically repeated three-note song resembles other *Ortalis* but delivery slower. **SS** None.

Colombian Chachalaca *Ortalis columbiana* `LC`
Guacharaca Colombiana
Locally common resident.

 L 56 cm (22"). Monotypic. Endemic. Dry to humid woodland, second growth, thickets and shrubby borders. Range now fragmented but survives in degraded habitat and settled areas if not persecuted. 300–2200 m. **ID** Scaly foreneck and breast, rufous tail tip. **Voice** Rhythmic three-note dawn chorus by pairs and groups is like other *Ortalis* but unusually harsh and loud. **SS** Only chachalaca in drier Cauca and Magdalena drainages.

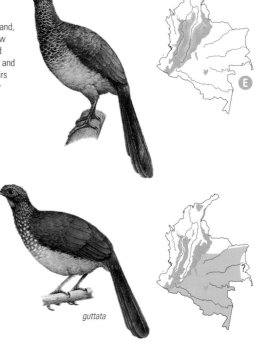

Speckled Chachalaca *Ortalis guttata* `LC`
Guacharaca Variable
Common resident.

 L 51 cm (20"). Race *guttata*. Humid lowland and foothill forest borders, tall river-edge vegetation, second growth on river islands. To 1500 m (occasionally higher). **ID** Small chachalaca; scaly or spotted foreparts and breast. **Voice** Dawn chorus as in other chachalacas but less vocal (seasonal?) than allies. Dawn choruses antiphonal, one singer uttering two harsh initial notes, a partner follows with triplet, "RAJ-RAJ'Rib-a-Dit" in seamless repetitive and rhythmic chorus; also other calls or partial choruses. **SS** Rufous-vented Chachalaca (overlap?).

guttata

[Variable Chachalaca *Ortalis motmot*] `LC`
Guacharaca Variable
Hypothetical.

 **L** 49 cm (19"). Race *motmot*. May occur along R Orinoco in extreme E Vichada and Guainía. Humid forest borders, second growth, river edges. To 200 m. **ID** From Speckled Chachalaca by contrasting dark rufous head, uniform greyish underparts (no scaling). **Voice** Dawn chorus loud rhythmic "WATCH'a'lak", repeatedly as in other chachalacas although less raucous, often less vocal. **AN** Little Chachalaca.

motmot

Nocturnal Curassow *Nothocrax urumutum* `LC`
Paují Nocturno
Uncommon resident (by voice).

 **L** 63 cm (25"). Monotypic. Tall remote lowland forest, especially hilly *terra firme*, occasionally *várzea*. To 500 m. Pre-dawn or dusk may feed on ground but rarely seen. **ID** Like small *Crax* but all rufous-chestnut; curly black crest, colourful bare ocular skin, red-orange bill. **Voice** A nocturnal voice; sings irregularly throughout night, especially after midnight (moonlit or dark) from mid-levels, or more often high, in large trees where exceedingly difficult to see; far-carrying song of extremely low-pitched humming notes, "hoou, hu-hu, huu-hu-hu… wUUT!", often followed by thin rising "whooooouu". **SS** None.

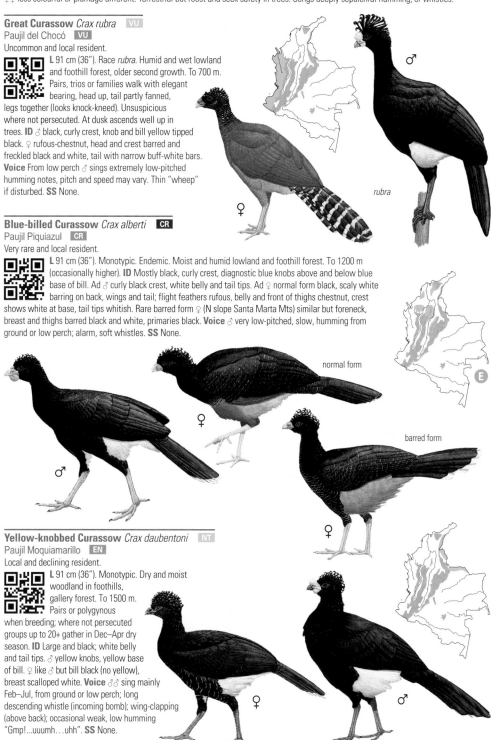

Genus *Crax* Largest cracids. Mostly black, curly crest, and base of bill, cere, sometimes forehead with colourful knobs or protuberances; ♀♀ less colourful or plumage different. Terrestrial but roost and seek safety in trees. Songs deeply sepulchral humming, or whistles.

Great Curassow *Crax rubra* VU

Paujil del Chocó VU

Uncommon and local resident.

L 91 cm (36"). Race *rubra*. Humid and wet lowland and foothill forest, older second growth. To 700 m. Pairs, trios or families walk with elegant bearing, head up, tail partly fanned, legs together (looks knock-kneed). Unsuspicious where not persecuted. At dusk ascends well up in trees. **ID** ♂ black, curly crest, knob and bill yellow tipped black. ♀ rufous-chestnut, head and crest barred and freckled black and white, tail with narrow buff-white bars. **Voice** From low perch ♂ sings extremely low-pitched humming notes, pitch and speed may vary. Thin "wheep" if disturbed. **SS** None.

rubra

Blue-billed Curassow *Crax alberti* CR

Paujil Piquiazul CR

Very rare and local resident.

L 91 cm (36"). Monotypic. Endemic. Moist and humid lowland and foothill forest. To 1200 m (occasionally higher). **ID** Mostly black, curly crest, diagnostic blue knobs above and below blue base of bill. Ad ♂ curly black crest, white belly and tail tips. Ad ♀ normal form black, scaly white barring on back, wings and tail; flight feathers rufous, belly and front of thighs chestnut, crest shows white at base, tail tips whitish. Rare barred form ♀ (N slope Santa Marta Mts) similar but foreneck, breast and thighs barred black and white, primaries black. **Voice** ♂ very low-pitched, slow, humming from ground or low perch; alarm, soft whistles. **SS** None.

normal form

E

barred form

Yellow-knobbed Curassow *Crax daubentoni* NT

Paujil Moquiamarillo EN

Local and declining resident.

L 91 cm (36"). Monotypic. Dry and moist woodland in foothills, gallery forest. To 1500 m. Pairs or polygynous when breeding; where not persecuted groups up to 20+ gather in Dec–Apr dry season. **ID** Large and black; white belly and tail tips. ♂ yellow knobs, yellow base of bill. ♀ like ♂ but bill black (no yellow), breast scalloped white. **Voice** ♂♂ sing mainly Feb–Jul, from ground or low perch; long descending whistle (incoming bomb); wing-clapping (above back); occasional weak, low humming "Gmp!...uuumh...uhh". **SS** None.

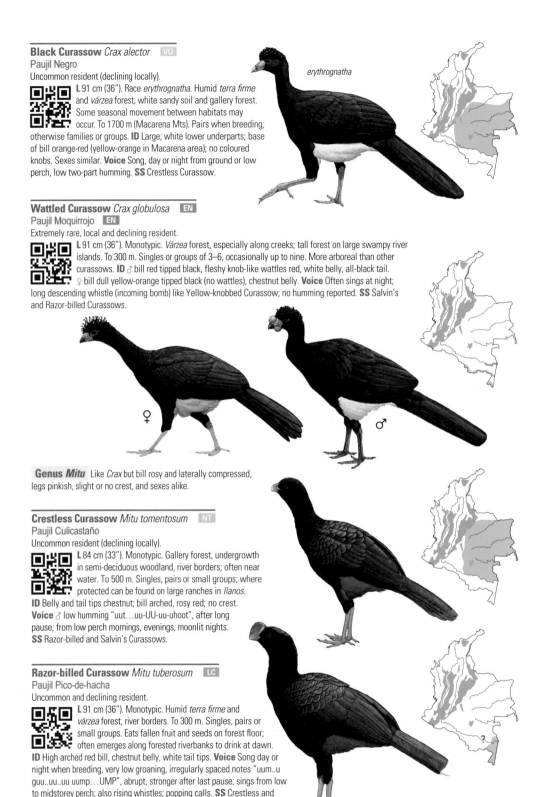

Black Curassow *Crax alector* VU
Paujil Negro
Uncommon resident (declining locally).

erythrognatha

L 91 cm (36"). Race *erythrognatha*. Humid *terra firme* and *várzea* forest, white sandy soil and gallery forest. Some seasonal movement between habitats may occur. To 1700 m (Macarena Mts). Pairs when breeding; otherwise families or groups. **ID** Large; white lower underparts; base of bill orange-red (yellow-orange in Macarena area); no coloured knobs. Sexes similar. **Voice** Song, day or night from ground or low perch, low two-part humming. **SS** Crestless Curassow.

Wattled Curassow *Crax globulosa* EN
Paujil Moquirrojo EN
Extremely rare, local and declining resident.

L 91 cm (36"). Monotypic. *Várzea* forest, especially along creeks; tall forest on large swampy river islands. To 300 m. Singles or groups of 3–6, occasionally up to nine. More arboreal than other curassows. **ID** ♂ bill red tipped black, fleshy knob-like wattles red, white belly, all-black tail. ♀ bill dull yellow-orange tipped black (no wattles), chestnut belly. **Voice** Often sings at night; long descending whistle (incoming bomb) like Yellow-knobbed Curassow; no humming reported. **SS** Salvin's and Razor-billed Curassows.

Genus *Mitu* Like *Crax* but bill rosy and laterally compressed, legs pinkish, slight or no crest, and sexes alike.

Crestless Curassow *Mitu tomentosum* NT
Paujil Culicastaño
Uncommon resident (declining locally).

L 84 cm (33"). Monotypic. Gallery forest, undergrowth in semi-deciduous woodland, river borders; often near water. To 500 m. Singles, pairs or small groups; where protected can be found on large ranches in *llanos*. **ID** Belly and tail tips chestnut; bill arched, rosy red; no crest. **Voice** ♂ low humming "uut…uu-UU-uu-uhoot", after long pause; from low perch mornings, evenings, moonlit nights. **SS** Razor-billed and Salvin's Curassows.

Razor-billed Curassow *Mitu tuberosum* LC
Paujil Pico-de-hacha
Uncommon and declining resident.

L 91 cm (36"). Monotypic. Humid *terra firme* and *várzea* forest, river borders. To 300 m. Singles, pairs or small groups. Eats fallen fruit and seeds on forest floor; often emerges along forested riverbanks to drink at dawn. **ID** High arched red bill, chestnut belly, white tail tips. **Voice** Song day or night when breeding, very low groaning, irregularly spaced notes "uum..u guu..uu..uu uump…UMP", abrupt, stronger after last pause; sings from low to midstorey perch; also rising whistles; popping calls. **SS** Crestless and Salvin's Curassows.

Salvin's Curassow *Mitu salvini* `LC`
Paujil Culiblanco
Uncommon and declining resident.

L 89 cm (35"). Monotypic. Humid *terra firme* and *várzea* forest. To 1100 m. Pairs or families take fallen fruit, seeds, some animal matter. Like other *Mitu*, roost and may rest in trees, usually not very high. **ID** Arched red bill, short curly crest, white belly and tail tips. **Voice** Very low humming or groaning song recalls Razor-billed Curassow but higher-pitched, final notes less emphatic; mostly at dawn or by night. **SS** Black Curassow.

Helmeted Curassow *Pauxi pauxi* `EN`
Paujil Copete-de-piedra `EN`
Rare and severely declining resident.

L 91 cm (36"). Races *gilliardi*[A], *pauxi*[B]. Humid and wet foothill and montane forest; dense vegetation in steep ravines. 700–1800 m. Pairs when breeding, otherwise small groups. Relatively unsuspicious if not persecuted, feeds on fallen fruit, seeds, some green plant material. **ID** Red bill, grey casque (casque smaller, *gilliardi*). ♀ (both races), similar to ♂, or head blackish, body brown finely barred and vermiculated buff and black, tail blackish tipped buff. **Voice** Song, long very low-pitched humming, "um…uUH a umm…umm…". **SS** Yellow-knobbed Curassow.

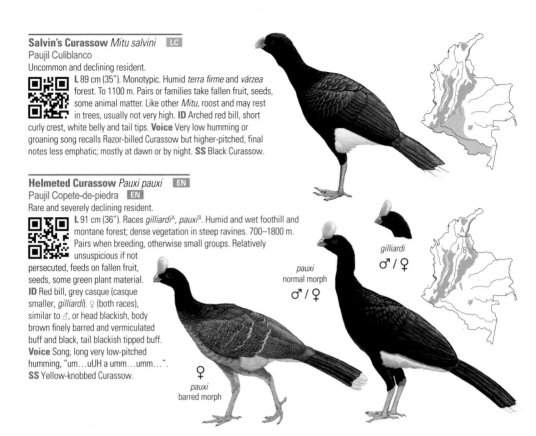

gilliardi
♂ / ♀

pauxi
normal morph
♂ / ♀

♀
pauxi
barred morph

ODONTOPHORIDAE
New World Quails
35 extant species, 10 in region

New World family of terrestrial species with strong legs, short rounded wings and brief explosive flights. Most Colombian species are shy montane forest-dwellers. Only Crested Bobwhite occurs in drier semi-open areas and it is seen far more than any other. All are primarily granivorous and nest on the ground.

Crested Bobwhite *Colinus cristatus* `LC`
Perdiz Chilindra
Common resident.

L 23 cm (9"). Races *decoratus*[A], *littoralis*[B], *cristatus*[C], *badius*[D], *leucotis*[E], *bogotensis*[F], *parvicristatus*[G]. Desert scrub, grassland, neglected pastures with brush and thickets. To 2500 m. Pairs when breeding, coveys rest of year. Runs quickly across openings, freezes to avoid detection; flushes explosively if pressed. **ID** Pointed crest (reduced in ♀); spotted below. **Voice** Vocal year-round, whistled upslurred "bob-white", first note weak; various weaker calls. **SS** Only quail in open areas.

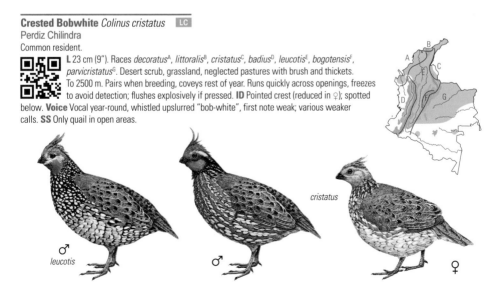

cristatus

♂
leucotis

♂

♀

Genus *Odontophorus* Robust forest-dwellers with short tails, sturdy legs and earth-tone colours; most have bare dark ocular skin (bright in a few). Infrequently seen, but their loud rhythmic duets often heard at dawn and dusk.

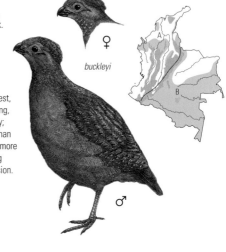

♀

buckleyi

♂

Marbled Wood-quail *Odontophorus gujanensis* NT
Perdiz Corcovada
Fairly common resident.

L 28 cm (11"). Races *marmoratus*A, *buckleyi*B. Floor of humid forest, especially cluttered undergrowth. To 1500 m. Pairs when breeding, coveys at other times. Freezes to avoid detection or creeps away; if pressed runs rapidly, flushes reluctantly. **ID** Plainer, browner than allies; large bare reddish ocular area. **Voice** Pairs give loud antiphonal duets more at dusk than dawn. Songs vary geographically; in Magdalena Valley, rollicking "ka-WE-KE wa"; E of Andes rapidly repeated "cor-cor-o'VAdo" or shorter version. **SS** Rufous-fronted Wood-quail.

melanotis

[Black-eared Wood-quail *Odontophorus melanotis*] LC
Perdiz Orejinegra
Hypothetical.

L 25 cm (10"). Race *melanotis*. Unrecorded; likely in humid forest near Cerro Pirre on Panama border. 300–1100 m (Panama). **ID** Crown and underparts rufous, throat and cheeks black. **Voice** Song, low hollow duet "co'WU'dō…" repeated rapidly.

Rufous-fronted Wood-quail *Odontophorus erythrops* LC
Perdiz Collareja
Uncommon resident.

L 28 cm (11"). Race *parambae*. Humid and wet lowland and foothill forest. To 1600 m. Pairs or small coveys freeze if close but scurry off through undergrowth at first opportunity. **ID** Chestnut head and underparts, black cheeks and throat separated by thin white collar; ♀ duller below. **Voice** Far-carrying antiphonal duet a few times at dawn; simple "po'eEK, po'eEK…" varied to "cho'wita, cho'wita…" repeated rapidly. **SS** Marbled Wood-quail.

parambae

Black-fronted Wood-quail *Odontophorus atrifrons* VU
Perdiz Carinegra NT
Fairly common resident (Santa Marta Mts), local elsewhere.

L 28 cm (11"). Races *atrifrons*A, *navai*B, *variegatus*C. Near-endemic (also extreme NW Venezuela). Humid montane forest, older second growth. 700–3100 m. Territorial pairs or groups to 12. **ID** Black forehead, face and throat, chestnut crown. **Voice** Exuberant rapidly repeated antiphonal duet of 3–4 notes "we-wee'WA-wert", or similar rhythmic variation, dawn and dusk. **SS** Occurs with no other wood-quail.

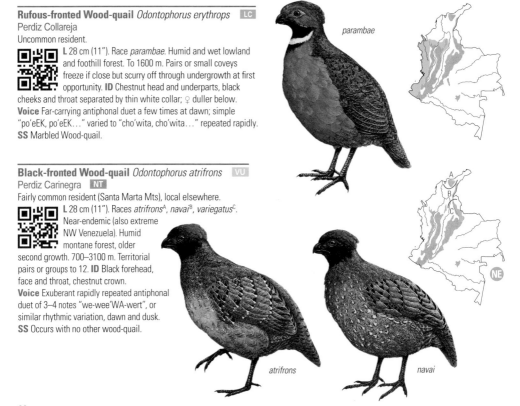

atrifrons

navai

NE

Chestnut Wood-quail *Odontophorus hyperythrus* NT
Perdiz Colorada NT

Fairly common but local resident.

 L 27 cm (10.5"). Monotypic. Endemic. Humid and wet montane forest. 1600–2800 m. Most widespread wood-quail in Colombian Andes. Pairs or groups to c. 9 may freeze when discovered but at first opportunity scurry away. **ID** Pale blue-tinged ocular area extends rearward. ♂ foreface, throat and underparts chestnut. ♀ like ♂ but mid-breast to belly grey. **Voice** At dawn pairs sing long (10–20-second) rollicking merry duets "orrit-chill'it…" or similar loud variation, only one bird may continue at end. Call, low descending "chur" repeated. **SS** Rufous-breasted Wood-quail.

Dark-backed Wood-quail *Odontophorus melanonotus* VU
Perdiz de Nariño EN

Resident (poorly known in Colombia).

 L 25 cm (10"). Monotypic. Near-endemic (also far NW Ecuador). Humid and wet montane forest. 1100–2200 m. Behaviour like other wood-quail. **ID** Notably dark and plain; dull dark blue ocular skin, chestnut throat and breast, no markings on head, throat or upperparts. **Voice** Rollicking antiphonal dawn chorus recalls other *Odontophorus*, especially Chestnut Wood-quail, loud rapidly repeated "ko'REE'ho…". **SS** Rufous-fronted Wood-quail.

Rufous-breasted Wood-quail *Odontophorus speciosus* NT
Perdiz Pechirrufo

Resident (few records).

 L 25 cm (10"). Race *soderstromii*. Humid and wet montane forest. 800–2000 m. **ID** Black throat, white-freckled superciliary (both sexes); ♂ chestnut underparts; ♀ mostly grey below, only chest rufous-chestnut. **Voice** Pairs give loud vigorous rhythmic duets at dawn or dusk that recall those of other wood-quail, e.g. rapidly repeated "CHEV-o'ree…" or "KEEo'ro're…" or variant. **SS** Chestnut and Marbled Wood-quails.

soderstromii

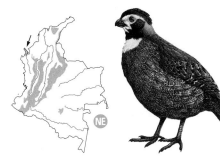

Tacarcuna Wood-quail *Odontophorus dialeucos* VU
Perdiz Katía EN

Poorly known resident.

L 23 cm (9"). Monotypic. Near-endemic (also extreme SE Panama). Humid montane forest of difficult access. 1050–1450 m (to 1700 m, Panama). **ID** Small; distinctive white ocular area, post-ocular, chin and crescent across throat, cinnamon nape. **Voice** Loud fast antiphonal dawn chorus recalls other wood-quail, 3–4-note "hu-hu'WEE-oo" or similar rhythmic variation over and over.

Gorgeted Wood-quail *Odontophorus strophium* `VU`
Perdiz Santandereana `EN`
Extremely local resident (range fragmented).

 L 25 cm (10"). Monotypic. Endemic. Humid and wet (mossy) montane forest, drier oak-dominated (*Quercus humboldtii*) forest. 1600–2050 m. **ID** Black face and throat, indistinct whitish eyebrow and chin mark, white throat-band, dark rufous below lightly spotted white. ♀ face and throat-band white, underparts greyish. **Voice** Energetic antiphonal dawn song recalls others of genus, rapidly repeated "WEE-e'ert", by pairs for up to 30+ seconds. **SS** No known overlap with other *Odontophorus*.

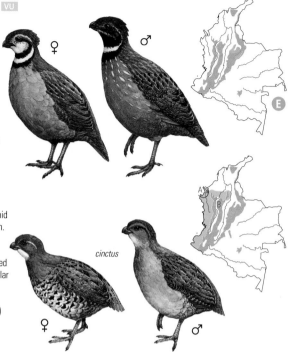

Tawny-faced Quail *Rhynchortyx cinctus* `LC`
Perdiz Selvática
Uncommon and local resident.

 L 19 cm (7.5"). Races *cinctus*[A], *australis*[B]. Humid and wet lowland and foothill forest. To 1000 m. Pairs; forest floor; inconspicuous, secretive and difficult to see. **ID** Quite small. ♂ bright tawny-orange face, dark post-ocular, grey chest, black-spotted wing-coverts. ♀ head and chest rusty brown, white post-ocular and throat, black-spotted wing-coverts, whitish lower underparts coarsely barred. **Voice** Most vocal at dusk, occasionally at night from low roost; slow (< 1 note/second) melancholy, slightly descending "puuu" whistles, vaguely tinamou-like, for a minute or more, often higher- or lower-pitched couplets near end. **SS** Rufous-fronted Wood-quail.

cinctus

ANHIMIDAE
Screamers
3 extant species, 2 in region

Small South American family of ancient lineage. Both genera, *Anhima* and *Chauna*, are large, heavy-bodied, superficially goose-like, and noted for their powerful voices. Anatomical peculiarities include wing spurs, thick sponge-like skin, plus absence of feather tracts and perforate nostrils. Marshes and wooded lakes; long unwebbed toes; do not swim. *Chauna* differ by bare facial skin; no frontal quill.

Horned Screamer *Anhima cornuta* `LC`
Aruco
Fairly common resident.

 L 89 cm (35"). Monotypic. Marshes, river edges, wooded lagoons, oxbows. To 500 m (1000 m, Cauca Valley). Vegetarian. Pairs or families forage in marshes; rest atop shrubs or high open tree limb; soar well. **ID** Enormous, mostly black; chicken-like bill, black scaling on white chest, black wing-linings, long 'unicorn-like' frontal quill. **Voice** Not forgotten once heard; powerful raucous gulping honks, "U-HOO, GULP-HOO... YOIK-YOK"; far-carrying calls (easily 1 km or more) echo across quiet lagoons. **SS** Northern Screamer.

Northern Screamer *Chauna chavaria* `NT`
Chavarrí `VU`
Local and declining resident.

 L 84 cm (33"). Monotypic. Near-endemic (also NW Venezuela). Marshes, lagoons, oxbows in open or semi-open areas; local in coastal marshes. To 200 m. Singles, pairs or small loose groups, rest atop bushes or high in trees near marshes. **ID** Large, blackish; white scarf around neck, small crest on nape, bare red ocular area and legs. **Voice** Gulping honks recall Horned Screamer but weaker; less vocal. **SS** Horned Screamer.

ANATIDAE
Ducks, Geese and Swans
165 extant species, 23 in region + 4 vagrants

Familiar worldwide family. Colombian species include residents and short-distance and boreal migrants, but few of latter are numerous. All have webbed feet and broad spatulate bills. Some feed by tipping up in shallow water and spring directly into the air. Others dive, feed in deep water and patter across water to get airborne.

Genus *Dendrocygna* Large, long-necked and long-legged. Social; seasonally in large flocks. Often fly to feeding areas at night. Sexes alike.

White-faced Whistling-duck
Dendrocygna viduata   LC
Iguasa Careta
Common resident.

L 46 cm (18"). Monotypic. Freshwater marshes, lagoons, flooded fields; infrequently brackish water. To 2700 m. Gregarious when not breeding; alert; regularly with other whistling-ducks. Seldom perches in trees; often forages at night. **ID** White face (frequently dirty); in flight wings all dark. **Voice** High reedy whistled "WEE-tee-de". **SS** Other whistling-ducks.

Black-bellied Whistling-duck *Dendrocygna autumnalis*   LC
Pisingo

Two subspecies in two subspecies groups; one in Colombia.

Southern Black-bellied Whistling-duck
Dendrocygna (autumnalis) autumnalis
Common resident.
L 56 cm (22"). One subspecies in group. Freshwater marshes, lagoons, flooded fields, brackish water and mangroves. Erratic to 2700 m (usually much lower). Large flocks gather at drying pools in *llanos* Dec–Apr; pairs breed with arrival of rains. Active, noisy day or night; often forages nocturnally. Only Colombian whistling-duck to regularly perch in trees. **ID** Rosy bill (grey, imm); white wing-band in flight. **Voice** Reedy whistle, "wissree" or longer "wee-tee-Wée-te-re". **SS** Imm Fulvous Whistling-duck.

Fulvous Whistling-duck *Dendrocygna bicolor*   LC
Iguasa María
Fairly common but declining resident.

L 48 cm (19"). Monotypic. Freshwater marshes, lagoons, flooded rice fields, shallow brackish water. To 2600 m (mainly lowlands). Singles, pairs or small groups with other ducks, especially other whistling-ducks, when not breeding. In severe decline due to pesticides and habit of nesting in rice fields. Forages day or night. **ID** Fulvous colour; in flight all-dark wings, white band at tail base. **Voice** High reedy "kur-dur" in flight. **SS** Other whistling-ducks.

Masked Duck *Nomonyx dominicus* `LC`
Pato Enmascarado
Local resident.

 L 33 cm (13"). Monotypic. Marshes; small freshwater lagoons with reeds and emergent vegetation. To 2700 m. Inconspicuous; pairs or families often remain hidden. Rather sedentary but periodically disperse. Floats low; dives to forage; spiky tail often held low. **ID** ♂ turquoise-blue bill, black foreface, obscure black spotting on back. ♀ two black facial stripes, mottled brown plumage. In flight white axillaries; small white patch in secondaries from above. **Voice** Quiet but displaying ♂♂ inflate neck and utter soft pigeon-like "ouu-goo-goo-ouu". **SS** ♀ Andean Duck.

Ruddy Duck *Oxyura jamaicensis* `LC`
Pato Rufo `EN`
Vagrant (Isla Providencia).

 L 41 cm (16"). Monotypic. Ad ♀, Oct 2001 (sight). Open bodies of fresh and brackish water. Conspicuous; often with other waterfowl. Forages by diving; spiky tail often held up. **ID** ♂ black head, large white cheek patch, blue bill. ♀ single dark stripe on sides of head. **SS** Masked Duck. **TN** Usually includes Andean Duck as a race.

Andean Duck *Oxyura ferruginea* `LC`
Pato Andino
Common resident.

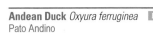 **L** 41 cm (16"). Monotypic. Deep open freshwater lakes. 2400–4000 m. Conspicuous. Pairs or loose groups, often with coots and other waterfowl, float low; forage by diving. Spiky tail often held up. **ID** ♂ head black or has highly variable amounts of white on sides of head (some near-identical to Ruddy Duck), blue bill. ♀ single dark stripe on cheeks. **SS** ♀ Masked Duck. **TN** Usually regarded as a race of Ruddy Duck (genetically close). Race *andina* (C & E Andes) merged with *ferruginea* of S Colombia.

'andina'

Black Scoter *Melanitta americana* `NT`
Negrón Americano
Vagrant (Pacific coast).

 L 48 cm (19"). Monotypic. Single record of seven birds offshore S of El Valle, Chocó, Feb 2013. Saltwater; dives in deep water. **ID** ♂ all black, yellow bill knob. ♀ grey, with blackish cap, pale cheeks, thin bill.

Red-breasted Merganser *Mergus serrator* LC
Serreta Mediana

Vagrant (Islas San Andrés and Providencia). L 58 cm (23"). Monotypic. One record each, Islas San Andrés (sight), Providencia and Santa Catalina (photos), Jan and Feb 2008, Nov 2017. Fresh or saltwater. Floats low, dives in deep water; typically in flocks. **ID** Long thin reddish bill. ♂ dark green head, shaggy crest, rufous chest. ♀ rufous head and neck becomes grey on chest, basal half of wing mostly white (both sexes).

Orinoco Goose *Oressochen jubatus* NT
Pato Carretero VU

Local and declining resident. L ♂ 69 cm (27"), ♀ 58 cm (23"). Monotypic. Freshwater marshes, riverbanks, sandbars; wet grassland in *llanos*. To 500 m (rarely 2600 m). Forms pairs (♂♂ fight) when breeding; otherwise small groups, generally not with other waterfowl. Conspicuous on ground or perched in open trees. Grazes on plant matter. Cavity nest low or high. **ID** 'Proud' upright posture; pale buff foreparts; small bill; reddish legs. **Voice** ♂ low reedy whistles (like whistling in barrel); ♀ low guttural "gur'rump" ('Wookie call'); both sexes utter purring or rolling "pur'r'r'ra" (context?). **TN** Formerly genus *Neochen*.

Muscovy Duck *Cairina moschata* LC
Pato Real

Rare resident W of Andes, uncommon E of Andes. L 76 cm (30"). Monotypic. Forested rivers, oxbows, lagoons; marshes in *llanos*. To 1000 m (rarely 2600 m). Often perches in trees; pairs when breeding, small groups at other times, sometimes with whistling-ducks. Semi-domesticated populations with variable amounts of white common throughout Andes. **ID** Large and black. ♂ white shoulders and underwing-coverts in flight. ♀ small white wing patch. Juv sooty black. **Voice** Rarely vocal.

American Comb Duck *Sarkidiornis sylvicola* LC
Pato Crestudo Americano EN

Rare and local resident. L ♂ 76 cm (30"), ♀ 56 cm (22"). Monotypic. Marshes; larger bodies of open water in *llanos*; waterholes in Guajira; rarely Andean lakes. To 500 m (vagrant, 3400 m). Singles, pairs or a few with large flocks of whistling-ducks in *llanos*; disperses in rainy season. Wary; readily perches in trees. **ID** ♂ large black comb on bill, black speckling on whitish head and underparts, wings all dark. ♀ smaller, no comb. **Voice** ♂ (rarely) whistled "churr"; ♀ grunts.

Torrent Duck *Merganetta armata* `LC`
Pato de Torrentes
Local resident.

L 43 cm (17"). Race *colombiana*. Rushing mountain streams with boulders. 1000–3500 m (Pacific slope to 300 m). Pairs loaf on boulders; inconspicuous foraging in fast clean water; avoid muddy silt-laden rivers that scour insect larvae food from stream bottom; large feet, soft bill, long stiff tail, narrow streamlined body facilitate swimming and diving expertly in turbulent water. **ID** ♂ boldly striped head and neck, red bill. ♀ chestnut underparts. Juv duller, paler; greyish above, white below, sides barred black.

adult

colombiana

♂

♀

juvenile

Southern Pochard *Netta erythrophthalma* `LC`
Pato Negro `CR`
Resident (few recent records).

L 51 cm (20"). Race *erythrophthalma*. Freshwater marshes, lakes. To 500 m (rarely 2600 m). Apparently never numerous; now virtually extinct in Colombia. Dives well, also dabbles or tips up to forage; may utilize rice fields. **ID** ♂ very dark, prominent white wing stripe in flight. ♀ patchy white face. **Voice** Soft quacks. **SS** Lesser Scaup, Ring-necked Duck.

erythrophthalma

♀

♂

Ring-necked Duck *Aythya collaris* `LC`
Pato Collarejo
Rare boreal migrant.

L 43 cm (17"). Monotypic. Fresh and brackish marshes and lakes. To 2600 m. Scattered records Caribbean islands and mainland; mainly deep water. **ID** ♂ black back, pale grey sides, white spur on shoulder, white outline around bill, white ring near tip (visible when close), grey flight feathers. ♀ dark cap, grey cheeks, white eye-ring, white at base of bill, faint shoulder spur. **SS** Lesser Scaup.

♀

♂

♂

Lesser Scaup *Aythya affinis* `LC`
Pato Canadiense
Rare to uncommon boreal migrant (Oct–Apr).

L 42 cm (16.5"). Monotypic. Deep freshwater lakes, brackish coastal marshes. To 3000 m. Small groups, alone or loosely associated with other ducks. **ID** ♂ black at both ends, pale grey back, white sides. ♀ dark brown head to breast, white at base of bill (no eye-ring). Head slightly peaked (♂ and ♀); in flight white wing stripe mainly on secondaries. **SS** Ring-necked Duck.

♀

♂

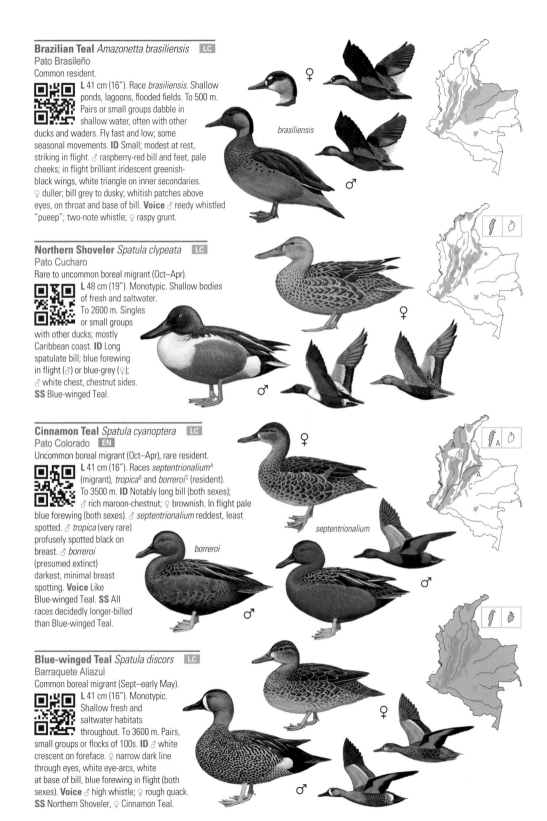

Brazilian Teal *Amazonetta brasiliensis* `LC`
Pato Brasileño
Common resident.

L 41 cm (16"). Race *brasiliensis*. Shallow ponds, lagoons, flooded fields. To 500 m. Pairs or small groups dabble in shallow water, often with other ducks and waders. Fly fast and low; some seasonal movements. **ID** Small; modest at rest, striking in flight. ♂ raspberry-red bill and feet, pale cheeks; in flight brilliant iridescent greenish-black wings, white triangle on inner secondaries. ♀ duller; bill grey to dusky; whitish patches above eyes, on throat and base of bill. **Voice** ♂ reedy whistled "pueep"; two-note whistle; ♀ raspy grunt.

brasiliensis

Northern Shoveler *Spatula clypeata* `LC`
Pato Cucharo
Rare to uncommon boreal migrant (Oct–Apr).

L 48 cm (19"). Monotypic. Shallow bodies of fresh and saltwater. To 2600 m. Singles or small groups with other ducks; mostly Caribbean coast. **ID** Long spatulate bill; blue forewing in flight (♂) or blue-grey (♀); ♂ white chest, chestnut sides. **SS** Blue-winged Teal.

Cinnamon Teal *Spatula cyanoptera* `LC` `EN`
Pato Colorado
Uncommon boreal migrant (Oct–Apr), rare resident.

L 41 cm (16"). Races *septentrionalium*[A] (migrant), *tropica*[B] and *borreroi*[C] (resident). To 3500 m. **ID** Notably long bill (both sexes); ♂ rich maroon-chestnut; ♀ brownish. In flight pale blue forewing (both sexes). ♂ *septentrionalium* reddest, least spotted. ♂ *tropica* (very rare) profusely spotted black on breast. ♂ *borreroi* (presumed extinct) darkest, minimal breast spotting. **Voice** Like Blue-winged Teal. **SS** All races decidedly longer-billed than Blue-winged Teal.

septentrionalium

borreroi

Blue-winged Teal *Spatula discors* `LC`
Barraquete Aliazul
Common boreal migrant (Sept–early May).

L 41 cm (16"). Monotypic. Shallow fresh and saltwater habitats throughout. To 3600 m. Pairs, small groups or flocks of 100s. **ID** ♂ white crescent on foreface. ♀ narrow dark line through eyes, white eye-arcs, white at base of bill, blue forewing in flight (both sexes). **Voice** ♂ high whistle; ♀ rough quack. **SS** Northern Shoveler, ♀ Cinnamon Teal.

Gadwall *Mareca strepera* `LC`
Pato Friso
Vagrant (Isla San Andrés).

L 43 cm (17"). Race *strepera*. Imm, Oct 2005. Shallow freshwater habitats. Feeds by tipping up. **ID** ♂ grey with black rear end. ♀ brownish; thin bill, orange only on sides; yellow legs. In flight both sexes show white patch on inner secondaries. **SS** ♀ Blue-winged Teal.

strepera

American Wigeon *Mareca americana* `LC`
Pato Americano
Rare boreal migrant (Oct–Apr).

L 51 cm (20"). Monotypic. Shallow fresh or brackish water. To 2600 m. Singles or small numbers, usually with other waterfowl. Feeds by up-ending. **ID** ♂ whitish cap, green mask, white at base of black rear end. ♀ grey-brown head, fine black line at base of short grey bill; pale tawny sides. In flight from above ♂ has broad white border to secondaries (narrower in ♀); both show white wing-linings. **SS** Boreal migrant ducks.

Mallard *Anas platyrhynchos* `LC`
Pato Real
Status unknown.

L 58 cm (23"). Race *platyrhynchos*. Fresh or brackish water. Mainland records introduced or domesticated birds, some now feral in Andes; verified wild bird records (?). To 2600 m. Readily hybridizes with domestic ducks. Wild birds most likely on Islas San Andrés and Providencia. **ID** ♂ bottle-green head, thin white neck-ring, chestnut breast, pale sides. ♀ orange bill with black across centre, speculum narrowly bordered white. **Voice** Familiar quack. **SS** Northern Shoveler.

platyrhynchos

White-cheeked Pintail *Anas bahamensis* `LC`
Pato Cariblanco `NT`
Fairly common but local resident.

L 43 cm (17"). Race *bahamensis*. Tidal marshes, mangroves, bays in Caribbean area; infrequent inland. To 2600 m. Handsome. Pairs or variable-sized groups dabble in shallow water or tip up; often with boreal migrant waterfowl and waders. Presumed resident but few breeding data. **ID** White cheeks and throat, red bill (less red, ♀), pointed tail; in flight (sometimes at rest) iridescent green secondaries bordered buff. **Voice** ♂ low whistle; ♀ soft quacks.

bahamensis

44

Northern Pintail *Anas acuta* `LC`
Pato Rabo-de-gallo
Rare boreal migrant.

 L 56 cm (22″). Monotypic. Shallow coastal marshes, bays; inland lakes. To 2600 m. On shore or in shallow water with other ducks. **ID** Large; ♂ long neck, brown head, curving white neck-stripe, long black needle tail. ♀ plain buffy-brown head, body slightly darker, bill dark, pointed tail shorter than ♂; white trailing edge on dark speculum (♂ and ♀). **Voice** ♂ mellow whistle; ♀ soft quack.

Yellow-billed Pintail *Anas georgica* `LC`
Pato Piquidorado `VU`

 Three subspecies in three subspecies groups; one in Colombia.

Yellow-billed Pintail *Anas (georgica) spinicauda*
Local resident.
L 61 cm (24″). Races *niceforoi*[A] (formerly 1000–3800 m), *spinicauda*[B] (2600–3300 m, Nariño). Inland lakes and marshes; race *niceforoi* extirpated from E Andes (Laguna de Tota) mid 1950s, Cauca Valley (Valle) records lack documentation. **ID** Large; warm brown (head paler); long neck; yellow bill with black ridge, dark green speculum bordered buff, underwing dark. Sexes similar. Smaller (51 cm; 20″) and darker (*niceforoi*). **Voice** ♂ trilled whistle; ♀ quacks.

Common Teal *Anas crecca* `LC`
Pato Aliverde

 Two subspecies in two subspecies groups; one in Colombia.

Green-winged Teal *Anas (crecca) carolinensis*
Rare boreal migrant.
L 36 cm (14″). One subspecies in group. No records of Eurasian *A. c. crecca*. Shallow fresh and brackish water. Few records. To 2600 m. Likely with other boreal migrant waterfowl. **ID** Small; wing speculum green, wing-linings white. ♂ chestnut head, green mask, vertical white bar on sides of chest. ♀ small, compact; dark brown, no white on face. **Voice** ♂ weak scratchy whistle; ♀ soft quack. **SS** ♀ Blue-winged Teal.

Andean Teal *Anas andium* `LC`
Cerceta Barcina
Fairly common resident.

 L 41 cm (16″). Races *altipetens*[A], *andium*[B]. High-Andean lakes, cold boggy marshes. 2600–4300 m. Pairs or small groups (not large flocks); rather wary; dabble in shallow water or stand on boggy shore. **ID** Small; almost featureless, dark head contrasts with paler body, bill blue-grey, underparts speckled; in flight green speculum bordered buff, white axillaries extend as band on underwing-coverts. **Voice** ♂ soft often double-noted whistle; ♀ quacks. **SS** Yellow-billed Pintail, ♀ Blue-winged Teal.

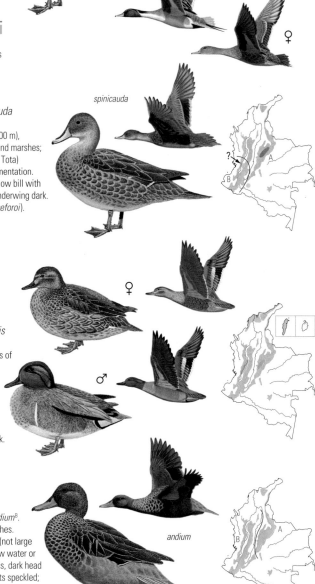

spinicauda

andium

45

PODICIPEDIDAE
Grebes
20 extant species, 3 in region + 1 extinct

A worldwide family of relatively small aquatic birds with lobed toes. Grebes are excellent swimmers and divers, but their legs are positioned too far rearward for walking on land; seldom seen in flight. Grebes become flightless for a short period during annual moult. Eat small fish and aquatic invertebrates.

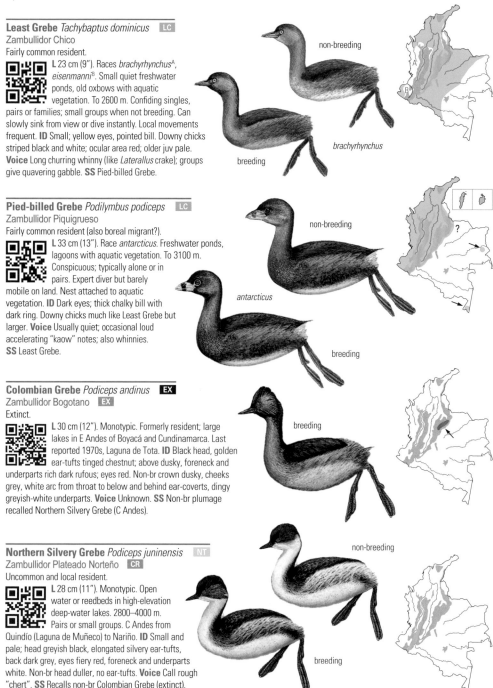

non-breeding

brachyrhynchus

breeding

non-breeding

antarcticus

breeding

breeding

non-breeding

breeding

Least Grebe *Tachybaptus dominicus* `LC`
Zambullidor Chico
Fairly common resident.
L 23 cm (9"). Races *brachyrhynchus*[A], *eisenmanni*[B]. Small quiet freshwater ponds, old oxbows with aquatic vegetation. To 2600 m. Confiding singles, pairs or families; small groups when not breeding. Can slowly sink from view or dive instantly. Local movements frequent. **ID** Small; yellow eyes, pointed bill. Downy chicks striped black and white; ocular area red; older juv pale. **Voice** Long churring whinny (like *Laterallus* crake); groups give quavering gabble. **SS** Pied-billed Grebe.

Pied-billed Grebe *Podilymbus podiceps* `LC`
Zambullidor Piquigrueso
Fairly common resident (also boreal migrant?).
L 33 cm (13"). Race *antarcticus*. Freshwater ponds, lagoons with aquatic vegetation. To 3100 m. Conspicuous; typically alone or in pairs. Expert diver but barely mobile on land. Nest attached to aquatic vegetation. **ID** Dark eyes; thick chalky bill with dark ring. Downy chicks much like Least Grebe but larger. **Voice** Usually quiet; occasional loud accelerating "kaow" notes; also whinnies. **SS** Least Grebe.

Colombian Grebe *Podiceps andinus* `EX`
Zambullidor Bogotano `EX`
Extinct.
L 30 cm (12"). Monotypic. Formerly resident; large lakes in E Andes of Boyacá and Cundinamarca. Last reported 1970s, Laguna de Tota. **ID** Black head, golden ear-tufts tinged chestnut; above dusky, foreneck and underparts rich dark rufous; eyes red. Non-br crown dusky, cheeks grey, white arc from throat to below and behind ear-coverts, dingy greyish-white underparts. **Voice** Unknown. **SS** Non-br plumage recalled Northern Silvery Grebe (C Andes).

Northern Silvery Grebe *Podiceps juninensis* `NT`
Zambullidor Plateado Norteño `CR`
Uncommon and local resident.
L 28 cm (11"). Monotypic. Open water or reedbeds in high-elevation deep-water lakes. 2800–4000 m. Pairs or small groups. C Andes from Quindío (Laguna de Muñeco) to Nariño. **ID** Small and pale; head greyish black, elongated silvery ear-tufts, back dark grey, eyes fiery red, foreneck and underparts white. Non-br head duller, no ear-tufts. **Voice** Call rough "chert". **SS** Recalls non-br Colombian Grebe (extinct).

46

PHOENICOPTERIDAE
Flamingos
6 extant species, 1 in region + 1 vagrant

Iconic group of pinkish, stilt-legged waders with partially webbed toes. In both Old and New World, usually in brackish or alkaline water. Unusual bill with comb-like lamellae is held upside-down to sift and strain water for tiny crustaceans and other invertebrates.

American Flamingo *Phoenicopterus ruber* `LC`
Flamenco Americano `EN`
Common but local resident.

 L 122 cm (48"). Monotypic. Shallow fresh or brackish water; coastal Guajira; rarely lower Magdalena Valley or inland. To 1000 m. Usually large groups; wary; flight strong, fast. Formerly bred in Colombia, now apparently only non-breeders from Bonaire or other Caribbean islands. **ID** Ad mostly pink; legs greyish pink, 'knees' redder; black flight feathers conspicuous in flight. Imm (to 3rd year) dull greyish white; bill and legs brownish. **Voice** Noisy honking and gabbling.

Chilean Flamingo *Phoenicopterus chilensis* `NT`
Flamenco Chileno
Vagrant.

L 94–104 cm (37–41"). Monotypic. Shallow alkaline, fresh or brackish water. One record of two, coastal SW Nariño, Jul 2018. **ID** Ad pinkish, folded wing carmine-red, flight feathers black (visible in flight); bill black, basal half pinkish ivory; legs dull bluish grey, conspicuous red 'knees'. Imm whitish (little or no pink); 'knees' dark (no red). **Voice** Low grunts; honking in flight. **SS** American Flamingo.

PHAETHONTIDAE
Tropicbirds
3 extant species, 2 in region

Small pelagic family of beautiful white seabirds with long ribbon-like central tail feathers. Found worldwide in warm tropical oceans; they dive for fish and nest in small colonies on sea cliffs, often on remote islands.

Red-billed Tropicbird *Phaethon aethereus* `LC`
Rabijunco Dorsibarrado
Rare or uncommon resident or seasonal visitor.

L 100 cm (39"). Race *mesonauta*. Apparently breeds on Isla Malpelo (Pacific) but not definitely present year-round; rare in Caribbean waters. Singles or pairs; highly pelagic; rarely seen from shore. Strong 'rowing' flight; swims well; plunge-dives for fish. **ID** Ad outer primaries black, bill red, back heavily barred black, long black line through eyes, white tail-streamers difficult to see. Juv bill pale. **SS** Royal Tern (p. 172), White-tailed Tropicbird.

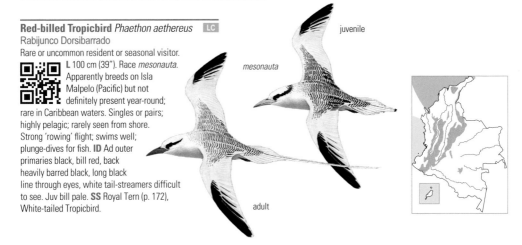

juvenile

mesonauta

adult

Red-tailed Tropicbird *Phaethon rubricauda* `LC`
Rabijunco Colirrojo
Status unknown.

L 89 cm (35"). Race *melanorhynchos*? Unconfirmed sight records (more in boreal autumn than boreal spring) in Colombian Pacific waters, 1980–95. Pelagic; mainly Indian and SW Pacific Oceans. **ID** Ad almost entirely white, outer primaries with a few black edges, short black eyestripe, red bill and tail-streamers. Juv bill blackish, forecrown white, upperparts and upperwing-coverts barred black, outer primaries black. **SS** Red-billed Tropicbird, Royal Tern (p. 172).

[White-tailed Tropicbird *Phaethon lepturus*] `LC`
Rabijunco Piquigualdo
Hypothetical.

L 76 cm (30"). Race *catesbyi*? Unverified sight record off Caribbean coast. Probably occurs singly far offshore. Wingbeats quick; plunge-dives for small oceanic prey. **ID** Ad smallest tropicbird; long black bar on upperwing-coverts, outer primaries mostly black, short black eyestripe, yellow-orange bill; white tail-streamers difficult to see. **Voice** Sharp tern-like calls. **SS** Royal Tern (p. 172), Red-billed Tropicbird.

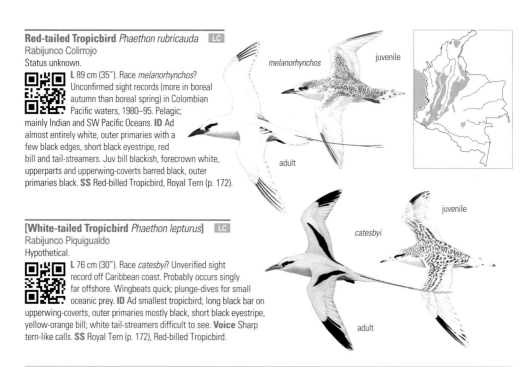

EURYPYGIDAE
Sunbittern
1 extant species, 1 in region

The Sunbittern is an exquisitely patterned Neotropical bird of elegant bearing and dainty halting movements. Sedentary, it is found along shady forest streams or pools of water. Bulky cup-like nest sited on a branch, usually near water.

Sunbittern *Eurypyga helias* `LC`
Garza del Sol

Three subspecies in three subspecies groups; two in Colombia.

Northern Sunbittern *Eurypyga (helias) major*
Uncommon and local resident.
L 51 cm (20"). One subspecies in group. **ID** Slightly larger, greyer above than Amazonian race, finer vermiculations above, mandible and legs orange-red (not yellowish).

Amazonian Sunbittern *Eurypyga (helias) helias*
Common (*llanos*) or uncommon (Amazonia) resident.
L 48 cm (19"). One subspecies in group. Damp leaf litter near water; quiet forest streams, pools; scarce along rocky foothill streams. To 800 m. Singles or pairs walk daintily at water's edge. Often wary; flushes in brief buoyant flight, showing colourful 'sunburst' wing pattern. **ID** Slender; bold head-stripes; thin bill; legs yellow. **Voice** Thin high melancholy whistle "wuuuuuuuuuu", easily imitated (recalls Cinereous Tinamou), may rise or fall slightly at end; trills and rattles in alarm.

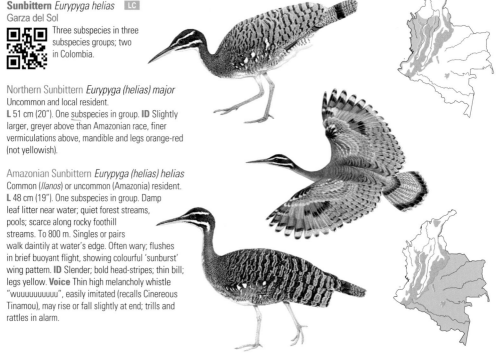

COLUMBIDAE
Pigeons and Doves
350 extant species, 36 in region + 1 vagrant + 1 introduced

Large cosmopolitan family of terrestrial and arboreal species. Colombian species are dull-coloured with soft dense plumage, plump bodies, small heads and a fleshy cere. They occur in every habitat from sea level to treeline; except pigeons, they mostly feed on the ground. Their simple but distinctive songs and calls are often helpful for identification. Some are conspicuous and easy to see, but quail-doves and a few others are difficult. Sexual dimorphism most obvious in ground-doves.

Rock Dove *Columba livia* LC
Paloma Doméstica
Common resident (introduced).

 L 32 cm (12.5"). Widespread feral pigeon of urban and settled areas. To 3000 m. Flocks; nests on buildings. **ID** Highly variable; can be pied, all dark brown, or mottled; most forms have pale or white rump; ancestral form pale grey with two large black bands on flight feathers. **Voice** Slow muffled series of low-pitched hoots. **SS** Native *Patagioenas* pigeons.

> **Genus *Patagioenas*** Arboreal pigeons; largest New World members of family. Squarish to slightly rounded tails. Forest and semi-open areas. Feed on berries and soft fruit.

White-crowned Pigeon
Patagioenas leucocephala NT
Paloma Coroniblanca NT
Common (Caribbean islands), rare (Caribbean coast) resident.

 **L** 34 cm (13.5"). Monotypic. Mangroves, dry coastal woodland, scattered trees. To 100 m. Singles or small groups perch high, often partly concealed; wary. **ID** Slate-grey with 'snowy' cap, white-tipped reddish bill. **Voice** Song low-pitched growling "whrruu…whoopoop wuu, wuupoop-wu…".

Scaled Pigeon *Patagioenas speciosa* LC
Paloma Escamada
Fairly common resident.

 L 32 cm (12.5"). Monotypic. Dry to humid forest borders, tall open woodland, coffee plantations, gallery forest. To 1400 m. Wary; solitary, in pairs or small groups, rarely large flocks. Perches high, mainly in canopy; flies high across large open areas. **ID** Scaly neck and underparts, red bill tipped white. **Voice** Slow drowsy "coo-OOOOaa…" c. 4 times. **SS** Pale-vented Pigeon.

Bare-eyed Pigeon *Patagioenas corensis* LC
Paloma Cardonera
Locally common resident.

 L 33 cm (13"). Monotypic. Desert scrub, especially with tall columnar cacti, dry semi-open brushland, mangroves. To 400 m. Singles, pairs or small to large flocks; arboreal, but sometimes forage on ground; perch atop tall cacti. Some seasonal movements; may gather in large flocks at roosts. **ID** Conspicuous white wing patch (in flight), black ring around bare ocular area imparts 'goggle-eyed' look, pale bill. **Voice** Slow cooing "cuooo…chuck'chuck cuóooo". **SS** Pale-vented Pigeon.

49

Southern Band-tailed Pigeon *Patagioenas albilinea* `LC`
Paloma Collareja Sureña
Common resident.

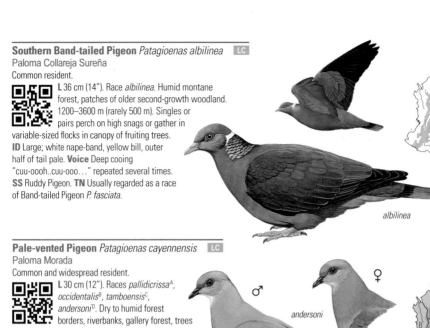

L 36 cm (14"). Race *albilinea*. Humid montane forest, patches of older second-growth woodland. 1200–3600 m (rarely 500 m). Singles or pairs perch on high snags or gather in variable-sized flocks in canopy of fruiting trees. **ID** Large; white nape-band, yellow bill, outer half of tail pale. **Voice** Deep cooing "cuu-oooh..cuu-ooo…" repeated several times. **SS** Ruddy Pigeon. **TN** Usually regarded as a race of Band-tailed Pigeon *P. fasciata*.

albilinea

Pale-vented Pigeon *Patagioenas cayennensis* `LC`
Paloma Morada
Common and widespread resident.

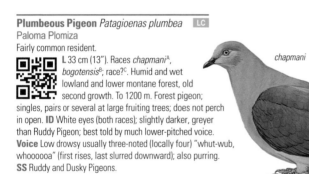

L 30 cm (12"). Races *pallidicrissa*[A], *occidentalis*[B], *tamboensis*[C], *andersoni*[D]. Dry to humid forest borders, riverbanks, gallery forest, trees in clearings. To 2100 m. Alone, in pairs or flocks; in afternoon gathers at waterholes during dry season. Commonest pigeon seen flying high over semi-open areas. **ID** Above vinaceous, head and rump grey, lower underparts whitish; eyes red. **Voice** Slow mournful cooing "coouu…co-woo, tu-coo, tu-coo" (up to eight phrases); purring "gurrrrooow". **SS** Scaled Pigeon.

♂   ♀   andersoni

Plumbeous Pigeon *Patagioenas plumbea* `LC`
Paloma Plomiza
Fairly common resident.

bogotensis

chapmani

L 33 cm (13"). Races *chapmani*[A], *bogotensis*[B]; race?[C]. Humid and wet lowland and lower montane forest, old second growth. To 1200 m. Forest pigeon; singles, pairs or several at large fruiting trees; does not perch in open. **ID** White eyes (both races); slightly darker, greyer than Ruddy Pigeon; best told by much lower-pitched voice. **Voice** Low drowsy usually three-noted (locally four) "whut-wub, whoooooa" (first rises, last slurred downward); also purring. **SS** Ruddy and Dusky Pigeons.

Ruddy Pigeon *Patagioenas subvinacea* `VU`
Paloma Colorada
Common resident.

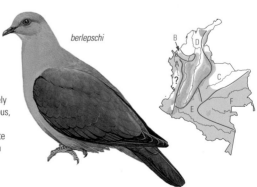

berlepschi

L 30 cm (12"). Races *berlepschi*[A], *ruberrima*[B], *zuliae*[C], *anolaimae*[D], *ogilviegranti*[E], *purpureotincta*[F]. Humid lowland and montane forest, borders, older second growth; foothills or higher W of Andes. To 2200 m (rarely 3000 m). Singles or pairs perch high in forest or at edge; inconspicuous, seldom completely in open; fly through (not above) canopy. **ID** Red eyes, uniform plumage; pay attention to voice. **Voice** Vocal; four-note "hit-the-FOWL-pole", or "what do YOU'know", an octave higher than Plumbeous Pigeon; loud purring. **SS** Plumbeous and Dusky Pigeons.

Short-billed Pigeon *Patagioenas nigrirostris* `LC`
Paloma Piquicorta
Uncommon resident.

 L 27 cm (10.5"). Monotypic. Humid lowland and lower montane forest. To 1500 m. Habits as Ruddy Pigeon. **ID** Very dark; short black bill, eyes reddish orange, eye-ring rose-red; best told from slightly larger Ruddy Pigeon by voice. Juv duller, eyes dark. **Voice** Rhythmic "WUUu, wuu-wa-wuuua", first note strongest, pause, rest quicker, second and last notes slightly higher, last often drawled; loud purring.

Dusky Pigeon *Patagioenas goodsoni* `LC`
Paloma Alirrufa
Fairly common resident.

 L 28 cm (11"). Monotypic. Near-endemic (also NW Ecuador). Wet lowland and foothill forest, borders, second growth. To 1100 m (rarely 1500 m). Singles or pairs, high in trees; inconspicuous but vocal and territorial; infrequently perches in open; flies within canopy, seldom above it. **ID** Smaller than allies; greyish head and chest, brownish belly, red eyes and eye-ring; rufous wing-linings show in flight. **Voice** Brisk rather high-pitched (for pigeon) "whoo, güü-güü", first note higher; mellow purring. **SS** Ruddy and Plumbeous Pigeons.

Genera *Geotrygon* and *Leptotrygon* Plump, short-tailed and semi-terrestrial pigeons of forest interior. Retiring and inconspicuous; forage on ground, but roost, nest, often sing from elevated perch. Most have dark malar line, iridescent nape feathers, bare coloured loral line and eye-ring. Flush quietly (cf. *Leptotila*).

Purple Quail-dove *Geotrygon purpurata* `EN`
Paloma-perdiz Morada
Uncommon (and local?) resident.

 L 22 cm (8.5"). Monotypic. Near-endemic (also NW Ecuador). Wet foothill and lower montane forest. 200–1400 m. Singles or pairs. Terrestrial; may flush to elevated perch. **ID** White forehead, broad white facial stripe, black malar, dark blue-grey crown, coppery tone to sides of neck, chest grey, lower underparts whitish. **Voice** From ground or low branch, low mournful whistled "wut…wuOOOuuuuu" (< 1 second), repeated at c. 3-second intervals, first note faint. **SS** Olive-backed Quail-dove. **TN** Formerly a race of Sapphire Quail-dove.

Sapphire Quail-dove *Geotrygon saphirina* `LC`
Paloma-perdiz Zafirina
Resident (few records).

 **L** 22 cm (8.5"). Race *saphirina*. Humid and wet lowland and foothill forest. 100–1450 m. **ID** Very like Purple Quail-dove but crown lighter, more blue-grey, chest paler grey; voice differs. **Voice** Song relatively high "ca'whooh…", recalls Purple Quail-dove but shorter or more variable in pitch and stress. **SS** Ruddy Quail-dove. **TN** Formerly included Purple Quail-dove.

saphirina

51

Ruddy Quail-dove *Geotrygon montana* `LC`
Paloma-perdiz Rojiza

Widespread resident in small numbers.
L 24 cm (9.5"). Race *montana*. Moist to humid forest, older second growth, light woodland, plantations. To 2000 m (rarely 2600 m). Singles or scattered pairs; terrestrial, unobtrusive; easily overlooked. If surprised hustles out of view on foot or flushes low with swerving flight to ground or low branch. Nomadism or local seasonal movements possible. **ID** Buff facial stripe, dark malar stripe, eye-ring and bill purplish red, eyes amber. ♀ face pattern less distinct; above duller, browner. **Voice** Low moaning "oooOOoou" from ground or low perch. **SS** Little Tinamou (p. 26).

montana

Violaceous Quail-dove *Geotrygon violacea* `LC`
Paloma-perdiz Violácea

Scarce, local and poorly known resident.
L 24 cm (9.5"). Races *albiventer*[A], *violacea*[B]. Humid foothill forest. 100–1650 m. Terrestrial; usually seen alone. **ID** Only Colombian quail-dove with no moustachial stripe; narrow whitish forecrown, foreface and throat, violet gloss on nape; purplish-red bill, lores and eye-ring; eyes yellow; underparts greyish. ♀ duller, less gloss. **Voice** Usually calls 2–8 m up in tree; low mellow "ooOOooou", recalls Grey-fronted Dove. **SS** Ruddy Quail-dove.

albiventer

violacea

Olive-backed Quail-dove *Leptotrygon veraguensis* `LC`
Paloma-perdiz Cariblanca

Uncommon resident.
L 24 cm (9.5"). Monotypic. Humid and wet lowland and hill forest. To 900 m. Singles or pairs; terrestrial, apt to freeze or walk away quietly rather than flush. **ID** Very dark, no iridescence; contrasting white forehead and facial stripe conspicuous even on dark forest floor; ♀ forecrown duller. **Voice** Less vocal (?) than other quail-doves; low nasal "thOOng", frog-like. **SS** Purple Quail-dove.

Genus *Leptotila* Semi-terrestrial, in forest or semi-open areas. Small white tail tips, bare red or blue eye-rings. Best told by voice, subtle plumage differences. Only two are common—White-tipped and Grey-fronted Doves.

decolor

verreauxi

White-tipped Dove *Leptotila verreauxi* `LC`
Tórtola Colipinta

Resident (the commonest *Leptotila*).
L 28 cm (11"). Races *verreauxi*[A], *hernandezi/decipiens*[B], *decolor*[C]. Dry forest, gallery forest, light woodland, Amazonian river islands, river edge clearings. To 2800 m. Singles or pairs walk hurriedly, bobbing head; flush quickly with audible wing noise to trees. **ID** Whitish forecrown turns greyish brown rearward; blue orbital ring (most areas) or dark red in *decolor* (colour inconsistent); white tail tips much like other *Leptotila*. **Voice** Deep hollow (blowing over bottle) "ub'uOOOOu", first note faint but two-note call (not single) diagnostic. **SS** Other *Leptotila*. **TN** Distribution and allocation of races unclear.

verreauxi

Caribbean Dove *Leptotila jamaicensis* `LC`
Tórtola Caribeña `CR`
Uncommon to fairly common resident (Isla San Andrés).

 L 28 cm (11"). Race *neoxena*. Dry woodland, shrubby partially open areas. To 100 m. **ID** Bare red orbital ring, vinaceous hindcrown and nape, white tail tips, cinnamon underwing-coverts. **Voice** Low hollow "UU, hoo-hoo-ho", first note higher-pitched. **SS** Only *Leptotila* on Isla San Andrés.

neoxena

Grey-chested Dove *Leptotila cassinii* `LC`
Tórtola Pechigris
Uncommon and local resident.

 L 25 cm (10"). Race *cassinii*. Humid lowland and foothill forest, treefalls, second growth, damp wooded borders. Singles or pairs forage mostly on ground; wary, hustle out of view or flush to tree. To 1000 m. **ID** Crown pale bluish grey, neck and chest grey; eyes yellow, eye-ring red; white tail tips smaller than White-tipped Dove. **Voice** Heard more than seen; notably long low "cooOOOoooh", stronger in middle. **SS** White-tipped Dove.

cassinii

♂

Tolima Dove *Leptotila conoveri* `EN`
Tórtola Tolimense `VU`
Uncommon and local resident.

 **L** 25 cm (10"). Monotypic. Endemic. Dry to humid montane forest, light woodland, borders. 1400–2500 m. Montane forest dove; singles or pairs forage on ground; venture into openings at forest edge in early morning. Calls from elevated perch, often fairly high. **ID** Grey crown, red orbital skin, rich pinkish-vinaceous breast contrasts with buff belly (belly whitish in other *Leptotila*), small white tail tips. **Voice** Single rising-falling "woOOOooo". **SS** White-tipped Dove (pale forecrown, whitish belly, breast much paler).

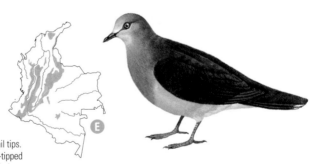

E

Grey-headed Dove *Leptotila plumbeiceps* `LC`
Tórtola Cabeciazul
Uncommon and local resident.

 L 27 cm (10.5"). Race *plumbeiceps*. Dry and moist forest, borders, light woodland. 600–2600 m. Behaviour like other *Leptotila*, flushes readily. **ID** Entire crown grey, cheeks tinged buff, breast pale pinkish buff, red orbital skin. **Voice** Very low-pitched brief "woOOoo", repeated more quickly than other *Leptotila*. **SS** White-tipped Dove; Grey-chested Dove (greyish chest; humid forest).

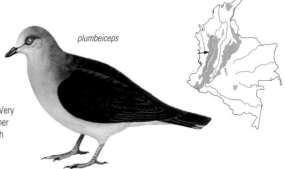

plumbeiceps

Grey-fronted Dove *Leptotila rufaxilla* LC
Tórtola Frentiblanca
Common resident.

 L 28 cm (11"). Races *pallidipectus*[A], *dubusi*[B].
Humid *terra firme* and *várzea* forest, old
second growth, gallery forest; ventures
briefly into clearings but typically inside forest.
To 800 m. Singles or pairs forage on ground, flush to trees; fly
low and fast across rivers, directly into forest. **ID** Forecrown pale
grey, darker grey rearwards, sides of head tinged buff, loral line
and eye-ring red. **Voice** ♂ and ♀ call from elevated perches, usually
not high; seasonally quite vocal; single "wooOOOoo", swells, fades;
♀ answers, higher-pitched. **SS** White-tipped Dove (not inside humid
forest; blue eye-ring in overlap area).

dubusi

Pallid Dove *Leptotila pallida* LC
Tórtola Pálida
Fairly common resident.

 L 25 cm (10"). Monotypic. Wet lowland and
especially foothill forest, older second growth,
borders. To 800 m. Singles or pairs forage on ground
mostly inside forest. Calls from elevated perches,
sometimes high. **ID** Bicoloured; white foreface, pale grey crown,
whitish underparts contrast with dark rufescent back and wings, red
eye-ring. **Voice** Heard more than seen; single low mournful
"woooOOOoo", recalls several other *Leptotila*. **SS** White-tipped Dove.

Genus *Zentrygon* Largest Colombian quail-doves. Montane, retiring, inconspicuous and
semi-terrestrial. Usually alone. Dark lines on hindneck. Flush without wing noise (unlike *Leptotila*).

White-throated Quail-dove *Zentrygon frenata* LC
Paloma-perdiz Bigotuda
Uncommon (overlooked?) resident.

 L 33 cm (13"). Race *bourcieri*. Humid and wet
montane forest. 900–2500 m. Singles or well-separated
pairs on forest floor, trails or edges of quiet roads at dawn;
if surprised hurries out of view or flushes to tree. **ID** Large;
pale grey forecrown darkens rearwards, cheeks buff, long black malar
line, dark greyish below, black neck lines. **Voice** Short low "whoOOp",
at 3–6-second intervals from well up in tree. **SS** Lined Quail-dove.

bourcieri

Lined Quail-dove *Zentrygon linearis* LC
Paloma-perdiz Lineada

 Two subspecies in two subspecies groups;
one in Colombia.

Lined Quail-dove *Zentrygon (linearis) linearis*
Locally common resident.
L 29 cm (11.5"). One subspecies in group. Humid and
wet montane forest. 1000–2500 m. **ID** Behaviour and
plumage as White-throated Quail-dove, differs in
forecrown cinnamon (not grey), underparts with buff
(not greyish) tones; slightly smaller. **Voice** Vocal
when breeding; low moaning "uuUUUuua" from perch
4–15 m up, throughout day. **TN** Race *infusca* (Santa Marta
Mts) not recognized.

♀

♂

Russet-crowned Quail-dove *Zentrygon goldmani* NT
Paloma-perdiz Cabecicanela VU
Uncommon (?) resident (few Colombian records).

 L 28 cm (11"). Race *goldmani*. Humid premontane and montane forest. 750–1600 m (rarely to 100 m). Behaviour like other *Zentrygon* quail-doves. **ID** Forecrown buff, rest of crown and nape rufous, cheeks buff, underparts grey. **Voice** From elevated perch, loud low "wOOoooou", abruptly swells, last part descending; songs often at slightly different pitch when two birds audible. **SS** Ruddy Quail-dove.

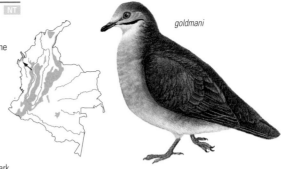

goldmani

Genus *Zenaida* Tails pointed or squarish; dark cheek mark (or marks); white or rufous tail tips. Only Eared Dove is common on mainland.

White-winged Dove *Zenaida asiatica* LC
Torcaza Aliblanca
Common (Islas San Andrés and Providencia), rare (Caribbean coast) resident.

 L 28 cm (11"). Race *asiatica*. Dry secondary woodland, scrub, mangroves, cultivated and urban areas. To 100 m. **ID** White wing patch always visible but conspicuous in flight; bare blue ocular area, dark malar spot; black primaries, squarish tail white-tipped. **Voice** Low slightly hoarse cooing "whohoo…hu..hoo", often given persistently. **SS** Caribbean Dove; Bare-eyed Pigeon.

asiatica

Eared Dove *Zenaida auriculata* LC
Torcaza Nagüiblanca
Common to abundant resident.

 L 25 cm (10.5"). Races *stenura*[A], *pentheria*[B], *antioquiae*[C], *caucae*[D], *hypoleuca*[E]. Arid to dry open or semi-open country, agricultural areas, towns and cities. To 3500 m. Singles, pairs or seasonally small to large flocks; fast direct flight. Can damage grain crops; locally hunted for sport. **ID** ♂ mid-crown bluish grey (dull brown, ♀), wedge-shaped tail tipped rufous (or white, *caucae*, *hypoleuca*), two black cheek marks, several black tertial spots. **Voice** Rather low, weak hoarse "wuu'uhUUhu..huu…ahu" or variations. **SS** Mourning Dove (accidental), *Leptotila* doves.

♂
stenura

♂
hypoleuca

Mourning Dove *Zenaida macroura* LC
Torcaza Plañidera
Vagrant.

 L 28 cm (11"). Race *marginella*? Dry semi-open areas. Small numbers winter S to dry C Panama; one old Cauca Valley record (1000 m). **ID** Single dark ear mark, long pointed white-tipped tail. **SS** Eared Dove (smaller; shorter tail, two facial marks), White-tipped Dove.

marginella

55

Genus _Columbina_ Smallest Colombian doves. Semi-terrestrial. Small groups in open, semi-open and settled areas. Short-tailed (except Scaled Dove). Rufous or black in primaries as they flush. ♂♂ usually brighter than ♀♀.

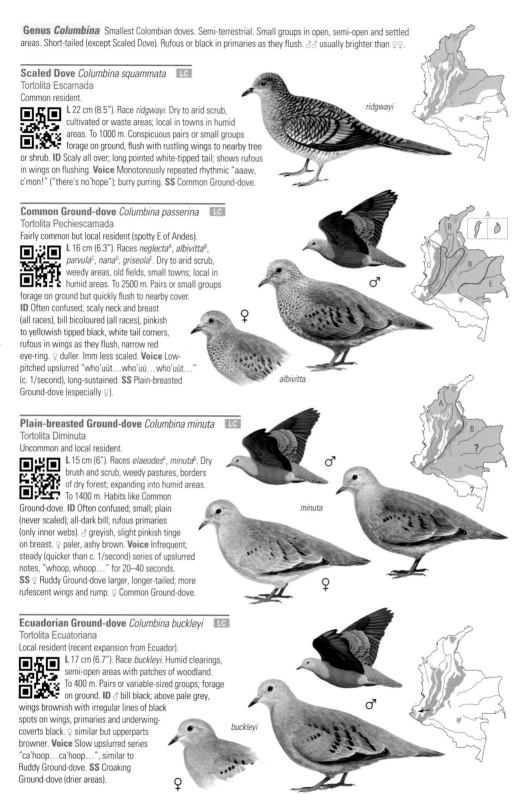

Scaled Dove _Columbina squammata_ `LC`
Tortolita Escamada
Common resident.

L 22 cm (8.5"). Race _ridgwayi_. Dry to arid scrub, cultivated or waste areas; local in towns in humid areas. To 1000 m. Conspicuous pairs or small groups forage on ground, flush with rustling wings to nearby tree or shrub. **ID** Scaly all over; long pointed white-tipped tail; shows rufous in wings on flushing. **Voice** Monotonously repeated rhythmic "aaaw, c'mon!" ("there's no'hope"); burry purring. **SS** Common Ground-dove.

ridgwayi

Common Ground-dove _Columbina passerina_ `LC`
Tortolita Pechiescamada
Fairly common but local resident (spotty E of Andes).

L 16 cm (6.3"). Races _neglecta_[A], _albivitta_[B], _parvula_[C], _nana_[D], _griseola_[E]. Dry to arid scrub, weedy areas, old fields, small towns; local in humid areas. To 2500 m. Pairs or small groups forage on ground but quickly flush to nearby cover. **ID** Often confused; scaly neck and breast (all races), bill bicoloured (all races), pinkish to yellowish tipped black, white tail corners, rufous in wings as they flush, narrow red eye-ring. ♀ duller. Imm less scaled. **Voice** Low-pitched upslurred "who'uút…who'uú…who'uút…" (c. 1/second), long-sustained. **SS** Plain-breasted Ground-dove (especially ♀).

♂

♀

albivitta

Plain-breasted Ground-dove _Columbina minuta_ `LC`
Tortolita Diminuta
Uncommon and local resident.

L 15 cm (6"). Races _elaeodes_[A], _minuta_[B]. Dry brush and scrub, weedy pastures, borders of dry forest; expanding into humid areas. To 1400 m. Habits like Common Ground-dove. **ID** Often confused; small; plain (never scaled); all-dark bill; rufous primaries (only inner webs). ♂ greyish, slight pinkish tinge on breast. ♀ paler, ashy brown. **Voice** Infrequent; steady (quicker than c. 1/second) series of upslurred notes, "whoop, whoop…" for 20–40 seconds. **SS** ♀ Ruddy Ground-dove larger, longer-tailed; more rufescent wings and rump. ♀ Common Ground-dove.

♂

minuta

♀

Ecuadorian Ground-dove _Columbina buckleyi_ `LC`
Tortolita Ecuatoriana
Local resident (recent expansion from Ecuador).

L 17 cm (6.7"). Race _buckleyi_. Humid clearings, semi-open areas with patches of woodland. To 400 m. Pairs or variable-sized groups; forage on ground. **ID** ♂ bill black; above pale grey, wings brownish with irregular lines of black spots on wings, primaries and underwing-coverts black. ♀ similar but upperparts browner. **Voice** Slow upslurred series "ca'hoop…ca'hoop…", similar to Ruddy Ground-dove. **SS** Croaking Ground-dove (drier areas).

buckleyi

♂

♀

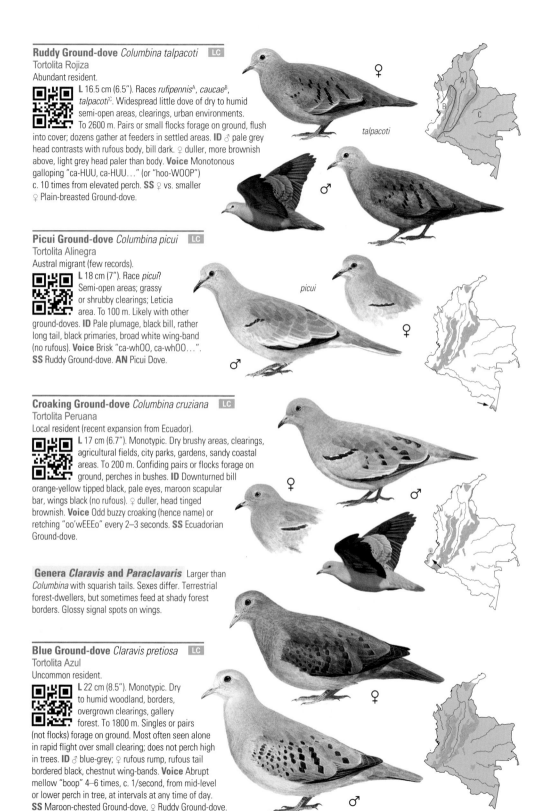

Ruddy Ground-dove *Columbina talpacoti* `LC`
Tortolita Rojiza
Abundant resident.

L 16.5 cm (6.5"). Races *rufipennis*[A], *caucae*[B], *talpacoti*[C]. Widespread little dove of dry to humid semi-open areas, clearings, urban environments. To 2600 m. Pairs or small flocks forage on ground, flush into cover; dozens gather at feeders in settled areas. **ID** ♂ pale grey head contrasts with rufous body, bill dark. ♀ duller, more brownish above, light grey head paler than body. **Voice** Monotonous galloping "ca-HUU, ca-HUU…" (or "hoo-WOOP") c. 10 times from elevated perch. **SS** ♀ vs. smaller ♀ Plain-breasted Ground-dove.

♀

talpacoti

♂

Picui Ground-dove *Columbina picui* `LC`
Tortolita Alinegra
Austral migrant (few records).

L 18 cm (7"). Race *picui*? Semi-open areas; grassy or shrubby clearings; Leticia area. To 100 m. Likely with other ground-doves. **ID** Pale plumage, black bill, rather long tail, black primaries, broad white wing-band (no rufous). **Voice** Brisk "ca-whOO, ca-whOO…". **SS** Ruddy Ground-dove. **AN** Picui Dove.

picui

♀

♂

Croaking Ground-dove *Columbina cruziana* `LC`
Tortolita Peruana
Local resident (recent expansion from Ecuador).

L 17 cm (6.7"). Monotypic. Dry brushy areas, clearings, agricultural fields, city parks, gardens, sandy coastal areas. To 200 m. Confiding pairs or flocks forage on ground, perches in bushes. **ID** Downturned bill orange-yellow tipped black, pale eyes, maroon scapular bar, wings black (no rufous). ♀ duller, head tinged brownish. **Voice** Odd buzzy croaking (hence name) or retching "oo'wEEEo" every 2–3 seconds. **SS** Ecuadorian Ground-dove.

♀

♂

Genera *Claravis* and *Paraclaravis* Larger than *Columbina* with squarish tails. Sexes differ. Terrestrial forest-dwellers, but sometimes feed at shady forest borders. Glossy signal spots on wings.

Blue Ground-dove *Claravis pretiosa* `LC`
Tortolita Azul
Uncommon resident.

L 22 cm (8.5"). Monotypic. Dry to humid woodland, borders, overgrown clearings, gallery forest. To 1800 m. Singles or pairs (not flocks) forage on ground. Most often seen alone in rapid flight over small clearing; does not perch high in trees. **ID** ♂ blue-grey; ♀ rufous rump, rufous tail bordered black, chestnut wing-bands. **Voice** Abrupt mellow "boop" 4–6 times, c. 1/second, from mid-level or lower perch in tree, at intervals at any time of day. **SS** Maroon-chested Ground-dove, ♀ Ruddy Ground-dove.

♀

♂

Maroon-chested Ground-dove
Paraclaravis mondetoura `LC`
Tortolita Chusquera
Rare resident, nomadic and irruptive.

 L 22 cm (8.5"). Race *mondetoura*. Dense *Chusquea* bamboo in cloud forest. 1200–3000 m (rarely 600 m). Seeks super-abundant but unpredictable seed crops of bamboo during die-offs, breeds rapidly and disperses. **ID** ♂ whitish foreface, plumage blue-grey, maroon chest patch, white tail tips. ♀ brown, warm buff below, rump, uppertail-coverts and tail rufescent, outer feathers blackish, tiny white tail corners. **Voice** Mellow "hwoop" c. 1/second for nearly a minute. **SS** Blue Ground-dove. **TN** Previously in *Claravis*.

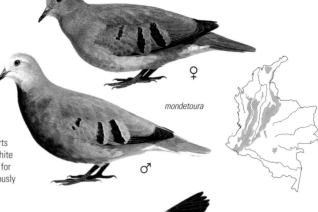

♀

mondetoura

♂

Black-winged Ground-dove *Metriopelia melanoptera* `LC`
Tortolita Paramuna
Local resident (S Nariño).

 L 23 cm (9"). Race *saturatior*. Páramo, dry grassy or shrubby slopes, barren rocky areas. 3000–4800 m. Pairs or small groups feed on ground; perch on rocks; wary, flush abruptly, fly fast on whistling wings. **ID** Wing bend white (conspicuous), black flight feathers and tail, bare orange-yellow spot in front of and below eye. ♀ duller. **Voice** Infrequent slow series of "rreee-up" phrases. **SS** Eared Dove.

saturatior

STEATORNITHIDAE
Oilbird
1 extant species, 1 in region

A distant nightjar relative, the Oilbird is gregarious and distinguished by its strong hooked bill, long rictal bristles, long stiff tail, and weak feet positioned far forward. Oilbirds pluck and swallow large fruit whole while hovering during nocturnal foraging bouts, the seeds later regurgitated. They locate fruit by smell and visual cues. The young quickly become very fat ('oily'), heavier than ads, only later acquire feathers.

Oilbird *Steatornis caripensis* `LC`
Guácharo
Widespread but local resident.

 L 48 cm (19"). Monotypic. Breeds in small to large colonies inside caves, occasionally shady cliffs. Disperses on post-breeding migration in search of food, some reaching dry deforested lowlands (e.g. Cauca Valley) where they often starve. To 3400 m. World's only nocturnal frugivore; eats large energy-rich high-fat content fruit. **ID** Rufous plumage dotted white; unusually long wings and tail. **Voice** Noisy, especially at caves; shrieks, snarls, snores; audible clicks (to human ears) enable echolocation in complete darkness. **SS** Cf. potoos.

NYCTIBIIDAE
Potoos

7 extant species, 6 in region

Unusual Neotropical family notable for cryptic plumage; perch motionless mimicking a tree stub during day. At night sally for flying insects, especially large moths. Their enormous eyes reflect orange-yellow in spotlights.

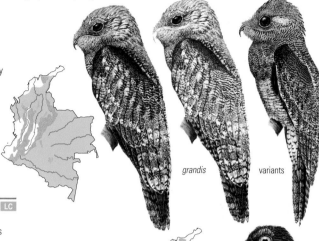

grandis   variants

Great Potoo *Nyctibius grandis* `LC`
Biemparado Grande

Common resident E of Andes, more local in N.

 L 53 cm (21"). Race *grandis*. Humid forest, wooded river borders, gallery forest. To 1000 m. Solitary and immobile by day, usually resting on high semi-open branch or stub. At night sallies from high open stump or forages during long rambling flights. **ID** Large; whitish with dark freckling and mottling; diagnostic narrow black lines border each tail-band. **Voice** Gruff, retching "BUAAAaa"; especially moonlit nights. **SS** Common and Long-tailed Potoos.

Long-tailed Potoo *Nyctibius aethereus* `LC`
Biemparado Rabilargo

 Three subspecies in two subspecies groups; one in Colombia.

Long-tailed Potoo *Nyctibius (aethereus) longicaudatus*

Uncommon and easily overlooked resident.

L 53 cm (21"). Races *chocoensis*[A], *longicaudatus*[B]. Inside humid and wet *terra firme* and transition forest. To 900 m. Immobile by day on low to mid-level perch in forest; sallies from higher stump at night. **ID** Large and dark; long graduated tail extends well beyond wingtips; may show pale shoulder patch; *chocoensis* darker. **Voice** Simple low "waa'ouuu" ("Ra'ul", descends-ascends), not loud, at well-spaced intervals. **SS** Common and Great Potoos.

longicaudatus

griseus

Common Potoo *Nyctibius griseus* `LC`
Biemparado Común

Widespread and common resident.

 L 36 cm (14"). Races *panamensis*[A], *griseus*[B]. Dry to humid forest; borders, gallery forest, *terra firme* and *várzea* river borders. To 2200 m. By day perches immobile and upright on open bare stump or branch, sometimes low; at night sallies from stub (usually lower than Great Potoo). **ID** Brownish but variable (light to dark); tail-bands lack crisp black borders of Great Potoo; wingtips almost reach tail tip. **Voice** Haunting melancholy series of slurred descending whistles, especially on moonlit nights. **SS** Great and Long-tailed Potoos.

variants

Andean Potoo *Nyctibius maculosus* `LC`
Biemparado Andino

Rare resident (few records).

 L 36 cm (14"). Monotypic. Humid upper montane forest, borders. 1800–2700 m (probably higher). Rests by day on open or partly obscured mid-level or higher stump or branch; at night sallies from higher exposed stub. **ID** Size of Common Potoo but dark brown to rufescent-brown (not greyish brown), whitish shoulder patch (not always obvious). **Voice** Call a slow, smoothly upslurred-downslurred "errrrrAAaaa". **SS** Common Potoo (lower elevations).

White-winged Potoo *Nyctibius leucopterus* LC
Biemparado Aliblanco
Rare or local resident (overlooked?).

 L 25–30 cm (10–12"). Monotypic. Audio recording (Xeno-canto), Aug 2019; R Yarí, E Caquetá. 200 m. May occur primarily in white sandy soil forest and tall scrub. **ID** Brownish grey with marbled black markings, prominent white wing-coverts, yellow eyes; considerably smaller than Common and Long-tailed Potoos. **Voice** Song, after dark, long low-pitched melancholy whistle (c. 4 seconds), slightly descending (1.8–1.5 kHz) "wuuuuuuuuuuuuaaaaa", easily imitated.

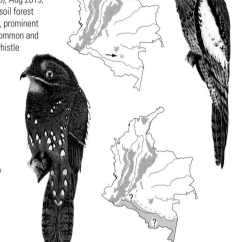

Rufous Potoo *Phyllaemulor bracteatus* LC
Biemparado Rufo
Resident (few records).

 L 27 cm (10.5"). Monotypic. Humid *várzea* and transition forest, less often *terra firme*. To 400 m. Poorly known; recent records from C Caquetá (near R Caquetá). Rests by day on low to mid-level perch inside forest. **ID** Small; plumage rufous spotted white; wedge of black pigment below pupil. **Voice** On moonlit nights, cackling or laugh-like "KA-Ka-ka-ka-ka-..." (c. 12 notes), stronger initially, very slightly descending; owl-like. **SS** Oilbird. **TN** Usually placed in genus *Nyctibius*.

CAPRIMULGIDAE
Nightjars
98 extant species, 21 in region

Worldwide family best known for cryptic plumage, crepuscular or nocturnal behaviour and insectivorous diets. Sexes similar but white markings in ♂ often replaced by buff in ♀. Identification usually requires checking multiple characters, including voice, for verification.

Genus *Chordeiles* Long narrow pointed wings (except Nacunda Nighthawk). Forage at dusk or later, fly at various heights, often high. Buoyant graceful wingbeats alternate with erratic 'gear-changing' swerves.

Nacunda Nighthawk *Chordeiles nacunda* LC
Chotacabras Collarejo
Fairly common resident (wet season) E of Andes, rare W of Andes.

 L 30 cm (12"). Races *coryi*[A] (resident), *nacunda*[B] (austral or intra-tropical migrant). Grassland and open areas. To 600 m; migrants locally higher. Migratory movements and breeding poorly understood. In *llanos* high-flying singles or loose flocks at dusk but often rest on open ground later at night. **ID** Largest nighthawk; mostly white below, white wing-band. **Voice** Not very vocal (in Colombia); low, frog-like "purrr'durrr". Quiet when foraging. **SS** Sand-colored Nighthawk.

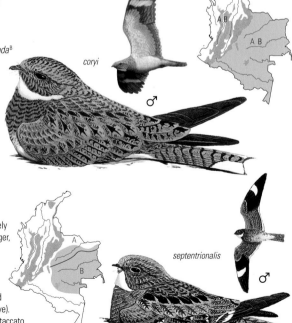

coryi

♂

Least Nighthawk *Chordeiles pusillus* LC
Chotacabras Enano
Fairly common but local resident.

 L 16.5 cm (6.5"). Races *septentrionalis*[A] (finely barred below; white vent), *esmeraldae*[B] (larger, entire underparts heavily barred; possibly migratory). Grassland, open areas with shrubs. To 300 m. Singles, pairs or loose groups fly at various heights from low to fairly high over open terrain at dusk; flight buoyant, erratic. **ID** Small; white wing-band near tip, whitish trailing edge to secondaries (mainly above). **Voice** Song (*septentrionalis*) from ground or bush, brisk staccato "tic'tic'tic'tic-tREE", rising at end. **SS** Lesser Nighthawk.

septentrionalis

♂

Common Nighthawk *Chordeiles minor* `LC`
Chotacabras Norteño
Common boreal passage migrant.

 L 23 cm (9"). Six or seven races (variation clinal?) possible but poorly documented. Loose high-flying groups at dawn or dusk; can occur almost anywhere, even large cities, over Amazonian rainforest; peak Mar–Apr and Sept–Nov. **ID** Wing-band nearer bend of wing than tip; at rest band diagonal across primaries, often hidden beneath tertials, flight feathers of extended wing uniform (no spots). **Voice** Occasional "purr" call; rarely vocal on migration. **SS** Lesser and Antillean Nighthawks.

minor

[Antillean Nighthawk *Chordeiles gundlachii*] `LC`
Chotacabras Antillano
Hypothetical.

 L 23 cm (9"). Monotypic. Scrub, partly wooded areas. To 100 m. Possibly a rare non-breeding passage migrant to Islas San Andrés and Providencia; one presumed sight record on latter, Apr 2018; none on mainland. **ID** Doubtfully separable from Common Nighthawk except by voice; at rest wingtips reach tail tip, pale tertials contrast with back, breast whitish, belly buff. **Voice** ♂ 2–6 rapid chattering or loosely staccato notes. **SS** Common and Lesser Nighthawks.

Lesser Nighthawk *Chordeiles acutipennis* `LC`
Chotacabras Chico
Fairly common (?) resident.

 L 20 cm (8"). Races *texensis*[A] (boreal migrant over W Colombia), *acutipennis*[B] (resident throughout, except Pacific lowlands), *crissalis*[C] (resident, Middle and upper Cauca Valley and upper Magdalena Valley), *aequatorialis*[D] (resident, only Pacific lowlands of Colombia south through W Ecuador). Drier partly open terrain. To 1000 m. Status and distribution of races complex, subject to revision. Flies low when foraging, high on migration. **ID** White (buff ♀) wing-band nearer tip than bend of wing; at rest band perpendicular (not diagonal) to primaries and extends beyond tertials; open wing shows buff-spotted flight feathers. **Voice** Purring trill. **SS** Common and Antillean Nighthawks.

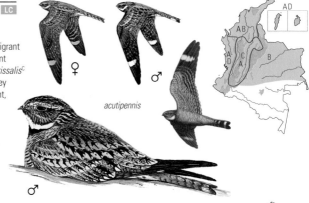

acutipennis

Sand-colored Nighthawk *Chordeiles rupestris* `LC`
Chotacabras Pechiblanco
Locally common resident.

 L 20 cm (8"). Races *xyostictus*[A] (verified?), *rupestris*[B]. Riverbanks, river islands, lake edges; village streetlights at dusk. To 400 m. Rests by day in small to large groups on ground, open sandbars, driftwood, fallen branches over water. Forages in loose flocks at dusk, periodically by night. Wingbeats deep; flight mechanical, less erratic than other *Chordeiles*. **ID** Bold wing pattern; white underwings and underparts. **Voice** Soft purring; bubbly sputters; guttural trills. **SS** Nacunda Nighthawk.

rupestris

Genus *Lurocalis* Short-tailed with fast, erratic bat-like flight; at rest wings extend beyond tail. The only New World caprimulgids that nest on high bare tree branches.

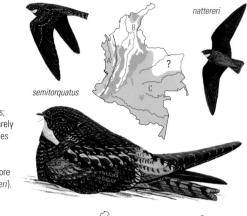

nattereri

semitorquatus

Short-tailed Nighthawk *Lurocalis semitorquatus* `LC`
Chotacabras Rabicorto
Uncommon and local resident.

L 20 cm (8"). Races *stonei*[A], *semitorquatus*[B], *nattereri*[C] (austral migrant?; resident). Humid lowland forest, borders; higher-elevation birds probably migrants? To c. 1000 m (rarely 1800 m). Rests on high forest branch by day. At dusk singles or pairs circle in fast erratic flight through or just above canopy or over clearings for a few minutes. **ID** Short tail, long wings; underparts dull rufous mottled dusky, wings entirely dark (*semitorquatus*) or brighter more contrasting pattern (*stonei*), also brighter, barring fainter below (*nattereri*). **Voice** High reedy upward-inflected "quiik, quiik…"; liquid "tuu-it" (*nattereri* in Argentina). **SS** Rufous-bellied Nighthawk.

Rufous-bellied Nighthawk *Lurocalis rufiventris* `LC`
Chotacabras Buchirrufo
Uncommon resident.

L 24 cm (9.5"). Monotypic. Humid montane forest and clearings. 1650–3000 m. Singles or pairs forage at dusk; weaving and circling in fast erratic flight through or just above forest canopy; seldom visible for long. **ID** Short tail, long all-dark wings, wing-linings and underparts (except chest) solid rufous; larger, more robust than Short-tailed Nighthawk. **Voice** In flight single hoarse whistles "wuck" or "tork"; longer descending "qua-QUEE-Quee, qua, qua". **SS** Short-tailed Nighthawk.

Genus *Nyctiprogne* Notably gregarious. Pointed all-dark wings. Vocalizations complex. More than one species involved.

Band-tailed Nighthawk *Nyctiprogne leucopyga* `LC`
Chotacabras Coliblanco

Five subspecies in two subspecies groups; both (?) in Colombia.

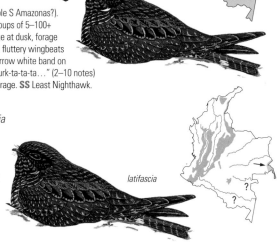

exigua

Band-tailed Nighthawk *Nyctiprogne (leucopyga) leucopyga*
Locally common resident (*llanos*).
L 18 cm (7"). Races *pallida*[A], *exigua*[B] (valid?), *majuscula* (possible S Amazonas?). White- and black-water lakes, rivers, riverbanks. To 400 m. Groups of 5–100+ roost above ground in riverbank and lake-edge thickets; emerge at dusk, forage at various heights, often low over or near water. Bat-like quick fluttery wingbeats alternate with short glides and swerves. **ID** Small; all dark, narrow white band on undertail (in spotlight). **Voice** Song (*pallida*) nasal frog-like "qurk-ta-ta-ta…" (2–10 notes) from ground or bush; soft "churk" or "werk-CHURK" as they forage. **SS** Least Nighthawk.

Rio Negro Nighthawk *Nyctiprogne (leucopyga) latifascia*
Status unknown.
L 18 cm (7"). Race *latifascia*. Possibly more associated with black-water rivers than Band-tailed Nighthawk; they co-occur locally. **ID** Darker than Band-tailed Nighthawk, less vermiculated, but reliably separated (in field) only by voice. **Voice** Call low staccato "t't't't'TRIP", last note stronger; steadily repeated c. 1 every 1.5 seconds; single harsh note; long-sustained staccato rattle from on or near ground. **TN** Recognized by vocal and molecular evidence; English name provisional.

latifascia

Nightjars Formerly *Caprimulgus*; now separated into *Nyctipolus, Systellura, Setopagis, Hydropsalis* and *Antrostomus* based on molecular data. Most share numerous similarities including broad rounded wings; fairly long tails and soft lax plumage. Voices often more diagnostic than plumage. ♀♀ confusing.

Blackish Nightjar *Nyctipolus nigrescens* `LC`
Guardacaminos Negruzco
Common resident (white-sand soil regions).
L 22 cm (8.5"). Monotypic. Savanna woodland borders, rock outcrops, *cerros*, boulders in rivers; rare or absent in lowland Amazonia. To 900 m (Andean foothills). Singles or pairs rest partly hidden under bush or in open on ground, log or blackish rock; after dark and before dawn sally short distances from ground or log.
ID Blackish; wings almost to tail tip, tertials contrastingly grey, tiny white wing-band, small white tail corners. ♀ no white. **Voice** Notably quiet; soft "pret!"; soft frog-like "puurrt…puurrt…" trills.

♂

?

Greater Band-winged Nightjar *Systellura longirostris* `LC`
Guardacaminos Andino
Fairly common and widespread resident.
L 22 cm (8.5"). Race *ruficervix*. Humid forest borders, road-cuts, open or bushy slopes, window ledges and roofs in cities. 1600–3600 m. Singles or pairs rest concealed by day. Sallies from ground, boulder or building after dark or makes short meandering sorties. **ID** Dark; white wing-band (buff, ♀), rufous nape, broad white terminal tail-band (or barred buff, ♀). **Voice** Thin high "seeeeert" or "seeEEEeert", squeezed out. **SS** Pauraque. **TN** Widespread South American species with 3–5 vocal and genetic groups.

♂

ruficervix

Genus *Nyctidromus* Larger, longer-tailed than allies; rounded wings; widespread.

Pauraque *Nyctidromus albicollis* `LC`
Bujío
Commonest resident nightjar in Colombia.
L 28 cm (11"). Races *gilvus*[A], *albicollis*[B]. Dry to humid forest edges, gallery forest, second-growth woodland. To 2600 m. Rests on fallen leaves just inside woodland or thicket by day. Sallies from ground, roadside or low perch after dark and before dawn; may make meandering sorties. **ID** Long-tailed; chestnut cheeks, buff-encircled black scapular spots, white wing-bands (buff, ♀), white in tail as flushes (no white, ♀); rare rufous morph mostly cinnamon (not greyish). **Voice** Vocal on moonlit nights; loud whistled "cuu-wheEEero"; numerous variations, especially at dusk. **SS** Overlaps many other nightjars but far commoner than all.

♀

♂

A

B

♂   *albicollis*

rufous morph

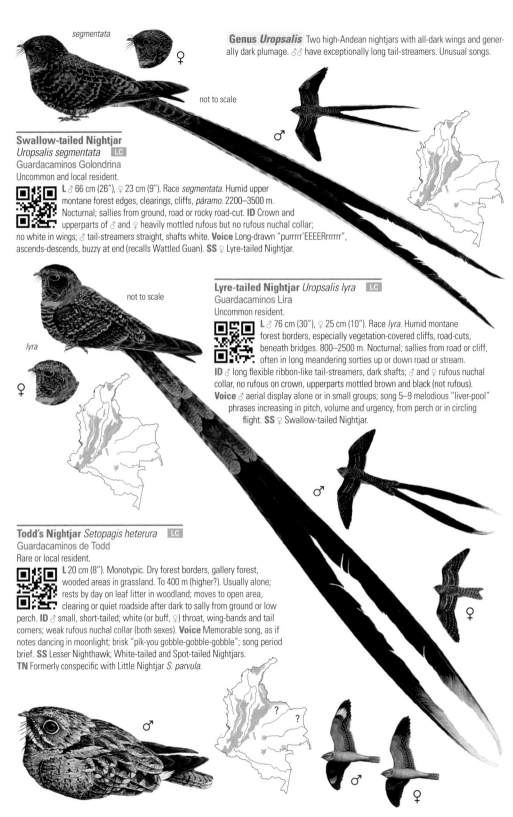

segmentata

♀

not to scale

Genus *Uropsalis* Two high-Andean nightjars with all-dark wings and generally dark plumage. ♂♂ have exceptionally long tail-streamers. Unusual songs.

♂

Swallow-tailed Nightjar
Uropsalis segmentata `LC`
Guardacaminos Golondrina
Uncommon and local resident.
L ♂ 66 cm (26"), ♀ 23 cm (9"). Race *segmentata*. Humid upper montane forest edges, clearings, cliffs, *páramo*. 2200–3500 m. Nocturnal; sallies from ground, road or rocky road-cut. **ID** Crown and upperparts of ♂ and ♀ heavily mottled rufous but no rufous nuchal collar; no white in wings; ♂ tail-streamers straight, shafts white. **Voice** Long-drawn "purrrrr'EEEERrrrrrr", ascends-descends, buzzy at end (recalls Wattled Guan). **SS** ♀ Lyre-tailed Nightjar.

not to scale

lyra

♀

Lyre-tailed Nightjar *Uropsalis lyra* `LC`
Guardacaminos Lira
Uncommon resident.
L ♂ 76 cm (30"), ♀ 25 cm (10"). Race *lyra*. Humid montane forest borders, especially vegetation-covered cliffs, road-cuts, beneath bridges. 800–2500 m. Nocturnal; sallies from road or cliff, often in long meandering sorties up or down road or stream. **ID** ♂ long flexible ribbon-like tail-streamers, dark shafts; ♂ and ♀ rufous nuchal collar, no rufous on crown, upperparts mottled brown and black (not rufous). **Voice** ♂ aerial display alone or in small groups; song 5–9 melodious "liver-pool" phrases increasing in pitch, volume and urgency, from perch or in circling flight. **SS** ♀ Swallow-tailed Nightjar.

♂

♀

Todd's Nightjar *Setopagis heterura* `LC`
Guardacaminos de Todd
Rare or local resident.
L 20 cm (8"). Monotypic. Dry forest borders, gallery forest, wooded areas in grassland. To 400 m (higher?). Usually alone; rests by day on leaf litter in woodland; moves to open area, clearing or quiet roadside after dark to sally from ground or low perch. **ID** ♂ small, short-tailed; white (or buff, ♀) throat, wing-bands and tail corners; weak rufous nuchal collar (both sexes). **Voice** Memorable song, as if notes dancing in moonlight; brisk "pík-you gobble-gobble-gobble"; song period brief. **SS** Lesser Nighthawk; White-tailed and Spot-tailed Nightjars. **TN** Formerly conspecific with Little Nightjar *S. parvula*.

♂

?   ?

♂

♀

Ladder-tailed Nightjar *Hydropsalis climacocerca* `LC`
Guardacaminos Rabilargo
Common resident.

L ♂ 28 cm (11"), ♀ 24 cm (9.5"). Race *climacocerca*. Brush and grass on sandy riverbanks, river island sandbars, lagoon edges. To 500 m. Roosts semi-concealed in piles of driftwood on sandbars or thickets near or over water. Sallies from ground or low stump after dark. **ID** ♂ flashes white wing-band, much white in tail. ♀ faint cinnamon wing-band, no white in tail. Either sex in flight by skinny shape, long crooked wings, long narrow tail. **Voice** Infrequent song of liquid "tsick!" notes. **SS** Pauraque.

climacocerca

White-tailed Nightjar *Hydropsalis cayennensis* `LC`
Guardacaminos Rastrojero
Fairly common resident.

L 22 cm (8.5"). Races *albicauda*[A], *insularis*[B], *aperta*[C], *cayennensis*[D]. Dry semi-open scrub in Andean foothills, marshes, grassland and scrub in *llanos*. To 2100 m. Roosts alone by day under bush or in weedy area; at night sallies from ground or in long-sustained low rambling flights. **ID** ♂ pale coloration, cinnamon nuchal collar, whitish throat, white wing-band, white tail borders, mostly white undertail. ♀ confusing; cinnamon nuchal collar, buff wing-band, dark barred tail (no white). **Voice** Thin high "spit-cheeeeuua", first note faint, last rising-falling. **SS** ♀ Spot-tailed and ♀ Todd's Nightjars.

cayennensis

Spot-tailed Nightjar *Hydropsalis maculicaudus* `LC`
Guardacaminos Rabimanchado
Uncommon resident (*llanos*), very local W of Andes.

L 20 cm (8"). Monotypic. Degraded areas of mixed grass and brush, savanna scrub. To 1200 m. Behaviour like White-tailed Nightjar. **ID** Small, short-tailed; buffier than allies. ♂ prominent white tail tips, no white wing-band, broad pale eyebrow, dusky cheeks with blackish 'eye sockets', rufous nuchal collar, 3–4 rows of buff spots on wings, chest with large prominent buff-white spots. ♀ like ♂ including dusky sides of head, spotted chest, terminal tail-band dingy grey. **Voice** Thin high "pit-swuueeét", weak, rising at end; vocal when breeding. **SS** White-tailed and Todd's Nightjars.

Genus *Nyctiphrynus* Two Colombian species (one either side of Andes) of deep forest interior. Dark plumage, with minor white spotting; rounded all-dark wings.

Choco Poorwill *Nyctiphrynus rosenbergi* `NT`
Guardacaminos del Chocó `NT`
Fairly common resident.

L 22 cm (8.5"). Monotypic. Near-endemic (also NW Ecuador). Inside humid and wet forest, especially foothills. To 900 m (higher?). Nocturnal; seems not to forage from roads; calls from elevated perch. **ID** Small, blackish, 2–3 conspicuous white wing spots. **Voice** Song whistled "wee'whuut", last note lower; or longer rising four- or five-note "wu-wu-wuu-whuut", recalls Pauraque. **SS** Pauraque (larger, paler). **TN** Formerly a race of Ocellated Poorwill.

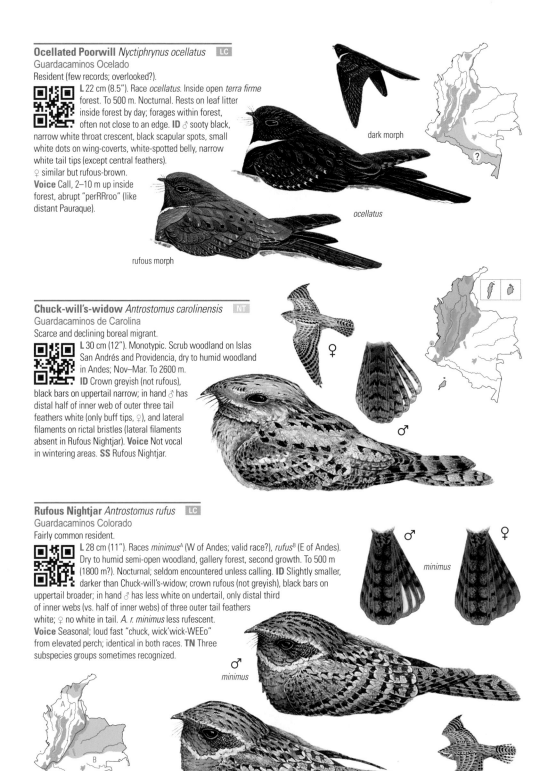

Ocellated Poorwill *Nyctiphrynus ocellatus* `LC`
Guardacaminos Ocelado
Resident (few records; overlooked?).

L 22 cm (8.5"). Race *ocellatus*. Inside open *terra firme* forest. To 500 m. Nocturnal. Rests on leaf litter inside forest by day; forages within forest, often not close to an edge. **ID** ♂ sooty black, narrow white throat crescent, black scapular spots, small white dots on wing-coverts, white-spotted belly, narrow white tail tips (except central feathers). ♀ similar but rufous-brown. **Voice** Call, 2–10 m up inside forest, abrupt "perRRroo" (like distant Pauraque).

dark morph

ocellatus

rufous morph

Chuck-will's-widow *Antrostomus carolinensis* `NT`
Guardacaminos de Carolina
Scarce and declining boreal migrant.

L 30 cm (12"). Monotypic. Scrub woodland on Islas San Andrés and Providencia, dry to humid woodland in Andes; Nov–Mar. To 2600 m. **ID** Crown greyish (not rufous), black bars on uppertail narrow; in hand ♂ has distal half of inner web of outer three tail feathers white (only buff tips, ♀), and lateral filaments on rictal bristles (lateral filaments absent in Rufous Nightjar). **Voice** Not vocal in wintering areas. **SS** Rufous Nightjar.

♀

♂

Rufous Nightjar *Antrostomus rufus* `LC`
Guardacaminos Colorado
Fairly common resident.

L 28 cm (11"). Races *minimus*[A] (W of Andes; valid race?), *rufus*[B] (E of Andes). Dry to humid semi-open woodland, gallery forest, second growth. To 500 m (1800 m?). Nocturnal; seldom encountered unless calling. **ID** Slightly smaller, darker than Chuck-will's-widow; crown rufous (not greyish), black bars on uppertail broader; in hand ♂ has less white on undertail, only distal third of inner webs (vs. half of inner webs) of three outer tail feathers white; ♀ no white in tail. *A. r. minimus* less rufescent. **Voice** Seasonal; loud fast "chuck, wick'wick-WEEo" from elevated perch; identical in both races. **TN** Three subspecies groups sometimes recognized.

♂   ♀

minimus

minimus

rufus

♂   *rufus*

♂

rufus

APODIDAE
Swifts

96 extant species, 17 in region

Highly aerial cosmopolitan family with dark plumage, stiff narrow wings and large eyes. Swifts (and hummingbirds) uniquely rotate their wings from the base, allowing the wing to remain fully extended and power the upstroke and downstroke. Swifts have weak feet, suitable for clinging, but not perching normally. Identification is challenging, often impossible; key points are wing shape, tail length, throat and rump shading (pale or dark). Status of many Colombian swifts poorly known due to unresolved taxonomy and lack of obvious field marks.

Genus *Cypseloides* Fairly large; long narrow wings; shorter-tailed than smaller *Chaetura*; plumage uniform blackish; difficult to identify.

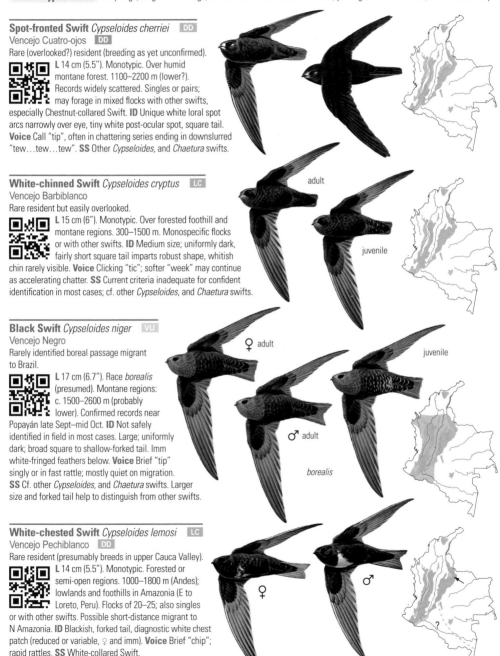

Spot-fronted Swift *Cypseloides cherriei* DD
Vencejo Cuatro-ojos DD
Rare (overlooked?) resident (breeding as yet unconfirmed).
L 14 cm (5.5"). Monotypic. Over humid montane forest. 1100–2200 m (lower?). Records widely scattered. Singles or pairs; may forage in mixed flocks with other swifts, especially Chestnut-collared Swift. **ID** Unique white loral spot arcs narrowly over eye, tiny white post-ocular spot, square tail. **Voice** Call "tip", often in chattering series ending in downslurred "tew…tew…tew". **SS** Other *Cypseloides*, and *Chaetura* swifts.

White-chinned Swift *Cypseloides cryptus* LC
Vencejo Barbiblanco
Rare resident but easily overlooked.
L 15 cm (6"). Monotypic. Over forested foothill and montane regions. 300–1500 m. Monospecific flocks or with other swifts. **ID** Medium size; uniformly dark, fairly short square tail imparts robust shape, whitish chin rarely visible. **Voice** Clicking "tic"; softer "week" may continue as accelerating chatter. **SS** Current criteria inadequate for confident identification in most cases; cf. other *Cypseloides*, and *Chaetura* swifts.

adult
juvenile

Black Swift *Cypseloides niger* VU
Vencejo Negro
Rarely identified boreal passage migrant to Brazil.
L 17 cm (6.7"). Race *borealis* (presumed). Montane regions: c. 1500–2600 m (probably lower). Confirmed records near Popayán late Sept–mid Oct. **ID** Not safely identified in field in most cases. Large; uniformly dark; broad square to shallow-forked tail. Imm white-fringed feathers below. **Voice** Brief "tip" singly or in fast rattle; mostly quiet on migration. **SS** Cf. other *Cypseloides*, and *Chaetura* swifts. Larger size and forked tail help to distinguish from other swifts.

♀ adult
juvenile
♂ adult
borealis

White-chested Swift *Cypseloides lemosi* LC
Vencejo Pechiblanco DD
Rare resident (presumably breeds in upper Cauca Valley).
L 14 cm (5.5"). Monotypic. Forested or semi-open regions. 1000–1800 m (Andes); lowlands and foothills in Amazonia (E to Loreto, Peru). Flocks of 20–25; also singles or with other swifts. Possible short-distance migrant to N Amazonia. **ID** Blackish, forked tail, diagnostic white chest patch (reduced or variable, ♀ and imm). **Voice** Brief "chip"; rapid rattles. **SS** White-collared Swift.

♀
♂

Genus *Streptoprocne* Largest Colombian swifts; tail notched. Typically fly high, occasionally quite low; short veering glides mixed with powerful wingbeats. Both species 'collared' and easy to identify.

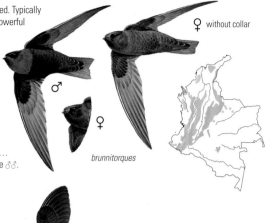

♀ without collar

♂

♀

brunnitorques

Chestnut-collared Swift *Streptoprocne rutila* `LC`
Vencejo Cuellirrojo
Common resident.

 L 14 cm (5.5"). Race *brunnitorques*. Over forested or semi-open areas, villages and towns; foothills or higher. 500–3000 m. Single-species flocks or with other swifts. **ID** Slightly forked tail. ♂ diagnostic chestnut collar (reduced or absent, ♀ and imm). **Voice** Buzzy "bzt… bzt…"; buzzy rattles. **SS** In highland swift flocks look for distinctive ♂♂. *Cypseloides*, especially larger Black Swift.

White-collared Swift *Streptoprocne zonaris* `LC`
Vencejo Collarejo
Common and widespread resident.

 L 20 cm (8"). Races *subtropicalis*[A], *altissima*[B] (breeds higher elevations). Both races presumably forage at all elevations. To 3500 m. Social. Monospecific flocks or with other swifts; 100s ride thermals to great heights in early morning. Powerful deceptively fast flight. Roost and nest behind mountain waterfalls; disperse far during day, even to Amazonian lowlands. **ID** Very large; white collar. Imm body plumage fringed white. **Voice** Often noisy; screeches, chittering; synchronous pulsating "ss'ree, ss'ree…" descending mountains at great speed.

subtropicalis

Genus *Chaetura* Small and dark; pale rump and/or uppertail-coverts contrast with darker body; throat pale or dark. Fast, stiff-winged flight alternates with brief glides. Taxonomy unresolved. Identification difficult, often impossible.

Band-rumped Swift *Chaetura spinicaudus* `LC`
Vencejo Culiblanco
Locally common resident.

aetherodroma

 L 11 cm (4.3"). Races *aetherodroma*[A], *latirostris*[B]. Humid lowlands and foothills. To 1800 m. Single-species flocks or with other *Chaetura*; often forages low. **ID** Small with slender profile; clean narrow white rump-band; mid-length square tail. **Voice** Call two-note "pseee-trr"; thin high "chit" singly, paired, or fast series. **SS** Grey-rumped Swift.

Grey-rumped Swift *Chaetura cinereiventris* `LC`
Vencejo Cenizo

 Seven subspecies in two subspecies groups; one in Colombia.

sclateri

Ashy-rumped Swift *Chaetura (cinereiventris) sclateri*
Vencejo Rabigrís
Fairly common E of Andes (presumed resident).
L 11 cm (4.3"). Races *occidentalis*[A], *schistacea*[B], *sclateri*[C]. Humid forest, semi-open lowland and lower montane regions. To 2000 m. Often in mixed *Chaetura* flocks. **ID** Small, relatively short-tailed; pale throat, contrasting grey (not white) rump (*sclateri*) or uniform grey below, less contrasting rump (*occidentalis*). **Voice** Brief "tsip" or "tic" notes; twittering. **SS** Other *Chaetura*. **TN** Race *occidentalis* often placed in separate subspecies group.

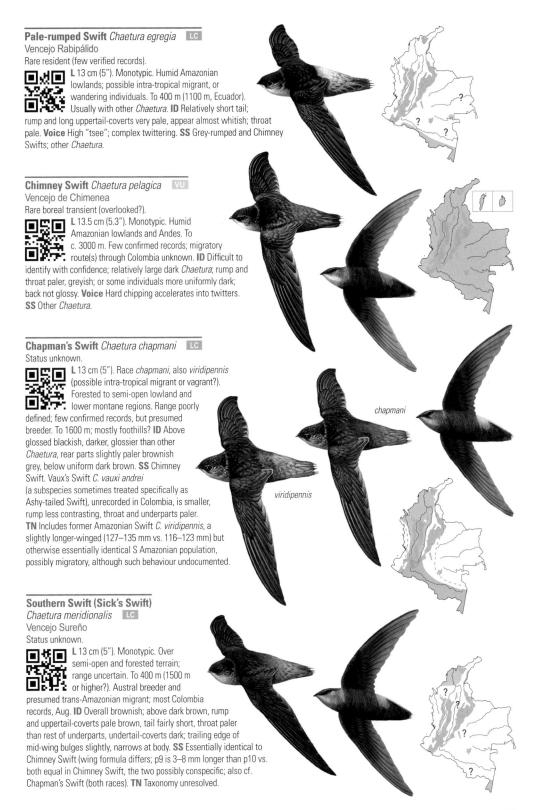

Pale-rumped Swift *Chaetura egregia* `LC`
Vencejo Rabipálido
Rare resident (few verified records).
L 13 cm (5"). Monotypic. Humid Amazonian lowlands; possible intra-tropical migrant, or wandering individuals. To 400 m (1100 m, Ecuador). Usually with other *Chaetura*. **ID** Relatively short tail; rump and long uppertail-coverts very pale, appear almost whitish; throat pale. **Voice** High "tsee"; complex twittering. **SS** Grey-rumped and Chimney Swifts; other *Chaetura*.

Chimney Swift *Chaetura pelagica* `VU`
Vencejo de Chimenea
Rare boreal transient (overlooked?).
L 13.5 cm (5.3"). Monotypic. Humid Amazonian lowlands and Andes. To c. 3000 m. Few confirmed records; migratory route(s) through Colombia unknown. **ID** Difficult to identify with confidence; relatively large dark *Chaetura*; rump and throat paler, greyish; or some individuals more uniformly dark; back not glossy. **Voice** Hard chipping accelerates into twitters. **SS** Other *Chaetura*.

Chapman's Swift *Chaetura chapmani* `LC`
Status unknown.
L 13 cm (5"). Race *chapmani*, also *viridipennis* (possible intra-tropical migrant or vagrant?). Forested to semi-open lowland and lower montane regions. Range poorly defined; few confirmed records, but presumed breeder. To 1600 m; mostly foothills? **ID** Above glossed blackish, darker, glossier than other *Chaetura*, rear parts slightly paler brownish grey, below uniform dark brown. **SS** Chimney Swift. Vaux's Swift *C. vauxi andrei* (a subspecies sometimes treated specifically as Ashy-tailed Swift), unrecorded in Colombia, is smaller, rump less contrasting, throat and underparts paler. **TN** Includes former Amazonian Swift *C. viridipennis*, a slightly longer-winged (127–135 mm vs. 116–123 mm) but otherwise essentially identical S Amazonian population, possibly migratory, although such behaviour undocumented.

chapmani

viridipennis

Southern Swift (Sick's Swift)
Chaetura meridionalis `LC`
Vencejo Sureño
Status unknown.
L 13 cm (5"). Monotypic. Over semi-open and forested terrain; range uncertain. To 400 m (1500 m or higher?). Austral breeder and presumed trans-Amazonian migrant; most Colombia records, Aug. **ID** Overall brownish; above dark brown, rump and uppertail-coverts pale brown, tail fairly short, throat paler than rest of underparts, undertail-coverts dark; trailing edge of mid-wing bulges slightly, narrows at body. **SS** Essentially identical to Chimney Swift (wing formula differs; p9 is 3–8 mm longer than p10 vs. both equal in Chimney Swift, the two possibly conspecific; also cf. Chapman's Swift (both races). **TN** Taxonomy unresolved.

Short-tailed Swift *Chaetura brachyura* `LC`
Vencejo Rabicorto

 Four subspecies in two subspecies groups; one in Colombia.

Short-tailed Swift *Chaetura (brachyura) brachyura*
Common resident.
L 11 cm (4.3"). Race *brachyura*. Over humid forest in Amazonia; dry semi-open terrain in N. To 1300 m (usually < 900 m). Flocks, often with other *Chaetura*; frequently flies high. **ID** Obviously short-tailed; very pale rear end; robust body; paddle-winged shape with bulging secondaries narrowing at body impart distinctive floppy flight. **Voice** Rapid chipping and twittering. **SS** Pale-rumped and Grey-rumped Swifts.

White-tipped Swift *Aeronautes montivagus* `LC`
Vencejo Pierniblanco
Fairly common but local resident.

 L 13 cm (5"). Race *montivagus*. Humid montane forest, clearings, canyons, buildings (nests under roofs); 400–2700 m; *cerros* in extreme E (to 300 m). Single-species flocks of 10–30, infrequently with other swifts; fly fast at low to moderate heights. **ID** Streamlined; throat, tail tips, flank patches, tips of inner secondaries white; longish tail with shallow fork. **Voice** Noisy ratchet-like buzzing or rattling accelerates, then slows and fades. **SS** Lesser Swallow-tailed Swift.

Pygmy Swift *Tachornis furcata* `LC`
Vencejo Enano `DD`
Fairly common resident.

 L 10 cm (4"). Race *furcata*. Moist forest, semi-open terrain, settled areas, towns with palms. To 800 m. Small monospecific flocks; fast twittering, zigzagging flight, often high over forest, semi-open or urban areas. Roosts and nests in tall palms (especially *Roystonea*). **ID** Small, slender; long forked tail held closed in point or spread during turns; dingy underparts. **Voice** Buzzy "bee, beez beez beez-be-be-be-b'b'b", trailing off. **AN** Pygmy Palm-swift.

Fork-tailed Palm-swift *Tachornis squamata* `LC`
Vencejo Palmero
Common resident.

 L 13 cm (5"). Race *semota*. Open or semi-open areas with *Mauritia* palms where roosts and nests. To 1000 m. Fast, buzzy flight, notably stiff-winged; circles at low or moderate heights. **ID** Slender; dingy below; long forked tail usually held closed in point. **Voice** Buzzy or ticking "d-z-z-z-z-z-z-z-z" and trills in flight. **SS** No overlap with Pygmy Swift. **AN** Neotropical Palm-swift.

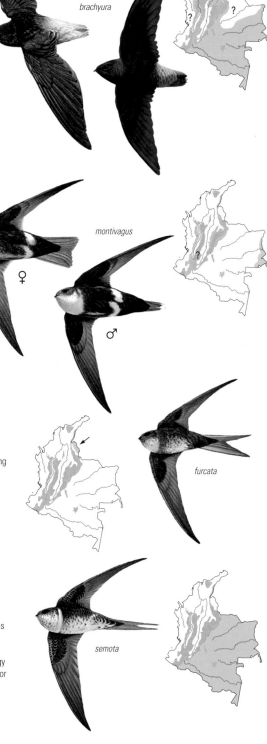

brachyura

montivagus
♀
♂

furcata

semota

Lesser Swallow-tailed Swift *Panyptila cayennensis* `LC`
Vencejo Rabihorcado
Uncommon resident.

 L 14 cm (5.5"). Race *cayennensis*. Forest or semi-open lowlands and foothills. To 1400 m. Alone, pairs, occasionally trios (never large monospecific flocks), sometimes loosely associated with other swifts. Flies high, typically higher than other swifts; erratic zigzag flight when foraging; fast wingbeats alternate with short glides. Unpredictable in occurrence. Felt-like tubular suspended nest. **ID** White throat continues as narrow nuchal collar, white flank patches, white tips to secondaries, long forked tail usually closed in point; tiny white pre-ocular spot. **Voice** Chittering notes. **SS** White-tipped Swift.

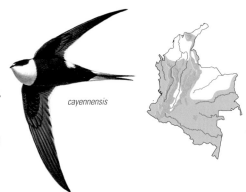

cayennensis

TROCHILIDAE
Hummingbirds
365 extant species, 163 in region

Hummingbirds are a large New World family with members in all terrestrial habitats from the lowlands to snowline. Peak diversity is reached in lower montane regions of the N Andes but still comprise a large proportion of the avifauna in cold treeline habitats. A family of superlatives, they have the fastest metabolism, fastest wingbeats, and are the only birds capable of flying backwards. They also are among the smallest birds and can regulate night-time body temperatures to conserve energy. Almost perpetually in motion, hummingbirds feed on nectar, supplemented by insects, and are important pollinators of many plants. Hummingbird foraging behaviour is varied and includes territorial species, trap-liners, filchers, low-nectar reward seekers, and nectar 'parasites'. Some gather in leks to sing and display, or employ aerial displays. Identification can be confusing. Iridescent plumage produces dramatic colour shifts, young ♂♂ often look like ♀, and their frantic movements make them difficult to see well. Bill lengths, tail shape and pattern, and features of head are helpful in identification, as is knowledge of distribution and elevation. Molecular data have dramatically altered hummingbird taxonomy.

Fiery Topaz *Topaza pyra* `LC`
Topacio Fúlgido
Local resident.

 L ♂ 19 cm (7.5"), ♀ 15 cm (6"); **B** 2.5 cm (1"). Races *pyra*[A], *amarun*[B]. Sandy soil forests, black-water river and stream borders, wet areas with *Mauritia* palms. To 400 m. Hovers over small streams for insects; visits flowers, eye level to canopy. **ID** ♂ black hood and chest surround metallic-green gorget, fiery red body, two elongated tail feathers, rufous wing-linings. ♀ ruby gorget, tail normal. Imm ♂ duller, tail plumes short. **Voice** Chattering song slows to "tchip" and wiry "pseet-seet" notes.

pyra

♂

♀

White-necked Jacobin *Florisuga mellivora* `LC`
Colibrí Nuquiblanco
Common resident.

 **L** 11.4 cm (4.5"); **B** 2 cm (0.8"). Race *mellivora*. Dry woodland, plantations, clearings, canopy and borders of humid forest. To 1900 m. Conspicuous. Often at large flowering trees; hovers in open for gnats. **ID** ♂ blue head, neck and throat, white on hindneck, lower underparts white, tail mostly white tipped black (older ♂♂ lose black tips). ♀ variable, recalls ♂ or, more often, scaled and spotted dusky on throat to breast, vent coarsely barred blackish. Imm variable, rufous malar and rump. **Voice** High "tseee". **SS** Scaly-breasted Hummingbird (p. 101).

mellivora

♂

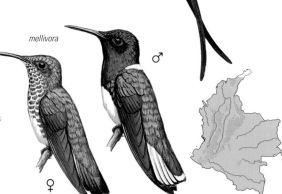

♀

Genus *Eutoxeres* Forest undergrowth; extremely decurved bills adapted for feeding at certain species of *Heliconia*; generally shy.

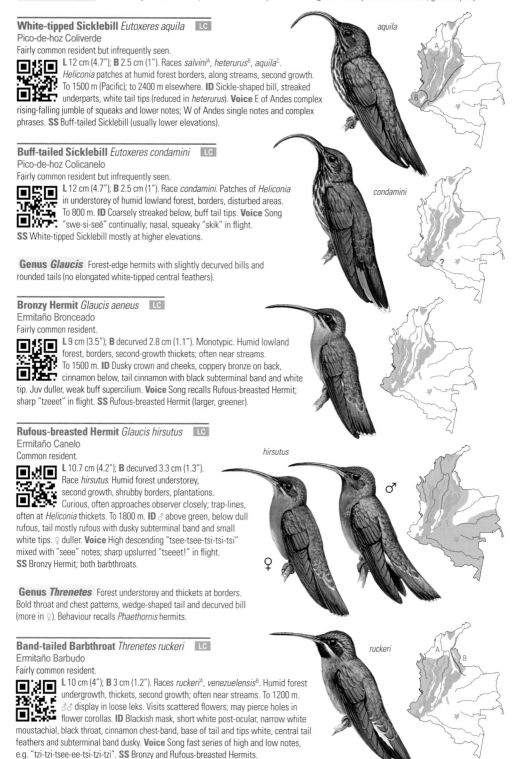

White-tipped Sicklebill *Eutoxeres aquila* LC
Pico-de-hoz Coliverde
Fairly common resident but infrequently seen.

aquila

L 12 cm (4.7"); **B** 2.5 cm (1"). Races *salvini*[A], *heterurus*[B], *aquila*[C]. *Heliconia* patches at humid forest borders, along streams, second growth. To 1500 m (Pacific); to 2400 m elsewhere. **ID** Sickle-shaped bill, streaked underparts, white tail tips (reduced in *heterurus*). **Voice** E of Andes complex rising-falling jumble of squeaks and lower notes; W of Andes single notes and complex phrases. **SS** Buff-tailed Sicklebill (usually lower elevations).

Buff-tailed Sicklebill *Eutoxeres condamini* LC
Pico-de-hoz Colicanelo
Fairly common resident but infrequently seen.

condamini

L 12 cm (4.7"); **B** 2.5 cm (1"). Race *condamini*. Patches of *Heliconia* in understorey of humid lowland forest, borders, disturbed areas. To 800 m. **ID** Coarsely streaked below, buff tail tips. **Voice** Song "swe-si-seé" continually; nasal, squeaky "skik" in flight. **SS** White-tipped Sicklebill mostly at higher elevations.

Genus *Glaucis* Forest-edge hermits with slightly decurved bills and rounded tails (no elongated white-tipped central feathers).

Bronzy Hermit *Glaucis aeneus* LC
Ermitaño Bronceado
Fairly common resident.

L 9 cm (3.5"); **B** decurved 2.8 cm (1.1"). Monotypic. Humid lowland forest, borders, second-growth thickets; often near streams. To 1500 m. **ID** Dusky crown and cheeks, coppery bronze on back, cinnamon below, tail cinnamon with black subterminal band and white tip. Juv duller, weak buff supercilium. **Voice** Song recalls Rufous-breasted Hermit; sharp "tzeeet" in flight. **SS** Rufous-breasted Hermit (larger, greener).

Rufous-breasted Hermit *Glaucis hirsutus* LC
Ermitaño Canelo
Common resident.

hirsutus

♂

L 10.7 cm (4.2"); **B** decurved 3.3 cm (1.3"). Race *hirsutus*. Humid forest understorey, second growth, shrubby borders, plantations. Curious, often approaches observer closely; trap-lines, often at *Heliconia* thickets. To 1800 m. **ID** ♂ above green, below dull rufous, tail mostly rufous with dusky subterminal band and small white tips. ♀ duller. **Voice** High descending "tsee-tsee-tsi-tsi-tsi" mixed with "seee" notes; sharp upslurred "tseeet!" in flight. **SS** Bronzy Hermit; both barbthroats.

♀

Genus *Threnetes* Forest understorey and thickets at borders. Bold throat and chest patterns, wedge-shaped tail and decurved bill (more in ♀). Behaviour recalls *Phaethornis* hermits.

Band-tailed Barbthroat *Threnetes ruckeri* LC
Ermitaño Barbudo
Fairly common resident.

ruckeri

L 10 cm (4"); **B** 3 cm (1.2"). Races *ruckeri*[A], *venezuelensis*[B]. Humid forest undergrowth, thickets, second growth; often near streams. To 1200 m. ♂♂ display in loose leks. Visits scattered flowers; may pierce holes in flower corollas. **ID** Blackish mask, short white post-ocular, narrow white moustachial, black throat, cinnamon chest-band, base of tail and tips white, central tail feathers and subterminal band dusky. **Voice** Song fast series of high and low notes, e.g. "tzi-tzi-tsee-ee-tsi-tzi-tzi". **SS** Bronzy and Rufous-breasted Hermits.

Pale-tailed Barbthroat *Threnetes leucurus* `LC`
Ermitaño Coliblanco

Five subspecies in two subspecies groups; one in Colombia.

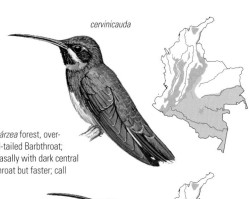

cervinicauda

Pale-tailed Barbthroat *Threnetes (leucurus) leucurus*
Uncommon resident.
L 10 cm (4"); **B** 3 cm (1.2"). Race *cervinicauda*. Humid *terra firme* and *várzea* forest, overgrown borders, thickets, second growth. To 700 m. Behaviour like Band-tailed Barbthroat; easily overlooked. **ID** ♂ throat blackish, chest-band rufous, tail white basally with dark central feathers and subterminal band. ♀ duller. **Voice** Like Band-tailed Barbthroat but faster; call sharp "tseet". **SS** Black-throated Hermit.

Genus *Phaethornis* Small to large; dull-plumaged. Low inside forest. Long decurved bills; long white-tipped central tail feathers. ♂♂ sing in leks. Forage by trap-lining. Timid.

Streak-throated Hermit *Phaethornis rupurumii* `LC`
Ermitaño Orinocense
Resident (few records).

L 9 cm (3.5"); **B** 2.5 cm (1"). Race *rupurumii*. Understorey in humid forest, borders; mainly white-sand regions. To 250 m. **ID** Fairly small; dusky mask, rufous-tinged rump, throat streaked dusky, chest smudged cinnamon, white central tail tips barely project. **Voice** ♂ at lek sings from low perch; repetitive squeaky song may vary individually or locally. **SS** Black-throated Hermit. **AN** Rupurumi Hermit.

rupurumii

Black-throated Hermit *Phaethornis atrimentalis* `LC`
Ermitaño Gorginegro
Common resident.

L 8.4 cm (3.3"); **B** 2.5 cm (1"). Race *atrimentalis*. Understorey of humid lowland forest, shrubby borders, second growth. To 500 m. **ID** Small; throat blackish, rump, breast and belly rusty; ♂ may show weakly indicated blackish line on breast. **Voice** ♂ on low perch at lek incessantly repeats short squeaky song, typically several single notes followed by 2+ rhythmic ones. **SS** Reddish and Grey-chinned Hermits. **TN** Formerly a race of Little Hermit *P. longuemareus*.

♂ atrimentalis

Stripe-throated Hermit *Phaethornis striigularis* `LC`
Ermitaño Gorgirrayado
Fairly common resident.

subrufescens

striigularis

L 9 cm (3.5"); **B** 2.3 cm (0.9").
Races *saturatus*[A],
subrufescens[B], *striigularis*[C].
Fairly dry to humid forest
understorey, shrubby borders, plantations.
To 1300 m. Trap-lines small scattered
flowers. **ID** Fairly small; white central
tail tips barely project. **Voice** ♂ at lek
incessantly repeats squeaky song from
low perch. **SS** Smallest hermit W of Andes.
TN Formerly a race of Little Hermit *P. longuemareus*.

saturatus

Grey-chinned Hermit *Phaethornis griseogularis* `LC`
Ermitaño Gorgigrís
Uncommon resident.

L 8.6 cm (3.4"); **B** 2.3 cm (0.9"). Race *griseogularis*. Understorey in humid foothill forest, shrubby borders. 500–1500 m. **ID** Very small; chin streaked or smudged dark grey (hard to see). ♂ obscure narrow black breast-band; ♀ no band. **Voice** ♂ at lek repeats squeaky song from low perch.
SS Black-throated and Reddish Hermits (both smaller; usually lower elevation).
TN Formerly a race of Little Hermit *P. longuemareus*.

♂

griseogularis

73

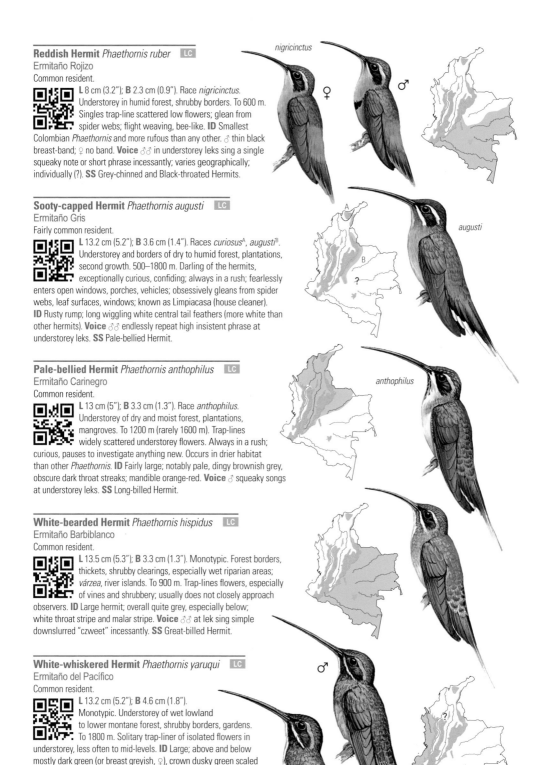

Reddish Hermit *Phaethornis ruber* LC
Ermitaño Rojizo
Common resident.

L 8 cm (3.2"); **B** 2.3 cm (0.9"). Race *nigricinctus*. Understorey in humid forest, shrubby borders. To 600 m. Singles trap-line scattered low flowers; glean from spider webs; flight weaving, bee-like. **ID** Smallest Colombian *Phaethornis* and more rufous than any other. ♂ thin black breast-band; ♀ no band. **Voice** ♂♂ in understorey leks sing a single squeaky note or short phrase incessantly; varies geographically; individually (?). **SS** Grey-chinned and Black-throated Hermits.

Sooty-capped Hermit *Phaethornis augusti* LC
Ermitaño Gris
Fairly common resident.

L 13.2 cm (5.2"); **B** 3.6 cm (1.4"). Races *curiosus*[A], *augusti*[B]. Understorey and borders of dry to humid forest, plantations, second growth. 500–1800 m. Darling of the hermits, exceptionally curious, confiding; always in a rush; fearlessly enters open windows, porches, vehicles; obsessively gleans from spider webs, leaf surfaces, windows; known as Limpiacasa (house cleaner). **ID** Rusty rump; long wiggling white central tail feathers (more white than other hermits). **Voice** ♂♂ endlessly repeat high insistent phrase at understorey leks. **SS** Pale-bellied Hermit.

Pale-bellied Hermit *Phaethornis anthophilus* LC
Ermitaño Carinegro
Common resident.

L 13 cm (5"); **B** 3.3 cm (1.3"). Race *anthophilus*. Understorey of dry and moist forest, plantations, mangroves. To 1200 m (rarely 1600 m). Trap-lines widely scattered understorey flowers. Always in a rush; curious, pauses to investigate anything new. Occurs in drier habitat than other *Phaethornis*. **ID** Fairly large; notably pale, dingy brownish grey, obscure dark throat streaks; mandible orange-red. **Voice** ♂ squeaky songs at understorey leks. **SS** Long-billed Hermit.

White-bearded Hermit *Phaethornis hispidus* LC
Ermitaño Barbiblanco
Common resident.

L 13.5 cm (5.3"); **B** 3.3 cm (1.3"). Monotypic. Forest borders, thickets, shrubby clearings, especially wet riparian areas; *várzea*, river islands. To 900 m. Trap-lines flowers, especially of vines and shrubbery; usually does not closely approach observers. **ID** Large hermit; overall quite grey, especially below; white throat stripe and malar stripe. **Voice** ♂♂ at lek sing simple downslurred "czweet" incessantly. **SS** Great-billed Hermit.

White-whiskered Hermit *Phaethornis yaruqui* LC
Ermitaño del Pacífico
Common resident.

L 13.2 cm (5.2"); **B** 4.6 cm (1.8"). Monotypic. Understorey of wet lowland to lower montane forest, shrubby borders, gardens. To 1800 m. Solitary trap-liner of isolated flowers in understorey, less often to mid-levels. **ID** Large; above and below mostly dark green (or breast greyish, ♀), crown dusky green scaled coppery buff, prominent post-ocular stripe buff, malar whitish (usually) or buff near bill, central throat stripe white to greyish, vent white. **Voice** ♂♂ sing squeaky "kree-u" and "seek" at understorey leks, some occupied year-round. **SS** Green Hermit.

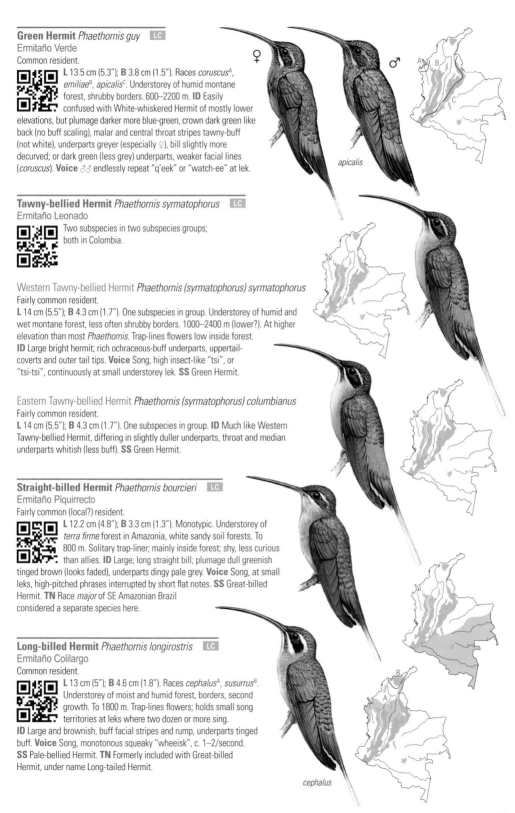

Green Hermit *Phaethornis guy* `LC`
Ermitaño Verde
Common resident.

L 13.5 cm (5.3"); **B** 3.8 cm (1.5"). Races *coruscus*[A], *emiliae*[B], *apicalis*[C]. Understorey of humid montane forest, shrubby borders. 600–2200 m. **ID** Easily confused with White-whiskered Hermit of mostly lower elevations, but plumage darker more blue-green, crown dark green like back (no buff scaling), malar and central throat stripes tawny-buff (not white), underparts greyer (especially ♀), bill slightly more decurved; or dark green (less grey) underparts, weaker facial lines (*coruscus*). **Voice** ♂♂ endlessly repeat "q'eek" or "watch-ee" at lek.

♀ ♂ apicalis

Tawny-bellied Hermit *Phaethornis syrmatophorus* `LC`
Ermitaño Leonado

Two subspecies in two subspecies groups; both in Colombia.

Western Tawny-bellied Hermit *Phaethornis (syrmatophorus) syrmatophorus*
Fairly common resident.
L 14 cm (5.5"); **B** 4.3 cm (1.7"). One subspecies in group. Understorey of humid and wet montane forest, less often shrubby borders. 1000–2400 m (lower?). At higher elevation than most *Phaethornis*. Trap-lines flowers low inside forest. **ID** Large bright hermit; rich ochraceous-buff underparts, uppertail-coverts and outer tail tips. **Voice** Song, high insect-like "tsi", or "tsi-tsi", continuously at small understorey lek. **SS** Green Hermit.

Eastern Tawny-bellied Hermit *Phaethornis (syrmatophorus) columbianus*
Fairly common resident.
L 14 cm (5.5"); **B** 4.3 cm (1.7"). One subspecies in group. **ID** Much like Western Tawny-bellied Hermit, differing in slightly duller underparts, throat and median underparts whitish (less buff). **SS** Green Hermit.

Straight-billed Hermit *Phaethornis bourcieri* `LC`
Ermitaño Piquirrecto
Fairly common (local?) resident.

L 12.2 cm (4.8"); **B** 3.3 cm (1.3"). Monotypic. Understorey of *terra firme* forest in Amazonia, white sandy soil forests. To 800 m. Solitary trap-liner; mainly inside forest; shy, less curious than allies. **ID** Large; long straight bill; plumage dull greenish tinged brown (looks faded), underparts dingy pale grey. **Voice** Song, at small leks, high-pitched phrases interrupted by short flat notes. **SS** Great-billed Hermit. **TN** Race *major* of SE Amazonian Brazil considered a separate species here.

Long-billed Hermit *Phaethornis longirostris* `LC`
Ermitaño Colilargo
Common resident.

L 13 cm (5"); **B** 4.6 cm (1.8"). Races *cephalus*[A], *susurrus*[B]. Understorey of moist and humid forest, borders, second growth. To 1800 m. Trap-lines flowers; holds small song territories at leks where two dozen or more sing. **ID** Large and brownish, buff facial stripes and rump, underparts tinged buff. **Voice** Song, monotonous squeaky "wheeisk", c. 1–2/second. **SS** Pale-bellied Hermit. **TN** Formerly included with Great-billed Hermit, under name Long-tailed Hermit.

cephalus

Great-billed Hermit *Phaethornis malaris* `LC`
Ermitaño Piquigrande

Six subspecies in two subspecies groups; one in Colombia.

Great-billed Hermit *Phaethornis (malaris) malaris*
Fairly common resident.
L 13 cm (5"); **B** 4.6 cm (1.8"). Races *insolitus*[A], *moorei*[B]. Undergrowth in humid lowland and foothill forest. To 1500 m. Behaviour like Long-billed Hermit. **ID** Large, overall brownish, long decurved bill; faint central throat stripe; or underparts paler and greyer, *moorei* (but races very similar). **Voice** ♂♂ tirelessly repeat simple "slee-up", or variation, c. 1.5 notes/second throughout much of day. **SS** Straight-billed and White-bearded Hermits. **TN** Formerly included with Long-billed Hermit, under name Long-tailed Hermit.

moorei

Green-fronted Lancebill *Doryfera ludovicae* `LC`
Pico-de-lanza Frentiverde
Locally fairly common resident.
L 11 cm (4.3"); **B** 3.6 cm (1.4"). Race *ludovicae*. Low to mid-strata in humid montane forest, shrubby borders, along mountain streams. 900–2700 m (occasionally lower or higher). Trap-lines scattered mostly epiphytic flowers with long tubular corollas including *Fuchsia*, Ericaceae, Loranthaceae, Rubiaceae. **ID** Long thin straight bill; overall dull and dark, reddish-bronze crown and nape, green forecrown (inconspicuous), bluish uppertail-coverts; rounded tail. ♀ duller, below greenish grey. **Voice** Song undescribed. **SS** Blue-fronted Lancebill.

ludovicae

Blue-fronted Lancebill *Doryfera johannae* `LC`
Pico-de-lanza Frentiazul
Uncommon resident.
L 9 cm (3.5"); **B** 2.8 cm (1.1"). Races *johannae*[A], *guianensis*[B] Guainía (?). Lower storey of humid forest, shrubby borders. 400–1600 m. Usually low; feeds from long tubular flowers; hovers for gnats. **ID** Like Green-fronted Lancebill but smaller, much darker, almost blackish below (especially ♂); generally lower elevation. ♀ bluish forecrown, greyer underparts. **Voice** Song undescribed. **SS** Green-fronted Lancebill.

johannae

Choco Daggerbill *Schistes albogularis* `LC`
Colibrí Piquicuña del Chocó
Uncommon resident.
L 9 cm (3.5"); short sharp-pointed **B** 1.5 cm (0.6"). Monotypic. Low inside humid montane forest, shrubby borders. 800–2600 m. Trap-lines low flowers, e.g. *Psammisia*, *Palicourea*, *Besleria*; partial nectar parasite, puncturing bases of flower corollas, taking nectar without transferring pollen; seldom at artificial feeders. **ID** Short bill. ♂ green throat, small blue-violet upper pectoral patch, larger white pectoral patches narrowly joined either side, white post-ocular, rump green, dark subterminal band, rounded tail. ♀ throat white. **Voice** High insect-like "sink". **TN** Formerly a race of Wedge-billed Hummingbird. **AN** Western Wedge-billed Hummingbird.

Geoffroy's Daggerbill *Schistes geoffroyi* `LC`
Colibrí Piquicuña
Uncommon resident.
L 9 cm (3.5"); short sharp-pointed **B** 1.5 cm (0.6"). Race *geoffroyi*. Low inside humid montane forest, shrubby borders. 600–2600 m. **ID** Like Choco Daggerbill but plumage duller (not glittering), white pectoral patches larger but not joined, post-ocular stripe longer, rump much more contrasting reddish copper. ♀ throat white speckled green. **SS** Ecuadorian Piedtail (p. 82). **TN** Formerly a race of Wedge-billed Hummingbird. **AN** Eastern Wedge-billed Hummingbird.

geoffroyi

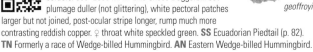

Genus *Colibri* Widespread montane hummingbirds; violet ear patches; dark subterminal tail-band; tireless singers; territorial.

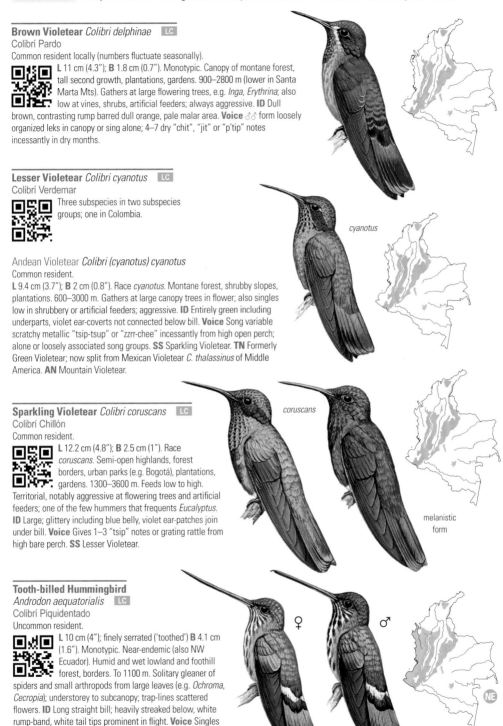

Brown Violetear *Colibri delphinae* `LC`
Colibrí Pardo
Common resident locally (numbers fluctuate seasonally).

L 11 cm (4.3"); **B** 1.8 cm (0.7"). Monotypic. Canopy of montane forest, tall second growth, plantations, gardens. 900–2800 m (lower in Santa Marta Mts). Gathers at large flowering trees, e.g. *Inga*, *Erythrina*; also low at vines, shrubs, artificial feeders; always aggressive. **ID** Dull brown, contrasting rump barred dull orange, pale malar area. **Voice** ♂♂ form loosely organized leks in canopy or sing alone; 4–7 dry "chit", "jit" or "p'tip" notes incessantly in dry months.

Lesser Violetear *Colibri cyanotus* `LC`
Colibrí Verdemar

Three subspecies in two subspecies groups; one in Colombia.

Andean Violetear *Colibri (cyanotus) cyanotus*
Common resident.
L 9.4 cm (3.7"); **B** 2 cm (0.8"). Race *cyanotus*. Montane forest, shrubby slopes, plantations. 600–3000 m. Gathers at large canopy trees in flower; also singles low in shrubbery or artificial feeders; aggressive. **ID** Entirely green including underparts, violet ear-coverts not connected below bill. **Voice** Song variable scratchy metallic "tsip-tsup" or "zzrr-chee" incessantly from high open perch; alone or loosely associated song groups. **SS** Sparkling Violetear. **TN** Formerly Green Violetear; now split from Mexican Violetear *C. thalassinus* of Middle America. **AN** Mountain Violetear.

cyanotus

Sparkling Violetear *Colibri coruscans* `LC`
Colibrí Chillón
Common resident.

L 12.2 cm (4.8"); **B** 2.5 cm (1"). Race *coruscans*. Semi-open highlands, forest borders, urban parks (e.g. Bogotá), plantations, gardens. 1300–3600 m. Feeds low to high. Territorial, notably aggressive at flowering trees and artificial feeders; one of the few hummers that frequents *Eucalyptus*. **ID** Large; glittery including blue belly, violet ear-patches join under bill. **Voice** Gives 1–3 "tsip" notes or grating rattle from high bare perch. **SS** Lesser Violetear.

coruscans

melanistic form

Tooth-billed Hummingbird
Androdon aequatorialis `LC`
Colibrí Piquidentado
Uncommon resident.

L 10 cm (4"); finely serrated ('toothed') **B** 4.1 cm (1.6"). Monotypic. Near-endemic (also NW Ecuador). Humid and wet lowland and foothill forest, borders. To 1100 m. Solitary gleaner of spiders and small arthropods from large leaves (e.g. *Ochroma*, *Cecropia*); understorey to subcanopy; trap-lines scattered flowers. **ID** Long straight bill; heavily streaked below, white rump-band, white tail tips prominent in flight. **Voice** Singles or 2–4 sing from low perches inside forest; repetitive three-note "tsi-tsée-tsek".

♀ ♂ `NE`

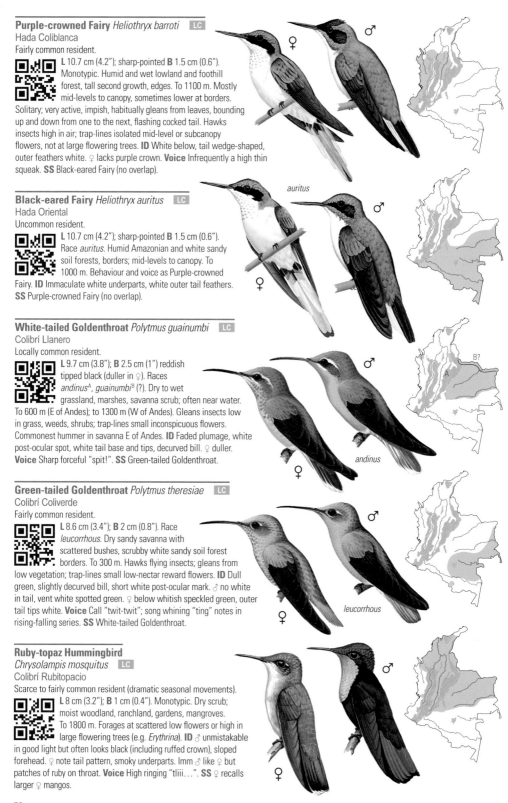

Purple-crowned Fairy *Heliothryx barroti* `LC`
Hada Coliblanca
Fairly common resident.
L 10.7 cm (4.2"); sharp-pointed **B** 1.5 cm (0.6"). Monotypic. Humid and wet lowland and foothill forest, tall second growth, edges. To 1100 m. Mostly mid-levels to canopy, sometimes lower at borders. Solitary; very active, impish, habitually gleans from leaves, bounding up and down from one to the next, flashing cocked tail. Hawks insects high in air; trap-lines isolated mid-level or subcanopy flowers, not at large flowering trees. **ID** White below, tail wedge-shaped, outer feathers white. ♀ lacks purple crown. **Voice** Infrequently a high thin squeak. **SS** Black-eared Fairy (no overlap).

Black-eared Fairy *Heliothryx auritus* `LC`
Hada Oriental
Uncommon resident.
L 10.7 cm (4.2"); sharp-pointed **B** 1.5 cm (0.6"). Race *auritus*. Humid Amazonian and white sandy soil forests, borders; mid-levels to canopy. To 1000 m. Behaviour and voice as Purple-crowned Fairy. **ID** Immaculate white underparts, white outer tail feathers. **SS** Purple-crowned Fairy (no overlap).

White-tailed Goldenthroat *Polytmus guainumbi* `LC`
Colibrí Llanero
Locally common resident.
L 9.7 cm (3.8"); **B** 2.5 cm (1") reddish tipped black (duller in ♀). Races *andinus*[A], *guainumbi*[B] (?). Dry to wet grassland, marshes, savanna scrub; often near water. To 600 m (E of Andes); to 1300 m (W of Andes). Gleans insects low in grass, weeds, shrubs; trap-lines small inconspicuous flowers. Commonest hummer in savanna E of Andes. **ID** Faded plumage, white post-ocular spot, white tail base and tips, decurved bill. ♀ duller. **Voice** Sharp forceful "spit!". **SS** Green-tailed Goldenthroat.

Green-tailed Goldenthroat *Polytmus theresiae* `LC`
Colibrí Coliverde
Fairly common resident.
L 8.6 cm (3.4"). Race *leucorrhous*. Dry sandy savanna with scattered bushes, scrubby white sandy soil forest borders. To 300 m. Hawks flying insects; gleans from low vegetation; trap-lines small low-nectar reward flowers. **ID** Dull green, slightly decurved bill, short white post-ocular mark. ♂ no white in tail, vent white spotted green. ♀ below whitish speckled green, outer tail tips white. **Voice** Call "twit-twit"; song whining "ting" notes in rising-falling series. **SS** White-tailed Goldenthroat.

Ruby-topaz Hummingbird
Chrysolampis mosquitus `LC`
Colibrí Rubitopacio
Scarce to fairly common resident (dramatic seasonal movements).
L 8 cm (3.2"); **B** 1 cm (0.4"). Monotypic. Dry scrub; moist woodland, ranchland, gardens, mangroves. To 1800 m. Forages at scattered low flowers or high in large flowering trees (e.g. *Erythrina*). **ID** ♂ unmistakable in good light but often looks black (including ruffed crown), sloped forehead. ♀ note tail pattern, smoky underparts. Imm ♂ like ♀ but patches of ruby on throat. **Voice** High ringing "tliii…". **SS** ♀ recalls larger ♀ mangos.

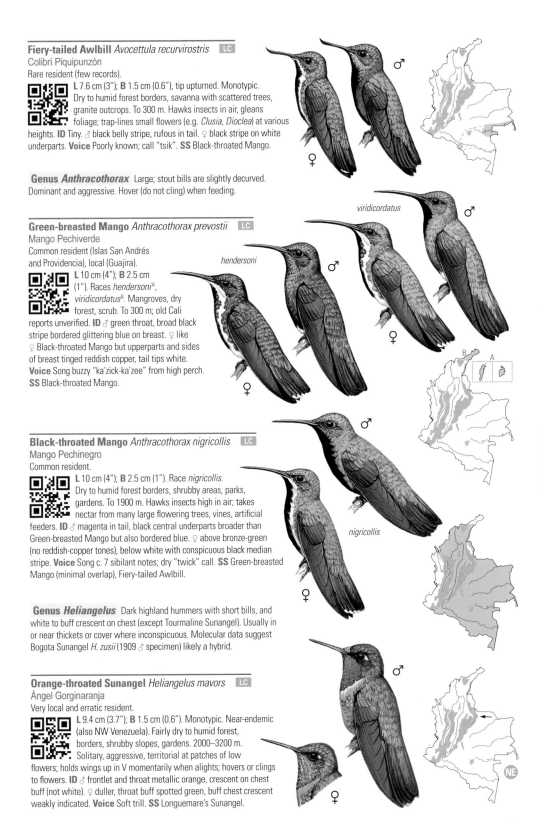

Fiery-tailed Awlbill *Avocettula recurvirostris* `LC`
Colibrí Piquipunzón
Rare resident (few records).
L 7.6 cm (3"); **B** 1.5 cm (0.6"), tip upturned. Monotypic.
Dry to humid forest borders, savanna with scattered trees,
granite outcrops. To 300 m. Hawks insects in air, gleans
foliage; trap-lines small flowers (e.g. *Clusia, Dioclea*) at various
heights. **ID** Tiny. ♂ black belly stripe, rufous in tail. ♀ black stripe on white
underparts. **Voice** Poorly known; call "tsik". **SS** Black-throated Mango.

Genus *Anthracothorax* Large; stout bills are slightly decurved.
Dominant and aggressive. Hover (do not cling) when feeding.

Green-breasted Mango *Anthracothorax prevostii* `LC`
Mango Pechiverde
Common resident (Islas San Andrés
and Providencia), local (Guajira).
L 10 cm (4"); **B** 2.5 cm
(1"). Races *hendersoni*[A],
viridicordatus[B]. Mangroves, dry
forest, scrub. To 300 m; old Cali
reports unverified. **ID** ♂ green throat, broad black
stripe bordered glittering blue on breast. ♀ like
♀ Black-throated Mango but upperparts and sides
of breast tinged reddish copper, tail tips white.
Voice Song buzzy "ka'zick-ka'zee" from high perch.
SS Black-throated Mango.

Black-throated Mango *Anthracothorax nigricollis* `LC`
Mango Pechinegro
Common resident.
L 10 cm (4"); **B** 2.5 cm (1"). Race *nigricollis*.
Dry to humid forest borders, shrubby areas, parks,
gardens. To 1900 m. Hawks insects high in air; takes
nectar from many large flowering trees, vines, artificial
feeders. **ID** ♂ magenta in tail, black central underparts broader than
Green-breasted Mango but also bordered blue. ♀ above bronze-green
(no reddish-copper tones), below white with conspicuous black median
stripe. **Voice** Song c. 7 sibilant notes; dry "twick" call. **SS** Green-breasted
Mango (minimal overlap), Fiery-tailed Awlbill.

Genus *Heliangelus* Dark highland hummers with short bills, and
white to buff crescent on chest (except Tourmaline Sunangel). Usually in
or near thickets or cover where inconspicuous. Molecular data suggest
Bogota Sunangel *H. zusii* (1909 ♂ specimen) likely a hybrid.

Orange-throated Sunangel *Heliangelus mavors* `LC`
Ángel Gorginaranja
Very local and erratic resident.
L 9.4 cm (3.7"); **B** 1.5 cm (0.6"). Monotypic. Near-endemic
(also NW Venezuela). Fairly dry to humid forest,
borders, shrubby slopes, gardens. 2000–3200 m.
Solitary, aggressive, territorial at patches of low
flowers; holds wings up in V momentarily when alights; hovers or clings
to flowers. **ID** ♂ frontlet and throat metallic orange, crescent on chest
buff (not white). ♀ duller, throat buff spotted green, buff chest crescent
weakly indicated. **Voice** Soft trill. **SS** Longuemare's Sunangel.

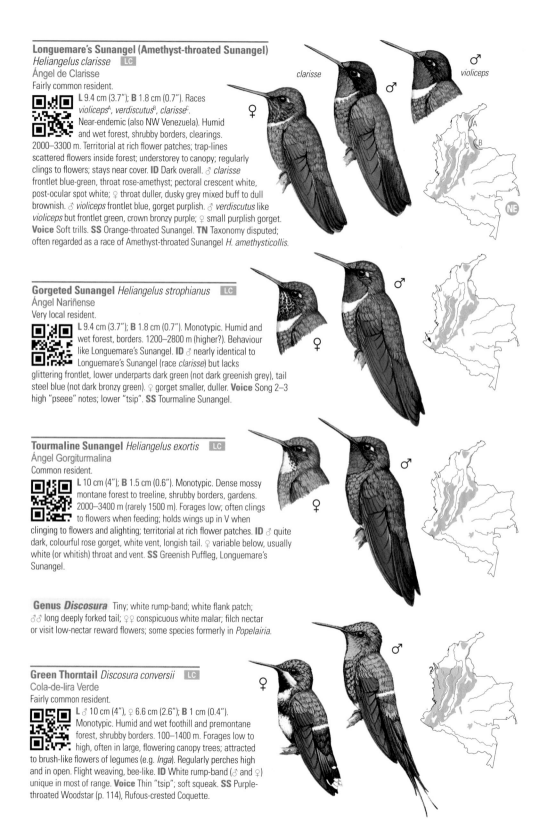

Longuemare's Sunangel (Amethyst-throated Sunangel)
Heliangelus clarisse LC
Ángel de Clarisse
Fairly common resident.

clarisse ♂ *violiceps* ♂

♀

L 9.4 cm (3.7"); **B** 1.8 cm (0.7"). Races *violiceps*[A], *verdiscutus*[B], *clarisse*[C]. Near-endemic (also NW Venezuela). Humid and wet forest, shrubby borders, clearings. 2000–3300 m. Territorial at rich flower patches; trap-lines scattered flowers inside forest; understorey to canopy; regularly clings to flowers; stays near cover. **ID** Dark overall. ♂ *clarisse* frontlet blue-green, throat rose-amethyst; pectoral crescent white, post-ocular spot white; ♀ throat duller, dusky grey mixed buff to dull brownish. ♂ *violiceps* frontlet blue, gorget purplish. ♂ *verdiscutus* like *violiceps* but frontlet green, crown bronzy purple; ♀ small purplish gorget. **Voice** Soft trills. **SS** Orange-throated Sunangel. **TN** Taxonomy disputed; often regarded as a race of Amethyst-throated Sunangel *H. amethysticollis*.

Gorgeted Sunangel *Heliangelus strophianus* LC
Ángel Nariñense
Very local resident.

♂

♀

L 9.4 cm (3.7"); **B** 1.8 cm (0.7"). Monotypic. Humid and wet forest, borders. 1200–2800 m (higher?). Behaviour like Longuemare's Sunangel. **ID** ♂ nearly identical to Longuemare's Sunangel (race *clarisse*) but lacks glittering frontlet, lower underparts dark green (not dark greenish grey), tail steel blue (not dark bronzy green). ♀ gorget smaller, duller. **Voice** Song 2–3 high "pseee" notes; lower "tsip". **SS** Tourmaline Sunangel.

Tourmaline Sunangel *Heliangelus exortis* LC
Ángel Gorgiturmalina
Common resident.

♂

♀

L 10 cm (4"); **B** 1.5 cm (0.6"). Monotypic. Dense mossy montane forest to treeline, shrubby borders, gardens. 2000–3400 m (rarely 1500 m). Forages low; often clings to flowers when feeding; holds wings up in V when clinging to flowers and alighting; territorial at rich flower patches. **ID** ♂ quite dark, colourful rose gorget, white vent, longish tail. ♀ variable below, usually white (or whitish) throat and vent. **SS** Greenish Puffleg, Longuemare's Sunangel.

Genus *Discosura* Tiny; white rump-band; white flank patch; ♂♂ long deeply forked tail; ♀♀ conspicuous white malar; filch nectar or visit low-nectar reward flowers; some species formerly in *Popelairia*.

Green Thorntail *Discosura conversii* LC
Cola-de-lira Verde
Fairly common resident.

♂

♀

L ♂ 10 cm (4"), ♀ 6.6 cm (2.6"); **B** 1 cm (0.4"). Monotypic. Humid and wet foothill and premontane forest, shrubby borders. 100–1400 m. Forages low to high, often in large, flowering canopy trees; attracted to brush-like flowers of legumes (e.g. *Inga*). Regularly perches high and in open. Flight weaving, bee-like. **ID** White rump-band (♂ and ♀) unique in most of range. **Voice** Thin "tsip"; soft squeak. **SS** Purple-throated Woodstar (p. 114), Rufous-crested Coquette.

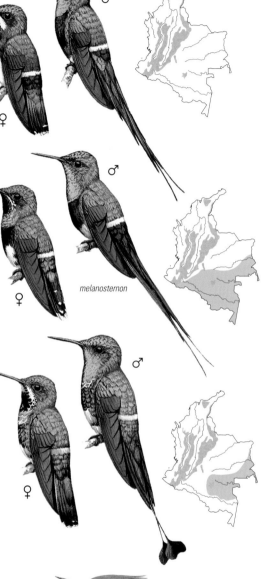

Wire-crested Thorntail *Discosura popelairii* NT
Cola-de-lira Guamero
Uncommon resident (sharp seasonal movements).

 L ♂ 11.4 cm (4.5"), ♀ 6.6 cm (2.6");
B 1.3 cm (0.5"). Monotypic. Canopy and
borders of humid forest, flowering shrubs
in clearings, gardens. 500–1600 m. Behaviour
as Green Thorntail. **ID** ♂ wispy recurved crest, white
rump-band and flank patch, long spiky outer tail feathers,
upperparts coppery green. ♀ short tail, white malar, flank
patch and rump-band, upperparts coppery green. **SS** Nearly
identical Black-bellied Thorntail (usually lower elevation).

Black-bellied Thorntail *Discosura langsdorffi* LC
Cola-de-lira Tronador
Uncommon resident (sharp seasonal movements).

 L ♂ 11.4 cm (4.5"), ♀ 6.6 mm (2.6");
B 1.3 cm (0.5"). Race *melanosternon*.
Canopy and borders of humid lowland forest.
To 400 m. Typically high in canopy at flowering
trees where overlooked; floating bee-like flight; regularly
perches on high open twigs. **ID** ♂ and ♀ very like respective
sexes of Wire-crested Thorntail but no crest, upperparts green
(no coppery tone). **SS** Racket-tipped Thorntail.

melanosternon

Racket-tipped Thorntail *Discosura longicaudus* LC
Cola-de-lira Raqueta
Rare (overlooked?) resident.

 L ♂ 12.2 cm (4.8"), ♀ 6.6 mm (2.6"); **B** 1.3 cm (0.5").
Monotypic. Canopy and borders of white sandy
soil forest around rocky outcrops. To 300 m.
Usually perches and feeds high at small flowers.
ID White rump-band (buff-white, ♀). ♂ racquet-tipped tail, gorget
glittering green, broad rusty-copper breast-band, belly whitish.
♀ white malar, central throat dusky, below mottled green
and rusty (or forecrown and underparts whitish mixed
orange-rufous below, sex?), tail light brown, broad dusky
subterminal band. **SS** Black-bellied Thorntail. **AN** Racket-tailed
Coquette (or Racket-tailed Thorntail).

Genus *Lophornis* Tiny. White rump-band, but no white flank
patch (cf. woodstars). ♂♂ ornamented, ♀♀ plainer and confusing.
Attracted to brush-like flowers of legumes.

Rufous-crested Coquette *Lophornis delattrei* LC
Coqueta Crestada
Uncommon, local and erratic resident.

 **L** 7 cm (2.7"); **B** 1 cm (0.4"), red tipped black.
Race *lessoni*. Humid forest borders, clearings,
flowering shrubs and trees (e.g. *Calliandra*, *Inga*)
in gardens. 500–2000 m. Bee-like flight; forages
eye level to canopy; filches nectar from territories of larger
species; visits small low-nectar reward flowers. **ID** White
rump-band. ♂ spiky rufous crest with few or no black-tipped
feathers at rear, white spots below gorget, tail mostly cinnamon-
rufous tipped dusky. ♀ very like ♀ Spangled Coquette but throat
usually richer buffy rufous, sometimes mixed brownish (palest
birds imm?), lower underparts bronzy green mixed buff to cinnamon.

lessoni

Spangled Coquette *Lophornis stictolophus* `LC`
Coqueta Coronada
Rare or uncommon (overlooked?) resident.

L 7 cm (2.7"); **B** red tipped black 1 cm (0.4").
Monotypic. Humid forest borders, shrubby clearings,
settled areas. 100–1300 m. Behaviour as Rufous-
crested Coquette. **ID** White rump-band. ♂ crest
bushy (not spiky) with obvious black-tipped feathers; tail as
Rufous-crested Coquette. ♀ throat variable, buffy white to whitish,
sometimes outlined dusky, belly greenish mixed buff to cinnamon.
SS Rufous-crested Coquette.

Butterfly Coquette (Festive Coquette)
Lophornis verreauxii `LC`
Coqueta Mariposa
Uncommon (overlooked?) resident.

L 7.6 cm (3"); **B** black 1 cm (0.4"). Race
verreauxii. Humid *terra firme* forest, white sandy
soil forest, borders, scrub. To 600 m. Perches and
feeds high in canopy at flowering trees, less often
low; bee-like flight. **ID** White rump-band. ♂ quite dark, flaring
white-spotted neck-tufts, underparts mostly green. ♀ broad
whitish malar streak, underparts greyish white mottled dusky.
SS Thorntails (*Discosura*), other coquettes. **TN** Often treated
as a race of Festive Coquette *L. chalybeus*.

verreauxii

Ecuadorian Piedtail *Phlogophilus hemileucurus* `VU`
Colibrí Ecuatoriano `NT`
Uncommon and local resident.

L 7.6 cm (3"); **B** 1.8 cm (0.7"). Monotypic. Shady undergrowth
inside humid forest. 600–1500 m. Solitary; inconspicuous at
low herbaceous and woody flowering plants. **ID** Tail
wedge-shaped, central feathers green, rest blue-black flashing
white at base and tips; throat mottled white, breast-band white, breast with
variable green discs. **Voice** ♂♂ sing in loose groups in understorey,
extremely high buzzy notes, sometimes twittering at end, "tzeee, tzeee…
titititititi". **SS** ♀ racket-tails (p. 95), Rufous-vented Whitetip (p. 96).

Speckled Hummingbird *Adelomyia melanogenys* `LC`
Colibrí Pechipunteado
Common resident.

L 8.4 cm (3.3"); **B** 1.5 cm (0.6"). Races
debellardiana[A] (valid?), *melanogenys*[B], *cervina*[C],
connectens[D], *maculata*[E], *sabinae*[F] (valid?).
Undergrowth inside humid and wet forest, shrubby
borders, gardens. 1000–2500 m. Often clings to flowers when
feeding; may steal nectar from holes in base of corollas.
ID Dull and brownish, face pattern recalls a hermit (*Phaethornis*),
throat speckling weak but varies with race (most in *melanogenys*,
least in *cervina*). **Voice** Pebbly "dt'dk" repeatedly; songs variable
(geographical?), some complex. **SS** ♀ *Chlorostilbon* emeralds.

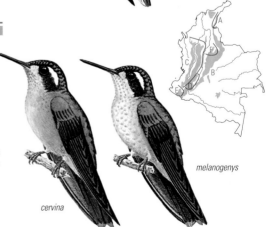

melanogenys

cervina

Genus *Aglaiocercus* Spectacular montane hummers. Long shimmering tails appear metallic (shorter in ♀♀); short bills. ♀♀ have white throat, cinnamon breast. Long suspended nest with dangling 'tail'.

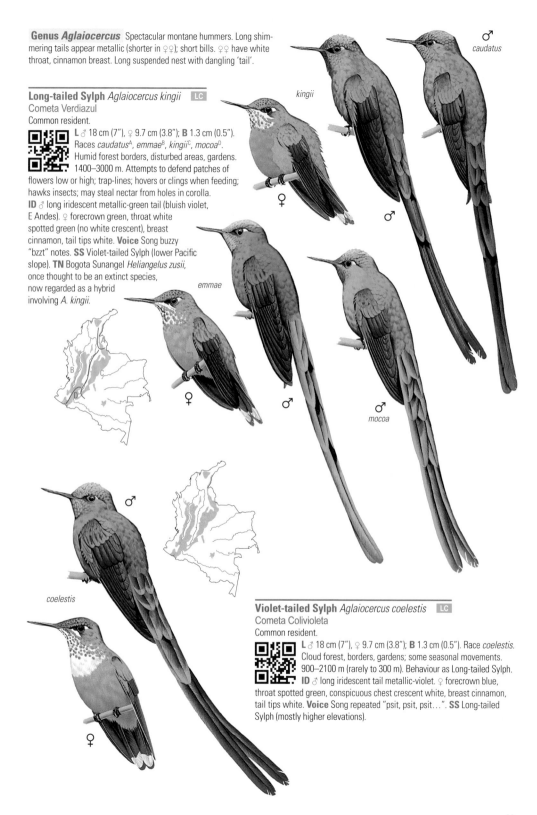

caudatus

kingii

Long-tailed Sylph *Aglaiocercus kingii* LC
Cometa Verdiazul
Common resident.

L ♂ 18 cm (7"), ♀ 9.7 cm (3.8"); **B** 1.3 cm (0.5"). Races *caudatus*[A], *emmae*[B], *kingii*[C], *mocoa*[D]. Humid forest borders, disturbed areas, gardens. 1400–3000 m. Attempts to defend patches of flowers low or high; trap-lines; hovers or clings when feeding; hawks insects; may steal nectar from holes in corolla. **ID** ♂ long iridescent metallic-green tail (bluish violet, E Andes). ♀ forecrown green, throat white spotted green (no white crescent), breast cinnamon, tail tips white. **Voice** Song buzzy "bzzt" notes. **SS** Violet-tailed Sylph (lower Pacific slope). **TN** Bogota Sunangel *Heliangelus zusii*, once thought to be an extinct species, now regarded as a hybrid involving *A. kingii*.

♀

emmae

♂

♀

♂

mocoa

♂

coelestis

Violet-tailed Sylph *Aglaiocercus coelestis* LC
Cometa Colivioleta
Common resident.

L ♂ 18 cm (7"), ♀ 9.7 cm (3.8"); **B** 1.3 cm (0.5"). Race *coelestis*. Cloud forest, borders, gardens; some seasonal movements. 900–2100 m (rarely to 300 m). Behaviour as Long-tailed Sylph. **ID** ♂ long iridescent tail metallic-violet. ♀ forecrown blue, throat spotted green, conspicuous chest crescent white, breast cinnamon, tail tips white. **Voice** Song repeated "psit, psit, psit…". **SS** Long-tailed Sylph (mostly higher elevations).

♀

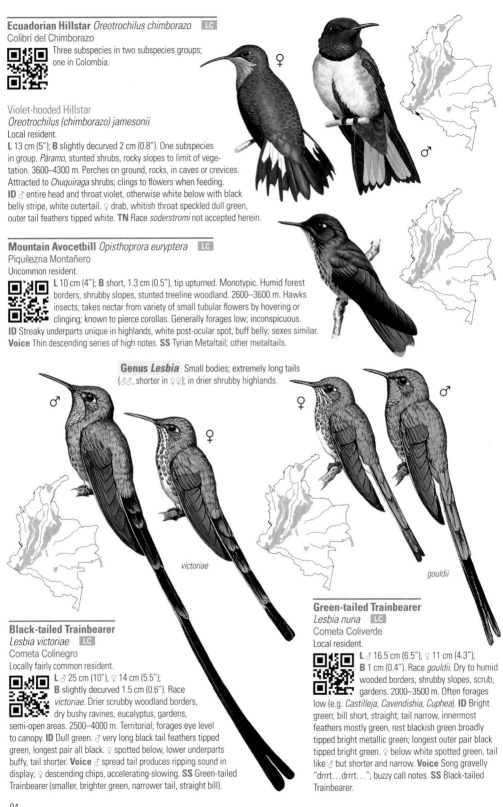

Ecuadorian Hillstar *Oreotrochilus chimborazo* `LC`
Colibrí del Chimborazo

Three subspecies in two subspecies groups; one in Colombia.

Violet-hooded Hillstar
Oreotrochilus (chimborazo) jamesonii
Local resident.

L 13 cm (5"); **B** slightly decurved 2 cm (0.8"). One subspecies in group. *Páramo*, stunted shrubs, rocky slopes to limit of vegetation. 3600–4300 m. Perches on ground, rocks, in caves or crevices. Attracted to *Chuquiraga* shrubs; clings to flowers when feeding. **ID** ♂ entire head and throat violet, otherwise white below with black belly stripe, white outertail. ♀ drab, whitish throat speckled dull green, outer tail feathers tipped white. **TN** Race *soderstromi* not accepted herein.

Mountain Avocetbill *Opisthoprora euryptera* `LC`
Piquilezna Montañero
Uncommon resident.

L 10 cm (4"); **B** short, 1.3 cm (0.5"), tip upturned. Monotypic. Humid forest borders, shrubby slopes, stunted treeline woodland. 2600–3600 m. Hawks insects; takes nectar from variety of small tubular flowers by hovering or clinging; known to pierce corollas. Generally forages low; inconspicuous. **ID** Streaky underparts unique in highlands, white post-ocular spot, buff belly; sexes similar. **Voice** Thin descending series of high notes. **SS** Tyrian Metaltail; other metaltails.

Genus *Lesbia* Small bodies; extremely long tails (♂♂, shorter in ♀♀); in drier shrubby highlands.

victoriae

gouldii

Black-tailed Trainbearer
Lesbia victoriae `LC`
Cometa Colinegro
Locally fairly common resident.

L ♂ 25 cm (10"), ♀ 14 cm (5.5"); **B** slightly decurved 1.5 cm (0.6"). Race *victoriae*. Drier scrubby woodland borders, dry bushy ravines, eucalyptus, gardens, semi-open areas. 2500–4000 m. Territorial; forages eye level to canopy. **ID** Dull green. ♂ very long black tail feathers tipped green, longest pair all black. ♀ spotted below, lower underparts buffy, tail shorter. **Voice** ♂ spread tail produces ripping sound in display; ♀ descending chips, accelerating-slowing. **SS** Green-tailed Trainbearer (smaller, brighter green, narrower tail, straight bill).

Green-tailed Trainbearer
Lesbia nuna `LC`
Cometa Coliverde
Local resident.

L ♂ 16.5 cm (6.5"), ♀ 11 cm (4.3"); **B** 1 cm (0.4"). Race *gouldii*. Dry to humid wooded borders, shrubby slopes, scrub, gardens. 2000–3500 m. Often forages low (e.g. *Castilleja*, *Cavendishia*, *Cuphea*). **ID** Bright green; bill short, straight; tail narrow, innermost feathers mostly green, rest blackish green broadly tipped bright metallic green; longest outer pair black tipped bright green. ♀ below white spotted green, tail like ♂ but shorter and narrow. **Voice** Song gravelly "drrrt…drrrt…"; buzzy call notes. **SS** Black-tailed Trainbearer.

Genus *Ramphomicron* Small high-elevation hummers with extremely short bills. Regularly cling to flowers when feeding.

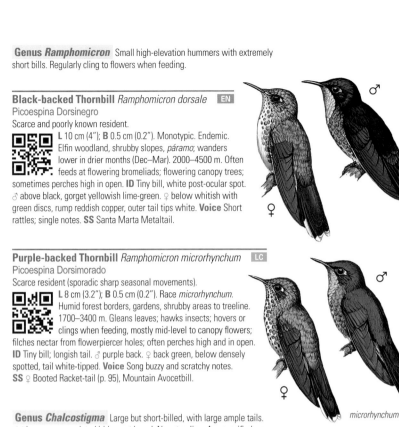

Black-backed Thornbill *Ramphomicron dorsale* EN
Picoespina Dorsinegro
Scarce and poorly known resident.

 L 10 cm (4"); **B** 0.5 cm (0.2"). Monotypic. Endemic. Elfin woodland, shrubby slopes, *páramo*; wanders lower in drier months (Dec–Mar). 2000–4500 m. Often feeds at flowering bromeliads; flowering canopy trees; sometimes perches high in open. **ID** Tiny bill, white post-ocular spot. ♂ above black, gorget yellowish lime-green. ♀ below whitish with green discs, rump reddish copper, outer tail tips white. **Voice** Short rattles; single notes. **SS** Santa Marta Metaltail.

Purple-backed Thornbill *Ramphomicron microrhynchum* LC
Picoespina Dorsimorado
Scarce resident (sporadic sharp seasonal movements).

 L 8 cm (3.2"); **B** 0.5 cm (0.2"). Race *microrhynchum*. Humid forest borders, gardens, shrubby areas to treeline. 1700–3400 m. Gleans leaves; hawks insects; hovers or clings when feeding, mostly mid-level to canopy flowers; filches nectar from flowerpiercer holes; often perches high and in open. **ID** Tiny bill; longish tail. ♂ purple back. ♀ back green, below densely spotted, tail white-tipped. **Voice** Song buzzy and scratchy notes. **SS** ♀ Booted Racket-tail (p. 95), Mountain Avocetbill.

microrhynchum

Genus *Chalcostigma* Large but short-billed, with large ample tails. ♂♂ have narrow pointed iridescent beard. Near treeline. An unverified record of Rufous-capped Thornbill *C. ruficeps* seems unlikely.

Blue-mantled Thornbill *Chalcostigma stanleyi* LC
Pico Espina Violeta
Rare resident (possibly Volcán Cumbal and Chiles).

 L 11.4 cm (4.5"); **B** 1 cm (0.4"). Race *stanleyi*. Humid elfin forest borders, patches of *Polylepis* woodland, *páramo*. 3000–4200 m (lower seasonally). Clings to flowers; forages on or near ground. **ID** ♂ sooty olive-brown, back with violet-blue reflections, narrow emerald beard tipped violet to pinkish lilac. ♀ no elongated beard, throat often streaked white, vent scaled whitish. **SS** Other *Chalcostigma*, Ecuadorian Metaltail.

stanleyi

Bronze-tailed Thornbill *Chalcostigma heteropogon* LC
Picoespina Bronceado
Fairly common but local resident.

 **L** ♂ 13 cm (5"), ♀ 10 cm (4"); **B** 1.3 cm (0.5"). Monotypic. Near-endemic (also W Venezuela). Stunted montane woodland, bushy areas, shrubby *páramo*. 2800–3900 m. Clings briefly as feeds, mostly at low flowers; aggressively guards small patches of flowers; also trap-lines and hawks insects. **ID** Dark; reddish-bronze rump, large tail, glittering gorget stripe. ♀ reduced gorget stripe. **SS** Tyrian Metaltail, ♀ Purple-backed Thornbill.

Rainbow-bearded Thornbill *Chalcostigma herrani* `LC`
Picoespina Arcoiris
Uncommon and local resident.

 L 11 cm (4.3"); **B** 1 cm (0.4"). Races *tolimae*[A], *herrani*[B]. Humid elfin woodland, borders, shrubby and rocky areas up to lower *páramo*. 2800–4000 m. Territorial; aggressive at patches of low flowers; also trap-lines; gleans foliage and tussock grass; clings to feed. **ID** Rufous forecrown, conspicuous white tail tips. ♂ spectacularly colourful beard stripe. ♀ no glittering beard, throat dull whitish spotted dusky. **SS** Blue-mantled Thornbill.

Genus *Oxypogon* High elevations. Wispy pointed crest, dark triangular face patch; and ♂♂ have colourful beard stripe. More insectivorous than allies. Strong affinity for *Espeletia* (Asteraceae). Marked seasonal movements.

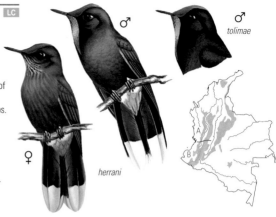

Blue-bearded Helmetcrest *Oxypogon cyanolaemus* `CR`
Barbudito Azul `EN`
Rare and declining resident (range largely inaccessible).

 L 12 cm (4.7"); **B** 0.8 cm (0.3"). Monotypic. Endemic. Treeline shrubs, *páramo*. 3050–4800 m. Behaviour similar to Green-bearded Helmetcrest. Habitat severely threatened by fire, deforestation, overgrazing; heavily dependent on *Libanothamnus occultus* (Asteraceae) as food source. **ID** Crest and tail shorter than other *Oxypogon*, sides of head dusky green, diagonal collar white, outer tail feathers mostly white. **TN** Previously a race of former Bearded Helmetcrest *O. guerinii*.

Green-bearded Helmetcrest *Oxypogon guerinii* `LC`
Barbudito Verde
Fairly common locally resident (e.g. Sumapaz National Park).

 L 11.4 cm (4.5"); **B** 0.8 cm (0.3"). Monotypic. Endemic. Shrubby ravines, *páramo* with *Espeletia* (Asteraceae). 3300–4600 m. Most numerous in *páramo* during rainy months. Feeds at low, even ground-level flowers by clinging, hovering or perching; takes insects from flowering *Espeletia* or gleaned from vegetation; often flies considerable distance between feeding and resting sites. **ID** ♂ whitish crest, green-tipped beard, blackish sides of head, diagonal whitish collar, flashes buff-white in tail. ♀ no beard or crest. **Voice** Rainy season song "peek…peek…peek…" for several minutes. **TN** Formerly regarded as a race of Bearded Helmetcrest *O. guerinii*.

Buffy Helmetcrest *Oxypogon stuebelii* `VU`
Barbudito Canelo `EN`
Fairly common resident (only on Nevado del Ruiz).

 L 11 cm (4.3"); **B** 0.8 cm (0.3"). Monotypic. Endemic. 3300–4800 m. **ID** Habits and plumage similar to Green-bearded Helmetcrest but smaller, buffier; ♂ throat stripe violet, crest buff (not white) and black. **Voice** Rainy season song, single "tsee" (c. 7 kHz) every 3–5 seconds. **TN** Formerly regarded as a race of Bearded Helmetcrest *O. guerinii*.

Genus *Metallura* Small highland hummers of shrubby borders. Iridescent tail colours vary with light. ♀♀ have varying amounts of buffy rufous below, especially throat.

Perija Metaltail *Metallura iracunda* `EN`
Metalura de Perijá `NT`
Fairly common but local resident.

 L 10 cm (4"); **B** 1 cm (0.4"). Monotypic. Near-endemic (also extreme NW Venezuela). Patches of elfin woodland, bushy ravines, *Swallenochloa* bamboo in *páramo*. 2400–3200 m. Seasonal elevational movements likely; has suffered severe habitat loss. **ID** White post-ocular spot. ♂ very dark almost blackish, glittering green throat stripe, long ample tail metallic wine-red. ♀ above like ♂ including tail, below buffy cinnamon, throat finely dotted green; rest of underparts boldly spotted green, dense on sides. **SS** Tyrian Metaltail ♂ smaller, greener, tail shorter; ♀ only throat and chest rufous.

Tyrian Metaltail *Metallura tyrianthina* `LC`
Metalura Colirroja

 Seven subspecies in six subspecies groups; two in Colombia.

Santa Marta Metaltail *Metallura (tyrianthina) districta*
Common resident.
L ♂ 8 cm (3.2"), ♀ 7.6 cm (3"); **B** 1 cm (0.4"). One subspecies in group. Near-endemic (also extreme NW Venezuela). 1900–3600 m. Measurements, habitat, behaviour and voice as Tyrian Metaltail. **ID** ♂ like Tyrian Metaltail but tail violet-blue. ♀ throat buffy rufous, breast unspotted. **SS** Santa Marta Blossomcrown (p. 101).

Tyrian Metaltail *Metallura (tyrianthina) tyrianthina*
Common resident.
L ♂ 8 cm (3.2"), ♀ 7.6 cm (3"); **B** 1 cm (0.4"). Races *tyrianthina*[A], *quitensis*[B]. Humid forest borders, shrubby areas. 1700–3600 m. Hovers or clings when feeding; uses small low-nectar reward flowers; may guard flower patches. Marked seasonal movements. Sexes sometimes segregated (only ♂♂ or only ♀♀ present). **ID** Learn this widespread species. ♂ small; below green, gorget glittering green, tail coppery rufous. ♀ tail like ♂ but outer feathers tipped white, throat and chest buffy rufous dotted green; or tail bronzy olive, *quitensis*. **Voice** Thin trills, squeaks. **SS** Other *Metallura*.

tyrianthina

Viridian Metaltail *Metallura williami* `LC`
Metalura Verde

 Four subspecies in four subspecies groups; three in Colombia.

Colombian Metaltail *Metallura (williami) recisa*
Uncommon resident.
L 8.6 cm (3.4"); **B** 1.3 cm (0.5"). One subspecies in group. Endemic. Stunted elfin woodland at treeline, brushy ravines and pre-*páramo*. 2800–3800 m. **ID** ♂ like ♂ Viridian Metaltail but tail above bronzy green to bronzy blue, undertail shining green. ♀ as in race *williami* (next page). **SS** Tyrian Metaltail.

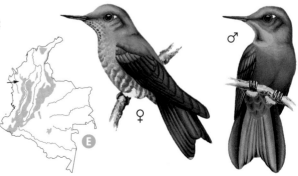

Viridian Metaltail
Metallura (williami) williami
Fairly common resident (S to S Cauca).
L 8.6 cm (3.4"); **B** 1.5 cm (0.6"). One subspecies
in group. Endemic. Stunted woodland borders at
treeline, shrubby ravines, low semi-open woody growth
in *páramo*. 2800–3800 m. Hovers at low to mid-height
flowers; territorial at small flower patches. **ID** ♂ shining
green, throat glittering green, tail above and especially
below purplish blue (cf. *recisa*, *primolina*), vent dull buff.
♀ below mottled green and buff, undertail tipped whitish.
SS Tyrian Metaltail, Glowing Puffleg (p. 89).

Ecuadorian Metaltail *Metallura (williami) primolina*
Uncommon resident (apparently only E Nariño).
L 8.6 cm (3.4"); **B** 1.5 cm (0.6"). One subspecies in group.
Elfin woodland borders, shrubby ravines, patches of low
woody growth in *páramo*. 2700–4000 m. **ID** ♂ like ♂
Viridian Metaltail but tail above bronze-green to dark
reddish purple, undertail shining green (like *recisa*).
♀ below mottled green and buff. **SS** Tyrian Metaltail;
Glowing Puffleg (p. 89).

Genus *Haplophaedia* Resemble *Eriocnemis* pufflegs
but duller; leg puffs smaller; more inside forest.

Greenish Puffleg *Haplophaedia aureliae* LC
Calzoncitos Verdoso
Fairly common resident.

 L 9 cm (3.6"); **B** 2 cm (0.8").
Races *floccus*[A], *caucensis*[B],
aureliae[C], *russata*[D]. Humid and
wet forest borders. 1500–3100 m,
seasonally lower. Gleans vegetation and hovers
at low to mid-level flowers inside forest, less at
edges; less pugnacious than *Eriocnemis* pufflegs.
ID Races vary: ♂ *caucensis* bright green, coppery-
tinged crown, large white leg puffs; other races
duller, leg puffs less conspicuous; coppery-rufous
uppertail-coverts (all races). ♀ duller, underparts
mottled. **Voice** A "tur-seet" repeatedly by ♂.
SS Hoary Puffleg.

russata

caucensis

aureliae

Hoary Puffleg *Haplophaedia lugens* NT
Calzoncitos del Pacífico NT
Uncommon (?) resident.

 L 9 cm (3.6"); **B** 1.8 cm (0.7"). Monotypic.
Near-endemic (mainly NW Ecuador). Wet
montane forest, dense wet scrub on
nutrient-poor ridges and steep slopes, second
growth. 1200–2000 m (locally to 2500 m). Feeds in dense
understorey or higher at small patches of short tubular flowers;
deforestation threatens. **ID** Dingiest puffleg, above dark green,
rump coppery rufous, below dull greenish grey, whitish leg puffs
small. **SS** Mostly below range of Greenish Puffleg.

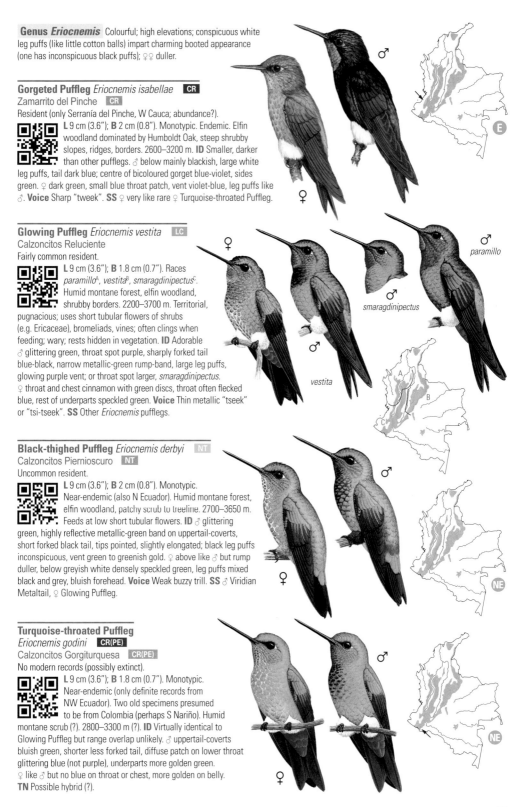

Genus *Eriocnemis* Colourful; high elevations; conspicuous white leg puffs (like little cotton balls) impart charming booted appearance (one has inconspicuous black puffs); ♀♀ duller.

Gorgeted Puffleg *Eriocnemis isabellae* `CR`
Zamarrito del Pinche `CR`
Resident (only Serranía del Pinche, W Cauca; abundance?).
L 9 cm (3.6"); **B** 2 cm (0.8"). Monotypic. Endemic. Elfin woodland dominated by Humboldt Oak, steep shrubby slopes, ridges, borders. 2600–3200 m. **ID** Smaller, darker than other pufflegs. ♂ below mainly blackish, large white leg puffs, tail dark blue; centre of bicoloured gorget blue-violet, sides green. ♀ dark green, small blue throat patch, vent violet-blue, leg puffs like ♂. **Voice** Sharp "tweek". **SS** ♀ very like rare ♀ Turquoise-throated Puffleg.

Glowing Puffleg *Eriocnemis vestita* `LC`
Calzoncitos Reluciente
Fairly common resident.
L 9 cm (3.6"); **B** 1.8 cm (0.7"). Races *paramillo*[A], *vestita*[B], *smaragdinipectus*[C]. Humid montane forest, elfin woodland, shrubby borders. 2200–3700 m. Territorial, pugnacious; uses short tubular flowers of shrubs (e.g. Ericaceae), bromeliads, vines; often clings when feeding; wary; rests hidden in vegetation. **ID** Adorable ♂ glittering green, throat spot purple, sharply forked tail blue-black, narrow metallic-green rump-band, large leg puffs, glowing purple vent; or throat spot larger, *smaragdinipectus*. ♀ throat and chest cinnamon with green discs, throat often flecked blue, rest of underparts speckled green. **Voice** Thin metallic "tseek" or "tsi-tseek". **SS** Other *Eriocnemis* pufflegs.

Black-thighed Puffleg *Eriocnemis derbyi* `NT`
Calzoncitos Piernioscuro `NT`
Uncommon resident.
L 9 cm (3.6"); **B** 2 cm (0.8"). Monotypic. Near-endemic (also N Ecuador). Humid montane forest, elfin woodland, patchy scrub to treeline. 2700–3650 m. Feeds at low short tubular flowers. **ID** ♂ glittering green, highly reflective metallic-green band on uppertail-coverts, short forked black tail, tips pointed, slightly elongated; black leg puffs inconspicuous, vent green to greenish gold. ♀ above like ♂ but rump duller, below greyish white densely speckled green, leg puffs mixed black and grey, bluish forehead. **Voice** Weak buzzy trill. **SS** ♂ Viridian Metaltail, ♀ Glowing Puffleg.

Turquoise-throated Puffleg
Eriocnemis godini `CR(PE)`
Calzoncitos Gorgiturquesa `CR(PE)`
No modern records (possibly extinct).
L 9 cm (3.6"); **B** 1.8 cm (0.7"). Monotypic. Near-endemic (only definite records from NW Ecuador). Two old specimens presumed to be from Colombia (perhaps S Nariño). Humid montane scrub (?). 2800–3300 m (?). **ID** Virtually identical to Glowing Puffleg but range overlap unlikely. ♂ uppertail-coverts bluish green, shorter less forked tail, diffuse patch on lower throat glittering blue (not purple), underparts more golden green. ♀ like ♂ but no blue on throat or chest, more golden on belly. **TN** Possible hybrid (?).

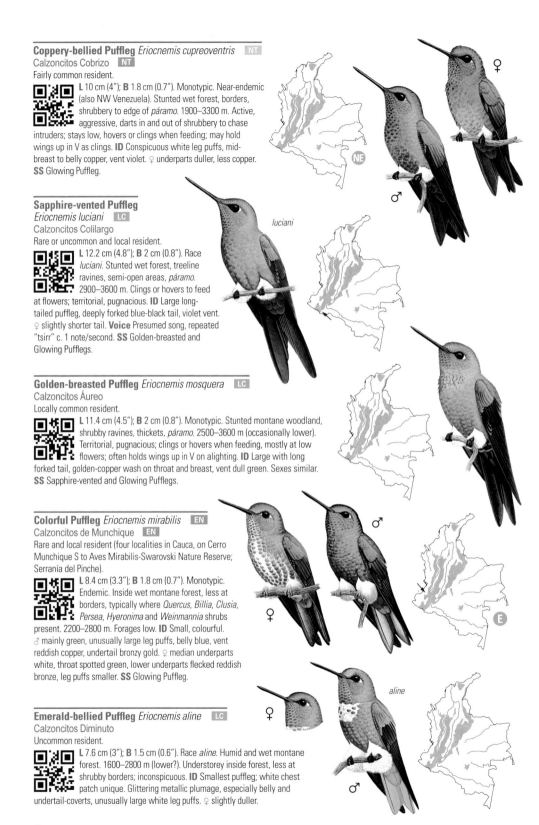

Coppery-bellied Puffleg *Eriocnemis cupreoventris* NT
Calzoncitos Cobrizo NT
Fairly common resident.

L 10 cm (4"); **B** 1.8 cm (0.7"). Monotypic. Near-endemic (also NW Venezuela). Stunted wet forest, borders, shrubbery to edge of *páramo*. 1900–3300 m. Active, aggressive, darts in and out of shrubbery to chase intruders; stays low, hovers or clings when feeding; may hold wings up in V as clings. **ID** Conspicuous white leg puffs, mid-breast to belly copper, vent violet. ♀ underparts duller, less copper. **SS** Glowing Puffleg.

Sapphire-vented Puffleg
Eriocnemis luciani LC
Calzoncitos Colilargo
Rare or uncommon and local resident.

L 12.2 cm (4.8"); **B** 2 cm (0.8"). Race *luciani*. Stunted wet forest, treeline ravines, semi-open areas, *páramo*. 2900–3600 m. Clings or hovers to feed at flowers; territorial, pugnacious. **ID** Large long-tailed puffleg, deeply forked blue-black tail, violet vent. ♀ slightly shorter tail. **Voice** Presumed song, repeated "tsirr" c. 1 note/second. **SS** Golden-breasted and Glowing Pufflegs.

Golden-breasted Puffleg *Eriocnemis mosquera* LC
Calzoncitos Áureo
Locally common resident.

L 11.4 cm (4.5"); **B** 2 cm (0.8"). Monotypic. Stunted montane woodland, shrubby ravines, thickets, *páramo*. 2500–3600 m (occasionally lower). Territorial, pugnacious; clings or hovers when feeding, mostly at low flowers; often holds wings up in V on alighting. **ID** Large with long forked tail, golden-copper wash on throat and breast, vent dull green. Sexes similar. **SS** Sapphire-vented and Glowing Pufflegs.

Colorful Puffleg *Eriocnemis mirabilis* EN
Calzoncitos de Munchique EN
Rare and local resident (four localities in Cauca, on Cerro Munchique S to Aves Mirabilis-Swarovski Nature Reserve; Serranía del Pinche).

L 8.4 cm (3.3"); **B** 1.8 cm (0.7"). Monotypic. Endemic. Inside wet montane forest, typically where *Quercus, Billia, Clusia, Persea, Hyeronima* and *Weinmannia* shrubs present. 2200–2800 m. Forages low. **ID** Small, colourful. ♂ mainly green, unusually large leg puffs, belly blue, vent reddish copper, undertail bronzy gold. ♀ median underparts white, throat spotted green, lower underparts flecked reddish bronze, leg puffs smaller. **SS** Glowing Puffleg.

Emerald-bellied Puffleg *Eriocnemis aline* LC
Calzoncitos Diminuto
Uncommon resident.

L 7.6 cm (3"); **B** 1.5 cm (0.6"). Race *aline*. Humid and wet montane forest. 1600–2800 m (lower?). Understorey inside forest, less at shrubby borders; inconspicuous. **ID** Smallest puffleg; white chest patch unique. Glittering metallic plumage, especially belly and undertail-coverts, unusually large white leg puffs. ♀ slightly duller.

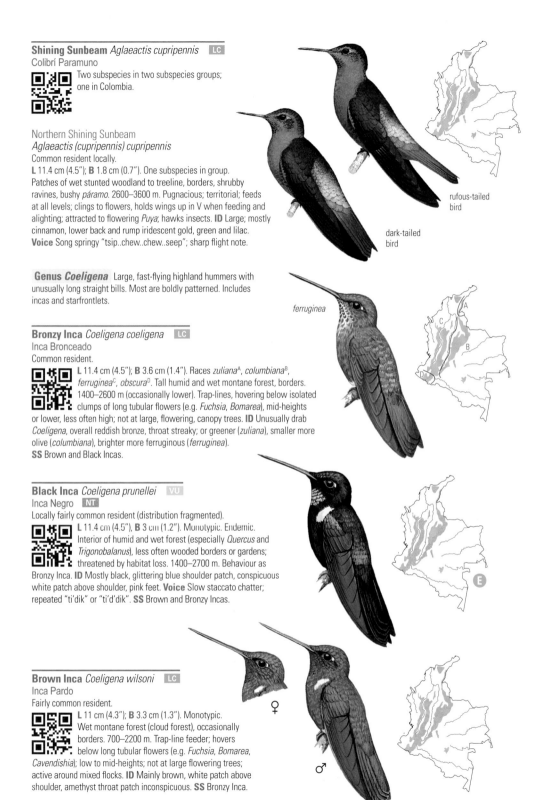

Shining Sunbeam *Aglaeactis cupripennis* `LC`
Colibrí Paramuno

Two subspecies in two subspecies groups; one in Colombia.

Northern Shining Sunbeam
Aglaeactis (cupripennis) cupripennis
Common resident locally.
L 11.4 cm (4.5"); **B** 1.8 cm (0.7"). One subspecies in group. Patches of wet stunted woodland to treeline, borders, shrubby ravines, bushy *páramo*. 2600–3600 m. Pugnacious; territorial; feeds at all levels; clings to flowers, holds wings up in V when feeding and alighting; attracted to flowering *Puya*; hawks insects. **ID** Large; mostly cinnamon, lower back and rump iridescent gold, green and lilac. **Voice** Song springy "tsip..chew..chew..seep"; sharp flight note.

rufous-tailed bird

dark-tailed bird

Genus *Coeligena* Large, fast-flying highland hummers with unusually long straight bills. Most are boldly patterned. Includes incas and starfrontlets.

ferruginea

Bronzy Inca *Coeligena coeligena* `LC`
Inca Bronceado
Common resident.
L 11.4 cm (4.5"); **B** 3.6 cm (1.4"). Races *zuliana*[A], *columbiana*[B], *ferruginea*[C], *obscura*[D]. Tall humid and wet montane forest, borders. 1400–2600 m (occasionally lower). Trap-lines, hovering below isolated clumps of long tubular flowers (e.g. *Fuchsia*, *Bomarea*), mid-heights or lower, less often high; not at large, flowering, canopy trees. **ID** Unusually drab *Coeligena*, overall reddish bronze, throat streaky; or greener (*zuliana*), smaller more olive (*columbiana*), brighter more ferruginous (*ferruginea*). **SS** Brown and Black Incas.

Black Inca *Coeligena prunellei* `VU`
Inca Negro `NT`
Locally fairly common resident (distribution fragmented).
L 11.4 cm (4.5"); **B** 3 cm (1.2"). Monotypic. Endemic. Interior of humid and wet forest (especially *Quercus* and *Trigonobalanus*), less often wooded borders or gardens; threatened by habitat loss. 1400–2700 m. Behaviour as Bronzy Inca. **ID** Mostly black, glittering blue shoulder patch, conspicuous white patch above shoulder, pink feet. **Voice** Slow staccato chatter; repeated "ti'dik" or "ti'd'dik". **SS** Brown and Bronzy Incas.

Brown Inca *Coeligena wilsoni* `LC`
Inca Pardo
Fairly common resident.
L 11 cm (4.3"); **B** 3.3 cm (1.3"). Monotypic. Wet montane forest (cloud forest), occasionally borders. 700–2200 m. Trap-line feeder; hovers below long tubular flowers (e.g. *Fuchsia*, *Bomarea*, *Cavendishia*); low to mid-heights; not at large flowering trees; active around mixed flocks. **ID** Mainly brown, white patch above shoulder, amethyst throat patch inconspicuous. **SS** Bronzy Inca.

♀

♂

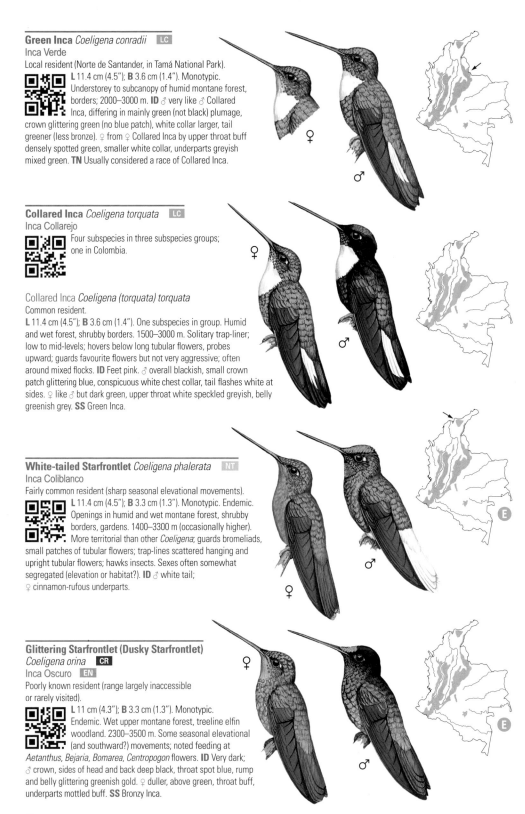

Green Inca *Coeligena conradii* `LC`
Inca Verde
Local resident (Norte de Santander, in Tamá National Park).
L 11.4 cm (4.5"); **B** 3.6 cm (1.4"). Monotypic.
Understorey to subcanopy of humid montane forest,
borders; 2000–3000 m. **ID** ♂ very like ♂ Collared
Inca, differing in mainly green (not black) plumage,
crown glittering green (no blue patch), white collar larger, tail
greener (less bronze). ♀ from ♀ Collared Inca by upper throat buff
densely spotted green, smaller white collar, underparts greyish
mixed green. **TN** Usually considered a race of Collared Inca.

Collared Inca *Coeligena torquata* `LC`
Inca Collarejo
Four subspecies in three subspecies groups;
one in Colombia.

Collared Inca *Coeligena (torquata) torquata*
Common resident.
L 11.4 cm (4.5"); **B** 3.6 cm (1.4"). One subspecies in group. Humid
and wet forest, shrubby borders. 1500–3000 m. Solitary trap-liner;
low to mid-levels; hovers below long tubular flowers, probes
upward; guards favourite flowers but not very aggressive; often
around mixed flocks. **ID** Feet pink. ♂ overall blackish, small crown
patch glittering blue, conspicuous white chest collar, tail flashes white at
sides. ♀ like ♂ but dark green, upper throat white speckled greyish, belly
greenish grey. **SS** Green Inca.

White-tailed Starfrontlet *Coeligena phalerata* `NT`
Inca Coliblanco
Fairly common resident (sharp seasonal elevational movements).
L 11.4 cm (4.5"); **B** 3.3 cm (1.3"). Monotypic. Endemic.
Openings in humid and wet montane forest, shrubby
borders, gardens. 1400–3300 m (occasionally higher).
More territorial than other *Coeligena*; guards bromeliads,
small patches of tubular flowers; trap-lines scattered hanging and
upright tubular flowers; hawks insects. Sexes often somewhat
segregated (elevation or habitat?). **ID** ♂ white tail;
♀ cinnamon-rufous underparts.

Glittering Starfrontlet (Dusky Starfrontlet)
Coeligena orina `CR`
Inca Oscuro `EN`
Poorly known resident (range largely inaccessible
or rarely visited).
L 11 cm (4.3"); **B** 3.3 cm (1.3"). Monotypic.
Endemic. Wet upper montane forest, treeline elfin
woodland. 2300–3500 m. Some seasonal elevational
(and southward?) movements; noted feeding at
Aetanthus, Bejaria, Bomarea, Centropogon flowers. **ID** Very dark;
♂ crown, sides of head and back deep black, throat spot blue, rump
and belly glittering greenish gold. ♀ duller, above green, throat buff,
underparts mottled buff. **SS** Bronzy Inca.

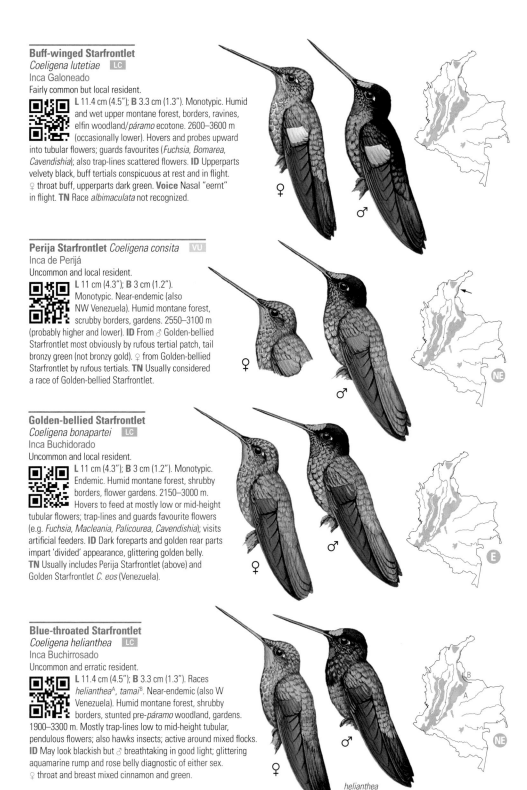

Buff-winged Starfrontlet
Coeligena lutetiae LC
Inca Galoneado
Fairly common but local resident.
L 11.4 cm (4.5"); **B** 3.3 cm (1.3"). Monotypic. Humid and wet upper montane forest, borders, ravines, elfin woodland/*páramo* ecotone. 2600–3600 m (occasionally lower). Hovers and probes upward into tubular flowers; guards favourites (*Fuchsia, Bomarea, Cavendishia*); also trap-lines scattered flowers. **ID** Upperparts velvety black, buff tertials conspicuous at rest and in flight. ♀ throat buff, upperparts dark green. **Voice** Nasal "eernt" in flight. **TN** Race *albimaculata* not recognized.

Perija Starfrontlet *Coeligena consita* VU
Inca de Perijá
Uncommon and local resident.
L 11 cm (4.3"); **B** 3 cm (1.2"). Monotypic. Near-endemic (also NW Venezuela). Humid montane forest, scrubby borders, gardens. 2550–3100 m (probably higher and lower). **ID** From ♂ Golden-bellied Starfrontlet most obviously by rufous tertial patch, tail bronzy green (not bronzy gold). ♀ from Golden-bellied Starfrontlet by rufous tertials. **TN** Usually considered a race of Golden-bellied Starfrontlet.

Golden-bellied Starfrontlet
Coeligena bonapartei LC
Inca Buchidorado
Uncommon and local resident.
L 11 cm (4.3"); **B** 3 cm (1.2"). Monotypic. Endemic. Humid montane forest, shrubby borders, flower gardens. 2150–3000 m. Hovers to feed at mostly low or mid-height tubular flowers; trap-lines and guards favourite flowers (e.g. *Fuchsia, Macleania, Palicourea, Cavendishia*); visits artificial feeders. **ID** Dark foreparts and golden rear parts impart 'divided' appearance, glittering golden belly. **TN** Usually includes Perija Starfrontlet (above) and Golden Starfrontlet *C. eos* (Venezuela).

Blue-throated Starfrontlet
Coeligena helianthea LC
Inca Buchirrosado
Uncommon and erratic resident.
L 11.4 cm (4.5"); **B** 3.3 cm (1.3"). Races *helianthea*[A], *tamai*[B]. Near-endemic (also W Venezuela). Humid montane forest, shrubby borders, stunted pre-*páramo* woodland, gardens. 1900–3300 m. Mostly trap-lines low to mid-height tubular, pendulous flowers; also hawks insects; active around mixed flocks. **ID** May look blackish but ♂ breathtaking in good light; glittering aquamarine rump and rose belly diagnostic of either sex. ♀ throat and breast mixed cinnamon and green.

helianthea

93

Mountain Velvetbreast *Lafresnaya lafresnayi* _{LC}
Colibrí Aterciopelado
Uncommon and erratic resident.

L 9.7 cm (3.8"); **B** decurved 2.5 cm (1"), longer in ♀. Races *liriope*[A], *lafresnayi*[B], *longirostris*[C], *saul*[D]. Inside humid and wet montane forest, bushy clearings, gardens. 2000–3700 m (rarely 1500 m). ♂ often territorial at rich flower patches; ♀ typically trap-lines scattered flowers; both sexes feed at low flowers with corollas that match bill shape; hawk insects. **ID** Decurved bill. ♂ black belly, white tail patches. ♀ underparts variable, usually buff spotted green on throat and sides (*lafresnayi*, *longirostris*) or whitish to faint buff (other races); tail patches buff. **SS** ♀ Buff-tailed Coronet.

Sword-billed Hummingbird *Ensifera ensifera* _{LC}
Colibrí Picoespada
Local resident.

L 14 cm (5.5"); **B** 10–12.2 cm (4–4.8"), slightly upturned; ♀ bill longer than ♂. Monotypic. Dry to wet upper montane forest, borders, shrubby pre-*páramo*, gardens. 2500–3500 m (occasionally to 1700 m). Trap-liner; feeds mostly by hovering and probing almost vertically into very long (usually) pendulous tubular flowers (especially *Brugmansia*, *Passiflora*, *Tacsonia*), usually fairly high. Flies fast; typically in view only briefly. **ID** Unmistakable; when perched bill tilted upward. **Voice** Trilled "trrr".

Great Sapphirewing
Pterophanes cyanopterus _{LC}
Alizafiro Grande
Fairly common resident.

L 16.3 cm (6.4"); **B** 3 cm (1.2"). Races *cyanopterus*[A], *caeruleus*[B], *peruvianus*[C]. Humid montane forest, borders, elfin woodland, patches of shrubs in *páramo*. 2600–3700 m. Guards territories or trap-lines; forages low to high at wide variety of tubular flowers by hovering, clinging or perching; active around mixed flocks. Flies very fast, often quite far; frequently engages in spectacular high aerial chases. **ID** Very large; feet pink. ♂ sapphire wings unique. ♀ only wing-coverts blue (not flight feathers), cinnamon-rufous underparts.

Genus *Boissonneaua* Robust territorial hummers of Andean mid-elevations. Short to mid-length bills. Contrasting colour in tail (buff, chestnut, white).

Buff-tailed Coronet *Boissonneaua flavescens* _{LC}
Colibrí Chupasavia
Common and widespread resident.

L 11.4 cm (4.5"); **B** 1.8 cm (0.7"). Races *flavescens*[A], *tinochlora*[B]. Humid montane forest, borders; feeders in gardens. Notably territorial, pugnacious; dominates most hummers at artificial feeders; hovers, or more often clings to flowers to feed; holds wings up in V when feeding and alighting; singles low at borders; in numbers at flowering canopy trees. 1500–3200 m. **ID** Buff wing-linings, buff in tail; ♀ duller below. **Voice** Song high "tsit" notes. **SS** Fawn-breasted Brilliant, ♀ Mountain Velvetbreast.

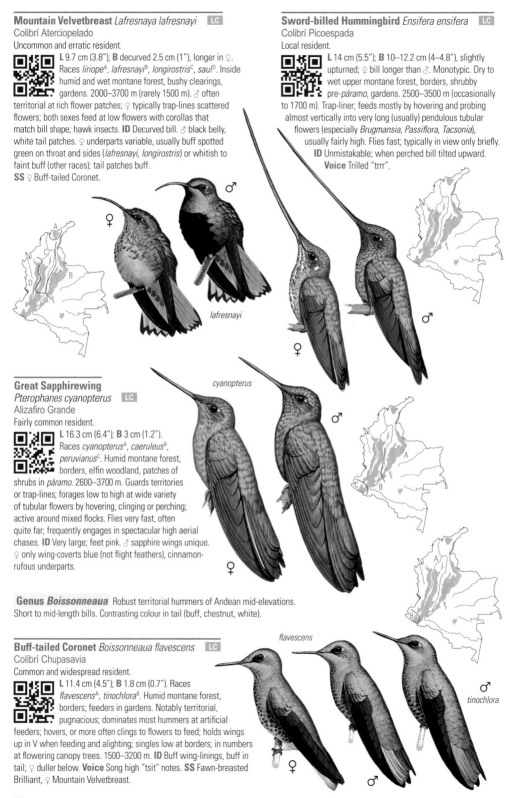

lafresnayi

cyanopterus

flavescens

tinochlora

Chestnut-breasted Coronet *Boissonneaua matthewsii* `LC`
Colibrí Pechicastaño
Uncommon and local resident.

 L 11.4 cm (4.5″); **B** 1.8 cm (0.7″). Monotypic. Humid montane forest, borders, shrubby clearings. 1200–2600 m. Behaviour like Buff-tailed Coronet. **ID** Chestnut breast and lower underparts diagnostic as is mostly chestnut tail.
SS Fawn-breasted Brilliant, Buff-tailed Coronet.

Velvet-purple Coronet *Boissonneaua jardini* `LC`
Colibrí Sietecolores
Rare to fairly common resident (seasonal or local movements).

 L 11 cm (4.3″); **B** 1.8 cm (0.7″). Monotypic. Near-endemic (also NW Ecuador). Wet montane forest (cloud forest), shrubby borders, flower gardens. 700–2300 m (more numerous above c. 1400 m). Habits as other *Boissonneaua*; holds wings in V when alighting; feeds at low- or mid-strata flowers; stays near or within cover; crown often ruffed. **ID** ♂ white in tail, blackish hood, spectacular colours often look black, rufous underwing-coverts. ♀ duller, crown lacks glitter, feathers of underparts slightly bluer (less purple) and fringed grey to greyish buff. **SS** Rufous-gaped Hillstar, Buff-tailed Coronet.

Booted Racket-tail *Ocreatus underwoodii* `LC`
Cola-de-raqueta Pierniblanco

 Eight subspecies in two subspecies groups; both in Colombia.

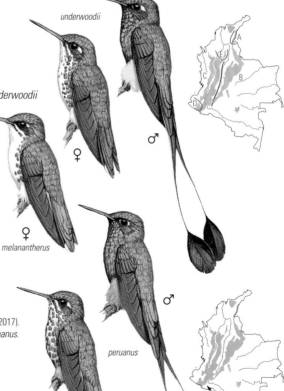

underwoodii

♂

♀

melanantherus

♀

♂

peruanus

♀

White-booted Racket-tail *Ocreatus (underwoodii) underwoodii*
Common resident.
L ♂ 12.2 cm (4.8″), ♀ 7.6 cm (3″); **B** 1.3 cm (0.5″). Races *discifer*[A], *underwoodii*[B], *incommodus*[C], *melanantherus*[D]; Serranía de San Lucas (undescribed race?[E]). Montane forest, borders, shrubby clearings, gardens. 1200–2600 m. Feeds low (e.g. *Palicourea*, *Impatiens*) to high at canopy flowers (e.g. *Inga*); flight weaving, wasp-like; filches nectar in territories of larger species. **ID** Tiny. ♂ large white leg puffs (or rufous, ssp. nov.?), long racket-tipped tail held up as feeds. ♀ leg puffs white, tail tipped white, underparts white variably spotted green on sides (most spotted *underwoodii*, least *melanantherus*). **Voice** Short trills; "tsit".
SS ♀ Purple-bibbed and Rufous-vented Whitetips.

Rufous-booted Racket-tail (Peruvian Racket-tail)
Ocreatus (underwoodii) addae
Local resident (photo c. 1400 m, San Martín, W Putumayo, 2017).
L ♂ 12.2 cm (4.8″), ♀ 7.6 cm (3″); **B** 1.3 cm (0.5″). Race *peruanus*. Montane forest, shrubby borders. 900–2200 m (Ecuador). **ID** ♂ leg puffs rufous. ♀ leg puffs buff, underparts heavily spotted. **SS** White-booted Racket-tail.

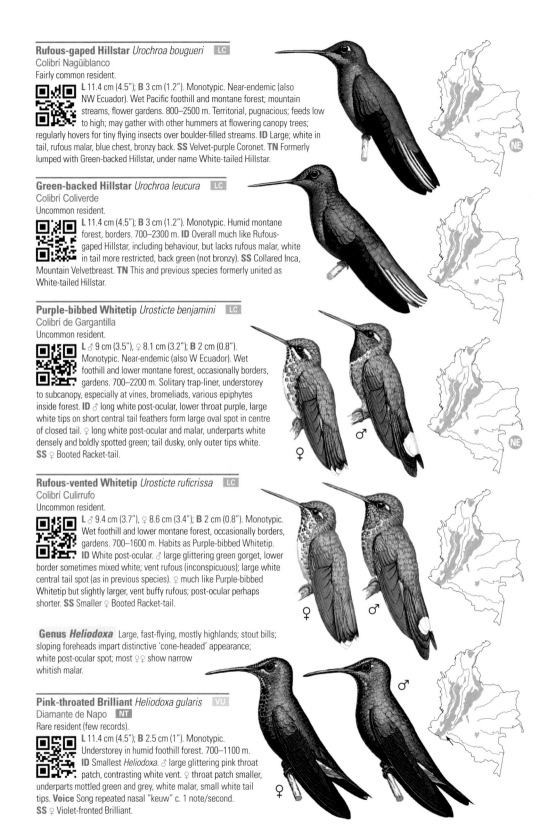

Rufous-gaped Hillstar *Urochroa bougueri* LC
Colibrí Nagüiblanco
Fairly common resident.

L 11.4 cm (4.5"); **B** 3 cm (1.2"). Monotypic. Near-endemic (also NW Ecuador). Wet Pacific foothill and montane forest; mountain streams, flower gardens. 800–2500 m. Territorial, pugnacious; feeds low to high; may gather with other hummers at flowering canopy trees; regularly hovers for tiny flying insects over boulder-filled streams. **ID** Large; white in tail, rufous malar, blue chest, bronzy back. **SS** Velvet-purple Coronet. **TN** Formerly lumped with Green-backed Hillstar, under name White-tailed Hillstar.

Green-backed Hillstar *Urochroa leucura* LC
Colibrí Coliverde
Uncommon resident.

L 11.4 cm (4.5"); **B** 3 cm (1.2"). Monotypic. Humid montane forest, borders. 700–2300 m. **ID** Overall much like Rufous-gaped Hillstar, including behaviour, but lacks rufous malar, white in tail more restricted, back green (not bronzy). **SS** Collared Inca, Mountain Velvetbreast. **TN** This and previous species formerly united as White-tailed Hillstar.

Purple-bibbed Whitetip *Urosticte benjamini* LC
Colibrí de Gargantilla
Uncommon resident.

L ♂ 9 cm (3.5"), ♀ 8.1 cm (3.2"); **B** 2 cm (0.8"). Monotypic. Near-endemic (also W Ecuador). Wet foothill and lower montane forest, occasionally borders, gardens. 700–2200 m. Solitary trap-liner, understorey to subcanopy, especially at vines, bromeliads, various epiphytes inside forest. **ID** ♂ long white post-ocular, lower throat purple, large white tips on short central tail feathers form large oval spot in centre of closed tail. ♀ long white post-ocular and malar, underparts white densely and boldly spotted green; tail dusky, only outer tips white. **SS** ♀ Booted Racket-tail.

Rufous-vented Whitetip *Urosticte ruficrissa* LC
Colibrí Culirrufo
Uncommon resident.

L ♂ 9.4 cm (3.7"), ♀ 8.6 cm (3.4"); **B** 2 cm (0.8"). Monotypic. Wet foothill and lower montane forest, occasionally borders, gardens. 700–1600 m. Habits as Purple-bibbed Whitetip. **ID** White post-ocular. ♂ large glittering green gorget, lower border sometimes mixed white; vent rufous (inconspicuous); large white central tail spot (as in previous species). ♀ much like Purple-bibbed Whitetip but slightly larger, vent buffy rufous; post-ocular perhaps shorter. **SS** Smaller ♀ Booted Racket-tail.

Genus *Heliodoxa* Large, fast-flying, mostly highlands; stout bills; sloping foreheads impart distinctive 'cone-headed' appearance; white post-ocular spot; most ♀♀ show narrow whitish malar.

Pink-throated Brilliant *Heliodoxa gularis* VU
Diamante de Napo NT
Rare resident (few records).

L 11.4 cm (4.5"); **B** 2.5 cm (1"). Monotypic. Understorey in humid foothill forest. 700–1100 m. **ID** Smallest *Heliodoxa*. ♂ large glittering pink throat patch, contrasting white vent. ♀ throat patch smaller, underparts mottled green and grey, white malar, small white tail tips. **Voice** Song repeated nasal "keuw" c. 1 note/second. **SS** ♀ Violet-fronted Brilliant.

Diamante Barbinegro
Scarce resident.

L 12.2 cm (4.8"); **B** 2.5 cm (1"). Monotypic. Shady lower levels, occasionally subcanopy inside humid forest, especially *terra firme*. To 1300 m. Poorly known.
ID ♂ very dark (usually looks black), black throat bordered below by narrow glittering purple patch, lower underparts black. ♀ purple on throat reduced, malar whitish. Imm like ♀ but malar rufous. **Voice** High descending trill. **SS** Pink-throated and Violet-fronted Brilliants.

Gould's Brilliant (Gould's Jewelfront)
Heliodoxa aurescens `LC`
Diamante Pechicastaño
Fairly common resident but infrequently seen.

L 12.2 cm (4.8"); **B** 2 cm (0.8"). Monotypic. Inside humid *terra firme* and transition forest, less in *várzea*. To 500 m (rarely 900 m). Trap-lines scattered understorey flowers, occasionally to subcanopy; ventures into shady clearings, light-gaps, along forest streams. **ID** Orange-rufous crescent on chest, forecrown purple (the 'jewelfront'), mostly rufous-chestnut tail. **Voice** Song continuous high "seee" notes.

Fawn-breasted Brilliant *Heliodoxa rubinoides* `LC`
Diamante Pechigamuza
Uncommon to locally common resident.

L 12.2 cm (4.8"); **B** 2.3 cm (0.9"). Races *rubinoides*[A], *aequatorialis*[B], *cervinigularis*[C]. Inside humid montane forest, borders. 1000–2600 m. Forages from lower levels to flowering canopy trees, shrubby gardens, artificial feeders. **ID** ♂ buff underparts, small pink throat spot, cinnamon underwing-coverts; *cervinigularis* much paler, whitish buff below. ♀ like ♂ but throat and chest speckled green (no pink spot), short whitish malar. **SS** Buff-tailed Coronet.

rubinoides

Green-crowned Brilliant *Heliodoxa jacula* `LC`
Diamante Frentiverde
Fairly common resident.

L ♂ 13 cm (5"), ♀ 11 cm (4.3"); **B** 2.3 cm (0.9"). Races *jacula*[A], *jamersoni*[B]. Humid and wet foothill to lower montane forest, borders. 500–2000 m. Low to mid-levels inside forest; visits feeders in shady clearings; inconspicuous. **ID** Large; dusky tail long for genus. ♂ green, forecrown glittering, small blue-violet throat spot. ♀ nearly identical to ♀ Violet-fronted Brilliant but no buff-tinge on lower underparts. Juv ♂ like ad but malar rufous. **SS** Violet-fronted Brilliant (both sexes very similar), Empress Brilliant.

jacula

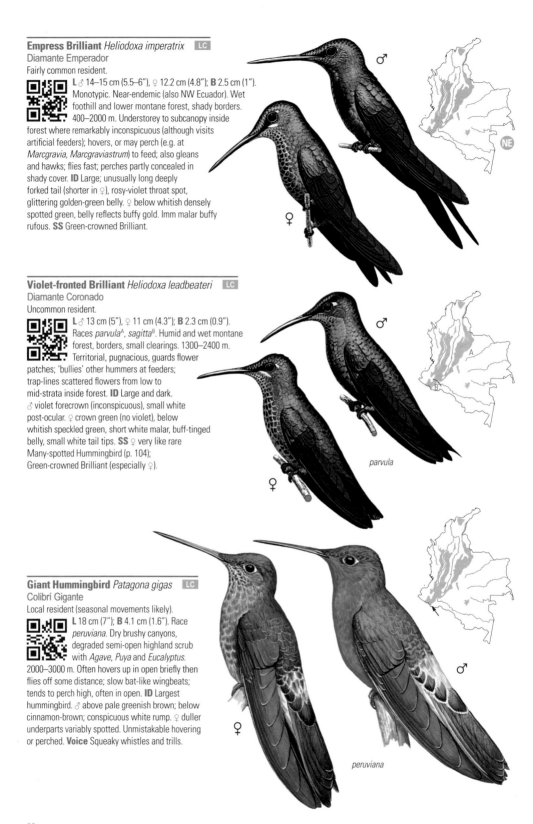

Empress Brilliant *Heliodoxa imperatrix* `LC`
Diamante Emperador
Fairly common resident.
L ♂ 14–15 cm (5.5–6"), ♀ 12.2 cm (4.8"); **B** 2.5 cm (1").
Monotypic. Near-endemic (also NW Ecuador). Wet
foothill and lower montane forest, shady borders.
400–2000 m. Understorey to subcanopy inside
forest where remarkably inconspicuous (although visits
artificial feeders); hovers, or may perch (e.g. at
Marcgravia, Marcgraviastrum) to feed; also gleans
and hawks; flies fast; perches partly concealed in
shady cover. **ID** Large; unusually long deeply
forked tail (shorter in ♀), rosy-violet throat spot,
glittering golden-green belly. ♀ below whitish densely
spotted green, belly reflects buffy gold. Imm malar buffy
rufous. **SS** Green-crowned Brilliant.

Violet-fronted Brilliant *Heliodoxa leadbeateri* `LC`
Diamante Coronado
Uncommon resident.
L ♂ 13 cm (5"), ♀ 11 cm (4.3"); **B** 2.3 cm (0.9").
Races *parvula*[A], *sagitta*[B]. Humid and wet montane
forest, borders, small clearings. 1300–2400 m.
Territorial, pugnacious, guards flower
patches; 'bullies' other hummers at feeders;
trap-lines scattered flowers from low to
mid-strata inside forest. **ID** Large and dark.
♂ violet forecrown (inconspicuous), small white
post-ocular. ♀ crown green (no violet), below
whitish speckled green, short white malar, buff-tinged
belly, small white tail tips. **SS** ♀ very like rare
Many-spotted Hummingbird (p. 104);
Green-crowned Brilliant (especially ♀).

parvula

Giant Hummingbird *Patagona gigas* `LC`
Colibrí Gigante
Local resident (seasonal movements likely).
L 18 cm (7"); **B** 4.1 cm (1.6"). Race
peruviana. Dry brushy canyons,
degraded semi-open highland scrub
with *Agave, Puya* and *Eucalyptus*.
2000–3000 m. Often hovers up in open briefly then
flies off some distance; slow bat-like wingbeats;
tends to perch high, often in open. **ID** Largest
hummingbird. ♂ above pale greenish brown; below
cinnamon-brown; conspicuous white rump. ♀ duller
underparts variably spotted. Unmistakable hovering
or perched. **Voice** Squeaky whistles and trills.

peruviana

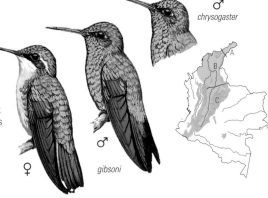

chrysogaster

Red-billed Emerald *Chlorostilbon gibsoni* `LC`
Esmeralda Piquirroja
Common resident (Guajira), less numerous elsewhere.

L 7.6 cm (3"); **B** 1.3 cm (0.5"). Races *nitens*[A], *chrysogaster*[B], *gibsoni*[C]. Desert scrub in N; dry to moist scrub woodland, borders, gardens further S. To 2300 m (upper Magdalena Valley); mainly below 500 m. **ID** Basal half of mandible reddish (often barely visible). ♂ small, glittering green; forked blue-black tail. ♀ dusky mask, whitish post-ocular, tail blue-black, outer tips whitish. *C. g. chrysogaster* larger; *nitens* has golden tinge to green plumage, less deeply forked tail. **Voice** Song, wiry trills. **SS** Western Emerald not definitely known to overlap in range; ♀♀ of the two essentially indistinguishable.

gibsoni

Blue-tailed Emerald *Chlorostilbon mellisugus* `LC`
Esmeralda Coliazul

Eight subspecies in two subspecies groups; both in Colombia.

Western Emerald *Chlorostilbon (mellisugus) melanorhynchus*
Esmeralda Occidental
Common resident.
L 7.6 cm (3"); **B** 1.3 cm (0.5"). Races *pumilus*[A] arid and semi-arid inter-Andean valleys; *melanorhynchus*[B] moist to humid shrubby areas, gardens. 650–2000 m. Trap-lines small low-nectar reward flowers (*Stachytarpheta*, *Lantana*); filches from larger hummers, especially at flowering canopy trees (*Inga*); steals nectar from holes in flower corollas; flight darting (not weaving). **ID** ♂ small, bill black, plumage glittering-green; tail blue-black, slightly forked. ♀ virtually identical to ♀ Red-billed Emerald. **Voice** Soft metallic "tsip"; song, weak scratchy. **SS** Best identified by range.

melanorhynchus

Blue-tailed Emerald
Chlorostilbon (mellisugus) mellisugus
Esmeralda Coliazul
Common resident.
L 7.6 cm (3"); **B** 1.3 cm (0.5"). Races *caribaeus*[A], *phoeopygus*[B]. Humid forest borders, shrubby areas, gardens. To 2000 m. **ID** ♂ small; glittering green, upper breast tinged blue, slightly forked blue-black tail. ♀ like ♀ Red-billed Emerald and most others of genus. **SS** Chiribiquete and Short-tailed Emeralds. **TN** Taxonomy and racial boundaries unresolved.

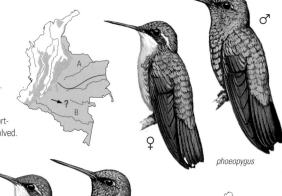

phoeopygus

Chiribiquete Emerald
Chlorostilbon olivaresi `LC`
Esmeralda de Chiribiquete
Common resident (only Serranía de Chiribiquete).

L 8.4 cm (3.3"); **B** 1.8 cm (0.7"). Monotypic. Endemic. Semi-open scrub, savanna, shrubby matorral atop low mesas. 250–600 m. Visits small low flowers (e.g. *Decagonocarpus*), hawks insects, gleans foliage. **ID** Larger, longer-billed than Blue-tailed Emerald, basal half of mandible red (trace in ♀). ♂ throat and upper breast glittering blue-green, slightly forked blue-black tail. ♀ like other *Chlorostilbon* but larger, tail bluish green (not blue-black). **SS** Blue-tailed Emerald.

Coppery Emerald *Chlorostilbon russatus*  LC
Esmeralda Cobriza
Fairly common resident.

 L 7.6 cm (3"); **B** 1.5 cm (0.6"). Monotypic. Near-endemic (also NW Venezuela). Shrubby borders, coffee plantations, gardens in semi-humid foothill and lower montane zones. 200–2200 m (rarely 2600 m). Trap-lines small low flowers or filches nectar from flowers in territories of larger hummers; hawks insects; gleans foliage. **ID** Upperparts tinged coppery green, more reddish-copper shoulders and tail. ♀ tail green with strong reddish-copper tinge, blackish subterminal band (especially from below), whitish tips. **SS** Red-billed Emerald.

Narrow-tailed Emerald *Chlorostilbon stenurus* LC
Esmeralda Colifina
Uncommon and poorly known resident.

 L 7.6 cm (3"); **B** 1.5 cm (0.6"). Race *stenurus*. Shrubby humid to semi-humid wooded borders, disturbed areas. 1000–2300 m. Trap-lines small low flowers and weedy shrubs like others of genus. **ID** ♂ green tail, outer three pairs of feathers very narrow, spiky (only 2 mm wide near tip), rest progressively broader. ♀ like other ♀ *Chlorostilbon* but tail greenish, outer pair of feathers only slightly narrowed, grey basally otherwise dark bluish green tipped white. **SS** Short-tailed Emerald.

stenurus

Short-tailed Emerald *Chlorostilbon poortmani* LC
Esmeralda Rabicorta

 Three subspecies in two subspecies groups; one in Colombia.

Short-tailed Emerald
Chlorostilbon (poortmani) poortmani
Fairly common but local resident.
L 7.6 cm (3"); **B** 1.5 cm (0.6"). Races *poortmani*[A], *euchloris*[B]. Near-endemic (also NW Venezuela). Semi-humid second growth, shrubby pastures, roadsides, gardens. 750–2700 m. Trap-liner of small low-nectar reward flowers. **ID** At rest, wings extend beyond greenish tail (both sexes). **SS** Narrow-tailed Emerald (mostly higher elevations), Red-billed Emerald.

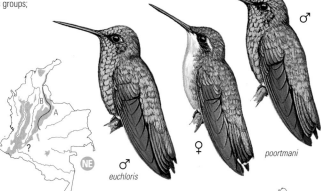

euchloris

poortmani

Violet-headed Hummingbird *Klais guimeti* LC
Colibrí Cabecivioleta
Uncommon resident.

 L 8 cm (3.2"); **B** 1.3 cm (0.5"). Races *merrittii*[A], *guimeti*[B]. Dry to humid forest; borders, shrubby areas, plantations. 400–1800 m. Forages at small low to mid-height flowers, filches nectar from territories of larger hummers; gleans from vines, trunks, foliage. **ID** Quite small; large white post-ocular spot, violet head (especially *merrittii*), whitish tail tips. ♀ similar but below pale grey, only crown violet. **Voice** ♂♂ in loose leks sing "pit-seet" tirelessly from high perches.

guimeti

Santa Marta Blossomcrown *Anthocephala floriceps* VU
Colibrí Cabecicastaño VU
Uncommon and local resident.

 L 9 cm (3.5"); **B** short 1.3 cm (0.5"). Monotypic. Endemic. Humid montane forest, borders, shrubby flower gardens. 600–2200 m. Trap-lines low flowers; attracted to non-native marmalade bush (*Streptosolen*) and vervain (*Stachytarpheta*) in gardens. **ID** Pale frontlet, rufous crown, white post-ocular spot, uppertail-coverts strongly tinged coppery buff, subterminal tail-band blackish, tail tips buff. ♀ crown bronzy green (no rufous). **Voice** ♂♂ in small understorey leks inside forest sing rapid metallic "tsip" notes. **SS** Speckled Hummingbird; beware other hummingbirds with pollen on forecrown. **TN** Formerly Blossomcrown.

Tolima Blossomcrown *Anthocephala berlepschi* VU
Colibrí Florido del Tolima VU
Uncommon resident.

L 9 cm (3.5"); **B** short 1.3 cm (0.5"). Monotypic. Endemic. Humid montane forest, borders, shrubby areas, highland gardens. 1200–2300 m. **ID** ♂ differs from ♂ Santa Marta Blossomcrown in larger pale frontlet, rufous on crown less extensive, rump bronze-green like back (only trace of buff), tail tips decidedly larger and white. ♀ also larger white tail tips. **SS** Speckled Hummingbird. **TN** Formerly regarded as race of *A. floriceps* (Blossomcrown).

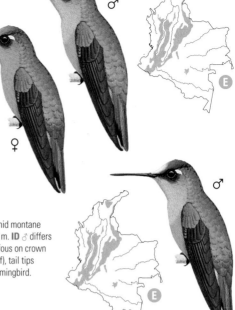

Scaly-breasted Hummingbird *Phaeochroa cuvierii* LC
Colibrí Pechiescamado
Uncommon and local resident.

 L 11.4 cm (4.5"); **B** 1.8 cm (0.7"), heavy, slightly decurved. Race *berlepschi*. Dry forest, semi-open scrub, mangroves, gardens. To 200 m. Territorial, pugnacious, dominates smaller hummers at flowering trees, shrubs and terrestrial bromeliads. Has thickened flat outer primary, curved like *Campylopterus* (but genetically unrelated). **ID** Large and dull, white tail corners, lower underparts tinged buff. **Voice** Loud variable mix of chips and trills. **SS** ♀ White-necked Jacobin (p. 71). **TN** Previously in *Campylopterus*. **AN** Scaly-breasted Sabrewing.

Genus *Campylopterus* Large and sturdy hummingbirds, with stout, slightly decurved bills, and outer two primaries ('sabres') curved, flattened and thick, especially in ♂♂ Lowland and montane habitats.

Grey-breasted Sabrewing *Campylopterus largipennis* LC
Ala-de-sable Pechigrís

Four subspecies in four subspecies groups; two in Colombia.

Amazonian Sabrewing *Campylopterus (largipennis) obscurus*
Fairly common resident.

L 13.5 cm (5.3"); **B** 2.8 cm (1.1"), decurved. Race *obscurus*. Inside humid *terra firme* and *várzea* forest, borders, second growth; lowlands and foothills, to 800 m. Commoner near Andes, rare (?) or local in extreme E. Visits *Heliconia* and scattered lower-strata flowers, occasionally at flowering canopy trees. **ID** Large; below uniformly grey, prominent greyish-white tail tips. **Voice** ♂♂ in loose leks sing sharp "tchip". **TN** Race *aequatorialis* (W Amazonia) here merged into very similar *obscurus* (EC Brazil S of Amazon).

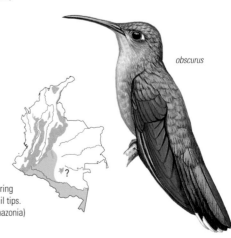

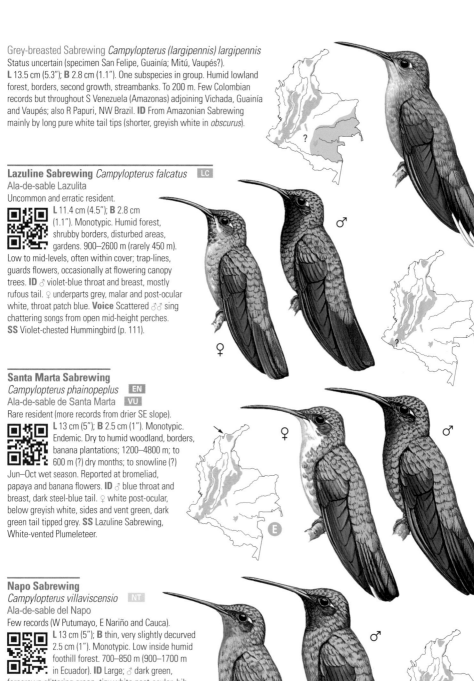

Grey-breasted Sabrewing *Campylopterus (largipennis) largipennis*
Status uncertain (specimen San Felipe, Guainía; Mitú, Vaupés?).
L 13.5 cm (5.3"); **B** 2.8 cm (1.1"). One subspecies in group. Humid lowland forest, borders, second growth, streambanks. To 200 m. Few Colombian records but throughout S Venezuela (Amazonas) adjoining Vichada, Guainía and Vaupés; also R Papuri, NW Brazil. **ID** From Amazonian Sabrewing mainly by long pure white tail tips (shorter, greyish white in *obscurus*).

Lazuline Sabrewing *Campylopterus falcatus* LC
Ala-de-sable Lazulita
Uncommon and erratic resident.
L 11.4 cm (4.5"); **B** 2.8 cm (1.1"). Monotypic. Humid forest, shrubby borders, disturbed areas, gardens. 900–2600 m (rarely 450 m). Low to mid-levels, often within cover; trap-lines, guards flowers, occasionally at flowering canopy trees. **ID** ♂ violet-blue throat and breast, mostly rufous tail. ♀ underparts grey, malar and post-ocular white, throat patch blue. **Voice** Scattered ♂♂ sing chattering songs from open mid-height perches. **SS** Violet-chested Hummingbird (p. 111).

Santa Marta Sabrewing
Campylopterus phainopeplus EN
Ala-de-sable de Santa Marta VU
Rare resident (more records from drier SE slope).
L 13 cm (5"); **B** 2.5 cm (1"). Monotypic. Endemic. Dry to humid woodland, borders, banana plantations; 1200–4800 m; to 600 m (?) dry months; to snowline (?) Jun–Oct wet season. Reported at bromeliad, papaya and banana flowers. **ID** ♂ blue throat and breast, dark steel-blue tail. ♀ white post-ocular, below greyish white, sides and vent green, dark green tail tipped grey. **SS** Lazuline Sabrewing, White-vented Plumeleteer.

Napo Sabrewing
Campylopterus villaviscensio NT
Ala-de-sable del Napo
Few records (W Putumayo, E Nariño and Cauca).
L 13 cm (5"); **B** thin, very slightly decurved 2.5 cm (1"). Monotypic. Low inside humid foothill forest. 700–850 m (900–1700 m in Ecuador). **ID** Large; ♂ dark green, forecrown glittering green, tiny white post-ocular, bib dark violet-blue, lower underparts greyish green, tail steel blue. ♀ below plain grey, sides mixed green, tail like ♂ but outer feathers narrowly tipped greyish white. **Voice** ♂ repeats "tslip…tseek…", long-sustained at understorey lek. **SS** Grey-breasted Sabrewing (large white tail corners), smaller ♀ Fork-tailed Woodnymph (p. 104).

Genus *Chalybura* Relatively large, white-vented hummers of forest or wooded borders. Bills slightly decurved.

White-vented Plumeleteer *Chalybura buffonii* `LC`
Colibrí de Buffon

Four subspecies in two subspecies groups; both in Colombia.

White-vented Plumeleteer *Chalybura (buffonii) buffonii*
Common resident.
L ♂ 11.4 cm (4.5"), ♀ 11 cm (4.3"); **B** 2.5 cm (1"). Races *micans*[A], *buffonii*[B], *aeneicauda*[C]. Humid forest, plantations, shrubby clearings, gardens. To 2000 m. Trap-lines low flowers at shady borders; gathers with other hummers at large flowering trees (e.g. *Inga, Erythrina*) where aggressive, territorial. **ID** Large; feet dark (cf. Bronze-tailed Plumeleteer). ♂ green, contrasting white vent, longish tail. ♀ below greyish white, contrasting white vent, pale tail tips. **Voice** Single "chip" or "tri-tick" as forages; weak trills. **SS** Bronze-tailed Plumeleteer.

Blue-bellied Plumeleteer *Chalybura (buffonii) caeruleogaster*
Common resident.
L ♂ 11.4 cm (4.5"), ♀ 11 cm (4.3"); **B** 2.5 cm (1"). One subspecies in group. Endemic. Humid forest borders, shrubby clearings. 400–1000 m (E slope of E Andes). **ID** ♂ like White-vented Plumeleteer but blue wash on breast (minimal on belly); ♀ similar to White-vented Plumeleteer. **SS** ♀ Fork-tailed Woodnymph.

Bronze-tailed Plumeleteer *Chalybura urochrysia* `LC`
Colibrí Colibronceado

Four subspecies in four subspecies groups; two in Colombia.

Blue-breasted Plumeleteer
Chalybura (urochrysia) isaurae
Status uncertain (Panama border).
L 10.7 cm (4.2"); **B** 2.5 cm (1"). One subspecies in group. Habitat, elevation and behaviour as in Green-breasted (*urochrysia*) race (below). **ID** Pink feet, pinkish mandible; ♂ throat and breast bluish, otherwise as White-vented Plumeleteer; ♀ below grey, tail tips whitish. **SS** White-vented Plumeleteer.

Green-breasted Plumeleteer
Chalybura (urochrysia) urochrysia
Fairly common resident.
L 10.7 cm (4.2"); **B** 2.5 cm (1"). One subspecies in group. Near-endemic (also extreme SE Panama and far NW Ecuador). Humid and wet forest, borders. To 1000 m. Trap-lines, mostly at lower levels inside or at edge of forest. **ID** Pink feet diagnostic, pinkish mandible, underparts green (no bluish tinge), white vent less conspicuous than White-vented Plumeleteer; ♀ below grey, tail tips whitish. **SS** White-vented Plumeleteer.

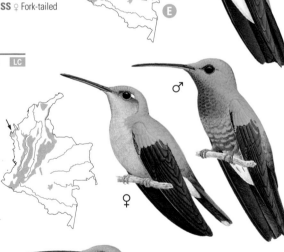

buffonii

♀ ♂

♂

♂ ♀

♀ ♂

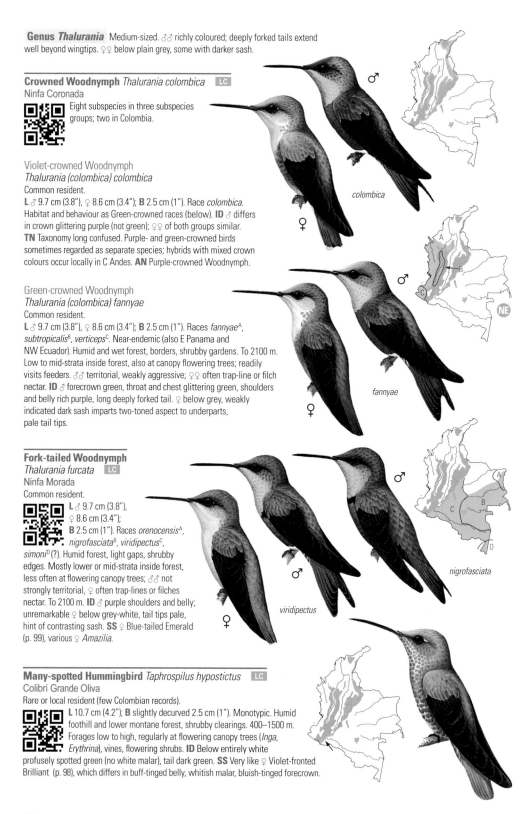

Genus *Thalurania* Medium-sized. ♂♂ richly coloured; deeply forked tails extend well beyond wingtips. ♀♀ below plain grey, some with darker sash.

Crowned Woodnymph *Thalurania colombica* `LC`
Ninfa Coronada

Eight subspecies in three subspecies groups; two in Colombia.

Violet-crowned Woodnymph
Thalurania (colombica) colombica
Common resident.
L ♂ 9.7 cm (3.8"), ♀ 8.6 cm (3.4"); **B** 2.5 cm (1"). Race *colombica*. Habitat and behaviour as Green-crowned races (below). **ID** ♂ differs in crown glittering purple (not green); ♀♀ of both groups similar. **TN** Taxonomy long confused. Purple- and green-crowned birds sometimes regarded as separate species; hybrids with mixed crown colours occur locally in C Andes. **AN** Purple-crowned Woodnymph.

colombica

Green-crowned Woodnymph
Thalurania (colombica) fannyae
Common resident.
L ♂ 9.7 cm (3.8"), ♀ 8.6 cm (3.4"); **B** 2.5 cm (1"). Races *fannyae*[A], *subtropicalis*[B], *verticeps*[C]. Near-endemic (also E Panama and NW Ecuador). Humid and wet forest, borders, shrubby gardens. To 2100 m. Low to mid-strata inside forest, also at canopy flowering trees; readily visits feeders. ♂♂ territorial, weakly aggressive; ♀♀ often trap-line or filch nectar. **ID** ♂ forecrown green, throat and chest glittering green, shoulders and belly rich purple, long deeply forked tail. ♀ below grey, weakly indicated dark sash imparts two-toned aspect to underparts, pale tail tips.

fannyae

Fork-tailed Woodnymph
Thalurania furcata `LC`
Ninfa Morada
Common resident.
L ♂ 9.7 cm (3.8"), ♀ 8.6 cm (3.4"); **B** 2.5 cm (1"). Races *orenocensis*[A], *nigrofasciata*[B], *viridipectus*[C], *simoni*[D] (?). Humid forest, light gaps, shrubby edges. Mostly lower or mid-strata inside forest, less often at flowering canopy trees; ♂♂ not strongly territorial, ♀ often trap-lines or filches nectar. To 2100 m. **ID** ♂ purple shoulders and belly; unremarkable ♀ below grey-white, tail tips pale, hint of contrasting sash. **SS** ♀ Blue-tailed Emerald (p. 99), various ♀ *Amazilia*.

viridipectus

nigrofasciata

Many-spotted Hummingbird *Taphrospilus hypostictus* `LC`
Colibrí Grande Oliva
Rare or local resident (few Colombian records).
L 10.7 cm (4.2"); **B** slightly decurved 2.5 cm (1"). Monotypic. Humid foothill and lower montane forest, shrubby clearings. 400–1500 m. Forages low to high, regularly at flowering canopy trees (*Inga*, *Erythrina*), vines, flowering shrubs. **ID** Below entirely white profusely spotted green (no white malar), tail dark green. **SS** Very like ♀ Violet-fronted Brilliant (p. 98), which differs in buff-tinged belly, whitish malar, bluish-tinged forecrown.

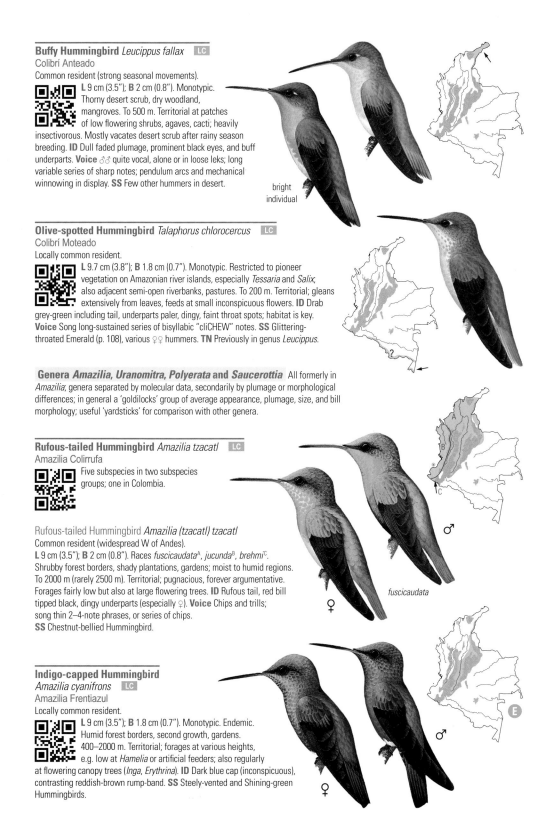

Buffy Hummingbird *Leucippus fallax* `LC`
Colibrí Anteado

Common resident (strong seasonal movements).

L 9 cm (3.5"); **B** 2 cm (0.8"). Monotypic. Thorny desert scrub, dry woodland, mangroves. To 500 m. Territorial at patches of low flowering shrubs, agaves, cacti; heavily insectivorous. Mostly vacates desert scrub after rainy season breeding. **ID** Dull faded plumage, prominent black eyes, and buff underparts. **Voice** ♂♂ quite vocal, alone or in loose leks; long variable series of sharp notes; pendulum arcs and mechanical winnowing in display. **SS** Few other hummers in desert.

bright
individual

Olive-spotted Hummingbird *Talaphorus chlorocercus* `LC`
Colibrí Moteado

Locally common resident.

L 9.7 cm (3.8"); **B** 1.8 cm (0.7"). Monotypic. Restricted to pioneer vegetation on Amazonian river islands, especially *Tessaria* and *Salix*; also adjacent semi-open riverbanks, pastures. To 200 m. Territorial; gleans extensively from leaves, feeds at small inconspicuous flowers. **ID** Drab grey-green including tail, underparts paler, dingy, faint throat spots; habitat is key. **Voice** Song long-sustained series of bisyllabic "cliCHEW" notes. **SS** Glittering-throated Emerald (p. 108), various ♀♀ hummers. **TN** Previously in genus *Leucippus*.

Genera *Amazilia, Uranomitra, Polyerata* and *Saucerottia* All formerly in *Amazilia*; genera separated by molecular data, secondarily by plumage or morphological differences; in general a 'goldilocks' group of average appearance, plumage, size, and bill morphology; useful 'yardsticks' for comparison with other genera.

Rufous-tailed Hummingbird *Amazilia tzacatl* `LC`
Amazilia Colirrufa

Five subspecies in two subspecies groups; one in Colombia.

Rufous-tailed Hummingbird *Amazilia (tzacatl) tzacatl*
Common resident (widespread W of Andes).
L 9 cm (3.5"); **B** 2 cm (0.8"). Races *fuscicaudata*[A], *jucunda*[B], *brehmi*[C]. Shrubby forest borders, shady plantations, gardens; moist to humid regions. To 2000 m (rarely 2500 m). Territorial; pugnacious, forever argumentative. Forages fairly low but also at large flowering trees. **ID** Rufous tail, red bill tipped black, dingy underparts (especially ♀). **Voice** Chips and trills; song thin 2–4-note phrases, or series of chips. **SS** Chestnut-bellied Hummingbird.

♂

♀

fuscicaudata

Indigo-capped Hummingbird
Amazilia cyanifrons `LC`
Amazilia Frentiazul

Locally common resident.

L 9 cm (3.5"); **B** 1.8 cm (0.7"). Monotypic. Endemic. Humid forest borders, second growth, gardens. 400–2000 m. Territorial; forages at various heights, e.g. low at *Hamelia* or artificial feeders; also regularly at flowering canopy trees (*Inga*, *Erythrina*). **ID** Dark blue cap (inconspicuous), contrasting reddish-brown rump-band. **SS** Steely-vented and Shining-green Hummingbirds.

♂

♀

Humboldt's Hummingbird (Humboldt's Sapphire)
Amazilia humboldtii LC
Zafiro de Humboldt
Fairly common resident (marked seasonal movements).

L 9 cm (3.5"); **B** 1.8 cm (0.7"). Monotypic. Near-endemic (also extreme SE Panama and NW Ecuador). Mangroves, especially *Pelliciera rhizophorae*, wet forest borders near coast. To 200 m. Forages at mid-heights or lower, often at small inconspicuous flowers, also *Heliconia*; hawks insects. **ID** Tail dark green. ♂ blue forecrown and throat, whitish lower breast and belly, bill mostly red tipped dusky. ♀ forecrown bluish, underparts white flecked green, mandible pinkish red basally. **Voice** ♂♂ sing from low perches in scattered leks. **SS** Blue-headed Sapphire (p. 109), ♀ Purple-chested and Blue-chested Hummingbirds. **TN** Also regularly placed in genus *Hylocharis*.

Andean Emerald *Uranomitra franciae* LC
Amazilia Andina

Three subspecies in two subspecies groups; both occur in region.

Ecuadorian Emerald *Uranomitra (franciae) viridiceps*
Common resident.
L 9.1 cm (3.6"); **B** 2 cm (0.8"). One subspecies in group. Humid lowland and foothill forest, borders. 100–1400 m (W Ecuador), below elevation of race *franciae* (Andean Emerald). **ID** ♂ like Andean Emerald but bill and tail shorter, crown glittering green (not blue); ♀ crown plain green. **TN** Often placed in *Amazilia* but differs genetically.

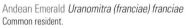

Andean Emerald *Uranomitra (franciae) franciae*
Common resident.
L 9.1 cm (3.6"); **B** 2.3 cm (0.9"). Race *franciae*. Endemic. Humid and wet montane forest, shrubby borders, gardens. 1000–2100 m. Trap-lines low or mid-level flowers; visits tall mass-flowering trees in forest or clearings where moderately territorial but subordinate to aggressive species. **ID** ♂ crown glittering blue, below immaculate white, green discs on sides, contrasting coppery-bronze uppertail-coverts. ♀ crown plain green. **Voice** Song complex high squeaks and trills. **TN** Often placed in *Amazilia* but differs genetically.

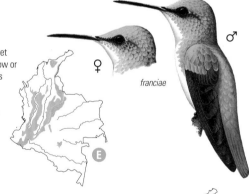

franciae

Blue-chested Hummingbird *Polyerata amabilis* LC
Amazilia Pechiazul
Common resident.

L 8.4 cm (3.3"); **B** 1.8 cm (0.7"). Monotypic. Shrubby borders of humid and wet forest, plantations and gardens. To 1000 m (rarely 1400 m). Forages mostly low at herbs and woody shrubs; trap-lines, but may guard patches of flowers. **ID** Overall dull, crown glittering green, violet-blue chest patch often indistinct, vent dingy greyish white. ♀ even duller below. **Voice** Loosely associated ♂♂ sing insistent squeaky songs. **SS** Purple-chested Hummingbird. **TN** Previously in *Amazilia*.

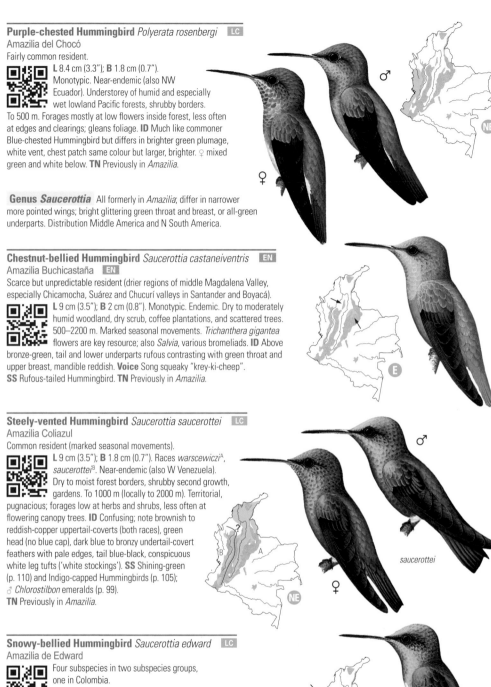

Purple-chested Hummingbird *Polyerata rosenbergi* `LC`
Amazilia del Chocó
Fairly common resident.

L 8.4 cm (3.3"); **B** 1.8 cm (0.7").
Monotypic. Near-endemic (also NW
Ecuador). Understorey of humid and especially
wet lowland Pacific forests, shrubby borders.
To 500 m. Forages mostly at low flowers inside forest, less often
at edges and clearings; gleans foliage. **ID** Much like commoner
Blue-chested Hummingbird but differs in brighter green plumage,
white vent, chest patch same colour but larger, brighter. ♀ mixed
green and white below. **TN** Previously in *Amazilia*.

Genus *Saucerottia* All formerly in *Amazilia*; differ in narrower
more pointed wings; bright glittering green throat and breast, or all-green
underparts. Distribution Middle America and N South America.

Chestnut-bellied Hummingbird *Saucerottia castaneiventris* `EN`
Amazilia Buchicastaña `EN`
Scarce but unpredictable resident (drier regions of middle Magdalena Valley,
especially Chicamocha, Suárez and Chucurí valleys in Santander and Boyacá).

L 9 cm (3.5"); **B** 2 cm (0.8"). Monotypic. Endemic. Dry to moderately
humid woodland, dry scrub, coffee plantations, and scattered trees.
500–2200 m. Marked seasonal movements. *Trichanthera gigantea*
flowers are key resource; also *Salvia*, various bromeliads. **ID** Above
bronze-green, tail and lower underparts rufous contrasting with green throat and
upper breast, mandible reddish. **Voice** Song squeaky "krey-ki-cheep".
SS Rufous-tailed Hummingbird. **TN** Previously in *Amazilia*.

Steely-vented Hummingbird *Saucerottia saucerottei* `LC`
Amazilia Coliazul
Common resident (marked seasonal movements).

L 9 cm (3.5"); **B** 1.8 cm (0.7"). Races *warscewiczi*[A],
saucerottei[B]. Near-endemic (also W Venezuela).
Dry to moist forest borders, shrubby second growth,
gardens. To 1000 m (locally to 2000 m). Territorial,
pugnacious; forages low at herbs and shrubs, less often at
flowering canopy trees. **ID** Confusing; note brownish to
reddish-copper uppertail-coverts (both races), green
head (no blue cap), dark blue to bronzy undertail-covert
feathers with pale edges, tail blue-black, conspicuous
white leg tufts ('white stockings'). **SS** Shining-green
(p. 110) and Indigo-capped Hummingbirds (p. 105);
♂ *Chlorostilbon* emeralds (p. 99).
TN Previously in *Amazilia*.

saucerottei

Snowy-bellied Hummingbird *Saucerottia edward* `LC`
Amazilia de Edward

Four subspecies in two subspecies groups,
one in Colombia.

Southern Snowy-bellied Hummingbird *Saucerottia (edward) edward* `LC`
Rare resident (perhaps seasonal; Panama border).
L 9 cm (3.5"); **B** 1.8 cm (0.7"). Race *edward*. Humid forest borders, semi-open areas,
gardens. To c. 700 m. Forages low, infrequent at canopy flowering trees. **ID** Green
breast sharply separated from white lower underparts, lower back and tail rufous.
SS Rufous-tailed Hummingbird. **TN** Previously in *Amazilia*.

edward

Green-bellied Hummingbird *Saucerottia viridigaster* `LC`
Amazilia Colimorada

Fairly common resident (only E slope of Andes).

 L 9 cm (3.5"); **B** 1.8 cm (0.7"). Race *viridigaster*. Near-endemic (also W Venezuela). Foothill and lower montane forest borders, coffee plantations, disturbed areas. 500–1800 m. Feeds at various heights, commonly gathers at flowering mid-level or canopy trees (especially *Inga, Erythrina*) where pugnacious, argumentative. **ID** All green, lower back, rump and uppertail-coverts brownish; ♀ dingy below. **Voice** Distinctive waif-like song "ta-da titi-da" ("titi" higher, quicker). **SS** Golden-tailed Sapphire. **TN** Previously in *Amazilia*.

viridigaster

Rufous-throated Sapphire *Hylocharis sapphirina* `LC`
Zafiro Barbirrufo

Uncommon resident (local or overlooked).

 L 9 cm (3.5"); **B** 2 cm (0.8"). Monotypic. Canopy and borders of humid forest, savanna woodland, scrub around rock outcrops. To 300 m. Forages at various heights, commonly high in flowering canopy trees. **ID** ♂ bill red tipped black, upper throat rufous (inconspicuous), lower throat and chest violet-blue, tail rufous. ♀ chin rufous, throat and breast white spotted blue and green, belly whitish, sides green. **SS** Golden-tailed Sapphire. **AN** Rufous-throated Hummingbird.

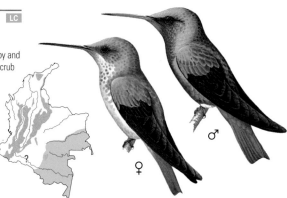

♂

♀

Glittering-throated Emerald *Chionomesa fimbriata* `LC`
Amazilia Buchiblanca

Common resident.

 L 9 cm (3.5"); **B** 1.8 cm (0.7"). Races *elegantissima*[A], *apicalis*[B], *fluviatilis*[C], *laeta*[D] (S Amazonas?). Wooded borders, gardens, semi-open, even urban areas. To 1100 m. Forages at almost any height at wide variety of flowering trees, shrubs and herbs; territorial, pugnacious. **ID** Narrow wedge of white on central underparts, prominent black eye in featureless face, dull red mandible; *fluviatilis* has bluish-tinged throat. **SS** Versicolored Emerald, Blue-chinned Sapphire (p. 110). **TN** Previously in *Amazilia*.

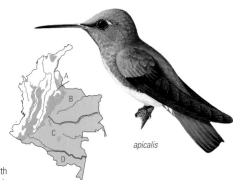

apicalis

Genus *Chrysuronia* United by molecular evidence. Medium-sized with slightly decurved bills (mandible often reddish). Most ♂♂ have blue on head and/or foreparts; ♀♀ mostly green with white median underparts.

Versicolored Emerald *Chrysuronia versicolor* `LC`
Amazilia Pechiblanca

Locally common resident (marked seasonal movements).

 L 9 cm (3.5"); **B** 2 cm (0.8"). Race *millerii*. Gallery forest borders, open or shrubby areas, savanna with scattered trees in *llanos*. To 600 m. Territorial; several regularly gather at large flowering trees, e.g. *Inga, Vochysia*, also at smaller flowering trees, e.g. *Calliandra*; or scatter and defend small flower patches, or hawk tiny insects. **ID** Crown usually glittering blue, sides of throat spotted blue, median throat and underparts white, flanks bronzy green, and mandible pinkish red. **SS** Glittering-throated Emerald. **TN** Previously in *Amazilia*.

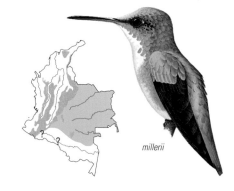

millerii

Blue-headed Sapphire *Chrysuronia grayi* `LC`
Zafiro Cabeciazul
Uncommon resident (marked seasonal movements).

 L 9 cm (3.5"); **B** 2 cm (0.8"). Monotypic. Near-endemic (also N Ecuador). Humid and wet forest borders, scattered trees in clearings, locally in dry to semi-humid areas and gardens. 600–2000 m (rarely 2600 m). Forages at various heights, often low including at artificial feeders. **ID** Dark blue tail; ♂ almost all-red bill, blue head; ♀ below white mottled green, mandible pinkish red. **SS** ♀ nearly identical to ♀ Humboldt's Hummingbird (p. 106) but occurs at higher elevations (no known overlap). **TN** Previously in *Hylocharis* (or *Amazilia*). **AN** Gray's Hummingbird.

Golden-tailed Sapphire *Chrysuronia oenone* `LC`
Zafiro Colidorado

 Three subspecies in two subspecies groups; one in Colombia.

Northern Golden-tailed Sapphire
Chrysuronia (oenone) oenone
Common resident (sharp seasonal movements).
L 9 cm (3.5"); **B** 1.8 cm (0.7"). One subspecies in group. Humid forest borders, coffee plantations, scattered trees in clearings. 100–1500 m. Quarrelsome ♂♂ forage low to high, gather at large flowering trees (e.g. *Erythrina*); ♀♀ often trap-line low at borders, also at canopy flowers. **ID** Rufous tail, narrow coppery-rufous uppertail-covert band (both sexes); ♂ head and throat violet-blue; ♀ dingy speckled underparts. **Voice** ♂ variable 'jerky' song from high open twig. **SS** Rufous-throated Sapphire. **TN** Race *josephinae* (S Amazonas?).

Sapphire-throated Hummingbird
Chrysuronia coeruleogularis `LC`
Colibrí Zafirino
Scarce and local resident.

 L 9 cm (3.5"); **B** 1.8 cm (0.7"). Races *confinis*^A, *coelina*^B. Mangroves, dry forest, scrub. To 100 m. Feeds mostly low or at mid-levels, occasionally at canopy flowers. **ID** ♂ malar area, gorget and breast deep glittering sapphire-blue, lower underparts green, mandible reddish. ♀ below white spotted green on sides, rump coppery, base of mandible reddish. **SS** Sapphire-bellied Hummingbird. **TN** Previously in *Lepidopyga*.

Sapphire-bellied Hummingbird *Chrysuronia lilliae* `CR`
Colibrí Manglero `EN`
Status unknown (few valid records).

 L 9.4 cm (3.7"); **B** 1.8 cm (0.7"), mandible reddish basally. Monotypic. Endemic. Mangroves, occasionally adjacent arid scrub. To 50 m. Forages at various heights but behaviour in general poorly known; also reported at flowering *Erythrina fusca*. **ID** Glittering deep violet-blue throat and breast becomes dark blue on lower underparts, forked tail steely blue-black. ♀ uncertain; possibly green with white median underparts. **SS** Sapphire-throated Hummingbird. **TN** Status as valid species questioned. Previously in *Lepidopyga*.

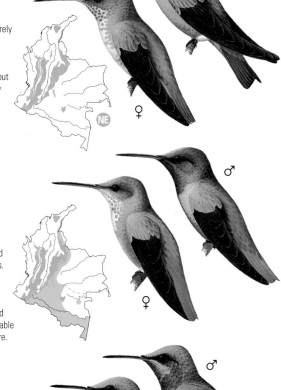

♂

♀

NE

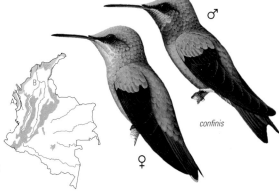

♂

♀

confinis

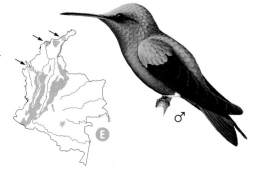

♂

E

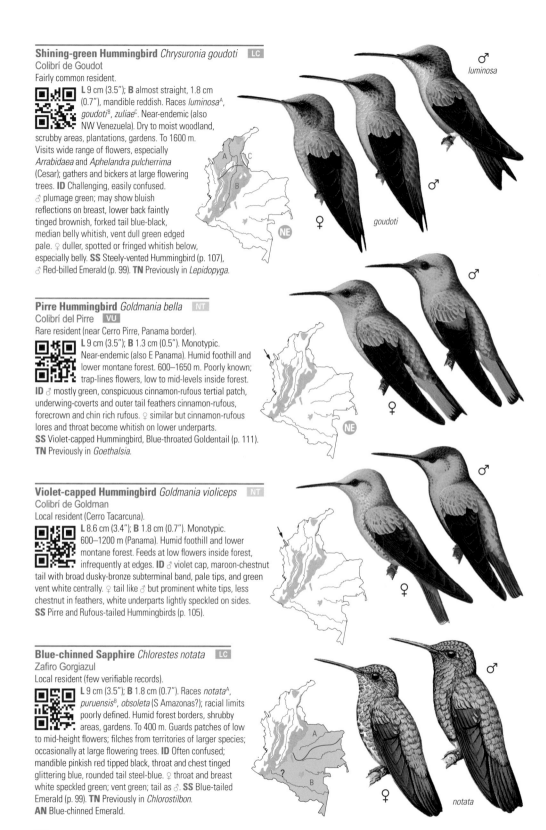

Shining-green Hummingbird *Chrysuronia goudoti* `LC`
Colibrí de Goudot
Fairly common resident.
L 9 cm (3.5"); **B** almost straight, 1.8 cm (0.7"), mandible reddish. Races *luminosa*[A], *goudoti*[B], *zuliae*[C]. Near-endemic (also NW Venezuela). Dry to moist woodland, scrubby areas, plantations, gardens. To 1600 m. Visits wide range of flowers, especially *Arrabidaea* and *Aphelandra pulcherrima* (Cesar); gathers and bickers at large flowering trees. **ID** Challenging, easily confused. ♂ plumage green; may show bluish reflections on breast, lower back faintly tinged brownish, forked tail blue-black, median belly whitish, vent dull green edged pale. ♀ duller, spotted or fringed whitish below, especially belly. **SS** Steely-vented Hummingbird (p. 107), ♂ Red-billed Emerald (p. 99). **TN** Previously in *Lepidopyga*.

Pirre Hummingbird *Goldmania bella* `NT`
Colibrí del Pirre `VU`
Rare resident (near Cerro Pirre, Panama border).
L 9 cm (3.5"); **B** 1.3 cm (0.5"). Monotypic. Near-endemic (also E Panama). Humid foothill and lower montane forest. 600–1650 m. Poorly known; trap-lines flowers, low to mid-levels inside forest. **ID** ♂ mostly green, conspicuous cinnamon-rufous tertial patch, underwing-coverts and outer tail feathers cinnamon-rufous, forecrown and chin rich rufous. ♀ similar but cinnamon-rufous lores and throat become whitish on lower underparts. **SS** Violet-capped Hummingbird, Blue-throated Goldentail (p. 111). **TN** Previously in *Goethalsia*.

Violet-capped Hummingbird *Goldmania violiceps* `NT`
Colibrí de Goldman
Local resident (Cerro Tacarcuna).
L 8.6 cm (3.4"); **B** 1.8 cm (0.7"). Monotypic. 600–1200 m (Panama). Humid foothill and lower montane forest. Feeds at low flowers inside forest, infrequently at edges. **ID** ♂ violet cap, maroon-chestnut tail with broad dusky-bronze subterminal band, pale tips, green vent white centrally. ♀ tail like ♂ but prominent white tips, less chestnut in feathers, white underparts lightly speckled on sides. **SS** Pirre and Rufous-tailed Hummingbirds (p. 105).

Blue-chinned Sapphire *Chlorestes notata* `LC`
Zafiro Gorgiazul
Local resident (few verifiable records).
L 9 cm (3.5"); **B** 1.8 cm (0.7"). Races *notata*[A], *puruensis*[B], *obsoleta* (S Amazonas?); racial limits poorly defined. Humid forest borders, shrubby areas, gardens. To 400 m. Guards patches of low to mid-height flowers; filches from territories of larger species; occasionally at large flowering trees. **ID** Often confused; mandible pinkish red tipped black, throat and chest tinged glittering blue, rounded tail steel-blue. ♀ throat and breast white speckled green; vent green; tail as ♂. **SS** Blue-tailed Emerald (p. 99). **TN** Previously in *Chlorostilbon*. **AN** Blue-chinned Emerald.

110

Violet-bellied Hummingbird *Chlorestes julie*
Colibrí Pechiverde
Uncommon and local resident.

 L 8 cm (3.2"); **B** 1.3 cm (0.5"). Races *panamensis*[A], *julie*[B], *feliciana*[C]. Dry to humid woodland, borders. Usually visits low or mid-level flowers, infrequently at flowering canopy trees. **ID** Quite small; ♂ mid-breast to vent violet-blue, tail rounded to wedge-shaped; ♀ below white, sides green, tail pale tipped. **Voice** Song thin high "kee-rrrrr". **SS** Crowned Woodnymph (p. 104). **TN** Previously in *Juliamyia*.

Blue-throated Goldentail *Chlorestes eliciae*
Zafiro Gorgiazul
Few records (Panama border).

 L 9 cm (3.5"); **B** 1.5 cm (0.6"). Race *earina*. Humid forest borders, shrubby clearings, mangroves. To 200 m. Feeds mostly at low flowers. **ID** ♂ black-tipped red bill, violet-blue throat, rump and tail contrasting coppery to golden-bronze. ♀ tail as ♂, underparts whitish, throat dotted blue, breast mostly green. **Voice** ♂'s song variable, from loose understorey lek. **SS** Rufous-tailed (p. 105) and Snowy-bellied Hummingbirds (p. 107); Sapphire-throated Hummingbird. **TN** Previously in *Hylocharis*.

White-chinned Sapphire *Chlorestes cyanus*
Zafiro Gorgiblanco
Locally common resident.

 L 9 cm (3.5"); **B** 2.3 cm (0.9"). Race *viridiventris*. Humid forest, borders, gallery forest, plantations, light woodland. To 1000 m. Forages from understorey to canopy, often with others at large flowering trees; aggressive and territorial. **ID** ♂ bright red bill tipped black, white chin difficult to see, violet-blue foreface, coppery-rufous rump-band. ♀ bill duller, rump like ♂, underparts white variably spotted green. **Voice** Solitary ♂♂ incessantly sing high insect-like phrases from bare subcanopy twig. **SS** Golden-tailed Sapphire. **TN** Previously in *Hylocharis*. Race *rostrata* (?) in S Amazonas.

Violet-chested Hummingbird *Sternoclyta cyanopectus*
Colibrí Grande de Cola Oliva
Rare resident (Tamá National Park, Venezuelan border).

 L 11.4 cm (4.5"); **B** stout, decurved 3 cm (1.2"). Monotypic. Humid forest borders, overgrown coffee plantations. Territorial, jealously guards patches of low flowers, especially *Heliconia*; rarely visits canopy. **ID** Large and robust, violet chest patch; ♀ below grey profusely spotted green, white tail tips. **Voice** Song, sharp "chit" notes mixed with squeaky trills. **SS** Violet-fronted Brilliant (p. 98), Lazuline Sabrewing (p. 102).

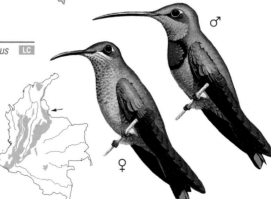

Long-billed Starthroat *Heliomaster longirostris* `LC`
Picudo Gorgiestrella
Uncommon and unpredictable resident.

 L 10 cm (4"); **B** 3.8 cm (1.5"). Race *longirostris*. Forest borders, open second growth, scattered trees in clearings. To 1500 m. Forages high, less often low; regularly perches high on open bare branch. Gathers with other hummers at flowering canopy trees; hovers high in open hawking insects. **ID** Long straight bill, white median stripe on lower back, ruby throat; ♀ duller, lacks blue forecrown.

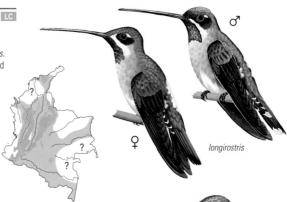

longirostris

[Blue-tufted Starthroat *Heliomaster furcifer*] `LC`
Picudo Buchiazul
Hypothetical (possible austral migrant).

 L 13 cm (5"); **B** 3 cm (1.2"). Monotypic. One report from Leticia (SE Amazonas). Probably forest borders. 100 m. Scrub, grassland and low woodland in Argentina. Perches high, often in open atop vegetation. **ID** Large with long bill. ♂ magenta throat patch, glittering dark blue underparts. ♀ dull, greyish below, white tail tips. **SS** Grey-breasted Sabrewing (p.101).

Genera *Chaetocercus, Calliphlox* and *Philodice* Tiny; white flank patch (no rump-band); ♂ has sharply pointed tail feathers, usually deeply forked tail. ♀ shorter blunt tail; underparts variably cinnamon with echo of ♂'s whitish post-ocular and pectoral collar; red gorget lacking or incomplete in juv ♂♂ and post-breeding (eclipse plumage) ad ♂♂.

White-bellied Woodstar *Chaetocercus mulsant* `LC`
Rumbito Buchiblanco
Common resident.

 L ♂ 7 cm (2.8"), ♀ 6.4 cm (2.5"); **B** 1.3 cm (0.5"). Monotypic. Forest borders, clearings with tall trees, gardens. 1500–3300 m. Forages low or high; regularly perches high on open bare twig; flight slow, weaving and bee-like. **ID** Either sex identified by white median and lower underparts. **SS** Gorgeted and Rufous-shafted Woodstars.

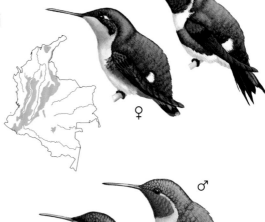

[Little Woodstar *Chaetocercus bombus*] `VU`
Rumbito Chico
Hypothetical (no confirmed records; possible in SW Nariño).

 L ♂ 6.4 cm (2.5"), ♀ 5.8 cm (2.3"); **B** 1.3 cm (0.5"). Monotypic. Borders of semi-humid woodland, clearings. To 1800 m (higher?). **ID** Tiny; ♂ buff chest collar unique, two long pointed feathers adjacent to central tail feathers. ♀ nearly identical to ♀ Gorgeted but paler. **SS** White-bellied and Gorgeted Woodstars.

Gorgeted Woodstar *Chaetocercus heliodor* `LC`
Rumbito Diminuto
Uncommon resident.

 L ♂ 6.4 cm (2.5"), ♀ 5.8 cm (2.3"); **B** 1.3 cm (0.5"). Races *heliodor, cleavesi* (E Nariño?). Humid forest borders, open second-growth woodland, gardens. 1200–3000 m. Forages at any height, but often perches high on open treetop twig; slow bee-like flight. **ID** ♂ magenta gorget flares rearward, dark green breast and belly (little or no white). ♀ rump cinnamon-rufous, tail cinnamon with dusky subterminal band, base may show green speckling; lower underparts rich cinnamon. **SS** Rufous-shafted and White-bellied Woodstars.

Santa Marta Woodstar *Chaetocercus astreans* `LC`
Rumbito de Santa Marta
Fairly common resident.

 L ♂ 6.4 cm (2.5"), ♀ 5.8 cm (2.3"); **B** 1.3 cm (0.5"). Monotypic. Endemic. Humid forest borders, coffee plantations, gardens. 800–2200 m. **ID** Only woodstar in Santa Marta Mts. ♂ very like Gorgeted Woodstar and formerly regarded as race of it; differs mainly in blue-green (not green) upperparts. ♀ much like ♀ Gorgeted Woodstar, but throat whitish (not buff), central tail feathers green (not all cinnamon).

Rufous-shafted Woodstar *Chaetocercus jourdanii* `LC`
Rumbito Colirrufo
Rare to uncommon resident (seasonal movements).

 L ♂ 7 cm (2.8"), ♀ 6.4 cm (2.5"); **B** 1.3 cm (0.5"). Race *andinus*. Montane forest borders, open second growth, gardens. 900–3000 m. **ID** ♂ rose-magenta gorget rounded (not flared rearward), deeply forked tail blackish with rufous shafts (rarely visible in field). ♀ much like ♀ Gorgeted Woodstar but lacks rufous rump-band, underparts darker, central tail feathers green. **SS** Gorgeted and White-bellied Woodstars.

Amethyst Woodstar *Calliphlox amethystina* `LC`
Rumbito Amatista
Uncommon and local resident.

 L ♂ 7 cm (2.8"), ♀ 6.4 cm (2.5"); **B** 1.3 cm (0.5"). Monotypic. Lowland and foothill forest borders, scrubby woodland, bushy savanna. To 1500 m. Feeds at many types of flowers including canopy trees; hawks tiny insects; perches high in open. **ID** Overlaps no other woodstar. ♂ much like *Chaetocercus* including white flank patch, but tail much longer, and deeply forked. ♀ whitish throat speckled green, white pectoral collar, orange-rufous sides, white median underparts, tail short, mostly green with dark subterminal band and buff tips.

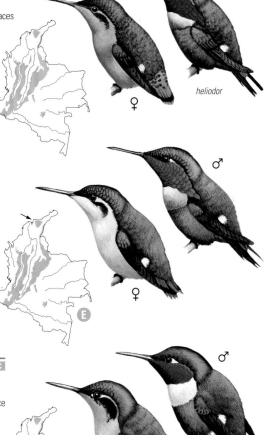

♀   ♂   *heliodor*

♀   ♂

♀   ♂   *andinus*

♀   ♂

Purple-throated Woodstar *Philodice mitchellii* `LC`
Rumbito Pechiblanco
Common resident (sharp seasonal movements).
L ♂ 7.6 cm (3"), ♀ 7 cm (2.8"); **B** 1.5 cm (0.6").
Monotypic. Humid and wet foothill and montane
forest, borders, gardens. 700–2200 m (rarely
sea level). Often perches high, forages low
or high at flowering shrubs and trees; filches nectar.
ID ♂ and ♀ very similar to smaller Amethyst Woodstar
(no overlap), differing in purple throat, rufous belly;
♀ buff-white throat, pectoral collar often faint,
greenish 'waistband', rufous lower underparts, tail
green with black subterminal band and buff tips.
SS White-bellied and Gorgeted Woodstars. **TN** Previously
in *Calliphlox*.

[Ruby-throated Hummingbird *Archilochus colubris*] `LC`
Colibrí Gorgirrubí
Hypothetical.
L 8 cm (3.2"); **B** 1.5 cm (0.6"). Monotypic. One possible sight
record (unconfirmed), Isla San Andrés. **ID** ♂ ruby throat, whitish
pectoral collar, dingy grey breast. ♀ below dull greyish white,
pectoral collar faint, tail green with broad black subterminal
band and white tips. **SS** Only resident hummer on island is very different
Green-breasted Mango.

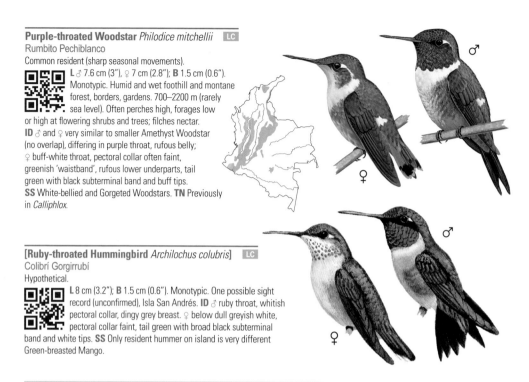

OPISTHOCOMIDAE
Hoatzin
1 extant species, 1 in region

The Hoatzin has one of the oldest unbranched ancestral histories of any modern bird, dating from nearly 65 million years. Its vegetarian diet is aided by microbes and bacterial fermentation (as in cattle), and it may fly poorly after ingesting heavy plant material. Young grow slowly, escape danger by dropping into water below the nest, but can clamber back up to safety using forewing claws that are lost with maturity.

Hoatzin *Opisthocomus hoazin* `LC`
Chenchena
Common but local resident.
L 64 cm (25"). Monotypic. Swampy backwaters,
oxbow lakes, galley forest riverbanks in *llanos*; local
in Amazonia, not white sandy soil forests. To 500 m.
Weak-flying groups, sometimes dozens, forage for
buds and leaves near or over water. Sedentary, sluggish,
suspicious, nest and feed rather low, but rest and roost higher.
ID Prehistoric appearance; dishevelled crest, blue facial skin,
rufous flight feathers, long buff-tipped tail. **Voice** When disturbed,
huffing and exhaling sounds as retreat deeper into swamps.

149 extant species, 20 in region

A cosmopolitan family of relatively similar anatomy but diverse behaviour. Family relationships between Old and New World groups remain unresolved. In general, cuckoos are slender-bodied, long-tailed and soft-plumaged. A few, such as anis, are conspicuous but most are retiring and heard more than seen. Breeding behaviour is varied, unconventional, and includes various forms of brood parasitism. In Colombia *Tapera* and *Dromococcyx* are parasitic, anis are communal nesters, and others generally raise their own young.

Genus *Crotophaga* Loose black plumage, with deep laterally compressed bills and long loose-jointed tails. Social behaviour well developed. Thermal regulation limited. Flight weak. Wide range of vocalizations but true song not obvious.

Greater Ani *Crotophaga major* LC
Garrapatero Grande

Common resident (local W of Andes; mainly Apr–Nov rainy season in *llanos*).

 L 48 cm (19"). Monotypic. Forested river edges, shrub-bordered lagoons. To 1200 m (rarely 2600 m). Groups of half-dozen to 100 or more sneak around low in shrubbery or occasionally higher, usually near water; when disturbed fly out low in single file. Notably catholic diet; may follow monkeys along river borders. Seasonal movements E of Andes poorly documented. **ID** White eyes, glossy plumage, 'broken nose' bill shape. **Voice** Huge variety of gurgling and 'pot-boiling' sounds.

Smooth-billed Ani *Crotophaga ani* LC
Garrapatero Piquiliso

Common and conspicuous resident.

 L 36 cm (14"). Monotypic. Humid forest borders, bushy pastures, cultivated areas; profits from deforestation. To 2600 m. Dishevelled groups huddle together in open in early morning; forage on or near ground, regularly around cattle. Flight weak, usually perches low. **ID** Blade-like arched bill forms small notch with forehead. **Voice** Noisy; rising squeal, "oooeeEEENK?". **SS** Groove-billed Ani (drier areas).

Groove-billed Ani *Crotophaga sulcirostris* LC
Garrapatero Piquiestriado

Common resident.

 L 30 cm (12"). Monotypic. Brush and scrub in dry and arid (not humid) regions. To 1200 m. Habits as Smooth-billed Ani, but found in drier habitats and less often perches in open; the two overlap locally. **ID** Easily confused. Bill much less arched than Smooth-billed Ani; note voice; maxilla grooves inconspicuous. **Voice** Forceful hissing "kiSSSSSyu". **SS** Smooth-billed Ani.

Striped Cuckoo *Tapera naevia* `LC`
Cuco Sin-fin

Fairly common resident.

L 30 cm (12"). Monotypic. Dry to humid wooded borders, shrubby clearings, semi-open terrain, and young river island vegetation in Amazonia. To 2000 m. Furtive; habitually raises and lowers crest and black alula feathers (like nervous tic). Forages on ground; sings from high, partly exposed, perch. Brood parasite, especially spinetails, other smaller birds. **ID** Rufous crest, streaked upperparts, long graduated tail. Juv duller, indistinct barring below. **Voice** Ventriloquial, heard more than seen; minor-key whistled "wuu-weee", second slightly higher, or 4–7 notes, "pee-pee-pee-PEEdee". **SS** Pheasant and Pavonine Cuckoos.

variant

Genus *Dromococcyx* Two exceedingly furtive cuckoos of dense lower vegetation that are heard far more than seen, but periods of vocalization are unpredictable. Both are brood parasites.

Pheasant Cuckoo *Dromococcyx phasianellus* `LC`
Cuco Faisán

Uncommon, local and secretive resident.

L 38 cm (15"). Monotypic. Thickets, undergrowth or on ground in dry to humid forest, shrubby second growth. To 1500 m. Short undulating flight, often with distinctive high wing lifts, almost always into thick cover. **ID** Small head, ample graduated tail, spotted foreneck and chest. **Voice** Song a three-part melancholy whistle "see-sée-weerrrrr", second note a half-tone higher, third quavering; calling seasonal. **SS** Pavonine Cuckoo.

Pavonine Cuckoo *Dromococcyx pavoninus* `LC`
Cuco Pavonino

Rare, secretive and local resident.

L 30 cm (12"). Monotypic. Moist to humid forest borders, vine thickets, dense second growth. 500–1800 m. Behaviour much like Pheasant Cuckoo. Brood parasite, host species include antbirds, furnariids, flycatchers and others. **ID** Broad graduated tail, throat and chest unstreaked buff. **Voice** Song seasonal; flat "püü pee, püü-pe'pe", first and third notes lower, rest a half-tone higher. **SS** Pheasant Cuckoo (especially their songs).

Genus *Neomorphus* Large terrestrial cuckoos of humid forest; wary, seldom seen; forage alone or utilize army ants, monkeys or peccaries as beaters to flush invertebrate and small vertebrae prey; natural history poorly known.

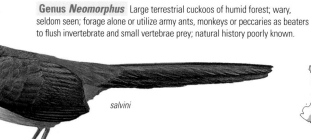

salvini

aequatorialis

Rufous-vented Ground-cuckoo *Neomorphus geoffroyi* `VU`
Cuco-terrestre Collarejo

Local and unpredictable resident.

L 50 cm (20"). Races *salvini*[A], *aequatorialis*[B]. Extensive humid *terra firme* and transition forest. To 1000 m. Terrestrial but may rest on log or low perch. Often follows army ants or large troops of Squirrel Monkeys. Agile, wary, runs rapidly. **ID** Recalls roadrunner (*Geococcyx*); strong pale yellowish bill, blue ocular skin, erectile crest, long tail, above bronze-brown (*salvini*) or bronze-green (*aequatorialis*), narrow black breast-band. **Voice** Listen for loud bill-snaps when foraging; infrequent song very low bovine-like moaning, slightly rising (300–400 Hz), lasting c. 2 seconds, repeated every 5–7 seconds.

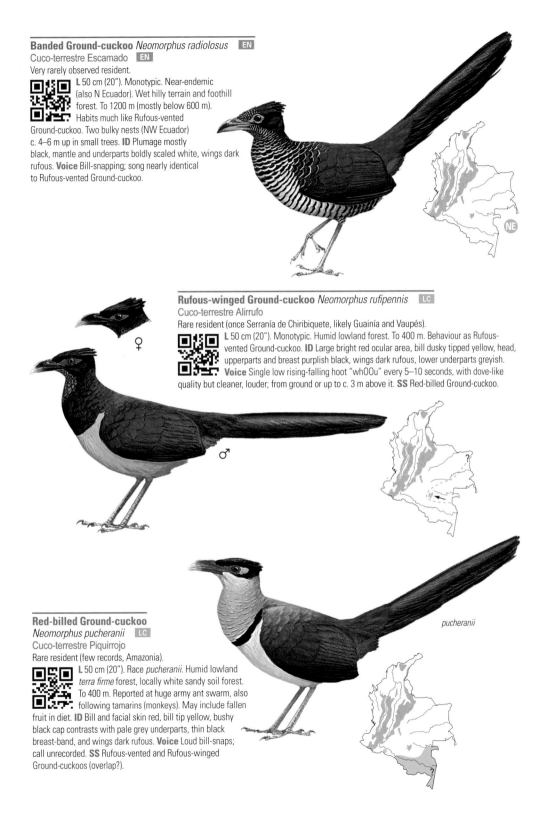

Banded Ground-cuckoo *Neomorphus radiolosus* `EN`
Cuco-terrestre Escamado `EN`
Very rarely observed resident.
L 50 cm (20"). Monotypic. Near-endemic (also N Ecuador). Wet hilly terrain and foothill forest. To 1200 m (mostly below 600 m). Habits much like Rufous-vented Ground-cuckoo. Two bulky nests (NW Ecuador) c. 4–6 m up in small trees. **ID** Plumage mostly black, mantle and underparts boldly scaled white, wings dark rufous. **Voice** Bill-snapping; song nearly identical to Rufous-vented Ground-cuckoo.

Rufous-winged Ground-cuckoo *Neomorphus rufipennis* `LC`
Cuco-terrestre Alirrufo
Rare resident (once Serranía de Chiribiquete, likely Guainía and Vaupés).
L 50 cm (20"). Monotypic. Humid lowland forest. To 400 m. Behaviour as Rufous-vented Ground-cuckoo. **ID** Large bright red ocular area, bill dusky tipped yellow, head, upperparts and breast purplish black, wings dark rufous, lower underparts greyish. **Voice** Single low rising-falling hoot "whOOu" every 5–10 seconds, with dove-like quality but cleaner, louder; from ground or up to c. 3 m above it. **SS** Red-billed Ground-cuckoo.

♀

♂

Red-billed Ground-cuckoo
Neomorphus pucheranii `LC`
Cuco-terrestre Piquirrojo
Rare resident (few records, Amazonia).
L 50 cm (20"). Race *pucheranii*. Humid lowland *terra firme* forest, locally white sandy soil forest. To 400 m. Reported at huge army ant swarm, also following tamarins (monkeys). May include fallen fruit in diet. **ID** Bill and facial skin red, bill tip yellow, bushy black cap contrasts with pale grey underparts, thin black breast-band, and wings dark rufous. **Voice** Loud bill-snaps; call unrecorded. **SS** Rufous-vented and Rufous-winged Ground-cuckoos (overlap?).

pucheranii

Genus *Coccycua* Relatively small cuckoos formerly in *Coccyzus*; the two Colombian residents differ markedly in habitat, behaviour and vocalizations; the third is a rare austral migrant.

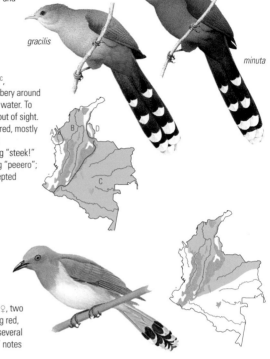

gracilis

minuta

Little Cuckoo *Coccycua minuta* LC
Cuco-ardilla Chico
Fairly common resident.

L 25 cm (10"). Races *panamensis*[A], *gracilis*[B], *minuta*[C], *barinensis*[D]. River-edge second growth, dense shrubbery around lakes, taller woody growth in marshes; usually near water. To 1600 m. Pairs forage low, peer slowly, keep mostly out of sight. **ID** Miniature of better-known Squirrel Cuckoo; eyes and eye-ring red, mostly rufous underparts W of Andes; or darker rufous-chestnut, *minuta*. **Voice** Many vocalizations, all infrequently uttered. Sharp scraping "steek!" (like static); rising nasal cackling, first note protracted; descending "peeero"; nasal meowing; soft "geep". **TN** Race *barinensis* not usually accepted (merged with *minuta*).

Dwarf Cuckoo *Coccycua pumila* LC
Cuco Enano
Uncommon (mainly May–Nov in *llanos*; intra-tropical migrant?).

L 22 cm (8.5"). Monotypic. Drier semi-open areas, ranchland with scattered trees, gallery forest borders. To 1000 m (rarely 2600 m). Solitary, sluggish, inconspicuous; forages at various heights, especially for caterpillars. Pairs and simultaneous polyandry (one ♀, two ♂♂) reported. **ID** Above grey, throat and chest dull rufous, eye-ring red, eye dark red, tail somewhat graduated. **Voice** Rather quiet. Call several dry grating churrs c. 2/second; rarely heard song c. 18 soft "kööa" notes at c. 2/second. **SS** Tropical Mockingbird (p. 443).

[Ash-colored Cuckoo *Coccycua cinerea*] LC
Cuco Cenizo
Hypothetical; possible austral migrant.

L 23 cm (9"). Monotypic. Unconfirmed sight record near Leticia, Amazonas, Jul 1975. Forest borders, semi-open areas. 100 m. Inconspicuous, somewhat furtive, movements deliberate. **ID** Lacks strong contrast; above pale brownish grey, eye-ring red, eye dark red, throat paler grey, breast and lower underparts whitish, tail tipped white, slightly graduated.

Squirrel-cuckoo *Piaya cayana* LC
Cuco-ardilla Común

Fourteen subspecies in three subspecies groups; all three in Colombia.

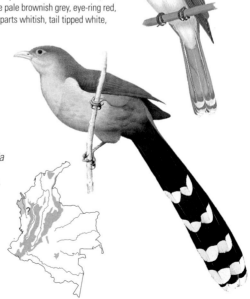

Middle American Squirrel-cuckoo *Piaya (cayana) thermophila*
Common resident.
L 43 cm (17"). One subspecies in group. Dry to humid forest borders, shrubby clearings. To 1500 m. **ID** Much like *nigricrissa* subspecies group (top of next page) but paler, especially lower underparts. **SS** Little Cuckoo.

Western Squirrel-cuckoo *Piaya (cayana) nigricrissa*
Common resident.
L 43 cm (17"). Races *nigricrissa*[A], *mehleri*[B]. Dry to humid
forest, borders, second growth. To 2800 m. Singles, pairs, alone
or with mixed flocks; bound up with squirrel-like hops through
branches, then launch out on downward glide. **ID** Eye-ring greenish
yellow (both races), plumage rufous, long graduated tail with white underside terminal spots; belly blackish, *mehleri*; or darker rufous-chestnut, lower
underparts blackish, *nigricrissa*. **Voice** Abrupt "gweep! ... waaeeeer"; loud
rattles; sharp "cheek"; infrequent song 30+ slow inflected whistles "wheep…
wheep…". **SS** Little Cuckoo.

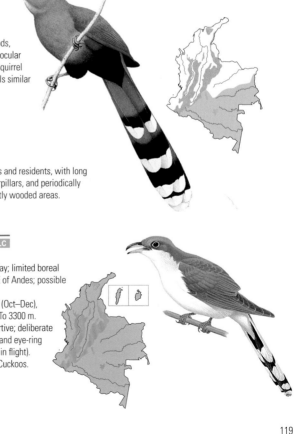

nigricrissa

Amazonian Squirrel-cuckoo *Piaya (cayana) cayana*
Common resident.
L 43 cm (17"). Races *circe*[A], *mesura*[B], *cayana*[C]. Humid
forest, borders, second growth. To 2200 m. **ID** Races
darker rufous than those W of Andes, eye-ring red (not
greenish yellow). **Voice** As in W races. **SS** Black-bellied
and Little Cuckoos.

mesura

Black-bellied Cuckoo *Piaya melanogaster* `LC`
Cuco-ardilla Buchinegro
Uncommon resident.

L 40 cm (16"). Monotypic. Canopy of humid
terra firme forest, white sandy soil forest.
To 700 m. Singles or pairs follow canopy
mixed-species flocks; feed on large arthropods,
caterpillars. **ID** Red bill, blue ocular skin, bare yellow pre-ocular
spot, grey cap, underparts more extensively rufous than Squirrel
Cuckoo. **Voice** Less vocal than Squirrel Cuckoo, some calls similar
but harsher, higher-pitched; rough "jjit-jjit-jjit"; song low
(c. 1.5 kHz) hollow "WEAK-walk" repeated, c. 1/second,
like distant Grey-cowled Wood-rail.

Genus *Coccyzus* Slender and agile, furtive migrants and residents, with long
graduated white-tipped tails. Feed heavily on bristly caterpillars, and periodically
shed stomach lining. Occasionally parasitic. Found in lightly wooded areas.

Yellow-billed Cuckoo *Coccyzus americanus* `LC`
Cuco Americano
Common (but declining) boreal passage migrant (Sept–May; limited boreal
winter resident E of Andes, northward migration mainly E of Andes; possible
breeding?).

L 30 cm (12"). Monotypic. Desert scrub in N (Oct–Dec),
forest borders, plantations, parks, gardens. To 3300 m.
Singles or small, loose migratory groups; furtive; deliberate
movements; flight swift, fluid. **ID** Mandible and eye-ring
yellow, underparts white, primaries rufous (most obvious in flight).
Voice Mostly quiet. **SS** Pearly-breasted and Dark-billed Cuckoos.

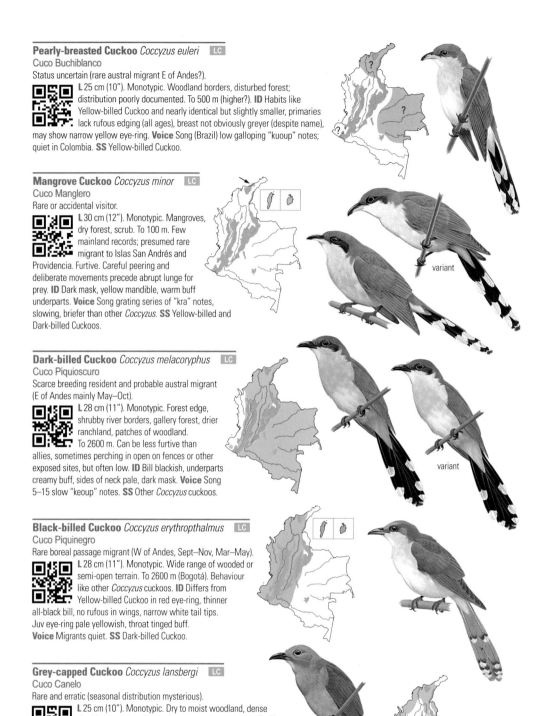

Pearly-breasted Cuckoo *Coccyzus euleri* `LC`
Cuco Buchiblanco
Status uncertain (rare austral migrant E of Andes?).
L 25 cm (10"). Monotypic. Woodland borders, disturbed forest; distribution poorly documented. To 500 m (higher?). **ID** Habits like Yellow-billed Cuckoo and nearly identical but slightly smaller, primaries lack rufous edging (all ages), breast not obviously greyer (despite name), may show narrow yellow eye-ring. **Voice** Song (Brazil) low galloping "kuoup" notes; quiet in Colombia. **SS** Yellow-billed Cuckoo.

Mangrove Cuckoo *Coccyzus minor* `LC`
Cuco Manglero
Rare or accidental visitor.
L 30 cm (12"). Monotypic. Mangroves, dry forest, scrub. To 100 m. Few mainland records; presumed rare migrant to Islas San Andrés and Providencia. Furtive. Careful peering and deliberate movements precede abrupt lunge for prey. **ID** Dark mask, yellow mandible, warm buff underparts. **Voice** Song grating series of "kra" notes, slowing, briefer than other *Coccyzus*. **SS** Yellow-billed and Dark-billed Cuckoos.

Dark-billed Cuckoo *Coccyzus melacoryphus* `LC`
Cuco Piquioscuro
Scarce breeding resident and probable austral migrant (E of Andes mainly May–Oct).
L 28 cm (11"). Monotypic. Forest edge, shrubby river borders, gallery forest, drier ranchland, patches of woodland. To 2600 m. Can be less furtive than allies, sometimes perching in open on fences or other exposed sites, but often low. **ID** Bill blackish, underparts creamy buff, sides of neck pale, dark mask. **Voice** Song 5–15 slow "keoup" notes. **SS** Other *Coccyzus* cuckoos.

Black-billed Cuckoo *Coccyzus erythropthalmus* `LC`
Cuco Piquinegro
Rare boreal passage migrant (W of Andes, Sept–Nov, Mar–May).
L 28 cm (11"). Monotypic. Wide range of wooded or semi-open terrain. To 2600 m (Bogotá). Behaviour like other *Coccyzus* cuckoos. **ID** Differs from Yellow-billed Cuckoo in red eye-ring, thinner all-black bill, no rufous in wings, narrow white tail tips. Juv eye-ring pale yellowish, throat tinged buff. **Voice** Migrants quiet. **SS** Dark-billed Cuckoo.

Grey-capped Cuckoo *Coccyzus lansbergi* `LC`
Cuco Canelo
Rare and erratic (seasonal distribution mysterious).
L 25 cm (10"). Monotypic. Dry to moist woodland, dense shrubbery; scattered records year-round, mostly near Pacific or Caribbean coasts; breeding unconfirmed. To 1000 m. Inconspicuous; numbers may fluctuate with caterpillar infestations, seasonal migrants from W Ecuador, or for unknown reasons. **ID** Cap grey, above dark rufous-brown, underparts cinnamon-buff, eye-ring yellow (occasionally grey), no mask. **Voice** Rapid hollow "cu-cu-cu-…" (6–8 notes). **SS** Dark-billed Cuckoo.

HELIORNITHIDAE
Finfoots
3 extant species, 1 in region

Small pantropical family of slender aquatic birds; they inhabit shady wooded streams and lake edges; have unwebbed but lobed feet; swim and dive expertly; and ♂♂ uniquely able to carry young in pouch under wing.

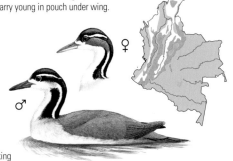

Sungrebe *Heliornis fulica* `LC`
Colimbo-selvático Americano
Fairly common resident.

L 30 cm (12"). Monotypic. Oxbow lakes and sluggish streams with abundant overhanging vegetation. To 500 m (rarely 2600 m). Wary; usually alone. Floats low, swims mostly beneath shady overhanging vegetation; if pressed flushes low over water, usually not far. Roosts on branch just above water. **ID** Like a small brown duck or grebe with black and white stripes on head and neck, bumblebee-coloured feet, reddish bill brightest when breeding; ♀ cinnamon cheeks. **Voice** Usually quiet but quite vocal when breeding; low hollow honking "eeyoó, eeyoó…" (2–4 notes).

RALLIDAE
Rails, Gallinules and Coots
142 extant species, 29 in region

A nearly worldwide family of mostly secretive aquatic species. Terrestrial habits, short tails, and slender laterally compressed bodies permit undetected movement through marsh vegetation or dense grass. All rails can swim, but only coots and gallinules regularly do so. Rails appear weak-flying but periodically disperse widely. Their diet includes invertebrate prey, fruits and seeds. Taxonomy of the family not fully resolved.

Speckled Rail *Coturnicops notatus* `LC`
Polluela Moteada `DD`
Rare (few records).

L 14 cm (5.5"). Monotypic. Wet or inundated grassland, flooded rice fields. To 400 m. Extremely furtive, reluctant to flush. May be irruptive, post-breeders perhaps disperse N from austral region (where known to breed) but movements little understood. **ID** Tiny; brownish black speckled white, eyes red, legs pale yellowish, in flight shows white patch on secondaries. **Voice** In Colombia probably silent; call (Argentina) "kooweee-CACK", first note higher, brief. **SS** Grey-breasted Crake. **AN** Speckled Crake.

Ocellated Crake *Micropygia schomburgkii* `LC`
Polluela Ocelada
Uncommon and local resident (seasonal movements likely).

L 14 cm (5.5"). Race *schomburgkii*. Dry to seasonally damp open or shrub-dotted grassland. To 500 m. Furtive; flushes low, legs dangling or raised, over grass, then quickly drops from view. **ID** Spotted upperparts, bright ochre underparts and vent, red legs. **Voice** High thin soft tinkling "t-t-t-t-…" (2–4 seconds), especially mornings and late evenings. **SS** Yellow-breasted Crake (habitat differs).

schomburgkii

Chestnut-headed Crake *Rufirallus castaneiceps* `LC`
Polluela Colorada
Fairly common resident (easily overlooked).

L 22 cm (9"). Race *coccineipes*. On ground in shrubby forest borders, Amerindian gardens, damp second-growth thickets; a land rail occasionally near water. To 1500 m. Retiring, slipping deftly through dense vegetation. **ID** Chestnut head and foreparts, greenish-yellow bill, coral-red legs. **Voice** Antiphonal duet loud, piercing "ti-too", answered or overlapped slightly by mate with "ti-turro", e.g. "ti-too, ti-turro…", long-sustained, fading. **SS** Black-banded Crake (smaller). **TN** Also placed in *Anurolimnas*.

coccineipes

Russet-crowned Crake *Rufirallus viridis* `LC`
Polluela Cabecirrufa
Local resident.

 L 15 cm (6"). Races *brunnescens*[A], *viridis*[B].
Dense thickets, overgrown clearings, tall grass,
Amerindian gardens; grass rail not usually associated with
water. To 1400 m. Furtive, inside dense vegetation and grass.
Terrestrial but sometimes climbs up in bushes. **ID** Red eyes, coral-red
legs, rufous-chestnut cap and underparts, grey face, no flanks barring;
brunnescens head and underparts paler. **Voice** Harsh descending,
whinny-like churr (up to c. 10 seconds), slowing. **SS** White-throated Crake
(W of Andes); Rufous-sided Crake (E of Andes). **TN** Also placed in *Anurolimnas*.

brunnescens

viridis

Genus *Laterallus* Small rails known as crakes with short thick bills
and tails often held cocked. Some near water, others away from it. Vocal
but furtive, remaining hidden in vegetation.

Rufous-sided Crake *Laterallus melanophaius* `LC`
Polluela Pechiblanca
Fairly common resident.

 L 15 cm (6"). Race *oenops*. Tall wet grass and marsh vegetation
at edges of oxbows or small bodies of freshwater. To 1000 m.
Furtive; rarely flushes. Forages at edge of water, occasionally walks
into open briefly but never far from cover. **ID** Rufous foreparts, white
median line on underparts, barred flanks, rufous undertail. **Voice** Heard far more than
seen. Song loud harsh descending churr often answered (or partly overlapped) by
mate; a high tinkling like Grey-breasted Crake. **SS** Black-banded Crake.

oenops

White-throated Crake *Laterallus albigularis* `LC`
Polluela Gorgiblanca
Common resident.

albigularis

 L 15 cm (6"). Races *albigularis*[A], *cerdaleus*[B].
Freshwater marshes, tall damp grass in clearings and
ditches, forest-edge thickets; can be some distance
from water. To 2000 m. Habits as Rufous-sided
Crake, but less closely tied to water. **ID** Rufous foreparts, white
throat, barred flanks and undertail (*albigularis*), or scarcely any throat
patch (*cerdaleus*). **Voice** Song loud descending churr similar
to Rufous-sided Crake, perhaps less harsh. **SS** Grey-breasted Crake.

cerdaleus

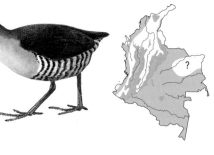

Grey-breasted Crake *Laterallus exilis* `LC`
Polluela Bicolor
Uncommon and local (easily overlooked) resident.

 L 14 cm (5.5"). Monotypic. Freshwater marshes,
seasonally flooded grass, dry grass in pastures and
clearings. To 1200 m (rarely 2800 m). Extremely
skulking, difficult to flush even when underfoot; likely more
widespread in *llanos* and elsewhere than records indicate. **ID** Bright rufous nape,
head to breast grey, flanks and vent barred, eyes red, bill grey, base of mandible
lime-green. **Voice** High metallic tinkling notes, often slower, hesitant
initially; loud harsh churring like Rufous-sided Crake. **SS** Paint-billed Crake;
rare Colombian Crake.

Black Rail *Laterallus jamaicensis* `EN`
Polluela Negra
Status unknown (no recent records).

 L 14 cm (5.5"). Race *jamaicensis* (?). Marshes and lagoon
edges; two old Colombian specimens without data,
possibly from Bogotá savanna. 2600 m (?). **ID** Blackish,
nape dull chestnut, back spotted and flanks barred with
white. **Voice** North American breeders, abrupt nasal "kic-kic'kerr".
SS Speckled Crake; downy black chicks of Blackish Rail.

jamaicensis

Genus *Rallus* Medium-sized rails of fresh- or saltwater marshes. Fairly long slightly decurved bill; legs dull red to pinkish. Often heard, infrequently seen.

Mangrove Rail *Rallus longirostris* `LC`
Rascón Manglero
Local resident (few records).

 L 33 cm (13"). Races *cypereti*ᴬ, *phelpsi*ᴮ. Coastal saltwater and brackish marshes, mangroves, mudflats at low tide. Usually remains hidden in marsh grass or mangroves; active at low tide. **ID** Large; above faded brown streaked dusky, below dull buff, flanks dusky narrowly barred white, mandible and legs dull orange. **Voice** Loud clattering "kek-kek-kek-…" gradually slowing. **SS** Rufous-necked Wood-rail. **TN** Formerly part of Clapper Rail *R. crepitans*.

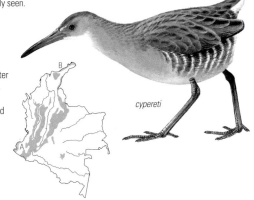

cypereti

Virginia Rail *Rallus limicola* `LC`
Rascón de Nariño

 Four subspecies in two subspecies groups; one in Colombia.

Ecuadorian Rail *Rallus (limicola) aequatorialis*
Local resident.
L 23 cm (9"). Race *aequatorialis* . High-elevation lakes. 2200–3000 m. Sedentary; tall aquatic reeds and marsh vegetation (e.g. Laguna la Cocha). **ID** Above brown streaked black, sides of head grey, loral area blackish, long red-orange bill tipped black, flanks and belly barred black and white. **Voice** Song harsh clattering "klik" notes (c. 6 notes/second) lasting 3–7 seconds; may begin as duet, end with single bird; unlike paired metallic notes of N birds. **SS** Sora.

aequatorialis

Bogota Rail *Rallus semiplumbeus* `EN`
Rascón Bogotano `EN`
Local resident (in decline due to wetland drainage and pollution).

 L 25 cm (10"). Race *semiplumbeus*. Endemic. Tall grass, reeds and rushes around lakes, lagoons in lower *páramo*. 2500–3600 m (rarely 2200 m). Sedentary; skulking, walks into openings at edges of marshes at dawn, but quickly retreats if disturbed. **ID** Reddish bill and legs, underparts grey, flanks barred. **Voice** Call (early morning) loud strident clatter; short piercing squeals; low throaty growls; piping notes. **SS** Sora.

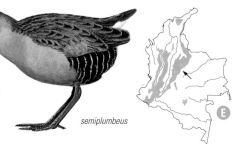

semiplumbeus

Ⓔ

Genus *Aramides* Large rails with strong greenish-yellow bills. Found in wooded areas, but usually near fresh or saltwater. Vocal at dawn and dusk. Only Grey-cowled Wood-rail is frequently seen.

Brown Wood-rail *Aramides wolfi* `VU`
Chilacoa Parda `VU`
Uncommon (possibly declining) resident.

 L 33 cm (13"). Monotypic. Pacific coast mangroves, swampy forest, riverine areas; mostly near coast. To 900 m. Sedentary, skulking, wary; forages for crabs during low tide. **ID** Large; mainly rufescent-brown, head grey, bill yellow-green, vent black, underwing-coverts chestnut barred black, legs coral-red. **Voice** Loud rhythmic, often long-sustained "chee-kock, chee-kock…ka, ka…" recalls Grey-cowled Wood-rail. **SS** Other *Aramides* wood-rails.

Grey-cowled Wood-rail *Aramides cajaneus* `LC`
Chilacoa Colinegra
Common resident.

 L 38 cm (15"). Race *cajaneus*. Forested streambanks in dry to wet regions, seasonal pools in *llanos*, mangroves. To 2300 m. Shy in forested regions; bolder, often in open in *llanos*. **ID** Large; contrasting earth-tone colours, grey head and neck, yellowish bill, coral-red legs. **Voice** Loud antiphonal duet pre-dawn, dusk or after dark, rhythmic "KEE-KAULK…" phrases ending in "KOOK-KOOK-…" series, long-sustained, slowing, single bird calling at end. **SS** Brown Wood-rail. **TN** Formerly included with Middle American birds and called Grey-necked Wood-rail.

Rufous-necked Wood-rail *Aramides axillaris* `LC`
Chilacoa Costera
Uncommon and local resident.

 L 30 cm (12"). Monotypic. Mangroves, coastal marshes, swampy riverbanks, occasionally dry to humid woodland inland from coast. To 1500 m. Secretive; most easily seen in mangroves (e.g. Tumaco) at low tide. **ID** Rufous head, neck and breast (no grey), bill yellow, patch on mantle blue-grey; otherwise recalls larger Grey-cowled Wood-rail. **Voice** Loud sharp series "keulp, keup…" (c. 2/second), mostly dawn and dusk; some vocalizations possibly antiphonal.

Uniform Crake *Amaurolimnas concolor* `LC`
Polluela Rufa
Uncommon or rare (overlooked?) resident.

 L 22 cm (8.5"). Races *guatemalensis*[A], *castaneus*[B]. Floor of damp lowland forest, forested streams, dense second-growth woodland, *Heliconia* thickets; apparently not mangroves. To 600 m; 1500 m (upper Magdalena Valley). **ID** Above uniform rufous-brown, below dull rufous, no barring, bill dull yellowish green, legs dusky pink. **Voice** Dawn or dusk, 6–20 soft upslurred whistled "tuuweet" notes, louder, then fading, c. 1/second or faster. **SS** Chestnut-headed Crake (may overlap race *castaneus*).

Ash-throated Crake *Mustelirallus albicollis* `LC`
Polluela Cienaguera
Fairly common resident E of Andes, local W of Andes.

 L 23 cm (9"). Race *typhoeca*. Damp grassy areas, drainage ditches, rice fields, freshwater marshes; seasonal movements need documentation. To 1800 m. Secretive but often in open near cover at dawn. **ID** Above brown streaked dusky, throat whitish, foreface and underparts pale grey, lower underparts barred black and white, bill greenish. **Voice** Loud fast vibrating (machine-gun) "d'd'd'd'd-ou", often over and over virtually without pause; far-carrying. **SS** Sora. **TN** Previously in *Porzana*.

Colombian Crake *Mustelirallus colombianus* `DD`
Polluela Pizarra `DD`
Enigmatic resident (records few, scattered).

 L 19 cm (7.5"). Races *ripleyi*[A], *colombianus*[B]. Near-endemic (also C Panama and NW Ecuador). Marshes, grassy pastures, forest edge thickets; not necessarily near water. To 200 m (to 1800 m above Cali, 1500–2100 m in Santa Marta Mts). Habits poorly known; may disperse widely (e.g. attracted to lighted windows at night); secretive, probably often undetected. **ID** Bill yellowish, red spot at base of mandible, head and underparts grey, unbarred flanks and lower underparts buff, wing-linings white. **Voice** Song unknown. **SS** Paint-billed and Grey-breasted Crakes. **TN** Previously in *Neocrex*.

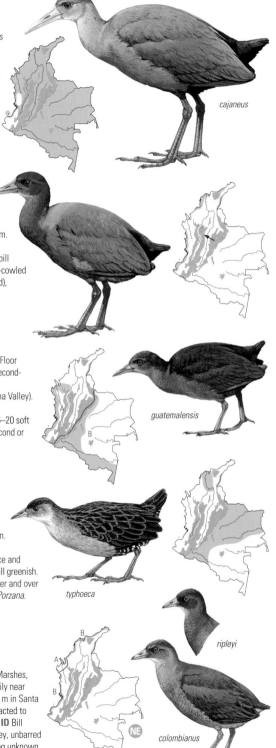

cajaneus

guatemalensis

typhoeca

ripleyi

colombianus

Paint-billed Crake *Mustelirallus erythrops* `LC`
Polluela Piquirroja

Records scattered but better known than Colombian Crake.

 L 19 cm (7.5"). Race *olivascens*. Freshwater marshes, wet grassy pastures, drainage ditches, rice fields; also away from water. To 600 m (E of Andes), to 2600 m (Sabana de Bogotá); marked seasonal dispersal, reported at lights at night. **ID** From Colombian Crake by red band around base of bill (not spot), flanks and lower underparts barred (not unbarred buff). **Voice** Up to 36 accelerating staccato "kjek" notes; frog-like, guttural. **SS** Grey-breasted Crake. **TN** Previously in *Neocrex*.

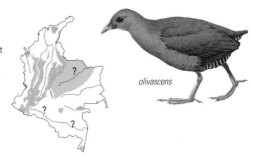

olivascens

Spotted Rail *Pardirallus maculatus* `LC`
Rascón Overo

 Two subspecies in two subspecies groups; one in Colombia.

Southern Spotted Rail *Pardirallus (maculatus) maculatus*
Uncommon and local resident.

L 25 cm (10"). One subspecies in group. Freshwater marshes, wet grass, flooded rice fields, grassy ditches. 400–2000 m. Secretive but may emerge in open at dawn; disperses with changes in water levels. **ID** Streaked and spotted black-and-white neck and underparts; greenish-yellow bill with red spot at base, legs red. **Voice** Squeals; raspy and guttural sounds.

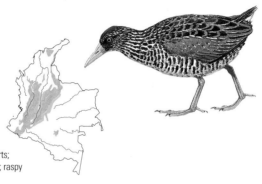

Blackish Rail *Pardirallus nigricans* `LC`
Rascón Negruzco

Uncommon and local resident.

 L 28 cm (11"). Races *caucae*[A], *nigricans*[B]. Tall wet grass around ponds and lakes in Andes. 500–2200 m. Not as secretive as many rails, often foraging in open but near cover. **ID** Fairly long lime-green bill, red legs, above uniform brown, head and underparts dark grey. **Voice** Wide range of vocalizations include metallic rattle, raptor-like "keeeeeaaa", squeals and whistles. **SS** Ash-throated Crake (limited overlap, in upper Cauca Valley).

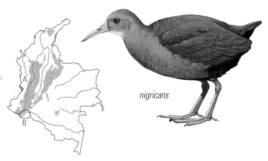

nigricans

Yellow-breasted Crake *Hapalocrex flaviventer* `LC`
Polluela de Antifaz

Local resident.

 L 14 cm (5.5"). Races *bangsi*[A], *flaviventer*[B]. Wet grass around ponds, floating vegetation in freshwater marshes (especially water hyacinth) and flooded fields; disperses with water level changes. To 1000 m. Secretive, emerges at dawn or late afternoon, may forage in open on floating vegetation for extended periods; occasionally flushes. **ID** Tiny; black-and-white head pattern, yellow-buff foreneck, barred flanks, yellowish legs. **Voice** Numerous infrequent vocalizations; little squeals, trills, odd mechanical notes. **SS** Ocellated Crake. **TN** Previously in *Porzana*.

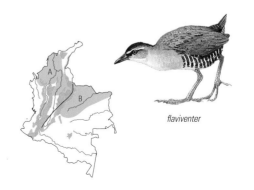

flaviventer

Black-banded Crake *Porzana fasciata* `LC`
Polluela Barrada
Uncommon resident.

 L 18 cm (7"). Monotypic. Tall wet grass and thickets in small forest clearings and riverbanks, Amazonian river islands; not always near water. To 500 m. Quite secretive; terrestrial, reluctant to flush but may climb up into shrubs. **ID** Head and underparts rufous, lower underparts barred black and rufous (no white), bill blackish, eyes red. **Voice** Long whinny-like churr recalls *Laterallus* but longer. **SS** Rufous-sided Crake. **TN** Taxonomy unresolved, but probably best placed in *Laterallus*; genus *Anurolimnas* sometimes employed.

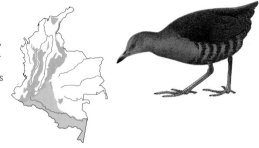

Sora *Porzana carolina* `LC`
Polluela Norteña
Fairly common boreal migrant.

 **L** 22 cm (8.5"). Monotypic. Fresh- and brackish-water marshes, rice fields, drainage ditches; mainly Nov–Apr, a few year-round; breeding (?). To 3000 m. Furtive but more easily seen than most rails; often forages in open near cover; numerous in some highland marshes. **ID** Small; black face surrounds short yellow bill, dark grey foreparts, and barred lower underparts. **Voice** Occasional nasal whinny; rising whistle; sharp notes. **SS** Spot-flanked Gallinule.

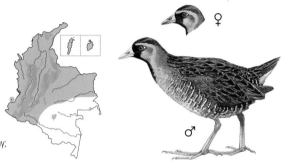

Purple Gallinule *Porphyrio martinicus* `LC`
Polla Azul
Common resident.

 L 33 cm (13"). Monotypic. Freshwater and brackish marshes, rice fields. To 3200 m. Most numerous in wet season in *llanos*. Conspicuous in tall marsh vegetation, often climbs up into open or perches atop bushes; infrequently swims, avoids open water; possible cooperative breeding. **ID** Bright purplish blue, red bill tipped yellow, legs yellow. Juv foreparts dull buff, wings tinged greenish blue, lower underparts white, bill dull. **Voice** Clucks and cackles, often in rapid series. **SS** Juv Azure Gallinule.

adult

juvenile

Azure Gallinule *Porphyrio flavirostris* `LC`
Polla Llanera
Uncommon (easily overlooked) resident.

 L 25 cm (10"). Monotypic. Flooded grassy margins of ponds, oxbows and rivers, rice fields. To 500 m (rarely 2600 m); numbers fluctuate seasonally. Perches atop grass stems or floating vegetation at dawn, otherwise hidden; flushes short distances, legs dangling; rarely swims or forages in open. **ID** Looks faded; pale azure head, neck and sides, bill greenish yellow, legs rich yellow. Juv dull brownish buff, paler below, blue wing edgings, dark rump and tail show in flight, bill dull grey. **Voice** Seldom vocal; plaintive whining. **SS** Juv Purple Gallinule.

Common Gallinule *Gallinula galeata* `LC`
Polla Gris

Common resident in lowlands, local in highlands.

 L 36 cm (14"). Races *pauxilla*, *cachinnans* (Caribbean islands?). Freshwater marshes, ponds and lakes with emergent vegetation. To 3300 m. Swims in open water, walks on floating vegetation or on shore; seeks cover in tall vegetation. Occasionally loose groups. Patters to get airborne. **ID** Red shield, red bill tipped pale yellow, sides white, red 'garters', white vent. Juv bill dull, plumage greyish brown, white on sides, white vent. **Voice** Deep "kuk"; cackles and clucks. **SS** Juv Purple Gallinule.

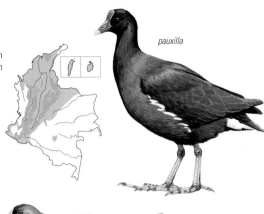

pauxilla

Spot-flanked Gallinule *Porphyriops melanops* `LC`
Polla Sabanera `EN`

Locally fairly common resident (declining).

 L 25 cm (10"). Race *bogotensis*. Small ponds and lagoons with reeds and emergent vegetation. 2300–3100 m. Conspicuous; swims in open, picking at water surface; seldom far from cover. Rarely seen walking; patters to get airborne. **ID** Lime-green bill, black foreface, uniform rufescent back, spotted flanks. **Voice** Hollow cackle-like burst of laughter. **SS** Sora. **TN** Previously in *Gallinula*.

bogotensis

American Coot *Fulica americana* `LC`
Focha Americana

Local boreal migrant, common resident.

 L 38 cm (15"). Race *americana*[A] (boreal migrant; Islas San Andrés and Providencia), *columbiana*[B] (resident). Highland lakes, ponds, urban parks; local in lowlands. To 3300 m. Gregarious; swims in open water, tips up or dives to feed; walks on land. **ID** Ad black head, dark grey body, white undertail, small dark red shield, chalky bill with faint dark ring. Juv no dark ring. **Voice** Noisy clucks, cackles; soft notes. **SS** Andean Coot. **TN** Includes variant Caribbean Coot ('*F. caribaea*') with bulbous shield; Caribbean coast and islands.

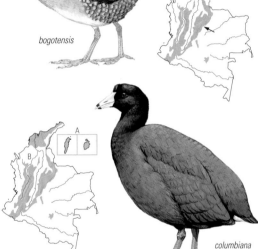

columbiana

Andean Coot (Slate-colored Coot) *Fulica ardesiaca* `LC`
Focha Andina

Locally common resident (Nariño).

 L 43 cm (17"). Race *atrura*. High-elevation lakes and marshes. 2200–3600 m. Behaviour as American Coot; vegetarian, up-ends or dives for *Chara*, *Elodea* etc. **ID** Like American Coot but larger, bill white (tinged yellowish when breeding), no dark ring, frontal shield larger; white shield and bill commonest but yellowish or white bill and yellow shield, and yellow bill with dark red shield combinations occur; undertail-coverts black (no white). **Voice** Cackles and clucks.

yellow-fronted shield

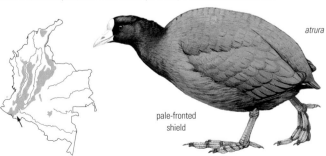

atrura

pale-fronted shield

red-fronted shield

PSOPHIIDAE
Trumpeters
6 extant species, 1 in region

A small Neotropical family of hunched terrestrial birds. They feed on fallen fruit, insects and small vertebrates including snakes, and are notable for their polyandrous cooperative breeding where multiple males copulate with a single female and help raise the young.

Grey-winged Trumpeter *Psophia crepitans* NT
Tente Aligrís
Uncommon resident.

L 53 cm (21"). Races *napensis*[A], *crepitans*[B]. Remote *terra firme* and transition forest. To 500 m. Groups of 5–15 run rapidly in alarm or flush to tree canopy; often kept as pets in Amerindian villages for their watchfulness. **ID** Hunched shape recalls guineafowl; velvet black head and neck with iridescent blue feathers, loose grey inner wing feathers cover lower back and short tail. **Voice** Song, given by several simultaneously on or near ground, deep rolling humming, gradually descending; loud harsh cackles in alarm. **SS White-winged Trumpeter** *P. leucoptera* reported near Leticia is likely a human-assisted escapee from S of Amazon; inner wing feathers white (not grey).

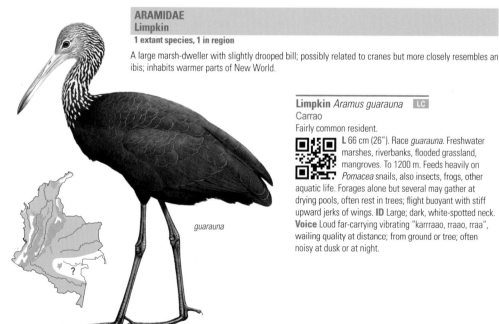

White-winged Trumpeter

napensis

crepitans

ARAMIDAE
Limpkin
1 extant species, 1 in region

A large marsh-dweller with slightly drooped bill; possibly related to cranes but more closely resembles an ibis; inhabits warmer parts of New World.

Limpkin *Aramus guarauna* LC
Carrao
Fairly common resident.

L 66 cm (26"). Race *guarauna*. Freshwater marshes, riverbanks, flooded grassland, mangroves. To 1200 m. Feeds heavily on *Pomacea* snails, also insects, frogs, other aquatic life. Forages alone but several may gather at drying pools, often rest in trees; flight buoyant with stiff upward jerks of wings. **ID** Large; dark, white-spotted neck. **Voice** Loud far-carrying vibrating "karrraao, rraao, rraa", wailing quality at distance; from ground or tree; often noisy at dusk or at night.

guarauna

SPHENISCIDAE
Penguins
18 extant species, 2 vagrants in region

A southern latitude family of flightless birds that needs little introduction; excellent swimmers and divers, propelling themselves through water with small flipper-like wings. Heavy-boned, densely feathered and lack feather tracts; sexes alike. Colombian records (all juv) apparently dispersing (or human-assisted?) individuals in poor physical condition.

Magellanic Penguin *Spheniscus magellanicus* `NT`
Pingüino de Magallanes
Vagrant.

L 70 cm (27"). Monotypic. Breeds Chile, Argentina and Falklands, mainly Sept–Apr. One record: juv ♂, mouth R Guapi, Cauca, Apr 1990 (photo and specimen), but perhaps least likely penguin in Colombian waters. **ID** Ad black face and throat encircled white, black bill, two black breast-bands, pink orbital and facial skin, flipper mostly white below, or with black markings. Juv variable, more diffuse pattern than ad.

Humboldt Penguin *Spheniscus humboldti* `VU`
Pingüino de Humboldt
Vagrant.

L 65 cm (25"). Monotypic. Breeds on islands in cold Humboldt Current waters off Peru and Chile. Pelagic when not breeding. One record (specimen), Isla Gorgona National Park. Some long-distance migratory or dispersal movements (mostly juv?) in Chile and Peru, but extremely rare N to Colombia. **ID** Black face and throat encircled by white, single black breast-band, heavy black bill, extensive pink facial skin and base of bill. Juv brownish foreface to breast.

adult

juvenile

[Galapagos Penguin *Spheniscus mendiculus*] `EN`
Pingüino de Galápagos
Hypothetical.

L 48 cm (19"). Monotypic. Unconfirmed record, presumed to be this species. Breeds in Galápagos but notably sedentary and population small. **ID** Small penguin; very thin white line encircles black face, may show white chin, underside of flippers black; plumage otherwise resembles Magellanic Penguin but uppermost breast-band obscure, much of mandible pale pinkish. Juv white face.

OCEANITIDAE
Southern Storm-petrels
9 extant species, 2 in region

The Oceanitidae are mostly Southern Hemisphere-breeding storm-petrels that were formerly united with northern-breeding Hydrobatidae. The two groups are morphologically similar, having tubular nostrils united into a single opening. They forage by pattering on the ocean with dangling legs (like walking on water), and picking small prey and oil from surface. Field identification is complex; pay attention to features associated with rump and tail.

White-vented Storm-petrel (Elliot's Storm-petrel)
Oceanites gracilis `DD`
Paíño de Elliot
Common seasonal visitor.

L 16 cm (6.3"). Race unknown. Cool pelagic waters; off coastal Nariño reportedly abundant in Sept. **ID** Quite small; crescent-shaped white rump, white belly patch (difficult to see), feet project slightly, underwing panel pale (but not white). **SS** White-bellied Storm-petrel.

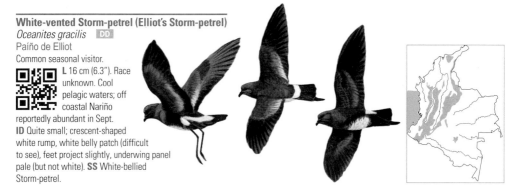

White-faced Storm-petrel *Pelagodroma marina* LC
Paíño Cariblanco

 Six subspecies in two subspecies groups; one in Colombia.

White-faced Storm-petrel *Pelagodroma (marina) marina*
Status unknown.
L 20 cm (8"). Race unknown. Six sight records (no photos) in Pacific Colombian waters (May 1990). Widespread pelagic species, which apparently appears in larger numbers in austral spring and autumn off W South America. **ID** Small; distinctive white frontlet and eyestripe, dark cheeks, white wing-linings and underparts. Above dark brown with pale upperwing-covert panel bordered white, forming broad whitish bar. Long legs (feet project). **SS** Phalaropes.

White-bellied Storm-petrel *Fregetta grallaria* LC
Paíño Ventriblanco

 Four subspecies in two subspecies groups; one perhaps occurs in Colombia.

segethi

[White-bellied Storm-petrel *Fregetta (grallaria) grallaria*]
Paíño Ventriblanco
Hypothetical; no confirmed record.
L 18 cm (7"). Race *segethi* (?). One sight record (1999), now believed to be within Ecuadorian (rather than Colombian) territorial waters, although doubtless occurs in latter. Highly pelagic, rarely near land. Known to associate with other seabirds, follows ships and dolphins. **ID** Small; squarish white rump patch, white underwing panel joins white lower underparts, feet do not project. **SS** White-vented Storm-petrel.

HYDROBATIDAE
Northern Storm-petrels
18 extant species, 6 in region

Primarily Northern Hemisphere-breeding storm-petrels formerly united with Oceanitidae. Morphology, behaviour and taxonomy discussed under Oceanitidae. Allocation of genera remains unresolved.

Band-rumped Storm-petrel *Hydrobates castro* LC
Paíño de Madeira
Common visitor.

 L 22 cm (8.5"). Monotypic. Known from numerous sight records off Isla Malpelo and Pacific waters of Nariño; recent published photos; also (undocumented) Caribbean reports. Highly pelagic, rarely near land; flight buoyant, direct. **ID** Deep rapid wingbeats alternate with short glides; all-dark plumage with broad white rump that extends onto sides, almost square tail, feet do not project. In hand note some white rump feathers tipped black. **SS** Leach's and Wedge-rumped Storm-petrels. **TN** Previously in *Oceanodroma*. **AN** Harcourt's Storm-petrel.

Black Storm-petrel *Hydrobates melania* LC
Paíño Oscuro
Uncommon boreal migrant (mainly Nov–Mar).

 **L** 23 cm (9"). Monotypic. Occurs in near-shore and warmer pelagic waters of Pacific; occasionally seen from shore. Flight smooth and graceful with deep slow wingbeats, frequent glides. Alone or loose groups, also with other storm-petrels including Least, Leach's and Wedge-rumped; regularly follows ships. **ID** Large, long-winged storm-petrel. Entirely sooty black with pale band on upperwing-coverts, tail deeply forked, black legs rather long. **SS** Markham's Storm-petrel; dark-rumped form of Leach's Storm-petrel. **TN** Previously in *Oceanodroma*.

Least Storm-petrel *Hydrobates microsoma* `LC`
Paíño Enano

Rare visitor (records scattered throughout year).

L 15 cm (6"). Monotypic. Highly pelagic over warmer Pacific waters, including NW Chocó, Gulf of Panamá and Isla Malpelo. Gregarious, often in flocks of 100s, regularly with Black and Wedge-rumped Storm-petrels. **ID** Smallest storm-petrel; all dark in flight, very short wedge-shaped (looks rounded) tail, feet do not project, pale band on upperwing-coverts obscure (often absent late in year); fluttery erratic bat-like flight. **SS** Black, Markham's and dark-rumped form of Leach's Storm-petrel all larger with forked tails. **TN** Previously in *Oceanodroma*.

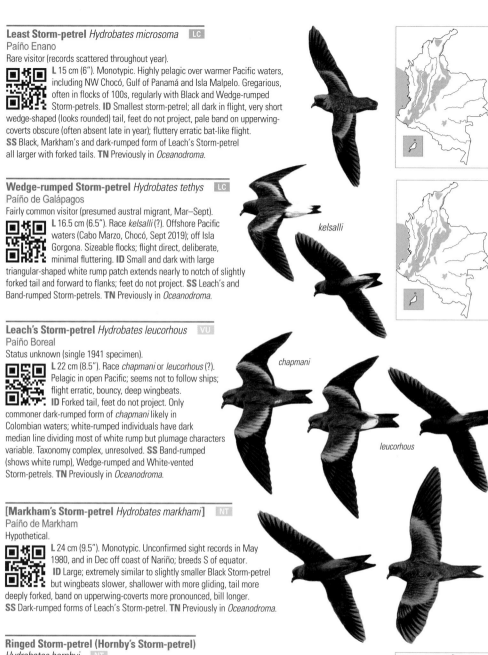

kelsalli

chapmani

leucorhous

Wedge-rumped Storm-petrel *Hydrobates tethys* `LC`
Paíño de Galápagos

Fairly common visitor (presumed austral migrant, Mar–Sept).

L 16.5 cm (6.5"). Race *kelsalli* (?). Offshore Pacific waters (Cabo Marzo, Chocó, Sept 2019); off Isla Gorgona. Sizeable flocks; flight direct, deliberate, minimal fluttering. **ID** Small and dark with large triangular-shaped white rump patch extends nearly to notch of slightly forked tail and forward to flanks; feet do not project. **SS** Leach's and Band-rumped Storm-petrels. **TN** Previously in *Oceanodroma*.

Leach's Storm-petrel *Hydrobates leucorhous* `VU`
Paíño Boreal

Status unknown (single 1941 specimen).

L 22 cm (8.5"). Race *chapmani* or *leucorhous* (?). Pelagic in open Pacific; seems not to follow ships; flight erratic, bouncy, deep wingbeats. **ID** Forked tail, feet do not project. Only commoner dark-rumped form of *chapmani* likely in Colombian waters; white-rumped individuals have dark median line dividing most of white rump but plumage characters variable. Taxonomy complex, unresolved. **SS** Band-rumped (shows white rump), Wedge-rumped and White-vented Storm-petrels. **TN** Previously in *Oceanodroma*.

[Markham's Storm-petrel *Hydrobates markhami*] `NT`
Paíño de Markham

Hypothetical.

L 24 cm (9.5"). Monotypic. Unconfirmed sight records in May 1980, and in Dec off coast of Nariño; breeds S of equator. **ID** Large; extremely similar to slightly smaller Black Storm-petrel but wingbeats slower, shallower with more gliding, tail more deeply forked, band on upperwing-coverts more pronounced, bill longer. **SS** Dark-rumped forms of Leach's Storm-petrel. **TN** Previously in *Oceanodroma*.

Ringed Storm-petrel (Hornby's Storm-petrel)
Hydrobates hornbyi `NT`
Paíño de Hornby

Status unknown.

L 22 cm (8.5"). Monotypic. One Jul 1979 specimen (Isla Gorgona) but reportedly 'common', early Sept, Isla Gorgona waters. Highly pelagic Humboldt Current species, usually far out at sea. Flight erratic; patters, dips, picks from ocean surface; deep wingbeats alternate with glides. Does not follow ships. **ID** Only South American storm-petrel all white below with dark breast-band; dark cap; grey back and rump; conspicuous pale upperwing-covert band, deeply forked tail, feet do not project. **TN** Previously in *Oceanodroma*.

DIOMEDEIDAE
Albatrosses
22 extant species, 2 vagrants in region

Albatrosses are large iconic seabirds with tube-nosed nostrils, exceptionally long narrow wings, and heavy hooked bills. Most are found in the Southern Hemisphere and are best known for their remarkable powers of flight. They remain at sea most of their lives except when breeding on islands. Cuttlefish comprise a large proportion of their diet.

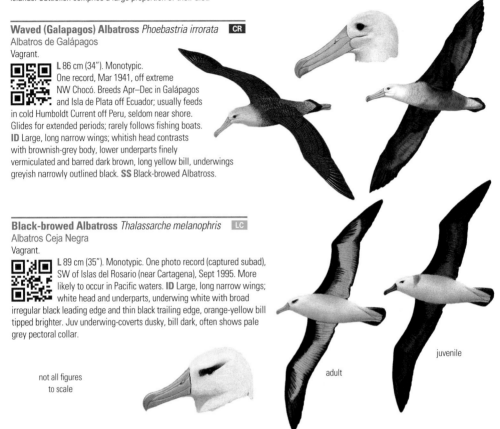

Waved (Galapagos) Albatross *Phoebastria irrorata* `CR`
Albatros de Galápagos
Vagrant.

L 86 cm (34"). Monotypic.
One record, Mar 1941, off extreme
NW Chocó. Breeds Apr–Dec in Galápagos
and Isla de Plata off Ecuador; usually feeds
in cold Humboldt Current off Peru, seldom near shore.
Glides for extended periods; rarely follows fishing boats.
ID Large, long narrow wings; whitish head contrasts
with brownish-grey body, lower underparts finely
vermiculated and barred dark brown, long yellow bill, underwings
greyish narrowly outlined black. **SS** Black-browed Albatross.

Black-browed Albatross *Thalassarche melanophris* `LC`
Albatros Ceja Negra
Vagrant.

L 89 cm (35"). Monotypic. One photo record (captured subad),
SW of Islas del Rosario (near Cartagena), Sept 1995. More
likely to occur in Pacific waters. **ID** Large, long narrow wings;
white head and underparts, underwing white with broad
irregular black leading edge and thin black trailing edge, orange-yellow bill
tipped brighter. Juv underwing-coverts dusky, bill dark, often shows pale
grey pectoral collar.

juvenile

not all figures
to scale

adult

PROCELLARIIDAE
Petrels and Shearwaters
95 extant species, 11 in region + 5 vagrants

Tube-nosed seabirds of open ocean; mostly vagrants to Colombian waters, and few if any will be seen from shore. In general, comprise two groups distinguished in part by manner of flight: shearwaters alternate fast stiff flaps with glides, usually relatively close to ocean surface. Gadfly petrels (*Pterodroma*) hold their wings slightly bent, often alternate arcs high over the water with low swoops into wave troughs. Both groups feed on squid and other marine life, and spend half or more of each year wandering at sea.

Cape Petrel *Daption capense* `LC`
Damero del Cabo
Vagrant.

capense

L 41 cm (16"). Race *capense* (?). One record, Oct 1981,
off Isla Gorgona (Cauca). Southern Hemisphere species,
follows cold currents into tropical latitudes, usually well
offshore; may follow ships; could be expected Apr–Oct.
ID Head to mantle black, upperwing mottled black and white, white
patch in primaries, from below white, underwing rimmed black.
AN Pintado Petrel.

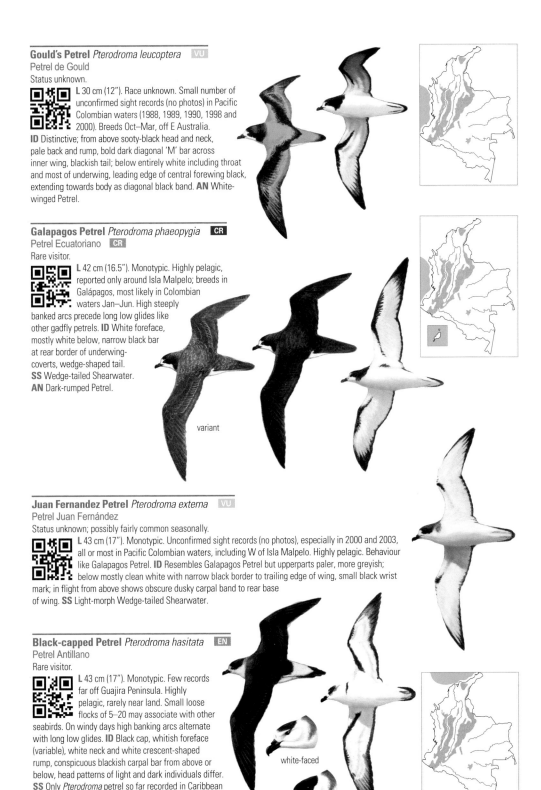

Gould's Petrel *Pterodroma leucoptera* VU
Petrel de Gould
Status unknown.

L 30 cm (12"). Race unknown. Small number of unconfirmed sight records (no photos) in Pacific Colombian waters (1988, 1989, 1990, 1998 and 2000). Breeds Oct–Mar, off E Australia.
ID Distinctive; from above sooty-black head and neck, pale back and rump, bold dark diagonal 'M' bar across inner wing, blackish tail; below entirely white including throat and most of underwing, leading edge of central forewing black, extending towards body as diagonal black band. **AN** White-winged Petrel.

Galapagos Petrel *Pterodroma phaeopygia* CR
Petrel Ecuatoriano CR
Rare visitor.

L 42 cm (16.5"). Monotypic. Highly pelagic, reported only around Isla Malpelo; breeds in Galápagos, most likely in Colombian waters Jan–Jun. High steeply banked arcs precede long low glides like other gadfly petrels. **ID** White foreface, mostly white below, narrow black bar at rear border of underwing-coverts, wedge-shaped tail. **SS** Wedge-tailed Shearwater. **AN** Dark-rumped Petrel.

variant

Juan Fernandez Petrel *Pterodroma externa* VU
Petrel Juan Fernández
Status unknown; possibly fairly common seasonally.

L 43 cm (17"). Monotypic. Unconfirmed sight records (no photos), especially in 2000 and 2003, all or most in Pacific Colombian waters, including W of Isla Malpelo. Highly pelagic. Behaviour like Galapagos Petrel. **ID** Resembles Galapagos Petrel but upperparts paler, more greyish; below mostly clean white with narrow black border to trailing edge of wing, small black wrist mark; in flight from above shows obscure dusky carpal band to rear base of wing. **SS** Light-morph Wedge-tailed Shearwater.

Black-capped Petrel *Pterodroma hasitata* EN
Petrel Antillano
Rare visitor.

L 43 cm (17"). Monotypic. Few records far off Guajira Peninsula. Highly pelagic, rarely near land. Small loose flocks of 5–20 may associate with other seabirds. On windy days high banking arcs alternate with long low glides. **ID** Black cap, whitish foreface (variable), white neck and white crescent-shaped rump, conspicuous blackish carpal bar from above or below; head patterns of light and dark individuals differ. **SS** Only *Pterodroma* petrel so far recorded in Caribbean Colombia. **AN** Capped Petrel.

white-faced

dark-faced

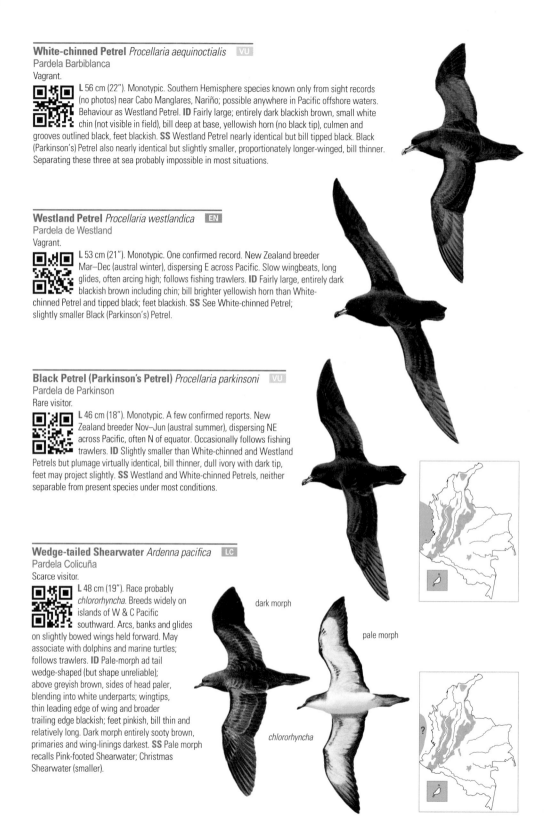

White-chinned Petrel *Procellaria aequinoctialis* `VU`
Pardela Barbiblanca
Vagrant.

L 56 cm (22"). Monotypic. Southern Hemisphere species known only from sight records (no photos) near Cabo Manglares, Nariño; possible anywhere in Pacific offshore waters. Behaviour as Westland Petrel. **ID** Fairly large; entirely dark blackish brown, small white chin (not visible in field), bill deep at base, yellowish horn (no black tip), culmen and grooves outlined black, feet blackish. **SS** Westland Petrel nearly identical but bill tipped black. Black (Parkinson's) Petrel also nearly identical but slightly smaller, proportionately longer-winged, bill thinner. Separating these three at sea probably impossible in most situations.

Westland Petrel *Procellaria westlandica* `EN`
Pardela de Westland
Vagrant.

L 53 cm (21"). Monotypic. One confirmed record. New Zealand breeder Mar–Dec (austral winter), dispersing E across Pacific. Slow wingbeats, long glides, often arcing high; follows fishing trawlers. **ID** Fairly large, entirely dark blackish brown including chin; bill brighter yellowish horn than White-chinned Petrel and tipped black; feet blackish. **SS** See White-chinned Petrel; slightly smaller Black (Parkinson's) Petrel.

Black Petrel (Parkinson's Petrel) *Procellaria parkinsoni* `VU`
Pardela de Parkinson
Rare visitor.

L 46 cm (18"). Monotypic. A few confirmed reports. New Zealand breeder Nov–Jun (austral summer), dispersing NE across Pacific, often N of equator. Occasionally follows fishing trawlers. **ID** Slightly smaller than White-chinned and Westland Petrels but plumage virtually identical, bill thinner, dull ivory with dark tip, feet may project slightly. **SS** Westland and White-chinned Petrels, neither separable from present species under most conditions.

Wedge-tailed Shearwater *Ardenna pacifica* `LC`
Pardela Colicuña
Scarce visitor.

L 48 cm (19"). Race probably *chlororhyncha*. Breeds widely on islands of W & C Pacific southward. Arcs, banks and glides on slightly bowed wings held forward. May associate with dolphins and marine turtles; follows trawlers. **ID** Pale-morph ad tail wedge-shaped (but shape unreliable); above greyish brown, sides of head paler, blending into white underparts; wingtips, thin leading edge of wing and broader trailing edge blackish; feet pinkish, bill thin and relatively long. Dark morph entirely sooty brown, primaries and wing-linings darkest. **SS** Pale morph recalls Pink-footed Shearwater; Christmas Shearwater (smaller).

dark morph

pale morph

chlororhyncha

Sooty Shearwater *Ardenna grisea* NT
Pardela Oscura
Common visitor.

L 46 cm (18"). Monotypic. Southern Hemisphere breeder mainly Sept or Oct–May; most numerous shearwater in Colombia, typically in flocks, and the only one frequently seen from shore. Rapid wingbeats alternate with low glides and sudden banked swerves. May rest on water. **ID** Medium-sized, slender wings; conspicuous silvery wing-linings contrast with dark plumage, long thin dark bill, dark legs. **SS** In Pacific waters Pink-footed Shearwater; darker Wedge-tailed Shearwater.

Pink-footed Shearwater *Ardenna creatopus* VU
Pardela Patirrosada
Rare visitor.

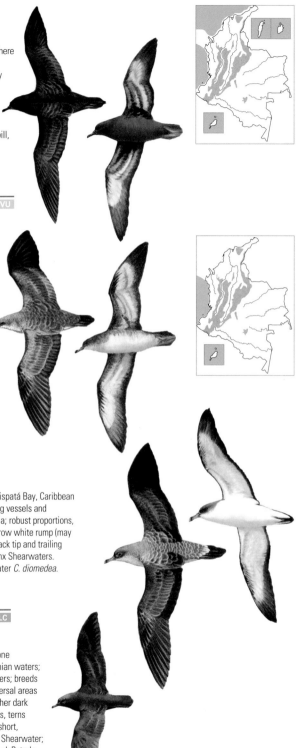

L 48 cm (19"). Monotypic. Various sight records, plus confirmed telemetry records (Oct) in Pacific Colombian waters; most likely Aug–Dec. Breeds off Chile; population small. Pelagic, less often offshore waters. Various-sized flocks may associate with other seabirds and dolphins; attracted to trawlers. Flight laboured. **ID** Sturdy bicoloured shearwater with broad wings, short tail, pinkish bill tipped black and pink feet. No dark 'M' pattern on brown upperwings, head and throat somewhat freckled; from below, base of primaries and secondaries pale but variable, flank mottling variable, undertail-coverts always dark. **SS** Pale-morph Wedge-tailed Shearwater slimmer, darker above, all-dark bill thinner.

Cory's Shearwater *Calonectris borealis* LC
Pardela Cenicienta
Vagrant.

L 53 cm (21"). Monotypic. One specimen, Cispatá Bay, Caribbean coast of Córdoba, May 2009. Follows fishing vessels and dolphins. **ID** Largest shearwater in Colombia; robust proportions, conspicuous yellow bill, greyish above, narrow white rump (may be absent), white below, underwing white with broad black tip and trailing edge. **SS** Sooty Shearwater; smaller Audubon's and Manx Shearwaters. **TN** Often considered conspecific with Scopoli's Shearwater *C. diomedea*.

[Christmas Shearwater *Puffinus nativitatis*] LC
Pardela de la Christmas
Hypothetical.

L 36 cm (14"). Monotypic. No records, but one unconfirmed report in adjacent W Panamanian waters; likely in Pacific Colombia seas. Pelagic waters; breeds on C & S Pacific islands; non-breeding dispersal areas poorly known. Flies low, wingbeats faster, stiffer than other dark shearwaters. Associates with other shearwaters, noddies, terns and dolphins. **ID** Small size; all-dark plumage, relatively short, slightly rounded wings, short tail, bill blackish. **SS** Sooty Shearwater; dark-morph Wedge-tailed Shearwater; Westland and Black Petrels (all larger).

Galapagos Shearwater *Puffinus subalaris* `LC`
Pardela de Galápagos
Rare visitor.

 L 30 cm (12"). Monotypic. Recorded in Pacific waters off NW Chocó (e.g. Cabo Marzo, photos, Sept). Occurs in both offshore and deeper pelagic waters. Joins other seabirds; follows small fishing boats. May rest on water. **ID** Note small size, thin bill, all dark above, white below but underwing quite variable, mostly dark to mostly white, axillaries usually white. **SS** Much smaller than any other 'bicoloured' shearwater in the Pacific. **TN** Has been considered a race of Audubon's Shearwater.

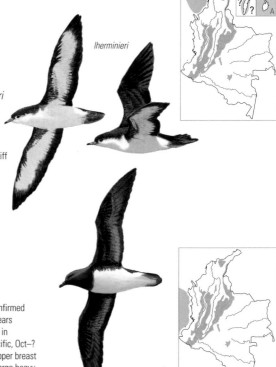

variant

Manx Shearwater *Puffinus puffinus* `LC`
Pardela Pintada
Boreal winter vagrant.

 L 33 cm (13"). Monotypic. Recorded off Isla San Andrés, mostly Nov–Mar; no Pacific records. Flies with stiff wingbeats and short glides on bowed wings. Alone or in small flocks, occasionally with whales or dolphins. **ID** Small; clean-cut black-and-white pattern, dark smudge on sides of neck, white undertail-coverts, can show small white crescent behind dark cheeks, pink feet. **SS** Very similar, but much commoner, Audubon's Shearwater has dark undertail-coverts, may have broader black outline on underwing.

Audubon's Shearwater *Puffinus lherminieri* `LC`
Pardela de Audubon

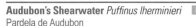 Three subspecies in three subspecies groups; one in Colombia.

lherminieri

Audubon's Shearwater *Puffinus (lherminieri) lherminieri*
Rare or seasonal.
L 33 cm (13"). Races *lherminieri*[A] breeds (presently?) on Crab Key, Isla Providencia; sometimes recognized *loyemilleri*[B] also possible. No Pacific records. Pelagic; joins other seabirds, rarely follows fishing boats. Flies with quick stiff wingbeats and short glides low over ocean. **ID** Small; clean-cut black-and-white pattern, 'capped' appearance, black undertail-coverts hard to see, short wings slightly rounded at tips, bill black; feet pinkish. **SS** Manx Shearwater.
TN NE Atlantic breeders sometimes separated as two other species, Barolo *P. baroli* and Boyd's Shearwaters *P. boydi*.

Tahiti Petrel *Pseudobulweria rostrata* `NT`
Pardela de Tahití
Status unknown; possibly seasonal far offshore.

 L 39 cm (15.5"). Race unknown. Numerous unconfirmed visual records (no photos) during five calendar years (1988–2000) in Colombian waters; also reported in Panamian/Colombian Bight. Breeds in South Pacific, Oct–? **ID** Medium-sized bicoloured petrel, upperparts and head to upper breast dark brown ('hooded' appearance), rest of underparts white, large heavy black bill, long narrow wings, underwings dark with white median line.

20 extant species, 3 in region

Storks are an ancient group of long-legged waders, found almost worldwide at warmer latitudes. All have bare facial skin and, unlike herons, fly with the neck outstretched. They have heavy bills, often soar to great heights, and are less dependent on water than herons.

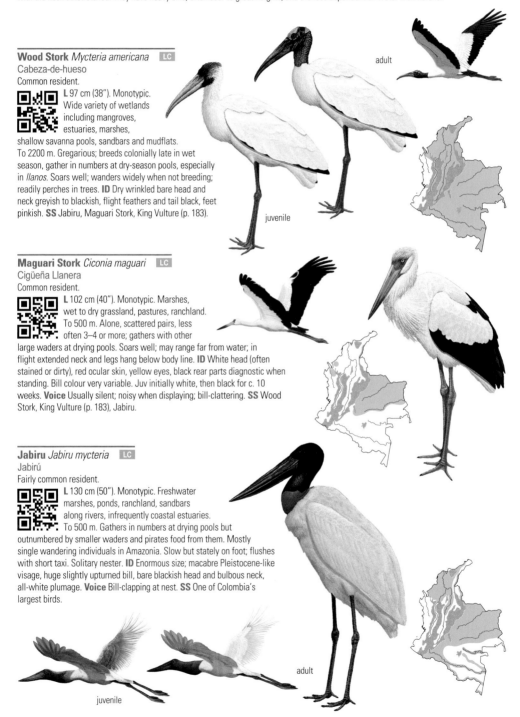

Wood Stork *Mycteria americana* `LC`
Cabeza-de-hueso
Common resident.
L 97 cm (38"). Monotypic. Wide variety of wetlands including mangroves, estuaries, marshes, shallow savanna pools, sandbars and mudflats. To 2200 m. Gregarious; breeds colonially late in wet season, gather in numbers at dry-season pools, especially in *llanos*. Soars well; wanders widely when not breeding; readily perches in trees. **ID** Dry wrinkled bare head and neck greyish to blackish, flight feathers and tail black, feet pinkish. **SS** Jabiru, Maguari Stork, King Vulture (p. 183).

adult

juvenile

Maguari Stork *Ciconia maguari* `LC`
Cigüeña Llanera
Common resident.
L 102 cm (40"). Monotypic. Marshes, wet to dry grassland, pastures, ranchland. To 500 m. Alone, scattered pairs, less often 3–4 or more; gathers with other large waders at drying pools. Soars well; may range far from water; in flight extended neck and legs hang below body line. **ID** White head (often stained or dirty), red ocular skin, yellow eyes, black rear parts diagnostic when standing. Bill colour very variable. Juv initially white, then black for c. 10 weeks. **Voice** Usually silent; noisy when displaying; bill-clattering. **SS** Wood Stork, King Vulture (p. 183), Jabiru.

Jabiru *Jabiru mycteria* `LC`
Jabirú
Fairly common resident.
L 130 cm (50"). Monotypic. Freshwater marshes, ponds, ranchland, sandbars along rivers, infrequently coastal estuaries. To 500 m. Gathers in numbers at drying pools but outnumbered by smaller waders and pirates food from them. Mostly single wandering individuals in Amazonia. Slow but stately on foot; flushes with short taxi. Solitary nester. **ID** Enormous size; macabre Pleistocene-like visage, huge slightly upturned bill, bare blackish head and bulbous neck, all-white plumage. **Voice** Bill-clapping at nest. **SS** One of Colombia's largest birds.

adult

juvenile

THRESKIORNITHIDAE
Ibises and Spoonbills
35 extant species, 8 in region

An ancient group found throughout much of the world's warmer regions. All have bare faces, long decurved bills and moderately long legs; spoonbills have straight flat, spoon-shaped bills and longer legs. All fly with necks outstretched; nest alone or in colonies.

adult

juvenile

caudatus

Roseate Spoonbill *Platalea ajaja* `LC`
Espátula Rosada
Common resident.

L 81 cm (32"). Monotypic. Mangroves, estuaries, marshes, wetlands and pools throughout *llanos*, rivers in forested areas. To 1000 m. Forages in shallow water by swinging bill side to side, sifting plankton-sized prey. Gathers in numbers at drying pools. Nests colonially in rainy season. **ID** 'Spoon bill' unmistakable, blood-red shoulders, amount of pink in plumage varies with age and breeding condition, head and bare parts colourful when breeding. Juv mostly whitish. **Voice** Usually silent.

Buff-necked Ibis *Theristicus caudatus* `LC`
Bandurria Aliblanca
Common resident.

L 76 cm (30"). Race *caudatus*. Savanna and ranchland in *llanos*, short grass, dry pastures, damp areas or pools but often far from water. To 1600 m. Singles, pairs or small loose groups forage mostly on dry ground. **ID** Goose-like shape; creamy-buff foreparts, white greater coverts, black belly. **Voice** Roosts in trees, often around ranch buildings; extremely noisy at dawn and in flight; loud nasal "KNACK-KNOCK" over and over; pre-dawn groups at roost chat in unforgettable rhythmic choruses, softly at first, then louder as others join.

Sharp-tailed Ibis *Cercibis oxycerca* `LC`
Tarotaro
Locally fairly common resident.

L 81 cm (32"). Monotypic. Muddy pools, flooded rice fields, damp grass. To 500 m. Mostly pairs or trios, not large flocks. Forages in usually bare relatively open areas, often near water. Flight slow, laboured, rather low as commutes long distances over open savanna. **ID** Large ibis; long tail, short legs (no projection behind tail), bare orange throat, orange-red facial skin and legs. **Voice** Vocal in flight; loud nasal bugled "TUUR-DEEE" (French ambulance sound) or truncated "TUT-TOOT" (second note higher), sometimes antiphonal.

Green Ibis *Mesembrinibis cayennensis* `LC`
Ibis Verde
Fairly common resident.

L 56 cm (22"). Monotypic. Forest ibis; shady riverbanks, forest borders and pools. Infrequently in open, rarely far from forest. To 800 m. Singles or loosely associated pairs; often perches in trees. Flies with stiff up-flicked wingbeats. **ID** Dark ibis, shows little colour, short legs do not project beyond tail, iridescent green hackles on neck, bare face and legs dull greenish. **Voice** At dusk or later, fast rolling low-pitched "kororkororkoro…" recalls Greater Ani. **SS** Juv Bare-faced Ibis.

Bare-faced Ibis *Phimosus infuscatus* `LC`
Coquito
Resident (commonest Colombian ibis).

 L 51 cm (20"). Race *berlepschi*. Dry to wet pastures, marshes, rice fields, lagoons, canals and ditches in urban areas. Small to large groups, sometimes 100s, occasionally singles. May forage around cattle or with other ibises. Forms string-like lines on long flights. **ID** Small, nondescript; bill, facial skin and legs pinkish but colours often dull or obscured by mud, short legs do not project behind tail. **Voice** Rather quiet; utters soft whispering calls when settling at evening roosts in wooded river borders. **SS** Green Ibis. **AN** Whispering Ibis.

White Ibis *Eudocimus albus* `LC`
Ibis Blanco
Common resident (sharp seasonal movements in *llanos*).

L 61 cm (24"). Race *ramobustorum* (perhaps better treated as monotypic). Mangroves, estuaries, coastal lagoons, freshwater marshes and lagoons. Occasional boreal migrant (or breeder?) on Caribbean islands. To 500 m. Habits similar to Scarlet Ibis and often with latter, but far less numerous. **ID** Mostly white, wingtips black, facial skin and bill pinkish red (partly blackish when breeding, or always pinkish in *llanos*?), legs pinkish. Juv identical to Scarlet Ibis, older birds progressively whiter, no pink. **Voice** Usually silent.

Scarlet Ibis *Eudocimus ruber* `LC`
Corocora
Common resident (seasonal movements in *llanos*).

L 61 cm (24"). Monotypic. Mangroves, estuaries, freshwater marshes, lagoons, wet areas in *llanos*. To 500 m (locally 1000 m). Numerous Dec–Jun dry season in *llanos* when large numbers gather at drying pools. Commutes long distances from roosting to feeding areas. **ID** Ad intense red on coast, much paler inland; black wingtips, bill and legs red, ad non-br duller. Juv above greyish brown, below whitish, no red; older birds first acquire pink on back. **Voice** Muffled sounds in flight and at roost. **SS** Juv White Ibis.

Glossy Ibis *Plegadis falcinellus* `LC`
Ibis Pico-de-hoz
Fairly common resident.

L 58 cm (23"). Monotypic. Marshes, lagoons, wet grassland, pastures. To 1000 m. Breeding unconfirmed (?); possible non-breeding intra-tropical migrant. Recorded virtually year-round in variable-sized flocks. Seasonal in some areas; far more numerous in C Venezuela. **ID** Long legs, glossy dark maroon plumage diagnostic but may look black, in flight legs and feet project behind tail. Non-br finely streaked. Juv duller. **SS** Bare-faced Ibis.

64 extant species, 22 in region

Herons and egrets comprise a worldwide family of slender, long-necked, long-legged waders with large pointed bills. They prey on fish, frogs and other aquatic life, and are much more closely tied to water than storks or ibises. Some are solitary, others gregarious although all of them tend to space themselves when foraging.

Rufescent Tiger-heron *Tigrisoma lineatum* `LC`
Vaco Colorado
Common resident.

 L 70 cm (28"). Race *lineatum*. Swampy lake edges, freshwater marshes, ponds, wooded streams (not fast-flowing water). To 800 m. Furtive and difficult to see in forested areas; conspicuous in *llanos* (especially dry season). Solitary; often flushes to tree in wooded areas; flight laboured. **ID** Long thick neck, stout dark bill (colour variable). Ad rufescent foreparts. Juv barred 'tiger plumage' retained 4–5 years. **Voice** Deep bovine-like "whoOOOOoo"; occasionally at night descending muffled hooting "WOO-HOO, WOO-Hoo, wóo-hoo, wóo-hoo…"; guttural alarm. **SS** Other juv tiger-herons.

Fasciated Tiger-heron *Tigrisoma fasciatum* `LC`
Vaco Cabecinegro
Uncommon resident.

 L 66 cm (26"). Race *salmoni*. Fast-flowing, clean mountain streams in humid foothills or higher. 300–2200 m. Stands alone on boulders, gravel bars or in shallow water; waits patiently for fish or aquatic prey. **ID** Ad recalls Bare-throated Tiger-heron; head, neck and upperparts slate-grey very finely barred black, throat whitish (feathered), belly greyish (not cinnamon). Juv (plumage retained c. 4 years) essentially identical to juv Rufescent Tiger-heron (bill colours of juvs of both species vary); best told by habitat, bill slightly shorter, thicker, three (not four) white tail-bands. **Voice** May flush with loud "kwok" notes.

Bare-throated Tiger-heron *Tigrisoma mexicanum* `LC`
Vaco Mejicano
Local resident.

 L 81 cm (32"). Monotypic. Forest streams, marshes, mangroves, brackish wetlands; nests in dry or humid woodland. To 200 m. Solitary; sometimes active at night; often perches in trees. **ID** Large tiger-heron; bare yellow throat (not always obvious) brightest when breeding, sides of head grey, neck buff with narrow black barring, lower underparts cinnamon-rufous. Juv from other tiger-herons by bare yellow throat (not feathered and white), dusky crown. **Voice** Croaking or frog-like calls; flushes with harsh "whuu, woh, woh, woh".

Agami Heron *Agamia agami* `VU`
Garza Agami
Uncommon and local resident.

 L 71 cm (28"). Monotypic. Easily overlooked. Shady forest streams, oxbows, gallery forest streams, occasionally mangroves. Solitary, stealthy; fishes by very slow wading, pausing beneath dense light-dappled vegetation or deep shade; not in open. To 500 m (vagrant 2600 m). **ID** Long neck, unusually long rapier-like bill. Ad stunning plumage; above slaty blue-green, shoulders maroon, underparts chestnut, wispy silver-blue foreneck plumes, white nuchal plumes when breeding. Juv drab greyish, belly whitish; ad plumage by third year. **Voice** Usually silent; low guttural or purring rattles when disturbed; frog-like snores; odd harsh notes.

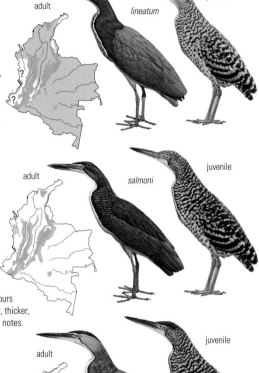

adult · *lineatum* · juvenile

adult · *salmoni* · juvenile

adult · juvenile

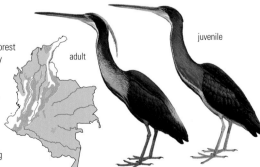

adult · juvenile

Boat-billed Heron *Cochlearius cochlearius* `LC`
Garza Cucharón

Five subspecies in two subspecies groups; both in Colombia.

Northern Boat-billed Heron
Cochlearius (cochlearius) zeledoni
Uncommon resident.
L 51 cm (20"). Race *panamensis*. Gulf of Urabá near Panama border. **ID** Like southern *cochlearius* but much darker, wings and back olive-grey (not white), underparts buffy rufous.

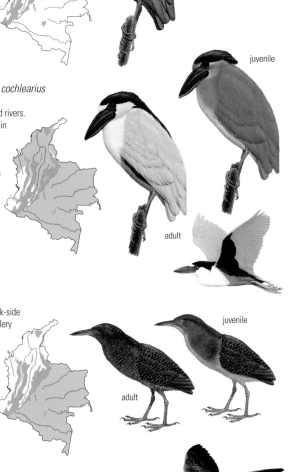

panamensis

juvenile

Southern Boat-billed Heron *Cochlearius (cochlearius) cochlearius*
Uncommon resident.
L 51 cm (20"). One subspecies in group. Mangroves, forested rivers. To 800 m (rarely 2600 m). Groups of up to 100+ roost by day in subcanopy vegetation near water. After dark fly to near or distant muddy feeding sites along wooded streams or open pools in grassland. Diet mostly fish; wary; flushes quickly at night. **ID** Shovel-like black bill; large black eyes, bowling-pin shape, crown and mantle black, otherwise white, rufous belly, black axillaries. Juv pale brown to rufescent-brown.
Voice Guttural "guuk" or "uuk"; flushes from day roost with chimpanzee-like "o-o-ou-ou-ah-ah-aa".
SS Black-crowned Night-heron.

adult

Zigzag Heron *Zebrilus undulatus* `NT`
Garza Zigzag
Very local resident.

L 30 cm (12"). Monotypic. Dense swampy creek-side vegetation, wet low-lying vegetation inside gallery forest, swampy oxbows (not open marshes). To 400 m. Solitary, secretive, on ground or low branch near or over water. **ID** Tiny dark heron; large-headed, short-legged, hunched shape. Ad above blackish with fine wavy buff barring, below paler. Juv foreface and underparts dark rufous, variable fine wavy blackish barring, legs dingy yellowish, eyes yellow.
Voice Call, from 1–3 m up, low hollow hooting or grunting "oooop" (drops in pitch), singly or slow series, c. 1/second.

juvenile

adult

Pinnated Bittern *Botaurus pinnatus* `LC`
Avetoro
Uncommon resident.

L 71 cm (28"). Race *pinnatus*. Shallow fresh- and brackish-water marshes with tall vegetation, flooded grassland, rice fields. Moves seasonally in *llanos* as marshes dry. To 1000 m (rarely 2600 m). Solitary, secretive; in alarm 'freezes' with bill pointed skyward or slowly creeps away; flushes reluctantly, flies slowly, does not alight in trees. **ID** Hindneck barred, back and wings streaked (not barred), in flight blackish flight feathers narrowly tipped buff.
Voice Infrequently vocal; deep rhythmic pumping "oong-ka-choonk!" far-carrying. **SS** Juv Rufescent Tiger-heron; juv Black-crowned Night-heron.

pinnatus

Stripe-backed Bittern *Ixobrychus involucris* LC
Avetorillo Estriado
Rare, local and erratic resident.

 L 33 cm (13"). Monotypic. Fresh- and brackish-water marshes with tall vegetation, rice fields, drainage ditches. Resident; possibly also local or short-distance migrant. Solitary, inconspicuous, easily overlooked; behaviour recalls Least Bittern. **ID** Upperparts boldly striped black and buff, below paler, lightly streaked, in flight shows broad rufous-tipped flight feathers. Juv resembles juv Least Bittern but back streaked. **Voice** Call from concealed perch; abrupt "huu" about once every two seconds; slow descending gurgle "g'u'u'u'a'a".

Least Bittern *Ixobrychus exilis* LC
Avetorillo Bicolor
Uncommon resident.

 L 30 cm (12"). Races *erythromelas*[A], *bogotensis*[B], *limoncochae* (Putumayo?); boreal migrant *exilis* in Cauca Valley (?). Freshwater marshes with tall vegetation. To 3100 m. Shy, secretive; if pressed 'freezes' with bill pointed up, creeps away or flushes but soon drops into cover. **ID** Small. Ad crown and back black (♂), or dusky to chestnut (♀); otherwise mostly cinnamon-rufous, narrow white scapular line, large tawny shoulder patch, blackish flight feathers. Juv like ♀ but duller. **Voice** Call, dawn and dusk, nasal hooting "hooh" at short intervals. **SS** Stripe-backed Bittern.

Black-crowned Night-heron *Nycticorax nycticorax* LC
Guaco Común
Common resident.

 L 64 cm (25"). Race *hoactli*. Mangroves; coastal and freshwater marshes, lagoons, wetlands, gallery forests. To 3200 m. Partly nocturnal, roosts by day in loose groups in wooded areas, also abroad by day. **ID** Chunky, hunched; in flight feet protrude. Ad crown and back black, wings grey, forehead and underparts white, eyes red. Juv brown broadly streaked whitish, wings spotted, underparts paler with broader, blurred streaking, eyes yellowish. **Voice** Low forced "wuuk!" or "quock!". **SS** Boat-billed Heron; juv Yellow-crowned Night-heron.

Yellow-crowned Night-heron *Nyctanassa violacea* LC
Guaco Manglero
Common resident on coasts, local inland.

L 66 cm (26"). Races *cayennensis*[A], *caliginis*[B], *violacea*[C] (boreal migrant). Mangroves, estuaries on both coasts. To 500 m. Partly nocturnal, small groups roost in wooded areas by day, also more frequently abroad by day than Black-crowned Night-heron. **ID** Longer legs, heavier bill than Black-crowned Night-heron. Ad head boldly striped, cheeks and nuchal plumes white, eyes orange-red. Juv darker than Black-crowned Night-heron, head, neck and underparts more finely streaked, back spotted, wing spots smaller. **Voice** Short "qwok".

erythromelas

♀   ♂

adult

hoactli

juvenile

cayennensis

adult

juvenile

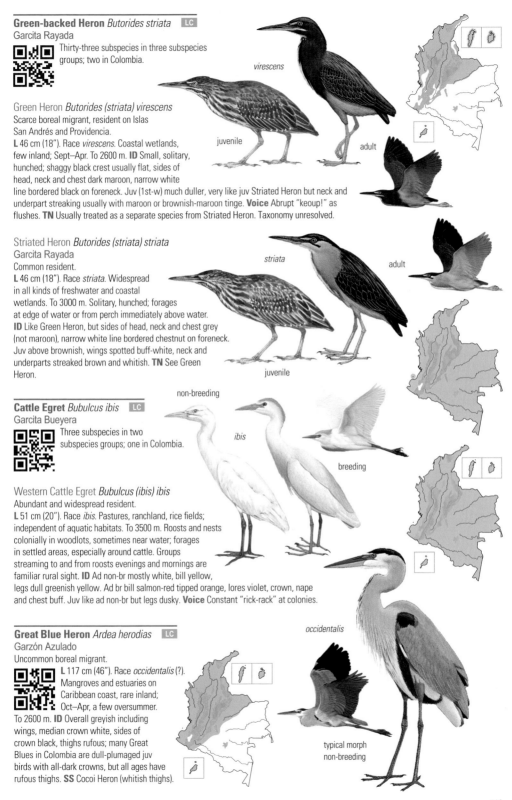

Green-backed Heron *Butorides striata* LC
Garcita Rayada

Thirty-three subspecies in three subspecies groups; two in Colombia.

Green Heron *Butorides (striata) virescens*
Scarce boreal migrant, resident on Islas San Andrés and Providencia.
L 46 cm (18"). Race *virescens*. Coastal wetlands, few inland; Sept–Apr. To 2600 m. **ID** Small, solitary, hunched; shaggy black crest usually flat, sides of head, neck and chest dark maroon, narrow white line bordered black on foreneck. Juv (1st-w) much duller, very like juv Striated Heron but neck and underpart streaking usually with maroon or brownish-maroon tinge. **Voice** Abrupt "keoup!" as flushes. **TN** Usually treated as a separate species from Striated Heron. Taxonomy unresolved.

virescens

juvenile

adult

Striated Heron *Butorides (striata) striata*
Garcita Rayada
Common resident.
L 46 cm (18"). Race *striata*. Widespread in all kinds of freshwater and coastal wetlands. To 3000 m. Solitary, hunched; forages at edge of water or from perch immediately above water. **ID** Like Green Heron, but sides of head, neck and chest grey (not maroon), narrow white line bordered chestnut on foreneck. Juv above brownish, wings spotted buff-white, neck and underparts streaked brown and whitish. **TN** See Green Heron.

striata

adult

juvenile

Cattle Egret *Bubulcus ibis* LC
Garcita Bueyera

Three subspecies in two subspecies groups; one in Colombia.

non-breeding

ibis

breeding

Western Cattle Egret *Bubulcus (ibis) ibis*
Abundant and widespread resident.
L 51 cm (20"). Race *ibis*. Pastures, ranchland, rice fields; independent of aquatic habitats. To 3500 m. Roosts and nests colonially in woodlots, sometimes near water; forages in settled areas, especially around cattle. Groups streaming to and from roosts evenings and mornings are familiar rural sight. **ID** Ad non-br mostly white, bill yellow, legs dull greenish yellow. Ad br bill salmon-red tipped orange, lores violet, crown, nape and chest buff. Juv like ad non-br but legs dusky. **Voice** Constant "rick-rack" at colonies.

Great Blue Heron *Ardea herodias* LC
Garzón Azulado
Uncommon boreal migrant.

L 117 cm (46"). Race *occidentalis* (?). Mangroves and estuaries on Caribbean coast, rare inland; Oct–Apr, a few oversummer. To 2600 m. **ID** Overall greyish including wings, median crown white, sides of crown black, thighs rufous; many Great Blues in Colombia are dull-plumaged juv birds with all-dark crowns, but all ages have rufous thighs. **SS** Cocoi Heron (whitish thighs).

occidentalis

typical morph
non-breeding

143

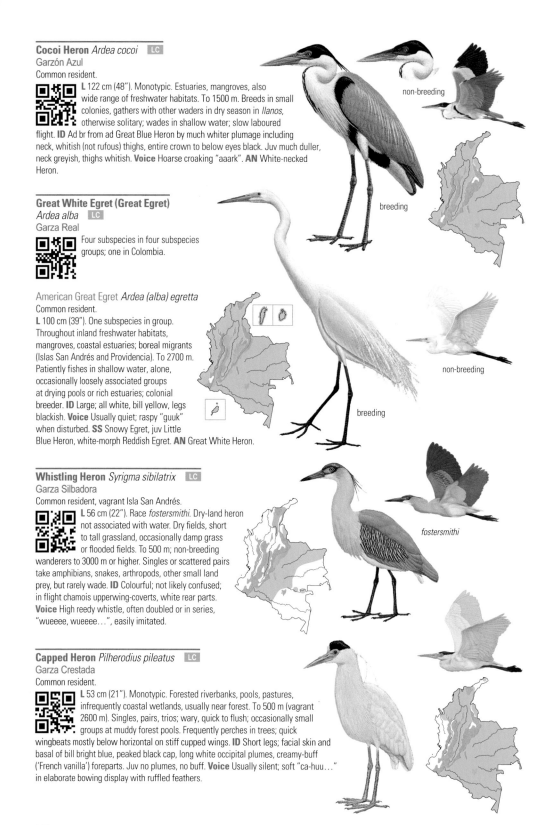

Cocoi Heron *Ardea cocoi* LC
Garzón Azul
Common resident.

L 122 cm (48"). Monotypic. Estuaries, mangroves, also wide range of freshwater habitats. To 1500 m. Breeds in small colonies, gathers with other waders in dry season in *llanos*, otherwise solitary; wades in shallow water; slow laboured flight. **ID** Ad br from ad Great Blue Heron by much whiter plumage including neck, whitish (not rufous) thighs, entire crown to below eyes black. Juv much duller, neck greyish, thighs whitish. **Voice** Hoarse croaking "aaark". **AN** White-necked Heron.

non-breeding

breeding

Great White Egret (Great Egret)
Ardea alba LC
Garza Real

Four subspecies in four subspecies groups; one in Colombia.

American Great Egret *Ardea (alba) egretta*
Common resident.
L 100 cm (39"). One subspecies in group. Throughout inland freshwater habitats, mangroves, coastal estuaries; boreal migrants (Islas San Andrés and Providencia). To 2700 m. Patiently fishes in shallow water, alone, occasionally loosely associated groups at drying pools or rich estuaries; colonial breeder. **ID** Large; all white, bill yellow, legs blackish. **Voice** Usually quiet; raspy "guuk" when disturbed. **SS** Snowy Egret, juv Little Blue Heron, white-morph Reddish Egret. **AN** Great White Heron.

non-breeding

breeding

Whistling Heron *Syrigma sibilatrix* LC
Garza Silbadora
Common resident, vagrant Isla San Andrés.

L 56 cm (22"). Race *fostersmithi*. Dry-land heron not associated with water. Dry fields, short to tall grassland, occasionally damp grass or flooded fields. To 500 m; non-breeding wanderers to 3000 m or higher. Singles or scattered pairs take amphibians, snakes, arthropods, other small land prey, but rarely wade. **ID** Colourful; not likely confused; in flight chamois upperwing-coverts, white rear parts. **Voice** High reedy whistle, often doubled or in series, "wueeee, wueeee…", easily imitated.

fostersmithi

Capped Heron *Pilherodius pileatus* LC
Garza Crestada
Common resident.

L 53 cm (21"). Monotypic. Forested riverbanks, pools, pastures, infrequently coastal wetlands, usually near forest. To 500 m (vagrant 2600 m). Singles, pairs, trios; wary, quick to flush; occasionally small groups at muddy forest pools. Frequently perches in trees; quick wingbeats mostly below horizontal on stiff cupped wings. **ID** Short legs; facial skin and basal of bill bright blue, peaked black cap, long white occipital plumes, creamy-buff ('French vanilla') foreparts. Juv no plumes, no buff. **Voice** Usually silent; soft "ca-huu…" in elaborate bowing display with ruffled feathers.

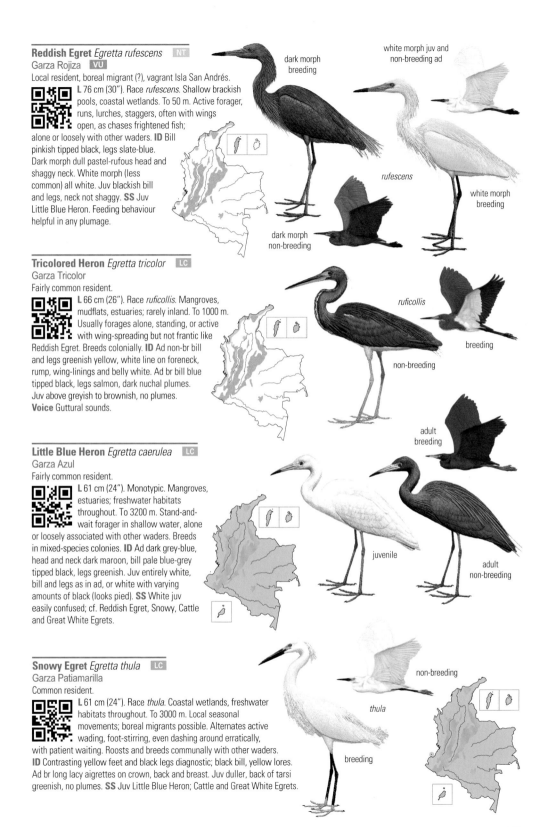

Reddish Egret *Egretta rufescens* NT
Garza Rojiza VU

Local resident, boreal migrant (?), vagrant Isla San Andrés.
L 76 cm (30"). Race *rufescens*. Shallow brackish pools, coastal wetlands. To 50 m. Active forager, runs, lurches, staggers, often with wings open, as chases frightened fish; alone or loosely with other waders. **ID** Bill pinkish tipped black, legs slate-blue. Dark morph dull pastel-rufous head and shaggy neck. White morph (less common) all white. Juv blackish bill and legs, neck not shaggy. **SS** Juv Little Blue Heron. Feeding behaviour helpful in any plumage.

dark morph breeding

white morph juv and non-breeding ad

rufescens

white morph breeding

dark morph non-breeding

Tricolored Heron *Egretta tricolor* LC
Garza Tricolor

Fairly common resident.
L 66 cm (26"). Race *ruficollis*. Mangroves, mudflats, estuaries; rarely inland. To 1000 m. Usually forages alone, standing, or active with wing-spreading but not frantic like Reddish Egret. Breeds colonially. **ID** Ad non-br bill and legs greenish yellow, white line on foreneck, rump, wing-linings and belly white. Ad br bill blue tipped black, legs salmon, dark nuchal plumes. Juv above greyish to brownish, no plumes. **Voice** Guttural sounds.

ruficollis

breeding

non-breeding

adult breeding

Little Blue Heron *Egretta caerulea* LC
Garza Azul

Fairly common resident.
L 61 cm (24"). Monotypic. Mangroves, estuaries; freshwater habitats throughout. To 3200 m. Stand-and-wait forager in shallow water, alone or loosely associated with other waders. Breeds in mixed-species colonies. **ID** Ad dark grey-blue, head and neck dark maroon, bill pale blue-grey tipped black, legs greenish. Juv entirely white, bill and legs as in ad, or white with varying amounts of black (looks pied). **SS** White juv easily confused; cf. Reddish Egret, Snowy, Cattle and Great White Egrets.

juvenile

adult non-breeding

Snowy Egret *Egretta thula* LC
Garza Patiamarilla

Common resident.
L 61 cm (24"). Race *thula*. Coastal wetlands, freshwater habitats throughout. To 3000 m. Local seasonal movements; boreal migrants possible. Alternates active wading, foot-stirring, even dashing around erratically, with patient waiting. Roosts and breeds communally with other waders.
ID Contrasting yellow feet and black legs diagnostic; black bill, yellow lores. Ad br long lacy aigrettes on crown, back and breast. Juv duller, back of tarsi greenish, no plumes. **SS** Juv Little Blue Heron; Cattle and Great White Egrets.

non-breeding

thula

breeding

145

PELECANIDAE
Pelicans
8 extant species, 1 in region + 1 vagrant

A small worldwide family of predominantly warmer latitudes. Best known for their huge pouched bills. Small groups are often seen flying in stately formation, alternating slow wingbeats with long glides just above coastal wave crests. Sea-cliff nesting colonies are sensitive to disturbance by human activity.

Brown Pelican *Pelecanus occidentalis* LC
Pelícano Pardo
Common resident.

L 132 cm (52"). Races *carolinensis*[A] (boreal migrant?), *occidentalis*[B], *murphyi*[C]. Rarely inland, vagrant to 3000 m. Conspicuous along coasts; plunge-dive in deep water or swim in cooperative groups in shallow water to capture fish. **ID** Unmistakable. Ad br hindneck chestnut, maxilla dark reddish brown, ad non-br head and neck whitish. Juv above greyish brown. **SS Peruvian Pelican** *P. thagus* of cold Humboldt Current, unrecorded but possible: ad like Brown Pelican but larger, back whitish or mottled white (not brownish grey), whitish (not greyish) upperwing-coverts; more red and blue on bill (breeders); juv variable white mottling on back.

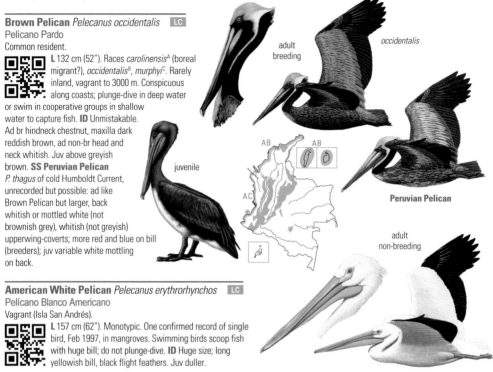

adult breeding · *occidentalis* · juvenile · Peruvian Pelican · adult non-breeding

American White Pelican *Pelecanus erythrorhynchos* LC
Pelícano Blanco Americano
Vagrant (Isla San Andrés).

L 157 cm (62"). Monotypic. One confirmed record of single bird, Feb 1997, in mangroves. Swimming birds scoop fish with huge bill; do not plunge-dive. **ID** Huge size; long yellowish bill, black flight feathers. Juv duller.

FREGATIDAE
Frigatebirds
5 extant species, 2 in region

Frigatebirds, or 'man-o'-war birds' are large, black, angular seabirds of tropical regions found nearly worldwide. Exceptionally agile and buoyant in the air, they cannot walk or swim and do not intentionally settle on water. Feed by snatching flying fish and squid from ocean surface, habitually pirate food, eggs and nestlings of other seabirds, also hatchling sea turtles and carrion; and occasionally wander inland.

Great Frigatebird *Fregata minor* LC
Fragata Alibandeada
Status unknown.

L 97 cm (38"). Race *ridgwayi*(?). Isla Malpelo in Pacific. **ID** Ad ♂ nearly identical to ♂ Magnificent Frigatebird, differing in more contrasting alar bar on upperwing, reddish to brown (not black) feet. Ad ♀ from ♀ Magnificent Frigatebird in white (not black) chin and throat, reddish (not blue) eye-ring (breeding only?), all-black axillaries (no white scaling at base). Juv variable amount of cinnamon (not white) on head to chest.

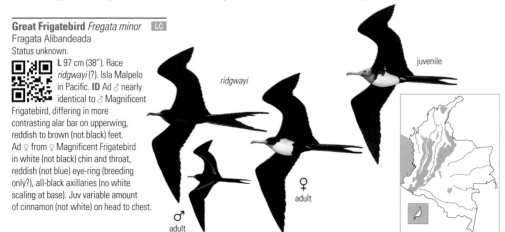

ridgwayi · juvenile · ♂ adult · ♀ adult

Magnificent Frigatebird *Fregata magnificens* `LC`
Fragata Magnífica
Common resident.

L 102 cm (40"). Race *rothschildi*. Coastal bays, harbours; usually within sight of land. Soars effortlessly, alone or in loose groups. Often follows fishing boats. Roosts mostly in mangroves; breeds in colonies on offshore islets. To 200 m. **ID** Long forked tail, long pointed wings bent at wrist. Ad ♂ black, bare red throat pouch inflates in display, feet blackish, faint alar 'brace' on upperwing. Ad ♀ like ♂ but broad white band across breast (throat black), diagnostic white scaling at base of axillaries. Youngest juv entire head to mid-breast white. **Voice** Grating gurgles and rattles at breeding colony. **SS** Great Frigatebird.

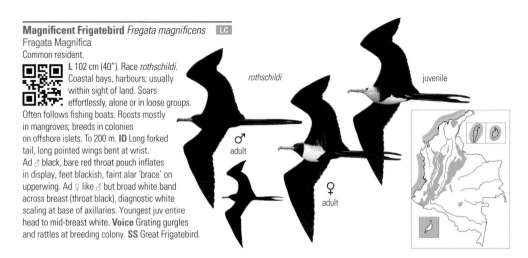

rothschildi   juvenile

♂
adult

♀
adult

SULIDAE
Gannets and Boobies
10 extant species, 6 in region

Large, sociable seabirds with angular proportions. Gannets occur in cold northern waters, boobies in warm tropical seas. Both groups breed in large colonies and capture fish in spectacular dives, plunging arrow-like into the sea. Four species breed on Colombia's islands, but only Brown Booby is regularly seen near mainland coasts.

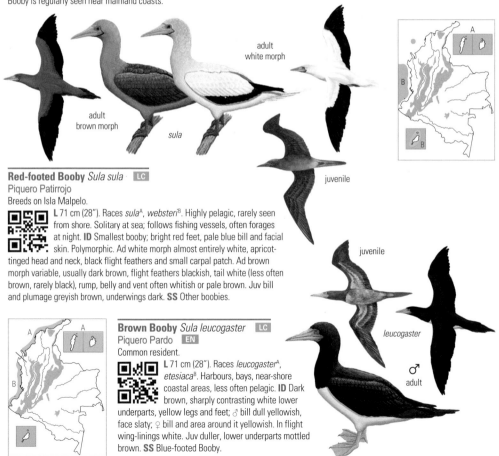

adult
white morph

adult
brown morph

sula

juvenile

Red-footed Booby *Sula sula* `LC`
Piquero Patirrojo
Breeds on Isla Malpelo.

L 71 cm (28"). Races *sula*[A], *websteri*[B]. Highly pelagic, rarely seen from shore. Solitary at sea; follows fishing vessels, often forages at night. **ID** Smallest booby; bright red feet, pale blue bill and facial skin. Polymorphic. Ad white morph almost entirely white, apricot-tinged head and neck, black flight feathers and small carpal patch. Ad brown morph variable, usually dark brown, flight feathers blackish, tail white (less often brown, rarely black), rump, belly and vent often whitish or pale brown. Juv bill and plumage greyish brown, underwings dark. **SS** Other boobies.

juvenile

leucogaster

Brown Booby *Sula leucogaster* `LC`
Piquero Pardo `EN`
Common resident.

L 71 cm (28"). Races *leucogaster*[A], *etesiaca*[B]. Harbours, bays, near-shore coastal areas, less often pelagic. **ID** Dark brown, sharply contrasting white lower underparts, yellow legs and feet; ♂ bill dull yellowish, face slaty; ♀ bill and area around it yellowish. In flight wing-linings white. Juv duller, lower underparts mottled brown. **SS** Blue-footed Booby.

♂
adult

Blue-footed Booby *Sula nebouxii* `LC`
Piquero Patiazul
Breeds on rocky sea cliffs on Isla Gorgonilla,
SW Pacific coast.

L 86 cm (34"). Race *nebouxii*.
Near-shore and offshore
waters, less often
pelagic. Social, often
flocks of 100s. **ID** Bright blue feet diagnostic,
head and neck white finely streaked brown,
rest of underparts white; in flight from below
wing-linings white with narrow black bar near
leading edge. Juv much darker, head, neck and
foreparts sooty brown, patch on mantle whitish,
wing-linings and lower underparts whitish, feet dull
blue-grey, bill dusky. **SS** Brown and Peruvian Boobies.

Peruvian Booby *Sula variegata* `LC`
Piquero Peruano
Uncommon resident (possibly common during
El Niño events).

L 74 cm (29"). Monotypic.
Near-shore and offshore waters, rarely
pelagic. Cold Humboldt Current species from
S. **ID** Recalls Blue-footed Booby but slightly
smaller; head, neck and underparts entirely white, back and
wings profusely dotted white, legs and feet dull blue-grey,
eyes red. Juv and imm very like respective ages of Blue-footed
Booby but duller, more uniform, no whitish patch on mantle.

Masked Booby *Sula dactylatra* `LC`
Piquero Enmascarado
Breeds on Islas San Andrés and Malpelo, elsewhere
non-breeding migrant from N (also S?).

L 86 cm (34"). Races *dactylatra*[A],
personata[B] (?). Highly
pelagic; more numerous
in Caribbean; does not
follow fishing trawlers. **ID** Large. Ad plumage
white, bill yellow to olive-yellow surrounded
black, legs dull orange-yellow, flight feathers
and tail black, in flight wing-linings white. Juv
dark brown head and neck recall ad Brown Booby
but differs in white nuchal collar, in flight from
below wing-linings white, dark carpal patch extends
as narrow dark line to body. **SS** Nazca Booby;
juv Blue-footed Booby.

Nazca Booby *Sula granti* `LC`
Piquero de Nazca `VU`
Breeds on Isla Malpelo.

L 84 cm (33"). Monotypic. Pelagic;
infrequent near Pacific coast (Cabo
Marzo, Chocó, photos Sept). Breeds on steep
cliffs, and may feed closer to colonies than
Masked Booby. **ID** Large; very like Masked Booby differing
in bill orange to pinkish (not yellow), becoming yellowish at
tip, legs dull olive, and central tail feathers white. Juv like juv
Masked (bills greyish in both species) but white collar narrower
and less complete, overall greyer brown. **Voice** Reedy whistles,
hisses and 'quacks' at breeding colony. **SS** Juv Blue-footed and
Brown Boobies. **TN** Formerly regarded as race of Masked Booby.

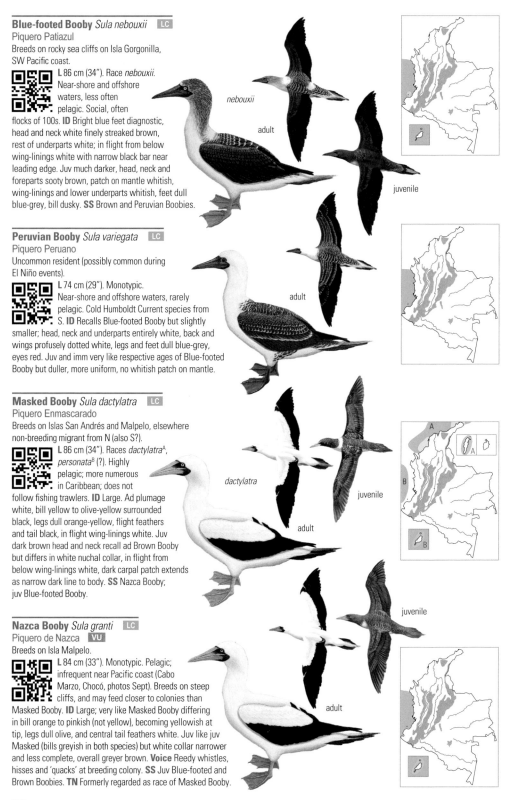

PHALACROCORACIDAE
Cormorants
34 extant species, 2 in region + 1 vagrant

A widespread and ancient lineage of aquatic birds found worldwide. They capture fish in underwater pursuit, float low in water, and patter to get airborne but are strong fliers. They often perch with wings spread wide to dry their non-waterproof plumage. Marine species nest colonially on rocky cliffs, freshwater species in trees. Generic placement of New World cormorants unresolved; traditionally *Phalacrocorax*.

Guanay Cormorant *Leucocarbo bougainvilliorum* NT
Guanay
Rare visitor.

L 74 cm (29"). Monotypic. Marine species occurring near shore to well out at sea. Breeds in cold Humboldt Current waters, disperses N irregularly in small numbers, possibly associated with El Niño events. **ID** Ad non-br blackish with unmistakable white central underparts, bare red face. Ad br similar but short crest, white plumes over eyes. Juv duller, tinged brownish. **SS** Neotropic Cormorant.

Double-crested Cormorant *Nannopterum auritum* LC
Cormorán Orejudo
Vagrant (Islas San Andrés and Providencia).

L 84 cm (33"). Race unknown. Sight records, Jan, Feb (Isla San Andrés), Oct (Isla Providencia). Freshwater and coastal habitats. To 100 m. **ID** Ad non-br orange chin patch rounded at rear, no white outline. Juv lores and gular patch orange-yellow, underparts pale brown. **SS** Easily confused with Neotropic Cormorant; ad and imm differ in larger size, shorter tail (most noticeable in flight), chin patch shape, and colour of lores.

Neotropic Cormorant *Nannopterum brasilianum* LC
Cormorán Neotropical
Common resident.

L 64 cm (25"). Race *brasilianum*. Freshwater and coastal habitats; more numerous inland, mainly lowlands but wanders widely. To 3400 m. **ID** Long tail (as long as neck); short bill. Ad br gular patch and facial skin dull orange-yellow (non-br duller), chin patch pointed at rear, outlined white. Juv breast dark brown, minimal orange on chin, no orange on lores, no white gular line. **Voice** Low grunting. **SS** On Caribbean islands cf. Double-crested Cormorant.

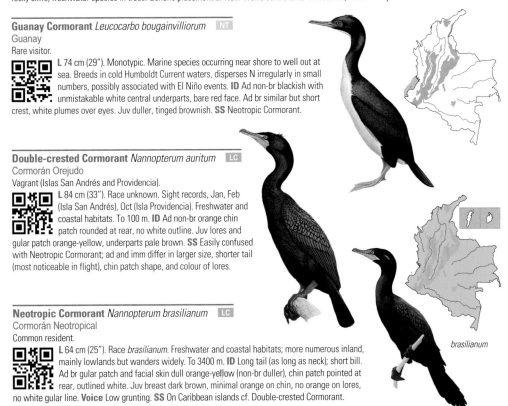

brasilianum

ANHINGIDAE
Darters
4 extant species, 1 in region

The Anhinga and Old World darters are a small family of mainly freshwater birds found nearly worldwide in warmer latitudes. They pursue fish underwater and spear them with their long pointed bill. Anhingas often swim with only their head and neck above the water, a habit earning them the name 'snakebird'. Their plumage is not waterproof, and they patter across the water surface to become airborne.

Anhinga *Anhinga anhinga* LC
Pato-aguja Americano
Fairly common resident.

L 86 cm (34"). Race *anhinga*. Freshwater lakes, oxbows, sluggish rivers, swamps; fewer in coastal habitats. To 1000 m (vagrant 3000 m). Often perches high in open on dead branch over water with wings held open to dry. Soars well, wings held flat. Boreal populations migratory. **ID** Slender; long skinny neck, pointed bill, long buff-tipped tail. ♂ mainly black, silvery-dotted wings, large silvery-grey shoulder patch. ♀ foreparts dingy greyish brown. Juv like ♀ but duller.

anhinga

♂

♀

BURHINIDAE
Thick-knees
10 extant species, 1 in region

A small but nearly worldwide family notably absent from North America, New Zealand and the Pacific. Usually just one species per region. Thick-knees have long legs, unusually large eyes and robust bodies. They resemble over-sized plovers but differ in their nocturnal behaviour and complete independence from water.

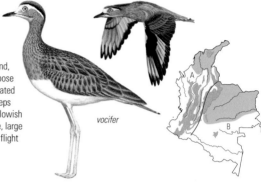

Double-striped Thick-knee *Burhinus bistriatus* `LC`
Alcaraván Venezolano
Local resident (easily overlooked).

L 46 cm (18"). Races *pediacus*[A], *vocifer*[B]. Dry grassland, pastures, open arid scrub. To 900 m. Singles, pairs, loose groups, rest on ground by day in sun, or shade of isolated tree but vigilant, moving away with quick graceful steps if pressed. Active and noisy after dark; taxi to take off. **ID** Long yellowish legs, cryptic plumage, white eyebrow bordered above by black line, large yellow eyes (black 'brow' forms 'frown' over eye in bright light); in flight white wing stripe, white on sides of tail. **Voice** Loud strident "kee-kee-kee…" recalls Southern Lapwing.

vocifer

HAEMATOPODIDAE
Oystercatchers
9 extant species, 1 in region

Small, nearly worldwide family found mostly along low- to mid-latitude sea coasts and inland in Patagonia. Oystercatchers are robust shorebirds with long chisel-tipped coral-red beaks used to open oysters and shellfish, and pry limpets from wave-washed rocks. They lack a hind toe.

American Oystercatcher *Haematopus palliatus* `LC`
Ostrero-pío Americano

Two subspecies in two subspecies groups; one in Colombia.

American Oystercatcher *Haematopus (palliatus) palliatus*
Local resident.
L 43 cm (17"). One subspecies in group. Sandy or gravel beaches, muddy or rocky tidal areas. To 100 m. Singles or pairs, conspicuous, generally apart from other shorebirds. **ID** Large black-and-white shorebird, red bill; white wing stripe and rump visible on flushing. **Voice** Sometimes noisy, shrill insistent whistled "kleee".

RECURVIROSTRIDAE
Avocets and Stilts
7 extant species, 1 in region + 1 vagrant

Small family of graceful waders that occur at shallow-water wetlands in warm to temperate regions. Notable for long, stilt-like legs, needle bills (stilts) or recurved bills (avocets) and bold patterns.

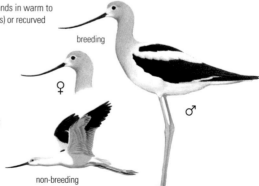

breeding

American Avocet *Recurvirostra americana* `LC`
Avoceta Americana
Vagrant (Caribbean islands and coast).

L 46 cm (18"). Monotypic. Shallow freshwater and coastal lagoons. Records May and Nov 2011 and Nov 2017, Isla Providencia, Oct 2019, Isla San Andrés; also Isla Salamanca (E of Barranquilla). Possible anywhere on Caribbean coast. **ID** Ad non-br large black-and-white wader, head and neck pale grey, long thin upturned bill, long grey legs. Ad br (unlikely) head, neck and breast orange-buff. **Voice** Far-carrying "kleek". **SS** Black-necked Stilt.

♀

♂

non-breeding

Black-winged Stilt *Himantopus himantopus* `LC`
Cigüeñuela Alinegra

Five subspecies in five subspecies groups; one in Colombia.

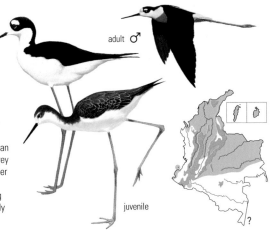

adult ♂

Black-necked Stilt *Himantopus (himantopus) mexicanus*
Common resident.

L 38 cm (15"). One subspecies in group. Brackish and freshwater lagoons, marshes. To 1500 m (rarely 2600 m or higher). Marked seasonal movements; mostly present last half of year on Caribbean islands. Pairs or small groups wade in shallow water, pick tiny prey from surface of water or mud. Breeds in small colonies. **ID** Slender elegant wader; long rosy legs, needle bill, lower back, rump and tail white; ♀ back tinged brownish. **Voice** Noisy; strident yelping "kek .. kek ..". **TN** Taxonomy unresolved; New World birds usually regarded as separate species.

juvenile

CHARADRIIDAE
Plovers

71 extant species, 10 in region

Worldwide family whose members recall sandpipers but are more robust and have shorter thicker bills. Found along seashores and other bodies of water but generally do not wade or probe mud; a few occur in short dry grassland or on sandbars. More than half of those found in Colombia are boreal migrants.

Grey Plover (Black-bellied Plover) *Pluvialis squatarola* `LC`
Chorlito Gris
Common boreal migrant.

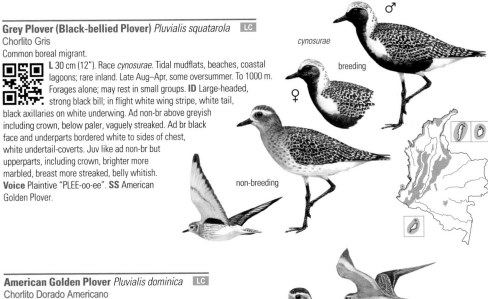

♂

cynosurae

breeding

♀

L 30 cm (12"). Race *cynosurae*. Tidal mudflats, beaches, coastal lagoons; rare inland. Late Aug–Apr, some oversummer. To 1000 m. Forages alone; may rest in small groups. **ID** Large-headed, strong black bill; in flight white wing stripe, white tail, black axillaries on white underwing. Ad non-br above greyish including crown, below paler, vaguely streaked. Ad br black face and underparts bordered white to sides of chest, white undertail-coverts. Juv like ad non-br but upperparts, including crown, brighter more marbled, breast more streaked, belly whitish. **Voice** Plaintive "PLEE-oo-ee". **SS** American Golden Plover.

non-breeding

American Golden Plover *Pluvialis dominica* `LC`
Chorlito Dorado Americano
Uncommon boreal passage migrant.

L 28 cm (11"). Monotypic. Short-grass fields, less often dry coastal mudflats; most records Sept–Dec, fewer Feb–Apr. To 3400 m. Singles or small groups.
ID All plumages resemble Grey Plover but slightly smaller, more delicate, head smaller, bill thinner. In flight tail dark, wings uniform, underwing plain grey (including axillaries). Ad br black undertail-coverts, broad white neck stripe. Juv dark cap, softly freckled breast, grey belly.
Voice High plaintive "QUEE'dle".

breeding

non-breeding

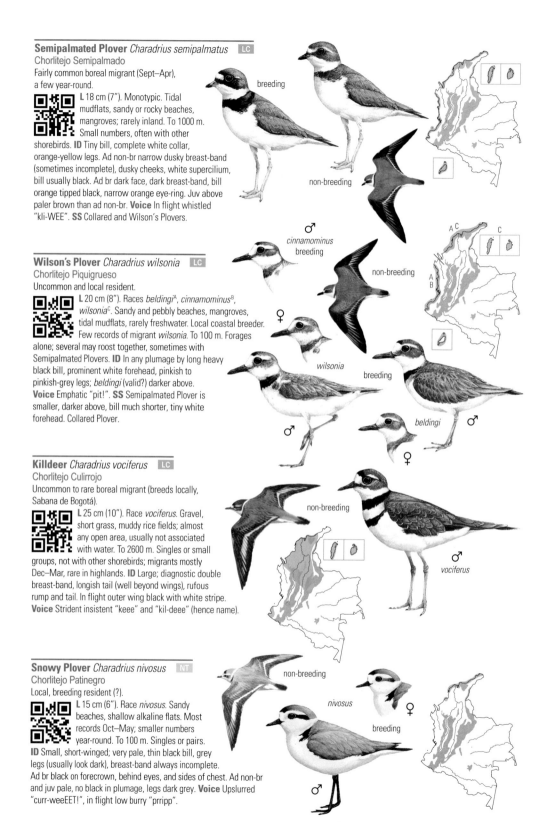

Semipalmated Plover *Charadrius semipalmatus* `LC`
Chorlitejo Semipalmado

Fairly common boreal migrant (Sept–Apr), a few year-round.

L 18 cm (7"). Monotypic. Tidal mudflats, sandy or rocky beaches, mangroves; rarely inland. To 1000 m. Small numbers, often with other shorebirds. **ID** Tiny bill, complete white collar, orange-yellow legs. Ad non-br narrow dusky breast-band (sometimes incomplete), dusky cheeks, white supercilium, bill usually black. Ad br dark face, dark breast-band, bill orange tipped black, narrow orange eye-ring. Juv above paler brown than ad non-br. **Voice** In flight whistled "kli-WEE". **SS** Collared and Wilson's Plovers.

breeding

non-breeding

Wilson's Plover *Charadrius wilsonia* `LC`
Chorlitejo Piquigrueso

Uncommon and local resident.

L 20 cm (8"). Races *beldingi*[A], *cinnamominus*[B], *wilsonia*[C]. Sandy and pebbly beaches, mangroves, tidal mudflats, rarely freshwater. Local coastal breeder. Few records of migrant *wilsonia*. To 100 m. Forages alone; several may roost together, sometimes with Semipalmated Plovers. **ID** In any plumage by long heavy black bill, prominent white forehead, pinkish to pinkish-grey legs; *beldingi* (valid?) darker above. **Voice** Emphatic "pit!". **SS** Semipalmated Plover is smaller, darker above, bill much shorter, tiny white forehead. Collared Plover.

♂ *cinnamominus* breeding

non-breeding

♀ *wilsonia*

wilsonia breeding

♂

beldingi ♂

♀

Killdeer *Charadrius vociferus* `LC`
Chorlitejo Culirrojo

Uncommon to rare boreal migrant (breeds locally, Sabana de Bogotá).

L 25 cm (10"). Race *vociferus*. Gravel, short grass, muddy rice fields; almost any open area, usually not associated with water. To 2600 m. Singles or small groups, not with other shorebirds; migrants mostly Dec–Mar, rare in highlands. **ID** Large; diagnostic double breast-band, longish tail (well beyond wings), rufous rump and tail. In flight outer wing black with white stripe. **Voice** Strident insistent "keee" and "kil-deee" (hence name).

non-breeding

♂ *vociferus*

Snowy Plover *Charadrius nivosus* `NT`
Chorlitejo Patinegro

Local, breeding resident (?).

L 15 cm (6"). Race *nivosus*. Sandy beaches, shallow alkaline flats. Most records Oct–May; smaller numbers year-round. To 100 m. Singles or pairs. **ID** Small, short-winged; very pale, thin black bill, grey legs (usually look dark), breast-band always incomplete. Ad br black on forecrown, behind eyes, and sides of chest. Ad non-br and juv pale, no black in plumage, legs dark grey. **Voice** Upslurred "curr-weeEET!", in flight low burry "prripp".

non-breeding

nivosus ♀

breeding

♂

Collared Plover *Charadrius collaris* `LC`
Chorlitejo Collarejo
Common resident.

L 15 cm (6"). Monotypic. Sand and gravel bars along larger rivers, mudflats, beaches, short grassy fields. Singles or pairs; marked seasonal movements, especially out of *llanos* during high water. **ID** Much like Semipalmated Plover. Ad br differs in no white collar on hindneck, dull pinkish legs, thinner all-black bill, cinnamon rear crown and nape. **Voice** Brief "pit" or "chit". **SS** Smallest, daintiest *Charadrius* plover and the only one regularly inland; Wilson's Plover.

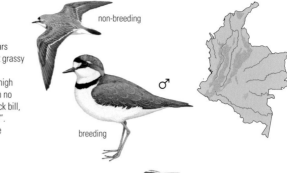

non-breeding

♂

breeding

Pied Lapwing *Hoploxypterus cayanus* `LC`
Pellar Playero
Common resident.

L 23 cm (9"). Monotypic. Sandbars on larger rivers, muddy borders to freshwater pools. To 500 m. Scattered pairs; marked seasonal movements during high water. Elegant little shorebird that stands erect, then runs ahead a short distance, stopping abruptly with a dip. **ID** Unmistakable; bold black-and-white pattern, red eye-ring and legs. **Voice** Flushes with soft reedy "whee-whuu"; chattered clicking "calee-calee-calee-…" in excitement. **TN** Usually in genus *Vanellus*.

Southern Lapwing *Vanellus chilensis* `LC`
Pellar Teru-teru

Four subspecies in two subspecies groups; one in Colombia.

cayennensis

Cayenne Lapwing *Vanellus (chilensis) cayennensis*
Common resident.
L 36 cm (14"). Race *cayennensis*. Short grassy fields, open areas, golf courses, airports; infrequently near water. To 3300 m. Singles, pairs, loosely associated groups; conspicuous, noisy, bold; quick to sound an alarm. Some seasonal movements in *llanos*. **ID** Rounded black-and-white wings, loose bounding flight, at rest black foreface, black chest, upperparts brownish grey. **Voice** Loud scolding "keek, keek …" and "kee, kee …" at slightest disturbance. **SS** Andean Lapwing.

Andean Lapwing *Vanellus resplendens* `LC`
Pellar Andino
Local and uncommon resident.

L 36 cm (14"). Monotypic. Dry fields, open dry to boggy terrain, *páramo*, lake shores. 2500–3800 m (usually > 3000 m). Singles, pairs, occasionally small groups; quieter, more sedate, and less conspicuous than Southern Lapwing. **ID** Wing and tail pattern like Southern Lapwing but upperparts dark bottle-green, no black on face or breast, pinkish legs shorter (feet do not project). **Voice** Recalls Southern Lapwing but higher-pitched, shrill, tern-like.

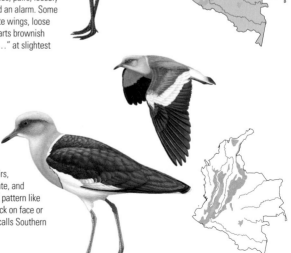

JACANIDAE
Jacanas
8 extant species, 1 in region

A small nearly worldwide family found in warmer latitudes. Jacanas are characterized by delicate proportions, extraordinarily long toes that enable them to walk over floating vegetation, a leathery frontal shield and small wing spur. New World species are polyandrous, ♂♂ incubate eggs and raise the precocial young.

Wattled Jacana *Jacana jacana*
Gallito-de-ciénaga Suramericano

Six subspecies in two subspecies groups; both in Colombia.

Black-backed Jacana *Jacana (jacana) hypomelaena*
Common resident.
L 23 cm (9"). One subspecies in group. Shallow freshwater marshes, coastal and inland wetlands. To 1000 m. **ID** Mostly black, bold lemon-yellow wings in fluttery butterfly-like flight. Juv similar to Chestnut-backed Jacana.

Chestnut-backed Jacana *Jacana (jacana) jacana*
Common resident.
L 23 cm (9"). Races *melanopygia*[A], *intermedia*[B], *scapularis*[C], *peruviana*[D], *jacana*[E] (?). Marshes, rice fields, oxbows and pools with floating vegetation. To 1400 m (rarely 2900 m). Conspicuous; walk in open on floating vegetation. Sharp-eyed, noisily mobs predators (anacondas; caimans). Flushes low over marsh, stiff quick wingbeats alternating with short glides as they scatter like bright yellow butterflies. **ID** Chestnut upperparts, yellow flight feathers. Juv striped head, white underparts. **Voice** Lifts wings when disturbed; loud complaining "kee-kick, kee-kick …" in protest.

intermedia

SCOLOPACIDAE
Sandpipers and allies
91 extant species, 34 in region + 2 vagrants

A large worldwide family notable for slender proportions and thin bills. Most species breed in pairs on the Arctic tundra or in boreal forest, but for the remainder of the year gather in flocks of 100s to 1000s along sea coasts or other lowland bodies of water. Identification is challenging and often requires recognizing the plumage stage, i.e. breeding, non-breeding, or juvenile, before accurate identification can be made. 1st-y birds often oversummer well S of breeding grounds.

Upland Sandpiper *Bartramia longicauda*
Correlimos Sabanero
Uncommon passage migrant.

L 30 cm (12"). Monotypic. Dry short grassland, pastures, burned fields, airfields; not associated with water. To 3500 m. Mostly Sept–Oct and Feb–May. Singles or small scattered groups; holds wing up stiffly upon alighting; erect posture. **ID** Cryptic plumage; thin neck, small head with prominent black eyes, thin yellowish bill, relatively long yellow legs. **Voice** Clear whistled "quip-ip-ip-ip" in flight. **SS** Buff-breasted Sandpiper (short legs).

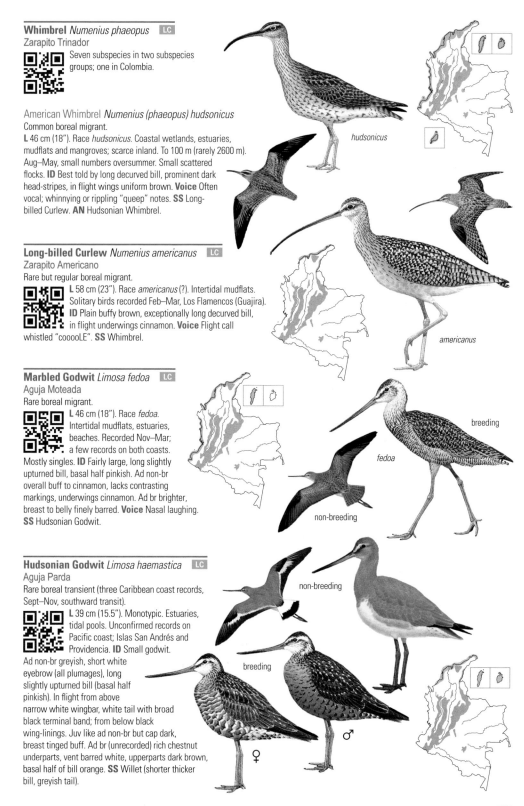

Whimbrel *Numenius phaeopus* `LC`
Zarapito Trinador

Seven subspecies in two subspecies groups; one in Colombia.

American Whimbrel *Numenius (phaeopus) hudsonicus*
Common boreal migrant.
L 46 cm (18"). Race *hudsonicus*. Coastal wetlands, estuaries, mudflats and mangroves; scarce inland. To 100 m (rarely 2600 m). Aug–May, small numbers oversummer. Small scattered flocks. **ID** Best told by long decurved bill, prominent dark head-stripes, in flight wings uniform brown. **Voice** Often vocal; whinnying or rippling "queep" notes. **SS** Long-billed Curlew. **AN** Hudsonian Whimbrel.

hudsonicus

Long-billed Curlew *Numenius americanus* `LC`
Zarapito Americano
Rare but regular boreal migrant.
L 58 cm (23"). Race *americanus* (?). Intertidal mudflats. Solitary birds recorded Feb–Mar, Los Flamencos (Guajira). **ID** Plain buffy brown, exceptionally long decurved bill, in flight underwings cinnamon. **Voice** Flight call whistled "cooooLE". **SS** Whimbrel.

americanus

Marbled Godwit *Limosa fedoa* `LC`
Aguja Moteada
Rare boreal migrant.
L 46 cm (18"). Race *fedoa*. Intertidal mudflats, estuaries, beaches. Recorded Nov–Mar; a few records on both coasts. Mostly singles. **ID** Fairly large, long slightly upturned bill, basal half pinkish. Ad non-br overall buff to cinnamon, lacks contrasting markings, underwings cinnamon. Ad br brighter, breast to belly finely barred. **Voice** Nasal laughing. **SS** Hudsonian Godwit.

breeding

fedoa

non-breeding

Hudsonian Godwit *Limosa haemastica* `LC`
Aguja Parda
Rare boreal transient (three Caribbean coast records, Sept–Nov, southward transit).
L 39 cm (15.5"). Monotypic. Estuaries, tidal pools. Unconfirmed records on Pacific coast; Islas San Andrés and Providencia. **ID** Small godwit. Ad non-br greyish, short white eyebrow (all plumages), long slightly upturned bill (basal half pinkish). In flight from above narrow white wingbar, white tail with broad black terminal band; from below black wing-linings. Juv like ad non-br but cap dark, breast tinged buff. Ad br (unrecorded) rich chestnut underparts, vent barred white, upperparts dark brown, basal half of bill orange. **SS** Willet (shorter thicker bill, greyish tail).

non-breeding

breeding

♂

♀

Ruddy Turnstone *Arenaria interpres* `LC`
Vuelvepiedras Rojizo
Common boreal migrant.

L 24 cm (9.5"). Race *morinella*. Rocky and sandy beaches, mudflats, harbours. Sept–May, smaller numbers oversummer. Variable-sized flocks of their own, or with other shorebirds. Flips pebbles and debris in search of prey. **ID** Ad non-br retains echo of bold tricoloured ad br plumage; dark chest, pale head. Juv duller, head and sides of throat pale. In all plumages short orange legs, short dark bill, bold striped wing pattern in flight. **Voice** In flight, short chuckling "tuk-tuk-i-tuk-tuk".

breeding

morinella

non-breeding

Red Knot *Calidris canutus* `NT`
Playero Rojizo
Uncommon boreal migrant.

L 27 cm (10.5"). Races *roselaari*, *rufa* (presumed). Intertidal mudflats, sandy beaches. Aug–May, a few oversummer. Singles or small groups, often with other shorebirds. **ID** Ad non-br relatively large compact *Calidris*, mostly grey, lower underparts whitish, flanks lightly barred, short dull yellowish legs, bill stout at base. In flight greyish-white rump and tail, narrow white wing stripe, uniformly pale grey underwing. Ad br above grey, below brick-red. **SS** Stilt Sandpiper; Dunlin.

non-breeding

breeding

rufa

Surfbird *Calidris virgata* `LC`
Chorlo de Rompientes
Scarce boreal migrant.

L 25 cm (10"). Monotypic. Rocky coasts and beaches. Scattered records, especially El Valle to Nuquí, Buenaventura Bay; late Aug–Apr (most records Sept–Oct). Singles or 2–3, sometimes with Ruddy Turnstones. **ID** Ad non-br mostly dark grey, belly whitish, sturdy yellow legs, bill black, yellowish at base; in flight white wing stripe (from above, mostly white below), white tail with black distal half. Ad br densely barred grey and white below, rusty wing-coverts. **SS** Wandering Tattler (p. 162).

non-breeding

breeding

Ruff *Calidris pugnax* `LC`
Combatiente
Eurasian vagrant.

L ♂ 28 cm (11"), ♀ 23 cm (9"). Monotypic. Shallow coastal or inland lagoons; two Caribbean coast sightings, one old 'Bogotá' specimen. **ID** Long yellowish legs, small head, humpbacked shape. Ad non-br short bill pale orange basally, whitish lores and frontlet, upperparts scaly. In flight underwings mostly white, basal half of tail white on sides, narrowly dark in centre forming white U around uppertail-coverts. Ad br ♂ (very unlikely), ruff black to rufous; ♀ smaller, variable. Juv like ad non-br but quite buffy. **SS** Size differences confusing. Pectoral Sandpiper; Lesser Yellowlegs.

non-breeding

♂

breeding

♀

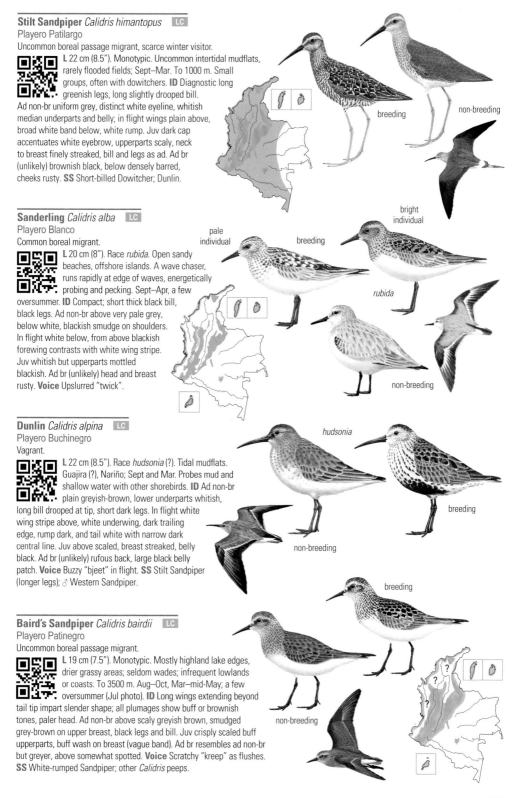

Stilt Sandpiper *Calidris himantopus* LC
Playero Patilargo
Uncommon boreal passage migrant, scarce winter visitor.
L 22 cm (8.5"). Monotypic. Uncommon intertidal mudflats, rarely flooded fields; Sept–Mar. To 1000 m. Small groups, often with dowitchers. **ID** Diagnostic long greenish legs, long slightly drooped bill. Ad non-br uniform grey, distinct white eyeline, whitish median underparts and belly; in flight wings plain above, broad white band below, white rump. Juv dark cap accentuates white eyebrow, upperparts scaly, neck to breast finely streaked, bill and legs as ad. Ad br (unlikely) brownish black, below densely barred, cheeks rusty. **SS** Short-billed Dowitcher; Dunlin.

breeding

non-breeding

bright individual

Sanderling *Calidris alba* LC
Playero Blanco
Common boreal migrant.
L 20 cm (8"). Race *rubida*. Open sandy beaches, offshore islands. A wave chaser, runs rapidly at edge of waves, energetically probing and pecking. Sept–Apr, a few oversummer. **ID** Compact; short thick black bill, black legs. Ad non-br above very pale grey, below white, blackish smudge on shoulders. In flight white below, from above blackish forewing contrasts with white wing stripe. Juv whitish but upperparts mottled blackish. Ad br (unlikely) head and breast rusty. **Voice** Upslurred "twick".

pale individual

breeding

rubida

non-breeding

Dunlin *Calidris alpina* LC
Playero Buchinegro
Vagrant.
L 22 cm (8.5"). Race *hudsonia* (?). Tidal mudflats. Guajira (?), Nariño; Sept and Mar. Probes mud and shallow water with other shorebirds. **ID** Ad non-br plain greyish-brown, lower underparts whitish, long bill drooped at tip, short dark legs. In flight white wing stripe above, white underwing, dark trailing edge, rump dark, and tail white with narrow dark central line. Juv above scaled, breast streaked, belly black. Ad br (unlikely) rufous back, large black belly patch. **Voice** Buzzy "bjeet" in flight. **SS** Stilt Sandpiper (longer legs); ♂ Western Sandpiper.

hudsonia

breeding

non-breeding

breeding

Baird's Sandpiper *Calidris bairdii* LC
Playero Patinegro
Uncommon boreal passage migrant.
L 19 cm (7.5"). Monotypic. Mostly highland lake edges, drier grassy areas; seldom wades; infrequent lowlands or coasts. To 3500 m. Aug–Oct, Mar–mid-May; a few oversummer (Jul photo). **ID** Long wings extending beyond tail tip impart slender shape; all plumages show buff or brownish tones, paler head. Ad non-br above scaly greyish brown, smudged grey-brown on upper breast, black legs and bill. Juv crisply scaled buff upperparts, buff wash on breast (vague band). Ad br resembles ad non-br but greyer, above somewhat spotted. **Voice** Scratchy "kreep" as flushes. **SS** White-rumped Sandpiper; other *Calidris* peeps.

non-breeding

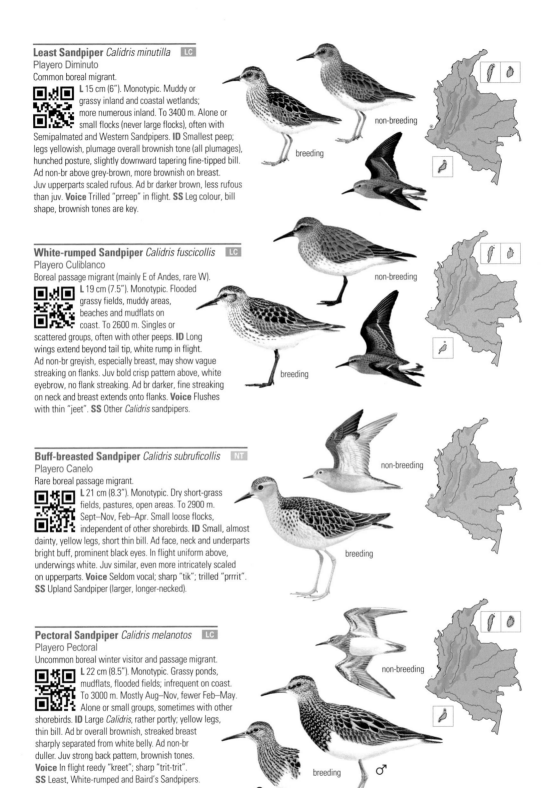

Least Sandpiper *Calidris minutilla* `LC`
Playero Diminuto
Common boreal migrant.
L 15 cm (6"). Monotypic. Muddy or grassy inland and coastal wetlands; more numerous inland. To 3400 m. Alone or small flocks (never large flocks), often with Semipalmated and Western Sandpipers. **ID** Smallest peep; legs yellowish, plumage overall brownish tone (all plumages), hunched posture, slightly downward tapering fine-tipped bill. Ad non-br above grey-brown, more brownish on breast. Juv upperparts scaled rufous. Ad br darker brown, less rufous than juv. **Voice** Trilled "prreep" in flight. **SS** Leg colour, bill shape, brownish tones are key.

non-breeding
breeding

White-rumped Sandpiper *Calidris fuscicollis* `LC`
Playero Culiblanco
Boreal passage migrant (mainly E of Andes, rare W).
L 19 cm (7.5"). Monotypic. Flooded grassy fields, muddy areas, beaches and mudflats on coast. To 2600 m. Singles or scattered groups, often with other peeps. **ID** Long wings extend beyond tail tip, white rump in flight. Ad non-br greyish, especially breast, may show vague streaking on flanks. Juv bold crisp pattern above, white eyebrow, no flank streaking. Ad br darker, fine streaking on neck and breast extends onto flanks. **Voice** Flushes with thin "jeet". **SS** Other *Calidris* sandpipers.

non-breeding
breeding

Buff-breasted Sandpiper *Calidris subruficollis* `NT`
Playero Canelo
Rare boreal passage migrant.
L 21 cm (8.3"). Monotypic. Dry short-grass fields, pastures, open areas. To 2900 m. Sept–Nov, Feb–Apr. Small loose flocks, independent of other shorebirds. **ID** Small, almost dainty, yellow legs, short thin bill. Ad face, neck and underparts bright buff, prominent black eyes. In flight uniform above, underwings white. Juv similar, even more intricately scaled on upperparts. **Voice** Seldom vocal; sharp "tik"; trilled "prrrit". **SS** Upland Sandpiper (larger, longer-necked).

non-breeding
breeding

Pectoral Sandpiper *Calidris melanotos* `LC`
Playero Pectoral
Uncommon boreal winter visitor and passage migrant.
L 22 cm (8.5"). Monotypic. Grassy ponds, mudflats, flooded fields; infrequent on coast. To 3000 m. Mostly Aug–Nov, fewer Feb–May. Alone or small groups, sometimes with other shorebirds. **ID** Large *Calidris*, rather portly; yellow legs, thin bill. Ad br overall brownish, streaked breast sharply separated from white belly. Ad non-br duller. Juv strong back pattern, brownish tones. **Voice** In flight reedy "kreet"; sharp "trit-trit". **SS** Least, White-rumped and Baird's Sandpipers.

non-breeding
breeding
♂
♀

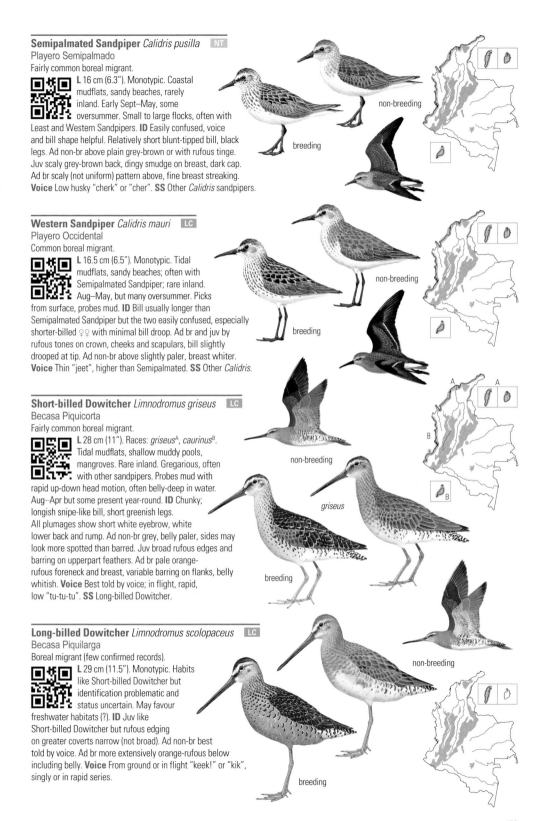

Semipalmated Sandpiper *Calidris pusilla* `NT`
Playero Semipalmado
Fairly common boreal migrant.
L 16 cm (6.3"). Monotypic. Coastal mudflats, sandy beaches, rarely inland. Early Sept–May, some oversummer. Small to large flocks, often with Least and Western Sandpipers. **ID** Easily confused, voice and bill shape helpful. Relatively short blunt-tipped bill, black legs. Ad non-br above plain grey-brown or with rufous tinge. Juv scaly grey-brown back, dingy smudge on breast, dark cap. Ad br scaly (not uniform) pattern above, fine breast streaking. **Voice** Low husky "cherk" or "cher". **SS** Other *Calidris* sandpipers.

non-breeding

breeding

Western Sandpiper *Calidris mauri* `LC`
Playero Occidental
Common boreal migrant.
L 16.5 cm (6.5"). Monotypic. Tidal mudflats, sandy beaches; often with Semipalmated Sandpiper; rare inland. Aug–May, but many oversummer. Picks from surface, probes mud. **ID** Bill usually longer than Semipalmated Sandpiper but the two easily confused, especially shorter-billed ♀♀ with minimal bill droop. Ad br and juv by rufous tones on crown, cheeks and scapulars, bill slightly drooped at tip. Ad non-br above slightly paler, breast whiter. **Voice** Thin "jeet", higher than Semipalmated. **SS** Other *Calidris*.

non-breeding

breeding

Short-billed Dowitcher *Limnodromus griseus* `LC`
Becasa Piquicorta
Fairly common boreal migrant.
L 28 cm (11"). Races: *griseus*[A], *caurinus*[B]. Tidal mudflats, shallow muddy pools, mangroves. Rare inland. Gregarious, often with other sandpipers. Probes mud with rapid up-down head motion, often belly-deep in water. Aug–Apr but some present year-round. **ID** Chunky; longish snipe-like bill, short greenish legs. All plumages show short white eyebrow, white lower back and rump. Ad non-br grey, belly paler, sides may look more spotted than barred. Juv broad rufous edges and barring on upperpart feathers. Ad br pale orange-rufous foreneck and breast, variable barring on flanks, belly whitish. **Voice** Best told by voice; in flight, rapid, low "tu-tu-tu". **SS** Long-billed Dowitcher.

non-breeding

griseus

breeding

Long-billed Dowitcher *Limnodromus scolopaceus* `LC`
Becasa Piquilarga
Boreal migrant (few confirmed records).
L 29 cm (11.5"). Monotypic. Habits like Short-billed Dowitcher but identification problematic and status uncertain. May favour freshwater habitats (?). **ID** Juv like Short-billed Dowitcher but rufous edging on greater coverts narrow (not broad). Ad non-br best told by voice. Ad br more extensively orange-rufous below including belly. **Voice** From ground or in flight "keek!" or "kik", singly or in rapid series.

non-breeding

breeding

Imperial Snipe *Gallinago imperialis* NT
Becasina Imperial DD
Status unknown.

L 30 cm (12"). Monotypic. One old 'Bogotá' specimen. Unconfirmed sight reports from Boyacá and Cundinamarca. Boggy *páramo*, damp elfin woodland near treeline. Crepuscular, look for it pre-dawn and dusk; c. 3000–3700 m. **ID** Upperparts barred and mottled rufous and black, darker, more rufescent than other snipes, no pale stripes on back, breast mottled, lower underparts dull whitish densely barred brown. **Voice** In Peru flight call "keekeekee"; display with long grating series and soft mechanical swooshing. **SS** Jameson's Snipe (striped back, no strong rufescent tones); Noble and Wilson's Snipes.

Jameson's Snipe *Gallinago jamesoni* LC
Becasina Andina
Local resident.

L 30 cm (12"). Monotypic. Boggy *páramo* with tall grass, moss, sedges. 3200–4000 m (2100–4200 m, Santa Marta Mts). In alarm freezes or scampers away; flushes in straight flight. **ID** Large dark highland snipe, heavy bill, entire underparts coarsely barred, weak head pattern, no rufous or white in tail. **Voice** Circling aerial display at dusk, sustained quivering winnowing (mechanical), louder as passes overhead, accompanied by loud vocal rapid "wic-a, wic-a…" in dive. **TN** Often regarded as race of Fuegian (Cordilleran) Snipe *G. stricklandii*. **AN** Andean Snipe.

Wilson's Snipe *Gallinago delicata* LC
Becasina Común
Fairly common boreal migrant.

L 27 cm (10.5"). Monotypic. Marshes, wet grass, boggy *páramo*. To 3900 m (mostly highlands). No confirmed records E of Andes; Jul–Mar. Probes shallow water and mud. No aerial displays in wintering areas. Not with other shorebirds. **ID** Basal half of bill pale, tip darker, legs yellowish. Near-identical to South American Snipe and doubtfully separable in field; in hand black bars on axillaries wider than white bars (reverse in South American Snipe), some measurements differ slightly; in flight toes do not project beyond tail, whitish tail tips. **Voice** Scratchy "chek" as flushes in rapid zigzag flight. **TN** Until recently considered conspecific with extralimital Common Snipe *G. gallinago*.

South American Snipe *Gallinago paraguaiae* LC
Becasina Suramericana

Two subspecies in two subspecies groups; one in Colombia.

South American Snipe *Gallinago (paraguaiae) paraguaiae*
Local resident.

L 25 cm (10"). One subspecies in group. Wet grass, marshes, muddy lagoon edges. To 400 m (higher?). Aerial winnowing displays, especially rainy May–Jul period in *llanos*, much like Wilson's Snipe, pre-dawn to well after dark, and may continue throughout day. **ID** Doubtfully separable in field from Wilson's Snipe; in hand black bars on axillaries narrower than white ones (reverse in Wilson's Snipe); the two generally separate by range and elevation. **SS** Giant Snipe. **AN** Paraguayan Snipe.

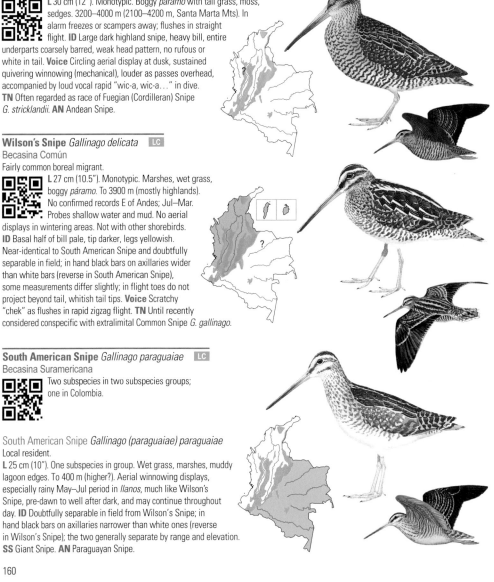

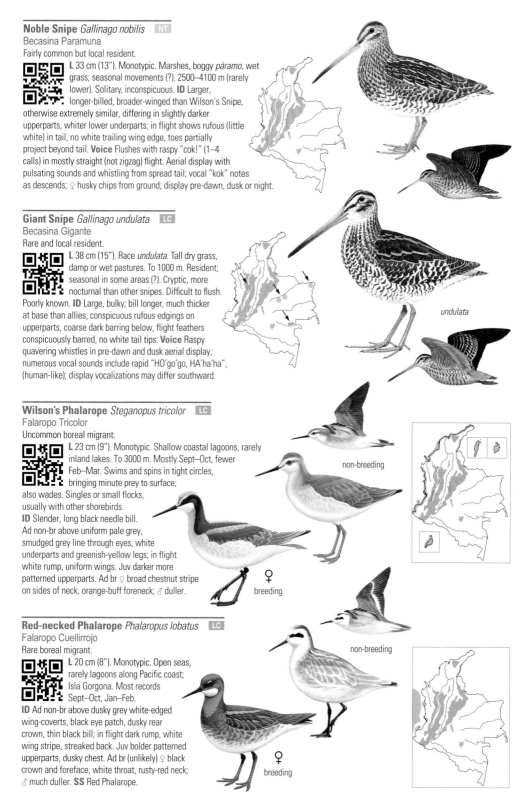

Noble Snipe *Gallinago nobilis* NT
Becasina Paramuna
Fairly common but local resident.

L 33 cm (13"). Monotypic. Marshes, boggy *páramo*, wet grass; seasonal movements (?). 2500–4100 m (rarely lower). Solitary, inconspicuous. **ID** Larger, longer-billed, broader-winged than Wilson's Snipe, otherwise extremely similar, differing in slightly darker upperparts, whiter lower underparts; in flight shows rufous (little white) in tail, no white trailing wing edge, toes partially project beyond tail. **Voice** Flushes with raspy "cok!" (1–4 calls) in mostly straight (not zigzag) flight. Aerial display with pulsating sounds and whistling from spread tail; vocal "kok" notes as descends; ♀ husky chips from ground; display pre-dawn, dusk or night.

Giant Snipe *Gallinago undulata* LC
Becasina Gigante
Rare and local resident.

L 38 cm (15"). Race *undulata*. Tall dry grass, damp or wet pastures. To 1000 m. Resident; seasonal in some areas (?). Cryptic, more nocturnal than other snipes. Difficult to flush. Poorly known. **ID** Large, bulky; bill longer, much thicker at base than allies, conspicuous rufous edgings on upperparts, coarse dark barring below, flight feathers conspicuously barred, no white tail tips. **Voice** Raspy quavering whistles in pre-dawn and dusk aerial display; numerous vocal sounds include rapid "HO'go'go, HA'ha'ha", (human-like); display vocalizations may differ southward.

undulata

Wilson's Phalarope *Steganopus tricolor* LC
Falaropo Tricolor
Uncommon boreal migrant.

L 23 cm (9"). Monotypic. Shallow coastal lagoons, rarely inland lakes. To 3000 m. Mostly Sept–Oct, fewer Feb–Mar. Swims and spins in tight circles, bringing minute prey to surface; also wades. Singles or small flocks, usually with other shorebirds. **ID** Slender, long black needle bill. Ad non-br above uniform pale grey, smudged grey line through eyes, white underparts and greenish-yellow legs; in flight white rump, uniform wings. Juv darker more patterned upperparts. Ad br ♀ broad chestnut stripe on sides of neck, orange-buff foreneck; ♂ duller.

non-breeding

♀
breeding

Red-necked Phalarope *Phalaropus lobatus* LC
Falaropo Cuellirrojo
Rare boreal migrant.

L 20 cm (8"). Monotypic. Open seas, rarely lagoons along Pacific coast; Isla Gorgona. Most records Sept–Oct, Jan–Feb. **ID** Ad non-br above dusky grey white-edged wing-coverts, black eye patch, dusky rear crown, thin black bill; in flight dark rump, white wing stripe, streaked back. Juv bolder patterned upperparts, dusky chest. Ad br (unlikely) ♀ black crown and foreface, white throat, rusty-red neck; ♂ much duller. **SS** Red Phalarope.

non-breeding

♀
breeding

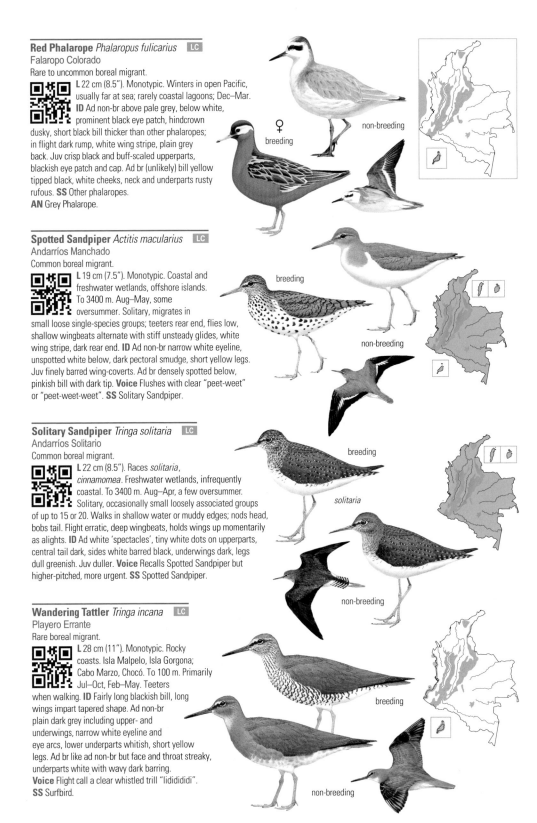

Red Phalarope *Phalaropus fulicarius* LC
Falaropo Colorado
Rare to uncommon boreal migrant.
L 22 cm (8.5"). Monotypic. Winters in open Pacific, usually far at sea; rarely coastal lagoons; Dec–Mar. **ID** Ad non-br above pale grey, below white, prominent black eye patch, hindcrown dusky, short black bill thicker than other phalaropes; in flight dark rump, white wing stripe, plain grey back. Juv crisp black and buff-scaled upperparts, blackish eye patch and cap. Ad br (unlikely) bill yellow tipped black, white cheeks, neck and underparts rusty rufous. **SS** Other phalaropes.
AN Grey Phalarope.

♀
breeding
non-breeding

Spotted Sandpiper *Actitis macularius* LC
Andarríos Manchado
Common boreal migrant.
L 19 cm (7.5"). Monotypic. Coastal and freshwater wetlands, offshore islands. To 3400 m. Aug–May, some oversummer. Solitary, migrates in small loose single-species groups; teeters rear end, flies low, shallow wingbeats alternate with stiff unsteady glides, white wing stripe, dark rear end. **ID** Ad non-br narrow white eyeline, unspotted white below, dark pectoral smudge, short yellow legs. Juv finely barred wing-coverts. Ad br densely spotted below, pinkish bill with dark tip. **Voice** Flushes with clear "peet-weet" or "peet-weet-weet". **SS** Solitary Sandpiper.

breeding
non-breeding

Solitary Sandpiper *Tringa solitaria* LC
Andarríos Solitario
Common boreal migrant.
L 22 cm (8.5"). Races *solitaria*, *cinnamomea*. Freshwater wetlands, infrequently coastal. To 3400 m. Aug–Apr, a few oversummer. Solitary, occasionally small loosely associated groups of up to 15 or 20. Walks in shallow water or muddy edges; nods head, bobs tail. Flight erratic, deep wingbeats, holds wings up momentarily as alights. **ID** Ad white 'spectacles', tiny white dots on upperparts, central tail dark, sides white barred black, underwings dark, legs dull greenish. Juv duller. **Voice** Recalls Spotted Sandpiper but higher-pitched, more urgent. **SS** Spotted Sandpiper.

breeding
solitaria
non-breeding

Wandering Tattler *Tringa incana* LC
Playero Errante
Rare boreal migrant.
L 28 cm (11"). Monotypic. Rocky coasts. Isla Malpelo, Isla Gorgona; Cabo Marzo, Chocó. To 100 m. Primarily Jul–Oct, Feb–May. Teeters when walking. **ID** Fairly long blackish bill, long wings impart tapered shape. Ad non-br plain dark grey including upper- and underwings, narrow white eyeline and eye arcs, lower underparts whitish, short yellow legs. Ad br like ad non-br but face and throat streaky, underparts white with wavy dark barring. **Voice** Flight call a clear whistled trill "lididididi". **SS** Surfbird.

breeding
non-breeding

Willet *Tringa semipalmata* `LC`
Playero Aliblanco

Common boreal migrant.

L 38 cm (15"). Races *semipalmata*[A] (Eastern), *inornata*[B] (Western). Tidal mudflats, mangroves, sandy and rocky beaches, offshore islands. Sept–Apr, many oversummer. Alone or small loose groups, roost or associate with other shorebirds. Strong buoyant flight. **ID** Large robust *Tringa*; stout blackish bill, blue-grey legs. Ad non-br plain grey, short whitish eyebrow, in flight bold black-and-white wings, white rump. Juv plainer and duller. Ad br scattered dark markings on upperparts, irregular barring below. Race *inornata* larger, paler, longer bill and legs. **Voice** Utters 1–3 loud ringing notes as flushes. **SS** Hudsonian Godwit. **TN** Races probably separate species.

Lesser Yellowlegs *Tringa flavipes* `LC`
Patiamarillo Chico

Common boreal migrant.

L 29 cm (10.5"). Monotypic. Coastal lagoons, wetlands, beaches; less numerous inland. To 3400 m. Aug–May, a few year-round. Active wader, noisy, often with Greater Yellowlegs. **ID** Slender, long yellow legs, white rump. Ad non-br similar to Greater Yellowlegs but smaller (size most apparent in direct comparison); key is shorter thinner straight all-dark bill. Juv smooth grey wash on chest. Ad br (unlikely) darker mottled upperparts, neck and chest, sides and flanks minimally barred. **Voice** Gives 1–3 loud "tew" notes, lower, weaker than Greater Yellowlegs.

Greater Yellowlegs *Tringa melanoleuca* `LC`
Patiamarillo Grande

Common boreal migrant.

L 36 cm (14"). Monotypic. Intertidal mudflats, mangroves and beaches; less numerous inland. To 3400 m. Aug–May, a few year-round. Active wader, noisy. **ID** Long yellow legs; much like Lesser Yellowlegs but larger (obvious in direct comparison); best told by longer heavier, slightly upturned bill (longer than head). Juv contrasting pale greyish base to bill (sometimes also ad non-br), finely streaked grey breast. Ad br much brighter, irregular dark barring on flanks. **Voice** Usually 3–4 loud "tew" notes.

LARIDAE
Gulls and Terns

100 extant species, 29 in region + 5 vagrants

Members of this large family occur predominantly on seacoasts, with a few on larger freshwater bodies. Generally gregarious and strong fliers. Most gulls in Colombia are boreal migrants. Gulls take 2–4 years to reach ad plumage and their various plumage stages are confusing. Terns by contrast reach ad plumage in only one or two years and, in Colombia, include breeding residents, migrants, and a few vagrants from southern regions.

Brown Noddy *Anous stolidus* `LC`
Tiñosa Parda

Common resident (at breeding colonies).

L 38 cm (15"). Races *stolidus*[A], *ridgwayi*[B], *galapagensis*[C] (verified records?). Nests in trees on islands off Pacific (Gorgona; Malpelo) and Caribbean (Las Rosas; San Andrés?) coasts. Away from colonies mostly pelagic, gregarious, rarely seen from shore. Rests on buoys, flotsam or ocean. Flies close to surface, splashes for small fish. **ID** Dark brown, white forehead blends into grey crown and nape, flight feathers and tail darker brown (two-toned wings); rounded tail. Juv duller brownish crown. **Voice** Grating croaks. **SS** Black Noddy.

Black Noddy *Anous minutus* LC
Tiñosa Negra
Local resident (rare in Caribbean).
L 36 cm (14"). Races *diamesus*[A], *americanus*[B]. Breeding reported Isla Malpelo (Isla Gorgona?). Habits as Brown Noddy but far fewer records. **ID** Very like Brown Noddy and often confused; differs in blackish (less brown) plumage, longer thinner, straight bill, slightly smaller size, in flight wings uniform. Juv more sharply contrasting white crown. **Voice** Like Brown Noddy.

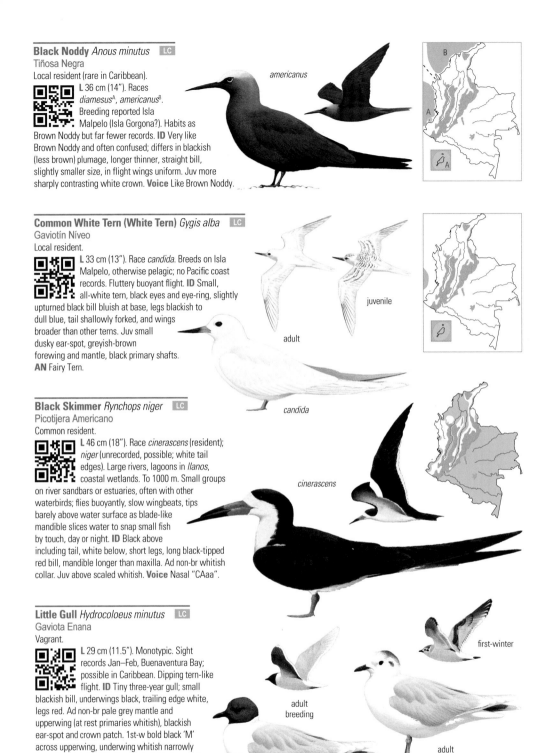

americanus

Common White Tern (White Tern) *Gygis alba* LC
Gaviotín Níveo
Local resident.
L 33 cm (13"). Race *candida*. Breeds on Isla Malpelo, otherwise pelagic; no Pacific coast records. Fluttery buoyant flight. **ID** Small, all-white tern, black eyes and eye-ring, slightly upturned black bill bluish at base, legs blackish to dull blue, tail shallowly forked, and wings broader than other terns. Juv small dusky ear-spot, greyish-brown forewing and mantle, black primary shafts. **AN** Fairy Tern.

juvenile

adult

candida

Black Skimmer *Rynchops niger* LC
Picotijera Americano
Common resident.
L 46 cm (18"). Race *cinerascens* (resident); *niger* (unrecorded, possible; white tail edges). Large rivers, lagoons in *llanos*, coastal wetlands. To 1000 m. Small groups on river sandbars or estuaries, often with other waterbirds; flies buoyantly, slow wingbeats, tips barely above water surface as blade-like mandible slices water to snap small fish by touch, day or night. **ID** Black above including tail, white below, short legs, long black-tipped red bill, mandible longer than maxilla. Ad non-br whitish collar. Juv above scaled whitish. **Voice** Nasal "CAaa".

cinerascens

Little Gull *Hydrocoloeus minutus* LC
Gaviota Enana
Vagrant.
L 29 cm (11.5"). Monotypic. Sight records Jan–Feb, Buenaventura Bay; possible in Caribbean. Dipping tern-like flight. **ID** Tiny three-year gull; small blackish bill, underwings black, trailing edge white, legs red. Ad non-br pale grey mantle and upperwing (at rest primaries whitish), blackish ear-spot and crown patch. 1st-w bold black 'M' across upperwing, underwing whitish narrowly tipped black, tail white tipped black. 2nd-w recalls ad non-br but underwing greyish (not black). Ad br head black.

first-winter

adult breeding

adult non-breeding

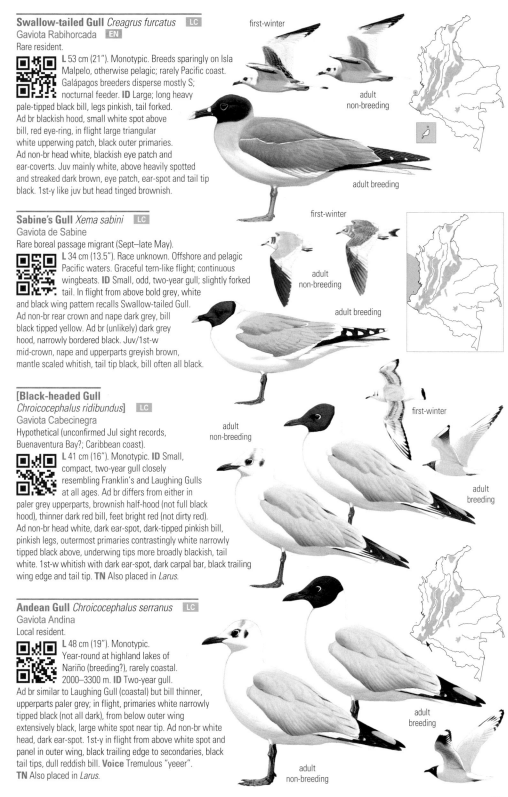

Swallow-tailed Gull *Creagrus furcatus* LC
Gaviota Rabihorcada EN
Rare resident.

L 53 cm (21"). Monotypic. Breeds sparingly on Isla Malpelo, otherwise pelagic; rarely Pacific coast. Galápagos breeders disperse mostly S; nocturnal feeder. **ID** Large; long heavy pale-tipped black bill, legs pinkish, tail forked. Ad br blackish hood, small white spot above bill, red eye-ring, in flight large triangular white upperwing patch, black outer primaries. Ad non-br head white, blackish eye patch and ear-coverts. Juv mainly white, above heavily spotted and streaked dark brown, eye patch, ear-spot and tail tip black. 1st-y like juv but head tinged brownish.

first-winter

adult
non-breeding

adult breeding

Sabine's Gull *Xema sabini* LC
Gaviota de Sabine
Rare boreal passage migrant (Sept–late May).

L 34 cm (13.5"). Race unknown. Offshore and pelagic Pacific waters. Graceful tern-like flight; continuous wingbeats. **ID** Small, odd, two-year gull; slightly forked tail. In flight from above bold grey, white and black wing pattern recalls Swallow-tailed Gull. Ad non-br rear crown and nape dark grey, bill black tipped yellow. Ad br (unlikely) dark grey hood, narrowly bordered black. Juv/1st-w mid-crown, nape and upperparts greyish brown, mantle scaled whitish, tail tip black, bill often all black.

first-winter

adult
non-breeding

adult breeding

[Black-headed Gull
Chroicocephalus ridibundus] LC
Gaviota Cabecinegra
Hypothetical (unconfirmed Jul sight records, Buenaventura Bay?; Caribbean coast).

L 41 cm (16"). Monotypic. **ID** Small, compact, two-year gull closely resembling Franklin's and Laughing Gulls at all ages. Ad br differs from either in paler grey upperparts, brownish half-hood (not full black hood), thinner dark red bill, feet bright red (not dirty red). Ad non-br head white, dark ear-spot, dark-tipped pinkish bill, pinkish legs, outermost primaries contrastingly white narrowly tipped black above, underwing tips more broadly blackish, tail white. 1st-w whitish with dark ear-spot, dark carpal bar, black trailing wing edge and tail tip. **TN** Also placed in *Larus*.

adult
non-breeding

first-winter

adult
breeding

Andean Gull *Chroicocephalus serranus* LC
Gaviota Andina
Local resident.

L 48 cm (19"). Monotypic. Year-round at highland lakes of Nariño (breeding?), rarely coastal. 2000–3300 m. **ID** Two-year gull. Ad br similar to Laughing Gull (coastal) but bill thinner, upperparts paler grey; in flight, primaries white narrowly tipped black (not all dark), from below outer wing extensively black, large white spot near tip. Ad non-br white head, dark ear-spot. 1st-y in flight from above white spot and panel in outer wing, black trailing edge to secondaries, black tail tips, dull reddish bill. **Voice** Tremulous "yeeer". **TN** Also placed in *Larus*.

adult
breeding

adult
non-breeding

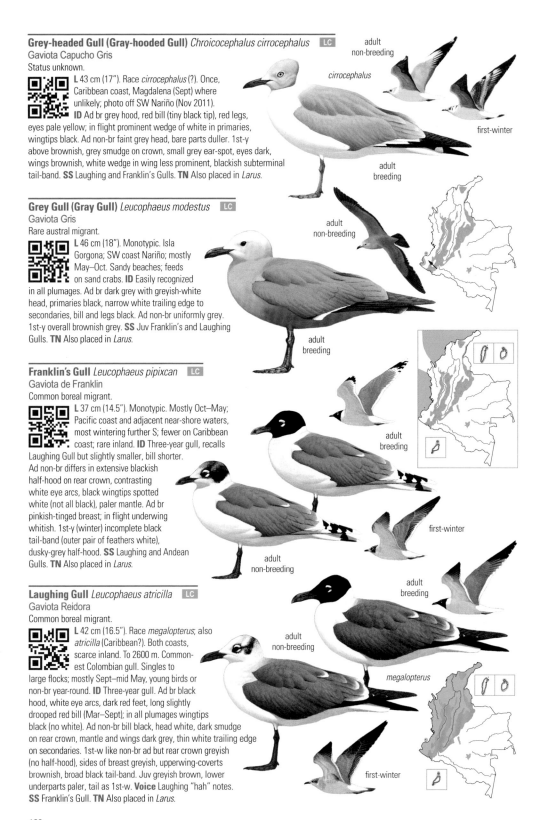

Grey-headed Gull (Gray-hooded Gull) *Chroicocephalus cirrocephalus* LC
Gaviota Capucho Gris
Status unknown.
L 43 cm (17"). Race *cirrocephalus*(?). Once, Caribbean coast, Magdalena (Sept) where unlikely; photo off SW Nariño (Nov 2011). **ID** Ad br grey hood, red bill (tiny black tip), red legs, eyes pale yellow; in flight prominent wedge of white in primaries, wingtips black. Ad non-br faint grey head, bare parts duller. 1st-y above brownish, grey smudge on crown, small grey ear-spot, eyes dark, wings brownish, white wedge in wing less prominent, blackish subterminal tail-band. **SS** Laughing and Franklin's Gulls. **TN** Also placed in *Larus*.

Grey Gull (Gray Gull) *Leucophaeus modestus* LC
Gaviota Gris
Rare austral migrant.
L 46 cm (18"). Monotypic. Isla Gorgona; SW coast Nariño; mostly May–Oct. Sandy beaches; feeds on sand crabs. **ID** Easily recognized in all plumages. Ad br dark grey with greyish-white head, primaries black, narrow white trailing edge to secondaries, bill and legs black. Ad non-br uniformly grey. 1st-y overall brownish grey. **SS** Juv Franklin's and Laughing Gulls. **TN** Also placed in *Larus*.

Franklin's Gull *Leucophaeus pipixcan* LC
Gaviota de Franklin
Common boreal migrant.
L 37 cm (14.5"). Monotypic. Mostly Oct–May; Pacific coast and adjacent near-shore waters, most wintering further S; fewer on Caribbean coast; rare inland. **ID** Three-year gull, recalls Laughing Gull but slightly smaller, bill shorter. Ad non-br differs in extensive blackish half-hood on rear crown, contrasting white eye arcs, black wingtips spotted white (not all black), paler mantle. Ad br pinkish-tinged breast; in flight underwing whitish. 1st-y (winter) incomplete black tail-band (outer pair of feathers white), dusky-grey half-hood. **SS** Laughing and Andean Gulls. **TN** Also placed in *Larus*.

Laughing Gull *Leucophaeus atricilla* LC
Gaviota Reidora
Common boreal migrant.
L 42 cm (16.5"). Race *megalopterus*; also *atricilla* (Caribbean?). Both coasts, scarce inland. To 2600 m. Commonest Colombian gull. Singles to large flocks; mostly Sept–mid May, young birds or non-br year-round. **ID** Three-year gull. Ad br black hood, white eye arcs, dark red feet, long slightly drooped red bill (Mar–Sept); in all plumages wingtips black (no white). Ad non-br bill black, head white, dark smudge on rear crown, mantle and wings dark grey, thin white trailing edge on secondaries. 1st-w like non-br ad but rear crown greyish (no half-hood), sides of breast greyish, upperwing-coverts brownish, broad black tail-band. Juv greyish brown, lower underparts paler, tail as 1st-w. **Voice** Laughing "hah" notes. **SS** Franklin's Gull. **TN** Also placed in *Larus*.

adult non-breeding
cirrocephalus
first-winter
adult breeding

adult non-breeding
adult breeding

adult breeding
first-winter
adult non-breeding

adult breeding
adult non-breeding
megalopterus
first-winter

Belcher's Gull *Larus belcheri* `LC`
Gaviota Sureña
Vagrant.

L 56 cm (22"). Monotypic. Austral breeder; most likely on Pacific coast, but photos of second-year Jan 2017, and subad Dec 2017, at Camarones, Guajira, on Caribbean coast. **ID** Large three-year gull. Ad br black tail-band, all-dark wingtips, red-tipped bill, bright yellow legs. Ad non-br dark brown head. 1st-y head and breast blackish brown, bill pale with black tip, black tail-band. **SS** Kelp Gull. **AN** Band-tailed Gull.

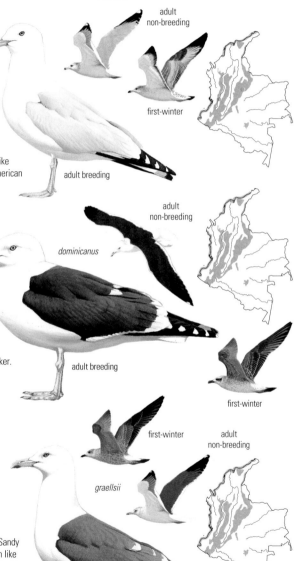

adult breeding

adult non-breeding

first-winter

Ring-billed Gull *Larus delawarensis* `LC`
Gaviota de Delaware
Rare boreal migrant.

L 46 cm (18"). Monotypic. Beaches and estuaries, Nov–Mar; rarely inland. **ID** Three-year gull. Ad br black ring on yellowish bill, pale grey mantle, yellow eyes and legs, black wingtips with small white tips. Ad non-br similar but brownish spots and streaks on crown and hindneck. 2nd-w like ad but neck and underparts more spotted and streaked, incomplete black subterminal tail-band, wingtips lack white. 1st-w dark eyes, pink bill tipped black, variable amount of brown on wings and tail, black tail-band. Juv like 1st-w but browner, dark spotting on wing-coverts. **SS** American Herring Gull; other imm gulls.

adult breeding

Kelp Gull *Larus dominicanus* `LC`
Gavión Cocinero
Very rare visitor.

L 61 cm (24"). Race *dominicanus* (?). Few records Nov–Mar, both coasts. Austral breeder. Beaches. **ID** Large four-year gull. Ad large; white head and tail, black mantle and wings, heavy yellow bill, red spot near tip, greenish-yellow legs, small white spots on wingtip. Juv brownish, bill black. 1st-y paler than juv, head and tail mostly white, tail with black band, legs greyish brown. 2nd-y similar but wings and back darker. **Voice** Laughing notes, accelerating. **SS** Belcher's, Great and Lesser Black-backed Gulls.

adult non-breeding

dominicanus

adult breeding

first-winter

Lesser Black-backed Gull *Larus fuscus* `LC`
Gaviota Sombría

Five subspecies in four subspecies groups; one in Colombia.

first-winter   adult non-breeding

graellsii

Lesser Black-backed Gull *Larus (fuscus) graellsii*
Rare but regular boreal visitor.
L 53 cm (21"). Race *graellsii* (?). W Palearctic species; Nov–early Apr, mainly Caribbean and SW Nariño coasts. Sandy beaches; estuaries. **ID** Medium-sized four-year gull; much like other dark-backed gulls. Ad br upperparts dark grey (not black), small white spots near tip of long wings, red spot on yellow bill, eyes and legs yellowish. Ad non-br similar but variable dark streaking on head and hindneck. 1st- and 2nd-y plumages recall larger Kelp Gull but legs yellow to pinkish (not greyish brown), tail whitish with broad dark band. **SS** American Herring and Great Black-backed Gulls.

adult breeding

Arctic Herring Gull (Herring Gull)
Larus smithsonianus (*Larus argentatus*) `LC`
Gaviota Argéntea del Ártico

Three subspecies in three subspecies groups; one in Colombia.

American Herring Gull (Herring Gull)
Larus (smithsonianus) smithsonianus
Occasional boreal visitor.
L 64 cm (25"). One subspecies in group. Dec–Mar; numerous records Caribbean and Pacific coasts, also Isla Gorgona (some unverified; more photo documentation needed). **ID** Large, variable, four-year gull; pink legs at all ages. Ad br pale grey upperparts, blackish primaries with small white tips, and red spot on yellow bill. Ad non-br variable brown streaking on head and neck. 1st-y and 2nd-y mostly dark tail, brownish body, black bill on youngest birds, pinkish with black tip by 2nd-w. **SS** Lesser Black-backed and Ring-billed Gulls. **TN** Taxonomy very complex. Often treated as part of European Herring Gull *L. argentatus*.

adult non-breeding

adult breeding

first-winter

Great Black-backed Gull *Larus marinus* `LC`
Gavión
Vagrant.

L 76 cm (30"). Monotypic. Beaches, mudflats; two (1st-y and 4th-y) Mar 2013 (photos), Los Flamencos, Guajira; one unconfirmed sight record Buenaventura Bay. **ID** Largest gull. In all plumages huge size, massive bill, pinkish legs distinctive. Ad br above slaty black, eyes yellow, narrow red orbital ring, black wingtips with large white spots. Ad non-br minor greyish smudges on crown. 1st-y bill black, plumage densely mottled whitish and brown, head, underparts and rump decidedly paler; in flight (from above) inner primaries paler, broad dark tail tip. 2nd-y above darker, greyish, bill pinkish tipped black. **SS** Kelp Gull (tiny wingtip spots, greenish-yellow legs); Lesser Black-backed Gull.

adult non-breeding

first-winter

adult breeding

Sooty Tern *Onychoprion fuscatus* `LC`
Gaviotín Oscuro
Breeds on Isla Malpelo, rare on Pacific coast, Caribbean coast (records?).

L 41 cm (16"). Races *fuscatus*[A], *crissalis*[B]. Pelagic when not breeding. Flight buoyant, near water surface. Flocks form over schools of fish; rarely alights on floating debris.
ID Ad br black above, snowy below, white forehead reaches to eyes; in flight white underwing-coverts contrast with dark flight feathers, long, deeply forked tail narrowly edged white. Ad non-br variable white-fringed upperparts. Juv/1st-y mainly blackish brown, lower underparts whitish, wings and upperparts spotted and barred white, tail shorter than ad. **Voice** Noisy "wide-a-wake" at breeding colony. **SS** Bridled Tern.

adult breeding

fuscatus

juvenile

Bridled Tern *Onychoprion anaethetus* `LC`
Gaviotín Embridado
Pantropical visitor.

L 38 cm (15"). Races *melanopterus*[A], *nelsoni*[B]. Coastal and offshore waters, less pelagic than Sooty Tern. Mainly Pacific coast; may breed on rocky islets off NW Chocó. Small groups. **ID** Ad mantle and wings dark grey (not blackish), cap black, narrow white forehead; from Sooty Tern (easily confused in flight) by more slender wings, more white on sides of tail, underwing more extensively white; often rests on floating debris. Juv/1st-y much paler than juv Sooty, head whitish, blackish postocular and nape, upperparts grey to brownish barred and scaled white, below white.

melanopterus

adult breeding

juvenile

168

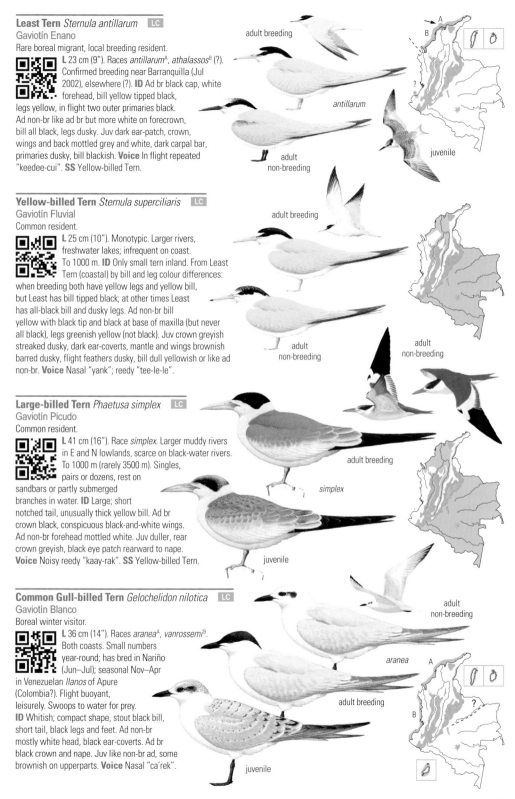

Least Tern *Sternula antillarum* LC
Gaviotín Enano

Rare boreal migrant, local breeding resident.
L 23 cm (9"). Races *antillarum*[A], *athalassos*[B] (?). Confirmed breeding near Barranquilla (Jul 2002), elsewhere (?). **ID** Ad br black cap, white forehead, bill yellow tipped black, legs yellow, in flight two outer primaries black. Ad non-br like ad br but more white on forecrown, bill all black, legs dusky. Juv dark ear-patch, crown, wings and back mottled grey and white, dark carpal bar, primaries dusky, bill blackish. **Voice** In flight repeated "keedee-cui". **SS** Yellow-billed Tern.

adult breeding

antillarum

adult non-breeding

juvenile

Yellow-billed Tern *Sternula superciliaris* LC
Gaviotín Fluvial

Common resident.
L 25 cm (10"). Monotypic. Larger rivers, freshwater lakes; infrequent on coast. To 1000 m. **ID** Only small tern inland. From Least Tern (coastal) by bill and leg colour differences: when breeding both have yellow legs and yellow bill, but Least has bill tipped black; at other times Least has all-black bill and dusky legs. Ad non-br bill yellow with black tip and black at base of maxilla (but never all black), legs greenish yellow (not black). Juv crown greyish streaked dusky, dark ear-coverts, mantle and wings brownish barred dusky, flight feathers dusky, bill dull yellowish or like ad non-br. **Voice** Nasal "yank"; reedy "tee-le-le".

adult breeding

adult non-breeding

adult non-breeding

Large-billed Tern *Phaetusa simplex* LC
Gaviotín Picudo

Common resident.
L 41 cm (16"). Race *simplex*. Larger muddy rivers in E and N lowlands, scarce on black-water rivers. To 1000 m (rarely 3500 m). Singles, pairs or dozens, rest on sandbars or partly submerged branches in water. **ID** Large; short notched tail, unusually thick yellow bill. Ad br crown black, conspicuous black-and-white wings. Ad non-br forehead mottled white. Juv duller, rear crown greyish, black eye patch rearward to nape. **Voice** Noisy reedy "kaay-rak". **SS** Yellow-billed Tern.

adult breeding

simplex

juvenile

Common Gull-billed Tern *Gelochelidon nilotica* LC
Gaviotín Blanco

Boreal winter visitor.
L 36 cm (14"). Races *aranea*[A], *vanrossemi*[B]. Both coasts. Small numbers year-round; has bred in Nariño (Jun–Jul); seasonal Nov–Apr in Venezuelan *llanos* of Apure (Colombia?). Flight buoyant, leisurely. Swoops to water for prey. **ID** Whitish; compact shape, stout black bill, short tail, black legs and feet. Ad non-br mostly white head, black ear-coverts. Ad br black crown and nape. Juv like non-br ad, some brownish on upperparts. **Voice** Nasal "ca'rek".

adult non-breeding

aranea

adult breeding

juvenile

169

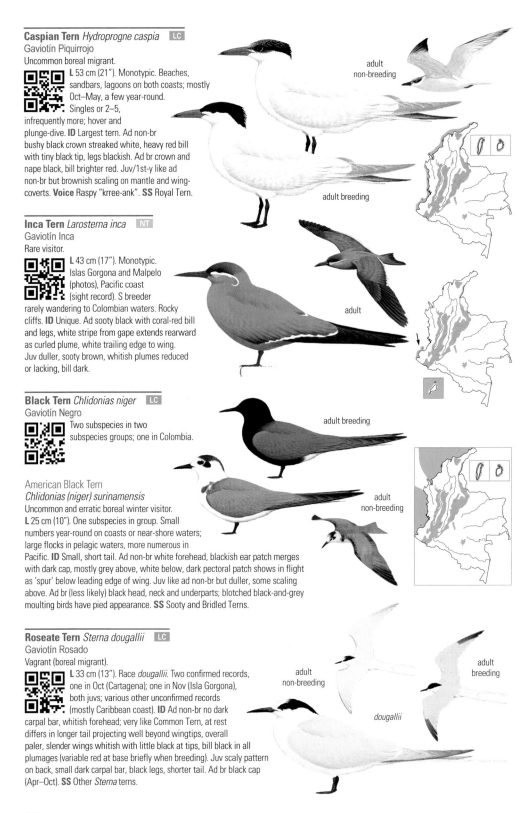

Caspian Tern *Hydroprogne caspia* LC
Gaviotín Piquirrojo
Uncommon boreal migrant.

L 53 cm (21"). Monotypic. Beaches, sandbars, lagoons on both coasts; mostly Oct–May, a few year-round. Singles or 2–5, infrequently more; hover and plunge-dive. **ID** Largest tern. Ad non-br bushy black crown streaked white, heavy red bill with tiny black tip, legs blackish. Ad br crown and nape black, bill brighter red. Juv/1st-y like ad non-br but brownish scaling on mantle and wing-coverts. **Voice** Raspy "krree-ank". **SS** Royal Tern.

adult non-breeding

adult breeding

Inca Tern *Larosterna inca* NT
Gaviotín Inca
Rare visitor.

L 43 cm (17"). Monotypic. Islas Gorgona and Malpelo (photos), Pacific coast (sight record). S breeder rarely wandering to Colombian waters. Rocky cliffs. **ID** Unique. Ad sooty black with coral-red bill and legs, white stripe from gape extends rearward as curled plume, white trailing edge to wing. Juv duller, sooty brown, whitish plumes reduced or lacking, bill dark.

adult

Black Tern *Chlidonias niger* LC
Gaviotín Negro

Two subspecies in two subspecies groups; one in Colombia.

adult breeding

American Black Tern
Chlidonias (niger) surinamensis
Uncommon and erratic boreal winter visitor.
L 25 cm (10"). One subspecies in group. Small numbers year-round on coasts or near-shore waters; large flocks in pelagic waters, more numerous in Pacific. **ID** Small, short tail. Ad non-br white forehead, blackish ear patch merges with dark cap, mostly grey above, white below, dark pectoral patch shows in flight as 'spur' below leading edge of wing. Juv like ad non-br but duller, some scaling above. Ad br (less likely) black head, neck and underparts; blotched black-and-grey moulting birds have pied appearance. **SS** Sooty and Bridled Terns.

adult non-breeding

Roseate Tern *Sterna dougallii* LC
Gaviotín Rosado
Vagrant (boreal migrant).

L 33 cm (13"). Race *dougallii*. Two confirmed records, one in Oct (Cartagena); one in Nov (Isla Gorgona), both juvs; various other unconfirmed records (mostly Caribbean coast). **ID** Ad non-br no dark carpal bar, whitish forehead; very like Common Tern, at rest differs in longer tail projecting well beyond wingtips, overall paler, slender wings whitish with little black at tips, bill black in all plumages (variable red at base briefly when breeding). Juv scaly pattern on back, small dark carpal bar, black legs, shorter tail. Ad br black cap (Apr–Oct). **SS** Other *Sterna* terns.

adult non-breeding

adult breeding

dougallii

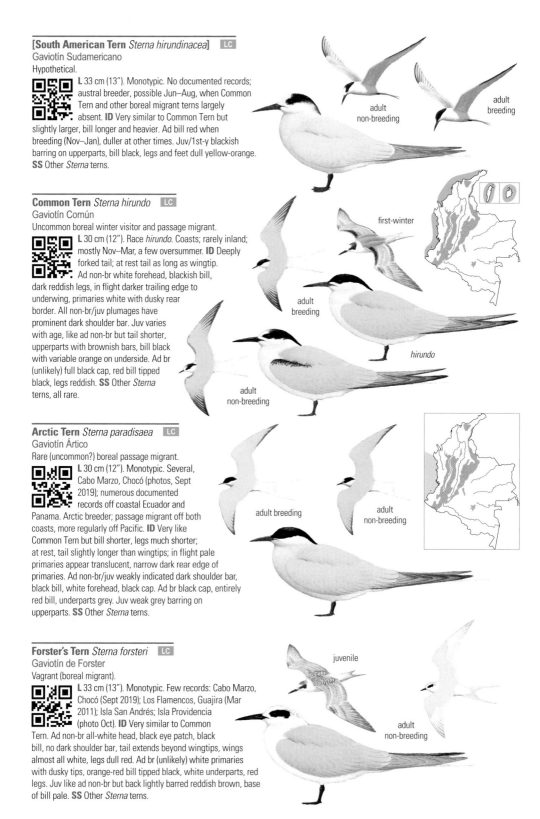

[South American Tern *Sterna hirundinacea*] `LC`
Gaviotín Sudamericano
Hypothetical.

L 33 cm (13"). Monotypic. No documented records; austral breeder, possible Jun–Aug, when Common Tern and other boreal migrant terns largely absent. **ID** Very similar to Common Tern but slightly larger, bill longer and heavier. Ad bill red when breeding (Nov–Jan), duller at other times. Juv/1st-y blackish barring on upperparts, bill black, legs and feet dull yellow-orange. **SS** Other *Sterna* terns.

adult
non-breeding

adult
breeding

Common Tern *Sterna hirundo* `LC`
Gaviotín Común
Uncommon boreal winter visitor and passage migrant.

L 30 cm (12"). Race *hirundo*. Coasts; rarely inland; mostly Nov–Mar, a few oversummer. **ID** Deeply forked tail; at rest tail as long as wingtip. Ad non-br white forehead, blackish bill, dark reddish legs, in flight darker trailing edge to underwing, primaries white with dusky rear border. All non-br/juv plumages have prominent dark shoulder bar. Juv varies with age, like ad non-br but tail shorter, upperparts with brownish bars, bill black with variable orange on underside. Ad br (unlikely) full black cap, red bill tipped black, legs reddish. **SS** Other *Sterna* terns, all rare.

first-winter

adult
breeding

hirundo

adult
non-breeding

Arctic Tern *Sterna paradisaea* `LC`
Gaviotín Ártico
Rare (uncommon?) boreal passage migrant.

L 30 cm (12"). Monotypic. Several, Cabo Marzo, Chocó (photos, Sept 2019); numerous documented records off coastal Ecuador and Panama. Arctic breeder; passage migrant off both coasts, more regularly off Pacific. **ID** Very like Common Tern but bill shorter, legs much shorter; at rest, tail slightly longer than wingtips; in flight pale primaries appear translucent, narrow dark rear edge of primaries. Ad non-br/juv weakly indicated dark shoulder bar, black bill, white forehead, black cap. Ad br black cap, entirely red bill, underparts grey. Juv weak grey barring on upperparts. **SS** Other *Sterna* terns.

adult breeding

adult
non-breeding

Forster's Tern *Sterna forsteri* `LC`
Gaviotín de Forster
Vagrant (boreal migrant).

L 33 cm (13"). Monotypic. Few records: Cabo Marzo, Chocó (Sept 2019); Los Flamencos, Guajira (Mar 2011); Isla San Andrés; Isla Providencia (photo Oct). **ID** Very similar to Common Tern. Ad non-br all-white head, black eye patch, black bill, no dark shoulder bar, tail extends beyond wingtips, wings almost all white, legs dull red. Ad br (unlikely) white primaries with dusky tips, orange-red bill tipped black, white underparts, red legs. Juv like ad non-br but back lightly barred reddish brown, base of bill pale. **SS** Other *Sterna* terns.

juvenile

adult
non-breeding

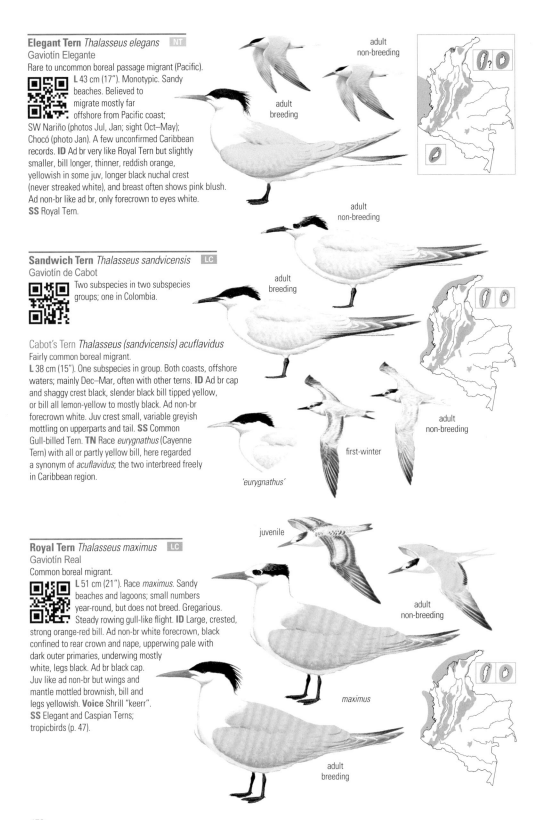

Elegant Tern *Thalasseus elegans* NT
Gaviotín Elegante
Rare to uncommon boreal passage migrant (Pacific).
L 43 cm (17"). Monotypic. Sandy
beaches. Believed to
migrate mostly far
offshore from Pacific coast;
SW Nariño (photos Jul, Jan; sight Oct–May);
Chocó (photo Jan). A few unconfirmed Caribbean
records. **ID** Ad br very like Royal Tern but slightly
smaller, bill longer, thinner, reddish orange,
yellowish in some juv, longer black nuchal crest
(never streaked white), and breast often shows pink blush.
Ad non-br like ad br, only forecrown to eyes white.
SS Royal Tern.

adult
non-breeding

adult
breeding

Sandwich Tern *Thalasseus sandvicensis* LC
Gaviotín de Cabot
Two subspecies in two subspecies
groups; one in Colombia.

adult
non-breeding

adult
breeding

Cabot's Tern *Thalasseus (sandvicensis) acuflavidus*
Fairly common boreal migrant.
L 38 cm (15"). One subspecies in group. Both coasts, offshore
waters; mainly Dec–Mar, often with other terns. **ID** Ad br cap
and shaggy crest black, slender black bill tipped yellow,
or bill all lemon-yellow to mostly black. Ad non-br
forecrown white. Juv crest small, variable greyish
mottling on upperparts and tail. **SS** Common
Gull-billed Tern. **TN** Race *eurygnathus* (Cayenne
Tern) with all or partly yellow bill, here regarded
a synonym of *acuflavidus*; the two interbreed freely
in Caribbean region.

adult
non-breeding

first-winter

'eurygnathus'

juvenile

Royal Tern *Thalasseus maximus* LC
Gaviotín Real
Common boreal migrant.
L 51 cm (21"). Race *maximus*. Sandy
beaches and lagoons; small numbers
year-round, but does not breed. Gregarious.
Steady rowing gull-like flight. **ID** Large, crested,
strong orange-red bill. Ad non-br white forecrown, black
confined to rear crown and nape, upperwing pale with
dark outer primaries, underwing mostly
white, legs black. Ad br black cap.
Juv like ad non-br but wings and
mantle mottled brownish, bill and
legs yellowish. **Voice** Shrill "keerr".
SS Elegant and Caspian Terns;
tropicbirds (p. 47).

adult
non-breeding

maximus

adult
breeding

7 extant species, 2 in region + 3 vagrants

Large predatory seabirds known for aerial piracy. Jaegers breed in northern polar regions, skuas in both north and south polar regions. Both groups are migratory and spend most of their time at sea when not breeding. Skuas have broad wings flexed at the wrist; those of jaegers longer, more pointed and falcon-like. All of them easily overtake gulls and terns, harassing them until they give up their food. The plumages of both groups are complex, especially those of juveniles and subadults, and photo documentation is important.

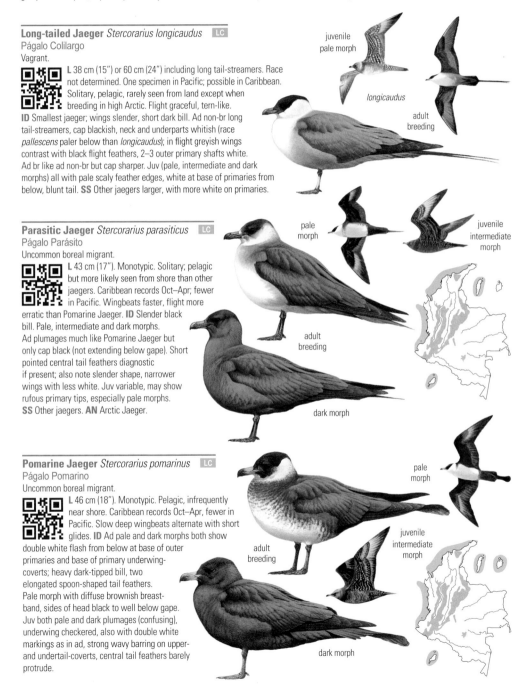

Long-tailed Jaeger *Stercorarius longicaudus* LC
Págalo Colilargo
Vagrant.

L 38 cm (15") or 60 cm (24") including long tail-streamers. Race not determined. One specimen in Pacific; possible in Caribbean. Solitary, pelagic, rarely seen from land except when breeding in high Arctic. Flight graceful, tern-like. **ID** Smallest jaeger; wings slender, short dark bill. Ad non-br long tail-streamers, cap blackish, neck and underparts whitish (race *pallescens* paler below than *longicaudus*); in flight greyish wings contrast with black flight feathers, 2–3 outer primary shafts white. Ad br like ad non-br but cap sharper. Juv (pale, intermediate and dark morphs) all with pale scaly feather edges, white at base of primaries from below, blunt tail. **SS** Other jaegers larger, with more white on primaries.

Parasitic Jaeger *Stercorarius parasiticus* LC
Págalo Parásito
Uncommon boreal migrant.

L 43 cm (17"). Monotypic. Solitary; pelagic but more likely seen from shore than other jaegers. Caribbean records Oct–Apr; fewer in Pacific. Wingbeats faster, flight more erratic than Pomarine Jaeger. **ID** Slender black bill. Pale, intermediate and dark morphs. Ad plumages much like Pomarine Jaeger but only cap black (not extending below gape). Short pointed central tail feathers diagnostic if present; also note slender shape, narrower wings with less white. Juv variable, may show rufous primary tips, especially pale morphs. **SS** Other jaegers. **AN** Arctic Jaeger.

Pomarine Jaeger *Stercorarius pomarinus* LC
Págalo Pomarino
Uncommon boreal migrant.

L 46 cm (18"). Monotypic. Pelagic, infrequently near shore. Caribbean records Oct–Apr, fewer in Pacific. Slow deep wingbeats alternate with short glides. **ID** Ad pale and dark morphs both show double white flash from below at base of outer primaries and base of primary underwing-coverts; heavy dark-tipped bill, two elongated spoon-shaped tail feathers. Pale morph with diffuse brownish breast-band, sides of head black to well below gape. Juv both pale and dark plumages (confusing), underwing checkered, also with double white markings as in ad, strong wavy barring on upper- and undertail-coverts, central tail feathers barely protrude.

Image labels: juvenile pale morph; *longicaudus*; adult breeding; pale morph; juvenile intermediate morph; adult breeding; dark morph; pale morph; juvenile intermediate morph; adult breeding; dark morph

Great Skua *Catharacta skua* `LC`
Págalo Grande
Vagrant.

 L 58 cm (23"). Monotypic. Pelagic. Breeds W Palearctic. Reported off coasts of Guajira and Atlántico (but few confirmed records); Pacific records (unlikely) need confirmation. Jan–May (?). **ID** Much like South Polar Skua but slightly larger, bill heavier, plumage more reddish brown, dark cap more contrasting, variable pale spotting and streaking on wings. **SS** South Polar Skua. **TN** Usually placed in *Stercorarius*.

pale morph

South Polar Skua *Catharacta maccormicki* `LC`
Págalo del Polo Sur
Vagrant.

 L 53 cm (21"). Monotypic. Mainly pelagic. Antarctic breeder. Unconfirmed sight records in Caribbean and Pacific waters, possibly Feb–Jul. **ID** Ad large and robust, hunchbacked shape, thick neck, heavy bill. Pale, intermediate and dark morphs all with short wedge-shaped tail, prominent white at base of primaries. Dark wings of pale morphs contrast with pale brown body. **SS** Great Skua. **TN** Usually placed in *Stercorarius*.

dark morph

TYTONIDAE
Barn-owls
16 extant species, 1 in region

This small, nearly worldwide, family differs from typical owls in having heart-shaped faces and longer legs feathered to the toes. Barn-owls feed heavily on small rodents and readily nest in old buildings. There are numerous species of barn-owls in the fossil record.

Common Barn-owl *Tyto alba* `LC`
Lechuza Común

 Twenty-eight subspecies in eight subspecies groups; one in Colombia.

American Barn-owl *Tyto (alba) furcata*
Locally common resident.
L 39 cm (15.5"). Races *guatemalae*[A] (?), *contempta*[B], unknown subspecies on Isla San Andrés (possibly introduced). Gallery forest borders, semi-open areas with scattered trees, towns. To 4000 m. Nocturnal. Singles or pairs roost in buildings or tree cavities by day. **ID** Ghostly pale owl; no ear-tufts, white heart-shaped facial disc, dark eyes. ♂ underparts white to light buff; ♀ usually more buff or tawny below. **Voice** Hisses, drawn-out screeches; scraping sounds; does not hoot. **SS** Buff-fronted Owl. **TN** Taxonomy unresolved.

contempta

220 extant species, 27 in region

A worldwide family of mostly nocturnal hunters. Owls have large heads and forward-facing eyes fixed in their orbits, but can rotate their heads nearly 270°. They have good vision day or night, extraordinarily acute hearing, and soft plumage that permits silent flight. Owls are monogamous but do not build a nest, instead they take over old hawk nests or occupy tree cavities.

Genus *Glaucidium* Colombia's smallest owls; diurnal and nocturnal. No ear-tufts, and black 'false eyes' on rear crown. Several have two colour morphs. Prey heavily on birds. Best told by voice and distribution.

Cloudforest Pygmy-owl *Glaucidium nubicola* VU
Buhíto Nubícola VU
Uncommon resident.

L 15 cm (6"). Monotypic. Near-endemic (also W Ecuador). Canopy of montane wet forest, occasionally borders. 1400–2000 m. **ID** Ad both rufous and dark morphs essentially identical to those of Andean Pygmy-owl but voice and elevational distribution differ; rufous morph usually unspotted. Juv unspotted dark brown head, upperparts and chest, sides rufous-brown, breast white lightly streaked brown. **Voice** One or two introductory notes, then paired "pu-pu" whistles for a minute or more; when excited notes quicker, less clearly paired.

Andean Pygmy-owl *Glaucidium jardinii* LC
Buhíto Andino
Uncommon resident.

L 15 cm (6"). Monotypic. Humid montane forest, elfin woodland to treeline. 2000–3500 m. Solitary; roosts partly concealed in vegetation. **ID** Dark morph brown, crown dotted white, whitish spotting on wing-coverts, irregular brown breast-band, sides blotched or with minor brownish barring, lower underparts streaked, tail blackish barred white. Rufous morph rufous (not brownish), few or no white dots on crown, tail rufous barred dusky. **Voice** A stutter, then long brisk series of evenly-spaced "pu" whistles. **SS** At higher elevation than other pygmy-owls.

rufous morph

dark morph

Central American Pygmy-owl *Glaucidium griseiceps* LC
Buhíto Cabecigrís
Fairly common but local (?) resident.

L 14.5 cm (5.7"). Race *rarum*. Humid lowland and foothill forest, borders, older second growth; subcanopy or lower. To 1500 m. **ID** Rufescent-brown, head greyish, tiny indistinct white dots on crown, incomplete brown breast-band, sides streaked, tail black barred white. **Voice** Call 3–5 whistled "tu" notes, c. 3/second; faster when disturbed. **SS** Mostly at lower elevations than other *Glaucidium*. **TN** Formerly a race of Least Pygmy-owl *G. minutissimum*. **AN** Choco Pygmy-owl.

rarum

Subtropical Pygmy-owl *Glaucidium parkeri* LC
Buhíto Subtropical
Local (overlooked?) resident.

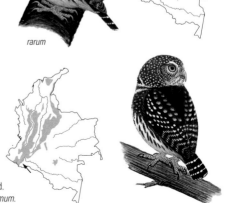

L 14.5 cm (5.7"). Monotypic. Subcanopy of humid montane forest, outlying ridges. 1200–1800 m (Putumayo and Cauca). **ID** Dark brown to greyish brown, crown profusely dotted white, scapulars and wing-coverts with large white spots, flight feathers barred white. **Voice** Low-pitched, slow whistled triplets (or 2–4 notes), "tu-tu-tu", repeated every 3–4 seconds, or increasingly spaced. **SS** Andean Pygmy-owl. **TN** Formerly a race of Least Pygmy-owl *G. minutissimum*.

Ferruginous Pygmy-owl *Glaucidium brasilianum* `LC`
Buhíto Ferrugíneo

 Twelve subspecies in two subspecies groups; one in Colombia.

rufous morph

grey morph

Ferruginous Pygmy-owl *Glaucidium (brasilianum) brasilianum*
Common resident.
L 16 cm (6.3"). Races *medianum*[A], *ucayalae*[B]. Desert scrub, dry to humid forest, gallery forest, semi-open areas. To 1200 m. Commonest in arid N; by far the most frequently seen pygmy-owl. Flies fast, flurry of wingbeats and a glide. Everywhere mobbed by small birds when discovered.
ID Rufous and grey morphs, but many intermediates, crown finely streaked, white to buff spots on scapulars and wing-coverts. **Voice** Call brisk whistled "tu" notes c. 2/second for up to a minute; easily imitated; chirrups and other notes.

ucayalae

[Amazonian Pygmy-owl *Glaucidium hardyi*] `LC`
Buhíto Amazónico
Hypothetical.

 L 14 cm (5.5"). Monotypic. Possible in S Amazonas. Rainforest interior (not edge). **ID** Like larger Ferruginous Pygmy-owl, but only brownish (no rufous) morph. **Voice** Soft fast "tutu..." whistles (ventriloqual).

Burrowing Owl *Athene cunicularia* `LC`
Mochuelo Conejo
Locally fairly common resident.

 L 23 cm (9"). Races *carrikeri*[A], *tolimae*[B]; S Amazonas race (?)[C]. Dry grassland, open scrub, sandy Amazonian river islands. To 1000 m. Partially diurnal, loose colonies; conspicuous pairs and families stand next to burrows or perch on nearby elevated sites; bob head when disturbed. **ID** Long-legged, round-headed, yellow eyes, furrowed brow, above brownish spotted white, below whitish to buff with variable coarse barring. Race *tolimae* darker, greyer, larger than *carrikeri*. **Voice** Not very vocal; ♂ soft hooting "coo-coooo"; both sexes raspy shrieking "kik"; screeches. **TN** Sometimes in *Speotyto*.

carrikeri

Buff-fronted Owl *Aegolius harrisii* `LC`
Búho Acanelado
Rare and very local resident.

 L 23 cm (9"). Race *harrisii*. Dry to moderately humid woodland, borders to treeline. 1300–3400 m. Solitary; nocturnal, mid-strata or lower. Infrequently heard or seen; poorly known. **ID** Small and handsome; above dark brown, tawny-buff face outlined black, underparts tawny. **Voice** Very fast quavering (bubbly) trill (c. 10 notes+/second) lasting 3–8 seconds or more, longer if disturbed. **SS** Striped and Short-eared Owls, both larger, paler.

harrisii

Stygian Owl *Asio stygius* `LC`
Búho Orejudo
Fairly common but local resident (easily overlooked).

 L 43 cm (17"). Race *robustus*. Light woodland, conifer plantations, groves of trees in semi-open areas, towns, urban parks. 400–3000 m. Nocturnal, roosts mid-levels or higher by day, typically close to trunks. **ID** Fairly large, blackish upperparts, upstanding black ear-tufts, whitish patch on forehead, orange-yellow eyes, coarse dark herringbone barring below. **Voice** Low "whoo" at intervals, cat-like scraping "wiiiap". **SS** Short-eared Owl.

robustus

Striped Owl *Asio clamator* `LC`
Búho Rayado

Uncommon to fairly common but local resident.

 L 38 cm (15"). Race *clamator*. Grassland, scrub or brush with scattered taller trees, light woodland, marshes (e.g. Sabana de Bogotá), Amazonian river islands, *várzea* borders. To 2600 m. Nocturnal, hunts from fence post or low to mid-level perch, roosts on ground, in marsh, or high in tree. **ID** Prominent ear-tufts, pale facial disc rimmed black, dark eyes, above brown to deep tawny, below whitish to buff, coarsely streaked. Juv plain cinnamon, inner facial disc white. **Voice** Not very vocal, whistled "wheeyoo", barks and yaps like small dog. **SS** Short-eared Owl.

clamator

Short-eared Owl *Asio flammeus* `LC`
Búho Campestre

 Eleven subspecies in two subspecies groups; one in Colombia.

Common Short-eared Owl *Asio (flammeus) flammeus*
Local resident.

L 38 cm (15"). Race *bogotensis*. Grassland in *llanos* (scarce), marshes, grassy pastures in highlands, *páramo*. 300–3500 m. Partially diurnal. Only Colombian owl likely to hunt in flight by day, especially at dusk, loose bounding flight, often perches in open close to ground, roosts in tall grass, reeds. **ID** Ear-tufts vestigial (looks earless), whitish to pale brown facial discs, blackish eye sockets, yellow eyes, streaked underparts. In flight whitish underwing shows black primary-covert mark. **Voice** Infrequent barks and squeals. **SS** Striped Owl (prominent ear-tufts).

bogotensis

Genus *Megascops* Small-bodied but large-headed owls with or without ear-tufts; their wings almost reach tail tip. Roost by day at low to moderate heights in foliage, moss or cavity. Feed heavily on large insects. Both sexes sing. Taxonomy poorly resolved.

Tropical Screech-owl *Megascops choliba* `LC`
Currucutú

Common resident.

 L 22 cm (8.5"). Races *luctisonus*[A], *cruciger*[B]. Light woodland, second growth, forest borders, parks and gardens, dry to humid areas. To 2800 m. Most commonly encountered small owl in Colombia. Singles or pairs, forage fairly low. **ID** Small ear-tufts, yellow eyes, whitish eyebrows, facial discs rimmed black, narrow dark streaks on underparts with short horizontal marks (cross-hatches). Both grey-brown and rufous morphs widespread. **Voice** Quite vocal, short tremulous trill with 1–3 abrupt notes at end, "purrrrrrrr bu boop!" with variations; when annoyed "taduú-taduú . . ." as flies off. **SS** Other *Megascops*.

grey-brown morph

rufous morph

cruciger

Bare-shanked Screech-owl *Megascops clarkii* `LC`
Autillo Manchado

Local resident.

L 24 cm (9.5"). Monotypic. Humid montane forest, borders; Cerro Tacarcuna. 1400–1500 m (1050–2100 m in Panama). **ID** Plain tawny to cinnamon facial discs, no black rims, underparts spotted. **Voice** Typically four slow, low-pitched whistled hoots "hu hu hu hu", or brief weaker first and last notes added, or longer more evenly spaced series. **SS** Tropical and Choco Screech-owls.

Rufescent Screech-owl *Megascops ingens* NA
Autillo Grande

Three subspecies may comprise two subspecies groups; if valid both in Colombia.

rufous morph

venezuelanus

brown morph

Rufescent Screech-owl
Megascops (ingens) ingens
Uncommon resident.
L 25 cm (10"). Races *ingens*[A], *venezuelanus*[B]. Humid and wet premontane and montane forest interior. 1100–2200 m. Forest mid-levels or lower. **ID** Large screech-owl, underparts of both brown and rufous morphs show a few dark shaft-streaks and fine cross-hatching, tiny ear-tufts, brownish facial discs (no black rim), dark brown eyes, whitish scapular spots, tarsus feathered. **Voice** Song, even-pitched series of tooting whistles "hu hu huhuhuhuhu . . ." c. 5–6/second for up to 15 seconds, initially soft, swelling, then fading, very like Cinnamon Screech-owl. **TN** Taxonomy confused and mapped range conjectural, considered to include Colombian Screech-owl (as here), sometimes also including Cinnamon Screech-owl, or all three treated as separate species.

Colombian Screech-owl *Megascops (ingens) colombianus*
Uncommon resident.
L 25 cm (10"). One subspecies in group. 1050–2200 m. **ID** Plumages, habits and vocalizations essentially identical to Rufescent Screech-owl. Differs presumably in lower tarsi bare (not fully feathered) and slightly longer (?), seems at best only a weakly indicated race of *M. ingens*. Mapped distribution conjectural.

Cinnamon Screech-owl *Megascops petersoni* LC
Autillo Canela
Few records (taxonomy poorly resolved).

L 23 cm (9"). Monotypic. Montane forest, borders. 1500–2300 m. **ID** Warm cinnamon-brown to buffy brown, eyebrows and facial discs cinnamon, obscure darker border to latter, underparts with dark shaft-streaks, tarsus feathered almost to toes. **Voice** Very similar to songs identified as Rufescent Screech-owl although marginally faster, c. 6–7 notes/second (speed varies with aggression?). **SS** Very like rufous examples of Rufescent Screech-owl, but slightly smaller, perhaps richer cinnamon, wings shorter (153–166 mm vs. 177–192 mm), song marginally faster. **TN** See Rufescent Screech-owl.

Tawny-bellied Screech-owl *Megascops watsonii* LC
Autillo Selvático

Two subspecies in two subspecies groups; one in Colombia.

Northern Tawny-bellied Screech-owl *Megascops (watsonii) watsonii*
Fairly common resident.
L 23 cm (9"). One subspecies in group. Inside humid *terra firme* and *várzea* forest, trees in clearings, around lodges. To 600 m. **ID** Small ear-tufts, facial discs narrowly rimmed black, amber eyes, plumage dark brown to tawny-rufous, underparts paler with narrow dark shaft-streaking finely cross-hatched. **Voice** Song ventriloquial, softly whistled low-pitched "wu" notes, 6–8/second, up to 30 seconds, gradually increasing in volume, then fading, sometimes faster in middle. Southern *usta* much slower, c. 3–4 notes/second, songs intermediate (clinal?) in N Peru and S Colombia. **SS** Tropical Screech-owl (not inside forest).

Choco Screech-owl *Megascops centralis* NA
Autillo del Chocó

Fairly common resident (mid-Magdalena Valley).

 L 21 cm (8.2"). Monotypic. Humid lowland and foothill forest, borders. To 1600 m. **ID** Smallest Colombian screech-owl, small ear-tufts, yellow eyes. Both brown and rufous morphs best told by voice, note whitish scapular spots, pale eyebrows, dusky facial rim faint or lacking, narrow shaft-streaks on underparts with fine cross-hatching. **Voice** Song a short slightly descending trill or purr, c. 30+ notes in 1.5 seconds. **TN** Has been included with vocally different Middle American Screech-owl *M. guatemalae.*

brown morph

rufous morph

Foothill Screech-owl *Megascops roraimae* NA
Autillo de Colina

Rare resident (few Colombian records).

 L 22 cm (8.5"). Race *napensis.* Humid foothill forest, borders. 600–1450 m (Ecuador). **ID** Small, greyish to buffy brown, vestigial ear-tufts, yellow eyes, no obvious facial disc markings, white scapular spots, underparts with narrow wavy dark barring (few vertical shaft-streaks). **Voice** Song, quavering dribbling toad-like trill "wuʹuʹuʹuʹuʹuʹu …", c. 12–16 notes/second for c. 3–6 seconds, initially soft, swells, then fades, faster than Northern Tawny-bellied Screech-owl. **SS** Tropical Screech-owl (black-rimmed face), Rufescent Screech-owl. **TN** Often included with Vermiculated Screech-owl *M. vermiculatus.*

napensis

Santa Marta Screech-owl *Megascops gilesi* VU
Autillo de Santa Marta

Locally common resident.

 L 22 cm (8.5"). Monotypic. Endemic. Humid montane forest, borders. 1800–2500 m. Lower levels to subcanopy, roosts in mid-level vine tangles. **ID** Vestigial ear-tufts, eyes yellow, morphs brown or rufous, lower underparts whitish to buffy white with a few dark shaft-streaks and fine cross-hatching. **Voice** Song short c. 2-second trill, c. 10 notes/second, rising slightly in pitch and volume, then slowing, fading. **SS** Tropical Screech-owl (mostly lower elevation). **TN** New taxon (described 2018).

brown morph

rufous morph

White-throated Screech-owl *Megascops albogularis* LC
Autillo Gorgiblanco

Fairly common resident.

 L 25 cm (10"). Races *obscurus*[A], *macabrus*[B], *albogularis*[C]. Moist (*Quercus*) to humid montane forest and borders to treeline. 2000–3500 m. Singles or pairs, mid-levels to subcanopy. **ID** Notably dark, vestigial ear-tufts, amber eyes, head and upperparts dark brown, no scapular spots, pale eyebrows, narrow white throat. **Voice** Song short tremulous or pulsating series of low whistles, c. 6–10 notes/second, in duet ♂ a few low-pitched, slow, hollow hoots, ♀ higher longer series, rhythmic tooting "pu pu púdu-púdu …" when excited. **SS** Higher elevation than other *Megascops.*

albogularis

Genus *Pulsatrix* Large owls; 'white spectacles'; dark chest; commanding voices.

Spectacled Owl *Pulsatrix perspicillata* `LC`
Búho de Anteojos

Six subspecies in two subspecies groups; one in Colombia.

Spectacled Owl *Pulsatrix (perspicillata) perspicillata*
Fairly common resident.
L 46 cm (18"). Races *chapmani*[A], *perspicillata*[B]. Dry to humid forest, borders, gallery forest, and large trees in towns. To 1400 m. Generally roosts fairly low by day, hunts higher at night; takes smaller vertebrates. **ID** White facial markings, white throat, dark brown breast-band, buff lower underparts. Juv white with black mask, dusky flight feathers. **Voice** Not forgotten once heard, low muffled hoots "BOO boo boo boo boo", weaker as descends, deep chuckling duets by pairs may end in higher-pitched maniacal 'laughter'. **SS** Band-bellied Owl.

juvenile

adult

perspicillata

Band-bellied Owl *Pulsatrix melanota* `LC`
Búho Barrado
Local resident.

L 38 cm (15"). Race *melanota*. Humid foothill and lower montane forest, borders. 500–1800 m. Occurs mostly above range of Spectacled Owl, behaviour similar. **ID** Facial pattern recalls larger Spectacled Owl but lower underparts broadly barred. Juv buff with black mask, dusky flight feathers. **Voice** Recalls Spectacled Owl but faster, higher-pitched, lacks deep booming resonance; also cat-like mewing.

juvenile

adult

melanota

Crested Owl *Lophostrix cristata* `LC`
Búho Crestado

Three subspecies in two subspecies groups; one in Colombia.

Southern Crested Owl
Lophostrix (cristata) cristata
Fairly common resident (Amazonia), local W of Andes.
L 41 cm (16"). Races *wedeli*[A], *cristata*[B]. Humid lowland forest. Singles or pairs roost low, 2–8 m up, ear-tufts erect. Hunts from canopy or subcanopy with ear-tufts flattened rearward. **ID** Long white eyebrows merge with white ear-tufts, amber-brown eyes. Polymorphic; above dark brown (or head mostly blackish) or pale rufescent, underparts paler, facial discs chestnut. Juv whitish, mask chestnut. **Voice** Calls well after dark; compresses wings as utters short throaty, frog-like "k'k'k'kkURR!". **TN** Middle American *stricklandi* has blackish head, chestnut facial disc, yellow eyes (N Middle America), faster call; S to NW Colombia (?).

pale morph

dark morph

cristata

Great Horned Owl *Bubo virginianus* `LC`
Búho Real
Local resident in Andes, fairly common in *llanos*.

L 56 cm (22"). Races *nigrescens*[A], *nacurutu*[B]. Dry to humid semi-open areas, isolated groves of trees, gallery forest and *páramo*. To c. 600 m (lowlands), or mostly 2500–4000 m in Andes, but scattered mid-elevation records in open inter-Andean valleys. Roosts in palms, tree stumps; trees around ranch buildings. Hunts from high perch, beginning just before full darkness. **ID** Largest, most powerful owl in Colombia. Prominent ear-tufts, amber-yellow eyes, facial discs rimmed black, V-shaped barring on underparts. **Voice** Deep hooting "whoo-whoo ... whoo, whoo-whoo", with variations; far-carrying.

nacurutu

Genus *Ciccaba* Round-headed, medium-sized owls without ear-tufts. Their vocalizations are often similar. Sometimes placed in *Strix*.

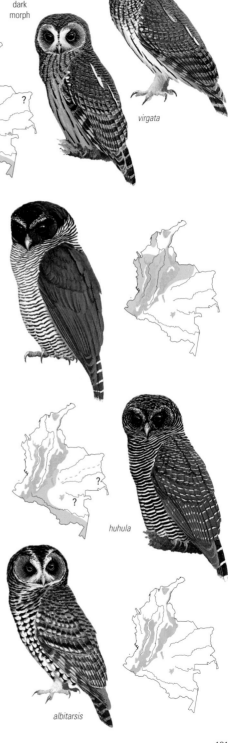

pale morph

dark morph

virgata

Mottled Owl *Ciccaba virgata* LC
Búho Moteado

Seven subspecies in three subspecies groups; one in Colombia.

Mottled Owl *Ciccaba (virgata) virgata*
Common resident.
L 36 cm (14"). Race *virgata*. Dry to humid forest, borders, second-growth woodland, woodlots in settled areas. To 2200 m. Pairs or families roost low in dense vegetation; hunt from high or low perch. Attracted to outdoor lights. **ID** Dark eyes, buff to white eyebrow, dark facial disc; colour of underparts varies from rich tawny buff to whitish coarsely streaked dark brown. Juv buff, dark mask, dusky flight feathers. **Voice** Call a low single or doubled "woOOOou", or several in succession; ♀ a dry cat-like scream. **SS** Rufous-banded Owl. **TN** Race *macconnelli* possible in extreme E Vichada and Guainía.

Black-and-white Owl *Ciccaba nigrolineata* LC
Búho Carinegro
Uncommon resident.

L 43 cm (17"). Monotypic. Dry to humid forest, borders, older second-growth woodland, large trees in settled areas. To 1500 m (locally 2000 m). Roosts by day high in trees or bamboo; attracted to outdoor lights. **ID** Bill yellow, eyebrows speckled white, facial disks, head and upperparts black, nape and underparts white, narrowly and evenly barred black. **Voice** Two very different vocalizations, both much like Black-banded Owl; territorial call a deep resonant "hu, hu, hu ... HOO-ah" with variations; high dry cat-like scream. **SS** Black-banded Owl.

Black-banded Owl *Ciccaba huhula* LC
Búho Negro
Uncommon resident (under-recorded?).

L 38 cm (15"). Race *huhula*. Humid lowland forest, borders. To 900 m (locally 2000 m). Roosts and hunts high in forest. **ID** Above black coarsely barred white, below black narrowly barred white (reverse of Black-and-white Owl), eyes dark, bill yellow. **Voice** Deep resonant hooting "hu, hu, hu, hu ... HOO", or single "HOO-ah" like Black-and-white Owl, various dry screams, meowing sounds, single gruff "woOOu", doubled or tripled (like Mottled Owl).

huhula

Rufous-banded Owl *Ciccaba albitarsis* LC
Búho Ocelado
Fairly common resident.

L 38 cm (15"). Race *albitarsis*. Humid and wet montane forest, borders, tall trees in clearings. Mid-level roost often on relatively open branch, higher when hunting, occasionally at outdoor lights. 1800–3000 m. **ID** Eyes dark amber brown, inner facial disc blackish, above coarsely marked rufous and brown, dark chest-band, underparts with large blocky silvery-white spots. Juv like juv Mottled Owl. **Voice** Variable; recalls previous two species but syncopation different, or rapid grumbling "hu-hu-hu-hu-hu,-hu-hu-hu ... HOOOah", last louder note after longer pause; single gruff "woOOu".

albitarsis

7 extant species, 6 in region

Large scavengers that feed on carrion, rarely live prey, and provide a valuable sanitation service. Soar effortlessly and, except American Black Vulture, can locate prey by olfaction as well as by sight. Bare unfeathered heads aid cleanliness. New World species not closely related to Old World vultures.

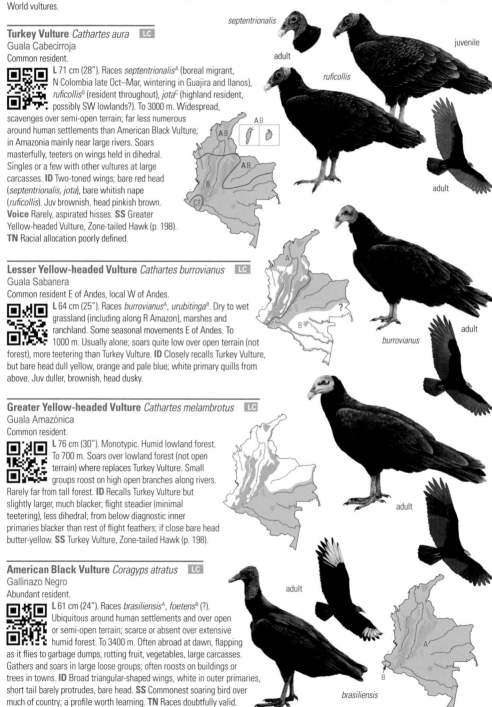

septentrionalis

adult

juvenile

ruficollis

adult

burrovianus

adult

adult

adult

adult

brasiliensis

Turkey Vulture *Cathartes aura* LC
Guala Cabecirroja
Common resident.

L 71 cm (28"). Races *septentrionalis*[A] (boreal migrant, N Colombia late Oct–Mar, wintering in Guajira and llanos), *ruficollis*[B] (resident throughout), *jota*[C] (highland resident, possibly SW lowlands?). To 3000 m. Widespread, scavenges over semi-open terrain; far less numerous around human settlements than American Black Vulture; in Amazonia mainly near large rivers. Soars masterfully, teeters on wings held in dihedral. Singles or a few with other vultures at large carcasses. **ID** Two-toned wings; bare red head (*septentrionalis*, *jota*), bare whitish nape (*ruficollis*). Juv brownish, head pinkish brown. **Voice** Rarely, aspirated hisses. **SS** Greater Yellow-headed Vulture, Zone-tailed Hawk (p. 198). **TN** Racial allocation poorly defined.

Lesser Yellow-headed Vulture *Cathartes burrovianus* LC
Guala Sabanera
Common resident E of Andes, local W of Andes.

L 64 cm (25"). Races *burrovianus*[A], *urubitinga*[B]. Dry to wet grassland (including along R Amazon), marshes and ranchland. Some seasonal movements E of Andes. To 1000 m. Usually alone; soars quite low over open terrain (not forest), more teetering than Turkey Vulture. **ID** Closely recalls Turkey Vulture, but bare head dull yellow, orange and pale blue; white primary quills from above. Juv duller, brownish, head dusky.

Greater Yellow-headed Vulture *Cathartes melambrotus* LC
Guala Amazónica
Common resident.

L 76 cm (30"). Monotypic. Humid lowland forest. To 700 m. Soars over lowland forest (not open terrain) where replaces Turkey Vulture. Small groups roost on high open branches along rivers. Rarely far from tall forest. **ID** Recalls Turkey Vulture but slightly larger, much blacker; flight steadier (minimal teetering), less dihedral; from below diagnostic inner primaries blacker than rest of flight feathers; if close bare head butter-yellow. **SS** Turkey Vulture, Zone-tailed Hawk (p. 198).

American Black Vulture *Coragyps atratus* LC
Gallinazo Negro
Abundant resident.

L 61 cm (24"). Races *brasiliensis*[A], *foetens*[B] (?). Ubiquitous around human settlements and over open or semi-open terrain; scarce or absent over extensive humid forest. To 3400 m. Often abroad at dawn, flapping as it flies to garbage dumps, rotting fruit, vegetables, large carcasses. Gathers and soars in large loose groups; often roosts on buildings or trees in towns. **ID** Broad triangular-shaped wings, white in outer primaries, short tail barely protrudes, bare head. **SS** Commonest soaring bird over much of country; a profile worth learning. **TN** Races doubtfully valid.

King Vulture *Sarcoramphus papa* `LC`
Rey de los Gallinazos
Uncommon resident.

L 81 cm (32"). Monotypic. Dry to humid forest, gallery forest and semi-open terrain. To c. 1500 m (rarely 3300 m). Large scavenger; shuns settled areas, most numerous in ranchland. Alone, occasionally 2–3, infrequently more at large carcasses where dominates, but outnumbered by, other vultures. Soars high on flat squarish-tipped wings. **ID** White body, black flight feathers and tail, colourful head, white eyes. Juv mainly brown; wing-linings soon paler than flight feathers, acquires white over four years. **SS** Wood Stork (p. 137).

Andean Condor *Vultur gryphus* `NT`
Cóndor Andino `CR`
Uncommon and very local resident.

L 122 cm (48"). Monotypic. High montane forest, semi-open terrain, *páramo*. Mostly 3000–5200 m; to 400 m on dry S slope of Santa Marta Mts. Iconic symbol of Andes; one of largest soaring birds. Singles, pairs or trios soar over canyons, cliffs, high open terrain in search of large carcasses. Roosts on cliffs; leaves when warm thermals provide lift. **ID** Upperwing-coverts silvery white, neck ruff white; in flight outer primaries bend upwards like long fingers. ♂ has dewlap, comb on head, red eyes; ♀ no comb or dewlap, eyes reddish brown.

PANDIONIDAE
Osprey
1 extant species, 1 in region

A nearly cosmopolitan fish-eating raptor closely related to hawks and eagles (Accipitridae). It differs in several anatomical features related to its foraging specialization, including leg musculature, dense oily plumage, equal-length toes, reversible outer toe, closable nostrils, and spines on the soles of the feet.

Osprey *Pandion haliaetus* `LC`
Águila Pescadora

Four subspecies in two subspecies groups; one in Colombia.

Western Osprey *Pandion (haliaetus) haliaetus*
Boreal migrant.
L 56 cm (22"). Race *carolinensis*. Freshwater and saltwater habitats throughout. To 3600 m. Mostly Oct–Apr, some (juv?) present year-round. Singles; perch in open; hover, plunge feet first into water for fish. Flight laboured, minimal gliding. **ID** Lanky shape, long narrow wings bent at wrist, mostly white head and underparts, black mask; ♀ sometimes shows minor streaking on breast. Juv has upper-parts feathers buff-edged; slight breast streaking. **Voice** Occasional high whistles "piu-piu...".

carolinensis

A worldwide family, the species notable for their hooked bills, strong feet and sharp claws. Range in size from tiny kites to massive eagles. English names often not indicative of natural groupings (e.g. kites). Large number of species and numerous plumages can be confusing. Learn the commonest species first, and their distributions and habitats. Range of measurements given reflects larger average size of ♀♀ and smaller size of ♂♂.

White-tailed Kite *Elanus leucurus* LC
Gavilán Maromero
Common resident.

 L 46–53 cm (18–21"). Race *leucurus*. Grassland, cultivated areas, farmland with scattered trees. To 3000 m. Profits from deforestation, especially in highlands, e.g. Sabana de Bogotá. Hovers, then plunges to ground for prey. **ID** Elegant, pointed wings, longish square tail, red eyes. Above pearl-grey, below white, shoulders black, small black underwing 'wrist' mark. Juv crown, back and chest tinged brownish. **Voice** Chirped "kewup". **SS** Somewhat gull-like at distance.

leucurus

Pearl Kite *Gampsonyx swainsonii* LC
Gavilancito Perlado
Uncommon and local resident.

 L 20–23 cm (8–9"). Races *leonae*[A], *magnus*[B]. Dry open terrain with trees and brush, arid scrub, waste areas in towns. Expanding into humid areas following deforestation. To 1000 m. Singles or pairs hunt from electric wires, poles, other elevated sites. **ID** Tiny, falcon-like and adorable, pointed wings; above blackish, below white, creamy-yellow cheeks, rusty thighs and sides, ruby eyes. **Voice** High metallic piping notes. **SS** Smallest Colombian raptor.

leonae

Grey-headed Kite *Leptodon cayanensis* LC
Aguililla Cabecigrís
Uncommon resident.

 L 46–53 cm (18–21"). Race *cayanensis*. Moist to humid *terra firme* forest, *várzea*, borders. To 1000 m. Soars on flat wings; advertises with calls and butterfly-like wing-flapping. Still-hunts, mostly reptiles in canopy. **ID** Ad black eyes, broad rounded wings, small dove-grey head, black wing-linings, pale flight feathers coarsely barred, broad tail-bands, legs not feathered to toes. Juv light morph dark eyes, orange-yellow cere and lores, head and underparts white, small black crown patch and post-ocular, underwings whitish, tail like ad. Juv dark morph like juv light morph, but head dusky, underparts heavily streaked dusky. **Voice** Aerial advertisement an odd 'skidding' "eed'lée'er". **SS** Black-and-white Hawk-eagle, Ornate Hawk-eagle.

adult

juvenile light morph

cayanensis

melanistic bird

Hook-billed Kite *Chondrohierax uncinatus* LC
Caracolero Piquiganchudo
Uncommon resident.

 L 41–46 cm (16–18"). Race *uncinatus*. Moist to humid lowland and montane forest, swampy areas, riparian woodland. To 2700 m. Soars on sunny mornings, usually not high. Preys on snails, other invertebrates, small vertebrates. Undertakes short-distance (?) migrations, especially in Amazonia. **ID** Wings bluntly rounded, narrow at base; broad bands on longish tail; large hooked bill imparts odd visage. Ad ♂ mostly grey, breast barred darker; lime-green eyes, greenish facial skin, yellowish

♂

♀

uncinatus

supraloral spot. In flight primaries coarsely barred. Ad ♀ upperparts dark brown, nuchal collar, neck and chest rufous, coarse rufous barring on breast. Rare melanistic birds all dark (both sexes). Juv whitish nuchal collar and neck, creamy underparts progressively barred with age. **Voice** Long fast chuckling "wi-i-i-i-i-i-i-i-i-i-uh!", rising then falling. **SS** Roadside Hawk.

forficatus

Swallow-tailed Kite *Elanoides forficatus* `LC`
Aguililla Tijereta
Common resident.

L 56–66 cm (22–26"). Race *forficatus*[A] (boreal migrant), *yetapa*[B] (resident and migrant, present c. Aug–Jan, from Central America). Humid lowland and montane forest, semi-open areas near forest. To 2600 m. Pairs and migrating or boreal wintering groups of 3–30. Flight languid, graceful; snatches large flying insects from air or canopy foliage, occasionally small vertebrates or fruit. Perches and roosts high, exposed. **ID** Mostly white, black flight feathers, long forked tail; shoulders purplish (*forficatus*), greenish (*yetapa*). Juv foreparts tinged buff. **Voice** Thin "k'weep, k'weep-weep".

Crested Eagle *Morphnus guianensis* `NT`
Águila Moñuda `NT`
Rarely seen, low-density resident.

L 79–89 cm (31–35"). Monotypic. Extensive humid and wet lowland and foothill forest. To 1000 m. Hunts within canopy, rarely soars low for brief periods. Preys on monkeys, other vertebrates, large birds. **ID** Single-pointed crest, eyes and lores blackish, broadly banded tail longer than Harpy Eagle. Ad light morph has coarse rufous or grey barring below; in flight wing-linings white. Ad dark morph (less common) above blackish, lower underparts white densely barred black, wing-linings greyish. Juv mostly whitish, small black mask, dark eyes, dusky flight feathers and tail. **Voice** High descending whistles. **SS** Ad Harpy Eagle larger, bifurcated crest, heavier bill, thicker tarsi, black chest-band, blackish wing-linings; juv Harpy lacks chest-band, wing-linings whitish.

light morph

dark morph

light morph

juvenile

Harpy Eagle *Harpia harpyja* `NT`
Águila Arpía `NT`
Rarely seen, low-density resident.

L 89–102 cm (35–40"). Monotypic. Extensive humid and wet lowland and foothill forest. To 1600 m. Hunts from subcanopy or canopy perch; flies at or below canopy height, does not soar. Fast and agile despite size. Preys on monkeys, sloths, other vertebrates, large birds. **ID** Ad black chest-band, shaggy bifurcated crest, massive tarsi. Juv whitish or pale grey, crest bushy, wing-linings whitish. Imm acquires ad plumage over several years. **Voice** Shrill metallic scream "PEE'EEeeerr", descending, c. 1.5 seconds, penetrating but not loud. **SS** Crested Eagle.

adult

Genus *Spizaetus* Large robust raptors, with long occipital crests, oval-shaped wings narrow at base (like heliconid butterfly), feathered tarsi, and long broadly banded tails. Advertise by soaring, calling and performing wing-flutters on sunny mornings. Hunt from perches inside forest.

Black Hawk-eagle *Spizaetus tyrannus* `LC`
Águila Iguanera
Fairly common resident (most frequent hawk-eagle).
L 64–71 cm (25–28"). Race *serus*. Humid lowland and montane forest, old second growth. To 2000 m. Soars high in slow circles on flat wings to advertise. **ID** Ad mostly black; in flight boldly barred outer flight feathers, rounded wings narrowed at base. Juv dark brown, white eyebrow and throat, narrowly streaked breast. **Voice** Advertising call a loud whistled "wheep-wheep-wheep-weHEEE-er" or shorter "puwhEEr", emphasis near end of call (reverse of Ornate Hawk-eagle). **SS** Juv Black-and-chestnut Eagle (higher elevations).

adult

serus

juvenile

Black-and-white Hawk-eagle *Spizaetus melanoleucus* `LC`
Águila Enmascarada
Uncommon and local resident.
L 56–61 cm (22–24"). Monotypic. Humid forest, borders. To 2000 m. Soars less than Black Hawk-eagle; occasionally perches in open, otherwise high inside forest. **ID** Small compact hawk-eagle, less oval wing shape nearer *Buteo* than *Spizaetus*, orange cere, black lores, yellow eyes, black crown patch forms slight crest, legs feathered to toes. Easily identified in flight by white leading edge of wing (like narrow headlights). Juv shoulders scaled whitish. **Voice** Shrill whistled "kree'oow". **SS** Juv light morph Grey-headed Kite, juv Ornate Hawk-eagle. **TN** Formerly in genus *Spizastur*.

Ornate Hawk-eagle *Spizaetus ornatus* `NT`
Águila Coronada
Fairly common but low-density resident.
L 58–64 cm (23–25"). Races *vicarius*[A], *ornatus*[B]. Humid lowland and premontane forest, borders, gallery forest. To 1500 m (rarely 2000 m). Soars lower than Black Hawk-eagle. **ID** Ad neck rufous; above black (little to no white barring on shoulders), underparts coarsely barred and spotted; cf. juv Grey-bellied Hawk (smaller, no crest, bare tarsi). Juv recalls ad Black-and-white Hawk-eagle but longer black crest, yellow (not orange) cere, barred flanks and thighs. **Voice** Loud rhythmic whistled "whit, wheEEeuuu, whep, whep, whep, whep", unlike Black Hawk-eagle emphasis near beginning, not end of call. **SS** Crested Eagle, Grey-headed Kite.

adult

juvenile

ornatus

Black-and-chestnut Eagle *Spizaetus isidori* `EN`
Águila Crestada `EN`
Uncommon to rare resident.
L 64–74 cm (25–29"). Monotypic. Humid and wet montane forest. 1600–3200 m (rarely lower). Soars low to high over forest; infrequently seen perched. **ID** Large and robust. Ad notably dark, spiked crest, chestnut underparts, in flight wing-linings chestnut, flight feathers pale with black tips, prominent whitish 'window' at base of outer primaries (above and below), broad black tip on longish tail. Juv undistinguished, much paler, above brownish, pale 'windows' in wings like ad, several broad tail-bands, plumage darker with age. **Voice** Low-pitched gull-like "kuaAAaa"; reedy whistled "kree, kee-kee". **SS** Juv Black Hawk-Eagle, juv Black Solitary Eagle, Black-chested Buzzard-eagle.

juvenile

adult

Double-toothed Kite *Harpagus bidentatus* LC
Gavilán Lagartero
Fairly common resident.

L 29–36 cm (11.5–14"). Races *fasciatus*[A], *bidentatus*[B]. Inside humid and wet lowland forest, tall second growth. To 1200 m. Rather unsuspicious; often follows monkeys, taking disturbed lizards and insects. Advertises by soaring, sometimes very high. **ID** In flight long-tailed shape recalls *Accipiter* but trailing edge of wing angled inward near body; conspicuous 'puffed' white undertail-coverts visible above or below. In all plumages white throat has vertical black central stripe; red to orange eyes; underparts extensively rufous (*bidentatus*) or less rufous, more barred (*fasciatus*). ♀ always more rufous below than ♂. Juv below whitish, variably streaked. **Voice** In flight thin high "peeeawee"; longer series of thin chirping notes. **SS** Plain-breasted and Roadside Hawks.

juvenile
adult
bidentatus

Rufous-thighed Kite *Harpagus diodon* LC
Elanio Muslirufo
Austral migrant (rare or overlooked?).

L 27–32 cm (10.5–12.5"). Monotypic. Humid lowland forest. Once, Puerto Nariño, Amazonas (photo, Jun 2019). To c. 200 m. **ID** Grey underparts, rufous thighs recall Bicolored Hawk but differs in black median throat stripe, inconspicuous double-notched maxilla, smaller size (♀ Bicolored much larger), redder eyes, uniform upperparts (Bicolored has contrasting dark crown). Juv resembles juv Double-toothed Kite; soon acquires rufous thighs.

adult

Genus *Circus* Long slender wings bent at wrist, long tail, and white rump. Beat low over fields and marshes, wings somewhat raised; take prey in sudden aerobatic pounce. Owl-like facial disc.

Long-winged Harrier *Circus buffoni* LC
Aguilucho Negro
Uncommon resident (very local W of Andes).

L 46–51 cm (18–24"). Monotypic. Wet pastures, marshes, grassland. To 1000 m. Like all harriers, an indefatigable hunter, quartering back and forth low over wet areas; occasionally soars. **ID** Large; plumage variable, always with white rump, contrasting grey primaries barred black, owl-like facial discs, multi-banded tail. Ad ♂ light morph upperparts and chest-band black, face black outlined white, lower underparts white. Ad ♀ light morph like ♂ but face, upperparts and chest brownish, below buff to whitish. Ad dark morph (both sexes) mostly sooty black, white eyebrow, may show tawny thighs. Juv light and dark morphs recall ad ♀, browner more steaked below, best identified by shape and behaviour. **SS** Northern Harrier (rare).

dark morph
♂
♂
light morph
♀
light morph
light morph

Northern Harrier *Circus hudsonius* LC
Aguilucho Pálido
Rare boreal migrant.

L 46–53 cm (18–21"). Monotypic. Few records, all W of Andes. To 2600 m. **ID** Conspicuous white rump (♂ and ♀). Ad ♂ pale grey with black wingtips, black-tipped secondaries; breast and belly whitish dotted rufous. Ad ♀ above brownish, short white eyebrow and line below eye, underparts buff streaked brown. Juv above like ♀, underparts unstreaked dull orange-rufous to buff; in flight dark head, dark inner secondaries. **SS** Long-winged Harrier.

♀
♂

Cinereous Harrier *Circus cinereus* `LC`
Aguilucho Cenizo `EN`

Uncommon resident in Nariño, rare in E Andes.

 L 43–51 cm (17–20"). Monotypic. *Páramo,* high-Andean grassland, marshes. 1700–3500 m (two widely separated areas). Lanky shape and behaviour as other harriers. **ID** Ad ♂ like ♂ Northern Harrier but breast and belly barred rufous. Ad ♀ above dark brown, neck and underparts barred rufous, rump white; in flight wings grey barred black. Juv like ♀ but darker, below mottled dark rufous. **SS** Northern Harrier.

Genus *Accipiter* Small to medium-sized, short rounded wings, long tails, long legs. Prey heavily on birds taken in speedy chase; soar infrequently, except Sharp-shinned Hawk. ♀♀ much larger than ♂♂. Identification often problematic.

Grey-bellied Hawk *Accipiter poliogaster* `NT`
Azor Selvático

Poorly known, possibly rare austral migrant.

L 43–51 cm (17–20"). Monotypic. Humid lowland forest, gallery forest. To 500 m. **ID** Ad large *Accipiter*. Crown and sides of head black, upperparts slightly contrasting slaty, tail black with four broad grey bars, below white, eyes, bare lores and ocular area bright orange to orange-yellow, underwings unbarred white. Juv very like ad Ornate Hawk-eagle, but smaller, no crest, tarsi bare. **Voice** Rapid cackling "kek-kek-kek-kek–kek–kek" slowing at end. **SS** Ad Slaty-backed Forest-falcon (p. 240; dark eyes, more extensive facial skin greenish yellow, upperparts uniform, underwings barred, narrow white tail bars). **AN** Grey-bellied Goshawk.

Sharp-shinned Hawk *Accipiter striatus* `LC`
Azor Cordillerano

Ten subspecies may comprise up to six subspecies groups; two in Colombia. Taxonomy unresolved.

Sharp-shinned Hawk *Accipiter (striatus) striatus*
Vagrant (boreal migrant).

L 23–34 cm (9–13.5"). Race *velox* (?). Once, Isla San Andrés.
ID Small *Accipiter*, square tail. Ad above dull blue-grey, below whitish variably barred rufous to tawny, eyes orange-red, cere and legs yellow; in flight leading edge of wing curved (not straight). Juv above brown, below coarsely streaked brown; by first year barred on thighs, tail narrowly tipped white, eyes yellowish.
Voice Single "chirp" notes; sharp "kew-kew-kew-kew-kew".
SS Cooper's Hawk.

Plain-breasted Hawk *Accipiter (striatus) ventralis*
Fairly common resident.

L 28–34 cm (11–13.5"). One subspecies in group. Humid montane forest, elfin woodland to treeline, woodlots, borders. 900–3500 m. Occasionally soars. **ID** Small. Ad plumage varies; thighs always rufous except rare all-dark morph. (1) above dark blue-grey, below cinnamon-rufous barred and spotted white, throat whitish; (2) underparts white with a few shaft-streaks; or (3) lower underparts tawny to chestnut. Juv like juv Sharp-shinned Hawk (above). **Voice** Cackling "kra-kra-kra-kra". **SS** Bicolored, Tiny and Cooper's Hawks, Great Thrush (p. 450). **TN** Race *ventralis* often regarded as a separate species.

Cooper's Hawk *Accipiter cooperii* LC
Azor de Cooper
Vagrant (boreal migrant).

 L 38–43 cm (15–17"). Monotypic. All records (visual and specimens) from mountains; Santa Marta (twice), also Cundinamarca and Tolima, 1200–3000 m. **ID** Medium-sized *Accipiter*, similar to paler forms of boreal migrant Sharp-shinned Hawk but always larger; differs in larger head, longer more rounded (not square-tipped) tail with broader white tip, in flight wings held straight (not pulled forward). Juv/1st-year above brownish, below white with thin dark streaks, eyes yellowish. **Voice** Cackling "ca-ca...".

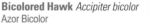

Bicolored Hawk *Accipiter bicolor* LC
Azor Bicolor

 Five subspecies in two subspecies groups; one in Colombia.

pale morph

dark morph

bicolor

Bicolored Hawk *Accipiter (bicolor) bicolor*
Uncommon resident.
L 36–43 cm (14–17"). Race *bicolor*. Dry to humid lowland and montane forest, borders, gallery forest, second growth. To 2400 m. **ID** Medium-sized; above dark grey, cap darker, underparts uniform pale grey (pale morph) to dark grey (dark morph), thighs always rufous, eyes yellow to orange, cere yellow. Juv variable; nuchal collar and underparts rich tawny to whitish, thighs rufous or mottled white. **Voice** Cackling "cak-cak-cak...". **SS** Ad Grey-bellied Hawk; compare juv to forest-falcons (p. 239).

Semicollared Hawk *Accipiter collaris* NT
Azor Collarejo NT
Rare resident.

  L 30–36 cm (12–14"). Monotypic. Humid and wet premontane and montane forest. 600–2000 m. Secretive but occasionally perches briefly in open. **ID** Small forest *Accipiter*. Ad resembles commoner ad Tiny Hawk (lower elevations) but eyes yellow (not red or orange), nearly complete whitish nuchal collar, underparts barring coarser (blackish ♂; brownish ♀), pale ear-coverts streaked blackish. Juv has rufous and grey morphs; both resemble respective morphs of Tiny Hawk but with buff-white nuchal collar. **Voice** Brief high-pitched "quee-kee-kee-kee", slightly rising.

juvenile brown morph

Tiny Hawk *Accipiter superciliosus* LC
Azor Diminuto

 L 22–27 cm (8.5–10.5"). Races *fontainieri*[A], *superciliosus*[B]. Humid and wet lowland and foothill forest. To 1500 m. Occasionally perches in open. Hunts small birds from understorey to canopy. **ID** Tiny. Ad ♂ above dark grey, eyes red, fine dense blackish barring on underparts. Ad ♀ and juv brown morph similar but browner; juv rufous morph rufous above, often also with barring, underparts finely barred rufous. Some ad (?) may retain rufous plumage. Race *fontainieri* smaller, barring coarser and blacker. **Voice** High thin "keer-keer...". **SS** Semicollared Hawk.

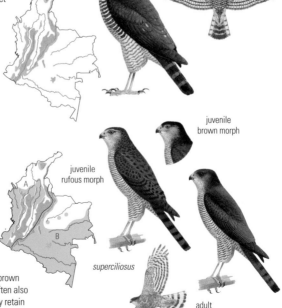

juvenile rufous morph

superciliosus

adult

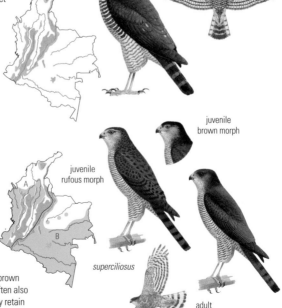

189

Black-collared Hawk *Busarellus nigricollis* LC
Gavilán Cienaguero
Common resident.

L 46–51 cm (18–20"). Race *nigricollis*. Mangroves, rivers, lagoons, almost any body of water with trees nearby. To 500 m. Confiding fishing hawk; singles or pairs perch on open branches near water, prey on fish and other aquatic life. Soars well, often low. **ID** Ad rufous plumage, whitish head, small black 'bow-tie'. Juv foreface whitish, rest of head streaked brownish, throat mottled blackish, lower underparts streaked and barred brown. **Voice** Odd slow nasal "na-a-a-a-a-a" (as if vomiting), clear rising "uuuueeeeeeeeEEE", downslurred "shreeeuuur". **SS** Savanna Hawk.

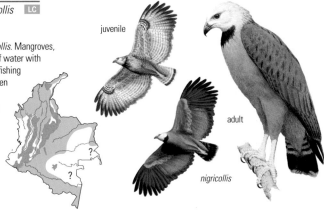

juvenile

adult

nigricollis

Crane Hawk *Geranospiza caerulescens* LC
Aguililla Zancona

Six subspecies in three subspecies groups; two in Colombia.

Blackish Crane Hawk *Geranospiza (caerulescens) nigra*
Uncommon resident.
L 43–51 cm (17–20"). Race *balzarensis*. To 800 m. **ID** Similar to Grey Crane (below) but darker, uniform slate-grey, usually with obscure white barring on lower underparts. **SS** Plumbeous Hawk, Common and Great Black Hawks.

balzarensis

Grey Crane Hawk
Geranospiza (caerulescens) caerulescens
Fairly common resident (especially *llanos*).
L 43–51 cm (17–20"). One subspecies in group. Dry to humid wooded or semi-open areas, gallery forest; often near water. To 700 m. Active versatile hunter from ground to treetops, uses long legs to reach into holes, crevices, hanging dead palm fronds for frogs, lizards, bats. **ID** Slender, small-headed, notably long legs and tail, red eyes and legs; in flight diagnostic white crescent on underside of primaries. Juv brownish, underparts coarsely streaked and barred, white underwing crescent like ad. **Voice** Clear downslurred whistle "WHEE'eer". **SS** Slate-colored Hawk, Slender-billed and Snail Kites.

Mississippi Kite *Ictinia mississippiensis* LC
Aguililla del Misisipí
Boreal passage migrant.

L 33–38 cm (13–15"). Monotypic. Can occur almost anywhere, even *páramo*. Oct–early Dec, Mar–Apr. To 3500 m. High-flying migratory flocks of up to 1000+ reported, largest in Apr on E Andean slope of Boyacá and Meta. **ID** Ad from similar Plumbeous Kite by paler grey head (almost whitish at distance), longer all-black tail (no bands), in flight from above diagnostic whitish secondaries, little or no rufous on underwing, legs yellowish. Juv variable; underparts and wing-linings streaked rufous, base of primaries whitish.

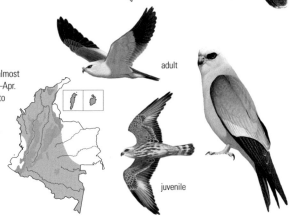

adult

juvenile

Plumbeous Kite *Ictinia plumbea* `LC`
Aguililla Plomiza

Common breeding resident and migrant.

L 33–38 cm (13–15"). Monotypic. Widespread over humid forest. To 2600 m. Singles, pairs or several. Regularly soars, often high, takes insects in air or snatched from canopy; perches high in open. Present year-round. Central American breeders move N Jan–Feb, return Aug–Oct, to or through W Colombia to Amazonia (?); movements poorly documented. **ID** Long pointed wings, base of primaries rufous, two narrow white tail-bands from below, legs reddish orange. Juv has underparts streaked grey, little or no rufous in primaries. **Voice** Rarely a weak twittering. **SS** Mississippi Kite.

juvenile

adult

Snail Kite *Rostrhamus sociabilis* `LC`
Caracolero Común

Common resident.

L 41–46 cm (16–18"). Race *sociabilis*. Freshwater marshes, wetlands, river borders. To 1000 m (rarely 2600 m). Pairs or small groups quarter low over marshes or perch low near water. Diet mainly *Pomacea* snails; moves seasonally in response to changing water levels and snail availability. Occasionally soars. **ID** Slender hooked bill, tail square, rump and tail base white, narrow tail tips white. Ad ♂ red cere, eyes and legs. Ad ♀ below heavily mottled and streaked, in flight whitish window in primaries, cere yellow. Juv like ♀ but paler. **SS** Slender-billed Kite.

♂

♀

sociabilis

Slender-billed Kite *Helicolestes hamatus* `LC`
Caracolero Negro

Fairly common but local resident.

L 36–41 cm (14–16"). Monotypic. Swampy forest, oxbows, *várzea*. To 700 m. Singles or pairs perch at various heights, regularly soar low for short periods. Feeds heavily on *Pomacea* snails. **ID** Chunky shape. Ad very slender hooked bill, cere, lores, eye-ring and legs red, conspicuous white eyes, short all-dark tail. In flight tail barely protrudes, wings broad. Juv brownish grey to slate-grey, underparts obscurely barred white, several narrow whitish tail-bands. **Voice** Nasal kazoo-like rising and falling "wheeeaaaaah". **SS** Snail Kite.

juvenile

adult

Roadside Hawk *Rupornis magnirostris* `LC`
Gavilán Caminero

Commonest Colombian raptor.

L 34–39 cm (13.5–15.5"). Race *magnirostris*. Dry to humid forest borders, semi-open terrain, settled areas. To 2600 m. Singles or pairs perch in open; soar and call incessantly on sunny mornings. Shallow wingbeats alternate with glides, shakes tail on alighting. **ID** Ad yellow cere and eyes, upperparts to chest greyish, underparts loosely barred pale rufous, in flight conspicuous rufous wing patch. Juv above brownish, below variably mottled, streaked or barred. **Voice** Angry buzzy "kzeeeeeer"; in flight long series of annoyed "kee-kee..." notes. **SS** Grey-lined and Broad-winged Hawks.

juvenile

adult

magnirostris

Harris's Hawk *Parabuteo unicinctus* `LC`
Gavilán Rabiblanco

Two subspecies in two subspecies groups; both in Colombia.

adult

Harris's Hawk *Parabuteo (unicinctus) harrisi*
Uncommon and quite local resident.
L 48–56 cm (19–22"). One subspecies in group. To 1500 m. Habitat, behaviour and plumage as Bay-winged Hawk. **ID** Like next subspecies, but no white scaling on lower underparts and thighs. Juv duller.

Bay-winged Hawk *Parabuteo (unicinctus) unicinctus*
Uncommon resident.
L 48–56 cm (19–22"). One subspecies in group. Desert scrub, grassland with brush and scattered trees, *llanos* (?). To 1700 m. Active; stoops from air on small prey or hunts from tree or cactus. Pairs or groups known to hunt and breed cooperatively (in Colombia?). Soars low for short periods. **ID** Ad lanky, long legs and tail, chestnut shoulders and thighs, rump and basal half of tail white, whitish belly. Juv dull, brownish, mottled and streaked below, rufous shoulders faint, primaries basally whitish from below. **Voice** Raspy scream; metallic scraping "squee'zit".

juvenile

adult

White-rumped Hawk *Parabuteo leucorrhous* `LC`
Gavilán Negro
Uncommon resident.

L 36–41 cm (14–16"). Monotypic. Humid and wet montane forest, borders.1700–2900 m. Alone or in pairs; most often seen soaring low over canopy. **ID** Small short-winged raptor, *Buteo*-like shape. In flight shows white rump and vent, whitish wing-linings contrast with black flight feathers, rufous thighs seldom visible. Juv dark brown, head, neck and underparts buff, heavily streaked and blotched brown and black. **Voice** Whistled "SPEEaa" in flight. **SS** Short-tailed and White-throated Hawks.

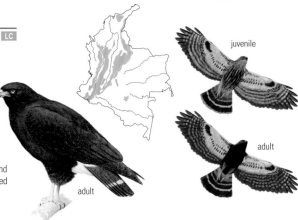

juvenile

adult

adult

Plumbeous Hawk *Cryptoleucopteryx plumbea* `VU`
Gavilán Pizarra `NT`
Uncommon and local resident.

L 36–38 cm (14–15"). Monotypic. Humid and wet lowland and foothill forest. To 800 m. Singles, inconspicuous inside forest at mid-levels or higher, perching quietly; does not soar. **ID** Small, chunky, short-winged. Ad slaty, single white tail-band, red eyes, orange cere and legs. In flight entire underwing white with black rear border. Juv lower underparts variably barred white, may show second tail-band. **Voice** Infrequent long (two-second) descending whistle "wheeeeeeeeur", ends abruptly. **SS** Slender-billed Kite, Crane Hawk.

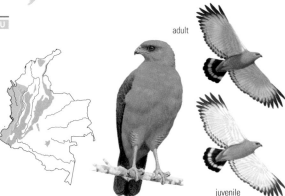

adult

juvenile

Genus *Buteogallus* Recently modified genus now united more by genetics than morphology; some similarities in juv plumages but ad plumage, size, wing and tail lengths, shape, and habitats vary widely.

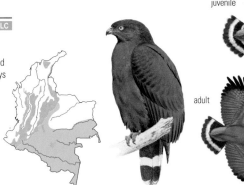

juvenile

adult

Slate-colored Hawk *Buteogallus schistaceus* `LC`
Gavilán Patirrojo
Common resident.

L 41–43 cm (16–17"). Monotypic. Swamp and *várzea* forest, borders, oxbows; almost always near water. To 500 m. Singles, sluggish, perches at various levels, sometimes quite low, infrequently soars. **ID** Broad-winged, short-tailed. Ad slaty black, single white tail-band, conspicuous red-orange cere and legs. Juv lower underparts and thighs barred white, underwings greyish with dark barring, and often a second tail-band. **Voice** Vocal; loud, piercing downslurred whistle "wheeeeeeaaah". **SS** Slender-billed Kite, Crane Hawk.

Common Black Hawk *Buteogallus anthracinus* `LC`
Cangrejero Negro

Five subspecies in two subspecies groups; both in Colombia.

anthracinus

adult

juvenile

Common Black Hawk
Buteogallus (anthracinus) anthracinus
Fairly common but local resident.
L 43–53 cm (17–21"). Race *anthracinus*. Mangroves (Caribbean coast), dry to humid woodland. To 500 m. Soars briefly, otherwise inconspicuous. **ID** Broad wings, short tail and tarsi. Ad single broad white tailband and narrow tip, thigh feathers black, from below small white patch at base of primaries, cere, base of bill and legs rich butter-yellow. Juv buff-white eyebrow, dusky line through eyes, below buff streaked and blotched dusky, 5–8 narrow dark tail-bands. **Voice** Perched or flying, high thin "spink-speenk-speenk-spink-spink-spink", rising and descending. **SS** Great Black Hawk.

subtilis

adult

Mangrove Black Hawk *Buteogallus (anthracinus) subtilis*
Fairly common resident.
L 42–51 cm (16.5–20"). Race *subtilis*. Mangroves, beach scrub on Pacific coast, offshore islands. To 100 m. **ID** Like Common Black Hawk but slightly smaller, larger white patches at base of outer primaries, rufous mottling on wings and belly may be more evident. **Voice** Like Common Black Hawk. **SS** Note restricted habitat. **TN** Now widely regarded as a well-marked subspecies.

Savanna Hawk *Buteogallus meridionalis* `LC`
Gavilán Sabanero
Common resident.

L 48–61 cm (19–24"). Monotypic. Ranchland, open terrain with scattered trees. Commonest in *llanos*. To 1000 m (rarely 1800 m). Singles or pairs perch in open on fence posts, treetops, shrubs or ground. Regularly soars; gathers at dry-season fires. **ID** Mostly dull rufous, long yellow legs. In flight unusually long broad wings (almost a flying wing), short black tail with white band; at rest wings reach beyond tail. Juv above brownish, head and underparts whitish streaked and barred throughout. Imm hint of rufous wings. **Voice** Shrill descending "keeeeeeeru". **SS** Shape and habitat are best clues. Black-collared Hawk.

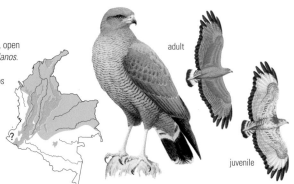

adult

juvenile

Great Black Hawk *Buteogallus urubitinga* LC
Cangrejero Grande

Two subspecies in two subspecies groups; one in Colombia.

Great Black Hawk
Buteogallus (urubitinga) urubitinga
Common resident E of Andes, fewer in N.
L 56–64 cm (22–25"). One subspecies in group.
Rivers and oxbows in humid forest, gallery forest, ranchland, mangroves. To 1000 m. Singles or pairs perch on open branches, shrubs, or roam afoot on ground, especially on muddy riverbanks and sandbars; take reptiles, smaller vertebrates, diet notably catholic. **ID** Large blackish raptor, dull yellowish cere, long yellow legs, basal half of tail white. Juv recalls juv Common Black Hawk but larger, more tail-bands (10–14 vs. 5–8). **Voice** High whistled scream "wheeeeeeeuur". **SS** Common Black Hawk.

juvenile

adult

Black Solitary Eagle *Buteogallus solitarius* NT
Águila Solitaria CR
Rare resident.

L 66–71 cm (26–28"). Race *solitarius*. Moist to wet foothill and montane forest. 700–2500 m (350 m, Santa Marta area). Singles or pairs soar high on flat wings, gliding over ridges, forested slopes.
ID All plumages much like Great Black Hawk, but decidedly greyer, more projecting slightly crested aquiline head, extremely short tail (barely protrudes) with single narrow white band, at rest wings extend beyond tail. Juv brownish blotched darker, longer unbanded tail, black terminal band obscure. **Voice** Infrequent rising whistle, a piercing "pi-pi...". **AN** Often known simply as Solitary Eagle.

juvenile

solitarius

adult

Barred Hawk *Morphnarchus princeps* LC
Gavilán Príncipe
Uncommon resident.

L 53–58 cm (21–23"). Monotypic. Humid and wet foothill and lower montane forest. 400–2200 m. Singles or pairs soar low above forest on sunny mornings. Perches and hunts inside forest where inconspicuous. **ID** Ad broad wings, single narrow white band on short tail, blackish upperparts and chest, finely barred pale lower underparts, dark eyes. In flight wing-linings pale grey. Juv white-edged mantle and shoulders. **Voice** Whistled scream "wheeeuuuu"; 30–40 short rapid whistles. **TN** Previously in genus *Leucopternis*.

Genus *Geranoaetus* Poorly defined genus morphologically; closely related to *Buteo* (and other genera). Species overall large; one notably short-tailed.

juvenile
pale morph

White-tailed Hawk *Geranoaetus albicaudatus* LC
Gavilán Coliblanco
Local resident.

L 51–61 cm (20–24"). Races *hypospodius*[A], *colonus*[B]. Dry savanna, ranchland, expanding into deforested highlands. To 2400 m. Singles or pairs; soar high, hover into wind on flat wings, perch in open, and gather at dry-season fires. **ID** In all ad plumages rump and tail white with black subterminal band; at rest broad wings project beyond tail. Ad pale morph head and upperparts grey (throat occasionally dark), underparts white, shoulders rufous, in flight, wing-linings whitish, inner primaries dusky. Ad dark morph sooty black, shoulders rufous. Juv pale morph blackish, tail pale, often has white chest patch. **SS** Variable Hawk.

dark morph

adult

adult

pale morph

colonus

Variable Hawk *Geranoaetus polyosoma* `LC`
Gavilán Variable

Two (four?) subspecies may comprise two subspecies groups; one in Colombia. Taxonomy unresolved.

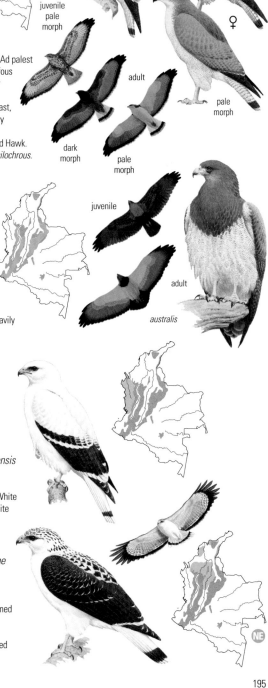

♂ pale morph

dark morph

juvenile pale morph

♀

Red-backed Hawk
Geranoaetus (polyosoma) polyosoma
Rare to uncommon resident.
L 48–61 cm (19–24"). One subspecies in group. Open or semi-open highlands, *páramo*. 1800–3800 m. Most records May–Sept (austral migrants?) but breeding reported. **ID** Very variable; all morphs have white tail and black subterminal band. Ad palest morph (commonest) much like White-tailed Hawk but ♂ lacks rufous shoulders; ♀ has back rufous (but not shoulders); both may show fine bars on breast. Ad dark morph notoriously variable, all sooty (tail as above) or also has rufous back, or rufous on back and breast, and variably barred below. Juv above mottled dark brown, usually pale or whitish eyebrow and cheeks, dark malar, below variable, usually with some bars. **SS** Separate with care from White-tailed Hawk. **TN** Some morphs (races?) sometimes split as Puna Hawk *G. poecilochrous*.

adult

pale morph

dark morph

pale morph

Black-chested Buzzard-eagle
Geranoaetus melanoleucus `LC`
Águila Paramuna
Fairly common resident.

L 61–69 cm (24–27"). Race *australis*. Dry to humid semi-open highlands, *páramo*, occasionally over humid forest. 2600–3800 m. Singles or pairs soar high on flat wings; perch on bushes, boulders, rocky slopes or ground. Stoops on birds, small mammals. **ID** Large; above greyish, chest black sharply separated from whitish underparts, wings broad at base, tapering outward (like flying wedge), extremely short tail. Juv heavily mottled and streaked buff and black, tail longer, wedge-shaped. **Voice** Piercing whistles.

juvenile

adult

australis

White Hawk *Pseudastur albicollis* `LC`
Gavilán Blanco

Four subspecies in four subspecies groups; three in Colombia.

Costa Rican White Hawk *Pseudastur (albicollis) costaricensis*
Uncommon and local resident.
L 46–51 cm (18–20"). One subspecies in group. N Chocó Pacific. To 1200 m (seldom higher). **ID** Much whiter than other races of White Hawk; head, back and shoulders entirely white, at rest single white band on black wings. Juv variable dark streaking on upperparts. **Voice** See Amazonian White Hawk.

Colombian White Hawk *Pseudastur (albicollis) williaminae*
Very local resident.
L 46–51 cm (18–20"). One subspecies in group. Near-endemic (also extreme NW Venezuela). Spottily distributed, mainly upper R Sinú, lower Cauca and middle Magdalena Valleys; most confirmed recent records in or close to Andean foothills or N base of Santa Marta Mts. Dry to humid forest. To 1400 m. **ID** Like Amazonian White Hawk but crown, back and shoulders black, heavily streaked and scalloped white; single white band on black wings.

`NE`

Amazonian White Hawk *Pseudastur (albicollis) albicollis*
Uncommon and local resident.
L 46–51 cm (18–20"). One subspecies in group. Humid
lowland and foothill forest. To 1400 m. Generally near
or in Andean foothills or sandy soil forests of extreme E.
Regularly soars over forest, perches inside it. **ID** Broad
rounded wings, short tail. Nape and mantle white with
narrow black shaft-streaks. At rest wings all black; in
flight from below largely white, tips black. Tail white,
broad black subterminal band. **Voice** Long (c. 2-second)
hoarse scream, slightly rising then falling (*costaricensis*);
cleaner, shorter, more piercing scream, sharply rising and
falling (*albicollis*); short metallic rising and falling
"pe'a" whistles.

[Grey-backed Hawk *Pseudastur occidentalis*] EN
Gavilán Espaldigrís
Hypothetical.

L 46–53 cm (18–21"). Monotypic. Unconfirmed
(but plausible) sight records in SW Nariño lowlands.
Probably to c. 1500 m. Humid forest. Behaviour like
White Hawk. **ID** Eyes dark, cere blue-grey, above dark
grey, crown and nape white variably streaked grey, tail white, with
broad black subterminal band. In flight only wingtips black. Juv similar
but above brownish grey, obscure dark barring on sides of breast.
Voice Hoarse screams (c. 1/second) in flight; recalls *costaricensis* race
of White Hawk but shorter.

Semiplumbeous Hawk *Leucopternis semiplumbeus* LC
Gavilán Gris
Uncommon resident.

L 33–36 cm (13–14"). Monotypic. Humid and wet
lowland and foothill forest. To 600 m (rarely
1000 m). Singles or pairs, generally inside forest;
does not soar. **ID** Small, bicoloured, bright orange
cere, yellow eyes, black tail with single white band and tip;
in flight from below wings mostly white. Juv above streaked
and spotted white, below minor dark shaft-streaks, 2–3 white
tail-bands, and bare parts dull. **Voice** Clear piercing scream
rising slightly, abruptly falling at end, "kweEEEa".

Black-faced Hawk *Leucopternis melanops* LC
Gavilán Carinegro
Rare to uncommon resident (local?).

L 38–43 cm (15–17"). Monotypic. Humid lowland forest.
To 500 m. Perches and hunts at various heights inside
forest. Inconspicuous, seldom perches in open; rarely if ever
soars. **ID** Resembles larger White Hawk, differs by bright
orange cere, small black mask, white head with thin dark shaft-streaks
on crown and nape, tail black, one white band, back and wing-coverts
spotted white. Juv two white tail-bands. **Voice** Single piercing whistle
(c. 1 second) "PZZeeyer" descending, forceful but fades.

Genus *Buteo* Widespread genus with broad wings and medium-length tail; a good 'yardstick' group for comparison with other raptors. Generally typical of forest borders and semi-open habitats; often soar.

Grey-lined Hawk *Buteo nitidus* `LC`
Gavilán Saraviado
Common resident.

L 38–43 cm (15–17"). Races *blakei*[A], *nitidus*[B]. Dry to humid forest borders, river edges, ranchland. To 800 m. Hunts from perch, or in agile pursuit, occasionally stoops in flight. Perches fairly high, regularly soars. **ID** Ad paler, greyer than Roadside Hawk; differs in black (not yellow) eyes, lightly barred upperparts, paler finely barred underparts (no rufous or brownish markings). In flight underwing pale (not rufous), one or more visible white tail-bands. Juv buff-white eyebrow, buff to white underparts coarsely spotted and blotched brown. **Voice** Loud clear "KEEeeeu", descending; weaker piping whistles. **TN** Previously in genus *Asturinus*. Formerly conspecific with Grey Hawk of Middle America.

Broad-winged Hawk *Buteo platypterus* `LC`
Gavilán Aliancho
Common boreal migrant.

L 38–46 cm (15–18"). Race *platypterus*. Sept–Apr. Moist to humid forest borders, clearings with scattered trees. To 2800 m (rarely higher). Numerous in Andes, far fewer in lowlands. Commonly perches at wooded borders; regularly soars, usually not high. **ID** Medium-sized. Ad underparts coarsely barred rufous-brown, numerous narrow white tail-bands; in flight, narrow black rim to whitish underwing. Juv duller, underparts streaked. **Voice** Calls from perch, high (c. 4.5 kHz) pure-whistled "w'eeeeeeeeEE", not raptor-like. **SS** Roadside Hawk.

White-throated Hawk *Buteo albigula* `LC`
Gavilán Gorgiblanco
Rare austral migrant.

L 41–48 cm (16–19"). Monotypic. Humid montane forest, *páramo*. 1700–3500 m. Mostly Apr–Oct. Often soars high. **ID** Ad dark head and cheeks (looks hooded), heavy rufous and black streaks and blotches on axillaries and sides of breast, sometimes lightly on lower breast. In flight pale flight feathers not strongly contrasting with wing-linings (sharp contrast in Short-tailed Hawk), minor dark-fringed markings at rear of wing-linings, whitish 'window' in outer primaries, wings longer, narrower than most *Buteo*, tail lacks strong barring. Juv browner, wing-linings and underparts somewhat mottled. **Voice** High thin scream, abruptly rising and falling.

Short-tailed Hawk *Buteo brachyurus* `LC`
Gavilán Rabicorto
Uncommon resident.

L 38–46 cm (15–18"). Race *brachyurus*. Open, semi-open and humid forest regions. To 1800 m (rarely 2500 m). Seen soaring much more than perched; often soars high. **ID** Ad pale morph (commonest) has upperparts blackish brown including neck- and sides of head (looks hooded), narrow white forehead, throat and underparts white. In flight, white wing-linings contrast with dark-barred flight feathers, tail has several obscure narrow dark bars. Ad dark morph (rare) overall blackish, tail like pale morph. In flight black wing-linings contrast sharply with pale flight feathers (reverse of pale morph). **Voice** Rarely, a high whistle. **SS** White-tailed and White-throated Hawks.

Swainson's Hawk *Buteo swainsoni* LC
Gavilán de Swainson
Common boreal passage migrant.

L 48–56 cm (19–22"). Monotypic. Over forested or semi-open terrain. To 3500 m. Sept–Nov, Feb–Mar; migrates broadly across mid-portion of E Andes, N half of C & W Andes. Small to huge flocks; 50–10,000+ over mid-Magdalena Valley (Mariquita) and C Andes in Antioquia. **ID** Ad pale morph (commonest) long narrow pointed wings, broad dark chest-band. In flight whitish wing-linings contrast with dark flight feathers, dark subterminal tail-band. Ad dark morph (rare) all brownish black including underwing, tail like pale morph. Intermediate morph (rare) dark chest-band, rufous-barred lower underparts. Juv heavily mottled below, dark blotches on chest-sides. **SS** Plumage variable; wing shape key.

intermediate morph

dark morph

pale morph

Zone-tailed Hawk *Buteo albonotatus* LC
Gavilán Gallinazo
Uncommon resident.

L 46–56 cm (18–22"). Monotypic. Dry open or semi-open areas, ranchland, also humid lowland and montane forest. To 2200 m (fewer to 3000 m). Singles or scattered pairs. Flight profile mimics Turkey Vulture including wings in dihedral and teetering. **ID** Black; two-toned wings, yellow cere and legs, 2–3 whitish tail-bands. Juv white-spotted, especially below, numerous narrow grey tail bars. **Voice** Long complaining scream, slightly descending. **SS** Turkey Vulture (p. 182), various dark-morph raptors.

juvenile

Red-tailed Hawk *Buteo jamaicensis* LC
Gavilán Colirrojo
Vagrant (or rare boreal migrant).

L 51–64 cm (20–25"). Race unknown. Few records (Nov, Jan, Mar), Santa Marta area, Andes. **ID** Large, robust; plumage variable. All ad plumages show rufous tail, except rare Harlan's form (unlikely). Juv below pale, belly heavily streaked, tail greyish and finely barred, wing-linings whitish, leading edge of carpal area dark, from above outer wing pale. **Voice** Raspy scream. **SS** Broad-winged Hawk.

adult

TROGONIDAE
Trogons
43 extant species, 14 in region

A virtually pantropical family that achieves peak diversity in humid Neotropical lowland and lower montane forests. Renowned for brilliant colours. Some, especially quetzals, are ranked among the world's most beautiful birds. The family is notable for soft, lax plumage, large eyes, short thick bills, weak feet and long, square-tipped graduated tails. They nest in natural or excavated cavities.

Genus *Pharomachrus* Glistening plumage, elongated upperwing-coverts, and uppertail-coverts longer than tail. Flight hurtling; swooping sally and brief hover, mostly for large-seeded fruits; more frugivorous than *Trogon*. Perch quietly for long periods. Songs slow, melancholy; cackle in agitation or prior to flight.

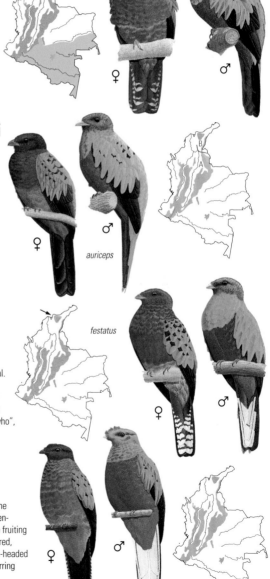

Pavonine Quetzal *Pharomachrus pavoninus* `LC`
Quetzal Amazónico
Uncommon and local resident.

 L 34 cm (13.5"). Monotypic. Humid *terra firme* and transition forest. To 600 m. Pairs, in mid-levels or subcanopy. Territory large. Mostly independent of mixed flocks; often wary. **ID** Bill red, undertail black (♂) or bill dusky red, undertail with a few whitish bars on outer feathers (♀). **Voice** Song a slow melancholy whistled "heeeeear'chok!..." repeated several times, especially at dawn as moves through forest.

Golden-headed Quetzal *Pharomachrus auriceps* `LC`
Quetzal Colinegro
Fairly common resident.

 L 34 cm (13.5"). Races *auriceps*[A], *hargitti*[B]. Humid and wet montane forest, tall second growth. 1050–2800 m. Mid-levels to subcanopy. Well-separated pairs, or several at fruiting trees, especially *Persea* and *Ocotea* (Lauraceae), sometimes with Crested Quetzals. **ID** Undertail slaty black, eyes reddish brown (both sexes), head may appear more brownish than golden (especially ♀), no frontal crest. **Voice** Slow whistled "whee'whEEEEo" (or "ka'whEEEEo") several times, melancholy, far-carrying. **SS** Crested Quetzal.

auriceps

White-tipped Quetzal *Pharomachrus fulgidus* `LC`
Quetzal Dorado
Fairly common resident.

 L 34 cm (13.5"). Race *festatus*. Humid montane forest, tall second growth, coffee plantations. 1400–2500 m. Behaviour as Golden-headed Quetzal. **ID** ♂ distal half of outer three tail feathers white (closed tail mostly white below). ♀ duller, especially head, outer tail feathers with variable white barring. **Voice** Song, especially first half of year, slow melancholy whistled "WHOOOOOou, ca'who", 4–6 times. **SS** Masked Trogon.

festatus

Crested Quetzal *Pharomachrus antisianus* `LC`
Quetzal Crestado
Uncommon resident.

 L 34 cm (13.5"). Monotypic. Humid and wet montane forest, borders. 1400–2700 m. Behaviour like Golden-headed Quetzal and sometimes joins it at favourite fruiting trees, but usually less numerous. **ID** ♂ eyes bright red, small frontal crest, closed tail white below. ♀ very like ♀ Golden-headed Quetzal but eyes reddish (not brown), tail with variable white barring (sometimes obscure) on outer feathers. **Voice** Slow steady "keeop-weEEeo", 3–6 times.

Genus *Trogon* Upright posture, long graduated square-tipped tails. ♂♂ have head and upperparts bluish to greenish; ♀♀ grey to brown, and undertail pattern usually differs. Take fruit and large insects during swooping sally and brief hover; flight headlong and undulating.

Slaty-tailed Trogon *Trogon massena* LC
Trogón Piquirrojo
Uncommon resident.

L 32 cm (12.5"). Races *hoffmanni*[A], *australis*[B]. Humid and wet forest, borders. To 1200 m. Loosely associated pairs in mid-levels to canopy; sometimes active around mixed flocks or troops of squirrel and capuchin monkeys. **ID** Large; from Choco Trogon by dark eyes, and Black-tailed Trogon by red on bill. **Voice** Song low nasal "cah" notes c. 2–3/second for up to c. 10+ seconds; occasionally gathers and calls in loose groups. **AN** Massena Trogon.

australis

Choco Trogon *Trogon comptus* LC
Trogón Ojiblanco
Fairly common resident.

L 32 cm (12.5"). Monotypic. Near-endemic (also NW Ecuador). Wet lowland and especially foothill forest, borders. 200–900 m (locally 1800 m). Pairs; midstorey or higher, sometimes with mixed flocks. **ID** Either sex identified by white eyes. **Voice** Slow series of c. 7–15 or more "coaw" notes, with up-down inflection, c. 2/second. **SS** Slaty-tailed Trogon (red bill), Black-tailed Trogon (narrow white chest-band).

Black-tailed Trogon *Trogon melanurus* LC
Trogón Colinegro

Four subspecies in two subspecies groups; both in Colombia.

Large-tailed Trogon *Trogon (melanurus) macroura*
Common resident.
L 32 cm (12.5"). One subspecies in group. Moist, humid and wet forest, borders, second growth. To 500 m. Behaviour as Black-tailed Trogon (race *melanurus*). **ID** Much like Slaty-tailed Trogon but bill yellow (not reddish). A few ♀♀ (juv?) show white markings on edge of tail. **Voice** Similar to *melanurus* (below). **SS** Choco Trogon (white eyes).

Black-tailed Trogon *Trogon (melanurus) melanurus*
Common resident.
L 32 cm (12.5"). Races *melanurus*[A], *eumorphus*[B] (S Amazonas?). Humid lowland forest, borders, old second growth. To 600 m. Loosely associated pairs in mid-levels to subcanopy, often with mixed flocks or troops of squirrel and capuchin monkeys. **ID** Either sex from other red-bellied Amazonian trogons by larger size, slaty-black undertail. **Voice** Song 20–30+ nasal, up-down inflected "wow" notes c. 2/second or faster; short chattering calls. **SS** Blue-crowned and Collared Trogons, Pavonine Quetzal.

melanurus

Green-backed Trogon *Trogon viridis* LC
Trogón Coliblanco
Commonest Amazonian trogon.

 L 29 cm (11.5"). Race *viridis*. Humid lowland and foothill forest. To 1200 m. **ID** ♂ from other yellow-bellied trogons by complete bluish eye-ring; ♀ complete greyish eye-ring, no white chest-band. **Voice** Song brisk "cowp" notes (c. 3–4/second) with sharp downward inflection; same pitch or first notes slightly higher, slightly accelerating initially; "chuck"; short chatters. **SS** Smaller ♀ Amazonian Trogon (broken greyish eye-ring). **TN** Formerly included *T. chionurus* and called White-tailed Trogon.

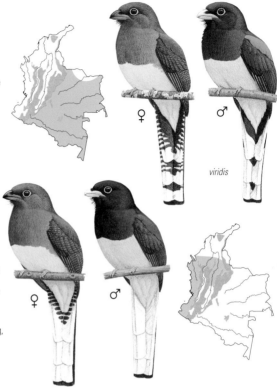

viridis

White-tailed Trogon *Trogon chionurus* LC
Trogón Coliblanco
Common resident.

 L 29 cm (11.5"). Monotypic. Humid forest, borders, second growth. To 1000 m. Pairs in mid-levels to subcanopy, occasionally low. **ID** ♂ complete bluish eye-ring, undertail white; ♀ complete grey eye-ring, tail narrowly barred white, with broad white tips. **Voice** Song faster than allies; a few "culp" notes accelerating into rapid (8+ notes/second) nasal "cua" notes; series may slightly descend and slow at end. Soft "chuck". **SS** Smaller ♀ Gartered Trogon (broken grey eye-ring, small white tail tips). **TN** See Green-backed Trogon.

Violaceous Trogon *Trogon violaceus* LC
Trogón Violáceo

 Six subspecies in three subspecies groups; two in Colombia. All three groups (including those below) now usually regarded as separate species.

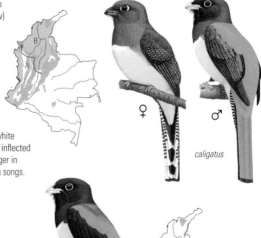

Gartered Trogon *Trogon (violaceus) caligatus*
Locally fairly common resident.
L 23 cm (9"). Races *concinnus*[A] (SW Nariño?), *caligatus*[B]. Dry to humid forest, borders, second growth, plantations. To 1400 m. **ID** Small; ♂ identified by complete yellow eye-ring, ♀ by broken greyish eye-ring, obscure white chest-band, fine white tail barring and small white tips. **Voice** Song, steady up-down inflected "qua" notes c. 4/second for several seconds; sometimes stronger in middle, but generally lacks acceleration of White-tailed Trogon songs. **SS** White-tailed and Black-throated Trogons.

caligatus

Amazonian Trogon *Trogon (violaceus) ramonianus*
Fairly common resident.
L 23 cm (9"). Race *ramonianus*. Humid forest, borders, second growth. To 600 m (higher?). Loosely associated pairs, upper understorey to subcanopy. **ID** Both sexes nearly identical to those of Gartered Trogon; ♂ crown glossier violet-blue (not blackish). **Voice** Songs like Gartered Trogon but marginally slower (c. 3 notes/second), sometimes strongly inflected as if each note doubled; song length variable. **SS** Green-backed and Black-throated Trogons.

ramonianus

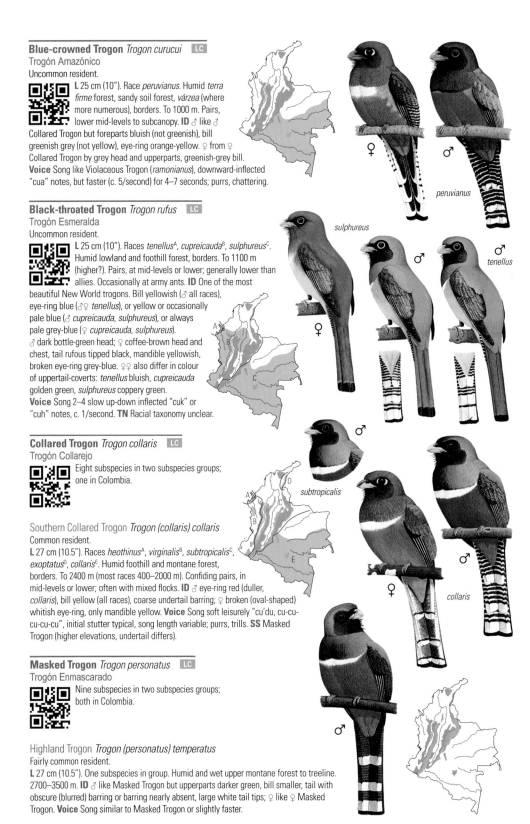

Blue-crowned Trogon *Trogon curucui* LC
Trogón Amazónico
Uncommon resident.

L 25 cm (10"). Race *peruvianus*. Humid *terra firme* forest, sandy soil forest, *várzea* (where more numerous), borders. To 1000 m. Pairs, lower mid-levels to subcanopy. **ID** ♂ like ♂ Collared Trogon but foreparts bluish (not greenish), bill greenish grey (not yellow), eye-ring orange-yellow. ♀ from ♀ Collared Trogon by grey head and upperparts, greenish-grey bill.
Voice Song like Violaceous Trogon (*ramonianus*), downward-inflected "cua" notes, but faster (c. 5/second) for 4–7 seconds; purrs, chattering.

peruvianus

Black-throated Trogon *Trogon rufus* LC
Trogón Esmeralda
Uncommon resident.

L 25 cm (10"). Races *tenellus*[A], *cupreicauda*[B], *sulphureus*[C]. Humid lowland and foothill forest, borders. To 1100 m (higher?). Pairs, at mid-levels or lower; generally lower than allies. Occasionally at army ants. **ID** One of the most beautiful New World trogons. Bill yellowish (♂ all races), eye-ring blue (♂♀ *tenellus*), or yellow or occasionally pale blue (♂ *cupreicauda*, *sulphureus*), or always pale grey-blue (♀ *cupreicauda*, *sulphureus*). ♂ dark bottle-green head; ♀ coffee-brown head and chest, tail rufous tipped black, mandible yellowish, broken eye-ring grey-blue. ♀♀ also differ in colour of uppertail-coverts: *tenellus* bluish, *cupreicauda* golden green, *sulphureus* coppery green.
Voice Song 2–4 slow up-down inflected "cuk" or "cuh" notes, c. 1/second. **TN** Racial taxonomy unclear.

sulphureus

♂ *tenellus*

Collared Trogon *Trogon collaris* LC
Trogón Collarejo

Eight subspecies in two subspecies groups; one in Colombia.

subtropicalis

Southern Collared Trogon *Trogon (collaris) collaris*
Common resident.
L 27 cm (10.5"). Races *heothinus*[A], *virginalis*[B], *subtropicalis*[C], *exoptatus*[D], *collaris*[E]. Humid foothill and montane forest, borders. To 2400 m (most races 400–2000 m). Confiding pairs, in mid-levels or lower; often with mixed flocks. **ID** ♂ eye-ring red (duller, *collaris*), bill yellow (all races), coarse undertail barring; ♀ broken (oval-shaped) whitish eye-ring, only mandible yellow. **Voice** Song soft leisurely "cu'du, cu-cu-cu-cu-cu", initial stutter typical, song length variable; purrs, trills. **SS** Masked Trogon (higher elevations, undertail differs).

collaris

Masked Trogon *Trogon personatus* LC
Trogón Enmascarado

Nine subspecies in two subspecies groups; both in Colombia.

Highland Trogon *Trogon (personatus) temperatus*
Fairly common resident.
L 27 cm (10.5"). One subspecies in group. Humid and wet upper montane forest to treeline. 2700–3500 m. **ID** ♂ like Masked Trogon but upperparts darker green, bill smaller, tail with obscure (blurred) barring or barring nearly absent, large white tail tips; ♀ like ♀ Masked Trogon. **Voice** Song similar to Masked Trogon or slightly faster.

Masked Trogon *Trogon (personatus) personatus*
Common resident.

L 25 cm (10"). Races *sanctaemartae*[A], *personatus*[B], *assimilis*[C]. Humid and wet montane forest, borders. 1400–2700 m (locally to 1000 m). **ID** ♂ (*sanctaemartae, personatus*) from ♂ Collared Trogon by much finer undertail barring, larger (blocky) white tail tips; ♀ by all-yellow bill, more prominent black mask, narrower undertail barring. Race *assimilis* closely resembles race *temperatus* (Highland Trogon). **Voice** Song (*personatus*) soft whistled "cawea…" of 4–8 notes, c. 1/second.

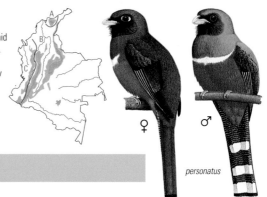

MOMOTIDAE
Motmots
14 extant species, 6 in region

personatus

Small Neotropical family, with peak diversity in N Central America. Best known for long racket-tipped tails, which are often swung mechanically from side to side. The rackets result from preening weak feather barbs, although a few races and species do not develop racket-tails. Motmots live in dry to humid forest, light woodland, and even desert scrub. They nest in burrows and are easily overlooked but for their hooting calls.

Tody Motmot *Hylomanes momotula* LC
Barranquero Colimocho
Very local resident (easily overlooked).

 L 18 cm (7"). Race *obscurus*. Humid forest understorey, damp ravines. To 1500 m. Singles or pairs perch hunched, relatively immobile, at mid-levels or lower; may flick tail side to side. Sally to foliage or ground for arthropods, small vertebrates. **ID** Chunky; rufous crown, black mask, white malar. **Voice** Loud resonant "kwa-kwa-…", c. 3–6 notes/second for up to ten seconds or more; low "whoop" recalls pygmy-owl.

obscurus

Whooping Motmot *Momotus subrufescens* LC
Barranquero Ferina
Common resident.

L 41 cm (16"). Races *conexus*[A], *subrufescens*[B], *spatha*[C], *osgoodi*[D], *olivaresi*[E]. Desert scrub, dry to humid forest borders, plantations. To 1200 m. Singles or pairs perch immobile, low to high, sally abruptly to foliage, limbs or ground for fruit, arthropods, small vertebrates; swing tail side to side when disturbed. **ID** Above dull green, eyebrow turquoise. Underparts colour clinal: greener in humid areas (*subrufescens, conexus*), paler (and smaller) in arid regions (*spatha*), darkest *osgoodi*. **Voice** Day call a brief single hoot "hooOOp"; *osgoodi* slightly more long-drawn. Pre-dawn hollow quavering "whu'r'r'r'r'r'r'o". **SS** Highland Motmot. **TN** Formerly part of Blue-crowned Motmot; race *reconditus* not recognized.

Amazonian Motmot
Momotus momota LC
Barranquero Coronado
Fairly common resident.

 **L** 41 cm (16"). Race *microstephanus*. Humid *terra firme* and *várzea* forest, borders, gallery forest, light woodland. To 1400 m. **ID** Like Whooping Motmot, but underparts more tawny; often perches high. **Voice** Primary day call a brief two-note "hoo'dup", first note longer, slightly rising, second truncated, dropping. Pre-dawn rapid quavering hoots. Both calls much like those of Rufous Motmot. **SS** Highland Motmot. **TN** Formerly part of Blue-crowned Motmot.

microstephanus

subrufescens

Highland Motmot (Andean Motmot)
Momotus aequatorialis LC
Barranquero Andino
Common resident.

L 48 cm (19"). Race *aequatorialis*. Humid forest borders, light woodland, settled areas. 1350–3000 m. Behaviour as Whooping Motmot. **ID** Quite large; below always tinged greenish, long tail, turquoise brow. **Voice** Day call a brief two-note "hudup", notes barely separated. Pre-dawn fast quavering series of hoots, sometimes by two birds. **SS** Whooping Motmot (lower elevation, little or no overlap). **TN** Formerly part of Blue-crowned Motmot.

Rufous Motmot *Baryphthengus martii* LC
Barranquero Pechicastaño
Fairly common resident.

L 46 cm (18"). Races *semirufus*^A, *martii*^B. Humid *terra firme* and transition forest, secondary woodland. To 1300 m. Singles or pairs; perch fairly high (*martii*) or low to high (*semirufus*); behaviour like Whooping Motmot, although both races confined to forest interior. **ID** Large; entire underparts to belly rufous; *martii* lacks rackets. **Voice** Primary day call an abrupt two-note "hoo'dup", nearly identical to Amazonian Motmot (higher-pitched?). Pre-dawn rolling bubbly hoots nearly identical to Amazonian Motmot. **SS** Broad-billed Motmot.

Broad-billed Motmot *Electron platyrhynchum* LC
Barranquero Piquigrueso

Six subspecies in two subspecies groups; both in Colombia.

Broad-billed Motmot *Electron (platyrhynchum) platyrhynchum*
Uncommon resident.
L 36 cm (14"). Races *platyrhynchum*^A, *minus*^B, *colombianum*^C. Humid lowland and hill forest. To 1400 m. Singles, scattered pairs, lower midstorey or subcanopy. Preys on wide range of arthropods, small vertebrates. **ID** Smaller, otherwise much like Rufous Motmot (W of Andes) including racket tail tips; differs in narrow greenish chin, rufous only to mid-breast, larger chest spots, green lower underparts. **Voice** Loud nasal honking "kuuuoonk!" a few times per minute, mainly dawn or late on sunny evenings. Duetting pair members call on slightly different pitches, but faster than lone bird. **SS** Rufous Motmot.

Plain-tailed Motmot *Electron (platyrhynchum) pyrrholaemum*
Uncommon resident.
L 36 cm (14"). Race *pyrrholaemum*. Humid transition and *terra firme* forest. To 1100 m. **ID** Differs from races W of Andes in no racket-tipped tail, larger bluish-green chin patch, darker rufous head and foreparts. **Voice** Like races W of Andes but smoother. **SS** Rufous Motmot larger, more extensively rufous below; different voice; both species E of Andes lack racket-tipped tails.

martii
pale variant

semirufus

aequatorialis

platyrhynchum

pyrrholaemum

A worldwide family. New World species, unlike elsewhere, are all closely tied to water. Characterized by large heads and outsized bills, they nest in burrows in banks, usually near water, and dive for fish. Perch and diving height when foraging are closely related to body size and habitat, the largest species perching highest and in open, the smallest close to water and within cover.

Genus *Megaceryle* Large grey-blue kingfishers with bushy crests; usually along larger, more open bodies of water.

Ringed Kingfisher *Megaceryle torquata* LC
Martín-pescador Grande
Common resident.

L 41 cm (16"). Race *torquata*. Fresh and brackish water throughout. To 2500 m (rarely higher). Singles or pairs perch high; dive for fish from heights without hovering. Often flies high overhead with unsteady wingbeats, moving between watercourses. In Amazonas may gather in loose nesting colonies on large exposed riverbanks. **ID** Large; ragged crest, chestnut underparts. **Voice** Coarse "kleck" in flight; rough rattle when disturbed. **SS** Belted Kingfisher.

Belted Kingfisher *Megaceryle alcyon* LC
Martín-pescador Norteño
Uncommon boreal migrant.

L 32 cm (12.5"). Monotypic. Mainly brackish and saltwater (in Colombia), especially mangroves, infrequent inland; Oct–Apr. To 100 m. Singles perch in open on wires or bare branches; hover before diving. **ID** Smaller than Ringed Kingfisher; ♂ has single bluish chest-band, ♀ one blue and one rufous chest-band. **Voice** Rattling calls higher-pitched, less harsh than Ringed Kingfisher.

Genus *Chloroceryle* Smaller kingfishers, with dark green upperparts and white or tawny collars. Lowlands; usually associated with shaded water, especially the three smaller species.

Amazon Kingfisher *Chloroceryle amazona* LC
Martín-pescador Matraquero
Common resident.

L 28 cm (11"). Monotypic. Rivers, streams and lagoons. To 1200 m. Singles or pairs perch fairly low, near or over water; fly low, plunge for fish, seldom hover. **ID** ♂ above dark oily green, no white on wings or tail (undertail has white barring), below white, broad rufous chest-band. ♀ no rufous, dark greenish patch on sides of breast, obscure white wing-covert dots. **Voice** Song loud, exuberant and rapid descending notes; also rattles. **SS** Green Kingfisher.

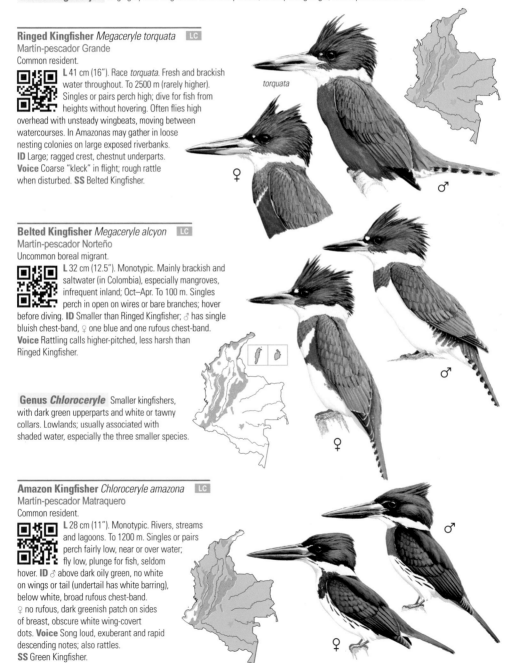

torquata

♀   ♂

♂

♀

♂

♀

205

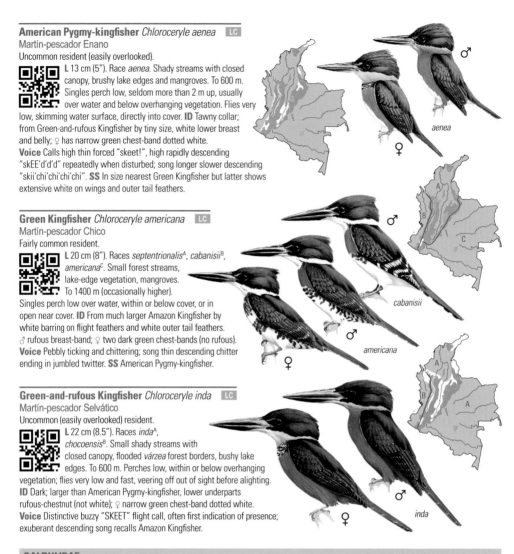

American Pygmy-kingfisher *Chloroceryle aenea* LC
Martín-pescador Enano
Uncommon resident (easily overlooked).
L 13 cm (5"). Race *aenea*. Shady streams with closed canopy, brushy lake edges and mangroves. To 600 m. Singles perch low, seldom more than 2 m up, usually over water and below overhanging vegetation. Flies very low, skimming water surface, directly into cover. **ID** Tawny collar; from Green-and-rufous Kingfisher by tiny size, white lower breast and belly; ♀ has narrow green chest-band dotted white. **Voice** Calls high thin forced "skeet!", high rapidly descending "skEE'd'd'd" repeatedly when disturbed; song longer slower descending "skii'chi'chi'chi". **SS** In size nearest Green Kingfisher but latter shows extensive white on wings and outer tail feathers.

Green Kingfisher *Chloroceryle americana* LC
Martín-pescador Chico
Fairly common resident.
L 20 cm (8"). Races *septentrionalis*[A], *cabanisii*[B], *americana*[C]. Small forest streams, lake-edge vegetation, mangroves. To 1400 m (occasionally higher). Singles perch low over water, within or below cover, or in open near cover. **ID** From much larger Amazon Kingfisher by white barring on flight feathers and white outer tail feathers. ♂ rufous breast-band; ♀ two dark green chest-bands (no rufous). **Voice** Pebbly ticking and chittering; song thin descending chitter ending in jumbled twitter. **SS** American Pygmy-kingfisher.

Green-and-rufous Kingfisher *Chloroceryle inda* LC
Martín-pescador Selvático
Uncommon (easily overlooked) resident.
L 22 cm (8.5"). Races *inda*[A], *chocoensis*[B]. Small shady streams with closed canopy, flooded *várzea* forest borders, bushy lake edges. To 600 m. Perches low, within or below overhanging vegetation; flies very low and fast, veering off out of sight before alighting. **ID** Dark; larger than American Pygmy-kingfisher, lower underparts rufous-chestnut (not white); ♀ narrow green chest-band dotted white. **Voice** Distinctive buzzy "SKEET" flight call, often first indication of presence; exuberant descending song recalls Amazon Kingfisher.

GALBULIDAE
Jacamars
19 extant species, 13 in region

Jacamars form a small Neotropical family, most diverse in Amazonia, and best known for their long pointed bills, shimmering metallic plumage and long tails. A few, however, are short-tailed and relatively dull-coloured. All sally rapidly for flying insects and occur in openings in wooded or partly open areas. Nest sites are burrows in the ground or holes in termitaries.

White-eared Jacamar *Galbalcyrhynchus leucotis* LC
Jacamar Orejiblanco
Locally common resident.
L 20 cm (8"). Monotypic. Forested stream-sides, second growth around oxbow lakes, young river island vegetation; rarely far from water. To 500 m. Pairs or groups of 3–8 perch on open bare branches, especially *Cecropia*; sally in big loops for flying insects. **ID** Reddish chestnut, white ear patch, pinkish kingfisher-like bill, pink feet. **Voice** Call piercing "pEEer", singly or series; song, often duet or chorus, thin chattering rising and falling trills.

Genus *Brachygalba* Small, short-tailed jacamars with long thin bills.

Brown Jacamar *Brachygalba lugubris* `LC`
Jacamar Lúgubre

Fairly common resident in white sandy soil regions (local in Amazonia).

L 18 cm (7"). Races *fulviventris*[A], *caquetae*[B]. Gallery forest, savanna woodland, forest canopy, river edges. To 1200 m. Pairs or small groups perch high on open bare snags at forest edge. **ID** Chunky; brown, foreface slightly paler, belly whitish (*caquetae*); or darker brown, belly buff (*fulviventris*). **Voice** Song high thin "p'p'pe'pe'pe'ple'ple'ple' plee, pleea, pleea" (c. 3 seconds), slowing, slightly descending at end. Call high "pii".

caquetae

fulviventris

Pale-headed Jacamar *Brachygalba goeringi* `LC`
Jacamar Cabeciblanco

Local resident.

L 18 cm (7"). Monotypic. Gallery forest especially along larger rivers, wooded borders, acacia scrub. To 500 m (higher?). Pairs or families sally to air from high open bare branches. **ID** Head contrasting pale greyish brown, central underparts white crossed by short chestnut band. **Voice** Call thin high "weet". Accelerating song ends in thin fast trill, "weet, weet, weet t'weet t'weet-t'weet'ti'ti'ti't't't'", often given simultaneously by pair. **SS** Brown Jacamar.

Dusky-backed Jacamar *Brachygalba salmoni* `LC`
Jacamar de Salmon

Uncommon, local and declining resident.

L 18 cm (7"). Monotypic. Near-endemic (also extreme SE Panama). Humid forest borders, small clearings, second growth with scattered trees and shrubs. To 600 m. Pairs or small families perch fairly high, sally to air from open branches. **ID** Small; dark, dusky-green chest-band, white (♂) or buff (♀) throat. **Voice** Song thin high trill much like others of genus. **SS** Rufous-tailed Jacamar (larger, perches lower).

♀

♂

`NE`

Genus *Galbula* Long thin bills; most species with long narrow graduated tail rounded at tip. Plumage iridescent. Sally into small openings for flying insects.

Yellow-billed Jacamar *Galbula albirostris* `LC`
Jacamar Piquidorado

Two subspecies in two subspecies groups; one (both?) in Colombia.

Yellow-billed Jacamar
Galbula (albirostris) albirostris

Status uncertain (few or no definite records?).

L 19 cm (7.5"). One subspecies in group. Habitat, behaviour and voice identical to Cerise-crowned Jacamar. **ID** From Cerise-crowned by crown more coppery blue (less coppery reddish), bill slightly shorter, basal third of maxilla and basal half or most of mandible yellow (extent variable), outer three tail feathers blackish green (not brownish). **SS** May meet or overlap Cerise-crowned in Vaupés, but status in Colombia requires confirmation; all records may refer to *G. a. chalcocephala*. **TN** Taxonomy unresolved; sometimes split as a species apart from Cerise-crowned.

♀

♂

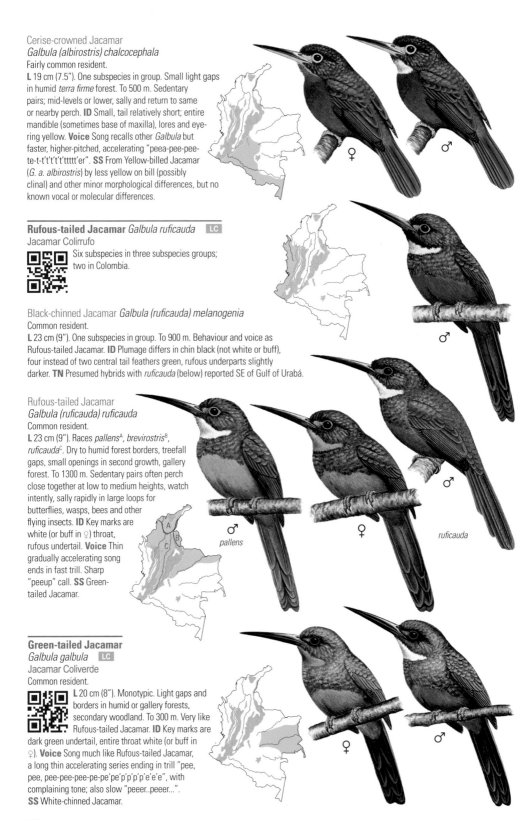

Cerise-crowned Jacamar
Galbula (albirostris) chalcocephala
Fairly common resident.
L 19 cm (7.5"). One subspecies in group. Small light gaps in humid *terra firme* forest. To 500 m. Sedentary pairs; mid-levels or lower, sally and return to same or nearby perch. **ID** Small, tail relatively short; entire mandible (sometimes base of maxilla), lores and eye-ring yellow. **Voice** Song recalls other *Galbula* but faster, higher-pitched, accelerating "peea-pee-pee-te-t-t't't't't'tttt'er". **SS** From Yellow-billed Jacamar (*G. a. albirostris*) by less yellow on bill (possibly clinal) and other minor morphological differences, but no known vocal or molecular differences.

Rufous-tailed Jacamar *Galbula ruficauda* `LC`
Jacamar Colirrufo

Six subspecies in three subspecies groups; two in Colombia.

Black-chinned Jacamar *Galbula (ruficauda) melanogenia*
Common resident.
L 23 cm (9"). One subspecies in group. To 900 m. Behaviour and voice as Rufous-tailed Jacamar. **ID** Plumage differs in chin black (not white or buff), four instead of two central tail feathers green, rufous underparts slightly darker. **TN** Presumed hybrids with *ruficauda* (below) reported SE of Gulf of Urabá.

Rufous-tailed Jacamar
Galbula (ruficauda) ruficauda
Common resident.
L 23 cm (9"). Races *pallens*[A], *brevirostris*[B], *ruficauda*[C]. Dry to humid forest borders, treefall gaps, small openings in second growth, gallery forest. To 1300 m. Sedentary pairs often perch close together at low to medium heights, watch intently, sally rapidly in large loops for butterflies, wasps, bees and other flying insects. **ID** Key marks are white (or buff in ♀) throat, rufous undertail. **Voice** Thin gradually accelerating song ends in fast trill. Sharp "peeup" call. **SS** Green-tailed Jacamar.

♂ *pallens*
♀
ruficauda

Green-tailed Jacamar
Galbula galbula `LC`
Jacamar Coliverde
Common resident.
L 20 cm (8"). Monotypic. Light gaps and borders in humid or gallery forests, secondary woodland. To 300 m. Very like Rufous-tailed Jacamar. **ID** Key marks are dark green undertail, entire throat white (or buff in ♀). **Voice** Song much like Rufous-tailed Jacamar, a long thin accelerating series ending in trill "pee, pee, pee-pee-pee-pe-pe'pe'p'p'p'e'e'e", with complaining tone; also slow "peeer..peeer...". **SS** White-chinned Jacamar.

208

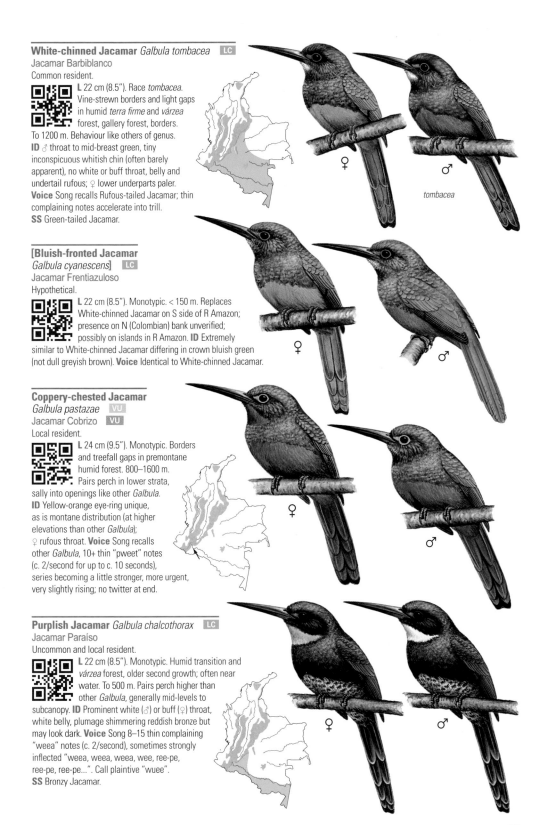

White-chinned Jacamar *Galbula tombacea* LC
Jacamar Barbiblanco
Common resident.

L 22 cm (8.5"). Race *tombacea*. Vine-strewn borders and light gaps in humid *terra firme* and *várzea* forest, gallery forest, borders. To 1200 m. Behaviour like others of genus. **ID** ♂ throat to mid-breast green, tiny inconspicuous whitish chin (often barely apparent), no white or buff throat, belly and undertail rufous; ♀ lower underparts paler. **Voice** Song recalls Rufous-tailed Jacamar; thin complaining notes accelerate into trill. **SS** Green-tailed Jacamar.

tombacea

[Bluish-fronted Jacamar *Galbula cyanescens*] LC
Jacamar Frentiazuloso
Hypothetical.

L 22 cm (8.5"). Monotypic. < 150 m. Replaces White-chinned Jacamar on S side of R Amazon; presence on N (Colombian) bank unverified; possibly on islands in R Amazon. **ID** Extremely similar to White-chinned Jacamar differing in crown bluish green (not dull greyish brown). **Voice** Identical to White-chinned Jacamar.

Coppery-chested Jacamar
Galbula pastazae VU
Jacamar Cobrizo VU
Local resident.

L 24 cm (9.5"). Monotypic. Borders and treefall gaps in premontane humid forest. 800–1600 m. Pairs perch in lower strata, sally into openings like other *Galbula*. **ID** Yellow-orange eye-ring unique, as is montane distribution (at higher elevations than other *Galbula*); ♀ rufous throat. **Voice** Song recalls other *Galbula*, 10+ thin "pweet" notes (c. 2/second for up to c. 10 seconds), series becoming a little stronger, more urgent, very slightly rising; no twitter at end.

Purplish Jacamar *Galbula chalcothorax* LC
Jacamar Paraíso
Uncommon and local resident.

L 22 cm (8.5"). Monotypic. Humid transition and *várzea* forest, older second growth; often near water. To 500 m. Pairs perch higher than other *Galbula*, generally mid-levels to subcanopy. **ID** Prominent white (♂) or buff (♀) throat, white belly, plumage shimmering reddish bronze but may look dark. **Voice** Song 8–15 thin complaining "weea" notes (c. 2/second), sometimes strongly inflected "weea, weea, weea, wee, ree-pe, ree-pe, ree-pe...". Call plaintive "wuee". **SS** Bronzy Jacamar.

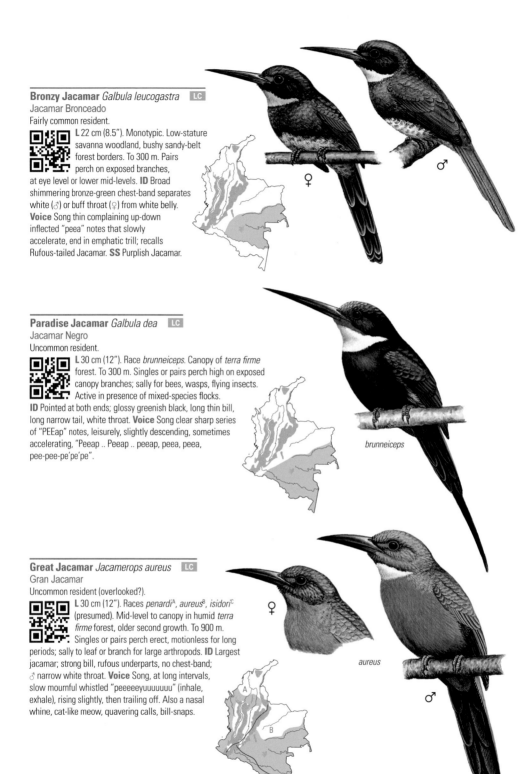

Bronzy Jacamar *Galbula leucogastra* `LC`
Jacamar Bronceado
Fairly common resident.
L 22 cm (8.5"). Monotypic. Low-stature savanna woodland, bushy sandy-belt forest borders. To 300 m. Pairs perch on exposed branches, at eye level or lower mid-levels. **ID** Broad shimmering bronze-green chest-band separates white (♂) or buff throat (♀) from white belly. **Voice** Song thin complaining up-down inflected "peea" notes that slowly accelerate, end in emphatic trill; recalls Rufous-tailed Jacamar. **SS** Purplish Jacamar.

♀

♂

Paradise Jacamar *Galbula dea* `LC`
Jacamar Negro
Uncommon resident.
L 30 cm (12"). Race *brunneiceps*. Canopy of *terra firme* forest. To 300 m. Singles or pairs perch high on exposed canopy branches; sally for bees, wasps, flying insects. Active in presence of mixed-species flocks. **ID** Pointed at both ends; glossy greenish black, long thin bill, long narrow tail, white throat. **Voice** Song clear sharp series of "PEEap" notes, leisurely, slightly descending, sometimes accelerating, "Peeap .. Peeap .. peeap, peea, peea, pee-pee-pe'pe'pe".

brunneiceps

Great Jacamar *Jacamerops aureus* `LC`
Gran Jacamar
Uncommon resident (overlooked?).
L 30 cm (12"). Races *penardi*[A], *aureus*[B], *isidori*[C] (presumed). Mid-level to canopy in humid *terra firme* forest, older second growth. To 900 m. Singles or pairs perch erect, motionless for long periods; sally to leaf or branch for large arthropods. **ID** Largest jacamar; strong bill, rufous underparts, no chest-band; ♂ narrow white throat. **Voice** Song, at long intervals, slow mournful whistled "peeeeeyuuuuuuu" (inhale, exhale), rising slightly, then trailing off. Also a nasal whine, cat-like meow, quavering calls, bill-snaps.

♀

aureus

♂

38 extant species, 26 in region

Small New World family that reaches greatest diversity in the Amazon Basin. Named for rotund shape, with large heads, strong cleft-hooked bills, short weak legs and lax puffy plumage. Classic 'sit-and-wait' foragers, they patiently watch for large prey. Most sing only a few times pre-dawn. Nests dug in termitaries or burrows in ground.

Genus _Notharchus_ Plumage mainly black and white. Mid-levels or canopy, often near borders.

White-necked Puffbird _Notharchus hyperrhynchus_ `LC`
Bobo de Collar

Rare to fairly common resident.

L 25 cm (10"). Race _hyperrhynchus_. Dry to humid forest, older second growth, borders, mostly _terra firme_ forest in Amazonia. To 1300 m. Usually seen alone on high branches in early morning, at times exposed, less so later in day. Sallies to foliage or branches. **ID** Large white forehead and eyebrow, broad white collar. **Voice** At dawn, long high frog-like purring trill "prrrrrrrrr..." (up to 15–20 notes/second) on same pitch, occasionally a few whistles at end. **SS** Other _Notharchus_.

hyperrhynchus

Black-breasted Puffbird _Notharchus pectoralis_ `LC`
Bobo Pechinegro

Uncommon resident.

L 22 cm (8.5"). Monotypic. Canopy of humid and wet forest, borders, secondary woodland. Behaviour much like White-necked Puffbird. To 1000 m. **ID** Entire crown black, large white ear patch. **Voice** Loud lengthy series of piercing "kwee" notes with raucous quality, slowing, ending in several doubled or syncopated notes, e.g. "kwee .... kweee-queer, kwee-queer, queer". **SS** Other _Notharchus_.

Brown-banded Puffbird _Notharchus ordii_ `LC`
Bobo Pechirrufo

Rare resident.

L 20 cm (8"). Monotypic. Mid-level to canopy in scrubby sandy-belt forest, borders, seasonally flooded woodland, scrub forest around rock outcrops. To 200 m. Curiously local. Behaviour like White-necked Puffbird. **ID** Resembles White-necked Puffbird but smaller, white forehead but no eyebrow, narrow black chest-band bordered below by broader brown band. **Voice** Often duets; loud wild, free-spirited, rhythmic "KUEEP!, KUEEP, kee-kee-kee-kee-kee, quaaa, kée-kée-quaaa, kée-kée-quaaa..." (up to 15 seconds). **SS** White-necked Puffbird.

Lesser Pied Puffbird _Notharchus subtectus_ `LC`
Bobo Coronado Pequeño

Common resident (Chocó).

L 15 cm (6"). Monotypic. Humid and wet forest, borders, secondary woodland. To 600 m. Singles or pairs sometimes perch in open at dawn, otherwise often in shady forest canopy. **ID** Very like birds in Amazonia (_tectus_) differing in crown with fewer white dots, chest-band narrower, minor biometrics. **Voice** Song high shrill rhythmic "peed'd-peed-peed-peed-it, peed-it, peed-it, peea pee pee, pee", accelerates, then slows, slightly descends. Call high "piiiia". **SS** White-necked Puffbird. **TN** Usually regarded as a race of _N. tectus_, with the single species known as Pied Puffbird.

Greater Pied Puffbird *Notharchus tectus* `LC`
Bobo Coronado

Rare to uncommon resident.

 L 16 cm (6.3"). Races *tectus*[A], *picatus*[B]. To 1000 m. Behaviour like birds W of Andes (previous page). **ID** Small; thin curved eyebrow, white-dotted crown, relatively broad chest-band, white patch on wings. **Voice** Song much like Lesser Pied Puffbird.

picatus

Genera *Cyphos*, *Nystactes* and *Bucco* (all formerly *Bucco*)
Inconspicuous. Bold head or forepart patterns; sombre earth-tone colours. Mid-strata or lower in humid lowland forest.

Chestnut-capped Puffbird *Cyphos macrodactylus* `LC`
Bobo Corbatín

Uncommon resident.

 L 16.5 cm (6.5"). Monotypic. *Várzea* forest borders, secondary woodland, treefall gaps in *terra firme*; usually near creeks or water. To 500 m. Quiet, unobtrusive singles, easily overlooked. Low to mid-levels, occasionally higher on open branch, e.g. *Cecropia*. **ID** Head pattern bold but colours subdued, chestnut crown, black mask bordered white, narrow chest-band, fine underparts barring. **Voice** Infrequently vocal; song thin high "puweeEEaa .. puweeEEaa.." c. 6 notes with 2–3-second pause between notes. **SS** Spotted Puffbird.

variant

Sooty-capped Puffbird *Nystactes noanamae* `NT`
Bobo de Noanamá `NT`

Notably local resident.

 L 18 cm (7"). Monotypic. Endemic. Wet forest borders, stream-sides; often in or near mangroves. To 150 m. Singles, mid-strata or lower, occasionally subcanopy. Like other puffbirds quiet, sluggish; flight fast, direct. **ID** Narrow white eyeline, white throat, broad blackish chest-band, scalloped lower underparts. **Voice** Infrequent song (mainly dawn) moderately high-pitched, starting fast (5–6 notes/second) but slowing, more emphatic at end "tuwee'tuwee'tuwee-tuwee-tuwee .... tuwe, tuwee...", up to 40 or more notes.

Spotted Puffbird *Nystactes tamatia* `LC`
Bobo Moteado

Uncommon and local resident.

L 19 cm (7.5"). Races *tamatia*[A], *pulmentum*[B]. Fairly low in shrubby *várzea* stream-sides in Amazonia, sandy soil forest borders in Guainía and Vaupés. To 300 m. Solitary, sluggish, inconspicuous. **ID** Long white subocular line bordered below by elongated black neck patch, throat tawny (or buff, *pulmentum*), boldly scalloped underparts. **Voice** Song a few times pre-dawn, brisk upward-inflected whistles "puwéep, puwéep..." (up to 30 notes in 15 seconds), soft, then stronger more inflected towards end. **SS** Chestnut-capped Puffbird.

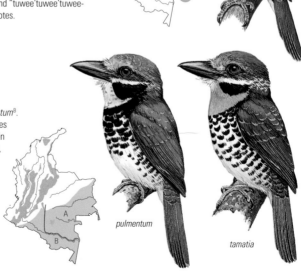

pulmentum

tamatia

Collared Puffbird *Bucco capensis* LC
Bobo Collarejo

Uncommon resident (often overlooked).

 L 19 cm (7.5"). Monotypic. Inside *terra firme* forest. To 500 m. Unsuspicious singles or pairs, usually mid-levels to subcanopy, infrequently at eye level; perch upright, motionless for long periods, more active around mixed flocks; sally to foliage and branches for large arthropods, small vertebrates. **ID** Bright red-orange bill, cinnamon-rufous head. **Voice** Pre-dawn song (sometimes pair members overlapping), leisurely whistled "cua-WILL, cua-will..." (Venezuela) or "cua-WILL chaw, cua-WILL chaw..." (Peru), half dozen or more phrases, recalls *Antrostomus* nightjar.

Genus *Nystalus* One barred species W of Andes, one streaked species E of Andes. Both high in forest; share vocal similarities.

Barred Puffbird *Nystalus radiatus* LC
Bobo Barrado

Fairly common resident.

rufous morph

 L 22 cm (8.5"). Monotypic. Dry forest, gallery forest, humid and wet forest borders, tall secondary woodland. To 1300 m. Usually seen alone in mid-levels to canopy; perches quietly for long periods. **ID** Brownish, some individuals mostly rufous; paler below, heavily barred, eyes yellow. **Voice** Song a few times at dawn, infrequent later, long-drawn ascending and descending wolf whistle "phweeeet-weeeuuuuu" (inhale, exhale), ventriloquial, human-like.

Striolated Puffbird *Nystalus striolatus* LC
Bobo Estriolado

 Three subspecies in two subspecies groups; one in Colombia.

Western Striolated Puffbird *Nystalus (striolatus) obamai*
Bobo Estriolado Occidental

Probably uncommon resident (first reported c. 2015).
L 20 cm (8"). One subspecies in group. Mid-levels to canopy of humid premontane forest. 800–1800 m (lower?). Well-separated pairs; sluggish, almost always first noted by voice. **ID** Throat and belly whitish, breast buff narrowly streaked black, bill greenish, eyes yellow. **Voice** Song, sometimes in duet, a slow melancholy "whip, whip'a-weeeee .. wheeuuuuu". Nasal, slightly rising in middle then, after distinct pause, descending. **SS** Black-streaked Puffbird. **TN** Striolated Puffbird is sometimes split into eastern (*striolatus*) and western (*obamai*) species.

Russet-throated Puffbird *Hypnelus ruficollis* LC
Bobo Punteado

Common resident.

 L 20 cm (8"). Races *decolor*[A], *ruficollis*[B], *coloratus*[C]. Arid scrub, dry forest, gallery forest, mangroves. To 1200 m. Pairs; more active, and decidedly more conspicuous than most puffbirds. Perches 1–8 m up, sallies to foliage, bark or ground for large arthropods, small vertebrates. **ID** Large dark bill, single chest-band, strong face pattern; *ruficollis* overall darker brown. **Voice** Song, mostly at dawn, by singles or pair members partly overlapping, a long rhythmic series of "wuduk" notes that gradually slows. **SS** Two-banded Puffbird.

decolor   ruficollis

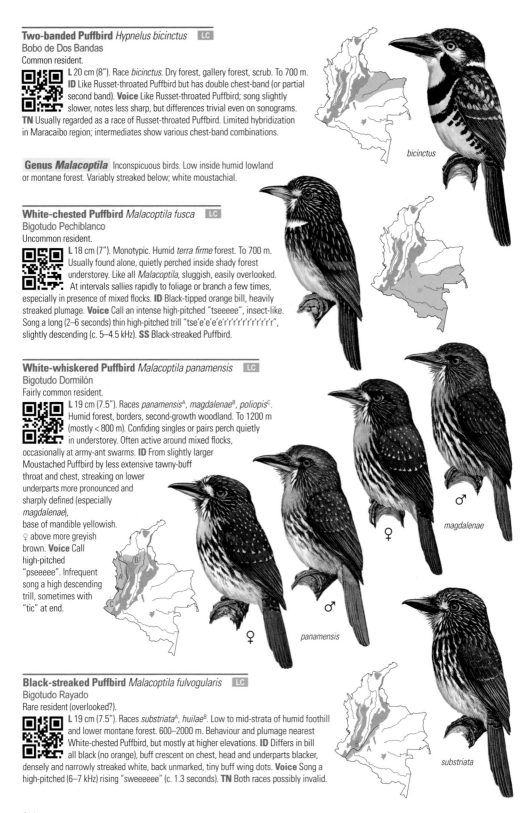

Two-banded Puffbird *Hypnelus bicinctus* `LC`
Bobo de Dos Bandas
Common resident.

L 20 cm (8"). Race *bicinctus*. Dry forest, gallery forest, scrub. To 700 m. **ID** Like Russet-throated Puffbird but has double chest-band (or partial second band). **Voice** Like Russet-throated Puffbird; song slightly slower, notes less sharp, but differences trivial even on sonograms. **TN** Usually regarded as a race of Russet-throated Puffbird. Limited hybridization in Maracaibo region; intermediates show various chest-band combinations.

Genus *Malacoptila* Inconspicuous birds. Low inside humid lowland or montane forest. Variably streaked below; white moustachial.

bicinctus

White-chested Puffbird *Malacoptila fusca* `LC`
Bigotudo Pechiblanco
Uncommon resident.

L 18 cm (7"). Monotypic. Humid *terra firme* forest. To 700 m. Usually found alone, quietly perched inside shady forest understorey. Like all *Malacoptila*, sluggish, easily overlooked. At intervals sallies rapidly to foliage or branch a few times, especially in presence of mixed flocks. **ID** Black-tipped orange bill, heavily streaked plumage. **Voice** Call an intense high-pitched "tseeeee", insect-like. Song a long (2–6 seconds) thin high-pitched trill "tse'e'e'e'e'r'r'r'r'r'r'r'r'r'r", slightly descending (c. 5–4.5 kHz). **SS** Black-streaked Puffbird.

White-whiskered Puffbird *Malacoptila panamensis* `LC`
Bigotudo Dormilón
Fairly common resident.

L 19 cm (7.5"). Races *panamensis*[A], *magdalenae*[B], *poliopis*[C]. Humid forest, borders, second-growth woodland. To 1200 m (mostly < 800 m). Confiding singles or pairs perch quietly in understorey. Often active around mixed flocks, occasionally at army-ant swarms. **ID** From slightly larger Moustached Puffbird by less extensive tawny-buff throat and chest, streaking on lower underparts more pronounced and sharply defined (especially *magdalenae*), base of mandible yellowish. ♀ above more greyish brown. **Voice** Call high-pitched "pseeeee". Infrequent song a high descending trill, sometimes with "tic" at end.

♂

♀

magdalenae

♀

♂

panamensis

Black-streaked Puffbird *Malacoptila fulvogularis* `LC`
Bigotudo Rayado
Rare resident (overlooked?).

L 19 cm (7.5"). Races *substriata*[A], *huilae*[B]. Low to mid-strata of humid foothill and lower montane forest. 600–2000 m. Behaviour and plumage nearest White-chested Puffbird, but mostly at higher elevations. **ID** Differs in bill all black (no orange), buff crescent on chest, head and underparts blacker, densely and narrowly streaked white, back unmarked, tiny buff wing dots. **Voice** Song a high-pitched (6–7 kHz) rising "sweeeeee" (c. 1.3 seconds). **TN** Both races possibly invalid.

substriata

Moustached Puffbird *Malacoptila mystacalis* `LC`
Bigotudo Canoso
Fairly common resident.

 L 20 cm (8"). Monotypic. Humid and wet montane forest, older second growth. 800–2200 m. Much like White-whiskered Puffbird, but usually at higher elevations. **ID** Bill blackish, base of mandible blue-grey (not yellowish). ♂ throat to mid-breast more extensively tawny-rufous, lower underparts whitish with little or no streaking, white arc behind eye. ♀ above duller greyish brown, lower underparts with blurred dark streaking. **Voice** Song infrequent high-pitched (6–7.5 kHz) "teeez, teeez…", 10–30 notes in 5–10 seconds (easily overlooked). Call a short high trill.

Lanceolated Monklet *Micromonacha lanceolata* `LC`
Bigotudo Lanceolado
Uncommon resident in Andes, rare or overlooked in Amazonia.

 L 13.5 cm (5.3"). Monotypic. Humid foothill and lower montane forest, borders, *terra firme* forest in W Amazonia. 100–2100 m. Singles or loosely associated pairs, mid-levels to subcanopy. Sluggish, often on relatively open branches but tiny, difficult to spot; at long intervals sallies to foliage and branches. **ID** Small; white spectacles (or white arc behind eye), white underparts boldly streaked black. **Voice** Infrequent 6–8-second song a moderately high (4–5 kHz) measured "sueet, sueet…", metallic; notes sharply upward-inflected and slightly accelerating. **SS** Nunlets.

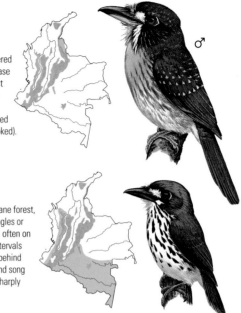

Genus *Nonnula* Small puffbirds; plain and brownish. Mostly low to mid-levels inside humid lowland forest; inconspicuous.

Rusty-breasted Nunlet *Nonnula rubecula* `LC`
Monjita Chica
Rare resident (overlooked).

 L 14 cm (5.5"). Race *simulatrix*, possibly *interfluvialis* (E Guainía). Humid lowland forest, sandy soil forest. To 200 m. Behaviour like Brown Nunlet. **ID** Plumage dull, very prominent white eye-ring, buff lores, whitish belly. **Voice** Infrequent song rather slow (c. 2 notes/second) up-down inflected whistles, "whEEa, whEEa…" on same pitch, but volume increasing. **SS** Only nunlet with white (not red) eye-ring. **TN** Allocation of races unresolved.

simulatrix

Brown Nunlet *Nonnula brunnea* `LC`
Monjita Parda
Uncommon resident.

 L 14 cm (5.5"). Monotypic. Humid *terra firme* forest, especially areas cluttered with vines. 200–600 m (?). Singles perch upright, low to midstorey levels, occasionally subcanopy, often on open branch; sally or move infrequently. More active in presence of mixed flocks. **ID** Dull red to pinkish eye-ring, uniform fulvous underparts. **Voice** Song nearly identical to Rusty-breasted Nunlet, steady (c. 2 notes/second) strongly up-down inflected whistles on same pitch, gradually stronger, c. 8–10 seconds. **SS** Rusty-breasted Nunlet (overlap?).

Rufous-capped Nunlet

Grey-cheeked Nunlet *Nonnula frontalis* `LC`
Monjita Canela
Uncommon resident.

 **L** 14 cm (5.5"). Races *stulta*[A], *pallescens*[B], *frontalis*[C]. Dry to humid forest (especially in large vine tangles), secondary woodland. To 1000 m. Lower levels to subcanopy. Singles, lethargic, confiding; more active when mixed flocks present. **ID** Tiny, large heavy bill, eye-ring red, lores, ocular area and cheeks grey, frontlet rufous. **Voice** Similar to Brown and Rusty-breasted Nunlets. **SS Rufous-capped Nunlet** *N. ruficapilla* (E Peru, W Brazil) possible in Amazonas or Putumayo; very like present species, crown darker, more chestnut.

pallescens

frontalis

White-faced Nunbird *Hapaloptila castanea* LC
Monjita Cariblanca
Rare to uncommon and local resident.

 L 24 cm (9.5"). Monotypic. Wet montane forest, occasionally borders. 700–2600 m. Singles, pairs, less often families. Mostly subcanopy, less often lower. Sluggish and inconspicuous; posture hunched. **ID** Large; puffy white forehead and upper throat, underparts tawny-rufous, eyes red. **Voice** Song flat or slightly rising low-pitched (1.5–2 kHz), hollow whistles "kauuu" (c. 1 note/2 seconds), up to 15 or more notes. Also gruff rattles. **SS** Moustached Puffbird.

Genus *Monasa* Slaty plumage; brightly coloured bills. Conspicuous in groups inside or at borders of humid lowland forest. Vocal, sing in choruses.

[Black Nunbird *Monasa atra*] LC
Monja Negra
Hypothetical.

 L 28 cm (11"). Monotypic. Unconfirmed but likely in extreme E Vichada and Guainía adjacent to R Orinoco. Humid forest borders, second growth, river edges (in Venezuela). Behaviour like other *Monasa*. **ID** Slate-grey plumage, coral-red bill, white wing patch (lesser wing-coverts). **Voice** Loud rollicking chorus "wheeer'pt-t-t-r-e-a-r" over and over.

Black-fronted Nunbird *Monasa nigrifrons* LC
Monjita Piquirroja
Common resident.

 L 28 cm (11"). Race *nigrifrons*. Humid *terra firme* and *várzea* forest borders, forest openings but not far inside tall forest. To 500 m. Pairs or up to six; lower levels to subcanopy. Regularly follows squirrel and capuchin monkeys, taking prey they disturb. **ID** Slaty black, coral-red bill. Juv yellowish bill. **Voice** Pairs or groups line up on prominent high branches, cheerfully singing loud boisterous choruses, especially late afternoon, with rollicking "cleeery", "curry" and trilled "tur'r'r'r'a" over and over. **SS** White-fronted Nunbird.

nigrifrons

White-fronted Nunbird *Monasa morphoeus* LC
Monjita Cantora
Fairly common resident.

 L 25 cm (10"). Races *fidelis*[A] (dusky), *pallescens*[B] (greyish), *sclateri*[C], *peruana*[D] (blackish). Subcanopy of humid *terra firme* and *várzea* forest in Amazonia; W of Andes (where Black-fronted Nunbird absent) also forest borders. To 1200 m (infrequently higher). Behaviour like Black-fronted Nunbird but consistently stays high; often with mixed flocks. **ID** Slaty (races vary), coral-red bill, white around bill. **Voice** Loud rollicking "dreary, dreary..." ending in frantic "dreary-me, dreary-me...", repeatedly given by singles, pairs or groups in unsynchronized rounds. Alarm several urgent "wuEEeo..." whistles, mimics alarm call of capuchin (*Cebus*) monkeys.

pallescens

Yellow-billed Nunbird
Monasa flavirostris LC
Monjita Piquiamarilla
Local resident in lowlands, commoner in foothills.

 **L** 24 cm (9.5"). Monotypic. Midstorey to subcanopy in *terra firme* and foothill forest, borders. To 1400 m. Pairs or small groups perch on fairly high branches. Quieter, less conspicuous than other nunbirds; more often independent of mixed flocks. **ID** Small *Monasa*, blacker plumage, thinner yellow bill, white scapulars (often hidden). **Voice** Loud rolling chattering chorus recalls other nunbirds. **SS** Juv Black-fronted Nunbird.

Swallow-winged Puffbird *Chelidoptera tenebrosa* LC
Monjita Culiblanca
Common resident.

L 15 cm (6"). Race *tenebrosa*. Forest and river borders, savanna and gallery forest borders. To 500 m. Singles or pairs perch on high exposed twigs atop canopy trees even in heat of day. Sallies high for flying insects, swoops back to perch, gliding on broad wings, more flycatcher-like than swallow-like. Digs nest holes in sandy banks. **ID** At rest appears all black, white rump in flight. **Voice** Not very vocal; weak piping and short descending trills.

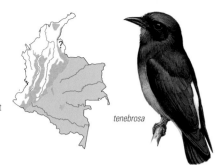

tenebrosa

RAMPHASTIDAE
Toucans
50 extant species, 22 in region

Toucans are iconic Neotropical birds best known for their large colourful bills. Pairs or groups feed on fruit, invertebrate and small vertebrate prey including nestlings and birds' eggs. They roost and nest in cavities, tail folded flat over their backs. Bills of ♂♂ are usually longer than those of ♀♀. Taxonomic allocation of species within the family remains controversial and unresolved.

Genus *Ramphastos* Large; white or yellow bibs. Two vocal groups, (1) large yelpers; (2) slightly smaller croakers; only one species, or one from each group is present in a region. Cavity nesters.

Yellow-throated Toucan *Ramphastos ambiguus* NT
Tucán Pechiamarillo

Three subspecies in two subspecies groups; both in Colombia.

abbreviatus

Chestnut-mandibled Toucan *Ramphastos (ambiguus) swainsonii*
Common resident.
L 53 cm (21"). Races *swainsonii*[A], *abbreviatus*[B]. Humid and wet lowland and lower montane forest, borders, older secondary woodland, trees in clearings. To 1500 m (rarely 2000 m). Pairs or several roam through canopy and forest mid-levels. **ID** Yellow bib, base of maxilla and all of mandible dark chestnut, facial skin yellowish green (both races). **Voice** Song, from high exposed perch, a loud rhythmic yelping "Dios te'de", second note-pair sometimes repeated; jerks bill and tail up with each call. **SS** Black-mandibled Toucan. **TN** Has been regarded as a species. Placement of *abbreviatus* controversial (some include it with Black-mandibled Toucan).

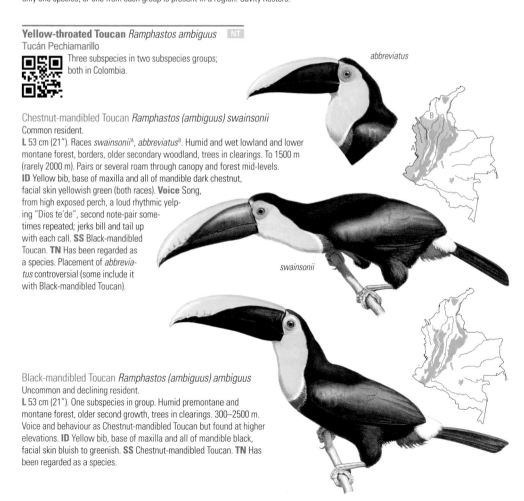

swainsonii

Black-mandibled Toucan *Ramphastos (ambiguus) ambiguus*
Uncommon and declining resident.
L 53 cm (21"). One subspecies in group. Humid premontane and montane forest, older second growth, trees in clearings. 300–2500 m. Voice and behaviour as Chestnut-mandibled Toucan but found at higher elevations. **ID** Yellow bib, base of maxilla and all of mandible black, facial skin bluish to greenish. **SS** Chestnut-mandibled Toucan. **TN** Has been regarded as a species.

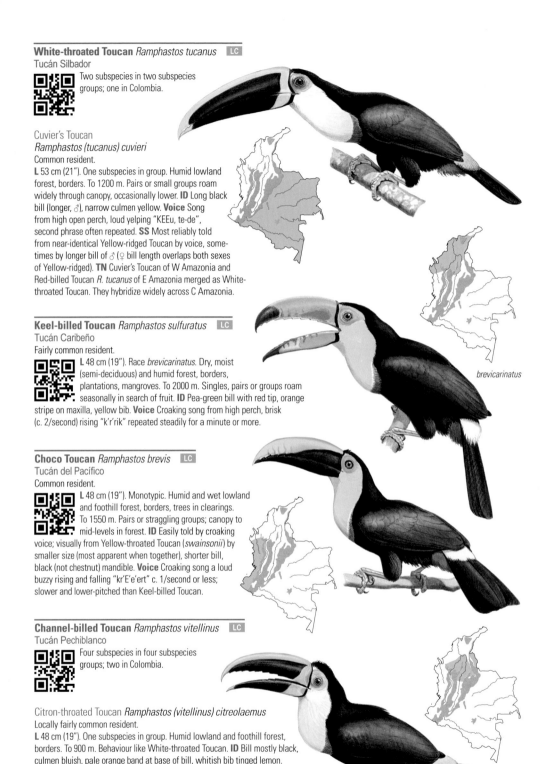

White-throated Toucan *Ramphastos tucanus* `LC`
Tucán Silbador

Two subspecies in two subspecies groups; one in Colombia.

Cuvier's Toucan
Ramphastos (tucanus) cuvieri
Common resident.
L 53 cm (21"). One subspecies in group. Humid lowland forest, borders. To 1200 m. Pairs or small groups roam widely through canopy, occasionally lower. **ID** Long black bill (longer, ♂), narrow culmen yellow. **Voice** Song from high open perch, loud yelping "KEEu, te-de", second phrase often repeated. **SS** Most reliably told from near-identical Yellow-ridged Toucan by voice, sometimes by longer bill of ♂ (♀ bill length overlaps both sexes of Yellow-ridged). **TN** Cuvier's Toucan of W Amazonia and Red-billed Toucan *R. tucanus* of E Amazonia merged as White-throated Toucan. They hybridize widely across C Amazonia.

Keel-billed Toucan *Ramphastos sulfuratus* `LC`
Tucán Caribeño
Fairly common resident.

L 48 cm (19"). Race *brevicarinatus*. Dry, moist (semi-deciduous) and humid forest, borders, plantations, mangroves. To 2000 m. Singles, pairs or groups roam seasonally in search of fruit. **ID** Pea-green bill with red tip, orange stripe on maxilla, yellow bib. **Voice** Croaking song from high perch, brisk (c. 2/second) rising "k'r'rik" repeated steadily for a minute or more.

brevicarinatus

Choco Toucan *Ramphastos brevis* `LC`
Tucán del Pacífico
Common resident.

L 48 cm (19"). Monotypic. Humid and wet lowland and foothill forest, borders, trees in clearings. To 1550 m. Pairs or straggling groups; canopy to mid-levels in forest. **ID** Easily told by croaking voice; visually from Yellow-throated Toucan (*swainsonii*) by smaller size (most apparent when together), shorter bill, black (not chestnut) mandible. **Voice** Croaking song a loud buzzy rising and falling "kr'E'e'ert" c. 1/second or less; slower and lower-pitched than Keel-billed Toucan.

Channel-billed Toucan *Ramphastos vitellinus* `LC`
Tucán Pechiblanco

Four subspecies in four subspecies groups; two in Colombia.

Citron-throated Toucan *Ramphastos (vitellinus) citreolaemus*
Locally fairly common resident.
L 48 cm (19"). One subspecies in group. Humid lowland and foothill forest, borders. To 900 m. Behaviour like White-throated Toucan. **ID** Bill mostly black, culmen bluish, pale orange band at base of bill, whitish bib tinged lemon. **Voice** Steadily repeated croaking or grinding "je'r'r'r'rp…je'r'r'r'rp…" like other croaking members of genus. **SS** Overlaps Yellow-throated Toucan ('yelper'), which has bright yellow bib. May meet Keel-billed Toucan locally but latter in drier or more open woodland. **TN** Occasionally given species status.

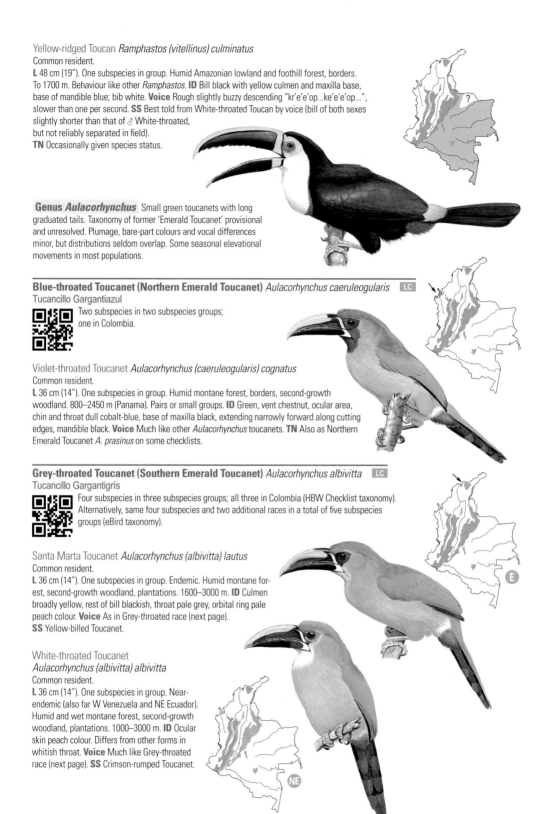

Yellow-ridged Toucan *Ramphastos (vitellinus) culminatus*
Common resident.
L 48 cm (19"). One subspecies in group. Humid Amazonian lowland and foothill forest, borders.
To 1700 m. Behaviour like other *Ramphastos*. **ID** Bill black with yellow culmen and maxilla base,
base of mandible blue; bib white. **Voice** Rough slightly buzzy descending "kr'e'e'op...ke'e'e'op...",
slower than one per second. **SS** Best told from White-throated Toucan by voice (bill of both sexes
slightly shorter than that of ♂ White-throated,
but not reliably separated in field).
TN Occasionally given species status.

Genus *Aulacorhynchus* Small green toucanets with long
graduated tails. Taxonomy of former 'Emerald Toucanet' provisional
and unresolved. Plumage, bare-part colours and vocal differences
minor, but distributions seldom overlap. Some seasonal elevational
movements in most populations.

Blue-throated Toucanet (Northern Emerald Toucanet) *Aulacorhynchus caeruleogularis* LC
Tucancillo Gargantiazul

Two subspecies in two subspecies groups;
one in Colombia.

Violet-throated Toucanet *Aulacorhynchus (caeruleogularis) cognatus*
Common resident.
L 36 cm (14"). One subspecies in group. Humid montane forest, borders, second-growth
woodland. 800–2450 m (Panama). Pairs or small groups. **ID** Green, vent chestnut, ocular area,
chin and throat dull cobalt-blue, base of maxilla black, extending narrowly forward along cutting
edges, mandible black. **Voice** Much like other *Aulacorhynchus* toucanets. **TN** Also as Northern
Emerald Toucanet *A. prasinus* on some checklists.

Grey-throated Toucanet (Southern Emerald Toucanet) *Aulacorhynchus albivitta* LC
Tucancillo Gargantigrís

Four subspecies in three subspecies groups; all three in Colombia (HBW Checklist taxonomy).
Alternatively, same four subspecies and two additional races in a total of five subspecies
groups (eBird taxonomy).

Santa Marta Toucanet *Aulacorhynchus (albivitta) lautus*
Common resident.
L 36 cm (14"). One subspecies in group. Endemic. Humid montane forest, second-growth woodland, plantations. 1600–3000 m. **ID** Culmen
broadly yellow, rest of bill blackish, throat pale grey, orbital ring pale
peach colour. **Voice** As in Grey-throated race (next page).
SS Yellow-billed Toucanet.

White-throated Toucanet
Aulacorhynchus (albivitta) albivitta
Common resident.
L 36 cm (14"). One subspecies in group. Near-
endemic (also far W Venezuela and NE Ecuador).
Humid and wet montane forest, second-growth
woodland, plantations. 1000–3000 m. **ID** Ocular
skin peach colour. Differs from other forms in
whitish throat. **Voice** Much like Grey-throated
race (next page). **SS** Crimson-rumped Toucanet.

Grey-throated Toucanet *Aulacorhynchus (albivitta) phaeolaemus*
Common resident.
L 36 cm (14"). Races *griseigularis*[A], *phaeolaemus*[B]. Endemic. Humid and wet montane forest, second-growth woodland, plantations. 1200–3000 m (seasonally lower). **ID** Mainly green, yellow of culmen extends over sides of bill, throat pale grey (*griseigularis*) or pale blue (*phaeolaemus*), ocular skin pale orange. **Voice** Low-pitched, guttural, grinding "graa'val, graa'val..." or "ruuek, ruuek...", c. 2 notes/second. Bill-clacking; other rough notes. **SS** Crimson-rumped Toucanet; possibly overlaps slightly with Groove-billed and Chestnut-tipped Toucanets. **AN** Greyish-throated Toucanet.

phaeolaemus

Crimson-rumped Toucanet *Aulacorhynchus haematopygus* `LC`
Tucancito Culirrojo
Fairly common resident.

L 36 cm (14"). Races *haematopygus*[A], *sexnotatus*[B]. Humid and wet premontane and montane forest, borders, older second growth. 800–2300 m (rarely 500 m). Pairs or several move in single file; forage at various levels, mostly well up inside forest. **ID** Bill blackish, base and culmen dark red, rump red, vent green, tail tips rufous. **Voice** Low-pitched guttural croaking "ra'a'ak..." or smoother higher-pitched, nasal "curank...", both < 2/second for a minute or more. **SS** Other *Aulacorhynchus*.

haematopygus

Groove-billed Toucanet *Aulacorhynchus sulcatus* `LC`
Tucancito Verde

Two subspecies in two subspecies groups; one in Colombia.

Yellow-billed Toucanet
Aulacorhynchus (sulcatus) calorhynchus
Common resident.
L 33 cm (13"). One subspecies in group. Humid montane forest, second growth, plantations, lightly wooded areas. 600–2000 m. Occurs mostly below elevational range of other 'green' toucanets in Santa Marta and Perijá Mts. **ID** Much of maxilla and patch at base of mandible yellow, undertail-coverts green (not rufous). **Voice** Song gruff "ruck, ruck..." like other *Aulacorhynchus*. **SS** Grey-throated Toucanet (race *albivitta*). **TN** Vocal and genetic data support merging this form with Groove-billed Toucanet *A. sulcatus*.

Chestnut-tipped Toucanet *Aulacorhynchus derbianus* `LC`
Tucancito Colicastaño
Rare and local resident.

L 36 cm (14"). Monotypic. Canopy of humid foothill and lower montane forest; only E slope of Andes near Ecuador. 600–1800 m. Singles or pairs, usually not in groups; least numerous *Aulacorhynchus* in Colombia. **ID** Bill and plumage much like Crimson-rumped Toucanet including chestnut tail tip, but lacks red rump. **Voice** Slow rough croaking "guak" notes. **SS** Occurs mostly at lower elevations than other *Aulacorhynchus*.

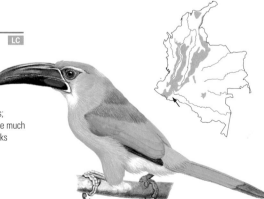

Genus *Andigena* Colourful high-Andean toucans. Singles or pairs; inconspicuous but sometimes perch in open. Calls loud and arresting, but infrequently given.

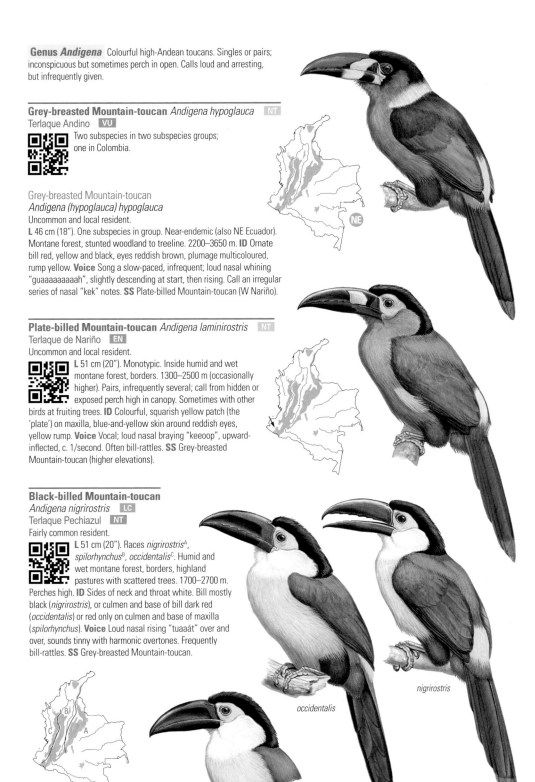

Grey-breasted Mountain-toucan *Andigena hypoglauca* NT
Terlaque Andino VU

Two subspecies in two subspecies groups; one in Colombia.

Grey-breasted Mountain-toucan
Andigena (hypoglauca) hypoglauca
Uncommon and local resident.
L 46 cm (18"). One subspecies in group. Near-endemic (also NE Ecuador). Montane forest, stunted woodland to treeline. 2200–3650 m. **ID** Ornate bill red, yellow and black, eyes reddish brown, plumage multicoloured, rump yellow. **Voice** Song a slow-paced, infrequent; loud nasal whining "guaaaaaaaaah", slightly descending at start, then rising. Call an irregular series of nasal "kek" notes. **SS** Plate-billed Mountain-toucan (W Nariño).

Plate-billed Mountain-toucan *Andigena laminirostris* NT
Terlaque de Nariño EN
Uncommon and local resident.
L 51 cm (20"). Monotypic. Inside humid and wet montane forest, borders. 1300–2500 m (occasionally higher). Pairs, infrequently several; call from hidden or exposed perch high in canopy. Sometimes with other birds at fruiting trees. **ID** Colourful, squarish yellow patch (the 'plate') on maxilla, blue-and-yellow skin around reddish eyes, yellow rump. **Voice** Vocal; loud nasal braying "keeoop", upward-inflected, c. 1/second. Often bill-rattles. **SS** Grey-breasted Mountain-toucan (higher elevations).

Black-billed Mountain-toucan
Andigena nigrirostris LC
Terlaque Pechiazul NT
Fairly common resident.
L 51 cm (20"). Races *nigrirostris*[A], *spilorhynchus*[B], *occidentalis*[C]. Humid and wet montane forest, borders, highland pastures with scattered trees. 1700–2700 m. Perches high. **ID** Sides of neck and throat white. Bill mostly black (*nigrirostris*), or culmen and base of bill dark red (*occidentalis*) or red only on culmen and base of maxilla (*spilorhynchus*). **Voice** Loud nasal rising "tuaaát" over and over, sounds tinny with harmonic overtones. Frequently bill-rattles. **SS** Grey-breasted Mountain-toucan.

occidentalis

nigrirostris

spilorhynchus

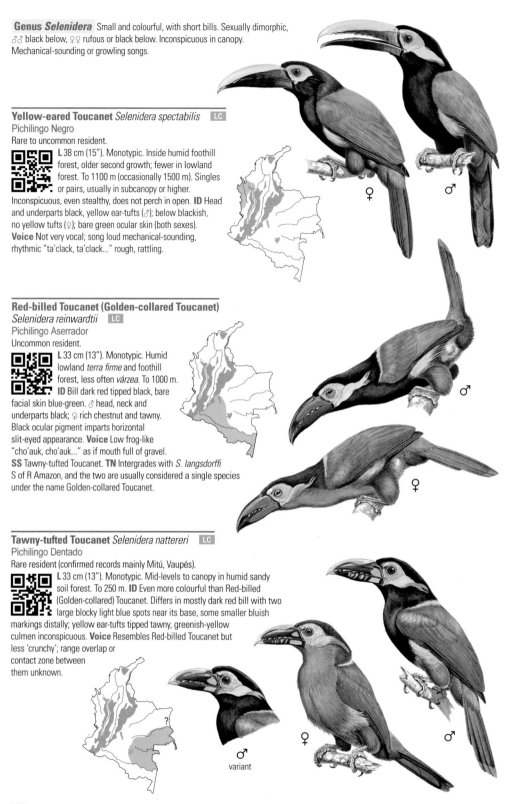

Genus *Selenidera* Small and colourful, with short bills. Sexually dimorphic, ♂♂ black below, ♀♀ rufous or black below. Inconspicuous in canopy. Mechanical-sounding or growling songs.

Yellow-eared Toucanet *Selenidera spectabilis* LC
Pichilingo Negro
Rare to uncommon resident.

L 38 cm (15"). Monotypic. Inside humid foothill forest, older second growth; fewer in lowland forest. To 1100 m (occasionally 1500 m). Singles or pairs, usually in subcanopy or higher. Inconspicuous, even stealthy, does not perch in open. **ID** Head and underparts black, yellow ear-tufts (♂); below blackish, no yellow tufts (♀); bare green ocular skin (both sexes). **Voice** Not very vocal; song loud mechanical-sounding, rhythmic "ta'clack, ta'clack..." rough, rattling.

Red-billed Toucanet (Golden-collared Toucanet)
Selenidera reinwardtii LC
Pichilingo Aserrador
Uncommon resident.

L 33 cm (13"). Monotypic. Humid lowland *terra firme* and foothill forest, less often *várzea*. To 1000 m. **ID** Bill dark red tipped black, bare facial skin blue-green. ♂ head, neck and underparts black; ♀ rich chestnut and tawny. Black ocular pigment imparts horizontal slit-eyed appearance. **Voice** Low frog-like "cho'auk, cho'auk..." as if mouth full of gravel. **SS** Tawny-tufted Toucanet. **TN** Intergrades with *S. langsdorffi* S of R Amazon, and the two are usually considered a single species under the name Golden-collared Toucanet.

Tawny-tufted Toucanet *Selenidera nattereri* LC
Pichilingo Dentado
Rare resident (confirmed records mainly Mitú, Vaupés).

L 33 cm (13"). Monotypic. Mid-levels to canopy in humid sandy soil forest. To 250 m. **ID** Even more colourful than Red-billed (Golden-collared) Toucanet. Differs in mostly dark red bill with two large blocky light blue spots near its base, some smaller bluish markings distally; yellow ear-tufts tipped tawny, greenish-yellow culmen inconspicuous. **Voice** Resembles Red-billed Toucanet but less 'crunchy'; range overlap or contact zone between them unknown.

♂ variant

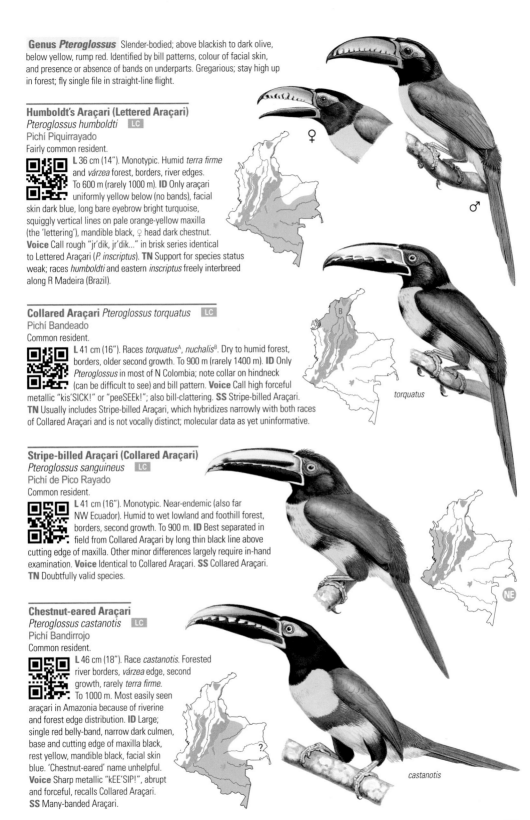

Genus *Pteroglossus* Slender-bodied; above blackish to dark olive, below yellow, rump red. Identified by bill patterns, colour of facial skin, and presence or absence of bands on underparts. Gregarious; stay high up in forest; fly single file in straight-line flight.

Humboldt's Araçari (Lettered Araçari)
Pteroglossus humboldti LC
Pichí Piquirrayado
Fairly common resident.

L 36 cm (14"). Monotypic. Humid *terra firme* and *várzea* forest, borders, river edges. To 600 m (rarely 1000 m). **ID** Only araçari uniformly yellow below (no bands), facial skin dark blue, long bare eyebrow bright turquoise, squiggly vertical lines on pale orange-yellow maxilla (the 'lettering'), mandible black, ♀ head dark chestnut. **Voice** Call rough "jr'dik, jr'dik..." in brisk series identical to Lettered Araçari (*P. inscriptus*). **TN** Support for species status weak; races *humboldti* and eastern *inscriptus* freely interbreed along R Madeira (Brazil).

Collared Araçari *Pteroglossus torquatus* LC
Pichí Bandeado
Common resident.

L 41 cm (16"). Races *torquatus*[A], *nuchalis*[B]. Dry to humid forest, borders, older second growth. To 900 m (rarely 1400 m). **ID** Only *Pteroglossus* in most of N Colombia; note collar on hindneck (can be difficult to see) and bill pattern. **Voice** Call high forceful metallic "kis'SICK!" or "peeSEEk!"; also bill-clattering. **SS** Stripe-billed Araçari. **TN** Usually includes Stripe-billed Araçari, which hybridizes narrowly with both races of Collared Araçari and is not vocally distinct; molecular data as yet uninformative.

torquatus

Stripe-billed Araçari (Collared Araçari)
Pteroglossus sanguineus LC
Pichí de Pico Rayado
Common resident.

L 41 cm (16"). Monotypic. Near-endemic (also far NW Ecuador). Humid to wet lowland and foothill forest, borders, second growth. To 900 m. **ID** Best separated in field from Collared Araçari by long thin black line above cutting edge of maxilla. Other minor differences largely require in-hand examination. **Voice** Identical to Collared Araçari. **SS** Collared Araçari. **TN** Doubtfully valid species.

NE

Chestnut-eared Araçari
Pteroglossus castanotis LC
Pichí Bandirrojo
Common resident.

L 46 cm (18"). Race *castanotis*. Forested river borders, *várzea* edge, second growth, rarely *terra firme*. To 1000 m. Most easily seen araçari in Amazonia because of riverine and forest edge distribution. **ID** Large; single red belly-band, narrow dark culmen, base and cutting edge of maxilla black, rest yellow, mandible black, facial skin blue. 'Chestnut-eared' name unhelpful. **Voice** Sharp metallic "kEE'SIP!", abrupt and forceful, recalls Collared Araçari. **SS** Many-banded Araçari.

castanotis

Many-banded Araçari *Pteroglossus pluricinctus* `LC`
Pichí Bibandeado
Uncommon to fairly common resident.

 L 43 cm (17"). Monotypic. Mid-levels and canopy of humid *terra firme* forest, less often *várzea* forest. To 900 m. **ID** Only araçari with two separated dark bands on underparts; facial skin blue. **Voice** Call brief metallic "PINK!", forceful, single-syllabled. **SS** Chestnut-eared Araçari.

Ivory-billed Araçari *Pteroglossus azara* `LC`
Pichí Pico-de-marfil

 Three subspecies in three subspecies groups; one in Colombia.

Yellow-billed Araçari (Ivory-billed Araçari)
Pteroglossus (azara) flavirostris
Pichí Piquiamarillo
Uncommon resident.
L 38 cm (15"). One subspecies in group. Humid *terra firme* and *várzea* forest, gallery forest, savanna woodland. To 800 m. **ID** Bill pale with variable lengthwise brownish smear on mandible, broad red and black bands on breast not separated. **Voice** Call a repeated rising "curEEE" as if in distress; grating notes often doubled. **SS** Chestnut-eared Araçari. **TN** Wide variation in bill appearance between subspecies.

CAPITONIDAE
New World Barbets
18 extant species, 8 in region

A small New World family, the species noted for their chunky shapes, short necks, short tarsi, heavy bills, prominent rictal bristles and colourful plumage. Genetically more closely related to toucans than to Old World barbets. Most are birds of forest canopy that occur in pairs, less often groups; eat both fruit and arthropods.

Genus *Capito* Large sturdy barbets with strong bills. Pairs, occasionally several, some regularly with mixed flocks. Buzzy straight-line flight on short wings.

Scarlet-crowned Barbet *Capito aurovirens* `LC`
Torito Coronado
Common resident.

 L 19 cm (7.5"). Monotypic. Canopy of *várzea* and swampy forest, river borders, lake edges; usually near water. To 600 m. Pairs are sluggish in canopy, usually independent of mixed flocks. **ID** Crown red (♂) or frosty white (♀), underparts butterscotch orange. **Voice** Call low rolling frog-like "cru'u, cru'u, cru'u…" c. 2 notes/second or less, given as leans forward, bill pointing down; slower than call of Lemon-throated Barbet. **SS** Gilded Barbet.

Spot-crowned Barbet *Capito maculicoronatus* `LC`
Torito Cabeciblanco
Common resident.

 L 18 cm (7"). Race *rubrilateralis*. Humid and wet lowland forest, borders, second growth. To 900 m. Pairs or trios, occasionally several; regularly follow canopy mixed flocks dominated by tanagers. **ID** No red on crown, white crown spots inconspicuous. ♂ underparts white, lower breast and belly heavily streaked black, flanks mixed red and black; ♀ throat and chest black. **Voice** Not very vocal. Call rough flat "chak"; infrequent song a rapid toad- or frog-like trill. **SS** Overlaps only Five-colored Barbet.

rubrilateralis

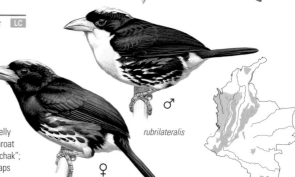

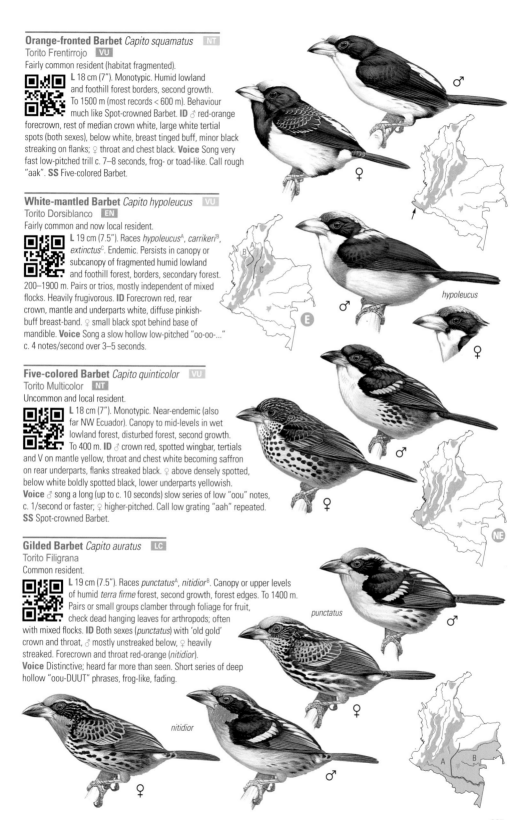

Orange-fronted Barbet *Capito squamatus* [NT]
Torito Frentirrojo [VU]

Fairly common resident (habitat fragmented).
L 18 cm (7"). Monotypic. Humid lowland and foothill forest borders, second growth. To 1500 m (most records < 600 m). Behaviour much like Spot-crowned Barbet. **ID** ♂ red-orange forecrown, rest of median crown white, large white tertial spots (both sexes), below white, breast tinged buff, minor black streaking on flanks; ♀ throat and chest black. **Voice** Song very fast low-pitched trill c. 7–8 seconds, frog- or toad-like. Call rough "aak". **SS** Five-colored Barbet.

White-mantled Barbet *Capito hypoleucus* [VU]
Torito Dorsiblanco [EN]

Fairly common and now local resident.
L 19 cm (7.5"). Races *hypoleucus*[A], *carrikeri*[B], *extinctus*[C]. Endemic. Persists in canopy or subcanopy of fragmented humid lowland and foothill forest, borders, secondary forest. 200–1900 m. Pairs or trios, mostly independent of mixed flocks. Heavily frugivorous. **ID** Forecrown red, rear crown, mantle and underparts white, diffuse pinkish-buff breast-band. ♀ small black spot behind base of mandible. **Voice** Song a slow hollow low-pitched "oo-oo-..." c. 4 notes/second over 3–5 seconds.

hypoleucus

Five-colored Barbet *Capito quinticolor* [VU]
Torito Multicolor [NT]

Uncommon and local resident.
L 18 cm (7"). Monotypic. Near-endemic (also far NW Ecuador). Canopy to mid-levels in wet lowland forest, disturbed forest, second growth. To 400 m. **ID** ♂ crown red, spotted wingbar, tertials and V on mantle yellow, throat and chest white becoming saffron on rear underparts, flanks streaked black. ♀ above densely spotted, below white boldly spotted black, lower underparts yellowish. **Voice** ♂ song a long (up to c. 10 seconds) slow series of low "oou" notes, c. 1/second or faster; ♀ higher-pitched. Call low grating "aah" repeated. **SS** Spot-crowned Barbet.

Gilded Barbet *Capito auratus* [LC]
Torito Filigrana

Common resident.
L 19 cm (7.5"). Races *punctatus*[A], *nitidior*[B]. Canopy or upper levels of humid *terra firme* forest, second growth, forest edges. To 1400 m. Pairs or small groups clamber through foliage for fruit, check dead hanging leaves for arthropods; often with mixed flocks. **ID** Both sexes (*punctatus*) with 'old gold' crown and throat, ♂ mostly unstreaked below, ♀ heavily streaked. Forecrown and throat red-orange (*nitidior*). **Voice** Distinctive; heard far more than seen. Short series of deep hollow "oou-DUUT" phrases, frog-like, fading.

punctatus

nitidior

225

Genus *Eubucco* Colourful; smaller than *Capito* and more active; bills more pointed.

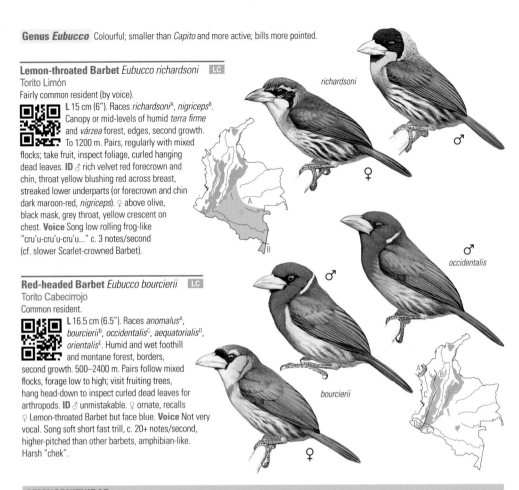

richardsoni

♂

♀

♂

occidentalis

♂

bourcierii

♀

Lemon-throated Barbet *Eubucco richardsoni* `LC`
Torito Limón
Fairly common resident (by voice).

L 15 cm (6"). Races *richardsoni*[A], *nigriceps*[B]. Canopy or mid-levels of humid *terra firme* and *várzea* forest, edges, second growth. To 1200 m. Pairs, regularly with mixed flocks; take fruit, inspect foliage, curled hanging dead leaves. **ID** ♂ rich velvet red forecrown and chin, throat yellow blushing red across breast, streaked lower underparts (or forecrown and chin dark maroon-red, *nigriceps*). ♀ above olive, black mask, grey throat, yellow crescent on chest. **Voice** Song low rolling frog-like "cru'u-cru'u-cru'u..." c. 3 notes/second (cf. slower Scarlet-crowned Barbet).

Red-headed Barbet *Eubucco bourcierii* `LC`
Torito Cabecirrojo
Common resident.

L 16.5 cm (6.5"). Races *anomalus*[A], *bourcierii*[B], *occidentalis*[C], *aequatorialis*[D], *orientalis*[E]. Humid and wet foothill and montane forest, borders, second growth. 500–2400 m. Pairs follow mixed flocks, forage low to high; visit fruiting trees, hang head-down to inspect curled dead leaves for arthropods. **ID** ♂ unmistakable. ♀ ornate, recalls ♀ Lemon-throated Barbet but face blue. **Voice** Not very vocal. Song soft short fast trill, c. 20+ notes/second, higher-pitched than other barbets, amphibian-like. Harsh "chek".

SEMNORNITHIDAE
Prong-billed Barbets
2 extant species, 1 in region

This small family is most closely related to New World barbets and toucans. In the past both species were sometimes included with barbets. The two species share bill morphology but otherwise are not very close genetically. Taxonomic placement unresolved.

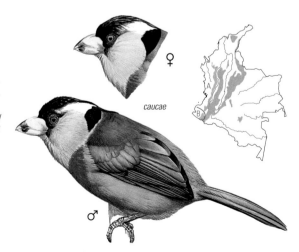

♀

caucae

♂

Toucan Barbet *Semnornis ramphastinus* `NT`
Compás `NT`
Fairly common resident.

 L 23 cm (9"). Races *caucae*[A], *ramphastinus*[B]. Mid-levels to canopy of wet montane forest, borders, older second growth. 900–2400 m. Pairs or small groups. Sluggish, perch quietly for protracted periods, so easily overlooked. Feeds heavily on fruit. Usually independent of mixed flocks. **ID** Multicoloured, thick pale bill tipped black, white eyebrow, grey throat and red belly. **Voice** Memorable loud resonant honking duet lasting up to 30 seconds, with ♂ and ♀ on different pitches and out of synch, producing distinct syncopation, recalling French ambulance.

Woodpeckers comprise a nearly worldwide family whose members are best known for hitching up trunks and limbs, and chiseling into wood to make nest cavities. Drum on wood rather than sing, and are endowed with shock-absorbing features that protect their brains when drilling and drumming. Most species drill into wood for wood-boring insects and extract them with their long barb-tipped tongues, although ants, fruit and even flying insects are taken by some species. All are cavity nesters.

Genus *Picumnus* Tiny twig specialists; singles or pairs, often with mixed flocks. ♂♂ crowns dotted red or yellow; ♀♀ dotted white. Tail pattern identical in all species. Song a high-pitched trill or slower descending series of high notes; also drum.

Bar-breasted Piculet *Picumnus aurifrons* LC
Carpinterito Frentidorado
Status uncertain (occurs S of R Amazon; N bank records need confirmation).

 L 9 cm (3.5"). Race *flavifrons* (possible S Amazonas). Borders of *várzea* forest, second growth, overgrown clearings. **ID** ♂ upperparts plain, chest barred (sometimes obscurely also on throat), rest of underparts coarsely streaked and spotted, crown dotted orange-yellow (or white in ♀).
Voice Short slow series of very high thin notes on same pitch.
SS Plain-breasted and Lafresnaye's Piculets.

flavifrons
♀
♂

Orinoco Piculet *Picumnus pumilus* LC
Carpinterito del Orinoco
Local and uncommon resident.

 L 10 cm (4"). Monotypic. Borders of white sandy soil forest, scrub and savanna woodland, gallery forest; often forages low. To 350 m. **ID** ♂ above uniform brownish olive, crown dotted and streaked yellow (or dotted white ♀), underparts whitish crisply and evenly barred black. **Voice** Call (?) c. 3 high-pitched, upward-inflected notes on same pitch. Song unconfirmed; short high trill (?). **SS** Lafresnaye's and Golden-spangled Piculets.

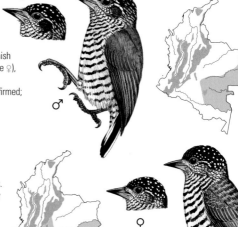
♀
♂

Lafresnaye's Piculet *Picumnus lafresnayi* LC
Carpinterito Barrado
Fairly common resident.

 L 9 cm (3.5"). Race *lafresnayi*. Humid forest borders, older overgrown second growth. Lowlands and foothills. To 1400 m (?). **ID** Only Colombian piculet with obviously barred (not spotted) upperparts, forecrown dotted red-orange, rear crown dotted white (or all dotted white in ♀), underparts yellowish white barred black. Sight records in Villavicencio area and Leticia need documentation.
Voice Song (c. 2 seconds) c. 5–8 very high-pitched, upward-inflected notes (c. 7.5–8.5 kHz) that descend slightly. Call rising "seek". **SS** Golden-spangled and Orinoco Piculets.

♀
lafresnayi
♂

Golden-spangled Piculet *Picumnus exilis* LC
Carpinterito Capirotado
Few records (recent photos).

 L 9 cm (3.5"). Race *undulatus*. Borders of sandy soil forest and savanna woodland, scrub. To 250 m. **ID** ♂ above olive-brown, feathers with yellowish margins giving spotted or scaled appearance, forecrown dotted red, rear crown white (or all dotted white ♀), underparts yellowish buff, throat finely barred, and rest of underparts narrowly barred blackish, more spotted on lower underparts. **Voice** Song (c. 2 seconds) 3–8 very high (7.5–8.5 kHz) upward-inflected notes lasting 1–3 seconds, slightly descending "seeeek, seeeek, seeee, see, se se" (very like Lafresnaye's Piculet). Call "seeek". **SS** Lafresnaye's and Orinoco Piculets.

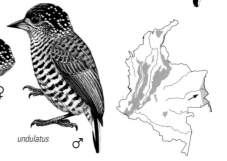
♀
undulatus
♂

227

Scaled Piculet *Picumnus squamulatus* `LC`
Carpinterito Escamado
Fairly common resident.

 L 9 cm (3.5"). Races *roehli*[A], *squamulatus*[B], *lovejoyi* (valid?) possible E Norte de Santander and Guajira. Dry forest borders, gallery forest, scrub. To 1600 m. **ID** ♂ above brown, below dingy white, scaled dusky throughout, forecrown dotted red, rear crown dotted white (or all dotted white ♀); or paler above and below (*roehli*), palest and lightly scaled below (*lovejoyi*). **Voice** Call 1–2 high "seek" notes. Song c. 4 high (8–8.5 kHz) thin upward-inflected "seek" notes, the series slowly descending. **SS** Expanding S into W Caquetá; cf. Lafresnaye's Piculet.

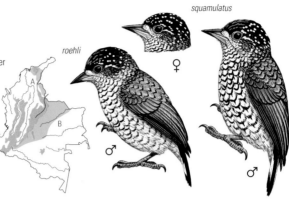

squamulatus

roehli

♀

♂

White-bellied Piculet *Picumnus spilogaster* `VU`
Carpinterito Ventriblanco
Local resident (first reported c. 2015).

 L 10 cm (4"). Race *orinocensis*. Semi-deciduous gallery forest, dry to moderately humid woodland borders, river island scrub. Photos, NE Vichada (Isla Santa Elena, R Orinoco). **ID** Relatively large piculet. ♂ crown black streaked red, rear crown dotted white; or crown dotted white ♀. Above pale greyish brown, uniform or lightly scaled dusky, inner remiges edged yellow-buff, below dull whitish, throat and chest sometimes faintly scaled. **Voice** Song long (c. 3 seconds) thin slightly descending trill "ti'eeeeeeeeeeeeeeeeeeeeeee".

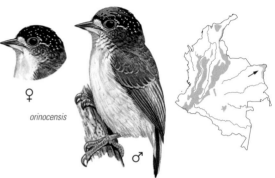

♀

orinocensis

♂

Rufous-breasted Piculet *Picumnus rufiventris* `LC`
Carpinterito Pechirrufo
Uncommon and local resident.

 L 10 cm (4"). Race *rufiventris*. Dense understorey of *várzea* and transition forest, borders, *Guadua* bamboo, young second growth, often near creeks; commoner in foothills. To 1100 m (higher?). Typically forages low (down to eye level). **ID** ♂ central crown black dotted red (dots obscure), underparts uniform rufous-chestnut; ♀ crown dotted white. **Voice** Song 2–3 very high-pitched (7.8–10 kHz) thin upward-inflected notes. Call, similar single notes. Drums more than other piculets.

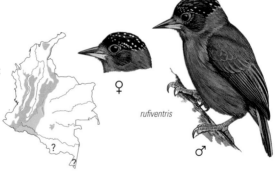

♀

rufiventris

♂

Plain-breasted Piculet *Picumnus castelnau* `LC`
Carpinterito Pechiblanco
Common resident.

 L 9 cm (3.5"). Monotypic. Young second growth bordering large rivers, nearby shrubby clearings, gardens; mid-stage successional vegetation (especially with *Cecropia*) on Amazonian river islands; usually near water. To 200 m. Forages at low to mid-levels, sometimes with mixed flocks. **ID** Easily identified by habitat and unmarked greyish-white underparts. ♂ black crown dotted red; ♀ solid black crown. **Voice** Song high (8–9 kHz) very fast descending trill, fading, c. 35 notes/1.5 seconds.

♀

♂

Olivaceous Piculet *Picumnus olivaceus* `LC`
Carpinterito Oliváceo
Fairly common resident.

 L 9 cm (3.5"). Races *flavotinctus*[A], *olivaceus*[B], *tachirensis*[C], *harterti*[D], *eisenmanni* (Venezuelan side Sierra de Perijá; Colombia?). Dry to humid forest borders, light woodland, shrubby second growth; mostly foothills or higher. To 1800 m (rarely 2500 m).
ID ♂ above plain olive, forecrown blackish dotted yellow-orange, rear crown dotted white (or all dotted white ♀), breast smudged dull olive (palest *flavotinctus*, darkest *olivaceus*), lower underparts tinged yellowish buff, obscurely streaked olive. **Voice** Song a high (6.8–7.8 kHz) thin fast descending trill (35–40 notes/2 seconds). **SS** Greyish Piculet.

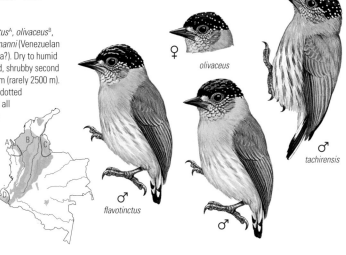

olivaceus

tachirensis

flavotinctus

Greyish Piculet *Picumnus granadensis* `LC`
Carpinterito Punteado
Fairly common resident.

 L 9 cm (3.5"). Races *antioquensis*[A], *granadensis*[B]. Endemic. Dry to humid forest borders, light woodland, shrubby second growth; foothills or higher. 300–2100 m.
ID ♂ uniform brownish grey above, crown black dotted yellow in front, white behind, underparts more or less uniform dingy grey (no streaking). ♀ crown dotted white. **Voice** Song a high (7–8 kHz) thin fast trill, descending, fading (30+ notes in two seconds). **SS** Range broadly overlaps Olivaceous Piculet but habitat separation (if any?) unclear.

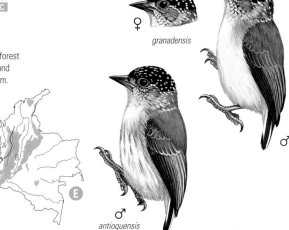

granadensis

antioquensis

Chestnut Piculet *Picumnus cinnamomeus* `LC`
Carpinterito Castaño
Fairly common resident.

 L 10 cm (4"). Races *cinnamomeus*[A], *persaturatus*[B], *perijanus* (NW base Perijá Mts?). Near-endemic (also NW Venezuela). Arid and semi-arid scrub, dry forest, scrubby woodland, mangroves. To 300 m. Pairs, sometimes with small mixed flocks. Forages at almost all heights and, like other piculets, is inconspicuous, but easier to see due to relatively open habitat.
ID Chestnut. ♂ blackish crown dotted yellow, ♀ forecrown buff; rest of crown blackish dotted white. **Voice** Song 7–8 high (6–6.6 kHz) thin "seet" notes, the series slightly descending in c. 1.2 seconds, or faster descending trill. Call 1–3 "seet" notes. Regularly drums.

cinnamomeus

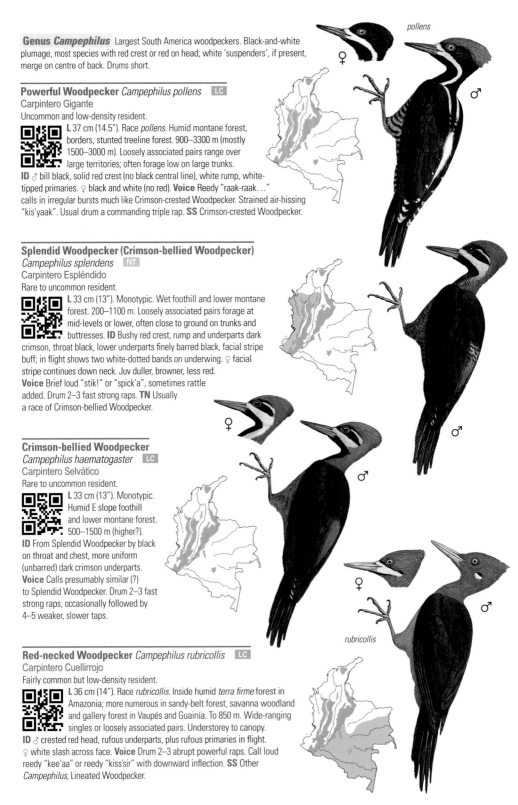

Genus *Campephilus* Largest South America woodpeckers. Black-and-white plumage, most species with red crest or red on head; white 'suspenders', if present, merge on centre of back. Drums short.

pollens

Powerful Woodpecker *Campephilus pollens* LC
Carpintero Gigante
Uncommon and low-density resident.
L 37 cm (14.5"). Race *pollens*. Humid montane forest, borders, stunted treeline forest. 900–3300 m (mostly 1500–3000 m). Loosely associated pairs range over large territories; often forage low on large trunks. **ID** ♂ bill black, solid red crest (no black central line), white rump, white-tipped primaries. ♀ black and white (no red). **Voice** Reedy "raak-raak…" calls in irregular bursts much like Crimson-crested Woodpecker. Strained air-hissing "kis'yaak". Usual drum a commanding triple rap. **SS** Crimson-crested Woodpecker.

Splendid Woodpecker (Crimson-bellied Woodpecker)
Campephilus splendens NT
Carpintero Espléndido
Rare to uncommon resident.
L 33 cm (13"). Monotypic. Wet foothill and lower montane forest. 200–1100 m. Loosely associated pairs forage at mid-levels or lower, often close to ground on trunks and buttresses. **ID** Bushy red crest, rump and underparts dark crimson, throat black, lower underparts finely barred black, facial stripe buff; in flight shows two white-dotted bands on underwing. ♀ facial stripe continues down neck. Juv duller, browner, less red. **Voice** Brief loud "stik!" or "spick'a", sometimes rattle added. Drum 2–3 fast strong raps. **TN** Usually a race of Crimson-bellied Woodpecker.

Crimson-bellied Woodpecker
Campephilus haematogaster LC
Carpintero Selvático
Rare to uncommon resident.
L 33 cm (13"). Monotypic. Humid E slope foothill and lower montane forest. 500–1500 m (higher?). **ID** From Splendid Woodpecker by black on throat and chest, more uniform (unbarred) dark crimson underparts. **Voice** Calls presumably similar (?) to Splendid Woodpecker. Drum 2–3 fast strong raps, occasionally followed by 4–5 weaker, slower taps.

rubricollis

Red-necked Woodpecker *Campephilus rubricollis* LC
Carpintero Cuellirrojo
Fairly common but low-density resident.
L 36 cm (14"). Race *rubricollis*. Inside humid *terra firme* forest in Amazonia; more numerous in sandy-belt forest, savanna woodland and gallery forest in Vaupés and Guainía. To 850 m. Wide-ranging singles or loosely associated pairs. Understorey to canopy. **ID** ♂ crested red head, rufous underparts, plus rufous primaries in flight. ♀ white slash across face. **Voice** Drum 2–3 abrupt powerful raps. Call loud reedy "kee'aa" or reedy "kiss'sir" with downward inflection. **SS** Other *Campephilus*, Lineated Woodpecker.

Crimson-crested Woodpecker

Campephilus melanoleucos `LC`

Carpintero Marcial

Common resident.

 L 36 cm (14"). Races *malherbii*[A], *melanoleucos*[B]. Dry to humid forest, borders, plantations, second growth, trees in clearings. To 2000 m. Pairs, occasionally families; low to high in woodland, less often outside forest. **ID** ♂ crested red head, white around base of bill. ♀ notably broad white cheek stripe, black divides red crest. **Voice** Drum 3–5 or more powerful raps, first two loudest (at distance sounds like double tap). Nasal reedy calls recall Red-necked Woodpecker. **SS** Lineated Woodpecker, Guayaquil Woodpecker (no overlap).

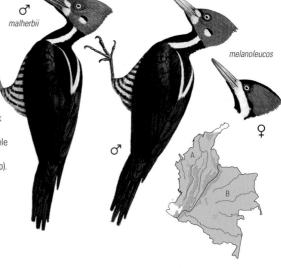

Guayaquil Woodpecker *Campephilus gayaquilensis* `NT`

Carpintero de Guayaquil `EN`

Local resident.

L 36 cm (14"). Monotypic. Dry to humid forest, borders, patchy disturbed woodland. To 800 m. **ID** Both sexes from Crimson-crested Woodpecker by brownish-tinged upperparts, variable buff barring on rump; ♂ no white around base of bill, ♀ solid red crest (no black). **Voice** Similar to Crimson-crested Woodpecker. **SS** Lineated Woodpecker.

Genus *Piculus* Medium-sized, with olive upperparts, yellow face or facial stripe, and banded or scalloped underparts. Upper levels inside lowland or foothill forest. None common.

White-throated Woodpecker *Piculus leucolaemus* `LC`

Carpintero Bigotudo

Uncommon resident (relatively few records).

 L 20 cm (8"). Monotypic. Mid-levels to canopy of humid lowland and foothill forest. To 1000 m. **ID** ♂ and ♀ have yellow cheek stripe, white throat, white (not olive-yellow) underparts prominently scalloped black. ♀ red only on nape, no red malar. **Voice** Short slightly descending air-expelling hiss; also 4–10 brisk, husky, reedy "reea-reea-..." calls. **SS** Golden-green Woodpecker has pale eyes, dark throat, underparts narrowly banded (not scalloped).

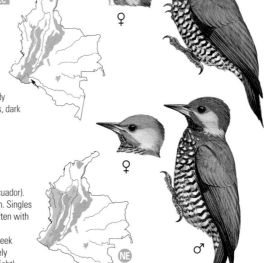

Lita Woodpecker *Piculus litae* `LC`

Carpintero de Litá

Uncommon and local (?) resident.

 L 18 cm (7"). Monotypic. Near-endemic (also NW Ecuador). Humid and wet lowland and foothill forest. To 800 m. Singles or pairs climb branches, mid-levels to subcanopy. Often with mixed flocks. **ID** Differs from allied White-throated Woodpecker (no overlap) by smaller size, much broader yellow cheek stripe (both sexes), white throat flecked black, chest olive obscurely spotted white; both species show rufous in primaries (mainly in flight). ♀ red nape band, no red malar. **Voice** Hissing "pessheer" very like White-throated Woodpecker. **TN** Formerly regarded as a race of White-throated Woodpecker.

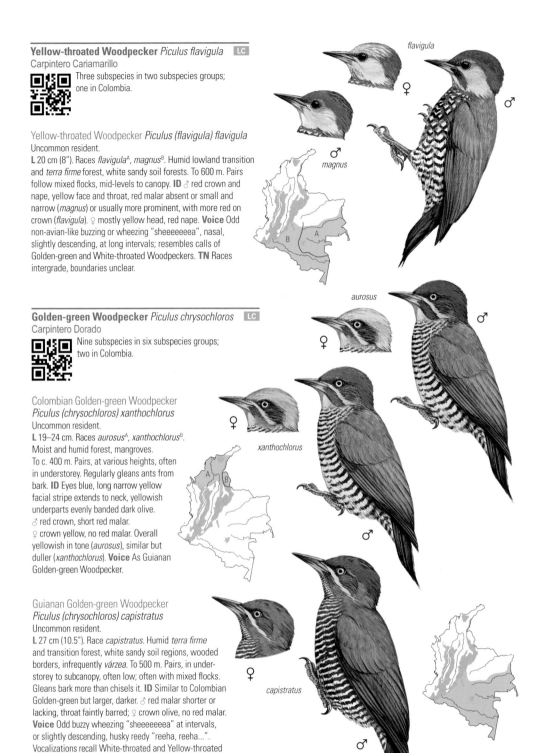

Yellow-throated Woodpecker *Piculus flavigula* `LC`
Carpintero Cariamarillo

Three subspecies in two subspecies groups; one in Colombia.

Yellow-throated Woodpecker *Piculus (flavigula) flavigula*
Uncommon resident.
L 20 cm (8"). Races *flavigula*[A], *magnus*[B]. Humid lowland transition and *terra firme* forest, white sandy soil forests. To 600 m. Pairs follow mixed flocks, mid-levels to canopy. **ID** ♂ red crown and nape, yellow face and throat, red malar absent or small and narrow (*magnus*) or usually more prominent, with more red on crown (*flavigula*). ♀ mostly yellow head, red nape. **Voice** Odd non-avian-like buzzing or wheezing "sheeeeeeea", nasal, slightly descending, at long intervals; resembles calls of Golden-green and White-throated Woodpeckers. **TN** Races intergrade, boundaries unclear.

Golden-green Woodpecker *Piculus chrysochloros* `LC`
Carpintero Dorado

Nine subspecies in six subspecies groups; two in Colombia.

Colombian Golden-green Woodpecker
Piculus (chrysochloros) xanthochlorus
Uncommon resident.
L 19–24 cm. Races *aurosus*[A], *xanthochlorus*[B]. Moist and humid forest, mangroves. To c. 400 m. Pairs, at various heights, often in understorey. Regularly gleans ants from bark. **ID** Eyes blue, long narrow yellow facial stripe extends to neck, yellowish underparts evenly banded dark olive. ♂ red crown, short red malar. ♀ crown yellow, no red malar. Overall yellowish in tone (*aurosus*), similar but duller (*xanthochlorus*). **Voice** As Guianan Golden-green Woodpecker.

Guianan Golden-green Woodpecker
Piculus (chrysochloros) capistratus
Uncommon resident.
L 27 cm (10.5"). Race *capistratus*. Humid *terra firme* and transition forest, white sandy soil regions, wooded borders, infrequently *várzea*. To 500 m. Pairs, in under-storey to subcanopy, often low; often with mixed flocks. Gleans bark more than chisels it. **ID** Similar to Colombian Golden-green but larger, darker. ♂ red malar shorter or lacking, throat faintly barred; ♀ crown olive, no red malar. **Voice** Odd buzzy wheezing "sheeeeeeea" at intervals, or slightly descending, husky reedy "reeha, reeha...". Vocalizations recall White-throated and Yellow-throated Woodpeckers.

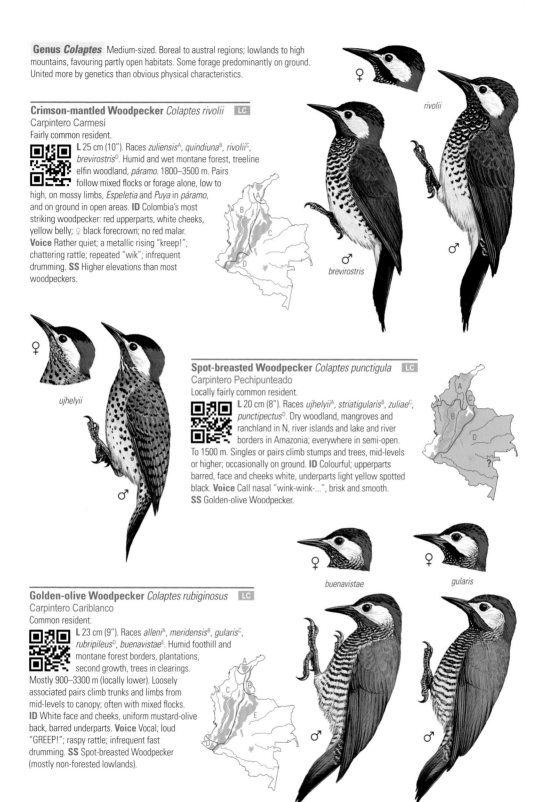

Genus *Colaptes* Medium-sized. Boreal to austral regions; lowlands to high mountains, favouring partly open habitats. Some forage predominantly on ground. United more by genetics than obvious physical characteristics.

rivolii

Crimson-mantled Woodpecker *Colaptes rivolii* LC
Carpintero Carmesí
Fairly common resident.

L 25 cm (10"). Races *zuliensis*[A], *quindiuna*[B], *rivolii*[C], *brevirostris*[D]. Humid and wet montane forest, treeline elfin woodland, *páramo*. 1800–3500 m. Pairs follow mixed flocks or forage alone, low to high, on mossy limbs, *Espeletia* and *Puya* in *páramo*, and on ground in open areas. **ID** Colombia's most striking woodpecker: red upperparts, white cheeks, yellow belly; ♀ black forecrown; no red malar. **Voice** Rather quiet; a metallic rising "kreep!"; chattering rattle; repeated "wik"; infrequent drumming. **SS** Higher elevations than most woodpeckers.

brevirostris

ujhelyii

Spot-breasted Woodpecker *Colaptes punctigula* LC
Carpintero Pechipunteado
Locally fairly common resident.

L 20 cm (8"). Races *ujhelyii*[A], *striatigularis*[B], *zuliae*[C], *punctipectus*[D]. Dry woodland, mangroves and ranchland in N, river islands and lake and river borders in Amazonia; everywhere in semi-open. To 1500 m. Singles or pairs climb stumps and trees, mid-levels or higher; occasionally on ground. **ID** Colourful; upperparts barred, face and cheeks white, underparts light yellow spotted black. **Voice** Call nasal "wink-wink-...", brisk and smooth. **SS** Golden-olive Woodpecker.

buenavistae

gularis

Golden-olive Woodpecker *Colaptes rubiginosus* LC
Carpintero Cariblanco
Common resident.

L 23 cm (9"). Races *alleni*[A], *meridensis*[B], *gularis*[C], *rubripileus*[D], *buenavistae*[E]. Humid foothill and montane forest borders, plantations, second growth, trees in clearings. Mostly 900–3300 m (locally lower). Loosely associated pairs climb trunks and limbs from mid-levels to canopy; often with mixed flocks. **ID** White face and cheeks, uniform mustard-olive back, barred underparts. **Voice** Vocal; loud "GREEP!"; raspy rattle; infrequent fast drumming. **SS** Spot-breasted Woodpecker (mostly non-forested lowlands).

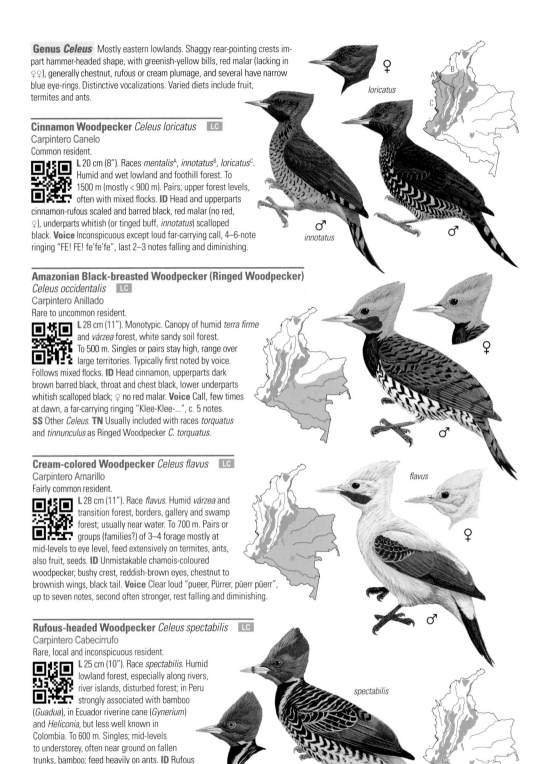

Genus *Celeus* Mostly eastern lowlands. Shaggy rear-pointing crests impart hammer-headed shape, with greenish-yellow bills, red malar (lacking in ♀♀), generally chestnut, rufous or cream plumage, and several have narrow blue eye-rings. Distinctive vocalizations. Varied diets include fruit, termites and ants.

loricatus

Cinnamon Woodpecker *Celeus loricatus* LC
Carpintero Canelo
Common resident.

L 20 cm (8"). Races *mentalis*[A], *innotatus*[B], *loricatus*[C]. Humid and wet lowland and foothill forest. To 1500 m (mostly < 900 m). Pairs; upper forest levels, often with mixed flocks. **ID** Head and upperparts cinnamon-rufous scaled and barred black, red malar (no red, ♀), underparts whitish (or tinged buff, *innotatus*) scalloped black. **Voice** Inconspicuous except loud far-carrying call, 4–6-note ringing "FE! FE! fe'fe'fe", last 2–3 notes falling and diminishing.

innotatus

Amazonian Black-breasted Woodpecker (Ringed Woodpecker)
Celeus occidentalis LC
Carpintero Anillado
Rare to uncommon resident.

L 28 cm (11"). Monotypic. Canopy of humid *terra firme* and *várzea* forest, white sandy soil forest. To 500 m. Singles or pairs stay high, range over large territories. Typically first noted by voice. Follows mixed flocks. **ID** Head cinnamon, upperparts dark brown barred black, throat and chest black, lower underparts whitish scalloped black; ♀ no red malar. **Voice** Call, few times at dawn, a far-carrying ringing "Klee-Klee-...", c. 5 notes. **SS** Other *Celeus*. **TN** Usually included with races *torquatus* and *tinnunculus* as Ringed Woodpecker *C. torquatus*.

Cream-colored Woodpecker *Celeus flavus* LC
Carpintero Amarillo
Fairly common resident.

L 28 cm (11"). Race *flavus*. Humid *várzea* and transition forest, borders, gallery and swamp forest; usually near water. To 700 m. Pairs or groups (families?) of 3–4 forage mostly at mid-levels to eye level, feed extensively on termites, ants, also fruit, seeds. **ID** Unmistakable chamois-coloured woodpecker; bushy crest, reddish-brown eyes, chestnut to brownish wings, black tail. **Voice** Clear loud "pueer, Pürrer, püerr püerr", up to seven notes, second often stronger, rest falling and diminishing.

flavus

Rufous-headed Woodpecker *Celeus spectabilis* LC
Carpintero Cabecirrufo
Rare, local and inconspicuous resident.

L 25 cm (10"). Race *spectabilis*. Humid lowland forest, especially along rivers, river islands, disturbed forest; in Peru strongly associated with bamboo (*Guadua*), in Ecuador riverine cane (*Gynerium*) and *Heliconia*, but less well known in Colombia. To 600 m. Singles; mid-levels to understorey, often near ground on fallen trunks, bamboo; feed heavily on ants. **ID** Rufous head, black chest, chestnut flight feathers, otherwise boldly scalloped buff and black. **Voice** Call "sqeeo'cua-cua-cua-cua-cua", first note higher, squealing. **SS** Amazonian Black-breasted (Ringed) Woodpecker.

spectabilis

Waved Woodpecker *Celeus undatus* `LC`
Carpinterito Ondulado
Fairly common resident.

 L 23 cm (9"). Races *grammicus*[A], *verreauxi*[B]. Humid *terra firme* and *várzea* forest in Amazonia, sandy-belt forest in extreme E. To 500 m. Singles or pairs at mid-levels or more often high in canopy, often with mixed flocks. **ID** Dark rufous-chestnut, chest and upper breast densely scalloped black, wing-coverts scaled black, rump yellow. **Voice** Heard more than seen; distinctive nasal rising then falling "curree-ho". **SS** Larger Chestnut Woodpecker lacks black markings. **TN** Often regarded as a species, Scale-breasted Woodpecker, distinct from E races of Waved Woodpecker.

Chestnut Woodpecker *Celeus elegans* `LC`
Carpintero Martillo

 Six subspecies may comprise two subspecies groups; one in Colombia.

Chestnut-crested Woodpecker
Celeus (elegans) jumanus
Fairly common resident.

L 28 cm (11"). Races *jumanus*[A], *citreopygius*[B]. Understorey to subcanopy of humid *terra firme* and *várzea* forest in Amazonia, white sandy soil forests. To 600 m. Singles, pairs or families often forage low, regularly with understorey mixed flocks, glean bark for ants, termites; pry loose bark, chisel wood, eat fruit. **ID** Uniform chestnut, rump yellow; ♀ no red malar. **Voice** Raspy "whEEjer" or hoarse "whAACHup", rising then falling. **SS** Waved Woodpecker. **TN** Racial boundary needs clarification.

Lineated Woodpecker *Hylatomus lineatus* `LC`
Carpintero Real
Common resident.

 L 36 cm (14"). Race *lineatus*. Dry to humid forest borders, disturbed woodland, clearings with scattered trees, plantations. To 2200 m. Singles or pairs hitch up live or decaying stumps, large trunks, limbs, low to high; chisel wood, scale bark, eat fruit; wary. **ID** Either sex identified by long narrow (not broad) white facial stripe, white shoulder stripes well separated. **Voice** Slow drum roll c. 8–15 raps; loud "weeka-weeka-..."; frequent "kip! whurrrr" (often in film backgrounds). **SS** Crimson-crested Woodpecker. **TN** Formerly *Dryocopus*.

Yellow-bellied Sapsucker *Sphyrapicus varius* `LC`
Carpintero Chupasavia
Rare boreal migrant (Islas San Andrés and Providencia) or vagrant (mainland).

 L 22 cm (8.5"). Monotypic. Forest borders, open montane woodland. Possible almost anywhere; breeds in North America. Drills lines of tiny holes for sap. To 2000 m. **ID** ♂ red forecrown and throat, white facial stripe, barred back, large white slash on lower border of wing. ♀ white throat. Juv (more likely than ad in Colombia) brownish, much duller, conspicuous white slash at lower border of wing. **Voice** Like soft pitiful cry of a kitten.

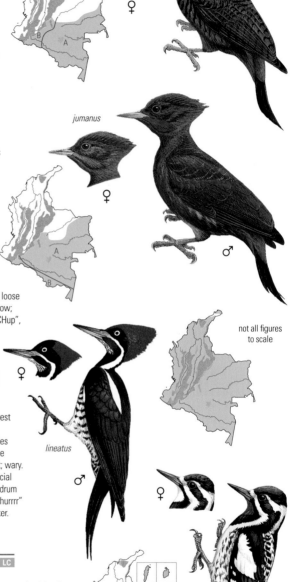

grammicus

jumanus

lineatus

not all figures to scale

Genus *Melanerpes* Boldly marked. Semi-open areas, often high up on bare branches. Some notably social, but not with mixed flocks.

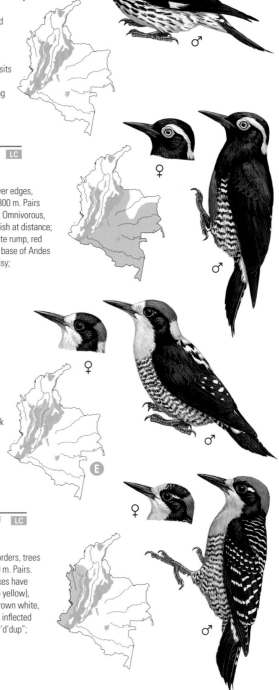

flavigula

Acorn Woodpecker *Melanerpes formicivorus* `LC`
Carpintero de Robledales
Common resident locally.

 L 20 cm (8"). Race *flavigula*. Dry to humid highland forest borders, especially with oak (*Quercus*); plantations, clearings with scattered trees. 1400–3000 m. Social; pairs or groups perch high on exposed bare stumps; may sally. Reported storing acorns, visits feeders. **ID** Clown-like face pattern, white throat (sometimes tinged yellowish) and rump, breast streaked, in flight white wing patch. **Voice** Raucous "R'Rack'up..." and "weeka..." repeated.

Yellow-tufted Woodpecker *Melanerpes cruentatus* `LC`
Carpintero Cejón
Common resident.

 L 20 cm (8"). Monotypic. Humid forest borders, river edges, clearings, settled areas with tall dead trees. To 1300 m. Pairs or social groups, conspicuous on high bare snags. Omnivorous, may sally or eat fruit. **ID** Colourful but looks blackish at distance; yellow eye-ring, long yellow post-ocular tufts join on nape, white rump, red belly. Birds lacking yellow tufts, or with partial tufts, occur at E base of Andes in Arauca, also E Vichada and Guainía (elsewhere?). **Voice** Noisy; "r'r'r'aack-up" and other calls similar to Acorn Woodpecker.

Beautiful Woodpecker *Melanerpes pulcher* `LC`
Carpintero Bonito `VU`
Local resident.

 L 20 cm (8"). Monotypic. Endemic. Openings in humid forest, borders, clearings, pastures with tall stumps or scattered dead trees. 150–1500 m. Singles or pairs, usually high on open dead branches and independent of mixed flocks. Often difficult to locate. **ID** Black mask, mid-crown red, nape yellow, central back and rump white, breast to belly white coarsely barred black, small red belly patch. **Voice** Call a loud nasal rising then falling "skWEup", typically in triplets; also churrs, rattles. **SS** Black-cheeked Woodpecker.

(E)

Black-cheeked Woodpecker *Melanerpes pucherani* `LC`
Carpintero de Antifaz
Common resident.

 L 20 cm (8"). Monotypic. Humid and wet forest borders, trees in clearings, second growth, settled areas. To 700 m. Pairs. **ID** Resembles Beautiful Woodpecker but both sexes have large white post-ocular patch. ♂ crown all red (no yellow), back black with messy white barring, only rump white; ♀ forecrown white, hindcrown red. **Voice** Call several loud nasal "sqirrrlee" notes, inflected upward, recalls Beautiful Woodpecker; brief rolling rising "chur'd'dup"; rattles; churrs. **SS** Beautiful Woodpecker (no known overlap).

Red-crowned Woodpecker *Melanerpes rubricapillus* `LC`
Carpintero Habado

Common and conspicuous resident.

 L 19 cm (7.5"). Race *rubricapillus*. Dry to humid forest borders, clearings with trees, plantations, gardens, mangroves. To 1700 m. Most commonly seen woodpecker across N half of country. Pairs climb low to high, usually in relatively open areas. **ID** Crisp black-and-white barred back, dingy whitish face and underparts. ♂ red crown and nape; ♀ paler yellow-orange patch only on nape. **Voice** Raspy "trrrr", often repeated; longer grating rattles; both sexes drum.

Genera *Leuconotopicus, Veniliornis* and *Dryobates* Taxonomy unsettled; some now place all *Veniliornis* in *Dryobates*. Colombian species small, above brownish, below barred (except Smoky-brown), red on crown.

Smoky-brown Woodpecker *Leuconotopicus fumigatus* `LC`
Carpintero Pardo

Fairly common resident.

 L 16.5 cm (6.5"). Race *fumigatus*. Humid montane forest borders, disturbed areas, coffee plantations. 1200–2800 m (locally 600 m). Rather inconspicuous, climbs low to fairly high, sometimes with mixed flocks. **ID** Only small uniformly brown woodpecker in mountains; in flight shows barred underwings. ♂ red cap. **Voice** Rough nasal rattle; wheezy "wicker...". **TN** Generic placement provisional. Previously in *Veniliornis* or *Picoides* then *Dryobates*.

Red-rumped Woodpecker *Veniliornis kirkii* `LC`
Carpintero Culirrojo

Common resident.

 L 16.5 cm (6.5"). Races *cecilii*[A], *continentalis*[B]. Dry to moderately humid woodland borders, plantations, parks, gardens, mangroves; few in Pacific region. To 1300 m. Behaviour like Smoky-brown Woodpecker but generally in drier woodland at lower elevations. **ID** Red rump is key (either sex) but often hard to see; evenly banded underparts, narrow yellow nuchal band. **Voice** Distinctive tinny clipped "ca-líck", sometimes repeatedly; short drum. **SS** Other *Veniliornis* (*Dryobates*) woodpeckers. **TN** Now often placed in *Dryobates*.

Little Woodpecker *Veniliornis passerinus* `LC`
Carpintero Ribereño

 Nine subspecies in two subspecies groups; one in Colombia.

Northern Little Woodpecker *Veniliornis (passerinus) passerinus*
Common resident.

L 16.5 cm (6.5"). Race *agilis*[A], *fidelis*[B]. Riverbanks, *várzea* borders, young second growth, *Gynerium* cane on river islands. To 1200 m. Singles or pairs, low in relatively open habitat (not inside tall forest), mostly independent of mixed flocks. **ID** From allies by habitat, weakly-defined whitish eyebrow and malar, no yellow on nape. **Voice** Call "wik, wik", often followed by sharp rapid "kik" notes; short drum. **SS** Red-stained and Red-rumped Woodpeckers.

Scarlet-backed Woodpecker *Veniliornis callonotus* `LC`
Carpintero Escarlata `EN`

Local and uncommon resident.

 L 15 cm (6"). Race *callonotus*. Dry to moist woodland and scrub in arid upper R Turbio (tributary of R Patía on Cauca/Nariño border). 600–1250 m (lower?). Singles or pairs forage mostly low, and not with mixed flocks. Colombian birds isolated from main population in W Ecuador and NW Peru. **ID** Only small woodpecker with scarlet back. **Voice** Brief (2–3-second) thin rapid rattle-trill (20+ notes/second); sharp "st-dik" alarm; short fast drum. **TN** Now often placed in *Dryobates*.

♀

rubricapillus

♂

♀

fumigatus

♂

A

B

♀

cecilii

♂

♂

agilis

♀

fidelis

♂

B

A

♀

callonotus

♂

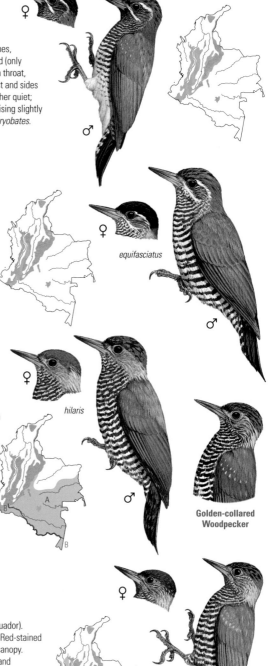

Yellow-vented Woodpecker *Veniliornis dignus* LC
Carpintero Buchiamarillo
Uncommon resident.

L 16.5 cm (6.5"). Race *dignus*. Inside humid and wet montane forest. 1200–2700 m. Singles or pairs, inconspicuous on smaller mid-level to canopy branches, regularly with mixed flocks. **ID** ♂ crown and nape red (only nape red, ♀), strong white eyebrow and moustachial line, blackish throat, sometimes shows buff markings on wing-coverts, yellowish breast and sides barred dusky, lower underparts bright unbarred yellow. **Voice** Rather quiet; rapid (c. 25 notes/second) nasal 3–4-second rattle-trill, stronger, rising slightly in middle. **SS** Bar-bellied Woodpecker. **TN** Now often placed in *Dryobates*.

dignus

Bar-bellied Woodpecker *Veniliornis nigriceps* LC
Carpintero Paramuno
Uncommon resident.

L 19 cm (7.5"). Race *equifasciatus*. Humid and wet montane forest, stunted woodland at treeline. 2500–3500 m. **ID** Generally at higher elevations than Yellow-vented Woodpecker with similar white supercilium and moustachial line. Differs in belly and undertail-coverts whitish (not yellow) and barred, wing-coverts unmarked, throat finely barred blackish, ♀ crown dusky brown, nape sometimes red. **Voice** Rather high (for a woodpecker) "keh'keh'keh'..." 7–25 or more notes, stronger as rises, then fades. **TN** Now often placed in *Dryobates*.

equifasciatus

Red-stained Woodpecker *Veniliornis affinis* LC
Carpintero Embridado
Fairly common resident.

L 19 cm (7.5"). Races *orenocensis*[A], *hilaris*[B]. Humid *terra firme* and *várzea* forest, borders, clearings with trees. To 1000 m. Singles or pairs, on trunks and small limbs high in canopy. Follows mixed flocks. **ID** Small; crown red (or brown, ♀), narrow yellow nuchal collar (occasionally absent), evenly barred underparts, tiny red shoulder stains seldom visible. **Voice** Call high thin rapid "ke'ke'ke'ke'..." recalls Bat Falcon. **SS** Little Woodpecker. **Golden-collared Woodpecker** *V. cassini* (S Venezuela) possible in Vichada, differs in tiny yellowish dots on lesser and median wing-coverts, yellow nuchal collar more distinct (?). **TN** Now often placed in *Dryobates*.

hilaris

Golden-collared Woodpecker

Choco Woodpecker *Veniliornis chocoensis* NT
Carpintero del Chocó NT
Rare resident (mainly foothills).

L 15 cm (6"). Monotypic. Near-endemic (also NW Ecuador). Wet forest. To 700 m (rarely 1000 m). Behaviour like Red-stained Woodpecker but mainly inside forest; mid-levels to canopy. **ID** Crown red (or brownish, ♀), face dusky narrowly and obscurely streaked buff-white, nape smudged yellow, uppertail-coverts narrowly barred buffy yellow, entire underparts whitish heavily barred blackish (dark bars wider than white bars), pale barring on chest often brownish buff. **Voice** High tinny "kip"; chattering rattles. **SS** Red-rumped Woodpecker. **TN** Now often placed in *Dryobates*.

NE

64 extant species, 18 in region

This heterogeneous group of Old and New World birds is not closely related to hawks, eagles and kites, except by raptorial foraging or scavenging behaviour, presumably through convergent evolution. Laughing Falcons are snake predators; forest-falcons are round-winged hunters inside forest; and true falcons are iconic, pointed-winged predators notable for high-speed aerial pursuit. With one exception, caracaras are omnivorous scavengers of open areas. The range of measurements given reflects the larger average size of ♀♀ compared to ♂♂.

Laughing Falcon *Herpetotheres cachinnans* LC
Halcón Reidor
Common resident.

L 46–56 cm (18–22"). Races *cachinnans*[A], *fulvescens*[B]. Dry to humid forest borders, trees in clearings, gallery forest. To 1500 m (rarely 2500 m). Perches upright for long periods in open trees, head often bowed. Flies with stiff rapid wingbeats and short glides. Preys heavily on snakes. **ID** Large-headed, short rounded wings, long tail; easily recognized by buff-white head and underparts, 'Panda Bear' mask. **Voice** Memorable far-carrying voice, a syncopated tirade, "gúa-co, gúa-co..." lasting several minutes, may end in muffled chuckling; especially early mornings and late evenings.

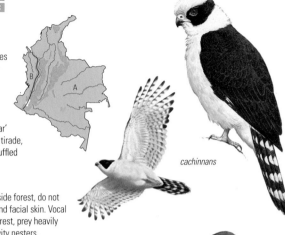

cachinnans

Genus *Micrastur* Furtive, solitary and fast-flying. Inside forest, do not soar. Long legs and long ample tail, extensive bare loral and facial skin. Vocal mainly at dawn and dusk. Larger species hunt higher in forest, prey heavily on birds; smaller species lower, diet more varied. Tree-cavity nesters.

Barred Forest-falcon *Micrastur ruficollis* LC
Halcón-montés Pajarero
Uncommon resident W of Andes, fewer in Amazonia.

L 33–38 cm (13–15"). Races *interstes*[A], *zonothorax*[B], *concentricus*[C]. Humid forest, older second growth. To 2500 m. **ID** Ad usually mainly grey (rarely rufous), with brown eyes, yellow cere, lores and facial skin, finely barred underparts, usually three white tail-bands. Juv variable; above brownish, nuchal collar whitish, face and underparts whitish to buff (rarely tawny), barring sparse, or lacking, occasionally heavily barred. **Voice** Pre-dawn "KELP" like bark of small dog, repeated tirelessly; also 3–6-note call, usually with pause after first note; cackling barks in excitement. **SS** Lined Forest-falcon.

adult
grey morph

adult
rufous morph

juvenile

Plumbeous Forest-falcon *Micrastur plumbeus* VU
Halcón-montés de Munchique EN
Rare resident (mainly Nariño).

L 30–36 cm (12–14"). Monotypic. Humid and wet foothill forest. 400–1000 m. **ID** Ad like Barred Forest-falcon but facial skin red-orange (not yellow), only single white tail-band, may show only sparse barring on underparts. Juv below whitish, barring apparently absent, faint or confined to sides, usually two white tail-bands. **Voice** Single loud "KELP" like Barred Forest-falcon but lower-pitched, more nasal; also longer 2–4-note yelp like Barred Forest-falcon, perhaps lower and faster. **TN** Taxonomic status uncertain.

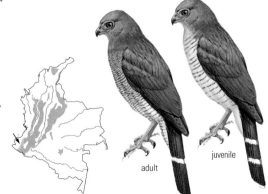

adult

juvenile

239

Lined Forest-falcon *Micrastur gilvicollis* `LC`
Halcón-montés Ojiblanco
Uncommon resident.

L 33–38 cm (13–15"). Monotypic. Inside humid *terra firme* forest. To 1500 m. In Amazonia, where overlaps Barred Forest-falcon, latter largely confined to second growth or *várzea*. Lined to forest interior. **ID** Ad from ad Barred Forest-falcon by white eyes, more orange (not yellowish) facial skin, little or no barring on lower underparts, and voice. Juv doubtfully separable from juv Barred Forest-falcon, but older stages may show white eyes. **Voice** At dawn, typically two- or three-note lamenting "kur, KYEER", second higher, stronger; agitated birds add third lower note or cackle. **SS** Buckley's Forest-falcon.

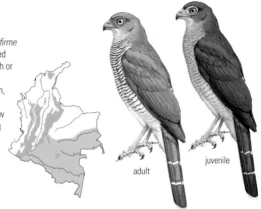

juvenile

adult

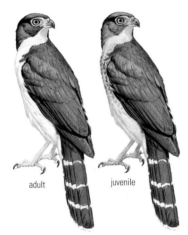

adult

juvenile

Slaty-backed Forest-falcon *Micrastur mirandollei* `LC`
Halcón-montés Pechiblanco
Rare resident.

L 41–46 cm (16–18"). Monotypic. Interior of tall humid forest. To 500 m. Mid-levels or higher. **ID** Large. Ad uniform slaty above (no white nuchal collar), yellow facial skin, brown to brownish-yellow eyes, underparts unmarked white to pale buff, occasionally minor dark shaft-streaking. Juv whitish underparts scalloped brown. **Voice** Pre-dawn and dusk, far-carrying slow series (15+ notes), initially soft, accelerating, louder, then slowing, last notes long-drawn, upward-inflected: "aa, aa, ah, ah-ah-aah-aah- ...., aah, cuaa, cuaao . cuaao". Short series of long-drawn single notes "uuuwa", nasal, complaining. **SS** Grey-bellied Hawk (p. 188; rare), juv Barred Forest-falcon.

Collared Forest-falcon *Micrastur semitorquatus* `LC`
Halcón-montés Collarejo
Uncommon resident.

L 48–61 cm (19–24"). Races *naso*[A], *semitorquatus*[B]. Dry to humid lowland forest, sandy-belt forest, borders, gallery forest. To 1000 m (rarely 2000 m). Large, low-density raptor, widespread across broad range of forest types; upper storeys. **ID** Light-morph ad above slaty black, facial skin yellow-green, eyes dark, four narrow tail-bands and tip (six bars on outermost feathers), white nuchal collar, curving black crescent from rear crown to sides of neck, white underparts. Buff morph is buff below. Black morph is all black, tail as above. Juv greenish facial skin, whitish to buff below, lightly to densely barred dark brown, long slightly rounded tail. **Voice** Assumes high open perch to call at dawn or dusk; single (or 2–3) far-carrying "cow" notes at well-spaced intervals; last note always louder after pause.

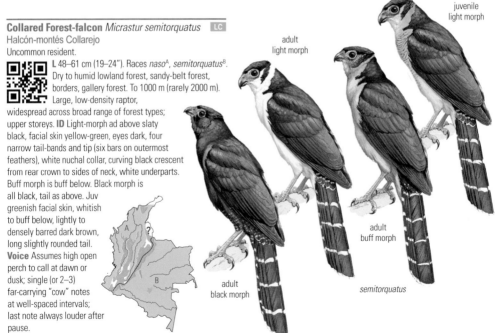

juvenile light morph

adult light morph

adult buff morph

adult black morph

semitorquatus

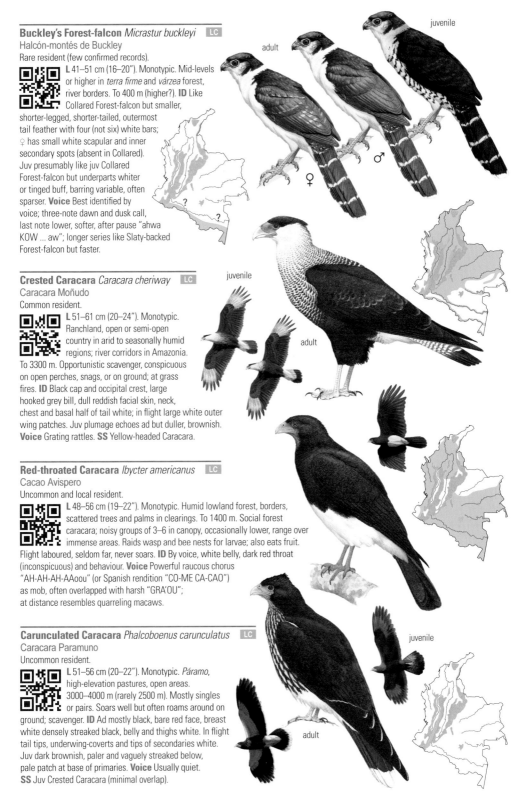

Buckley's Forest-falcon *Micrastur buckleyi* LC
Halcón-montés de Buckley
Rare resident (few confirmed records).

L 41–51 cm (16–20"). Monotypic. Mid-levels or higher in *terra firme* and *várzea* forest, river borders. To 400 m (higher?). **ID** Like Collared Forest-falcon but smaller, shorter-legged, shorter-tailed, outermost tail feather with four (not six) white bars; ♀ has small white scapular and inner secondary spots (absent in Collared). Juv presumably like juv Collared Forest-falcon but underparts whiter or tinged buff, barring variable, often sparser. **Voice** Best identified by voice; three-note dawn and dusk call, last note lower, softer, after pause "ahwa KOW ... aw"; longer series like Slaty-backed Forest-falcon but faster.

Crested Caracara *Caracara cheriway* LC
Caracara Moñudo
Common resident.

L 51–61 cm (20–24"). Monotypic. Ranchland, open or semi-open country in arid to seasonally humid regions; river corridors in Amazonia. To 3300 m. Opportunistic scavenger, conspicuous on open perches, snags, or on ground; at grass fires. **ID** Black cap and occipital crest, large hooked grey bill, dull reddish facial skin, neck, chest and basal half of tail white; in flight large white outer wing patches. Juv plumage echoes ad but duller, brownish. **Voice** Grating rattles. **SS** Yellow-headed Caracara.

Red-throated Caracara *Ibycter americanus* LC
Cacao Avispero
Uncommon and local resident.

L 48–56 cm (19–22"). Monotypic. Humid lowland forest, borders, scattered trees and palms in clearings. To 1400 m. Social forest caracara; noisy groups of 3–6 in canopy, occasionally lower, range over immense areas. Raids wasp and bee nests for larvae; also eats fruit. Flight laboured, seldom far, never soars. **ID** By voice, white belly, dark red throat (inconspicuous) and behaviour. **Voice** Powerful raucous chorus "AH-AH-AH-AAoou" (or Spanish rendition "CO-ME CA-CAO") as mob, often overlapped with harsh "GRA'OU"; at distance resembles quarreling macaws.

Carunculated Caracara *Phalcoboenus carunculatus* LC
Caracara Paramuno
Uncommon resident.

L 51–56 cm (20–22"). Monotypic. *Páramo*, high-elevation pastures, open areas. 3000–4000 m (rarely 2500 m). Mostly singles or pairs. Soars well but often roams around on ground; scavenger. **ID** Ad mostly black, bare red face, breast white densely streaked black, belly and thighs white. In flight tail tips, underwing-coverts and tips of secondaries white. Juv dark brownish, paler and vaguely streaked below, pale patch at base of primaries. **Voice** Usually quiet. **SS** Juv Crested Caracara (minimal overlap).

Yellow-headed Caracara *Milvago chimachima* `LC`
Pigua
Common resident.

L 41–46 cm (16–18"). Race *cordata*. Dry to humid ranchland, open terrain, riverbanks; expanding with deforestation. To 2500 m. Singles or pairs, perch on open treetops, posts, or roam afoot along roadsides, riverbanks, pastures. Scavenges almost anything edible; watches for disturbed prey while riding backs of capybaras and cattle. **ID** Yellow facial skin, black streak behind eye, head, neck and underparts cream to buff, whitish primary patch conspicuous in flight, whitish tail has broad black tip. Juv brownish, head and underparts streaked and mottled, unkempt. **Voice** Harsh descending scream, scratchy. **SS** Crested Caracara, juv Grey-lined Hawk (p. 197).

adult

juvenile

cordata

Black Caracara *Daptrius ater* `LC`
Cacao Negro
Fairly common resident.

L 43–48 cm (17–19"). Monotypic. Sandbars along larger Amazonian rivers, gallery or sandy-belt forests, savannas. To 600 m. Small lightweight scavenger of open areas E of Andes. Singles, pairs, families of 3–4 patrol sandy riverbanks on foot for carrion, nestlings, insects and fruit. Perches high in trees; flies over forest (rarely soars). **ID** Slender wings, bare bright orange (or yellow, juv) facial skin, white tail base. **Voice** Scratchy descending scream "kraaaaaaaa".

juvenile

adult

Genus *Falco* Long pointed wings, fairly long tails. Fast-flying. Eyes always dark (unlike *Accipiter*). ♀♀ significantly larger than ♂♂. Almost worldwide.

American Kestrel *Falco sparverius* `LC`
Cernícalo Americano
Uncommon and local resident.

L 23–28 cm (9–11"). Races *isabellinus*[A], *ochraceus*[B], *caucae*[C], *aequatorialis*[D], *sparverius*[E] (boreal migrant). Dry to humid, open or semi-open terrain; lowlands to mountains. To 3200 m. Solitary except when breeding. Perches well up in open, habitually bobs tail; hovers before stooping. **ID** Races vary; all identified by bold head pattern, streaked or spotted underparts. ♂♂ bluish wings, rufous back, rufous tail tipped black; ♀♀ black barring on rufous back and tail. **Voice** Shrill frantic "killy, killy...", high-pitched. **TN** Distribution of races poorly known.

♂

♀

♂

sparverius

Merlin *Falco columbarius* `LC`
Esmerejón
Uncommon boreal migrant.

L 25–33 cm (10–13"). Races *columbarius*, *richardsoni* (?). Ranchland, open terrain with scattered trees, wooded borders. To 3400 m. Singles perch low, less often in open. Flight fast, usually low in pursuit of small birds or other prey. **ID** Small. ♂ dull bluish, underparts streaked, undertail-coverts buff, dark evenly banded tail, weak moustache and post-auricular mark (face pattern weakly indicated); in flight wings dark above and below. ♀ above dull brownish blue. Juv like ad ♀. **Voice** Shrill accelerating notes.

♀

♂

columbarius

Bat Falcon *Falco rufigularis* `LC`
Halcón Murcielaguero
Fairly common resident.

L 23–30 cm (9–12"). Races *petoensis*[A], *rufigularis*[B]. Dry to humid forest and river borders, clearings with tall trees, mangroves. To 1600 m (rarely 2600 m). Singles or pairs perch high on open treetop stumps. Sally rapidly in pursuit of birds, flying insects, butterflies, dragonflies, at dusk especially for bats and birds flying to roosts. **ID** Small (especially ♂), broad black 'vest' finely barred white, upper edge almost straight, minor rufous at sides of throat and sides of neck (especially *petoensis*), little or none above chest; or overall throat whiter (*rufigularis*). Juv duller, throat buff. **Voice** High shrill "ke-ke-ke…", recalls American Kestrel and Red-stained Woodpecker. **SS** Orange-breasted Falcon.

Orange-breasted Falcon *Falco deiroleucus* `NT`
Halcón Colorado `DD`
Rare and local resident.

L 33–38 cm (13–15"). Monotypic. Humid forest, borders; mostly foothills, often near cliffs; local in Amazonian lowlands. To 2500 m. Perches high, often exposed. Pursues birds in swift, strong flight. **ID** Like Bat Falcon (especially ♀) but larger, black vest narrower, U-shaped across top, white barring coarser (more conspicuous), white throat contrasts with orange-rufous on sides of neck and above chest; also (with experience) bulkier shape, larger head, shorter tail, stronger tarsi and feet. **Voice** Rapid complaining chatter, "ka-ka…" perched or in flight.

Aplomado Falcon *Falco femoralis* `LC`
Halcón Plomizo
Uncommon resident.

L 36–43 cm (14–17"). Races *femoralis*[A], *pichinchae*[B]. Dry to moderately humid open or semi-open terrain. To 2800 m (rarely 3500 m). Singles or separated pair members perch in trees or shrubs, generally lower than Bat Falcon, often very low, even on ground. Pursues birds and other prey in low powerful flight. **ID** Rangy with long tail and long narrow wings. Ad white head-band, white throat and chest, black 'unbuttoned vest'; in flight from above trailing edge of secondaries white. Juv similar, dark brown (not bluish), chest streaky. **Voice** High thin notes.

Peregrine Falcon *Falco peregrinus* `LC`
Halcón Peregrino
Uncommon boreal migrant and perhaps resident.

L 38–51 cm (15–20"). Races *tundrius*[A], *anatum*[B] (boreal migrants), *cassini*[C] (resident ?). Can occur anywhere but mainly open areas; rivers in Amazonia. To 3500 m. Perches on ground, sea cliff, high in tree, or on man-made structures. Renowned for powerful flight, high-speed dives; preys on birds overtaken in flight. **ID** Large, 'muscular'; broad tapering wings, black cap. Plumage blue-grey, prominent 'sideburns', underparts buff to whitish (*anatum*, *cassini*), or paler, with narrow black sideburns (*tundrius*). Juv above dark brown, dusky moustachial streak, below whitish streaked brown. **Voice** Raspy "keee". **SS** Aplomado Falcon, Merlin.

anatum   juvenile

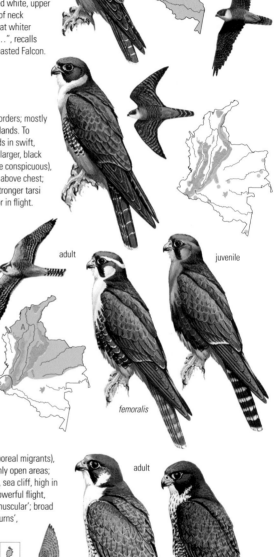

rufigularis

adult   juvenile

femoralis

adult

tundrius   *cassini*

anatum

375 extant species, 57 in region

Iconic family primarily of tropical latitudes. Colombian species range from tiny to immense, and modestly attired to flagrantly colourful, although green predominates. In general noisy, social, believed to mate for life, and notable for thick hooked bills and yoke-toed feet. They feed on fruit, seeds, and sometimes flowers, all often manipulated with their feet. Except tiny *Forpus* and *Touit* parrotlets, sexes are similar (to human eyes). Various species occur from steamy lowland forests to high cold *páramos*; all are cavity nesters. The fates of many are now entwined with humans and they have suffered heavily from deforestation and the cagebird trade. Anyone who has witnessed these magnificent birds winging through dawn's rising mists, or listened to the raucous cries of pairs streaming out from roosts, will likely never again view them in cages with anything but sadness.

Genus *Touit* Small, chunky; long uppertail-coverts conceal colourful short square tail; wings often with patches of bright colour. Compact flocks fly high in straight lines on long-distance commutes, or in rapid swerving flight at canopy level.

Lilac-tailed Parrotlet *Touit batavicus* `LC`
Periquito Sietecolores
Status (?), irruptive or seasonal (from Venezuela?).

 L 16.5 cm (6.5"). Monotypic. Humid foothill and lower montane forest. 200–1700 m. Single-species flocks of 3–20+, stealthy and silent in treetops, or compact, high- and fast-flying flocks that are often just specks in sky. Breeding unconfirmed but likely. **ID** Colourful (especially tail) but colours hard to see. Back and wings black, broad greenish-yellow wing-band includes tertials. **Voice** Soft continuous chatter in flight. **SS** Barred Parakeet.

Scarlet-shouldered Parrotlet *Touit huetii* `VU`
Periquito Frentinegro
Uncommon resident.

 L 16 cm (6.3"). Monotypic. Humid lowland and foothill forest, sandy-belt forest. To 700 m (seasonally higher?). Breed in pairs, otherwise flocks of c. 3–50+. Silent, stealthy in fruiting trees; call moments prior to departing. Rapid treetop-level flight or compact flocks high overhead. **ID** Bill yellowish, eye-ring whitish, forecrown black, upperwing-coverts dark blue; in flight bend of wing and underwing-coverts red, magenta in tail hard to see. **Voice** Soft bisyllabic "touit" or "reenk"; continuous chatter in flocks.

Blue-fronted Parrotlet *Touit dilectissimus* `LC`
Periquito Alirrojo
Uncommon to locally fairly common resident.

 L 17 cm (6.7"). Monotypic. Humid and wet foothill and lower montane forest. 100–1700 m (mostly > 600 m). Pairs or flocks of 3–15, silent in canopy or mid-levels, occasionally low inside forest; fly fast, fearlessly twisting and turning through forest, briefly over treetops, less often steady flight high overhead. **ID** Red eyestripe; in flight flashes red and yellow (♂) or yellow (♀) underwing. **Voice** Soft nasal whining "tuu'eet" continuously given in flight.

Sapphire-rumped Parrotlet *Touit purpuratus* `LC`
Periquito Zafiro
Uncommon resident.

 L 17 cm (6.7"). Race *viridiceps*. Humid *terra firme* and *várzea* forest, second growth, forest clearings, Amerindian gardens. To 400 m. Pairs or groups to c. 15, fly fast at or below canopy height as cross rivers and plunge directly into forest. **ID** Few good marks. At rest brown scapulars, no eye-ring; in flight green underwings, blue rump or red in tail seldom visible. **Voice** Call a low-pitched nasal "kaaya" or "hoya" like small bicycle horn. **SS** Scarlet-shouldered and Spot-winged Parrotlets.

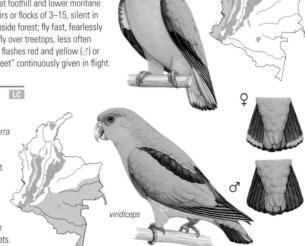

viridiceps

Spot-winged Parrotlet *Touit stictopterus* `VU`
Periquito Alipunteado `VU`
Uncommon and local resident.

 L 18 cm (7"). Monotypic. Humid foothill and lower montane forest. 500–1700 m (records to 2400 m); formerly W slope of W Andes N to Fusagasugá, Sumapaz (extirpated?). Pairs or small groups, stealthy, silent when feeding inside forest, mid-levels to subcanopy; fly fast through or just above canopy. **ID** ♂ wing-coverts dusky brown spotted buff, small orange forewing spot (outermost greater coverts); ♀ mainly green, wing-coverts plain green or obscurely spotted dusky, no orange, foreface tinged yellowish. **Voice** Chattering call resembles Orange-chinned Parakeet. **SS** Barred Parakeet.

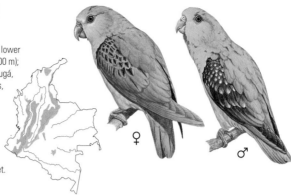

♀

♂

Genus *Bolborhynchus* Small, green, highland parakeets, with blunt swollen bills and short wedge-shaped tails that project beyond the wings.

Barred Parakeet *Bolborhynchus lineola* `LC`
Periquito Barrado
Uncommon resident.

 L 18 cm (7"). Race *tigrinus*. Humid montane forest, borders, older second growth; affinity for bamboo when seeding. 1600–3000 m. Almost always seen in compact, high-flying flocks (specks in sky) of 3–100+, commuting long distances in straight purposeful flight, on rapid steady wingbeats. Circle and call repeatedly before alighting, then disappear in silence. **ID** Above dark olive-green, below brighter green, finely barred blackish throughout (hard to see). **Voice** High shrill chatter. **SS** Rufous-fronted Parakeet, *Touit* parrotlets.

tigrinus

Rufous-fronted Parakeet *Bolborhynchus ferrugineifrons* `VU`
Periquito Frentirrufo `VU`
Very local resident.

 L 20 cm (8"). Monotypic. Endemic. Stunted treeline woodland and scrub, tussock grass on cliffs, *páramo*. 3200–4100 m. Small flocks roost and nest on cliffs, at dawn fly off to forage in *páramo* (*Espeletia* flowers, seeds) or open ground. **ID** Green, rufous frontlet diagnostic but inconspicuous, dusky bill, wedge-shaped tail. **Voice** Shrill chatter recalls *Brotogeris*. **SS** Barred Parakeet (lower).

E

Genus *Brotogeris* Small and green with short pointed tails. Buzzy wingbeats alternate with brief closed-wing freefall, producing jerky erratic flight. Mainly in lowlands. Remain active during heat of day.

Tui Parakeet *Brotogeris sanctithomae* `LC`
Periquito Cabeciamarillo
Common resident (riverine).

 L 16.5 cm (6.5"). Race *sanctithomae*. River islands, *várzea* borders, second growth along Amazon and adjacent tributaries, oxbows; never far from water. To 300 m. Chattering flocks roost on large river islands with other parakeets, especially White-winged Parakeets; at dawn fly off with much commotion to feed, separating into pairs or small groups. **ID** Conspicuous yellow forecrown, dusky-red bill, whitish eyes, no blue in wings. **Voice** Shrill raspy chatter. **SS** Cobalt-winged Parakeet.

sanctithomae

245

White-winged Parakeet *Brotogeris versicolurus* `LC`
Periquito Aliblanco
Common to locally abundant resident.

 L 23 cm (9"). Monotypic. River islands, *várzea* forest, second growth along Amazon and adjacent tributaries, oxbows; usually near water. To 300 m. Roosts on river islands (especially in *Gynerium* cane), palms in towns, sometimes in huge flocks; disperse daily in large groups. **ID** Yellow and white in wings conspicuous, unique in flight. **Voice** Noisy; constant shrill chatter in flight and at roost. **AN** Previously called Canary-winged Parakeet when lumped with Yellow-chevroned Parakeet *B. chiriri*.

Orange-chinned Parakeet *Brotogeris jugularis* `LC`
Periquito Bronceado
Common resident.

 L 18 cm (7"). Races *jugularis*[A], *exsul*[B]. Dry to semi-humid woodland, partly deforested or cultivated areas, gallery forest, shady parks in towns; local in Pacific lowlands. To 1400 m. Lively pairs when breeding, otherwise small chattering flocks. Flies in fits and starts on erratic trajectory. Forages fairly high in trees for seeds, fruits, blossoms. **ID** Bronzy-brown shoulders, small orange chin patch. **Voice** Shrill chatter, unmusical to human ears. **SS** Cobalt-winged Parakeet (overlap?).

Cobalt-winged Parakeet *Brotogeris cyanoptera* `LC`
Periquito Aliazul
Common resident.

 L 20 cm (8"). Race *cyanoptera*. Canopy of *terra firme* and *várzea* forest, gallery forest, river borders, scattered trees in clearings. To 1000 m. Behaviour like Orange-chinned Parakeet. Small to large flocks along Amazonian rivers; visits riverside clay banks (*salados*) with other psittacines. **ID** Forecrown dull yellowish, eyes dark, bill pale, inconspicuous orange chin patch, flight feathers and central tail feathers dark blue (mainly visible in flight). **Voice** Shrill chatter like allies. **SS** Tui Parakeet, Orange-chinned Parakeet (overlap?).

Genus *Pyrilia* Medium-sized, square-tailed parrots. Colourful contrasting head, bend of wing red, axillaries red (one exception) and dark blue primaries. Deep wingbeats like *Pionus*.

Brown-hooded Parrot *Pyrilia haematotis* `LC`
Cotorra Cabeciparda
Uncommon resident.

 L 22 cm (8.5"). Race *coccinicollaris*. Humid lowland to lower montane forest, borders, and clearings with scattered trees. To 1200 m. Pairs or small groups in canopy, quiet and stealthy when feeding; rapid headlong, somewhat unsteady flight. **ID** Contrasting brown head, white ocular ring, red ear patch, in flight blue remiges and red axillaries. **Voice** Flight call screechy bi- or multisyllabic "skree-ree"; various mostly unmusical sounds. **SS** Blue-headed Parrot.

Saffron-headed Parrot *Pyrilia pyrilia* `NT`
Cotorra Cariamarilla `NT`
Uncommon, local and unpredictable resident.

 L 24 cm (9.5"). Monotypic. Humid and wet lowland and foothill forest, borders, tall second growth. To 900 m. Singles, pairs or small flocks fly fast, weaving through forest canopy or rapidly crossing small clearings, calling as they go; flight appears unsteady, pitching from side to side; stealthy and quiet perched. **ID** Yellow head unique. Flashes yellow bend of wing, red axillaries in flight. **Voice** Flight call scraping "sheeweek" like Orange-cheeked Parrot; single high "keek!" when perched.

jugularis

cyanoptera

coccinicollaris

Rose-faced Parrot *Pyrilia pulchra* `LC`
Cotorra Carirrosada
Fairly common resident.

 L 23 cm (9"). Monotypic. Humid and wet lowland to lower montane forest, borders, clearings with trees, papayas and plantains in gardens. To 1200 m. Pairs or small groups of 3–10 on treetop snags or lower. Flight fast, somewhat rolling; quiet and stealthy when feeding. **ID** Rose face enclosed by thin black line resembles no other species. Red shoulder in flight. **Voice** Harsh shrieking "chuuk-skreek" or variations in flight.

Orange-cheeked Parrot *Pyrilia barrabandi* `NT`
Cotorra Cabecinegra
Uncommon resident.

 L 25 cm (10"). Race *barrabandi*. Humid *terra firme* and *várzea* forest, occasionally riverine or forest clay banks (*salados*). To 500 m. Pairs or groups of 4–10 fly at canopy height or lower, rarely perch fully in open. Flight trajectory fast, direct with side to side rocking motion. **ID** Colourful; black head, orange malar patch, red underwing-coverts in flight. **Voice** Rather quiet; distinctive but infrequent flight call 'mushy' upward-inflected "chu'wink". **SS** Scarlet-shouldered Parrotlet (p. 244).

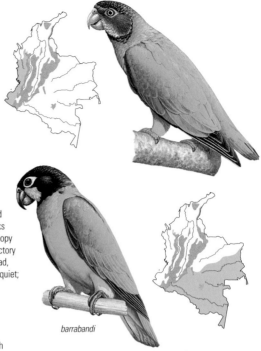

barrabandi

Genus *Hapalopsittaca* Broad-winged and short-tailed, much like *Pionus* but undertail-coverts green (not red). Only in montane forest, and distributions fragmented.

Rusty-faced Parrot *Hapalopsittaca amazonina* `VU`
Cotorra Montañera `VU`
Uncommon and local resident.

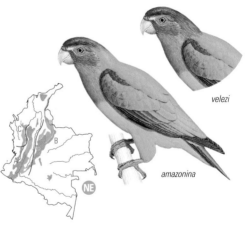

velezi

 L 23 cm (9"). Races *velezi*[A], *amazonina*[B], ssp. nov.?[C]. Near-endemic (also W Venezuela). Wet epiphyte-rich montane forest, borders, trees in clearings. 2000–3000 m. Pairs or groups to c. 25 fly high over forest, feed quietly inside canopy, but may rest on exposed high snags. **ID** Looks unkempt; foreface smudged brownish red, throat stained red, bend of wing and underwing-coverts red, shoulders bluish, primaries dark blue (*amazonina*), or head duller, rear crown olive (not green) (*velezi*), or head to chest paler, brownish (ssp. nov.). **Voice** Flight call a metallic screeching "shrEEnk"; perched a bisyllabic "EEreek" (metal scraping metal). **SS** Indigo-winged and Bronze-winged Parrots.

amazonina

Indigo-winged Parrot *Hapalopsittaca fuertesi* `CR`
Cotorra Aliazul `CR`
Rare and very local resident.

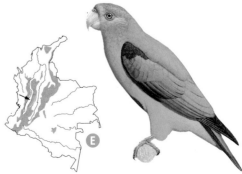 **L** 23 cm (9"). Monotypic. Endemic. Epiphyte-rich humid and wet upper montane forest, stunted treeline woodland. 2600–3500 m. Small flocks of 7–15, feed preferentially on mistletoe berries of *Antidaphne*. **ID** Recalls Rusty-faced Parrot but plainer, crown light blue, face and sides of head olive-yellow, bend of wing and underwing-coverts red, primaries ultramarine blue, secondaries blue-green, base of tail dark red (difficult). **Voice** Flight call a nasal grating "krraa". **AN** Fuertes's Parrot.

Genus *Pionus* Medium-sized, short square tails, red undertail-coverts, and characteristic deep wingbeats mostly below horizontal plane of body. Harsh high-pitched vocalizations. Dusky Parrot *Pionus fuscus*, of Guianan Shield region, previously listed for Perijá Mts based on presumed record from Airoca (= Hiroca or Eroca), Cesar, at 1200 m is likely an error (or extirpated). Recalls Bronze-winged Parrot (no overlap) but darker, more purplish plum. No verified records.

Red-billed Parrot *Pionus sordidus* [LC]
Cotorra Piquirroja
Common resident (disjunct distribution).

 L 28 cm (11"). Races *saturatus*[A] (Santa Marta highlands), *ponsi*[B] (Santa Marta foothills and Perijá Mts), *corallinus*[C], *mindoensis*[D]. Canopy of semi-humid to humid foothill and lower montane forest, borders, clearings, coffee plantations. 200–2400 m. Closely recalls Blue-headed Parrot but generally at higher elevations. **ID** Reddish bill, head variably bluish to greenish mottled white imparting unkempt appearance; or overall darker, duller green (*saturatus*). **Voice** Like Blue-headed Parrot.

White-capped Parrot (Speckle-faced Parrot)
Pionus seniloides [LC]
Cotorra Coroniblanca
Uncommon resident.

L 28 cm (11"). Monotypic. Humid and wet montane forest almost to treeline, clearings with trees. 1600–3100 m. Pairs or small groups in canopy, range widely; seasonal or local movements. **ID** White crown, extensive whitish speckling on face imparts unkempt appearance, red undertail-coverts. **Voice** Harsh scraping flight call recalls *Psittacara* or *Aratinga*. **SS** Red-billed and Rusty-faced Parrots. **TN** Called Speckle-faced Parrot *P. tumultuosus* when merged with 'plum-crowned' birds of S Peru and Bolivia.

Blue-headed Parrot *Pionus menstruus* [LC]
Cotorra Cabeciazul
Common resident.

L 25 cm (10"). Races *rubrigularis*[A], *menstruus*[B]. Humid lowland and foothill forest, older second growth, clearings with trees, plantations. To 1600 m. Singles, pairs or raucous free-wheeling flocks of 5–20, occasionally 100+, often perch high on exposed snag or palm spike; forage quietly in canopy, depart noisily. **ID** Blue head and throat, pinkish spot on bill, red vent. **Voice** Noisy. Shrieking metallic "schweenk!" constantly heard in flight. **SS** Red-billed Parrot.

Bronze-winged Parrot *Pionus chalcopterus* [LC]
Cotorra Oscura
Fairly common resident (seasonally nomadic).

 L 28 cm (11"). Monotypic. Humid montane forest, borders, partially deforested areas with scattered trees, coffee plantations, orchards. 1400–2400 m (rarely 500–2800 m). Behaviour much like Blue-headed Parrot but quieter, less conspicuous. Pairs or small flocks fly at canopy height or higher; extremely deep wingbeats. **ID** Dark navy blue but often looks blackish, shoulders dark bronze-brown, bill pale, scaly whitish throat, red vent. **Voice** Similar to Blue-headed Parrot.

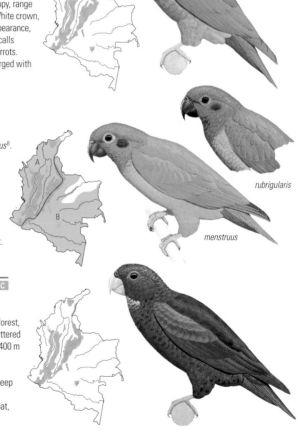

saturatus

corallinus

rubrigularis

menstruus

Short-tailed Parrot *Graydidascalus brachyurus* `LC`
Cotorra Colicorta

Common resident (restricted habitat).

 L 24 cm (9.5"). Monotypic. Amazonian river islands, *várzea* and second growth along Amazon and nearby tributaries; never far from large rivers; scattered records along R Putumayo and Caquetá. To 400 m. Pairs or small groups, gregarious, conspicuous, quite noisy; fly low and fast over canopy, perch semi-exposed in treetops; feed in canopy. **ID** Block-headed, all green, blackish bill, dark orbital ring extends forward as 'frown' line over lores; in flight chunky, short-tailed. **Voice** Loud raucous shrieks, squeals; varied repertoire, always harsh, grating and unpleasant to human ears.

Genus *Amazona* Large, green, squarish-tailed, most with red or orange wing patch. Flight strong, and high on longer commutes; wingbeats shallow, stiff and rapid. Pairs stay together within flocks. Mainly lowlands. Distinctive flight calls; complex gurgling songs.

Northern Festive Amazon *Amazona bodini* `NT`
Lora Festiva Norteña

Fairly common resident.

 L 36 cm (14"). Monotypic. Oxbows and gallery forest along large rivers. To 300 m. **ID** Differs from Southern Festive Amazon in green (not bluish) outer flight feathers, blue-tinged (not green) cheeks, post-ocular area green (not pale blue). **SS** See under Southern Festive Amazon. **TN** Northern (Orinocan) and Southern (Amazonian) forms usually regarded as races of Festive Amazon *A. festiva*. Separation lacks genetic confirmation. **AN** Festive Parrot.

Southern Festive Amazon *Amazona festiva* `NT`
Lora Festiva

Fairly common resident.

 L 36 cm (14"). Monotypic. Closely associated with large rivers, *várzea* forest, oxbows, old river island vegetation. To 300 m. **ID** Bill blackish, narrow dark red frontlet extends narrowly through lores to eyes (forms permanent frown). **Voice** Odd nasal laughing "ooínk-ooínk" and "wah-wah" in flight; gurgling and carolling notes often human-like. **SS** From other *Amazona* by blaze of red up rump and back (hard to see), voice, and absence of red in wings. **AN** Festive Parrot.

Red-lored Amazon (Red-lored Parrot)
Amazona autumnalis `LC`
Lora Frentirroja

Fairly common resident.

 L 36 cm (14"). Race *salvini*. Humid and wet lowland and foothill forest, borders, adjacent clearings. To 1000 m (mostly below 500 m). Behaviour like other *Amazona* parrots. **ID** Red frontlet, crown scaled blue (hard to see), otherwise green, red speculum. **Voice** Flight call a harsh shrieking "oorák" or "kalink" repeatedly. **SS** Other *Amazona*.

salvini

Yellow-crowned Amazon (Yellow-crowned Parrot)
Amazona ochrocephala `LC`
Lora Cabeciamarilla
Fairly common resident.

 L 36 cm (14"). Races *panamensis*[A], *ochrocephala*[B], *nattereri*[C]. Wide variety of dry to humid lowland forests, borders, gallery forest. To 500 m (locally 1000 m). Declining W of Andes. **ID** Yellow crown patch (size varies), narrow (not wide) bare eye-ring, red at bend of wing. **Voice** Flight call a loud throaty "curr-oww" (or "bow-wow") repeatedly. Like all *Amazona*, song a complex repertoire of gurgling and falsetto notes at dawn and dusk; captives are uncanny mimics. **SS** Southern Mealy and Orange-winged Amazons.

Scaly-naped Amazon (Scaly-naped Parrot)
Amazona mercenarius `LC`
Lora Andina
Fairly common resident (local and declining).

 L 36 cm (14"). Race *canipalliata*. Humid montane forest. Flies high over open highlands. 1500–3600 m. Pairs within very high-flying flocks may commute long distances, even between Andean ranges, or move seasonally. **ID** Lacks strong marks but only *Amazona* at high elevations, red wing speculum small or absent, scaly nape and red at tail base hard to see. **Voice** Flight call "kalé" or "chaléek"; higher, shriller, faster than lowland allies. **SS** White-capped Parrot.

Southern Mealy Amazon (Mealy Parrot)
Amazona farinosa `NT`
Lora Real
Locally common resident.

 L 38 cm (15"). Monotypic. Humid lowland forest, borders. To 1000 m (rarely 1600 m). **ID** Largest *Amazona*, large bare pale orbital ring, yellow crown patch variable in size or absent, distal half of tail yellowish, nape pale, scaly. **Voice** Flight call a loud "chó'op", last syllable swallowed. Rambling dawn and dusk song of semi-musical gurgles, gargled trills and falsetto notes. **TN** Central American birds, previously considered separate species, differ in minor plumage details; separation lacks molecular confirmation.

Orange-winged Amazon (Orange-winged Parrot)
Amazona amazonica `LC`
Lora Amazónica
Local resident W of Andes, common E of Andes.

 L 33 cm (13"). Monotypic. Dry to humid forest, especially *várzea*, river borders, semi-open areas with *Mauritia* palms; local in mangroves. To 1500 m. **ID** Small (for *Amazona*), best mark is yellow cheek patch. **Voice** Noisy; flight call an endlessly repeated screechy "cm'quick" or "cm'quick-quick", high-pitched, unmusical. **SS** Other *Amazona*.

ochrocephala

canipalliata

Genus *Forpus* Tiny and cute, short wedge-shaped tail and stubby bill. Most ♂♂ show blue on wings and rump. Flight undulating, erratic, seldom long-sustained. Usually only one species in an area, except Amazonia.

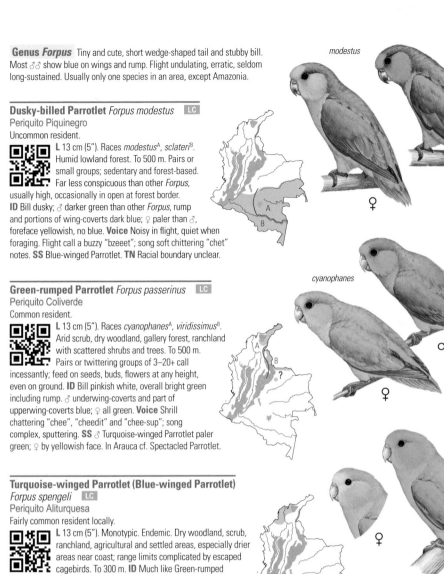

modestus

cyanophanes

crassirostris

Dusky-billed Parrotlet *Forpus modestus* LC
Periquito Piquinegro
Uncommon resident.

 L 13 cm (5"). Races *modestus*[A], *sclateri*[B]. Humid lowland forest. To 500 m. Pairs or small groups; sedentary and forest-based. Far less conspicuous than other *Forpus*, usually high, occasionally in open at forest border. **ID** Bill dusky; ♂ darker green than other *Forpus*, rump and portions of wing-coverts dark blue; ♀ paler than ♂, foreface yellowish, no blue. **Voice** Noisy in flight, quiet when foraging. Flight call a buzzy "bzeeet"; song soft chittering "chet" notes. **SS** Blue-winged Parrotlet. **TN** Racial boundary unclear.

Green-rumped Parrotlet *Forpus passerinus* LC
Periquito Coliverde
Common resident.

L 13 cm (5"). Races *cyanophanes*[A], *viridissimus*[B]. Arid scrub, dry woodland, gallery forest, ranchland with scattered shrubs and trees. To 500 m. Pairs or twittering groups of 3–20+ call incessantly; feed on seeds, buds, flowers at any height, even on ground. **ID** Bill pinkish white, overall bright green including rump. ♂ underwing-coverts and part of upperwing-coverts blue; ♀ all green. **Voice** Shrill chattering "chee", "cheedit" and "chee-sup"; song complex, sputtering. **SS** ♂ Turquoise-winged Parrotlet paler green; ♀ by yellowish face. In Arauca cf. Spectacled Parrotlet.

Turquoise-winged Parrotlet (Blue-winged Parrotlet)
Forpus spengeli LC
Periquito Aliturquesa
Fairly common resident locally.

L 13 cm (5"). Monotypic. Endemic. Dry woodland, scrub, ranchland, agricultural and settled areas, especially drier areas near coast; range limits complicated by escaped cagebirds. To 300 m. **ID** Much like Green-rumped Parrotlet but paler green. ♂ rump light blue, part of greater wing-coverts violet-blue, underwing-coverts dark blue. ♀ no blue, foreface yellowish. **Voice** Incessant shrill chatter like Green-rumped Parrotlet. **TN** Possibly a race of Blue-winged or Green-rumped Parrotlet; taxonomy unsettled.

Blue-winged Parrotlet *Forpus xanthopterygius* LC
Periquito Azulejo
Fairly common resident.

L 13 cm (5"). Race *crassirostris*. Humid forest borders, river edges, overgrown clearings, young river island vegetation in Amazonia. To 500 m. **ID** Bill pale. ♂ has parts of upperwing-coverts, secondaries and rump blue. ♀ similar but no blue. **Voice** Calls incessantly; high buzzy "zeet", twittering "zidit" and "zididit" in flight and perched. **SS** Dusky-billed Parrotlet.

Spectacled Parrotlet *Forpus conspicillatus* `LC`
Periquito de Anteojos
Common to abundant resident.

 L 13 cm (5"). Races *conspicillatus*[A], *metae*[B], *caucae*[C]. Commonest *Forpus* in Colombia. Drier semi-open and cultivated areas, ranchland, towns; clearings, wooded borders. To 2000 m (locally 2500 m). Cute, chattering, confiding; pairs or twittering little groups feed on seeds on ground, in weeds, or on fruit, buds and flowers higher up. **ID** Pale bill. ♂ bright green, blue wash around eyes, rump, part of wings and underwing-coverts blue (or less blue around eyes, *metae*). ♀ paler green, no blue, underparts yellowish green. **Voice** High jangling "chit" and "chidit" constantly. **SS** In Arauca cf. Green-rumped Parrotlet; in Caribbean Turquoise-winged Parrotlet. Birds in SW Nariño likely escaped cagebirds.

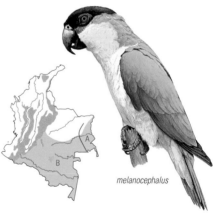

conspicillatus

♀ ♂ *metae*

Pacific Parrotlet *Forpus coelestis* `LC`
Periquito Pacífico
Local resident, with recent (c. 2014) northward range expansion.

 L 13 cm (5"). Monotypic. Drier semi-open areas, scrub, wooded borders. To 500 m. **ID** Pale bill. ♂ duller more greyish green above than allies, back of head bluish, foreface tinged yellow. ♀ distinctly yellowish foreface and underparts. **Voice** Constant chatter like other *Forpus*. **SS** Spectacled Parrotlet.

♂

♀

Genus *Pionites* Chunky shape, large head, short squarish tail, bold contrasting colours, and white belly. Unusual vocalizations.

Black-headed Parrot *Pionites melanocephalus* `LC`
Lora Pechiblanca
Fairly common resident.

 L 23 cm (9"). Races *melanocephalus*[A], *pallidus*[B]. Canopy of *terra firme* and *várzea* forest, sandy-belt forest (common). To 600 m. Flocks of 3–10 fly fast, through or skimming over canopy; perch on high snags early morning. Otherwise easily overlooked but for odd calls. **ID** Blackish bill, black cap, yellow throat, apricot-yellow nape, underparts mostly white. **Voice** Flight call a high squealing "SKEEEa, SKEEEa"; perched gives varied piping whistles, metallic and electronic sounds, often at long intervals. **SS** Black-legged Parrot (?). **TN** Racial boundary uncertain.

melanocephalus

Black-legged Parrot (White-bellied Parrot)
Pionites xanthomerius `LC`
Lora Patinegra
Rare resident.

 L 23 cm (9"). Monotypic. Photo and sight records of flocks in *várzea* forest on Isla Ronda (Colombian side of Amazon) near Leticia (2008, 2011, 2019). Canopy of *terra firme* and especially *várzea* forest. To 100 m. Widespread on S (Peruvian) side of Amazon, but not known to be established on N (Colombian mainland) bank of river. **ID** From Black-headed Parrot by whitish bill; crown, as well as nape, apricot-yellow. **Voice** Like Black-headed Parrot. **TN** Usually regarded as a race of White-bellied Parrot *P. leucogaster*.

Red-fan Parrot *Deroptyus accipitrinus* LC
Lora Gavilana

Two subspecies in two subspecies groups; one in Colombia.

Northern Red-fan Parrot *Deroptyus (accipitrinus) accipitrinus*
Lora Gavilana Norteña
Uncommon resident.
L 36 cm (14"). One subspecies in group. Tall humid forest on white sandy soil, black-water areas, local in floodplain and lateritic upland soils; tolerates some forest disturbance. To 300 m. Pairs or groups of 3–7 perch on high exposed branches, fly low over canopy in curious undulating flap-and-sail flight; feed inside canopy. **ID** Large hawk-like head, long tail, whitish forecrown, colourful fan-like crest often depressed. **Voice** Noisy in flight, "chack" notes followed by 1–5 squealing "tak, tak KEEya, KEEya" phrases; at rest chatters, whistles, raspy bugle-like "yaag" notes; nasal honking "naaaaaaaa-unk".

Genus *Pyrrhura* Slender-bodied, long tapering bluntly rounded tail mostly reddish, primaries blue. Compact noisy flocks fly fast, twisting through canopy. Taxonomy unresolved.

Sinu Parakeet (Painted Parakeet) *Pyrrhura subandina* CR(PE)
Perico del Sinú
Possibly extinct resident (no recent records).

L 25 cm (10"). Monotypic. Endemic. Probably moist to humid forest, borders, clearings with trees. 100–? m. Poorly known; factors causing decline likely include deforestation. **ID** Differs from Perija Parakeet (*caeruleiceps*) by entire crown dusky maroon (not blue), cheek patch buff (not white), narrow red line on forehead and extending down narrowly below eye much more restricted, and malar area dull blue-green (not bluish). **Voice** Unknown. **TN** Often regarded as a subspecies of Painted Parakeet *P. picta*.

Perija Parakeet (Todd's Parakeet)
Pyrrhura caeruleiceps EN
Perico de Perijá
Local resident (poorly known).

L 23 cm (9"). Races *caeruleiceps*[A], *pantchenkoi*[B] (doubtfully distinct). Near-endemic (also Venezuelan side of Sierra de Perijá). Semi-deciduous to humid foothill and montane forest, patchy second growth, disturbed woodland. 400–2200 m. Small flocks; behaviour like Maroon-tailed Parakeet. **ID** Forecrown light blue, nape brownish blue, lores, area around eye and cheeks red, patch at rear of cheeks white, narrow malar area bluish. **Voice** Strident "pik-pik" in flight. **SS** Not known to overlap other *Pyrrhura*. **TN** Often regarded as a subspecies of Painted Parakeet *P. picta*.

Santa Marta Parakeet *Pyrrhura viridicata* EN
Periquito de Santa Marta EN
Uncommon resident (unpredictable, declining).

L 25 cm (10"). Monotypic. Endemic. Humid montane forest, borders, adjacent clearings. 1800–3000 m. Flocks of 3–25+ often roost at predictable sites; disperse rapidly and noisily at dawn. Quiet when feeding, utter soft calls prior to flight. **ID** Mostly green, distal half of outer tail feathers dark red, narrow red frontlet, ear-coverts spot reddish, bend of wing extensively red or red mixed yellow, variable red flecking on head and throat, irregular orange-red breast-band; bill pale. **Voice** Screeching squeals in flight. **SS** Scarlet-fronted Parakeet.

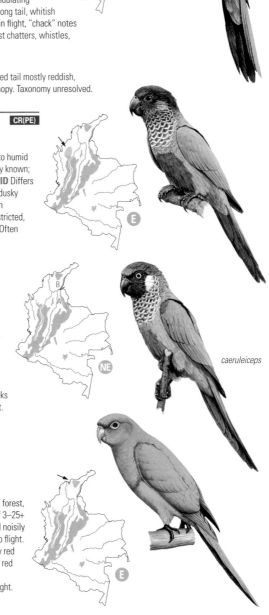

caeruleiceps

Maroon-tailed Parakeet *Pyrrhura melanura* `LC`
Periquito Colirrojo

 Five subspecies in three subspecies groups; all three in Colombia.

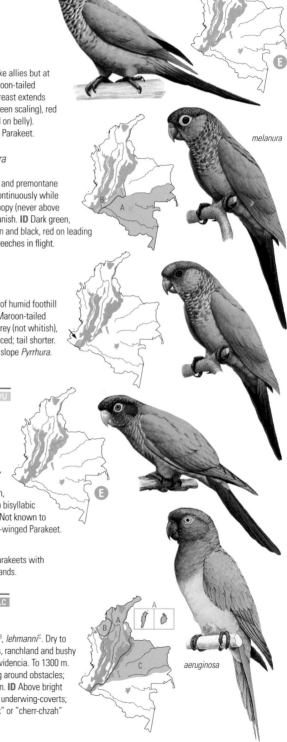

melanura

Huila Parakeet *Pyrrhura (melanura) chapmani*
Uncommon resident.
L 28 cm (11"). One subspecies in group. Endemic. Habitat like allies but at higher elevations. 1600–2800 m. **ID** Closely resembles Maroon-tailed Parakeet (race *melanura*), but decidedly larger, scaling on breast extends completely around neck, crown mostly brown (little or no green scaling), red wing patch smaller, larger red belly patch (vs. almost no red on belly). **TN** Sometimes treated as a species. **AN** Upper Magdalena Parakeet.

Maroon-tailed Parakeet *Pyrrhura (melanura) melanura*
Uncommon resident.
L 25 cm (10"). Races *melanura*[A], *souancei*[B]. Humid lowland and premontane forest, borders. To 1900 m. Small tight flocks of 3–12 call continuously while threading their way rapidly through forest subcanopy or canopy (never above it); immediately become silent on alighting, then seem to vanish. **ID** Dark green, tail dark maroon-red, ocular ring whitish, crown mixed green and black, red on leading edge of wing conspicuous in flight. **Voice** Harsh grating screeches in flight.

Choco Parakeet *Pyrrhura (melanura) pacifica*
Perico del Chocó
Uncommon resident.
L 23 cm (9"). One subspecies in group. Canopy and borders of humid foothill and lower montane forest. 250–1750 m (Ecuador). **ID** Like Maroon-tailed group (*melanura*) but plumage darker green, eye-ring dark grey (not whitish), forehead green (not blackish), breast scaling narrower, reduced; tail shorter. **Voice** As Maroon-tailed *melanura* (above). **SS** Only Pacific slope *Pyrrhura*. **TN** Sometimes treated as separate species.

Brown-breasted Parakeet *Pyrrhura calliptera* `VU`
Periquito Aliamarillo `VU`
Uncommon and local (declining).

 L 23 cm (9"). Monotypic. Endemic. Humid montane forest, borders, adjacent clearings, elfin woodland to treeline. 1700–3400 m. **ID** Colourful, especially in flight; bend of wing, upper- and underwing-coverts yellow mixed orange-red, throat and chest dark brown scalloped buff to pinkish brown, ear-coverts patch, belly patch and tail dull red. **Voice** Harsh bisyllabic "chee'jit", a screeching cacophony from flocks in flight. **SS** Not known to overlap other *Pyrrhura*. Scarlet-fronted Parakeet. **AN** Flame-winged Parakeet.

Genera *Eupsittula* and *Aratinga* Medium-sized parakeets with long pointed tails and a conspicuous bare orbital ring. Lowlands.

Brown-throated Parakeet *Eupsittula pertinax* `LC`
Perico Carisucio
Common and conspicuous resident.

 L 25 cm (10"). Races *aeruginosa*[A], *griseipecta*[B], *lehmanni*[C]. Dry to arid woodland, scrub, mangroves, urban areas, ranchland and bushy savanna. Introduced Islas San Andrés and Providencia. To 1300 m. Noisy flocks of 3–15 fly fast and low, swerving around obstacles; rest atop shrubs, small trees or cacti; flush at slightest alarm. **ID** Above bright green, pale brownish foreparts ('dirty face'), in flight yellow underwing-coverts; races vary in foreparts colour. **Voice** Rough scraping "chzak" or "cherr-chzah" in flight. **TN** Formerly placed in *Aratinga*.

aeruginosa

Dusky-headed Parakeet *Aratinga weddellii* `LC`
Perico Canoso
Common resident.

 L 28 cm (11"). Monotypic. Humid Amazonian lowlands, mainly *várzea* forest borders, river edges, tall stumps and second growth around swampy oxbows; usually near water. To 600 m. Pairs or small flocks to c. 10, perch in open, fly fairly low over forest, visit clay banks (*salados*), feed heavily on *Erythrina* blossoms. **ID** Plain, pale brownish-grey head, pale grey eyes, no wing colour in flight. **Voice** Nasal whining bisyllabic notes in flight. **SS** White-eyed Parakeet.

Red-bellied Macaw *Orthopsittaca manilatus* `LC`
Guacamaya Buchirroja
Locally common resident.

 L 51 cm (20"). Monotypic. Associated with *Mauritia* palms (roosting, nesting, palm nut food) in swampy seasonally flooded Amazonian forest, or mixed savanna, gallery and sandy soil forest. To 600 m. Pairs when breeding, otherwise flocks of 5–100+. May commute long distances between feeding and roosting sites. Flight smooth, steady, wingbeats rapid. **ID** Prominent yellowish facial skin, yellow-gold underwing, red belly difficult to see. **Voice** Flight call a high reedy strained "graEE'reek", rising in middle, complaining, not raucous. **SS** Chestnut-fronted Macaw, White-eyed Parakeet.

Genus *Ara* Large, colourful Neotropical icons; bare cheeks and facial skin; long pointed tails; massive bills. Formerly included smaller, less colourful *Orthopsittaca* and *Diopsittaca*.

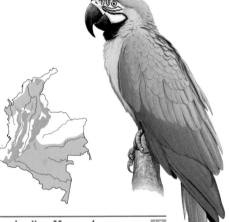

militaris

Blue-and-yellow Macaw *Ara ararauna* `LC`
Guacamaya Azuliamarilla
Local and declining resident.

 L 84 cm (33"). Monotypic. Gallery forest, *várzea* and swamp forest, floodplains with *Mauritia* palms; usually near water, less so in NW; generally far from settled areas. To 500 m (rarely 1200 m). At dawn and dusk pairs, trios or small groups fly long distances between roosting and feeding sites; by day rest or argue among themselves in large canopy trees. **ID** Usually unmistakable but in low evening light easily confused at distance with Scarlet, and Red-and-green Macaw; calls helpful. **Voice** Smoother, slightly nasal, least raucous of large macaws, softer "gr'a'a'k".

Military Macaw *Ara militaris* `VU`
Guacamaya Verde `VU`
Uncommon and local resident.

L 71 cm (28"). Race *militaris*. Dry deciduous and semi-deciduous forest, riparian woodland, seasonally in humid forest. To 2000 m (usually much lower). Seasonal or sporadic in many areas; movements not well documented, but crosses low passes in E Andes between W Caquetá and E Huila. Pairs, trios or groups to c. 25+; behaviour like other *Ara*. **ID** Best identified by range from very similar Great Green Macaw (which see). **Voice** Flight call a loud harsh bisyllabic "graA'a", rising then falling.

ambiguus

macao

Great Green Macaw
Ara ambiguus `EN`
Guacamaya Verdelimón `EN`
Rare and very local resident
(status in S Nariño?).

L 89 cm (35"). Races *ambiguus*[A],
guayaquilensis[B] (valid race?). Humid
and wet lowland and foothill forest.
Has suffered from extensive deforestation,
especially banana cultivation in NW. To 600 m (higher?).
Pairs, trios, small groups. **ID** From Military Macaw (range
overlap?) by larger size, paler yellow-green plumage
(especially back, wing-coverts and inner flight feathers),
rump paler blue, basal half of central tail feathers orange-
red, not brownish red. **Voice** Doubtfully separable from
Military Macaw; flight calls slightly longer, flatter.

Scarlet Macaw *Ara macao* `LC`
Guacamaya Macao
Fairly common resident (local W of Andes).

L 89 cm (35"). Race *macao*.
Humid transition and *várzea*
forest (less in *terra firme*) in
Amazonia, sandy-belt forest
(strong seasonal movements), gallery forest
in *llanos*, dry to humid forest and ranchland
in N. To 700 m. **ID** Bare facial skin and cheeks
(no feather lines), yellow median and greater
upperwing-coverts, in flight tail proportionately longer than in Red-and-green Macaw
and wiggles during flight. **Voice** Loudest
harshest macaw vocally. In flight, call
rasping white noise, with little structure;
perched, wide range of gruff calls.

Red-and-green Macaw
Ara chloropterus `LC`
Guacamaya Rojiverde
Uncommon and local resident.

L 94 cm (37"). Monotypic. Humid
terra firme forest in Amazonia,
gallery forest in *llanos*, local in dry
to humid forest in N. To 500 m. Pairs,
trios or small flocks. Visits riverbank clay licks
(*salados*) during dry months in S Amazonia (Peru;
Colombia?). **ID** Larger-bodied, darker red than Scarlet
Macaw, median and greater upperwing-coverts
green, bare face with lines of red feathers. In flight
tail proportionately shorter than Scarlet Macaw and
held steady (no wiggle). **Voice** Loud harsh flight call
resembles Scarlet Macaw but often with buried falsetto
overtone. **AN** Green-winged Macaw.

Chestnut-fronted Macaw *Ara severus* `LC`
Guacamaya Cariseca
Fairly common to common resident locally.

L 48 cm (19"). Monotypic. Mostly forest
borders in humid lowlands, ranchland,
gallery forest and *Mauritia* palms in
semi-open areas. To 600 m. Pairs and small
flocks, commute between roosting and feeding sites,
perch on exposed snags early morning and late evening.
ID Mid-sized macaw; bare face, in flight wings blue from
above, reddish below, bright red at 'wrist', chestnut
'forehead' inconspicuous. **Voice** Flight call scratchy
'fingernails-on-blackboard', grating, weaker than large
Ara. Song at dusk complex, rambling, rather musical.
SS Red-bellied Macaw.

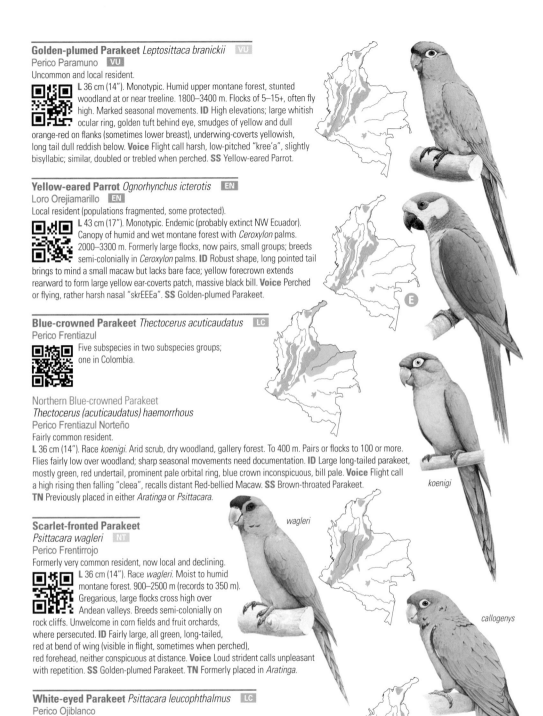

Golden-plumed Parakeet *Leptosittaca branickii* VU
Perico Paramuno VU

Uncommon and local resident.

L 36 cm (14"). Monotypic. Humid upper montane forest, stunted woodland at or near treeline. 1800–3400 m. Flocks of 5–15+, often fly high. Marked seasonal movements. **ID** High elevations; large whitish ocular ring, golden tuft behind eye, smudges of yellow and dull orange-red on flanks (sometimes lower breast), underwing-coverts yellowish, long tail dull reddish below. **Voice** Flight call harsh, low-pitched "kree'a", slightly bisyllabic; similar, doubled or trebled when perched. **SS** Yellow-eared Parrot.

Yellow-eared Parrot *Ognorhynchus icterotis* EN
Loro Orejiamarillo EN

Local resident (populations fragmented, some protected).

L 43 cm (17"). Monotypic. Endemic (probably extinct NW Ecuador). Canopy of humid and wet montane forest with *Ceroxylon* palms. 2000–3300 m. Formerly large flocks, now pairs, small groups; breeds semi-colonially in *Ceroxylon* palms. **ID** Robust shape, long pointed tail brings to mind a small macaw but lacks bare face; yellow forecrown extends rearward to form large yellow ear-coverts patch, massive black bill. **Voice** Perched or flying, rather harsh nasal "skrEEEa". **SS** Golden-plumed Parakeet.

Blue-crowned Parakeet *Thectocerus acuticaudatus* LC
Perico Frentiazul

Five subspecies in two subspecies groups; one in Colombia.

Northern Blue-crowned Parakeet
Thectocerus (acuticaudatus) haemorrhous
Perico Frentiazul Norteño

Fairly common resident.

L 36 cm (14"). Race *koenigi*. Arid scrub, dry woodland, gallery forest. To 400 m. Pairs or flocks to 100 or more. Flies fairly low over woodland; sharp seasonal movements need documentation. **ID** Large long-tailed parakeet, mostly green, red undertail, prominent pale orbital ring, blue crown inconspicuous, bill pale. **Voice** Flight call a high rising then falling "cleea", recalls distant Red-bellied Macaw. **SS** Brown-throated Parakeet.
TN Previously placed in either *Aratinga* or *Psittacara*.

koenigi

Scarlet-fronted Parakeet
Psittacara wagleri NT
Perico Frentirrojo

Formerly very common resident, now local and declining.

L 36 cm (14"). Race *wagleri*. Moist to humid montane forest. 900–2500 m (records to 350 m). Gregarious, large flocks cross high over Andean valleys. Breeds semi-colonially on rock cliffs. Unwelcome in corn fields and fruit orchards, where persecuted. **ID** Fairly large, all green, long-tailed, red at bend of wing (visible in flight, sometimes when perched), red forehead, neither conspicuous at distance. **Voice** Loud strident calls unpleasant with repetition. **SS** Golden-plumed Parakeet. **TN** Formerly placed in *Aratinga*.

wagleri

callogenys

White-eyed Parakeet *Psittacara leucophthalmus* LC
Perico Ojiblanco

Common resident.

L 36 cm (14"). Races *nicefori*[A], *callogenys*[B]. Borders of humid lowland forest, river edges, gallery forest, semi-open areas. To 500 m. Gregarious; flocks often fly high in long morning and evening commutes from roosting and feeding sites, overflying tall forest and open areas. Breeds in tall dead trunks, especially around old oxbows. **ID** Large, long-tailed, green, conspicuous red-and-yellow underwing-coverts, large bare whitish orbital ring (the 'white' eye). **Voice** Loud and screechy; some calls rough, others nasal; constant shrill chatter in flight. **SS** Dusky-headed Parakeet. **TN** Formerly placed in *Aratinga*.

SAPAYOIDAE
Sapayoa
1 extant species, 1 in region

The single unremarkable-looking member of this family has had a checkered taxonomic history, having been aligned with manakins, Old World broadbills, and more recently placed in its own family for lack of clear genetic affinities.

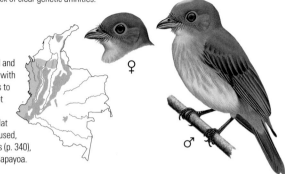

♀

♂

Sapayoa *Sapayoa aenigma* `LC`
Saltarín Piquigrueso
Uncommon and local resident.

L 15 cm (6"). Monotypic. Understorey of humid and wet forest. To c. 1000 m. Alone or sometimes with mixed flocks. Posture relatively upright; sallies to foliage. **ID** Broad flat bill. Plumage nondescript olive, wings and tail slightly darker, throat and belly tinged yellowish; ♂ concealed yellow crown-stripe. **Voice** Weak flat trill c. 1.5 seconds, fades, slightly descends. **SS** Easily confused, confirm by voice; larger, longer-tailed than most ♀ manakins (p. 340), Green Manakin (p. 343), flatbills (p. 369). **AN** Broad-billed Sapayoa.

THAMNOPHILIDAE
Typical Antbirds
241 extant species, 121 in region

This large Neotropical family is most diverse in Amazonia, but its members are found from sea level to the treeline. Recent genetic work has resulted in massive realignments of traditional genera within the family and the introduction of many novel genera. All terrestrial species are now placed either in separate families, e.g. antpittas in Grallariidae, antthrushes in Formicariidae, or with gnateaters in Conopophagidae. Despite taxonomic tinkering, the family remains endlessly fascinating and its species truly iconic Neotropical birds. None of them feeds on ants, despite their name, and only about 10% of species are associated with ants, these mainly by following marauding army ants, and preying on arthropods fleeing the attacking ants. To pursue a nomadic food source, these species have, in some cases, evolved novel breeding systems. All other antbirds pursue more traditional breeding and foraging strategies, and feed almost entirely on insects. Many antbirds were named by northern ornithologists who knew comparatively little about these birds, and chose names for them based on their perceived resemblance to familiar Northern Hemisphere birds, hence antshrikes, antwrens, antvireos, and so on. Songs of antbirds are largely unvarying, the result of a primitive vocal anatomy compared to true songbirds. Nevertheless, their songs are often loud and distinctive, both sexes sing, and frequently song is the only indication of their presence. Anyone wishing to see antbirds needs to pay attention to their songs.

Genus *Euchrepomis* Small, brightly coloured, and warbler-like with thin bill, moderately long tail, and orange-rufous rump or scapular patch. Usually with mixed flocks. All previously in *Terenura*.

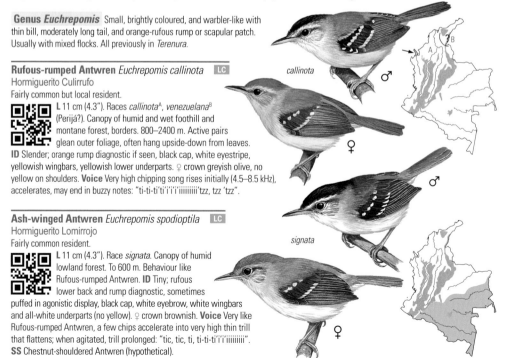

callinota

♂

♀

♂

signata

♀

Rufous-rumped Antwren *Euchrepomis callinota* `LC`
Hormiguerito Culirrufo
Fairly common but local resident.

L 11 cm (4.3"). Races *callinota*[A], *venezuelana*[B] (Perijá?). Canopy of humid and wet foothill and montane forest, borders. 800–2400 m. Active pairs glean outer foliage, often hang upside-down from leaves. **ID** Slender; orange rump diagnostic if seen, black cap, white eyestripe, yellowish wingbars, yellowish lower underparts. ♀ crown greyish olive, no yellow on shoulders. **Voice** Very high chipping song rises initially (4.5–8.5 kHz), accelerates, may end in buzzy notes: "ti-ti-ti'ti'i'i'i'iiiiiiii'tzz, tzz 'tzz".

Ash-winged Antwren *Euchrepomis spodioptila* `LC`
Hormiguerito Lomirrojo
Fairly common resident.

L 11 cm (4.3"). Race *signata*. Canopy of humid lowland forest. To 600 m. Behaviour like Rufous-rumped Antwren. **ID** Tiny; rufous lower back and rump diagnostic, sometimes puffed in agonistic display, black cap, white eyebrow, white wingbars and all-white underparts (no yellow). ♀ crown brownish. **Voice** Very like Rufous-rumped Antwren, a few chips accelerate into very high thin trill that flattens; when agitated, trill prolonged: "tic, tic, ti, ti-ti-ti'i'i'iiiiiiiii". **SS** Chestnut-shouldered Antwren (hypothetical).

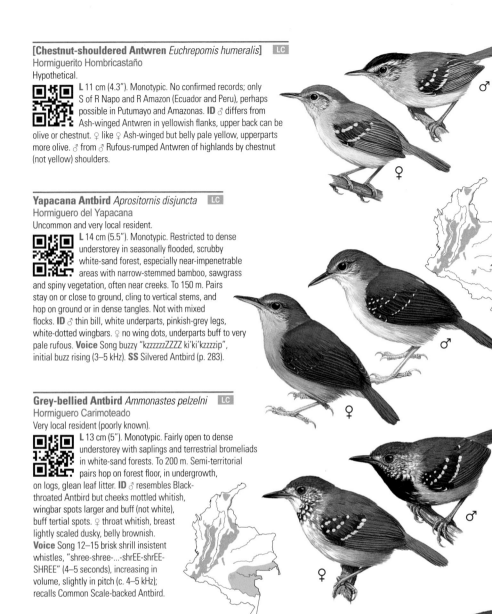

[Chestnut-shouldered Antwren *Euchrepomis humeralis*] `LC`
Hormiguerito Hombricastaño
Hypothetical.

L 11 cm (4.3"). Monotypic. No confirmed records; only S of R Napo and R Amazon (Ecuador and Peru), perhaps possible in Putumayo and Amazonas. **ID** ♂ differs from Ash-winged Antwren in yellowish flanks, upper back can be olive or chestnut. ♀ like ♀ Ash-winged but belly pale yellow, upperparts more olive. ♂ from ♂ Rufous-rumped Antwren of highlands by chestnut (not yellow) shoulders.

Yapacana Antbird *Aprositornis disjuncta* `LC`
Hormiguero del Yapacana
Uncommon and very local resident.

L 14 cm (5.5"). Monotypic. Restricted to dense understorey in seasonally flooded, scrubby white-sand forest, especially near-impenetrable areas with narrow-stemmed bamboo, sawgrass and spiny vegetation, often near creeks. To 150 m. Pairs stay on or close to ground, cling to vertical stems, and hop on ground or in dense tangles. Not with mixed flocks. **ID** ♂ thin bill, white underparts, pinkish-grey legs, white-dotted wingbars. ♀ no wing dots, underparts buff to very pale rufous. **Voice** Song buzzy "kzzzzzzZZZZ ki'ki'kzzzzip", initial buzz rising (3–5 kHz). **SS** Silvered Antbird (p. 283).

Grey-bellied Antbird *Ammonastes pelzelni* `LC`
Hormiguero Carimoteado
Very local resident (poorly known).

L 13 cm (5"). Monotypic. Fairly open to dense understorey with saplings and terrestrial bromeliads in white-sand forests. To 200 m. Semi-territorial pairs hop on forest floor, in undergrowth, on logs, glean leaf litter. **ID** ♂ resembles Black-throated Antbird but cheeks mottled whitish, wingbar spots larger and buff (not white), buff tertial spots. ♀ throat whitish, breast lightly scaled dusky, belly brownish. **Voice** Song 12–15 brisk shrill insistent whistles, "shree-shree-...-shrEE-shrEE-SHREE" (4–5 seconds), increasing in volume, slightly in pitch (c. 4–5 kHz); recalls Common Scale-backed Antbird.

Black-throated Antbird *Myrmophylax atrothorax* `LC`
Hormiguero Gorginegro
Common resident.

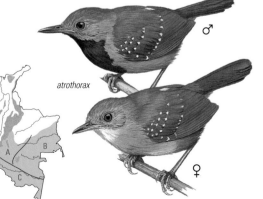

atrothorax

L 14 cm (5.5"). Races *metae*[A], *atrothorax*[B], *tenebrosa*[C]. Grassy thickets at edge of *terra firme* and low-lying forest, well-lit treefalls, grassy savanna-woodland borders. To 500 m. Pairs or families, noisy, excitable, skulk in grass or thickets, near ground, adept at staying hidden, use horizontal or diagonal perches (infrequently vertical). **ID** ♂ upperparts brown, below iron grey with black throat, white-dotted wingbars. ♀ whitish throat, orange-rufous breast. **Voice** Song intense "pe'pee, pee-pee-pee-pee". Slightly rising; sharp "PSEEyap!"; rattles; chips. **SS** Grey-bellied Antbird.

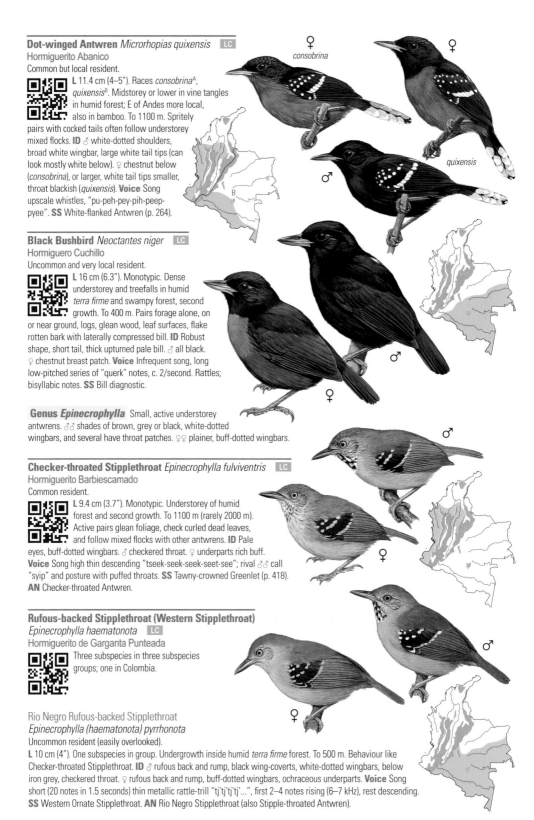

Dot-winged Antwren *Microrhopias quixensis* LC
Hormiguerito Abanico

Common but local resident.

L 11.4 cm (4–5"). Races *consobrina*[A], *quixensis*[B]. Midstorey or lower in vine tangles in humid forest; E of Andes more local, also in bamboo. To 1100 m. Spritely pairs with cocked tails often follow understorey mixed flocks. **ID** ♂ white-dotted shoulders, broad white wingbar, large white tail tips (can look mostly white below). ♀ chestnut below (*consobrina*), or larger, white tail tips smaller, throat blackish (*quixensis*). **Voice** Song upscale whistles, "pu-peh-pey-pih-peep-pyee". **SS** White-flanked Antwren (p. 264).

♀
consobrina

♀

♂

quixensis

Black Bushbird *Neoctantes niger* LC
Hormiguero Cuchillo

Uncommon and very local resident.

L 16 cm (6.3"). Monotypic. Dense understorey and treefalls in humid *terra firme* and swampy forest, second growth. To 400 m. Pairs forage alone, on or near ground, logs, glean wood, leaf surfaces, flake rotten bark with laterally compressed bill. **ID** Robust shape, short tail, thick upturned pale bill. ♂ all black. ♀ chestnut breast patch. **Voice** Infrequent song, long low-pitched series of "querk" notes, c. 2/second. Rattles; bisyllabic notes. **SS** Bill diagnostic.

♂

♀

Genus *Epinecrophylla* Small, active understorey antwrens. ♂♂ shades of brown, grey or black, white-dotted wingbars, and several have throat patches. ♀♀ plainer, buff-dotted wingbars.

♂

Checker-throated Stipplethroat *Epinecrophylla fulviventris* LC
Hormiguerito Barbiescamado

Common resident.

L 9.4 cm (3.7"). Monotypic. Understorey of humid forest and second growth. To 1100 m (rarely 2000 m). Active pairs glean foliage, check curled dead leaves, and follow mixed flocks with other antwrens. **ID** Pale eyes, buff-dotted wingbars. ♂ checkered throat. ♀ underparts rich buff. **Voice** Song high thin descending "tseek-seek-seek-seet-see"; rival ♂♂ call "syip" and posture with puffed throats. **SS** Tawny-crowned Greenlet (p. 418). **AN** Checker-throated Antwren.

♀

Rufous-backed Stipplethroat (Western Stipplethroat)
Epinecrophylla haematonota LC
Hormiguerito de Garganta Punteada

Three subspecies in three subspecies groups; one in Colombia.

♂

Rio Negro Rufous-backed Stipplethroat
Epinecrophylla (haematonota) pyrrhonota
Uncommon resident (easily overlooked).

♀

L 10 cm (4"). One subspecies in group. Undergrowth inside humid *terra firme* forest. To 500 m. Behaviour like Checker-throated Stipplethroat. **ID** ♂ rufous back and rump, black wing-coverts, white-dotted wingbars, below iron grey, checkered throat. ♀ rufous back and rump, buff-dotted wingbars, ochraceous underparts. **Voice** Song short (20 notes in 1.5 seconds) thin metallic rattle-trill "tj'tj'tj'…", first 2–4 notes rising (6–7 kHz), rest descending. **SS** Western Ornate Stipplethroat. **AN** Rio Negro Stipplethroat (also Stipple-throated Antwren).

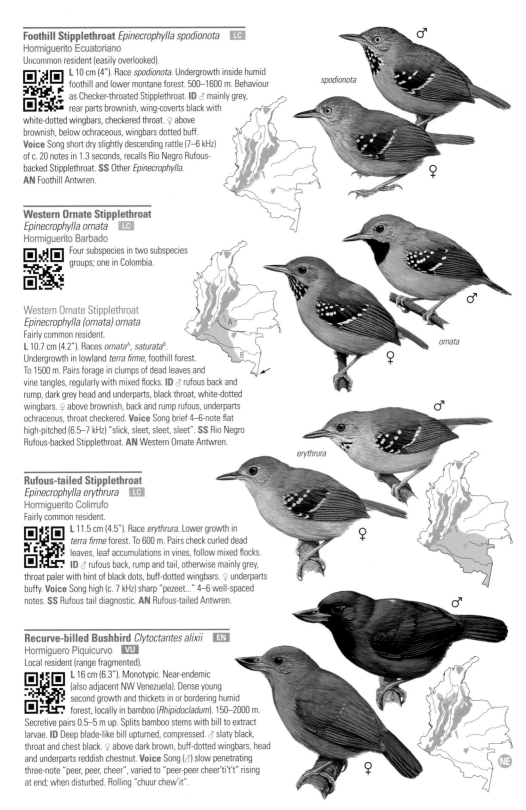

Foothill Stipplethroat *Epinecrophylla spodionota* `LC`
Hormiguerito Ecuatoriano

Uncommon resident (easily overlooked).

L 10 cm (4"). Race *spodionota*. Undergrowth inside humid foothill and lower montane forest. 500–1600 m. Behaviour as Checker-throated Stipplethroat. **ID** ♂ mainly grey, rear parts brownish, wing-coverts black with white-dotted wingbars. ♀ above brownish, below ochraceous, wingbars dotted buff. **Voice** Song short dry slightly descending rattle (7–6 kHz) of c. 20 notes in 1.3 seconds, recalls Rio Negro Rufous-backed Stipplethroat. **SS** Other *Epinecrophylla*. **AN** Foothill Antwren.

spodionota

♂

♀

Western Ornate Stipplethroat
Epinecrophylla ornata `LC`
Hormiguerito Barbado

Four subspecies in two subspecies groups; one in Colombia.

Western Ornate Stipplethroat
Epinecrophylla (ornata) ornata
Fairly common resident.

L 10.7 cm (4.2"). Races *ornata*[A], *saturata*[B]. Undergrowth in lowland *terra firme*, foothill forest. To 1500 m. Pairs forage in clumps of dead leaves and vine tangles, regularly with mixed flocks. **ID** ♂ rufous back and rump, dark grey head and underparts, black throat, white-dotted wingbars. ♀ above brownish, back and rump rufous, underparts ochraceous, throat checkered. **Voice** Song brief 4–6-note flat high-pitched (6.5–7 kHz) "slick, sleet, sleet, sleet". **SS** Rio Negro Rufous-backed Stipplethroat. **AN** Western Ornate Antwren.

ornata

♂

♀

Rufous-tailed Stipplethroat
Epinecrophylla erythrura `LC`
Hormiguerito Colirrufo

Fairly common resident.

L 11.5 cm (4.5"). Race *erythrura*. Lower growth in *terra firme* forest. To 600 m. Pairs check curled dead leaves, leaf accumulations in vines, follow mixed flocks. **ID** ♂ rufous back, rump and tail, otherwise mainly grey, throat paler with hint of black dots, buff-dotted wingbars. ♀ underparts buffy. **Voice** Song high (c. 7 kHz) sharp "pezeet..." 4–6 well-spaced notes. **SS** Rufous tail diagnostic. **AN** Rufous-tailed Antwren.

erythrura

♂

♀

Recurve-billed Bushbird *Clytoctantes alixii* `EN`
Hormiguero Piquicurvo `VU`

Local resident (range fragmented).

L 16 cm (6.3"). Monotypic. Near-endemic (also adjacent NW Venezuela). Dense young second growth and thickets in or bordering humid forest, locally in bamboo (*Rhipidocladum*). 150–2000 m. Secretive pairs 0.5–5 m up. Splits bamboo stems with bill to extract larvae. **ID** Deep blade-like bill upturned, compressed. ♂ slaty black, throat and chest black. ♀ above dark brown, buff-dotted wingbars, head and underparts reddish chestnut. **Voice** Song (♂) slow penetrating three-note "peer, peer, cheer", varied to "peer-peer cheer'ti't't" rising at end; when disturbed. Rolling "chuur chew'it".

♂

♀

`NE`

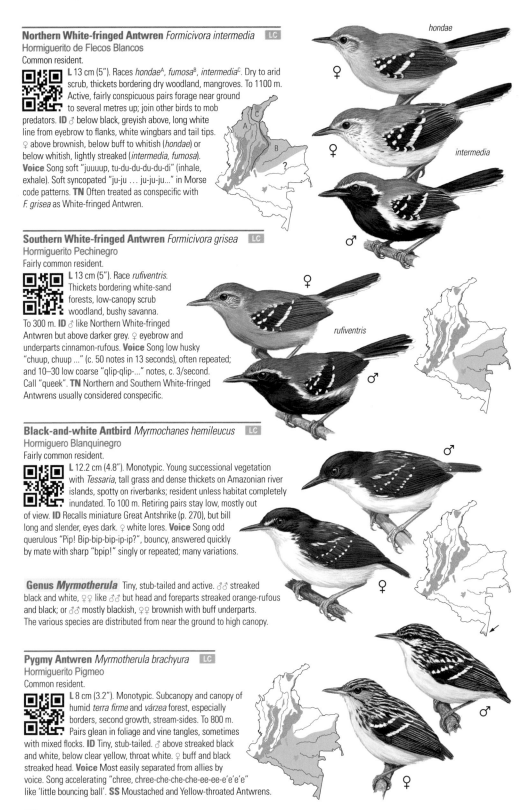

Northern White-fringed Antwren *Formicivora intermedia* `LC`
Hormiguerito de Flecos Blancos
Common resident.

L 13 cm (5"). Races *hondae*[A], *fumosa*[B], *intermedia*[C]. Dry to arid scrub, thickets bordering dry woodland, mangroves. To 1100 m. Active, fairly conspicuous pairs forage near ground to several metres up; join other birds to mob predators. **ID** ♂ below black, greyish above, long white line from eyebrow to flanks, white wingbars and tail tips. ♀ above brownish, below buff to whitish (*hondae*) or below whitish, lightly streaked (*intermedia*, *fumosa*). **Voice** Song soft "juuuup, tu-du-du-du-du-di" (inhale, exhale). Soft syncopated "ju-ju … ju-ju-ju…" in Morse code patterns. **TN** Often treated as conspecific with *F. grisea* as White-fringed Antwren.

hondae

intermedia

Southern White-fringed Antwren *Formicivora grisea* `LC`
Hormiguerito Pechinegro
Fairly common resident.

L 13 cm (5"). Race *rufiventris*. Thickets bordering white-sand forests, low-canopy scrub woodland, bushy savanna. To 300 m. **ID** ♂ like Northern White-fringed Antwren but above darker grey. ♀ eyebrow and underparts cinnamon-rufous. **Voice** Song low husky "chuup, chuup …" (c. 50 notes in 13 seconds), often repeated; and 10–30 low coarse "qlip-qlip-…" notes, c. 3/second. Call "queek". **TN** Northern and Southern White-fringed Antwrens usually considered conspecific.

rufiventris

Black-and-white Antbird *Myrmochanes hemileucus* `LC`
Hormiguero Blanquinegro
Fairly common resident.

L 12.2 cm (4.8"). Monotypic. Young successional vegetation with *Tessaria*, tall grass and dense thickets on Amazonian river islands, spotty on riverbanks; resident unless habitat completely inundated. To 100 m. Retiring pairs stay low, mostly out of view. **ID** Recalls miniature Great Antshrike (p. 270), but bill long and slender, eyes dark. ♀ white lores. **Voice** Song odd querulous "Pip! Bip-bip-bip-ip-ip?", bouncy, answered quickly by mate with sharp "bpip!" singly or repeated; many variations.

Genus *Myrmotherula* Tiny, stub-tailed and active. ♂♂ streaked black and white, ♀♀ like ♂♂ but head and foreparts streaked orange-rufous and black; or ♂♂ mostly blackish, ♀♀ brownish with buff underparts. The various species are distributed from near the ground to high canopy.

Pygmy Antwren *Myrmotherula brachyura* `LC`
Hormiguerito Pigmeo
Common resident.

L 8 cm (3.2"). Monotypic. Subcanopy and canopy of humid *terra firme* and *várzea* forest, especially borders, second growth, stream-sides. To 800 m. Pairs glean in foliage and vine tangles, sometimes with mixed flocks. **ID** Tiny, stub-tailed. ♂ above streaked black and white, below clear yellow, throat white. ♀ buff and black streaked head. **Voice** Most easily separated from allies by voice. Song accelerating "chree, chree-che-che-che-ee-ee-e'e'e'e" like 'little bouncing ball'. **SS** Moustached and Yellow-throated Antwrens.

Moustached Antwren *Myrmotherula ignota* `LC`
Hormiguerito de Griscom
Fairly common resident.

L 8 cm (3.2"). Races *ignota*[A], *obscura*[B]. Subcanopy of humid *terra firme* forest, borders, treefalls; more inside forest than Pygmy Antwren. To 900 m. Behaviour like Pygmy Antwren. **ID** ♂ from ♀ Pygmy Antwren by blacker crown and upperparts (black streaking wider), broader and more conspicuous moustachial line, and ♀ more extensive buff on throat and chest (*ignota*); or ♂ even blacker above, ♀ foreparts buffier (*obscura*). **Voice** Song (*obscura*) resembles Pygmy Antwren but slower (c. 3 notes/second), steady, slightly accelerating, descending at end. Song (*ignota*) marginally higher-pitched. **TN** Amazonian *obscura* formerly treated as a separate species, Short-billed Antwren.

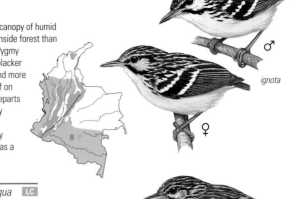

ignota

Yellow-throated Antwren *Myrmotherula ambigua* `LC`
Hormiguerito Barbiamarillo
Local resident.

L 8.6 cm (3.4"). Monotypic. Canopy and subcanopy of white-sand forest. To 300 m. Active pairs high in vine tangles, regularly with mixed flocks. **ID** Best told by voice. ♂ very like ♂ Pygmy Antwren, differing in yellow (not white) throat. ♀ from ♀ Pygmy Antwren by yellowish (not white) throat. **Voice** Song 10–15 leisurely paced, low-pitched (for *Myrmotherula*) notes, 2.5 kHz, penetrating, same pitch, no acceleration "weeup, weeup..." or "teeup..." at rate of fewer than c. 2 notes/second.

Guianan Streaked Antwren *Myrmotherula surinamensis* `VU`
Hormiguerito Rayado
Status uncertain (records?).

L 9.4 cm (3.7"). Monotypic. Thickets and vine tangles overhanging lakes, small streams, less often humid forest borders. To 300 m. **ID** ♂ much like ♂ Amazonian Streaked Antwren (best separated by voice). ♀ like ♀ Amazonian Streaked Antwren but no thin black malar line, foreface, throat and chest unstreaked or with only minor shaft-streaks. **Voice** Bubbly song of 6–8 notes rising-falling in steps quickly; recalls Amazonian Streaked Antwren but faster, more notes, "tu-tu-HEE-HEE-he-he-ha" repeatedly. Long vibrating trill; short breezy "weet-weet-weet-weet". **SS** Also Cherrie's Antwren.

Amazonian Streaked Antwren *Myrmotherula multostriata* `LC`
Hormiguerito Estriado
Common resident.

L 9.4 cm (3.7"). Monotypic. Thickets and vine tangles overhanging oxbow lakes and small streams. To 300 m. Active, pairs, fairly low to mid-levels, not with mixed flocks. **ID** ♂ streaked black and white, two white wingbars. ♀ head and nape orange-rufous streaked black, throat to breast ochraceous with thin shaft-streaks. **Voice** Song c. 5 notes, rising-falling quickly, "tu-tee-HEE-hu-hu" over and over. Dry rattling trill; brief "chee-pu". **SS** Guianan Streaked Antwren, Cherrie's Antwren.

Pacific Antwren *Myrmotherula pacifica* `LC`
Hormiguerito del Pacífico
Common resident.

 L 9.4 cm (3.7"). Monotypic. Low in second growth and vine tangles at humid wooded borders (not associated with water), overgrown clearings, gardens. To 1200 m. Pairs glean actively in foliage, mid-levels or lower, usually away from mixed flocks. **ID** ♂ streaked black and white. ♀ head and neck orange-rufous finely streaked black, underparts paler and unstreaked. **Voice** Song evenly spaced dry chattering, "chit-chit-chit-chit-che-che-che..." of 12+ notes, rising initially.

Cherrie's Antwren *Myrmotherula cherriei* `LC`
Hormiguerito de Cherrie
Fairly common but local resident.

 L 9.4 cm (3.7"). Monotypic. Seasonally flooded low scrub forest on white sandy soil, shrubby borders of sandy riverine woodland. To 500 m. Pairs, low to mid-levels, sometimes with mixed flocks. **ID** Much like Guianan Streaked Antwren. ♂ black streaking much coarser, reaching to belly. ♀ crown pale buff, entire head finely streaked black, underparts, including belly, buff heavily streaked black. **Voice** Song, fast even-paced rattle, ascends, swells then flattens "trtrtrddddddddddddddd", with hard mechanical quality. **SS** Amazonian Streaked Antwren.

Stripe-chested Antwren *Myrmotherula longicauda* `LC`
Hormiguerito Pechirrayado
Local resident (few records).

 L 9.4 cm (3.7"). Race *soderstromi*. Shrubby borders of humid forest, vine-laden second growth. Foothills, c. 400–1400 m. Singles or pairs forage at mid-levels, sometimes with mixed flocks. **ID** ♂ streaked black and white, throat and mid-breast to belly white. ♀ head and upperparts streaked buff and black, throat to mid-breast unstreaked rich ochraceous, mid-breast to belly white. **Voice** Song c. 10 slow couplets, "chee'dip, chee'dip...", low-pitched, monotonously repeated. **SS** Amazonian Streaked Antwren.

White-flanked Antwren *Myrmotherula axillaris* `LC`
Hormiguerito Flanquiblanco
Common resident.

 L 10 cm (4"). Races *albigula*[A], *melaena*[B]. Mid-levels or lower in humid lowland and foothill forest, old second growth. To 1000 m. Restless territorial pairs persistently wing-flick, flashing white flanks as forage. Often with mixed flocks. **ID** ♂ white wingbars and shoulder dots, white flanks. ♀ buff wingbars, underparts pale buff, white flanks. **Voice** Song 6–10 measured descending whistles: "pyee, pee, piy, pey, puh, pu". Call "cheep-do" (W of Andes); nasal "nyaa-wop" (E of Andes). **SS** Flank patches diagnostic.

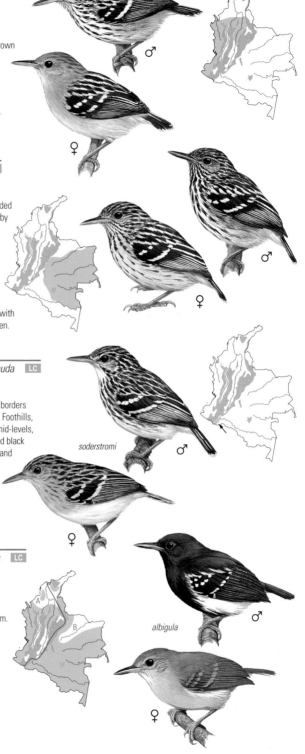

soderstromi

albigula

Slaty Antwren *Myrmotherula schisticolor*
Hormiguerito Pizarroso
Common resident (easily overlooked).

 L 10 cm (4"). Three races: *schisticolor*[A], *sanctaemartae*[B], *interior*[C]. Inside shady humid montane forest. 900–2300 m (rarely 400 m). Pairs or 3–4 work quietly 0.5–4 m up in undergrowth, sometimes with small mixed flocks. **ID** ♂ blackish (*schisticolor* blackest), throat and chest black, 2–3 white-dotted wingbars. ♀ plain, above greyish olive, below dull cinnamon; or above greyer (*sanctaemartae*, *interior*). **Voice** Nasal squeezed "myaa-a"; short "tee-up". Infrequent song 2–3 slow even-pitch whistles "swEErt, swEErt, swEErt" or longer series. **SS** Plain-winged Antwren; other grey *Myrmotherula* occur lower.

Rio Suno Antwren *Myrmotherula sunensis*
Hormiguerito del Churuyaco
Rare resident (few records).

 L 9 cm (3.5"). Race *sunensis*. Low to mid-level inside humid *terra firme* forest, locally *várzea*. To 500 m. Look for it in understorey mixed flocks. **ID** ♂ like Slaty Antwren (*interior*) but slightly paler (less black), smaller, shorter-tailed. ♀ not readily separated from ♀ Slaty but browner above, paler cinnamon below. The two species are unlikely to occur together. **Voice** Song 2–5 clear high, rising-falling notes "puEE'sa, puEE'sa, puEE'sa", energetic. **SS** Long-winged Antwren.

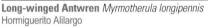

Long-winged Antwren *Myrmotherula longipennis*
Hormiguerito Alilargo
Fairly common resident.

 L 10 cm (4"). Race *longipennis*. Low to mid-level inside *terra firme* and *várzea* forest. To 500 m. Singles, pairs, families, flick wings, mostly perch-glean 2–8 m up, with mixed flocks containing other antwrens. **ID** ♂ dark grey, black bib to centre of chest, three white wingbars, white scapular fringes and tail tips. ♀ above brownish, wing-coverts tinged and tipped rufescent, throat to mid-breast yellowish buff, below contrasting whitish. **Voice** Song thin burry slightly rising "chewey-chewey-chewee-chee", leisurely, c. 10 notes in c. 5 seconds, insistent. **SS** Rio Suno Antwren, ♀ Grey Antwren.

Plain-winged Antwren *Myrmotherula behni*
Hormiguerito Cerrero
Rare and local resident (few records).

 L 9.4 cm (3.7"). Race *behni*. Undergrowth inside humid foothill and lower montane forest. 800–1600 m. Pairs, low to mid-levels (1–10 m up) with mixed flocks. Often inspects dead hanging leaves. **ID** ♂ dark grey, black bib, only *Myrmotherula* with no white in plumage. ♀ few marks; above olivaceous brown, tail more dusky, throat whitish, underparts dull olive-buff (no obvious ochraceous tones), but best known by company she keeps. **Voice** Song (Venezuela) slightly descending, 7–11 soft notes "fee-fee ...". **SS** Slaty Antwren.

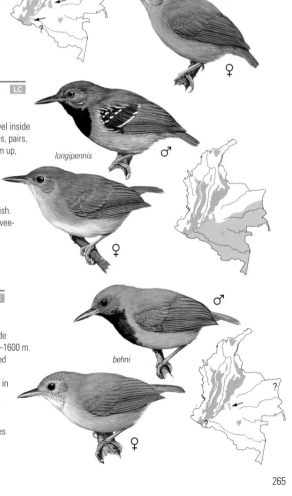

Grey Antwren *Myrmotherula menetriesii* `LC`
Hormiguerito Murino
Common resident.

L 9.4 cm (3.7"). Race *pallida*. Mid-level to subcanopy inside *terra firme* and *várzea* forest. Pairs follow mixed flocks, generally forage higher than other grey-plumaged *Myrmotherula*. Habitually twitches tail to side. **ID** ♂ uniform light grey, wing-coverts black tipped white forming three wingbars, tail tipped white. ♀ paler than most allies, distinctly greyish above, uniform ochraceous below. **Voice** Song (*pallida*) 9–12 soft timid "reee" notes steadily rising in pitch (2.5–4 kHz). **SS** ♀ Long-winged Antwren.

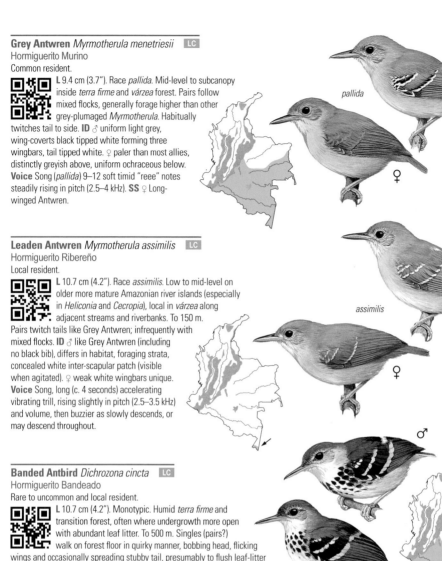

pallida ♂

♀

Leaden Antwren *Myrmotherula assimilis* `LC`
Hormiguerito Ribereño
Local resident.

L 10.7 cm (4.2"). Race *assimilis*. Low to mid-level on older more mature Amazonian river islands (especially in *Heliconia* and *Cecropia*), local in *várzea* along adjacent streams and riverbanks. To 150 m. Pairs twitch tails like Grey Antwren; infrequently with mixed flocks. **ID** ♂ like Grey Antwren (including no black bib), differs in habitat, foraging strata, concealed white inter-scapular patch (visible when agitated). ♀ weak white wingbars unique. **Voice** Song, long (c. 4 seconds) accelerating vibrating trill, rising slightly in pitch (2.5–3.5 kHz) and volume, then buzzier as slowly descends, or may descend throughout.

assimilis ♂

♀

Banded Antbird *Dichrozona cincta* `LC`
Hormiguerito Bandeado
Rare to uncommon and local resident.

L 10.7 cm (4.2"). Monotypic. Humid *terra firme* and transition forest, often where undergrowth more open with abundant leaf litter. To 500 m. Singles (pairs?) walk on forest floor in quirky manner, bobbing head, flicking wings and occasionally spreading stubby tail, presumably to flush leaf-litter insects. **ID** Cute, unlikely to be confused; tiny. Streaked breast, bold buff wing-bands, white rump. **Voice** Song long (10–15 seconds) slow, barely rising (3–3.5 kHz) series of soft whistles "reeeEE, reeEE...". **SS** Ringed Antpipit (p. 365).

♂

♀

Plain-throated Antwren *Isleria hauxwelli* `LC`
Hormiguerito Culipinto
Fairly common resident.

L 9.7 cm (3.8"). Race *suffusa*. Humid *terra firme* and transition forest, less in *várzea*. To 600 m. Pairs or families cling to vertical saplings, near ground to 2 m up; seldom with mixed flocks, sometimes with army ants. **ID** ♂ only antwren with bold white tertial and tail spots. ♀ buff tertial and tail spots, cinnamon-rufous underparts. **Voice** Song, 6–12 thin rising (c. 5 kHz) "sueee" notes, slowly increasing in intensity. Harsh rattle alarm. **SS** Common Scale-backed Antbird (p. 281). **TN** Formerly in genus *Myrmotherula*.

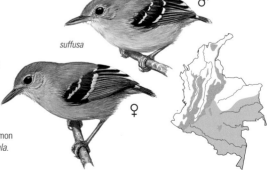

♂

suffusa

♀

Genus *Thamnomanes* Longish tails; upright postures. ♂♂ plain grey, ♀♀ rather two-toned below. Prominent members of understorey bird flocks.

Dusky-throated Antshrike
Thamnomanes ardesiacus LC
Hormiguero Grisazul
Fairly common resident.
L 14 cm (5.5"). Races *ardesiacus*[A], *obidensis*[B]. Humid *terra firme* and *várzea* forest. Pairs perch upright in understorey, sally to foliage like flycatchers; almost always in mixed flocks, especially with Cinereous Antshrikes, but less conspicuous. **ID** Best told by voice and behaviour. ♂ black throat hard to see. ♀ drab, whitish throat, dull tawny breast. **Voice** Song, sharply ascending raspy, grinding "jaaw, jaaw, jaw, jay, juu, ju,ju,ju j-j-j", ends abruptly. Loud sharp "skéeap"; buzzy snarling "juueeer"; no loud rattle. **SS** Cinereous Antshrike.

obidensis
ardesiacus

Cinereous Antshrike *Thamnomanes caesius* LC
Hormiguero Cenizo
Fairly common to common resident.
L 14 cm (5.5"). Race *glaucus*. Humid lowland forest. To 500 m. Behaviour much like Dusky-throated Antshrike but noisier, perches higher, more conspicuous; acts as sentinel in understorey flocks. **ID** Listen for voice. ♂ plain grey. ♀ throat pale grey, chest brownish grey sharply separated from orange-rufous breast. **Voice** Constant dialogue of low whistles "wert-wert", and loud staccato rattles "d'd'd'd'd'd'd" invariably indicate an understorey bird flock. Song several slow wheezy whistles accelerating into bubbly trill "squeet … wheet, wheet, wheesp wheesp whees whe we we e-e-e-e-u-u-u-r". **SS** Dusky-throated Antshrike.

glaucus

Pearly Antshrike *Megasticus margaritatus* LC
Hormiguero Perlado
Uncommon and local resident.
L 14 cm (5.5"). Monotypic. White-sand forest, older second growth; rare and local in *terra firme* forests of other soil types. To 500 m. Pairs or families, mostly alone, forest mid-levels; often sally to foliage. **ID** ♂ grey, bold white wing-covert, tertial and tail spots, pale eyes. ♀ similar but spots buff, above brownish, head brownish grey, underparts tawny cinnamon. **Voice** Song 3–4 clear leisurely whistles, followed by 4–5 slightly lower, faster grating notes. **SS** Amazonian Antshrike (p. 275).

Genus *Dysithamnus* Larger than *Myrmotherula* antwrens, but smaller than *Thamnophilus* antshrikes. Chunky, large-headed and short-tailed; horizontal posture. Gleaners (no sallying), with deliberate movements; low inside forest; mostly in foothills.

Plain Antvireo *Dysithamnus mentalis* LC
Hormiguero Tiznado
Common resident.
L 11.4 cm (4.5"). Races *suffusus*[A], *extremus*[B], *viridis*[C], *semicinereus*[D], *napensis*[E], *aequatorialis*[F]. Humid foothill and lower montane forest. 600–2200 m (rarely 300 m). Pairs, alone or with mixed flocks. **ID** ♂ pale below, dusky cheeks, weakly indicated white wingbars. ♀ chestnut crown, white eye-ring, dusky cheeks, below faintly yellowish white; or lower underparts strongly tinged yellow (*viridis*). **Voice** Song soft nasal accelerating roll ('bouncing ball'), higher-pitched than *Thamnophilus*, descends, weakens. Call nasal "nyet". **SS** Spot-crowned Antvireo.

semicinereus
extremus

Spot-crowned Antvireo *Dysithamnus puncticeps* `LC`
Hormiguero Coronipunteado
Common resident.

 L 11.4 cm (4.5"). Monotypic. Humid and wet Pacific slope foothills, local in lowlands. To 1100 m. **ID** Greyish-white eyes. ♂ white-spotted crown and wingbars, faint streaking on chest. ♀ crown dull rufous dotted blackish, buff-dotted wingbars, below buff, chest faintly streaked. **Voice** Song series of soft tremulous accelerating ('bouncing ball') notes, descends, weakens. **SS** Plain Antvireo.

Bicolored Antvireo *Dysithamnus occidentalis* `VU`
Hormiguero Occidental `VU`
Uncommon and local resident.

 L 14 cm (5.5"). Race *occidentalis*. Wet lower montane and montane Pacific slope forest; W Nariño records (and race involved) need confirmation. 900–2200 m. Inconspicuous, pairs glean foliage in dense undergrowth, usually not with mixed flocks. **ID** ♂ sooty black, white-dotted wing-coverts. ♀ quite dark with chestnut crown, buff-white wing dots, faint whitish throat streaking. **Voice** Song, c. 12 low husky "cheeur" notes, stronger in middle, accelerating (little 'bouncing ball'), weakening near end. Soft descending "churr". **SS** Uniform Antshrike (p. 275; larger).

occidentalis

White-streaked Antvireo
Dysithamnus leucostictus `VU`
Hormiguero Cabecipunteado
Rare or uncommon resident (poorly known).

 L 13 cm (5"). Race *leucostictus*. Undergrowth of humid foothill and montane forest; SE slope of Andes. 900–2000 m. Behaviour like congeners; sometimes with mixed flocks. **ID** ♂ slaty, white-fringed wing-coverts, black bib, breast with a few white shaft-streaks. ♀ chestnut crown, reddish-brown upperparts, face and underparts iron grey extensively streaked white. **Voice** Leisurely song of 5–7 low-pitched whistles descending throughout; recalls *Trogon*. **SS** Uniform Antshrike (p. 275).

leucostictus

Genus *Herpsilochmus* Well-marked grey, white and black plumage, prominent white eyebrows, white wingbars, and white tail tips. Both sexes sing, otherwise inconspicuous, usually in canopy.

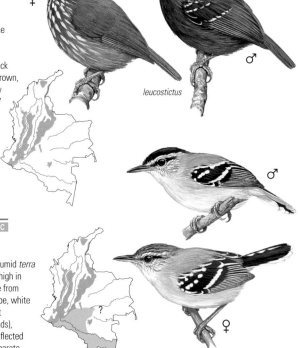

Dugand's Antwren *Herpsilochmus dugandi* `LC`
Hormiguerito de Dugand
Uncommon resident (easily overlooked).

L 11 cm (4.3"). Monotypic. Canopy of tall humid *terra firme* forest. To 600 m. Pairs glean foliage high in canopy, follow mixed flocks; difficult to see from ground. **ID** ♂ black cap, long white eyestripe, white wingbars, underparts, tail tips. ♀ crown chestnut, breast buff-white. **Voice** Song short (15–20 notes in c. 2 seconds), accelerating, "chew, chew, chu'chu'ch'...", downward-inflected notes like little 'bouncing ball'. ♀ higher-pitched. **SS** Separate Spot-backed Antwren by voice (but minimal range overlap).

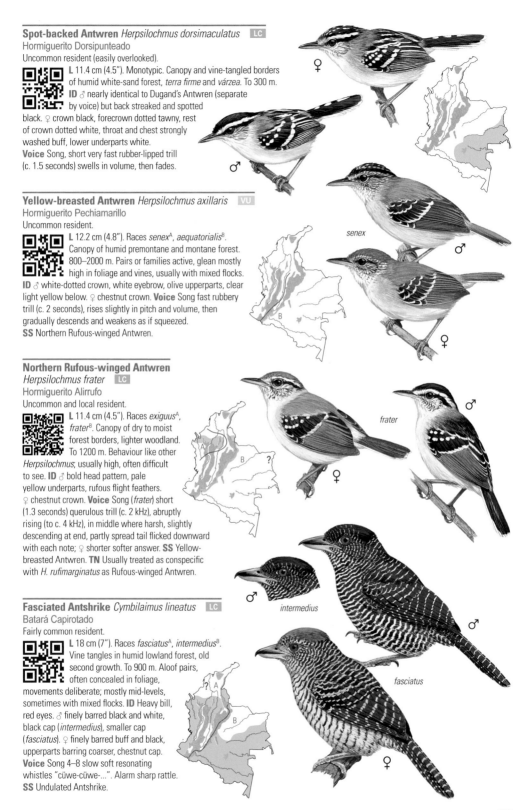

Spot-backed Antwren *Herpsilochmus dorsimaculatus* `LC`
Hormiguerito Dorsipunteado
Uncommon resident (easily overlooked).
L 11.4 cm (4.5"). Monotypic. Canopy and vine-tangled borders of humid white-sand forest, *terra firme* and *várzea*. To 300 m. **ID** ♂ nearly identical to Dugand's Antwren (separate by voice) but back streaked and spotted black. ♀ crown black, forecrown dotted tawny, rest of crown dotted white, throat and chest strongly washed buff, lower underparts white. **Voice** Song, short very fast rubber-lipped trill (c. 1.5 seconds) swells in volume, then fades.

Yellow-breasted Antwren *Herpsilochmus axillaris* `VU`
Hormiguerito Pechiamarillo
Uncommon resident.
L 12.2 cm (4.8"). Races *senex*[A], *aequatorialis*[B]. Canopy of humid premontane and montane forest. 800–2000 m. Pairs or families active, glean mostly high in foliage and vines, usually with mixed flocks. **ID** ♂ white-dotted crown, white eyebrow, olive upperparts, clear light yellow below. ♀ chestnut crown. **Voice** Song fast rubbery trill (c. 2 seconds), rises slightly in pitch and volume, then gradually descends and weakens as if squeezed. **SS** Northern Rufous-winged Antwren.

senex

Northern Rufous-winged Antwren
Herpsilochmus frater `LC`
Hormiguerito Alirrufo
Uncommon and local resident.
L 11.4 cm (4.5"). Races *exiguus*[A], *frater*[B]. Canopy of dry to moist forest borders, lighter woodland. To 1200 m. Behaviour like other *Herpsilochmus*; usually high, often difficult to see. **ID** ♂ bold head pattern, pale yellow underparts, rufous flight feathers. ♀ chestnut crown. **Voice** Song (*frater*) short (1.3 seconds) querulous trill (c. 2 kHz), abruptly rising (to c. 4 kHz), in middle where harsh, slightly descending at end, partly spread tail flicked downward with each note; ♀ shorter softer answer. **SS** Yellow-breasted Antwren. **TN** Usually treated as conspecific with *H. rufimarginatus* as Rufous-winged Antwren.

frater

Fasciated Antshrike *Cymbilaimus lineatus* `LC`
Batará Capirotado
Fairly common resident.
L 18 cm (7"). Races *fasciatus*[A], *intermedius*[B]. Vine tangles in humid lowland forest, old second growth. To 900 m. Aloof pairs, often concealed in foliage, movements deliberate; mostly mid-levels, sometimes with mixed flocks. **ID** Heavy bill, red eyes. ♂ finely barred black and white, black cap (*intermedius*), smaller cap (*fasciatus*). ♀ finely barred buff and black, upperparts barring coarser, chestnut cap. **Voice** Song 4–8 slow soft resonating whistles "cüwe-cüwe-...". Alarm sharp rattle. **SS** Undulated Antshrike.

intermedius

fasciatus

Great Antshrike *Taraba major* LC
Batará Grande

Ten subspecies in two subspecies groups; both in Colombia.

Western Great Antshrike
Taraba (major) transandeanus
Fairly common resident.
L 20 cm (8"). Races *obscurus*[A], *transandeanus*[B], *granadensis*[C]. Shrubby forest borders, overgrown clearings. To 1400 m (rarely 1800 m). Pairs keep to themselves, stay hidden 1–5 m up in dense undergrowth. **ID** Heavy black bill, shaggy crest, fire-red eyes. ♂ above black, three dotted white wingbars, below all white; or vent grey (*granadensis*). ♀ above mostly rufous; or face blackish (*granadensis*). **Voice** Song slowly accelerating ('bouncing ball') series of nasal chuckling notes "Cuk, cuk, cuk-cuk-...", nasal snarling "waaa" at end varies.

Eastern Great Antshrike *Taraba (major) major*
Fairly common resident.
L 20 cm (8"). Races *semifasciatus*[A], *melanurus*[B]. Shrubby *várzea* forest borders, overgrown clearings, river edges, Amazonian river islands. To 600 m. **ID** From western races by three solid white wingbars, white undertail-coverts, white tips on tail (from below). **Voice** Songs much like western forms, and like them may differ in note speed, song length, and terminal snarl (longer, brief or absent). **TN** Taxonomy needs re-evaluation; differences between eastern and western forms minor.

obscurus

♂

♀

♂

melanurus

♀

Undulated Antshrike *Frederickena unduliger* LC
Batará Ondulado

Four subspecies in two subspecies groups; only one definitely in Colombia.

Fulvous Antshrike *Frederickena (unduliger) fulva*
Batará Leonado
Rare or local resident.
L 23 cm (9"). One subspecies in group. Dense undergrowth inside humid *terra firme* forest and older second growth. To 500 m. Skulking pairs; often not very vocal, furtive and difficult to see. **ID** Heavy black bill. ♂ sooty black finely barred white, bushy crest. ♀ warm rusty brown, fine wavy black barring. **Voice** Song, 8–14 emphatic rising whistles in c. 6 seconds (like whistling for dog) "wuee, wuEE, wuEE...", on same pitch. **SS** Fasciated Antshrike, Undulated Antshrike (?).

Undulated Antshrike *Frederickena (unduliger) unduliger*
Batará Ondulado
Status uncertain.
L 23 cm (9"). Race *unduliger*. Listed (in error?) for extreme E Vaupés (where presumably possible). Sandy soil forests? (*unduliger*). **ID** Very like Fulvous Antshrike, differing in wavy barring of ♀ marginally brighter. **Voice** Song similar to *fulva* but faster, slightly rising; notes upslurred in *fulva*, more rounded up-down in *unduliger*. **TN** Molecular confirmation of taxonomic status needed.

♂

♀

♀

unduliger

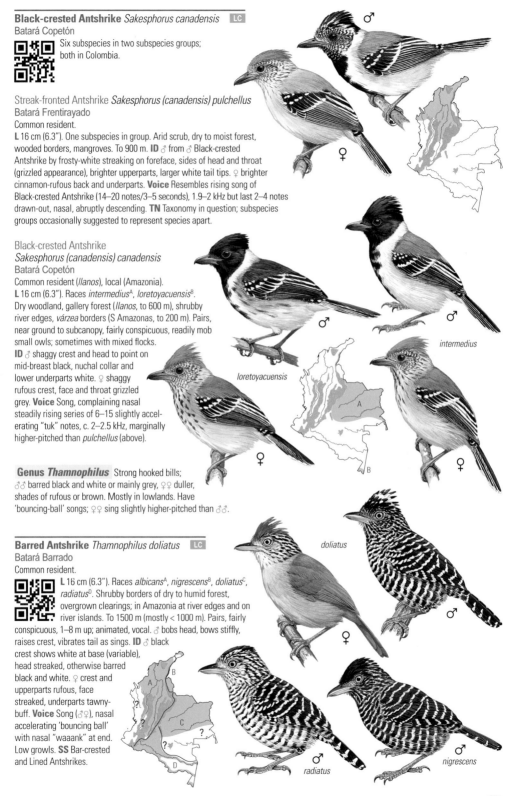

Black-crested Antshrike *Sakesphorus canadensis* LC
Batará Copetón

Six subspecies in two subspecies groups;
both in Colombia.

Streak-fronted Antshrike *Sakesphorus (canadensis) pulchellus*
Batará Frentirayado
Common resident.
L 16 cm (6.3"). One subspecies in group. Arid scrub, dry to moist forest,
wooded borders, mangroves. To 900 m. **ID** ♂ from ♂ Black-crested
Antshrike by frosty-white streaking on foreface, sides of head and throat
(grizzled appearance), brighter upperparts, larger white tail tips. ♀ brighter
cinnamon-rufous back and underparts. **Voice** Resembles rising song of
Black-crested Antshrike (14–20 notes/3–5 seconds), 1.9–2 kHz but last 2–4 notes
drawn-out, nasal, abruptly descending. **TN** Taxonomy in question; subspecies
groups occasionally suggested to represent species apart.

Black-crested Antshrike
Sakesphorus (canadensis) canadensis
Batará Copetón
Common resident (*llanos*), local (Amazonia).
L 16 cm (6.3"). Races *intermedius*[A], *loretoyacuensis*[B].
Dry woodland, gallery forest (*llanos*, to 600 m), shrubby
river edges, *várzea* borders (S Amazonas, to 200 m). Pairs,
near ground to subcanopy, fairly conspicuous, readily mob
small owls; sometimes with mixed flocks.
ID ♂ shaggy crest and head to point on
mid-breast black, nuchal collar and
lower underparts white. ♀ shaggy
rufous crest, face and throat grizzled
grey. **Voice** Song, complaining nasal
steadily rising series of 6–15 slightly accelerating "tuk" notes, c. 2–2.5 kHz, marginally
higher-pitched than *pulchellus* (above).

loretoyacuensis

intermedius

Genus *Thamnophilus* Strong hooked bills;
♂♂ barred black and white or mainly grey, ♀♀ duller,
shades of rufous or brown. Mostly in lowlands. Have
'bouncing-ball' songs; ♀♀ sing slightly higher-pitched than ♂♂.

Barred Antshrike *Thamnophilus doliatus* LC
Batará Barrado
Common resident.

L 16 cm (6.3"). Races *albicans*[A], *nigrescens*[B], *doliatus*[C],
radiatus[D]. Shrubby borders of dry to humid forest,
overgrown clearings; in Amazonia at river edges and on
river islands. To 1500 m (mostly < 1000 m). Pairs, fairly
conspicuous, 1–8 m up; animated, vocal. ♂ bobs head, bows stiffly,
raises crest, vibrates tail as sings. **ID** ♂ black
crest shows white at base (variable),
head streaked, otherwise barred
black and white. ♀ crest and
upperparts rufous, face
streaked, underparts tawny-
buff. **Voice** Song (♂♀), nasal
accelerating 'bouncing ball'
with nasal "waaank" at end.
Low growls. **SS** Bar-crested
and Lined Antshrikes.

doliatus

radiatus

nigrescens

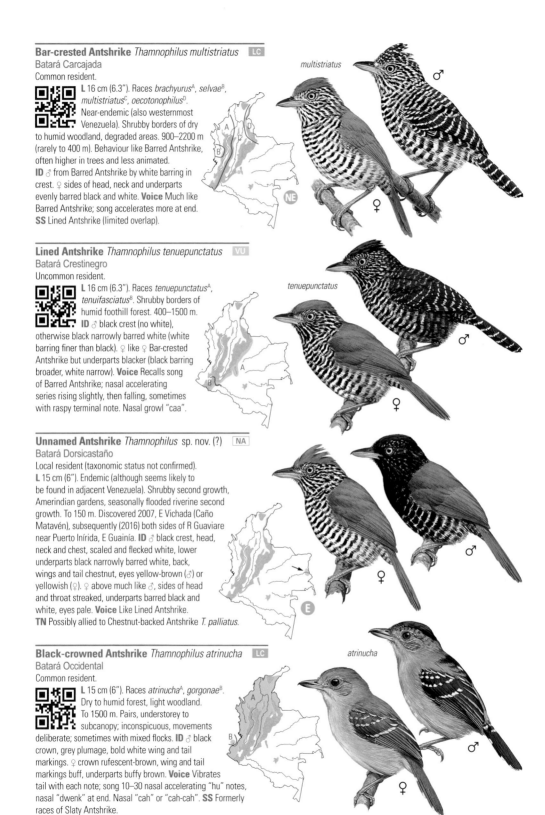

Bar-crested Antshrike *Thamnophilus multistriatus* `LC`
Batará Carcajada
Common resident.

multistriatus ♂

L 16 cm (6.3"). Races *brachyurus*[A], *selvae*[B], *multistriatus*[C], *oecotonophilus*[D]. Near-endemic (also westernmost Venezuela). Shrubby borders of dry to humid woodland, degraded areas. 900–2200 m (rarely to 400 m). Behaviour like Barred Antshrike, often higher in trees and less animated. **ID** ♂ from Barred Antshrike by white barring in crest. ♀ sides of head, neck and underparts evenly barred black and white. **Voice** Much like Barred Antshrike; song accelerates more at end. **SS** Lined Antshrike (limited overlap).

♀

Lined Antshrike *Thamnophilus tenuepunctatus* `VU`
Batará Crestinegro
Uncommon resident.

tenuepunctatus

L 16 cm (6.3"). Races *tenuepunctatus*[A], *tenuifasciatus*[B]. Shrubby borders of humid foothill forest. 400–1500 m. **ID** ♂ black crest (no white), otherwise black narrowly barred white (white barring finer than black). ♀ like ♀ Bar-crested Antshrike but underparts blacker (black barring broader, white narrow). **Voice** Recalls song of Barred Antshrike; nasal accelerating series rising slightly, then falling, sometimes with raspy terminal note. Nasal growl "caa".

♂

♀

Unnamed Antshrike *Thamnophilus* sp. nov. (?) `NA`
Batará Dorsicastaño
Local resident (taxonomic status not confirmed). L 15 cm (6"). Endemic (although seems likely to be found in adjacent Venezuela). Shrubby second growth, Amerindian gardens, seasonally flooded riverine second growth. To 150 m. Discovered 2007, E Vichada (Caño Matavén), subsequently (2016) both sides of R Guaviare near Puerto Inírida, E Guainía. **ID** ♂ black crest, head, neck and chest, scaled and flecked white, lower underparts black narrowly barred white, back, wings and tail chestnut, eyes yellow-brown (♂) or yellowish (♀). ♀ above much like ♂, sides of head and throat streaked, underparts barred black and white, eyes pale. **Voice** Like Lined Antshrike. **TN** Possibly allied to Chestnut-backed Antshrike *T. palliatus*.

♂

♀

Black-crowned Antshrike *Thamnophilus atrinucha* `LC`
Batará Occidental
Common resident.

atrinucha

L 15 cm (6"). Races *atrinucha*[A], *gorgonae*[B]. Dry to humid forest, light woodland. To 1500 m. Pairs, understorey to subcanopy; inconspicuous, movements deliberate; sometimes with mixed flocks. **ID** ♂ black crown, grey plumage, bold white wing and tail markings. ♀ crown rufescent-brown, wing and tail markings buff, underparts buffy brown. **Voice** Vibrates tail with each note; song 10–30 nasal accelerating "hu" notes, nasal "dwenk" at end. Nasal "cah" or "cah-cah". **SS** Formerly races of Slaty Antshrike.

♂

♀

Plain-winged Antshrike *Thamnophilus schistaceus* LC
Batará Pizarra

Three subspecies in two subspecies groups; both in Colombia.

Tefe Antshrike
Thamnophilus (schistaceus) heterogynus
Status unknown.
L 15 cm (6"). One subspecies in group. White-sand forests of Vaupés. **ID** Reddish eyes. ♂ uniform dark grey (no black cap). ♀ above dull rufous-brown, below paler, more ochraceous. **Voice** Nasal song (c. 8 notes/2.5 seconds), nearly identical to Plain-winged Antshrike, last few notes hurried, last descends: "ank . ank . ank . ank . ank, ank, ank, rac'keer". **SS** Mouse-colored Antshrike.

Plain-winged Antshrike
Thamnophilus (schistaceus) schistaceus
Fairly common resident.
L 15 cm (6"). Race *capitalis*. Humid lowland *terra firme* and especially *várzea* forest, infrequently borders. Sluggish pairs, mid- or lower levels, often with mixed flocks. **ID** Reddish eyes. ♂ uniform slate-grey, cap black, no wing dots. ♀ above drab olive-brown, contrasting rufous crown, below olive-buff. **Voice** Song (c. 6 notes/2.5 seconds) nasal lazy "ank, ank, ank, rac'keer", characteristic hiccup near end, last note hurried and downslurred. **SS** Mouse-colored Antshrike. **TN** Song of Tefe Antshrike (*heterogynus*; above) slightly faster, lower-pitched.

Mouse-colored Antshrike *Thamnophilus murinus* LC
Batará Ratón

Uncommon to fairly common resident.
L 15 cm (6"). Races *murinus*[A], *canipennis*[B]. White-sand forests, local in hilly *terra firme* forest in Amazonia. To 600 m. Pairs forage methodically, mid-levels or lower, sometimes with mixed flocks.
ID Eyes grey (usually) to brown, much like Plain-winged Antshrike. Look for ♂'s brownish-tinged wings (or greyish, *canipennis*), whitish-dotted wingbars, paler grey underparts, greyish-white belly. ♀ weakly contrasting chestnut brown crown, brownish wings and tail, faint buff-dotted wingbars. **Voice** Song, much like Plain-winged Antshrike, slightly accelerating series of up to 15 notes, last 1–2 briefer, higher-pitched (not abruptly dropping).

Black Antshrike *Thamnophilus nigriceps* LC
Batará Negro

Fairly common resident locally.
L 15 cm (6"). Monotypic. Humid lowland and foothill forest, borders. To c. 600 m (rarely 1400 m). Pairs forage at deliberate pace, mid-levels or lower, mostly independent of mixed flocks. **ID** ♂ uniform black, slight crest. ♀ unique, above rufous-brown, head and underparts black streaked buff. **Voice** Song, nasal slightly accelerating "kuok, kuok, kuok-ku-ku-ku-ku", tail flicked down with each note. Hollow "peero"; nasal growl.

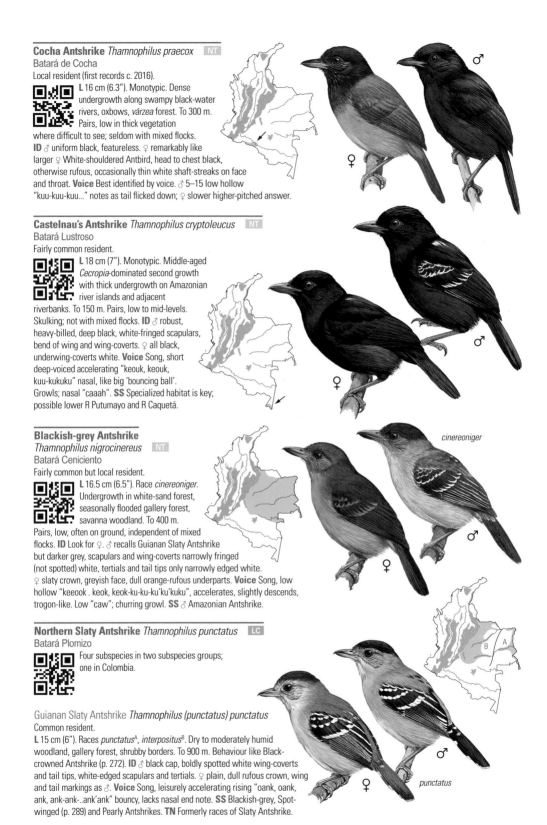

Cocha Antshrike *Thamnophilus praecox* NT
Batará de Cocha
Local resident (first records c. 2016).
L 16 cm (6.3"). Monotypic. Dense undergrowth along swampy black-water rivers, oxbows, *várzea* forest. To 300 m. Pairs, low in thick vegetation where difficult to see; seldom with mixed flocks. **ID** ♂ uniform black, featureless. ♀ remarkably like larger ♀ White-shouldered Antbird, head to chest black, otherwise rufous, occasionally thin white shaft-streaks on face and throat. **Voice** Best identified by voice. ♂ 5–15 low hollow "kuu-kuu-kuu..." notes as tail flicked down; ♀ slower higher-pitched answer.

Castelnau's Antshrike *Thamnophilus cryptoleucus* NT
Batará Lustroso
Fairly common resident.
L 18 cm (7"). Monotypic. Middle-aged *Cecropia*-dominated second growth with thick undergrowth on Amazonian river islands and adjacent riverbanks. To 150 m. Pairs, low to mid-levels. Skulking; not with mixed flocks. **ID** ♂ robust, heavy-billed, deep black, white-fringed scapulars, bend of wing and wing-coverts. ♀ all black, underwing-coverts white. **Voice** Song, short deep-voiced accelerating "keouk, keouk, kuu-kukuku" nasal, like big 'bouncing ball'. Growls; nasal "caaah". **SS** Specialized habitat is key; possible lower R Putumayo and R Caquetá.

Blackish-grey Antshrike
Thamnophilus nigrocinereus NT
Batará Ceniciento
Fairly common but local resident.
L 16.5 cm (6.5"). Race *cinereoniger*. Undergrowth in white-sand forest, seasonally flooded gallery forest, savanna woodland. To 400 m.
Pairs, low, often on ground, independent of mixed flocks. **ID** Look for ♀. ♂ recalls Guianan Slaty Antshrike but darker grey, scapulars and wing-coverts narrowly fringed (not spotted) white, tertials and tail tips only narrowly edged white. ♀ slaty crown, greyish face, dull orange-rufous underparts. **Voice** Song, low hollow "keeook . keok, keok-ku-ku-ku'ku'kuku", accelerates, slightly descends, trogon-like. Low "caw"; churring growl. **SS** ♂ Amazonian Antshrike.

Northern Slaty Antshrike *Thamnophilus punctatus* LC
Batará Plomizo
Four subspecies in two subspecies groups; one in Colombia.

Guianan Slaty Antshrike *Thamnophilus (punctatus) punctatus*
Common resident.
L 15 cm (6"). Races *punctatus*[A], *interpositus*[B]. Dry to moderately humid woodland, gallery forest, shrubby borders. To 900 m. Behaviour like Black-crowned Antshrike (p. 272). **ID** ♂ black cap, boldly spotted white wing-coverts and tail tips, white-edged scapulars and tertials. ♀ plain, dull rufous crown, wing and tail markings as ♂. **Voice** Song, leisurely accelerating rising "oank, oank, ank, ank-ank-..ank'ank" bouncy, lacks nasal end note. **SS** Blackish-grey, Spot-winged (p. 289) and Pearly Antshrikes. **TN** Formerly races of Slaty Antshrike.

cinereoniger

punctatus

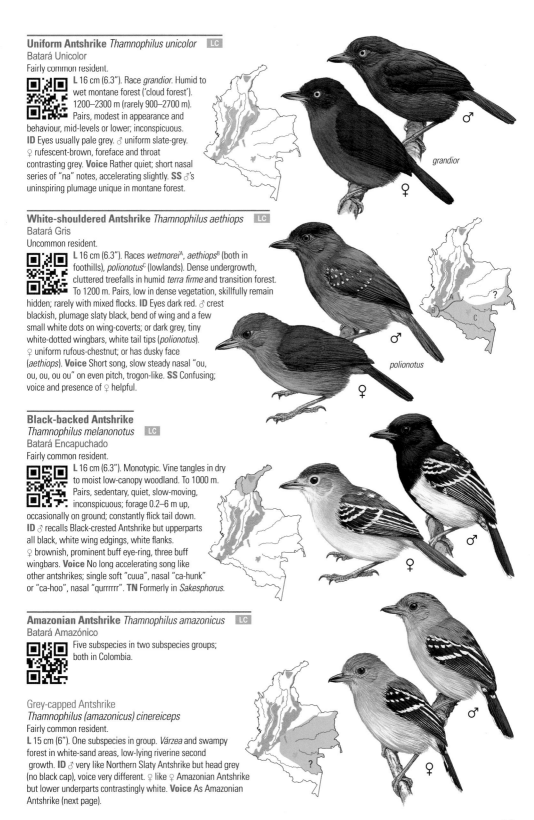

Uniform Antshrike *Thamnophilus unicolor* `LC`
Batará Unicolor

Fairly common resident.

L 16 cm (6.3"). Race *grandior*. Humid to wet montane forest ('cloud forest'). 1200–2300 m (rarely 900–2700 m). Pairs, modest in appearance and behaviour, mid-levels or lower; inconspicuous. **ID** Eyes usually pale grey. ♂ uniform slate-grey. ♀ rufescent-brown, foreface and throat contrasting grey. **Voice** Rather quiet; short nasal series of "na" notes, accelerating slightly. **SS** ♂'s uninspiring plumage unique in montane forest.

grandior

♂

♀

White-shouldered Antshrike *Thamnophilus aethiops* `LC`
Batará Gris

Uncommon resident.

L 16 cm (6.3"). Races *wetmorei*[A], *aethiops*[B] (both in foothills), *polionotus*[C] (lowlands). Dense undergrowth, cluttered treefalls in humid *terra firme* and transition forest. To 1200 m. Pairs, low in dense vegetation, skillfully remain hidden; rarely with mixed flocks. **ID** Eyes dark red. ♂ crest blackish, plumage slaty black, bend of wing and a few small white dots on wing-coverts; or dark grey, tiny white-dotted wingbars, white tail tips (*polionotus*). ♀ uniform rufous-chestnut; or has dusky face (*aethiops*). **Voice** Short song, slow steady nasal "ou, ou, ou, ou ou" on even pitch, trogon-like. **SS** Confusing; voice and presence of ♀ helpful.

♂

polionotus

♀

Black-backed Antshrike
Thamnophilus melanonotus `LC`
Batará Encapuchado

Fairly common resident.

L 16 cm (6.3"). Monotypic. Vine tangles in dry to moist low-canopy woodland. To 1000 m. Pairs, sedentary, quiet, slow-moving, inconspicuous; forage 0.2–6 m up, occasionally on ground; constantly flick tail down. **ID** ♂ recalls Black-crested Antshrike but upperparts all black, white wing edgings, white flanks. ♀ brownish, prominent buff eye-ring, three buff wingbars. **Voice** No long accelerating song like other antshrikes; single soft "cuua", nasal "ca-hunk" or "ca-hoo", nasal "qurrrrrr". **TN** Formerly in *Sakesphorus*.

♀

♂

Amazonian Antshrike *Thamnophilus amazonicus* `LC`
Batará Amazónico

Five subspecies in two subspecies groups; both in Colombia.

Grey-capped Antshrike
Thamnophilus (amazonicus) cinereiceps
Fairly common resident.

L 15 cm (6"). One subspecies in group. *Várzea* and swampy forest in white-sand areas, low-lying riverine second growth. **ID** ♂ very like Northern Slaty Antshrike but head grey (no black cap), voice very different. ♀ like ♀ Amazonian Antshrike but lower underparts contrastingly white. **Voice** As Amazonian Antshrike (next page).

♂

♀

Amazonian Antshrike
Thamnophilus (amazonicus) amazonicus
Fairly common resident.
L 15 cm (6"). Race *amazonicus*. Black-water
várzea in Amazonian, nutrient-poor sandy soil
areas, borders. To 500 m. Pairs, mid-levels
or lower, often independent of mixed flocks.
ID ♂ like Northern Slaty Antshrike including
black cap (but voice differs). ♀ crown rufous-
chestnut, otherwise head, neck and underparts
orange-rufous. **Voice** Rapid accelerating roll, swelling
in volume, then slowing; fanned tail vibrates with each
note. **SS** If in doubt look for ♀ or note voice and habitat.

amazonicus
♂
♀

Spiny-faced Antshrike *Xenornis setifrons* VU
Hormiguero de Tacarcuna VU
Rare and local resident.

L 15 cm (6"). Monotypic. Undergrowth in humid
foothill and premontane forest. 150–600 m
(higher?). Pairs, fairly active, often with
mixed flocks; use horizontal and vertical
perches, sally to foliage. **ID** Greyish eyes. ♂ above
brownish spotted and streaked buff, spotted buff
wingbars, underparts dark grey. ♀ above much
like ♂, below paler, brownish, somewhat streaked.
Voice Often quiet; song c. 4–10 thin notably high notes
(c. 3/second), rising in pitch (3.5–5.5 kHz). Call descending
"teeeaaar"; or "chak". **AN** Speckled Antshrike.

♀
♂

Genus *Cercomacra* Mid-sized, slender-billed, slender-bodied,
with longish graduated white-tipped tails. In dense low shrubbery,
or (one species) high vine tangles. Formerly included *Cercomacroides*.

Grey Antbird *Cercomacra cinerascens* LC
Hormiguero Nagüiblanco
Common resident.

L 15 cm (6"). Race *cinerascens*. Mid-level and
canopy vine tangles in humid lowland forest,
older second growth. To 800 m. Pairs, stay high
in massive vine tangles where often heard but
difficult to see. **ID** ♂ faint white-dotted wingbars, white
tail tips (also often faint). ♀ plain and dull, underparts buffy
ochre. **Voice** Song, rising-falling "crook-shank..." repeated
several times, best clue to its presence. **SS** See *Cercomacroides*.

cinerascens
♂
♀

Jet Antbird *Cercomacra nigricans* LC
Hormiguero Yeguá
Locally common resident.
L 14.7 cm (5.8"). Monotypic. Shrubby borders
of dry to humid forest, vine-tangled second
growth, often near water or in low-lying
areas. To 1500 m. Pairs skulk, low to
mid-levels, often difficult to see. **ID** ♂ black, white
wingbars and shoulders, bold white tail tips from
below. ♀ dark grey, throat to mid-breast streaked and
freckled white. **Voice** ♂ song, harsh halting "chék-off,
chék-off..." (second note swallowed); in duet ♀ may overlap
with gravelly "karump, karump...", producing antiphonal
"chék-kor-rump...".

♂
♀

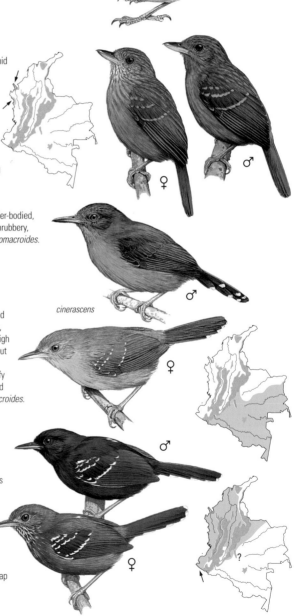

Northern Chestnut-tailed Antbird (Zimmer's Antbird)
Sciaphylax castanea `LC`
Hormiguero Colicastaño Norteño
Uncommon and local resident (few records).

 L 13 cm (5"). Race *centunculorum*. Undergrowth in humid lowland forest. To 500 m (higher southward). Pairs, on or close to ground in thickets, old treefalls; not with mixed flocks. **ID** ♂ grey head, black bib, buff-white wingbars, rufous rump and tail. ♀ browner, throat and chest orange-rufous. **Voice** Song, 4–6 thin notes (3–4 kHz), gradually upscale, hurried at end: "teeeee, teeee, tee-te-te'te".

centunculorum

Genus *Cercomacroides* Thin-billed and slender-bodied, with longish graduated tails. Grey to blackish; concealed white inter-scapular patch. ♂♂ quite similar; ♀♀ dull rufous to ochraceous below. Usually not with mixed flocks. Best identified by voice. Pairs sing partly overlapping duets.

Blackish Antbird *Cercomacroides nigrescens* `LC`
Hormiguero Ceniciento
Status uncertain (few records).

 L 15 cm (6"). Race *aequatorialis*. Dense thickets, shrubby forest borders, second growth in foothills of Putumayo/Nariño border. Probably c. 600–1500 m. Pairs, low, often near ground; retiring. **ID** ♂ blackish grey, obscure white fringing on wing-coverts. ♀ above olive-brown, tail blackish, forehead, face and underparts orange-rufous. **Voice** Song, ♂ single low note, then stronger, accelerating, slightly descending rattling "querk...CUE, Cue, cu-cu-cu-cu'cu'cu"; ♀ answers with softer whistles. **SS** Riparian Antbird.

aequatorialis

Riparian Antbird *Cercomacroides fuscicauda* `LC`
Hormiguero Ribereño
Fairly common resident (restricted habitat).

L 15 cm (6"). Monotypic. Damp seasonally flooded thickets with cane (*Gynerium*) and *Heliconia*, wet areas along creeks. To 500 m. Skulking pairs. **ID** ♂ marginally paler but inseparable from Blackish Antbird except by voice. ♀ from ♀ Blackish by voice, crown not contrasting strongly with sides of head. **Voice** Song, ♂ loud "bal-PEEEeeeeer", second part trilled, louder, gradually descending, slightly buzzy as ♀ sings overlapping rising series of 6–7 notes, "pier, pier, pier...". **SS** Blackish Antbird. **TN** Formerly a race of Blackish Antbird.

Parker's Antbird *Cercomacroides parkeri* `LC`
Hormiguero de Parker
Local resident.

L 15 cm (6"). Monotypic. Endemic. Thickets in regenerating light gaps, shrubby borders of humid and wet montane forest. 1100–2200 m. **ID** Much like Dusky Antbird (including behaviour), but voice and elevational distribution differ; ♀ brighter, more orange-rufous below. **Voice** Loose rattling song recalls Dusky Antbird but higher-pitched, notes downward-inflected; first 2–3 of series usually rise, rest gradually quicken, then decline in pitch and volume; ♀ often overlaps ♂ midway with rattling notes. **TN** Formerly a race of Dusky Antbird.

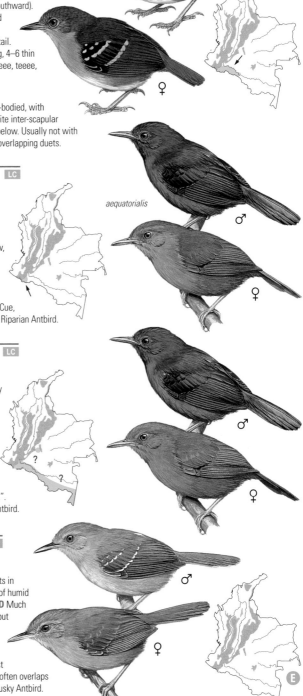

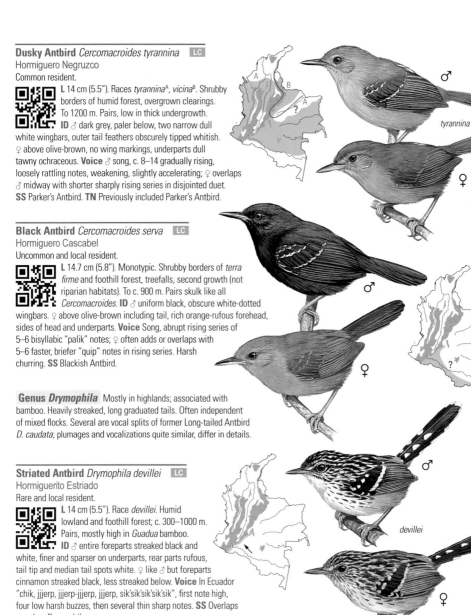

Dusky Antbird *Cercomacroides tyrannina* `LC`
Hormiguero Negruzco
Common resident.

L 14 cm (5.5"). Races *tyrannina*[A], *vicina*[B]. Shrubby borders of humid forest, overgrown clearings. To 1200 m. Pairs, low in thick undergrowth. **ID** ♂ dark grey, paler below, two narrow dull white wingbars, outer tail feathers obscurely tipped whitish. ♀ above olive-brown, no wing markings, underparts dull tawny ochraceous. **Voice** ♂ song, c. 8–14 gradually rising, loosely rattling notes, weakening, slightly accelerating; ♀ overlaps ♂ midway with shorter sharply rising series in disjointed duet. **SS** Parker's Antbird. **TN** Previously included Parker's Antbird.

tyrannina
♂
♀

Black Antbird *Cercomacroides serva* `LC`
Hormiguero Cascabel
Uncommon and local resident.

L 14.7 cm (5.8"). Monotypic. Shrubby borders of *terra firme* and foothill forest, treefalls, second growth (not riparian habitats). To c. 900 m. Pairs skulk like all *Cercomacroides*. **ID** ♂ uniform black, obscure white-dotted wingbars. ♀ above olive-brown including tail, rich orange-rufous forehead, sides of head and underparts. **Voice** Song, abrupt rising series of 5–6 bisyllabic "palik" notes; ♀ often adds or overlaps with 5–6 faster, briefer "quip" notes in rising series. Harsh churring. **SS** Blackish Antbird.

♂
♀

Genus *Drymophila* Mostly in highlands; associated with bamboo. Heavily streaked, long graduated tails. Often independent of mixed flocks. Several are vocal splits of former Long-tailed Antbird *D. caudata*; plumages and vocalizations quite similar, differ in details.

Striated Antbird *Drymophila devillei* `LC`
Hormiguerito Estriado
Rare and local resident.

L 14 cm (5.5"). Race *devillei*. Humid lowland and foothill forest; c. 300–1000 m. Pairs, mostly high in *Guadua* bamboo. **ID** ♂ entire foreparts streaked black and white, finer and sparser on underparts, rear parts rufous, tail tip and median tail spots white. ♀ like ♂ but foreparts cinnamon streaked black, less streaked below. **Voice** In Ecuador "chik, jjjerp, jjjerp-jjjerp, jjjerp, sik'sik'sik'sik'sik", first note high, four low harsh buzzes, then several thin sharp notes. **SS** Overlaps no other *Drymophila*.

♂
devillei
♀

Klages's Antbird *Drymophila klagesi* `LC`
Hormiguerito Rabilargo
Fairly common but local resident.

L 15 cm (6"). Monotypic. *Chusquea* bamboo in humid montane forest, occasionally away from bamboo. 1500–2700 m (lower). **ID** Like East Andean Antbird but throat to mid-breast have fewer black shaft-streaks. **Voice** Unusual, but very like Santa Marta Antbird. ♂ two bouncy notes, then two higher louder wheezy asthmatic phrases "chuet, chuet, pa-FJEEE-jit, pa-FJEEE-jit"; midway in song ♀ adds soft descending "tu, tu, tu, tu, tu" in loose overlapping duet. **SS** Overlaps no other *Drymophila*.

♂
♀

Santa Marta Antbird *Drymophila hellmayri* NT
Hormiguerito de Santa Marta
Common resident.

L 15 cm (6"). Monotypic. Endemic. Native and non-native bamboo in humid montane forest, occasionally away from bamboo. 800–2150 m. **ID** Both sexes very like respective sexes of East Andean Antbird, but tail dusky rufous with black subterminal band; ♂ median rear crown blackish. **Voice** Vocally similar to other *Drymophila*, nearly identical to Klages's; ♀ may overlap midway with softer descending note and harsh end note. **SS** Overlaps no other *Drymophila*.

East Andean Antbird *Drymophila caudata* NT
Hormiguerito Rabilargo
Fairly common resident.

L 15 cm (6"). Monotypic. Endemic. Range fragmented, only E Andes (W Santander, upper Magdalena Valley). Humid montane forest with *Chusquea* bamboo, c. 1500–2700 m. **ID** ♂ foreparts to mid-back and mid-breast heavily streaked black and white, rear parts tawny-rufous, tail blackish boldly tipped white (no white central spots), mid-crown to hindcrown black. ♀ foreparts streaked cinnamon and black. **Voice** Song much like other *Drymophila*; ♂ differs from Klages's and Santa Marta Antbirds principally in 4–6 (not two) introductory notes. **SS** Not known to overlap other *Drymophila*.

Streak-headed Antbird
Drymophila striaticeps LC
Hormiguerito Rabilargo
Fairly common resident.

L 15 cm (6"). Races *striaticeps*[A], *occidentalis*[B]. *Chusquea* bamboo in humid montane forest, c. 1400–2800 m. **ID** ♂ and ♀ essentially identical to respective sexes of East Andean Antbird but ♂ lacks black on rear crown. **Voice** Much like others of genus (cf. Klages's Antbird); song has 4–6 (rather than two) rising introductory notes like East Andean Antbird; ♀ differences minor. **SS** Not known to overlap other *Drymophila*.

Genus *Hypocnemis* Relatively small, chunky, and short-tailed. Markings handsome but not crisp. Lower levels inside forest. Raspy songs.

Yellow-browed Antbird *Hypocnemis hypoxantha* LC
Hormiguero Cejiamarillo
Uncommon resident.

L 13 cm (5"). Race *hypoxantha*. Undergrowth inside humid *terra firme* forest. To 500 m. Pairs 1–10 m up inside forest, inconspicuous, infrequently with mixed flocks. **ID** Bright yellow eyebrow, rich yellow underparts streaked black at sides. **Voice** Song descending series of 5–10 notes, initially clean but progressively rougher, more raspy; tonal quality recalls Peruvian Warbling-antbird but slower. **SS** Peruvian Warbling-antbird. **AN** Yellow-browed Antwarbler.

striaticeps

hypoxantha

Imeri Warbling-antbird *Hypocnemis flavescens* `LC`
Hormiguero Cantarín
Fairly common resident.

 L 13 cm (5"). Monotypic. Undergrowth and treefall gaps inside humid white-sand forest, savanna woodland. To 300 m. **ID** Much like Peruvian Warbling-antbird but upperparts paler, throat and chest usually tinged yellow, streaking minimal or lacking except at sides; ♀ duller. **Voice** ♂ song resembles Peruvian Warbling-antbird; 8–10 notes on same pitch (not descending), last three raspy, louder and slowing. ♀ answers with softer descending series. Call semi-musical nasal "wheeu'd-d-d". **TN** Formerly a race of Warbling-antbird *H. cantator*. **AN** Imeri Antwarbler.

Peruvian Warbling-antbird *Hypocnemis peruviana* `LC`
Hormiguero Peruano
Common resident.

 L 13 cm (5"). Race *saturata*. Undergrowth, treefall gaps, creek-sides in humid lowland forest. **ID** ♂ head and back heavily streaked black, throat white liberally streaked and spotted black. ♀ duller, browner. **Voice** ♂ song, c. 8–10 notes on same pitch or slightly descending with last 5–6 raspy. **SS** Imeri Warbling-antbird. **TN** Formerly a race of Warbling-antbird *H. cantator*. **AN** Peruvian Antwarbler.

saturata

Ocellated Antbird *Phaenostictus mcleannani* `LC`
Hormiguero Ocelado
Uncommon resident.

 L 20 cm (8"). Races *mcleannani*[A], *pacificus*[B]. Undergrowth in humid and wet lowland and foothill forest, tall second growth. To 900 m. Wary, suspicious, obligate army ant follower. Singles, pairs or family clans cling to vertical saplings, drop to ground, dominate other ant followers. **ID** Bare blue facial skin, orange-rufous collar, spotted plumage, pink legs. **Voice** Song, long series of whistles, ascending, then descending, rough at end: "pee, pee, pee, pee,-pee-le-te'e'e'e'e'e'pe peer peer charr".

mcleannani

White-plumed Antbird *Pithys albifrons* `LC`
Hormiguero Empenachado
Common resident (ant swarms).

 L 13 cm (5"). Race *peruvianus*. Undergrowth in humid *terra firme* forest in Amazonian and white-sand areas. To 1100 m. Obligate army ant follower, often many together at swarms but wary (be patient). Clings to vertical saplings, darts to ground. **ID** Two upstanding white tufts plus white 'beard', black head, chestnut collar and underparts, bright yellow legs. **Voice** Song, high descending "seeeer". Buzzy "chirr" when disturbed or alarmed.

peruvianus

Common Scale-backed Antbird *Willisornis poecilinotus* `LC`
Hormiguero Escamado
Fairly common resident.

L 13.5 cm (5.3"). Races *duidae*[A], *lepidonota*[B]. Undergrowth in humid *terra firme* forest. To 800 m. Singles, pairs, confiding, attend army ant swarms where dominated by larger species; frequently also away from swarms. **ID** ♂ back, wing-coverts and tertials scalloped white (conspicuous), white central tail spots. ♀ white markings like ♂, head cinnamon-rufous, duller below (*duidae*) or head and underparts dull rufous-brown (*lepidonota*). **Voice** Song, c. 10 slow quavering "preeeeee" whistles, each a half-tone above previous. **SS** *Hylophylax* antbirds.

duidae

♂

♀

lepidonota

Black-spotted Bare-eye *Phlegopsis nigromaculata* `LC`
Hormiguero Caripelado
Fairly common resident.

L 19 cm (7.5"). Race *nigromaculata*. Undergrowth in *várzea* and transition forest, less common in *terra firme*, very local in white-sand regions. To 500 m. Pairs or families; obligate army ant follower, dominant at swarms. Wary, difficult to approach. **ID** Bare red ocular area, back and wing-coverts brown spotted black, and flight feathers and tail rufous-chestnut. **Voice** Heard far more than seen; song, 2–4 notes, each lower than preceding "skreeeup . zeeeew . zeeeeew", last two harsh, buzzy. Alarm descending "chirr".

nigromaculata

Reddish-winged Bare-eye *Phlegopsis erythroptera* `LC`
Hormiguero Pavo
Rare to uncommon resident.

L 19 cm (7.5"). Race *erythroptera*. Undergrowth in *terra firme* forest. To 500 m. Pairs or families; obligate army ant follower. Notably wary, secretive. **ID** Bare red ocular skin. ♂ white scallops on back and wing-coverts, rufous wingbars, flight feathers mostly rufous. ♀ head and underparts rufescent-brown, two bold white wingbars, tertials tipped white. **Voice** Song, descending series of 4–6 rising-falling notes "skee, skea, skeer, skeer .. skeeea", (4–3 kHz), penetrating, almost squealing, then buzzy, slowing at end. Call descending "PEuur".

erythroptera

♂

♀

Bicolored Antbird *Gymnopithys bicolor* `LC`
Hormiguero Bicolor
Fairly common resident.

L 14.5 cm (5.7"). Races *bicolor*[A], *daguae*[B], *aequatorialis*[C], *ruficeps*[D]. To 900 m. Undergrowth in humid and wet forest, old second growth. Singles, pairs or several; obligate army ant follower. Wary but habituate with patience; cling to vertical saplings. **ID** Bare ocular area grey to pale blue, grey post-ocular, or post-ocular and cheeks black (*ruficeps*). **Voice** Usually first noted by song or alarm. Song, rapid rising-falling series of ringing whistles "whee, whee, WHE WHE-we-pe'pe'pe'pe'p'p". Alarm, harsh descending "jiiiir"; loud "chip-ip".

ruficeps

aequatorialis

bicolor

White-cheeked Antbird *Gymnopithys leucaspis* `LC`
Hormiguero Cariblanco
Fairly common resident.

 L 14.5 cm (5.7"). Races *leucaspis*[A], *castaneus*[B], *lateralis*[C]. Undergrowth in humid lowland and foothill forest. To 900 m. **ID** Much like Bicolored Antbird (W of Andes); bare ocular ring pale blue, black band through eyes and down neck to flanks, lower cheeks white. **Voice** Recalls Bicolored Antbird, songs may show more variation. **TN** Has been treated as conspecific with Bicolored Antbird.

leucaspis

Chestnut-crested Antbird
Rhegmatorhina cristata `LC`
Hormiguero Colorado
Uncommon resident.

 L 15 cm (6"). Monotypic. Dense undergrowth in humid sandy soil forests of Vaupés region. To 250 m. Singles, pairs or families; obligate army ant swarm follower. Quite wary. **ID** Bare light blue ocular area ('goggle-eyed'), bushy crest, black face, chestnut plumage. ♀ less crested, dark marks on back. **Voice** Song initially rises in pitch and volume, last few notes descend and fade: "wer, weEER WEEER, WEer, weer, wer, we". Alarm low buzzy "chirr".

♂

♀

Hairy-crested Antbird
Rhegmatorhina melanosticta `LC`
Hormiguero Crestado

 Three subspecies in two subspecies groups; one in Colombia.

melanosticta

Hairy-crested Antbird
Rhegmatorhina (melanosticta) melanosticta
Uncommon resident.
L 15 cm (6"). Race *melanosticta*. Undergrowth, mainly humid *terra firme* forest. To 700 m. Behaviour as Chestnut-crested Antbird. **ID** ♂ bushy greyish-white crest, bare bluish ocular ring (like 'goggles'), black face, above dark brown, nuchal collar and underparts paler. ♀ black spotting on back and wing-coverts. Juv spotted back, dusky crown. **Voice** Song 5–7 slow whistles, "weeeeeeer, weer, weer, weer, weeeeeeaar", first and last notes long drawn, series slightly rising then falling. Call "chip-it"; alarm buzzy "churr".

♂

♀

Spotted Antbird *Hylophylax naevioides* `LC`
Hormiguero Collarejo
Fairly common resident.

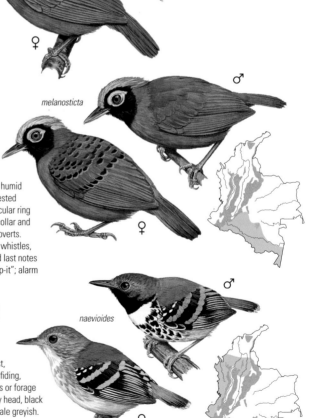

naevioides

L 11.4 cm (4.5"). Race *naevioides*. Undergrowth inside humid and wet forest, old second growth. To 1000 m. Pairs, confiding, cling to saplings, follow army ant swarms or forage independent of them. **ID** Attractively patterned. ♂ grey head, black throat, bold necklace on white breast. ♀ duller, head pale greyish. **Voice** Song, high, rhythmic "puweety, weety weety weety, weety, weety", first note rises, rest gradually descend. Alarm buzzy "chirr"; sharp "peep".

♂

♀

Spot-backed Antbird *Hylophylax naevius* `LC`
Hormiguero de Gargantilla
Fairly common resident.

 L 11.4 cm (4.5"). Race *naevius*.
Undergrowth in humid lowland and foothill forest, especially dense cluttered understorey, old second growth. To 1100 m. Behaviour like Spotted Antbird. **ID** ♂ grey head, black throat, bold necklace on white underparts, back spotted white. ♀ duller, throat white (not black), reduced black necklace on buff underparts, wingbars and spots on back buff (not white). **Voice** Rhythmic song recalls Spotted Antbird but more variable (5–12 couplets), initial couplet emphatic, first 2–3 couplets rise, rest gradually descend: "pée-be, pée-be, PEE-BE, PEE-be, pée-be ...". Soft buzzy "shiiiir" alarm. **SS** Dot-backed Antbird.

naevius

Dot-backed Antbird *Hylophylax punctulatus* `LC`
Hormiguero Dorsipunteado
Uncommon and local resident.

 L 11.4 cm (4.5"). Monotypic. Undergrowth in *várzea* forest, black-water streams. To 400 m. Pairs, often wary, cling to saplings or perch 0.5–4 m up; not with mixed flocks or army ants. **ID** Much like Spot-backed Antbird. ♂ differs in diagnostic greyish-white cheeks, dark (not pink) tarsi, black (not rufescent) tail, but spots on rump difficult to see. ♀ similar but throat white with black malar. **Voice** Song, emphatic series of rising-falling couplets "weE'PEo!", c. 1 couplet/second or slower. Call descending "peeap"; sharp "pip'pip". **SS** Spot-backed Antbird.

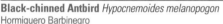

Black-chinned Antbird *Hypocnemoides melanopogon* `LC`
Hormiguero Barbinegro
Common resident.

 L 12.2 cm (4.8"). Race *melanopogon*. Stream-sides in *várzea* forest, gallery forest, poorly drained white-sand forest. To 500 m. Confiding pairs forage alone, very low over water, below shrubby vegetation; rarely far from water. **ID** ♂ grey, black throat, three white-fringed wingbars, tail minutely tipped white. ♀ underparts whitish clouded grey. **Voice** Song, accelerating "psheep, psheep, eep ep-ep-e-e-e'e'e' weep-weep-jeep-jeep", slowing, raspy at end. Alarm "pée'chup".
SS Silvered Antbird, also Band-tailed Antbird (p. 553).

melanopogon

Silvered Antbird *Sclateria naevia* `LC`
Hormiguero Plateado
Common resident.

L 15 cm (6"). Race *argentata*. Edge of oxbow lakes, stream-sides, *Mauritia* palm swamps. To 500 m. Pairs, alone, on ground at water's edge or very low in vegetation near or over water; glean from surface of water. **ID** ♂ long bill, pink legs, greyish-white underparts, and tiny white-dotted wingbars. ♀ above brownish, sides of face, breast and flanks pale rufous-brown. **Voice** Song loud ringing crescendo, accelerates, then diminishes: "tweep twep, tip-tip-tip-tip-ti'ti'ti'ti'Tl'Tl'Tl' Tl'ti'ti'ti'i'iiiii" (c. 4 seconds). Bubbly "pup'pup"; alarm "chit-it". **SS** Black-chinned Antbird.

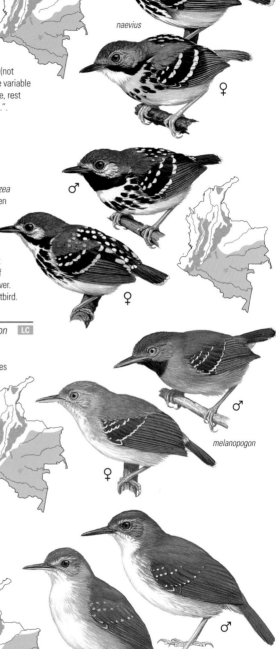
argentata

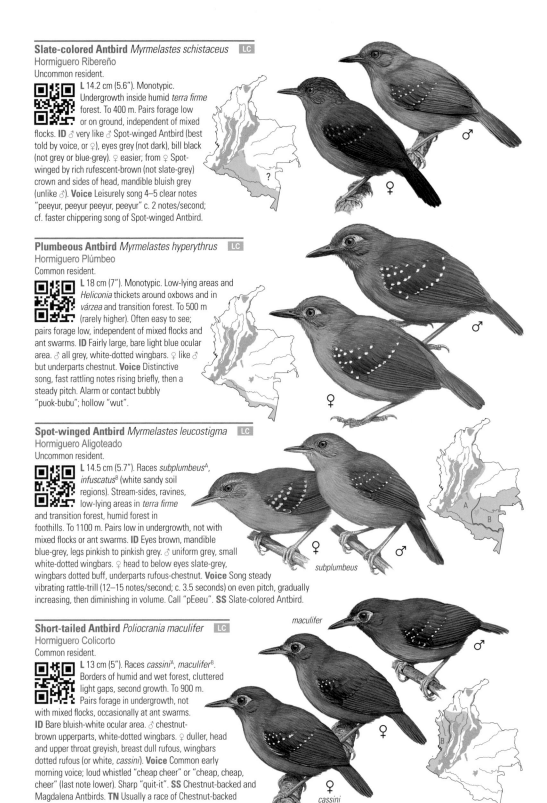

Slate-colored Antbird *Myrmelastes schistaceus* `LC`
Hormiguero Ribereño
Uncommon resident.

L 14.2 cm (5.6"). Monotypic. Undergrowth inside humid *terra firme* forest. To 400 m. Pairs forage low or on ground, independent of mixed flocks. **ID** ♂ very like ♂ Spot-winged Antbird (best told by voice, or ♀), eyes grey (not dark), bill black (not grey or blue-grey). ♀ easier; from ♀ Spot-winged by rich rufescent-brown (not slate-grey) crown and sides of head, mandible bluish grey (unlike ♂). **Voice** Leisurely song 4–5 clear notes "peeyur, peeyur peeyur, peeyur" c. 2 notes/second; cf. faster chippering song of Spot-winged Antbird.

Plumbeous Antbird *Myrmelastes hyperythrus* `LC`
Hormiguero Plúmbeo
Common resident.

L 18 cm (7"). Monotypic. Low-lying areas and *Heliconia* thickets around oxbows and in *várzea* and transition forest. To 500 m (rarely higher). Often easy to see; pairs forage low, independent of mixed flocks and ant swarms. **ID** Fairly large, bare light blue ocular area. ♂ all grey, white-dotted wingbars. ♀ like ♂ but underparts chestnut. **Voice** Distinctive song, fast rattling notes rising briefly, then a steady pitch. Alarm or contact bubbly "puok-bubu"; hollow "wut".

Spot-winged Antbird *Myrmelastes leucostigma* `LC`
Hormiguero Aligoteado
Uncommon resident.

L 14.5 cm (5.7"). Races *subplumbeus*[A], *infuscatus*[B] (white sandy soil regions). Stream-sides, ravines, low-lying areas in *terra firme* and transition forest, humid forest in foothills. To 1100 m. Pairs low in undergrowth, not with mixed flocks or ant swarms. **ID** Eyes brown, mandible blue-grey, legs pinkish to pinkish grey. ♂ uniform grey, small white-dotted wingbars. ♀ head to below eyes slate-grey, wingbars dotted buff, underparts rufous-chestnut. **Voice** Song steady vibrating rattle-trill (12–15 notes/second; c. 3.5 seconds) on even pitch, gradually increasing, then diminishing in volume. Call "pEeeu". **SS** Slate-colored Antbird.

subplumbeus

Short-tailed Antbird *Poliocrania maculifer* `LC`
Hormiguero Colicorto
Common resident.

L 13 cm (5"). Races *cassini*[A], *maculifer*[B]. Borders of humid and wet forest, cluttered light gaps, second growth. To 900 m. Pairs forage in undergrowth, not with mixed flocks, occasionally at ant swarms. **ID** Bare bluish-white ocular area. ♂ chestnut-brown upperparts, white-dotted wingbars. ♀ duller, head and upper throat greyish, breast dull rufous, wingbars dotted rufous (or white, *cassini*). **Voice** Common early morning voice; loud whistled "cheap cheer" or "cheap, cheap, cheer" (last note lower). Sharp "quit-it". **SS** Chestnut-backed and Magdalena Antbirds. **TN** Usually a race of Chestnut-backed Antbird; species status needs confirmation.

maculifer

cassini

Chestnut-backed Antbird *Poliocrania exsul* `LC`
Hormiguero Dorsicastaño
Common resident (Panama border).

 L 13 cm (5"). Race *niglarus*. Shrubby borders of humid and wet forest, cluttered light gaps, second growth. To 900 m. Behaviour and voice identical to Short-tailed Antbird. **ID** From ♂ and ♀ Short-tailed Antbird by lack of wing dots (presence or absence variable), tail slightly longer. **TN** See Short-tailed Antbird.

Stub-tailed Antbird *Sipia berlepschi* `LC`
Hormiguero Colimocho
Fairly common but local resident.

 L 13.2 cm (5.2"). Monotypic. Near-endemic (also far NW Ecuador). Lowland and foothill wet forest, especially treefalls, light gaps. To 400 m (rarely higher). Pairs, close to ground, occasionally at army ant swarms. **ID** Eyes reddish brown. ♂ uniformly black, semi-concealed white inter-scapular patch. ♀ 2–3 white-dotted wingbars, underparts spotted white. **Voice** Song 7–10 slow downslurred notes, series slightly lower in middle "chik, chu, chu…chú, chú". Call metallic "si'lik". **SS** Esmeraldas Antbird.

Esmeraldas Antbird *Sipia nigricauda* `LC`
Hormiguero de Esmeraldas
Uncommon resident.

 L 14 cm (5.5"). Monotypic. Undergrowth in humid and wet forest (mainly foothills), especially dense vegetation in ravines. 150–1250 m. Pairs, hop on ground, logs, cling to saplings, occasionally at ant swarms; retiring, inconspicuous. **ID** Red eyes. ♂ sooty black, 2–3 white-dotted wingbars. ♀ back, wings and tail dark reddish brown, buff- (or white-) dotted wingbars, throat scaled white. **Voice** Weak song, short thin, high-pitched (5–6 kHz) "eek-eek, seek-seek-seek, seet", triplet lower, final note or two highest. Downslurred "jeer".

Magdalena Antbird *Sipia palliata* `NT`
Hormiguero del Magdalena
Local resident.

L 14 cm (5.5"). Monotypic. Near-endemic (also adjacent W Venezuela). Dense cluttered undergrowth in humid lowland forest, especially hill or broken forest. To 1100 m. Behaviour like Esmeraldas Antbird. **ID** ♂ recalls ♂ Short-tailed Antbird (race *cassini*) but lacks bare ocular skin, underparts grey with black throat. ♀ almost identical to ♀ Esmeraldas Antbird, but duller rufous rear parts. **Voice** Weak song, high (4.5–6 kHz) thin intense "see, ee-ee-ee-ee, eek", first note slightly lower, last highest. Call descending "jeeurp". **SS** Esmeraldas Antbird (no overlap).

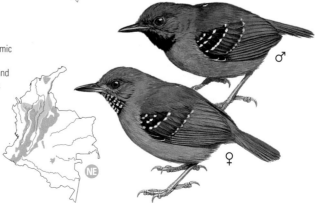

285

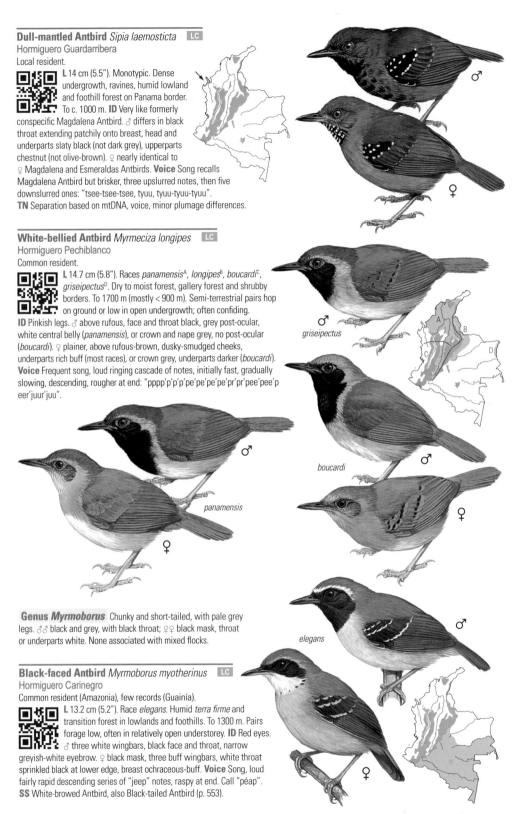

Dull-mantled Antbird *Sipia laemosticta* `LC`
Hormiguero Guardarribera
Local resident.
L 14 cm (5.5"). Monotypic. Dense undergrowth, ravines, humid lowland and foothill forest on Panama border. To c. 1000 m. **ID** Very like formerly conspecific Magdalena Antbird. ♂ differs in black throat extending patchily onto breast, head and underparts slaty black (not dark grey), upperparts chestnut (not olive-brown). ♀ nearly identical to ♀ Magdalena and Esmeraldas Antbirds. **Voice** Song recalls Magdalena Antbird but brisker, three upslurred notes, then five downslurred ones: "tsee-tsee-tsee, tyuu, tyuu-tyuu-tyuu". **TN** Separation based on mtDNA, voice, minor plumage differences.

White-bellied Antbird *Myrmeciza longipes* `LC`
Hormiguero Pechiblanco
Common resident.
L 14.7 cm (5.8"). Races *panamensis*[A], *longipes*[B], *boucardi*[C], *griseipectus*[D]. Dry to moist forest, gallery forest and shrubby borders. To 1700 m (mostly < 900 m). Semi-terrestrial pairs hop on ground or low in open undergrowth; often confiding. **ID** Pinkish legs. ♂ above rufous, face and throat black, grey post-ocular, white central belly (*panamensis*), or crown and nape grey, no post-ocular (*boucardi*). ♀ plainer, above rufous-brown, dusky-smudged cheeks, underparts rich buff (most races), or crown grey, underparts darker (*boucardi*). **Voice** Frequent song, loud ringing cascade of notes, initially fast, gradually slowing, descending, rougher at end: "pppp'p'p'p'pe'pe'pe'pe'pr'pr'pee'pee'p eer'juur'juu".

griseipectus

boucardi

panamensis

Genus *Myrmoborus* Chunky and short-tailed, with pale grey legs. ♂♂ black and grey, with black throat; ♀♀ black mask, throat or underparts white. None associated with mixed flocks.

Black-faced Antbird *Myrmoborus myotherinus* `LC`
Hormiguero Carinegro
Common resident (Amazonia), few records (Guainía).
L 13.2 cm (5.2"). Race *elegans*. Humid *terra firme* and transition forest in lowlands and foothills. To 1300 m. Pairs forage low, often in relatively open understorey. **ID** Red eyes. ♂ three white wingbars, black face and throat, narrow greyish-white eyebrow. ♀ black mask, three buff wingbars, white throat sprinkled black at lower edge, breast ochraceous-buff. **Voice** Song, loud fairly rapid descending series of "jeep" notes, raspy at end. Call "péap". **SS** White-browed Antbird, also Black-tailed Antbird (p. 553).

elegans

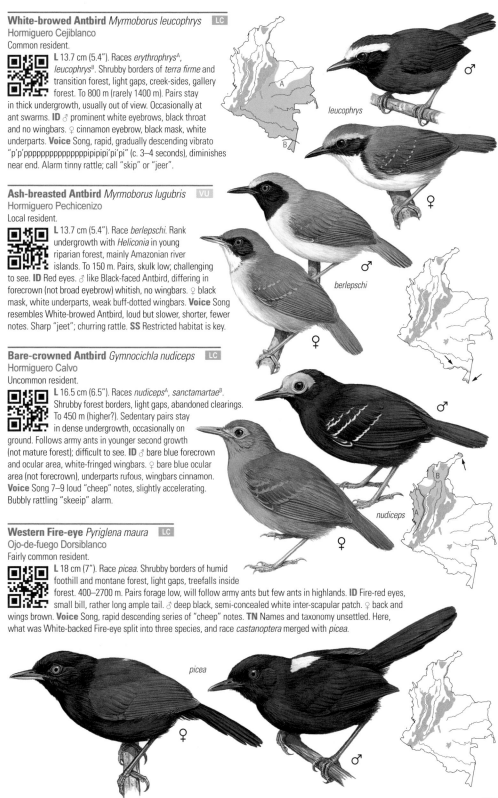

White-browed Antbird *Myrmoborus leucophrys* LC
Hormiguero Cejiblanco
Common resident.
L 13.7 cm (5.4"). Races *erythrophrys*[A], *leucophrys*[B]. Shrubby borders of *terra firme* and transition forest, light gaps, creek-sides, gallery forest. To 800 m (rarely 1400 m). Pairs stay in thick undergrowth, usually out of view. Occasionally at ant swarms. **ID** ♂ prominent white eyebrows, black throat and no wingbars. ♀ cinnamon eyebrow, black mask, white underparts. **Voice** Song, rapid, gradually descending vibrato "p'p'ppppppppppppppppipipipi'pi'pi" (c. 3–4 seconds), diminishes near end. Alarm tinny rattle; call "skip" or "jeer".

leucophrys

Ash-breasted Antbird *Myrmoborus lugubris* VU
Hormiguero Pechicenizo
Local resident.
L 13.7 cm (5.4"). Race *berlepschi*. Rank undergrowth with *Heliconia* in young riparian forest, mainly Amazonian river islands. To 150 m. Pairs, skulk low; challenging to see. **ID** Red eyes. ♂ like Black-faced Antbird, differing in forecrown (not broad eyebrow) whitish, no wingbars. ♀ black mask, white underparts, weak buff-dotted wingbars. **Voice** Song resembles White-browed Antbird, loud but slower, shorter, fewer notes. Sharp "jeet"; churring rattle. **SS** Restricted habitat is key.

berlepschi

Bare-crowned Antbird *Gymnocichla nudiceps* LC
Hormiguero Calvo
Uncommon resident.
L 16.5 cm (6.5"). Races *nudiceps*[A], *sanctamartae*[B]. Shrubby forest borders, light gaps, abandoned clearings. To 450 m (higher?). Sedentary pairs stay in dense undergrowth, occasionally on ground. Follows army ants in younger second growth (not mature forest); difficult to see. **ID** ♂ bare blue forecrown and ocular area, white-fringed wingbars. ♀ bare blue ocular area (not forecrown), underparts rufous, wingbars cinnamon. **Voice** Song 7–9 loud "cheep" notes, slightly accelerating. Bubbly rattling "skeeip" alarm.

nudiceps

Western Fire-eye *Pyriglena maura* LC
Ojo-de-fuego Dorsiblanco
Fairly common resident.
L 18 cm (7"). Race *picea*. Shrubby borders of humid foothill and montane forest, light gaps, treefalls inside forest. 400–2700 m. Pairs forage low, will follow army ants but few ants in highlands. **ID** Fire-red eyes, small bill, rather long ample tail. ♂ deep black, semi-concealed white inter-scapular patch. ♀ back and wings brown. **Voice** Song, rapid descending series of "cheep" notes. **TN** Names and taxonomy unsettled. Here, what was White-backed Fire-eye split into three species, and race *castanoptera* merged with *picea*.

picea

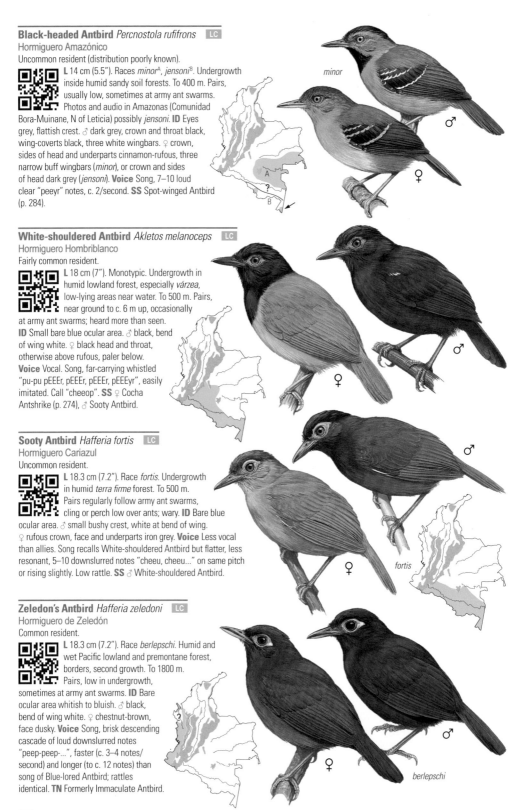

Black-headed Antbird *Percnostola rufifrons* `LC`
Hormiguero Amazónico
Uncommon resident (distribution poorly known).
L 14 cm (5.5"). Races *minor*[A], *jensoni*[B]. Undergrowth inside humid sandy soil forests. To 400 m. Pairs, usually low, sometimes at army ant swarms. Photos and audio in Amazonas (Comunidad Bora-Muinane, N of Leticia) possibly *jensoni*. **ID** Eyes grey, flattish crest. ♂ dark grey, crown and throat black, wing-coverts black, three white wingbars. ♀ crown, sides of head and underparts cinnamon-rufous, three narrow buff wingbars (*minor*), or crown and sides of head dark grey (*jensoni*). **Voice** Song, 7–10 loud clear "peeyr" notes, c. 2/second. **SS** Spot-winged Antbird (p. 284).

minor

White-shouldered Antbird *Akletos melanoceps* `LC`
Hormiguero Hombriblanco
Fairly common resident.
L 18 cm (7"). Monotypic. Undergrowth in humid lowland forest, especially *várzea*, low-lying areas near water. To 500 m. Pairs, near ground to c. 6 m up, occasionally at army ant swarms; heard more than seen. **ID** Small bare blue ocular area. ♂ black, bend of wing white. ♀ black head and throat, otherwise above rufous, paler below. **Voice** Vocal. Song, far-carrying whistled "pu-pu pEEEr, pEEEr, pEEEr, pEEEyr", easily imitated. Call "cheeop". **SS** ♀ Cocha Antshrike (p. 274), ♂ Sooty Antbird.

Sooty Antbird *Hafferia fortis* `LC`
Hormiguero Cariazul
Uncommon resident.
L 18.3 cm (7.2"). Race *fortis*. Undergrowth in humid *terra firme* forest. To 500 m. Pairs regularly follow army ant swarms, cling or perch low over ants; wary. **ID** Bare blue ocular area. ♂ small bushy crest, white at bend of wing. ♀ rufous crown, face and underparts iron grey. **Voice** Less vocal than allies. Song recalls White-shouldered Antbird but flatter, less resonant, 5–10 downslurred notes "cheeu, cheeu..." on same pitch or rising slightly. Low rattle. **SS** ♂ White-shouldered Antbird.

fortis

Zeledon's Antbird *Hafferia zeledoni* `LC`
Hormiguero de Zeledón
Common resident.
L 18.3 cm (7.2"). Race *berlepschi*. Humid and wet Pacific lowland and premontane forest, borders, second growth. To 1800 m. Pairs, low in undergrowth, sometimes at army ant swarms. **ID** Bare ocular area whitish to bluish. ♂ black, bend of wing white. ♀ chestnut-brown, face dusky. **Voice** Song, brisk descending cascade of loud downslurred notes "peep-peep-...", faster (c. 3–4 notes/second) and longer (to c. 12 notes) than song of Blue-lored Antbird; rattles identical. **TN** Formerly Immaculate Antbird.

berlepschi

Blue-lored Antbird *Hafferia immaculata* `LC`
Hormiguero de Nariz Azul
Common resident.
L 18.3 cm (7.2"). Races
immaculata[A], *concepcion*[B]
(in W Andes only on E slope).
Undergrowth from humid foothill
to montane forest, old second growth.
300–2000 m. Behaviour like Zeledon's Antbird
but fewer ant swarms at higher elevations.
ID Essentially identical to Zeledon's Antbird.
Voice Song recalls Zeledon's Antbird but slower
(c. 2 notes/second), shorter (c. 4–6 notes).
SS Differs from Zeledon's Antbird in distribution
and song. **TN** Formerly Immaculate Antbird.

immaculata

Northern Wing-banded Antbird (Buff-banded Antbird)
Myrmornis stictoptera `LC`
Hormiguero Alifranjeado Norteño
Rare resident (few records).
L 16.5 cm (6.5"). Monotypic. To 400 m
(1200 m, Panama). **ID** Chunky, short
legs, rudimentary tail, bare blue ocular
skin. ♂ three narrow buff wingbars, black-and-
white freckling behind eye and on neck (not encircling throat).
♀ small orange-buff throat. **Voice** Like Southern Wing-banded
(below) but song longer, slightly higher-pitched and accelerating.
TN Taxonomy unresolved. Usually regarded as conspecific with
torquata as Wing-banded Antbird.

Southern Wing-banded Antbird *Myrmornis torquata* `LC`
Hormiguero Alifranjeado Sureño
Rare resident (few records).
L 16.5 cm (6.5"). Monotypic. Floor of
humid *terra firme* forest, lowlands,
foothills, shady slopes. To 900 m.
Sedentary, inconspicuous,
singles or pairs hop in deliberate manner,
toss leaves; often flick both wings.
ID From northern *stictoptera* (above) by
lighter brighter plumage, black-and-
white scaling on neck encircles throat
in both sexes. ♀ larger rufous throat
patch. **Voice** Song, long (c. 5 seconds),
brittle, slowly rising series of "wueep" notes.
Call "chirrrr". **TN** See Northern Wing-banded Antbird.

♀
occipitalis

Spot-winged Antshrike *Pygiptila stellaris* `LC`
Hormiguero Alipunteado
Fairly common resident.
L 14 cm (5.5"). Races *occipitalis*[A], *maculipennis*[B],
stellaris[C]. Mid-levels to canopy in humid
lowland forest. To 500 m. Foraging pairs
hustle in foliage, habitually with mixed flocks.
ID Chunky, short-tailed, large-headed, heavy-billed. ♂ grey,
black crown, white-dotted wingbars. ♀ flight feathers
edged rufous, face and underparts dull ochraceous (face
of *occipitalis* more contrasting). **Voice** Song, short
vibrating trill ends in ringing note "t-t-t-t'treer!" often
steadily repeated up to ten times. **TN** Race *maculipennis*
may not be valid.

stellaris

♀

Russet Antshrike *Thamnistes anabatinus* `LC`
Hormiguero Bermejo

Six subspecies in two subspecies groups; both in Colombia.

Tawny Antshrike
Thamnistes (anabatinus) anabatinus
Hormiguero Bermejo Leonado
Fairly common resident.
L 14.7 cm (5.8"). Races *coronatus*[A], *intermedius*[B]. Humid foothill and lower montane forest, borders; local in lowlands. 100–1500 m. Pairs, mid-levels or higher in foliage and epiphytes; often with mixed flocks. **ID** Strong bill, buff eyestripe, dark line through eyes, wings and tail rufous. **Voice** Infrequent song, c. 7–8 sharply downward-inflected notes (c. 2 seconds). High forced "sit, tseeú-tseeú-...". **SS** Buff-fronted Foliage-gleaner (p. 324). **TN** Both subspecies groups usually treated within Russet Antshrike, but distinct from Rufescent Antshrike *T. rufescens* of S Andes. However, some propose separating birds E & W of Andes.

Andean Antshrike *Thamnistes (anabatinus) aequatorialis*
Hormiguero Bermejo Andino
Uncommon resident.
L 14.7 cm (5.8"). Races *gularis*[A] (?), *aequatorialis*[B]. Humid foothill and lower montane forest, borders. 400–2000 m. **ID** Like previous subspecies group but upperparts rufescent-brown (not olive-brown). **Voice** Infrequent song, unlike western birds, thinner, faster, sharper (c. 1.2 seconds), "tic'tsik'tsik-tsik tsik'tsk", first and last notes lower, weaker; series slightly rising-falling (c. 5.5–7.5 kHz). **SS** Recalls a foliage-gleaner. **TN** See Tawny Antshrike (above).

aequatorialis

CONOPOPHAGIDAE
Gnateaters
12 extant species, 4 in region

This small, exclusively Neotropical family comprises species found in the lowlands and highlands of South America. *Conopophaga* are chunky forest understorey birds notable for their rotund shape, wee tails and small silvery rear-projecting ear-tufts (like winged hat of Roman deity Mercury). *Pittasoma*, formerly placed with antbirds, are larger and resemble boldly patterned antpittas.

Chestnut-belted Gnateater *Conopophaga aurita* `LC`
Zumbador Pechirrufo
Uncommon resident.

L 13 cm (5"). Races *inexpectata*[A], *occidentalis*[B]. Undergrowth of humid *terra firme* forest. To 500 m. Cute but inconspicuous. Singles or pairs perch or cling low on saplings, often sally to ground; incidental at army ants. **ID** Plump, nearly tailless, pale blue legs. ♂ face and throat black, chest rusty, prominent white post-ocular. ♀ face and throat orange-rufous, long white post-ocular line, chin and belly pale. **Voice** Song, loose metallic rattle, initially rising slightly in pitch.

inexpectata

Chestnut-crowned Gnateater *Conopophaga castaneiceps* `LC`
Zumbador Pechigrís
Uncommon resident.

L 13.2 cm (5.2"). Races *chocoensis*[A], *castaneiceps*[B]. Undergrowth in humid and wet premontane and montane forest, treefalls. 700–2100 m. Inconspicuous, pairs perch or cling 0.2–3 m up, sally to foliage or ground, move frequently. **ID** Long bluish legs. ♂ rufous cap, bright white post-ocular tuft, face and underparts dark grey. ♀ head to breast rufous, post-ocular tuft duller. **Voice** Song not loud, infrequent, mostly at dawn; raspy slightly rising rattle, sometimes 1–2 notes follow. Alarm raspy metallic "chek"; wings whirr in flight.

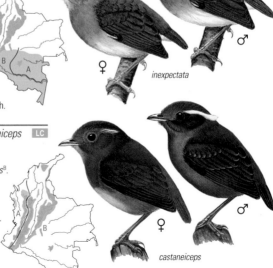

castaneiceps

Black-crowned Pittasoma (Black-crowned Antpitta)
Pittasoma michleri LC
Tororoí Pechiescamado
Uncommon and local resident.

L 18 cm (7"). Race *michleri*. Undergrowth inside humid forest. To 400 m (higher?). Singles or pairs, hop or bound over forest floor and on logs, often at army ant swarms. **ID** Very heavy bill; black crown, bold black-scalloped underparts. ♀ less black on throat. **Voice** Song, metallic "pik" or "dink" notes, c. 3–4/second, steadily for a minute or more. Call rapid clatter; harsh metallic "wak".

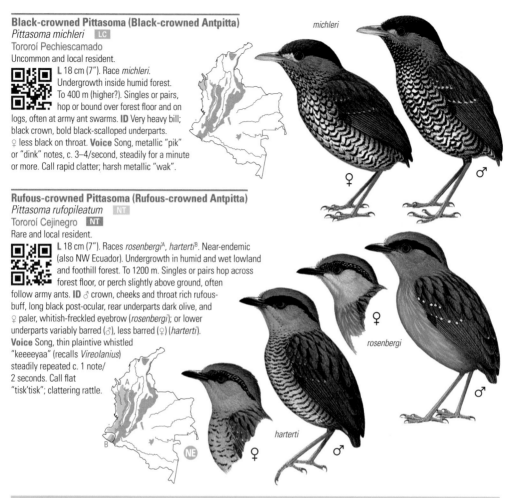

michleri

♀

♂

Rufous-crowned Pittasoma (Rufous-crowned Antpitta)
Pittasoma rufopileatum NT
Tororoí Cejinegro NT
Rare and local resident.

L 18 cm (7"). Races *rosenbergi*[A], *harterti*[B]. Near-endemic (also NW Ecuador). Undergrowth in humid and wet lowland and foothill forest. To 1200 m. Singles or pairs hop across forest floor, or perch slightly above ground, often follow army ants. **ID** ♂ crown, cheeks and throat rich rufous-buff, long black post-ocular, rear underparts dark olive, and ♀ paler, whitish-freckled eyebrow (*rosenbergi*); or lower underparts variably barred (♂), less barred (♀) (*harterti*). **Voice** Song, thin plaintive whistled "keeeeyaa" (recalls *Vireolanius*) steadily repeated c. 1 note/ 2 seconds. Call flat "tisk'tisk"; clattering rattle.

♀

rosenbergi

♂

harterti

♂

NE

GRALLARIIDAE
Antpittas
55 extant species, 33 in region

Grallariidae are rotund terrestrial birds whose shapes have been described as 'eggs on legs'. Formerly included with antbirds in Formicariidae, all are shy, retiring, usually requiring patience to see, although several are now easily observed at feeding sites.

Genus *Grallaria* Plump and virtually tailless, with long legs. Terrestrial; attractive earth-tone colours. Springy hops alternate with running. Heard far more than seen, but occasionally in open at dawn. Most diverse in Andean forests.

Undulated Antpitta *Grallaria squamigera* LC
Tororoí Ondulado
Uncommon resident (by voice).

L 23 cm (9"). Race *squamigera*. Undergrowth in humid and wet montane forest. 2100–3500 m. Singles, retiring, appear in small openings at dawn; hop, then pause bolt upright to stare or flick leaves. **ID** Large; crown and nape grey, loral spot buffy, black submalar borders white throat, underparts yellow-ochraceous thickly scalloped black. **Voice** At dawn, from log or low perch, hollow vibrating ('rubber-lipped') rising "hühühühühühühühü hú hú", slowing, notes enunciated at end. **SS** Giant Antpitta.

squamigera

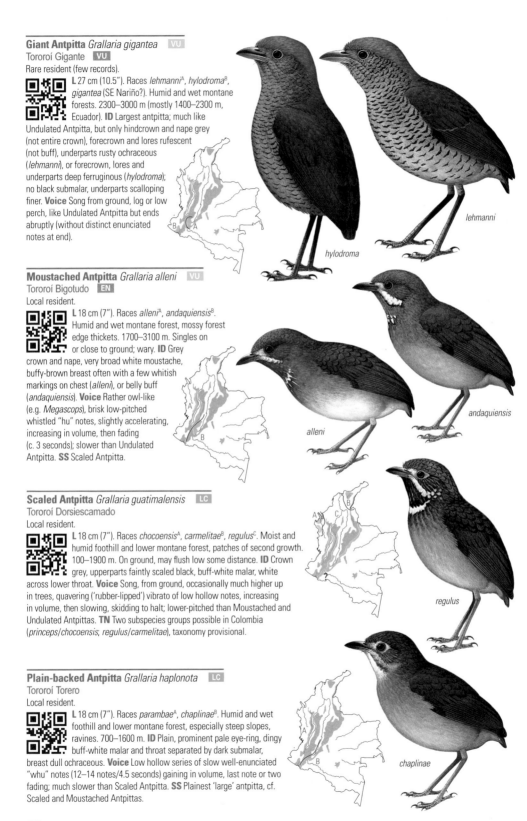

Giant Antpitta *Grallaria gigantea* `VU`
Tororoí Gigante `VU`
Rare resident (few records).

L 27 cm (10.5"). Races *lehmanni*[A], *hylodroma*[B], *gigantea* (SE Nariño?). Humid and wet montane forests. 2300–3000 m (mostly 1400–2300 m, Ecuador). **ID** Largest antpitta; much like Undulated Antpitta, but only hindcrown and nape grey (not entire crown), forecrown and lores rufescent (not buff), underparts rusty ochraceous (*lehmanni*), or forecrown, lores and underparts deep ferruginous (*hylodroma*); no black submalar, underparts scalloping finer. **Voice** Song from ground, log or low perch, like Undulated Antpitta but ends abruptly (without distinct enunciated notes at end).

hylodroma

lehmanni

Moustached Antpitta *Grallaria alleni* `VU`
Tororoí Bigotudo `EN`
Local resident.

L 18 cm (7"). Races *alleni*[A], *andaquiensis*[B]. Humid and wet montane forest, mossy forest edge thickets. 1700–3100 m. Singles on or close to ground; wary. **ID** Grey crown and nape, very broad white moustache, buffy-brown breast often with a few whitish markings on chest (*alleni*), or belly buff (*andaquiensis*). **Voice** Rather owl-like (e.g. *Megascops*), brisk low-pitched whistled "hu" notes, slightly accelerating, increasing in volume, then fading (c. 3 seconds); slower than Undulated Antpitta. **SS** Scaled Antpitta.

alleni

andaquiensis

Scaled Antpitta *Grallaria guatimalensis* `LC`
Tororoí Dorsiescamado
Local resident.

L 18 cm (7"). Races *chocoensis*[A], *carmelitae*[B], *regulus*[C]. Moist and humid foothill and lower montane forest, patches of second growth. 100–1900 m. On ground, may flush low some distance. **ID** Crown grey, upperparts faintly scaled black, buff-white malar, white across lower throat. **Voice** Song, from ground, occasionally much higher up in trees, quavering ('rubber-lipped') vibrato of low hollow notes, increasing in volume, then slowing, skidding to halt; lower-pitched than Moustached and Undulated Antpittas. **TN** Two subspecies groups possible in Colombia (*princeps/chocoensis*; *regulus/carmelitae*), taxonomy provisional.

regulus

Plain-backed Antpitta *Grallaria haplonota* `LC`
Tororoí Torero
Local resident.

L 18 cm (7"). Races *parambae*[A], *chaplinae*[B]. Humid and wet foothill and lower montane forest, especially steep slopes, ravines. 700–1600 m. **ID** Plain, prominent pale eye-ring, dingy buff-white malar and throat separated by dark submalar, breast dull ochraceous. **Voice** Low hollow series of slow well-enunciated "whu" notes (12–14 notes/4.5 seconds) gaining in volume, last note or two fading; much slower than Scaled Antpitta. **SS** Plainest 'large' antpitta, cf. Scaled and Moustached Antpittas.

chaplinae

Ochre-striped Antpitta *Grallaria dignissima* LC
Tororoí Estriado
Rare resident (few records, Putumayo; likely in Amazonas).
L 19 cm (7.5"). Monotypic. Dense undergrowth and cluttered gaps in humid *terra firme* and transition forest. To 400 m. **ID** Prominent pale area in front of and behind eye, throat to mid-breast bright orange-rufous, lower underparts streaked black and white, virtually tailless. **Voice** Song, low-pitched whistled "wü-wüüüüooo", melancholy, second note slightly descending; or single-noted "wüüüüooo". Call fast vibrating trill, slightly descending.

Chestnut-crowned Antpitta *Grallaria ruficapilla* LC
Tororoí Comprapán
Commonest antpitta in Colombian Andes.
L 20 cm (8"). Races *perijana*[A], *ruficapilla*[B]. Dense borders, cluttered light gaps in humid and wet montane forest. 1200–3200 m. Easier to see than allies. **ID** Large, bold pattern; rufous head, white throat, white underparts streaked black (*ruficapilla*), less streaked (*perijana*). **Voice** Vocal. Song, clear whistled "wü, paaw, puuee", second note lowest, third upslurred; Spanish renditions include "compra pan", "compadre", "seco estoy". Two-note song reported in Serranía de los Yariguíes. Call (local) loud downslurred whistle.

ruficapilla

perijana

Santa Marta Antpitta *Grallaria bangsi* VU
Tororoí de Santa Marta VU
Fairly common resident.
L 18 cm (7"). Monotypic. Endemic. Cluttered understorey inside humid montane forest, adjacent second growth, forest border thickets. 1500–2800 m (seldom lower). **ID** Large pale eye-ring, tawny throat, whitish underparts narrowly streaked olive-brown. **Voice** Song, especially dawn and dusk, loud upslurred "hüb, white". Call, high metallic scraping "skrEEK" rising (unlike other *Grallaria*).

Cundinamarca Antpitta *Grallaria kaestneri* EN
Tororoí de Cundinamarca EN
Local resident (several sites near Cundinamarca/Meta border).
L 18 cm (7"). Monotypic. Endemic. Dense undergrowth in humid montane forest, older second growth, disturbed forest. 1700–2700 m. **ID** Dull brownish, whitish eye-ring, mottled whitish throat, liberally streaked white chest (narrower, sparser below), pale bill, and cinnamon wing-linings. **Voice** Song, rather high (2.8–3.5 kHz) piercing whistled "peu . peeu, pweep", pause after brief first note, next two progressively higher and stronger.

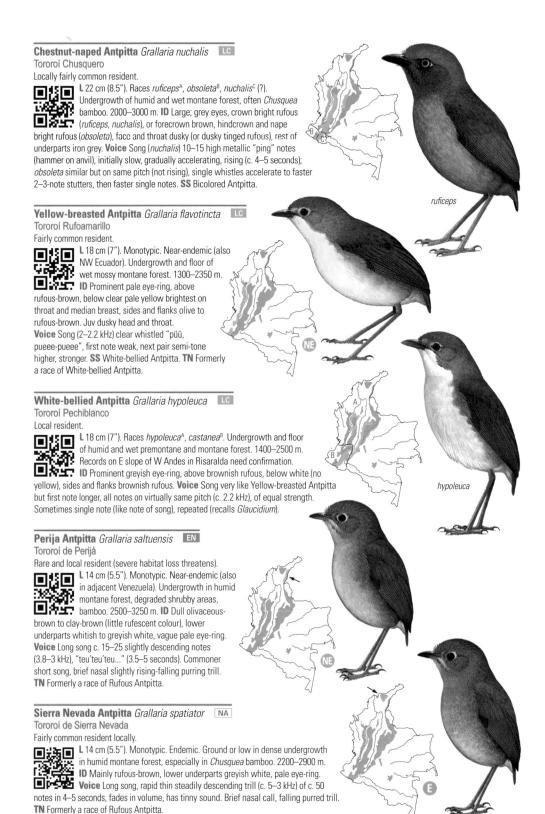

Chestnut-naped Antpitta *Grallaria nuchalis* `LC`
Tororoí Chusquero
Locally fairly common resident.
L 22 cm (8.5"). Races *ruficeps*[A], *obsoleta*[B], *nuchalis*[C] (?). Undergrowth of humid and wet montane forest, often *Chusquea* bamboo. 2000–3000 m. **ID** Large; grey eyes, crown bright rufous (*ruficeps, nuchalis*), or forecrown brown, hindcrown and nape bright rufous (*obsoleta*), face and throat dusky (or dusky tinged rufous), rest of underparts iron grey. **Voice** Song (*nuchalis*) 10–15 high metallic "ping" notes (hammer on anvil), initially slow, gradually accelerating, rising (c. 4–5 seconds); *obsoleta* similar but on same pitch (not rising), single whistles accelerate to faster 2–3-note stutters, then faster single notes. **SS** Bicolored Antpitta.

ruficeps

Yellow-breasted Antpitta *Grallaria flavotincta* `LC`
Tororoí Rufoamarillo
Fairly common resident.
L 18 cm (7"). Monotypic. Near-endemic (also NW Ecuador). Undergrowth and floor of wet mossy montane forest. 1300–2350 m. **ID** Prominent pale eye-ring, above rufous-brown, below clear pale yellow brightest on throat and median breast, sides and flanks olive to rufous-brown. Juv dusky head and throat. **Voice** Song (2–2.2 kHz) clear whistled "püü, pueee-pueee", first note weak, next pair semi-tone higher, stronger. **SS** White-bellied Antpitta. **TN** Formerly a race of White-bellied Antpitta.

White-bellied Antpitta *Grallaria hypoleuca* `LC`
Tororoí Pechiblanco
Local resident.
L 18 cm (7"). Races *hypoleuca*[A], *castanea*[B]. Undergrowth and floor of humid and wet premontane and montane forest. 1400–2500 m. Records on E slope of W Andes in Risaralda need confirmation. **ID** Prominent greyish eye-ring, above brownish rufous, below white (no yellow), sides and flanks brownish rufous. **Voice** Song very like Yellow-breasted Antpitta but first note longer, all notes on virtually same pitch (c. 2.2 kHz), of equal strength. Sometimes single note (like note of song), repeated (recalls *Glaucidium*).

hypoleuca

Perija Antpitta *Grallaria saltuensis* `EN`
Tororoí de Perijá
Rare and local resident (severe habitat loss threatens).
L 14 cm (5.5"). Monotypic. Near-endemic (also in adjacent Venezuela). Undergrowth in humid montane forest, degraded shrubby areas, bamboo. 2500–3250 m. **ID** Dull olivaceous-brown to clay-brown (little rufescent colour), lower underparts whitish to greyish white, vague pale eye-ring. **Voice** Long song c. 15–25 slightly descending notes (3.8–3 kHz), "teu'teu'teu..." (3.5–5 seconds). Commoner short song, brief nasal slightly rising-falling purring trill. **TN** Formerly a race of Rufous Antpitta.

Sierra Nevada Antpitta *Grallaria spatiator* `NA`
Tororoí de Sierra Nevada
Fairly common resident locally.
L 14 cm (5.5"). Monotypic. Endemic. Ground or low in dense undergrowth in humid montane forest, especially in *Chusquea* bamboo. 2200–2900 m. **ID** Mainly rufous-brown, lower underparts greyish white, pale eye-ring. **Voice** Long song, rapid thin steadily descending trill (c. 5–3 kHz) of c. 50 notes in 4–5 seconds, fades in volume, has tinny sound. Brief nasal call, falling purred trill. **TN** Formerly a race of Rufous Antpitta.

Muisca Antpitta *Grallaria rufula* NA
Tororoí Muisca
Local resident.

 L 14 cm (5.5"). Monotypic. Endemic. Ground or undergrowth in humid montane forest, stunted treeline woodland, dense shrubbery in *páramo*. 1850–3800 m. **ID** Overall rufous-brown, belly slightly paler; identify by range and vocalizations. **Voice** Long song, 6–8 near identical slow "tuu" notes, c. 1/second or slower, same pitch (c. 3.5 kHz) or slight decline at end. Short two-part song, harsh rattle-trill followed by slightly lower, weaker burry trill "tjjjjjjj . diiiii". Both vocalizations very like Bicolored Antpitta. **TN** Formerly a race of Rufous Antpitta.

Bicolored Antpitta *Grallaria rufocinerea* VU
Tororoí Rufocenizo VU
Local resident.

 L 16.5 cm (6.5"). Races *rufocinerea*[A], *romeroana*[B]. Near-endemic (also NE Ecuador). Dense undergrowth in humid and wet montane forest. 2000–3100 m. Retiring and difficult to see. **ID** Pale eye-ring, head, throat and upperparts rufous-brown sharply demarcated from grey lower underparts. **Voice** Long song (*rufocinerea*) 6–12+ short piercing whistles, same pitch or slightly descending, "tee, tee, tee...", c. 1 note/second. Short song, single long-drawn (1–1.5 seconds) flat or slightly rising whistle "tueeeeeeea". **SS** Chestnut-naped Antpitta (larger). **TN** Plumages differ, but close vocally and genetically to Muisca Antpitta.

Chami Antpitta *Grallaria alvarezi* NA
Tororoí Chamí
Local resident.
L 14 cm (5.5"). Monotypic. Endemic. Ground or low in dense humid and wet montane forest undergrowth to treeline. 2350–3650 m. **ID** Rich deep reddish brown (brighter than allies), slightly paler belly. **Voice** Long song, fast trill of c. 50 notes in c. 3 seconds, slightly descending (3–2.5 kHz), slowing, weaker near end. Short song, single note followed by 4–5 rapid notes, each one inflected up-down (2 kHz), or two raspy notes (alarm?). **TN** Formerly a race of Rufous Antpitta.

Equatorial Antpitta *Grallaria saturata* NA
Tororoí Ecuatorial
Uncommon to fairly common resident.
L 14 cm (5.5"). Monotypic. Habitat as Chami Antpitta. C Andes; isolated population in Iguaque massif (E Andes) of SW Santander and W Boyacá. 2550–3650 m. **ID** Overall reddish brown, underparts paler with yellowish-brown tone. **Voice** Long song, c. 19–20 notes in c. 2 seconds (3 kHz), flat, slightly stronger initially. Short song variable, in C Andes two metallic notes (hammer striking anvil), or single note, a pause, then 4–5 quicker diminishing metallic notes; or second part slightly trilled, or both parts trilled, first rising, second lower and buzzy, "taaeee . djjjjjjjjj". **TN** Formerly a race of Rufous Antpitta.

Northern Tawny Antpitta *Grallaria alticola* LC
Tororoí Leonado del Norte
Common resident.

L 17 cm (6.7"). Monotypic. Endemic. Stunted treeline woodland, shrubs and grass in *páramo*. 2800–4000 m. **ID** Like western *quitensis* (next page) but slightly smaller, above browner, bill shorter, underparts more extensively mottled whitish; voice quite different. **Voice** Song, typically 4–5 notes (not three), loud "queek, kuaa, kuee'beet" ("quick, draw, hur-bert") or more rhythmic "queek, kuaa, kuee-be'beek", or last three notes alone. Call higher, thin descending "keeeurp" (4–3 kHz). **TN** This and the next species usually treated as one species (Tawny Antpitta *G. quitensis*).

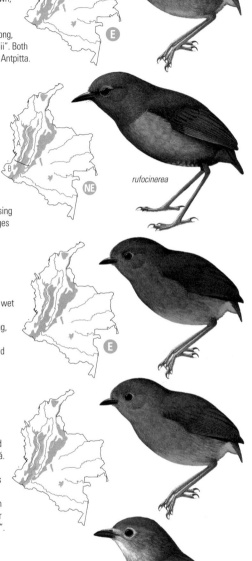

rufocinerea

Western Tawny Antpitta *Grallaria quitensis* `LC`
Tororoí Leonado
Common resident.

 L 18 cm (7"). Monotypic. Stunted treeline woodland, shrubs, grass, small openings in *páramo*; tolerates some disturbance. 2800–4000 m. Conspicuous, confiding, easy-to-see antpitta; often bounds into open in broad daylight. **ID** Rather plain, lores and ocular area whitish, above pale greyish brown, below pale tawny-buff somewhat mottled whitish. Juv duller, head paler, spotted. **Voice** Song, simple husky "took, tuu-tuu", first note slightly higher; occasionally two-note variants. Loud descending blurred "keeyurp" when disturbed. **TN** See Northern Tawny Antpitta.

Urrao Antpitta *Grallaria fenwickorum* `CR`
Tororoí de Urrao `EN`
Local resident (discovered 2010).

 L 16.5 cm (6.5"). Monotypic. Endemic. Undergrowth in humid upper montane forest, especially with *Chusquea* bamboo, treefall gaps. 2500–3300 m. Tiny range; threatened by deforestation, livestock grazing, fires. **ID** Plain, large grey eye-ring and lores, head and throat pale cinnamon-brown, lower underparts grey vaguely scalloped. **Voice** Song (3–3.5 kHz) fairly high for antpitta, like piccolo "pe .. pee, peet", pause after first note, succeeding notes higher. Call metallic scraping "skreet", slightly rising. **TN** Scientific name disputed; also known as *G. urraoensis* (author's preference).

Brown-banded Antpitta *Grallaria milleri* `VU`
Tororoí de Miller `EN`
Fairly common but very local resident.

 L 16.5 cm (6.5"). Races *milleri*[A], *gilesi*[B] (probably extinct, differs minimally). Endemic. Undergrowth in humid montane forest. 1900–3100 m. **ID** Small; above rufescent-brown, below greyish white, broad brownish band across chest, sides and flanks. **Voice** Song, recalls Urrao Antpitta but faster, no obvious pause after first note, "peeap-peee-peet", first note slightly stronger and longer, last brief. Call nasal scraping "skaank", dropping at start, then rising. **SS** Slate-crowned Antpitta (p. 299).

Genus *Hylopezus* Lowlands. Like *Grallaria* but smaller, bold eye-ring ('wide-eyed' appearance), and streaked underparts. Often perch above ground; sway body side to side when singing.

Streak-chested Antpitta *Hylopezus perspicillatus* `LC`
Tororoí de Anteojos
Uncommon resident.

 L 14 cm (5.5"). Races *perspicillatus*[A], *pallidior*[B], *periophthalmicus*[C]. Undergrowth in humid forest borders, old treefalls, gaps inside forest. To 1200 m. Singles, retiring, on ground to several metres up. **ID** Grey crown, bold buff eye-ring, streaked breast, whitish belly. **Voice** Persistent singer from log or elevated perch. Song (*perspicillatus, periophthalmicus*) leisurely melancholy whistled "dah-DEH-dee-dee-dee, deh'a, deh'a", first note lowest, second loudest, rest melancholy, slowing, gradually falling as if in sad resignation. **SS** Thicket Antpitta. **TN** Taxonomy unresolved.

milleri

perspicillatus

Spotted Antpitta *Hylopezus macularius* LC
Tororoí Carimanchado

Four subspecies in three subspecies groups; one in Colombia.

Spotted Antpitta *Hylopezus (macularius) macularius*
Rare resident.

L 14 cm (5.5"). Race *dilutus*. Undergrowth inside humid forest. To 150 m. Singles, shy, retiring; move with quick springy hops and run-hops on leafy forest floor, pauses, stares and flicks leaves. **ID** Grey crown, large orange-buff eye-ring, streaked chest, tawny flanks, legs and mandible pink. **Voice** Sings, dawn and dusk, usually from just above ground, a low hollow rhythmic "wü-wü-whút, wü-whút-whút" (Puerto Inírida); stronger "whút" notes impart 'beat' or syncopation to song. Guttural "cu-cu-...". Some geographical variation. **TN** Some authors split Spotted Antpitta into three species.

dilutus

Thicket Antpitta *Hylopezus dives* LC
Tororoí Buchifulvo
Locally common resident.

L 16.5 cm (6.5"). Race *barbacoae*. Dense thickets, borders, light gaps in humid and wet forest. To 900 m. Behaviour like Spotted Antpitta. **ID** Grey crown and nape, prominent whitish eye arcs before and behind eye, whitish throat, rest of underparts tawny orange, with coarse blurred dark streaking on breast, pink legs. **Voice** Song, throughout day, 4–12 brisk mellow whistles, series rising slightly (1.5–2 kHz), last notes on same pitch: "oh-oh-ou-oü-oü-üü-üü-üü". **SS** Streak-chested Antpitta. **TN** Previously a race of White-lored Antpitta.

barbacoae

White-lored Antpitta *Hylopezus fulviventris* LC
Tororoí Buchicanelo
Rare or uncommon resident.

L 15 cm (6"). Races *caquetae*[A], *fulviventris*[B] (S Putumayo?). Thickets at borders of low-lying forest, dense overgrown clearings. 150–400 m. **ID** Recalls Spotted Antpitta but crown darker grey, conspicuous white lores, large white post-ocular spot (incomplete eye-ring) and no wingbars. **Voice** Song, 3–5 very low painful "ouup" hoots as if in distress, a little quicker than c. 1/second. Also faster slightly accelerating series of c. 10+ low hollow notes. **SS** Spotted Antpitta. **TN** See Thicket Antpitta.

caquetae

Thrush-like Antpitta *Myrmothera campanisona* LC
Tororoí Campanero

Six subspecies in two subspecies groups; one in Colombia.

signata

Thrush-like Antpitta
Myrmothera (campanisona) campanisona
Fairly common resident (by voice).

L 15 cm (6"). Races *modesta*[A], *dissors*[B], *signata*[C]. Old treefalls in humid *terra firme* forest. To 1000 m. Singles, pairs, sedentary, widely separated, on or close to ground in very dense vegetation. Devilishly hard to see. **ID** Above plain brown, below greyish white with darker blurred streaking, white arc behind eye; or more brownish below (*modesta*). **Voice** Song 4–8 very low hollow whistles, increasing in volume, then fading, "wuh-wuH-WUH-WUH-Wuh-wu", or shorter, first note prolonged. **SS** White-lored Antpitta.

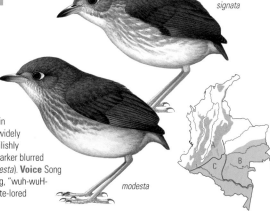

modesta

Genus *Grallaricula* Miniatures of *Grallaria*; tiny, virtually tailless. Usually perch some distance above ground, but often sally to ground briefly. Large dark eyes. Vocalizations varied.

mindoensis

flavirostris

Ochre-breasted Antpitta *Grallaricula flavirostris* NT
Tororoí Piquigualdo
Very local resident (overlooked).

L 11 cm (4.3"). Races *brevis*[A], *ochraceiventris*[B], *mindoensis*[C], *flavirostris*[D]. Wet foothill to montane forest. 500–2200 m. Inconspicuous, sedentary pairs, 1–7 m up in dark understorey, occasionally higher; sally to foliage, branches or ground. **ID** Tiny; streaked below, tawny eye-ring and loral spot, underparts ochraceous variably streaked dusky. **Voice** Not very vocal. Song, brief weak moderately high (c. 3–4 kHz) up-down slurred "weeu" at well-spaced intervals, of variable tone and pitch. Longer series of even-pitched whistles reported.

Hooded Antpitta *Grallaricula cucullata* VU
Tororoí Cabecirrufo NT
Local (?) or overlooked resident.

L 11.4 cm (4.5"). Races *venezuelana*[A], *cucullata*[B]. Near-endemic (also extreme W Venezuela). Understorey inside humid montane forest; known distribution fragmented, perhaps formerly more widespread. 1500–2700 m. Often about eye level, short quick movements difficult to follow. **ID** Bill orange-yellow, entire head and throat orange-rufous, below greyish white. **Voice** Not very vocal. Song, at lengthy intervals, brief moderately high (4–4.5 kHz) up-down slurred whistle "ueeeaa", soft but penetrating; recalls *G. flavirostris* but higher-pitched.

cucullata

Unnamed Antpitta *Grallaricula* sp. nov. (?) NA
Tororoí Bailador
Very local resident (discovered 2019; Farallones National Park).
L 11.4 cm (4.5"). Monotypic. Endemic. Understorey of humid montane forest; known from single area in Valle, W Andes. **ID** Above brown, crown and nape rufescent, large buff-white arc before and behind eye, white malar bordered black, median throat white, breast and sides white heavily scaled dusky and spotted white. **Voice** Call, high "skeeet", with upward inflection at end. **AN** Like many antpittas, often rotates body side to side, hence Tororoí Bailador (Dancing Antpitta).

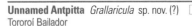

♂

♀

Rusty-breasted Antpitta *Grallaricula ferrugineipectus* LC
Tororoí Ferruginoso
Fairly common resident (Santa Marta Mts), local elsewhere.

L 11.4 cm (4.5"). Races *ferrugineipectus*[A], *rara*[B], ssp.? (W slope of C Andes, Caldas). Cluttered undergrowth in humid forest, often in bamboo. 800–2200 m. Singles, retiring, 0.5–6 m up. **ID** Indistinct buff loral patch, prominent buff arc behind eye, narrow white crescent below lower throat (*ferrugineipectus*), or darker, white crescent faint (*rara*). **Voice** Persistent singer, especially early rainy season. Song (both races) rapid even-paced, slightly rising "kwa'kwa'kwa ... kue'kue'kua" (c. 18–20 notes in c. 2 seconds), second half stronger, declines at end.

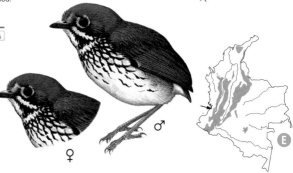

rara

ferrugineipectus

Slate-crowned Antpitta *Grallaricula nana*
Tororoí Enano
Uncommon resident.

 L 11.4 cm (4.5"). Races *occidentalis*[A], *nana*[B], *hallsi*[C], *nanitaea*[D]. Undergrowth in wet (mossy) montane forest, especially in bamboo. 1700–3350 m (to 1300 m, Pacific slope). Perches 0.5–10 m up. **ID** Recalls Rusty-breasted Antpitta but differs in grey crown, rufous loral patch, paler underparts. **Voice** Especially early rainy season. Fife-like song runs a little upscale, then a long arcing descent "we'e'e'ti'ti'ti'ti'ti'ti'ti'ti'te'te'te'e'e'e" (c. 25 notes in c. 2 seconds), moderately high (3–3.9 kHz), penetrating, ventriloquial. Some songs (*hallsi*) briefer, notes blurred.

nana

Crescent-faced Antpitta *Grallaricula lineifrons*
Tororoí Medialuna
Local resident.

 L 12.2 cm (4.8"). Monotypic. Undergrowth in wet (mossy) montane forest, especially with *Chusquea* bamboo. 2800–3700 m (higher?). Inconspicuous in undergrowth; difficult to see, but habituated at a feeding site in Caldas. **ID** Ornate and adorable. Bold white facial crescent and post-ocular, heavily streaked underparts. **Voice** Spirited, high piping song (3–4.4 kHz) "ti-ti-ti-ti-ti-ti-ti-d-d-d-d-d-e" gradually rising, then flattens, (c. 13–20 notes in 2–3 seconds); slower than *G. nana*.

RHINOCRYPTIDAE
Tapaculos
59 extant species, 19 in region

An exclusively Neotropical family believed to have evolved in dry S South America. Although a small number still occur there, the family is now most diverse in the Andes where recent rapid speciation in the genus *Scytalopus* has resulted in many closely related, extremely similar species. All species in the family are semi-terrestrial and retain a movable nasal flap, the operculum, a feature perhaps more helpful in dry dusty Patagonia than in humid Andean regions.

Rusty-belted Tapaculo *Liosceles thoracicus*
Tapaculo Collarejo
Fairly common resident.

 L 19 cm (7.5"). Races *erithacus*[A], *dugandi*[B] (distinct?). *Terra firme* and transition forest. To 1000 m. Terrestrial, walks alone on leafy forest floor or on fallen logs, tail often slightly cocked; wary, suspicious (playback helps). **ID** Long-tailed; white bib with rusty-ochre stain. **Voice** Heard more than seen. Song, often from log, a low hollow whistled "koouk .. ku . ku, ku, ku, ku, ku..." on same pitch, volume fades (c. 12–20 notes/5–6 seconds), slight pause after initial note.

dugandi

Ocellated Tapaculo *Acropternis orthonyx*
Tapaculo Ocelado
Uncommon resident.

 L 23 cm (9"). Race *orthonyx*. Dense undergrowth in humid and wet montane forest, often in bamboo (*Chusquea*). 2300–3600 m. Spectacular but retiring (needs patience to see), hops heavily on ground or low in vegetation, vigorously scratches leaf litter (both feet together), often at same location for several minutes. **ID** Large; spotted plumage and bright rufous foreparts unmistakable. **Voice** Heard far more than seen. Call at dawn, loud piercing whistle "quEEEow", far-carrying. When disturbed, strident whistled "kueee!", jay-like "KEEa".

orthonyx

Ash-colored Tapaculo *Myornis senilis* `LC`
Tapaculo Cenizo
Uncommon resident.

 L 14 cm (5.5"). Monotypic. Dense undergrowth in humid and wet montane forest, often in *Chusquea* bamboo. 2000–3500 m. Hops on or near ground; easily overlooked but for loud vocalizations. **ID** Large; plain grey, longish tail, cinnamon-tinged vent. Juv rufous-brown, paler below, dark wavy rear-part barring. **Voice** Song variable, loud series of measured "skeop" notes may accelerate slightly, changes to couplets or triplets, or merges into fast descending trill or series of trills. **SS** *Scytalopus* tapaculos.

Genus *Scytalopus* Quintessential little dark birds. All are extremely similar, semi-terrestrial, skulking but strongly territorial, and vocalize randomly throughout day. Identified by voice, elevation and range (not visual clues), a task made easier because usually only 2–3 occur together, and songs (but not necessarily alarm calls or other vocalizations) of most are distinctive. Some vocalizations of ♀♀ may differ from those of ♂♂. Both sexes may approach playback without singing. In general, ♀♀ slightly browner than ♂♂; juv brownish with varying amounts of rufous and dusky barring.

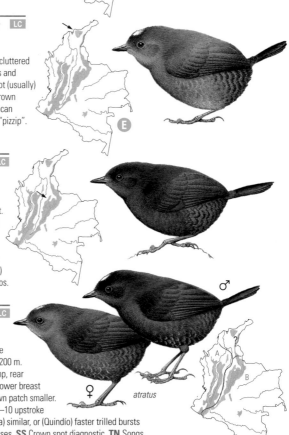

Blackish Tapaculo *Scytalopus latrans* `LC`
Tapaculo Negruzco
Fairly common resident.

 L 13 cm (5"). Race *latrans*. Ground or undergrowth in humid montane forest, borders, bamboo, bushy second growth. 2100–3500 m. **ID** ♂ blackish grey; ♀ slightly paler, lower underparts brownish. **Voice** Song, relatively slow "tock" or "querk" (like rough barking sound) repeated c. 3–4 times/second for up to a minute. Low upward-inflected "wik".

Santa Marta Tapaculo *Scytalopus sanctaemartae* `LC`
Tapaculo Buchirrufo `VU`
Common resident.

 L 13.2 cm (5.2"). Monotypic. Endemic. Dense cluttered undergrowth in moist to humid forest, borders and ravines. 700–1950 m. **ID** White forecrown spot (usually) is key, rump and lower underparts chestnut-brown barred black. **Voice** Song, fast trill c. 15–17 notes/second, can continue 30+ seconds. Call, harsh angry-sounding metallic "pizzip". **SS** Brown-rumped Tapaculo (higher elevation).

Long-tailed Tapaculo *Scytalopus micropterus* `LC`
Tapaculo Ecuatorial
Local resident.

 L 13.5 cm (5.3"). Monotypic. Dense undergrowth inside or at edge of humid forest. 1200–2800 m. **ID** Large, relatively long-tailed (for *Scytalopus*), blackish grey. **Voice** Song, slow series of harsh couplets "rach'up...", c. 2 couplets/second, for sometimes a minute or more; repetitive pattern produces distinct beat or syncopation. **SS** Range (elevation) overlaps White-crowned, Blackish and Spillmann's Tapaculos.

White-crowned Tapaculo *Scytalopus atratus* `LC`
Tapaculo Cabeciblanco
Fairly common resident.

 L 13 cm (5"). Races *confusus*[A], *atratus*[B]. Dense undergrowth in gaps or forest borders. 900–2200 m. **ID** ♂ *atratus* blackish; white crown patch, rump, rear flanks and belly reddish brown barred dusky, lower breast and belly with whitish-tipped feathers; *confusus* paler, crown patch smaller. **Voice** Song (*atratus*) short frog-like one-second bursts of 8–10 upstroke notes (c. 2.5 kHz) with 1–2-second pauses; *confusus* (Tolima) similar, or (Quindío) faster trilled bursts of c. 12 upstroke notes in 0.6 seconds with one-second pauses. **SS** Crown spot diagnostic. **TN** Songs in Colombia and Ecuador unlike those in Venezuela and Peru. Race *nigricans* possible (Perijá Mts).

Tacarcuna Tapaculo *Scytalopus panamensis* VU
Tapaculo Cejiblanco VU
Locally common resident.

 L 13 cm (5"). Monotypic. Near-endemic (also adjacent Panama). Dense undergrowth in gaps, humid forest borders. 1050–1500 m. **ID** Slaty black, long narrow white eyestripe, pale grey throat, rufous-brown rump, rear flanks and belly barred dusky.
Voice Song, long series of up-down inflected notes, initially fast (10–12 notes/second) and weak, gradually slowing to c. 5/second but increasing in volume. Call 2–5 loud sharp notes in little bursts.
SS Choco Tapaculo (lower elevation). **AN** Pale-throated Tapaculo.

Choco Tapaculo *Scytalopus chocoensis* LC
Tapaculo del Chocó
Common resident.

 L 11.4 cm (4.5"). Monotypic. Near-endemic (also far SE Panama and NW Ecuador). Dense undergrowth and gaps in steep wet forest. 250–1250 m (1340–1465 m in adjacent Panama).
ID Essentially identical to many other *Scytalopus*; slaty black, rear parts dark reddish brown barred dusky. **Voice** Song, long (5–30 seconds), a few quick lower-pitched notes then settles into slower pace of c. 3 up-down inflected notes/second. **SS** At lower elevations than Narino and Tatama Tapaculos.

Magdalena Tapaculo *Scytalopus rodriguezi* EN
Tapaculo del Bajo Magdalena VU

 Two subspecies in separate subspecies groups; both in Colombia.

Yariguies Tapaculo *Scytalopus (rodriguezi) yariguiorum*
Tapaculo de los Yariguíes
Status undetermined.
L 12.2 cm (4.8"). One subspecies in group. Endemic. Dense undergrowth around treefall gaps, humid forest borders. 1800–2200 m (lower?). **ID** Much like Upper Magdalena Tapaculo but darker, blackish grey, shorter-tailed. **Voice** Recalls Upper Magdalena Tapaculo but lower-pitched, slightly faster. **SS** Occurs with White-crowned and Long-tailed Tapaculos (both vocally different). **TN** An incipient species.

Upper Magdalena Tapaculo *Scytalopus (rodriguezi) rodriguezi*
Tapaculo del Magdalena
Local resident.
L 12.2 cm (4.8"). One subspecies in group. Endemic. Dense undergrowth in treefall gaps, shrubby humid forest borders. 2000–2300 m (elevational limits probably broader). **ID** Dark slate-grey, lower underparts chestnut barred dusky. **Voice** Simple song of 10–100+ notes, c. 4–5/second, with strong downward inflection, often preceded by short introductory note, e.g. "peer'chuuk'chuuk'chuuk...". **AN** Magdalena Tapaculo.

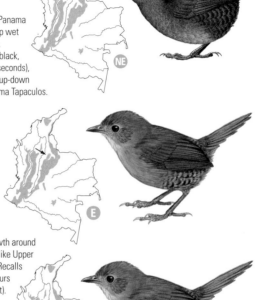

Stiles's Tapaculo *Scytalopus stilesi* LC
Tapaculo de Stiles EN
Local resident.

L 12.2 cm (4.8"). Monotypic. Endemic. Dense undergrowth in humid forest. 1400–2200 m. **ID** ♂ slaty black, rump brownish, lower underparts chestnut barred dusky. ♀ paler grey, especially throat and breast, wings brownish, legs paler. **Voice** Song, series of very rapid frog-like trills in bursts of 20–35 notes/second at intervals of c. 1 second. **SS** Range overlaps locally with White-crowned and Blackish Tapaculos; Spillmann's Tapaculo (mostly higher).

Tatama Tapaculo *Scytalopus alvarezlopezi* NT
Tapaculo de Tatamá
Locally common resident.

 L 12.2 cm (4.8"). Monotypic. Endemic. Undergrowth in wet Pacific slope forest; locally on adjacent E slope of W Andes. 1300–1800 m. **ID** Slaty black, rump tinged brownish, flanks and lower underparts chestnut obscurely barred dusky. **Voice** Unusual song, continuous bursts of low-pitched rattle-trills (c. 8–15 notes/0.35–0.75 seconds) with 0.1-second breaks between bursts "dddddd dddddd…" for a minute or more; frog-like. **SS** Occurs above Choco Tapaculo, below Spillmann's Tapaculo, overlaps Narino Tapaculo. **TN** Discovered 1992. **AN** Alto Pisones Tapaculo.

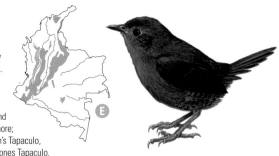

Narino Tapaculo *Scytalopus vicinior* LC
Tapaculo de Nariño
Common resident.

 L 12.2 cm (4.8"). Monotypic. Near-endemic (also NW Ecuador). Habitat as Tatama Tapaculo but at higher elevations; only Pacific slope. 1700–2100 m (verifiable records lower?). **ID** Indistinguishable from Spillmann's Tapaculo except by voice. **Voice** Song variable, typically long series of even-paced notes (c. 5–7 notes/second), or introductory note followed by softer notes gradually increasing in volume. Scold, short rattles, and "kik" notes. **SS** Spillmann's Tapaculo (mostly highest elevations, much faster songs), Tatama Tapaculo (frog-like songs), Choco Tapaculo (lower elevations, slower songs).

Brown-rumped Tapaculo *Scytalopus latebricola* NT
Tapaculo Ratón
Common resident.

 L 13 cm (5"). Monotypic. Endemic. Dense undergrowth at borders or gaps in humid forest, shrubby low-stature second growth, *Chusquea* bamboo. 2200–3700 m. **ID** Overall greyish (not slaty), throat pale grey, rump brownish, lower underparts rufous-brown (plain or lightly barred). **Voice** Song, several nasal introductory "qeeyop" notes increase in speed, abruptly accelerate into very fast trill (c. 20–25 notes/second). Call, short fast trills; scold, brief nasal descending buzz "bzzert". **SS** Santa Marta Tapaculo (lower elevations).

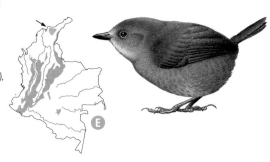

Perija Tapaculo *Scytalopus perijanus* VU
Tapaculo de Perijá VU
Fairly common resident.

 L 12.2 cm (4.8"). Monotypic. Near-endemic (also adjacent Venezuela). Dense undergrowth at borders of humid forest, elfin woodland, shrubby bushes and bamboo in *páramo*, patches of shrubs. 1600–3225 m (mostly 2500–3000 m). **ID** Nearly identical to Brown-rumped Tapaculo; barring on rear parts faint or lacking. **Voice** Complex, variable. Song, generally short bursts of slow churring trills (8–10 notes/0.5–0.8 seconds), or (in agnostic encounters) trills ascend in pitch (like little rising waves of sound), or bursts descend; trills repeated with only short (0.5–3-second) pauses. **TN** New species (described 2015).

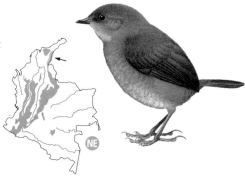

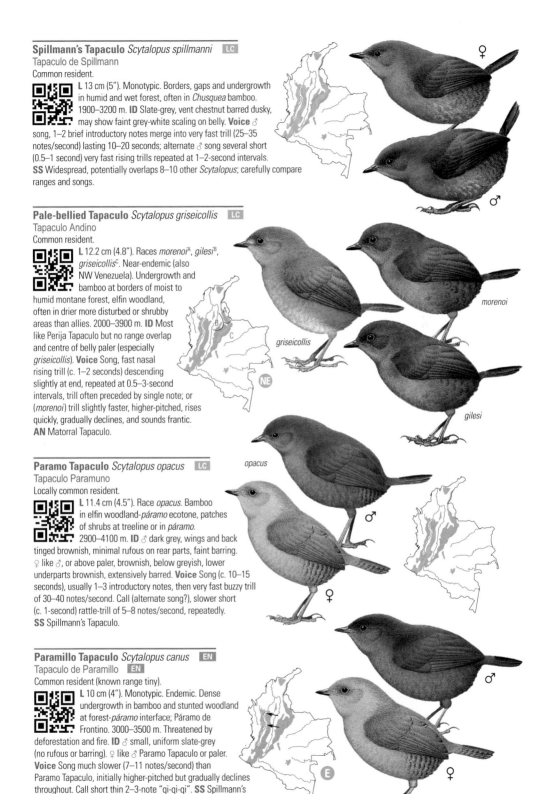

Spillmann's Tapaculo *Scytalopus spillmanni* `LC`
Tapaculo de Spillmann
Common resident.

L 13 cm (5"). Monotypic. Borders, gaps and undergrowth in humid and wet forest, often in *Chusquea* bamboo. 1900–3200 m. **ID** Slate-grey, vent chestnut barred dusky, may show faint grey-white scaling on belly. **Voice** ♂ song, 1–2 brief introductory notes merge into very fast trill (25–35 notes/second) lasting 10–20 seconds; alternate ♂ song several short (0.5–1 second) very fast rising trills repeated at 1–2-second intervals. **SS** Widespread, potentially overlaps 8–10 other *Scytalopus*; carefully compare ranges and songs.

Pale-bellied Tapaculo *Scytalopus griseicollis* `LC`
Tapaculo Andino
Common resident.

L 12.2 cm (4.8"). Races *morenoi*[A], *gilesi*[B], *griseicollis*[C]. Near-endemic (also NW Venezuela). Undergrowth and bamboo at borders of moist to humid montane forest, elfin woodland, often in drier more disturbed or shrubby areas than allies. 2000–3900 m. **ID** Most like Perija Tapaculo but no range overlap and centre of belly paler (especially *griseicollis*). **Voice** Song, fast nasal rising trill (c. 1–2 seconds) descending slightly at end, repeated at 0.5–3-second intervals, trill often preceded by single note; or (*morenoi*) trill slightly faster, higher-pitched, rises quickly, gradually declines, and sounds frantic. **AN** Matorral Tapaculo.

Paramo Tapaculo *Scytalopus opacus* `LC`
Tapaculo Paramuno
Locally common resident.

L 11.4 cm (4.5"). Race *opacus*. Bamboo in elfin woodland-*páramo* ecotone, patches of shrubs at treeline or in *páramo*. 2900–4100 m. **ID** ♂ dark grey, wings and back tinged brownish, minimal rufous on rear parts, faint barring. ♀ like ♂, or above paler, brownish, below greyish, lower underparts brownish, extensively barred. **Voice** Song (c. 10–15 seconds), usually 1–3 introductory notes, then very fast buzzy trill of 30–40 notes/second. Call (alternate song?), slower short (c. 1-second) rattle-trill of 5–8 notes/second, repeatedly. **SS** Spillmann's Tapaculo.

Paramillo Tapaculo *Scytalopus canus* `EN`
Tapaculo de Paramillo `EN`
Common resident (known range tiny).

L 10 cm (4"). Monotypic. Endemic. Dense undergrowth in bamboo and stunted woodland at forest-*páramo* interface; Páramo de Frontino. 3000–3500 m. Threatened by deforestation and fire. **ID** ♂ small, uniform slate-grey (no rufous or barring). ♀ like ♂ Paramo Tapaculo or paler. **Voice** Song much slower (7–11 notes/second) than Paramo Tapaculo, initially higher-pitched but gradually declines throughout. Call short thin 2–3-note "qi-qi-qi". **SS** Spillmann's Tapaculo. **TN** Formerly treated as conspecific with Paramo Tapaculo.

morenoi

griseicollis

gilesi

opacus

FORMICARIIDAE
Ground-antbirds
12 extant species, 8 in region

Small group of terrestrial 'antbirds' found in humid lowland and montane forests from Mexico to Amazonia. The family presently comprises two genera, *Formicarius* and *Chamaeza*, both originally included with other antbirds. DNA studies, however, revealed that species in these genera were not closely related to other antbirds, leading eventually to the present three-family arrangement (typical antbirds, antpittas, and ground-antbirds) with *Pittasoma* moved to yet another family, the Conopophagidae.

Genus *Formicarius* Plump, terrestrial; walk with jaunty gait and cocked tail. Sing from ground or log; challenging to see.

Rufous-capped Antthrush *Formicarius colma* LC
Gallito Cuellirrojo
Fairly common resident.

L 18 cm (7"). Race *colma*. Undergrowth in humid *terra firme* and transition forest. To 500 m. Usually seen singly. Walks lightly with cocked tail and bobbing head, pausing to flick leaves aside. Occasionally at army ant swarms. Responds to playback by flying in close to eye-level perch, rather than by walking. **ID** ♂ rufous crown, black face and underparts. ♀ (also imm?) usually white-dotted throat. **Voice** Song, from ground to c. 4 m up, quavering glissando, faltering slightly, then gradually rising "wu-u-er-er-u-u-u-u-u-u-u-u-u" (c. 4 seconds). Call, sharp "KEET!". **SS** Black-faced Antthrush.

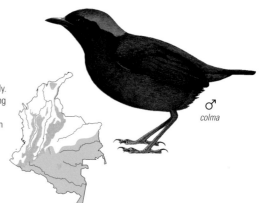

♂
colma

Black-faced Antthrush *Formicarius analis* LC
Gallito Carinegro

Eleven subspecies in two subspecies groups; both in Colombia.

Northern Black-faced Antthrush
Formicarius (analis) hoffmanni
Formicario Enmascarado del Norte
Uncommon but somewhat local resident.
L 18 cm (7"). Races *panamensis*[A], *virescens*[B], *griseoventris*[C], *saturatus*[D]. Humid lowland and foothill forest, older second growth. To 1200 m. Behaviour as Rufous-capped Antthrush but approaches on foot (not flying). **ID** Face and throat black, below grey. **Voice** Song, loud emphatic whistle (c. 2 kHz) followed, after pause, by 2–5 briefer, slightly lower-pitched whistles "WHE! . wü, wü, wü". Alarm, loud clipped "churlip!". **TN** Race *saturatus* often placed with southern *analis* group, but voice and distribution align with this primarily Central American subspecies group. Here, Mayan Antthrush *F. moniliger* treated at species level.

saturatus

panamensis

Southern Black-faced Antthrush *Formicarius (analis) analis*
Formicario Enmascarado del Sur
Common resident.
L 18 cm (7"). Races *connectens*[A], *zamorae*[B] (?). Undergrowth in humid *terra firme* forest; mainly second growth and *várzea* where Rufous-capped Antthrush present. To 1000 m. **ID** Like northern races but underparts darker, vent brighter, and chestnut neck patch faint or lacking. **Voice** Song (*zamorae*) recalls northern races but faster: "WHE! . wi-wi-wü-wü-wü-...", 10–15 run-together notes after pause, rising slightly, then gradually falling and fading. **SS** Rufous-capped Antthrush.

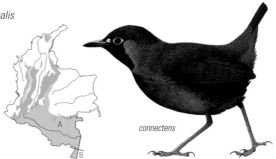

connectens

Black-headed Antthrush *Formicarius nigricapillus* `LC`
Gallito Cabecinegro
Fairly common resident.

 L 18 cm (7"). Race *destructus*. Dense undergrowth in wet lowland and foothill forest. To 900 m (rarely 1400 m). Singles walk with deliberate gait on forest floor, tail up, head bobbing; pause, flick leaves, may follow ant swarms. With patience approaches playback. **ID** Head and most of underparts black, vent chestnut. **Voice** Song, eerie quavering glissando of 30+ notes sliding upscale, slowing at end. **SS** Like black replica of Black-faced Antthrush (minimal overlap).

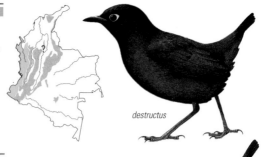

destructus

Rufous-breasted Antthrush *Formicarius rufipectus* `LC`
Gallito Pechirrufo
Uncommon resident.

 L 19 cm (7.5"). Races *rufipectus*[A], *carrikeri*[B], *lasallei*[C], *thoracicus*[D] (?). Thick undergrowth in humid and wet premontane and montane forest. 1100–2200 m. Behaviour like Black-headed Antthrush but even harder to see. **ID** Face and throat black, crown and underparts dark rufous (*carrikeri*), or crown blackish nearly like face (*thoracicus*). **Voice** Song (2 kHz), flat insipid whistled "wü, üü", second note same pitch or semi-tone higher. Alarm, coarse low "quik-quik-..." of c. 3–8 notes.

carrikeri

lasallei

Genus *Chamaeza* Robust, with stubby cocked tail and short bill. Cryptic plumage, strongly patterned underparts. Terrestrial inside shady forest. Wary, heard far more than seen.

Short-tailed Antthrush *Chamaeza campanisona* `LC`
Tovaca Campanera

 Twelve subspecies in five subspecies groups; one in Colombia.

Colombian Short-tailed Antthrush
Chamaeza (campanisona) columbiana
Local resident.
L 20 cm (8"). One subspecies in group. Endemic. Humid foothill and montane forest. 600–2050 m. Forest recluse always noted first by voice. Widely scattered pairs; alert, jaunty attitude as thread their way on foot through cluttered undergrowth. **ID** Resembles Scalloped Antthrush but differs in voice, lower-elevational range, tiny buff-white tail tips. **Voice** Sings from ground or log; 10–20 slowly accelerating rising "whoo" whistles, abruptly followed by several slower, falling, strongly inflected and trogon-like "woop" notes. **TN** Circum-Amazonian distribution suggest several species possibly involved, but voices rather similar.

Striated Antthrush *Chamaeza nobilis* `LC`
Tovaca Estriada

Three subspecies in two subspecies groups; one in Colombia.

Western Striated Antthrush *Chamaeza (nobilis) nobilis*
Uncommon resident (widely separated pairs).
L 23 cm (9"). Race *rubida*. Floor of humid *terra firme* forest. To 500 m (higher?). **ID** Resembles Short-tailed and Scalloped Antthrushes but larger, whiter below, always lower elevation; similar furtive behaviour. **Voice** Dramatic song, from on or near ground, long accelerating series of low hollow "who" notes, abruptly ending with several slower inflected "whoop" notes, recalls Short-tailed Antthrush but much longer (10–15 seconds). Call liquid "quik!". **AN** Noble Antthrush.

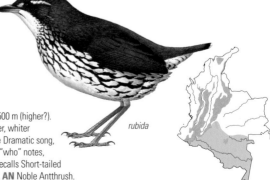

rubida

Scalloped Antthrush (Schwartz's Antthrush)
Chamaeza turdina LC
Tovacá Turdino
Uncommon resident.

turdina

 L 19 cm (7.5"). Race *turdina*. Floor of humid and wet montane forest. 1500–2800 m. **ID** From Short-tailed Antthrush by voice; differs in slightly smaller size, all-dark tail, more scalloped underparts.
Voice Song, incredibly long (to 50 seconds) series of whistled "cu" notes (2–3/second) without pause, gains slightly in pitch and volume throughout. Also loud abrupt descending series of "cuk" notes slowing, laugh-like, may merge into long song (above); either song may end in chuckling notes, e.g. "…cu-cu-towak, wak, wak". Alarm "ble'blink".

Barred Antthrush *Chamaeza mollissima* LC
Tovaca Barrada
Rare to uncommon resident.

mollissima

L 20 cm (8"). Race *mollissima*. Dense mossy forest floor in montane forest. 1600–3100 m. Behaviour like other *Chamaeza* but even harder to see. **ID** Finely barred eyebrow and underparts are key; shape (short legs, hunched posture) and behaviour (always walks) unlike antpittas. **Voice** Song, long series (up to 25 seconds) of low hollow "cuh" notes that increase in volume and pitch, ends abruptly (no descending notes). **SS** Darker, generally higher elevation than other *Chamaeza*.

FURNARIIDAE
Ovenbirds
331 extant species, 118 in region

This large, fascinating family becomes most diverse from Amazonia southward. Many species are notable for their unusual nests, which rank among the most remarkable in the Western Hemisphere, and range from domed mud 'ovens' to enormous stick nests, sometimes with long tubular entrances. Earth-tone colours predominate and plumage differences between species are often slight. The recent addition of woodcreepers (subfamily Dendrocolaptinae) only adds to identification difficulties, and is compounded by many controversial and unresolved taxonomic issues.

Genus *Sclerurus* Furtive, with dark plumage. Forest understorey, inconspicuous, often perversely coy but songs distinctive. Hop on ground, pause to toss leaves (hence name). Legs short; bills slender, slightly decurved. Burrow nests. None follow mixed flocks.

Tawny-throated Leaftosser *Sclerurus mexicanus* LC
Raspahojas Picudo

Seven subspecies in up to seven subspecies groups; three in Colombia. A fourth (*pullus*) may occur on Panama border (Cerro Tacarcuna). Taxonomy unresolved; all vocally rather similar.

Andean Tawny-throated Leaftosser *Sclerurus (mexicanus) andinus*
Uncommon resident.
L 15 cm (6"). One subspecies in group. Near-endemic (also extreme NW Venezuela and NW Ecuador). Damp shady undergrowth in humid premontane and montane forest; c. 500–2000 m (elevational range needs confirmation). **ID** Rufous-brown to chestnut-brown, tawny throat obviously paler, rump paler, tail contrasting blackish; distinguish from allies by voice and range. **Voice** Song, c. 5–9 faster, sharply up-down inflected notes in three seconds "peEEir, peEEir…" gradually descending (c. 5–4 kHz). Call sharp "spik". **TN** This and the following two subspecies groups sometimes treated as one group (Southern Tawny-throated Leaftosser).

Dusky Tawny-throated Leaftosser *Sclerurus (mexicanus) obscurior*
Uncommon resident.
L 15 cm (6"). One subspecies in group. Chocó-Pacific lowlands, to c. 1100 m (higher?). **ID** Like *andinus* race (above) but darker, duskier, lacking contrast between upperparts and rump; distinguish by voice and range. **Voice** Song, up to c. 8 flat to slightly upslurred "squeeik" notes in leisurely, gradually descending series (c. 5.5–4 kHz in 2.5 seconds). Call, sharp metallic "spik!".

Amazonian Tawny-throated Leaftosser
Sclerurus (mexicanus) peruvianus
Uncommon resident.
L 15 cm (6"). One subspecies in group. To 2000 m. **ID** Like *andinus*
race (previous page) but little or no contrast between rump and tail;
best identified by voice and range. **Voice** Song, lazier, more musical
than previous two forms but much like *andinus* in tonal quality,
"suweee, suweee, ...", c. 7–10+ notes in c. 3–4 seconds, slightly
descending (4–3 kHz). **TN** Sometimes *peruvianus* is treated as
forming a single subspecies group with *S. m. macconnelli* (Guianan
Tawny-throated Leaftosser).

Short-billed Leaftosser *Sclerurus rufigularis* `LC`
Raspahojas Piquicorto
Uncommon resident.

 L 15 cm (6"). Races *brunnescens*[A],
fulvigularis[B] (SE Guainía?). To 500 m
(1800 m, Macarena Mts). Undergrowth
and floor of humid *terra firme* forest.
Behaviour typical of genus. **ID** Very like Amazonian
Tawny-throated Leaftosser (*peruvianus*) but bill
shorter and straight, indistinct tawny eyebrow.
Best identified by song. **Voice** Song, high, thin penetrating series
of 10–20 "pee" notes that descend then ascend, finally level out
and slow. Call sharp metallic "skreep!". **SS** Black-tailed Leaftosser.

fulvigularis

brunnescens

Scaly-throated Leaftosser *Sclerurus guatemalensis* `LC`
Raspahojas Medialuna
Uncommon resident.

 L 16.5 cm (6.5"). Races *salvini*[A], *ennosiphyllus*[B].
Undergrowth and floor of moist to moderately
humid (not wet middle Chocó) forest in lowlands
and foothills. To 1250 m. Behaviour typical of
genus. **ID** Whitish throat diagnostic (hard to see), lacks
contrasting rump. **Voice** Song, 10–12 high rapid notes,
descending slightly, then ascending and accelerating; often
given over and over. Call, sharp "pik!". **SS** Dusky Tawny-throated
Leaftosser.

salvini

Black-tailed Leaftosser *Sclerurus caudacutus* `LC`
Raspahojas Colinegro
Uncommon resident.

 L 18 cm (7"). Race *brunneus*. Humid *terra firme*
forest. To 500 m. Behaviour typical of genus.
ID Uniformly dark, throat whitish (hard to see),
long straight bill. **Voice** Song, 10–12 loud,
emphatic "spink" notes, gradually falling in pitch, slowing
slightly at end. **SS** Short-billed Leaftosser.

brunneus

Grey-throated Leaftosser *Sclerurus albigularis* `NT`
Raspahojas Collarejo
Fairly common resident (Santa Marta), rare to uncommon elsewhere.

 L 16.5 cm (6.5"). Races *propinquus*[A], *albigularis*[B].
Undergrowth and floor of humid foothill and lower montane
forest. 500–2100 m. Behaviour typical of genus. **ID** Grey
throat, rufous chest (*propinquus*), or more rufescent
above (*albigularis*). **Voice** Distinctive song, 4–6 nasal rising notes
"quee, quee, queet, queeek", trills and chattering added when disturbed.
SS Amazonian Tawny-throated Leaftosser.

albigularis

Spot-throated Woodcreeper
Certhiasomus stictolaemus LC
Trepatroncos del Putumayo
Rare to uncommon resident (distribution poorly known).

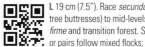 **L** 19 cm (7.5"). Race *secundus*. Low (even on tree buttresses) to mid-levels in humid *terra firme* and transition forest. Singles or pairs follow mixed flocks; unobtrusive, easily overlooked. **ID** Fairly small, thin bill; minimal short dot-like streaking on throat and chest, even less on sides of head. **Voice** Song, short fast chattering rattle-trill, descends slightly, then steadily ascends (c. 2 seconds). **SS** Wedge-billed Woodcreeper (short bill), larger Southern Long-tailed Woodcreeper.

secundus

Southern Long-tailed Woodcreeper
Deconychura pallida NT
Trepatroncos Rabilargo del Sur
Resident (few records).

 L 19–21 cm (7.5–8.2"). Race *connectens*. Low in humid lowland forest. To 300 m (higher?). **ID** Mid-length straight bill. ♂ larger than ♀, longish tail imparts slender appearance; thin buff eyestripe, short narrow spot-like streaking on face, throat and chest, back plain. **Voice** Unusual song (*connectens*) c. 6–10 clear leisurely whistles in c. 4–5 seconds, each distinctly lower than preceding one; melancholy, unlike allies. **SS** Various *Xiphorhynchus* woodcreepers, Spot-throated Woodcreeper.

connectens

Little Long-tailed Woodcreeper
Deconychura typica LC
Trepatroncos Rabilargo Pequeño
Uncommon resident.

 **L** 20 cm (8"). Races *darienensis*[A], *minor*[B]. Mid- and lower-levels in humid lowland and foothill forest. To 1300 m. Singles or pairs follow mixed flocks. **ID** Much like Southern Long-tailed (below) but underparts spotted (not streaked). **Voice** Song, long (up to 12 seconds) series of "chit" notes accelerating, rising a little in pitch and volume, then slows, declines in volume, ends with 4–5 well-spaced notes. **SS** Southern Spotted Woodcreeper. **TN** Southern *connectens* (below) usually included with present races as Long-tailed Woodcreeper *D. longicauda*.

darienensis

Olivaceous Woodcreeper *Sittasomus griseicapillus* LC
Trepatroncos Oliváceo

Fifteen subspecies in 5–6 subspecies groups (taxonomy dependent); three in Colombia. Taxonomy provisional and debated; may involve multiple species (two recognized by one checklist).

Greyish Woodcreeper *Sittasomus (griseicapillus) griseus*
Uncommon resident.
L 16.5 cm (6.5"). Races *sylvioides*[A], *perijanus*[B], *tachirensis*[C]. Wide range of dry, moist and humid forests, borders, second growth. To 2000 m. Singles or pairs follow mixed flocks, at various heights, but generally mid-levels or higher. Hitches jerkily up trunks and large limbs. **ID** Small; plain, greyish olive, wings and tail chestnut. All races show buff wing-stripe in flight. **Voice** Song (2.5–4.2 kHz), very fast smoothly rising-falling (bell-curve) trill, with buzzy or flat thin tone, c. 2.5 seconds. **SS** Wedge-billed Woodcreeper.

sylvioides

Pacific Olivaceous Woodcreeper
Sittasomus (griseicapillus) aequatorialis
Uncommon resident.
L 16.5 cm (6.5"). One subspecies in group. Dry, moist and humid forest borders, second growth, light or disturbed woodland; perhaps expanding N with partial deforestation. To c. 1500 m (higher?). Behaviour as *griseus* group (previous page). **ID** Best separated from *griseus* group by voice, and isolated range. **Voice** Song, short (2–2.5 seconds) fast, smoothly rising-falling (c. 1.5–2.5 KHz) trill "prrrrRRRRRrrrrrrrrrr" of 35+ notes, louder in middle then fading; recalls *griseus* group (previous page), but lower-pitched, 'heavier' tone.

Amazonian Olivaceous Woodcreeper
Sittasomus (griseicapillus) griseicapillus
Uncommon resident.
L 17 cm (6.7"). Race *amazonus*. Mostly mid-levels or lower inside humid forest, borders, second growth. To 1100 m. **ID** Like *griseus* species group (previous page), but slightly larger, head and underparts darker more plain grey. **Voice** Song, measured series of 6–15 notes "pu-pu-pu-pu-pwe-pwe-pwe, pu", steadily rising, last note or two dropping at end. **AN** Amazonian Woodcreeper.

amazonus

Genus *Dendrocincla* Medium-sized with uniform plumage (no stripes or spots). Some species associated with army ant swarms.

Tyrannine Woodcreeper *Dendrocincla tyrannina* `LC`
Trepatroncos Cordillerano
Rare to uncommon resident.
L 25 cm (10"). Races *tyrannina*[A], *hellmayri*[B]. Humid montane forest, borders. 1900–3200 m (1500 m, Pacific slope). Singles, alone or with mixed flocks; mid-levels; not with army ants (few at high elevations). **ID** Long black bill, plumage uniform olive-brown. **Voice** Infrequent song, long 10–20 seconds, rapid accelerating chattering trill, rising slightly, but quickly slowing at end. Call loud stuttering "bl'b'b'b". **SS** Plain-brown Woodcreeper (lower elevation).

tyrannina

White-chinned Woodcreeper *Dendrocincla merula* `LC`
Trepatroncos Barbiblanco
Seven subspecies in two subspecies groups; one in Colombia.

Southern White-chinned Woodcreeper
Dendrocincla (merula) castanoptera
Rare to very uncommon resident.
L 18 cm (7"). Race *bartletti*. Undergrowth in humid *terra firme* and *várzea* forest, sandy soil forests. To 500 m. Singles or pairs, almost always at army ant swarms; wary, difficult to see, stay very low. **ID** Eyes grey to bluish, plumage uniform rufescent-brown, only central throat white (inconspicuous), loral area pale, otherwise sides of head uniform (no dark malar or pale cheek). **Voice** Harsh staccato 2–3-note "st'st'st'". Song, abrupt rippling semi-musical "w'w'wup", rising. **SS** Often confused with Plain-brown Woodcreeper.

bartletti

Ruddy Woodcreeper *Dendrocincla homochroa* LC
Trepatroncos Colorado
Rare and local resident.

 L 20 cm (8"). Races *ruficeps*[A], *meridionalis*[B]. Moist to humid lowland and foothill forest, borders, scattered trees in clearings. To 1800 m (mostly < 800 m). Singles follow mixed flocks, occasionally 2–3 at army ant swarms; mid-levels or lower. **ID** Uniform rufescent-brown, crown brighter rufous than body. **Voice** Song, descending churring rattle (c. 2.5 seconds), chattering, spilled out; long rattling over ants. Call, buzzy meowing. **SS** Plain-brown Woodcreeper.

meridionalis

Wedge-billed Woodcreeper
Glyphorynchus spirurus LC
Trepatroncos Pico-de-cuña

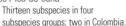 Thirteen subspecies in four subspecies groups; two in Colombia.

Northern Wedge-billed Woodcreeper
Glyphorynchus (spirurus) pectoralis
Common resident.

L 14 cm (5.5"). Races *pallidulus*[A], *subrufescens*[B], *integratus*[C]. Humid lowland and lower montane forest. To 2100 m (mostly < 1200 m). Singles or pairs follow mixed-species flocks. Low to mid-levels, occasionally subcanopy. Jerky and mechanical as hitches up large trunks. **ID** Smallest woodcreeper, stubby wedge-shaped bill. **Voice** Commonest call, often repeated, dry sneezing "chief" or "chief beef!". Brief dawn song, 8–20 clear brisk little warbles "chu-uu-we-we-we-weet" rising sharply.

pallidulus

Plain-brown Woodcreeper *Dendrocincla fuliginosa* LC
Trepatroncos Pardo

 Twelve subspecies in two subspecies groups; one in Colombia.

Plain-brown Woodcreeper
Dendrocincla (fuliginosa) meruloides
Common resident.

L 20 cm (8"). Races *ridgwayi*[A], *lafresnayei*[B], *barinensis*[C], *phaeochroa*[D]. Mid-levels or lower in humid lowland to montane forest, borders, older second growth. To 1800 m. Persistent army ant follower, often several at large swarms; clings low on trunks, drops to ground; away from swarms follows mixed flocks. **ID** Uniform dull brown, ill-defined dusky malar line, pale ear-coverts. **Voice** Song, over ants, long-sustained bubbly or purring rattle, pitch and volume rising and falling. Normal song (c. 3 seconds) rapid descending rattle (3–2.5 kHz). **SS** White-chinned Woodcreeper.

ridgwayi

Central Wedge-billed Woodcreeper
Glyphorynchus (spirurus) spirurus
Common resident.

L 14 cm (5.5"). Race *rufigularis*. To 1450 m. Habitat and behaviour as previous group. **ID** As northern races (left). **Voice** Song, also similar but slower than northern races, c. 4–12 wheezy upward-inflected notes, slowly ascending "wee-wee-wee-wheet" or longer "too-e too-e tu-tu-tu-tue'tue'twu'tweetwee", burry quality. **SS** Amazonian Olivaceous and Spot-throated Woodcreepers.

rufigularis

Cinnamon-throated Woodcreeper
Dendrexetastes rufigula `LC`
Trepatronco Piquidorado
Fairly common resident.

L 25 cm (10"). Race *devillei*. Subcanopy and canopy of humid *terra firme* and *várzea* forest, borders, trees in clearings. To 500 m (rarely 900 m). Singles or pairs, alone or with mixed flocks, climb trunks and high limbs, also clamber in terminal foliage, even hang upside-down, like *Philydor* foliage-gleaners. **ID** Thick greenish bill is key; uniform plumage, necklace inconspicuous. **Voice** Song (c. 3 seconds), pre-dawn and dusk, loud staccato rattle with wild ripping quality, accelerates, then slowly skids to halt.

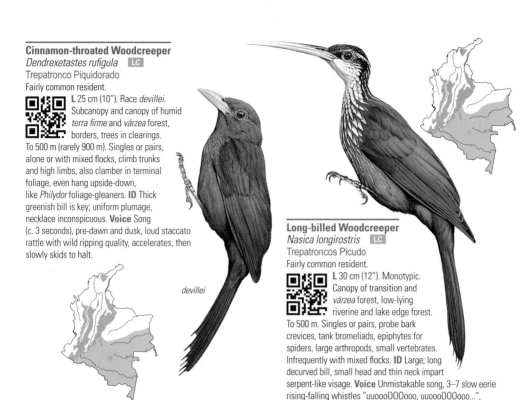

devillei

Long-billed Woodcreeper
Nasica longirostris `LC`
Trepatroncos Picudo
Fairly common resident.

L 30 cm (12"). Monotypic. Canopy of transition and *várzea* forest, low-lying riverine and lake edge forest. To 500 m. Singles or pairs, probe bark crevices, tank bromeliads, epiphytes for spiders, large arthropods, small vertebrates. Infrequently with mixed flocks. **ID** Large; long decurved bill, small head and thin neck impart serpent-like visage. **Voice** Unmistakable song, 3–7 slow eerie rising-falling whistles "uuooo000ooo, uuooo000ooo...", raptor-like, low (2 kHz), easily imitated. Harsh stuttering calls.

Genera *Dendrocolaptes* and *Hylexetastes* Large, strong-billed; often have combinations of barring and spotting. Some regularly follow army ant swarms.

Western Barred Woodcreeper
(Northern Barred Woodcreeper)
Dendrocolaptes sanctithomae `LC`
Trepatroncos del Magdalena
Uncommon resident.

L 27 cm (10.5"). Race *sanctithomae*. Humid lowland and foothill forest. To 900 m (rarely 1200 m). Singles, pairs or several follow army ant swarms where aggressive, dominant; cling low on trunks and saplings, higher away from ants. **ID** Bill and lores blackish, crown often ruffed, head and underparts barred, back and wing-covert barring fainter. **Voice** Song, dawn and dusk c. 4–10 strongly upslurred whistles, slightly rising in pitch "oweé, oweé, owé, owe-we-we-we-weet", last notes weaker, higher or omitted. **SS** Eastern Barred Woodcreeper. **TN** Taxonomy unsettled; Western and Eastern Barred Woodcreepers often treated as subspecies groups of Northern Barred Woodcreeper *D. sanctithomae*.

Eastern Barred Woodcreeper
(Northern Barred Woodcreeper)
Dendrocolaptes punctipectus `VU`
Trepatroncos Barrado Oriental
Uncommon resident.

L 28 cm (11"). Monotypic. To 1000 m. Habitat and behaviour as Western Barred. **ID** As Western Barred Woodcreeper but marginally larger, chin and throat mottled, less barred. **Voice** Song differs slightly; first several notes flat (not upslurred), rest somewhat overslurred, at least initially in narrower frequency range, overall maximum frequency lower. **SS** Western Barred Woodcreeper doubtfully separable in field (except by range). **TN** See previous species.

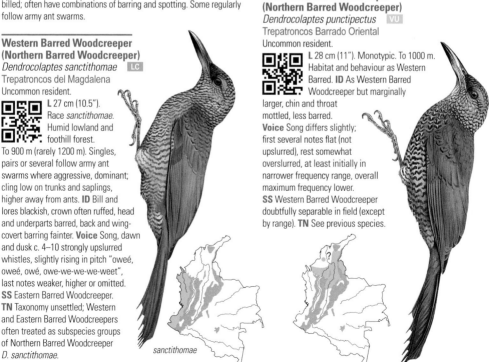

sanctithomae

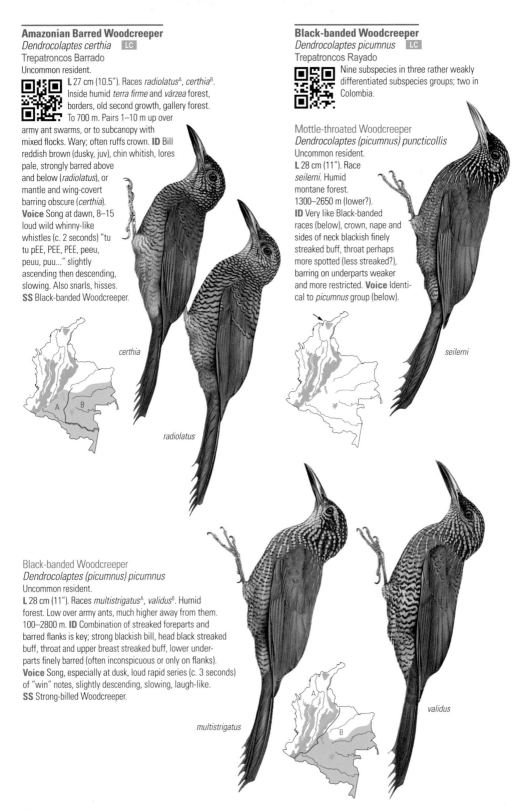

Amazonian Barred Woodcreeper
Dendrocolaptes certhia LC
Trepatroncos Barrado
Uncommon resident.

L 27 cm (10.5"). Races *radiolatus*[A], *certhia*[B]. Inside humid *terra firme* and *várzea* forest, borders, old second growth, gallery forest. To 700 m. Pairs 1–10 m up over army ant swarms, or to subcanopy with mixed flocks. Wary; often ruffs crown. **ID** Bill reddish brown (dusky, juv), chin whitish, lores pale, strongly barred above and below (*radiolatus*), or mantle and wing-covert barring obscure (*certhia*). **Voice** Song at dawn, 8–15 loud wild whinny-like whistles (c. 2 seconds) "tu tu pEE, PEE, peeu, peuu, puu..." slightly ascending then descending, slowing. Also snarls, hisses. **SS** Black-banded Woodcreeper.

certhia

radiolatus

Black-banded Woodcreeper
Dendrocolaptes (picumnus) picumnus
Uncommon resident.
L 28 cm (11"). Races *multistrigatus*[A], *validus*[B]. Humid forest. Low over army ants, much higher away from them. 100–2800 m. **ID** Combination of streaked foreparts and barred flanks is key; strong blackish bill, head black streaked buff, throat and upper breast streaked buff, lower underparts finely barred (often inconspicuous or only on flanks). **Voice** Song, especially at dusk, loud rapid series (c. 3 seconds) of "win" notes, slightly descending, slowing, laugh-like. **SS** Strong-billed Woodcreeper.

multistrigatus

Black-banded Woodcreeper
Dendrocolaptes picumnus LC
Trepatroncos Rayado

Nine subspecies in three rather weakly differentiated subspecies groups; two in Colombia.

Mottle-throated Woodcreeper
Dendrocolaptes (picumnus) puncticollis
Uncommon resident.
L 28 cm (11"). Race *seilerni*. Humid montane forest. 1300–2650 m (lower?). **ID** Very like Black-banded races (below), crown, nape and sides of neck finely streaked buff, throat perhaps more spotted (less streaked?), barring on underparts weaker and more restricted. **Voice** Identical to *picumnus* group (below).

seilerni

validus

312

Bar-bellied Woodcreeper *Hylexetastes stresemanni* `LC`
Trepatronco Pico de Barba
Rare resident (few records).

L 29 cm (11.5"). Race *insignis*. Humid *terra firme* forest. To 300 m. Singles, wary, follow army ant swarms, or ascend to subcanopy with mixed flocks. **ID** Large and robust, strong reddish bill, head and upperparts unstreaked, broad dark malar bordered above by a few whitish markings, below by whitish throat, minor white chest streaking, lower underparts barred. **Voice** Song, 5–8 falling-rising phrases, same pitch or slightly descending, "jow'wie, jow'wie…", mushy (not clean). **SS** Amazonian Barred and Black-banded Woodcreepers.

Strong-billed Woodcreeper
Xiphocolaptes promeropirhynchus `LC`
Trepatroncos Gigante

Up to 25 subspecies in three or more subspecies groups; two in Colombia.

Andean Strong-billed Woodcreeper
Xiphocolaptes (promeropirhynchus) promeropirhynchus
Fairly common resident (Santa Marta Mts), uncommon elsewhere.

L 30.5 cm (12"). Races *sanctaemartae*[A], *rostratus*[B], *virgatus*[C], *promeropirhynchus*[D], *macarenae*[E], *ignotus*[F]. Humid and wet montane forest; c. 500–3000 m. Singles or pairs, forage high at tank bromeliads and epiphytes (especially *sanctaemartae*), less often low, regularly with mixed flocks. **ID** Blackish bill long and heavy, slightly decurved, blackish malar stripe, minor barring on lower underparts (except *sanctaemartae*). **Voice** Song, dawn and dusk, 8–10 slow, painfully strained (almost herniated) couplets "Reee'per, Reee'per…", the series descending; c. 1/second. **SS** Black-banded Woodcreeper. **TN** Race *fortis* known only from type specimen (thought to be from N Colombia or Venezuela) not certainly valid?

Amazonian Strong-billed Woodcreeper
Xiphocolaptes (promeropirhynchus) orenocensis
Uncommon resident.

L 32 cm (12.5"). Race *orenocensis*. Mid-levels to canopy in *terra firme* and *várzea* forest. To 800 m. **ID** Much like Andean forms (above) but bill paler than some Andean races, malar stripe and eyebrow faint or lacking; overall more rufescent (especially below). **Voice** Like Andean forms but a little faster and crisper. **SS** Black-banded Woodcreeper.

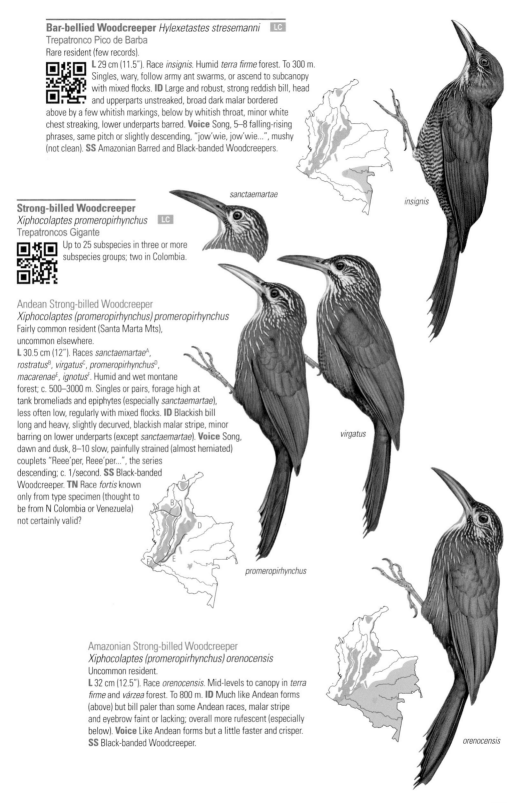

sanctaemartae

insignis

virgatus

promeropirhynchus

orenocensis

Genus *Xiphorhynchus* Large, taxonomically confusing group (perhaps over-split for field observers). Note bill shape and length, distribution of streaking, and voice. Several taxa not reliably separated in field; even molecular data are conflicting. Some voices geographically variable.

Striped Woodcreeper *Xiphorhynchus obsoletus* `LC`
Trepatroncos Listado
Fairly common resident.

 L 20 cm (8"). Races *notatus*[A], *palliatus*[B]. *Várzea* and swampy forest, especially low-lying areas along forested creek banks, gallery forest; almost always near water. To 500 m. Singles or pairs, usually low, infrequent even at mid-levels; generally inconspicuous. **ID** Above and below prominently streaked including entire back.
Voice Song, harsh staccato rattle-trill, initially descending slightly, then ascending throughout. **SS** Medium size and streaking on back are key points.

palliatus

Line-crowned Woodcreeper
Xiphorhynchus (ocellatus) beauperthuysii
Trepatroncos Lineocoronado
Status unknown.
L 20 cm (8"). Race *beauperthuysii*. Mid-levels or lower in humid *terra firme* and *várzea* forest, borders, sandy soil forest. To 500 m. **ID** Nearly identical to Tschudi's group (above), best told by voice (and genetics); may differ in crown having more line-like (not dotted) buff markings (?). **Voice** Song, dawn and dusk, slightly descending trill, then ascending for most of duration, accelerating at end; also whinnying trill with emphatic squeak at end "t'r'r'r'r'r'a'a'a'a'eik". Call descending "teeew". **SS** Elegant Woodcreeper. **TN** Taxonomy confused, with all three subspecies groups sometimes treated at species level; true Ocellated Woodcreeper possibly only S of R Amazon.

beauperthuysii

Ocellated Woodcreeper *Xiphorhynchus ocellatus* `LC`
Trepatroncos Ocelado

 Seven subspecies in three subspecies groups; two in Colombia.

Tschudi's Woodcreeper
Xiphorhynchus (ocellatus) chunchotambo
Trepatroncos de Tschudi
Status unknown.
L 20 cm (8"). Race *napensis*. Humid forest, often in *Guadua* bamboo, older second growth; more numerous in foothills. **ID** Fine buff spotting on crown becomes thin teardrop-shaped streaking on rear crown and nape, buff shaft-streaks on upper back, lower throat with lines of black-edged buff spots. **Voice** Song, rapid descending series of nasal notes, emphatic at end "whe-whe-whe-whe-whe-chéchéché cheow", or either part separately. Call slurred "kleer!". **TN** See Line-crowned Woodcreeper (below).

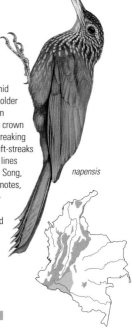

napensis

Elegant Woodcreeper
Xiphorhynchus elegans `LC`
Trepatroncos Elegante
Fairly common resident.

 L 20 cm (8"). Races *buenavistae*[A], *ornatus*[B]. Low and mid-strata in *terra firme* forest, less in *várzea*. To 500 m. Singles or pairs, usually with mixed flocks. **ID** Best told by voice; breast and mantle with teardrop spotting. **Voice** Song, long (2.5–5 seconds) brisk, gradually descending series of "tchu" notes, thinner, weaker at end, or sometimes repeated without clear break. Call, short staccato rattles; rising whines. **SS** Ocellated Woodcreeper. **TN** Taxonomic history complex, confused, subject to revision; formerly included with Spix's Woodcreeper *X. spixii* (both races).

ornatus

Cocoa Woodcreeper *Xiphorhynchus susurrans* LC
Trepatroncos Cacao

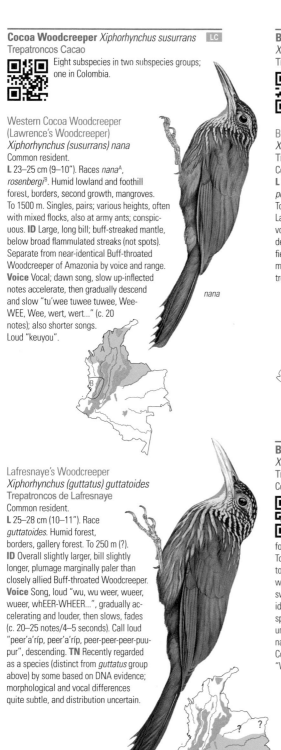

Eight subspecies in two subspecies groups; one in Colombia.

Western Cocoa Woodcreeper
(Lawrence's Woodcreeper)
Xiphorhynchus (susurrans) nana
Trepatroncos Cacao
Common resident.
L 23–25 cm (9–10"). Races *nana*[A], *rosenbergi*[B]. Humid lowland and foothill forest, borders, second growth, mangroves. To 1500 m. Singles, pairs; various heights, often with mixed flocks, also at army ants; conspicuous. **ID** Large, long bill; buff-streaked mantle, below broad flammulated streaks (not spots). Separate from near-identical Buff-throated Woodcreeper of Amazonia by voice and range. **Voice** Vocal; dawn song, slow up-inflected notes accelerate, then gradually descend and slow "tu'wee tuwee tuwee, Wee-WEE, Wee, wert, wert..." (c. 20 notes); also shorter songs. Loud "keuyou".

nana

Lafresnaye's Woodcreeper
Xiphorhynchus (guttatus) guttatoides
Trepatroncos de Lafresnaye
Common resident.
L 25–28 cm (10–11"). Race *guttatoides*. Humid forest, borders, gallery forest. To 250 m (?). **ID** Overall slightly larger, bill slightly longer, plumage marginally paler than closely allied Buff-throated Woodcreeper. **Voice** Song, loud "wu, wu weer, wueer, wueer, whEER-WHEER...", gradually accelerating and louder, then slows, fades (c. 20–25 notes/4–5 seconds). Call loud "peer'a'ríp, peer'a'ríp, peer-peer-peer-puu-pur", descending. **TN** Recently regarded as a species (distinct from *guttatus* group above) by some based on DNA evidence; morphological and vocal differences quite subtle, and distribution uncertain.

guttatoides

Buff-throated Woodcreeper
Xiphorhynchus guttatus LC
Trepatroncos Silbador

Eight subspecies in up to three subspecies groups; two in Colombia.

Buff-throated Woodcreeper
Xiphorhynchus (guttatus) guttatus
Trepatroncos Silbador
Common resident.
L 23–25 cm (9–10"). Race *polystictus*. Humid forest, borders. To 1000 m. **ID** Nearly identical to Lafresnaye's group (below), no vocal or morphological criteria definitively separate them in the field; separation at present based on molecular evidence. **TN** Occasionally treated as a species.

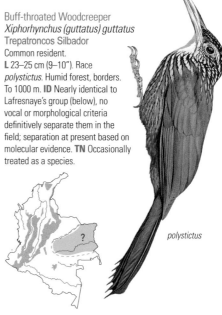

polystictus

Black-striped Woodcreeper
Xiphorhynchus lachrymosus LC
Trepatroncos Lacrimoso
Common (Pacific) or uncommon resident (Magdalena Valley).

L 23 cm (9").
Races *lachrymosus*[A], *alarum*[B]. Humid and wet forest borders, trees in clearings. To 1500 m. Singles and pairs, mid-strata to subcanopy, sometimes with mixed flocks or ant swarms. **ID** Easily identified by bold buff spot-like streaks on back and underparts. **Voice** Song, long-drawn, nasal smoothly descending whinny. Commonest call (3–4 notes), loud emphatic "WEE, WE-pa-pa".

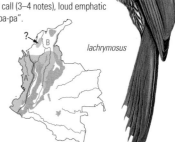

lachrymosus

Southern Spotted Woodcreeper

Xiphorhynchus aequatorialis LC

Trepatroncos Punteado Sureño

Fairly common resident.

 L 23 cm (9"). Races *insolitus*[A], *aequatorialis*[B]. Humid and wet foothill and premontane forest. 200–1600 m (rarely 2100 m). Pairs, mid-strata or higher, hitch up trunks or underside of mossy branches. Follows mixed flocks. **ID** Crown blackish obscurely dotted buff, prominent buff eye-ring, minimal fine streaking on mantle, underparts spotted. **Voice** Song 3–4 quavering whinnies, each lower than previous, "d'd'd'dddrear, d'd'd'dddrear, d'd'd'dddrrear", often with 2–3 brief "whew" notes added. **SS** Olive-backed Woodcreeper. **TN** Often treated as conspecific with *X. erythropygius* of Middle America as Spotted Woodcreeper.

aequatorialis

Olive-backed Woodcreeper

Xiphorhynchus triangularis LC

Trepatroncos Perlado

Fairly common resident.

L 23 cm (9"). Race *triangularis*. Humid and wet mossy montane forest. 1500–2700 m (rarely 400 m, Pacific slope). **ID** Much like Southern Spotted Woodcreeper but mostly at higher elevations; differs in voice, more obviously spotted crown, less streaking on mantle, throat and eye-ring more whitish than buff. **Voice** Infrequent song, single short quavering whinny expanding in volume, then fading (c. 1.3 seconds). Call sharp loud "qEEoo".

triangularis

Straight-billed Woodcreeper *Dendroplex picus* LC

Trepatroncos Pico-de-lanza

 Thirteen subspecies in two subspecies groups; both (if recognized) in Colombia, but all forms vocally identical.

Plain-throated Woodcreeper

Dendroplex (picus) picirostris

Common resident.

L 20 cm (8"). Races *extimus*[A], *dugandi*[B], *picirostris*[C]. Desert scrub, mangroves, dry to moist forest borders. To 600 m. Singles or pairs, usually low and conspicuous, often with mixed flocks. **ID** Whitish dagger-like bill, extensive whitish on foreface, throat and chest. **Voice** Song (3–4 seconds) a few brief notes and nasal colourless accelerating whinny, dropping slightly in pitch then slowing. Also inflected "pfew" notes gradually slowing and dropping.

picirostris

Straight-billed Woodcreeper *Dendroplex (picus) picus*

Common resident.

L 20 cm (8"). Races *saturatior*[A], *duidae*[B], *picus*[C]. Gallery forest in *llanos*; in Amazonia, river edges, river islands, *várzea* borders, second growth; generally fairly open areas. To 500 m. **ID** Bill shape and voice are key; straight pale grey bill (not as whitish as *picirostris* group), pointed dagger-like shape. **Voice** Identical to *picirostris* group. **SS** Zimmer's Woodcreeper (best separated by voice), Striped Woodcreeper. **TN** Distribution of races unclear.

duidae   *picus*

Zimmer's Woodcreeper *Dendroplex kienerii*
Trepatroncos de Zimmer
Fairly common resident locally.

 L 20 cm (8"). Monotypic. *Várzea* forest streambanks, smaller rivers, lagoon borders; seldom far from water. **ID** Nearly identical to Straight-billed Woodcreeper and they may occur together. Zimmer's differs in browner (less rufescent) lesser wing-coverts, more line-like (less spotted) streaking, but much more reliably identified by voice. **Voice** Song (c. 3 seconds), fast evenly descending whirring trill (does not rise at end): "wh'r'r'r'r'r'r'r'r'r'u'u'u". **SS** Striped Woodcreeper.

Red-billed Scythebill
Campylorhamphus trochilirostris LC
Guadañero Rojizo

Twelve subspecies in four subspecies groups; two (not universally recognized) in Colombia.

Northern Red-billed Scythebill
Campylorhamphus (trochilirostris) venezuelensis
Rare to uncommon and local resident.
L 23 cm (9"); **B** 6.4 cm (2.5"). Races *brevipennis*[A], *venezuelensis*[B], *napensis*[C] (valid records?). Dry to humid woodland, borders, second growth; gallery forests (*llanos*). 100–1600 m. Probes crevices, epiphytes; in dry areas often quite low; follows mixed flocks. **ID** Bill reddish to reddish brown, crisper more extensive streaking on back than Brown-billed Scythebill (habitat and elevation also usually differ). **Voice** Song, fast descending whinny-like crescendo of 10–25 notes, becoming louder, slower at end; also slow descending series of c. 5 notes. Call or alarm (?) loud vibrating sharply rising trill (c. 2 seconds) "str'r'r'e'e'e'e'ek!".

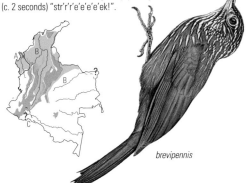

brevipennis

Genus *Campylorhamphus* Long decurved bills (hence 'scythebill'). Occur at various heights mostly inside forest (in Colombia); wary. Identification of species confusing.

Brown-billed Scythebill *Campylorhamphus pusillus* LC
Guadañero Estriado
Uncommon resident.

L 22 cm (8.5"); **B** 5.1 cm (2"). Races *tachirensis*[A], *pusillus*[B], *guapiensis*[C] (W Cauca, doubtfully distinct). Humid and wet foothill and montane forest. 300–2500 m. Singles, inconspicuous, mid-strata or higher with mixed flocks; probe moss. **ID** Bill reddish brown to dusky, not reliably different from Red-billed Scythebill; buff streaking duller, less extensive, throat buff (not whitish). **Voice** Song, soft melancholy wailing, tremulous "twe-twe-wEO-WEO-weo-we-we-we-we-we", louder in middle, often repeated without break. **SS** Curve-billed Scythebill (no known range overlap).

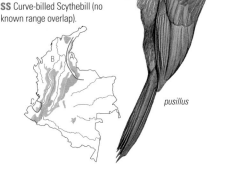

pusillus

Western Red-billed Scythebill
Campylorhamphus (trochilirostris) thoracicus
Rare resident.
L 23 cm (9"); **B** 6.4 cm (2.5"). Race *thoracicus*. Humid forest borders, semi-open second growth, plantations. To 800 m (Ecuador). **ID** Indistinguishable in field from other races, except perhaps vocally. **Voice** Described (?) as a shorter, descending, slowing series of whistles "tuwee-tuwee-toowa-tew-tew". **TN** Taxonomy unresolved.

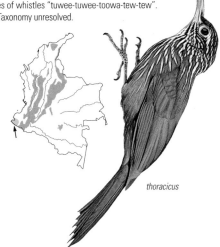

thoracicus

Curve-billed Scythebill
Campylorhamphus procurvoides
Guadañero Punteado
Rare resident (range poorly known, most records
E Vaupés and E Guainía).

 **L** 23 cm (9"); **B** 5.1 cm (2"). Race
sanus . Humid *terra firme* forest;
várzea (E Guainía). To 500 m. **ID** From Red-billed
Scythebill by essentially unstreaked mantle and
back, slightly more olivaceous (not rufescent) underparts,
in hand underpart streaking lacks
thin black edges. **Voice** Song
(*sanus*, E Venezuela), melancholy
lamenting "kuweee, kuwee, kwee
wee-we-d'd'ddddddddddd", ending
abruptly in a harsh chattering rattle on
same pitch. Strident "sti'dik" call.

sanus

Greater Scythebill *Drymotoxeres pucheranii* NT
Guadañero Cariblanco NT
Rare low-density resident.

 L 29 cm (11.5);
B 5.6 cm (2.2").
Monotypic. Humid and wet
montane forest. 2000–2800 m
(once 900 m, Pacific slope). Singles, inconspicuous, low to mid-levels, sometimes with mixed
flocks. **ID** Large; pale bill, whitish
eyestripe and malar, narrow buff
streaking confined to nape.
Voice Song (?),
long rising whine
followed by one
or several shorter whining
notes, sometimes sharp note
at end; also descending whinny.
Call (?), loud, rising "kaweek".

Genus *Lepidocolaptes* Fairly small, slender; bill thinner,
more decurved (sometimes slightly reddish) than most other
woodcreepers. Species separate by range and elevation

Duida Woodcreeper *Lepidocolaptes duidae* LC
Trepatroncos Duida
Uncommon (overlooked?) resident.

L 19 cm (7.5"). Monotypic. Tall humid lowland
forest including sandy soil areas, borders.
To 1000 m (Putumayo). Singles or pairs, mostly
subcanopy or canopy with mixed-species
flocks, hitch up high branches, often keeping on undersides.
ID Small; upperparts uniform brown, thin decurved
bill, crisp black-edged streaking on
underparts. **Voice** Song, c. 15 clear
high notes starting slowly,
accelerating downscale, faster at end
"teer, teer, peer, peer-peer-pe-pe'pe'p'p'p'p",
with becard-like quality. **SS** Overlaps
no other *Lepidocolaptes*.
TN Formerly a race of
Lineated Woodcreeper
L. albolineatus.

Streak-headed Woodcreeper
Lepidocolaptes souleyetii LC
Trepatroncos Campestre
Common resident.

L 20 cm (8"). Races *lineaticeps*[A], *littoralis*[B],
esmeraldae[C]. Forest borders, light open
woodland, plantations,
clearings with trees, gallery
forest; dry to moist regions. To 1800 m. Singles
or pairs, low to fairly high, usually easy to see,
follows small mixed flocks. **ID** Slender delicate
proportions, thin decurved
bill, crown finely streaked,
underparts streaking distinct
but plumage overall pale,
faded. **Voice** Song, short
descending trill, chattering,
thin, nasal. **SS** Montane
Woodcreeper (higher, montane
forest).

lineaticeps

Montane Woodcreeper *Lepidocolaptes lacrymiger* `LC`
Trepatroncos Montañero

Nine subspecies in two subspecies groups; both groups (if valid) in Colombia.

Northern Montane Woodcreeper
Lepidocolaptes (lacrymiger) lacrymiger
Common resident.
L 19 cm (7.5"). Races *sanctaemartae*[A], *lacrymiger*[B], *sneiderni*[C]. Humid and wet montane forest (cloud forest), borders, stunted treeline woodland. 1500–3400 m (rarely 1200 m). Singles or pairs, mid-levels to canopy, habitually with mixed flocks. **ID** Small; thin decurved bill, crown spotted, underparts with crisp black-edged line-like streaks, mantle and back unstreaked. **Voice** Infrequent song, extremely high thin, rising, wispy "tsip, tsip tsip sit-sit-sit-seet-seet-seet-seet". **SS** Unique at high elevations.

lacrymiger

Southern Montane Woodcreeper
Lepidocolaptes (lacrymiger) warscewiczi
Common resident.
L 19 cm (7.5"). Races *frigidus*[A], *aequatorialis*[B]. **ID** Very like northern races but slightly darker and more rufescent above and below, minor streaking on back, underparts streaking deeper buff-edged (but not tipped) black. No vocal differences documented. **TN** Doubtfully valid subspecies group.

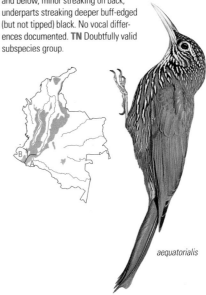

aequatorialis

Genera *Xenops* and *Microxenops* Cute and industrious, with slightly upturned bills (except Slender-billed). Busily flake off bark from dry twigs; acrobatically hang upside-down.

Plain Xenops *Xenops genibarbis* `LC`
Xenops Parduzco

Ten subspecies in two subspecies groups; both in Colombia.

Northwestern Plain Xenops *Xenops (genibarbis) mexicanus*
Common resident.
L 12.2 cm (4.8"). Races *littoralis*[A], *olivaceus*[B], *neglectus*[C]. Dry to humid forest, second growth, light woodland, plantations. To 2000 m. **ID** Small; white eyestripe and malar, area around throat somewhat streaked. **Voice** Song (*littoralis*), brisk bubbly trill (c. 7 kHz) of 6–15+ notes on same pitch or slight dip, then gradually ascending. **SS** Streaked Xenops (higher elevation, streaked). **TN** White-throated Xenops *X. minutus* (S Atlantic Forest), treated here as a separate species, usually considered a third subspecies group of Plain Xenops.

littoralis

Southeastern Plain Xenops
Xenops (genibarbis) genibarbis
Common resident.
L 12.2 cm (4.8"). Races *remoratus*[A], *ruficaudus*[B], *obsoletus* (Putumayo, Amazonas?). Humid lowland *terra firme* and *várzea* forest, foothills. To 1900 m. **ID** Similar to *mexicanus* subspecies group, but throat duller, chest with only obsolete streaking. **Voice** Song variable, c. 10+ flat dry chattering "chit" notes slowing at end (*remoratus*), or shorter series of 6–10 shrill chattering notes, hesitant, then a little faster, descending slightly towards end (*obsoletus*), or brief series of c. 6–7 shrill notes on same pitch (6 kHz) or sharply ascending (3–6.5 kHz). **TN** See *mexicanus* subspecies group.

ruficaudus

Streaked Xenops *Xenops rutilus* `LC`
Xenops Estriado
Fairly common resident.

 L 11.4 cm (4.5"). Races *phelpsi*[A], *perijanus*[B], *heterurus*[C], *incomptus*[D] (?). Humid and wet montane forest, borders. 1400–2900 m. **ID** Mandible upturned, whitish eyebrow and malar, otherwise streaked above and below. **Voice** Brief song (*heterurus*), 4–7 weak chattering notes, slightly rising, then falling; or (after playback) same pitch or slightly descending. **SS** Streaky plumage and montane elevations are key.

heterurus

Slender-billed Xenops *Xenops tenuirostris* `LC`
Xenops Picofino
Uncommon (overlooked?) resident.

 L 10.7 cm (4.2"). Race *acutirostris*. Humid lowland and foothill forest. To 650 m. Singles or pairs follow canopy or subcanopy mixed flocks. **ID** White eyebrow and malar, streaked above and below, bill straight, slender and comparatively long (difficult to see if high overhead). **Voice** Song (c. 7 kHz), 3–4 high insistent notes "sit-sit-sit-sit". **SS** Rufous-tailed Xenops; near-identical Streaked Xenops (highlands) has upturned bill.

acutirostris

Point-tailed Palmcreeper *Berlepschia rikeri* `LC`
Trepapalmas de Cola Puntiaguda
Very local resident.

 L 20 cm (8"). Monotypic. *Mauritia* palm groves in wet grassland or *várzea* forest. To 300 m. Rarely or never far from *Mauritia*. Pairs or families hide in canopy of palms; forage by clambering around, mostly at base and on underside of fronds. **ID** Bright rufous, head, nape and underparts streaked black and white. **Voice** Song, a few times at dawn or dusk, strident upward-inflected series (c. 5–7 seconds) of nasal notes (7–8 notes/second) "kreek-kreek-kreek-...", loud, penetrating, very slightly rising, then level; also rattles. **AN** Palmcreeper.

Rufous-tailed Xenops *Microxenops milleri* `LC`
Xenops Escamado
Uncommon (overlooked?) resident.

 L 10 cm (4"). Monotypic. Humid *terra firme* forest, less in *várzea*. To 500 m (locally 1000 m). Singles or pairs, canopy or subcanopy, habitually with mixed flocks. **ID** Bill straight, no white malar, head, back and underparts broadly streaked, diagnostic all-rufous tail difficult to verify. **Voice** Song, short thin very fast trill "brrrrrEEEErrr", quickly rises in pitch and volume, then descends slightly. **SS** Slender-billed Xenops, Streaked Xenops (overlap?). **TN** Previously in *Xenops*.

Genus *Pseudocolaptes* English name highlights elongated buff to white cheek feathers. Forage in accumulated debris within tank bromeliads in cloud forests.

Pacific Tuftedcheek *Pseudocolaptes johnsoni* `LC`
Trepamusgos Barbablanca del Pacífico
Uncommon resident.

 L 20 cm (8"). Monotypic. Near-endemic (also NW Ecuador). Wet premontane and montane forest. 700–2000 m. Pairs, lower mid-levels to canopy with fast-moving mixed flocks; inconspicuous, seldom affording more than brief views. **ID** From Streaked Tuftedcheek (minimal overlap) by unstreaked back, buff-tinged (not white) cheek-tufts, dingy throat, blurry spotting (less scaled) on chest, richer rufous-chestnut plumage; none of this easy to verify. **Voice** Song, metallic, chattering rising rattle-trill, abruptly ending in descending buzz: "chi'ch't't't't'e'e'bzzzzuuu". Call "spik". **TN** Usually considered conspecific with Buffy Tuftedcheek *P. lawrencii* of S Central America.

Streaked Tuftedcheek
Pseudocolaptes boissonneauii `LC`
Trepamusgos Barbiblanco Rayado
Fairly common resident.

 L 20 cm (8"). Races *meridae*[A], *boissonneauii*[B], *oberholseri* (Nariño?). Wet montane forest (cloud forest). 1700–3200 m. **ID** Conspicuous white flaring cheek-tufts, white throat, buff streaking on back, chest somewhat scaly. **Voice** Song, one to several sharp "spik" notes (sometimes followed by brief pause) and rather high-pitched penetrating, slightly descending rattle: "spik! . spik! spik! te-t-t-t-t-t-t-t-e-e-e-e". Call "spik".

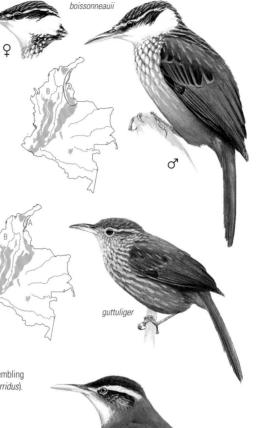

boissonneauii

♀

♂

Rusty-winged Barbtail *Premnornis gutguliger* `LC`
Corretroncos Alirrufo
Uncommon resident (inconspicuous).

 L 14 cm (5.5"). Races *venezuelanus*[A], *gutguliger*[B]. Humid montane forest. 1600–2700 m. Quiet dark little bird, easily overlooked in dim undergrowth. Singles follow mixed flocks, hop and probe in mossy tangles like small foliage-gleaners. **ID** Underparts heavily streaked, wings and tail rufous. **Voice** Infrequent song (variable?), high fairly rapid "tsit" notes on same pitch (c. 7 kHz), or long very high trill (c. 8 kHz), or sharp "tsip!" followed by very high notes, louder and more emphatic at end. **SS** Lineated Foliage-gleaner.

gutguliger

Genus *Furnarius* Builders of conspicuous domed mud nests resembling ovens ('horneros'). Short tail, strong legs, pale wing-band (except *F. torridus*). Semi-terrestrial; usually associated with water.

Pale-billed Hornero *Furnarius torridus* `LC`
Hornero Piquiclaro
Rare and local resident.

 L 18 cm (7"). Monotypic. Dense undergrowth on seasonally flooded river islands in R Amazon; local on mainland in dense *várzea* borders. To 150 m. Singles in rank vegetation, on or near ground; wary, inconspicuous; not around habitations. **ID** Above dark chestnut, below brown, eyestripe and throat whitish, bill and legs greyish pink, no pale wing-band in flight. **Voice** Song (4–5 seconds), very like Pale-legged Hornero, but slightly faster, staccato. **AN** Bay Hornero.

Pale-legged Hornero *Furnarius leucopus* `LC`
Hornero Patiamarillo
Common resident.

 L 18 cm (7"). Race *tricolor*. Várzea borders, river islands, river-edge second growth, damp shady areas, often around habitations. To 150 m. Singles or pairs, walk jauntily, forage on ground. Conspicuous mud nests well up in open trees. **ID** Above rufous, long white eyestripe, below whitish to buff-white, pale wing-band in flight. **Voice** Song (3–4 seconds), loud clattering that decreases slightly in pitch, gradually slowing. **SS** Other *Furnarius*.

tricolor

Caribbean Hornero *Furnarius longirostris* `LC`
Hornero del Caribe

Fairly common resident locally.

 L 16.5 cm (6.5"). Races *longirostris*[A], *endoecus*[B]. Dry woodland, desert scrub, ranchland, patches of trees and brush; less closely associated with water than allies. To 600 m. Singles or pairs on or close to ground, often wary, walk with jaunty gait, occasionally in open; flip fallen leaves. **ID** Bright cinnamon-rufous. Much like Pale-legged Hornero but crown paler grey, underparts richer buff. **Voice** Closely resembles Pale-legged Hornero. **SS** Usually a race of Pale-legged Hornero.

Pacific Hornero *Furnarius cinnamomeus* `LC`
Hornero del Pacífico

Fairly common resident (range expansion from Ecuador).

 L 19 cm (7.5"). Monotypic. Moist to humid wooded borders, scrub, agricultural and urban areas. To 200 m (likely higher as range expands). **ID** Much like Pale-legged Hornero but slightly larger, eyes yellow, crown and face paler, underparts whitish (only trace of buff). **Voice** Song very like Pale-legged Hornero but slower, less deceleration, pitch nearly constant. **TN** Often regarded as a race of Pale-legged Hornero.

Lesser Hornero *Furnarius minor* `LC`
Hornero Chico

Fairly common resident.

 L 15 cm (6"). Monotypic. Sandbars, driftwood, grass and young regrowth vegetation on young Amazonian river islands; riverbanks during high water. To 150 m. **ID** Very like Pale-legged Hornero, but smaller, duller, underparts dingier, legs greyish (not pale), bill dusky. **Voice** Song recalls Pale-legged Hornero, loud initially but flatter and brittle, less resonant; does not decelerate.

Sharp-tailed Streamcreeper *Lochmias nematura* `LC`
Saltarocas Punteado

Rare and local resident.

 L 15 cm (6"). Races *nelsoni*[A], *sororius*[B] (Panama border?). Undergrowth and mossy rocks beside forested mountain streams. 1000–2200 m. Singles or pairs, hop on ground, boulders or in tangled mossy vegetation near streams; generally quiet (hard to hear over stream noise), retiring, inconspicuous. **ID** Dark brown, white-spotted underparts, rather long thin bill. **Voice** Song (c. 2.5 seconds), urgent little nasal trill, rising, then falling. Call, abrupt dry 3–4-note chattering "ji'ji'i". **SS** Spotted Barbtail (p. 330). **AN** Streamcreeper.

Genus *Cinclodes* Large genus best represented in austral region; high-Andean open habitats (in Colombia). Semi-terrestrial. Prominent wing-band in flight. Nest in burrows.

Chestnut-winged Cinclodes *Cinclodes albidiventris* `LC`
Cíncodes Colirrufo

Local resident.

 L 22 cm (7.5"). Race *oreobates*. *Páramo*, damp or wet semi-open areas near treeline. 3200–4400 m. Singles or pairs walk or hop on ground, pause with tail cocked, probe damp areas, grass and soil for arthropods. **ID** Bill relatively thin, short, virtually straight (cf. Stout-billed Cinclodes); breast greyish buff mottled whitish. **Voice** Song, rapid rattling trill often with upraised flapping wings. **SS** Stout-billed Cinclodes (minimal overlap). **TN** Called Bar-winged Cinclodes prior to split from southern allies.

longirostris

sororius

oreobates

Stout-billed Cinclodes *Cinclodes excelsior* `LC`
Cínclodes Cavador
Fairly common resident.

 L 22 cm (8.5"). Races *columbianus*[A], *excelsior*[B]. Open or bushy *páramo*, grassy areas near treeline, usually near water or boggy areas. 3200–5200 m. Behaviour like Chestnut-winged Cinclodes; often perches exposed, on rocks, post or bush tops. **ID** Often confused with slightly smaller Chestnut-winged Cinclodes (very little overlap) but bill decidedly thicker, longer, clearly decurved; underparts often somewhat darker. **Voice** Song (2–3 seconds), thin high trill quickly rising, flattens, then descends: "t'r'r're'e'e'e'e'u'u". Call, loud raptor-like descending "KEeu".

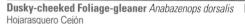

excelsior

Dusky-cheeked Foliage-gleaner *Anabazenops dorsalis* `LC`
Hojarasquero Cejón
Rare resident (few Colombian records).

 L 18.5 cm (7.3"). Monotypic. Dense forest borders, second growth, usually in tall *Guadua* bamboo and cane. 200–1000 m. Singles or pairs remain hidden in cluttered vegetation, low to mid-levels. Usually noted first by voice. Sometimes with mixed flocks. **ID** Prominent white eye-ring, post-ocular and throat. **Voice** Low husky series of "cluck" or "chlok" notes, soft, then louder. Low rattle often long-sustained. **SS** Olive-backed Foliage-gleaner (p. 329). **AN** Bamboo or Crested Foliage-gleaner.

Genus *Philydor* Rather small slender foliage-gleaners. Forest mid-levels to subcanopy, a few lower. Lack streaking (cf. *Anabacerthia*); identification challenging.

Cinnamon-rumped Foliage-gleaner *Philydor pyrrhodes* `LC`
Hojarasquero Colorado
Uncommon resident.

 L 17 cm (6.7"). Monotypic. Dense understorey to mid-levels in humid *terra firme*, *várzea* and sandy soil forests, often near streams, ravines, wet areas with many understorey palms. To 700 m. Usually singles, wary, sometimes with mixed flocks. **ID** Bright cinnamon rump and tail, ochraceous underparts, slaty wings. **Voice** Song, short fast steadily rising trill with purring quality; alternate song (?) long-sustained low rattling (30+ seconds). **SS** No other Amazonian foliage-gleaner is so bright and contrasting.

Slaty-winged Foliage-gleaner *Philydor fuscipenne* `LC`
Hojarasquero Alinegro

 Two subspecies in two subspecies groups; one in Colombia.

Rufous-backed Foliage-gleaner
Philydor (fuscipenne) erythronotum
Rare (Pacific coast) or uncommon resident
(mid-Magdalena Valley).
L 17 cm (6.7"). One subspecies in group. Near-endemic (also E Panama and W Ecuador). Humid lowland and premontane forest. To 1600 m. Singles or pairs, understorey to mid-levels; active, energetic, often with mixed flocks. **ID** Cinnamon eyestripe, blackish wings, rich buffy-ochraceous underparts. **Voice** Brief squeezed trills of 5–8 high notes. Song (?) longer (1.5 seconds) lower-pitched rattle. **SS** Contrasting plumage unique in range.

Rufous-rumped Foliage-gleaner *Philydor erythrocercum* `LC`
Hojarasquero Anteado

Five subspecies in two subspecies groups;
one in Colombia.

Rufous-rumped Foliage-gleaner
Philydor (erythrocercum) erythrocercum
Fairly common resident.
L 17 cm (6.7"). Races *suboles*[A], *subfulvum*[B]. Humid *terra firme* forest,
fewer in *várzea*. To 850 m (*subfulvum*). Singles or pairs, mid-levels or lower;
active, check curled dead leaves, regularly with lower-level mixed flocks. **ID** Both
races extremely similar to Rufous-tailed Foliage-gleaner (see), but differ in essentially
uniform, unstreaked breast; rump colour rarely discernible. **Voice** Infrequent song
(< 2 seconds), chattering rattle "pa-pu-tu'TRE-TRE-TRE-TER-tu-pa", rising, middle
notes highest and strongest, dropping at end. Call metallic "chink".

subfulvum

erythropterum

Chestnut-winged Foliage-gleaner
Philydor erythropterum `LC`
Hojarasquero Alirrojo
Fairly common resident.

L 19 cm (7.5"). Race *erythropterum*. Humid *terra firme* and
transition forest, sandy soil forest. To 500 m. Singles, less often
pairs; high mid-level to canopy with mixed flocks; active, searches
foliage, checks curled dead leaves. **ID** Smooth clean-cut plumage,
contrasting rufous wings and tail, no streaking, short pale eyebrow. **Voice** Song
(2–3 seconds), very fast trill, same pitch or slightly descending (4–3 kHz), less
often slightly ascending. Call metallic "chink!". **SS** Chestnut-winged Hookbill.

Buff-fronted Foliage-gleaner *Philydor rufum* `LC`
Hojarasquero Ocráceo
Uncommon and local resident.

panerythrum

L 19 cm (7.5"). Races *panerythrum*[A], *riveti*[B].
Humid premontane and montane forest, borders.
900–2000 m. Singles or pairs regularly follow mixed flocks
in canopy; active, check terminal foliage, accumulated
dead leaf clusters, hanging dead leaves. **ID** Dark grey crown, bright
ochraceous eyebrow and underparts (especially throat), rather long
rufous tail, dull rufous wings. **Voice** Song (*riveti*), rather loose metallic
(but not resonant) rattle, slightly descending (5.5–4.5 kHz).
SS Russet Antshrike (p. 290).

riveti

Genera *Anabacerthia* and *Syndactyla* Rather small lightweight
foliage-gleaners, occur low or high in forest. Several are streaked or show
weak streaking on underparts. All follow mixed flocks.

Montane Foliage-gleaner *Anabacerthia striaticollis* `LC`
Hojarasquero Montañero
Common resident.

L 16.5 cm (6.5"). Races *anxia*[A], *perijana*[B], *striaticollis*[C],
montana[D]. Humid montane forest, borders, older second
growth. 1000–2700 m. By far commonest foliage-gleaner
in Colombian Andes. Singles or pairs, mid-levels or higher;
easy to see. **ID** Large buff-white 'spectacles' and post-ocular mark,
breast streaking weak or lacking, tail rufous; or breast streaking more
evident (*anxia*). **Voice** Infrequent song, slow series of incisive raspy
"chink" or "chek" notes. Call, same note singly. **SS** Scaly-throated Foliage-gleaner.

striaticollis

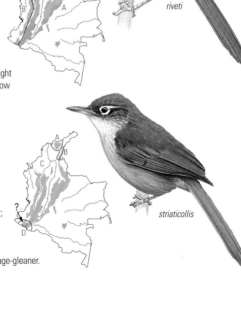

Scaly-throated Foliage-gleaner *Anabacerthia variegaticeps* LC
Hojarasquero del Pacífico

Three subspecies in two subspecies groups; one in Colombia.

Spot-breasted Foliage-gleaner
Anabacerthia (variegaticeps) temporalis
Uncommon resident.
L 19 cm (7.5"). One subspecies in group. Humid and wet foothill and montane forest. 700–2200 m. Singles or pairs, low mid-strata to canopy; active, acrobatic, rummages in epiphytes, accumulated leaf debris and scans outer foliage. **ID** Bright ochraceous 'spectacles', whitish throat finely scaled dusky, blurred ochre streaking on breast. **Voice** Infrequent song, a few slow "tjeet!" notes, followed by a slightly longer faster series of same. Call, single "tjeet!". **SS** Montane Foliage-gleaner. **AN** Spectacled Foliage-gleaner.

Rufous-tailed Foliage-gleaner *Anabacerthia ruficaudata* LC
Hojarasquero Colirrufo
Fairly common resident.

L 18 cm (7"). Race *flavipectus*. Humid *terra firme* forest. To 600 m. Very like Rufous-rumped Foliage-gleaner but forages higher, mainly with subcanopy and canopy mixed flocks, searches dead leaves. **ID** Differs in ill-defined blurred streaking on upper breast, brownish (not rufous) rump (seldom verifiable in field) and voice. **Voice** Dawn song, a few sputtering "put" notes abruptly changing to a loose chattering unmusical rattle (c. 8 notes/second) wavering somewhat in pitch. **TN** Formerly in *Philydor*.

flavipectus

Lineated Foliage-gleaner *Syndactyla subalaris* LC
Hojarasquero Listado
Fairly common resident.

L 18 cm (7"). Races *tacarcunae*[A], *subalaris*[B], *striolata*[C]. Humid and wet montane forest. 1300–2700 m (to 900 m, Pacific slope). Singles or pairs, often with mixed flocks. Dark lower levels inside tangled mossy vegetation; inconspicuous. **ID** Easily confused. Bill thin, head, mantle and underparts (except throat) narrowly streaked buff (*subalaris*) or streaking paler, slightly broader (*striolata*). **Voice** Song, harsh ratchet-like accelerating "cjak . . cjak . cjak-czak-zak-zak-zak-ck'ck'ck'ck" (may add notes at end). Rough "cjak" call. **SS** Striped and Flammulated Treehunters; woodhaunters (p. 328).

subalaris

Chestnut-winged Hookbill *Ancistrops strigilatus* LC
Pico-de-gancho Alicastaño
Fairly common resident.

L 19 cm (7.5"). Monotypic. Humid *terra firme* and transition forest. To 500 m. Singles or pairs, habitually with mid-level or canopy mixed flocks. Searches vine tangles, dead leaves, foliage near trunks, less in outer foliage. **ID** Narrow eyebrow, yellow-buff streaking above and below, contrasting rufous wings and tail, bill hook inconspicuous. **Voice** Call harsh "bzzt". Song, short (2–3 seconds) fast rising trill (2–3 kHz); after playback longer rapid or slow rattles to 30 seconds. **SS** Chestnut-winged Foliage-gleaner.

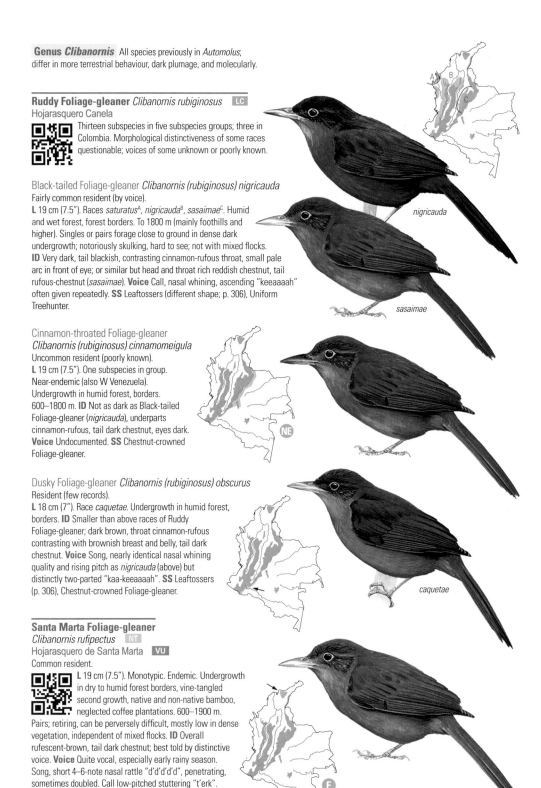

Genus *Clibanornis* All species previously in *Automolus*; differ in more terrestrial behaviour, dark plumage, and molecularly.

Ruddy Foliage-gleaner *Clibanornis rubiginosus* LC
Hojarasquero Canela

Thirteen subspecies in five subspecies groups; three in Colombia. Morphological distinctiveness of some races questionable; voices of some unknown or poorly known.

Black-tailed Foliage-gleaner *Clibanornis (rubiginosus) nigricauda*
Fairly common resident (by voice).
L 19 cm (7.5"). Races *saturatus*[A], *nigricauda*[B], *sasaimae*[C]. Humid and wet forest, forest borders. To 1800 m (mainly foothills and higher). Singles or pairs forage close to ground in dense dark undergrowth; notoriously skulking, hard to see; not with mixed flocks. **ID** Very dark, tail blackish, contrasting cinnamon-rufous throat, small pale arc in front of eye; or similar but head and throat rich reddish chestnut, tail rufous-chestnut (*sasaimae*). **Voice** Call, nasal whining, ascending "keeaaaah" often given repeatedly. **SS** Leaftossers (different shape; p. 306), Uniform Treehunter.

Cinnamon-throated Foliage-gleaner
Clibanornis (rubiginosus) cinnamomeigula
Uncommon resident (poorly known).
L 19 cm (7.5"). One subspecies in group. Near-endemic (also W Venezuela). Undergrowth in humid forest, borders. 600–1800 m. **ID** Not as dark as Black-tailed Foliage-gleaner (*nigricauda*), underparts cinnamon-rufous, tail dark chestnut, eyes dark. **Voice** Undocumented. **SS** Chestnut-crowned Foliage-gleaner.

Dusky Foliage-gleaner *Clibanornis (rubiginosus) obscurus*
Resident (few records).
L 18 cm (7"). Race *caquetae*. Undergrowth in humid forest, borders. **ID** Smaller than above races of Ruddy Foliage-gleaner; dark brown, throat cinnamon-rufous contrasting with brownish breast and belly, tail dark chestnut. **Voice** Song, nearly identical nasal whining quality and rising pitch as *nigricauda* (above) but distinctly two-parted "kaa-keeaaaah". **SS** Leaftossers (p. 306), Chestnut-crowned Foliage-gleaner.

Santa Marta Foliage-gleaner
Clibanornis rufipectus NT
Hojarasquero de Santa Marta VU
Common resident.

L 19 cm (7.5"). Monotypic. Endemic. Undergrowth in dry to humid forest borders, vine-tangled second growth, native and non-native bamboo, neglected coffee plantations. 600–1900 m. Pairs; retiring, can be perversely difficult, mostly low in dense vegetation, independent of mixed flocks. **ID** Overall rufescent-brown, tail dark chestnut; best told by distinctive voice. **Voice** Quite vocal, especially early rainy season. Song, short 4–6-note nasal rattle "d'd'd'd'd", penetrating, sometimes doubled. Call low-pitched stuttering "t'erk". **TN** Previously included in Ruddy Foliage-gleaner.

nigricauda

sasaimae

NE

caquetae

E

Genus *Thripadectes* Large, strong-billed foliage-gleaners; even more robust than *Automolus*; at lower levels inside forest. Wary, but several have loud arresting vocalizations.

Uniform Treehunter *Thripadectes ignobilis* `LC`
Hojarasquero Buchioscuro
Uncommon resident.

L 19 cm (7.5"). Monotypic. Humid and wet Pacific slope premontane and montane forest, borders. 600–2200 m. Usually singles; mossy vegetation, mid-level or lower; furtive but easier to see than other *Thripadectes*. Occasionally with mixed flocks. **ID** Plain and dark, short thick bill, dark rufescent-brown, small buff post-ocular, weak buff streaking on throat and chest. **Voice** Song, 6–8 thin tinny clipped "sklip" notes, series slightly rising (4.5–5 kHz). Call "klip". **SS** Striped and Streak-capped Treehunters.

Flammulated Treehunter *Thripadectes flammulatus* `LC`
Hojarasquero Grande
Uncommon resident.

L 24 cm (9.5"). Race *flammulatus*. Undergrowth in humid and wet montane forest, especially in *Chusquea* bamboo. 1400–3100 m (mostly > 2000 m). Usually solitary, skulks in dense vegetation, wary, often difficult to see; generally apart from mixed flocks. **ID** Black and buff streaking broader, much bolder than any other furnariid. **Voice** Song (c. 2–3 seconds), loud staccato ticking rattle "st't't't't't'..." (c. 4.5 kHz), same pitch or slightly rising. **SS** Striped Treehunter, Lineated Foliage-gleaner (smaller, thin bill).

flammulatus

Striped Treehunter *Thripadectes holostictus* `LC`
Hojarasquero Mediano
Uncommon resident.

L 20 cm (8"). Races *striatidorsus*[A], *holostictus*[B] (the two differ minimally). Undergrowth in humid montane forest, especially with *Chusquea* bamboo, shrubby forest borders. 1700–3150 m (locally 900 m, Pacific slope). **ID** Much like Flammulated Treehunter but smaller, ground colour brown to dusky brown (not black), streaking blurred (not crisp). **Voice** Song, hard rattle-trill recalls Flammulated Treehunter but shorter, c. 10 notes/1 second, with distinct rising-falling pattern; shrill. Call abrupt run-together "st'd'dik", rising; also single "skip" notes. **SS** Lineated Foliage-gleaner.

holostictus

Streak-capped Treehunter
Thripadectes virgaticeps `LC`
Hojarasquero Difuso
Fairly common and local resident.

L 22 cm (8.5"). Races *magdalenae*[A], *sclateri*[B], *sumaco*[C], *virgaticeps*[D]. Humid montane forest, especially dense borders. 1200–2500 m. Dense understorey; generally the most frequently seen *Thripadectes* in Colombia because of nest burrows dug in road-cuts. **ID** Back unstreaked, crown finely streaked buff, throat to chest streaked buff. **Voice** Song, emphatic but measured (1.5–2-second) series of 3–6 thin chips "chep, chuwip-chuwip..." (4 kHz). Call, low abrupt stuttered "ju'dut". **SS** Black-billed Treehunter.

sclateri

Black-billed Treehunter *Thripadectes melanorhynchus* `LC`
Hojarasquero Negruzco
Uncommon resident.

 L 20 cm (8"). Race *striaticeps*. Undergrowth of humid montane forest and borders. 1000–1900 m. Behaviour like other *Thripadectes*. **ID** Crown and sides of head dusky brown streaked buff, mantle and back brown streaked buff, throat rich buff scaled and streaked black, fine buff shaft-streaks on chest. **Voice** Song, loud almost yelping (rising-falling notes) "skiiop-skiiop" in pairs, triplets or quadruplets with only brief pauses. Call, low "chuck". **SS** Streak-capped and Striped Treehunters (both usually higher elevation).

Genus *Automolus* Large and robust; low inside forest. Wary, suspicious (some exceedingly so), in dense vegetation. Earth-toned rufescent and brown colours.

Chestnut-crowned Foliage-gleaner
Automolus rufipileatus `LC`
Hojarasquero Ojirrojo
Uncommon resident (by voice).

 L 19 cm (7.5"). Race *consobrinus*. Lowland river-edge second growth, transition and *várzea* forest, humid foothill second growth. To 750 m. Notoriously skulking, often perversely difficult; dense tangles at lower levels. Singles, occasionally with mixed understorey flocks. **ID** Eyes greyish yellow to orange-yellow, crown chestnut, otherwise slightly paler rufous-chestnut above and below. **Voice** Dawn song (c. 1 second), loud, nasal rattling trill "t'dddddddddd", slightly descending, over and over. Call, low harsh "tchop". **SS** Ruddy Foliage-gleaner (E slope races).

Brown-rumped Foliage-gleaner
Automolus melanopezus `LC`
Hojarasquero Rojizo
Rare resident (few records).

 L 20 cm (8"). Monotypic. Humid transition forest especially with *Guadua* bamboo, dense vegetation in low-lying or swampy areas. 250–500 m (Ecuador). Singles, mid- to low levels inside forest; often unreasonably wary and difficult. Occasionally with understorey mixed flocks (Peru). **ID** Eyes orange-red; notably uniform, tail rufous, throat tawny ochraceous, brighter on sides (malar area). **Voice** Song, two whistles followed by short chattering rattle, "wheet! wheet! 'wr'rrrrrrrr", speed of rattle varies. **SS** Chestnut-crowned Foliage-gleaner.

Western Woodhaunter *Automolus virgatus* `LC`
Hojarasquero Amazónico
Uncommon resident (easily overlooked).

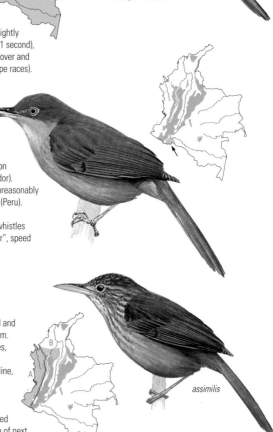 **L** 18 cm (7"). Races *assimilis*[A], *cordobae*[B]. Humid and wet lowland and lower montane forest. To 1700 m. Singles, undergrowth to mid-levels, vines, tangles, leaf accumulations, often near trunks. Furtive; sometimes with mixed flocks. **ID** Longish bill, narrow buff eyeline, back unstreaked, head and underparts streaking dull, blurred, brighter on chest, throat unmarked buff. **Voice** Song, steady nasal "skank-skank-...", c. 3 notes/second, hammering, sometimes long-continued. **SS** Lineated Foliage-gleaner, Striped Treehunter. **TN** Formerly in *Hyloctistes*. Often regarded as race of next species under name Striped Woodhaunter.

striaticeps

consobrinus

assimilis

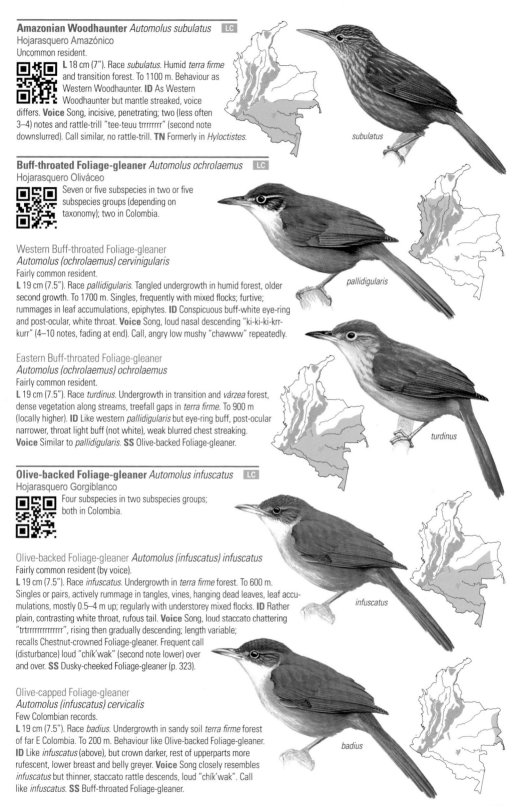

Amazonian Woodhaunter *Automolus subulatus* `LC`
Hojarasquero Amazónico
Uncommon resident.

L 18 cm (7"). Race *subulatus*. Humid *terra firme* and transition forest. To 1100 m. Behaviour as Western Woodhaunter. **ID** As Western Woodhaunter but mantle streaked, voice differs. **Voice** Song, incisive, penetrating; two (less often 3–4) notes and rattle-trill "tee-teuu trrrrrrrr" (second note downslurred). Call similar, no rattle-trill. **TN** Formerly in *Hyloctistes*.

subulatus

Buff-throated Foliage-gleaner *Automolus ochrolaemus* `LC`
Hojarasquero Oliváceo

Seven or five subspecies in two or five subspecies groups (depending on taxonomy); two in Colombia.

Western Buff-throated Foliage-gleaner
Automolus (ochrolaemus) cervinigularis
Fairly common resident.
L 19 cm (7.5"). Race *pallidigularis*. Tangled undergrowth in humid forest, older second growth. To 1700 m. Singles, frequently with mixed flocks; furtive; rummages in leaf accumulations, epiphytes. **ID** Conspicuous buff-white eye-ring and post-ocular, white throat. **Voice** Song, loud nasal descending "ki-ki-ki-krr-kurr" (4–10 notes, fading at end). Call, angry low mushy "chawww" repeatedly.

pallidigularis

Eastern Buff-throated Foliage-gleaner
Automolus (ochrolaemus) ochrolaemus
Fairly common resident.
L 19 cm (7.5"). Race *turdinus*. Undergrowth in transition and *várzea* forest, dense vegetation along streams, treefall gaps in *terra firme*. To 900 m (locally higher). **ID** Like western *pallidigularis* but eye-ring buff, post-ocular narrower, throat light buff (not white), weak blurred chest streaking. **Voice** Similar to *pallidigularis*. **SS** Olive-backed Foliage-gleaner.

turdinus

Olive-backed Foliage-gleaner *Automolus infuscatus* `LC`
Hojarasquero Gorgiblanco

Four subspecies in two subspecies groups; both in Colombia.

Olive-backed Foliage-gleaner *Automolus (infuscatus) infuscatus*
Fairly common resident (by voice).
L 19 cm (7.5"). Race *infuscatus*. Undergrowth in *terra firme* forest. To 600 m. Singles or pairs, actively rummage in tangles, vines, hanging dead leaves, leaf accu-mulations, mostly 0.5–4 m up; regularly with understorey mixed flocks. **ID** Rather plain, contrasting white throat, rufous tail. **Voice** Song, loud staccato chattering "trtrrrrrrrrrrrrr", rising then gradually descending; length variable; recalls Chestnut-crowned Foliage-gleaner. Frequent call (disturbance) loud "chík'wak" (second note lower) over and over. **SS** Dusky-cheeked Foliage-gleaner (p. 323).

infuscatus

Olive-capped Foliage-gleaner
Automolus (infuscatus) cervicalis
Few Colombian records.
L 19 cm (7.5"). Race *badius*. Undergrowth in sandy soil *terra firme* forest of far E Colombia. To 200 m. Behaviour like Olive-backed Foliage-gleaner. **ID** Like *infuscatus* (above), but crown darker, rest of upperparts more rufescent, lower breast and belly greyer. **Voice** Song closely resembles *infuscatus* but thinner, staccato rattle descends, loud "chík'wak". Call like *infuscatus*. **SS** Buff-throated Foliage-gleaner.

badius

Spotted Barbtail *Premnoplex brunnescens* `LC`
Corretroncos Barranquero
Common resident.

 L 14 cm (5.5"). Races *brunnescens*[A], *coloratus*[B], *albescens*[C].
Undergrowth in humid and wet montane forest. 1200–3000 m (to
800 m, Pacific slope). Inconspicuous singles or pairs clamber around
(no tail support) low in dark mossy tangles, vines and on trunks;
sometimes with mixed flocks; confiding. **ID** Chunky; above dark mummy-brown,
throat tawny-buff, brown underparts densely spotted buff. **Voice** Rather quiet.
Song, very high descending (8–7 kHz) fast (almost buzzy) flat trill (c. 1 second)
"teeeeeeea"; or 12–14 very high (8.5–5.5 kHz) notes in leisurely descending
series (*coloratus*). **TN** Race *coloratus* perhaps specifically distinct; *albescens* not
consistently recognized.

coloratus

brunnescens

Genus *Margarornis* Climb high trunks and limbs. Varying amounts
of spotting on underparts. Calls and songs extremely high-pitched.

Fulvous-dotted Treerunner *Margarornis stellatus* `NT`
Corretroncos Barbiblanco `NT`
Uncommon resident.

 L 15 cm (6"). Monotypic. Near-endemic (also NW Ecuador).
Humid and wet premontane and montane forest. 1200–2400 m.
Singles or pairs quietly hitch up epiphyte-laden trunks and
branches, mid-levels to canopy, rarely away from mixed flocks.
ID Bill pale; overall rich rufous, white throat, sprinkle of tiny black-encircled
white dots on chest (inconspicuous). **Voice** Infrequent (overlooked?) song,
brief rising-falling trill "t ti'ti'ti'ti't" (8–8.5 kHz), first and last notes lower.
Call, exceeding high-pitched (9 kHz) "stit" notes; 2–4-note trills (c. 10 kHz).
AN Star-chested Treerunner.

Pearled Treerunner *Margarornis squamiger* `LC`
Corretroncos Perlado

 Three subspecies in two subspecies groups;
one in Colombia.

Northern Pearled Treerunner
Margarornis (squamiger) perlatus
Fairly common resident.
L 16 cm (6.3"). Race *perlatus*. Humid and wet montane forest, elfin forest,
Polylepis at treeline. 1600–3500 m (mostly > 2000 m). Charming singles
or pairs follow mixed flocks, hitch up trunks, along undersides of high
epiphyte-laden branches, and occasionally work outer foliage like small
foliage-gleaners. Easy to see. **ID** Creeper-like but none so handsome; above
bright rufous, below with beautiful pearly spots. **Voice** Quiet. Extremely
high-pitched (8–10 kHz) single, double or tripled "tsit" notes. Short "trrrt-trrrt"
trills may be song.

perlatus

Beautiful Treerunner *Margarornis bellulus* `NT`
Subepalos Bonito `VU`
Rare resident (adjacent Panama, found in 2017 in Colombia).

L 15 cm (6"). Monotypic. Mid-levels to canopy of
humid montane forest. 1050 m (900–1580 m, Panama).
Behaviour as Pearled Treerunner. **ID** Like Pearled
Treerunner but overall duller, upperparts
olive-tinged (not bright rufous), smaller and fewer spots on
underparts. **Voice** High "tseep!".

Andean Tit-spinetail *Leptasthenura andicola*
Coludito Paramuno
Fairly common resident.

L 16.5 cm (6.5"). Races *extima*[A], *exterior*[B], *andicola*[C]. Shrubby *páramo* with *Espeletia* (Asteraceae) and *Polylepis*, scattered shrubs, brushy ravines. 3000–4500 m. Singles or pairs acrobatically work over shrubs, often hang upside-down, fly low across open spaces; sometimes loosely associated with a few other birds. **ID** Unusually long spiky double-pointed tail, dark cap, heavily streaked above and below. **Voice** High thin "ti" and "tic" notes. Song, descending tinkling trill. When disturbed chattering rattle-trills.

andicola

exterior

Plain Thornbird (Rufous-fronted Thornbird)
Phacellodomus inornatus LC
Espinero Liso
Common resident.

L 16 cm (6.3"). Race *castilloi*. Ranchland with scattered trees, gallery forest borders. To 1000 m. Pairs or families (helpers), forage in outer foliage of large spreading trees (*Pithecellobium*), bushes or ground. Active, industrious, obsessively collects sticks for large (to 2 m), conspicuous, multi-chambered nests. **ID** Wren-like but longer-tailed, very plain, habits, habitat, voice and ubiquitous nests helpful clues. **Voice** Noisy. Song, bright chipper series of loud "chit" notes, accelerating, then slowing, declining, and often enthusiastically joined by mate. **TN** Taxonomy unresolved; traditionally treated as conspecific with *P. rufifrons* (Rufous-fronted Thornbird) of S & E South America.

castilloi

White-browed Spinetail *Hellmayrea gularis* LC
Chamicero Cejiblanco
Uncommon resident (easily overlooked).

L 13.2 cm (5.2"). Races *gularis*[A], *brunneidorsalis*[B] . Dense mossy undergrowth at borders of montane forest, elfin woodland with *Chusquea* bamboo. 2300–3500 m. Usually found singly, low or on ground. Quiet, inconspicuous; infrequently with mixed flocks. **ID** Short-tailed, sharp white eyebrow, white throat. **Voice** Song, a few high notes accelerating into short flat trill. **SS** *Cinnycerthia* wrens (p. 439). **TN** Subspecies taxonomy unsettled; *cinereiventris* (if valid) apparently confined to Venezuela (not E Andes of Colombia).

gularis

Genus *Asthenes* Treeline/*páramo* (in Colombia). Two with long frayed tails; two with rufous wing stripes; dark orange to whitish chin patches. Previously comprised two genera.

quindiana

Many-striped Canastero *Asthenes flammulata* LC
Canastero Flamulado
Common resident locally.

L 15 cm (6"). Races *multostriata*[A], *quindiana*[B], *flammulata*[C]. Grassy slopes and *páramo* with tussock grass and scattered shrubs. 2800–4200 m. Forages out of view on ground or in grass and shrubs; sings from atop a shrub. **ID** Attractive, heavily streaked, rufous wing-band (in flight), rufous-edged tail, orange-buff chin spot; similar but foreface paler (*multostriata*). **Voice** Song (c. 4 seconds), thin high trill initially accelerating and increasing in pitch, then attenuating. **SS** Streak-backed Canastero, Andean Tit-Spinetail.

multostriata

331

Streak-backed Canastero *Asthenes wyatti* `LC`
Canastero Rayado

 Twelve subspecies in two subspecies groups; one in Colombia.

wyatti

Streak-backed Canastero *Asthenes (wyatti) wyatti*
Fairly common resident.
L 15 cm (6"). Races *sanctaemartae*[A], *phelpsi*[B], *wyatti*[C]. Drier *páramo*, grass and shrubs almost to snowline. 3100–4400 m (to 2400 m, *sanctaemartae*). Semi-terrestrial, but sings from exposed bush top; furtive singles flush off low, quickly dive into cover, run rapidly between bushes and grass tufts. **ID** Dingy and brown, rufous wing-band (in flight), rufous outer tail feathers; underparts greyer, bill longer (*sanctaemartae*). **Voice** Song, short flat rapidly accelerating trill "wu'wu'ur'ur'd'd'dddd!". **SS** Many-striped Canastero.

sanctaemartae

Perija Thistletail *Asthenes perijana* `EN`
Chamicero de Perijá `EN`
Local and uncommon resident.

 L 21 cm (8.2"). Monotypic. Near-endemic (also adjacent Venezuela). Scrub-scattered *páramo* with tall grass and frailejones (*Espeletia, Libanothamnus*), treeline elfin woodland, *Chusquea* bamboo. 2950–3400 m.
ID Plain and dull, long frayed tail (like old broom), white eye-ring, short whitish eyebrow, cinnamon-orange chin spot. **Voice** Song (c. 2.5 seconds), 6–8 notes steadily rising in pitch, abruptly accelerating into short chattering metallic trill: "wu, wu, we, we, pe, pee, pee'p'eeeer". Call, clear rising-falling "fweeo".
TN Formerly in genus *Schizoeaca*.

`NE`

fumigata

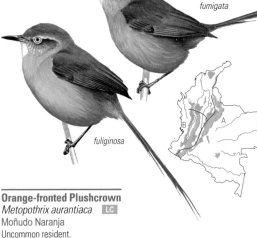

fuliginosa

White-chinned Thistletail
Asthenes fuliginosa `LC`
Chamicero Andino
Fairly common resident.

 **L** 18 cm (7"). Races *fuliginosa*[A], *fumigata*[B], race? Shrubby *páramo*, stunted woodland borders near treeline. 2300–3600 m. Singles or pairs forage acrobatically in shrubs; if flushed quickly dive back into cover. **ID** Very long frayed tail (like old broom), white eye-ring, short white eyebrow; or darker above, browner below (*fumigata*). **Voice** Song, from elevated perch, long (c. 4 seconds) gradually rising series of notes accelerating into fast squeezed trill: "squee, squee, sque, st'st't't't'tttttttttt".
TN Formerly in genus *Schizoeaca*.

Orange-fronted Plushcrown
Metopothrix aurantiaca `LC`
Moñudo Naranja
Uncommon resident.
L 11.4 cm (4.5"). Monotypic. Second growth on river-edge floodplains, canopy of wooded borders, trees in clearings, gardens; locally in foothills. To 700 m. Pairs or families (helpers?), active, warbler-like, acrobatically glean foliage. Large, conspicuous, ball-like stick nest. **ID** Resembles a parulid warbler; small, orange legs, orange forehead, yellow face and throat. **Voice** Apparent song, two to several very high (8 kHz) thin "tseek" or "tink!" notes. **SS** ♀ Northern Yellow Warbler (p. 488), Orange-headed Tanager (p. 526).

Double-banded Greytail *Xenerpestes minlosi* `LC`
Trapecista Gris
Rare and local resident.

 L 11.4 cm (4.5"). Races *umbraticus*[A], *minlosi*[B]. Near-endemic (also SE Panama and NW Ecuador). Mainly humid foothill forest, tall second growth. To 900 m; records spotty, clustered (better documentation needed). Pairs or small groups actively glean foliage, mid-levels to canopy, sometimes with mixed flocks. **ID** Eyes reddish, broad white eyebrow, narrow white wingbars, underparts whitish, vent dingy. **Voice** Song long, very high-pitched (c. 8 kHz) buzzing trill, insect-like. **SS** Easily (often?) confused. Recalls several boreal migrant warblers (Bay-breasted, Cerulean and Blackpoll; all thinner-billed; pp. 488, 486 and 489), various small flycatchers, vireos (p. 416).

minlosi

striaticollis

Spectacled Prickletail *Siptornis striaticollis* `LC`
Musguero de Anteojos `NT`
Rare or uncommon resident.

 L 11.4 cm (4.5"). Races *striaticollis*[A], *nortoni*[B] (?). Mid-levels to canopy in humid premontane and montane forest. 1300–2400 m. Singles, pairs, climb and hitch along branches like a barbtail (*Premnoplex*, p. 330), follow mixed flocks. **ID** Recalls Streaked Xenops (p. 320) but upperparts unstreaked, bill thin and straight, conspicuous white eye-ring and post-ocular. Race *nortoni* (more streaking on throat and chest, less white on face) possible W Putumayo/ Nariño. **Voice** Song (Ecuador), high dry chipping trill (c. 2 seconds). **TN** Race *nortoni* possibly invalid and species therefore monotypic.

nortoni

Genus *Thripophaga* Streaked and/or spotted, some with orange chin patch, and tail lacks protruding spines (hence 'softtail') except Speckled Spinetail.

Speckled Spinetail *Thripophaga gutturata* `LC`
Chamicero Punteado
Uncommon and local resident.

 L 13.2 cm (5.2"). Monotypic. Humid lowland *terra firme*, transition and *várzea* forest. To 500 m. Singles or pairs, low mid-levels to subcanopy in tangles, vines, epiphytes, hanging dead leaf clusters; often with mixed flocks. **ID** Speckled underparts, rufous cap, wings and tail, pale eyebrow; up close yellowish eyes. **Voice** Infrequent song, very high thin "tsee, tsit, tsit, tsit, tsit", first note or two slightly lower-pitched; hummingbird-like. **SS** Orinoco Softtail (rare). **TN** Formerly in *Cranioleuca*.

Orinoco Softtail *Thripophaga cherriei* `VU`
Rabiblando del Orinoco
Local resident (first reported 2012).

L 16 cm (6.3"). Monotypic. Near-endemic (also adjacent Venezuela). Dense vine tangles in seasonally flooded riverine forest. To 150 m. Pairs, infrequently with mixed flocks, near ground in shady understorey to low mid-levels. Inconspicuous but not furtive. **ID** Eyes dark yellow, bill sharp-pointed, thin buff eyeline, rufous tail, orange-rufous chin patch, sides of head, throat and breast brown with narrow drop-like buff streaking. **Voice** Song (4–8 seconds), long loose chattering rattle, slightly accelerating, attenuating, often overlapped by mate. **SS** Speckled Spinetail.

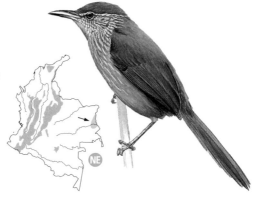

Genus *Cranioleuca* Small, plain, mostly arboreal (a few occur low); tail shorter than *Synallaxis*. Large ball- or pyramid-shaped mossy nests.

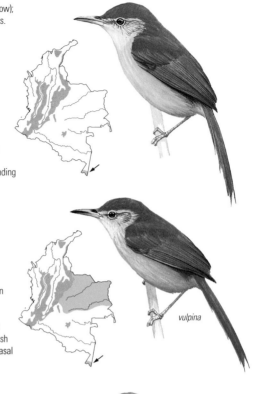

Parker's Spinetail *Cranioleuca vulpecula*   LC
Chamicero de Parker
Locally common resident.

 L 15.7 cm (6"). Monotypic. Mainly cane (*Gynerium*) and *Tessaria* (Asteraceae) on young sandy Amazonian river islands, adjacent riverbanks. 100 m. Pairs, at various heights, but typically hidden. **ID** Large *Cranioleuca*, much like Rusty-backed Spinetail and best separated by voice; differs in slightly heavier bill, whiter throat and breast, duller eyebrow. **Voice** Song, a few low throaty notes accelerating into slightly descending rattle-trill: "chu, chu, chu-chu'chu'ch'r'r'rrrrr" (recalls Rusty-backed Spinetail). Call, sharp staccato single or doubled notes.

Rusty-backed Spinetail *Cranioleuca vulpina*   LC
Chamicero Ribereño
Common resident.

 L 14.7 cm (5.8"). Race *vulpina*. Low vegetation near or overhanging streams and lake edges, gallery forest, open seasonally flooded areas (Amazonia). To 400 m. Pairs or families stay close, 1–7 m up in vines and tangled shrubbery. Inconspicuous but not furtive, sometimes with small mixed flocks. **ID** Rufous-brown, weak dingy white eyeline, below dingy greyish white. **Voice** Song, often as overlapping duet (not antiphonal), loud nasal chuckling, descending "kuee-kuee-kuee-quaa-quaa-qua-quaquaqua". Call "kuee-kuee". **SS** Yellow-chinned Spinetail, Parker's Spinetail.

vulpina

Red-faced Spinetail *Cranioleuca erythrops*   LC
Chamicero Rubicundo
Common resident.

 L 14.7 cm (5.8"). Race *griseigularis*. Humid premontane and montane forest, borders, older second growth. 1000–2200 m (to 700 m, Pacific slope). Singles or pairs, habitually with mixed flocks, in upper mid-levels to canopy. Active, conspicuous. **ID** Key mark is rufous on crown and face, wings and tail rufous. Juv less rufous on head, faint buff eyebrow. **Voice** Song, brief (1.5 seconds) high thin bouncy trill, 10–15 notes, descending.

griseigularis

Ash-browed Spinetail *Cranioleuca curtata*   VU
Chamicero Capirotado
Uncommon and local resident.

 L 15 cm (6"). Races *curtata*[A], *cisandina*[B]. Subcanopy and canopy of humid montane forest, borders, older second growth. 700–2500 m. Behaviour like Red-faced Spinetail. **ID** Undistinguished; solid rufous crown, weak greyish eyestripe, rufous wings and tail, throat dingy whitish, faint pale streaking on chest. Juv face and underparts ochraceous rufous. **Voice** High thin bouncy trill recalls Red-faced Spinetail but rises slightly, then gradually descends, strongest in middle. **SS** Crested Spinetail.

curtata

Streak-capped Spinetail *Cranioleuca hellmayri* `LC`
Chamicero Coronado

Common resident (Santa Marta Mts), rare (Serranía de Perijá; confirmation needed).

 L 15 cm (6"). Monotypic. Near-endemic (specimen and sightings from adjacent Venezuela). Humid montane forest, borders, older second growth. 1600–3000 m (rarely lower). Behaviour like Red-faced Spinetail. **ID** Streaked crown, whitish eyes, whitish eyebrow, crisp but inconspicuous crown streaking. **Voice** Song, short bouncy sharply descending squeaky trill (7–4 kHz), first few notes very high, much stronger; or may slightly ascend, then descend; recalls Red-faced Spinetail. **SS** Crested Spinetail (Perijá Mts).

Crested Spinetail *Cranioleuca subcristata* `LC`
Chamicero Copetón

Common resident.

 L 14 cm (5.5"). Races *subcristata*[A], *fuscivertex*[B] (?). Humid foothill and lower montane forest, older second growth. 400–1600 m. Behaviour like Red-faced Spinetail. **ID** Little evident crest, but bill pinkish, eyes greyish, crown streaked black, indistinct pale eyeline, wings and tail rufous. **Voice** Song a few high bouncy notes (7–5 kHz) accelerating and dropping in pitch, or series sometimes rises, then descends in attenuated trill; recalls other *Cranioleuca*. **SS** Ash-browed Spinetail.

Genera *Mazaria* and *Certhiaxis* Both occur low in shrubby semi-open areas; always associated with water. *Mazaria* closely resembles, and was previously placed in, *Synallaxis*, but voice very different.

White-bellied Spinetail *Mazaria propinqua* `LC`
Chamicero Buchiblanco

Fairly common resident.

 L 15 cm (6"). Monotypic. Early-successional vegetation on young Amazonian river islands; mainly grass mixed with *Tessaria*, *Salix* and bushes. To 150 m. Singles or pairs, skulking, difficult to see, seldom perching in open. Disperse during seasonal flooding. **ID** Undistinguished; crown plain (no rufous), whitish throat with blackish feather bases (throat can look either black or mostly whitish), underparts brownish grey, only central belly whitish. **Voice** Song, an unusual harsh, grating clatter, sometimes accelerating into rattle-trill, may slow to extended dribble of rough notes. **SS** Dark-breasted Spinetail (p. 339).

Yellow-chinned Spinetail *Certhiaxis cinnamomeus* `LC`
Chamicero Barbiamarillo

Common resident (N and *llanos*), local (Amazonas).

 L 15 cm (6"). Races *fuscifrons*[A], *marabinus*[B], *pallidus*[C]. Shallow marshes, wetlands, lagoon edges, mangroves; always near water. To 500 m. Conspicuous; pairs hop on ground, in grass or bushes, often pick prey from water surface. **ID** Above rufous, indistinct pale eyebrow, whitish below, yellow chin inconspicuous. **Voice** Vocal; harsh churring rattle, often given simultaneously by pair, and irregular ticking like winding an old watch. **SS** Red-and-white Spinetail (Amazonas).

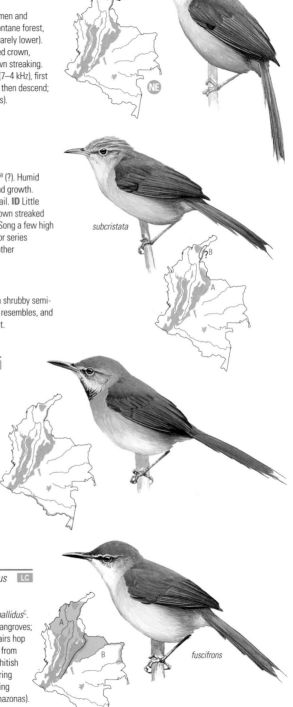

subcristata

fuscifrons

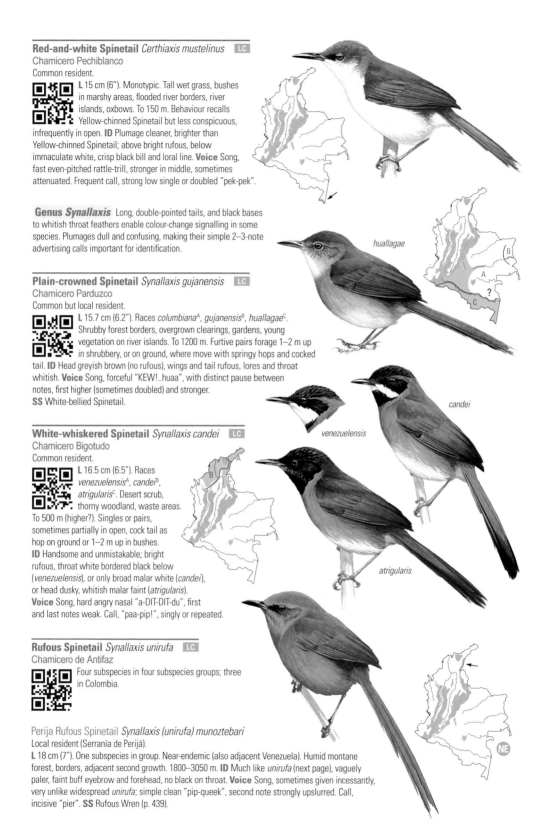

Red-and-white Spinetail *Certhiaxis mustelinus* `LC`
Chamicero Pechiblanco
Common resident.

L 15 cm (6"). Monotypic. Tall wet grass, bushes in marshy areas, flooded river borders, river islands, oxbows. To 150 m. Behaviour recalls Yellow-chinned Spinetail but less conspicuous, infrequently in open. **ID** Plumage cleaner, brighter than Yellow-chinned Spinetail; above bright rufous, below immaculate white, crisp black bill and loral line. **Voice** Song, fast even-pitched rattle-trill, stronger in middle, sometimes attenuated. Frequent call, strong low single or doubled "pek-pek".

Genus *Synallaxis* Long, double-pointed tails, and black bases to whitish throat feathers enable colour-change signalling in some species. Plumages dull and confusing, making their simple 2–3-note advertising calls important for identification.

Plain-crowned Spinetail *Synallaxis gujanensis* `LC`
Chamicero Parduzco
Common but local resident.

L 15.7 cm (6.2"). Races *columbiana*[A], *gujanensis*[B], *huallagae*[C]. Shrubby forest borders, overgrown clearings, gardens, young vegetation on river islands. To 1200 m. Furtive pairs forage 1–2 m up in shrubbery, or on ground, where move with springy hops and cocked tail. **ID** Head greyish brown (no rufous), wings and tail rufous, lores and throat whitish. **Voice** Song, forceful "KEW!..huaa", with distinct pause between notes, first higher (sometimes doubled) and stronger. **SS** White-bellied Spinetail.

huallagae

White-whiskered Spinetail *Synallaxis candei* `LC`
Chamicero Bigotudo
Common resident.

L 16.5 cm (6.5"). Races *venezuelensis*[A], *candei*[B], *atrigularis*[C]. Desert scrub, thorny woodland, waste areas. To 500 m (higher?). Singles or pairs, sometimes partially in open, cock tail as hop on ground or 1–2 m up in bushes. **ID** Handsome and unmistakable; bright rufous, throat white bordered black below (*venezuelensis*), or only broad malar white (*candei*), or head dusky, whitish malar faint (*atrigularis*). **Voice** Song, hard angry nasal "a-DIT-DIT-du", first and last notes weak. Call, "paa-pip!", singly or repeated.

candei

venezuelensis

atrigularis

Rufous Spinetail *Synallaxis unirufa* `LC`
Chamicero de Antifaz

Four subspecies in four subspecies groups; three in Colombia.

Perija Rufous Spinetail *Synallaxis (unirufa) munoztebari*
Local resident (Serranía de Perijá).
L 18 cm (7"). One subspecies in group. Near-endemic (also adjacent Venezuela). Humid montane forest, borders, adjacent second growth. 1800–3050 m. **ID** Much like *unirufa* (next page), vaguely paler, faint buff eyebrow and forehead, no black on throat. **Voice** Song, sometimes given incessantly, very unlike widespread *unirufa*; simple clean "pip-queek", second note strongly upslurred. Call, incisive "pier". **SS** Rufous Wren (p. 439).

`NE`

Merida Rufous Spinetail *Synallaxis (unirufa) meridana*
Local resident (Norte de Santander).
L 18 cm (7"). One subspecies in group. Habitat and behaviour like next group. **ID** Much as *unirufa* (below) but slightly paler, black feather bases on throat more visible, tail slightly longer. **Voice** Song resembles *unirufa* but with longer series of identical notes on same pitch, and less upslurred. **SS** Rufous Wren (p. 439).

Colombian Rufous Spinetail *Synallaxis (unirufa) unirufa*
Common resident.
L 18 cm (7"). One subspecies in group. Humid and wet montane forest, stunted woodland near treeline. 1700–3200 m (rarely higher). Pairs or families move through cluttered undergrowth and *Chusquea* bamboo inside forest, generally low, out of view; sometimes with mixed flocks. **ID** Slender, bright rufous, bill and lores black, throat feathers black basally (visible if raised). **Voice** Song, incisive nasal upslurred "ka-queeéik", thinner "queeeik" or "quee-quee-queéik". Low "churr" in alarm. **SS** Rufous (p. 439) and Sharpe's Wrens (p. 440).

Rusty-headed Spinetail *Synallaxis fuscorufa* `VU`
Chamicero Serrano `NT`
Common resident (Santa Marta Mts).
L 14 cm (7"). Monotypic. Endemic. Humid montane forest (especially shrubby borders), overgrown clearings. 2000–3000 m (rarely 900 m). Pairs or families move around near ground to c. 6 m up, mostly out of view in vine tangles, brambles, thickets. Less furtive than many *Synallaxis*. **ID** Unmistakable; entire head, neck and upper breast orange-rufous. **Voice** Song, at times tirelessly repeated, a nasal "dit-dit-du", last note lower.

Stripe-breasted Spinetail *Synallaxis cinnamomea* `LC`
Chamicero Listado
Fairly common resident.
L 14 cm (5.5"). Races *cinnamomea*[A], *aveledoi*[B]. Thickets, vine tangles, overgrown treefall gaps inside or at edge of humid forest, neglected coffee plantations, dry shrubbery. 700–2100 m. Notoriously skulking. 'Peevish' singles or pairs hop on ground, scratch leaves, or move up in bushes, but stay within cover, offering only brief views; incidental around mixed flocks. **ID** Streaked underparts diagnostic. **Voice** Vocal in rainy seasons, otherwise sporadic. Rather high nasal, "keep, going", first note higher, second drops then bounces. Call, a soft whining "peeeur".

cinnamomea

Ruddy Spinetail *Synallaxis rutilans* `LC`
Chamicero Colorado
Seven subspecies in two subspecies groups; one in Colombia.

Ruddy Spinetail *Synallaxis (rutilans) rutilans*
Rare to uncommon resident.
L 15 cm (6"). Races *dissors*[A], *caquetensis*[B]. Undergrowth, old treefalls inside humid *terra firme* forest. To 500 m. Furtive singles or pairs hop in leaf litter on ground, or close to it; call from slightly elevated perch. Not with mixed flocks. **ID** Rufous-chestnut, small black throat, black lores, dusky tail. Juv duller. **Voice** Song (*caquetensis*), persistently repeated "chik-waaa", last note rises, second lower; *dissors* similar, second note flatter. **SS** Chestnut-throated Spinetail. **TN** Taxonomy unresolved.

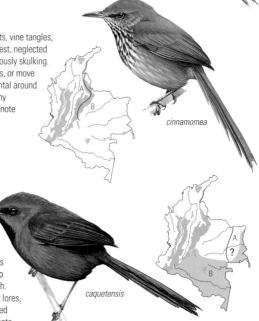

caquetensis

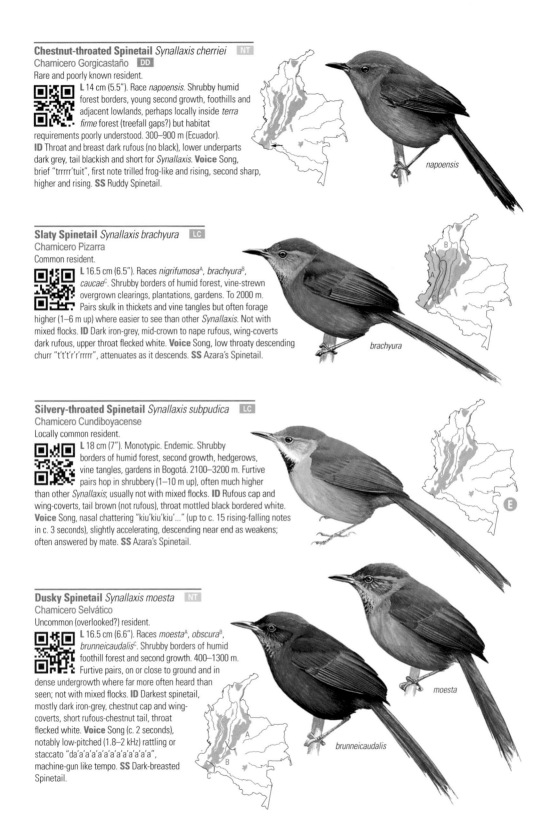

Chestnut-throated Spinetail *Synallaxis cherriei* NT
Chamicero Gorgicastaño DD
Rare and poorly known resident.
L 14 cm (5.5"). Race *napoensis*. Shrubby humid forest borders, young second growth, foothills and adjacent lowlands, perhaps locally inside *terra firme* forest (treefall gaps?) but habitat requirements poorly understood. 300–900 m (Ecuador). **ID** Throat and breast dark rufous (no black), lower underparts dark grey, tail blackish and short for *Synallaxis*. **Voice** Song, brief "trrrrr'tuit", first note trilled frog-like and rising, second sharp, higher and rising. **SS** Ruddy Spinetail.

napoensis

Slaty Spinetail *Synallaxis brachyura* LC
Chamicero Pizarra
Common resident.
L 16.5 cm (6.5"). Races *nigrifumosa*[A], *brachyura*[B], *caucae*[C]. Shrubby borders of humid forest, vine-strewn overgrown clearings, plantations, gardens. To 2000 m. Pairs skulk in thickets and vine tangles but often forage higher (1–6 m up) where easier to see than other *Synallaxis*. Not with mixed flocks. **ID** Dark iron-grey, mid-crown to nape rufous, wing-coverts dark rufous, upper throat flecked white. **Voice** Song, low throaty descending churr "t't't'r'r'rrrrr", attenuates as it descends. **SS** Azara's Spinetail.

brachyura

Silvery-throated Spinetail *Synallaxis subpudica* LC
Chamicero Cundiboyacense
Locally common resident.
L 18 cm (7"). Monotypic. Endemic. Shrubby borders of humid forest, second growth, hedgerows, vine tangles, gardens in Bogotá. 2100–3200 m. Furtive pairs hop in shrubbery (1–10 m up), often much higher than other *Synallaxis*; usually not with mixed flocks. **ID** Rufous cap and wing-coverts, tail brown (not rufous), throat mottled black bordered white. **Voice** Song, nasal chattering "kiu'kiu'kiu'..." (up to c. 15 rising-falling notes in c. 3 seconds), slightly accelerating, descending near end as weakens; often answered by mate. **SS** Azara's Spinetail.

E

Dusky Spinetail *Synallaxis moesta* NT
Chamicero Selvático
Uncommon (overlooked?) resident.
L 16.5 cm (6.6"). Races *moesta*[A], *obscura*[B], *brunneicaudalis*[C]. Shrubby borders of humid foothill forest and second growth. 400–1300 m. Furtive pairs, on or close to ground and in dense undergrowth where far more often heard than seen; not with mixed flocks. **ID** Darkest spinetail, mostly dark iron-grey, chestnut cap and wing-coverts, short rufous-chestnut tail, throat flecked white. **Voice** Song (c. 2 seconds), notably low-pitched (1.8–2 kHz) rattling or staccato "da'a'a'a'a'a'a'a'a'a'a'a", machine-gun like tempo. **SS** Dark-breasted Spinetail.

moesta

brunneicaudalis

Dark-breasted Spinetail *Synallaxis albigularis* `LC`
Chamicero Amazónico
Common resident.

 L 15.7 cm (6.2"). Races *rodolphei*[A], *albigularis*[B]. Shrubby clearings, overgrown pastures, tall grass, cane (*Gynerium*) and bushy second growth on river islands and riverbanks; often near water or wet areas. To 1600 m (rarely higher). Behaviour recalls Dusky Spinetail but not associated with forest borders; probably expanding with deforestation. **ID** Rufous cap and wing-coverts, wings and tail brownish, forehead, face and underparts greyish, throat black bordered white. **Voice** Song, short low "dit, dudududu", often incessantly.

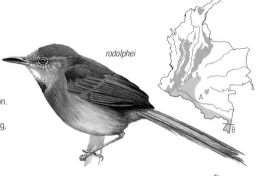

rodolphei

Rio Orinoco Spinetail *Synallaxis beverlyae* `NT`
Chamicero del Río Orinoco
Local resident.

 L 16.5 cm (6.5"). Monotypic. Scrub, dense vines and low vegetation on semi-permanent and ephemeral islands in R Orinoco, occasionally riverbanks. To 100 m. Pairs skulk in cover, near ground to 3–4 m up; sing partially exposed. **ID** Plumage (but not voice) resembles Pale-breasted Spinetail; differs in eyes yellowish, marginally paler facial area and underparts. **Voice** Song, short "pik, pt-pt-pt", first stronger, rest after slight pause, or three to several quicker notes added "pik, pt-pt-pt-pt, pkpkpk". Trill when excited. **SS** Pale-breasted Spinetail.

Pale-breasted Spinetail *Synallaxis albescens* `LC`
Chamicero Pálido
Common resident.

 L 16.5 cm (6.5"). Races *hypoleuca*[A], *littoralis*[B], *insignis*[C], *perpallida*[D], *occipitalis*[E], *nesiotis*[F], *josephinae*[G], race? Dry to moderately humid semi-open areas with scattered shrubs, waste areas, thickets. To 2100 m. Skulking, most easily seen at dawn when sings partly exposed in bush top. **ID** Eyes dark, most of crown and shoulders rufous, tail rather long, dingy greyish brown, whitish throat with black feather bases (signals black in aggression). **Voice** Song, buzzy "wait'here" or "wit'tee", often given incessantly. **SS** Rio Orinoco Spinetail (voice and eye colour differ).

occipitalis

latitabunda

Azara's Spinetail *Synallaxis azarae* `LC`
Chamicero Piscuís

 Nine subspecies in three subspecies groups; one in Colombia.

Elegant Spinetail *Synallaxis (azarae) elegantior*
Common resident.

L 16.5 cm (6.5"). Races *elegantior*[A], *media*[B]. Shrubby borders of dry to humid montane forest, regenerating clearings, bushy roadsides; profits from deforestation. 1400–3000 m. Another skulking, furtive *Synallaxis*, forages near ground to 3–4 m up; vocal. **ID** Resembles Pale-breasted Spinetail but tail longer, rufous (not brownish); voice differs. **Voice** Song, thin high "pip-squeak" or "mac-white". **TN** Northern races in past regarded as a separate species based on voice (now refuted) and two fewer tail feathers.

elegantior

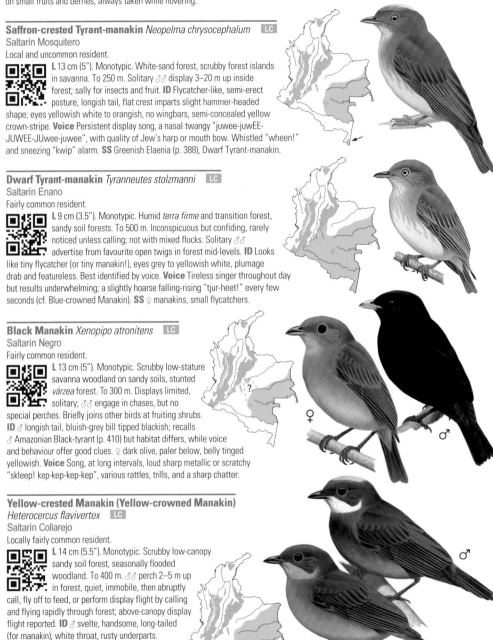

PIPRIDAE
Manakins
52 extant species, 21 in region

A Neotropical family that achieves peak diversity in lowland forests. They are small forest birds with short round bills, chunky bodies, and large eyes. Most males are brightly coloured but females are drab. Bright males—the boys of *La dolce vita*—are renowned for their remarkable displays, often performed at communal leks inside forest. Females are 'single mothers', undertaking all nesting duties alone. Manakins feed heavily on small fruits and berries, always taken while hovering.

Saffron-crested Tyrant-manakin *Neopelma chrysocephalum* LC
Saltarín Mosquitero
Local and uncommon resident.
L 13 cm (5"). Monotypic. White-sand forest, scrubby forest islands in savanna. To 250 m. Solitary ♂♂ display 3–20 m up inside forest; sally for insects and fruit. **ID** Flycatcher-like, semi-erect posture, longish tail, flat crest imparts slight hammer-headed shape; eyes yellowish white to orangish, no wingbars, semi-concealed yellow crown-stripe. **Voice** Persistent display song, a nasal twangy "juwee-juwEE-JUWEE-JUwee-juwee", with quality of Jew's harp or mouth bow. Whistled "wheen!" and sneezing "kwip" alarm. **SS** Greenish Elaenia (p. 388), Dwarf Tyrant-manakin.

Dwarf Tyrant-manakin *Tyranneutes stolzmanni* LC
Saltarín Enano
Fairly common resident.
L 9 cm (3.5"). Monotypic. Humid *terra firme* and transition forest, sandy soil forests. To 500 m. Inconspicuous but confiding, rarely noticed unless calling; not with mixed flocks. Solitary ♂♂ advertise from favourite open twigs in forest mid-levels. **ID** Looks like tiny flycatcher (or tiny manakin!), eyes grey to yellowish white, plumage drab and featureless. Best identified by voice. **Voice** Tireless singer throughout day but results underwhelming; a slightly hoarse falling-rising "tjur-heet!" every few seconds (cf. Blue-crowned Manakin). **SS** ♀ manakins, small flycatchers.

Black Manakin *Xenopipo atronitens* LC
Saltarín Negro
Fairly common resident.
L 13 cm (5"). Monotypic. Scrubby low-stature savanna woodland on sandy soils, stunted *várzea* forest. To 300 m. Displays limited, solitary; ♂♂ engage in chases, but no special perches. Briefly joins other birds at fruiting shrubs. **ID** ♂ longish tail, bluish-grey bill tipped blackish; recalls ♂ Amazonian Black-tyrant (p. 410) but habitat differs, while voice and behaviour offer good clues. ♀ dark olive, paler below, belly tinged yellowish. **Voice** Song, at long intervals, loud sharp metallic or scratchy "skleep! kep-kep-kep-kep", various rattles, trills, and a sharp chatter.

Yellow-crested Manakin (Yellow-crowned Manakin)
Heterocercus flavivertex LC
Saltarín Collarejo
Locally fairly common resident.
L 14 cm (5.5"). Monotypic. Scrubby low-canopy sandy soil forest, seasonally flooded woodland. To 400 m. ♂♂ perch 2–5 m up in forest, quiet, immobile, then abruptly call, fly off to feed, or perform display flight by calling and flying rapidly through forest; above-canopy display flight reported. **ID** ♂ svelte, handsome, long-tailed (for manakin); white throat, rusty underparts. ♀ duller, throat greyish. **Voice** Advertise (perch or flight) with loud explosive "speeeeeeeeeEEEEEits-spit-cheeeeeeeeu" (rises, stutters or hiccups, then falls). Shorter "speeeee"; high thin trilled "t't't't't't't".

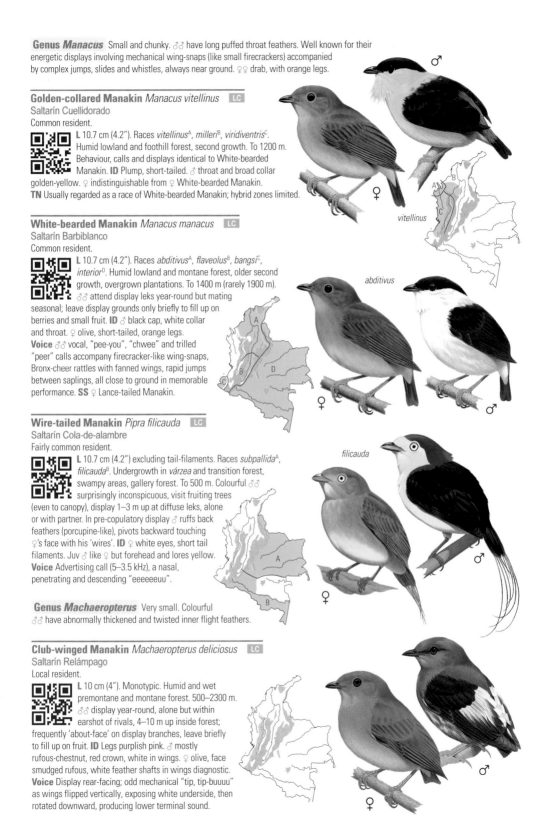

Genus *Manacus* Small and chunky. ♂♂ have long puffed throat feathers. Well known for their energetic displays involving mechanical wing-snaps (like small firecrackers) accompanied by complex jumps, slides and whistles, always near ground. ♀♀ drab, with orange legs.

Golden-collared Manakin *Manacus vitellinus* `LC`
Saltarín Cuellidorado
Common resident.
L 10.7 cm (4.2"). Races *vitellinus*[A], *milleri*[B], *viridiventris*[C]. Humid lowland and foothill forest, second growth. To 1200 m. Behaviour, calls and displays identical to White-bearded Manakin. **ID** Plump, short-tailed. ♂ throat and broad collar golden-yellow. ♀ indistinguishable from ♀ White-bearded Manakin.
TN Usually regarded as a race of White-bearded Manakin; hybrid zones limited.

vitellinus

White-bearded Manakin *Manacus manacus* `LC`
Saltarín Barbiblanco
Common resident.
L 10.7 cm (4.2"). Races *abditivus*[A], *flaveolus*[B], *bangsi*[C], *interior*[D]. Humid lowland and montane forest, older second growth, overgrown plantations. To 1400 m (rarely 1900 m). ♂♂ attend display leks year-round but mating seasonal; leave display grounds only briefly to fill up on berries and small fruit. **ID** ♂ black cap, white collar and throat. ♀ olive, short-tailed, orange legs.
Voice ♂♂ vocal, "pee-you", "chwee" and trilled "peer" calls accompany firecracker-like wing-snaps, Bronx-cheer rattles with fanned wings, rapid jumps between saplings, all close to ground in memorable performance. **SS** ♀ Lance-tailed Manakin.

abditivus

Wire-tailed Manakin *Pipra filicauda* `LC`
Saltarín Cola-de-alambre
Fairly common resident.
L 10.7 cm (4.2") excluding tail-filaments. Races *subpallida*[A], *filicauda*[B]. Undergrowth in *várzea* and transition forest, swampy areas, gallery forest. To 500 m. Colourful ♂♂ surprisingly inconspicuous, visit fruiting trees (even to canopy), display 1–3 m up at diffuse leks, alone or with partner. In pre-copulatory display ♂ ruffs back feathers (porcupine-like), pivots backward touching ♀'s face with his 'wires'. **ID** ♀ white eyes, short tail filaments. Juv ♂ like ♀ but forehead and lores yellow.
Voice Advertising call (5–3.5 kHz), a nasal, penetrating and descending "eeeeeeuu".

filicauda

Genus *Machaeropterus* Very small. Colourful ♂♂ have abnormally thickened and twisted inner flight feathers.

Club-winged Manakin *Machaeropterus deliciosus* `LC`
Saltarín Relámpago
Local resident.
L 10 cm (4"). Monotypic. Humid and wet premontane and montane forest. 500–2300 m. ♂♂ display year-round, alone but within earshot of rivals, 4–10 m up inside forest; frequently 'about-face' on display branches, leave briefly to fill up on fruit. **ID** Legs purplish pink. ♂ mostly rufous-chestnut, red crown, white in wings. ♀ olive, face smudged rufous, white feather shafts in wings diagnostic.
Voice Display rear-facing; odd mechanical "tip, tip-buuuu" as wings flipped vertically, exposing white underside, then rotated downward, producing lower terminal sound.

Striolated Manakin *Machaeropterus striolatus* LC
Saltarín Rayado Occidental

Common (but easily overlooked) resident.

L 9 cm (3.5"). Races *zulianus*[A], *antioquiae*[B], *striolatus*[C]. Low to mid-levels in humid forest, second growth. 250–1700 m (*antioquiae*) or to 1100 m (*striolatus*). Inconspicuous except at fruiting trees. **ID** ♂ olive, red cap, swirling pinkish-red striped underparts. ♀ blurred reddish-brown streaking on breast. **Voice** ♂'s advertising call (all races), delicate little "pit-sink", last note stronger. Mechanical buzz while rotating rapidly in presence of ♀. **AN** Western Striped Manakin.

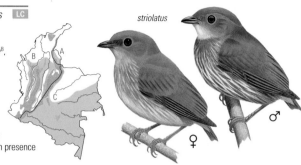

striolatus

♂

♀

Genera *Pseudopipra* (formerly *Dixiphia*), *Ceratopipra* and *Lepidothrix* All formerly placed in *Pipra*; and quick, short-tailed and inconspicuous. ♂♂ largely black but cap, sometimes also rump or eye colours differ. ♀♀ greenish. Advertising ♂♂ not in visual contact, but stay within auditory range of rivals. Taxonomy unresolved.

White-crowned Manakin *Pseudopipra pipra* LC
Saltarín Cabeciblanco

Thirteen subspecies in seven subspecies groups; four in Colombia. Previously placed in *Dixiphia*. Advertising calls of races *bolivari* and *unica* (Colombian White-crowned Manakin) differ markedly. Only *unica* and *coracina* appear to have similar advertising calls.

♀
minima

Western White-crowned Manakin *Pseudopipra (pipra) anthracina*
Local resident.

L 10 cm (4"). Race *minima*. Lower levels inside humid and wet foothill and lower montane forest. 400–1200 m. Behaviour as Northern White-crowned Manakin. **ID** As Northern White-crowned; ♀ has contrasting grey crown and sides of head, red eyes. **Voice** ♂ advertising call a shrill buzzy "shureeee!" that rises dramatically; lacks 'mushy' harshness of other races.

Colombian White-crowned Manakin *Pseudopipra (pipra) unica*
Local (?) resident.

L 10 cm (4"). Races *bolivari*[A], *unica*[B]. Endemic. Habitat and behaviour as next subspecies group. **ID** Both sexes as Andean race *coracina*. **Voice** ♂ advertising call (*unica*) essentially similar to race *coracina* (below). Advertising call *bolivari* (near Anorí, Antioquia) clear whistled "whuuu-u-wheet!" with first, drawn-out note lowest, middle sharply rising, last highest, strongest and very slightly rising; the only Colombian race with clean whistled call (all others burry or somewhat harsh).

♂
unica

Andean White-crowned Manakin *Pseudopipra (pipra) coracina*
Local (?) resident.

L 10 cm (4"). One subspecies in group. Undergrowth in humid premontane forest. c. 700–1600 m (elevational limits not well defined). **ID** Like Northern White-crowned Manakin (below); ♀'s crown and sides of head more clearly contrasting greyish, eyes red. **Voice** ♂ advertising call rather low-pitched 'mushy'/harsh "buuuuujip!" (abruptly rising at end), nearly identical to race *unica* (above), but very unlike lowland *pipra* and western races *minima* and *bolivari*.

♂

♀

Northern White-crowned Manakin
Pseudopipra (pipra) pipra
Locally common resident.

L 10 cm (4"). One subspecies in group. Undergrowth in humid lowland forest, sandy soil forests. To 1260 m. ♂♂ audible to competitors in dispersed leks. **ID** ♂ glossy black, white crown and nape, red eyes. ♀ and 1st-y ♂ olive-green to grey-green, crown usually greyish but variable, eyes red. **Voice** ♂ advertising call, rather harsh buzzy/hissing "scheeeeer" (descending, or locally flat). **SS** ♀ grey-tinged crown, reddish eyes diagnostic.

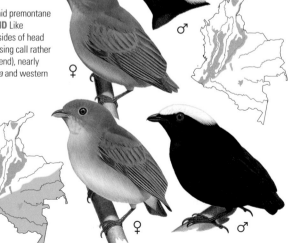

♀

♂

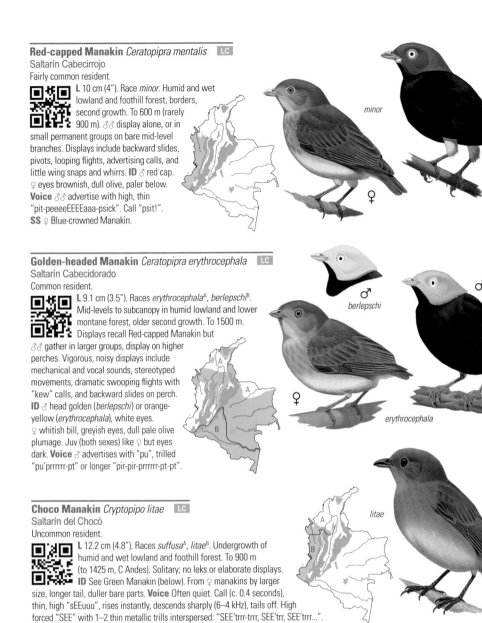

Red-capped Manakin *Ceratopipra mentalis* `LC`
Saltarín Cabecirrojo
Fairly common resident.

L 10 cm (4"). Race *minor*. Humid and wet lowland and wet lowland and foothill forest, borders, second growth. To 600 m (rarely 900 m). ♂♂ display alone, or in small permanent groups on bare mid-level branches. Displays include backward slides, pivots, looping flights, advertising calls, and little wing snaps and whirrs. **ID** ♂ red cap. ♀ eyes brownish, dull olive, paler below. **Voice** ♂♂ advertise with high, thin "pit-peeeeEEEEaaa-psick". Call "psit!". **SS** ♀ Blue-crowned Manakin.

minor

♀

♂

Golden-headed Manakin *Ceratopipra erythrocephala* `LC`
Saltarín Cabecidorado
Common resident.

L 9.1 cm (3.5"). Races *erythrocephala*[A], *berlepschi*[B]. Mid-levels to subcanopy in humid lowland and lower montane forest, older second growth. To 1500 m. Displays recall Red-capped Manakin but ♂♂ gather in larger groups, display on higher perches. Vigorous, noisy displays include mechanical and vocal sounds, stereotyped movements, dramatic swooping flights with "kew" calls, and backward slides on perch. **ID** ♂ head golden (*berlepschi*) or orange-yellow (*erythrocephala*), white eyes. ♀ whitish bill, greyish eyes, dull pale olive plumage. Juv (both sexes) like ♀ but eyes dark. **Voice** ♂ advertises with "pu", trilled "pu'prrrrrr-pt" or longer "pir-pir-prrrrrr-pt-pt".

♂

berlepschi

♂

♀

erythrocephala

Choco Manakin *Cryptopipo litae* `LC`
Saltarín del Chocó
Uncommon resident.

L 12.2 cm (4.8"). Races *suffusa*[A], *litae*[B]. Undergrowth of humid and wet lowland and foothill forest. To 900 m (to 1425 m, C Andes). Solitary; no leks or elaborate displays. **ID** See Green Manakin (below). From ♀ manakins by larger size, longer tail, duller bare parts. **Voice** Often quiet. Call (c. 0.4 seconds), thin, high "sEEuuu", rises instantly, descends sharply (6–4 kHz), tails off. High forced "SEE" with 1–2 thin metallic trills interspersed: "SEE'trrr-trrr, SEE'trr, SEE'trrr...". **SS** Sapayoa (p. 258). **TN** Usually included with Green Manakin.

litae

Green Manakin *Cryptopipo holochlora* `LC`
Saltarín Verde
Uncommon resident.

L 12.2 cm (4.8"). Race *holochlora*. Undergrowth in humid foothill forest. 400–1400 m. **ID** Legs grey, indistinct pale eye-ring, above bright grass green, below olive, belly paler soft yellow. **Voice** Quiet. Advertising call, high (5 kHz) rising "sueee" at 2–3-second intervals. **SS** Blue-backed Manakin, other ♀♀ manakins smaller. **TN** Usually includes Choco Manakin.

holochlora

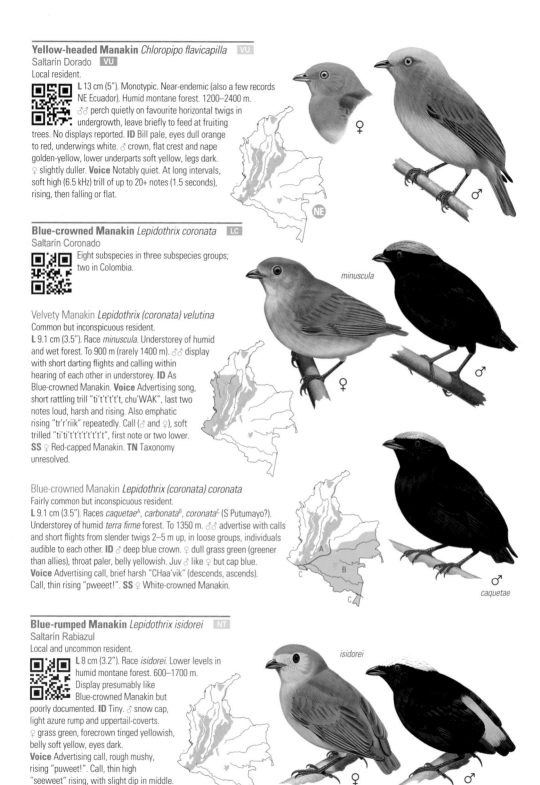

Yellow-headed Manakin *Chloropipo flavicapilla* `VU`
Saltarín Dorado `VU`
Local resident.

L 13 cm (5"). Monotypic. Near-endemic (also a few records NE Ecuador). Humid montane forest. 1200–2400 m. ♂♂ perch quietly on favourite horizontal twigs in undergrowth, leave briefly to feed at fruiting trees. No displays reported. **ID** Bill pale, eyes dull orange to red, underwings white. ♂ crown, flat crest and nape golden-yellow, lower underparts soft yellow, legs dark. ♀ slightly duller. **Voice** Notably quiet. At long intervals, soft high (6.5 kHz) trill of up to 20+ notes (1.5 seconds), rising, then falling or flat.

Blue-crowned Manakin *Lepidothrix coronata* `LC`
Saltarín Coronado

Eight subspecies in three subspecies groups; two in Colombia.

Velvety Manakin *Lepidothrix (coronata) velutina*
Common but inconspicuous resident.
L 9.1 cm (3.5"). Race *minuscula*. Understorey of humid and wet forest. To 900 m (rarely 1400 m). ♂♂ display with short darting flights and calling within hearing of each other in understorey. **ID** As Blue-crowned Manakin. **Voice** Advertising song, short rattling trill "ti't't't't't, chu'WAK", last two notes loud, harsh and rising. Also emphatic rising "tr'r'riik" repeatedly. Call (♂ and ♀), soft trilled "ti'ti'ti't't't't't't't", first note or two lower. **SS** ♀ Red-capped Manakin. **TN** Taxonomy unresolved.

Blue-crowned Manakin *Lepidothrix (coronata) coronata*
Fairly common but inconspicuous resident.
L 9.1 cm (3.5"). Races *caquetae*[A], *carbonata*[B], *coronata*[C] (S Putumayo?). Understorey of humid *terra firme* forest. To 1350 m. ♂♂ advertise with calls and short flights from slender twigs 2–5 m up, in loose groups, individuals audible to each other. **ID** ♂ deep blue crown. ♀ dull grass green (greener than allies), throat paler, belly yellowish. Juv ♂ like ♀ but cap blue. **Voice** Advertising call, brief harsh "CHaa'vik" (descends, ascends). Call, thin rising "pweeet!". **SS** ♀ White-crowned Manakin.

Blue-rumped Manakin *Lepidothrix isidorei* `NT`
Saltarín Rabiazul
Local and uncommon resident.

L 8 cm (3.2"). Race *isidorei*. Lower levels in humid montane forest. 600–1700 m. Display presumably like Blue-crowned Manakin but poorly documented. **ID** Tiny. ♂ snow cap, light azure rump and uppertail-coverts. ♀ grass green, forecrown tinged yellowish, belly soft yellow, eyes dark. **Voice** Advertising call, rough mushy, rising "puweet!". Call, thin high "seeweet" rising, with slight dip in middle. **SS** ♀ White-crowned Manakin (red eyes).

minuscula

caquetae

isidorei

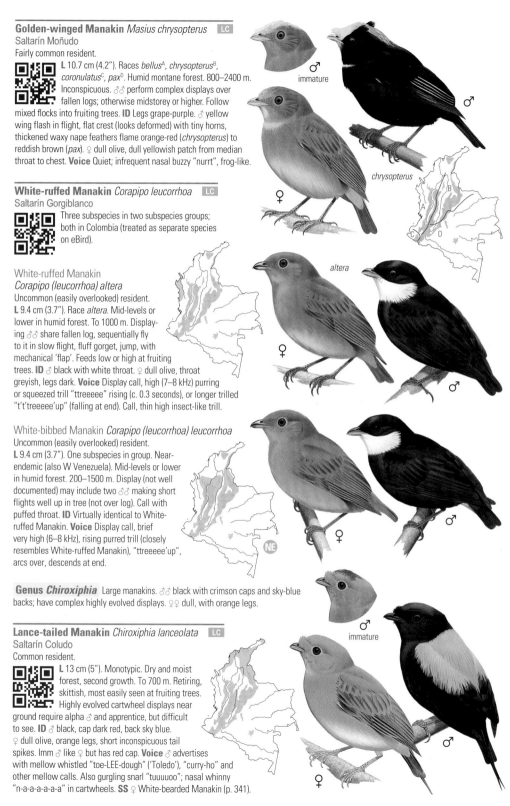

Golden-winged Manakin *Masius chrysopterus* `LC`
Saltarín Moñudo
Fairly common resident.

L 10.7 cm (4.2"). Races *bellus*[A], *chrysopterus*[B], *coronulatus*[C], *pax*[D]. Humid montane forest. 800–2400 m. Inconspicuous. ♂♂ perform complex displays over fallen logs; otherwise midstorey or higher. Follow mixed flocks into fruiting trees. **ID** Legs grape-purple. ♂ yellow wing flash in flight, flat crest (looks deformed) with tiny horns, thickened waxy nape feathers flame orange-red (*chrysopterus*) to reddish brown (*pax*). ♀ dull olive, dull yellowish patch from median throat to chest. **Voice** Quiet; infrequent nasal buzzy "nurrt", frog-like.

immature

♂

♀

chrysopterus

White-ruffed Manakin *Corapipo leucorrhoa* `LC`
Saltarín Gorgiblanco

Three subspecies in two subspecies groups; both in Colombia (treated as separate species on eBird).

White-ruffed Manakin
Corapipo (leucorrhoa) altera
Uncommon (easily overlooked) resident.
L 9.4 cm (3.7"). Race *altera*. Mid-levels or lower in humid forest. To 1000 m. Displaying ♂♂ share fallen log, sequentially fly to it in slow flight, fluff gorget, jump, with mechanical 'flap'. Feeds low or high at fruiting trees. **ID** ♂ black with white throat. ♀ dull olive, throat greyish, legs dark. **Voice** Display call, high (7–8 kHz) purring or squeezed trill "ttreeeee" rising (c. 0.3 seconds), or longer trilled "t't'treeeee'up" (falling at end). Call, thin high insect-like trill.

altera

♀

♂

White-bibbed Manakin *Corapipo (leucorrhoa) leucorrhoa*
Uncommon (easily overlooked) resident.
L 9.4 cm (3.7"). One subspecies in group. Near-endemic (also W Venezuela). Mid-levels or lower in humid forest. 200–1500 m. Display (not well documented) may include two ♂♂ making short flights well up in tree (not over log). Call with puffed throat. **ID** Virtually identical to White-ruffed Manakin. **Voice** Display call, brief very high (6–8 kHz), rising purred trill (closely resembles White-ruffed Manakin), "ttreeeee'up", arcs over, descends at end.

♀

♂

Genus *Chiroxiphia* Large manakins. ♂♂ black with crimson caps and sky-blue backs; have complex highly evolved displays. ♀♀ dull, with orange legs.

Lance-tailed Manakin *Chiroxiphia lanceolata* `LC`
Saltarín Coludo
Common resident.

L 13 cm (5"). Monotypic. Dry and moist forest, second growth. To 700 m. Retiring, skittish, most easily seen at fruiting trees. Highly evolved cartwheel displays near ground require alpha ♂ and apprentice, but difficult to see. **ID** ♂ black, cap dark red, back sky blue. ♀ dull olive, orange legs, short inconspicuous tail spikes. Imm ♂ like ♀ but has red cap. **Voice** ♂ advertises with mellow whistled "toe-LEE-dough" ('Toledo'), "curry-ho" and other mellow calls. Also gurgling snarl "tuuuuoo"; nasal whinny "n-a-a-a-a-a-a" in cartwheels. **SS** ♀ White-bearded Manakin (p. 341).

immature

♂

♀

♂

Blue-backed Manakin *Chiroxiphia pareola* `LC`
Saltarín Dorsiazul

Uncommon and local resident.

L 13 cm (5"). Race *napensis*. Lower levels in humid *terra firme* forest. To 600 m. Wary, difficult to see. **ID** ♂ and ♀ like respective sexes of Lance-tailed Manakin, but no tail spikes. Imm ♂ like ♀ but has red cap. **Voice** ♂ wide range of calls. Loud human-like whistled "WEEO-WEET!"; ♂♂ in chorus, loud whistled "chuEET" and "wich'CHEER" given repeatedly. During cartwheel display, ♂♂ utter frog-like nasal buzzy "eerrrrrr" repeatedly. **SS** Green Manakin.

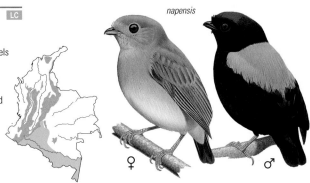

napensis

♀   ♂

COTINGIDAE
Cotingas
67 extant species, 34 in region

A heterogeneous New World family whose taxonomic relationships seem to be forever in flux. All are forest-based and all of them eat some fruit—several are almost entirely frugivorous. The family includes some of the most beautiful birds in the American tropics. Breeding systems range from monogamy (a few) to polygamy in lekking species. Much of what is known about their breeding and mating systems is due to the pioneering work of Barbara & David Snow and Alexander Skutch.

Scaled Fruiteater *Ampelioides tschudii* `LC`
Frutero Escamado

Local and unpredictable resident.

L 20 cm (8"). Monotypic. Mid-levels to canopy in humid foothill and montane forest, older second growth. 650–2700 m. Mainly singles or pairs, inconspicuous, hop sluggishly among epiphytes; diet mostly fruit; follow canopy mixed flocks. **ID** Plump, short-tailed; patchy plumage. ♂ black head, whitish throat, scaly plumage. ♀ similar but head olive-green. **Voice** Loud raptor-like whistle "weeeeEEEEaaa", fading, descending at end; lower-pitched than *Pipreola*.

♂

♀

Genus *Pipreola* Plump, short-tailed, sluggish and inconspicuous; montane, and highly frugivorous. Vocalizations extremely high-pitched. Predominantly green and yellow, bill and legs usually red to red-orange; ♀♀ duller, confusing.

Fiery-throated Fruiteater *Pipreola chlorolepidota* `NT`
Frutero Pigmeo `NT`

Rare (overlooked?) resident.

L 12.2 cm (4.8"). Monotypic. Humid foothill and lower montane forest. 600–1500 m. Pairs perch quietly, mid-levels or lower, sometimes with mixed flocks. **ID** Tiny; yellow eyes. ♂ bright green, fiery throat. ♀ wavy green-and-yellow barred underparts. **Voice** Very high (7–8 kHz) weak, rather forced "pzeEEeet", slightly rising-falling. Call, high "tsi". **SS** Smallest, least numerous fruiteater. ♀ Andean Mourner (p. 363), ♀ Swallow Tanager (p. 508).

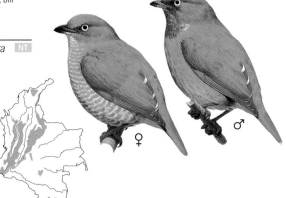

♀   ♂

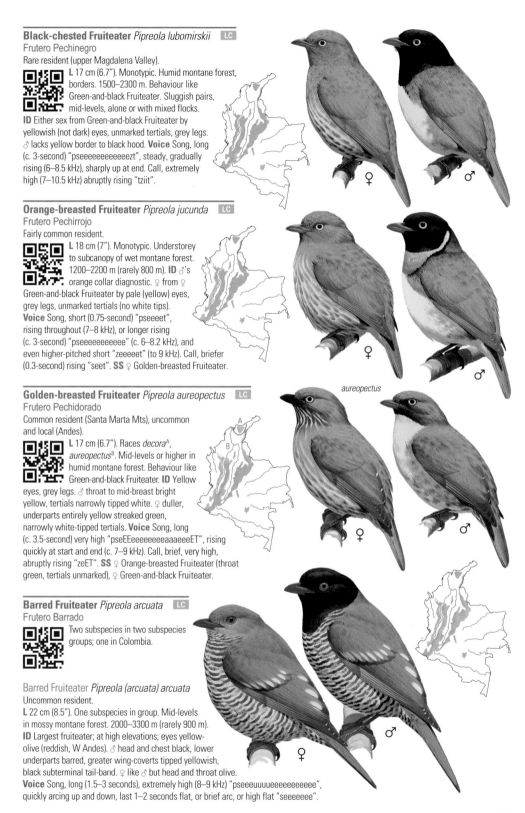

Black-chested Fruiteater *Pipreola lubomirskii* LC
Frutero Pechinegro

Rare resident (upper Magdalena Valley).

L 17 cm (6.7"). Monotypic. Humid montane forest, borders. 1500–2300 m. Behaviour like Green-and-black Fruiteater. Sluggish pairs, mid-levels, alone or with mixed flocks. **ID** Either sex from Green-and-black Fruiteater by yellowish (not dark) eyes, unmarked tertials, grey legs. ♂ lacks yellow border to black hood. **Voice** Song, long (c. 3-second) "pseeeeeeeeeeezt", steady, gradually rising (6–8.5 kHz), sharply up at end. Call, extremely high (7–10.5 kHz) abruptly rising "tziit".

Orange-breasted Fruiteater *Pipreola jucunda* LC
Frutero Pechirrojo

Fairly common resident.

L 18 cm (7"). Monotypic. Understorey to subcanopy of wet montane forest. 1200–2200 m (rarely 800 m). **ID** ♂'s orange collar diagnostic. ♀ from Green-and-black Fruiteater by pale (yellow) eyes, grey legs, unmarked tertials (no white tips). **Voice** Song, short (0.75-second) "pseeeet", rising throughout (7–8 kHz), or longer rising (c. 3-second) "pseeeeeeeeee" (c. 6–8.2 kHz), and even higher-pitched short "zeeeet" (to 9 kHz). Call, briefer (0.3-second) rising "seet". **SS** ♀ Golden-breasted Fruiteater.

Golden-breasted Fruiteater *Pipreola aureopectus* LC
Frutero Pechidorado

aureopectus

Common resident (Santa Marta Mts), uncommon and local (Andes).

L 17 cm (6.7"). Races *decora*[A], *aureopectus*[B]. Mid-levels or higher in humid montane forest. Behaviour like Green-and-black Fruiteater. **ID** Yellow eyes, grey legs. ♂ throat to mid-breast bright yellow, tertials narrowly tipped white. ♀ duller, underparts entirely yellow streaked green, narrowly white-tipped tertials. **Voice** Song, long (c. 3.5-second) very high "pseEEeeeeeeeeaaaeeeET", rising quickly at start and end (c. 7–9 kHz). Call, brief, very high, abruptly rising "zeET". **SS** ♀ Orange-breasted Fruiteater (throat green, tertials unmarked), ♀ Green-and-black Fruiteater.

Barred Fruiteater *Pipreola arcuata* LC
Frutero Barrado

Two subspecies in two subspecies groups; one in Colombia.

Barred Fruiteater *Pipreola (arcuata) arcuata*
Uncommon resident.

L 22 cm (8.5"). One subspecies in group. Mid-levels in mossy montane forest. 2000–3300 m (rarely 900 m). **ID** Largest fruiteater; at high elevations; eyes yellow-olive (reddish, W Andes). ♂ head and chest black, lower underparts barred, greater wing-coverts tipped yellowish, black subterminal tail-band. ♀ like ♂ but head and throat olive. **Voice** Song, long (1.5–3 seconds), extremely high (8–9 kHz) "pseeeuuuueeeeeeeeeee", quickly arcing up and down, last 1–2 seconds flat, or brief arc, or high flat "seeeeeee".

Green-and-black Fruiteater *Pipreola riefferii* `LC`
Frutero Verdinegro

Six subspecies in three subspecies groups; one in Colombia.

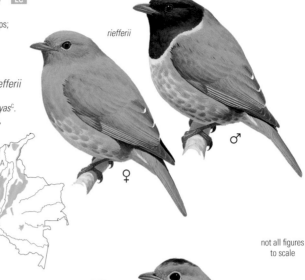

riefferii

Green-and-black Fruiteater *Pipreola (riefferii) riefferii*
Commonest Colombian fruiteater.
L 20 cm (8"). Races *riefferii*[A], *occidentalis*[B], *chachapoyas*[C].
Mid-levels or lower in humid and wet montane forest,
borders, secondary woodland. 1400–2800 m (rarely
3200 m). Pairs or 3–6, lethargic, unsuspicious,
often with mixed flocks. **ID** Orange-red bill
and legs, dark eyes, white-tipped tertials.
♂ black hood bordered yellow. ♀ olive-
green, breast yellow flammulated green.
Voice Song (2–3 seconds), extremely high
(8–9 kHz) "ti-ti-ti-ti-ti-ti-ti-ti-seeeeeeeeea"
rising-falling. Flat (c. 2.5–20 seconds)
"ti-ti-ti…".

not all figures
to scale

Grey-tailed Piha *Snowornis subalaris* `NT`
Guardabosque Coligrís
Uncommon and inconspicuous resident.

L 23 cm (9"). Monotypic. Mid-levels or lower
in humid foothill and premontane forest.
c. 600–1500 m. Singles, movements
deliberate, perch erect; hover-glean fruit
and glean insects, occasionally with mixed flocks. **ID** Grey
eye-ring, faint yellow shaft-streaks on breast, rear parts
and tail grey. ♀ similar to ♂ but semi-concealed black
coronal patch smaller or lacking. **Voice** Call, at long
intervals, clear whistled "weeeeWEET!", rising at end,
human-like. **SS** Olivaceous Piha.

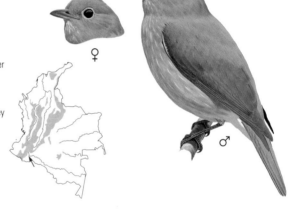

Olivaceous Piha *Snowornis cryptolophus* `LC`
Guardabosque Oliva
Uncommon to fairly common resident.

L 23 cm (9"). Races *mindoensis*[A], *cryptolophus*[B].
Mid-levels or lower in humid and wet montane forest.
900–2500 m. Singles, less often pairs, perch erect,
peer sluggishly, flutter to foliage for insects, hover
for fruit, often with mixed flocks. **ID** Short dark bill, yellowish
eye-ring, bend of wing and underwing-coverts yellow.
♀ similar to ♂ but lacks semi-concealed black coronal patch.
Nestlings look like large bristly caterpillars. **Voice** Rarely
vocal; a brief rattle, and low "chuck". **SS** Grey-tailed Piha
(lower elevations, little overlap).

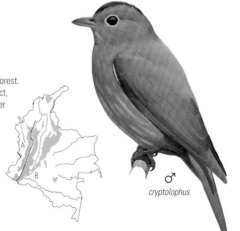

cryptolophus

sanguinolentus

Genus *Rupicola* Icons of beauty. ♂♂ display at leks, the Andean species forming noisy groups in trees in large mountain ravines, but the Guianan species largely silently in beams of sunshine on forest floor (some ♂♂ watch from trees). ♀♀ choose ♂♂ for copulation but are 'single mothers'. Nests difficult of access. Long nestling period.

Andean Cock-of-the-rock *Rupicola peruvianus* LC
Gallito-de-roca Andino
Local resident.

L 33 cm (13"). Races *sanguinolentus*[A], *aequatorialis*[B]. Humid montane forest, steep river canyons. 500–2400 m. Up to 15 polygamous ♂♂ in permanent mid-level leks, display early mornings, also late afternoon matinees. Wary, suspicious but will habituate at lek if unmolested. Eat large nutritious fruits. Mud-and-moss nest on inaccessible rock cliff, boulder, etc. **ID** Robust. ♂ unmistakable. ♀ reddish brown, lumpy; small crest, eyes orange; or blue-white (*aequatorialis*). Imm ♂ like ♀ or slighter redder, eyes amber to yellow. **Voice** Noisy at leks. Advertising calls, harsh "jurrrrrreE!", rough nasal "urr-ur-ur…", chanting "kip-kip-kip…"; become frantic when ♀ present.

Guianan Cock-of-the-rock *Rupicola rupicola* LC
Gallito-de-roca Guyanés
Local resident.

L ♂ 29 cm (11.5"), ♀ 28 cm (11"). Monotypic. Sandy soil forest in areas with large rock outcrops. To 300 m. Behaviour recalls Andean species but leks can be larger. Display on ground. **ID** ♂ smaller but even gaudier, more orange than Andean species. ♀ uniform brown, small lumpy crest. **Voice** Commonest call at or away from lek arena, loud, crowing "GET-REEAL"; silent during actual display. When foraging, drawn-out "qaaaOWW" at intervals. ♀ rarely a high "quEEeo" and "quaao".

Black-necked Red Cotinga *Phoenicircus nigricollis* LC
Cotinga Roja
Rare and local resident (mostly S of R Caquetá).

L ♂ 23 cm (9"), ♀ 24 cm (9.5"). Monotypic. Mid-levels to subcanopy of humid *terra firme* forest. To 400 m. Wary, difficult to see. Polygamous ♂♂ scatter singly (within earshot) over wide area; in early morning, bow, expose brilliant rump, call sporadically, often several answer in vocal outbursts. **ID** ♂ unmistakable. ♀ pattern echoes ♂ but throat and upperparts olive-brown. **Voice** Call sharp squeaking bark "skEEya!" at variable intervals. Wings whistle in flight.

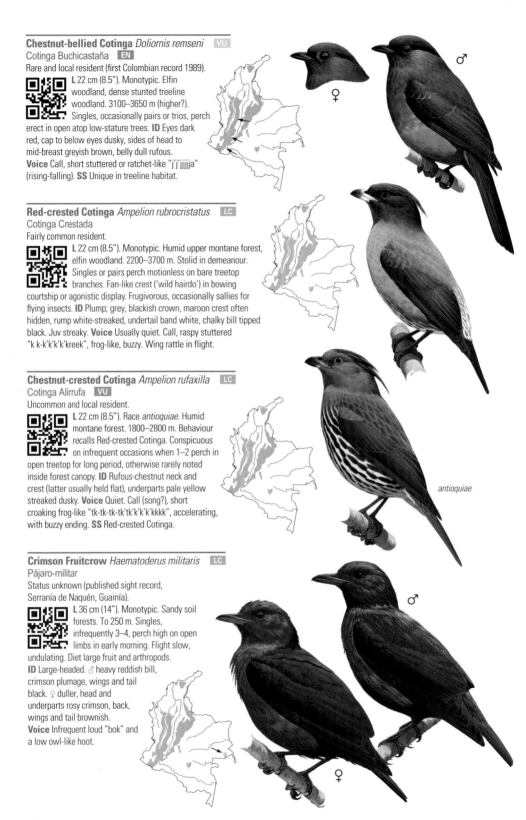

Chestnut-bellied Cotinga *Doliornis remseni* VU
Cotinga Buchicastaña EN

Rare and local resident (first Colombian record 1989). **L** 22 cm (8.5"). Monotypic. Elfin woodland, dense stunted treeline woodland. 3100–3650 m (higher?). Singles, occasionally pairs or trios, perch erect in open atop low-stature trees. **ID** Eyes dark red, cap to below eyes dusky, sides of head to mid-breast greyish brown, belly dull rufous. **Voice** Call, short stuttered or ratchet-like "j'j'jjjjja" (rising-falling). **SS** Unique in treeline habitat.

Red-crested Cotinga *Ampelion rubrocristatus* LC
Cotinga Crestada

Fairly common resident. **L** 22 cm (8.5"). Monotypic. Humid upper montane forest, elfin woodland. 2200–3700 m. Stolid in demeanour. Singles or pairs perch motionless on bare treetop branches. Fan-like crest ('wild hairdo') in bowing courtship or agonistic display. Frugivorous, occasionally sallies for flying insects. **ID** Plump; grey, blackish crown, maroon crest often hidden, rump white-streaked, undertail band white, chalky bill tipped black. Juv streaky. **Voice** Usually quiet. Call, raspy stuttered "k k-k'k'k'k'kreek", frog-like, buzzy. Wing rattle in flight.

Chestnut-crested Cotinga *Ampelion rufaxilla* LC
Cotinga Alirrufa VU

Uncommon and local resident. **L** 22 cm (8.5"). Race *antioquiae*. Humid montane forest. 1800–2800 m. Behaviour recalls Red-crested Cotinga. Conspicuous on infrequent occasions when 1–2 perch in open treetop for long period, otherwise rarely noted inside forest canopy. **ID** Rufous-chestnut neck and crest (latter usually held flat), underparts pale yellow streaked dusky. **Voice** Quiet. Call (song?), short croaking frog-like "tk-tk-tk-tk'tk'k'k'kkkk", accelerating, with buzzy ending. **SS** Red-crested Cotinga.

antioquiae

Crimson Fruitcrow *Haematoderus militaris* LC
Pájaro-militar

Status unknown (published sight record, Serranía de Naquén, Guainía). **L** 36 cm (14"). Monotypic. Sandy soil forests. To 250 m. Singles, infrequently 3–4, perch high on open limbs in early morning. Flight slow, undulating. Diet large fruit and arthropods. **ID** Large-headed. ♂ heavy reddish bill, crimson plumage, wings and tail black. ♀ duller, head and underparts rosy crimson, back, wings and tail brownish. **Voice** Infrequent loud "bok" and a low owl-like hoot.

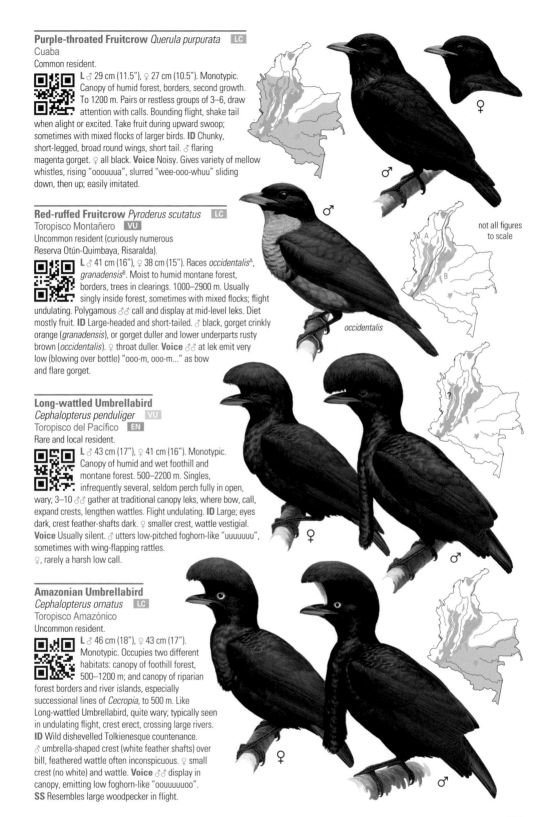

Purple-throated Fruitcrow *Querula purpurata* `LC`
Cuaba

Common resident.

L ♂ 29 cm (11.5″), ♀ 27 cm (10.5″). Monotypic. Canopy of humid forest, borders, second growth. To 1200 m. Pairs or restless groups of 3–6, draw attention with calls. Bounding flight, shake tail when alight or excited. Take fruit during upward swoop; sometimes with mixed flocks of larger birds. **ID** Chunky, short-legged, broad round wings, short tail. ♂ flaring magenta gorget. ♀ all black. **Voice** Noisy. Gives variety of mellow whistles, rising "ooouuua", slurred "wee-ooo-whuu" sliding down, then up; easily imitated.

♀

♂

Red-ruffed Fruitcrow *Pyroderus scutatus* `LC`
Toropisco Montañero `VU`

Uncommon resident (curiously numerous Reserva Otún-Quimbaya, Risaralda).

L ♂ 41 cm (16″), ♀ 38 cm (15″). Races *occidentalis*[A], *granadensis*[B]. Moist to humid montane forest, borders, trees in clearings. 1000–2900 m. Usually singly inside forest, sometimes with mixed flocks; flight undulating. Polygamous ♂♂ call and display at mid-level leks. Diet mostly fruit. **ID** Large-headed and short-tailed. ♂ black, gorget crinkly orange (*granadensis*), or gorget duller and lower underparts rusty brown (*occidentalis*). ♀ throat duller. **Voice** ♂♂ at lek emit very low (blowing over bottle) "ooo-m, ooo-m…" as bow and flare gorget.

♂

not all figures to scale

occidentalis

Long-wattled Umbrellabird
Cephalopterus penduliger `VU`
Toropisco del Pacífico `EN`

Rare and local resident.

L ♂ 43 cm (17″), ♀ 41 cm (16″). Monotypic. Canopy of humid and wet foothill and montane forest. 500–2200 m. Singles, infrequently several, seldom perch fully in open, wary; 3–10 ♂♂ gather at traditional canopy leks, where bow, call, expand crests, lengthen wattles. Flight undulating. **ID** Large; eyes dark, crest feather-shafts dark. ♀ smaller crest, wattle vestigial. **Voice** Usually silent. ♂ utters low-pitched foghorn-like "uuuuuuu", sometimes with wing-flapping rattles. ♀, rarely a harsh low call.

♀

♂

Amazonian Umbrellabird
Cephalopterus ornatus `LC`
Toropisco Amazónico

Uncommon resident.

L ♂ 46 cm (18″), ♀ 43 cm (17″). Monotypic. Occupies two different habitats: canopy of foothill forest, 500–1200 m; and canopy of riparian forest borders and river islands, especially successional lines of *Cecropia*, to 500 m. Like Long-wattled Umbrellabird, quite wary; typically seen in undulating flight, crest erect, crossing large rivers. **ID** Wild dishevelled Tolkienesque countenance. ♂ umbrella-shaped crest (white feather shafts) over bill, feathered wattle often inconspicuous. ♀ small crest (no white) and wattle. **Voice** ♂♂ display in canopy, emitting low foghorn-like "oouuuuuoo". **SS** Resembles large woodpecker in flight.

♀

♂

Capuchinbird *Perissocephalus tricolor* `LC`
Pájaro Capuchino
Local resident.

 L 36 cm (14"). Monotypic. Canopy of sandy soil forests. To 250 m. Forages alone, wandering widely in canopy for fruit, taken with short upward swoops; also arthropods. At leks, 3–15 or more advertise at dawn or later. **ID** Bald head imparts small-headed, hump-backed appearance to this unforgettable, bob-tailed bird. When calling perch erect, raise neck ruff, cock tail, fluff two orange-feathered puff-balls beneath tail (like tail-lights). Underparts rusty. **Voice** Advertising call, loud growling "grrrraaaaaaaaoooooooo" like distant chainsaw, preceded by air hissing (inhaling) sound.

Rufous Piha *Lipaugus unirufus* `LC`
Guardabosque Rufo
Uncommon resident.

 L 23 cm (9"). Races *unirufus*[A], *castaneotinctus*[B]. Mid-levels in humid forest. To 1000 m (rarely 1500 m). Solitary or small loose groups. Lethargic, inconspicuous; sally for arthropods and fruit. No true leks or pair formation. **ID** Cinnamon rufous, throat paler, mandible pale basally. **Voice** At long intervals, loud, explosive "PEEouu" or "QUIR'a", other whistles; often in response to loud noise. **SS** Much like Rufous Mourner (p. 402) and best separated by voice; mourner has more angular shape, longer tail, flatter crown (not rounded). Also Speckled Mourner (p. 362).

unirufus

Screaming Piha *Lipaugus vociferans* `LC`
Guardabosque Chillón
Common resident.

 L 25 cm (10"). Monotypic. Mid-levels or lower in humid *terra firme* and transition forest. To 600 m. ♂♂ gather at leks containing 10–80+ birds, individuals audible, sometimes visible to competitors; attract ♀♀ through sheer vocal power (yelling matches!). Diet mostly fruit. **ID** Thrush-sized, plain grey, orange mouth lining. **Voice** Iconic Amazonian voice. Advertising ♂♂ give 1–4 hesitant growling whistles, leading to explosive whip-cracking ear-splitting "wuur...wuur... wuEE, WHEE-u!", sometimes only growling "wuur". Calls throughout day, and much of year.

Chestnut-capped Piha *Lipaugus weberi* `CR`
Guardabosque Antioqueño `CR`
Local resident (new species, described 2001).

 L 24 cm (9.5"). Monotypic. Endemic. Mid-levels or higher in humid premontane forest. 1400–2000 m. Singles, inconspicuous, lethargic; no pair formation. ♂♂ advertise from scattered territories (no leks). Not with mixed flocks. **ID** Dark grey, small chestnut crown patch, cinnamon wash on lower underparts. **Voice** Advertising call, loud piercing "SCREE'AAK" (abrupt, rising-falling). Nasal "gluck" and mechanical wing-whirr.

E

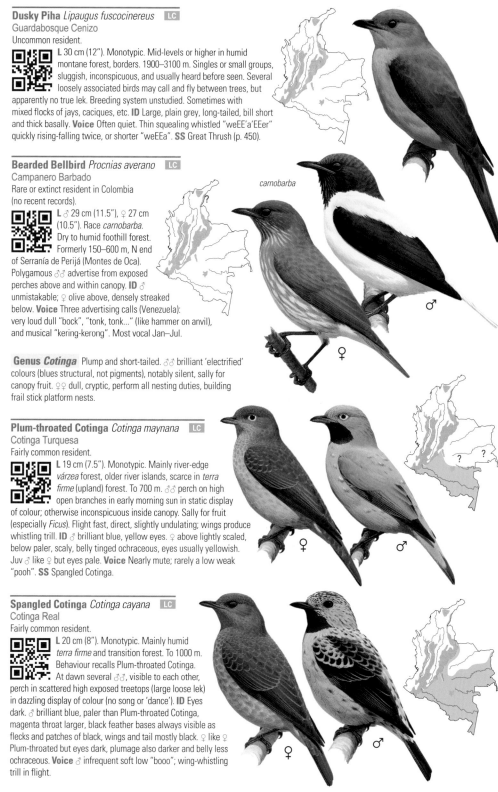

Dusky Piha *Lipaugus fuscocinereus* `LC`
Guardabosque Cenizo

Uncommon resident.

L 30 cm (12"). Monotypic. Mid-levels or higher in humid montane forest, borders. 1900–3100 m. Singles or small groups, sluggish, inconspicuous, and usually heard before seen. Several loosely associated birds may call and fly between trees, but apparently no true lek. Breeding system unstudied. Sometimes with mixed flocks of jays, caciques, etc. **ID** Large, plain grey, long-tailed, bill short and thick basally. **Voice** Often quiet. Thin squealing whistled "weEE'a'EEer" quickly rising-falling twice, or shorter "weEEa". **SS** Great Thrush (p. 450).

Bearded Bellbird *Procnias averano* `LC`
Campanero Barbado

Rare or extinct resident in Colombia (no recent records).

L ♂ 29 cm (11.5"), ♀ 27 cm (10.5"). Race *carnobarba*. Dry to humid foothill forest. Formerly 150–600 m, N end of Serranía de Perijá (Montes de Oca). Polygamous ♂♂ advertise from exposed perches above and within canopy. **ID** ♂ unmistakable; ♀ olive above, densely streaked below. **Voice** Three advertising calls (Venezuela): very loud dull "bock", "tonk, tonk..." (like hammer on anvil), and musical "kering-kerong". Most vocal Jan–Jul.

carnobarba

Genus *Cotinga* Plump and short-tailed. ♂♂ brilliant 'electrified' colours (blues structural, not pigments), notably silent, sally for canopy fruit. ♀♀ dull, cryptic, perform all nesting duties, building frail stick platform nests.

Plum-throated Cotinga *Cotinga maynana* `LC`
Cotinga Turquesa

Fairly common resident.

L 19 cm (7.5"). Monotypic. Mainly river-edge *várzea* forest, older river islands, scarce in *terra firme* (upland) forest. To 700 m. ♂♂ perch on high open branches in early morning sun in static display of colour; otherwise inconspicuous inside canopy. Sally for fruit (especially *Ficus*). Flight fast, direct, slightly undulating; wings produce whistling trill. **ID** ♂ brilliant blue, yellow eyes. ♀ above lightly scaled, below paler, scaly, belly tinged ochraceous, eyes usually yellowish. Juv ♂ like ♀ but eyes pale. **Voice** Nearly mute; rarely a low weak "pooh". **SS** Spangled Cotinga.

Spangled Cotinga *Cotinga cayana* `LC`
Cotinga Real

Fairly common resident.

L 20 cm (8"). Monotypic. Mainly humid *terra firme* and transition forest. To 1000 m. Behaviour recalls Plum-throated Cotinga. At dawn several ♂♂, visible to each other, perch in scattered high exposed treetops (large loose lek) in dazzling display of colour (no song or 'dance'). **ID** Eyes dark. ♂ brilliant blue, paler than Plum-throated Cotinga, magenta throat larger, black feather bases always visible as flecks and patches of black, wings and tail mostly black. ♀ like ♀ Plum-throated but eyes dark, plumage also darker and belly less ochraceous. **Voice** ♂ infrequent soft low "booo"; wing-whistling trill in flight.

Blue Cotinga *Cotinga nattererii* `LC`
Cotinga Azul
Uncommon resident.
L 18.5 cm (7.3"). Monotypic. Canopy of humid lowland and foothill forest, second growth. To 500 m (rarely 1600 m). Behaviour as Spangled Cotinga but displays apparently solitary. Several may gather at fruit trees. **ID** Unique in range; round dove-like head, small black bill. ♂ brilliant blue-purple throat and large patch on breast and upper belly. ♀ brown, scaled and spotted dark brown, cinnamon underwing-coverts. **Voice** Virtually silent; wing whirr in flight.

Purple-breasted Cotinga *Cotinga cotinga* `LC`
Cotinga Pechimorada
Uncommon and local resident.
L 18 cm (7"). Monotypic. Humid sandy soil forests. To 300 m. ♂♂ perch on high exposed branches under canopy at dawn, ♀♀ for briefer periods, otherwise both inconspicuous in canopy. Diet fruit; not with mixed flocks. **ID** ♂ deep cobalt-blue, throat to belly purple. ♀ above dark brown narrowly scaled buff, below paler, heavily scaled buff. **Voice** Seldom vocal. ♂ soft "preeeer" and wing whirr in flight. **SS** ♀ Spangled Cotinga.

Purple-throated Cotinga
Porphyrolaema porphyrolaema `LC`
Cotinga Degollada
Rare (overlooked?) resident.
L 18.5 cm (7.3"). Monotypic. Canopy of humid *várzea* forest, scarce in *terra firme*. To 500 m. Less numerous than Amazonian *Cotinga*. ♂♂ (especially) and ♀♀ perch on open treetop branches dawn and dusk, sometimes with Plum-throated Cotinga and other frugivores at large fruiting trees, e.g. *Ficus*. **ID** ♂ white wing slash, white below, small purple throat. ♀ orange-rufous throat and vent, rest of underparts buff finely barred dusky. **Voice** Infrequent loud "WHEEEEER" and a softer descending whistle.

Bare-necked Fruitcrow
Gymnoderus foetidus `LC`
Frutero Vulturino
Common resident.
L ♂ 38 cm (15"), ♀ 33 cm (13"). Monotypic. Humid *várzea* forest, especially near rivers, local in sandy soil areas. To 500 m. Often seen in slow flight, very high over large rivers or forest. Singles or several in fruiting trees, and often roost in groups in large isolated trees. **ID** Vulturine appearance, fairly large, thin bare neck. ♂ silvery upperwing surface flashes in flight. ♀ less ornate. **Voice** No verified voice known. **SS** Shape diagnostic.

Pompadour Cotinga *Xipholena punicea*
Cotinga Pompadour

Locally fairly common resident.

L 20 cm (8"). Monotypic. Humid, nutrient-poor white-sand forest with savanna or rock outcrops. To 300 m. ♂♂ perch on high exposed branches early morning and late afternoon, sometimes several simultaneously when engage in brief chases; ♀♀ up briefly. **ID** Stunning ♂ unmistakable; in flight white wings twinkle against dark foliage. Plump grey ♀ recalls a thrush; note white eyes, short tail, white wing edgings. Juv like ♀ but eyes dark. **Voice** Usually silent. Rarely abrupt frog-like rattle.

Black-tipped Cotinga *Carpodectes hopkei*
Cotinga Blanca

Fairly common resident.

L 22 cm (8.5"). Monotypic. Near-endemic (also extreme SE Panama and NW Ecuador). Wet lowland and foothill forest, borders, second growth, mangroves. To 450 m (rarely 900 m). Most easily seen early morning when ♂♂ assume high open sunny perches, otherwise inconspicuous in canopy. Several may gather at fruiting trees; occasionally sally for flying insects during mass emergences. **ID** Eyes dark red. ♂ white, tiny black tips on primaries and inner tail feathers. ♀ greyish, white wing edgings. **Voice** Rarely, a rough low "chak". **AN** White Cotinga.

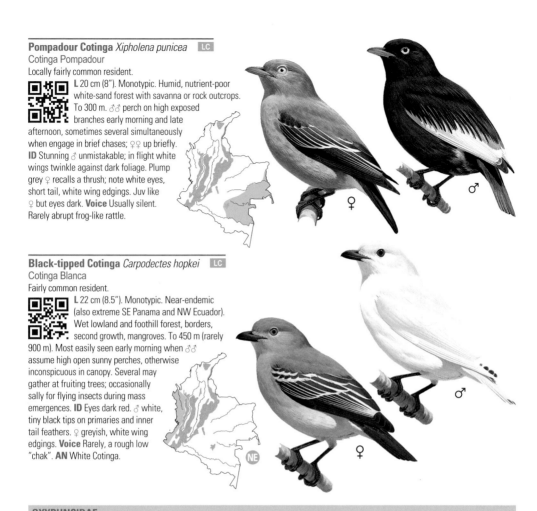

OXYRUNCIDAE
Sharpbill

1 extant species, 1 in region

The relationships of the Sharpbill have long been controversial. Current genetic evidence finds no strong support linking it to any modern-day bird family, although it appears closer to *Onychorhynchus* (royal flycatchers) than any other genus.

Sharpbill *Oxyruncus cristatus*
Picoagudo

Local resident (distribution fragmented).

L 18 cm (7"). Races *brooksi* (?)[A], unknown (?)[B]. Humid foothill and premontane forest. 800–1600 m. Inconspicuous in canopy, usually with mixed flocks. Quite active, even hanging upside-down for arthropod prey; also fruit. **ID** Plump; semi-concealed red crest, pointed bill, orange eyes, spotted underparts. **Voice** Song, at long intervals, long-drawn, buzzy trill, descending slightly, "beeeeeeeuuuuu'u'u'a'a"; alone or in loosely associated song leks. **SS** Speckled Tanager (p. 543).

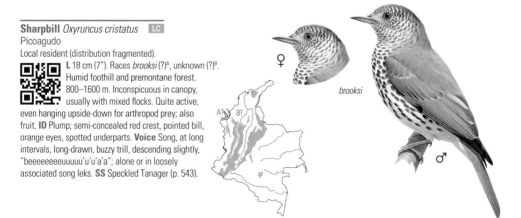

brooksi

Members of this small newly erected family were formerly included with flycatchers, subsequently placed in Tityridae, and more recently separated in their own family based on strong genetic evidence.

Northern Royal Flycatcher *Onychorhynchus mexicanus* `LC`
Atrapamoscas-real Norteño
Locally fairly common resident.

 L 16.5 cm (6.5"). Race *fraterculus*. Dry to moist forest, old second growth, often along shady streams. To 1200 m (1400+ m, Perijá). Singles or pairs, sally for large arthropods low inside forest, infrequent with mixed flocks; long (to 1.5 m) pendant nest low over stream. **ID** Remarkable but rarely seen crest (scarlet ♂, orange ♀) normally lays flat, projecting rearward, imparts hammerhead shape. Long bill, plumage warm brown, underparts buff, rump and tail cinnamon, buff-dotted wingbars. **Voice** Call, nasal jacamar-like "KEE'yup". **SS** Brownish Twistwing (p. 369). **TN** Royal flycatchers variously treated as 1–4 species, but differ only slightly in plumage.

Amazonian Royal Flycatcher *Onychorhynchus coronatus* `LC`
Atrapamoscas-real Amazónico
Uncommon and local resident (few records).

 L 16 cm (6.3"). Race *castelnaui*. Humid lowland forest including *várzea*, low-lying areas and sandy soil zones. To 500 m (higher?). **ID** Like Northern Royal Flycatcher but marginally smaller, underparts slightly more barred, throat buff (not whitish), tail chestnut-rufous (not cinnamon). **Voice** Abrupt "KEEE'yup", identical to previous species.

Ruddy-tailed Flycatcher *Terenotriccus erythrurus* `LC`
Atrapamoscas Colirrufo
Common resident.

 L 10 cm (4"). Races *fulvigularis*[A], *venezuelensis*[B], *signatus*[C]. Mid-levels in humid lowland and foothill forest. To 1200 m. Singles or pairs, regularly with mixed flocks, perch erect. Movements abrupt, chase leaf-hoppers in rapid aerobatic sallies to foliage or air. **ID** Tiny; large black eyes, slight crest, short bill, prominent rictal bristles, yellow legs. **Voice** Call, high weak "teeu-TEEP", second note higher. Song, high timid whistles "keeek, keeek, eek-eek-eek-eek-eek", accelerating, pitch and volume diminishing, or rising-falling "wi-wi-wi, keek...". **SS** Cinnamon Manakin-tyrant (p. 363).

Genus *Myiobius* Yellow rump, black tail, unusually large eyes, and long rictal bristles enclosing bill like basket. Extremely aerobatic but minimally vocal; their tail fanning, wing-drooping foraging behaviour recalls Old World fantails (*Rhipidura*).

Tawny-breasted Flycatcher *Myiobius villosus* `LC`
Atrapamoscas Leonado
Rare to uncommon resident (range fragmented).

 L 14.7 cm (5.8"). Races *villosus*[A], *schaeferi*[B], *clarus*[C]. Undergrowth in humid foothill and lower montane forest. 800–2100 m. Fast-moving, hard-to-observe. Behaviour as Sulphur-rumped Flycatcher. **ID** Barely differs from other *Myiobius*. Note distribution, higher elevations, slightly larger size, marginally darker above (browner, no olive tinge), no eye-ring, more extensive tawny-brown on underparts (chest to mid-breast and sides). ♀ crown patch cinnamon (or absent). **Voice** Quiet; undistinctive weak "espit".

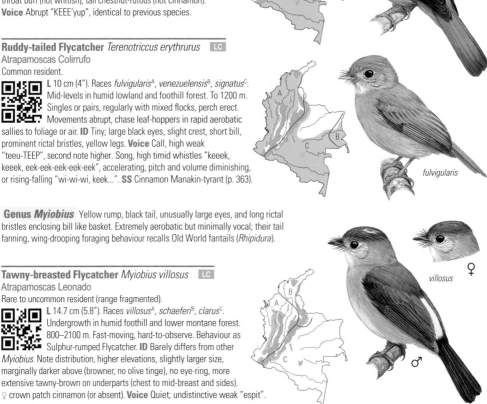

fraterculus

castelnaui

fulvigularis

♀

villosus

♂

Sulphur-rumped Flycatcher *Myiobius sulphureipygius* `LC`
Atrapamoscas Culiamarillo
Fairly common resident.

 L 13 cm (5″). Races *aureatus*[A], *semiflavus*[B]. Humid and wet lowland, foothill and premontane forest. To 1000 m. Singles or pairs, extremely active, fast-moving, fan tail, droop wings, pivot and sally acrobatically in lower strata of forest; regularly with mixed flocks. **ID** Yellow rump, light tawny wash on chest, narrow whitish eye-ring; note range and elevation. **Voice** Sharp "spit". **SS** Tawny-breasted Flycatcher (mostly higher elevations), Black-tailed Flycatcher. **TN** Race *semiflavus* usually included with Whiskered Flycatcher from E of Andes, but the two species are still sometimes treated as one.

aureatus

Whiskered Flycatcher *Myiobius barbatus* `LC`
Atrapamoscas Bigotudo

 Four subspecies in two subspecies groups; one in Colombia.

Whiskered Flycatcher *Myiobius (barbatus) barbatus*
Uncommon and local resident.
L 13 cm (5″). Race *barbatus*. Lower levels in humid *terra firme* forest. To 600 m.
ID Only regularly occurring *Myiobius* E of Andes in Colombia; note narrow whitish eye-ring, greyish-olive breast-band (no tawny or buff tones). Black-tailed Flycatcher (overlap?) differs in dull buff breast, and drier habitats. **Voice** Like Sulphur-rumped Flycatcher. **TN** See Sulphur-rumped Flycatcher.

barbatus

Black-tailed Flycatcher *Myiobius atricaudus* `LC`
Atrapamoscas Colinegro

 Seven subspecies in two subspecies groups; one in Colombia.

Black-tailed Flycatcher *Myiobius (atricaudus) atricaudus*
Local resident (W of Andes, Amazonia?).
L 13 cm (5″). Races *atricaudus*[A], *adjacens*[B] (few verified records).
Dry and moist secondary woodland, humid forest borders, arid Pacific slope valleys (Dagua, Patía), dry woodland or *várzea* borders (?) E of Andes. To 1500 m.
Behaviour like Sulphur-rumped Flycatcher. **ID** Most like Whiskered Flycatcher, but chest tinged dull buff, eye-ring faint. **Voice** Wiry "wit"; sharp abruptly rising-falling "skEap" (c. 4–8 kHz).

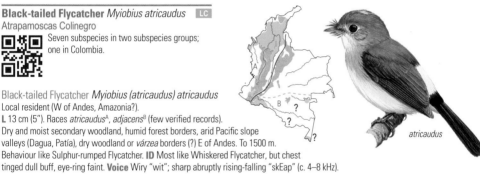

atricaudus

TITYRIDAE
Tityras, Becards, Schiffornises and Mourners
39 extant species, 22 in region

A recently erected family based on molecular genetic data. Endemic to the Neotropics. At present includes c. 40 species formerly considered tyrant-flycatchers, manakins or cotingas. Inclusion of some genera controversial, and further revision is likely.

White-browed Purpletuft *Iodopleura isabellae* `LC`
Cotinga Diminuta
Fairly common (but unpredictable) resident.

 L 12 cm (4.7″). Race *isabellae*. Canopy of humid *terra firme* and *várzea* forest, borders. To 500 m. Pairs or groups of 3–6 perch bolt upright on exposed bare treetop twigs, sally for flying insects, take fruit; occasionally low at forest border fruiting shrubs. **ID** Tiny, cute and round, long wings; crescent on foreface, post-ocular, and rump white, purple hard to see (unless displaying). **Voice** Weak trilled "tre'e'e'd", shrill "eeeEE", high rattle.

isabellae

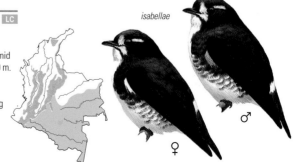

♂

♀

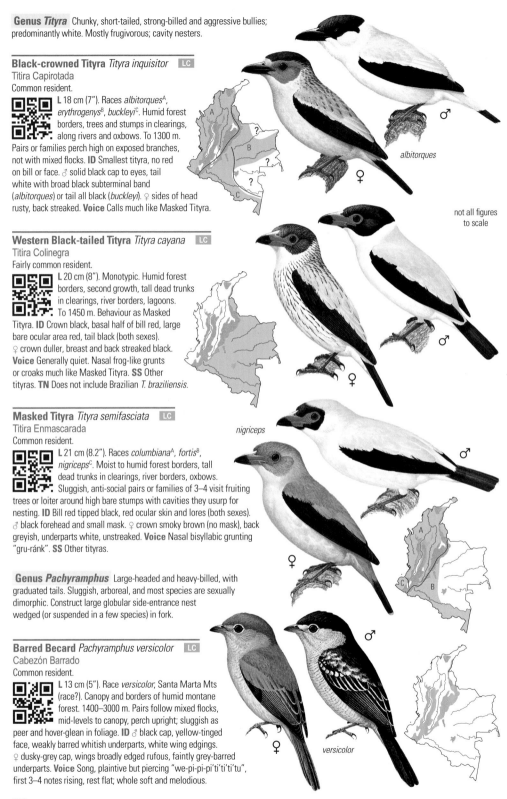

Genus *Tityra* Chunky, short-tailed, strong-billed and aggressive bullies; predominantly white. Mostly frugivorous; cavity nesters.

Black-crowned Tityra *Tityra inquisitor* `LC`
Titira Capirotada
Common resident.

L 18 cm (7"). Races *albitorques*[A], *erythrogenys*[B], *buckleyi*[C]. Humid forest borders, trees and stumps in clearings, along rivers and oxbows. To 1300 m. Pairs or families perch high on exposed branches, not with mixed flocks. **ID** Smallest tityra, no red on bill or face. ♂ solid black cap to eyes, tail white with broad black subterminal band (*albitorques*) or tail all black (*buckleyi*). ♀ sides of head rusty, back streaked. **Voice** Calls much like Masked Tityra.

albitorques

not all figures to scale

Western Black-tailed Tityra *Tityra cayana* `LC`
Titira Colinegra
Fairly common resident.

L 20 cm (8"). Monotypic. Humid forest borders, second growth, tall dead trunks in clearings, river borders, lagoons. To 1450 m. Behaviour as Masked Tityra. **ID** Crown black, basal half of bill red, large bare ocular area red, tail black (both sexes). ♀ crown duller, breast and back streaked black. **Voice** Generally quiet. Nasal frog-like grunts or croaks much like Masked Tityra. **SS** Other tityras. **TN** Does not include Brazilian *T. braziliensis*.

Masked Tityra *Tityra semifasciata* `LC`
Titira Enmascarada
Common resident.

nigriceps

L 21 cm (8.2"). Races *columbiana*[A], *fortis*[B], *nigriceps*[C]. Moist to humid forest borders, tall dead trunks in clearings, river borders, oxbows. Sluggish, anti-social pairs or families of 3–4 visit fruiting trees or loiter around high bare stumps with cavities they usurp for nesting. **ID** Bill red tipped black, red ocular skin and lores (both sexes). ♂ black forehead and small mask. ♀ crown smoky brown (no mask), back greyish, underparts white, unstreaked. **Voice** Nasal bisyllabic grunting "gru-ránk". **SS** Other tityras.

Genus *Pachyramphus* Large-headed and heavy-billed, with graduated tails. Sluggish, arboreal, and most species are sexually dimorphic. Construct large globular side-entrance nest wedged (or suspended in a few species) in fork.

Barred Becard *Pachyramphus versicolor* `LC`
Cabezón Barrado
Common resident.

L 13 cm (5"). Race *versicolor*; Santa Marta Mts (race?). Canopy and borders of humid montane forest. 1400–3000 m. Pairs follow mixed flocks, mid-levels to canopy, perch upright; sluggish as peer and hover-glean in foliage. **ID** ♂ black cap, yellow-tinged face, weakly barred whitish underparts, white wing edgings. ♀ dusky-grey cap, wings broadly edged rufous, faintly grey-barred underparts. **Voice** Song, plaintive but piercing "we-pi-pi-pi'ti'ti'ti'tu", first 3–4 notes rising, rest flat; whole soft and melodious.

versicolor

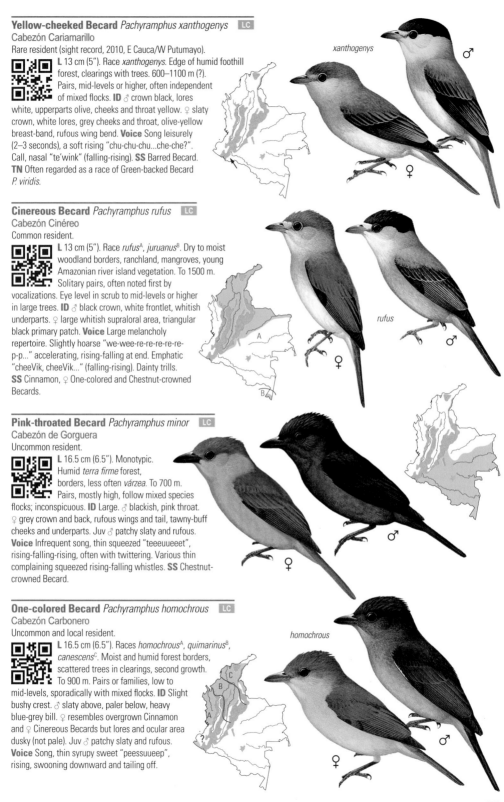

Yellow-cheeked Becard *Pachyramphus xanthogenys* `LC`
Cabezón Cariamarillo
Rare resident (sight record, 2010, E Cauca/W Putumayo).

xanthogenys

L 13 cm (5"). Race *xanthogenys*. Edge of humid foothill forest, clearings with trees. 600–1100 m (?). Pairs, mid-levels or higher, often independent of mixed flocks. **ID** ♂ crown black, lores white, upperparts olive, cheeks and throat yellow. ♀ slaty crown, white lores, grey cheeks and throat, olive-yellow breast-band, rufous wing bend. **Voice** Song leisurely (2–3 seconds), a soft rising "chu-chu-chu...che-che?". Call, nasal "te'wink" (falling-rising). **SS** Barred Becard. **TN** Often regarded as a race of Green-backed Becard *P. viridis*.

Cinereous Becard *Pachyramphus rufus* `LC`
Cabezón Cinéreo
Common resident.

L 13 cm (5"). Race *rufus*ᴬ, *juruanus*ᴮ. Dry to moist woodland borders, ranchland, mangroves, young Amazonian river island vegetation. To 1500 m. Solitary pairs, often noted first by vocalizations. Eye level in scrub to mid-levels or higher in large trees. **ID** ♂ black crown, white frontlet, whitish underparts. ♀ large whitish supraloral area, triangular black primary patch. **Voice** Large melancholy repertoire. Slightly hoarse "we-wee-re-re-re-re-re-p-p..." accelerating, rising-falling at end. Emphatic "cheeVik, cheeVik..." (falling-rising). Dainty trills. **SS** Cinnamon, ♀ One-colored and Chestnut-crowned Becards.

rufus

Pink-throated Becard *Pachyramphus minor* `LC`
Cabezón de Gorguera
Uncommon resident.

L 16.5 cm (6.5"). Monotypic. Humid *terra firme* forest, borders, less often *várzea*. To 700 m. Pairs, mostly high, follow mixed species flocks; inconspicuous. **ID** Large. ♂ blackish, pink throat. ♀ grey crown and back, rufous wings and tail, tawny-buff cheeks and underparts. Juv ♂ patchy slaty and rufous. **Voice** Infrequent song, thin squeezed "teeeuueeet", rising-falling-rising, often with twittering. Various thin complaining squeezed rising-falling whistles. **SS** Chestnut-crowned Becard.

One-colored Becard *Pachyramphus homochrous* `LC`
Cabezón Carbonero
Uncommon and local resident.

homochrous

L 16.5 cm (6.5"). Races *homochrous*ᴬ, *quimarinus*ᴮ, *canescens*ᶜ. Moist and humid forest borders, scattered trees in clearings, second growth. To 900 m. Pairs or families, low to mid-levels, sporadically with mixed flocks. **ID** Slight bushy crest. ♂ slaty above, paler below, heavy blue-grey bill. ♀ resembles overgrown Cinnamon and ♀ Cinereous Becards but lores and ocular area dusky (not pale). Juv ♂ patchy slaty and rufous. **Voice** Song, thin syrupy sweet "peessuueep", rising, swooning downward and tailing off.

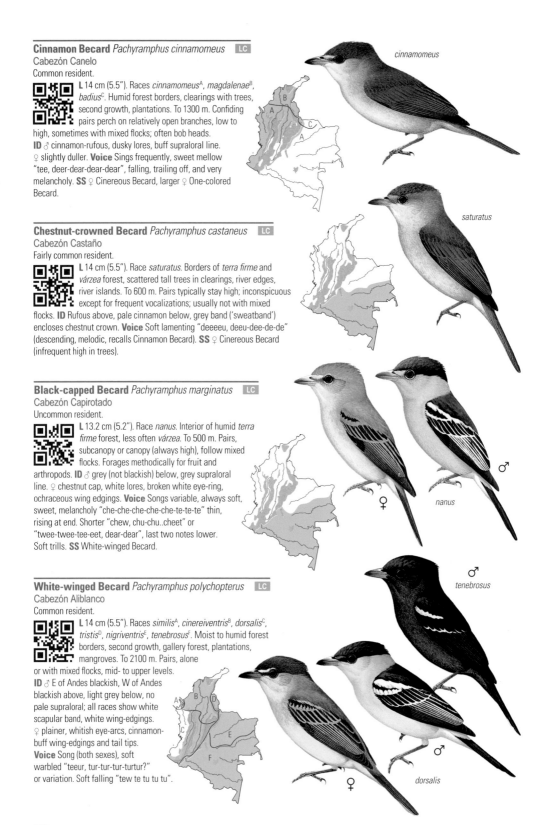

Cinnamon Becard *Pachyramphus cinnamomeus* `LC`
Cabezón Canelo
Common resident.

L 14 cm (5.5"). Races *cinnamomeus*[A], *magdalenae*[B], *badius*[C]. Humid forest borders, clearings with trees, second growth, plantations. To 1300 m. Confiding pairs perch on relatively open branches, low to high, sometimes with mixed flocks; often bob heads. **ID** ♂ cinnamon-rufous, dusky lores, buff supraloral line. ♀ slightly duller. **Voice** Sings frequently, sweet mellow "tee, deer-dear-dear-dear", falling, trailing off, and very melancholy. **SS** ♀ Cinereous Becard, larger ♀ One-colored Becard.

cinnamomeus

Chestnut-crowned Becard *Pachyramphus castaneus* `LC`
Cabezón Castaño
Fairly common resident.

L 14 cm (5.5"). Race *saturatus*. Borders of *terra firme* and *várzea* forest, scattered tall trees in clearings, river edges, river islands. To 600 m. Pairs typically stay high; inconspicuous except for frequent vocalizations; usually not with mixed flocks. **ID** Rufous above, pale cinnamon below, grey band ('sweatband') encloses chestnut crown. **Voice** Soft lamenting "deeeeu, deeu-dee-de-de" (descending, melodic, recalls Cinnamon Becard). **SS** ♀ Cinereous Becard (infrequent high in trees).

saturatus

Black-capped Becard *Pachyramphus marginatus* `LC`
Cabezón Capirotado
Uncommon resident.

L 13.2 cm (5.2"). Race *nanus*. Interior of humid *terra firme* forest, less often *várzea*. To 500 m. Pairs, subcanopy or canopy (always high), follow mixed flocks. Forages methodically for fruit and arthropods. **ID** ♂ grey (not blackish) below, grey supraloral line. ♀ chestnut cap, white lores, broken white eye-ring, ochraceous wing edgings. **Voice** Songs variable, always soft, sweet, melancholy "che-che-che-che-che-te-te-te" thin, rising at end. Shorter "chew, chu-chu..cheet" or "twee-twee-tee-eet, dear-dear", last two notes lower. Soft trills. **SS** White-winged Becard.

♀ *nanus* ♂

White-winged Becard *Pachyramphus polychopterus* `LC`
Cabezón Aliblanco
Common resident.

L 14 cm (5.5"). Races *similis*[A], *cinereiventris*[B], *dorsalis*[C], *tristis*[D], *nigriventris*[E], *tenebrosus*[F]. Moist to humid forest borders, second growth, gallery forest, plantations, mangroves. To 2100 m. Pairs, alone or with mixed flocks, mid- to upper levels. **ID** ♂ E of Andes blackish, W of Andes blackish above, light grey below, no pale supraloral; all races show white scapular band, white wing-edgings. ♀ plainer, whitish eye-arcs, cinnamon-buff wing-edgings and tail tips. **Voice** Song (both sexes), soft warbled "teeur, tur-tur-tur-turtur?" or variation. Soft falling "tew te tu tu tu".

tenebrosus

♂

♀ *dorsalis* ♂

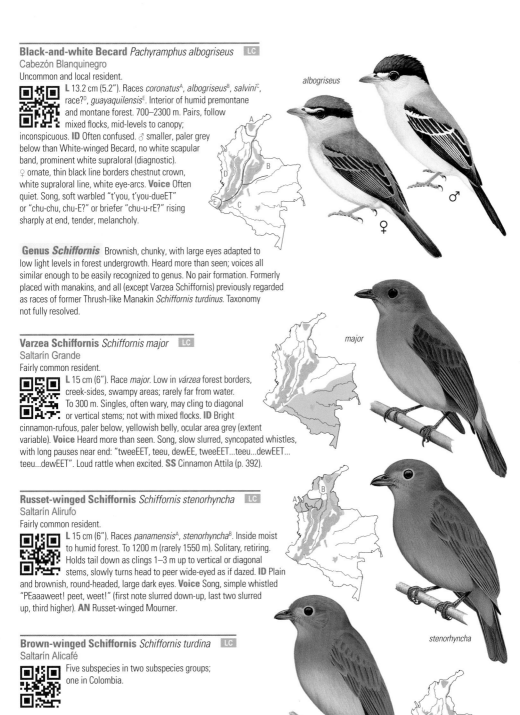

Black-and-white Becard *Pachyramphus albogriseus* `LC`
Cabezón Blanquinegro
Uncommon and local resident.

L 13.2 cm (5.2"). Races *coronatus*[A], *albogriseus*[B], *salvini*[C], race?[D], *guayaquilensis*[E]. Interior of humid premontane and montane forest. 700–2300 m. Pairs, follow mixed flocks, mid-levels to canopy; inconspicuous. **ID** Often confused. ♂ smaller, paler grey below than White-winged Becard, no white scapular band, prominent white supraloral (diagnostic). ♀ ornate, thin black line borders chestnut crown, white supraloral line, white eye-arcs. **Voice** Often quiet. Song, soft warbled "t'you, t'you-dueET" or "chu-chu, chu-E?" or briefer "chu-u-rE?" rising sharply at end, tender, melancholy.

albogriseus

♂

♀

Genus *Schiffornis* Brownish, chunky, with large eyes adapted to low light levels in forest undergrowth. Heard more than seen; voices all similar enough to be easily recognized to genus. No pair formation. Formerly placed with manakins, and all (except Varzea Schiffornis) previously regarded as races of former Thrush-like Manakin *Schiffornis turdinus*. Taxonomy not fully resolved.

Varzea Schiffornis *Schiffornis major* `LC`
Saltarín Grande
Fairly common resident.

L 15 cm (6"). Race *major*. Low in *várzea* forest borders, creek-sides, swampy areas; rarely far from water. To 300 m. Singles, often wary, may cling to diagonal or vertical stems; not with mixed flocks. **ID** Bright cinnamon-rufous, paler below, yellowish belly, ocular area grey (extent variable). **Voice** Heard more than seen. Song, slow slurred, syncopated whistles, with long pauses near end: "tweeEET, teeu, dewEE, tweeEET...teeu...dewEET...teeu...dewEET". Loud rattle when excited. **SS** Cinnamon Attila (p. 392).

major

Russet-winged Schiffornis *Schiffornis stenorhyncha* `LC`
Saltarín Alirufo
Fairly common resident.

L 15 cm (6"). Races *panamensis*[A], *stenorhyncha*[B]. Inside moist to humid forest. To 1200 m (rarely 1550 m). Solitary, retiring. Holds tail down as clings 1–3 m up to vertical or diagonal stems, slowly turns head to peer wide-eyed as if dazed. **ID** Plain and brownish, round-headed, large dark eyes. **Voice** Song, simple whistled "PEaaaweet! peet, weet!" (first note slurred down-up, last two slurred up, third higher). **AN** Russet-winged Mourner.

Brown-winged Schiffornis *Schiffornis turdina* `LC`
Saltarín Alicafé

Five subspecies in two subspecies groups; one in Colombia.

stenorhyncha

Amazonian Brown-winged Schiffornis
Schiffornis (turdina) amazonum
Uncommon resident.

L 15 cm (6"). Race *amazonum*. Humid *terra firme* forest, white-sand forest. To 1100 m. Behaviour as Russet-winged Schiffornis. **ID** Like previous species. **Voice** Song, clear sweet whistled "peeeeeeer, puree, puHEET", first note drawn-out, second rises slightly, last abruptly upslurred. **SS** Larger than ♀ manakins, smaller than thrushes. **AN** Western Brown-winged Mourner.

amazonum

Foothill Schiffornis *Schiffornis aenea* `LC`
Llorón de Colina
Uncommon resident.

L 15 cm (6"). Monotypic. Humid premontane forest. About 1100–1800 m (Ecuador), 850 m (Colombia). **ID** As Russet-winged Schiffornis. **Voice** Song, slurred whistle "peeEEaaaaaEEee'et-et", slides up-down-up, then quickly followed by two brief lower whistles; or first note separated and lower than the slurred up-down phrases. Change in pitch small. **SS** Brown-winged Schiffornis. **AN** Foothill Mourner.

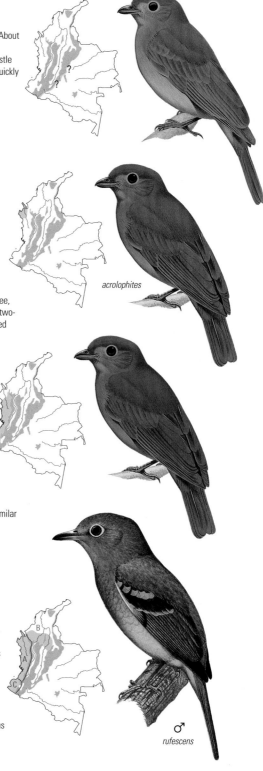

Northern Schiffornis *Schiffornis veraepacis* `LC`
Saltarín Occidental

Four subspecies in two subspecies groups; both in Colombia.

Northern Schiffornis *Schiffornis (veraepacis) veraepacis*
Uncommon resident.
L 15 cm (6"). Race *acrolophites*. Undergrowth in humid foothill and premontane forest. About 100–1200 m. **ID** As Russet-winged Schiffornis; reliably separated in field only by voice. **Voice** Song (Panama, 750 m) c. 3 seconds, thin melancholy whistled "peeee-eee, ee-ee-ee, tee-eeeet...eeeet", mostly on same pitch, first and fifth two-part phrases very slightly rising, rest monotones. **SS** Russet-winged Schiffornis. **AN** Northern Mourner.

acrolophites

Choco Schiffornis *Schiffornis (veraepacis) rosenbergi*
Uncommon resident.
L 15 cm (6"). One subspecies in group. Humid and wet lowland forest. To 500 m. **ID** As Russet-winged Schiffornis. **Voice** Song, clear whistled "tuuuuuuuuWEET, gEET!". Call, "tuuueet" sliding up. **SS** Russet-winged Schiffornis. **AN** Choco Mourner.

Genus *Laniocera* Previously placed in Tyrannidae, then Cotingidae. Two species, one east and one west of Andes, with similar voices and behaviour, but strikingly different plumages.

Speckled Mourner *Laniocera rufescens* `LC`
Plañidera Manchada
Rare to uncommon resident.

L 20 cm (8"). Races *rufescens*[A], *griseigula*[B], *tertia*[C]. Humid lowland forest, often near streams or ravines. To 500 m (locally 1000 m). ♂♂ inconspicuous and solitary, sings from mid-level perches, often for years at same sites. **ID** Above cinnamon-rufous, paler below, indistinct scalloping and spotting on chest, 2–3 cinnamon wingbars on dusky wing-coverts, semi-concealed yellow pectoral tufts. ♀ similar but usually lacks ♂'s hidden yellow pectoral tufts. **Voice** Song, at intervals throughout day, 10–15 slurred singsong phrases, "teEEa-yee", penetrating, hypnotic and drowsy. **SS** Rufous Mourner (p. 402), Rufous Piha (p. 352).

♂
rufescens

Cinereous Mourner *Laniocera hypopyrra* `LC`
Plañidera Ceniza
Uncommon resident.

L 20 cm (8"). Monotypic. Humid *terra firme* forest, especially on sandy soil. To 500 m (locally 700 m). Behaviour recalls Speckled Mourner. Solitary ♂♂, or a few well-separated individuals in traditional song leks for years, sing from low or mid-level perches at intervals throughout day. **ID** Plain grey, orange-spotted wingbars, semi-concealed orange-yellowish pectoral tufts. Juv variable orange-spotted underparts. **Voice** Song, 10–15 high thin monotonously singsong "seea-weh" phrases, c. 1/second, hypnotic, ventriloquial, insect-like.

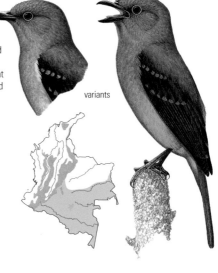

variants

buckleyi

♂

♀

Andean Mourner (Andean Laniisoma)
Laniisoma buckleyi `NT`
Lanisoma Andina
Rare and local resident.

L 18 cm (7"). Races *venezuelense*[A], *buckleyi*[B]. Humid foothill forest (E Boyacá). 700 m (400–1350 m, Ecuador). Singles, various levels inside forest, quiet and inconspicuous. **ID** ♂ black cap, yellow below, dark barring on sides. ♀ plain olive above, below yellow entirely barred dusky. Juv rufous wingbars. **Voice** Song, very high thin (7 kHz) "piiiiuuuuiiiiii" (c. 1 second), pitch sags in middle, not loud. **SS** ♀ Fiery-throated Fruiteater (p. 346). **TN** Race *venezuelense* often not recognized. Split of isolated Brazilian population also probably not warranted. Shrike-like Cotinga is name often used when *buckleyi* is lumped with SE Brazilian *L. elegans*.

TYRANNIDAE
Tyrant-flycatchers
449 extant species, 209 in region + 3 vagrants

Large Western Hemisphere family, which is most diverse in the warm tropics. While migrants from both boreal and austral regions sally to air for insects, tropical latitude residents employ a wide range of behaviours in pursuit of both arthropods and fruit. For some genera, field identification is complex; knowledge of voice, behaviour, habitat, elevation and shape must be taken into account. Monogamy predominates, but in a few species no pair bonds are formed. Nests range from tiny well-formed cups (e.g. *Elaenia*) to pendant structures (e.g. *Tolmomyias*), the latter sometimes pirated by Piratic Flycatchers. A few are cavity nesters.

Cinnamon Manakin-tyrant *Neopipo cinnamomea* `LC`
Atrapamoscas-saltarín Canelo
Rare or local resident (easily overlooked).

cinnamomea

L 9 cm (3.5"). Race *cinnamomea*. Humid *terra firme* forest, especially white-sand forests. To 600 m. Singles, in forest mid-levels. **ID** Tiny; very like Ruddy-tailed Flycatcher (p. 356), differing in shorter tail, hunched posture, dusky legs, narrow rounded bill, no rictal bristles, rounded greyish crown (concealed yellow patch). **Voice** Little piping song (4–5 seconds), like piccolo "pe, pa pe pe-pee-fee-fee-feaa-feaa-feaa-feaa", second note lowest, next few rise, last half falls, overall leisurely. **TN** Formerly in Pipridae. **AN** Cinnamon Neopipo.

Genus *Platyrinchus* Tiny, inconspicuous and stub-tailed, with very wide flat bills (wider than long), large eyes, and large blocky heads. Movements darting, forage by upward strikes, 'scooping' prey from underside of foliage. Semi-concealed crown patches in ♂♂, usually lacking in ♀♀.

Cinnamon-crested Spadebill *Platyrinchus saturatus* `LC`
Pico-de-pala Rufo
Rare resident (few records).

L 9.4 cm (3.7"). Race *saturatus*. Humid *terra firme* forest, especially dense undergrowth in white-sand forest. To 300 m. Like other *Platyrinchus*, perches low, mostly < 1.5 m up; active as mixed flocks pass.
ID Drab; whitish lores and ocular area, white throat contrasts with brownish breast. **Voice** Song, curious bursts of slow squeaking or scraping rattles "ka-keek-keek-keek-keek", surprisingly harsh. Call "squik!" (sometimes doubled). **SS** Golden-crowned Spadebill.

saturatus

Western White-throated Spadebill *Platyrinchus albogularis* `LC`
Pico-de-pala Gargantiblanco Occidental
Fairly common resident.

L 9.5 cm (3.8"). Races *neglectus*[A], *albogularis*[B], *perijanus*[C]. Low in undergrowth, dry to humid foothill and montane forest; possibly gallery forests in Arauca. Mostly 900–2000 m (lower, Pacific slope). Singles or pairs, most active when mixed flocks overhead; perch quietly, abruptly dart to underside of foliage to snap insect prey. **ID** Brownish, strong facial pattern, contrasting white throat, buff breast. **Voice** Song, fairly high buzzy or bubbly trill, "pe'e'e'e'e'e'e'e'e't" (c. 1.5 seconds), steadily rising. Call, emphatic "squik!". **SS** Golden-crowned Spadebill.

albogularis

Golden-crowned Spadebill *Platyrinchus coronatus* `LC`
Pico-de-pala Coronado
Fairly common (variable) resident.

L 8.6 cm (3.4"). Races *superciliaris*[A], *coronatus*[B]. Undergrowth in humid and wet forest. To 900 m. Behaviour like Western White-throated Spadebill but often perches a little higher (1–6 m up) in more open understorey. **ID** Black-bordered crown, yellowish underparts, prominent face pattern. **Voice** Frequent song, high-pitched weak insect-like buzzy trill "se'e'e'e'e'r'r'r're'e'e" (7.5–6.5 kHz), slightly descending, then ascending, 1–3 sharp "pip" notes sometimes added. **SS** Western White-throated Spadebill.

coronatus

Yellow-throated Spadebill *Platyrinchus flavigularis* `LC`
Pico-de-pala Gorgiamarillo
Rare and local resident.

 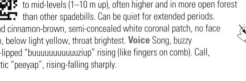

L 10 cm (4"). Races *vividus*[A], *flavigularis*[B]. Humid and wet montane forest. 1400–2300 m. Singles or pairs, in understorey to mid-levels (1–10 m up), often higher and in more open forest than other spadebills. Can be quiet for extended periods.
ID Head cinnamon-brown, semi-concealed white coronal patch, no face pattern, below light yellow, throat brightest. **Voice** Song, buzzy rubber-lipped "buuuuuuuuuuuziup" rising (like fingers on comb). Call, emphatic "peeyap", rising-falling sharply.

flavigularis

White-crested Spadebill *Platyrinchus platyrhynchos* `LC`
Pico-de-pala Canelo
Local resident.

 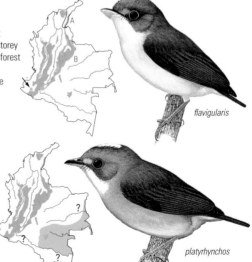

L 11.4 cm (4.5"). Race *platyrhynchos*. Mainly white-sand *terra firme* forest. To 300 m. Singles, 1–5 m up inside forest, more conspicuous than other spadebills.
ID Largest spadebill; head grey, white coronal streak, no face pattern, throat white, lower underparts cinnamon-buff.
Voice Frequent call, sharp "pEap" or "skEEap". Less frequent song (c. 2 seconds), buzzy rubber-lipped (fingers on comb) "buuuuuuurrrree, preeeer" (slowly rising, 2–3.5 kHz, quickly falling).

platyrhynchos

Wing-barred Piprites *Piprites chloris* `LC`
Saltarín Oliva

Seven subspecies in two subspecies groups; one (or both?) in Colombia.

chlorion

Grey-breasted Piprites *Piprites (chloris) chlorion*
Status unknown.
L 14 cm (5.5"). Race *chlorion*. Humid *terra firme* forest. To 250 m.
ID As *chloris* group (below), but underparts mostly light grey (not yellowish).
Voice As Wing-barred Piprites. **TN** Weakly supported subspecies group;
distribution in Colombia needs confirmation. **AN** Formerly Wing-barred Manakin.

Wing-barred Piprites *Piprites (chloris) chloris*
Uncommon to fairly common resident.
L 14 cm (5.5"). Races *perijana*[A], *antioquiae*[B], *tschudii*[C]. Humid
lowland and foothill forest. 100–1700 m. Usually noted first
by voice. Singles, mid-levels to subcanopy, often with mixed
flocks. **ID** Plump, round-headed and short-tailed; large black
eyes and prominent white-tipped tertials. All races have
yellow lores, eye-ring, throat and wingbars (one bold),
greyish nuchal collar, dull yellow underparts (or breast
yellowish tinged olive, *tschudii*). **Voice** Song, leisurely
nasal whistled (curlew-like) "kuep..kuep, kuep, kuee'di'le..
kuep?", warbled in middle. **SS** Becard- or manakin-like.

tschudii

antioquiae

Bronze-olive Pygmy-tyrant *Pseudotriccus pelzelni* `LC`
Tiranuelo Broncioliva
Fairly common but inconspicuous resident.

L 11.4 cm (4.5"). Races *berlepschi*[A], *annectens*[B],
pelzelni[C]. Undergrowth in humid and wet montane
forest. 700–2500 m. Usually singly, close to ground;
sallies to underside of leaves, not with mixed
flocks. **ID** Uniform dark olive, red eyes, cinnamon wing
edgings, creamy throat and belly (or browner, *annectens*).
Voice Infrequent song, high metallic trill "piiiiiiiiiizeet" abruptly
rising at end. Short flat dry trill slightly descending. Bill snaps; wing rattles.
SS Habitat and elevation good clues for this plain dark little bird.

pelzelni

Rufous-headed Pygmy-tyrant *Pseudotriccus ruficeps* `LC`
Tiranuelo Encapuchado
Uncommon resident.

L 11 cm (4.3"). Monotypic. Dense undergrowth in humid and wet
montane forest, borders. 1400–3200 m. Singles, near ground to
3 m up, actively sally up to underside of foliage but out of sight
within or beneath vegetation. Not with mixed flocks. **ID** Rufous
head and throat, dark rufous wings and tail. **Voice** Song, shrill flat or descending
trill; or longer slightly falling-rising trill, sometimes with emphatic note or two at
end. Surprisingly loud bill snaps.

Ringed Antpipit *Corythopis torquatus* `LC`
Atrapamoscas Collarejo
Uncommon resident (heard more than seen).

L 14 cm (5.5"). Races *sarayacuensis*[A],
anthoides[B]. Humid *terra firme* and
transition forest. To 500 m. Singles, walk
rapidly on forest floor, on logs, or pause
momentarily 1–2 m up. Jumps up to snap prey from
underside of leaves; teeters body, bobs head. **ID** White
underparts, black necklace on chest (not apparent if
walking away). **Voice** Song, mainly at dawn, shrill quickly
whistled "peeur-prayer", first note descends, second rebounds.

sarayacuensis

Genus *Phylloscartes* Small, slender, arboreal tyrannulets with prominent wingbars, and long tail usually held cocked. Regularly with mixed flocks. May flip up a wing briefly (in 'salute'). Has included *Pogonotriccus*.

Ecuadorian Tyrannulet *Phylloscartes gualaquizae* NT
Tiranuelo Ecuatoriano
Uncommon resident (recently confirmed in Colombia).
L 11.4 cm (4.5"). Monotypic. Humid premontane forest, borders. 700–1300 m. Singles or pairs, mid-levels to subcanopy. **ID** Bill all dark, crown light grey, weak white eyeline and eye-ring, whitish cheeks dusky at edges (but no obvious dark crescent), yellow wingbars, throat whitish, rest of underparts clear yellow, chest tinged olive. **Voice** Song, short falling-rising trill, sometimes with sputtering or rattled notes added: "tiiiiiaaeeEP" and "tiiiii, t't't't". **SS** Plumbeous-crowned Tyrannulet (p. 389; shorter bill, ear-covert crescent), White-fronted Tyrannulet (p. 388).

Rufous-browed Tyrannulet *Phylloscartes superciliaris* LC
Tiranuelo de Visera
Uncommon resident (distribution fragmented).
L 11.4 cm (4.5"). Races *palloris*[A], *griseocapillus*[B]. Local in humid premontane and montane forest, edges, plantations. 1000–2000 m (rarely 600 m). Pairs or little families, mid-levels to subcanopy, follow mixed flocks; spritely, active, chattery. **ID** White cheeks outlined black, narrow rufous frontlet to behind eyes. **Voice** Vocal; little "swick" and "squeet" notes; longer "swee-swee-swee". **SS** Behaviour recalls a gnatcatcher.

palloris

Genus *Pogonotriccus* Small and quick, perch erect, tail down, and often raise a wing (little 'salute'); habitually with mixed flocks. Prominent dark crescent-shaped ear-coverts patch on grizzled face, and yellowish to ochraceous wingbars. Sometimes merged into *Phylloscartes*.

Variegated Bristle-tyrant *Pogonotriccus poecilotis* LC
Atrapamoscas Variegado
Uncommon resident.
L 11 cm (4.3"). Monotypic. Mid-levels to subcanopy of humid montane forest, borders. 1500–2400 m. Singles or pairs with mixed flocks, upright posture, sally or flit to foliage. **ID** Mandible orange-yellow, bright tawny-buff wingbars, grizzled face with dusky ear patch. **Voice** Dawn song, long-continued sharp chips mixed with short rattle-trills. Foraging birds give chattering trills and chips. **SS** Bold wingbars diagnostic.

Marble-faced Bristle-tyrant *Pogonotriccus ophthalmicus* LC
Atrapamoscas Marmóreo
Common resident.
L 11.4 cm (4.5"). Race *ophthalmicus*. Mid-levels or subcanopy of humid and wet montane forest. 1500–2400 m. Pairs or families follow mixed flocks, perch upright. **ID** Short bill, greyish crown, grizzled face, dusky ear-covert crescent, yellowish wingbars. **Voice** Song, high shrill falling-rising trill, preceded and followed by one to several high notes: "tti, tiiiiiaaaaiiiiii'pit'pit pit, pit". Call, high "cheet!". **SS** Slaty-capped Flycatcher (p. 368; larger, longer bill and tail), Ashy-headed Tyrannulet (p. 389).

ophthalmicus

Antioquia Bristle-tyrant *Pogonotriccus lanyoni* EN
Tiranuelo Antioqueño EN
Local resident.

L 11 cm (4.3"). Monotypic. Endemic. Humid lowland and foothill forest. 250–1100 m. Behaviour typical of genus. **ID** Greyish crown, faint broken white eye-ring, whitish supraloral area, yellowish-white face with indistinct dusky ear-coverts (barely evident on some), yellowish wingbars, and soft yellow underparts. **Voice** Song (c. 1.5 seconds), high slightly descending chattering rattle (8–10 notes) followed by 3–4 slower, successively higher "chit" notes. **SS** Marble-faced Bristle-tyrant (higher elevations), Slaty-capped Flycatcher (larger, with longer bill).

Spectacled Bristle-tyrant *Pogonotriccus orbitalis* LC
Atrapamoscas de Anteojos
Local resident (W Putumayo).

L 11.4 cm (4.5"). Monotypic. Humid foothill and lower montane forest, c. 700–1300 m. Behaviour like other *Pogonotriccus*. **ID** Mandible pale, crown greyish, prominent white eye-ring but narrow indistinct dark ear-covert crescent, two yellowish-white wingbars, underparts yellowish tinged olive. **Voice** Song, weak piping series of brisk rising notes: "pi-pi-pi-pe-pe-pee-pee-peet". **SS** Ecuadorian Tyrannulet, Slaty-capped Flycatcher.

Genus *Mionectes* Slender, narrow bill, with few or no rictal bristles. Diet mostly small fruit taken while hovering; often quickly flick up one wing. Formerly in genus *Pipromorpha*.

Streak-necked Flycatcher
Mionectes striaticollis LC
Atrapamoscas Estriado
Common but inconspicuous resident.

L 13.5 cm (5.3"). Races *columbianus*ᴬ, *viridiceps*ᴮ. Humid montane forest. 1300–2700 m (usually above 1600 m). Timid singles perch hunched, nod head, nervously flick wings; briefly active with mixed flocks or other birds at fruiting trees (e.g. *Trema*, *Clusia*, *Miconia*). **ID** Prominent white post-ocular spot; head, neck and throat grey (or greyish olive, *viridiceps*), finely streaked yellowish to mid-breast, unstreaked yellow belly. **Voice** Usually silent. ♂♂ sing in loose understorey leks; song, exceeding high (6–9 kHz) wiry stream of hummingbird-like notes (c. 1–2/second), as sway head and body back and forth with bill open to expose orange mouth lining, or lower-pitched (c. 5 kHz) in *viridiceps*. **SS** Olive-striped Flycatcher.

viridiceps

columbianus

Olive-striped Flycatcher *Mionectes galbinus* LC
Atrapamoscas Oliváceo

Four subspecies in two subspecies groups; both in Colombia, although poorly differentiated.

Western Olive-striped Flycatcher *Mionectes (galbinus) galbinus*
Common resident.
L 13.5 cm (5.3"). Races *galbinus*ᴬ, *hederaceus*ᴮ. Humid lowland and lower montane forest. 100–1800 m (mostly foothills or higher), rarely 2400 m. **ID** Prominent white post-ocular spot, plumage mainly olive, sides of head and underparts with blurred yellowish streaking, belly less streaked. **Voice** Usually silent. ♂ at lek sings exceedingly high (9–10 kHz) "tseei, tseei..." (notes upslurred, slightly varied in pitch). **SS** Streak-necked Flycatcher (higher elevations, finer streaking, greyer head).

hederaceus

Eastern Olive-striped Flycatcher
Mionectes (galbinus) venezuelensis
Common resident.
L 13.5 cm (5.3"). Races *venezuelensis*[A], *fasciaticollis*[B]. Humid foothill and lower montane forest. c. 400–1800 m. **ID** Very like western forms, but both races slightly darker olive above (especially *fasciaticollis*); below richer yellow. **Voice** Song like western races, possibly longer-sustained, pitch more even. **SS** Streak-necked Flycatcher.

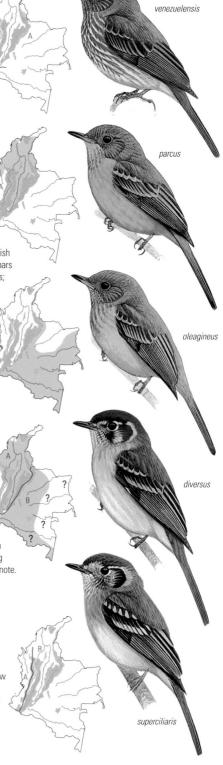

venezuelensis

Ochre-bellied Flycatcher *Mionectes oleagineus* `LC`
Atrapamoscas Ocráceo

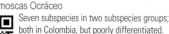

Seven subspecies in two subspecies groups; both in Colombia, but poorly differentiated.

Ochre-bellied Flycatcher *Mionectes (oleagineus) assimilis*
Common resident.
L 13.5 cm (5.3"). Races *parcus*[A], *pacificus*[B]. Humid lowland, foothill and lower montane forest. To 1700 m. Solitary, quirky, inconspicuous inside forest. ♂ sings 2–6 m up, alone or in dispersed leks, frequently flicks up a wing, raises tiny crest. Maintains small territories, or behaves as subordinate satellite, or as floater; displays complex. **ID** Bill thin, mandible pinkish basally, mouth lining yellow, upperparts dull olive (like tarnished copper), wingbars ochraceous, and lower underparts burnt orange. **Voice** Persistent singer on leks; chirps, twitters, little sneezing "choo" and "pitchóo" notes.

parcus

Oleaginous Flycatcher *Mionectes (oleagineus) oleagineus*
Common resident.
L 13.5 cm (5.3"). Race *oleagineus*. Humid lowland, foothill and lower montane forest. Behaviour as previous group. **ID** Nearly identical to *assimilis* subspecies group (above). **Voice** Also similar but detailed comparison lacking. **TN** Basis for separation as subspecies group needs reevaluation.

oleagineus

Genus *Leptopogon* Grizzled face, dark crescent-shaped ear-coverts patch (faint in some); larger, longer-tailed, and distinctly longer- and heavier-billed than *Pogonotriccus*. Perch upright; often raise one wing in 'salute'.

Sepia-capped Flycatcher *Leptopogon amaurocephalus* `LC`
Atrapamoscas Sepia
Fairly common resident.
L 14 cm (5.5"). Races *diversus*[A], *peruvianus*[B]. Undergrowth in moist and humid forest, light woodland, plantations, gallery forest; frequently along streams. To 900 m. **ID** Closely resembles Slaty-capped Flycatcher but facial area buffy white (not grizzled grey and white), cap sepia-brown contrasting with olive back, wingbars buff (not yellowish white). **Voice** Song, scraping chattering rattle, descending; also short stuttering chatter, either often preceded by sharp note. **SS** Slaty-capped Flycatcher (higher elevations).

diversus

Slaty-capped Flycatcher *Leptopogon superciliaris* `LC`
Atrapamoscas Orejinegro
Common resident.
L 14 cm (5.5"). Races *transandinus*[A], *superciliaris*[B] (both races variable, doubtfully distinct). Humid and wet foothill and montane forest, borders, second growth. 500–2100 m. Singles or pairs follow mixed flocks at low to mid-levels, sally to foliage. **ID** Crown dark grey, indistinct whitish eyeline, face grey grizzled whitish, dark crescent-shaped ear-coverts patch, prominent yellowish-spotted wingbars. **Voice** Frequent sneezing "Ah'chew" (or "hít'you"); descending "tt-t-e-e-e" trill; sharp emphatic "skEET'de'e'e'er!". **SS** Sepia-capped Flycatcher.

superciliaris

Rufous-breasted Flycatcher *Leptopogon rufipectus* `LC`
Atrapamoscas Pechirrufo
Uncommon resident.

 L 14 cm (5.5"). Monotypic. Humid montane forest (except Pacific slope?). 1500–2700 m. Singles or pairs follow mixed flocks, perch erect at mid-levels; sally-glean from foliage. **ID** Face, sides of head, throat and chest rufous, cheeks faintly grizzled, dusky ear patch. **Voice** Advertising call 1–5 loud, squeaky "spik" notes like child's squeeze toy, typically at long intervals. **SS** Rufous foreparts diagnostic.

Brownish Twistwing *Cnipodectes subbrunneus* `LC`
Atrapamoscas Zumbador
Uncommon and local resident.

 L ♂ 18 cm (7"), ♀ 15 cm (6"). Races subbrunneus[A], minor[B]. Undergrowth in humid lowland forest. To 1200 m (to 700 m E of Andes). Singles are sedentary, not with mixed flocks, often raise up a wing in slow stretch. Function of ♂'s thick twisted outer primaries uncertain. **ID** Eyes brown to orange, mandible pale, plumage brown, rear parts more rufescent and belly yellowish white. **Voice** Persistent call (all areas), emphatic "KUEER!" or "KUEER KUEER", occasionally trebled, often preceded by loud bill snaps. **SS** Royal flycatchers (p. 356).

♂ *minor*   ♂ *subbrunneus*

Genus *Rhynchocyclus* Large-headed and large-eyed; exceptionally wide flat bill, with pale mandible and prominent rictal bristles. Dull plumage. Inconspicuous; lethargic, perch quietly, roll head upwards or side to side, as if dazed. Sally upwards to foliage; often with mixed flocks.

Eye-ringed Flatbill *Rhynchocyclus brevirostris* `LC`
Picoplano de Anteojos
Few records (Colombian range remote).

 L 15 cm (6"). Race *hellmayri*. Humid foothill and lower montane forest, c. 700–1500 m. **ID** Prominent white eye-ring, dark olive upperparts, wing-coverts and flight feathers obscurely edged yellow-olive, throat to mid-breast olive with blurred streaking merging into yellowish belly. **Voice** Presumed song (Mexico), 2–3 very high rising buzzes "peeeeez, bzzzu, bzzu", each slightly higher, briefer than preceding. **SS** Mostly at higher elevations than Western Olivaceous Flatbill.

hellmayri

Western Olivaceous Flatbill (Olivaceous Flatbill)
Rhynchocyclus aequinoctialis (*Rhynchocyclus olivaceus*) `LC`
Picoplano Oliváceo
Fairly common resident.

 L 15 cm (6"). Races bardus[A], mirus[B], flavus[C], tamborensis[D], aequinoctialis[E]. Humid lowland and foothill forest, borders, *várzea* (scarce or absent in sandy soil areas). To 600 m (rarely 1400 m). **ID** Prominent white eye-ring; very like Eye-ringed Flatbill (best separated by voice), but overall paler olive, underparts paler greyish olive, wing-coverts and flight feathers edged yellowish. **Voice** Dawn song E & W of Andes, 5–15 clear rising, accelerating whistles: "tree, tree-wee-wee-we-we-e-e". **SS** Pacific Flatbill. **TN** Does not include Eastern Olivaceous Flatbill *R. olivaceus* (Venezuela to SE Brazil).

aequinoctialis

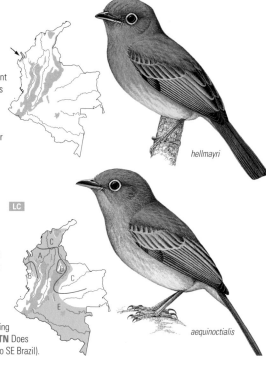

Pacific Flatbill *Rhynchocyclus pacificus* LC
Picoplano Chocoano
Fairly common resident.

 L 15 cm (6"). Monotypic. Near-endemic (also NW Ecuador). Wet lowland and foothill forest, old second growth. To 600 m (rarely 1200 m). **ID** Much like Eye-ringed and Western Olivaceous Flatbills, differing from both in darker olive plumage, including streaking on breast, greyer and less prominent eye-ring, wing-coverts edged ochraceous (more conspicuous than Western Olivaceous Flatbill). **Voice** Song, at dawn, 5–8 clear whistles "peee, pee, pee, tee, tee, tee-teer", slightly descending and accelerating. **SS** Fulvous-breasted Flatbill (higher elevations). **TN** Formerly a race of Eye-ringed Flatbill.

Fulvous-breasted Flatbill *Rhynchocyclus fulvipectus* LC
Picoplano Pectoral
Fairly common resident.

 L 15 cm (6"). Monotypic. Humid premontane and montane forest. 700–2100 m. **ID** Much like Pacific Flatbill but occurs at higher elevations; throat to mid-breast tawny (not olive). Both have greyish eye-rings, wing-coverts edged ochraceous. **Voice** Call (or song?), single buzzy sharply rising "suzzzzet", medium-pitched (3–5 kHz), or with two low, introductory 'grace-notes' "tay-twe-suzzzzet". **SS** Western Olivaceous Flatbill.

Genus *Tolmomyias* Broad flat bill (but not as wide as *Platyrinchus* and *Rhynchocyclus*), pale lores, pale mandible (except Grey-crowned and Ochre-lored), yellowish wingbars, and yellow-edged flight feathers. Perch semi-upright, tail slightly cocked. Taxonomy confusing; identify by combination of habitat, voice and plumage. Usually called flycatchers.

Yellow-olive Flatbill (Yellow-olive Flycatcher)
Tolmomyias sulphurescens LC
Picoplano Azufrado
Commonest *Tolmomyias*.

exortivus

 L 14 cm (5.5"). Races *flavoolivaceus*[A], *asemus*[B], *exortivus*[C], *confusus*[D]. Dry to humid forest borders (not inside forest), wooded riparian edges and plantations. To 1200 m (locally 1800 m). Singles or pairs, mid-levels or lower, sometimes with mixed flocks. **ID** Largest *Tolmomyias*; eyes grey (usually) to brown, crown grey (or greyish olive, *exortivus*, *asemus*), narrow whitish supraloral and eye-ring, hint of dusky ear-coverts (or ear-coverts darker, *confusus*). **Voice** Song may vary geographically; *confusus* typically 2–3 sharp notes, "psst!..psst!...psst!", often at long intervals. **SS** Other *Tolmomyias*.

Orange-eyed Flatbill (Orange-eyed Flycatcher)
Tolmomyias traylori LC
Picoplano Ojinaranja
Uncommon and local resident.

 L 13.5 cm (5.3"). Monotypic. Mid-levels in *várzea* forest, borders, low-lying riparian forest; distribution poorly known. To 500 m. Singles or pairs, sometimes with mixed flocks. **ID** Resembles Yellow-olive Flatbill but slightly smaller, buff wash on face, orange eyes, yellower underparts. **Voice** Best identified by voice. Song, typically three (from 2–7) shrill buzzy or hoarse whistles "zuwe zweet"..zweET..zweeET!" growing stronger, more urgent, notes upslurred. Call "pweea" (rising-falling). **SS** Other *Tolmomyias*.

Yellow-margined Flatbill (Yellow-margined Flycatcher)
Tolmomyias assimilis LC
Picoplano Aliamarillo

Eight subspecies in two subspecies groups; one in Colombia.

neglectus

Yellow-margined Flatbill *Tolmomyias (assimilis) assimilis*
Fairly common resident.
L 13 cm (5"). Races *neglectus*[A], *obscuriceps*[B]. Mid-levels and subcanopy in tall humid forest. To 700 m. **ID** Easily confused; much like smaller Grey-crowned Flatbill but grey crown less contrasting, wingbars obscure, lower mandible entirely pale, eyes dark (not pale), (up close or in hand) pale area at base of primaries. Larger Yellow-olive Flatbill (not inside forest) has more contrasting grey crown, dark ear-coverts patch (lacking in Yellow-margined). **Voice** Song (?), three asthmatic (wheezy) rising whistles c. 2–3 seconds apart "weeeu...weeeu...weee". Also 1–2 distinctive rising-falling "zweeeu" notes, and flatter "weeu". **AN** Zimmer's Flatbill.

Yellow-winged Flatbill *Tolmomyias flavotectus* LC
Picoplano Aliamarillo
Fairly common resident.

L 13 cm (5"). Monotypic. Mid-levels to canopy in humid and wet lowland forest. To 800 m. **ID** Much like races of Yellow-margined Flatbill E of Andes but greater wing-coverts more broadly edged yellow, wingbars obscure. **Voice** Song, 3–5 thin sharp notes "pzip,..pzip, zip, pzip" with distinct pause after first note, rest brisk. **SS** Larger Yellow-olive Flatbill (not inside forest) lacks trim clean-cut appearance, has dark ear-coverts patch, often ruffed crown. **TN** Usually considered a race of Yellow-margined Flatbill.

Grey-crowned Flatbill (Grey-crowned Flycatcher)
Tolmomyias poliocephalus LC
Picoplano Diminuto
Common resident.

poliocephalus

L 11.7 cm (4.6"). Race *poliocephalus*. Canopy and borders of humid lowland forest; commonest in sandy soil forest. To 700 m. Regularly with canopy mixed flocks or in crowns of emergent trees (e.g. *Ceiba*). **ID** Smaller, and generally higher in forest than other *Tolmomyias*; yellowish eyes, whitish supraloral mark, contrasting grey crown, and mandible tipped dark (pale in other *Tolmomyias*). **Voice** Persistent singer at dawn, 3–7 leisurely, slightly husky whistles "tee...tee..teea..teeawe..teeaweep", somewhat variable, usually accelerating, stronger at end. **SS** Yellow-margined Flatbill.

Olive-faced Flatbill (Yellow-breasted Flycatcher)
Tolmomyias viridiceps LC
Picoplano Carioliváceo
Uncommon resident.

viridiceps

L 13 cm (5"). Race *viridiceps*. River islands, young river-edge vegetation, overgrown clearings, forest borders. To 500 m. Singles or pairs, not very high, often away from mixed flocks. **ID** Plainest *Tolmomyias*; eyes dark, crown and upperparts olive (no grey), face plain, below yellow, breast tinged olive. **Voice** Song, 2–5 shrill whistles "zep..zep...zeep...zweep!... zweep!", initially timid, stronger more confident, rising at end. **TN** Usually considered conspecific with *T. flaviventris* (Yellow-breasted Flycatcher).

371

Ochre-lored Flatbill (Yellow-breasted Flycatcher)
Tolmomyias flaviventris LC
Picoplano Pechiamarillo
Common resident.

 L 13 cm (5"). Race *aurulentus*. Dry, moist and humid forest borders, plantations, urban parks, gallery forest. To 800 m. Singles or pairs, mid-levels to subcanopy, sometimes with small mixed flocks. **ID** Prominent black eyes, above bright yellowish olive, supraloral spot and eye-ring ochre, yellowish wingbars, below bright yellow with faint ochre-tinged throat and chest. **Voice** Song, 3–5 penetrating whistles "sweeEP!...sweeEP!...sweeEP!". Call "sweeEP!". **TN** See previous species.

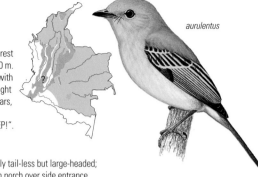

aurulentus

Genus *Myiornis* Tiny (among the smallest passerines), virtually tail-less but large-headed; in flight resembles a large bee or beetle. 'Trashy' hanging nest with porch over side entrance.

Black-capped Pygmy-tyrant *Myiornis atricapillus* LC
Tiranuelo Capirotado
Common (but easily overlooked) resident.

 L 7 cm (2.7"). Monotypic. Humid and wet forest, borders, tall second growth. To 900 m. Singles or pairs are sedentary; perch quietly at mid-levels, dart off to snap prey from nearby leaf but flight also can be slow, buzzy, insect-like. Infrequently with mixed flocks. **ID** Black cap, white spectacles, white breast, yellow-tinged belly. **Voice** Rarely noticed unless calling; weak trilled "eeeek" or "creek", sometimes repeatedly, like cricket or frog!

Short-tailed Pygmy-tyrant *Myiornis ecaudatus* LC
Tiranuelo Colimocho
Fairly common resident.

 L 7 cm (2.7"). Race *miserabilis*. Humid forest, borders, tall second growth. To 500 m. **ID** Cap grey, otherwise as Black-capped Pygmy-tyrant. **Voice** Like Black-capped Pygmy-tyrant; cricket-like soft trilled "eeeeek!", sometimes changing to series of short squeaky "creek" notes. Also chirp-like squeaks. All vocalizations easily overlooked.

miserabilis

Genus *Oncostoma* Two plain little flycatchers with an unusually thick bent bill. Weak toad-like trilled calls.

Northern Bentbill *Oncostoma cinereigulare* LC
Piquitorcido Cinéreo
Status uncertain (record possibly invalid).

 L 10 cm (4"). Monotypic. Known from one old specimen (1965) from lowlands of Chigorodó, Antioquia, 400–600 km E of its known range in Panama. **ID** Very like Southern Bentbill and doubtfully separable in field. Northern Bentbill differs in greyish-white (instead of yellowish-white) throat and chest, with obscure greyish (rather than slightly olive) streaking, crown perhaps greyer (less olive). **Voice** Like Southern Bentbill.

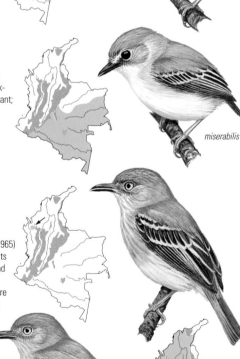

Southern Bentbill *Oncostoma olivaceum* LC
Piquitorcido Oliváceo
Fairly common resident (easily overlooked).

L 9.7 cm (3.8"). Monotypic. Thickets and low vine tangles in second growth, borders of moist to humid forest. To 1000 m. Singles or pairs perch quietly inside thickets, sally abruptly to foliage or twigs, occasionally take small berries. **ID** Told by pale eyes and odd thickened bill (looks almost deformed). **Voice** Weak toad-like purring trill "prrrrrr" or "gurrrrr", nasal, like amphibian or insect. **SS** Northern Bentbill.

Genus *Lophotriccus* Small and inconspicuous; mostly in lower growth. Ornate crests usually held flat; loud calls and trills. ♂♂ solitary; apparently no pair formation. ♀♀ have shorter crests. Not with mixed flocks.

squamaecrista

Scale-crested Pygmy-tyrant *Lophotriccus pileatus* `LC`
Tiranuelo Crestibarrado
Common resident.

 L 10 cm (4"). Races *luteiventris*[A], *santaeluciae*[B], *squamaecrista*[C]. Thickets, shrubby borders of humid foothill and montane forest, second growth. 500–2400 m. Singles, mid-strata or lower; scattered solitary ♂♂ call (no leks). **ID** Eyes yellowish, rufous-edged black crest feathers held flat (protrude rearward), spread fan-like (rare) imparts fierce countenance, underparts yellowish white obscurely streaked olive. **Voice** Frequent calls betray its presence; remarkably loud (for small bird), metallic "preet", "pic" or "trik", sometimes accelerating, like winding old watch; minor geographical differences.

Double-banded Pygmy-tyrant *Lophotriccus vitiosus* `LC`
Tiranuelo Alibarrado
Fairly common resident.

 L 10 cm (4"). Race *affinis*. Low at borders of *terra firme* forest, treefall gaps, second growth. To 500 m. **ID** Eyes pale, crest of black feathers edged grey usually laid flat, yellowish wingbars, below pale yellowish with blurred olive streaking. **Voice** Advertising call, slightly descending trill (c. 1 second) "dzzzzzzr" fast or slower (like winding watch). Also a rough buzzy "drazzzzzer", rising at start. **SS** Helmeted Pygmy-tyrant, White-eyed Tody-tyrant.

affinis

Helmeted Pygmy-tyrant *Lophotriccus galeatus* `LC`
Tiranuelo Empenachado
Common resident.

 L 10 cm (4"). Monotypic. Humid sandy soil forest, savanna woodland and second growth; less often at forest edges and swamp forest. To 400 m. Alone in middle stories, usually slightly higher than Double-banded Pygmy-tyrant. **ID** From very similar Double-banded Pygmy-tyrant, by crown feathers narrower and more elongated, making crest less conspicuous; wingbars less noticeable; underparts whiter, especially belly, with more distinct streaking; tail longer. **Voice** Series of 4–10 dry staccato "pik" or "trik" notes, sometimes ending in warbled phrase, pattern similar to Double-banded but not as loud; sometimes sings constantly throughout heat of day. **SS** In SE Colombia, see Double-banded. Slightly larger White-eyed Tody-tyrant lacks crest, has an eye-ring and more conspicuous wingbars.

Pale-eyed Pygmy-tyrant *Atalotriccus pilaris* `LC`
Tiranuelo Ojiamarillo
Common resident.

 L 10.7 cm (4.2"). Races *pilaris*[A], *griseiceps*[B]. Desert scrub, dry and moist forest, dry brushy areas. To 1200 m (rarely 2000 m). Inconspicuous, mid-levels or lower, sometimes active around small mixed flocks; hover-glean or sally-strike underside of foliage. **ID** Recalls Pearly-vented Tody-tyrant but smaller, eyes whitish (not orange), upperparts olive (not brownish), and vocalizations differ. **Voice** Dry "tic" notes; nasal trills (sings through its nose) of variable length, "tic-tttttttttttt", sometimes loud. **SS** Slender-billed Tyrannulet (p. 381).

griseiceps

pilaris

Genus *Hemitriccus* Small; most have pale eyes, faintly streaked underparts, moderately broad bills; active around mixed flocks but don't follow them. A taxonomically complex group.

White-eyed Tody-tyrant *Hemitriccus zosterops* LC
Picochato Ojiblanco
Uncommon or local resident.

zosterops

L 10.7 cm (4.2"). Race *zosterops*. Inside humid lowland *terra firme* forest. To 500 m. Singles, perch semi-erect, mid-levels or slightly lower; inconspicuous. **ID** Confusing. White eyes, base of bill pinkish, small whitish supraloral mark, weak yellowish-white wingbars, below whitish, belly tinged yellowish, indistinct streaking on breast. **Voice** Pay attention to voice. Primary song, loud sharp series "pik, pik-pik" or longer series of "pik" notes, sometimes tirelessly. When agitated hard rattles, sputtering "pik" notes. **SS** Often confused with Pale-eyed Pygmy-tyrant but habitats differ and pygmy-tyrant utters nasal trills.

Joao's Tody-tyrant (Johannes's Tody-tyrant)
Hemitriccus iohannis LC
Picochato Amazónico
Rare resident (few records).

L 10.7 cm (4.2"). Monotypic. Mid-level vine tangles in humid older second growth in transitional or seasonally flooded areas. To 400 m. Sedentary, singles or pairs. **ID** Confusing. Eyes yellowish white, indistinct greyish lores and eye-ring, above drab olive, two indistinct yellowish wingbars and edges, throat whitish, rest of underparts dull yellowish, throat and breast with some blurred olive streaking. **Voice** Best identified by distinctive song, a single note followed by slightly rising, staccato, slow nasal trill "tuu't'u'r'r'r'r'r'r'r'r". Single "tu" notes. **SS** White-eyed and Stripe-necked Tody-tyrants. **TN** Formerly a race of Stripe-necked Tody-tyrant.

Stripe-necked Tody-tyrant *Hemitriccus striaticollis* LC
Picochato Rayado
Uncommon and local resident.

striaticollis

L 10.7 cm (4.2"). Race *striaticollis*. Shrubby thickets, forest borders, overgrown clearings; restricted (?) distribution. To 400 m. Singles or pairs, fairly low. **ID** Much like Joao's Tody-tyrant but lores, short narrow eyeline and eye-ring better defined and white, wing-coverts and edges olive (no wingbars), throat white, breast yellow, streaking sharper, bolder, much better defined. **Voice** Call, brief husky rising "puwEET!" or upslurred "kuEK-kuEK!". Song 1–2 rising notes and short rattle-trill "puit-puit d'd'd".

Pearly-vented Tody-tyrant *Hemitriccus margaritaceiventer* LC
Picochato Perlado
Common resident.

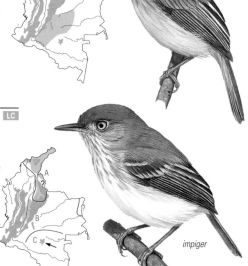

L 11.4 cm (4.5"). Races *impiger*[A], *septentrionalis*[B], *chiribiquetensis*[C], E Vichada (race?). Thickets in arid scrub, dry brush, thorny *Acacia* woodland. To 1100 m. Singles or pairs perch-glean or flit to foliage, below eye level to crowns of low vegetation. **ID** Eyes orange-yellow (darker, juv). Resembles Pale-eyed Pygmy-tyrant but larger, longer bill, orange-yellow eyes (not whitish), brown (not olive) upperparts, hint of streaking on chest; above browner (*impiger*). **Voice** Distinctive sharp "tuk, tuk quéek, quéek". Quick falling-rising "tic-tic- tic-tuk-tuk-tuk-tic-tic". Stuttering notes ending in rattle "quick, tuk-tuk-kw'e'e'e'e". Descending trill "tick'rrrrrr"; low rattle-trill "trrrrrrr".

impiger

Pelzeln's Tody-tyrant *Hemitriccus inornatus* `LC`
Picochato de Pelzeln

Local resident (recent, 2017, audio confirmation, Puerto Inírida).

L 10 cm (4"). Monotypic. Low-canopy scrub (*campina*) woodland, within which it typically keeps to the tallest sections. To 250 m (?). **ID** May occur with Helmeted Pygmy-tyrant and/or White-eyed Tody-tyrant, and similar to both; best confirmed by voice and occurrence in lower, scrubbier woodland (not forest), wingbars whitish (not yellowish). **Voice** Song, low-pitched (2.8–3 kHz) hard emphatic "tic, tic, tic'ti't't't"; some songs shorter or longer but short accelerating rattle-trill at end characteristic. Call, 1–4 slow "tic" notes.

Black-throated Tody-tyrant *Hemitriccus granadensis* `LC`
Picochato Carinegro

Fairly common resident.

L 10 cm (4"). Races *lehmanni*[A], *intensus*[B], *granadensis*[C], *andinus*[D]. Humid and wet montane forest, borders, second growth. 1800–3000 m (rarely 3500 m). Singles or pairs, quiet, inconspicuous, mid-levels or lower; active when mixed flocks present but does not join them. **ID** Large whitish (buff, *lehmanni*) loral area, ocular area and frontlet impart bare-faced appearance, black throat wraps rearward to cheeks, and no wingbars. **Voice** Low gravelly stuttering "dut't't, dut't't". Low flat "tuck, peet peet" with 2–4 "peet" notes (*lehmanni*). Also short slow trills and single notes (*granadensis*). Calls vary geographically.

lehmanni

granadensis

Buff-throated Tody-tyrant *Hemitriccus rufigularis* `NT`
Picochato Gorgirrufo

Rare resident (few records, Orito, Putumayo).

L 11.4 cm (4.5"). Monotypic. 1000 m (1000–1500 m, Ecuador). Mid-levels or lower in humid montane forest borders, treefall gaps, stunted vegetation on outlying ridges (Ecuador, Peru). **ID** Rather plain, eyes yellowish, throat and sides of neck buff, chest faintly greyish-smudged, no wingbars, belly white. **Voice** Song (call?), 2–10 or more slightly hoarse upslurred "kweep" notes. Burry "kip-kip, kweep". **SS** Above elevational range of other *Hemitriccus*.

Genus *Poecilotriccus* Plump, bills narrower and slightly shorter than *Todirostrum*. Thicket-dwellers; usually noted first by their soft calls and low trills. Not with mixed flocks.

Rufous-crowned Tody-flycatcher *Poecilotriccus ruficeps* `LC`
Tiranuelo Coronado

Fairly common resident.

L 9.7 cm (3.8"). Races *ruficeps*[A], *melanomystax*[B], *rufigenis*[C]. Shrubby montane forest borders, bushy pastures, thickets in gardens. 1500–2700 m. Inconspicuous, pairs stay out of sight 0.5–4 m up; movements abrupt, brief upward sally-strikes to foliage. **ID** Plump, large head; colourful head pattern, cheeks buff outlined black, throat white (*melanomystax*), or cheeks less clearly outlined black at lower edge (*ruficeps*) or crown, cheeks and throat dull rufous, with no black (*rufigenis*). **Voice** Soft stuttering "pa'treer, pít-pit-pit" or "pip'prrrrrr" (like shuffling cards), sometimes in loose duets. Call, flat "chak". **TN** More than one species perhaps involved (*rufigenis* very plain-headed).

ruficeps

rufigenis

melanomystax

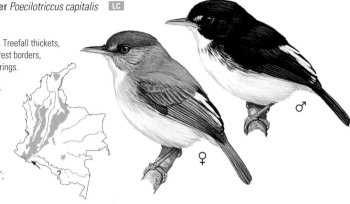

Black-and-white Tody-flycatcher *Poecilotriccus capitalis* LC
Tiranuelo Blanquinegro
Uncommon and local resident.

L 9.7 cm (3.8"). Monotypic. Treefall thickets, vine-tangled *terra firme* forest borders, undergrowth in bushy clearings. 300–1100 m (all records in foothills). Sedentary pairs generally stay out of sight 1–10 m up. **ID** Mandible orange-yellow. ♂ above black, below white, white eye-ring, yellowish wing bend and tertials. ♀ above olive, crown rufous, face and chest grey, tertials like ♂. **Voice** Advertising call "stik, tuk-tuk-tuk" (first note higher); "stik stik"; short stuttering rattles and trills.

Rusty-fronted Tody-flycatcher *Poecilotriccus latirostris* LC
Espatulilla Rubicunda
Fairly common resident.

L 9.7 cm (3.8"). Races *mituensis*[A], *caniceps*[B]. Dense thickets at borders of humid forest, overgrown clearings. To 500 m (locally 900 m). Singles or pairs, near ground to 3 m up; inconspicuous and difficult to see. Not with mixed flocks. **ID** Rusty-buff forehead and facial area, whitish underparts. **Voice** Advertising call, low frog-like "tik, trrrrr", latter part rolled, descending, gravelly. **SS** Potentially confusing, but rarely noted except by distinctive voice.

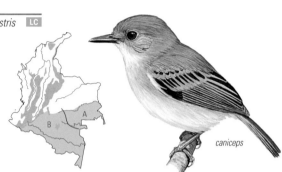

caniceps

Slate-headed Tody-flycatcher *Poecilotriccus sylvia* LC
Espatulilla Rastrojera
Common resident.

L 9.7 cm (3.8"). Races *superciliaris*[A], *griseolus*[B]. Dry to humid scrub, shrubby borders, young second growth, roadside thickets; gallery forest in *llanos*. To 1200 m. Sedentary pairs, near ground to 6 m up, inconspicuous, usually noted first by voice. **ID** Grey head, white spectacles, bright golden wingbars and edges, white underparts. **Voice** Easily overlooked call, soft low "tik", varied to "tic, tjurrr" (last part like swallowed trill); sometimes trill repeated several times. Recalls Rusty-fronted Tody-flycatcher but last part faster.

griseolus

Golden-winged Tody-flycatcher *Poecilotriccus calopterus* LC
Espatulilla Alidorada
Uncommon and local resident.

L 9.7 cm (3.8"). Monotypic. Shrubby forest borders, roadside thickets; most records in or near foothills. 300–1200 m. Sedentary, inconspicuous pairs stay hidden, near ground to 5 m up. Not with mixed flocks. **ID** Black head, olive upperparts, white throat, yellow breast and belly, chestnut wing bend, broad yellow greater wing-coverts band. **Voice** Rather quiet. Advertising call, low sputtering "churr, jrrrrr" given repeatedly. Rapid-paced alternating duets "d'jrr, d'jrr, d'jrr-d'jrr…".

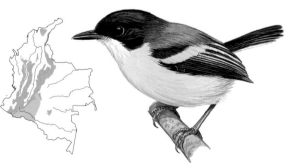

Genus *Todirostrum* Small and colourful, with narrow cocked tails, long flat and narrow bills. Much more arboreal than *Poecilotriccus*. 'Bright', high-pitched, piping calls, and sprightly behaviour.

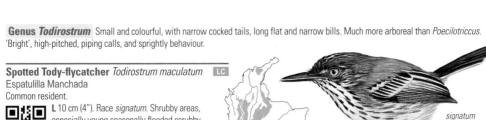

Spotted Tody-flycatcher *Todirostrum maculatum* `LC`
Espatulilla Manchada
Common resident.

L 10 cm (4"). Race *signatum*. Shrubby areas, especially young seasonally flooded scrubby second growth, gardens, river islands, riverfronts in towns. To 500 m. Pairs, easy to see, eye level or sometimes much higher. **ID** Orange-yellow eyes, greyish head, white loral spot, white throat and yellow underparts finely dotted and streaked black. **Voice** Advertising call, loud energetic "PEEP!" or "peek", singly, doubled or rapid duets "pe'peek, pe'peek..." or "peek d-dit, peek d-dit...". **SS** Common Tody-flycatcher.

signatum

sclateri

Common Tody-flycatcher *Todirostrum cinereum* `LC`
Espatulilla Común
Common resident.

L 9.7 cm (3.8"). Races *cinereum*[A], *sclateri*[B], *peruanum* (Putumayo?). Dry to humid shrubby habitats, forest borders, trees in parks, gardens. To 2200 m. Most familiar *Todirostrum*. Pairs are confiding, engaging; wag cocked tails and sidle up branches, flit to underside of foliage. Mid-levels or lower. **ID** Eyes yellow (dark, juv), forecrown blackish, below bright yellow including throat (or throat white, *sclateri*). **Voice** Quite vocal; loud bright "peept!" (singly or repeated); short bursts of high (5–6 kHz) trills "te'e'e'e" recalling Tropical Kingbird.

cinereum

Black-headed Tody-flycatcher *Todirostrum nigriceps* `LC`
Espatulilla Cabecinegra
Fairly common resident (inconspicuous).

L 9 cm (3.5"). Monotypic. Humid forest borders, older second growth. To 1000 m. Less frequently seen than Common Tody-flycatcher. Singles or pairs, invariably high overhead in canopy. Easily detected by voice but difficult to see well. Not with mixed flocks. **ID** Easily confused with Common Tody-flycatcher but eyes always dark, head black, back yellowish olive, throat white; voice differs. **Voice** Advertising song, high (6 kHz) "teek, teek..." given 5–15 times, almost two/second.

[Painted Tody-flycatcher *Todirostrum pictum*] `LC`
Espatulilla Pintada
Hypothetical.

L 9 cm (3.5"). Monotypic. Occurs on Venezuelan side of border with Vichada and Guainía; as yet no confirmed Colombian records but likely. Canopy of tall lowland forest, especially borders, tall trees in clearings. **ID** Much like Yellow-browed Tody-flycatcher, differing in head to below eyes all black (no yellow brow), otherwise similar including voice.

Yellow-browed Tody-flycatcher *Todirostrum chrysocrotaphum* `LC`
Espatulilla Collareja
Common but easily overlooked resident.

L 9 cm (3.5"). Race *guttatum*. Borders of tall humid forest, old second growth, clearings with tall trees. To 500 m. Pairs stay in canopy where inconspicuous, difficult to see well. Not with mixed flocks. **ID** Head glossy black, white supraloral spot, long broad yellow eyebrow, back olive, throat white, breast to belly yellow, bold black breast streaking. **Voice** Much like Black-headed Tody-flycatcher. Series of high "teek..." notes, easily overlooked. **SS** Painted Tody-flycatcher.

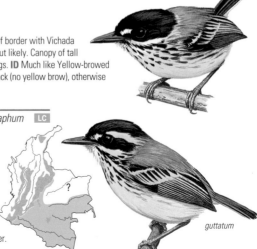

guttatum

Eastern Ornate Flycatcher *Myiotriccus phoenicurus* `LC`
Atrapamoscas Adornado Oriental
Common resident.

 L 11.7 cm (4.6"). Race *phoenicurus*. Humid and wet forest. 800–1300 m (to 2000 m, Ecuador). **ID** Like next species but slightly larger, tail all rufous, inner flight feathers edged rufous, white pre-ocular spots join or nearly join (not distinctly separated). **Voice** Presumably like Western Ornate. **TN** Usually regarded as a subspecies of Ornate Flycatcher *M. ornatus*.

phoenicurus

Western Ornate Flycatcher *Myiotriccus ornatus* `LC`
Atrapamoscas Ornado
Common resident.

 L 11.4 cm (4.5"). Races *stellatus*[A], *ornatus*[B]. Humid and wet foothill and montane forest, treefalls, mossy ravines. 600–2300 m (rarely 400 m). Sedentary pairs perch upright, mid-levels or lower, sally in acrobatic loops to air or foliage. **ID** Large white pre-ocular spots (like false eyes) usually well separated, yellow rump and belly, basal half of tail rufous, rest blackish. **Voice** Call, high penetrating "peeet!". Dawn song, high "cheet..chi..chi'chi'chi'chi'chi", slightly descending and run together. **TN** Usually includes eastern *phoenicurus*.

ornatus

Handsome Flycatcher *Nephelomyias pulcher* `LC`
Atrapamoscas Elegante
Locally fairly common resident.

 L 11.4 cm (4.5"). Races *pulcher*[A], *bellus*[B]. Humid and wet montane forest. 1500–2600 m (to 800 m, Pacific slope). Pairs or groups of 3–8 follow mixed flocks, mid-strata or higher. Posture horizontal to semi-erect; sallies to foliage. **ID** Compact and short-tailed. Grey cap (concealed rufous coronal patch, ♂), bold cinnamon wingbars, orange-rufous chest, lower underparts creamy-yellow (*bellus*), or slightly smaller, chest and wingbars paler ochre (*pulcher*). **Voice** Call, high insistent "tsit" or "tsit-tsit". **SS** Flavescent Flycatcher (p. 406). **TN** Previously in genus *Myiophobus*.

pulcher

♀

♂

♂

bellus

Cinnamon Flycatcher *Pyrrhomyias cinnamomeus* `LC`
Atrapamoscas Canelo

 Six subspecies in three subspecies groups; two in Colombia.

Santa Marta Cinnamon Flycatcher
Pyrrhomyias (cinnamomeus) assimilis
Common resident.

L 13 cm (5"). One subspecies in group. Endemic. **ID** Like Andean forms, but brighter cinnamon including crown, back, wings and tail; rump-band paler. **Voice** Similar to Andean forms.

E

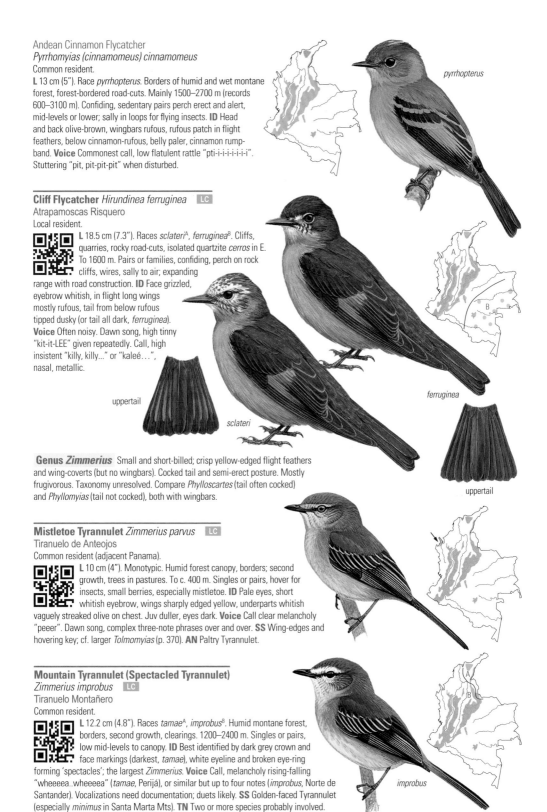

Andean Cinnamon Flycatcher
Pyrrhomyias (cinnamomeus) cinnamomeus
Common resident.
L 13 cm (5"). Race *pyrrhopterus*. Borders of humid and wet montane forest, forest-bordered road-cuts. Mainly 1500–2700 m (records 600–3100 m). Confiding, sedentary pairs perch erect and alert, mid-levels or lower; sally in loops for flying insects. **ID** Head and back olive-brown, wingbars rufous, rufous patch in flight feathers, below cinnamon-rufous, belly paler, cinnamon rump-band. **Voice** Commonest call, low flatulent rattle "pti-i-i-i-i-i-i-i". Stuttering "pit, pit-pit-pit" when disturbed.

pyrrhopterus

Cliff Flycatcher *Hirundinea ferruginea* LC
Atrapamoscas Risquero
Local resident.
L 18.5 cm (7.3"). Races *sclateri*[A], *ferruginea*[B]. Cliffs, quarries, rocky road-cuts, isolated quartzite *cerros* in E. To 1600 m. Pairs or families, confiding, perch on rock cliffs, wires, sally to air; expanding range with road construction. **ID** Face grizzled, eyebrow whitish, in flight long wings mostly rufous, tail from below rufous tipped dusky (or tail all dark, *ferruginea*). **Voice** Often noisy. Dawn song, high tinny "kit-it-LEE" given repeatedly. Call, high insistent "killy, killy..." or "kaleé...", nasal, metallic.

uppertail

sclateri

ferruginea

uppertail

Genus *Zimmerius* Small and short-billed; crisp yellow-edged flight feathers and wing-coverts (but no wingbars). Cocked tail and semi-erect posture. Mostly frugivorous. Taxonomy unresolved. Compare *Phylloscartes* (tail often cocked) and *Phyllomyias* (tail not cocked), both with wingbars.

Mistletoe Tyrannulet *Zimmerius parvus* LC
Tiranuelo de Anteojos
Common resident (adjacent Panama).
L 10 cm (4"). Monotypic. Humid forest canopy, borders; second growth, trees in pastures. To c. 400 m. Singles or pairs, hover for insects, small berries, especially mistletoe. **ID** Pale eyes, short whitish eyebrow, wings sharply edged yellow, underparts whitish vaguely streaked olive on chest. Juv duller, eyes dark. **Voice** Call clear melancholy "peeer". Dawn song, complex three-note phrases over and over. **SS** Wing-edges and hovering key; cf. larger *Tolmomyias* (p. 370). **AN** Paltry Tyrannulet.

Mountain Tyrannulet (Spectacled Tyrannulet)
Zimmerius improbus LC
Tiranuelo Montañero
Common resident.
L 12.2 cm (4.8"). Races *tamae*[A], *improbus*[B]. Humid montane forest, borders, second growth, clearings. 1200–2400 m. Singles or pairs, low mid-levels to canopy. **ID** Best identified by dark grey crown and face markings (darkest, *tamae*), white eyeline and broken eye-ring forming 'spectacles'; the largest *Zimmerius*. **Voice** Call, melancholy rising-falling "wheeeea..wheeeea" (*tamae*, Perijá), or similar but up to four notes (*improbus*, Norte de Santander). Vocalizations need documentation; duets likely. **SS** Golden-faced Tyrannulet (especially *minimus* in Santa Marta Mts). **TN** Two or more species probably involved.

improbus

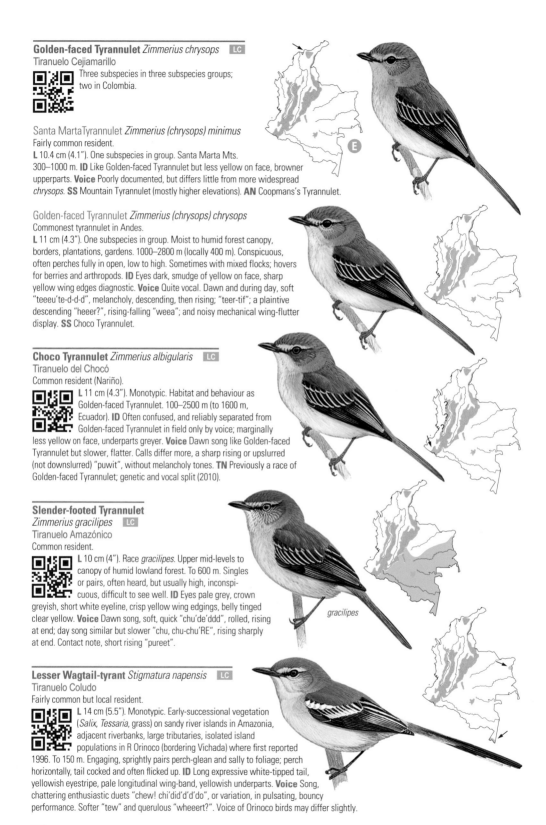

Golden-faced Tyrannulet *Zimmerius chrysops* `LC`
Tiranuelo Cejiamarillo

Three subspecies in three subspecies groups; two in Colombia.

Santa MartaTyrannulet *Zimmerius (chrysops) minimus*
Fairly common resident.
L 10.4 cm (4.1"). One subspecies in group. Santa Marta Mts. 300–1000 m. **ID** Like Golden-faced Tyrannulet but less yellow on face, browner upperparts. **Voice** Poorly documented, but differs little from more widespread *chrysops*. **SS** Mountain Tyrannulet (mostly higher elevations). **AN** Coopmans's Tyrannulet.

Golden-faced Tyrannulet *Zimmerius (chrysops) chrysops*
Commonest tyrannulet in Andes.
L 11 cm (4.3"). One subspecies in group. Moist to humid forest canopy, borders, plantations, gardens. 1000–2800 m (locally 400 m). Conspicuous, often perches fully in open, low to high. Sometimes with mixed flocks; hovers for berries and arthropods. **ID** Eyes dark, smudge of yellow on face, sharp yellow wing edges diagnostic. **Voice** Quite vocal. Dawn and during day, soft "teeeu'te-d-d-d", melancholy, descending, then rising; "teer-tif"; a plaintive descending "heeer?", rising-falling "weea"; and noisy mechanical wing-flutter display. **SS** Choco Tyrannulet.

Choco Tyrannulet *Zimmerius albigularis* `LC`
Tiranuelo del Chocó
Common resident (Nariño).

L 11 cm (4.3"). Monotypic. Habitat and behaviour as Golden-faced Tyrannulet. 100–2500 m (to 1600 m, Ecuador). **ID** Often confused, and reliably separated from Golden-faced Tyrannulet in field only by voice; marginally less yellow on face, underparts greyer. **Voice** Dawn song like Golden-faced Tyrannulet but slower, flatter. Calls differ more, a sharp rising or upslurred (not downslurred) "puwit", without melancholy tones. **TN** Previously a race of Golden-faced Tyrannulet; genetic and vocal split (2010).

Slender-footed Tyrannulet
Zimmerius gracilipes `LC`
Tiranuelo Amazónico
Common resident.

L 10 cm (4"). Race *gracilipes*. Upper mid-levels to canopy of humid lowland forest. To 600 m. Singles or pairs, often heard, but usually high, inconspicuous, difficult to see well. **ID** Eyes pale grey, crown greyish, short white eyeline, crisp yellow wing edgings, belly tinged clear yellow. **Voice** Dawn song, soft, quick "chu'de'ddd", rolled, rising at end; day song similar but slower "chu, chu-chu'RE", rising sharply at end. Contact note, short rising "pureet".

gracilipes

Lesser Wagtail-tyrant *Stigmatura napensis* `LC`
Tiranuelo Coludo
Fairly common but local resident.

L 14 cm (5.5"). Monotypic. Early-successional vegetation (*Salix*, *Tessaria*, grass) on sandy river islands in Amazonia, adjacent riverbanks, large tributaries, isolated island populations in R Orinoco (bordering Vichada) where first reported 1996. To 150 m. Engaging, sprightly pairs perch-glean and sally to foliage; perch horizontally, tail cocked and often flicked up. **ID** Long expressive white-tipped tail, yellowish eyestripe, pale longitudinal wing-band, yellowish underparts. **Voice** Song, chattering enthusiastic duets "chew! chi'did'd'd'do", or variation, in pulsating, bouncy performance. Softer "tew" and querulous "wheeert?". Voice of Orinoco birds may differ slightly.

Genus *Inezia* Narrow bill, longish slightly cocked tail and horizontal posture. Confusing, somewhat diverse in appearance; identify with care. Taxonomically united partly by skull and syringeal characters.

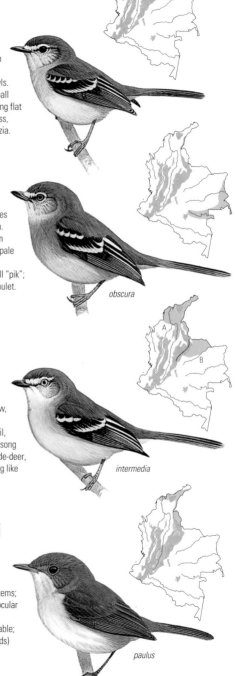

obscura

intermedia

paulus

Slender-billed Tyrannulet *Inezia tenuirostris* LC
Tiranuelo Diminuto
Common resident.

L 9.4 cm (3.7"). Monotypic. Desert scrub, thorn woodland, mangrove borders. To 500 m. Fidgety, confiding little imp with horizontal posture, short slightly cocked tail, mostly 1–5 m up in *Acacia* scrub. Perch-gleans or hover-gleans; mobs small owls. **ID** Mainly Guajira (W to Barranquilla). Best identified by combination of small size, blurred eyebrow, wingbars, yellowish belly and trilled song. **Voice** Song flat dry trill "tleeeeee'e'e'e'e'e'e", thin and attenuated. **SS** Southern Beardless, Pale-tipped and Mouse-colored Tyrannulets (p. 389). **AN** Slender-billed Inezia.

Amazonian Tyrannulet *Inezia subflava* LC
Tiranuelo Pantanero
Uncommon resident.

L 12 cm (4.7"). Race *obscura*. Forested streambanks, lake edges and shrubby openings in low-lying areas near water. To 300 m. Pairs, usually low (0.5–2 m up). **ID** Not reliably separated from Pale-tipped Tyrannulet by plumage, and eyes of both species pale (but juvs dark); voices differ. **Voice** Song, by ♂, brief "pee-chew", ♀ faster "kutup" or "kut'ter'nup", often repeated in rapid rhythmic duet. Call "pik"; dry rattle (0.5–2 seconds). **TN** Formerly conspecific with Pale-tipped Tyrannulet. **AN** Amazonian Inezia.

Pale-tipped Tyrannulet *Inezia caudata* LC
Tiranuelo Colipinto
Fairly common resident.

L 12 cm (4.7"). Races *intermedia*[A], *caudata*[B]. Dry to moist woodland, scrub, gallery forest, seasonally flooded areas. To 400 m. Pairs, flick tail up, often perch-glean or sally quite low, usually away from mixed flocks. **ID** White 'spectacles' impart clean-cut appearance, white eyes, white wingbars, longish white-tipped tail, throat and chest tinged yellowish buff, belly soft yellow. **Voice** Vocal. Day song descending "TEEP! tee-de-dear"; longer, lazy descending "peep, pe-de-de-de-deer, deer, deer" recalls Southern Beardless Tyrannulet, often in duet. Dawn song like day songs but faster. **AN** Pale-tipped Inezia.

Tawny-crowned Pygmy-tyrant *Euscarthmus meloryphus* LC
Tiranuelo Pico-de-tuna
Locally common resident.

L 10.2 cm (4"). Race *paulus*. Dry weedy thickets, scrub, waste ground. To 1000 m (locally 1800 m). Singles, heard more than seen, being reluctant to leave cover. Often clings to vertical stems; perch-gleans 0.1–2 m up. **ID** Plain, faded brown, tawny-buff ocular area, large black eyes, slight peaked crest, and weak cinnamon wingbars. **Voice** Advertising songs (often given obsessively through heat of day) variable; abrupt run-together "pit'cher", or "pit'chup", or dry scratchy (0.2–0.5 seconds) "rrrit'A'ter" (Santander, Guajira), longer (0.8 seconds) dry ratchet-like "rrrrrrrrich'A'Ter" (Tolima); locust-like.

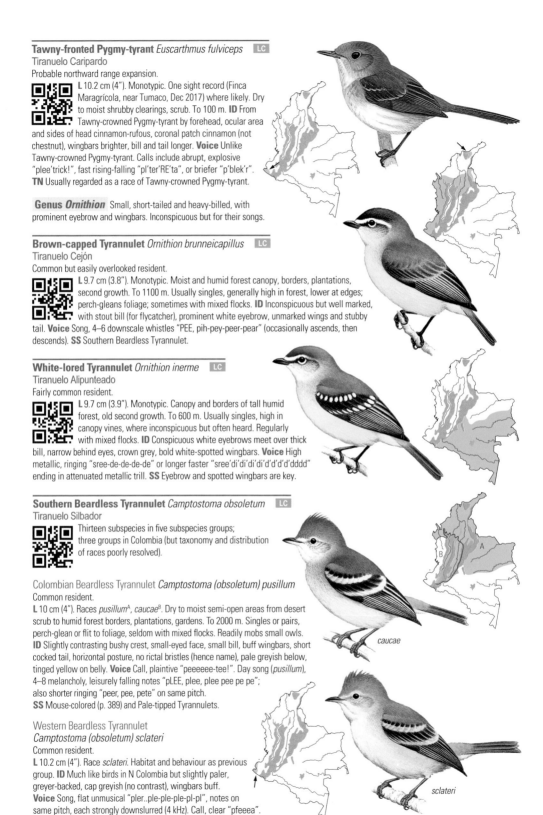

Tawny-fronted Pygmy-tyrant *Euscarthmus fulviceps* `LC`
Tiranuelo Caripardo

Probable northward range expansion.

L 10.2 cm (4"). Monotypic. One sight record (Finca Maragrícola, near Tumaco, Dec 2017) where likely. Dry to moist shrubby clearings, scrub. To 100 m. **ID** From Tawny-crowned Pygmy-tyrant by forehead, ocular area and sides of head cinnamon-rufous, coronal patch cinnamon (not chestnut), wingbars brighter, bill and tail longer. **Voice** Unlike Tawny-crowned Pygmy-tyrant. Calls include abrupt, explosive "plee'trick!", fast rising-falling "pl'ter'RE'ta", or briefer "p'blek'r". **TN** Usually regarded as a race of Tawny-crowned Pygmy-tyrant.

Genus *Ornithion* Small, short-tailed and heavy-billed, with prominent eyebrow and wingbars. Inconspicuous but for their songs.

Brown-capped Tyrannulet *Ornithion brunneicapillus* `LC`
Tiranuelo Cejón

Common but easily overlooked resident.

L 9.7 cm (3.8"). Monotypic. Moist and humid forest canopy, borders, plantations, second growth. To 1100 m. Usually singles, generally high in forest, lower at edges; perch-gleans foliage; sometimes with mixed flocks. **ID** Inconspicuous but well marked, with stout bill (for flycatcher), prominent white eyebrow, unmarked wings and stubby tail. **Voice** Song, 4–6 downscale whistles "PEE, pih-pey-peer-pear" (occasionally ascends, then descends). **SS** Southern Beardless Tyrannulet.

White-lored Tyrannulet *Ornithion inerme* `LC`
Tiranuelo Alipunteado

Fairly common resident.

L 9.7 cm (3.9"). Monotypic. Canopy and borders of tall humid forest, old second growth. To 600 m. Usually singles, high in canopy vines, where inconspicuous but often heard. Regularly with mixed flocks. **ID** Conspicuous white eyebrows meet over thick bill, narrow behind eyes, crown grey, bold white-spotted wingbars. **Voice** High metallic, ringing "sree-de-de-de-de" or longer faster "sree'di'di'di'di'd'd'd'dddd" ending in attenuated metallic trill. **SS** Eyebrow and spotted wingbars are key.

Southern Beardless Tyrannulet *Camptostoma obsoletum* `LC`
Tiranuelo Silbador

Thirteen subspecies in five subspecies groups; three groups in Colombia (but taxonomy and distribution of races poorly resolved).

Colombian Beardless Tyrannulet *Camptostoma (obsoletum) pusillum*
Common resident.

L 10 cm (4"). Races *pusillum*[A], *caucae*[B]. Dry to moist semi-open areas from desert scrub to humid forest borders, plantations, gardens. To 2000 m. Singles or pairs, perch-glean or flit to foliage, seldom with mixed flocks. Readily mobs small owls. **ID** Slightly contrasting bushy crest, small-eyed face, small bill, buff wingbars, short cocked tail, horizontal posture, no rictal bristles (hence name), pale greyish below, tinged yellow on belly. **Voice** Call, plaintive "peeeeee-tee!". Day song (*pusillum*), 4–8 melancholy, leisurely falling notes "pLEE, plee, plee pee pe pe"; also shorter ringing "peer, pee, pete" on same pitch. **SS** Mouse-colored (p. 389) and Pale-tipped Tyrannulets.

caucae

Western Beardless Tyrannulet
Camptostoma (obsoletum) sclateri
Common resident.

L 10.2 cm (4"). Race *sclateri*. Habitat and behaviour as previous group. **ID** Much like birds in N Colombia but slightly paler, greyer-backed, cap greyish (no contrast), wingbars buff. **Voice** Song, flat unmusical "pler..ple-ple-ple-pl-pl", notes on same pitch, each strongly downslurred (4 kHz). Call, clear "pfeeea".

sclateri

Olive Beardless Tyrannulet *Camptostoma (obsoletum) olivaceum*
Fairly common resident.

L 10 cm (4"). One subspecies in group. Humid forest canopy, borders, second growth, gardens; river islands in Amazonia. Generally in more forested habitats, often found higher, and is less conspicuous than races W of Andes. To 500 m (rarely 1200 m). **ID** Differs from Western Beardless (previous page) in darker more olive upperparts (cap not contrasting), whitish (not buff) wingbars, yellowish underparts. **Voice** Song, rapid descending (c. 5–3 kHz) ringing "PEER-p'p'p'p'p'p". Call, single plaintive "pleee" or "p'peeeee, peer", melancholy.

Genus *Elaenia* A large and conspicuous group of difficult-to-identify species. Small-headed, usually with slight to prominent crest, and semi-concealed white crown patch (except Rufous-crowned Elaenia), whitish wingbars, roundish peg-like bill, upright posture, and no rictal bristles. Glean and browse in shrubby areas; not with mixed flocks. A few are austral migrants.

Rufous-crowned Elaenia *Elaenia ruficeps* LC
Elenia Crestirrufa
Uncommon resident.

L 14.5 cm (5.7"). Monotypic. Scrubby woodland borders, white-sand savannas with scattered shrubs and small fire-resistant trees (*Curatella, Byrsonima*). To 400 m. Scattered pairs, never numerous. Perch up to sing, but otherwise inconspicuous as perch-glean in foliage. **ID** Rufous crown patch (look carefully) in rear-projecting crest, variable dark breast streaking. **Voice** Infrequent song, odd 'mushy' ticking or rattling "rr'tt'tt'tt'tt'tt'tt'tt'td'd'd", low-pitched and mechanical-sounding, attenuates, or may end abruptly. **SS** Plain-crested Elaenia.

Plain-crested Elaenia *Elaenia cristata* LC
Elenia Crestada
Uncommon and local resident.

L 14.5 cm (5.7"). Race *cristata*. Savanna with scattered bushes, scrubby fire-resistant trees, dry brush. To 300 m. Singles or pairs, often perch in open. **ID** Drab and undistinguished; small crest projects rearward, no crown patch (may need time to verify), base of mandible pinkish, whitish wingbars. **Voice** Dawn song, a snappy rolling "cheV'a'rear" or "CHEE'beer-ip", second note descending, buzzy. Day song, low gravelly "peeu, peeu, p'pr'pr're'bit, pi'pi'pi" (three parts). Various soft notes. **SS** Lesser Elaenia.

cristata

Mottle-backed Elaenia *Elaenia gigas* LC
Elenia Gigante
Uncommon (mostly May–Dec in lowlands; non-breeding).

L 19 cm (7.5"). Monotypic. Humid forest borders, regenerating landslides, second growth on river islands, river borders. 300–600 m (to 1400 m, Ecuador). Conspicuous, often perches in open. May breed mainly (?) in foothills. **ID** Large; easily identified by upstanding bifurcated crest (like miniature Harpy Eagle) with white in centre, mantle and back dappled. **Voice** Loud upslurred "wur'eet" or "pueent!". Short buzzy trill "bjeeet".

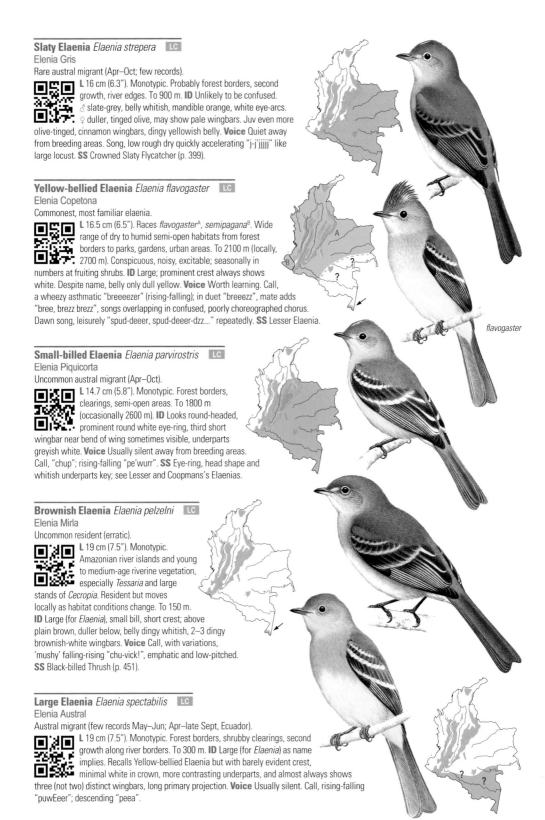

Slaty Elaenia *Elaenia strepera* `LC`
Elenia Gris
Rare austral migrant (Apr–Oct; few records).

L 16 cm (6.3"). Monotypic. Probably forest borders, second growth, river edges. To 900 m. **ID** Unlikely to be confused. ♂ slate-grey, belly whitish, mandible orange, white eye-arcs. ♀ duller, tinged olive, may show pale wingbars. Juv even more olive-tinged, cinnamon wingbars, dingy yellowish belly. **Voice** Quiet away from breeding areas. Song, low rough dry quickly accelerating "j-j'jjjjj" like large locust. **SS** Crowned Slaty Flycatcher (p. 399).

Yellow-bellied Elaenia *Elaenia flavogaster* `LC`
Elenia Copetona
Commonest, most familiar elaenia.

L 16.5 cm (6.5"). Races *flavogaster*[A], *semipagana*[B]. Wide range of dry to humid semi-open habitats from forest borders to parks, gardens, urban areas. To 2100 m (locally, 2700 m). Conspicuous, noisy, excitable; seasonally in numbers at fruiting shrubs. **ID** Large; prominent crest always shows white. Despite name, belly only dull yellow. **Voice** Worth learning. Call, a wheezy asthmatic "breeeezer" (rising-falling); in duet "breeezz", mate adds "bree, brezz brezz", songs overlapping in confused, poorly choreographed chorus. Dawn song, leisurely "spud-deeer, spud-deeer-dzz…" repeatedly. **SS** Lesser Elaenia.

flavogaster

Small-billed Elaenia *Elaenia parvirostris* `LC`
Elenia Piquicorta
Uncommon austral migrant (Apr–Oct).

L 14.7 cm (5.8"). Monotypic. Forest borders, clearings, semi-open areas. To 1800 m (occasionally 2600 m). **ID** Looks round-headed, prominent round white eye-ring, third short wingbar near bend of wing sometimes visible, underparts greyish white. **Voice** Usually silent away from breeding areas. Call, "chup"; rising-falling "pe'wurr". **SS** Eye-ring, head shape and whitish underparts key; see Lesser and Coopmans's Elaenias.

Brownish Elaenia *Elaenia pelzelni* `LC`
Elenia Mirla
Uncommon resident (erratic).

L 19 cm (7.5"). Monotypic. Amazonian river islands and young to medium-age riverine vegetation, especially *Tessaria* and large stands of *Cecropia*. Resident but moves locally as habitat conditions change. To 150 m. **ID** Large (for *Elaenia*), small bill, short crest; above plain brown, duller below, belly dingy whitish, 2–3 dingy brownish-white wingbars. **Voice** Call, with variations, 'mushy' falling-rising "chu-vick!", emphatic and low-pitched. **SS** Black-billed Thrush (p. 451).

Large Elaenia *Elaenia spectabilis* `LC`
Elenia Austral
Austral migrant (few records May–Jun; Apr–late Sept, Ecuador).

L 19 cm (7.5"). Monotypic. Forest borders, shrubby clearings, second growth along river borders. To 300 m. **ID** Large (for *Elaenia*) as name implies. Recalls Yellow-bellied Elaenia but with barely evident crest, minimal white in crown, more contrasting underparts, and almost always shows three (not two) distinct wingbars, long primary projection. **Voice** Usually silent. Call, rising-falling "puwEeer"; descending "peea".

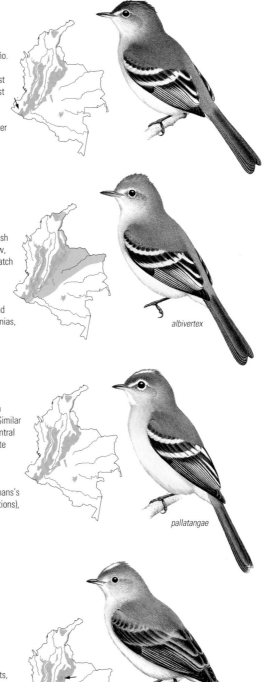

Coopmans's Elaenia *Elaenia brachyptera* `LC`
Elenia de Coopmans

Few records (visual and sound recordings).

 L 13.5 cm (5.3"). Monotypic. c. 700–2000 m (1370 m, W of Andes in Nariño), likely also E of Andes in Nariño. **ID** Very like Lesser Elaenia, differing in voice and molecularly. **Voice** Dawn song, W slope foothills, fast (0.75 seconds) "cheer'cha'b'r'R'R'er", the first note descending, rest fast rising-falling trill; dawn song, E slope foothills (Ecuador) sharply rising-falling (0.25 seconds) "p'fd'd'dup". Whistled call, thin steeply rising-falling "pEEo"; rattle call also reported. **SS** Lesser Elaenia. **TN** Formerly a race of Lesser Elaenia.

Lesser Elaenia *Elaenia chiriquensis* `LC`
Elenia Chica

Uncommon resident.

 L 14 cm (5.5"). Race *albivertex*. Overgrown clearings, shrubby areas with scattered trees. To 2200 m (mostly above c. 400 m). **ID** Confusing. Above brownish grey, below paler greyish white vaguely tinged yellow, belly more yellowish, small crest, semi-concealed white coronal patch (can be absent or small), indistinct white eye-ring, two white wingbars. **Voice** Call (*albivertex*), low husky "p'chure", abruptly drops then rises (0.3 seconds); dawn song, fast (0.75 seconds) "churEE'ba'ba'ba'reet", first and last note rising, middle rattling and low. **SS** Distinguish carefully from Sierran and White-crested Elaenias, and by voice from Coopmans's Elaenia.

albivertex

Sierran Elaenia *Elaenia pallatangae* `LC`
Elenia Serrana

Fairly common resident.

 L 14.7 cm (5.8"). Race *pallatangae*. Humid semi-open highlands, shrubby forest borders. 1600–2800 m. **ID** Similar to Lesser Elaenia, including slight crest and white central crown patch. Differs in narrow broken yellowish-white eye-ring, browner upperparts, and much more obviously yellow underparts throughout. **Voice** Dawn song, simple almost warbled "peeu'weet", first note drops, second higher, steadily repeated at c. 1/second or faster. Call, rising-falling "peEEo" (much like Coopmans's Elaenia). **SS** Lesser and Coopmans's Elaenias (mostly lower elevations), White-crested Elaenia (same elevations or higher).

pallatangae

White-crested Elaenia *Elaenia albiceps* `LC`
Elenia Buchiblanca

 Six subspecies in three subspecies groups; one in Colombia.

White-crested Elaenia *Elaenia (albiceps) albiceps*
Uncommon (?) resident.

L 14.7 cm (5.8"). Races *griseigularis* (resident), *chilensis* (austral migrant); indistinguishable in field. Dry to humid semi-open habitats, shrubby forest borders. 2100–3000 m (*griseigularis*); *chilensis* largely unknown (once?, La Mesa, near Bogotá). May not vocalize. **ID** Closely resembles Lesser Elaenia but at higher elevations. Differs in larger white central crown patch, eye-ring less distinct, wings and tail darker, lower underparts whiter, or flanks and vent with yellowish tinge. **Voice** Dawn song (*griseigularis*), falling-rising "jew'weet" repeatedly; call "beeu", slightly hoarse, dropping. **SS** Sierran, Lesser and Coopmans's Elaenias.

griseigularis

Mountain Elaenia *Elaenia frantzii* `LC`
Elenia Montañera

Four subspecies in two subspecies groups; one in Colombia.

Southern Mountain Elaenia *Elaenia (frantzii) pudica*
Common resident.
L 14 cm (5.5"). Races *pudica*[A], *browni*[B]. Humid montane forest borders, clearings with shrubs and trees. 1500–3000 m (to 3600 m, Santa Marta Mts). **ID** Undistinguished. Looks more olive (less brown) than allies. Note rounded head without crest (no white crown patch), wingbars, weak eye-ring, and highland range. **Voice** Dawn song, breezy "WEeu'tic" repeatedly; call, clear "peeeer"; also "pfeeit! ch-weer" and buzzy "freeer". **TN** Subspecies groups based on dawn song differences.

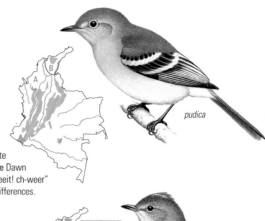

pudica

Caribbean Elaenia *Elaenia martinica* `LC`
Elenia Caribeña

Seven subspecies in two subspecies groups; one in Colombia.

Chinchorro Elaenia *Elaenia (martinica) cinerescens*
Common resident (only Islas San Andrés and Providencia).
L 16.5 cm (6.5"). Race *cinerescens*. Dry woodland, semi-open areas, mangroves. **ID** Resembles slightly larger Yellow-bellied Elaenia (mainland only) but crest smaller and often held depressed, belly paler, base of mandible orange. **Voice** Dawn song, sharp up-down-up, slurred "pee-a-ree, trrrr" followed by 1–2 short rattles. Call, clear whistled "puREEaa" (rising-falling).

cinerescens

Yellow-crowned Tyrannulet *Tyrannulus elatus* `LC`
Tiranuelo Coronado
Common resident.

L 10.7 cm (4.2"). Monotypic. Top of canopy of humid lowland forest, borders, shrubby clearings, plantations, gardens, especially in citrus. To 1600 m. Singles or pairs, perch quietly, often in open; hover-glean berries and insects. Not with mixed flocks. **ID** Tiny, plump, short-tailed; very short bill; bold white wingbars, short indistinct whitish eyebrow, flaring golden-yellow crest seldom visible. **Voice** Common voice; brief little rising-falling 'wolf whistle', "wee-wheer" or "pree-teer" given throughout day. **SS** Southern Beardless Tyrannulet (p. 382), *Zimmerius* tyrannulets (p. 379).

Genus *Myiopagis* Smaller than *Elaenia*, usually darker-capped, with concealed yellow or white crown patch, and longish tail.

Amazonian Grey Elaenia *Myiopagis cinerea* `LC`
Elenia Gris Amazónica
Rare or uncommon and local resident.

L 13 cm (5"). Monotypic. Humid lowland and foothill forest. To 500 m. Pairs, invariably high in forest, where inconspicuous and often with mixed flocks. **ID** ♂ mostly grey, whitish below, blackish wings, white wingbars and edges, white coronal stripe. ♀ above olive, head greyish, yellowish coronal patch, wings like ♂ but edges tinged yellowish, lower underparts yellowish. **Voice** Song, 1–3 descending "seet" notes followed by high fast bubbly descending series of c. 25–30 notes/2.5 seconds. **SS** ♀ brighter than Forest Elaenia. **TN** Usually includes Choco forms as single species.

Choco Grey Elaenia *Myiopagis parambae* `LC`
Elenia Gris del Chocó
Uncommon resident.

 L 13 cm (5"). Race *parambae*. Humid and wet lowland forest. To 1000 m. **ID** ♀ has white coronal patch like ♂, otherwise like Amazonian birds (previous page) differing only in minor shades. **Voice** Song recalls Amazonian Grey Elaenia but shorter (c. 8–20 notes), with up to four well-spaced initial notes. **SS** ♀ very like Foothill Elaenia; Forest Elaenia. **TN** Species status unresolved.

parambae

♂

♀

Foothill Elaenia *Myiopagis olallai* `LC`
Elenia de Piedemonte
Status uncertain (disjunct distribution).

 L 12.2 cm (4.8"). Races *coopmansi*[A], *incognita*[B], *olallai*[C]. Moist and humid premontane forest, borders. 900–1500 m. **ID** Above olive, crown greyish, concealed white crown patch, pale yellow wingbars, throat white, rest of underparts yellow, breast tinged olive. **Voice** Song, c. 2–4 introductory notes followed by a fast (14 notes/second) rising trill (c. 2 seconds), reverse of both Grey Elaenias (above). **SS** Remarkably like ♀ Choco Grey Elaenia but generally at higher elevations; Forest Elaenia. **TN** Recently described (2000) 'cryptic' species.

olallai

Forest Elaenia *Myiopagis gaimardii* `LC`
Elenia Selvática
Common resident.

 L 13.2 cm (5.2"). Races *macilvainii*[A], *bogotensis*[B], *guianensis*[C]. Dry to humid forest, old second growth. To 1100 m. Singles or pairs perch semi-erect, in mid-levels or higher. Inconspicuous but vocal (worth learning song), often with mixed flocks. **ID** Easily confused. Base of mandible pinkish, short indistinct whitish eyeline, unkempt somewhat grizzled greyish face, concealed white coronal stripe, wingbars dull yellowish, breast pale yellowish clouded and vaguely streaked olive, belly pale yellow. **Voice** Advertising song, brief "pil'dwEET!", the second note sharply rising; dawn song more complex.

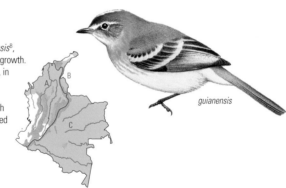

guianensis

Yellow-crowned Elaenia *Myiopagis flavivertex* `LC`
Elenia Coroniamarilla
Local resident (few records, but probably overlooked).

 **L** 12.7 cm (5"). Monotypic. Undergrowth in *várzea* forest, swampy areas, often near or over water. To 300 m. Singles, 1–6 m up, confiding. **ID** Much like Forest Elaenia (including wingbars, pinkish base of bill) but concealed crown patch yellow (not white), overall darker, more greyish olive, especially below, no breast streaking. **Voice** Best located by voice. Song, at long intervals (hard to track down), low-pitched (2–4 kHz) hoarse explosive "PEEr, PEE-JE-jew", first note lower, rest slightly higher-pitched, piercing, and often accelerating.

Greenish Elaenia *Myiopagis viridicata* `LC`
Elenia Verdosa

Ten subspecies in two subspecies groups; one in Colombia.

Greenish Elaenia *Myiopagis (viridicata) viridicata*
Fairly common resident; also austral and Central American migrants (?).
L 13.2 cm (5.2"). Races *accola*[A], *pallens*[B], *zuliae*[C], *restricta*[D] (valid records?), *implacens*[E]. Scattered old records E of Andes need confirmation. Dry to moist forest, dry scrub, plantations. To 1200 m. Singles, sometimes with mixed flocks, mid-levels or lower. **ID** Resembles commoner Forest Elaenia but no wingbars, cleaner face (not grizzled) and concealed crown patch yellow (not white); also by voice, drier habitat, lower strata in vegetation. **Voice** Commonest call, harsh, buzzy "jeeeet!" or "skzeet!"; dawn song repeated "peer-ee...".

zuliae

Yellow Tyrannulet *Capsiempis flaveola* `LC`
Tiranuelo Amarillo
Fairly common resident.

L 11.4 cm (4.5"). Races *leucophrys*[A], *cerula*[B], *magnirostris*[C]. Shrubby borders of dry to humid forest, overgrown clearings, bamboo (Putumayo and Caquetá); curiously local (?) E of Andes. To 1300 m. Sedentary pairs or families, fairly low, inconspicuous but vigorously defend small territories. Not with mixed flocks. **ID** Above olive-yellow, white to yellowish-white supercilium, yellowish wingbars, bright yellow underparts. **Voice** Lively rhythmic duet "pít'ti'keek" ("pretty'cake"), repeated rapidly by pair members; soft nasal toad-like trill "trrrrrrrrrr".

cerula

leucophrys

Genus *Phyllomyias* A confusing genus; bill short, tail generally not cocked; perch semi-erect, some frequently wing-lift, and several show dark ear-coverts crescent. Hover-glean, sally or flit up to foliage.

White-fronted Tyrannulet *Phyllomyias zeledoni* `LC`
Tiranuelo de Zeledón

Five subspecies in two subspecies groups; one in Colombia.

leucogonys

White-fronted Tyrannulet *Phyllomyias (zeledoni) leucogonys*
Rare and local resident.
L 11.4 cm (4.5"). Races *wetmorei*[A], *leucogonys*[B]. Canopy and borders of humid forest, older second growth. 500–1900 m. Singles, mid-levels or higher, sluggish; sometimes with mixed flocks. **ID** Eyes pale orange-yellow, short stout bill, narrow white forehead (frontlet) extends back to eyes, base of mandible pinkish, head grey (no dark ear-coverts patch), pale yellowish wingbars, whitish throat. **Voice** Song, 8–10 high leisurely buzzy notes "PEEza, PEEza..." (c. 2 notes/second), forceful. Call, high (6.5–7.5 kHz) thin rising-falling "sEEa". **SS** Easily confused; compare other *Phyllomyias*, also *Tolmomyias* (p. 370), *Zimmerius* (p. 379) and *Pogonotriccus* (p. 366). **TN** Often regarded as a race of Rough-legged Tyrannulet *P. burmeisteri*.

Sooty-headed Tyrannulet *Phyllomyias griseiceps* `LC`
Tiranuelo Cabecigrís
Common resident.

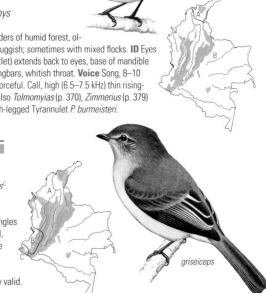
L 11 cm (4.3"). Races *cristatus*[A], *caucae*[B], *griseiceps*[C]. Borders of moist to humid forest, second growth, plantations, clearings; mainly foothills or higher. To 1800 m. Inconspicuous, non-forest tyrannulet; singles or pairs, at various heights, seldom with mixed flocks. **ID** Tiny bill, dark eyes; best identified by voice, lack of obvious wingbars, pale edgings mainly on tertials. **Voice** Often noted by voice. Song, snappy rhythmic "whit!, wheet-wheet-wheéu", with minor geographical variation. **TN** Races *caucae* and *cristatus* doubtfully valid.

griseiceps

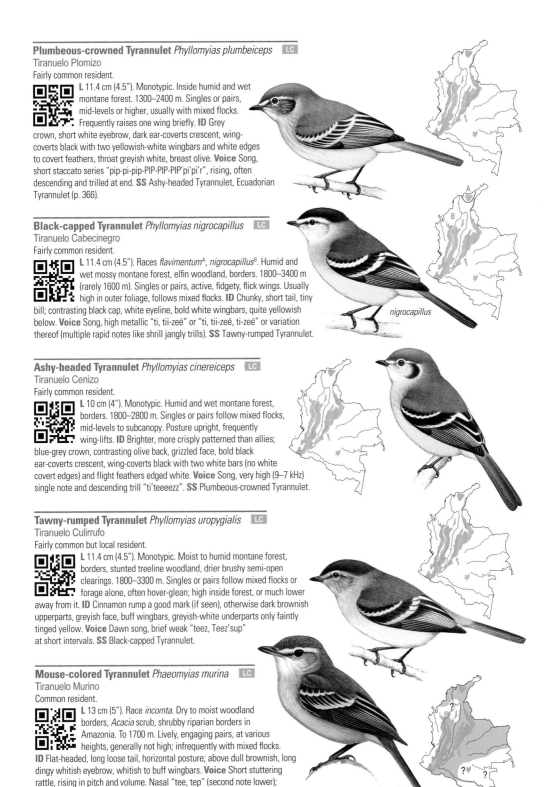

Plumbeous-crowned Tyrannulet *Phyllomyias plumbeiceps* LC
Tiranuelo Plomizo
Fairly common resident.

L 11.4 cm (4.5"). Monotypic. Inside humid and wet montane forest. 1300–2400 m. Singles or pairs, mid-levels or higher, usually with mixed flocks. Frequently raises one wing briefly. **ID** Grey crown, short white eyebrow, dark ear-coverts crescent, wing-coverts black with two yellowish-white wingbars and white edges to covert feathers, throat greyish white, breast olive. **Voice** Song, short staccato series "pip-pi-pip-PIP-PIP-PIP'pi'pi'r", rising, often descending and trilled at end. **SS** Ashy-headed Tyrannulet, Ecuadorian Tyrannulet (p. 366).

Black-capped Tyrannulet *Phyllomyias nigrocapillus* LC
Tiranuelo Cabecinegro
Fairly common resident.

L 11.4 cm (4.5"). Races *flavimentum*[A], *nigrocapillus*[B]. Humid and wet mossy montane forest, elfin woodland, borders. 1800–3400 m (rarely 1600 m). Singles or pairs, active, fidgety, flick wings. Usually high in outer foliage, follows mixed flocks. **ID** Chunky, short tail, tiny bill; contrasting black cap, white eyeline, bold white wingbars, quite yellowish below. **Voice** Song, high metallic "ti, tii-zeé" or "ti, tii-zeé, ti-zeé" or variation thereof (multiple rapid notes like shrill jangly trills). **SS** Tawny-rumped Tyrannulet.

nigrocapillus

Ashy-headed Tyrannulet *Phyllomyias cinereiceps* LC
Tiranuelo Cenizo
Fairly common resident.

L 10 cm (4"). Monotypic. Humid and wet montane forest, borders. 1800–2800 m. Singles or pairs follow mixed flocks, mid-levels to subcanopy. Posture upright, frequently wing-lifts. **ID** Brighter, more crisply patterned than allies; blue-grey crown, contrasting olive back, grizzled face, bold black ear-coverts crescent, wing-coverts black with two white bars (no white covert edges) and flight feathers edged white. **Voice** Song, very high (9–7 kHz) single note and descending trill "ti'teeeezz". **SS** Plumbeous-crowned Tyrannulet.

Tawny-rumped Tyrannulet *Phyllomyias uropygialis* LC
Tiranuelo Culirrufo
Fairly common but local resident.

L 11.4 cm (4.5"). Monotypic. Moist to humid montane forest, borders, stunted treeline woodland, drier brushy semi-open clearings. 1800–3300 m. Singles or pairs follow mixed flocks or forage alone, often hover-glean; high inside forest, or much lower away from it. **ID** Cinnamon rump a good mark (if seen), otherwise dull brownish upperparts, greyish face, buff wingbars, greyish-white underparts only faintly tinged yellow. **Voice** Dawn song, brief weak "teez, Teez'sup" at short intervals. **SS** Black-capped Tyrannulet.

Mouse-colored Tyrannulet *Phaeomyias murina* LC
Tiranuelo Murino
Common resident.

L 13 cm (5"). Race *incomta*. Dry to moist woodland borders, *Acacia* scrub, shrubby riparian borders in Amazonia. To 1700 m. Lively, engaging pairs, at various heights, generally not high; infrequently with mixed flocks. **ID** Flat-headed, long loose tail, horizontal posture; above dull brownish, long dingy whitish eyebrow, whitish to buff wingbars. **Voice** Short stuttering rattle, rising in pitch and volume. Nasal "tee, tep" (second note lower); complex dawn song, with occasional duets. **SS** Drab, distinctive features subtle; focus on shape, plumage and voice.

incomta

Genus *Mecocerculus* Andean genus, with flattish bill, bold wingbars and supercilium. Tail length and behaviour vary; posture horizontal to semi-erect. Pairs, families and groups of 6–8, all regularly with mixed flocks.

White-tailed Tyrannulet *Mecocerculus poecilocercus* LC
Tiranuelo Coliblanco
Uncommon resident.

L 11.4 cm (4.5"). Monotypic. Subcanopy and canopy of humid and wet montane forest, old second growth. 1600–2800 m. Small, active, almost parulid-like; horizontal posture. **ID** Grey crown, white eyestripe, yellowish-white wingbars and edges, pale yellow rump (hard to see), outer two tail feathers mostly white (undertail looks white). **Voice** Song, high (6–7 kHz) leisurely descending "seeeit, pseeit, pseeit", occasionally more notes. Call, high rising "pseet". **SS** White-banded Tyrannulet (generally at higher elevations).

White-banded Tyrannulet *Mecocerculus stictopterus* LC
Tiranuelo Colilargo
Common resident.

L 13 cm (5"). Race *stictopterus*. Humid and wet montane forest, stunted treeline woodland. 1800–3600 m. Pairs or groups of half dozen or more follow mixed flocks. Active, low to high, glean and sally short distances to foliage. **ID** Trim, clean-cut; bold white eyebrows and wingbars, grey crown. **Voice** Sharp staccato notes. Bubbly rising-falling trill with sharp notes or trills preceding or following. Call, buzzy rising "pzeet". **SS** White-tailed Tyrannulet (lower elevations, more inside forest).

stictopterus

White-throated Tyrannulet *Mecocerculus leucophrys* LC
Tiranuelo Gorgiblanco
Common resident.

L 14.7 cm (5.8"). Races *notatus*[A], *setophagoides*[B], *montensis*[C], *rufomarginatus*[D]. Humid and wet montane forest, elfin woodland, borders. 2600–3600 m. Characteristic species of high montane mixed flocks. Confiding pairs or groups, perch semi-erect, flit to foliage, glean parulid-like and hang upside-down. Mid-levels or higher, often low at borders. **ID** Notable geographical variation. Puffy white throat, long expressive droopy tail flicked up. **Voice** Vocal, sputtering "pri'i'it", "pur'r'r'r'-prit" and "pit-pit-pit"; at dawn repetitive energetic "ch'd'dik, ch'd'dik, ch'd'dik, chew". **TN** Plumage and behaviour atypical of genus; race *montensis* often merged with *nigriceps*.

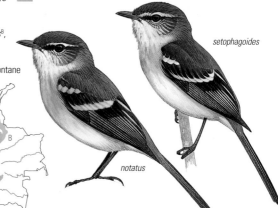

setophagoides

notatus

Sulphur-bellied Tyrannulet *Mecocerculus minor* LC
Tiranuelo Azufrado
Uncommon and local resident.

L 12 cm (4.7"). Monotypic. Humid and wet montane forest, especially borders, broken, patchy or younger woodland. 1600–2700 m (locally 1100 m). Singles or pairs, alone or with mixed flocks; mid-levels to canopy. **ID** Greyish crown, white eyestripe, two broad buff wingbars, yellow underparts, breast tinged olive. **Voice** Call, low coarse rapid "stu'du'du"; higher, squeakier, slightly descending "squee-ke-ke-ke-qua, skip!". **SS** Ecuadorian Tyrannulet (p. 366).

Tufted Tit-tyrant *Anairetes parulus* LC
Cachudito Paramuno

Fairly common resident.

 L 11 cm (4.3"). Race *aequatorialis*. Bushy borders of dry to humid upper montane woodland, shrubby *páramo*. 2400–3600 m. Inconspicuous pairs actively work through tops of dense shrubs, sometimes with mixed flocks; glean, flutter and sally in foliage. **ID** Tiny and heavily streaked, pale eyes, thin recurved crest, white wingbars. **Voice** Short medium-pitched (4–5 kHz) chattering or bubbly trills and chittering notes; at dawn or during day, thin "sqee'dit". **SS** Agile Tit-tyrant.

Bearded Tachuri *Polystictus pectoralis* NT
Tachuri Barbado VU

Very local resident.

 L 10 cm (4"). Races *bogotensis*[A] (extinct; formerly Sabana de Bogotá and upper Dagua Valley), *brevipennis*[B]. Tall grass or grass with scattered shrubs. To 2600 m. Inconspicuous, flushes low in erratic or zigzag manner, then drops from view. Pair formation unconfirmed. Threatened by fires, loss of grassland habitat. **ID** Tiny, breast and sides buff. ♂ blackish head, throat and shaggy crest flecked white. ♀ crown greyish streaked black. **Voice** Soft "pee-wee". ♂ display song (Brazil) as flies up, 4–5 quick notes rising up scale and low wing-buzz "p'pe'te'te'brrrrr"; or without wing buzz from perch.

Subtropical Doradito *Pseudocolopteryx acutipennis* LC
Doradito Lagunero CR

Very local and easily overlooked resident.

 L 10.5 cm (4"). Monotypic. Resident (no known austral migrants). Marshes, reeds (*Scirpus, Typha*), wet shrubby pastures. 1500–3000 m. Loose colonies; inconspicuous, perch up on reeds for brief periods, otherwise stay hidden. **ID** Small, thin black bill, above olive, below bright yellow, indistinct olive wingbars. **Voice** Rather quiet. Display song 3–4 rough scratchy or buzzy notes, and louder mechanical wing-whirring "czzek, czzek...plurrrp". **SS** ♀ American Yellow Warbler (p. 488).

Torrent Tyrannulet *Serpophaga cinerea* LC
Tiranuelo Salta-arroyo

Common resident.

 L 11.2 cm (4.4"). Race *cinerea*. Boulder-filled montane streams. 400–3200 m (rarely 100 m). Sprightly, alert pairs, perch on boulders in streams, sally in small circles to rock surface or air, occasionally venture into nearby pastures. **ID** Unmistakable. Plump, short-tailed; crown, sides of head, wings and tail black, otherwise pale grey to whitish. **Voice** Loud "seek" audible above stream noise. Song, thin, high "seek! ti'ti'ti'ti'ti".

River Tyrannulet *Serpophaga hypoleuca* LC
Tiranuelo Ribereño

Local resident.

 L 10.7 cm (4.2"). Races *venezuelana*[A], *hypoleuca*[B]. Early successional scrub (*Tessaria, Salix*) and river edges on Amazonian and Orinocan river islands and riverbanks; near water in seasonally flooded scrub, thorny brush and weeds in *llanos* (likely in Arauca, Vichada). To 100 m. Scattered pairs or trios, active, restless, gnatcatcher-like but longish tail not cocked. 0.3–5 m up in shrubs. **ID** Small, slender; blackish cap to below eyes, flat crest conceals white coronal stripe, mostly white below. **Voice** Thin weak "see-blik!"; "tsit"; chattering duet "p'dit p'dit'p'dit" and bubbly "pik-up, pik-up..."; sputtering rattle ending in sharp "chit" notes.

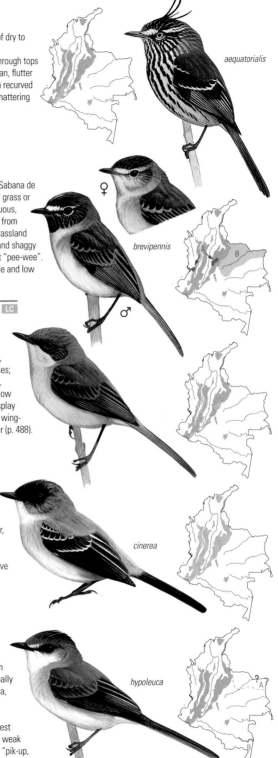

aequatorialis

♀

brevipennis

♂

cinerea

hypoleuca

391

Agile Tit-tyrant *Uromyias agilis* LC
Cachudito Rabilargo
Fairly common resident.

 L 13 cm (5"). Monotypic. Humid upper montane forest, borders, elfin forest, often in *Chusquea* bamboo. 2500–3500 m. Cute pairs or small parties, eye level to canopy of smaller trees, follow mixed flocks, perch upright, tail down, and actively flit to foliage. **ID** Flat crest, white eyebrows, heavily streaked, dark eyes, no wingbars. **Voice** Weak contact notes and trills. Song, exuberant jumble of trills and sharp notes. **SS** Tufted Tit-Tyrant. **TN** Formerly in genus *Anairetes*.

Short-tailed Field-tyrant *Muscigralla brevicauda* LC
Dormilona Colicorta
Rare visitor (few records).

 L 11.4 cm (4.5"). Monotypic. Open dry areas with or without scattered bushes. To 100 m. Terrestrial, runs rapidly, pauses, stands erect on long 'stilt' legs; occasionally in a bush. **ID** Unmistakable: extremely short tail (looks tailless), white supraloral, rufous rump, pale underparts, belly tinged yellowish. **Voice** Song (in air or perched), "chit" notes and short (mechanical?) buzz.

Genus *Attila* Large head with strong hooked bill. Vocal but notably inconspicuous. Wooded regions, especially in Amazonia.

Cinnamon Attila *Attila cinnamomeus* LC
Atila Acanelado
Locally common resident.

 L 19.8 cm (7.8"). Monotypic. Swamp and *várzea* forest, borders of oxbows, low-lying areas. To 600 m. Singles, mid-levels, not with mixed flocks. Sluggish, holds tail down, sometimes unsuspicious. **ID** Bill black, above rufous, paler below, contrasting blackish wings. **Voice** Vocal. Dawn song, rising whistled, "weery, weery, weery weery". Also (dawn or later), long drowsy whistled "pu-puEEEeeeear", rising quickly, slowly descending, raptor-like, over and over. **SS** Bright-rumped Attila.

Ochraceous Attila *Attila torridus* VU
Atila Ocráceo VU
Uncommon resident.

L 20 cm (8"). Monotypic. Moist to humid forest borders, second growth, plantations. To 200 m (to 1500 m, Ecuador). Singles, less often pairs, usually noted first by voice, at mid-levels or higher. **ID** Above cinnamon, rump yellowish, contrasting blackish wings, below ochraceous-yellow. **Voice** Call, slow whistled "wueEEer" (raptor-like). Song, variable length (often long) series of whistled "weep" notes, on same pitch (c. 2.5 kHz), first note or two hesitant, last descending. **SS** Bright-rumped Attila (rufous morph), other *Attila*.

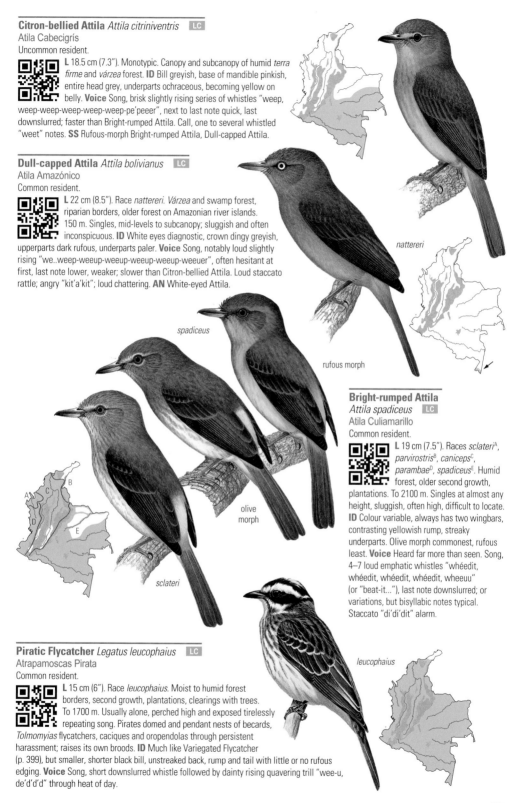

Citron-bellied Attila *Attila citriniventris* LC
Atila Cabecigrís
Uncommon resident.

L 18.5 cm (7.3"). Monotypic. Canopy and subcanopy of humid *terra firme* and *várzea* forest. **ID** Bill greyish, base of mandible pinkish, entire head grey, underparts ochraceous, becoming yellow on belly. **Voice** Song, brisk slightly rising series of whistles "weep, weep-weep-weep-weep-weep-pe'peeer", next to last note quick, last downslurred; faster than Bright-rumped Attila. Call, one to several whistled "weet" notes. **SS** Rufous-morph Bright-rumped Attila, Dull-capped Attila.

Dull-capped Attila *Attila bolivianus* LC
Atila Amazónico
Common resident.

L 22 cm (8.5"). Race *nattereri*. *Várzea* and swamp forest, riparian borders, older forest on Amazonian river islands. 150 m. Singles, mid-levels to subcanopy; sluggish and often inconspicuous. **ID** White eyes diagnostic, crown dingy greyish, upperparts dark rufous, underparts paler. **Voice** Song, notably loud slightly rising "we..weep-weeup-weeup-weeup-weeup-weeuer", often hesitant at first, last note lower, weaker; slower than Citron-bellied Attila. Loud staccato rattle; angry "kit'a'kit"; loud chattering. **AN** White-eyed Attila.

nattereri

spadiceus

rufous morph

Bright-rumped Attila
Attila spadiceus LC
Atila Culiamarillo
Common resident.

L 19 cm (7.5"). Races *sclateri*[A], *parvirostris*[B], *caniceps*[C], *parambae*[D], *spadiceus*[E]. Humid forest, older second growth, plantations. To 2100 m. Singles at almost any height, sluggish, often high, difficult to locate. **ID** Colour variable, always has two wingbars, contrasting yellowish rump, streaky underparts. Olive morph commonest, rufous least. **Voice** Heard far more than seen. Song, 4–7 loud emphatic whistles "whéedit, whéedit, whéedit, whéedit, wheeuu" (or "beat-it..."), last note downslurred; or variations, but bisyllabic notes typical. Staccato "di'di'dit" alarm.

olive morph

sclateri

Piratic Flycatcher *Legatus leucophaius* LC
Atrapamoscas Pirata
Common resident.

L 15 cm (6"). Race *leucophaius*. Moist to humid forest borders, second growth, plantations, clearings with trees. To 1700 m. Usually alone, perched high and exposed tirelessly repeating song. Pirates domed and pendant nests of becards, *Tolmomyias* flycatchers, caciques and oropendolas through persistent harassment; raises its own broods. **ID** Much like Variegated Flycatcher (p. 399), but smaller, shorter black bill, unstreaked back, rump and tail with little or no rufous edging. **Voice** Song, short downslurred whistle followed by dainty rising quavering trill "wee-u, de'd'd'd" through heat of day.

leucophaius

Genus *Ramphotrigon* Despite name, bill not as wide as *Rhynchocyclus* flatbills or *Tolmomyias* flycatchers. Distinctive vocalizations. Forest interior; tree-cavity nesters.

Large-headed Flatbill *Ramphotrigon megacephalum* `LC`
Picoplano Cabezón
Uncommon resident (disjunct distribution).

 L 13.5 cm (5.3"). Races *venezuelense*[A], *pectorale*[B]. *Guadua* bamboo especially in or near foothill forest. To 1300 m (upper Magdalena Valley). Solitary, quiet and inconspicuous; usually noted first by voice. Perches upright, fairly low. Seldom with mixed flocks. **ID** Short white eyebrow widest over lores, white lower eye-arc, ochraceous wingbars, underparts yellowish and vaguely streaked. **Voice** Song, soft whistled "whée-whoo" (inhale, exhale), first note slightly higher. **SS** Voice and bamboo habitat key.

venezuelense

Rufous-tailed Flatbill *Ramphotrigon ruficauda* `LC`
Picoplano Colirrufo
Fairly common resident.

 L 16 cm (6.3"). Monotypic. Relatively open mid-levels in humid *terra firme* and *várzea* forest, including on sandy soils. To 600 m. Sedentary singles or pairs, sluggish, sometimes around mixed flocks but doesn't follow them. **ID** Whitish eyeline and eye-arcs, flight feathers mostly rufous, tail all rufous. **Voice** Song, sporadically during day, melancholy slurred, low-pitched whistle, gradually rises, slight dip or wobble in middle, then last briefer part flat or descending: "wuuuuueeeaauuu".

Dusky-tailed Flatbill *Ramphotrigon fuscicauda* `LC`
Picoplano Alibarrado
Rare resident (once, W Putumayo, 1969).

 L 16 cm (6.3"). Monotypic. Humid lowland forest, especially low-lying areas with dense understorey and *Guadua* bamboo. To 600 m. Mid-levels or lower, inconspicuous and difficult to see, even with playback. **ID** Broken white eye-ring, cinnamon-rufous wingbars and edges, tail edged rufous, throat and breast streaked olive and yellow. **Voice** Song, loud up-down slurred whistle, chatter and several quick short descending whistles slowing at end: "WHEEr'tttt'PEER-peer-peer, peeu". Single slurred falling-rising whistle "PEEerweEEP".

Great Kiskadee *Pitangus sulphuratus* `LC`
Bichofué
Common resident.

 L 22 cm (8.5"). Races *rufipennis*[A], *caucensis*[B], *trinitatis*[C] (distribution?), *sulphuratus*[D]. Ubiquitous around habitations, urban areas, clearings, lake and river borders in forested areas (except Pacific coast where recently found and local). To 2600 m. Needs no introduction; noisy, brash, conspicuously public character everywhere. Forages on wide array of food. **ID** Broad-shouldered and short-tailed; strong bill, white band encircles head, and wing and tail feathers edged rufous (less on *trinitatis*, *caucensis*). **Voice** Perhaps most widely recognized voice in the country; loud exuberant "Cristofué" or "KISS-ka-DEE", or briefer "ka-DEE!". **SS** Boat-billed Flycatcher.

sulphuratus

rufipennis

Lesser Kiskadee *Philohydor lictor* LC
Bichofué Chico

Common resident (E of Andes), fewer W of Andes.

 L 18 cm (7"). Races *panamense*[A], *lictor*[B]. Rarely far from water. Wooded lagoons, borders of sluggish streams, ponds, mangroves. To 500 m. Quieter, more sedate than Great Kiskadee. Pairs or families always perch low over or near water. **ID** Told by long slender bill and voice; plumage like numerous other 'look-alike' flycatchers. **Voice** Commonest call (unlike Great Kiskadee) wheezy "SQUEEZE'ME, Ba'by!" or briefer "SQUEEZE, me!" (or "SQUEE-be"); greet with excited "ca-déde" fluttering wings and ruffing crown. **SS** Rusty-margined Flycatcher (p. 397). **TN** Sometimes placed in *Pitangus*.

lictor

Cattle Tyrant *Machetornis rixosa* LC
Sirirí Bueyero

Common resident (expanding range).

 L 19 cm (7.5"). Races *flavigularis*[A], *obscurodorsalis*[B]. Drier semi-open terrain, cattle pastures, ranch buildings, lawns, urban parks. To 2000 m (recorded 3200 m). Conspicuous, terrestrial when foraging, otherwise perches on bushes, buildings, rooftops; ride backs of cattle, horses, capybaras, drop to ground for arthropods. **ID** Red eyes, long legs, sandy upperparts, concealed flame crown patch. **Voice** Calls, thin, squeaky; dawn song short trilled "t'te'te'ree" (recalls Tropical Kingbird but higher-pitched).

flavigularis

Sulphury Flycatcher *Tyrannopsis sulphurea* LC
Sirirí Colimocho

Local and uncommon resident.

 L 20 cm (8"). Monotypic. Associated with *Mauritia* palms. To 500 m. Solitary pairs perch erect, quiet and inconspicuous in *Mauritia*; sally to air or fly off to hover-glean small fruit. **ID** Except voice, deceptively like Tropical Kingbird but smaller, foreparts darker, bill shorter, and smudged greyish-brown area surrounds white throat. **Voice** At long intervals, abrupt strident screech "zhrEEEEEEEE!, zhr-zhrEEEEEEEE!" by pairs (recalls electric bug-zapper). Song, similar high blurred trills "zhr'dek... zhr'r'r'e'k...zhr'dek'dek...", like pulses of electric energy.

Boat-billed Flycatcher *Megarynchus pitangua* LC
Bichofué Picudo

 Six subspecies in three subspecies groups; two in Colombia.

Northern Boat-billed Flycatcher *Megarynchus (pitangua) mexicanus*
Common resident.

L 23 cm (9"). Race *mexicanus*. **ID** Very like southern *pitangua* race but upperparts brighter more greenish olive (less brownish olive), no rufous edges to flight feathers. **Voice** Complaining calls differ only slightly from southern *pitangua*, being longer, but individual notes briefer and faster. Rattle call flatter, with longer emphasized note at end. **TN** Taxonomic implications of differences need evaluation.

mexicanus

395

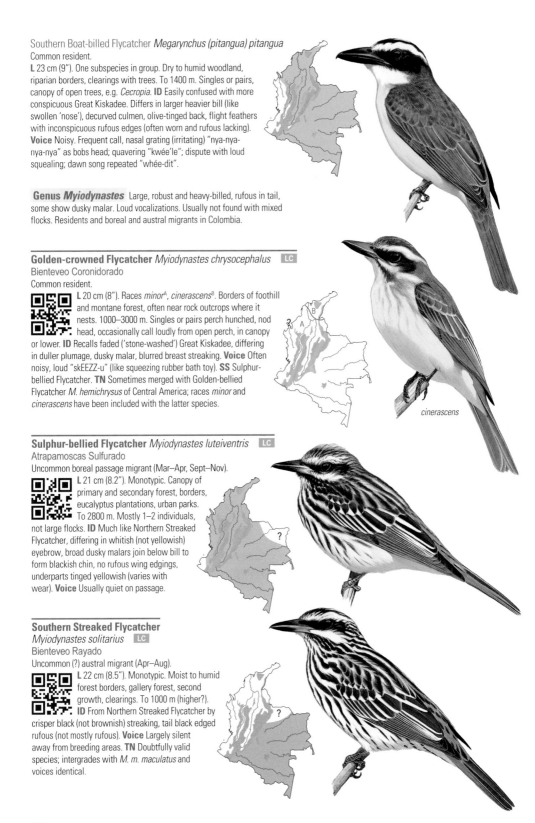

Southern Boat-billed Flycatcher *Megarynchus (pitangua) pitangua*
Common resident.
L 23 cm (9"). One subspecies in group. Dry to humid woodland,
riparian borders, clearings with trees. To 1400 m. Singles or pairs,
canopy of open trees, e.g. *Cecropia*. **ID** Easily confused with more
conspicuous Great Kiskadee. Differs in larger heavier bill (like
swollen 'nose'), decurved culmen, olive-tinged back, flight feathers
with inconspicuous rufous edges (often worn and rufous lacking).
Voice Noisy. Frequent call, nasal grating (irritating) "nya-nya-
nya-nya" as bobs head; quavering "kwée'le"; dispute with loud
squealing; dawn song repeated "whée-dit".

Genus *Myiodynastes* Large, robust and heavy-billed, rufous in tail,
some show dusky malar. Loud vocalizations. Usually not found with mixed
flocks. Residents and boreal and austral migrants in Colombia.

Golden-crowned Flycatcher *Myiodynastes chrysocephalus* `LC`
Bienteveo Coronidorado
Common resident.
L 20 cm (8"). Races *minor*[A], *cinerascens*[B]. Borders of foothill
and montane forest, often near rock outcrops where it
nests. 1000–3000 m. Singles or pairs perch hunched, nod
head, occasionally call loudly from open perch, in canopy
or lower. **ID** Recalls faded ('stone-washed') Great Kiskadee, differing
in duller plumage, dusky malar, blurred breast streaking. **Voice** Often
noisy, loud "skEEZZ-u" (like squeezing rubber bath toy). **SS** Sulphur-
bellied Flycatcher. **TN** Sometimes merged with Golden-bellied
Flycatcher *M. hemichrysus* of Central America; races *minor* and
cinerascens have been included with the latter species.

cinerascens

Sulphur-bellied Flycatcher *Myiodynastes luteiventris* `LC`
Atrapamoscas Sulfurado
Uncommon boreal passage migrant (Mar–Apr, Sept–Nov).
L 21 cm (8.2"). Monotypic. Canopy of
primary and secondary forest, borders,
eucalyptus plantations, urban parks.
To 2800 m. Mostly 1–2 individuals,
not large flocks. **ID** Much like Northern Streaked
Flycatcher, differing in whitish (not yellowish)
eyebrow, broad dusky malars join below bill to
form blackish chin, no rufous wing edgings,
underparts tinged yellowish (varies with
wear). **Voice** Usually quiet on passage.

Southern Streaked Flycatcher
Myiodynastes solitarius `LC`
Bienteveo Rayado
Uncommon (?) austral migrant (Apr–Aug).
L 22 cm (8.5"). Monotypic. Moist to humid
forest borders, gallery forest, second
growth, clearings. To 1000 m (higher?).
ID From Northern Streaked Flycatcher by
crisper black (not brownish) streaking, tail black edged
rufous (not mostly rufous). **Voice** Largely silent
away from breeding areas. **TN** Doubtfully valid
species; intergrades with *M. m. maculatus* and
voices identical.

Northern Streaked Flycatcher
Myiodynastes maculatus
Sirirí Rayado
Common resident.

 L 22 cm (8.5"). Races *difficilis*[A], *nobilis*[B], *chapmani*[C], *insolens* (probable migrant, distribution unknown, from N Central America, Sept–Feb?). Dry to humid woodland, borders, second growth, clearings. To 1600 m. Singles or pairs, on open branches, mid-levels or higher; sometimes with mixed flocks. **ID** Forehead and eyebrow tinged yellowish, streaking blurred (brownish, not crisp blackish), tail mostly rufous. **Voice** Loud "squEE-zik!"; sharp "teep!"; dawn song rapid rhythmic "WEET, wiggle-your-feet!" repeatedly. **SS** Southern Streaked Flycatcher. **TN** Usually includes austral migrant *solitarius*.

Genus *Myiozetetes* Confusing 'lookalikes' of kiskadees but smaller, bill much shorter, and eyebrows do not encircle crown. Common and conspicuous (except Dusky-chested Flycatcher). Sally to air or ground, hover-glean or employ sally strikes to foliage; take insects and fruit. Large messy roofed nests with side entrances, often sited near wasp nests.

Rusty-margined Flycatcher *Myiozetetes cayanensis*
Suelda Crestinegra
Common resident.

 L 18 cm (7"). Races *hellmayri*[A], *rufipennis*[B]. Moist to humid forest borders, semi-open areas, gardens; absent from most of Amazonia. To 2200 m. Lively energetic pairs and families perch in open atop shrubs or trees. **ID** Often confused with Social Flycatcher but has blackish (not dull dusky) cheeks, brownish (not olive) tone to back, no obvious wingbars, weak wing-covert edgings, overall brighter plumage, sometimes by rufous primary edges (but juv Social has buff-rufous edges). **Voice** Most easily identified from Social Flycatcher by voice: long melancholy whining "peeeeeea" or "wheeeeeea"; duet and greet with exuberant "puuuureeeEET-EET-EET!" and "tuWEET, cheat! cheat! cheat!".

Social Flycatcher *Myiozetetes similis*
Suelda Social
Uncommon resident (W of Andes), commoner in E.

 L 18 cm (7"). Races *columbianus*[A], *similis*[B]. Drier wooded borders, shrubby clearings W of Andes (where seasonal in some areas), forest borders, river margins, gardens E of Andes. To 1300 m. **ID** Very like Rusty-margined Flycatcher (see above), even concealed coronal patches barely differ (red-orange in Social, yellow-orange in Rusty-margined). **Voice** Commonest call, dry "chiit", often doubled or in rapid series; pairs duet or greet with high rolling "chit't't't't't't" in high-energy bursts, mixed with sharp notes.

Grey-capped Flycatcher
Myiozetetes granadensis
Suelda Cabecigrís
Common resident.

 L 17 cm. Races *occidentalis*[A], *obscurior*[B]. Shrubby humid forest borders, overgrown clearings, top of forest canopy. To 1200 m. Pairs or families perch low to high, always conspicuous. **ID** Grey head, whitish forehead extends to just over pale grey-brown eyes, dusky grey cheeks. **Voice** Noisy. Sharp "kip!"; "kip, kip, kip-it!" or variations, some calls recall Social Flycatcher but more nasal. **SS** Other *Myiozetetes* and allies have bolder head patterns. **TN** Racial distributions unclear.

difficilis

rufipennis

similis

obscurior

Dusky-chested Flycatcher *Myiozetetes luteiventris* LC
Sirirí Pechirrayado
Uncommon (overlooked?) resident.

L 15 cm (6"). Race *luteiventris*. Borders and top of humid forest canopy, treefall gaps. To 600 m. Not as conspicuous as other *Myiozetetes*; lacks bold head pattern. Pairs stay quite high, close together; not with mixed flocks. Sally to air, take fruit. **ID** Small, whitish throat faintly streaked grey, otherwise yellow below with blurred breast streaks. **Voice** Nasal meowing whining "neeeuw", softer "neea", rapid "neea-ne-wit!"; some calls resemble Grey-capped Flycatcher but more nasal, petulant. **SS** Sulphury Flycatcher.

luteiventris

Genus *Conopias* Resemble *Myiozetetes* but bill longer, eyebrow encircles crown and claw of middle toe unusually long (note habits). Nest in tree cavity or old oropendola nest.

White-ringed Flycatcher *Conopias albovittatus* LC
Suelda Aureolada
Fairly common resident.

L 16.5 cm (6.5"). Race *albovittatus*. Top of canopy and borders of wet forest, trees in clearings. To 900 m. Pairs or families typically stay high, stand on top of canopy leaves, sally to foliage or air; active around mixed flocks. **ID** Unlike *Myiozetetes*, white eyebrow broader, completely enclosing crown, no buff or rufous wing edges; voice differs. **Voice** Call, rattling trill "que-l'e'e'e'e'e", medium-high (4.5–5 kHz); thin squealing "squee'leeeeee".

albovittatus

Yellow-throated Flycatcher *Conopias parvus* LC
Suelda Gargantiamarilla
Fairly common resident.

L 16.5 cm (6.5"). Monotypic. To 400 m. Top of canopy and borders of humid forest in Amazonia, sandy soil forest in Vaupés/Guainía. Behaviour like White-ringed Flycatcher. **ID** Broad white eyebrow encircles head, and long bill. **Voice** Call, repeated bursts of rolling rattle-trills "tuwe'le'le'le'le", bubbly and lower-pitched than White-ringed Flycatcher. **SS** Social and Rusty-margined Flycatchers. **TN** Formerly a race of White-ringed Flycatcher.

Lemon-browed Flycatcher *Conopias cinchoneti* VU
Suelda Cejiamarilla
Fairly common (local?) resident.

L 16.5 cm (6.5"). Race *icterophrys*. Humid and wet foothill and montane forest, borders. 400–2200 m. Pairs, families or small groups, stand atop leaves in high canopy; call, move around restlessly, sally to foliage or air. Often with mixed flocks, ranges over large areas. **ID** Key marks are voice, long bill and bold yellow (not white) eyebrow encircling crown. **Voice** Call, loud high (5 kHz) tinny trills often given over and over. **SS** Rusty-margined Flycatcher.

icterophrys

White-bearded Flycatcher *Phelpsia inornata* `LC`
Suelda Simple
Local resident (*llanos*).

 L 18 cm (7"). Monotypic. Ranchland, around habitations, groves of trees, gallery forest. To 300 m. Pairs or families perch low to high, sally to air, foliage or ground. Quieter, less conspicuous than allies. **ID** Resembles Rusty-margined Flycatcher, but easily identified by large puffy-headed shape, puffed throat, and bill that seems too small; if in doubt listen to duet. **Voice** Sporadic morning duets, vigorous staccato "CHEE'ter, CHEE'ter...", up to 12 couplets accompanied by bowing and wing-flapping.

Variegated Flycatcher *Empidonomus varius* `LC`
Atrapamoscas Veteado

 Two subspecies in two subspecies groups; both in Colombia.

[Northern Variegated Flycatcher] *Empidonomus (varius) rufinus*
Hypothetical.

L 18 cm (7"). One subspecies in group. Habitat and behaviour as austral migrant form (below). Northern *rufinus* resident in Venezuela; no records in E Colombia but possible (breeder or seasonal). **ID** Like southern *varius* but duller, paler, less streaked below (some only vaguely streaked); bill, wing and tail measurements smaller. **Voice** Usually quiet; thin "zuree" or "zreeetee" (Guyana). **TN** Taxonomic status needs review.

Southern Variegated Flycatcher
Empidonomus (varius) varius
Fairly common austral migrant E of Andes, scarce Magdalena Valley (Apr–Sept).
L 19 cm (7.5"). One subspecies in group. Canopy and borders of humid lowland forest, gallery forest, urban parks. To 600 m. **ID** Basal half of mandible pinkish. Migrant and resident races both much like smaller Piratic Flycatcher (including concealed yellow crown patch) but larger, longer-tailed, back streaked, wing fringes brighter, rump and tail feathers broadly edged rufous, underparts streaking blacker and sharper. **Voice** Usually silent. **SS** Streaked Flycatchers (p. 396).

Crowned Slaty Flycatcher
Griseotyrannus aurantioatrocristatus `LC`
Atrapamoscas Coronidorado
Uncommon austral migrant (late Mar–late Oct).

 L 18 cm (7"). Race *aurantioatrocristatus*. Canopy and borders of lowland and foothill forest, tall trees in clearings; mainly E of Andes. To 900 m (occasional 2700 m). Solitary, perches in open treetops, sallying to air, returning to same perch. **ID** Plain, slender, flat-headed; above brown, crown black, semi-concealed yellow crown patch, narrow dusky mask, grey eyebrow and underparts. Juv belly tinged yellow. **Voice** Silent on non-breeding grounds. **TN** Often placed in genus *Empidonomus*.

aurantioatrocristatus

Genus *Tyrannus* Large and conspicuous, perch in open, often pugnacious; quintessential 'flycatching' behaviour (aerial hawkers). None occurs inside forest. Several are austral or boreal migrants.

Snowy-throated Kingbird *Tyrannus niveigularis* LC
Sirirí Sureño

Uncommon post-breeding migrant (from W Ecuador, Jul–Oct).

 L 19 cm (7.5"). Monotypic. Dry to humid wooded borders, clearings, second growth. To 500 m (rarely 1600 m). Singles, perch in open; may defend non-breeding feeding territory. **ID** Resembles Tropical Kingbird, but slightly smaller, back greyish (not olive), tail nearly square-tipped, throat pure white, chest pale grey, breast bright yellow (vs. greyish-white throat grading into olive chest). **Voice** Calls and trills thinner than Tropical Kingbird.

White-throated Kingbird *Tyrannus albogularis* LC
Sirirí Brasileño

Fairly common austral migrant (Apr–Sept).

 L 21 cm (8.2"). Monotypic. Second growth along or near Amazonian rivers; fewer along other large rivers. To 400 m. Perches in open, sallies to air; often with austral migrant Tropical Kingbirds. **ID** Easily overlooked. Like Tropical Kingbird (especially paler juv) but brighter, head paler grey (dusky mask contrasts strongly), back bright olive, throat pure white (not greyish) contrasting with bright yellow underparts (no olive wash on chest). **Voice** Higher and squeakier than Tropical Kingbird.

Tropical Kingbird *Tyrannus melancholicus* LC
Sirirí Común

Common resident (austral migrants, Jun–Aug, in Amazonia, poorly documented).

 L 22 cm (8.5"). Races *satrapa*ᴬ, *melancholicus*ᴮ. In all kinds of open or semi-open habitats including urban areas, dry to humid regions. To 1800 m (fewer 3100 m). Singles or pairs, perch conspicuously in open, sally to air in agile pursuit of insects, hover for small fruit. **ID** So numerous its shape, size and appearance should be memorized for comparison with other species. Head grey, mask dusky, back greyish olive, pale throat grades into olive-washed chest, notched tail. **Voice** Noisy; shrill twittering trills usually the first pre-dawn song.

melancholicus

Eastern Kingbird *Tyrannus tyrannus* LC
Sirirí Norteño

Common boreal passage migrant (mostly Sept–Nov, Feb–early May).

L 22 cm (8.5"). Monotypic. Forest and river borders, clearings, urban areas, and semi-open areas throughout. To 3200 m. Singles or flocks, sometimes large (500+), often migrating by day. Mostly frugivorous and timid during migration (unlike when breeding); regularly with migrating Fork-tailed Flycatchers in Amazonia. **ID** Black cap to below eyes, tail black broadly tipped white, and white underparts. **Voice** Usually quiet. **SS** Juv and moulting Fork-tailed Flycatchers.

Grey Kingbird *Tyrannus dominicensis* `LC`
Sirirí Gris
Common Caribbean migrant (Sept–Apr), a few year-round.

L 23 cm (9"). Race *dominicensis*. Drier open or semi-open habitats, ranchland. Breeds locally in *llanos*. To 1500 m (recorded 3000 m). Singles, pairs, occasionally small flocks; perch in open, sally to air. **ID** Large-headed, heavy black bill; above grey, black mask, wing-coverts and flight feathers edged white (no bars), below white. Juv rusty-edged wing-coverts and tail. **Voice** Shrill "pitch-chir'r'r'e". **SS** Eastern Kingbird, Fork-tailed Flycatcher.

Scissor-tailed Flycatcher
Tyrannus forficatus `LC`
Tijereta Rosada
Vagrant or rare boreal overshoot.

L ♂ 33 cm (13"), ♀ 29 cm (11.5"). Monotypic. Two published records: Santander (Jan 2010), NW Chocó (Dec 2018). Open or semi-open areas; perches in open. **ID** Pearl grey, whitish below, wings black edged white, long outer tail feathers white tipped black, salmon-red axillaries (in flight), orange-buff flanks. ♀ and juv duller, shorter-tailed. **Voice** Likely silent; nasal "kip". **SS** Fork-tailed Flycatcher.

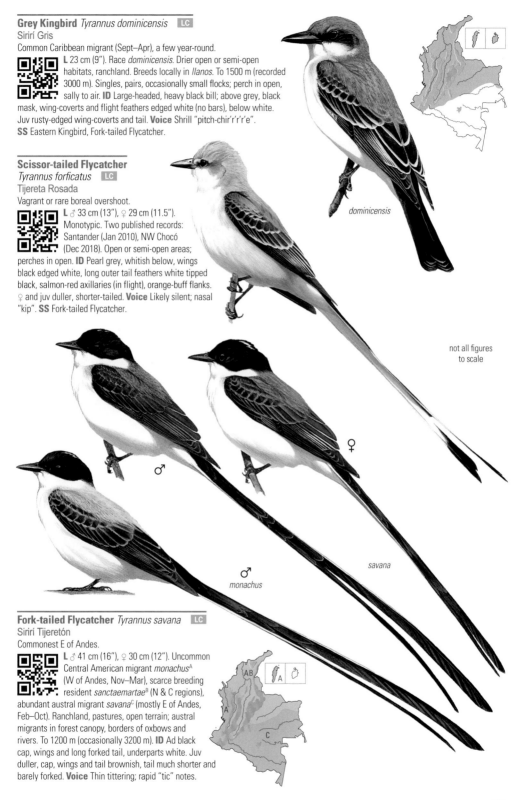

dominicensis

not all figures
to scale

♀

♂
monachus

♂

savana

Fork-tailed Flycatcher *Tyrannus savana* `LC`
Sirirí Tijeretón
Commonest E of Andes.

L ♂ 41 cm (16"), ♀ 30 cm (12"). Uncommon Central American migrant *monachus*[A] (W of Andes, Nov–Mar), scarce breeding resident *sanctaemartae*[B] (N & C regions), abundant austral migrant *savana*[C] (mostly E of Andes, Feb–Oct). Ranchland, pastures, open terrain; austral migrants in forest canopy, borders of oxbows and rivers. To 1200 m (occasionally 3200 m). **ID** Ad black cap, wings and long forked tail, underparts white. Juv duller, cap, wings and tail brownish, tail much shorter and barely forked. **Voice** Thin tittering; rapid "tic" notes.

401

Genus _Rhytipterna_ Grey or rufous, with hooked bill tip and prominent rictal bristles. Perch upright, sally to foliage or perch-glean; nests and nesting behaviour largely unknown.

rosenbergi

Rufous Mourner _Rhytipterna holerythra_ LC
Plañidera Rufa
Uncommon resident.

L 20 cm (8"). Races _holerythra_[A], _rosenbergi_[B]. Humid and wet lowland and foothill forest. To 1100 m. Singles, mid-levels to subcanopy inside forest, perch quietly, sally for large arthropods; sometimes with mixed flocks. **ID** Base of mandible pinkish. Very like Rufous Piha (p. 352) but slightly smaller, bill thinner, head less rounded; easiest by voice. **Voice** Call, slow melancholy rising-falling, whistled "wheeeep, wheeeur" recalls Barred Puffbird. Song, 3–4 quicker slurred whistles. **SS** Speckled Mourner (p. 362).

Greyish Mourner _Rhytipterna simplex_ LC
Plañidera Grisácea
Fairly common resident.

frederici

L 20 cm (8"). Race _frederici._ Humid lowland forest. To 700 m. Behaviour like Rufous Mourner. **ID** Eyes reddish to reddish brown; plain grey, marginally paler below, hint of yellowish on belly (doubtful aid in field). Juv (also ♀?) fulvous-edged wings and tail. **Voice** Song, slowly rising series of brisk whistles, louder, slower at end, or ends abruptly: "wu-u-u-u-u-u-u-u-u-u-wu-wuuer!". **SS** Screaming Piha (p. 352) larger, slightly paler, bill marginally heavier, eyes grey-brown.

juvenile ♂

Pale-bellied Mourner _Rhytipterna immunda_ LC
Plañidera Sabanera
Uncommon and local resident.

L 19 cm (7.5"). Monotypic. Savanna woodland, borders, scrub in white-sand regions. To 300 m. Singles or separated pair members, eye level or higher; sluggish, sally to foliage. **ID** Resembles slender pale _Myiarchus_ in demeanour and appearance; bill short and dark, upperparts pale greyish brown, below pale grey, belly tinged yellow, indistinct greyish wingbars, primaries and tail narrowly edged rufous. **Voice** Song, abruptly rising-falling whistle "püüweEE, chew". **SS** From various _Myiarchus_ by duller plumage, slender, and short-legged proportions, greyer rounded head (no crest).

Genus _Sirystes_ Resemble _Myiarchus_ in shape but have distinctive black and pearly white plumage. In forest canopy. Both previously regarded as races of Sirystes _S. sibilator._

Choco Sirystes _Sirystes albogriseus_ LC
Atrapamoscas Silbador
Uncommon and local resident.

L 19 cm (7.5"). Monotypic. Humid lowland forest. To 500 m. Singles or pairs, high in canopy and often difficult to see from ground. **ID** Often shows bushy crest. Much like White-rumped Sirystes, but wing-coverts and flight feathers prominently edged white, back greyer, tail tips white. **Voice** Loud "chip-hrip-hrip", often in long, irregular rapid series.

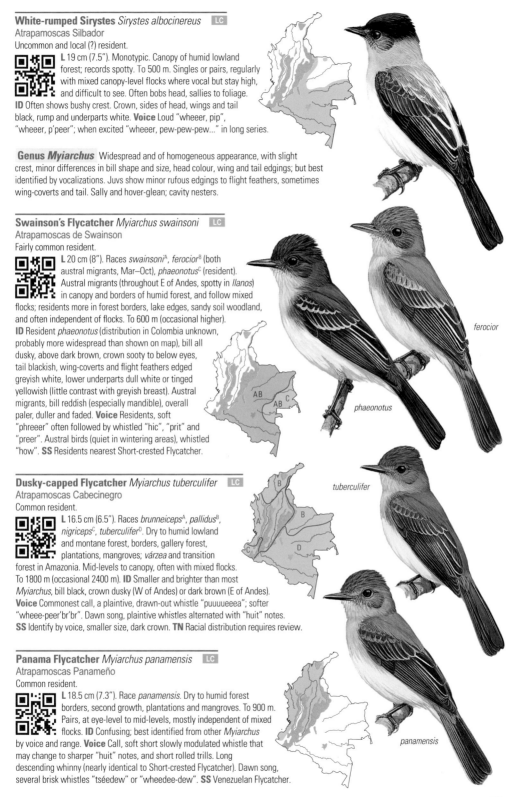

White-rumped Sirystes *Sirystes albocinereus* `LC`
Atrapamoscas Silbador
Uncommon and local (?) resident.

L 19 cm (7.5"). Monotypic. Canopy of humid lowland forest; records spotty. To 500 m. Singles or pairs, regularly with mixed canopy-level flocks where vocal but stay high, and difficult to see. Often bobs head, sallies to foliage. **ID** Often shows bushy crest. Crown, sides of head, wings and tail black, rump and underparts white. **Voice** Loud "wheeer, pip", "wheeer, p'peer"; when excited "wheeer, pew-pew-pew..." in long series.

Genus *Myiarchus* Widespread and of homogeneous appearance, with slight crest, minor differences in bill shape and size, head colour, wing and tail edgings; but best identified by vocalizations. Juvs show minor rufous edgings to flight feathers, sometimes wing-coverts and tail. Sally and hover-glean; cavity nesters.

Swainson's Flycatcher *Myiarchus swainsoni* `LC`
Atrapamoscas de Swainson
Fairly common resident.

L 20 cm (8"). Races *swainsoni*[A], *ferocior*[B] (both austral migrants, Mar–Oct), *phaeonotus*[C] (resident). Austral migrants (throughout E of Andes, spotty in *llanos*) in canopy and borders of humid forest, and follow mixed flocks; residents more in forest borders, lake edges, sandy soil woodland, and often independent of flocks. To 600 m (occasional higher). **ID** Resident *phaeonotus* (distribution in Colombia unknown, probably more widespread than shown on map), bill all dusky, above dark brown, crown sooty to below eyes, tail blackish, wing-coverts and flight feathers edged greyish white, lower underparts dull white or tinged yellowish (little contrast with greyish breast). Austral migrants, bill reddish (especially mandible), overall paler, duller and faded. **Voice** Residents, soft "phreeer" often followed by whistled "hic", "prit" and "preer". Austral birds (quiet in wintering areas), whistled "how". **SS** Residents nearest Short-crested Flycatcher.

ferocior

phaeonotus

Dusky-capped Flycatcher *Myiarchus tuberculifer* `LC`
Atrapamoscas Cabecinegro
Common resident.

L 16.5 cm (6.5"). Races *brunneiceps*[A], *pallidus*[B], *nigriceps*[C], *tuberculifer*[D]. Dry to humid lowland and montane forest, borders, gallery forest, plantations, mangroves; *várzea* and transition forest in Amazonia. Mid-levels to canopy, often with mixed flocks. To 1800 m (occasional 2400 m). **ID** Smaller and brighter than most *Myiarchus*, bill black, crown dusky (W of Andes) or dark brown (E of Andes). **Voice** Commonest call, a plaintive, drawn-out whistle "puuuueeea"; softer "whee-peer'br'br". Dawn song, plaintive whistles alternated with "huit" notes. **SS** Identify by voice, smaller size, dark crown. **TN** Racial distribution requires review.

tuberculifer

Panama Flycatcher *Myiarchus panamensis* `LC`
Atrapamoscas Panameño
Common resident.

L 18.5 cm (7.3"). Race *panamensis*. Dry to humid forest borders, second growth, plantations and mangroves. To 900 m. Pairs, at eye-level to mid-levels, mostly independent of mixed flocks. **ID** Confusing; best identified from other *Myiarchus* by voice and range. **Voice** Call, soft short slowly modulated whistle that may change to sharper "huit" notes, and short rolled trills. Long descending whinny (nearly identical to Short-crested Flycatcher). Dawn song, several brisk whistles "tséedew" or "wheedee-dew". **SS** Venezuelan Flycatcher.

panamensis

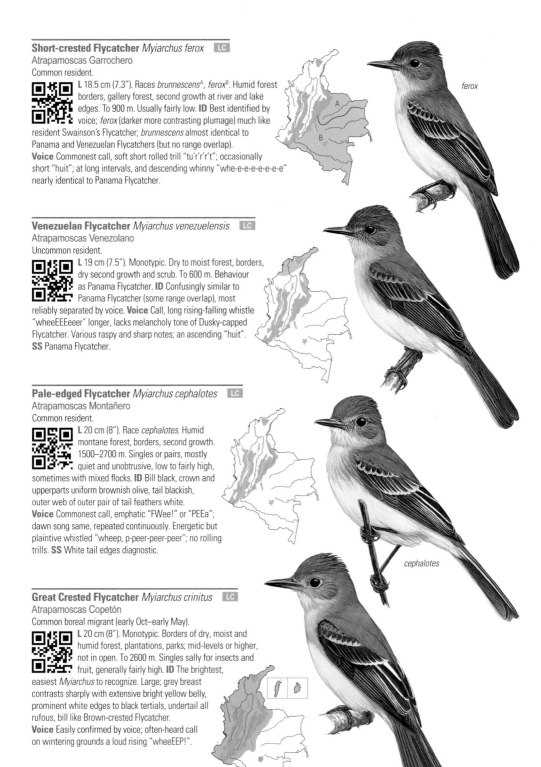

Short-crested Flycatcher *Myiarchus ferox* LC
Atrapamoscas Garrochero
Common resident.

L 18.5 cm (7.3"). Races *brunnescens*[A], *ferox*[B]. Humid forest borders, gallery forest, second growth at river and lake edges. To 900 m. Usually fairly low. **ID** Best identified by voice; *ferox* (darker more contrasting plumage) much like resident Swainson's Flycatcher; *brunnescens* almost identical to Panama and Venezuelan Flycatchers (but no range overlap). **Voice** Commonest call, soft short rolled trill "tu'r'r'r't"; occasionally short "huit"; at long intervals, and descending whinny "whe-e-e-e-e-e-e" nearly identical to Panama Flycatcher.

ferox

Venezuelan Flycatcher *Myiarchus venezuelensis* LC
Atrapamoscas Venezolano
Uncommon resident.

L 19 cm (7.5"). Monotypic. Dry to moist forest, borders, dry second growth and scrub. To 600 m. Behaviour as Panama Flycatcher. **ID** Confusingly similar to Panama Flycatcher (some range overlap), most reliably separated by voice. **Voice** Call, long rising-falling whistle "wheeEEEeeer" longer, lacks melancholy tone of Dusky-capped Flycatcher. Various raspy and sharp notes; an ascending "huit". **SS** Panama Flycatcher.

Pale-edged Flycatcher *Myiarchus cephalotes* LC
Atrapamoscas Montañero
Common resident.

L 20 cm (8"). Race *cephalotes*. Humid montane forest, borders, second growth. 1500–2700 m. Singles or pairs, mostly quiet and unobtrusive, low to fairly high, sometimes with mixed flocks. **ID** Bill black, crown and upperparts uniform brownish olive, tail blackish, outer web of outer pair of tail feathers white. **Voice** Commonest call, emphatic "FWee!" or "PEEa"; dawn song same, repeated continuously. Energetic but plaintive whistled "wheep, p-peer-peer-peer"; no rolling trills. **SS** White tail edges diagnostic.

cephalotes

Great Crested Flycatcher *Myiarchus crinitus* LC
Atrapamoscas Copetón
Common boreal migrant (early Oct–early May).

L 20 cm (8"). Monotypic. Borders of dry, moist and humid forest, plantations, parks; mid-levels or higher, not in open. To 2600 m. Singles sally for insects and fruit, generally fairly high. **ID** The brightest, easiest *Myiarchus* to recognize. Large; grey breast contrasts sharply with extensive bright yellow belly, prominent white edges to black tertials, undertail all rufous, bill like Brown-crested Flycatcher. **Voice** Easily confirmed by voice; often-heard call on wintering grounds a loud rising "wheeEEP!".

Brown-crested Flycatcher *Myiarchus tyrannulus* `LC`
Atrapamoscas Crestipardo

Seven subspecies in four subspecies groups; one in Colombia.

tyrannulus

Southern Brown-crested Flycatcher
Myiarchus (tyrannulus) tyrannulus
Common resident.
L 20 cm (8"). Race *tyrannulus*. Arid scrub, dry to moist woodland, borders, gallery forest, mangroves. To 1000 m. Singles or pairs, conspicuous, at eye level or higher. **ID** Heavy black bill, base of mandible pinkish, bushy brown crown, primaries edged rufous (faint when worn), inner webs of all but central pair of tail feathers rufous (conspicuous from below). **Voice** Vocal. Commonest calls, sharp inflected "whit!", rolling "pr-pr'r'r'r't!" repeatedly; no long whistles. Dawn song, whistled rolling "WHEE'p'peer". **SS** Great Crested Flycatcher.

Apical Flycatcher *Myiarchus apicalis* `LC`
Atrapamoscas Apical
Fairly common but local resident.

L 19 cm (7.5"). Monotypic. Endemic. Dry forest, borders, brushy ranchland with scattered trees. 400–2300 m. Pairs, usually well above ground. **ID** Like many other *Myiarchus* but bushy crown darker than back, tail has fairly broad diagnostic whitish tip. **Voice** Commonest call, stuttering rising-falling rolled trill "whir'R'R'r r'r'r", rather high-pitched, squealing; given repeatedly when excited.

Long-tailed Tyrant *Colonia colonus* `LC`
Atrapamoscas Rabijunco
Common resident.

L ♂ 25 cm (10"), ♀ 20 cm (8"), including tail-streamers. Races *leuconota*[A], *fuscicapillus*[B]. Humid forest borders, small openings, treefall gaps, almost always with large rotten trunk or stub, especially with bee colonies. To 1200 m (rarely 1800 m). Confiding, sedentary pairs or families perch in open on dead trunks; seldom venture far; sally to air, feed heavily on bees and other flying insects. Cavity nester. **ID** Unmistakable; long tail-streamers (shorter ♀), frosty forehead and brows, white central back and rump. **Voice** Call, soft rising "wheeet" (like Barn Swallow) as flicks tail; longer "wee-ta..." series.

Genus *Myiophobus* Small and inconspicuous; resemble *Empidonax* but darker, with concealed coronal patch and wingbars. Several are poorly known, some possibly not closely related.

Mouse-grey Flycatcher *Myiophobus crypterythrus* `LC`
Atrapamoscas Grisáceo
Fairly common resident.

L 12.2 cm (4.8"). Monotypic. Shrubby forest borders, overgrown clearings, scrub. To 1500 m. Behaviour like Bran-colored Flycatcher. **ID** Above dull brownish grey, whitish supraloral mark, bold buff wingbars, streaked underparts. ♀ coronal patch small or lacking. **Voice** Day song, a fast thin "whee-b-b-b-b-b-b", higher-pitched (4–5 kHz), flatter than Bran-colored Flycatcher. Dawn song, slow, well-spaced "we'dt" phrase. **TN** Usually regarded as a race of Bran-colored Flycatcher.

leuconota   ♀

405

Bran-colored Flycatcher *Myiophobus fasciatus* LC
Atrapamoscas Pechirrayado
Fairly common resident.

 L 12.2 cm (4.8"). Race *fasciatus*. Dry to humid shrubby forest borders, degraded or overgrown slopes, thickets. 600–2200 m (200 m, Vichada). Singles or (less often) pairs, inconspicuous, perch low, usually out of sight or only briefly in open.
ID Above bright cinnamon-rufous ('bran color'), buffy-rufous wingbars, streaked underparts. **Voice** Day song, a fast, musical "whee-be-be-be-be-be-be" with pattern and tempo of Mouse-grey Flycatcher but lower-pitched (2–3 kHz), richer; also at faster tempo. **SS** Colour, wingbars and streaks diagnostic.

Flavescent Flycatcher *Myiophobus flavicans* LC
Atrapamoscas Amarillento
Common resident.

 L 13 cm (5"). Races *flavicans*[A], *perijanus*[B]. Humid montane forest, borders. 1500–2700 m. Singles or pairs perch erect, at mid-levels or lower; quiet, unobtrusive, and generally not with mixed flocks. **ID** Lacks strong features. Bill all dark, broken yellowish-white eye-ring, weak yellowish supraloral mark, concealed yellow coronal stripe (lacking, ♀), buffy wingbars, below yellowish, chest vaguely streaked olive. **Voice** Call, sharp "tsink"; dawn song, rhythmic "ka'whik" repeatedly; chattering "pik" notes. **SS** Note elevation, habitat, subtle plumage features.

Orange-crested Flycatcher *Myiophobus phoenicomitra* LC
Atrapamoscas Coronirrufo
Uncommon (local or overlooked?) resident.

 L 13 cm (5"). Races *litae*[A], *phoenicomitra*[B]. Lower levels in wet foothill and premontane forest. Mostly 500–1600 m. **ID** Resembles better known Flavescent Flycatcher (higher elevations), differing in upperparts darker olive, eye-ring complete but faint, no supraloral mark, wingbars brighter ochre-rufous, concealed coronal patch usually orange (rarely yellow; lacking ♀), mandible pale. **Voice** Song, weak high (7–8 kHz) 3–4-note "pit-sít-sít-tsu", middle notes stronger, slightly higher (*litae*); or 2–3 notes, series rising (*phoenicomitra*).

[Roraiman Flycatcher *Myiophobus roraimae*] LC
Atrapamoscas de Roraima
Hypothetical.

 L 13.5 cm (5.3"). Race unknown. Possible in low-stature sandy soil forest in Vaupés or Guainía, although elevations probably too low. Often included on previous Colombian lists, but no verifiable records. **ID** Small, brownish and *Empidonax*-like; strong rufous-buff wingbars and wing edgings, weak yellowish eye-ring, yellowish underparts, brighter belly, olive-tinged breast. **Voice** Song, 2–3 brief high metallic trills (c. 6–8 kHz), each higher than preceding one, then longer descending trill; also chatter-like variations.

Genera *Silvicultrix* and *Ochthoeca* Two high-Andean genera; puffy-headed with tiny bills, most have long white eyebrows and erect posture. *Silvicultrix* occur in thickets. All species often placed in *Ochthoeca*.

Crowned Chat-tyrant *Silvicultrix frontalis* LC
Pitajo Coronado

 Four subspecies in two subspecies groups; one in Colombia.

Crowned Chat-tyrant *Silvicultrix (frontalis) frontalis*
Uncommon (easily overlooked) resident.
L 13 cm (5"). Races *albidiadema*[A], *frontalis*[B]. Upper montane forest, elfin woodland, treeline thickets. 2300–3600 m. Retiring, quiet, inconspicuous low in dense understorey, occasionally with small mixed flocks. **ID** Long white eyebrow, narrow yellow frontlet (or frontlet all white, *albidiadema*), no wingbars, grey underparts. **Voice** Song, high (7–5 kHz) weak descending trill lasting c. 3 seconds.

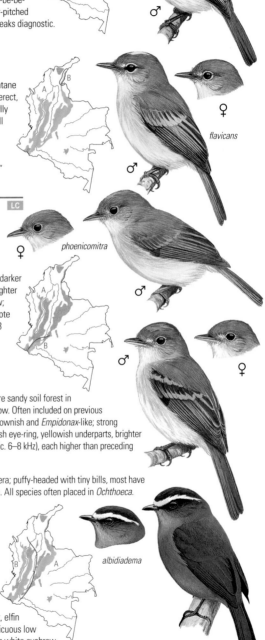

♀
fasciatus
♂

♀
flavicans
♂

♀
phoenicomitra
♂

♂
♀

albidiadema
frontalis

Yellow-bellied Chat-tyrant *Silvicultrix diadema* LC
Pitajo de Diadema
Fairly common resident.

L 12.2 cm (4.8"). Races *jesupi*[A], *rubellula*[B], *diadema*[C], *gratiosa*[D]. Undergrowth in humid and wet montane forest. 1700–3100 m. Rather confiding, quiet and inconspicuous; commoner at lower elevations. **ID** Long yellow eyebrow, yellow underparts, wingbars obscure (or somewhat brighter and rufescent, *rubellula*, *gratiosa*). **Voice** Dawn song, thin delicate little trill running upscale "prrrreeeeeeeee" (like fingers on a comb), or running downscale (*diadema*), or higher-pitched trill rising quickly, descending slowly (*jesupi*, *gratiosa*).

gratiosa

diadema

Slaty-backed Chat-tyrant *Ochthoeca cinnamomeiventris* LC
Pitajo Torrentero
Fairly common resident.

L 12.2 cm (4.8"). Monotypic. Humid montane forest, steep ravines above small Andean streams. 1600–3000 m. Sedentary pairs in undergrowth, sally and return to perch; not with mixed flocks. **ID** Small, chunky blackish bird with large elongated white false eye-spots, lower underparts chestnut. **Voice** Penetrating rising-falling whistle "sweeeeeeaaa", drawn-out, audible above stream noise; may add 3–4 "tseét" notes to song at dawn. **TN** Treated here as a separate species from Blackish *O. nigrita* and Chestnut-belted Chat-tyrants *O. thoracica*.

Rufous-breasted Chat-tyrant *Ochthoeca rufipectoralis* LC
Pitajo Pechirrufo
Fairly common resident.

L 13 cm (5"). Races *poliogastra*[A], *rubicundula*[B], *rufopectus*[C], *obfuscata*[D]. Humid upper montane forest, roadside borders, gaps, elfin woodland. 2000–3600 m. Attractive; quiet pairs stay close together, perch upright, eye level to mid-levels, often in open where conspicuous. Sallies to air or foliage; active when mixed flocks nearby. **ID** Long white eyebrows, large rufous chest patch. **Voice** Song, often as duet, bouncy chattering "ch-brrr, ch-brrr..."; soft "cleeoo-pt-pt-pt..."; dawn song, leisurely but tireless "wheet, weEa".

obfuscata

poliogastra

Brown-backed Chat-tyrant *Ochthoeca fumicolor* LC
Pitajo Ahumado
Common resident.

L 15 cm (6"). Races *fumicolor*[A], *brunneifrons*[B], *ferruginea*[C]. Elfin woodland borders, semi-open highlands, shrubby *páramo*. 2500–3800 m. Quiet but conspicuous pairs perch upright in open, sally to ground or air, usually staying together. **ID** Long whitish to buffy eyebrows, rufous wingbars (lower more prominent), cinnamon-rufous underparts (brightest, *ferruginea*). **Voice** Infrequent duet, rapidly repeated unmusical chatty phrases "chít't'pip" or "chit, chít't'pit", rhythmic (*fumicolor*), with geographical variation. Dawn song, simple high "fweet" repeated.

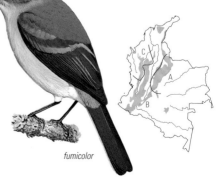

fumicolor

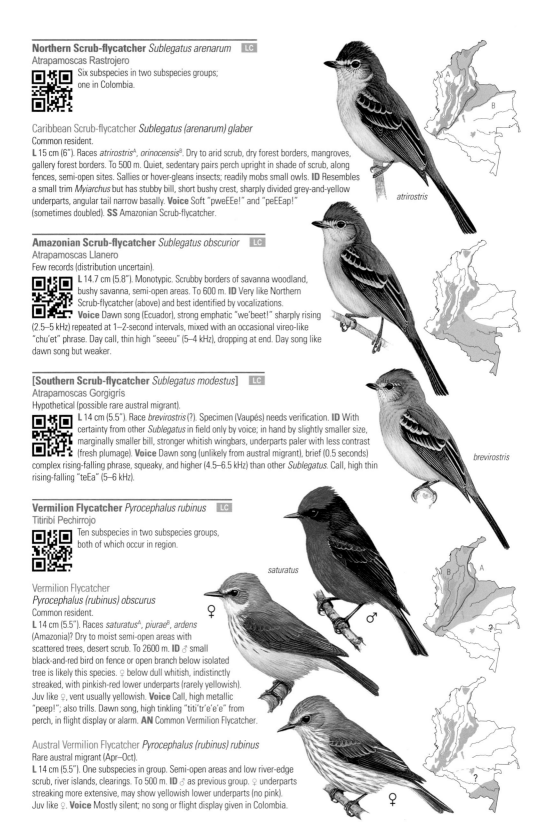

Northern Scrub-flycatcher *Sublegatus arenarum* `LC`
Atrapamoscas Rastrojero

Six subspecies in two subspecies groups; one in Colombia.

Caribbean Scrub-flycatcher *Sublegatus (arenarum) glaber*
Common resident.
L 15 cm (6"). Races *atrirostris*[A], *orinocensis*[B]. Dry to arid scrub, dry forest borders, mangroves, gallery forest borders. To 500 m. Quiet, sedentary pairs perch upright in shade of scrub, along fences, semi-open sites. Sallies or hover-gleans insects; readily mobs small owls. **ID** Resembles a small trim *Myiarchus* but has stubby bill, short bushy crest, sharply divided grey-and-yellow underparts, angular tail narrow basally. **Voice** Soft "pweEEe!" and "peEEap!" (sometimes doubled). **SS** Amazonian Scrub-flycatcher.

atrirostris

Amazonian Scrub-flycatcher *Sublegatus obscurior* `LC`
Atrapamoscas Llanero
Few records (distribution uncertain).

L 14.7 cm (5.8"). Monotypic. Scrubby borders of savanna woodland, bushy savanna, semi-open areas. To 600 m. **ID** Very like Northern Scrub-flycatcher (above) and best identified by vocalizations.
Voice Dawn song (Ecuador), strong emphatic "we'beet!" sharply rising (2.5–5 kHz) repeated at 1–2-second intervals, mixed with an occasional vireo-like "chu'et" phrase. Day call, thin high "seeeu" (5–4 kHz), dropping at end. Day song like dawn song but weaker.

[Southern Scrub-flycatcher *Sublegatus modestus*] `LC`
Atrapamoscas Gorgigrís
Hypothetical (possible rare austral migrant).

L 14 cm (5.5"). Race *brevirostris* (?). Specimen (Vaupés) needs verification. **ID** With certainty from other *Sublegatus* in field only by voice; in hand by slightly smaller size, marginally smaller bill, stronger whitish wingbars, underparts paler with less contrast (fresh plumage). **Voice** Dawn song (unlikely from austral migrant), brief (0.5 seconds) complex rising-falling phrase, squeaky, and higher (4.5–6.5 kHz) than other *Sublegatus*. Call, high thin rising-falling "teEa" (5–6 kHz).

brevirostris

Vermilion Flycatcher *Pyrocephalus rubinus* `LC`
Titiribí Pechirrojo

Ten subspecies in two subspecies groups, both of which occur in region.

Vermilion Flycatcher
Pyrocephalus (rubinus) obscurus
Common resident.
L 14 cm (5.5"). Races *saturatus*[A], *piurae*[B], *ardens* (Amazonia)? Dry to moist semi-open areas with scattered trees, desert scrub. To 2600 m. **ID** ♂ small black-and-red bird on fence or open branch below isolated tree is likely this species. ♀ below dull whitish, indistinctly streaked, with pinkish-red lower underparts (rarely yellowish). Juv like ♀, vent usually yellowish. **Voice** Call, high metallic "peep!"; also trills. Dawn song, high tinkling "titi'tr'e'e'e" from perch, in flight display or alarm. **AN** Common Vermilion Flycatcher.

saturatus

♀

♂

Austral Vermilion Flycatcher *Pyrocephalus (rubinus) rubinus*
Rare austral migrant (Apr–Oct).
L 14 cm (5.5"). One subspecies in group. Semi-open areas and low river-edge scrub, river islands, clearings. To 500 m. **ID** ♂ as previous group. ♀ underparts streaking more extensive, may show yellowish lower underparts (no pink). Juv like ♀. **Voice** Mostly silent; no song or flight display given in Colombia.

♀

Genus *Fluvicola* Small, with pied plumage and rounded tails. Rarely far from water.

Pied Water-tyrant *Fluvicola pica* `LC`
Viudita Blanquinegra
Common resident.

 L 13.5 cm (5.3"). Monotypic. Mangroves, freshwater ponds, marshes. To 1100 m. Engaging pairs perch low over water, on floating vegetation, or on ground at water's edge. Leap, flutter up, or run to snap flying prey. Constantly spread and flick tail down. **ID** ♂ chunky, with head, scapulars, underparts and rump white, rest of plumage black. ♀ rear crown and back mixed brownish. Juv duller. **Voice** Calls, a weak nasal "dreéap!" (sometimes as jumps up) or soft "pick". Song, buzzy "choo-wer".

Masked Water-tyrant *Fluvicola nengeta* `LC`
Viudita Enmascarada
Local resident (SW Nariño).

atripennis

 L 13.5 cm (5.3"). Race *atripennis*. Habitat and behaviour as Pied Water-tyrant. Recent range expansion from NW Ecuador (c. 2011). To 300 m. **ID** Differs most obviously from Pied Water-tyrant in black stripe through eyes, all-white crown and nape, white base to tail. **Voice** Call, sharp "curt!" or "curt'it"; chatter in duet.

White-headed Marsh-tyrant *Arundinicola leucocephala* `LC`
Monjita Pantanera
Common resident.

 **L** 13 cm (5"). Monotypic. Freshwater marshes, ponds, grassy riverbanks, river islands. To 600 m. Conspicuous, pairs perch upright atop shrubs and grass, typically over or near water. **ID** Large-headed. ♂ dark chocolate, white slightly crested head, mandible orange-yellow. ♀ above ashy brown, wings and tail dusky, forecrown, sides of head, and underparts whitish, prominent black eyes. **Voice** Usually quiet; a high sharp "sedik!". **SS** ♀ Pied Water-tyrant.

Genus *Knipolegus* Three or four species in Colombia (taxonomy-dependent); all remarkably quiet and inconspicuous. Lowland species are sexually dimorphic, with pale blue-grey bills, and all-black ♂♂.

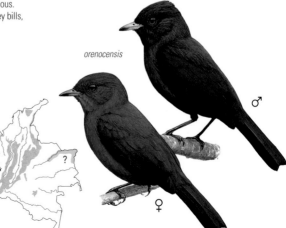

orenocensis

Riverside Tyrant *Knipolegus orenocensis* `LC`
Viudita Playera
Uncommon and local resident.

 L 15 cm (6"). Race *orenocensis*. Semi-open scrub and weedy areas in *llanos*, early-successional vegetation on riverbanks and river islands. To 200 m. Singles or pairs, inconspicuous, 0.5–5 m up; sally to grass, foliage, or ground. **ID** Bill blue-grey tipped black. ♂ slaty black; recalls ♂ Amazonian Black-tyrant (of seasonally flooded gallery forest and borders) but larger, duller, with more erect posture, slight crest. ♀ above olive-grey, below paler, faint breast and flank streaking. **Voice** Call, soft "peEEo". **SS** Amazonian Black-tyrant.

Sclater's Riverside Tyrant *Knipolegus sclateri*  LC
Viudita Ribereña
Local resident.

 L 15 cm (6"). Monotypic. Semi-open scrub and early-successional vegetation on Amazonian riverbanks, river islands. To 150 m. Behaviour like Riverside Tyrant. **ID** ♂ dull black. ♀ above dark olive-grey, wings and tail dusky, rump faintly rufescent, weak buff wingbars, below paler with weak olive-grey streaking. **Voice** Call, incisive "pik". Song, quick liquid "pik, pik'a'tuk". Short vertical flight display includes mechanical buzz at peak. **SS** Amazonian Black-tyrant. **TN** Usually regarded as a race of Riverside Tyrant. **AN** Sclater's Black-tyrant.

Amazonian Black-tyrant *Knipolegus poecilocercus*  LC
Viudita Renegrida
Fairly common but local resident.

 L 13 cm (5"). Monotypic. Seasonally flooded gallery forest in *llanos*; *várzea* and riverine forest in Amazonia. To 400 m. **ID** Small. ♂ bill blue-grey tipped black, plumage glossy black. ♀ bill brownish, eye-ring greyish, wingbars buff, rump rufous, tail broadly edged rufous, underparts dull buff-white, coarse blurred streaking coalesces on breast. **Voice** Solitary ♂♂ perch 0.5–2 m up on open shady branch or vine near water; advertise with weak "see-sa'lick" or buzzy "bzzEEa" during vertical jump of 0.2–0.3 m. **SS** Black Manakin (p. 340).

Rufous-tailed Tyrant *Knipolegus poecilurus*  LC
Viudita Ojirroja
Uncommon and local resident.

 L 14.7 cm (5.8"). Race *poecilurus*[A], race?[B]. Humid montane forest borders, clearings, highland pastures with trees and shrubs. 1400–3100 m. Alone or in pairs, perch upright at various heights, often in open (even on fences). **ID** Conspicuous red eyes, tail dusky (rufous-edged inner webs most visible in flight), dull buff wingbars, dull cinnamon belly. **Voice** Very quiet; rarely short "trrrrt" trill, or more complex phrase in vertical aerial display.

poecilurus

Yellow-browed Tyrant *Satrapa icterophrys*  LC
Atrapamoscas Cejiamarillo
Uncommon resident (possibly seasonal, mostly Jan–Jul).

 L 16 cm (6.3"). Monotypic. Ranchland, savanna, pastures with scattered trees, gallery forest borders. To 500 m. Breeds sparingly, Jun–Sept, in Venezuelan *llanos* (Colombia?); austral birds migratory. Mostly singles, perch upright in trees and shrubs, sally to foliage (less to air). **ID** Trim, clean-cut; broad yellow eyebrow, dusky mask, bright yellow underparts. ♀ slightly duller. **Voice** Notably quiet. Song, fast sharply rising "p'p'p'pi'pr'reep" (kingbird-like). Call, a rising "pueep!".

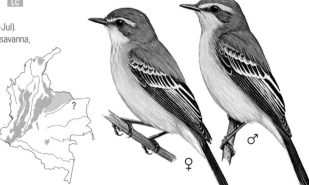

Genus *Muscisaxicola* Terrestrial. Mostly high-Andean or austral regions. Often wary; run on open ground. Slender, with short bills, long legs, and blackish tails edged white, which are often flicked open. Notably quiet, with confusingly similar plumages; separated by size, subtle head pattern and colour differences.

Little Ground-tyrant *Muscisaxicola fluviatilis* LC
Dormilona Fluvial
Uncommon seasonal resident (austral migrant?).

 L 14 cm (5.5"). Monotypic. Sandbars in R Amazon and on river islands; mostly Jun–Nov (Colombia; Loreto, NE Peru) during lower-water period. 100 m. Singles (pairs?) run fast, then pause bolt upright on sand, driftwood or bush. Breeding undocumented. **ID** Small and nondescript, buff breast fades to whitish belly, pale tail edges. **Voice** Weak rising "peeeép". **SS** Drab Water-tyrant.

Spot-billed Ground-tyrant *Muscisaxicola maculirostris* LC
Dormilona Chica   EN
Uncommon and local resident.

 L 14.5 cm (5.7"). Races *niceforoi* (resident, records mainly Dec–Jul), *rufescens* (possible austral migrant to Nariño). Drier highlands with bare slopes, ploughed fields, short grass, scattered shrubs; lakeshores. 2600–3600 m (rarely lower). Runs on ground, may perch atop small shrub. **ID** Small and drab, indistinct whitish eyebrow, base of mandible yellowish (the 'spot', difficult to see), faint wingbars, vague breast streaking. **Voice** Song (in aerial display), weak staccato "tic..tic, tic-tic'trEEa", last part rising sharply.

White-browed Ground-tyrant *Muscisaxicola albilora* LC
Dormilona Cejiblanca
Vagrant (Isla Gorgona, 1987).

 L 18 cm (7"). Monotypic. Possible rare austral migrant to dry grassy and rocky highlands and *páramo* in S Nariño (numerous records, N Ecuador). Above c. 2800 m. **ID** Upperparts greyish brown, long well-defined but narrow and inconspicuous white eyebrow, dull brownish cap, brighter more rufous rear crown (not sharply defined).
Voice Unlikely to be heard in Colombia. **SS** Plain-capped Ground-tyrant.

Plain-capped Ground-tyrant *Muscisaxicola alpinus* LC
Dormilona Cenicienta
Local resident.

 L 19 cm (7.5"). Races *columbianus*[A], *quesadae*[B], *alpinus*[C]. Drier open *páramo*, rocky slopes to snowline. 3200–4500 m. Terrestrial, singles, pairs or scattered loosely associated groups run rapidly, pause abruptly, stand erect on ground, rock or other slightly elevated site. Often flicks wings and tail. Flight swift and strong on long wings. **ID** Closely recalls rare White-browed Ground-tyrant, but has shorter, broader white supraloral stripe, and plainer browner crown lacking rufous. **Voice** Rarely a weak "tic".

Red-rumped Bush-tyrant
Cnemarchus erythropygius LC
Atrapamoscas Culirrojo
Uncommon and local resident.

 L 23 cm (9"). Races *orinomus*[A], *erythropygius*[B]. *Páramo*, semi-open highland pastures, open areas around habitations. 3000–3900 m. Singles or pairs, sometimes wary, but perch in open atop shrubs, low trees, fence posts, wires, buildings; sally to ground for prey. **ID** Large handsome flycatcher; small bill, unmistakable whitish face, and orange-rufous rump, lower underparts and most of tail (except central feathers and tip). **Voice** Call, loud fairly high-pitched rising-falling whistle "pEEEu".

niceforoi

alpinus

erythropygius

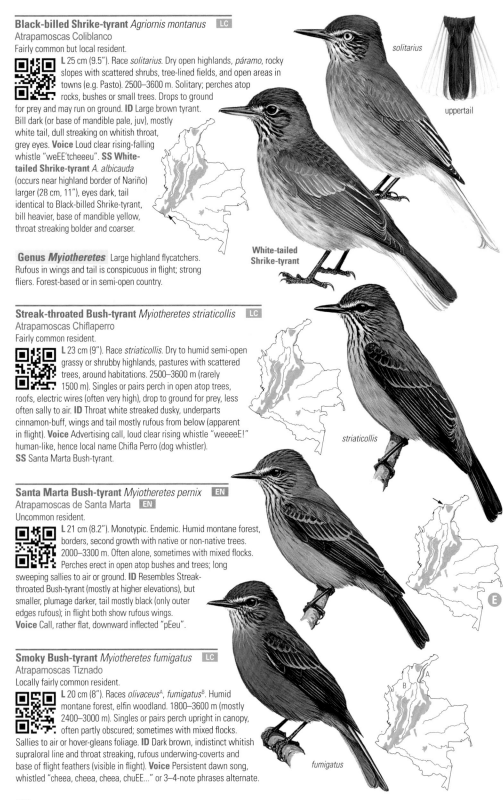

Black-billed Shrike-tyrant *Agriornis montanus* LC
Atrapamoscas Coliblanco
Fairly common but local resident.

L 25 cm (9.5"). Race *solitarius*. Dry open highlands, *páramo*, rocky slopes with scattered shrubs, tree-lined fields, and open areas in towns (e.g. Pasto). 2500–3600 m. Solitary; perches atop rocks, bushes or small trees. Drops to ground for prey and may run on ground. **ID** Large brown tyrant. Bill dark (or base of mandible pale, juv), mostly white tail, dull streaking on whitish throat, grey eyes. **Voice** Loud clear rising-falling whistle "weEE'tcheeeu". **SS** White-tailed Shrike-tyrant *A. albicauda* (occurs near highland border of Nariño) larger (28 cm, 11"), eyes dark, tail identical to Black-billed Shrike-tyrant, bill heavier, base of mandible yellow, throat streaking bolder and coarser.

solitarius

uppertail

White-tailed Shrike-tyrant

Genus *Myiotheretes* Large highland flycatchers. Rufous in wings and tail is conspicuous in flight; strong fliers. Forest-based or in semi-open country.

Streak-throated Bush-tyrant *Myiotheretes striaticollis* LC
Atrapamoscas Chiflaperro
Fairly common resident.

L 23 cm (9"). Race *striaticollis*. Dry to humid semi-open grassy or shrubby highlands, pastures with scattered trees, around habitations. 2500–3600 m (rarely 1500 m). Singles or pairs perch in open atop trees, roofs, electric wires (often very high), drop to ground for prey, less often sally to air. **ID** Throat white streaked dusky, underparts cinnamon-buff, wings and tail mostly rufous from below (apparent in flight). **Voice** Advertising call, loud clear rising whistle "weeeeE!" human-like, hence local name Chifla Perro (dog whistler). **SS** Santa Marta Bush-tyrant.

striaticollis

Santa Marta Bush-tyrant *Myiotheretes pernix* EN
Atrapamoscas de Santa Marta EN
Uncommon resident.

L 21 cm (8.2"). Monotypic. Endemic. Humid montane forest, borders, second growth with native or non-native trees. 2000–3300 m. Often alone, sometimes with mixed flocks. Perches erect in open atop bushes and trees; long sweeping sallies to air or ground. **ID** Resembles Streak-throated Bush-tyrant (mostly at higher elevations), but smaller, plumage darker, tail mostly black (only outer edges rufous); in flight both show rufous wings. **Voice** Call, rather flat, downward inflected "pEeu".

E

Smoky Bush-tyrant *Myiotheretes fumigatus* LC
Atrapamoscas Tiznado
Locally fairly common resident.

L 20 cm (8"). Races *olivaceus*[A], *fumigatus*[B]. Humid montane forest, elfin woodland. 1800–3600 m (mostly 2400–3000 m). Singles or pairs perch upright in canopy, often partly obscured; sometimes with mixed flocks. Sallies to air or hover-gleans foliage. **ID** Dark brown, indistinct whitish supraloral line and throat streaking, rufous underwing-coverts and base of flight feathers (visible in flight). **Voice** Persistent dawn song, whistled "cheea, cheea, cheea, chuEE..." or 3–4-note phrases alternate.

fumigatus

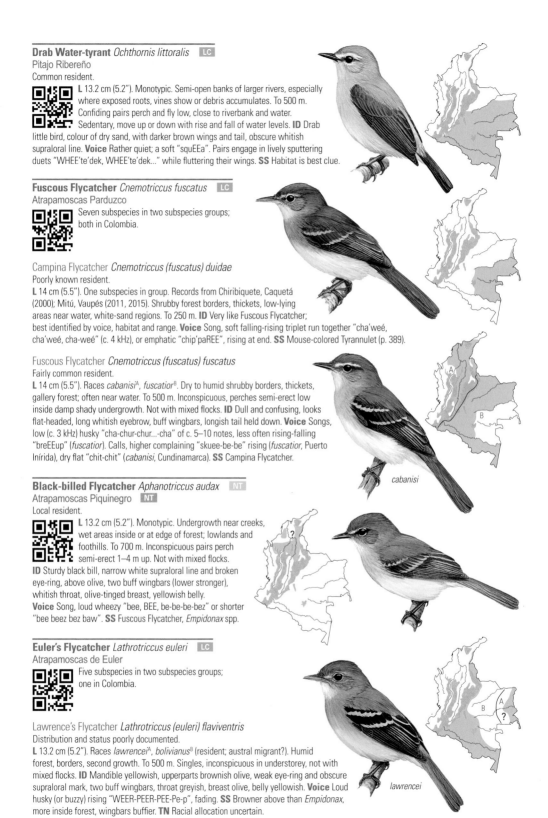

Drab Water-tyrant *Ochthornis littoralis* `LC`
Pitajo Ribereño
Common resident.

L 13.2 cm (5.2"). Monotypic. Semi-open banks of larger rivers, especially where exposed roots, vines show or debris accumulates. To 500 m. Confiding pairs perch and fly low, close to riverbank and water. Sedentary, move up or down with rise and fall of water levels. **ID** Drab little bird, colour of dry sand, with darker brown wings and tail, obscure whitish supraloral line. **Voice** Rather quiet; a soft "squEEa". Pairs engage in lively sputtering duets "WHEE'te'dek, WHEE'te'dek..." while fluttering their wings. **SS** Habitat is best clue.

Fuscous Flycatcher *Cnemotriccus fuscatus* `LC`
Atrapamoscas Parduzco

Seven subspecies in two subspecies groups; both in Colombia.

Campina Flycatcher *Cnemotriccus (fuscatus) duidae*
Poorly known resident.
L 14 cm (5.5"). One subspecies in group. Records from Chiribiquete, Caquetá (2000); Mitú, Vaupés (2011, 2015). Shrubby forest borders, thickets, low-lying areas near water, white-sand regions. To 250 m. **ID** Very like Fuscous Flycatcher; best identified by voice, habitat and range. **Voice** Song, soft falling-rising triplet run together "cha'weé, cha'weé, cha–weé" (c. 4 kHz), or emphatic "chip'paREE", rising at end. **SS** Mouse-colored Tyrannulet (p. 389).

Fuscous Flycatcher *Cnemotriccus (fuscatus) fuscatus*
Fairly common resident.
L 14 cm (5.5"). Races *cabanisi*[A], *fuscatior*[B]. Dry to humid shrubby borders, thickets, gallery forest; often near water. To 500 m. Inconspicuous, perches semi-erect low inside damp shady undergrowth. Not with mixed flocks. **ID** Dull and confusing, looks flat-headed, long whitish eyebrow, buff wingbars, longish tail held down. **Voice** Songs, low (c. 3 kHz) husky "cha-chur-chur...-cha" of c. 5–10 notes, less often rising-falling "breEEup" (*fuscatior*). Calls, higher complaining "skuee-be-be" rising (*fuscatior*, Puerto Inírida), dry flat "chit-chit" (*cabanisi*, Cundinamarca). **SS** Campina Flycatcher.

cabanisi

Black-billed Flycatcher *Aphanotriccus audax* `NT`
Atrapamoscas Piquinegro `NT`
Local resident.

L 13.2 cm (5.2"). Monotypic. Undergrowth near creeks, wet areas inside or at edge of forest; lowlands and foothills. To 700 m. Inconspicuous pairs perch semi-erect 1–4 m up. Not with mixed flocks. **ID** Sturdy black bill, narrow white supraloral line and broken eye-ring, above olive, two buff wingbars (lower stronger), whitish throat, olive-tinged breast, yellowish belly. **Voice** Song, loud wheezy "bee, BEE, be-be-be-bez" or shorter "bee beez bez baw". **SS** Fuscous Flycatcher, *Empidonax* spp.

Euler's Flycatcher *Lathrotriccus euleri* `LC`
Atrapamoscas de Euler

Five subspecies in two subspecies groups; one in Colombia.

Lawrence's Flycatcher *Lathrotriccus (euleri) flaviventris*
Distribution and status poorly documented.
L 13.2 cm (5.2"). Races *lawrencei*[A], *bolivianus*[B] (resident; austral migrant?). Humid forest, borders, second growth. To 500 m. Singles, inconspicuous in understorey, not with mixed flocks. **ID** Mandible yellowish, upperparts brownish olive, weak eye-ring and obscure supraloral mark, two buff wingbars, throat greyish, breast olive, belly yellowish. **Voice** Loud husky (or buzzy) rising "WEER-PEER-PEE-Pe-p", fading. **SS** Browner above than *Empidonax*, more inside forest, wingbars buffier. **TN** Racial allocation uncertain.

lawrencei

413

Tufted Flycatcher *Mitrephanes phaeocercus* `LC`
Atrapamoscas Moñudo

Five subspecies in three subspecies groups;
one in Colombia.

Choco Tufted Flycatcher *Mitrephanes (phaeocercus) berlepschi*
Local resident.

L 13 cm (5"). Races *eminulus*[A] (valid?), *berlepschi*[B]. Near-endemic (also extreme SE Panama and NW Ecuador). Borders of humid and wet lowland and foothill forest. 100–1200 m. Singles or pairs, perky, confiding, pewee-like with alert erect posture; mid-levels. Sallies to air, returns to same perch, quivers tail as alights. Not with mixed flocks. **ID** Small, with pointed crest, olive breast tinged ochraceous, lower underparts yellow. **Voice** Call, 4–7 bubbly "pik" notes as quivers tail. Song, snappy "p-pe'pe'pe'pe'pEET", first note lower, last stronger and rising.

Black Phoebe *Sayornis nigricans* `LC`
Atrapamoscas Cuidapuentes

Six subspecies in two subspecies groups;
one in Colombia.

White-winged Phoebe *Sayornis (nigricans) latirostris*
Common resident.

L 17.3 cm (6.8"). Race *angustirostris*. Streams, rivers, bridges, edges of ponds, around habitations in foothills and mountains but rarely far from water. 100–2800 m. Conspicuous, confiding pairs perch on boulders in rushing torrents, on nearby vegetation, fences or wires. Sallies to air, less to ground. Flicks tail up. **ID** Sooty black, with white wing-coverts, wingbars, wing edgings and belly. **Voice** Not very vocal; descending "tseeu"; song (c. 1 note/1.5 seconds) similar but more prolonged "tseeeeu".

Genus *Empidonax* Small, extremely similar species breeding in North America; several winter S to South America. Differences in colour and pattern subtle and overlapping; most are reliably identified by voice, but only Acadian regularly vocalizes in Colombia; all have pale mandibles.

Acadian Flycatcher *Empidonax virescens* `LC`
Atrapamoscas Verdoso

Common boreal migrant (late Aug–Apr).

L 14 cm (5.5"). Monotypic. Moist and humid forest interior, borders, old second growth, plantations. To 2800 m (mainly < 1200 m). Singles perch upright, mid-levels or lower, sally to foliage or air. Not with mixed flocks. **ID** Yellowish mandible, olive upperparts, narrow complete whitish eye-ring, two whitish wingbars, long primary extension, whitish throat, greyish-olive tinged breast, whitish or faintly yellow-tinged lower underparts. Juv lower underparts more yellowish, wingbars buffy. **Voice** Best identified by voice. Calls persistently throughout day, a dry rising "fweep!". **SS** The only consistently vocal boreal migrant *Empidonax*.

Yellow-bellied Flycatcher *Empidonax flaviventris* `LC`
Atrapamoscas Buchiamarillo

Rare boreal migrant.

L 13.5 cm (5.3"). Monotypic. Photo, Acandí, Chocó (Oct 2014); Isla San Andrés (2015, 2018). Probably overlooked. Disturbed and wooded edges. **ID** Overall yellowish olive, complete eye-ring, short bill, strong olive-tinged breast, wings and tail shorter than allies; only *Empidonax* likely in Colombia that usually has yellowish throat. **Voice** Call, clear "tuwee", but seldom heard away from breeding areas. **SS** Other *Empidonax*, especially Acadian Flycatcher.

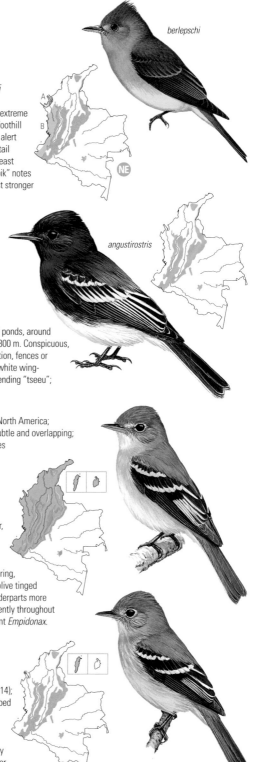

berlepschi

angustirostris

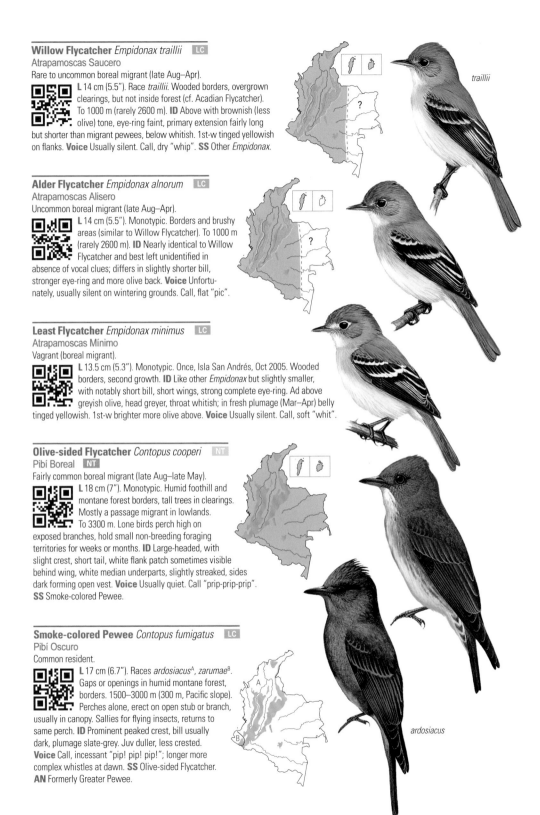

Willow Flycatcher *Empidonax traillii* `LC`
Atrapamoscas Saucero

Rare to uncommon boreal migrant (late Aug–Apr).
L 14 cm (5.5"). Race *traillii*. Wooded borders, overgrown clearings, but not inside forest (cf. Acadian Flycatcher). To 1000 m (rarely 2600 m). **ID** Above with brownish (less olive) tone, eye-ring faint, primary extension fairly long but shorter than migrant pewees, below whitish. 1st-w tinged yellowish on flanks. **Voice** Usually silent. Call, dry "whip". **SS** Other *Empidonax*.

traillii

Alder Flycatcher *Empidonax alnorum* `LC`
Atrapamoscas Alisero

Uncommon boreal migrant (late Aug–Apr).
L 14 cm (5.5"). Monotypic. Borders and brushy areas (similar to Willow Flycatcher). To 1000 m (rarely 2600 m). **ID** Nearly identical to Willow Flycatcher and best left unidentified in absence of vocal clues; differs in slightly shorter bill, stronger eye-ring and more olive back. **Voice** Unfortunately, usually silent on wintering grounds. Call, flat "pic".

Least Flycatcher *Empidonax minimus* `LC`
Atrapamoscas Mínimo

Vagrant (boreal migrant).
L 13.5 cm (5.3"). Monotypic. Once, Isla San Andrés, Oct 2005. Wooded borders, second growth. **ID** Like other *Empidonax* but slightly smaller, with notably short bill, short wings, strong complete eye-ring. Ad above greyish olive, head greyer, throat whitish; in fresh plumage (Mar–Apr) belly tinged yellowish. 1st-w brighter more olive above. **Voice** Usually silent. Call, soft "whit".

Olive-sided Flycatcher *Contopus cooperi* `NT`
Pibí Boreal `NT`

Fairly common boreal migrant (late Aug–late May).
L 18 cm (7"). Monotypic. Humid foothill and montane forest borders, tall trees in clearings. Mostly a passage migrant in lowlands. To 3300 m. Lone birds perch high on exposed branches, hold small non-breeding foraging territories for weeks or months. **ID** Large-headed, with slight crest, short tail, white flank patch sometimes visible behind wing, white median underparts, slightly streaked, sides dark forming open vest. **Voice** Usually quiet. Call "prip-prip-prip". **SS** Smoke-colored Pewee.

Smoke-colored Pewee *Contopus fumigatus* `LC`
Pibí Oscuro

Common resident.
L 17 cm (6.7"). Races *ardosiacus*[A], *zarumae*[B]. Gaps or openings in humid montane forest, borders. 1500–3000 m (300 m, Pacific slope). Perches alone, erect on open stub or branch, usually in canopy. Sallies for flying insects, returns to same perch. **ID** Prominent peaked crest, bill usually dark, plumage slate-grey. Juv duller, less crested. **Voice** Call, incessant "pip! pip! pip!"; longer more complex whistles at dawn. **SS** Olive-sided Flycatcher. **AN** Formerly Greater Pewee.

ardosiacus

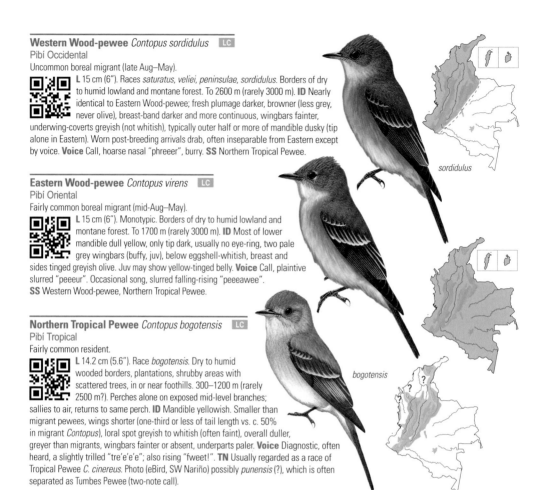

Western Wood-pewee *Contopus sordidulus* `LC`
Pibí Occidental

Uncommon boreal migrant (late Aug–May).

L 15 cm (6"). Races *saturatus, veliei, peninsulae, sordidulus*. Borders of dry to humid lowland and montane forest. To 2600 m (rarely 3000 m). **ID** Nearly identical to Eastern Wood-pewee; fresh plumage darker, browner (less grey, never olive), breast-band darker and more continuous, wingbars fainter, underwing-coverts greyish (not whitish), typically outer half or more of mandible dusky (tip alone in Eastern). Worn post-breeding arrivals drab, often inseparable from Eastern except by voice. **Voice** Call, hoarse nasal "phreeer", burry. **SS** Northern Tropical Pewee.

sordidulus

Eastern Wood-pewee *Contopus virens* `LC`
Pibí Oriental

Fairly common boreal migrant (mid-Aug–May).

L 15 cm (6"). Monotypic. Borders of dry to humid lowland and montane forest. To 1700 m (rarely 3000 m). **ID** Most of lower mandible dull yellow, only tip dark, usually no eye-ring, two pale grey wingbars (buffy, juv), below eggshell-whitish, breast and sides tinged greyish olive. Juv may show yellow-tinged belly. **Voice** Call, plaintive slurred "peeeur". Occasional song, slurred falling-rising "peeeawee". **SS** Western Wood-pewee, Northern Tropical Pewee.

Northern Tropical Pewee *Contopus bogotensis* `LC`
Pibí Tropical

Fairly common resident.

L 14.2 cm (5.6"). Race *bogotensis*. Dry to humid wooded borders, plantations, shrubby areas with scattered trees, in or near foothills. 300–1200 m (rarely 2500 m?). Perches alone on exposed mid-level branches; sallies to air, returns to same perch. **ID** Mandible yellowish. Smaller than migrant pewees, wings shorter (one-third or less of tail length vs. c. 50% in migrant *Contopus*), loral spot greyish to whitish (often faint), overall duller, greyer than migrants, wingbars fainter or absent, underparts paler. **Voice** Diagnostic, often heard, a slightly trilled "tre'e'e'e"; also rising "fweet!". **TN** Usually regarded as a race of Tropical Pewee *C. cinereus*. Photo (eBird, SW Nariño) possibly *punensis* (?), which is often separated as Tumbes Pewee (two-note call).

bogotensis

VIREONIDAE
Vireos

64 extant species, 25 in region

Relatively small New World songbirds. Arboreal leaf-gleaners, with sturdy slightly hooked to strongly hooked bills, and rather plain plumage (except shrike-vireos and peppershrikes). Forest or wooded habitats; several are migratory. Some more easily identified by song than plumage.

Genus *Cyclarhis* Large-headed, with heavy hooked bill, rufous eyebrow and pale orange eyes; tireless singers.

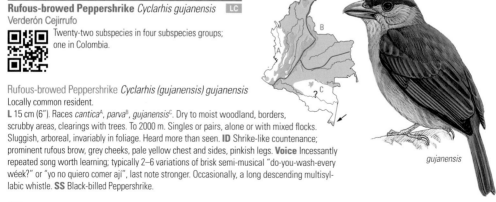

Rufous-browed Peppershrike *Cyclarhis gujanensis* `LC`
Verderón Cejirrufo

Twenty-two subspecies in four subspecies groups; one in Colombia.

Rufous-browed Peppershrike *Cyclarhis (gujanensis) gujanensis*
Locally common resident.

L 15 cm (6"). Races *cantica*[A], *parva*[B], *gujanensis*[C]. Dry to moist woodland, borders, scrubby areas, clearings with trees. To 2000 m. Singles or pairs, alone or with mixed flocks. Sluggish, arboreal, invariably in foliage. Heard more than seen. **ID** Shrike-like countenance; prominent rufous brow, grey cheeks, pale yellow chest and sides, pinkish legs. **Voice** Incessantly repeated song worth learning; typically 2–6 variations of brisk semi-musical "do-you-wash-every wéek?" or "yo no quiero comer ají", last note stronger. Occasionally, a long descending multisyllabic whistle. **SS** Black-billed Peppershrike.

gujanensis

Black-billed Peppershrike *Cyclarhis nigrirostris* `LC`
Verderón Piquinegro
Uncommon resident.

L 15 cm (6"). Races *nigrirostris*[A], *atrirostris*[B]. Humid montane forest borders. 1600–2700 m. Behaviour like previous species. **ID** Recalls Rufous-browed Peppershrike but plumage with colder grey and olive appearance, black bill (not horn-grey), short dark maroon eyebrow, olive cheeks (not grey), grey-white below (or greyer, *atrirostris*). **Voice** Song like commoner Rufous-browed Peppershrike but richer, more melodious, next-to-last syllable usually strongest.

atrirostris

nigrirostris

Genus *Hylophilus* Small, fairly slender conical bills (but heavier than Parulidae) and usually pale (whitish to grey) eyes. All regularly hang upside-down from leaf tips. Simple repetitive songs. Mostly in scrub or forest edge.

Scrub Greenlet *Hylophilus flavipes* `LC`
Verderón Rastrojero
Common resident.

L 11.4 cm (4.5"). Races *flavipes*[A], *melleus*[B], *galbanus*[C]. Desert scrub, dry to moist forest borders, degraded areas. To 1500 m. Singles or pairs, sometimes with mixed flocks of insectivores. Mid-levels; restless leaf-gleaner. **ID** Drab little bird of dry areas; pinkish bill, faded plumage, white eyes (or dark, juv?). **Voice** Frequent song, a penetrating "turee, turee, turee…" (2–5 notes/second for several seconds). Harsh nasal scolding. **SS** Golden-fronted Greenlet, Tennessee Warbler (p. 484).

flavipes

Grey-chested Greenlet *Hylophilus semicinereus* `LC`
Verderón Pechigrís
Uncommon (easily overlooked) resident.

L 12 cm (4.7"). Race *viridiceps*. Sight records (photos?). Mid-levels to canopy in shrubby riverine vegetation, adjacent *várzea* forest; mainly along larger Amazonian and white-sand rivers. To 300 m. With mixed flocks in vine-laden outer foliage. **ID** Undistinguished; mandible pinkish, eyes grey to whitish, rear crown greyish, underparts light grey tinged yellowish on sides of chest (no breast-band). **Voice** Notably vocal at dawn; song a repetitive downslurred "peeer, peeer, peeer…" 20+ notes, c. 1/ second. **SS** Other *Hylophilus*.

viridiceps

Lemon-chested Greenlet *Hylophilus griseiventris* `LC`
Verderón Pechiamarillo
Uncommon and local (?) resident.

L 13 cm (5"). Race *aemulus*. Humid *terra firme* and *várzea* forest, older second growth. To 400 m. Mid-levels to canopy, alone or with mixed flocks; restless. **ID** Broad greenish-yellow breast-band, eyes pale (or dark, juv?). **Voice** Song, 6–10 penetrating "chewee-chewee-chewee..." notes, c. 3/second, on same pitch or becoming gradually stronger. **SS** Brown-headed and Dusky-capped Greenlets. **TN** Usually regarded as a race of *H. thoracicus*.

aemulus

Brown-headed Greenlet *Hylophilus brunneiceps* `LC`
Verderón Amazónico
Uncommon resident.

L 11.4 cm (4.5"). Monotypic. Savanna woodland, low-canopy scrub forest in sandy soil black-water areas, borders of riverine and *várzea* forest. To 300 m. Active, mid-levels or higher, alone or with mixed flocks. **ID** Drab and confusing. Eyes grey to dark brown, mandible pinkish, above olive with slightly contrasting brownish crown, legs pale. **Voice** Song, series of downward-inflected notes "peeeern, peeeern, peeeern…" c. 1/second. Twittering and varied notes when agitated. **SS** Dusky-capped Greenlet.

Genus *Vireolanius* Strong hooked bills like peppershrikes, bold facial pattern and predominantly yellow or green below. Dwell in leafy canopy where heard far more than seen.

mutabilis

eximius

Yellow-browed Shrike-vireo *Vireolanius eximius* `LC`
Verderón Cejiamarillo
Uncommon and local resident.

 L 14 cm (5.5"). Races *eximius*[A], *mutabilis*[B]. Near-endemic (also far E Panama and NW Venezuela). Humid lowland and foothill forest, tall trees in coffee plantations. To 1800 m. Usually encountered singly, but may follow flocks high in canopy. Sluggish, difficult to see. **ID** Plumage resembles other Colombian *Vireolanius* but brighter green, crown and nape bluish, eyes reddish brown (not lime-green). **Voice** Song, rapid flat four-note "puee-puee-puee-puee" (c. 1 second), tirelessly repeated every 2–3 seconds. **TN** Race *mutabilis* doubtfully distinct.

Slaty-capped Shrike-vireo *Vireolanius leucotis* `LC`
Verderón Coroniplomizo
Uncommon resident.

 L 14.5 cm (5.7"). Race *leucotis*. Tall humid foothill forest. 300–1500 m (lowland records?). Behaviour like Pale-legged Shrike-vireo. **ID** Yellow eyebrow and underparts, white stripe below eye (usually), lime-green eyes, dark grey legs. **Voice** Song, slightly descending whistled "heeer" c. 1/second, monotonously repeated. **TN** Usually includes Pacific slope *V. mikettae*.

leucotis

Pale-legged Shrike-vireo (Slaty-capped Shrike-vireo)
Vireolanius mikettae (*Vireolanius* [*leucotis*] *mikettae*) `LC`
Verderón Real
Common (by voice) resident.

 L 14.5 cm (5.7"). Monotypic. Humid and wet Pacific foothill forest. 200–1800 m (rarely 2100 m). Sluggish, stays high in canopy foliage, often heard, difficult to see. Diligently follows mixed flocks. **ID** Bold eyebrow, spot below eye and underparts yellow, eyes lime-green, legs flesh-pink. **Voice** Much like allied Slaty-capped Shrike-vireo but notes nearly flat (not descending); monotonously repeated, penetrating "eeeer". **TN** Usually regarded as a race of Slaty-capped Shrike-vireo.

Genus *Tunchiornis* Recalls other greenlets (*Hylophilus*, *Pachysylvia*) but vocalizations differ. Eyes light or dark. Usually fairly low (not high) inside forest.

Tawny-crowned Greenlet *Tunchiornis ochraceiceps* `LC`
Verderón Leonado
Common (but easily overlooked) resident.

 L 12 cm (4.7"). Races *bulunensis*[A], *ferrugineifrons*[B]. Fairly low inside humid and wet lowland and foothill forest. To 800 m. Restless, habitually clings upside-down to leaves like many greenlets; follows mixed flocks. **ID** Tawny-rufous forecrown, otherwise uniform olive above, underparts faintly tinged yellow, eyes grey. **Voice** Best identified by voice: a clear descending "pueeeeeeeer" (recalls gnatwrens); upward-inflected meowing; a harsh nasal "nya" scold. **SS** ♀ Plain Antvireo (p. 267); other forest greenlets usually in canopy.

ferrugineifrons

418

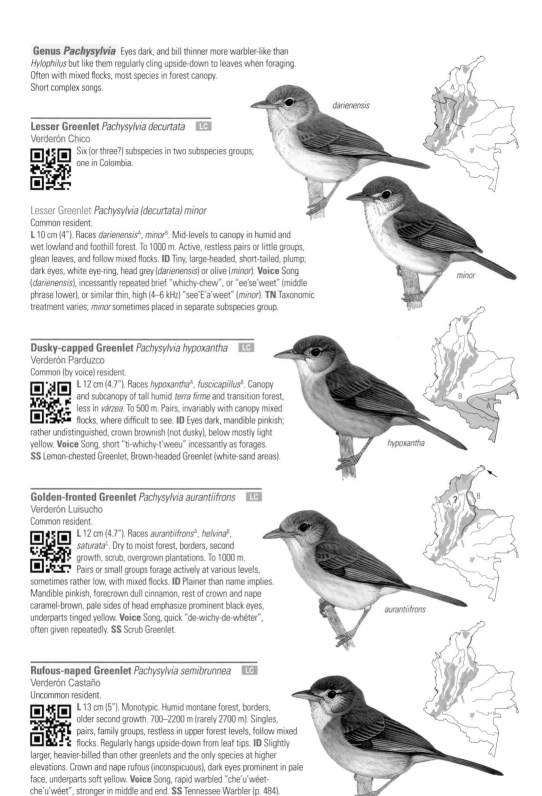

Genus *Pachysylvia* Eyes dark, and bill thinner more warbler-like than *Hylophilus* but like them regularly cling upside-down to leaves when foraging. Often with mixed flocks, most species in forest canopy. Short complex songs.

darienensis

Lesser Greenlet *Pachysylvia decurtata* LC
Verderón Chico

Six (or three?) subspecies in two subspecies groups; one in Colombia.

minor

Lesser Greenlet *Pachysylvia (decurtata) minor*
Common resident.
L 10 cm (4"). Races *darienensis*[A], *minor*[B]. Mid-levels to canopy in humid and wet lowland and foothill forest. To 1000 m. Active, restless pairs or little groups, glean leaves, and follow mixed flocks. **ID** Tiny, large-headed, short-tailed, plump; dark eyes, white eye-ring, head grey (*darienensis*) or olive (*minor*). **Voice** Song (*darienensis*), incessantly repeated brief "whichy-chew", or "ee'se'weet" (middle phrase lower), or similar thin, high (4–6 kHz) "see'E'a'weet" (*minor*). **TN** Taxonomic treatment varies; *minor* sometimes placed in separate subspecies group.

Dusky-capped Greenlet *Pachysylvia hypoxantha* LC
Verderón Parduzco
Common (by voice) resident.
L 12 cm (4.7"). Races *hypoxantha*[A], *fuscicapillus*[B]. Canopy and subcanopy of tall humid *terra firme* and transition forest, less in *várzea*. To 500 m. Pairs, invariably with canopy mixed flocks, where difficult to see. **ID** Eyes dark, mandible pinkish; rather undistinguished, crown brownish (not dusky), below mostly light yellow. **Voice** Song, short "ti-whichy-t'weeu" incessantly as forages. **SS** Lemon-chested Greenlet, Brown-headed Greenlet (white-sand areas).

hypoxantha

Golden-fronted Greenlet *Pachysylvia aurantiifrons* LC
Verderón Luisucho
Common resident.
L 12 cm (4.7"). Races *aurantiifrons*[A], *helvina*[B], *saturata*[C]. Dry to moist forest, borders, second growth, scrub, overgrown plantations. To 1000 m. Pairs or small groups forage actively at various levels, sometimes rather low, with mixed flocks. **ID** Plainer than name implies. Mandible pinkish, forecrown dull cinnamon, rest of crown and nape caramel-brown, pale sides of head emphasize prominent black eyes, underparts tinged yellow. **Voice** Song, quick "de-wichy-de-whéter", often given repeatedly. **SS** Scrub Greenlet.

aurantiifrons

Rufous-naped Greenlet *Pachysylvia semibrunnea* LC
Verderón Castaño
Uncommon resident.
L 13 cm (5"). Monotypic. Humid montane forest, borders, older second growth. 700–2200 m (rarely 2700 m). Singles, pairs, family groups, restless in upper forest levels, follow mixed flocks. Regularly hangs upside-down from leaf tips. **ID** Slightly larger, heavier-billed than other greenlets and the only species at higher elevations. Crown and nape rufous (inconspicuous), dark eyes prominent in pale face, underparts soft yellow. **Voice** Song, rapid warbled "che'u'wéet-che'u'wéet", stronger in middle and end. **SS** Tennessee Warbler (p. 484).

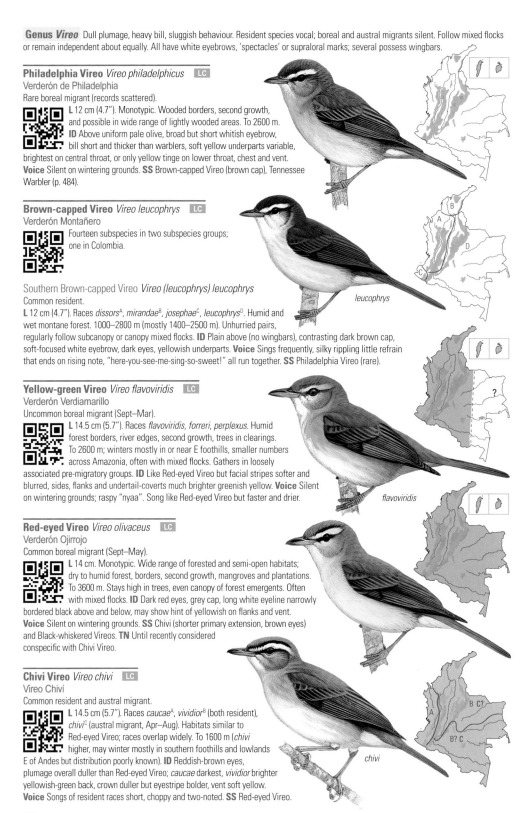

Genus *Vireo* Dull plumage, heavy bill, sluggish behaviour. Resident species vocal; boreal and austral migrants silent. Follow mixed flocks or remain independent about equally. All have white eyebrows, 'spectacles' or supraloral marks; several possess wingbars.

Philadelphia Vireo *Vireo philadelphicus* `LC`
Verderón de Philadelphia
Rare boreal migrant (records scattered).

L 12 cm (4.7"). Monotypic. Wooded borders, second growth, and possible in wide range of lightly wooded areas. To 2600 m. **ID** Above uniform pale olive, broad but short whitish eyebrow, bill short and thicker than warblers, soft yellow underparts variable, brightest on central throat, or only yellow tinge on lower throat, chest and vent. **Voice** Silent on wintering grounds. **SS** Brown-capped Vireo (brown cap), Tennessee Warbler (p. 484).

Brown-capped Vireo *Vireo leucophrys* `LC`
Verderón Montañero

Fourteen subspecies in two subspecies groups; one in Colombia.

Southern Brown-capped Vireo *Vireo (leucophrys) leucophrys*
Common resident.
L 12 cm (4.7"). Races *dissors*[A], *mirandae*[B], *josephae*[C], *leucophrys*[D]. Humid and wet montane forest. 1000–2800 m (mostly 1400–2500 m). Unhurried pairs, regularly follow subcanopy or canopy mixed flocks. **ID** Plain above (no wingbars), contrasting dark brown cap, soft-focused white eyebrow, dark eyes, yellowish underparts. **Voice** Sings frequently, silky rippling little refrain that ends on rising note, "here-you-see-me-sing-so-sweet!" all run together. **SS** Philadelphia Vireo (rare).

leucophrys

Yellow-green Vireo *Vireo flavoviridis* `LC`
Verderón Verdiamarillo
Uncommon boreal migrant (Sept–Mar).

L 14.5 cm (5.7"). Races *flavoviridis, forreri, perplexus*. Humid forest borders, river edges, second growth, trees in clearings. To 2600 m; winters mostly in or near E foothills, smaller numbers across Amazonia, often with mixed flocks. Gathers in loosely associated pre-migratory groups. **ID** Like Red-eyed Vireo but facial stripes softer and blurred, sides, flanks and undertail-coverts much brighter greenish yellow. **Voice** Silent on wintering grounds; raspy "nyaa". Song like Red-eyed Vireo but faster and drier.

flavoviridis

Red-eyed Vireo *Vireo olivaceus* `LC`
Verderón Ojirrojo
Common boreal migrant (Sept–May).

L 14 cm. Monotypic. Wide range of forested and semi-open habitats; dry to humid forest, borders, second growth, mangroves and plantations. To 3600 m. Stays high in trees, even canopy of forest emergents. Often with mixed flocks. **ID** Dark red eyes, grey cap, long white eyeline narrowly bordered black above and below, may show hint of yellowish on flanks and vent. **Voice** Silent on wintering grounds. **SS** Chivi (shorter primary extension, brown eyes) and Black-whiskered Vireos. **TN** Until recently considered conspecific with Chivi Vireo.

Chivi Vireo *Vireo chivi* `LC`
Vireo Chiví
Common resident and austral migrant.

L 14.5 cm (5.7"). Races *caucae*[A], *vividior*[B] (both resident), *chivi*[C] (austral migrant, Apr–Aug). Habitats similar to Red-eyed Vireo; races overlap widely. To 1600 m (*chivi* higher, may winter mostly in southern foothills and lowlands E of Andes but distribution poorly known). **ID** Reddish-brown eyes, plumage overall duller than Red-eyed Vireo; *caucae* darkest, *vividior* brighter yellowish-green back, crown duller but eyestripe bolder, vent soft yellow. **Voice** Songs of resident races short, choppy and two-noted. **SS** Red-eyed Vireo.

chivi

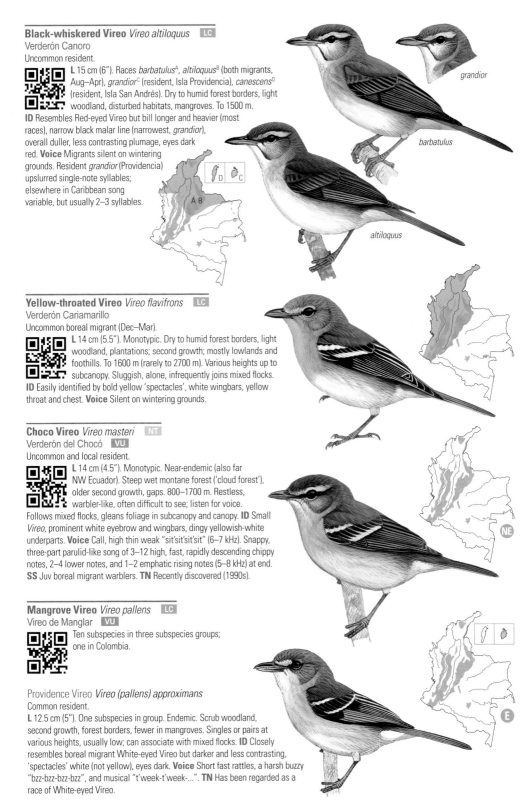

Black-whiskered Vireo *Vireo altiloquus* `LC`
Verderón Canoro
Uncommon resident.

L 15 cm (6"). Races *barbatulus*[A], *altiloquus*[B] (both migrants, Aug–Apr), *grandior*[C] (resident, Isla Providencia), *canescens*[D] (resident, Isla San Andrés). Dry to humid forest borders, light woodland, disturbed habitats, mangroves. To 1500 m.
ID Resembles Red-eyed Vireo but bill longer and heavier (most races), narrow black malar line (narrowest, *grandior*), overall duller, less contrasting plumage, eyes dark red. **Voice** Migrants silent on wintering grounds. Resident *grandior* (Providencia) upslurred single-note syllables; elsewhere in Caribbean song variable, but usually 2–3 syllables.

grandior

barbatulus

altiloquus

Yellow-throated Vireo *Vireo flavifrons* `LC`
Verderón Cariamarillo
Uncommon boreal migrant (Dec–Mar).

L 14 cm (5.5"). Monotypic. Dry to humid forest borders, light woodland, plantations; second growth; mostly lowlands and foothills. To 1600 m (rarely to 2700 m). Various heights up to subcanopy. Sluggish, alone, infrequently joins mixed flocks.
ID Easily identified by bold yellow 'spectacles', white wingbars, yellow throat and chest. **Voice** Silent on wintering grounds.

Choco Vireo *Vireo masteri* `NT`
Verderón del Chocó `VU`
Uncommon and local resident.

L 14 cm (4.5"). Monotypic. Near-endemic (also far NW Ecuador). Steep wet montane forest ('cloud forest'), older second growth, gaps. 800–1700 m. Restless, warbler-like, often difficult to see; listen for voice. Follows mixed flocks, gleans foliage in subcanopy and canopy. **ID** Small *Vireo*, prominent white eyebrow and wingbars, dingy yellowish-white underparts. **Voice** Call, high thin weak "sit'sit'sit'sit" (6–7 kHz). Snappy, three-part parulid-like song of 3–12 high, fast, rapidly descending chippy notes, 2–4 lower notes, and 1–2 emphatic rising notes (5–8 kHz) at end.
SS Juv boreal migrant warblers. **TN** Recently discovered (1990s).

Mangrove Vireo *Vireo pallens* `LC`
Vireo de Manglar `VU`

Ten subspecies in three subspecies groups; one in Colombia.

Providence Vireo *Vireo (pallens) approximans*
Common resident.

L 12.5 cm (5"). One subspecies in group. Endemic. Scrub woodland, second growth, forest borders, fewer in mangroves. Singles or pairs at various heights, usually low; can associate with mixed flocks. **ID** Closely resembles boreal migrant White-eyed Vireo but darker and less contrasting, 'spectacles' white (not yellow), eyes dark. **Voice** Short fast rattles, a harsh buzzy "bzz-bzz-bzz-bzz", and musical "t'week-t'week-...". **TN** Has been regarded as a race of White-eyed Vireo.

421

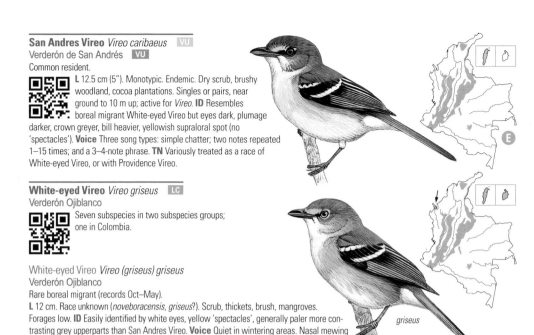

San Andres Vireo *Vireo caribaeus* VU
Verderón de San Andrés VU

Common resident.

L 12.5 cm (5"). Monotypic. Endemic. Dry scrub, brushy woodland, cocoa plantations. Singles or pairs, near ground to 10 m up; active for *Vireo*. **ID** Resembles boreal migrant White-eyed Vireo but eyes dark, plumage darker, crown greyer, bill heavier, yellowish supraloral spot (no 'spectacles'). **Voice** Three song types: simple chatter; two notes repeated 1–15 times; and a 3–4-note phrase. **TN** Variously treated as a race of White-eyed Vireo, or with Providence Vireo.

White-eyed Vireo *Vireo griseus* LC
Verderón Ojiblanco

Seven subspecies in two subspecies groups; one in Colombia.

White-eyed Vireo *Vireo (griseus) griseus*
Verderón Ojiblanco

Rare boreal migrant (records Oct–May).

L 12 cm. Race unknown (*noveboracensis, griseus*?). Scrub, thickets, brush, mangroves. Forages low. **ID** Easily identified by white eyes, yellow 'spectacles', generally paler more contrasting grey upperparts than San Andres Vireo. **Voice** Quiet in wintering areas. Nasal mewing note. **TN** Providence and San Andres Vireos sometimes regarded as races of present species.

griseus

CORVIDAE
Crows and Jays
130 extant species, 8 in region

Nearly worldwide family whose members are generally commoner and more conspicuous in northern latitudes. Only jays occur in South America. They can scold noisily, but more often are quiet and stealthy. They travel in small groups that typically contain younger birds of previous generations that behave as helpers to breeding pairs.

Genus *Cyanolyca* High montane species; slender, attractive blue-and-black plumage, black mask. Quiet, inconspicuous and easily overlooked. Omnivorous diet includes more arthropods than fruit.

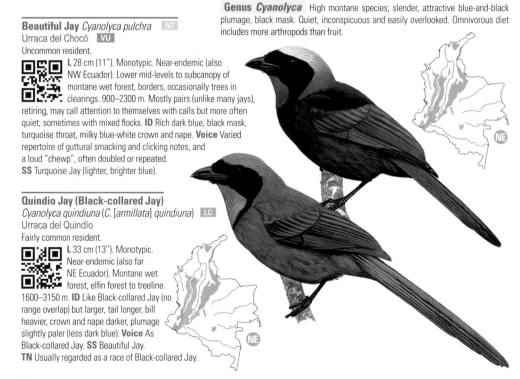

Beautiful Jay *Cyanolyca pulchra* NT
Urraca del Chocó VU

Uncommon resident.

L 28 cm (11"). Monotypic. Near-endemic (also NW Ecuador). Lower mid-levels to subcanopy of montane wet forest, borders, occasionally trees in clearings. 900–2300 m. Mostly pairs (unlike many jays), retiring, may call attention to themselves with calls but more often quiet; sometimes with mixed flocks. **ID** Rich dark blue; black mask, turquoise throat, milky blue-white crown and nape. **Voice** Varied repertoire of guttural smacking and clicking notes, and a loud "chewp", often doubled or repeated. **SS** Turquoise Jay (lighter, brighter blue).

Quindio Jay (Black-collared Jay)
Cyanolyca quindiuna (*C.* [*armillata*] *quindiuna*) LC
Urraca del Quindío

Fairly common resident.

L 33 cm (13"). Monotypic. Near-endemic (also far NE Ecuador). Montane wet forest, elfin forest to treeline. 1600–3150 m. **ID** Like Black-collared Jay (no range overlap) but larger, tail longer, bill heavier, crown and nape darker, plumage slightly paler (less dark blue). **Voice** As Black-collared Jay. **SS** Beautiful Jay. **TN** Usually regarded as a race of Black-collared Jay.

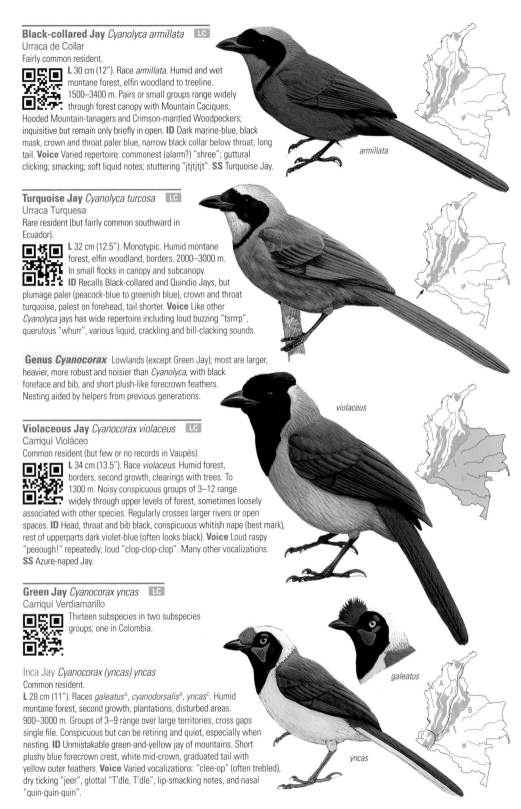

Black-collared Jay *Cyanolyca armillata* `LC`
Urraca de Collar
Fairly common resident.

L 30 cm (12"). Race *armillata*. Humid and wet montane forest, elfin woodland to treeline. 1500–3400 m. Pairs or small groups range widely through forest canopy with Mountain Caciques, Hooded Mountain-tanagers and Crimson-mantled Woodpeckers; inquisitive but remain only briefly in open. **ID** Dark marine-blue, black mask, crown and throat paler blue, narrow black collar below throat, long tail. **Voice** Varied repertoire: commonest (alarm?) "shree"; guttural clicking; smacking; soft liquid notes; stuttering "jtjtjtjt". **SS** Turquoise Jay.

armillata

Turquoise Jay *Cyanolyca turcosa* `LC`
Urraca Turquesa
Rare resident (but fairly common southward in Ecuador).

L 32 cm (12.5"). Monotypic. Humid montane forest, elfin woodland, borders. 2000–3000 m. In small flocks in canopy and subcanopy. **ID** Recalls Black-collared and Quindio Jays, but plumage paler (peacock-blue to greenish blue), crown and throat turquoise, palest on forehead, tail shorter. **Voice** Like other *Cyanolyca* jays has wide repertoire including loud buzzing "tsrrrp", querulous "whurr", various liquid, crackling and bill-clacking sounds.

Genus *Cyanocorax* Lowlands (except Green Jay); most are larger, heavier, more robust and noisier than *Cyanolyca*, with black foreface and bib, and short plush-like forecrown feathers. Nesting aided by helpers from previous generations.

violaceus

Violaceous Jay *Cyanocorax violaceus* `LC`
Carriquí Violáceo
Common resident (but few or no records in Vaupés).

L 34 cm (13.5"). Race *violaceus*. Humid forest, borders, second growth, clearings with trees. To 1300 m. Noisy conspicuous groups of 3–12 range widely through upper levels of forest, sometimes loosely associated with other species. Regularly crosses larger rivers or open spaces. **ID** Head, throat and bib black, conspicuous whitish nape (best mark), rest of upperparts dark violet-blue (often looks black). **Voice** Loud raspy "peeough!" repeatedly; loud "clop-clop-clop". Many other vocalizations. **SS** Azure-naped Jay.

Green Jay *Cyanocorax yncas* `LC`
Carriquí Verdiamarillo

Thirteen subspecies in two subspecies groups; one in Colombia.

Inca Jay *Cyanocorax (yncas) yncas*
Common resident.

L 28 cm (11"). Races *galeatus*[A], *cyanodorsalis*[B], *yncas*[C]. Humid montane forest, second growth, plantations, disturbed areas. 900–3000 m. Groups of 3–9 range over large territories, cross gaps single file. Conspicuous but can be retiring and quiet, especially when nesting. **ID** Unmistakable green-and-yellow jay of mountains. Short plushy blue forecrown crest, white mid-crown, graduated tail with yellow outer feathers. **Voice** Varied vocalizations: "clee-op" (often trebled), dry ticking "jeer", glottal "T'dle, T'dle", lip-smacking notes, and nasal "quin-quin-quin".

galeatus

yncas

423

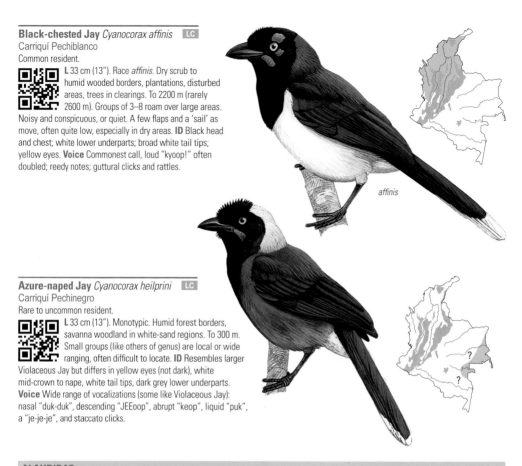

Black-chested Jay *Cyanocorax affinis* LC
Carriquí Pechiblanco
Common resident.

 L 33 cm (13"). Race *affinis*. Dry scrub to
humid wooded borders, plantations, disturbed
areas, trees in clearings. To 2200 m (rarely
2600 m). Groups of 3–8 roam over large areas.
Noisy and conspicuous, or quiet. A few flaps and a 'sail' as
move, often quite low, especially in dry areas. **ID** Black head
and chest; white lower underparts; broad white tail tips;
yellow eyes. **Voice** Commonest call, loud "kyoop!" often
doubled; reedy notes; guttural clicks and rattles.

affinis

Azure-naped Jay *Cyanocorax heilprini* LC
Carriquí Pechinegro
Rare to uncommon resident.

L 33 cm (13"). Monotypic. Humid forest borders,
savanna woodland in white-sand regions. To 300 m.
Small groups (like others of genus) are local or wide
ranging, often difficult to locate. **ID** Resembles larger
Violaceous Jay but differs in yellow eyes (not dark), white
mid-crown to nape, white tail tips, dark grey lower underparts.
Voice Wide range of vocalizations (some like Violaceous Jay):
nasal "duk-duk", descending "JEEoop", abrupt "keop", liquid "puk",
a "je-je-je", and staccato clicks.

ALAUDIDAE
Larks

92 extant species, 1 in region

Large almost exclusively Old World family, commonest in grasslands of dry to arid regions, with just one species in the Americas. Notable for cryptic plumages; terrestrial, run or walk.

Horned Lark *Eremophila alpestris* LC
Alondra Cornuda EN

Twenty-eight subspecies in seven subspecies groups;
one in Colombia.

Colombian Horned Lark *Eremophila (alpestris) peregrina*
Local and declining resident.
L 15 cm (6"). One subspecies in group. Endemic. Short-grass pastures,
bare or sparsely vegetated fields, airport runways. 2500–3200 m.
Singles, pairs or scattered small groups; terrestrial, with short-legged
crouching posture. Flight low and dipping. **ID** Drooping black mask,
black chest crescent, tiny black 'horns', yellow-tinged face (♀ paler).
In flight tail black, edges white. **Voice** A few faint notes and complex
tinkling warble that rises in pitch. **TN** Colombian *peregrina* sometimes
included with North American races in the *alpestris* group.

DONACOBIIDAE
Donacobius
1 extant species, 1 in region

An enigmatic species that has, at various times, been placed with wrens or mimids, but which molecular studies have revealed belongs in a family of its own. Its genetic affinities may be closest to some Old World warblers (Locustellidae).

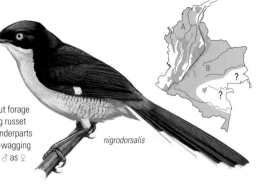

Black-capped Donacobius
Donacobius atricapilla `LC`
Cucarachero de Laguna
Common resident.

L 22 cm (8.5"). Races *brachypterus*[A], *nigrodorsalis*[B]. Marshes, lake edges, wet shrubby pastures. To 1000 m (occasionally higher). Engaging jesters of marshy areas, perch conspicuously atop bushes or tall grass to duet, but forage on or near ground. **ID** Unmistakable. Eyes yellow, head black becoming russet brown on back, white wing patch, long graduated white-tipped tail, underparts creamy buff. **Voice** Loud whistled calls; antiphonal duets include tail-wagging display, with slow liquid "whot-whot-whot..." (or "whick-whick...") by ♂ as ♀ gives scratchy "jeeeeer, jeeeeer...". **AN** Donacobius.

nigrodorsalis

HIRUNDINIDAE
Swallows and Martins
89 extant species, 17 in region + 2 vagrants

Swallows and martins are a nearly worldwide group, many having lived in close association with humans since the dawn of history. Their stream-lined bodies, long pointed wings and wide gapes are adaptations for capturing food on the wing. Swallows differ from swifts in having flexible wings, buoyant manoeuvrable flight, and the ability to perch normally. Many are migratory, and most are gregarious to varying degrees. Nesting is often colonial, in holes, burrows, open or enclosed globular mud nests. Molecular data now place many genera on a firmer taxonomic footing.

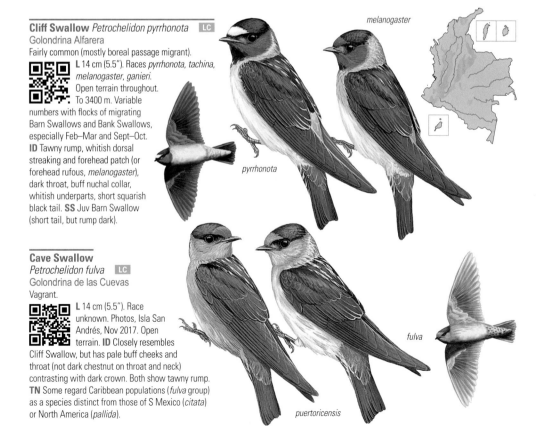

Cliff Swallow *Petrochelidon pyrrhonota* `LC`
Golondrina Alfarera
Fairly common (mostly boreal passage migrant).

L 14 cm (5.5"). Races *pyrrhonota*, *tachina*, *melanogaster*, *ganieri*. Open terrain throughout. To 3400 m. Variable numbers with flocks of migrating Barn Swallows and Bank Swallows, especially Feb–Mar and Sept–Oct. **ID** Tawny rump, whitish dorsal streaking and forehead patch (or forehead rufous, *melanogaster*), dark throat, buff nuchal collar, whitish underparts, short squarish black tail. **SS** Juv Barn Swallow (short tail, but rump dark).

melanogaster

pyrrhonota

Cave Swallow
Petrochelidon fulva `LC`
Golondrina de las Cuevas
Vagrant.

L 14 cm (5.5"). Race unknown. Photos, Isla San Andrés, Nov 2017. Open terrain. **ID** Closely resembles Cliff Swallow, but has pale buff cheeks and throat (not dark chestnut on throat and neck) contrasting with dark crown. Both show tawny rump. **TN** Some regard Caribbean populations (*fulva* group) as a species distinct from those of S Mexico (*citata*) or North America (*pallida*).

fulva

puertoricensis

Barn Swallow *Hirundo rustica* `LC`
Golondrina Tijereta

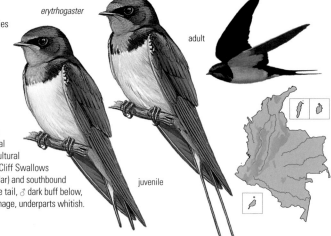

erytrhogaster

adult

Eight subspecies in two subspecies groups; one in Colombia.

American Barn Swallow
Hirundo (rustica) erythrogaster
Common boreal winter visitor and passage migrant (late Aug–May).
L 15 cm (6"). Race *erythrogaster*. Open terrain. To 3400 m. Large passage flocks, smaller boreal wintering flocks. Fly low, especially over agricultural fields; gather in large numbers with Bank and Cliff Swallows along rivers in Amazonia during north- (Feb–Mar) and southbound (Sept–Oct) migration. **ID** Ad long forked needle tail, ♂ dark buff below, ♀ whitish below. Juv short-tailed, ragged plumage, underparts whitish. **Voice** Soft "tweed".

juvenile

Bank Swallow *Riparia riparia* `LC`
Golondrina Ribereña

Sporadically common boreal passage migrant W of Andes, large numbers E of Andes (Sept–Oct and Feb–Mar), winter resident in small numbers throughout.

riparia

L 13 cm (5"). Race *riparia*. Open terrain, usually with other migrant swallows. To 3400 m. **ID** Small, above brown, below white with narrow dark breast-band, white of throat wraps onto sides of neck, narrow notched tail, underwing-coverts darker than flight feathers. **SS** Juv Barn Swallow, Brown-chested Martin. **AN** Collared Sand Martin (Old World).

Genus *Tachycineta* Small and bicoloured, glossy blue-black above and white below. Notched or sharply forked tails. Several have white rumps or white on sides of rump. Often near water.

Tree Swallow *Tachycineta bicolor* `LC`
Golondrina Bicolor

Vagrant (Isla San Andrés; once, Antioquia, Aug).
L 14.5 cm (5.7"). Monotypic. Open terrain, often near water. To 2800 m. Records Aug–Jan, alone or with other swallows. **ID** ♂ above glossy greenish blue, below white, uniformly dark underwing-coverts, squarish to slightly notched tail. ♀ duller (no gloss). Juv above dark brown, darker contrasting cheeks, faint dusky chest-band. **SS** Bank Swallow.

[Violet-green Swallow *Tachycineta thalassina*] `LC`
Golondrina Verdivioleta

Hypothetical (one unconfirmed sight record, Santa Marta Mts).
L 13.5 cm (5.3"). Race presumably *thalassina*. Open terrain or open woodland. 2200 m. **ID** Ad ♂ crown and upperparts glossy bottle-green, rump and short tail glossed purplish, line above eyes, cheeks, underparts and sides of rump white. ♀ above duller, less white on face, white-edged tertials. Juv above dark brown including cheeks, below dingy white. **SS** Tree Swallow.

thalassina

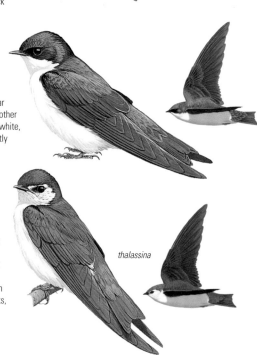

[Bahama Swallow *Tachycineta cyaneoviridis*] `EN`
Golondrina de Bahamas
Hypothetical (one unconfirmed sight record, coastal Guajira).

 L 14.7 cm (5.8"). Monotypic. Open or semi-open terrain. **ID** Ad ♂ above bright oily green including long deeply forked tail, blackish eyeline, cheeks, underparts and underwing-coverts white, flight feathers dusky. ♀ similar (including white underwing-coverts) but duller above. Juv similar but above dusky brown, tail shorter.

[Mangrove Swallow *Tachycineta albilinea*] `LC`
Golondrina Manglera
Hypothetical.

 L 13 cm (5"). Monotypic. Low above ground near water. Sea level. Resident, E Panama; unconfirmed sight records in NW Colombia. **ID** Ad ♂ above glossy blue-green, short white eyeline, white rump, dark underwing-coverts contrast with paler flight feathers, tertials often edged white. ♀ duller. **SS** Easily confused with White-winged Swallow (no white eyeline, much more white on secondaries).

White-winged Swallow *Tachycineta albiventer* `LC`
Golondrina Aliblanca
Common resident.

 L 14 cm (5.5"). Monotypic. Almost always near or over rivers, lakes or bodies of water. To 1000 m. Conspicuous, perches on snags or partly submerged driftwood in water; flies low over water. Nests in cavities over water. **ID** Ad ♂ above dark glossy greenish blue, rump and underparts white, tertials, inner secondaries and upperwing-coverts broadly edged white. ♀ duller. Juv above brownish, less white on wings. **SS** Mangrove Swallow.

Genus *Progne* Large swallows (known as martins), which often fly high (except Brown-chested Martin). Tail fairly long and shallowly forked (except Southern Martin). Migratory forms gather and roost in large numbers. Several represent identification challenges and photo documentation is encouraged; the sexes usually differ. Taxonomy not fully resolved.

Brown-chested Martin *Progne tapera* `LC`
Golondrina Sabanera
Common austral migrant E of Andes, fewer W of Andes (Mar–Sept), and local resident.

 L 18 cm (7") resident *tapera*, or 18.5 cm (7.3") austral migrant *fusca*. Open riverbanks, lakes, savanna with scattered trees, often near water. To 1200 m (infrequently 3000 m). Resident pairs nest singly in cavities; austral migrants in small to large flocks (may reach Caribbean islands?). Perches in open on snags, wires, fallen branches in water. **ID** Below white, brownish chest-band, long white undertail-coverts conspicuous in flight (*tapera*), or similar but darker chest-band crossed by irregular vertical band of brown spots (*fusca*). **Voice** Rich gurgling sounds.

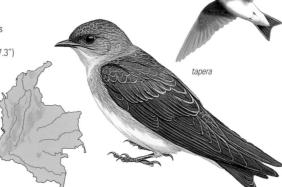

tapera

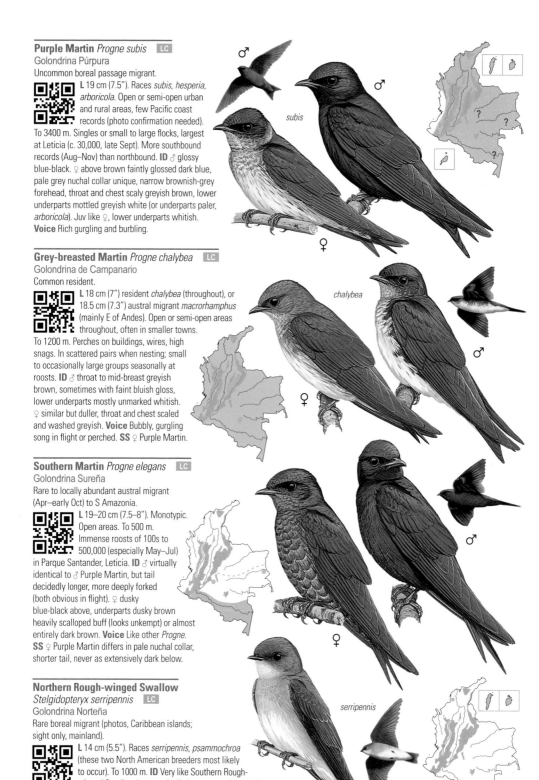

Purple Martin *Progne subis* `LC`
Golondrina Púrpura
Uncommon boreal passage migrant.

L 19 cm (7.5"). Races *subis, hesperia, arboricola*. Open or semi-open urban and rural areas, few Pacific coast records (photo confirmation needed). To 3400 m. Singles or small to large flocks, largest at Leticia (c. 30,000, late Sept). More southbound records (Aug–Nov) than northbound. **ID** ♂ glossy blue-black. ♀ above brown faintly glossed dark blue, pale grey nuchal collar unique, narrow brownish-grey forehead, throat and chest scaly greyish brown, lower underparts mottled greyish white (or underparts paler, *arboricola*). Juv like ♀, lower underparts whitish. **Voice** Rich gurgling and burbling.

subis

Grey-breasted Martin *Progne chalybea* `LC`
Golondrina de Campanario
Common resident.

L 18 cm (7") resident *chalybea* (throughout), or 18.5 cm (7.3") austral migrant *macrorhamphus* (mainly E of Andes). Open or semi-open areas throughout, often in smaller towns. To 1200 m. Perches on buildings, wires, high snags. In scattered pairs when nesting; small to occasionally large groups seasonally at roosts. **ID** ♂ throat to mid-breast greyish brown, sometimes with faint bluish gloss, lower underparts mostly unmarked whitish. ♀ similar but duller, throat and chest scaled and washed greyish. **Voice** Bubbly, gurgling song in flight or perched. **SS** ♀ Purple Martin.

chalybea

Southern Martin *Progne elegans* `LC`
Golondrina Sureña
Rare to locally abundant austral migrant (Apr–early Oct) to S Amazonia.

L 19–20 cm (7.5–8"). Monotypic. Open areas. To 500 m. Immense roosts of 100s to 500,000 (especially May–Jul) in Parque Santander, Leticia. **ID** ♂ virtually identical to ♂ Purple Martin, but tail decidedly longer, more deeply forked (both obvious in flight). ♀ dusky blue-black above, underparts dusky brown heavily scalloped buff (looks unkempt) or almost entirely dark brown. **Voice** Like other *Progne*. **SS** ♀ Purple Martin differs in pale nuchal collar, shorter tail, never as extensively dark below.

Northern Rough-winged Swallow
Stelgidopteryx serripennis `LC`
Golondrina Norteña
Rare boreal migrant (photos, Caribbean islands; sight only, mainland).

L 14 cm (5.5"). Races *serripennis, psammochroa* (these two North American breeders most likely to occur). To 1000 m. **ID** Very like Southern Rough-winged Swallow but marginally larger, rump brown like back (not whitish), tail squarish, throat dusky brown (not cinnamon-buff). Juv cinnamon-edged wing-coverts, throat tinged pinkish buff.

serripennis

Southern Rough-winged Swallow *Stelgidopteryx ruficollis* `LC`
Golondrina Barranquera
Common resident.

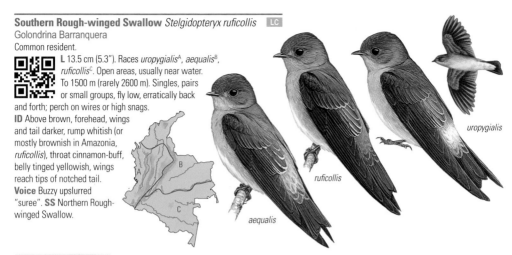

L 13.5 cm (5.3"). Races *uropygialis*[A], *aequalis*[B], *ruficollis*[C]. Open areas, usually near water. To 1500 m (rarely 2600 m). Singles, pairs or small groups, fly low, erratically back and forth; perch on wires or high snags. **ID** Above brown, forehead, wings and tail darker, rump whitish (or mostly brownish in Amazonia, *ruficollis*), throat cinnamon-buff, belly tinged yellowish, wings reach tips of notched tail. **Voice** Buzzy upslurred "suree". **SS** Northern Rough-winged Swallow.

uropygialis

ruficollis

aequalis

Genus *Pygochelidon* Relatively small bicoloured swallows, genetically close but otherwise differ in habitat and elevation.

Blue-and-white Swallow *Pygochelidon cyanoleuca* `LC`
Golondrina Blanquiazul

Three subspecies in two subspecies groups; both in Colombia.

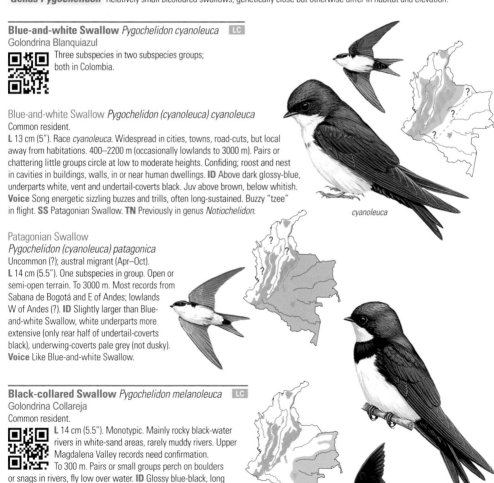

Blue-and-white Swallow *Pygochelidon (cyanoleuca) cyanoleuca*
Common resident.
L 13 cm (5"). Race *cyanoleuca*. Widespread in cities, towns, road-cuts, but local away from habitations. 400–2200 m (occasionally lowlands to 3000 m). Pairs or chattering little groups circle at low to moderate heights. Confiding; roost and nest in cavities in buildings, walls, in or near human dwellings. **ID** Above dark glossy-blue, underparts white, vent and undertail-coverts black. Juv above brown, below whitish. **Voice** Song energetic sizzling buzzes and trills, often long-sustained. Buzzy "tzee" in flight. **SS** Patagonian Swallow. **TN** Previously in genus *Notiochelidon*.

cyanoleuca

Patagonian Swallow
Pygochelidon (cyanoleuca) patagonica
Uncommon (?); austral migrant (Apr–Oct).
L 14 cm (5.5"). One subspecies in group. Open or semi-open terrain. To 3000 m. Most records from Sabana de Bogotá and E of Andes; lowlands W of Andes (?). **ID** Slightly larger than Blue-and-white Swallow, white underparts more extensive (only rear half of undertail-coverts black), underwing-coverts pale grey (not dusky). **Voice** Like Blue-and-white Swallow.

Black-collared Swallow *Pygochelidon melanoleuca* `LC`
Golondrina Collareja
Common resident.

L 14 cm (5.5"). Monotypic. Mainly rocky black-water rivers in white-sand areas, rarely muddy rivers. Upper Magdalena Valley records need confirmation. To 300 m. Pairs or small groups perch on boulders or snags in rivers, fly low over water. **ID** Glossy blue-black, long deeply forked black tail, white below with narrow black chest collar, black vent and undertail-coverts, blackish-brown underwing-coverts. **Voice** Short buzzes and trills. **SS** White-banded Swallow.

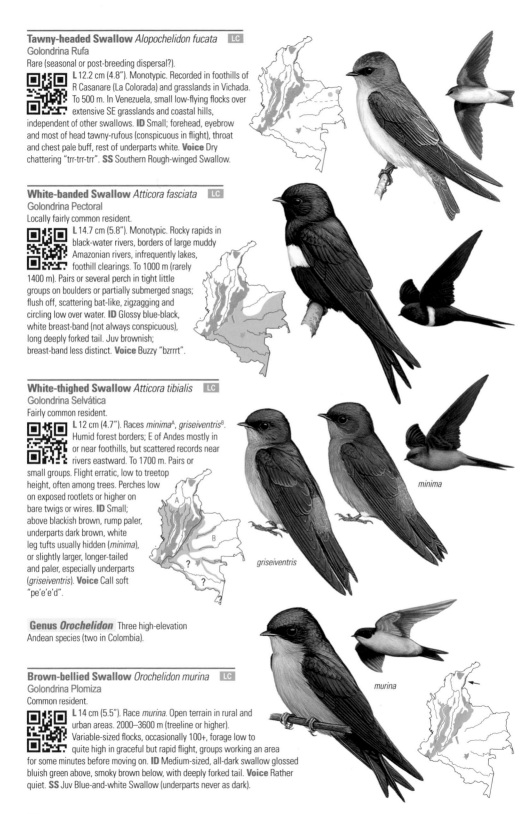

Tawny-headed Swallow *Alopochelidon fucata* `LC`
Golondrina Rufa

Rare (seasonal or post-breeding dispersal?).
L 12.2 cm (4.8"). Monotypic. Recorded in foothills of R Casanare (La Colorada) and grasslands in Vichada. To 500 m. In Venezuela, small low-flying flocks over extensive SE grasslands and coastal hills, independent of other swallows. **ID** Small; forehead, eyebrow and most of head tawny-rufous (conspicuous in flight), throat and chest pale buff, rest of underparts white. **Voice** Dry chattering "trr-trr-trr". **SS** Southern Rough-winged Swallow.

White-banded Swallow *Atticora fasciata* `LC`
Golondrina Pectoral

Locally fairly common resident.
L 14.7 cm (5.8"). Monotypic. Rocky rapids in black-water rivers, borders of large muddy Amazonian rivers, infrequently lakes, foothill clearings. To 1000 m (rarely 1400 m). Pairs or several perch in tight little groups on boulders or partially submerged snags; flush off, scattering bat-like, zigzagging and circling low over water. **ID** Glossy blue-black, white breast-band (not always conspicuous), long deeply forked tail. Juv brownish; breast-band less distinct. **Voice** Buzzy "bzrrrt".

White-thighed Swallow *Atticora tibialis* `LC`
Golondrina Selvática

Fairly common resident.
L 12 cm (4.7"). Races *minima*[A], *griseiventris*[B]. Humid forest borders; E of Andes mostly in or near foothills, but scattered records near rivers eastward. To 1700 m. Pairs or small groups. Flight erratic, low to treetop height, often among trees. Perches low on exposed rootlets or higher on bare twigs or wires. **ID** Small; above blackish brown, rump paler, underparts dark brown, white leg tufts usually hidden (*minima*), or slightly larger, longer-tailed and paler, especially underparts (*griseiventris*). **Voice** Call soft "pe'e'e'd".

griseiventris

minima

Genus *Orochelidon* Three high-elevation Andean species (two in Colombia).

Brown-bellied Swallow *Orochelidon murina* `LC`
Golondrina Plomiza

Common resident.
L 14 cm (5.5"). Race *murina*. Open terrain in rural and urban areas. 2000–3600 m (treeline or higher). Variable-sized flocks, occasionally 100+, forage low to quite high in graceful but rapid flight, groups working an area for some minutes before moving on. **ID** Medium-sized, all-dark swallow glossed bluish green above, smoky brown below, with deeply forked tail. **Voice** Rather quiet. **SS** Juv Blue-and-white Swallow (underparts never as dark).

murina

Pale-footed Swallow *Orochelidon flavipes* LC
Golondrina Paramuna

Local (easily overlooked) resident.

 L 12.2 cm (4.8"). Monotypic. Humid montane forest, borders. 2000–3400 m (usually above 2500 m). Pairs or small groups fly rapidly back and forth low over forest canopy or forested roads. Flight erratic; rests on high bare twigs. **ID** Very like Blue-and-white Swallow (both have pale feet), but differs in dull cinnamon throat, dark sides and flanks (both hard to see), trilled vocalizations, and usually at higher elevations away from settled areas. **Voice** Crisp crackling "tszeet" and soft trilled "tr'e'e'e'e'd", both unlike Blue-and-white Swallow.

POLIOPTILIDAE
Gnatcatchers
15 extant species, 6 in region

A small New World family. Gnatcatchers are spritely, hyperactive little insectivores of dry scrub or canopy of dry to humid forest. They are notable for their slender bodies, long tails, and grey, black and white plumage. Gnatwrens are equally slender with even longer bills, but shorter tails, and more sombre attire. They inhabit forest understorey; only Long-billed Gnatwren occurs higher up.

Collared Gnatwren *Microbates collaris* LC
Curruca Collareja

Uncommon resident.

 L 10.7 cm (4.2"). Races *collaris*[A], *perlatus*[B], *colombianus*[C]. Undergrowth in *terra firme* forest, commonest in white-sand forests. To 700 m. Pairs, perky, animated, constantly wagging cocked tails, but often difficult to see. Flit to foliage or pick small prey from curled dead leaves and vegetation; especially active when mixed flocks pass. **ID** Long thin bill, bold face pattern (less white, *perlatus*), white underparts, black chest-band. **Voice** Song, high thin "eeeeeeeeea" repeatedly; harsh scolding "jipp". **SS** Tawny-faced Gnatwren.

collaris

Tawny-faced Gnatwren *Microbates cinereiventris* LC
Curruca Rubicunda

Locally fairly common resident.

 L 10.7 cm (4.2"). Races *semitorquatus*[A], *cinereiventris*[B], *albapiculus*[C], *magdalenae*[D], *unicus*[E], *hormotus*[F]. Humid forest undergrowth. To 1300 m. Behaviour like Collared Gnatwren. **ID** Wren-like, brownish, with short tail, bright cinnamon sides of head, thin black malar line (black post-ocular, *cinereiventris*), variable dark chest streaking. **Voice** Song, high thin "teeeeeea" repeatedly; harsh scolding and chattering. **SS** Collared Gnatwren. **TN** Races *albapiculus* and *unicus* doubtfully valid. **AN** Half-collared Gnatwren.

cinereiventris

Long-billed Gnatwren *Ramphocaenus melanurus* LC
Curruca Picuda

 Fifteen subspecies in three subspecies groups; two in Colombia.

Long-billed Gnatwren *Ramphocaenus (melanurus) rufiventris*
Fairly common resident.

L 13 cm (5"). Races *rufiventris*[A], *griseodorsalis*[B]. High vine tangles in dry, moist and humid forest. To 1800 m. Skinny little bird, like animated skeleton with wiggling cocked tail. Active pairs or families pick tiny prey from curled dead leaves or live foliage; sometimes with mixed flocks. **ID** Long thin bill, buff face and sides, white throat and median underparts. **Voice** Complex. In general both races sing chattering songs that vary in pitch, c. 2.5–4 kHz. **TN** Taxonomy unresolved.

rufiventris

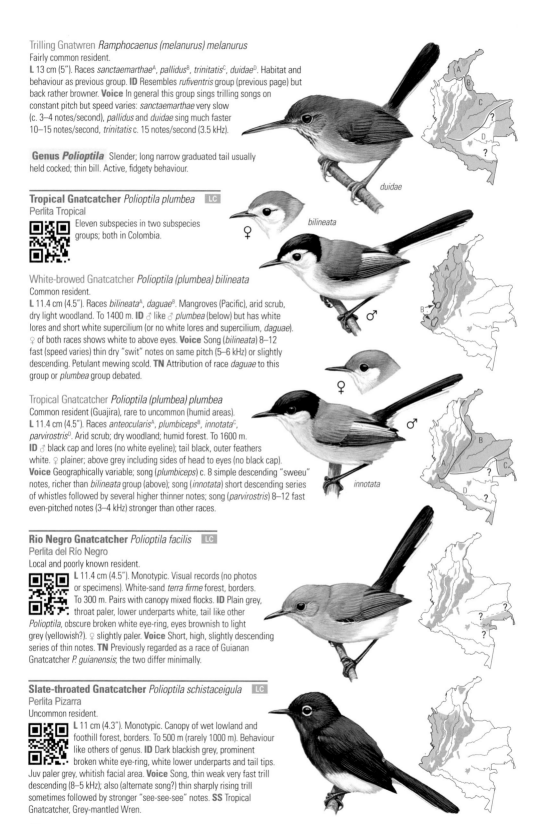

Trilling Gnatwren *Ramphocaenus (melanurus) melanurus*
Fairly common resident.
L 13 cm (5"). Races *sanctaemarthae*[A], *pallidus*[B], *trinitatis*[C], *duidae*[D]. Habitat and behaviour as previous group. **ID** Resembles *rufiventris* group (previous page) but back rather browner. **Voice** In general this group sings trilling songs on constant pitch but speed varies: *sanctaemarthae* very slow (c. 3–4 notes/second), *pallidus* and *duidae* sing much faster 10–15 notes/second, *trinitatis* c. 15 notes/second (3.5 kHz).

Genus *Polioptila* Slender; long narrow graduated tail usually held cocked; thin bill. Active, fidgety behaviour.

duidae

bilineata

Tropical Gnatcatcher *Polioptila plumbea* `LC`
Perlita Tropical

Eleven subspecies in two subspecies groups; both in Colombia.

White-browed Gnatcatcher *Polioptila (plumbea) bilineata*
Common resident.
L 11.4 cm (4.5"). Races *bilineata*[A], *daguae*[B]. Mangroves (Pacific), arid scrub, dry light woodland. To 1400 m. **ID** ♂ like ♂ *plumbea* (below) but has white lores and short white supercilium (or no white lores and supercilium, *daguae*). ♀ of both races shows white to above eyes. **Voice** Song (*bilineata*) 8–12 fast (speed varies) thin dry "swit" notes on same pitch (5–6 kHz) or slightly descending. Petulant mewing scold. **TN** Attribution of race *daguae* to this group or *plumbea* group debated.

Tropical Gnatcatcher *Polioptila (plumbea) plumbea*
Common resident (Guajira), rare to uncommon (humid areas).
L 11.4 cm (4.5"). Races *anteocularis*[A], *plumbiceps*[B], *innotata*[C], *parvirostris*[D]. Arid scrub; dry woodland; humid forest. To 1600 m. **ID** ♂ black cap and lores (no white eyeline); tail black, outer feathers white. ♀ plainer; above grey including sides of head to eyes (no black cap). **Voice** Geographically variable; song (*plumbiceps*) c. 8 simple descending "sweeu" notes, richer than *bilineata* group (above); song (*innotata*) short descending series of whistles followed by several higher thinner notes; song (*parvirostris*) 8–12 fast even-pitched notes (3–4 kHz) stronger than other races.

innotata

Rio Negro Gnatcatcher *Polioptila facilis* `LC`
Perlita del Río Negro
Local and poorly known resident.
L 11.4 cm (4.5"). Monotypic. Visual records (no photos or specimens). White-sand *terra firme* forest, borders. To 300 m. Pairs with canopy mixed flocks. **ID** Plain grey, throat paler, lower underparts white, tail like other *Polioptila*, obscure broken white eye-ring, eyes brownish to light grey (yellowish?). ♀ slightly paler. **Voice** Short, high, slightly descending series of thin notes. **TN** Previously regarded as a race of Guianan Gnatcatcher *P. guianensis*; the two differ minimally.

Slate-throated Gnatcatcher *Polioptila schistaceigula* `LC`
Perlita Pizarra
Uncommon resident.
L 11 cm (4.3"). Monotypic. Canopy of wet lowland and foothill forest, borders. To 500 m (rarely 1000 m). Behaviour like others of genus. **ID** Dark blackish grey, prominent broken white eye-ring, white lower underparts and tail tips. Juv paler grey, whitish facial area. **Voice** Song, thin weak very fast trill descending (8–5 kHz); also (alternate song?) thin sharply rising trill sometimes followed by stronger "see-see-see" notes. **SS** Tropical Gnatcatcher, Grey-mantled Wren.

93 extant species, 35 in region

Wrens are primarily New World in distribution, and most diverse in Central and South America. With few exceptions, they are small, thin-billed and brownish in plumage, often with dark barring on the wings and tail. As a group they are active, fidgety 'busybodies', and often skulking. Many are wonderful singers, noted for their precise antiphonal duets. Most build domed nests with side entrances.

Genus *Microcerculus* Small, with dark plumage and stubby cocked tails. Partly terrestrial inside humid forest. Clear pure-tone whistles; difficult to see.

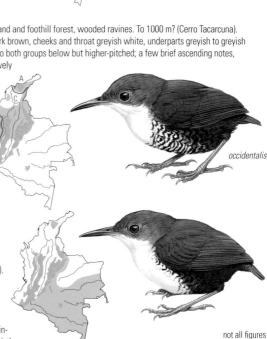

luscinia

Scaly-breasted Wren *Microcerculus marginatus* `LC`
Cucarachero Ruiseñor Sureño

Six subspecies in three subspecies groups; all three in Colombia. Taxonomy unsettled.

Whistling Wren *Microcerculus (marginatus) luscinia*
Status unknown.
L 10.7 cm (4.2"). Race *luscinia*. Thick undergrowth in humid lowland and foothill forest, wooded ravines. To 1000 m? (Cerro Tacarcuna).
ID Chunky, virtually tailless, with long slender bill; upperparts dark brown, cheeks and throat greyish white, underparts greyish to greyish brown, flanks brown, breast faintly scaled dusky. **Voice** Similar to both groups below but higher-pitched; a few brief ascending notes, then a protracted series of piercing whistles becoming progressively lower and agonizingly slow at end.

Scaly-breasted Wren
Microcerculus (marginatus) squamulatus
Fairly common resident.
L 10.7 cm (4.2"). Races *corrasus*[A], *occidentalis*[B], *squamulatus*[C]. Humid lowland and foothill forest. To 1200 m (locally higher). Behaviour like Amazonian Scaly-breasted Wren. **ID** Like Amazonian Scaly-breasted Wren but more variably scaled below. **Voice** Like other Scaly-breasted Wrens.

occidentalis

Amazonian Scaly-breasted Wren
Microcerculus (marginatus) marginatus
Fairly common resident.
L 10.7 cm (4.2"). One subspecies in group. Humid lowland and foothill forest, *terra firme* in Amazonia. To 1100 m (rarely 1600 m). Furtive, always on or close to ground. Hops on logs or walks on ground (often beneath tangles) while teetering rear end. **ID** Dark, almost tailless with long slender bill; underparts white, sides, flanks and belly dark brown or mottled dark brown. Juv heavily scaled dusky. **Voice** A few quick high notes followed by increasingly slower, fractionally descending series of pure-tone whistles, last notes after long pauses of 5–10 seconds, or first high notes sometimes omitted.

not all figures
to scale

minor

Grey-mantled Wren *Odontorchilus branickii* `LC`
Cucarachero Dorsigrís
Rare to uncommon and local resident.

L 13 cm (5"). Races *minor*[A], *branickii*[B]. Canopy of humid and wet lower montane forest. 800–1500 m. Singles or pairs actively hop along large mossy, epiphyte-covered limbs (not terminal foliage), usually with mixed flocks. **ID** Recalls a gnatcatcher. Long cocked tail barred (barring stronger, *branickii*), overall grey above, white below. **Voice** W of Andes weak high thin trill of 10–20 notes/second (7–8.5 kHz) over 1.5 seconds, or E of Andes trill slower, c. 5–7 notes/second, and slightly lower-pitched. **SS** Double-banded Greytail (p. 333), Tropical Gnatcatcher.

branickii

433

Genus *Troglodytes* Small, brownish and rather plain, with short cocked tails. Inquisitive. One is widespread and common, but others less numerous or rare.

House Wren *Troglodytes aedon* `LC`
Cucarachero Común

Approximately thirty-one subspecies in four (or five) subspecies groups (taxonomy-dependent); one in Colombia.

Southern House Wren *Troglodytes (aedon) musculus*
Common resident.
L 11.4 cm (4.5"). Races *atopus*[A], *striatulus*[B], *columbae*[C], *effutitus*[D], *clarus*[E], *albicans*[F], *inquietus*[G]. Semi-open habitats from lowlands to above treeline; in Amazonia, river borders and small clearings. To 3400 m. Cheerful industrious pairs, often around habitations. Cocked tail; active, inquisitive. **ID** Small and brownish, without strong field marks; dark barring on wings and tail, faint buff eyebrow. **Voice** Spirited, bubbly or gurgling song year-round. **SS** Mountain Wren. **TN** Morphological and acoustic differences between most subspecies subtle.

columbae

Ochraceous Wren *Troglodytes ochraceus* `LC`
Cucarachero Ocre
Uncommon (?) resident.

L 10.7 cm (4.2"). Race *festinus*. Humid montane forest. About 900–2450 m. Mid-levels to subcanopy inside forest. Forages actively in moss and epiphytes, often with mixed flocks. First Colombian record, Cerro Tacarcuna (Cuchillo del Lago), Aug 2010. **ID** Recalls Mountain Wren but buffier, prominent ochre eyestripe, dusky line through eyes, whitish belly. **Voice** Song, extremely complex rapid jumble of semi-musical notes, often ends in descending trill. **SS** House Wren.

festinus

Mountain Wren *Troglodytes solstitialis* `LC`
Cucarachero Montaraz
Uncommon to fairly common resident.

L 10.7 cm (4.2"). Races *solitarius*[A], *solstitialis*[B]. Humid and wet montane forest. 1500–3600 m. Singles, pairs or little families, actively explore mossy limbs and epiphytes from low mid-levels to canopy in dense forest. Active in presence of mixed flocks. **ID** Small, mostly rufous-buff, prominent buff eyestripe. **Voice** Songs vary geographically, high (7–8 kHz) complex jumble of tinkling notes and brief trills. **SS** House Wren.

solstitialis

Santa Marta Wren *Troglodytes monticola* `CR`
Cucarachero de Santa Marta `EN`
Rare and extremely local resident.

L 10 cm (4"). Monotypic. Endemic. Elfin woodland borders, treeline scrub, *páramo*. 3200–4600 m. Poorly known. Tiny remote range (mostly within Sierra Nevada National Park), requires multi-day expedition to reach. Threatened by often illegal wood-cutting, burning and overgrazing; possibly fewer than 250 individuals remain. **ID** Like Mountain Wren including buff eyestripe and ruddy foreparts, but differs in entire rear parts densely barred. **Voice** Call, high chittering "chi'dit" (disturbance). Song, high complex rapid jumble of notes that generally descends.

Genus *Cistothorus* Small, with streaked backs and cocked tails. Inhabit tall grass and shrubs, mostly at high elevations. Taxonomy not resolved.

Grass Wren *Cistothorus platensis* `LC`
Cucarachero Paramuno

 Nineteen subspecies in eight subspecies groups; two in Colombia.

Venezuelan Wren *Cistothorus (platensis) alticola*
Status unknown.
L 10 cm (4"). One subspecies in group. Damp grass in or near *páramo*. 3200–3800 m (Santa Marta Mts). **ID** Like *aequatorialis* race (below) but paler, eyestripe less obvious, shorter wing and tail measurements. **Voice** Song, long cheerful series of buzzes, bubbly chatters, rattles, and short staccato phrases. **SS** Santa Marta Wren. **TN** Taxonomy unresolved.

Paramo Wren *Cistothorus (platensis) aequatorialis*
Locally common resident.
L 10 cm (4"). Races *aequatorialis*[A], lowlands, Meta[B] (race?). Tall damp grass and bushes. Wee little bird that hides in tall grass, flushes weakly on fluttering wings, soon drops from view. Partly colonial; sings from bush tops. **ID** Above rufescent; buff-white streaks on back, eyebrow obscure, wings and notably short tail barred, below buff-white. **Voice** Geographically variable; complex sustained songs of chuckling notes, churrs, chattering rattles and buzzes, often trills at end. **SS** Apolinar's Wren. **TN** Taxonomy unresolved; races *tolimae* and *tamae* not recognized here.

aequatorialis

Apolinar's Wren *Cistothorus apolinari* `EN`
Cucarachero de Apolinar `CR`

 Two subspecies in two subspecies groups; both in Colombia.

Apolinar's Wren *Cistothorus (apolinari) apolinari*
Local resident (numbers declining due to habitat loss and contamination).
L 12.2 cm (4.8"). One subspecies in group. Endemic. Cattails (*Typha*) and reeds (*Scirpus*) in lake-edge marshes. Largest colonies Laguna de Tota and Laguna de Fúquene. 2500–3100 m. Pairs, sing and scold as cling semi-exposed to reeds, otherwise hidden. **ID** Buff-white dorsal streaks, greyish eyebrow, whitish throat, buff underparts, rufescent flanks. **Voice** Song by singles, sometimes pairs or families simultaneously, rhythmic but scratchy, sawing bubbly phrases mixed with gravelly churrs, harsh rattles. Call, rough churring. **SS** Grass Wren.

Sumapaz Wren *Cistothorus (apolinari) hernandezi*
Local resident.
L 12.2 cm (4.8"). One subspecies in group. Endemic. Shrubby and boggy *páramo*, Sumapaz National Park (Laguna Chisacá), especially with *Espeletia*, dwarf *Chusquea tessellata*, shrubby *Diplostephium*, 3800–3900 m; also Sierra Nevada del Cocuy National Park (Nevado Güicán), Boyacá (c. 4000 m). **ID** Like Apolinar's Wren but underparts whiter, weak buff tinge on flanks. **Voice** Similar to Apolinar's Wren but larger repertoire (at least 11 song types). ♀ sings, often initiating song; some songs antiphonal.

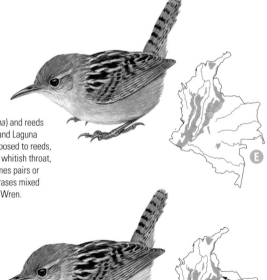

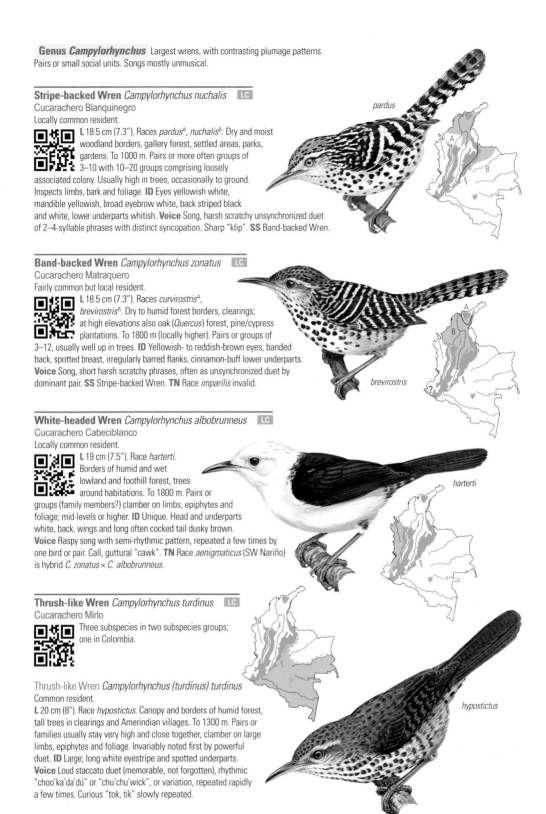

Genus *Campylorhynchus* Largest wrens, with contrasting plumage patterns. Pairs or small social units. Songs mostly unmusical.

Stripe-backed Wren *Campylorhynchus nuchalis* `LC`
Cucarachero Blanquinegro
Locally common resident.
L 18.5 cm (7.3"). Races *pardus*[A], *nuchalis*[B]. Dry and moist woodland borders, gallery forest, settled areas, parks, gardens. To 1000 m. Pairs or more often groups of 3–10 with 10–20 groups comprising loosely associated colony. Usually high in trees, occasionally to ground. Inspects limbs, bark and foliage. **ID** Eyes yellowish white, mandible yellowish, broad eyebrow white, back striped black and white, lower underparts whitish. **Voice** Song, harsh scratchy unsynchronized duet of 2–4-syllable phrases with distinct syncopation. Sharp "klip". **SS** Band-backed Wren.

pardus

Band-backed Wren *Campylorhynchus zonatus* `LC`
Cucarachero Matraquero
Fairly common but local resident.
L 18.5 cm (7.3"). Races *curvirostris*[A], *brevirostris*[B]. Dry to humid forest borders, clearings; at high elevations also oak (*Quercus*) forest, pine/cypress plantations. To 1800 m (locally higher). Pairs or groups of 3–12, usually well up in trees. **ID** Yellowish- to reddish-brown eyes, banded back, spotted breast, irregularly barred flanks, cinnamon-buff lower underparts. **Voice** Song, short harsh scratchy phrases, often as unsynchronized duet by dominant pair. **SS** Stripe-backed Wren. **TN** Race *imparilis* invalid.

brevirostris

White-headed Wren *Campylorhynchus albobrunneus* `LC`
Cucarachero Cabeciblanco
Locally common resident.
L 19 cm (7.5"). Race *harterti*. Borders of humid and wet lowland and foothill forest, trees around habitations. To 1800 m. Pairs or groups (family members?) clamber on limbs, epiphytes and foliage; mid-levels or higher. **ID** Unique. Head and underparts white, back, wings and long often cocked tail dusky brown. **Voice** Raspy song with semi-rhythmic pattern, repeated a few times by one bird or pair. Call, guttural "cawk". **TN** Race *aenigmaticus* (SW Nariño) is hybrid *C. zonatus* × *C. albobrunneus*.

harterti

Thrush-like Wren *Campylorhynchus turdinus* `LC`
Cucarachero Mirlo
Three subspecies in two subspecies groups; one in Colombia.

Thrush-like Wren *Campylorhynchus (turdinus) turdinus*
Common resident.
L 20 cm (8"). Race *hypostictus*. Canopy and borders of humid forest, tall trees in clearings and Amerindian villages. To 1300 m. Pairs or families usually stay very high and close together, clamber on large limbs, epiphytes and foliage. Invariably noted first by powerful duet. **ID** Large; long white eyestripe and spotted underparts. **Voice** Loud staccato duet (memorable, not forgotten), rhythmic "choo'ka'da'dú" or "chu'chu'wick", or variation, repeated rapidly a few times. Curious "tok, tik" slowly repeated.

hypostictus

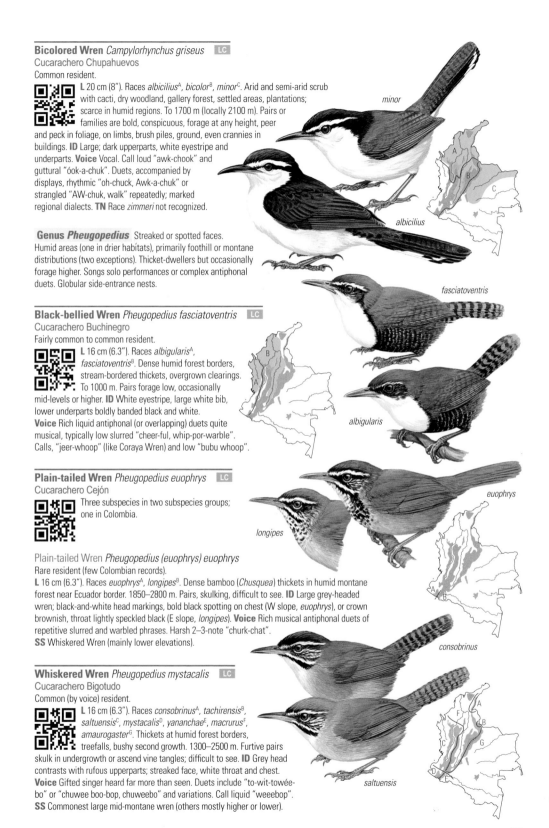

Bicolored Wren *Campylorhynchus griseus* `LC`
Cucarachero Chupahuevos
Common resident.

L 20 cm (8"). Races *albicilius*[A], *bicolor*[B], *minor*[C]. Arid and semi-arid scrub with cacti, dry woodland, gallery forest, settled areas, plantations; scarce in humid regions. To 1700 m (locally 2100 m). Pairs or families are bold, conspicuous, forage at any height, peer and peck in foliage, on limbs, brush piles, ground, even crannies in buildings. **ID** Large; dark upperparts, white eyestripe and underparts. **Voice** Vocal. Call loud "awk-chook" and guttural "óok-a-chuk". Duets, accompanied by displays, rhythmic "oh-chuck, Awk-a-chuk" or strangled "AW-chuk, walk" repeatedly; marked regional dialects. **TN** Race *zimmeri* not recognized.

minor

albicilius

Genus *Pheugopedius* Streaked or spotted faces. Humid areas (one in drier habitats), primarily foothill or montane distributions (two exceptions). Thicket-dwellers but occasionally forage higher. Songs solo performances or complex antiphonal duets. Globular side-entrance nests.

Black-bellied Wren *Pheugopedius fasciatoventris* `LC`
Cucarachero Buchinegro
Fairly common to common resident.

L 16 cm (6.3"). Races *albigularis*[A], *fasciatoventris*[B]. Dense humid forest borders, stream-bordered thickets, overgrown clearings. To 1000 m. Pairs forage low, occasionally mid-levels or higher. **ID** White eyestripe, large white bib, lower underparts boldly banded black and white. **Voice** Rich liquid antiphonal (or overlapping) duets quite musical, typically low slurred "cheer-ful, whip-por-warble". Calls, "jeer-whoop" (like Coraya Wren) and low "bubu whoop".

fasciatoventris

albigularis

Plain-tailed Wren *Pheugopedius euophrys* `LC`
Cucarachero Cejón

Three subspecies in two subspecies groups; one in Colombia.

euophrys

longipes

Plain-tailed Wren *Pheugopedius (euophrys) euophrys*
Rare resident (few Colombian records).

L 16 cm (6.3"). Races *euophrys*[A], *longipes*[B]. Dense bamboo (*Chusquea*) thickets in humid montane forest near Ecuador border. 1850–2800 m. Pairs, skulking, difficult to see. **ID** Large grey-headed wren; black-and-white head markings, bold black spotting on chest (W slope, *euophrys*), or crown brownish, throat lightly speckled black (E slope, *longipes*). **Voice** Rich musical antiphonal duets of repetitive slurred and warbled phrases. Harsh 2–3-note "churk-chat". **SS** Whiskered Wren (mainly lower elevations).

consobrinus

Whiskered Wren *Pheugopedius mystacalis* `LC`
Cucarachero Bigotudo
Common (by voice) resident.

L 16 cm (6.3"). Races *consobrinus*[A], *tachirensis*[B], *saltuensis*[C], *mystacalis*[D], *yananchae*[E], *macrurus*[F], *amaurogaster*[G]. Thickets at humid forest borders, treefalls, bushy second growth. 1300–2500 m. Furtive pairs skulk in undergrowth or ascend vine tangles; difficult to see. **ID** Grey head contrasts with rufous upperparts; streaked face, white throat and chest. **Voice** Gifted singer heard far more than seen. Duets include "to-wit-towée-bo" or "chuwee boo-bop, chuweebo" and variations. Call liquid "weeebop". **SS** Commonest large mid-montane wren (others mostly higher or lower).

saltuensis

437

Coraya Wren *Pheugopedius coraya* LC
Cucarachero Amazónico
Fairly common resident.

 L 15 cm (6"). Races *caurensis*[A], *griseipectus*[B]. Thickets at borders of *terra firme* and *várzea* forest, treefalls, younger second growth. To 600 m. **ID** White eyestripe, broad black malar, black face with minor white streaking on cheeks. **Voice** Short but vivacious antiphonal duets with many variations; longer loud "peeeur", then 4–7 rapid hammering "chu" notes; or introductory notes variable, may descend, ascend or both (geographical?). Also slower "eeeeou, peeou-peeou-peeou". **TN** Racial boundaries unclear.

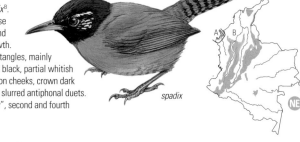
griseipectus

Sooty-headed Wren *Pheugopedius spadix* LC
Cucarachero Cabecinegro
Fairly common resident.

 L 15 cm (6"). Races *xerampelinus*[A], *spadix*[B]. Near-endemic (also far SE Panama). Dense undergrowth in humid and wet foothill and lower montane forest, older second growth. 400–2100 m (higher?). Pairs, alone, low in dark mossy tangles, mainly inside forest (not borders). **ID** Sides of head and throat black, partial whitish eyestripe, white lower eye-arc, minor white streaking on cheeks, crown dark grey, chest dark rufous. **Voice** Pairs sing loud complex slurred antiphonal duets. Distinctive call, sad "tee-dooo" or "chur-dóo, chur-dáw", second and fourth notes lower.

spadix

NE

Colombian Wren (Speckle-breasted Wren)
Pheugopedius columbianus LC
Cucarachero Jaspeado Colombiano
Local resident.

 L 13.2 cm (5.2"). Monotypic. Endemic. Understorey to subcanopy in moist to moderately humid foothill and lower montane forest and borders. 600–2000 m. Undergrowth but often ranges into dense vine tangles high overhead. **ID** Relatively small; speckled face and spotted and barred underparts unique. **Voice** Variable but short antiphonal duets recall others of genus. Call, thin rising trill (like fingers on comb), similar to Rufous-breasted Wren. **TN** Often regarded as a race of Speckle-breasted Wren *P. sclateri*.

E

Rufous-breasted Wren *Pheugopedius rutilus* LC
Cucarachero Pechirrufo
Common resident.

 L 14 cm (5.5"). Races *laetus*[A], *interior*[B], *hypospodius*[C]. Shrubby thickets and vine tangles at edge of dry to moist foothill and lower montane forest, coffee plantations. To 1900 m. Pairs or families, a little less furtive than some wrens. Sometimes moves from undergrowth into mid-level vines. Methodically peer and poke in accumulations of dead leaves and curled hanging dead leaves, or hop up through vines near trunks where sometimes fairly easy to observe. **ID** Speckled 'salt-and-pepper' face, rufous chest. **Voice** Antiphonal duets varied and vigorous but lack rich mellow quality of allies. Songs notable for many slurred notes given in rollicking up-tempo manner, phrases repeated 2–3 times, e.g. "too-see-HEEear to-see, to-see-HEEear to-see", then changing. Calls, rising "chip-reeeez" and thin waif-like rising trill (like fingers on comb).

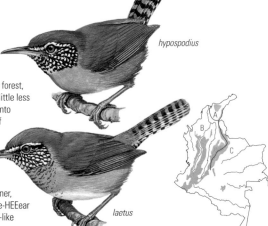
hypospodius

laetus

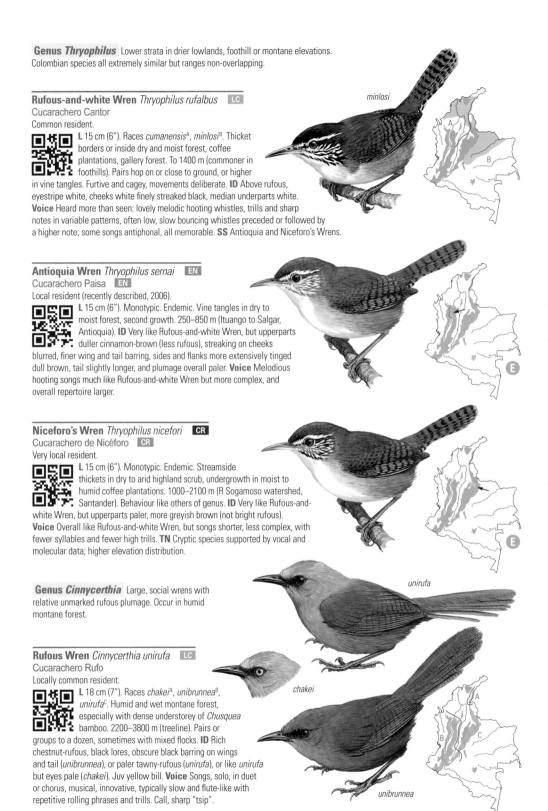

Genus *Thryophilus* Lower strata in drier lowlands, foothill or montane elevations. Colombian species all extremely similar but ranges non-overlapping.

Rufous-and-white Wren *Thryophilus rufalbus* LC
Cucarachero Cantor
Common resident.

minlosi

L 15 cm (6"). Races *cumanensis*[A], *minlosi*[B]. Thicket borders or inside dry and moist forest, coffee plantations, gallery forest. To 1400 m (commoner in foothills). Pairs hop on or close to ground, or higher in vine tangles. Furtive and cagey, movements deliberate. **ID** Above rufous, eyestripe white, cheeks white finely streaked black, median underparts white. **Voice** Heard more than seen: lovely melodic hooting whistles, trills and sharp notes in variable patterns, often low, slow bouncing whistles preceded or followed by a higher note; some songs antiphonal, all memorable. **SS** Antioquia and Niceforo's Wrens.

Antioquia Wren *Thryophilus sernai* EN
Cucarachero Paisa EN
Local resident (recently described, 2006).

L 15 cm (6"). Monotypic. Endemic. Vine tangles in dry to moist forest, second growth. 250–850 m (Ituango to Salgar, Antioquia). **ID** Very like Rufous-and-white Wren, but upperparts duller cinnamon-brown (less rufous), streaking on cheeks blurred, finer wing and tail barring, sides and flanks more extensively tinged dull brown, tail slightly longer, and plumage overall paler. **Voice** Melodious hooting songs much like Rufous-and-white Wren but more complex, and overall repertoire larger.

Niceforo's Wren *Thryophilus nicefori* CR
Cucarachero de Nicéforo CR
Very local resident.

L 15 cm (6"). Monotypic. Endemic. Streamside thickets in dry to arid highland scrub, undergrowth in moist to humid coffee plantations. 1000–2100 m (R Sogamoso watershed, Santander). Behaviour like others of genus. **ID** Very like Rufous-and-white Wren, but upperparts paler, more greyish brown (not bright rufous). **Voice** Overall like Rufous-and-white Wren, but songs shorter, less complex, with fewer syllables and fewer high trills. **TN** Cryptic species supported by vocal and molecular data; higher elevation distribution.

Genus *Cinnycerthia* Large, social wrens with relative unmarked rufous plumage. Occur in humid montane forest.

unirufa

Rufous Wren *Cinnycerthia unirufa* LC
Cucarachero Rufo
Locally common resident.

chakei

L 18 cm (7"). Races *chakei*[A], *unibrunnea*[B], *unirufa*[C]. Humid and wet montane forest, especially with dense understorey of *Chusquea* bamboo. 2200–3800 m (treeline). Pairs or groups to a dozen, sometimes with mixed flocks. **ID** Rich chestnut-rufous, black lores, obscure black barring on wings and tail (*unibrunnea*), or paler tawny-rufous (*unirufa*), or like *unirufa* but eyes pale (*chakei*). Juv yellow bill. **Voice** Songs, solo, in duet or chorus, musical, innovative, typically slow and flute-like with repetitive rolling phrases and trills. Call, sharp "tsip".

unibrunnea

439

Sharpe's Wren *Cinnycerthia olivascens* `LC`
Cucarachero Sepia
Fairly common resident.

L 18 cm (7"). Races *olivascens*[A], *bogotensis*[B]. Undergrowth of humid and wet montane forest. 1500–3100 m. Behaviour like Rufous Wren, but more often in pairs or smaller groups. **ID** Browner (less rufous) than Rufous Wren, especially below, wing and tail barring more distinct (*bogotensis*), or slightly darker brown, some individuals with white forecrown (*olivascens*). **Voice** Pairs or several in antiphonal or overlapping chorus. Musical whistles and trills recall Rufous Wren; repetitive phrases often much longer. Call, harsh "jud'it".

Genus *Cantorchilus* Forest borders or inside forest. In pairs, notable for antiphonal duets and loud energetic calls, but mostly remain hidden from view.

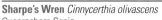

variant

olivascens

bogotensis

Stripe-throated Wren *Cantorchilus leucopogon* `LC`
Cucarachero del Chocó
Scarce and local resident.

L 12 cm (4.7"). Races *grisescens*[A], *leucopogon*[B]. Cluttered understorey in humid and wet forest, old second growth. To 900 m. Pairs, unlike many allies, often with mixed understorey flocks. **ID** Small wren, throat sharply streaked black and white, underparts buff (*leucopogon*), or above greyer and overall paler (*grisescens*). **Voice** Solo song, rather flat rapid "easy'a-wert" over and over; antiphonal duet more complex but repetitive. Single slow, "tee... tee...". **SS** Buff-breasted Wren.

leucopogon

grisescens

Buff-breasted Wren *Cantorchilus leucotis* `LC`
Cucarachero Anteado
Locally common resident.

L 14 cm (5.5"). Races *galbraithii*[A], *leucotis*[B], *collinus*[C], *venezuelanus*[D], *zuliensis*[E], *bogotensis*[F], *peruanus*[G]. Shrubby streamside thickets from arid N to humid Amazonia, usually near water; in Amazonia always along creeks and watercourses. To 600 m. Obstinately skulking pairs, difficult to see, usually low, often near ground. **ID** Plain; white eyebrow, streaked face, white throat, rest of underparts buff. **Voice** Loud energetic duets recall other wrens but looser, less musical. Simple duets repetitive, complex ones less so. Call, loud incisive "chit-cho" or "chit, chit-cho", last syllable lower; varied to "pssEE-CHOO!".

leucotis

Bay Wren *Cantorchilus nigricapillus* `LC`
Cucarachero Ribereño

Seven subspecies in two subspecies groups; one in Colombia.

Southern Bay Wren *Cantorchilus (nigricapillus) nigricapillus*
Fairly common resident.
L 15 cm (6"). Races *schottii*[A], *connectens*[B]. Rank thickets at humid and wet forest borders, streamsides, dense second growth. To 1800 m (rare above 1400 m). **ID** Beautiful richly patterned wren, bold black-and-white head markings; only Colombian wren with finely barred underparts. **Voice** Songs, most vigorous, energetic and rapid of family. Solos include "sst sst-churrr"; loud ringing "hist-t-whíp". Loud fast (often staccato) antiphonal duets repeated a few times, then abruptly change.

schottii

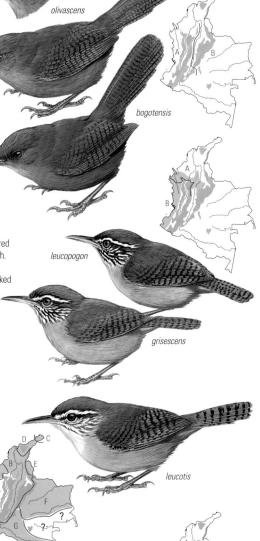

Genus *Henicorhina* Small with short cocked tails. Inhabit tangled understorey
and thickets, where usually remain hidden but inquisitive. Sing loud antiphonal duets.

White-breasted Wood-wren *Henicorhina leucosticta* `LC`
Cucarachero Pechiblanco

Thirteen races in 3–4 subspecies groups; two or three in Colombia. Plumage, vocal and DNA data indicate substantial variation
within groups, and some races (and groups) perhaps invalid, with disagreement as to allocation of races to groups. Arrangement
below conditional and does not account for biogeographical barriers that might isolate populations.

Choco White-breasted Wood-wren *Henicorhina (leucosticta) inornata*
Common resident.
L 10.7 cm (4.2"). Races *eucharis*[A], *inornata*[B]. Near-endemic (also extreme
NW Ecuador). Humid lowland and foothill forest. To c. 700 m (rarely 1600 m).
ID Similar to races in N Colombia and Amazonia (below) but crown slightly
browner, either blackish brown (*eucharis*) or chestnut-brown (*inornata*),
but plumage differences minimal in all Colombian forms. **Voice** Songs
of various races and subgroups remain unevaluated, but all broadly
similar. Repertoire W of Andes perhaps more complex than in Amazonia.
SS Grey-breasted Wood-wren. **TN** Taxonomy unresolved; comprehensive molecular study badly needed.

Amazonian White-breasted Wood-wren
Henicorhina (leucosticta) leucosticta
Common resident.
L 10 cm (4"). Races *darienensis*[A], *albilateralis*[B],
hauxwelli[C]. Humid lowland *terra firme* and foothill
forest. To 1100 m. Pairs hop on fallen logs or in
tangles, on or close to ground. Independent of mixed
flocks, furtive but curious. **ID** Very like races above but
eyestripe white, face streaked black and white, crown black
(*darienensis*, *hauxwelli*) or dark brown (*albilateralis*), underparts
white (no grey). **Voice** Pairs sing solo or in duet; songs energetic, E of
Andes perhaps briefer and less complex than W of Andes, often with several rapidly
repeated notes, e.g. "cheery-cheery-chée", "we-per-chee, purty-choo", "gear-hurry",
"SKEET, purty-purty-purty". Scold with churrs or rattles. **TN** Taxonomy unresolved.

Grey-breasted Wood-wren *Henicorhina leucophrys* `LC`
Cucarachero Pechigrís
Common resident.

L 10.7 cm (4.2"). Races *collina*[A], *bangsi*[B], *manastarae*[C],
tamae[D], *brunneiceps*[E], *leucophrys*[F], Serranía de
San Lucas (race?), Andean slope E Nariño (race?).
Humid montane forest, c. 1000–2900 m (locally
400 m). Inquisitive, sedentary; like allied White-breasted Wood-wren
but less often on ground. Pokes around low in thickets and mossy tangles.
ID Throat whitish or streaked. From other *Henicorhina* by grey underparts,
different voice, largely non-overlapping distribution. **Voice** Pairs sing solo
or antiphonal duets year-round; songs longer, usually 3–6 notes, more
complex than White-breasted Wood-wrens, but geographical and local
variation extensive. **TN** Taxonomy unsettled.

Hermit Wood-wren *Henicorhina anachoreta* `NT`
Cucarachero Ermitaño
Common resident.

L 10.7 cm (4.2"). Monotypic. Endemic. Dense borders and
gaps in humid upper montane forest. Santa Marta Mts.
2000–3600 m. **ID** Cryptic species, not reliably separated
in field by plumage or morphology (many characters
overlap) from Grey-breasted Wood-wren. Even songs barely differ, on average
higher-pitched, frequency range greater, but field identification based on song
requires care (reliable?). Best identified by distribution as presumably only this taxon occurs
above 2300 m (on Cuchillo de San Lorenzo) and only *bangsi* race of Grey-breasted below
c. 2000 m; both (?) in between. **TN** Formerly a subspecies of Grey-breasted Wood-wren.

inornata

albilateralis

hauxwelli

leucophrys

brunneiceps

Munchique Wood-wren *Henicorhina negreti* `VU`
Cucarachero de Munchique `VU`
Locally fairly common resident.

L 10.7 cm (4.2"). Monotypic. Endemic. Undergrowth in wet mossy montane forest. 2200–2650 m. **ID** Generally at higher elevations than Grey-breasted Wood-wren and in wetter forest; face and throat streaking may be stronger (more checkered), but always best identified by dramatically different vocalizations. **Voice** Pairs sing solos or antiphonal duets, high-pitched, tinkling, fife- or piccolo-like in quality, in many patterns with longer phrases of 6–12 notes sometimes repeated up to ten times. **TN** Discovered 1978; described 2003.

Genus *Cyphorhinus* Large wrens, with keeled slightly arched culmen and dark earth-tone colours. Found on or near ground inside humid forest. Melodious songs.

Northern Chestnut-breasted Wren
Cyphorhinus dichrous `LC`
Cucarachero Flautista
Local resident.

L 15 cm (6"). Monotypic. Mossy undergrowth in wet montane forest. 1100–2600 m (Pacific slope to 700 m). Often perversely difficult to see; singles or pairs hop on ground, on logs or in undergrowth. **ID** Lacks barring, underparts orange-rufous, narrow bluish eye-ring. **Voice** Not a persistent singer; hauntingly beautiful flute-like songs (numerous patterns), typically 2–4 minor-key notes, one per second or slower, ascend, descend or alternate in hypnotic half-tone steps. **TN** Usually regarded as a race of *C. thoracicus*.

Song Wren *Cyphorhinus phaeocephalus* `LC`
Cucarachero Gaitero
Uncommon resident.

L 14 cm (5.5"). Races *lawrencii*[A], *propinquus*[B], *chocoanus*[C], *phaeocephalus*[D]. Undergrowth inside humid and wet forest. To 1200 m. Semi-terrestrial pairs or families of 2–5. **ID** Bare pale blue ocular area, wings and tail barred, face and throat to mid-breast orange-rufous, rarely chin or throat whitish. **Voice** Unusual song of guttural churrs, pot-boiling sounds and melodic fluty whistles with dramatic changes in pitch, "ong cutta, cutta, whong cutta cutta, glut WHOO HEE...". Scolding "churr".

Musician Wren *Cyphorhinus arada* `LC`
Cucarachero Musical

Six subspecies in six subspecies groups; two in Colombia.

Imeri Musician Wren *Cyphorhinus (arada) transfluvialis*
Uncommon resident.
L 14 cm (5.5"). One subspecies in group. Undergrowth in humid *terra firme* forest, especially white-sand areas. To 1200 m. **ID** Like *salvini* race (below) but paler, forecrown orange-rufous, eyebrow brighter. **Voice** Songs resemble *salvini*. **TN** Distribution of this and next race unclear.

Napo Musician Wren *Cyphorhinus (arada) salvini*
Uncommon resident.
L 14 cm (5.5"). One subspecies in group. Humid *terra firme* forest, scarce in *várzea*. To 1200 m. Semi-terrestrial singles or pairs, furtive in undergrowth or on ground; invariably detected first by voice. **ID** Above dark brown; foreparts, short obscure postocular, throat and breast orange-rufous, narrow bluish eye-ring, wings and tail barred. **Voice** Memorable song flute-like, mostly antiphonal, more complex and musical than Song Wren, mixing low guttural churring with delightful musical notes in high-low jumps that seem random but are often repeated many times.

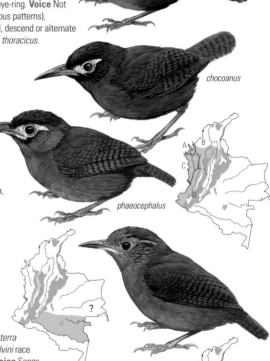

chocoanus

phaeocephalus

CINCLIDAE
Dippers
5 extant species, 1 in region

Dippers are a small family of aquatic passerines. Well adapted for life in or near water, they are short-tailed and chunky with dense plumage, strong legs, a musty odour, movable nostril cover, well-developed nictitating membrane, and a large oil gland. All are confined to rocks and boulders along cold mountain streams. South American species do not dive or walk underwater unlike northern species.

White-capped Dipper *Cinclus leucocephalus* `LC`
Mirlo-acuático Suramericano

Three subspecies in three subspecies groups; two in Colombia.

Santa Marta Dipper *Cinclus (leucocephalus) rivularis*
Rare resident (few records).
L 16 cm (6.3"). One subspecies in group. Endemic. Mountain streams. 650–2800 m (probably higher). Behaviour as next race. **ID** Like race *leuconotus* (below) but paler, greyish brown, only crown and throat white, both flecked and speckled dark grey, no white on back or breast. **Voice** Unrecorded. Probably similar to wide-ranging Andean forms.

White-capped Dipper *Cinclus (leucocephalus) leuconotus*
Fairly common resident.
L 15 cm (6"). One subspecies in group. Boulder-strewn Andean streams, sometimes surprisingly small. 600–3900 m (to 300 m, Pacific slope). Forages at edges of rushing mountain streams, occasionally wades. **ID** Blackish brown, with crown, patch on back and throat to belly white. **Voice** Song, loud, shrill piercing trill, easily heard above river noise. Buzzy "zre'e'e'e'e'd" in flight. **AN** White-backed Dipper, White-bellied Dipper.

MIMIDAE
Mockingbirds and Thrashers
34 extant species, 2 in region

Small New World family beloved for their cheerful songs and some also for their powers of vocal mimicry; most are slender-bodied and long-tailed.

Grey Catbird *Dumetella carolinensis* `LC`
Pájaro Gato Gris
Scarce boreal migrant (Nov–Mar).

L 20 cm (8"). Monotypic. Dry to humid woodland, damp thickets, shady areas. To 2100 m. Solitary; stays in thick vegetation, forages on or close to ground. **ID** Dark grey, black cap, blackish tail, rufous undertail-coverts. **Voice** Nasal cat-like mewing. Complex jumbled song unlikely to be heard on wintering grounds.

Tropical Mockingbird
Mimus gilvus `LC`
Sinsonte Común
Common resident.

L 23 cm (9"). Races *magnirostris*[A], *tolimensis*[B], *melanopterus*[C]. Dry to humid brushy areas, plantations; settled areas, parks, gardens. To 2800 m. Singles or pairs are conspicuous, territorial, quick to mob. Flight buoyant; often forages on ground, lifts tail. Eats fruit and insects. **ID** Long tail tipped white, chalky eyestripe, narrow dusky mask. **Voice** Energetic singer of long rambling choppy phrases and husky notes, some repeated "you're a chéater…dirty-dirty…chéater…chipa-chipa…" and so on. Does not mimic.

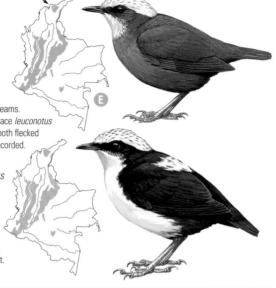

magnirostris

melanopterus

176 extant species, 30 in region

This large, nearly worldwide family is most numerous in the Old World. Among North American breeders, many are long-distance migrants that reach or pass through Colombia each year. South American species, however, are non-migratory. Some members of the family, especially *Turdus*, are well known and live comfortably in settled areas from the lowlands to treeline, while others such as nightingale-thrushes and solitaires are shy forest- or thicket-dwellers in montane regions. Many species have pleasing songs, although a few have atonal or unmusical vocalizations.

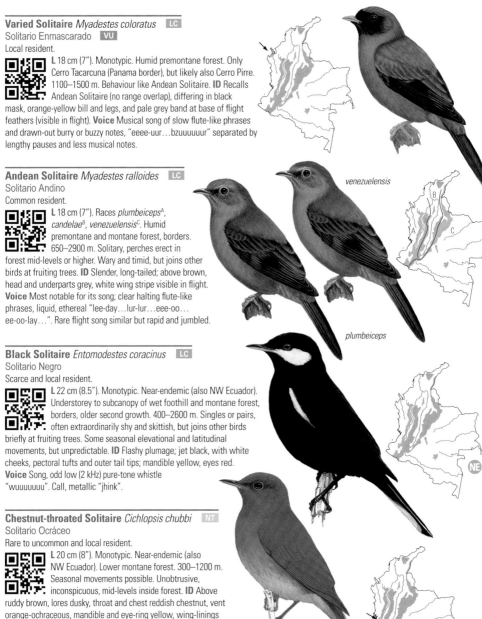

venezuelensis

plumbeiceps

Varied Solitaire *Myadestes coloratus* LC
Solitario Enmascarado VU
Local resident.

L 18 cm (7"). Monotypic. Humid premontane forest. Only Cerro Tacarcuna (Panama border), but likely also Cerro Pirre. 1100–1500 m. Behaviour like Andean Solitaire. **ID** Recalls Andean Solitaire (no range overlap), differing in black mask, orange-yellow bill and legs, and pale grey band at base of flight feathers (visible in flight). **Voice** Musical song of slow flute-like phrases and drawn-out burry or buzzy notes, "eeee-uur…bzuuuuuur" separated by lengthy pauses and less musical notes.

Andean Solitaire *Myadestes ralloides* LC
Solitario Andino
Common resident.

L 18 cm (7"). Races *plumbeiceps*[A], *candelae*[B], *venezuelensis*[C]. Humid premontane and montane forest, borders. 650–2900 m. Solitary, perches erect in forest mid-levels or higher. Wary and timid, but joins other birds at fruiting trees. **ID** Slender, long-tailed; above brown, head and underparts grey, white wing stripe visible in flight. **Voice** Most notable for its song; clear halting flute-like phrases, liquid, ethereal "lee-day…lur-lur…eee-oo… ee-oo-lay…". Rare flight song similar but rapid and jumbled.

Black Solitaire *Entomodestes coracinus* LC
Solitario Negro
Scarce and local resident.

L 22 cm (8.5"). Monotypic. Near-endemic (also NW Ecuador). Understorey to subcanopy of wet foothill and montane forest, borders, older second growth. 400–2600 m. Singles or pairs, often extraordinarily shy and skittish, but joins other birds briefly at fruiting trees. Some seasonal elevational and latitudinal movements, but unpredictable. **ID** Flashy plumage; jet black, with white cheeks, pectoral tufts and outer tail tips; mandible yellow, eyes red. **Voice** Song, odd low (2 kHz) pure-tone whistle "wuuuuuuu". Call, metallic "jhink".

Chestnut-throated Solitaire *Cichlopsis chubbi* NT
Solitario Ocráceo
Rare to uncommon and local resident.

L 20 cm (8"). Monotypic. Near-endemic (also NW Ecuador). Lower montane forest. 300–1200 m. Seasonal movements possible. Unobtrusive, inconspicuous, mid-levels inside forest. **ID** Above ruddy brown, lores dusky, throat and chest reddish chestnut, vent orange-ochraceous, mandible and eye-ring yellow, wing-linings orange-buff. Juv buff-spotted wing-coverts. **Voice** Often quiet. Song, mainly at dawn, recalls Andean Solitaire but less musical; choppy high-low 4–5-note phrases typically end with variable rising or falling flourish. **TN** Usually regarded as an isolated race of Rufous-brown Solitaire *C. leucogenys* but differs in minor aspects of plumage and voice (descending vs. ascending call).

Wood Thrush *Hylocichla mustelina* NT
Zorzal de Bosque
Rare boreal visitor.

 L 19.5 cm (7.7"). Monotypic. Inside humid forest, second growth. Known from small number of records, but possible elsewhere in N. To 1700 m. Quiet and solitary. Forages mostly on ground; opportunistically follows army ants. **ID** Rich reddish brown, brightest on crown and mantle, underparts white boldly spotted black. **Voice** Call, staccato "pit-pit-pit". Lovely flute-like song only heard on northern breeding grounds. **SS** Larger, brighter and more boldly marked than *Catharus* thrushes.

Genus *Catharus* Timid, retiring and inconspicuous, their songs range from lovely and flute-like to squeaky and unmusical. Resident species in Andes, and drabber boreal migrants throughout. On or close to ground, except Swainson's Thrush.

Swainson's Thrush *Catharus swainsoni* LC
Zorzal Buchipecoso
Common boreal winter resident and passage migrant (Oct–Apr).

 L 18 cm (7"). Races *incanus, swainsoni, appalachiensis*. Moist to humid forest, second growth, plantations. Commonest W of Andes. To 3300 m. Singles or loosely associated groups, visit fruiting trees, timidly flutter for fruit, stare wide-eyed, flee to cover. Low to high but seldom on ground. **ID** Warm buff lores and eye-ring suggest spectacles, buffy-brown cheeks, buff tinge and dusky speckling on throat and chest. **Voice** Call, soft "whit". Pre-migratory birds sing short weak versions of beautiful flute-like, upward-spiralling song.

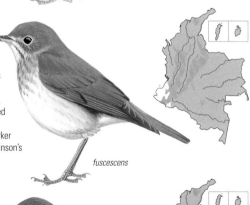

swainsoni

Veery *Catharus fuscescens* LC
Zorzal Rojizo
Scarce boreal passage migrant (Sept–Nov, Mar).

 L 18 cm (7"). Races *salicicola, subpallidus, fuscescens, fuliginosus*. Forest edge, wooded areas. To 3000 m. Migratory routes poorly known (more records NW Chocó lowlands than elsewhere), possible elliptical circuit through Brazilian Amazon. Shy, inconspicuous; often on ground. **ID** Rich reddish brown above, grey lores, buff wash on weakly speckled chest, basal half of mandible yellow; *salicicola* above olive brown; *subpallidus* duller, browner, breast spots more defined; *fuliginosus* darker brown, larger sharper breast spots. **Voice** Quiet on passage. **SS** Swainson's and Grey-cheeked Thrushes.

fuscescens

Grey-cheeked Thrush *Catharus minimus* LC
Zorzal Carigrís
Fairly common boreal passage migrant (small numbers overwinter, Oct–early May).

L 18 cm (7"). Races *aliciae, minimus*. Humid forest, shade-coffee plantations, thickets, second growth. Wintering birds more inside foothill and premontane forest to c. 1500 m; passage migrants to 3000 m. Inconspicuous, singles or loosely associated parties, on or near ground, infrequently fruiting shrubs. **ID** Lacks warm buff tones of Swainson's Thrush, no obvious eye-ring, cold grey cheeks, above drab brown, dusky speckling on chest. **Voice** Quiet on passage.

minimus

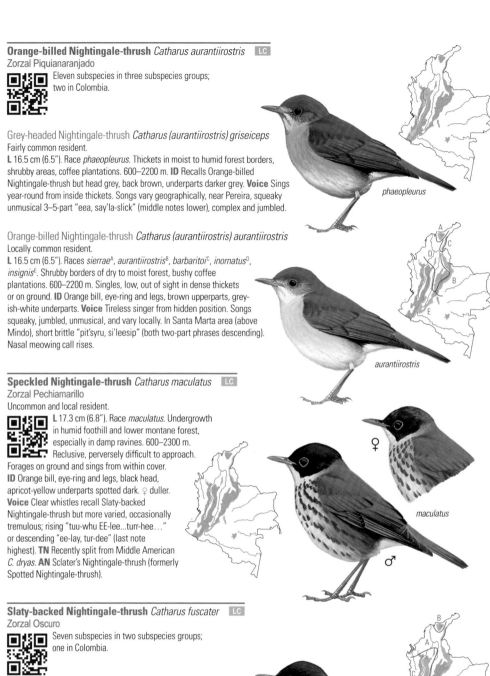

Orange-billed Nightingale-thrush *Catharus aurantiirostris* `LC`
Zorzal Piquianaranjado

Eleven subspecies in three subspecies groups;
two in Colombia.

Grey-headed Nightingale-thrush *Catharus (aurantiirostris) griseiceps*
Fairly common resident.
L 16.5 cm (6.5"). Race *phaeopleurus*. Thickets in moist to humid forest borders,
shrubby areas, coffee plantations. 600–2200 m. **ID** Recalls Orange-billed
Nightingale-thrush but head grey, back brown, underparts darker grey. **Voice** Sings
year-round from inside thickets. Songs vary geographically, near Pereira, squeaky
unmusical 3–5-part "eea, say'la-slick" (middle notes lower), complex and jumbled.

phaeopleurus

Orange-billed Nightingale-thrush *Catharus (aurantiirostris) aurantiirostris*
Locally common resident.
L 16.5 cm (6.5"). Races *sierrae*[A], *aurantiirostris*[B], *barbaritoi*[C], *inornatus*[D],
insignis[E]. Shrubby borders of dry to moist forest, bushy coffee
plantations. 600–2200 m. Singles, low, out of sight in dense thickets
or on ground. **ID** Orange bill, eye-ring and legs, brown upperparts, greyish-white underparts. **Voice** Tireless singer from hidden position. Songs
squeaky, jumbled, unmusical, and vary locally. In Santa Marta area (above
Mindo), short brittle "pit'syru, si'leesip" (both two-part phrases descending).
Nasal meowing call rises.

aurantiirostris

Speckled Nightingale-thrush *Catharus maculatus* `LC`
Zorzal Pechiamarillo
Uncommon and local resident.

L 17.3 cm (6.8"). Race *maculatus*. Undergrowth
in humid foothill and lower montane forest,
especially in damp ravines. 600–2300 m.
Reclusive, perversely difficult to approach.
Forages on ground and sings from within cover.
ID Orange bill, eye-ring and legs, black head,
apricot-yellow underparts spotted dark. ♀ duller.
Voice Clear whistles recall Slaty-backed
Nightingale-thrush but more varied, occasionally
tremulous; rising "tuu-whu EE-lee...turr-hee..."
or descending "ee-lay, tur-dee" (last note
highest). **TN** Recently split from Middle American
C. dryas. **AN** Sclater's Nightingale-thrush (formerly
Spotted Nightingale-thrush).

♀

maculatus

♂

Slaty-backed Nightingale-thrush *Catharus fuscater* `LC`
Zorzal Oscuro

Seven subspecies in two subspecies groups;
one in Colombia.

Slaty-backed Nightingale-thrush *Catharus (fuscater) fuscater*
Fairly common resident.
L 18 cm (7"). Races *fuscater*[A], *sanctaemartae*[B], *opertaneus*[C]. Humid and wet
montane forest. 600–2800 m. Singles, on or close to ground, shy and almost
unapproachable (like phantom in undergrowth). Rarely ventures into openings;
occasionally at *Labidus* army ant swarms. **ID** Bill, eye-ring and legs orange, eyes
white, above blackish slate, head blackest, belly whitish. **Voice** Lovely song,
haunting, ethereal 2–3-note phrases (evokes old rusty gate), e.g. "eer-lee" or
"ur-eee-lee", last note higher (*sanctaemartae*). **SS** Spotted Nightingale-thrush.

fuscater

Genus _Turdus_ Familiar, widespread, large thrushes with strong legs. Some are common in settled areas, others shy forest-dwellers. Identification often difficult; note habitat, distribution, vocalizations, subtle colour shading and bare-part colours. Juvs often somewhat spotted and wing-coverts tipped rufous.

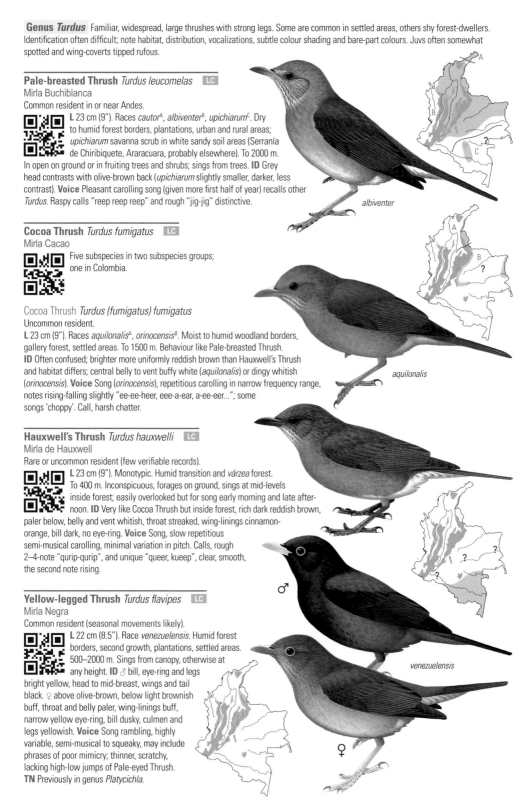

Pale-breasted Thrush _Turdus leucomelas_ LC
Mirla Buchiblanca
Common resident in or near Andes.

L 23 cm (9"). Races _cautor_[A], _albiventer_[B], _upichiarum_[C]. Dry to humid forest borders, plantations, urban and rural areas; _upichiarum_ savanna scrub in white sandy soil areas (Serranía de Chiribiquete, Araracuara, probably elsewhere). To 2000 m. In open on ground or in fruiting trees and shrubs; sings from trees. **ID** Grey head contrasts with olive-brown back (_upichiarum_ slightly smaller, darker, less contrast). **Voice** Pleasant carolling song (given more first half of year) recalls other _Turdus_. Raspy calls "reep reep reep" and rough "jig-jig" distinctive.

albiventer

Cocoa Thrush _Turdus fumigatus_ LC
Mirla Cacao

Five subspecies in two subspecies groups; one in Colombia.

Cocoa Thrush _Turdus (fumigatus) fumigatus_
Uncommon resident.
L 23 cm (9"). Races _aquilonalis_[A], _orinocensis_[B]. Moist to humid woodland borders, gallery forest, settled areas. To 1500 m. Behaviour like Pale-breasted Thrush. **ID** Often confused; brighter more uniformly reddish brown than Hauxwell's Thrush and habitat differs; central belly to vent buffy white (_aquilonalis_) or dingy whitish (_orinocensis_). **Voice** Song (_orinocensis_), repetitious carolling in narrow frequency range, notes rising-falling slightly "ee-ee-heer, eee-a-ear, a-ee-eer..."; some songs 'choppy'. Call, harsh chatter.

aquilonalis

Hauxwell's Thrush _Turdus hauxwelli_ LC
Mirla de Hauxwell
Rare or uncommon resident (few verifiable records).

L 23 cm (9"). Monotypic. Humid transition and _várzea_ forest. To 400 m. Inconspicuous, forages on ground, sings at mid-levels inside forest; easily overlooked but for song early morning and late afternoon. **ID** Very like Cocoa Thrush but inside forest, rich dark reddish brown, paler below, belly and vent whitish, throat streaked, wing-linings cinnamon-orange, bill dark, no eye-ring. **Voice** Song, slow repetitious semi-musical carolling, minimal variation in pitch. Calls, rough 2–4-note "qurip-qurip", and unique "queer, kueep", clear, smooth, the second note rising.

♂

Yellow-legged Thrush _Turdus flavipes_ LC
Mirla Negra
Common resident (seasonal movements likely).

L 22 cm (8.5"). Race _venezuelensis_. Humid forest borders, second growth, plantations, settled areas. 500–2000 m. Sings from canopy, otherwise at any height. **ID** ♂ bill, eye-ring and legs bright yellow, head to mid-breast, wings and tail black. ♀ above olive-brown, below light brownish buff, throat and belly paler, wing-linings buff, narrow yellow eye-ring, bill dusky, culmen and legs yellowish. **Voice** Song rambling, highly variable, semi-musical to squeaky, may include phrases of poor mimicry; thinner, scratchy, lacking high-low jumps of Pale-eyed Thrush. **TN** Previously in genus _Platycichla_.

venezuelensis

♀

447

Lawrence's Thrush *Turdus lawrencii* LC
Mirla Amazónica

Uncommon and local resident.

 L 23 cm (9"). Monotypic. Humid *terra firme* and *várzea* forest. To 500 m. ♂♂ sing from rainforest canopy. Forages on ground inside forest or visits fruiting trees. **ID** ♂ bill, eye-ring and legs bright yellow, throat streaked, underparts warm buffy brown. ♀ dusky bill, inconspicuous yellow eye-ring, paler below than ♂. **Voice** Renowned for unsurpassed powers of vocal mimicry. ♂♂ sing loud uninterrupted strings of near-perfect renditions of songs or portions of songs of almost any bird it hears (> 50 species reported in single song bouts!). Occasional random notes. **SS** ♀ Hauxwell's Thrush (no eye-ring).

Pale-vented Thrush *Turdus obsoletus* LC
Mirla Selvática

Rare to uncommon and local resident.

 L 23 cm (9"). Races *obsoletus*[A], *parambanus*[B], *colombianus*[C]. Interior of humid and wet foothill and lower montane forest, less at borders, clearings. 400–1500 m (seasonally lower?). **ID** Overall rufous-brown, throat paler, lightly streaked; best identified by contrasting white belly and vent. **Voice** Song (*parambanus*), brisk musical carolling (no churrs or trills), repetitive, narrow 2–3 kHz range. Calls, slow rising "bzeeeek" and low "wuk". **SS** Often confused; cf. Pale-breasted and Black-billed Thrushes (neither inside forest).

obsoletus

White-throated Thrush *Turdus assimilis* LC
Mirla Gorguiblanca

 Eleven or 14 subspecies (taxonomy-dependent) in two subspecies groups; one in Colombia.

Dagua Thrush *Turdus (assimilis) daguae*
Mirla de Dagua

Uncommon resident.

L 22 cm (8.5"). One subspecies in group. Mainly inside humid lowland and foothill forest; also borders, second growth, trees in clearings. To 900 m (higher?). Forages on ground in forest, regularly in mid-level or canopy fruiting trees. **ID** Yellow eye-ring, white throat streaked black, conspicuous white crescent on chest, bill dull brownish yellow. **Voice** Song lethargic carolling of slurred 2–3-note phrases, with hypnotic sing-song pattern. One call (of many), harsh buzzy "bzeeeyet". **TN** Taxonomy unresolved. Dagua Thrush sometimes treated as a race of next species.

White-necked Thrush *Turdus albicollis* LC
Mirla Collareja

 Seven subspecies in two subspecies groups; one in Colombia.

Grey-flanked Thrush *Turdus (albicollis) phaeopygus*
Fairly common resident.

L 23 cm (9"). Races *phaeopygoides*[A], *phaeopygus*[B]. Humid *terra firme* and *várzea* forest; also white-sand forest (common). To 1500 m. Sings from elevated perch, forages on ground or in fruiting trees, and may attend army ants. **ID** Looks dark-headed, bill blackish, base of lower mandible yellow, eye-ring yellow, throat white heavily streaked black, narrow white chest crescent, otherwise greyish below. **Voice** Carolling song melodious but lazy, repetitive, hypnotic. Call, rough "jjig-wig" or "jjig-wig-wig".

phaeopygoides

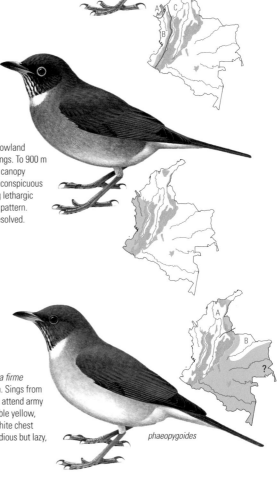

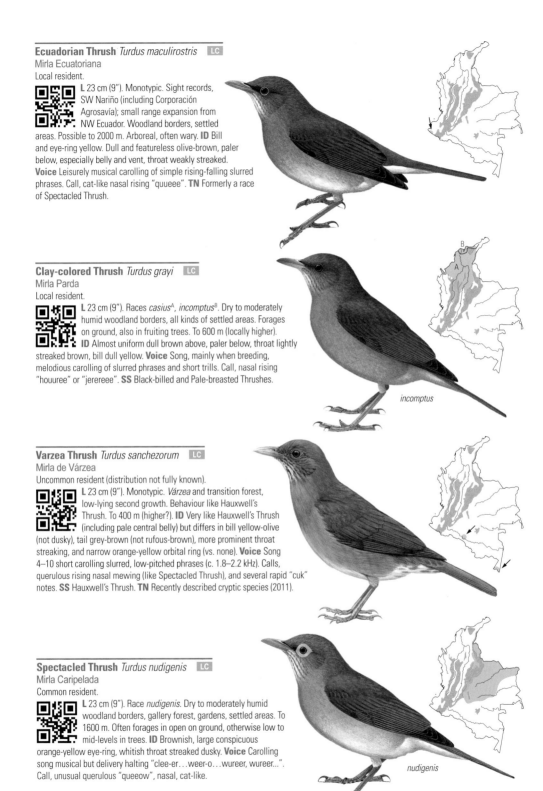

Ecuadorian Thrush *Turdus maculirostris* `LC`
Mirla Ecuatoriana
Local resident.

L 23 cm (9"). Monotypic. Sight records, SW Nariño (including Corporación Agrosavía); small range expansion from NW Ecuador. Woodland borders, settled areas. Possible to 2000 m. Arboreal, often wary. **ID** Bill and eye-ring yellow. Dull and featureless olive-brown, paler below, especially belly and vent, throat weakly streaked. **Voice** Leisurely musical carolling of simple rising-falling slurred phrases. Call, cat-like nasal rising "quueee". **TN** Formerly a race of Spectacled Thrush.

Clay-colored Thrush *Turdus grayi* `LC`
Mirla Parda
Local resident.

L 23 cm (9"). Races *casius*[A], *incomptus*[B]. Dry to moderately humid woodland borders, all kinds of settled areas. Forages on ground, also in fruiting trees. To 600 m (locally higher). **ID** Almost uniform dull brown above, paler below, throat lightly streaked brown, bill dull yellow. **Voice** Song, mainly when breeding, melodious carolling of slurred phrases and short trills. Call, nasal rising "houuree" or "jerereee". **SS** Black-billed and Pale-breasted Thrushes.

incomptus

Varzea Thrush *Turdus sanchezorum* `LC`
Mirla de Várzea
Uncommon resident (distribution not fully known).

L 23 cm (9"). Monotypic. *Várzea* and transition forest, low-lying second growth. Behaviour like Hauxwell's Thrush. To 400 m (higher?). **ID** Very like Hauxwell's Thrush (including pale central belly) but differs in bill yellow-olive (not dusky), tail grey-brown (not rufous-brown), more prominent throat streaking, and narrow orange-yellow orbital ring (vs. none). **Voice** Song 4–10 short carolling slurred, low-pitched phrases (c. 1.8–2.2 kHz). Calls, querulous rising nasal mewing (like Spectacled Thrush), and several rapid "cuk" notes. **SS** Hauxwell's Thrush. **TN** Recently described cryptic species (2011).

Spectacled Thrush *Turdus nudigenis* `LC`
Mirla Caripelada
Common resident.

L 23 cm (9"). Race *nudigenis*. Dry to moderately humid woodland borders, gallery forest, gardens, settled areas. To 1600 m. Often forages in open on ground, otherwise low to mid-levels in trees. **ID** Brownish, large conspicuous orange-yellow eye-ring, whitish throat streaked dusky. **Voice** Carolling song musical but delivery halting "clee-er…weer-o…wureer, wureer…". Call, unusual querulous "queeow", nasal, cat-like.

nudigenis

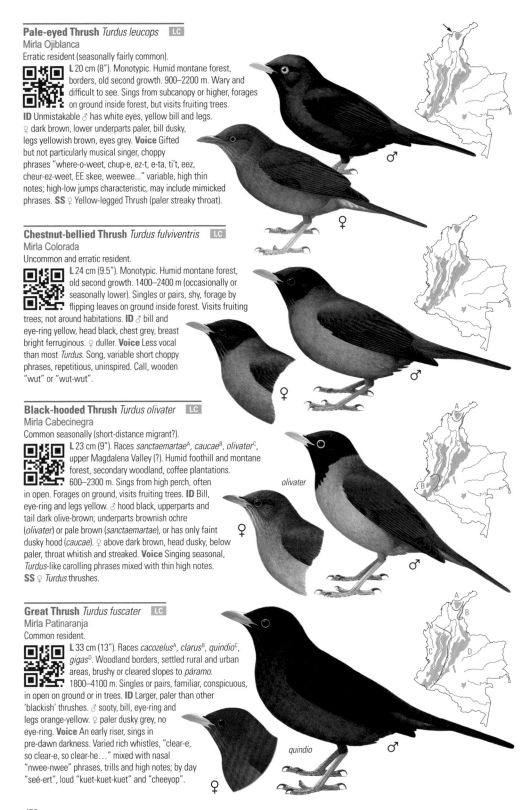

Pale-eyed Thrush *Turdus leucops* `LC`
Mirla Ojiblanca
Erratic resident (seasonally fairly common).
L 20 cm (8"). Monotypic. Humid montane forest, borders, old second growth. 900–2200 m. Wary and difficult to see. Sings from subcanopy or higher, forages on ground inside forest, but visits fruiting trees. **ID** Unmistakable ♂ has white eyes, yellow bill and legs. ♀ dark brown, lower underparts paler, bill dusky, legs yellowish brown, eyes grey. **Voice** Gifted but not particularly musical singer, choppy phrases "where-o-weet, chup-e, ez-t, e-ta, ti't, eez, cheur-ez-weet, EE skee, weewee..." variable, high thin notes; high-low jumps characteristic, may include mimicked phrases. **SS** ♀ Yellow-legged Thrush (paler streaky throat).

Chestnut-bellied Thrush *Turdus fulviventris* `LC`
Mirla Colorada
Uncommon and erratic resident.
L 24 cm (9.5"). Monotypic. Humid montane forest, old second growth. 1400–2400 m (occasionally or seasonally lower). Singles or pairs, shy, forage by flipping leaves on ground inside forest. Visits fruiting trees; not around habitations. **ID** ♂ bill and eye-ring yellow, head black, chest grey, breast bright ferruginous. ♀ duller. **Voice** Less vocal than most *Turdus*. Song, variable short choppy phrases, repetitious, uninspired. Call, wooden "wut" or "wut-wut".

Black-hooded Thrush *Turdus olivater* `LC`
Mirla Cabecinegra
Common seasonally (short-distance migrant?).
L 23 cm (9"). Races *sanctaemartae*[A], *caucae*[B], *olivater*[C], upper Magdalena Valley (?). Humid foothill and montane forest, secondary woodland, coffee plantations. 600–2300 m. Sings from high perch, often in open. Forages on ground, visits fruiting trees. **ID** Bill, eye-ring and legs yellow. ♂ hood black, upperparts and tail dark olive-brown; underparts brownish ochre (*olivater*) or pale brown (*sanctaemartae*), or has only faint dusky hood (*caucae*). ♀ above dark brown, head dusky, below paler, throat whitish and streaked. **Voice** Singing seasonal, *Turdus*-like carolling phrases mixed with thin high notes. **SS** ♀ *Turdus* thrushes.

olivater

Great Thrush *Turdus fuscater* `LC`
Mirla Patinaranja
Common resident.
L 33 cm (13"). Races *cacozelus*[A], *clarus*[B], *quindio*[C], *gigas*[D]. Woodland borders, settled rural and urban areas, brushy or cleared slopes to *páramo*. 1800–4100 m. Singles or pairs, familiar, conspicuous, in open on ground or in trees. **ID** Larger, paler than other 'blackish' thrushes. ♂ sooty, bill, eye-ring and legs orange-yellow. ♀ paler dusky grey, no eye-ring. **Voice** An early riser, sings in pre-dawn darkness. Varied rich whistles, "clear-e, so clear-e, so clear-he..." mixed with nasal "nwee-nwee" phrases, trills and high notes; by day "seé-ert", loud "kuet-kuet-kuet" and "cheeyop".

quindio

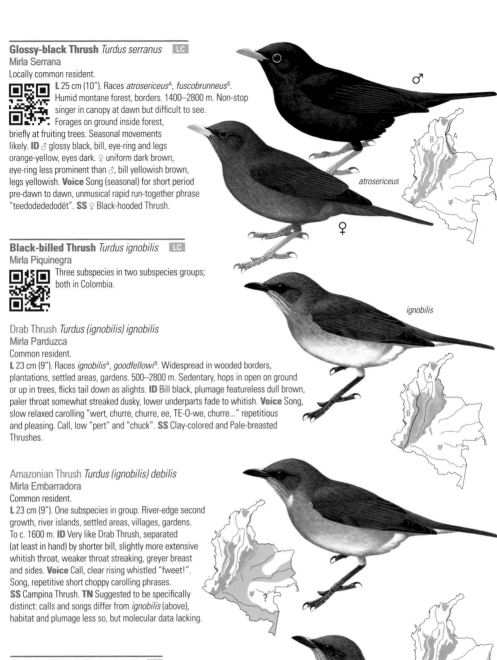

Glossy-black Thrush *Turdus serranus* `LC`
Mirla Serrana
Locally common resident.

L 25 cm (10"). Races *atrosericeus*[A], *fuscobrunneus*[B]. Humid montane forest, borders. 1400–2800 m. Non-stop singer in canopy at dawn but difficult to see. Forages on ground inside forest, briefly at fruiting trees. Seasonal movements likely. **ID** ♂ glossy black, bill, eye-ring and legs orange-yellow, eyes dark. ♀ uniform dark brown, eye-ring less prominent than ♂, bill yellowish brown, legs yellowish. **Voice** Song (seasonal) for short period pre-dawn to dawn, unmusical rapid run-together phrase "teedodededodét". **SS** ♀ Black-hooded Thrush.

atrosericeus

♂

♀

Black-billed Thrush *Turdus ignobilis* `LC`
Mirla Piquinegra

Three subspecies in two subspecies groups; both in Colombia.

ignobilis

Drab Thrush *Turdus (ignobilis) ignobilis*
Mirla Parduzca
Common resident.

L 23 cm (9"). Races *ignobilis*[A], *goodfellowi*[B]. Widespread in wooded borders, plantations, settled areas, gardens. 500–2800 m. Sedentary, hops in open on ground or up in trees, flicks tail down as alights. **ID** Bill black, plumage featureless dull brown, paler throat somewhat streaked dusky, lower underparts fade to whitish. **Voice** Song, slow relaxed carolling "wert, churre, churre, ee, TE-O-we, churre..." repetitious and pleasing. Call, low "pert" and "chuck". **SS** Clay-colored and Pale-breasted Thrushes.

Amazonian Thrush *Turdus (ignobilis) debilis*
Mirla Embarradora
Common resident.

L 23 cm (9"). One subspecies in group. River-edge second growth, river islands, settled areas, villages, gardens. To c. 1600 m. **ID** Very like Drab Thrush, separated (at least in hand) by shorter bill, slightly more extensive whitish throat, weaker throat streaking, greyer breast and sides. **Voice** Call, clear rising whistled "fweet!". Song, repetitive short choppy carolling phrases. **SS** Campina Thrush. **TN** Suggested to be specifically distinct: calls and songs differ from *ignobilis* (above), habitat and plumage less so, but molecular data lacking.

Campina Thrush *Turdus arthuri* `LC`
Mirla de Campina
Fairly common (?) resident.

L 23 cm. Monotypic. Restricted to bushy savanna and low-canopy scrub (*matorral*) on white sandy soils. To 400 m. **ID** Separation from *debilis* race of Black-billed Thrush based on molecular evidence and habitat separation in areas of known overlap (Puerto Inírida, Guainía; Araracuara, Caquetá); plumage differences minimal, slightly greyer underparts with white confined to median belly and vent, stronger throat streaks (?). **Voice** Needs confirmation (like Black-billed Thrush?). **SS** Black-billed Thrush (race *debilis*). **TN** Prior to 2019 regarded as a race of *T. ignobilis*.

BOMBYCILLIDAE
Waxwings
3 extant species, 1 in region

Small crested passerines with black mask and yellow-tipped tails. Name derives from red wax-like tips to their secondaries, the result of dense concentrations of pigment from fruit they eat. Social, usually in flocks.

Cedar Waxwing *Bombycilla cedrorum* `LC`
Ampelis Americano
Occasional boreal migrant.

 L 18.5 cm (7.3"). Race *cedrorum*. Can occur in almost any forested or semi-open habitat; records in Colombia (and South America) all associated with El Niño years or its onset, suggesting depressed fruit availability in N may promote dispersal. **ID** Sleek brown plumage, angular black mask, crest, and yellow-tipped tail. **Voice** Extremely high (8–9 kHz) "eeeeeee".

cedrorum

ESTRILDIDAE
Waxbills
141 extant species, 2 introduced

A family of Old World tropical regions and Australasia. Small, seed-eating birds with thick bills and varied, often colourful, plumage. Widely kept as cagebirds; often introduced in warmer latitudes.

Tricoloured Munia *Lonchura malacca* `LC`
Monjita Tricolor
Introduced (established locally in Cauca and Magdalena Valleys).

 L 12 cm (4.7"). Monotypic. Escaped cagebird; native to Indian Subcontinent. Range expanding. Rice fields, tall grass and brush. Pairs or small groups. **ID** Thick whitish bill, black head and throat, chestnut upperparts, white below, large black patch from breast to vent. **TN** Chestnut Munia sometimes regarded as a race of present species.

Chestnut Munia *Lonchura atricapilla* `LC`
Monjita Castaña
Introduced (local in Cauca Valley and around Ibague, Neiva, Magdalena Valley).

 L 12 cm (4.7"). Race unknown. Escaped cagebird; native of S & SE Asia. Brushy and grassy regions, rice fields. Often with Tricoloured Munia, and they are known to interbreed. **ID** Like Tricoloured Munia but underparts rufous-chestnut (no white), black belly patch smaller.

PASSERIDAE
Old World Sparrows
43 extant species, 1 introduced

Small group of sturdy seed-eating birds native to the Old World, some of which are now widely introduced.

House Sparrow *Passer domesticus* `LC`
Copetón Europeo
Local introduced resident (mainly coastal cities).

 L 15 cm (6"). Race *domesticus*? Present since at least 1979 (Buenaventura), now locally on both coasts. Noisy, gregarious, aggressive pest capable of spreading, although more successful in colder higher latitudes. **ID** ♂ grey crown, dull rufous nape, whitish cheeks and black bib, single white wingbar. ♀ plain, stout yellowish-grey bill, streaked back, dingy buff to whitish underparts, weak eyebrow and wingbar. **Voice** Noisy, monotonous husky chirping.

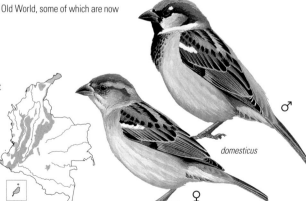

♂

domesticus

♀

Nearly worldwide family of ground-dwelling birds found in grasslands and *páramo*. Pipits have slender bills, long hindclaws, and streaky cryptically patterned plumage.

Buff-bellied Pipit (American Pipit) *Anthus rubescens* LC
Bisbita Norteamericana
Vagrant (Isla San Andrés).

 L 16.5 cm (6.5"). Race *rubescens*? Open areas, fields and pastures. Walks or runs, weaves through grass. **ID** Ad non-br grey-brown upperparts faintly streaked, two wingbars, buff eyebrow, thin black malar, and underparts dingy buff-white streaked dusky. Ad br (unlikely) brighter buff underparts, streaking faint. **Voice** Flight call, thin "sip'it".

rubescens

non-breeding

Yellowish Pipit *Anthus lutescens* LC
Bisbita Sabanera
Locally fairly common resident.

 L 14 cm (5.5"). Race *lutescens*. Grassland in *llanos*, sandy soil savannas. To 500 m. Pairs or loosely associated groups, crouch to avoid detection or flush off in bounding flight, often quite high and far. **ID** Above buff-brown streaked dusky, white outer tail feathers, streaky underparts tinged yellowish. **Voice** Buzzy song from ground or overhead as circles or parachutes earthward, a few nasal notes and long descending buzz "tsit'sit'sit'tiz-bzzzzzeeeeeeuuuuuu". Flushes with "chit-chit".

lutescens

Paramo Pipit *Anthus bogotensis* LC
Bisbita Paramuna
Local resident.

 L 15 cm (6"). Race *bogotensis*. Grassy pastures, short grass in *páramo*. 3100–3800 m. Singles or scattered pairs, territorial, inconspicuous, walk in bare areas, hide in grass, crouch to avoid detection or flush up, often flying far away. **ID** Streaky above, spotted on breast, streaked at sides; white tail edges. **Voice** Sings from rock or ground, or in display flight. Song variable, short or long, typically a slurred note and high "sit" notes, buzzes and jumbled high notes at end.

bogotensis

FRINGILLIDAE
Finches
211 extant species, 24 in region

Nearly worldwide family whose species composition has changed markedly as a result of molecular studies. The family now includes the colourful and exclusively Neotropical chlorophonias and euphonias, as well as siskins, several genera with massive seed-cracking bills, or crossed bills, and Hawaiian honeycreepers with thin decurved probing bills. All species feed mainly or exclusively on vegetable matter, either seeds, fruit or nectar, and also feed their young on them, usually in regurgitated form. As a group they are the most widely distributed of the nine-primaried oscine passerines, and also include some of the most endangered.

Genus *Chlorophonia* Small, plump, brightly coloured, mostly emerald-green frugivorous passerines; ad ♂♂ are brighter, but usually outnumbered by ♀-plumaged birds. Some short-distance seasonal movements occur.

Yellow-collared Chlorophonia *Chlorophonia flavirostris* LC
Clorofonia Collareja
Locally fairly common resident.

L 10.2 cm (4"). Monotypic. Near-endemic (also extreme E Panama and NW Ecuador). Wet foothill and lower montane forest, borders; erratic in lowlands. 100–1900 m (rarely higher). Pairs or groups of 3–30, occasionally 80+, wander alone, visit fruiting trees; follow mixed flocks but inconspicuous. Feeds on small berries, e.g. *Miconia* and mistletoe, mid-levels or higher. **ID** Colourful, green and yellow, with white eyes, salmon-orange bill and legs. ♀ and juv duller, no yellow collar. **Voice** Soft "pek", and plaintive "pleeeeee" perched or in flight. Song, buzzy rattle and high notes.

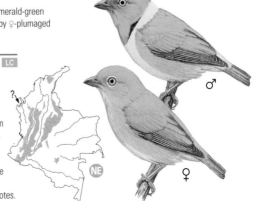

♂

♀

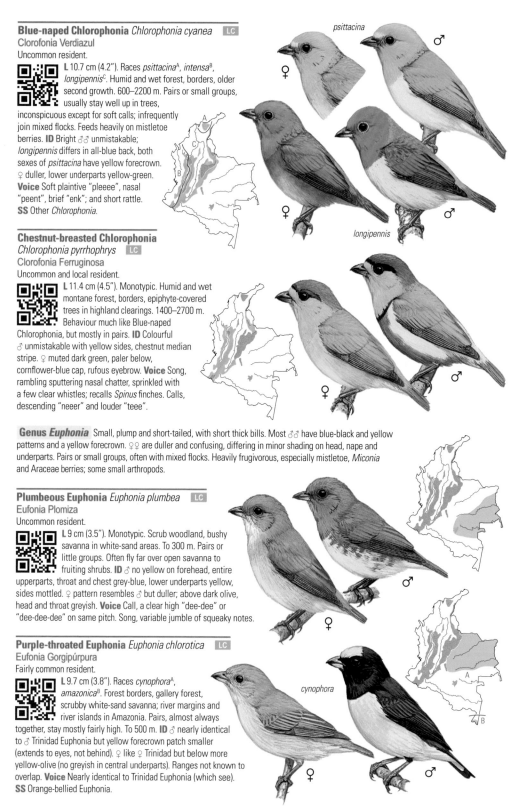

Blue-naped Chlorophonia *Chlorophonia cyanea* `LC`
Clorofonia Verdiazul
Uncommon resident.

L 10.7 cm (4.2"). Races *psittacina*[A], *intensa*[B], *longipennis*[C]. Humid and wet forest, borders, older second growth. 600–2200 m. Pairs or small groups, usually stay well up in trees, inconspicuous except for soft calls; infrequently join mixed flocks. Feeds heavily on mistletoe berries. **ID** Bright ♂♂ unmistakable; *longipennis* differs in all-blue back, both sexes of *psittacina* have yellow forecrown. ♀ duller, lower underparts yellow-green. **Voice** Soft plaintive "pleeee", nasal "peent", brief "enk"; and short rattle. **SS** Other *Chlorophonia*.

psittacina

longipennis

Chestnut-breasted Chlorophonia
Chlorophonia pyrrhophrys `LC`
Clorofonia Ferruginosa
Uncommon and local resident.

L 11.4 cm (4.5"). Monotypic. Humid and wet montane forest, borders, epiphyte-covered trees in highland clearings. 1400–2700 m. Behaviour much like Blue-naped Chlorophonia, but mostly in pairs. **ID** Colourful ♂ unmistakable with yellow sides, chestnut median stripe. ♀ muted dark green, paler below, cornflower-blue cap, rufous eyebrow. **Voice** Song, rambling sputtering nasal chatter, sprinkled with a few clear whistles; recalls *Spinus* finches. Calls, descending "neeer" and louder "teee".

Genus *Euphonia* Small, plump and short-tailed, with short thick bills. Most ♂♂ have blue-black and yellow patterns and a yellow forecrown. ♀♀ are duller and confusing, differing in minor shading on head, nape and underparts. Pairs or small groups, often with mixed flocks. Heavily frugivorous, especially mistletoe, *Miconia* and Araceae berries; some small arthropods.

Plumbeous Euphonia *Euphonia plumbea* `LC`
Eufonia Plomiza
Uncommon resident.

L 9 cm (3.5"). Monotypic. Scrub woodland, bushy savanna in white-sand areas. To 300 m. Pairs or little groups. Often fly far over open savanna to fruiting shrubs. **ID** ♂ no yellow on forehead, entire upperparts, throat and chest grey-blue, lower underparts yellow, sides mottled. ♀ pattern resembles ♂ but duller; above dark olive, head and throat greyish. **Voice** Call, a clear high "dee-dee" or "dee-dee-dee" on same pitch. Song, variable jumble of squeaky notes.

Purple-throated Euphonia *Euphonia chlorotica* `LC`
Eufonia Gorgipúrpura
Fairly common resident.

L 9.7 cm (3.8"). Races *cynophora*[A], *amazonica*[B]. Forest borders, gallery forest, scrubby white-sand savanna; river margins and river islands in Amazonia. Pairs, almost always together, stay mostly fairly high. To 500 m. **ID** ♂ nearly identical to ♂ Trinidad Euphonia but yellow forecrown patch smaller (extends to eyes, not behind). ♀ like ♀ Trinidad but below more yellow-olive (no greyish in central underparts). Ranges not known to overlap. **Voice** Nearly identical to Trinidad Euphonia (which see). **SS** Orange-bellied Euphonia.

cynophora

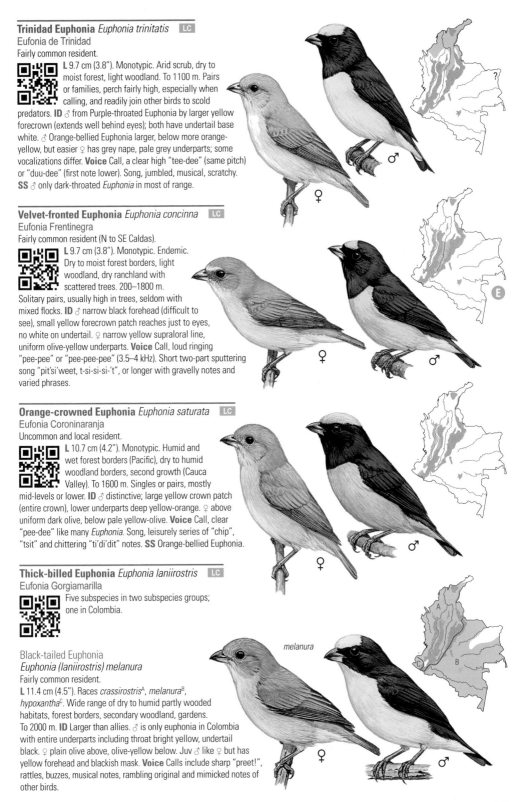

Trinidad Euphonia *Euphonia trinitatis* LC
Eufonia de Trinidad
Fairly common resident.

L 9.7 cm (3.8"). Monotypic. Arid scrub, dry to moist forest, light woodland. To 1100 m. Pairs or families, perch fairly high, especially when calling, and readily join other birds to scold predators. **ID** ♂ from Purple-throated Euphonia by larger yellow forecrown (extends well behind eyes); both have undertail base white. ♂ Orange-bellied Euphonia larger, below more orange-yellow, but easier ♀ has grey nape, pale grey underparts; some vocalizations differ. **Voice** Call, a clear high "tee-dee" (same pitch) or "duu-dee" (first note lower). Song, jumbled, musical, scratchy. **SS** ♂ only dark-throated *Euphonia* in most of range.

Velvet-fronted Euphonia *Euphonia concinna* LC
Eufonia Frentinegra
Fairly common resident (N to SE Caldas).

L 9.7 cm (3.8"). Monotypic. Endemic. Dry to moist forest borders, light woodland, dry ranchland with scattered trees. 200–1800 m. Solitary pairs, usually high in trees, seldom with mixed flocks. **ID** ♂ narrow black forehead (difficult to see), small yellow forecrown patch reaches just to eyes, no white on undertail. ♀ narrow yellow supraloral line, uniform olive-yellow underparts. **Voice** Call, loud ringing "pee-pee" or "pee-pee-pee" (3.5–4 kHz). Short two-part sputtering song "pit'si'weet, t-si-si-si-'t", or longer with gravelly notes and varied phrases.

Orange-crowned Euphonia *Euphonia saturata* LC
Eufonia Coroninaranja
Uncommon and local resident.

L 10.7 cm (4.2"). Monotypic. Humid and wet forest borders (Pacific), dry to humid woodland borders, second growth (Cauca Valley). To 1600 m. Singles or pairs, mostly mid-levels or lower. **ID** ♂ distinctive; large yellow crown patch (entire crown), lower underparts deep yellow-orange. ♀ above uniform dark olive, below pale yellow-olive. **Voice** Call, clear "pee-dee" like many *Euphonia*. Song, leisurely series of "chip", "tsit" and chittering "ti'di'dit" notes. **SS** Orange-bellied Euphonia.

Thick-billed Euphonia *Euphonia laniirostris* LC
Eufonia Gorgiamarilla

Five subspecies in two subspecies groups; one in Colombia.

Black-tailed Euphonia
Euphonia (laniirostris) melanura
Fairly common resident.
L 11.4 cm (4.5"). Races *crassirostris*[A], *melanura*[B], *hypoxantha*[C]. Wide range of dry to humid partly wooded habitats, forest borders, secondary woodland, gardens. To 2000 m. **ID** Larger than allies. ♂ is only euphonia in Colombia with entire underparts including throat bright yellow, undertail black. ♀ plain olive above, olive-yellow below. Juv ♂ like ♀ but has yellow forehead and blackish mask. **Voice** Calls include sharp "preet!", rattles, buzzes, musical notes, rambling original and mimicked notes of other birds.

melanura

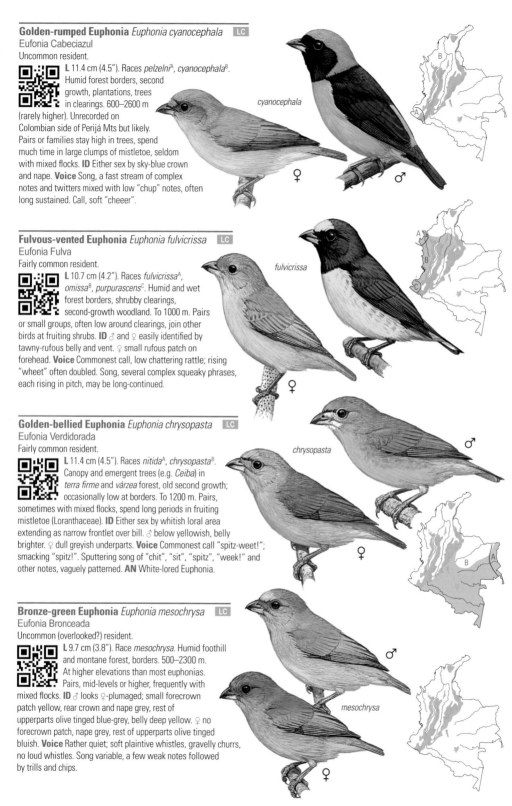

Golden-rumped Euphonia *Euphonia cyanocephala* `LC`
Eufonia Cabeciazul
Uncommon resident.

L 11.4 cm (4.5"). Races *pelzelni*[A], *cyanocephala*[B]. Humid forest borders, second growth, plantations, trees in clearings. 600–2600 m (rarely higher). Unrecorded on Colombian side of Perijá Mts but likely. Pairs or families stay high in trees, spend much time in large clumps of mistletoe, seldom with mixed flocks. **ID** Either sex by sky-blue crown and nape. **Voice** Song, a fast stream of complex notes and twitters mixed with low "chup" notes, often long sustained. Call, soft "cheeer".

cyanocephala

♀

♂

Fulvous-vented Euphonia *Euphonia fulvicrissa* `LC`
Eufonia Fulva
Fairly common resident.

L 10.7 cm (4.2"). Races *fulvicrissa*[A], *omissa*[B], *purpurascens*[C]. Humid and wet forest borders, shrubby clearings, second-growth woodland. To 1000 m. Pairs or small groups, often low around clearings, join other birds at fruiting shrubs. **ID** ♂ and ♀ easily identified by tawny-rufous belly and vent. ♀ small rufous patch on forehead. **Voice** Commonest call, low chattering rattle; rising "wheet" often doubled. Song, several complex squeaky phrases, each rising in pitch, may be long-continued.

fulvicrissa

♀

Golden-bellied Euphonia *Euphonia chrysopasta* `LC`
Eufonia Verdidorada
Fairly common resident.

L 11.4 cm (4.5"). Races *nitida*[A], *chrysopasta*[B]. Canopy and emergent trees (e.g. *Ceiba*) in *terra firme* and *várzea* forest, old second growth; occasionally low at borders. To 1200 m. Pairs, sometimes with mixed flocks, spend long periods in fruiting mistletoe (Loranthaceae). **ID** Either sex by whitish loral area extending as narrow frontlet over bill. ♂ below yellowish, belly brighter. ♀ dull greyish underparts. **Voice** Commonest call "spitz-weet!"; smacking "spitz!". Sputtering song of "chit", "sit", "spitz", "week!" and other notes, vaguely patterned. **AN** White-lored Euphonia.

chrysopasta

♂

♀

Bronze-green Euphonia *Euphonia mesochrysa* `LC`
Eufonia Bronceada
Uncommon (overlooked?) resident.

L 9.7 cm (3.8"). Race *mesochrysa*. Humid foothill and montane forest, borders. 500–2300 m. At higher elevations than most euphonias. Pairs, mid-levels or higher, frequently with mixed flocks. **ID** ♂ looks ♀-plumaged; small forecrown patch yellow, rear crown and nape grey, rest of upperparts olive tinged blue-grey, belly deep yellow. ♀ no forecrown patch, nape grey, rest of upperparts olive tinged bluish. **Voice** Rather quiet; soft plaintive whistles, gravelly churrs, no loud whistles. Song variable, a few weak notes followed by trills and chips.

♂

mesochrysa

♀

White-vented Euphonia *Euphonia minuta* `LC`
Eufonia Culiblanca
Fairly common resident.

L 9.7 cm (3.8"). Races *humilis*[A], *minuta*[B]. Canopy of humid lowland and foothill forest. To 1000 m. Pairs or little groups stay high, follow mixed flocks or spend much time in mistletoe (Loranthaceae) often with other euphonias. **ID** Small *Euphonia*. ♂ tiny yellow forecrown patch, white belly, vent and base of undertail. ♀ above light olive, no forecrown patch, lower underparts whitish like ♂. **Voice** Call, simple whistled "bree"; sputtering song resembles that of Golden-bellied Euphonia.

♂ *humilis*

minuta

♀

♂

Tawny-capped Euphonia
Euphonia anneae `LC`
Eufonia Cabecirrufa
Status unknown.

L 11 cm (4.3"). Race *rufivertex*. Canopy and edge of mossy foothill forest, lower in shrubby clearings, treefall gaps. 400–1700 m. **ID** ♂ tawny-rufous cap, white undertail-coverts and undertail base. ♀ olive above with tawny-rufous forecrown, greyish central underparts. **Voice** Call, downslurred "seerp"; various churrs. Song, mix of thin notes, slurs, trills and sharp notes. **SS** Tawny cap diagnostic.

rufivertex

♀

♂

Orange-bellied Euphonia *Euphonia xanthogaster* `LC`
Eufonia Buchinaranja
Commonest euphonia in Andes, fewer in Amazonian lowlands.

L 11 cm (4.3"). Races *chocoensis*[A], *exsul*[B], *badissima*[C], *oressinoma*[D], *brevirostris*[E], *dilutior*[F]. Humid and wet foothill and montane forest, borders, second growth. To 2300 m (rarely 2600 m). Pairs, low at fruiting shrubs, higher inside forest and regularly follow mixed flocks. Diet mostly fruit (*Miconia, Cecropia, Anthurium*). **ID** ♂ rufous cap (*badissima*) or large yellow cap (other races), rich yellow underparts (not obviously 'orange-bellied'), white undertail base. ♀ grey rear crown and nape. **Voice** Calls, "dee-dee-deet" (last higher), nasal "jew-jew" and gravelly rattles. Song, rambling notes. **TN** Several races poorly differentiated.

♂

chocoensis

♀

Rufous-bellied Euphonia *Euphonia rufiventris* `LC`
Eufonia Buchirrufa
Uncommon resident.

L 11.4 cm (4.5"). Race *rufiventris*. Canopy and borders of lowland forest. To 900 m (occasionally higher). Amazonian species, typically high in canopy or emergent trees; pairs, regularly with mixed flocks. **ID** ♂ upperparts, head and throat glossy navy-blue (no yellow crown patch), lower underparts deep burnt orange. ♀ forecrown yellowish, rear crown greyish, median breast to mid-belly grey, but best identified by deep tawny-orange vent and undertail-coverts. **Voice** Call, slow harsh gravelly rattles.

rufiventris

♂

♀

Genus *Spinus* Small, social seed-eating finches with conical bills and notched tails. Forest borders and semi-open areas, mostly at high elevations in Colombia. Siskins have yellow wing-bands (except Red Siskin), goldfinches white wing-bands. Frequent seasonal movements.

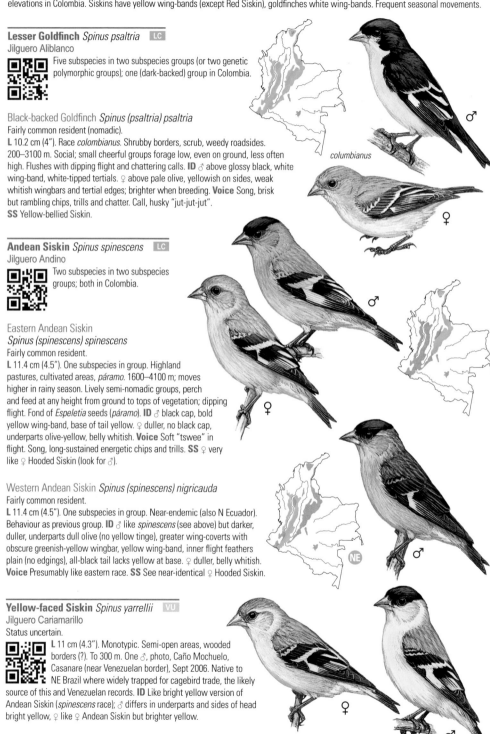

Lesser Goldfinch *Spinus psaltria* `LC`
Jilguero Aliblanco

Five subspecies in two subspecies groups (or two genetic polymorphic groups); one (dark-backed) group in Colombia.

Black-backed Goldfinch *Spinus (psaltria) psaltria*
Fairly common resident (nomadic).
L 10.2 cm (4"). Race *colombianus*. Shrubby borders, scrub, weedy roadsides. 200–3100 m. Social; small cheerful groups forage low, even on ground, less often high. Flushes with dipping flight and chattering calls. **ID** ♂ above glossy black, white wing-band, white-tipped tertials. ♀ above pale olive, yellowish on sides, weak whitish wingbars and tertial edges; brighter when breeding. **Voice** Song, brisk but rambling chips, trills and chatter. Call, husky "jut-jut-jut". **SS** Yellow-bellied Siskin.

columbianus

Andean Siskin *Spinus spinescens* `LC`
Jilguero Andino

Two subspecies in two subspecies groups; both in Colombia.

Eastern Andean Siskin
Spinus (spinescens) spinescens
Fairly common resident.
L 11.4 cm (4.5"). One subspecies in group. Highland pastures, cultivated areas, *páramo*. 1600–4100 m; moves higher in rainy season. Lively semi-nomadic groups, perch and feed at any height from ground to tops of vegetation; dipping flight. Fond of *Espeletia* seeds (*páramo*). **ID** ♂ black cap, bold yellow wing-band, base of tail yellow. ♀ duller, no black cap, underparts olive-yellow, belly whitish. **Voice** Soft "tswee" in flight. Song, long-sustained energetic chips and trills. **SS** ♀ very like ♀ Hooded Siskin (look for ♂).

Western Andean Siskin *Spinus (spinescens) nigricauda*
Fairly common resident.
L 11.4 cm (4.5"). One subspecies in group. Near-endemic (also N Ecuador). Behaviour as previous group. **ID** ♂ like *spinescens* (see above) but darker, duller, underparts dull olive (no yellow tinge), greater wing-coverts with obscure greenish-yellow wingbar, yellow wing-band, inner flight feathers plain (no edgings), all-black tail lacks yellow at base. ♀ duller, belly whitish. **Voice** Presumably like eastern race. **SS** See near-identical ♀ Hooded Siskin.

`NE`

Yellow-faced Siskin *Spinus yarrellii* `VU`
Jilguero Cariamarillo
Status uncertain.

L 11 cm (4.3"). Monotypic. Semi-open areas, wooded borders (?). To 300 m. One ♂, photo, Caño Mochuelo, Casanare (near Venezuelan border), Sept 2006. Native to NE Brazil where widely trapped for cagebird trade, the likely source of this and Venezuelan records. **ID** Like bright yellow version of Andean Siskin (*spinescens* race); ♂ differs in underparts and sides of head bright yellow, ♀ like ♀ Andean Siskin but brighter yellow.

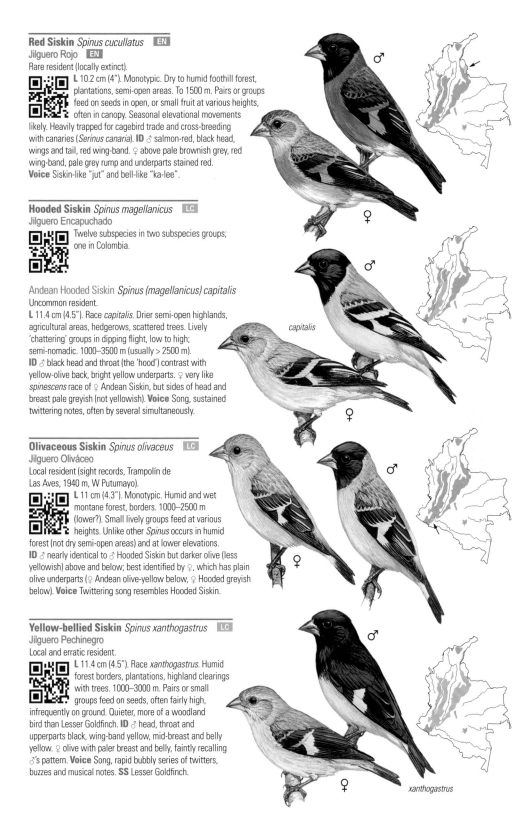

Red Siskin *Spinus cucullatus* EN
Jilguero Rojo EN
Rare resident (locally extinct).

L 10.2 cm (4"). Monotypic. Dry to humid foothill forest, plantations, semi-open areas. To 1500 m. Pairs or groups feed on seeds in open, or small fruit at various heights, often in canopy. Seasonal elevational movements likely. Heavily trapped for cagebird trade and cross-breeding with canaries (*Serinus canaria*). **ID** ♂ salmon-red, black head, wings and tail, red wing-band. ♀ above pale brownish grey, red wing-band, pale grey rump and underparts stained red. **Voice** Siskin-like "jut" and bell-like "ka-lee".

Hooded Siskin *Spinus magellanicus* LC
Jilguero Encapuchado

Twelve subspecies in two subspecies groups; one in Colombia.

Andean Hooded Siskin *Spinus (magellanicus) capitalis*
Uncommon resident.
L 11.4 cm (4.5"). Race *capitalis*. Drier semi-open highlands, agricultural areas, hedgerows, scattered trees. Lively 'chattering' groups in dipping flight, low to high; semi-nomadic. 1000–3500 m (usually > 2500 m). **ID** ♂ black head and throat (the 'hood') contrast with yellow-olive back, bright yellow underparts. ♀ very like *spinescens* race of ♀ Andean Siskin, but sides of head and breast pale greyish (not yellowish). **Voice** Song, sustained twittering notes, often by several simultaneously.

Olivaceous Siskin *Spinus olivaceus* LC
Jilguero Oliváceo
Local resident (sight records, Trampolín de Las Aves, 1940 m, W Putumayo).

L 11 cm (4.3"). Monotypic. Humid and wet montane forest, borders. 1000–2500 m (lower?). Small lively groups feed at various heights. Unlike other *Spinus* occurs in humid forest (not dry semi-open areas) and at lower elevations. **ID** ♂ nearly identical to ♂ Hooded Siskin but darker olive (less yellowish) above and below; best identified by ♀, which has plain olive underparts (♀ Andean olive-yellow below, ♀ Hooded greyish below). **Voice** Twittering song resembles Hooded Siskin.

Yellow-bellied Siskin *Spinus xanthogastrus* LC
Jilguero Pechinegro
Local and erratic resident.

L 11.4 cm (4.5"). Race *xanthogastrus*. Humid forest borders, plantations, highland clearings with trees. 1000–3000 m. Pairs or small groups feed on seeds, often fairly high, infrequently on ground. Quieter, more of a woodland bird than Lesser Goldfinch. **ID** ♂ head, throat and upperparts black, wing-band yellow, mid-breast and belly yellow. ♀ olive with paler breast and belly, faintly recalling ♂'s pattern. **Voice** Song, rapid bubbly series of twitters, buzzes and musical notes. **SS** Lesser Goldfinch.

capitalis

xanthogastrus

RHODINOCICHLIDAE
Thrush-tanager
1 extant species, 1 in region

The single species in this family has had a confused taxonomic history. Molecular data indicate that it is not closely related to any other nine-primaried oscine lineage.

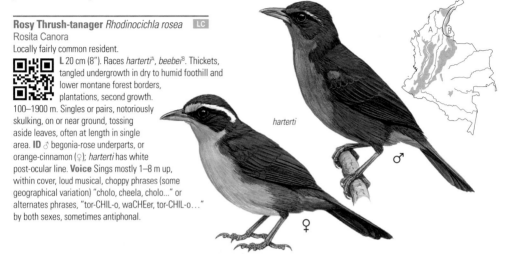

Rosy Thrush-tanager *Rhodinocichla rosea* `LC`
Rosita Canora
Locally fairly common resident.

L 20 cm (8"). Races *harterti*[A], *beebei*[B]. Thickets, tangled undergrowth in dry to humid foothill and lower montane forest borders, plantations, second growth. 100–1900 m. Singles or pairs, notoriously skulking, on or near ground, tossing aside leaves, often at length in single area. **ID** ♂ begonia-rose underparts, or orange-cinnamon (♀); *harterti* has white post-ocular line. **Voice** Sings mostly 1–8 m up, within cover, loud musical, choppy phrases (some geographical variation) "cholo, cheela, cholo..." or alternates phrases, "tor-CHIL-o, waCHEer, tor-CHIL-o..." by both sexes, sometimes antiphonal.

harterti

♂

♀

PASSERELLIDAE
New World Sparrows
145 extant species, 38 in region + 2 vagrants

Recently erected New World family of nine-primaried oscines based on molecular data, which indicate that these species are more closely related to each other than to species in various other families where they were previously placed. Occupy a broad array of habitats. Plumages drabber, more streaked and cryptic at northern latitudes, bolder with patches of colour in some tropical genera. Feed on fruit and seeds. Mostly monogamous.

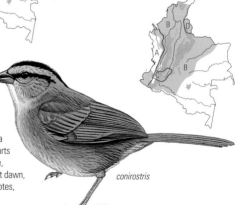

Tocuyo Sparrow *Arremonops tocuyensis* `LC`
Pinzón de Tocuyo `NT`
Uncommon and local resident.

L 13 cm (5"). Monotypic. Dry to arid scrub, dry woodland and thickets. To 300 m. Singles or pairs forage low or on ground. **ID** Like Black-striped Sparrow but smaller and paler, crown-stripes whitish (not grey), underparts more extensively whitish, often buff-tinged on breast. **Voice** Not especially vocal (seasonal?). Song, from low perch at dawn, short, musical, variable, typically three-parted "te, te, te, tsee'sweeu-sweeu-sweeu" or "tsu tsu, sEEuu-ti'ti'ti'ti", middle part often higher, last sometimes chattering.

Black-striped Sparrow *Arremonops conirostris* `LC`
Pinzón Conirrostro
Fairly common resident.

L 16.5 cm (6.5"). Races *striaticeps*[A], *conirostris*[B], *inexpectatus*[C], *umbrinus*[D]. Shrubby borders, thickets, plantations in dry to humid areas. To 1600 m. Retiring, semi-terrestrial singles or pairs, hop on ground, but ascend a few metres in vegetation to sing. **ID** Black and grey head-stripes, upperparts brownish olive, below whitish, chest and sides tinged grey; or above olive, below greyer (*umbrinus*). **Voice** Songs (geographically variable), mainly at dawn, individuals typically with two or more variations, a few slow sputtering notes, then longer accelerating series. **SS** Tocuyo Sparrow.

conirostris

Grasshopper Sparrow *Ammodramus savannarum* LC
Sabanero Grillo EN
Local and declining resident.

 L 12.2 cm (4.8"). Race *caucae*. Open grassy areas in upper Cauca and Patía watersheds. 500–1600 m, locally (Imués, Nariño) to c. 2600 m. Sings exposed from grass or weed stem, otherwise hides on ground; if flushed soon drops into grass. **ID** Ad flat-headed; white median crown-stripe, buffy lores, narrow white eye-ring, plain buff underparts. Juv streaked necklace. **Voice** North American birds sing high "tik-tuk" followed by insect-like buzz (9–10 kHz); also complex rapid jumble of high notes.

caucae

Grassland Sparrow *Ammodramus humeralis* LC
Sabanero Rayado
Common resident in *llanos*, local elsewhere.

 L 13 cm (5"). Races *pallidulus*^A, *humeralis*^B. Savannas, grassy pastures. To 1400 m (higher?). Forages out of sight on ground, runs quickly; sings from grass stem, shrub or fence wire. Flushes low, soon drops into grass. **ID** Plain; greyish sides of head and neck, white eye-ring, yellow supraloral (not entire eyebrow), chestnut inner flight feathers (conspicuous). Juv buffier with streaky necklace. **Voice** Dainty song variable (geographical?); delicate musical "tic-JEEE-wic'wazeee" or "ee-beezz, slip-slow-EEE".

humeralis

Yellow-browed Sparrow *Ammodramus aurifrons* LC
Sabanero Zumbador
Common resident.

 L 13 cm (5"). Races *apurensis*^A, *cherriei*^B, *tenebrosus*^C, *aurifrons*^D. Grassy and bushy semi-open areas, sandbars and grassy Amazonian riverbanks. Profits from deforestation. To 1600 m. Easiest *Ammodramus* sparrow: singles or pairs, conspicuous, hop in open on ground, and sing from ground or low perch. **ID** Recalls Grassland Sparrow but entire eyebrow, lower eye-arc and malar area yellow, also lacks eye-ring and chestnut tertials, and note different habitats. **Voice** Song (telephone busy signal) "tic, zzzzz, zzzzz, zzzzz", first note (or two) faint; often through heat of day.

aurifrons

Tanager Finch *Oreothraupis arremonops* LC
Gorrión Tangarino VU
Fairly common (but easily overlooked) resident.

 L 20 cm (8"). Monotypic. Near-endemic (also NW Ecuador). Dense undergrowth in wet montane forest. 1700–2500 m. Pairs or families, retiring, hop sluggishly on mossy logs, in cluttered thickets, leaf litter on ground. Not with mixed flocks. **ID** Bold white stripes on black head, above brownish rufous, underparts orange-rufous. **Voice** Song variable, sole or duet; several high rising accelerating notes (6–10 kHz), then slower insistent ones on same pitch "t't't't't'ti'tsee'tsee'tsee't see'see'tsee'tsee" (3–4 seconds). Call, high (9–10 kHz) "puet".

NE

461

Genus *Chlorospingus* Previously called bush-tanagers and placed in Thraupidae. Small, dull and mainly olive, several with pale eyes. Understorey to low canopy inside or at edges of forest. Form noisy fussy groups, integral components of mixed flocks. Diet arthropods, fruit, and mashed flower parts for nectar.

nigriceps

flavopectus

Common Chlorospingus *Chlorospingus flavopectus* `LC`
Montero Ojiblanco

Twenty-six subspecies in nine subspecies groups; two in Colombia. Taxonomic rearrangements and name changes inevitable.

Yellow-breasted Chlorospingus
Chlorospingus (flavopectus) flavopectus
Common resident.
L 14.7 cm (5.8"). Races *flavopectus*[A], *trudis*[B], *nigriceps*[C], *exitelus*[D], *macarenae*[E], *olsoni*[F], *phaeocephalus*[G] (both slopes S Nariño?).
Understorey to subcanopy of humid and wet montane forest, borders.
1000–2800 m. Pairs or groups are vocal and often dominate mixed flocks.
ID Confusing; head dusky to greyish, darker than body (or blackish, *nigriceps*), throat whitish, chest and sides yellowish, eyes dark (*flavopectus, trudis, macarenae*) or yellowish (most other races),conspicuous white post-ocular (lacking, *exitelus*); or duller plumage, throat dotted buff (*nigriceps, exitelus, phaeocephalus*).
Voice Sings incessantly at dawn, stream of "chit", "chid-it" and "chup" notes.
Constant "chip" notes while foraging. **SS** Other *Chlorospingus*.
AN Yellow-breasted Bush-tanager (older name).

phaeocephalus

Common Chlorospingus
Chlorospingus (flavopectus) venezuelanus
Common resident.
L 14.7 cm (5.8"). Races *jacqueti*[A], *eminens*[B], *ponsi*[C]. Understorey to subcanopy of humid and wet mossy montane forest, borders.
1000–2700 m. **ID** Much like Yellow-breasted Chlorospingus (above), but head dusky brown to greyish brown, conspicuous post-ocular spot white, throat white to buff (white in *eminens*, greyish white *jacqueti*, buffy *ponsi*).
Voice Similar to Yellow-breasted Chlorospingus. **SS** Other *Chlorospingus*.
AN Common Bush-tanager (older name).

ponsi

Tacarcuna Chlorospingus *Chlorospingus tacarcunae* `LC`
Montero de Tacarcuna `NT`
Local resident.

L 14 cm (5.5"). Monotypic. Humid montane forest. Only Cerro Tacarcuna, Panama border. 700–1500 m. Behaviour like other *Chlorospingus* (see above). **ID** Best identified by uniform dull olive head and upperparts (no white post-ocular), yellowish throat and chest, more greenish yellow on sides, whitish belly, whitish or pale orange eyes (dark, juv). **Voice** Call, forceful slightly descending "tseeeu!". **SS** Overlaps no other *Chlorospingus* (Pirre Chlorospingus closest). **AN** Tacarcuna Bush-tanager (older name).

Pirre Chlorospingus *Chlorospingus inornatus* `LC`
Montero de Pirre `VU`
Local but fairly common resident (only sight records).

L 14–15 cm (5.5–6"). Monotypic. Near-endemic (also adjacent Panama). Wet montane forest. Only Alto de Nique, Panama border. 800–1550 m (commoner above 1200 m).
Behaviour like other *Chlorospingus*, although reported to forage high. **ID** Closely recalls Tacarcuna Chlorospingus (pale eyes, yellow underparts, no white post-ocular) but differs in dark grey to dusky-grey head contrasting with olive upperparts. **Voice** Thin high buzzy "spEEtza", "tsip" or "chuweet?".
SS Overlaps no other *Chlorospingus*. **AN** Pirre Bush-tanager (older name).

Dusky Chlorospingus *Chlorospingus semifuscus* `LC`
Montero Grisáceo

Two subspecies in two subspecies groups; both in Colombia.

Northern Dusky Chlorospingus *Chlorospingus (semifuscus) livingstoni*
Fairly common resident.
L 14.5 cm. One subspecies in group. Endemic. Pacific slope wet montane forest with bamboo (S to W Cauca). 1200–2500 m (rarely lower). Behaviour like other *Chlorospingus*; monospecific groups (up to 15–20), or more often smaller numbers with mixed flocks. **ID** Dull and dark; above dark olive, crown and sides of head dark grey, underparts paler grey, eyes pale yellow, infrequently has small white postocular spot. **Voice** Song poorly documented (like southern form?). **SS** Darkest *Chlorospingus*. **AN** Northern Dusky Bush-tanager (older name).

Southern Dusky Chlorospingus
Chlorospingus (semifuscus) semifuscus
Fairly common resident.
L 15 cm (6"). One subspecies in group. Wet mossy montane forest with bamboo. 1200–2500 m. **ID** Very like Northern Dusky Chlorospingus but crown more brownish grey, eyes orange-red. **Voice** Dawn song, high "chit" notes accelerating into bursts of short fast rattle-trills. Call, high chips and trills. Reported to form song leks, where birds incessantly repeat high "chit" (c. 2/second). **AN** Southern Dusky Bush-tanager (older name).

Short-billed Chlorospingus *Chlorospingus parvirostris* `LC`
Montero Bigotudo
Fairly common resident.

L 14.7 cm (5.8"). Race *huallagae*. Low to mid- strata in humid and wet forest, borders. 1400–2100 m. Behaviour like other *Chlorospingus*; pairs or small groups with mixed flocks and congeners, especially Yellow-throated Chlorospingus. **ID** Not obviously 'short-billed' but flaring mustard-yellow sides of throat distinctive; eyes pale grey. **Voice** Dawn song, leisurely, seemingly random rising-falling notes (4–6 kHz). **AN** Yellow-whiskered Chlorospingus, Short-billed Bush-tanager (older name).

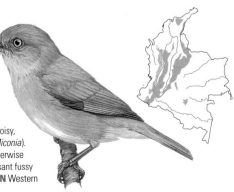

huallagae

Yellow-throated Chlorospingus *Chlorospingus flavigularis* `LC`
Montero Gorgiamarillo

Two subspecies in two subspecies groups; both in Colombia.

Western Yellow-throated Chlorospingus
Chlorospingus (flavigularis) marginatus
Common resident.
L 14 cm (5.5"). One subspecies in group. Understorey to subcanopy of Pacific slope humid and wet foothill and lower montane forest, borders, second growth. 600–2000 m (rarely 300 m). Groups of a dozen or more, noisy, usually with mixed flocks. Heavily frugivorous, especially melastomes (*Miconia*). **ID** Only *Chlorospingus* in its range with contrasting all-yellow throat. Otherwise underparts brownish grey, eyes greyish to brownish yellow. **Voice** Incessant fussy "chip" notes when foraging. Dawn song, similar repeated "tsit" notes. **AN** Western Yellow-throated Bush-tanager (older name).

Eastern Yellow-throated Chlorospingus
Chlorospingus (flavigularis) flavigularis
Fairly common resident.
L 14 cm (5.5"). One subspecies in group. Humid foothill and lower montane forest, borders, second growth. 600–2000 m. **ID** Behaviour and appearance much like western *marginatus* (previous page); underparts plain grey (greyer than western race), eyes brownish orange (E slope) or white (N Antioquia). **Voice** Dawn song, unlike western race, slower repetitive series of falling-rising "tsuu-seet..." notes. **SS** Short-billed Chlorospingus (commoner at higher elevations). **AN** Eastern Yellow-throated Bush-tanager (older name).

Ashy-throated Chlorospingus *Chlorospingus canigularis* `LC`
Montero Pectoral

Five subspecies in two subspecies groups; one in Colombia.

Ashy-throated Chlorospingus *Chlorospingus (canigularis) canigularis*
Uncommon to fairly common resident.
L 14 cm (5.5"). Races *canigularis*[A], *conspicillatus*[B], *signatus*[C]. Humid montane forest. 1000–2600 m. Regularly forages in subcanopy, higher than other *Chlorospingus*, in pairs or small groups. **ID** Grey head contrasts with bright olive back, well-defined yellow breast-band, dark eyes. Smallest, most slender-billed *Chlorospingus*. Race *signatus* (E Nariño) has white post-ocular streak. **Voice** Song, staccato trills mixed with "chit" notes. **SS** Common Chlorospingus (all races) duller, breast-band diffuse. **AN** Ashy-throated Bush-tanager (older name).

canigularis

Genus *Arremon* Plumage diverse, drab and dark, or shows bolder patches of colour; sexes alike. Pairs, low or semi-terrestrial, always retiring. Songs thinner, much higher-pitched than *Atlapetes*. Several previously placed in *Buarremon* or *Atlapetes*.

Sooty-faced Finch *Arremon crassirostris* `LC`
Pinzón Tiznado
Local resident.

L 16.5 cm (6.5"). Monotypic. Only Cerro Tacarcuna, Panama border. Habitat and behaviour as Olive Finch. c. 600–2350 m. **ID** From Olive Finch by conspicuous white malar, central lower underparts yellow. **Voice** Leisurely song, a complex jumble of very high-pitched (6–10 kHz) rising-falling, slurred "sip", "seet" and "seea" notes, often prolonged. Call, lower (6–7 kHz) "pee-pseeet", second note higher. **TN** Formerly in genus *Lysurus*.

Olive Finch *Arremon castaneiceps* `NT`
Pinzón Oliva

Uncommon (and easily overlooked) resident.

L 15 cm (6"). Monotypic. Dense understorey in humid and wet foothill and lower montane forest. 750–2200 m. Skulking semi-terrestrial pairs flick wings, hop sluggishly on ground, in dense vegetation, damp ravines; more active when mixed flocks overhead. **ID** Chestnut crown and nape, dark grey face and throat. **Voice** Song, a prolonged leisurely series of very high-pitched (7–10.5 kHz) rising-falling and slurred notes; recalls Sooty-faced Finch but rising notes more slurred. Call, high rattle-trill. **TN** Formerly in genus *Lysurus*.

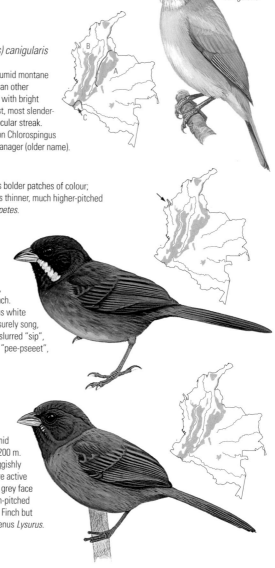

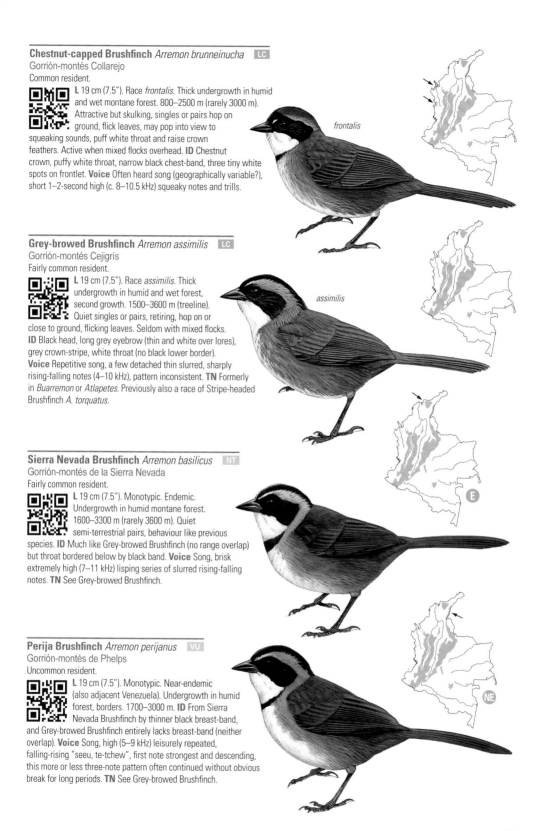

Chestnut-capped Brushfinch *Arremon brunneinucha* `LC`
Gorrión-montés Collarejo
Common resident.
L 19 cm (7.5"). Race *frontalis*. Thick undergrowth in humid
and wet montane forest. 800–2500 m (rarely 3000 m).
Attractive but skulking, singles or pairs hop on
ground, flick leaves, may pop into view to
squeaking sounds, puff white throat and raise crown
feathers. Active when mixed flocks overhead. **ID** Chestnut
crown, puffy white throat, narrow black chest-band, three tiny white
spots on frontlet. **Voice** Often heard song (geographically variable?),
short 1–2-second high (c. 8–10.5 kHz) squeaky notes and trills.

frontalis

Grey-browed Brushfinch *Arremon assimilis* `LC`
Gorrión-montés Cejigrís
Fairly common resident.
L 19 cm (7.5"). Race *assimilis*. Thick
undergrowth in humid and wet forest,
second growth. 1500–3600 m (treeline).
Quiet singles or pairs, retiring, hop on or
close to ground, flicking leaves. Seldom with mixed flocks.
ID Black head, long grey eyebrow (thin and white over lores),
grey crown-stripe, white throat (no black lower border).
Voice Repetitive song, a few detached thin slurred, sharply
rising-falling notes (4–10 kHz), pattern inconsistent. **TN** Formerly
in *Buarremon* or *Atlapetes*. Previously also a race of Stripe-headed
Brushfinch *A. torquatus*.

assimilis

Sierra Nevada Brushfinch *Arremon basilicus* `NT`
Gorrión-montés de la Sierra Nevada
Fairly common resident.
L 19 cm (7.5"). Monotypic. Endemic.
Undergrowth in humid montane forest.
1600–3300 m (rarely 3600 m). Quiet
semi-terrestrial pairs, behaviour like previous
species. **ID** Much like Grey-browed Brushfinch (no range overlap)
but throat bordered below by black band. **Voice** Song, brisk
extremely high (7–11 kHz) lisping series of slurred rising-falling
notes. **TN** See Grey-browed Brushfinch.

E

Perija Brushfinch *Arremon perijanus* `VU`
Gorrión-montés de Phelps
Uncommon resident.
L 19 cm (7.5"). Monotypic. Near-endemic
(also adjacent Venezuela). Undergrowth in humid
forest, borders. 1700–3000 m. **ID** From Sierra
Nevada Brushfinch by thinner black breast-band,
and Grey-browed Brushfinch entirely lacks breast-band (neither
overlap). **Voice** Song, high (5–9 kHz) leisurely repeated,
falling-rising "seeu, te-tchew", first note strongest and descending,
this more or less three-note pattern often continued without obvious
break for long periods. **TN** See Grey-browed Brushfinch.

NE

465

Black-headed Brushfinch *Arremon atricapillus* `LC`
Gorrión-montés Cabecinegra
Uncommon and local (overlooked?) resident.

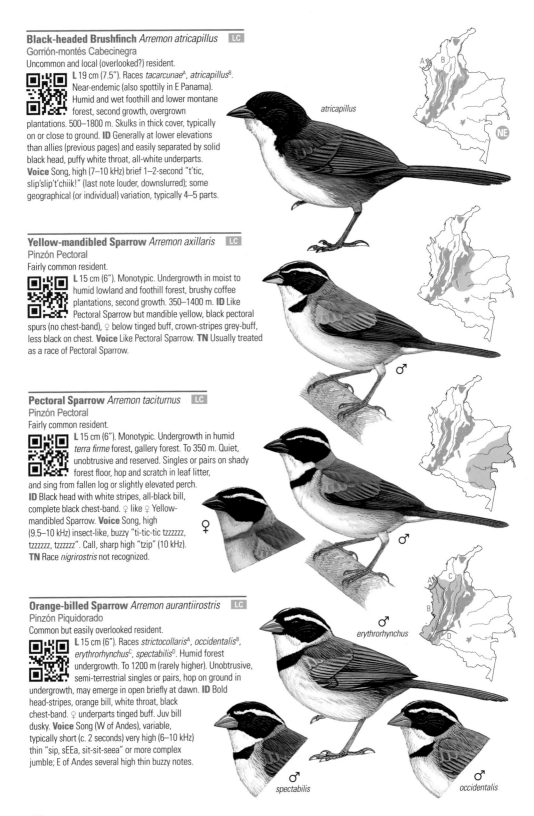

L 19 cm (7.5"). Races *tacarcunae*[A], *atricapillus*[B].
Near-endemic (also spottily in E Panama).
Humid and wet foothill and lower montane
forest, second growth, overgrown
plantations. 500–1800 m. Skulks in thick cover, typically
on or close to ground. **ID** Generally at lower elevations
than allies (previous pages) and easily separated by solid
black head, puffy white throat, all-white underparts.
Voice Song, high (7–10 kHz) brief 1–2-second "t'tic,
slip'slip't'chiik!" (last note louder, downslurred); some
geographical (or individual) variation, typically 4–5 parts.

atricapillus

Yellow-mandibled Sparrow *Arremon axillaris* `LC`
Pinzón Pectoral
Fairly common resident.

L 15 cm (6"). Monotypic. Undergrowth in moist to
humid lowland and foothill forest, brushy coffee
plantations, second growth. 350–1400 m. **ID** Like
Pectoral Sparrow but mandible yellow, black pectoral
spurs (no chest-band), ♀ below tinged buff, crown-stripes grey-buff,
less black on chest. **Voice** Like Pectoral Sparrow. **TN** Usually treated
as a race of Pectoral Sparrow.

♂

Pectoral Sparrow *Arremon taciturnus* `LC`
Pinzón Pectoral
Fairly common resident.

L 15 cm (6"). Monotypic. Undergrowth in humid
terra firme forest, gallery forest. To 350 m. Quiet,
unobtrusive and reserved. Singles or pairs on shady
forest floor, hop and scratch in leaf litter,
and sing from fallen log or slightly elevated perch.
ID Black head with white stripes, all-black bill,
complete black chest-band. ♀ like ♀ Yellow-
mandibled Sparrow. **Voice** Song, high
(9.5–10 kHz) insect-like, buzzy "ti-tic-tic tzzzzzz,
tzzzzzz, tzzzzzz". Call, sharp high "tzip" (10 kHz).
TN Race *nigrirostris* not recognized.

♀

♂

Orange-billed Sparrow *Arremon aurantiirostris* `LC`
Pinzón Piquidorado
Common but easily overlooked resident.

L 15 cm (6"). Races *strictocollaris*[A], *occidentalis*[B],
erythrorhynchus[C], *spectabilis*[D]. Humid forest
undergrowth. To 1200 m (rarely higher). Unobtrusive,
semi-terrestrial singles or pairs, hop on ground in
undergrowth, may emerge in open briefly at dawn. **ID** Bold
head-stripes, orange bill, white throat, black
chest-band. ♀ underparts tinged buff. Juv bill
dusky. **Voice** Song (W of Andes), variable,
typically short (c. 2 seconds) very high (6–10 kHz)
thin "sip, sEEa, sit-sit-seea" or more complex
jumble; E of Andes several high thin buzzy notes.

♂
erythrorhynchus

♂
spectabilis

♂
occidentalis

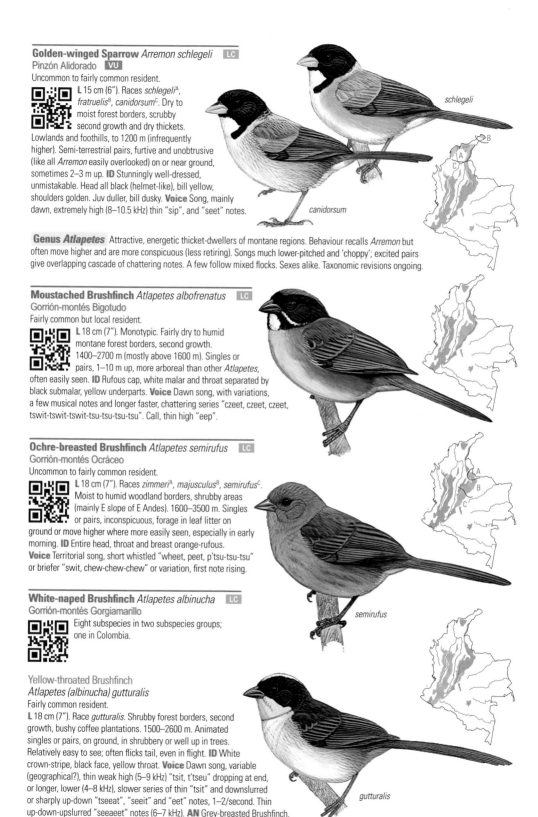

Golden-winged Sparrow *Arremon schlegeli* `LC`
Pinzón Alidorado `VU`
Uncommon to fairly common resident.
L 15 cm (6"). Races *schlegeli*[A], *fratruelis*[B], *canidorsum*[C]. Dry to moist forest borders, scrubby second growth and dry thickets. Lowlands and foothills, to 1200 m (infrequently higher). Semi-terrestrial pairs, furtive and unobtrusive (like all *Arremon* easily overlooked) on or near ground, sometimes 2–3 m up. **ID** Stunningly well-dressed, unmistakable. Head all black (helmet-like), bill yellow, shoulders golden. Juv duller, bill dusky. **Voice** Song, mainly dawn, extremely high (8–10.5 kHz) thin "sip", and "seet" notes.

schlegeli

canidorsum

Genus *Atlapetes* Attractive, energetic thicket-dwellers of montane regions. Behaviour recalls *Arremon* but often move higher and are more conspicuous (less retiring). Songs much lower-pitched and 'choppy'; excited pairs give overlapping cascade of chattering notes. A few follow mixed flocks. Sexes alike. Taxonomic revisions ongoing.

Moustached Brushfinch *Atlapetes albofrenatus* `LC`
Gorrión-montés Bigotudo
Fairly common but local resident.
L 18 cm (7"). Monotypic. Fairly dry to humid montane forest borders, second growth. 1400–2700 m (mostly above 1600 m). Singles or pairs, 1–10 m up, more arboreal than other *Atlapetes*, often easily seen. **ID** Rufous cap, white malar and throat separated by black submalar, yellow underparts. **Voice** Dawn song, with variations, a few musical notes and longer faster, chattering series "czeet, czeet, czeet, tswit-tswit-tswit-tsu-tsu-tsu-tsu". Call, thin high "eep".

Ochre-breasted Brushfinch *Atlapetes semirufus* `LC`
Gorrión-montés Ocráceo
Uncommon to fairly common resident.
L 18 cm (7"). Races *zimmeri*[A], *majusculus*[B], *semirufus*[C]. Moist to humid woodland borders, shrubby areas (mainly E slope of E Andes). 1600–3500 m. Singles or pairs, inconspicuous, forage in leaf litter on ground or move higher where more easily seen, especially in early morning. **ID** Entire head, throat and breast orange-rufous. **Voice** Territorial song, short whistled "wheet, peet, p'tsu-tsu-tsu" or briefer "swit, chew-chew-chew" or variation, first note rising.

White-naped Brushfinch *Atlapetes albinucha* `LC`
Gorrión-montés Gorgiamarillo
Eight subspecies in two subspecies groups; one in Colombia.

semirufus

Yellow-throated Brushfinch
Atlapetes (albinucha) gutturalis
Fairly common resident.
L 18 cm (7"). Race *gutturalis*. Shrubby forest borders, second growth, bushy coffee plantations. 1500–2600 m. Animated singles or pairs, on ground, in shrubbery or well up in trees. Relatively easy to see; often flicks tail, even in flight. **ID** White crown-stripe, black face, yellow throat. **Voice** Dawn song, variable (geographical?), thin weak high (5–9 kHz) "tsit, t'tseu" dropping at end, or longer, lower (4–8 kHz), slower series of thin "tsit" and downslurred or sharply up-down "tseeat", "seeit" and "eet" notes, 1–2/second. Thin up-down-upslurred "seeaeet" notes (6–7 kHz). **AN** Grey-breasted Brushfinch.

gutturalis

Santa Marta Brushfinch *Atlapetes melanocephalus* `LC`
Gorrión-montés de Santa Marta
Common resident.
L 17 cm (6.7"). Monotypic. Endemic. Humid forest borders, shrubby second growth, coffee plantations, gardens. 700–3000 m. Singles, pairs or families on ground to 10 m up. Often bold, inquisitive and conspicuous; readily habituates to humans. **ID** Black head, silvery cheeks, yellow underparts. **Voice** Dawn song, over and over, brief "cheet, chew'it", first note higher, last rebounds, or "cheet, cheet, chew'it". Duet, during day, short fast rattle and slower cascade of chattering and buzzy notes.

Pale-naped Brushfinch *Atlapetes pallidinucha* `LC`
Gorrión-montés Cabeciblanco
Common resident.
L 18 cm (7"). Races *pallidinucha*[A], *papallactae*[B]. Shrubby humid and wet forest border thickets, elfin woodland to or above treeline. 2400–3700 m (locally 2000 m). Inquisitive pairs stay low, mostly out of sight, but will pop up in open briefly. Unlike most allies, regularly with mixed flocks. **ID** Forecrown and crown-stripe cinnamon becoming white rearward (or yellowish becoming white rearward, *papallactae*). **Voice** Dawn song, prolonged brisk buzzy and chattering notes mixed with little trills, over wide frequency range (4–9 kHz).

Yellow-headed Brushfinch *Atlapetes flaviceps* `EN`
Gorrión-montés de Anteojos `VU`
Locally fairly common resident.
L 18 cm (7"). Monotypic. Endemic. Shrubby borders of humid forest, overgrown pastures, younger second growth. 1300–2450 m. Pairs or families forage mostly low and within cover, but will ascend well up in trees. Often sing from higher exposed positions, especially at dawn. **ID** Entire head and underparts yellow. **Voice** Dawn song (Tolima), sharp insistent "speets-speets, spit-tu-chu" with briefer fragments mixed between songs, or mate may join in exuberant chattering duet.

Dusky-headed Brushfinch *Atlapetes fuscoolivaceus* `NT`
Gorrión-montés Oliváceo `VU`
Fairly common resident (restricted range).
L 18 cm (7"). Monotypic. Endemic. Bushy overgrown pastures, shrubby forest borders; tolerant of considerable disturbance. 1500–2400 m. Like Yellow-headed Brushfinch forages low, but also moves higher, partly in open where relatively easy to see. Sometimes with mixed flocks. **ID** Plain dusky olive above, yellowish below, brightest on throat, thin black malar line. **Voice** Song, brief insistent 3–4-note "peeu-peeu peet'it" (parulid-like) or mate joins to produce fast chattering duet.

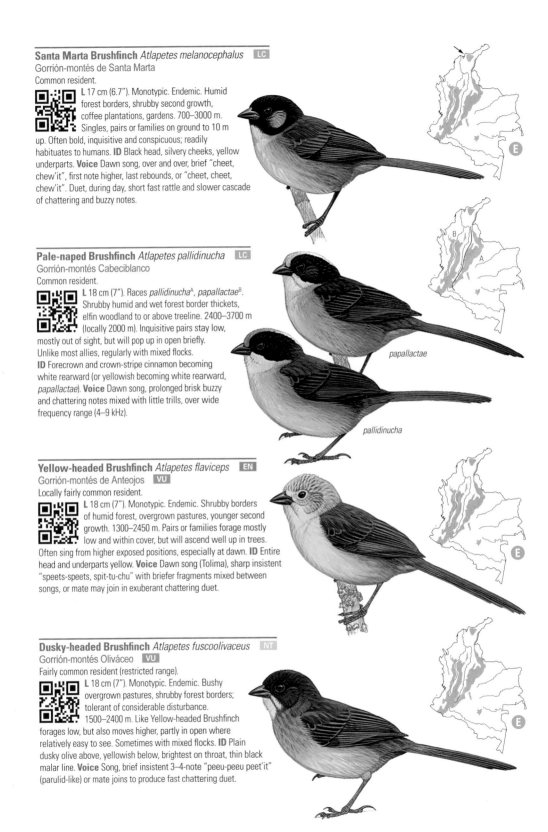

papallactae

pallidinucha

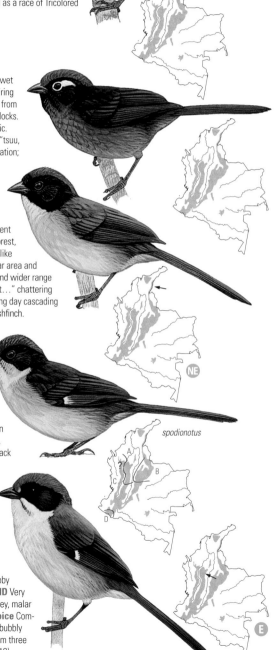

Choco Brushfinch *Atlapetes crassus* `LC`
Gorrión-montés del Chocó
Common resident.

L 17 cm (6.7"). Monotypic. Shrubby borders of humid and wet forest, gaps in steep broken forest; W slope of W Andes (E slope locally). 400–2000 m. Pairs or families forage low, also move higher where easier to see, briefly join mixed flocks. **ID** Broad crown-stripe 'old gold', sides of head black, underparts dull yellow. **Voice** Dawn song, thin insistent "seeit, seeit, swit-swit-swit" and short rattle-trill or variation. Day song, longer and more complex. **TN** Often treated as a race of Tricolored Brushfinch *A. tricolor*.

White-rimmed Brushfinch *Atlapetes leucopis* `LC`
Gorrión-montés Parduzco
Uncommon resident.

L 18 cm (7"). Monotypic. Dense shrubby borders of wet montane forest, elfin woodland. 1800–3000 m. Retiring and difficult to see, on or near ground. Rarely away from thick low cover, occasionally glimpsed with mixed flocks. **ID** Chestnut crown, bold white eye-ring and post-ocular diagnostic. **Voice** Song (Putumayo), loud clear, rather low-pitched (3–4 kHz) "tsuu, wee, wee, chu-chu", first and last two notes downslurred, or variation; only minor variation in pitch.

Black-fronted Brushfinch *Atlapetes nigrifrons* `NT`
Gorrión-montés de Perijá
Local resident (Serranía de Perijá).

L 18 cm (7"). Monotypic. Near-endemic (also adjacent Venezuela). Shrubby borders of moist and humid forest, patchy low second growth. 1100–2850 m. **ID** Very like Yellow-breasted Brushfinch, but forehead, submalar area and chin black, no white wing patch, ear-coverts often tinged grey, and wider range of vocalizations. **Voice** Three-part dawn song, "tk, chit, chit, chit…" chattering "swit'swit'swit…" and faster trill with numerous variations. During day cascading chatters. **TN** Usually regarded as a race of Yellow-breasted Brushfinch.

Yellow-breasted Brushfinch
Atlapetes latinuchus `LC`
Gorrión-montés Cabecirrufo
Locally fairly common resident.

L 18 cm (7"). Races *elaeoprorus*[A], *yariguierum*[B], *caucae*[C], *spodionotus*[D]. Shrubby humid forest borders, regenerating second growth. 1600–3700 m. More arboreal and conspicuous than some *Atlapetes*. **ID** Crown and nape rufous, sides of head black, underparts yellow, small white wing spot, and may show thin black malar; or no wing spot (*yariguierum*); or wing spot inconsistent, malar indistinct (*spodionotus*). **Voice** Exuberant complex multi-part song of trills, semi-musical notes, rising-falling phrases and chatters; varies geographically. **TN** Formerly part of Rufous-naped Brushfinch *A. rufinucha*.

spodionotus

Antioquia Brushfinch *Atlapetes blancae* `CR`
Gorrión-montés Antioqueño `CR(PE)`
Rare and local resident.

L 19.5 cm (7.7"). Monotypic. Endemic. Humid shrubby borders, remnant woodland edges. 2200–2800 m. **ID** Very like Slaty Brushfinch but larger, underparts paler grey, malar line faint, chestnut crown broader, voice differs. **Voice** Complex song of trills, chattering, rising-falling and slurred notes, in bubbly energetic phrases. **SS** Slaty Brushfinch. **TN** Described (2007) from three old specimens; believed extinct, but rediscovered, Antioquia (2018).

Slaty Brushfinch *Atlapetes schistaceus* `LC`
Gorrión-montés Pizarra
Common resident.

L 18 cm (7"). Races *fumidus*[A], *tamae*[B], *schistaceus*[C]. Shrubby borders of humid and wet montane forest, stunted woodland to treeline. 1800–3800 m. Handsome pairs or families forage out of view in dense vegetation but often move higher for fruit or to sing. Most easily seen with mixed flocks. **ID** Rusty crown and nape, mainly black sides of head, dark grey upperparts, white throat, most of underparts grey. **Voice** Dawn song, short "tsuu, tsweet-tsweet", first note downslurred; solos or poorly coordinated duets of trills, chatters and high notes. **SS** Antioquia Brushfinch.

Rufous-collared Sparrow *Zonotrichia capensis* `LC`
Gorrión Copetón
Very common resident.

L 14 cm (5.5"). Races *costaricensis*[A] (settled highlands including agricultural areas, hedgerows, gardens, urban areas, 500–3800 m), *roraimae*[B] (scarce and local in lowland scrub, bushy sandy soil savanna, to 700 m). Familiar, friendly, ubiquitous little 'pensioner' of dooryards throughout Andes. Forages on ground, sings from elevated perch. **ID** Grey-and-black striped head, rufous nape, and streaky sparrow back. Juv duller, finely streaked above and below. **Voice** Dozens of geographical dialects but everywhere easily recognized; typically 1–2 slurred whistles with or without ending trill.

Savannah Sparrow *Passerculus sandwichensis* `LC`
Vagrant (boreal migrant, Isla San Andrés).

L 14 cm (5.5"). Race presumably *sandwichensis*. Once, Oct 2001. Open grassy or partially bare fields, brushy borders. **ID** Variable; heavily streaked above and below, dark eyeline and malar, usually shows prominent yellow lores, small pale conical bill.

Lincoln's Sparrow *Melospiza lincolnii* `LC`
Gorrión de Lincoln
Vagrant (boreal migrant).

L 13 cm (5.2"). Race *lincolnii*? Records: Isla San Andrés, Nov 2010 and Oct 2017; near Ocaña, Norte de Santander, Mar 2017. Thickets and borders. **ID** Broad grey eyebrow and sides of head, buff eye-ring, broad buff malar bordered black below, streaked back, dull rufous wings, buff breast and sides with crisp black streaking, whitish central lower underparts.

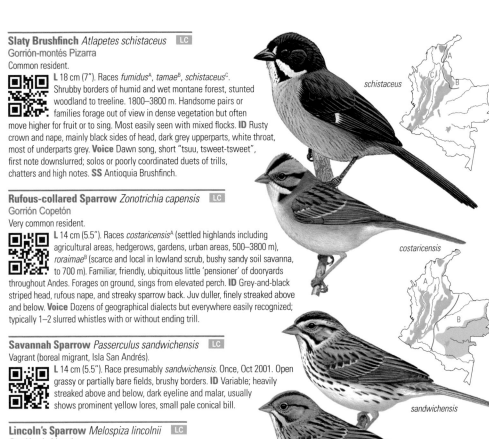

schistaceus

costaricensis

sandwichensis

lincolnii

ICTERIDAE
New World Blackbirds
114 extant species, 43 in region

Members of this new World family have sharp-pointed bills and strong legs and feet, but otherwise differ greatly in size and plumage. Icterids are most diverse in tropical regions, but migratory species occur in both northern and southern latitudes. Sexes usually similar in tropical species, but ♂ caciques and oropendolas are dramatically larger than ♀♀. Orioles have melodious songs, caciques and oropendolas complex, liquid songs. Breeding is solitary, parasitic (a few) or colonial, with polygamy predominating in colonial species, which are notable for their long conspicuous nests suspended from isolated trees.

Bobolink *Dolichonyx oryzivorus* `LC`
Tordo Arrocero
Erratic boreal passage migrant (Sept–Nov, Mar–May).

L 18 cm (7"). Monotypic. Rice fields, pastures, open areas. To 2600 m. Small to large flocks. Most of population believed to pass through Colombia twice annually between boreal breeding and austral wintering areas. **ID** Sharp-pointed tail feathers. Non-br ♂ and ♀ buffy brown, streaked dark on crown, upperparts and sides, below plain buff. Juv similar but sides unstreaked. Br ♂ below black, rear crown yellowish buff, scapular bar, lower back and rump white. **Voice** Call, sharp "ink".

♂ breeding

♀/♂ non-breeding

Eastern Meadowlark *Sturnella magna* `NT`
Chirlobirlo

 Sixteen subspecies in three subspecies groups; one in Colombia.

Eastern Meadowlark *Sturnella (magna) magna*
Common resident (profits from deforestation).
L 23 cm (9"). Races *meridionalis*[A] (larger and darker; highlands), *paralios*[B], *praticola*[C] (smaller, less streaked below, less white in tail; lowlands). Grasslands, sea level to *páramo*. To 3500 m. Singles or scattered pairs, flush in sputtering flight, flashing white in tail. Sings from fence post or elevated open perch, but forages hidden in grass. **ID** Long sharp-pointed bill; above streaky, below yellow, black V on chest. **Voice** Song, clear sweet "see-eer, see-yuuu", slurred, descending. Rough rattle in flight.

Red-breasted Meadowlark *Leistes militaris* `LC`
Soldadito

Common resident (profits from deforestation).
 L 18.5 cm (7.3"). Monotypic. Cattle pastures, tall grassland, airstrips. To 2100 m. Singles, pairs or small flocks. ♂ sings from fence post or elevated perch, then drops into tall grass. Breeding loosely colonial. **ID** Ad ♂ throat and breast bright red, above black scaled buff in fresh plumage (buff wears off). ♀ streaky, brownish, reddish wash on breast. **Voice** Song, 1–3 unmusical notes and buzzy trill "eslik'rLEEEEEZ" or two buzzes on different pitches; short aerial song with display. Call, "pleek".
AN Red-breasted Blackbird.

Peruvian Meadowlark *Leistes bellicosus* `LC`
Turpial Belicoso

Local resident (recent northward range expansion).
 L 20 cm (8"). Race *bellicosus*. Dry to wet grassy pastures, agricultural areas. To 500 m. Feeds on ground but perches up. Gregarious, especially when not breeding. **ID** Long pointed bill, white eyebrow. ♂ red breast; ♀ streaked greyish brown above and below, chest tinged pinkish red. **Voice** Song variable (perched or in air), 1–5 wheezy notes and short buzz.

Yellow-billed Cacique *Amblycercus holosericeus* `LC`
Arrendajo Negro

Three subspecies in two subspecies groups; both in Colombia.

Lowland Yellow-billed Cacique *Amblycercus (holosericeus) holosericeus*
Local resident.
L ♂ 23 cm (9"), ♀ 22 cm (8.5"). Races *holosericeus*[A] (much of range perhaps no longer occupied), *flavirostris*[B]. Understorey in humid lowland and foothill forest, dense second growth. To 1500 m. Secretive and skulking; pairs or families stay low, out of view, follow mixed flocks, best glimpsed flying low across openings. Cup (not hanging pouch) nest. **ID** Plain black, yellow eyes, ivory-yellow bill.
Voice Sporadic loud rough grating churrs and rattles; ringing series of whistles. **SS** Highland Yellow-billed Cacique. **AN** Western Yellow-billed Cacique.

meridionalis

uppertail

♂

♀

bellicosus

♀

♂

holosericeus

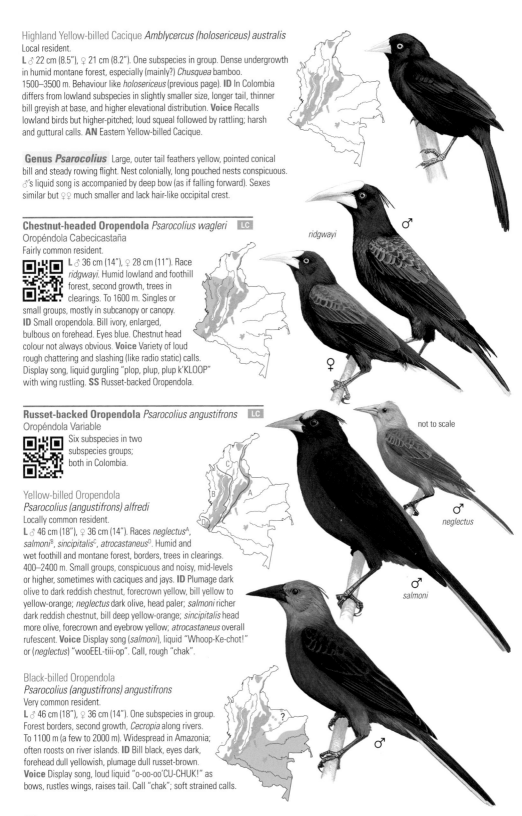

Highland Yellow-billed Cacique *Amblycercus (holosericeus) australis*
Local resident.
L ♂ 22 cm (8.5"), ♀ 21 cm (8.2"). One subspecies in group. Dense undergrowth in humid montane forest, especially (mainly?) *Chusquea* bamboo. 1500–3500 m. Behaviour like *holosericeus* (previous page). **ID** In Colombia differs from lowland subspecies in slightly smaller size, longer tail, thinner bill greyish at base, and higher elevational distribution. **Voice** Recalls lowland birds but higher-pitched; loud squeal followed by rattling; harsh and guttural calls. **AN** Eastern Yellow-billed Cacique.

Genus *Psarocolius* Large, outer tail feathers yellow, pointed conical bill and steady rowing flight. Nest colonially, long pouched nests conspicuous. ♂'s liquid song is accompanied by deep bow (as if falling forward). Sexes similar but ♀♀ much smaller and lack hair-like occipital crest.

Chestnut-headed Oropendola *Psarocolius wagleri* `LC`
Oropéndola Cabecicastaña
Fairly common resident.
L ♂ 36 cm (14"), ♀ 28 cm (11"). Race *ridgwayi*. Humid lowland and foothill forest, second growth, trees in clearings. To 1600 m. Singles or small groups, mostly in subcanopy or canopy. **ID** Small oropendola. Bill ivory, enlarged, bulbous on forehead. Eyes blue. Chestnut head colour not always obvious. **Voice** Variety of loud rough chattering and slashing (like radio static) calls. Display song, liquid gurgling "plop, plup, plup k'KLOOP" with wing rustling. **SS** Russet-backed Oropendola.

ridgwayi

♂

♀

Russet-backed Oropendola *Psarocolius angustifrons* `LC`
Oropéndola Variable
Six subspecies in two subspecies groups; both in Colombia.

not to scale

Yellow-billed Oropendola
Psarocolius (angustifrons) alfredi
Locally common resident.
L ♂ 46 cm (18"), ♀ 36 cm (14"). Races *neglectus*[A], *salmoni*[B], *sincipitalis*[C], *atrocastaneus*[D]. Humid and wet foothill and montane forest, borders, trees in clearings. 400–2400 m. Small groups, conspicuous and noisy, mid-levels or higher, sometimes with caciques and jays. **ID** Plumage dark olive to dark reddish chestnut, forecrown yellow, bill yellow to yellow-orange; *neglectus* dark olive, head paler; *salmoni* richer dark reddish chestnut, bill deep yellow-orange; *sincipitalis* head more olive, forecrown and eyebrow yellow; *atrocastaneus* overall rufescent. **Voice** Display song (*salmoni*), liquid "Whoop-Ke-chot!" or (*neglectus*) "wooEEL-tiii-op". Call, rough "chak".

♂

neglectus

♂

salmoni

Black-billed Oropendola
Psarocolius (angustifrons) angustifrons
Very common resident.
L ♂ 46 cm (18"), ♀ 36 cm (14"). One subspecies in group. Forest borders, second growth, *Cecropia* along rivers. To 1100 m (a few to 2000 m). Widespread in Amazonia; often roosts on river islands. **ID** Bill black, eyes dark, forehead dull yellowish, plumage dull russet-brown. **Voice** Display song, loud liquid "o-oo-oo'CU-CHUK!" as bows, rustles wings, raises tail. Call "chak"; soft strained calls.

♂

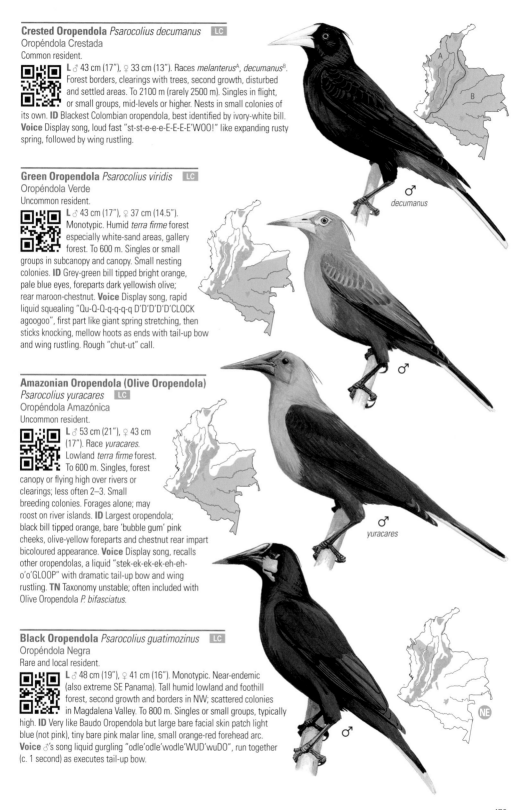

Crested Oropendola *Psarocolius decumanus* `LC`
Oropéndola Crestada
Common resident.

L ♂ 43 cm (17"), ♀ 33 cm (13"). Races *melanterus*[A], *decumanus*[B]. Forest borders, clearings with trees, second growth, disturbed and settled areas. To 2100 m (rarely 2500 m). Singles in flight, or small groups, mid-levels or higher. Nests in small colonies of its own. **ID** Blackest Colombian oropendola, best identified by ivory-white bill. **Voice** Display song, loud fast "st-st-e-e-e-E-E-E-E'WOO!" like expanding rusty spring, followed by wing rustling.

♂
decumanus

Green Oropendola *Psarocolius viridis* `LC`
Oropéndola Verde
Uncommon resident.

L ♂ 43 cm (17"), ♀ 37 cm (14.5"). Monotypic. Humid *terra firme* forest especially white-sand areas, gallery forest. To 600 m. Singles or small groups in subcanopy and canopy. Small nesting colonies. **ID** Grey-green bill tipped bright orange, pale blue eyes, foreparts dark yellowish olive; rear maroon-chestnut. **Voice** Display song, rapid liquid squealing "Qu-Q-Q-q-q-q-q D'D'D'D'CLOCK agoogoo", first part like giant spring stretching, then sticks knocking, mellow hoots as ends with tail-up bow and wing rustling. Rough "chut-ut" call.

♂

Amazonian Oropendola (Olive Oropendola)
Psarocolius yuracares `LC`
Oropéndola Amazónica
Uncommon resident.

L ♂ 53 cm (21"), ♀ 43 cm (17"). Race *yuracares*. Lowland *terra firme* forest. To 600 m. Singles, forest canopy or flying high over rivers or clearings; less often 2–3. Small breeding colonies. Forages alone; may roost on river islands. **ID** Largest oropendola; black bill tipped orange, bare 'bubble gum' pink cheeks, olive-yellow foreparts and chestnut rear impart bicoloured appearance. **Voice** Display song, recalls other oropendolas, a liquid "stek-ek-ek-ek-eh-eh-o'o'GLOOP" with dramatic tail-up bow and wing rustling. **TN** Taxonomy unstable; often included with Olive Oropendola *P. bifasciatus*.

♂
yuracares

Black Oropendola *Psarocolius guatimozinus* `LC`
Oropéndola Negra
Rare and local resident.

L ♂ 48 cm (19"), ♀ 41 cm (16"). Monotypic. Near-endemic (also extreme SE Panama). Tall humid lowland and foothill forest, second growth and borders in NW; scattered colonies in Magdalena Valley. To 800 m. Singles or small groups, typically high. **ID** Very like Baudo Oropendola but large bare facial skin patch light blue (not pink), tiny bare pink malar line, small orange-red forehead arc. **Voice** ♂'s song liquid gurgling "odle'odle'wodle'WUD'wuDO", run together (c. 1 second) as executes tail-up bow.

♂

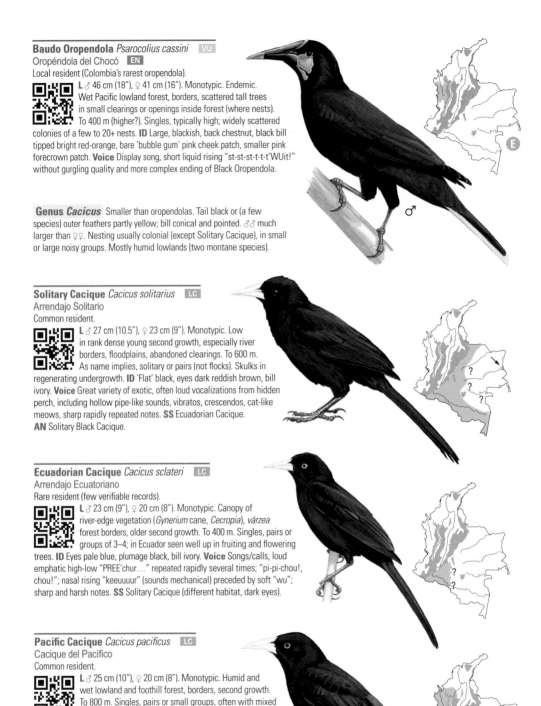

Baudo Oropendola *Psarocolius cassini* `VU`
Oropéndola del Chocó `EN`
Local resident (Colombia's rarest oropendola).
L ♂ 46 cm (18"), ♀ 41 cm (16"). Monotypic. Endemic.
Wet Pacific lowland forest, borders, scattered tall trees
in small clearings or openings inside forest (where nests).
To 400 m (higher?). Singles, typically high; widely scattered
colonies of a few to 20+ nests. **ID** Large, blackish, back chestnut, black bill
tipped bright red-orange, bare 'bubble gum' pink cheek patch, smaller pink
forecrown patch. **Voice** Display song, short liquid rising "st-st-st-t-t-t'WUit!"
without gurgling quality and more complex ending of Black Oropendola.

Genus *Cacicus* Smaller than oropendolas. Tail black or (a few
species) outer feathers partly yellow; bill conical and pointed. ♂♂ much
larger than ♀♀. Nesting usually colonial (except Solitary Cacique), in small
or large noisy groups. Mostly humid lowlands (two montane species).

Solitary Cacique *Cacicus solitarius* `LC`
Arrendajo Solitario
Common resident.
L ♂ 27 cm (10.5"), ♀ 23 cm (9"). Monotypic. Low
in rank dense young second growth, especially river
borders, floodplains, abandoned clearings. To 600 m.
As name implies, solitary or pairs (not flocks). Skulks in
regenerating undergrowth. **ID** 'Flat' black, eyes dark reddish brown, bill
ivory. **Voice** Great variety of exotic, often loud vocalizations from hidden
perch, including hollow pipe-like sounds, vibratos, crescendos, cat-like
meows, sharp rapidly repeated notes. **SS** Ecuadorian Cacique.
AN Solitary Black Cacique.

Ecuadorian Cacique *Cacicus sclateri* `LC`
Arrendajo Ecuatoriano
Rare resident (few verifiable records).
L ♂ 23 cm (9"), ♀ 20 cm (8"). Monotypic. Canopy of
river-edge vegetation (*Gynerium* cane, *Cecropia*), várzea
forest borders, older second growth. To 400 m. Singles, pairs or
groups of 3–4; in Ecuador seen well up in fruiting and flowering
trees. **ID** Eyes pale blue, plumage black, bill ivory. **Voice** Songs/calls, loud
emphatic high-low "PREE'chur…" repeated rapidly several times; "pi-pi-chou!,
chou!"; nasal rising "keeuuuur" (sounds mechanical) preceded by soft "wu";
sharp and harsh notes. **SS** Solitary Cacique (different habitat, dark eyes).

Pacific Cacique *Cacicus pacificus* `LC`
Cacique del Pacífico
Common resident.
L ♂ 25 cm (10"), ♀ 20 cm (8"). Monotypic. Humid and
wet lowland and foothill forest, borders, second growth.
To 800 m. Singles, pairs or small groups, often with mixed
flocks, Purple-throated Fruitcrows etc. Nests alone or in
small colonies. **ID** Black, red rump (often hidden), ivory bill, icy blue eyes.
Voice Calls varied; loud downslurred "eurp" repeatedly, loud "peeur",
other downslurred notes. **TN** Usually regarded as a race of Scarlet-rumped
Cacique *C. microrhynchus* of Central America (voices differ).

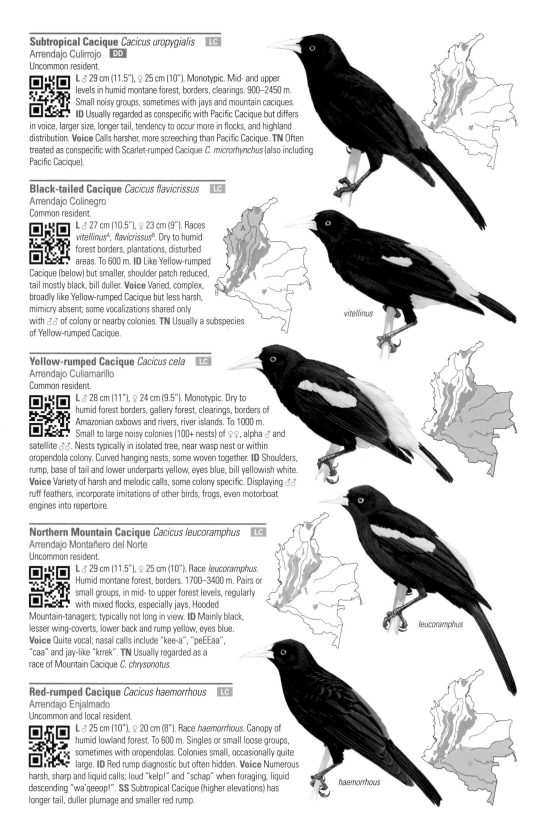

Subtropical Cacique *Cacicus uropygialis* `LC`
Arrendajo Culirrojo `DD`
Uncommon resident.

L ♂ 29 cm (11.5"), ♀ 25 cm (10"). Monotypic. Mid- and upper
levels in humid montane forest, borders, clearings. 900–2450 m.
Small noisy groups, sometimes with jays and mountain caciques.
ID Usually regarded as conspecific with Pacific Cacique but differs
in voice, larger size, longer tail, tendency to occur more in flocks, and highland
distribution. **Voice** Calls harsher, more screeching than Pacific Cacique. **TN** Often
treated as conspecific with Scarlet-rumped Cacique *C. microrhynchus* (also including
Pacific Cacique).

Black-tailed Cacique *Cacicus flavicrissus* `LC`
Arrendajo Colinegro
Common resident.

L ♂ 27 cm (10.5"), ♀ 23 cm (9"). Races
vitellinus[A], *flavicrissus*[B]. Dry to humid
forest borders, plantations, disturbed
areas. To 600 m. **ID** Like Yellow-rumped
Cacique (below) but smaller, shoulder patch reduced,
tail mostly black, bill duller. **Voice** Varied, complex,
broadly like Yellow-rumped Cacique but less harsh,
mimicry absent; some vocalizations shared only
with ♂♂ of colony or nearby colonies. **TN** Usually a subspecies
of Yellow-rumped Cacique.

vitellinus

Yellow-rumped Cacique *Cacicus cela* `LC`
Arrendajo Culiamarillo
Common resident.

L ♂ 28 cm (11"), ♀ 24 cm (9.5"). Monotypic. Dry to
humid forest borders, gallery forest, clearings, borders of
Amazonian oxbows and rivers, river islands. To 1000 m.
Small to large noisy colonies (100+ nests) of ♀♀, alpha ♂ and
satellite ♂♂. Nests typically in isolated tree, near wasp nest or within
oropendola colony. Curved hanging nests, some woven together. **ID** Shoulders,
rump, base of tail and lower underparts yellow, eyes blue, bill yellowish white.
Voice Variety of harsh and melodic calls, some colony specific. Displaying ♂♂
ruff feathers, incorporate imitations of other birds, frogs, even motorboat
engines into repertoire.

Northern Mountain Cacique *Cacicus leucoramphus* `LC`
Arrendajo Montañero del Norte
Uncommon resident.

L ♂ 29 cm (11.5"), ♀ 25 cm (10"). Race *leucoramphus*.
Humid montane forest, borders. 1700–3400 m. Pairs or
small groups, in mid- to upper forest levels, regularly
with mixed flocks, especially jays, Hooded
Mountain-tanagers; typically not long in view. **ID** Mainly black,
lesser wing-coverts, lower back and rump yellow, eyes blue.
Voice Quite vocal; nasal calls include "kee-a", "peEEaa",
"caa" and jay-like "krrek". **TN** Usually regarded as a
race of Mountain Cacique *C. chrysonotus*.

leucoramphus

Red-rumped Cacique *Cacicus haemorrhous* `LC`
Arrendajo Enjalmado
Uncommon and local resident.

L ♂ 25 cm (10"), ♀ 20 cm (8"). Race *haemorrhous*. Canopy of
humid lowland forest. To 600 m. Singles or small loose groups,
sometimes with oropendolas. Colonies small, occasionally quite
large. **ID** Red rump diagnostic but often hidden. **Voice** Numerous
harsh, sharp and liquid calls; loud "kelp!" and "schap" when foraging; liquid
descending "wa'qeeop!". **SS** Subtropical Cacique (higher elevations) has
longer tail, duller plumage and smaller red rump.

haemorrhous

Casqued Cacique *Cacicus oseryi* LC
Oropéndola Cascuda
Few records (Amazonas; Putumayo?).

 L ♂ 36 cm (14"), ♀ 29 cm (11.5"). Monotypic. Humid *várzea*, transition and *terra firme* forest. To 300 m. Smaller groups (3–12+) in tall forest canopy; one of few caciques to nest colonially inside forest. **ID** Olive-yellow throat and chest, swollen casque on forehead, relatively short pale bill, blue eyes. **Voice** Noisy. Startlingly loud harsh "CH'RAK" and descending "EEOP!". Display call, loud buzzy descending "CHUuuuu". **SS** Olive Oropendola. **TN** Formerly Casqued Oropendola *Clypicterus oseryi*.

Band-tailed Cacique *Cacicus latirostris* LC
Oropéndola de Cola Bandeada
Scarce and local resident.

 L ♂ 33 cm (13"), ♀ 25 cm (10"). Monotypic. *Várzea* forest borders, creeks, *Cecropia* on river islands. To 300 m. Small groups, often with other caciques and oropendolas. **ID** Eyes blue. Resembles Yellow-rumped Cacique but mainly black (no yellow shoulders or rump), tail yellow, with central feathers and terminal band black (looks mostly yellow from below). **Voice** Calls, rough "chuck!" and "chewop". Display call, liquid swallowed "cheer'fol"; gurgling sounds. **TN** Formerly Band-tailed Oropendola *Ocyalus latirostris*.

Genus *Icterus* Colourful yellow or orange plumage with sharp-pointed bills and long tails. Sexes similar in resident species, differ in boreal migrants. Musical songs. Lightly wooded lowlands (one montane). Diet varied but fond of nectar. Build woven pendant nests (except troupials).

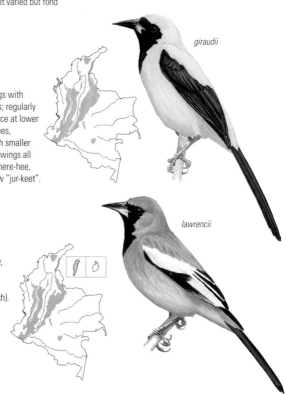

giraudii

Yellow-backed Oriole *Icterus chrysater* LC
Turpial Montañero
Common resident (highlands).

L 22 cm (8.5"). Race *giraudii*. Highland clearings with scattered trees, plantations, woodland borders; regularly uses introduced *Eucalyptus*. 500–2800 m (scarce at lower elevations). Pairs, groups of 3–4, well up in trees, inspect foliage, take fruit and nectar. **ID** Often confused with smaller lowland Yellow Oriole, but entire foreface and throat black, wings all black. **Voice** Often heard musical song of loud whistles "where-hee, who-hee, who-hee, ha-heet, wita-wita". Also, jerky high-low "jur-keet".

lawrencii

Jamaican Oriole *Icterus leucopteryx* LC
Turpial Jamaiquino CR
Common resident (only Isla San Andrés).

L 22 cm (8.5"). Race *lawrencii*. **ID** Olive-yellow, black foreface and throat, wings black, large white patch on wing-coverts, flight feathers edged white. Juv two white wingbars (no patch). **Voice** Short musical whistles "you cheat, you cheat" or "cheat-you", most vocal Oct–Jun. **SS** ♀ Baltimore Oriole.

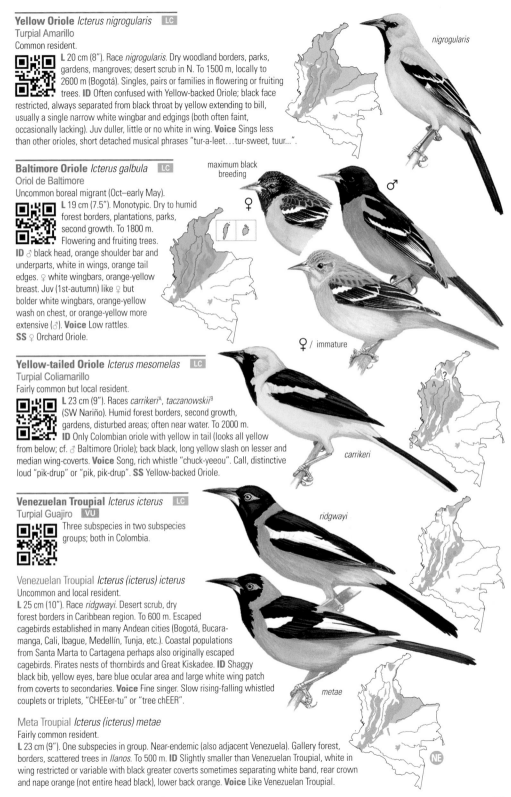

Yellow Oriole *Icterus nigrogularis* LC
Turpial Amarillo
Common resident.

L 20 cm (8"). Race *nigrogularis*. Dry woodland borders, parks, gardens, mangroves; desert scrub in N. To 1500 m, locally to 2600 m (Bogotá). Singles, pairs or families in flowering or fruiting trees. **ID** Often confused with Yellow-backed Oriole; black face restricted, always separated from black throat by yellow extending to bill, usually a single narrow white wingbar and edgings (both often faint, occasionally lacking). Juv duller, little or no white in wing. **Voice** Sings less than other orioles, short detached musical phrases "tur-a-leet…tur-sweet, tuur…".

nigrogularis

Baltimore Oriole *Icterus galbula* LC
Oriol de Baltimore
Uncommon boreal migrant (Oct–early May).

L 19 cm (7.5"). Monotypic. Dry to humid forest borders, plantations, parks, second growth. To 1800 m. Flowering and fruiting trees. **ID** ♂ black head, orange shoulder bar and underparts, white in wings, orange tail edges. ♀ white wingbars, orange-yellow breast. Juv (1st-autumn) like ♀ but bolder white wingbars, orange-yellow wash on chest, or orange-yellow more extensive (♂). **Voice** Low rattles. **SS** ♀ Orchard Oriole.

maximum black breeding

♀

♂

♀ / immature

Yellow-tailed Oriole *Icterus mesomelas* LC
Turpial Coliamarillo
Fairly common but local resident.

L 23 cm (9"). Races *carrikeri*[A], *taczanowskii*[B] (SW Nariño). Humid forest borders, second growth, gardens, disturbed areas; often near water. To 2000 m. **ID** Only Colombian oriole with yellow in tail (looks all yellow from below; cf. ♂ Baltimore Oriole); back black, long yellow slash on lesser and median wing-coverts. **Voice** Song, rich whistle "chuck-yeeou". Call, distinctive loud "pik-drup" or "pik, pik-drup". **SS** Yellow-backed Oriole.

carrikeri

Venezuelan Troupial *Icterus icterus* LC
Turpial Guajiro VU

Three subspecies in two subspecies groups; both in Colombia.

ridgwayi

Venezuelan Troupial *Icterus (icterus) icterus*
Uncommon and local resident.
L 25 cm (10"). Race *ridgwayi*. Desert scrub, dry forest borders in Caribbean region. To 600 m. Escaped cagebirds established in many Andean cities (Bogotá, Bucaramanga, Cali, Ibague, Medellín, Tunja, etc.). Coastal populations from Santa Marta to Cartagena perhaps also originally escaped cagebirds. Pirates nests of thornbirds and Great Kiskadee. **ID** Shaggy black bib, yellow eyes, bare blue ocular area and large white wing patch from coverts to secondaries. **Voice** Fine singer. Slow rising-falling whistled couplets or triplets, "CHEEer-tu" or "tree chEER".

metae

Meta Troupial *Icterus (icterus) metae*
Fairly common resident.
L 23 cm (9"). One subspecies in group. Near-endemic (also adjacent Venezuela). Gallery forest, borders, scattered trees in *llanos*. To 500 m. **ID** Slightly smaller than Venezuelan Troupial, white in wing restricted or variable with black greater coverts sometimes separating white band, rear crown and nape orange (not entire head black), lower back orange. **Voice** Like Venezuelan Troupial.

477

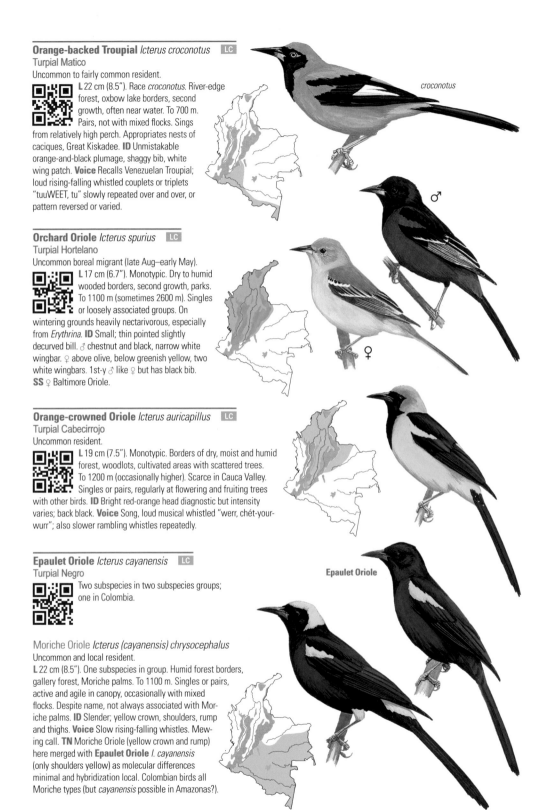

Orange-backed Troupial *Icterus croconotus* `LC`
Turpial Matico

Uncommon to fairly common resident.

L 22 cm (8.5"). Race *croconotus*. River-edge forest, oxbow lake borders, second growth, often near water. To 700 m. Pairs, not with mixed flocks. Sings from relatively high perch. Appropriates nests of caciques, Great Kiskadee. **ID** Unmistakable orange-and-black plumage, shaggy bib, white wing patch. **Voice** Recalls Venezuelan Troupial; loud rising-falling whistled couplets or triplets "tuuWEET, tu" slowly repeated over and over, or pattern reversed or varied.

croconotus

♂

Orchard Oriole *Icterus spurius* `LC`
Turpial Hortelano

Uncommon boreal migrant (late Aug–early May).

L 17 cm (6.7"). Monotypic. Dry to humid wooded borders, second growth, parks. To 1100 m (sometimes 2600 m). Singles or loosely associated groups. On wintering grounds heavily nectarivorous, especially from *Erythrina*. **ID** Small; thin pointed slightly decurved bill. ♂ chestnut and black, narrow white wingbar. ♀ above olive, below greenish yellow, two white wingbars. 1st-y ♂ like ♀ but has black bib. **SS** ♀ Baltimore Oriole.

♀

Orange-crowned Oriole *Icterus auricapillus* `LC`
Turpial Cabecirrojo

Uncommon resident.

L 19 cm (7.5"). Monotypic. Borders of dry, moist and humid forest, woodlots, cultivated areas with scattered trees. To 1200 m (occasionally higher). Scarce in Cauca Valley. Singles or pairs, regularly at flowering and fruiting trees with other birds. **ID** Bright red-orange head diagnostic but intensity varies; back black. **Voice** Song, loud musical whistled "werr, chét-your-wurr"; also slower rambling whistles repeatedly.

Epaulet Oriole *Icterus cayanensis* `LC`
Turpial Negro

Two subspecies in two subspecies groups; one in Colombia.

Epaulet Oriole

Moriche Oriole *Icterus (cayanensis) chrysocephalus*
Uncommon and local resident.

L 22 cm (8.5"). One subspecies in group. Humid forest borders, gallery forest, Moriche palms. To 1100 m. Singles or pairs, active and agile in canopy, occasionally with mixed flocks. Despite name, not always associated with Moriche palms. **ID** Slender; yellow crown, shoulders, rump and thighs. **Voice** Slow rising-falling whistles. Mewing call. **TN** Moriche Oriole (yellow crown and rump) here merged with **Epaulet Oriole** *I. cayanensis* (only shoulders yellow) as molecular differences minimal and hybridization local. Colombian birds all Moriche types (but *cayanensis* possible in Amazonas?).

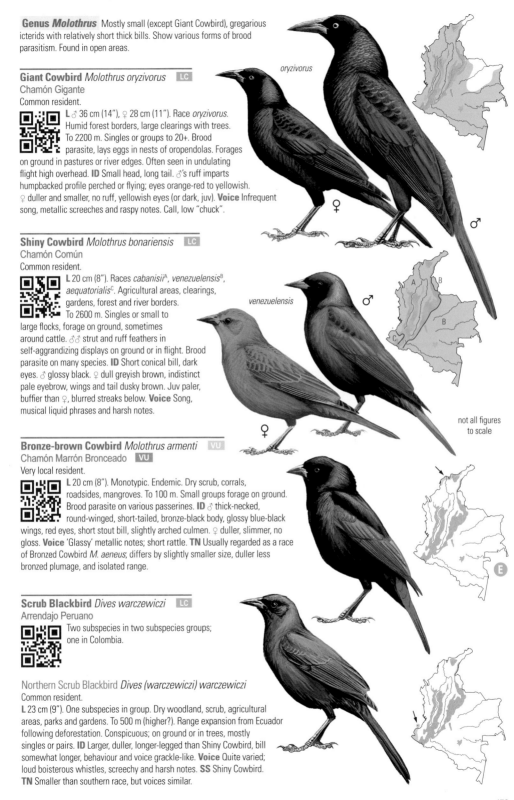

Genus *Molothrus* Mostly small (except Giant Cowbird), gregarious icterids with relatively short thick bills. Show various forms of brood parasitism. Found in open areas.

oryzivorus

Giant Cowbird *Molothrus oryzivorus* `LC`
Chamón Gigante
Common resident.

L ♂ 36 cm (14"), ♀ 28 cm (11"). Race *oryzivorus*. Humid forest borders, large clearings with trees. To 2200 m. Singles or groups to 20+. Brood parasite, lays eggs in nests of oropendolas. Forages on ground in pastures or river edges. Often seen in undulating flight high overhead. **ID** Small head, long tail. ♂'s ruff imparts humpbacked profile perched or flying; eyes orange-red to yellowish. ♀ duller and smaller, no ruff, yellowish eyes (or dark, juv). **Voice** Infrequent song, metallic screeches and raspy notes. Call, low "chuck".

♀ ♂

Shiny Cowbird *Molothrus bonariensis* `LC`
Chamón Común
Common resident.

L 20 cm (8"). Races *cabanisii*[A], *venezuelensis*[B], *aequatorialis*[C]. Agricultural areas, clearings, gardens, forest and river borders. To 2600 m. Singles or small to large flocks, forage on ground, sometimes around cattle. ♂♂ strut and ruff feathers in self-aggrandizing displays on ground or in flight. Brood parasite on many species. **ID** Short conical bill, dark eyes. ♂ glossy black. ♀ dull greyish brown, indistinct pale eyebrow, wings and tail dusky brown. Juv paler, buffier than ♀, blurred streaks below. **Voice** Song, musical liquid phrases and harsh notes.

venezuelensis ♂

♀

not all figures to scale

Bronze-brown Cowbird *Molothrus armenti* `VU`
Chamón Marrón Bronceado `VU`
Very local resident.

L 20 cm (8"). Monotypic. Endemic. Dry scrub, corrals, roadsides, mangroves. To 100 m. Small groups forage on ground. Brood parasite on various passerines. **ID** ♂ thick-necked, round-winged, short-tailed, bronze-black body, glossy blue-black wings, red eyes, short stout bill, slightly arched culmen. ♀ duller, slimmer, no gloss. **Voice** 'Glassy' metallic notes; short rattle. **TN** Usually regarded as a race of Bronzed Cowbird *M. aeneus*; differs by slightly smaller size, duller less bronzed plumage, and isolated range.

Scrub Blackbird *Dives warczewiczi* `LC`
Arrendajo Peruano

Two subspecies in two subspecies groups; one in Colombia.

Northern Scrub Blackbird *Dives (warczewiczi) warczewiczi*
Common resident.

L 23 cm (9"). One subspecies in group. Dry woodland, scrub, agricultural areas, parks and gardens. To 500 m (higher?). Range expansion from Ecuador following deforestation. Conspicuous; on ground or in trees, mostly singles or pairs. **ID** Larger, duller, longer-legged than Shiny Cowbird, bill somewhat longer, behaviour and voice grackle-like. **Voice** Quite varied; loud boisterous whistles, screechy and harsh notes. **SS** Shiny Cowbird. **TN** Smaller than southern race, but voices similar.

479

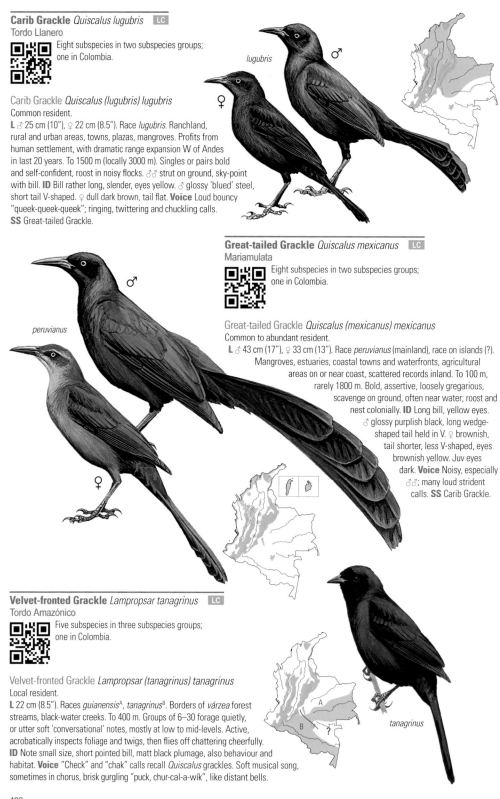

Carib Grackle *Quiscalus lugubris* LC
Tordo Llanero

Eight subspecies in two subspecies groups; one in Colombia.

lugubris

♂

♀

Carib Grackle *Quiscalus (lugubris) lugubris*
Common resident.
L ♂ 25 cm (10"), ♀ 22 cm (8.5"). Race *lugubris*. Ranchland, rural and urban areas, towns, plazas, mangroves. Profits from human settlement, with dramatic range expansion W of Andes in last 20 years. To 1500 m (locally 3000 m). Singles or pairs bold and self-confident, roost in noisy flocks. ♂♂ strut on ground, sky-point with bill. **ID** Bill rather long, slender, eyes yellow. ♂ glossy 'blued' steel, short tail V-shaped. ♀ dull dark brown, tail flat. **Voice** Loud bouncy "queek–queek–queek"; ringing, twittering and chuckling calls. **SS** Great-tailed Grackle.

♂

peruvianus

♀

Great-tailed Grackle *Quiscalus mexicanus* LC
Mariamulata

Eight subspecies in two subspecies groups; one in Colombia.

Great-tailed Grackle *Quiscalus (mexicanus) mexicanus*
Common to abundant resident.
L ♂ 43 cm (17"), ♀ 33 cm (13"). Race *peruvianus* (mainland), race on islands (?). Mangroves, estuaries, coastal towns and waterfronts, agricultural areas on or near coast, scattered records inland. To 100 m, rarely 1800 m. Bold, assertive, loosely gregarious, scavenge on ground, often near water; roost and nest colonially. **ID** Long bill, yellow eyes. ♂ glossy purplish black, long wedge-shaped tail held in V. ♀ brownish, tail shorter, less V-shaped, eyes brownish yellow. Juv eyes dark. **Voice** Noisy, especially ♂♂; many loud strident calls. **SS** Carib Grackle.

Velvet-fronted Grackle *Lampropsar tanagrinus* LC
Tordo Amazónico

Five subspecies in three subspecies groups; one in Colombia.

Velvet-fronted Grackle *Lampropsar (tanagrinus) tanagrinus*
Local resident.
L 22 cm (8.5"). Races *guianensis*[A], *tanagrinus*[B]. Borders of *várzea* forest streams, black-water creeks. To 400 m. Groups of 6–30 forage quietly, or utter soft 'conversational' notes, mostly at low to mid-levels. Active, acrobatically inspects foliage and twigs, then flies off chattering cheerfully. **ID** Note small size, short pointed bill, matt black plumage, also behaviour and habitat. **Voice** "Check" and "chak" calls recall *Quiscalus* grackles. Soft musical song, sometimes in chorus, brisk gurgling "puck, chur-cal-a-wík", like distant bells.

tanagrinus

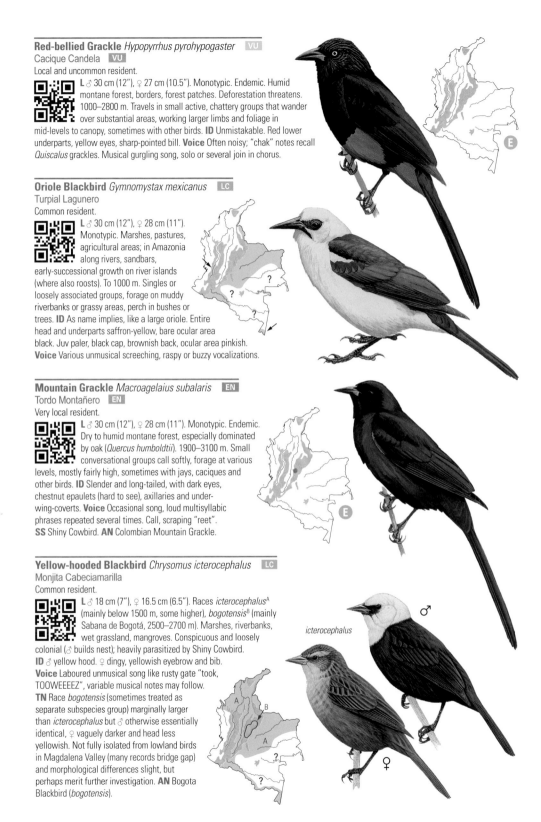

Red-bellied Grackle *Hypopyrrhus pyrohypogaster* VU
Cacique Candela VU
Local and uncommon resident.

L ♂ 30 cm (12"), ♀ 27 cm (10.5"). Monotypic. Endemic. Humid montane forest, borders, forest patches. Deforestation threatens. 1000–2800 m. Travels in small active, chattery groups that wander over substantial areas, working larger limbs and foliage in mid-levels to canopy, sometimes with other birds. **ID** Unmistakable. Red lower underparts, yellow eyes, sharp-pointed bill. **Voice** Often noisy; "chak" notes recall *Quiscalus* grackles. Musical gurgling song, solo or several join in chorus.

Oriole Blackbird *Gymnomystax mexicanus* LC
Turpial Lagunero
Common resident.

L ♂ 30 cm (12"), ♀ 28 cm (11"). Monotypic. Marshes, pastures, agricultural areas; in Amazonia along rivers, sandbars, early-successional growth on river islands (where also roosts). To 1000 m. Singles or loosely associated groups, forage on muddy riverbanks or grassy areas, perch in bushes or trees. **ID** As name implies, like a large oriole. Entire head and underparts saffron-yellow, bare ocular area black. Juv paler, black cap, brownish back, ocular area pinkish. **Voice** Various unmusical screeching, raspy or buzzy vocalizations.

Mountain Grackle *Macroagelaius subalaris* EN
Tordo Montañero EN
Very local resident.

L ♂ 30 cm (12"), ♀ 28 cm (11"). Monotypic. Endemic. Dry to humid montane forest, especially dominated by oak (*Quercus humboldtii*). 1900–3100 m. Small conversational groups call softly, forage at various levels, mostly fairly high, sometimes with jays, caciques and other birds. **ID** Slender and long-tailed, with dark eyes, chestnut epaulets (hard to see), axillaries and under-wing-coverts. **Voice** Occasional song, loud multisyllabic phrases repeated several times. Call, scraping "reet". **SS** Shiny Cowbird. **AN** Colombian Mountain Grackle.

Yellow-hooded Blackbird *Chrysomus icterocephalus* LC
Monjita Cabeciamarilla
Common resident.

L ♂ 18 cm (7"), ♀ 16.5 cm (6.5"). Races *icterocephalus*[A] (mainly below 1500 m, some higher), *bogotensis*[B] (mainly Sabana de Bogotá, 2500–2700 m). Marshes, riverbanks, wet grassland, mangroves. Conspicuous and loosely colonial (♂ builds nest); heavily parasitized by Shiny Cowbird. **ID** ♂ yellow hood. ♀ dingy, yellowish eyebrow and bib. **Voice** Laboured unmusical song like rusty gate "took, TOOWEEEEZ", variable musical notes may follow. **TN** Race *bogotensis* (sometimes treated as separate subspecies group) marginally larger than *icterocephalus* but ♂ otherwise essentially identical, ♀ vaguely darker and head less yellowish. Not fully isolated from lowland birds in Magdalena Valley (many records bridge gap) and morphological differences slight, but perhaps merit further investigation. **AN** Bogota Blackbird (*bogotensis*).

icterocephalus

♂

♀

Small active birds with thin, sharp-pointed bills. Most species colourful and arboreal, a few terrestrial and modestly attired. Two groups occur in Colombia: (1) long-distance boreal migrants, and (2) residents. Boreal migrants are smaller, more delicately proportioned, more colourful (in breeding plumage), sexually dimorphic, and juvenile plumages also usually differ; their high-pitched songs are not heard in Colombia (and so not described). Residents comprise fewer species, but all are slightly larger, sexes similar, and some genera differ little in appearance from tanagers.

Ovenbird *Seiurus aurocapilla* LC
Reinita Hornera
Common boreal migrant (islands), rare (mainland),
Oct–Mar.

 L 15 cm (6"). Race *aurocapilla*. Dry to moderately humid forest interior. To 1500 m. Alone, unobtrusive and inconspicuous, mainly on forest floor, walks with head-bobbing gait, tail often raised. **ID** Large eyes, bold eye-ring, dull orange crown-stripe bordered black, streaked underparts. **Voice** Dry "chip". **SS** Northern Waterthrush.

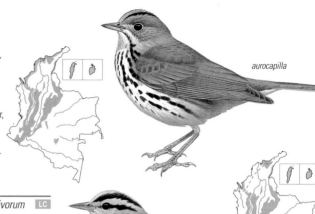

aurocapilla

Worm-eating Warbler *Helmitheros vermivorum* LC
Reinita Gusanera
Fairly common boreal migrant (islands), vagrant (mainland; Santa Marta foothills, Gulf of Urabá).

 L 13.5 cm (5.3"). Monotypic. Understorey of dry to humid woodland, plantations. To 1200 m. Forages low, gleans arthropods from dead hanging leaves and in vine tangles. **ID** Plain; bold head-stripes, rather short broad tail. **Voice** Mostly quiet.

Louisiana Waterthrush *Parkesia motacilla* LC
Reinita de Luisiana
Rare boreal migrant (most verified records near Caribbean coast, Oct–Mar?).

 L 15 cm (6"). Monotypic. Damp areas, small streams in wooded areas. **ID** Very similar to far commoner Northern Waterthrush, but has slightly larger bill, broader white eyebrow (especially behind eye), usually buff-tinged flanks, pinkish legs, sparser brown streaking on white underparts, and bobs short tail slowly, mostly side to side. Inland records need documentation.

Northern Waterthrush *Parkesia noveboracensis* LC
Reinita Acuática
Common boreal migrant (islands and mainland, Sept–late Apr).

L 15 cm (6"). Races *notabilis*, *noveboracensis*. Mangroves, small streams, damp areas in dry to humid forest. To 3000 m. **ID** Much like rare Louisiana Waterthrush, but has smaller bill, long narrow uniform-width eyebrow, denser underparts streaking, eyebrow and underparts tinged yellowish (occasionally whitish), throat finely streaked (hard to see), dull legs, and bobs longer tail and rear parts more rapidly up and down.

noveboracensis

Golden-winged Warbler *Vermivora chrysoptera*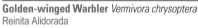
Reinita Alidorada
Very rare boreal migrant (islands), uncommon (mainland),
late Sept–early Apr.

 L 12.2 cm (4.8"). Monotypic. Moderately dry
to humid foothill and montane forest, borders,
light woodland, plantations. To 2500 m. Singles,
regularly in upper forest levels with mixed flocks.
ID Ad ♂ greyish, forecrown yellow, conspicuous black mask and
throat, large yellow wing patch. ♀ and juv duller, mask and
throat greyish.

Blue-winged Warbler *Vermivora cyanoptera* LC
Reinita Aliazul
Rare boreal migrant (Isla San Andrés; Providencia?),
vagrant (Santa Marta and coastal region).

 L 12.2 cm (4.8"). Monotypic. Dry to humid
woodland borders. To 1200 m. May occur with
mixed flocks. **ID** Ad ♂ bright yellow forehead and
underparts, black line through eye, blue-grey wings,
two white wingbars, white vent. ♀ duller. **TN** Formerly *V. pinus*.

Black-and-white Warbler *Mniotilta varia* LC
Cebrita Trepadora
Common boreal migrant (islands and mainland, Sept–early Apr).

 **L** 13.5 cm (5.3"). Monotypic. Mostly humid foothill
and montane forest, borders, plantations. To 3000 m.
Hitches, creeper-like, around trunks and larger limbs,
in lower levels to subcanopy; 1–2 per mixed flock.
ID Ad br ♂ boldly streaked black and white above and below, black
cheeks. ♀ duller, much less streaked below, thin black post-ocular
line. **SS** Ad ♂ Blackpoll Warbler (p. 489).

Prothonotary Warbler *Protonotaria citrea* LC
Reinita Cabecidorada
Common boreal migrant (Caribbean coast, fewer Pacific
coast), scarce inland (Sept–early Apr).

 L 14 cm (5.5"). Monotypic.
Mangroves, dry to humid
woodland, generally near
water. To 1500 m
(occasionally higher). Stays in
understorey, sometimes with mixed
flocks. **ID** Ad ♂ brilliant golden-yellow
head and underparts, white vent, bill
and eyes black, wings grey. ♀ duller,
less yellow below.

Swainson's Warbler
Limnothlypis swainsonii LC
Reinita de Swainson
Rare to uncommon boreal migrant (islands),
vagrant (Santa Marta area?).

 L 14 cm (5.5"). Monotypic. Understorey
or ground in dry to moist woodland.
Lowlands or foothills. **ID** Ad above uniform
brown, crown rusty with flattish forecrown,
pale eyebrow, less distinct dark eyeline, fairly long bill
(for parulid), dingy grey-white underparts tinged lemon.
Sexes similar. **SS** Worm-eating Warbler.

Tennessee Warbler *Leiothlypis peregrina* `LC`
Reinita Verderona
Common boreal migrant W of Andes (Oct–early May).
L 12.2 cm (4.8"). Monotypic. Canopy of dry to humid woodland borders, second growth, coffee plantations, gardens. Often visits flowering trees for nectar, regularly with mixed flocks.
ID Confusing. Ad br ♂ grey crown contrasts with olive back, narrow white superciliary, sharp-pointed bill, whitish underparts. ♀ duller, crown less contrasting, foreparts tinged yellow. 1st-w even plainer, faint yellowish eyebrow, underparts yellowish, two thin pale wingbars, undertail whitish. **SS** 1st-w Cerulean Warbler (p. 486).

Nashville Warbler *Leiothlypis ruficapilla* `LC`
Reinita de Nashville
Rare and erratic boreal migrant (San Andrés), vagrant (mainland).
L 12.2 cm (4.8"). Race *ruficapilla*? Isla San Andrés (three records), E Andes (photo, Laguna de Fúquene, Cundinamarca). Dry to humid woodland. **ID** Ad ♂ contrasting grey head, white eye-ring, yellow underparts. ♀ similar but duller, less yellow on underparts but vent yellow. Juv like dull ♀, wings olive. **SS** Rare 1st-w Connecticut Warbler.

Connecticut Warbler *Oporornis agilis* `LC`
Reinita Pechigrís
Rare boreal passage migrant (mainland; islands?), Sept–Nov, Apr–early May.
L 13.2 cm (5.2"). Monotypic. Could occur almost anywhere; solitary. Dense thickets; secretive on or near ground where walks. Winters in Amazonia but region poorly defined; low in dense young second growth on river islands (Peru).
ID Complete white eye-ring in all plumages. Ad ♂ grey hood, olive upperparts, long yellow undertail-coverts nearly reach tail tip. ♀ duller. 1st-w hood and upperparts brownish. **SS** Mourning Warbler.

Genus *Geothlypis* (yellowthroats) Skulk in tall grass and thickets, ♂♂ have black masks. ♀♀ nondescript. Molecular data now place some former *Oporornis* in *Geothlypis*.

Masked Yellowthroat *Geothlypis aequinoctialis* `LC`
Reinita Enmascarada
Two subspecies in two subspecies groups; one in Colombia.

Masked Yellowthroat
Geothlypis (aequinoctialis) aequinoctialis
Locally fairly common resident.
L 13.2 cm (5.2"). One subspecies in group. Overgrown grassy clearings, damp grass, marshes, flooded ditches. To 1500 m. More engaging than Olive-crowned Yellowthroat; skulks, but pops up in open to scold or sing. **ID** ♂ like ♂ Olive-crowned Yellowthroat (no range overlap) but crown grey, black mask smaller. ♀ faint yellowish eyeline, otherwise like ♀ Olive-crowned Yellowthroat.
Voice Song, complex musical "tee-chee-chee, teeche weet, teecheweet" with variations. Husky "chup" call.

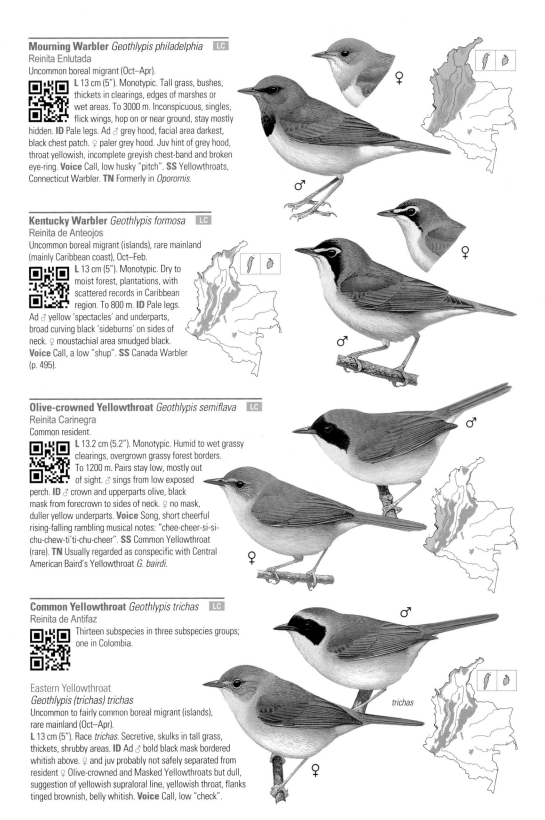

Mourning Warbler *Geothlypis philadelphia* `LC`
Reinita Enlutada
Uncommon boreal migrant (Oct–Apr).
L 13 cm (5"). Monotypic. Tall grass, bushes, thickets in clearings, edges of marshes or wet areas. To 3000 m. Inconspicuous, singles, flick wings, hop on or near ground, stay mostly hidden. **ID** Pale legs. Ad ♂ grey hood, facial area darkest, black chest patch. ♀ paler grey hood. Juv hint of grey hood, throat yellowish, incomplete greyish chest-band and broken eye-ring. **Voice** Call, low husky "pitch". **SS** Yellowthroats, Connecticut Warbler. **TN** Formerly in *Oporornis*.

Kentucky Warbler *Geothlypis formosa* `LC`
Reinita de Anteojos
Uncommon boreal migrant (islands), rare mainland (mainly Caribbean coast), Oct–Feb.
L 13 cm (5"). Monotypic. Dry to moist forest, plantations, with scattered records in Caribbean region. To 800 m. **ID** Pale legs. Ad ♂ yellow 'spectacles' and underparts, broad curving black 'sideburns' on sides of neck. ♀ moustachial area smudged black. **Voice** Call, a low "shup". **SS** Canada Warbler (p. 495).

Olive-crowned Yellowthroat *Geothlypis semiflava* `LC`
Reinita Carinegra
Common resident.
L 13.2 cm (5.2"). Monotypic. Humid to wet grassy clearings, overgrown grassy forest borders. To 1200 m. Pairs stay low, mostly out of sight. ♂ sings from low exposed perch. **ID** ♂ crown and upperparts olive, black mask from forecrown to sides of neck. ♀ no mask, duller yellow underparts. **Voice** Song, short cheerful rising-falling rambling musical notes: "chee-cheer-si-si-chu-chew-ti'ti-chu-cheer". **SS** Common Yellowthroat (rare). **TN** Usually regarded as conspecific with Central American Baird's Yellowthroat *G. bairdi*.

Common Yellowthroat *Geothlypis trichas* `LC`
Reinita de Antifaz
Thirteen subspecies in three subspecies groups; one in Colombia.

Eastern Yellowthroat
Geothlypis (trichas) trichas
Uncommon to fairly common boreal migrant (islands), rare mainland (Oct–Apr).
L 13 cm (5"). Race *trichas*. Secretive, skulks in tall grass, thickets, shrubby areas. **ID** Ad ♂ bold black mask bordered whitish above. ♀ and juv probably not safely separated from resident ♀ Olive-crowned and Masked Yellowthroats but dull, suggestion of yellowish supraloral line, yellowish throat, flanks tinged brownish, belly whitish. **Voice** Call, low "check".

trichas

Hooded Warbler *Setophaga citrina* `LC`
Reinita Encapuchada

Uncommon boreal migrant (islands), rare mainland (Oct–early May).

 L 13 cm (5"). Monotypic. Low in thickets, dry to humid wooded areas, forest borders. To 1000 m (rarely higher). Most photo-documented records involve ♂♂. **ID** Ad ♂ black crown and throat encircle yellow forehead and face; tail mostly white below, often flicked open. ♀ suggestion of black crown encircling rear face, little or no black on throat. 1st-w no black, with face, cheeks and underparts yellow, tail as ad.

American Redstart *Setophaga ruticilla* `LC`
Candelita Norteña

Common boreal migrant (Aug–early May).

 L 13 cm (5"). Monotypic. Dry to humid wooded areas, plantations, parks, mangroves. Mostly below 1500 m (occasionally 3000 m). Hyperactive, alone or with mixed flocks. Fans and raises tail to startle insects. **ID** Ad ♂ black, bright orange patches in wings and tail. ♀ head grey, pectoral patch, wing-band and base of tail yellow. 1st-y ♂ like ♀ but pectoral patches orange, may show patches of black.

Cape May Warbler *Setophaga tigrina* `LC`
Reinita Atigrada

Rare boreal migrant (islands and mainland), also Isla Malpelo (once).

 L 11.4 cm (4.5"). Monotypic. Forest borders, plantations, mangroves, often in flowering trees. **ID** Ad br ♂ rusty-red ear patch encircled by yellow, white wing-coverts, yellow underparts streaked black. ♀ much paler, greyish cheeks enclosed by pale yellow, wing-coverts tipped white, streaked underparts tinged yellow. 1st-w ♂ and ♀ recall respective ad but much duller, hint of yellow on sides of neck, weaker streaking below.

Cerulean Warbler *Setophaga cerulea* `NT`
Reinita Cerúlea

Very rare boreal migrant (islands), uncommon W of Andes, fairly common E slope of E Andes.

 L 12.2 cm (4.8"). Monotypic. Humid forest, borders, second growth, coffee plantations. Mostly 500–2200 m. Singles forage in canopy, often with mixed flocks. Small groups gather prior to northbound migration. **ID** Ad br ♂ porcelain blue, white wingbars, narrow chest-band, streaked sides. ♀ duller, no chest-band, streaks fainter, blurred. 1st-w pale eyestripe, blue-green upperparts, white wingbars, underparts tinged yellow. **SS** 1st-w Blackburnian Warbler.

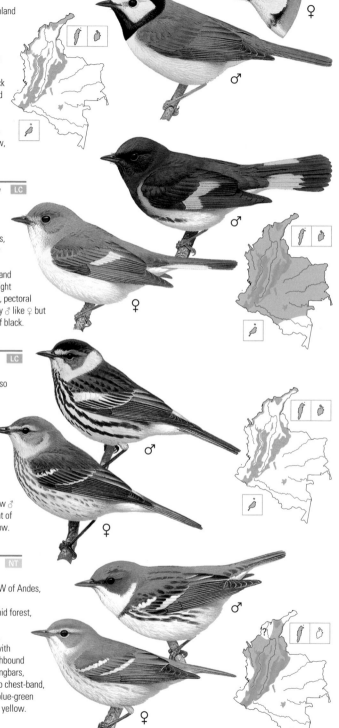

Northern Parula *Setophaga americana* LC
Reinita Norteña

Uncommon boreal migrant (islands), rare mainland.

 L 11.4 cm (4.5"). Monotypic. Dry woodland. **ID** Ad ♂ above blue-grey, broken white eye-ring, dark smudged chest-band. ♀ duller, chest-band weaker. 1st-y like ♀ but wingbars reduced, less yellow below, no chest-band. **SS** Tropical Parula.

Tropical Parula *Setophaga pitiayumi* LC
Reinita Tropical

 Eight subspecies in two subspecies groups; one in Colombia.

Tropical Parula *Setophaga (pitiayumi) pitiayumi*
Common resident.

L 11.4 cm (4.5"). Races *inornata*[A] (includes *nana*), *pacifica*[B], *pitiayumi*[C], *alarum*[D] (?). Dry to humid forest borders, light woodland, plantations. To 2700 m (mostly foothills to mid-elevations). Pairs forage actively, high in trees, follow mixed flocks. **ID** Ad ♂ much like Northern Parula (usually two wingbars, sometimes single or vestigial bar), but face dark (no white eye-arcs), chest plain orange-yellow. ♀ duller. **Voice** Energetic song, a few buzzy notes accelerating into rising buzzy trill. **SS** Northern Parula.

pitiayumi

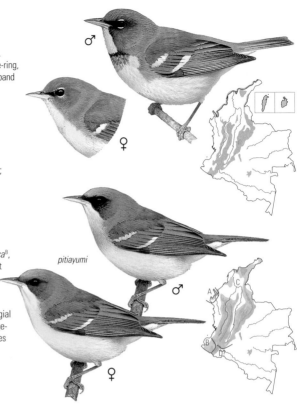

Magnolia Warbler *Setophaga magnolia* LC
Reinita Magnolia

Fairly common boreal migrant (Islas San Andrés and Providencia), rare mainland.

 L 13 cm (5"). Monotypic. Dry to humid wooded areas. Caribbean coast, rarely inland or to 1700 m. **ID** In all plumages, yellow rump and white tail panels diagnostic. Ad br ♂ unmistakable black-and-yellow pattern, white wing and tail panels, boldly streaked underparts. ♀ like ♂ but duller, face mask dark grey. Non-br ♂ above olive streaked dusky, white wing panel reduced to narrow white bars. 1st-w from non-br ♂ by white eye-ring, unstreaked underparts.

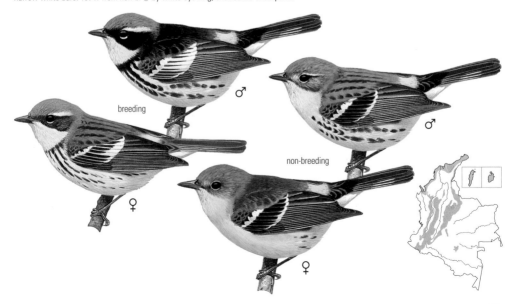

breeding

non-breeding

Bay-breasted Warbler *Setophaga castanea* `LC`
Reinita Castaña

Uncommon boreal migrant (islands), common W of Andes (Oct–late Apr).

L 14 cm (5.5"). Monotypic. Humid forest borders, older second growth, light woodland. To 1200 m. Singles, usually in canopy with mixed flocks. **ID** Ad br ♂ quite dark, large buff neck patch, chestnut underparts. ♀ much duller, head dingy, buff neck patch, touch of chestnut on sides. Non-br ♂ above olive, white wingbars, chestnut wash on flanks. 1st-w throat and breast tinged buffy yellow, neck olive, flanks and vent buff, legs dusky. **SS** 1st-w Blackpoll Warbler.

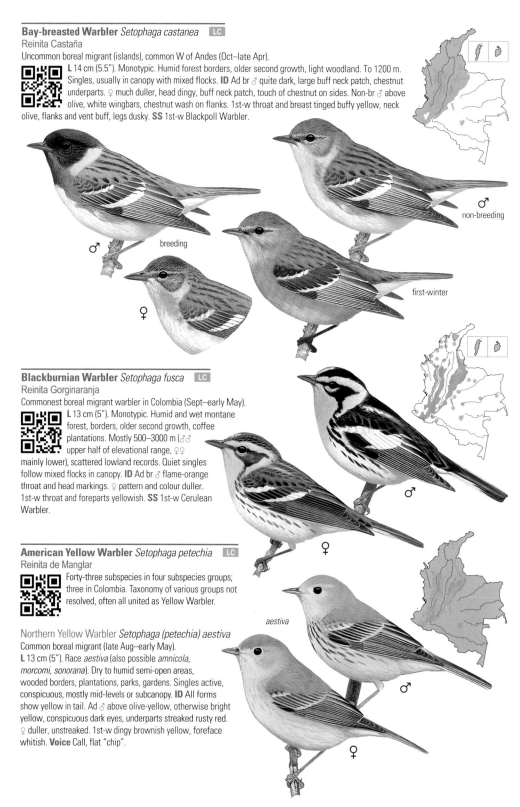

breeding

♂

♀

♂
non-breeding

first-winter

Blackburnian Warbler *Setophaga fusca* `LC`
Reinita Gorginaranja

Commonest boreal migrant warbler in Colombia (Sept–early May).

L 13 cm (5"). Monotypic. Humid and wet montane forest, borders, older second growth, coffee plantations. Mostly 500–3000 m (♂♂ upper half of elevational range, ♀♀ mainly lower), scattered lowland records. Quiet singles follow mixed flocks in canopy. **ID** Ad br ♂ flame-orange throat and head markings. ♀ pattern and colour duller. 1st-w throat and foreparts yellowish. **SS** 1st-w Cerulean Warbler.

♂

♀

American Yellow Warbler *Setophaga petechia* `LC`
Reinita de Manglar

Forty-three subspecies in four subspecies groups; three in Colombia. Taxonomy of various groups not resolved, often all united as Yellow Warbler.

Northern Yellow Warbler *Setophaga (petechia) aestiva*
Common boreal migrant (late Aug–early May).
L 13 cm (5"). Race *aestiva* (also possible *amnicola, morcomi, sonorana*). Dry to humid semi-open areas, wooded borders, plantations, parks, gardens. Singles active, conspicuous, mostly mid-levels or subcanopy. **ID** All forms show yellow in tail. Ad ♂ above olive-yellow, otherwise bright yellow, conspicuous dark eyes, underparts streaked rusty red. ♀ duller, unstreaked. 1st-w dingy brownish yellow, foreface whitish. **Voice** Call, flat "chip".

aestiva

♂

♀

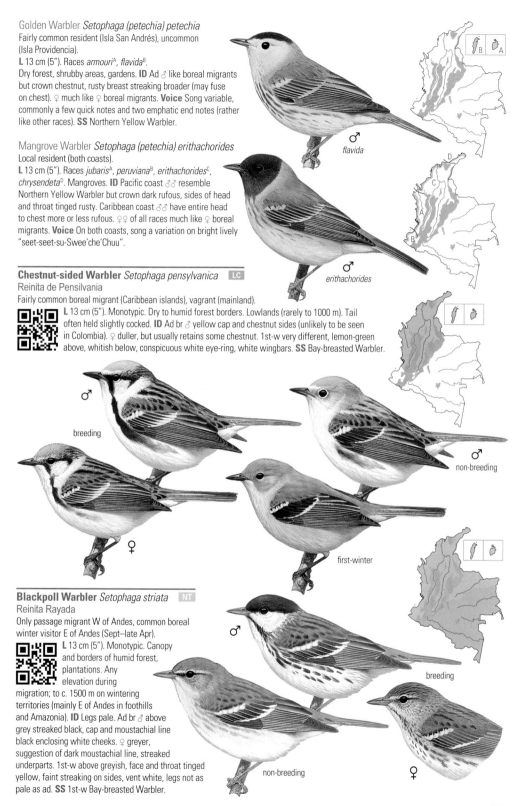

Golden Warbler *Setophaga (petechia) petechia*
Fairly common resident (Isla San Andrés), uncommon (Isla Providencia).
L 13 cm (5"). Races *armouri*[A], *flavida*[B].
Dry forest, shrubby areas, gardens. **ID** Ad ♂ like boreal migrants but crown chestnut, rusty breast streaking broader (may fuse on chest). ♀ much like ♀ boreal migrants. **Voice** Song variable, commonly a few quick notes and two emphatic end notes (rather like other races). **SS** Northern Yellow Warbler.

flavida

Mangrove Warbler *Setophaga (petechia) erithachorides*
Local resident (both coasts).
L 13 cm (5"). Races *jubaris*[A], *peruviana*[B], *erithachorides*[C], *chrysendeta*[D]. Mangroves. **ID** Pacific coast ♂♂ resemble Northern Yellow Warbler but crown dark rufous, sides of head and throat tinged rusty. Caribbean coast ♂♂ have entire head to chest more or less rufous. ♀♀ of all races much like ♀ boreal migrants. **Voice** On both coasts, song a variation on bright lively "seet-seet-su-Swee'che'Chuu".

♂
erithachorides

Chestnut-sided Warbler *Setophaga pensylvanica* `LC`
Reinita de Pensilvania
Fairly common boreal migrant (Caribbean islands), vagrant (mainland).
L 13 cm (5"). Monotypic. Dry to humid forest borders. Lowlands (rarely to 1000 m). Tail often held slightly cocked. **ID** Ad br ♂ yellow cap and chestnut sides (unlikely to be seen in Colombia). ♀ duller, but usually retains some chestnut. 1st-w very different, lemon-green above, whitish below, conspicuous white eye-ring, white wingbars. **SS** Bay-breasted Warbler.

♂
breeding

♂
non-breeding

♀

first-winter

Blackpoll Warbler *Setophaga striata* `NT`
Reinita Rayada
Only passage migrant W of Andes, common boreal winter visitor E of Andes (Sept–late Apr).
L 13 cm (5"). Monotypic. Canopy and borders of humid forest, plantations. Any elevation during migration; to c. 1500 m on wintering territories (mainly E of Andes in foothills and Amazonia). **ID** Legs pale. Ad br ♂ above grey streaked black, cap and moustachial line black enclosing white cheeks. ♀ greyer, suggestion of dark moustachial line, streaked underparts. 1st-w above greyish, face and throat tinged yellow, faint streaking on sides, vent white, legs not as pale as ad. **SS** 1st-w Bay-breasted Warbler.

♂
breeding

non-breeding

♀

Black-throated Blue Warbler *Setophaga caerulescens* `LC`
Reinita Negriazul

Rare boreal migrant (islands), vagrant (mainland).

L 13 cm (5"). Race unknown. Almost any wooded habitat; a few undocumented sight records inland. **ID** Ad br ♂ trim blue, black and white pattern. ♀ above brown, below buff, cheeks darker, whitish eyeline and lower eye-arc, small white wing spot (diagnostic, often faint). 1st-w like ♀ but paler, buffier, has darker cheeks, wing spot usually absent. **SS** Tennessee Warbler (p. 484).

Palm Warbler *Setophaga palmarum* `LC`
Reinita Palmera

Two subspecies in two subspecies groups; one in Colombia.

Western Palm Warbler
Setophaga (palmarum) palmarum

Rare to uncommon boreal migrant (islands), vagrant (mainland).

L 13 cm (5"). One subspecies in group. Borders of light woodland, bushy partly open areas. Semi-terrestrial; constantly bobs tail up and down. Sometimes loosely associated with other birds. **ID** Sexes similar. Ad br pale brown, crown rufous, dark eyeline, throat and vent yellow, sides variably streaked. Non-br paler, with little or no rufous on crown, narrow pale eyebrow, dark eyeline, underparts dingy, little or no blurred streaking, yellowish vent. **SS** Prairie Warbler.

breeding

non-breeding

[Pine Warbler *Setophaga pinus*] `LC`
Reinita del Pino

Hypothetical (unverified sight record, Santa Marta Mts, Nov 2002; records on Caribbean islands?).

L 13 cm (5"). Race unknown. **ID** ♂ weak yellow 'spectacles', two white wingbars, blurred olive steaks on dull yellow breast, whitish belly. ♀ much duller. 1st-w very drab greyish brown, weak wingbars, dark cheeks contrast whitish throat.

Yellow-rumped Warbler *Setophaga coronata* `LC`
Reinita Culiamarilla

Five subspecies in four subspecies groups (sometimes treated as two or more species); one in Colombia.

Myrtle Warbler *Setophaga (coronata) coronata*
Reinita Coronada

Uncommon boreal migrant (islands), vagrant (mainland).
L 13.2 cm (5.2"). Race *coronata*? Wooded areas, borders, plantations. **ID** Ad br ♂ (unlikely) black cheeks, white throat, black necklace, streaked sides, yellow pectoral patch. ♀/non-br ♂ much duller than br ♂, with less yellow on sides. 1st-w similar but little or no yellow on sides of chest; dingy brown, conspicuous yellow rump, cheeks darker than crown, throat pale, weak streaking on chest and sides. **Voice** Call, flat "chip". **TN** *S. c. auduboni* (unrecorded but possible; has been treated as separate species) ad yellow throat, no contrasting dark cheeks; 1st-w like Yellow-rumped but dingier, vague streaking, cheeks brownish like crown.

non-breeding

coronata

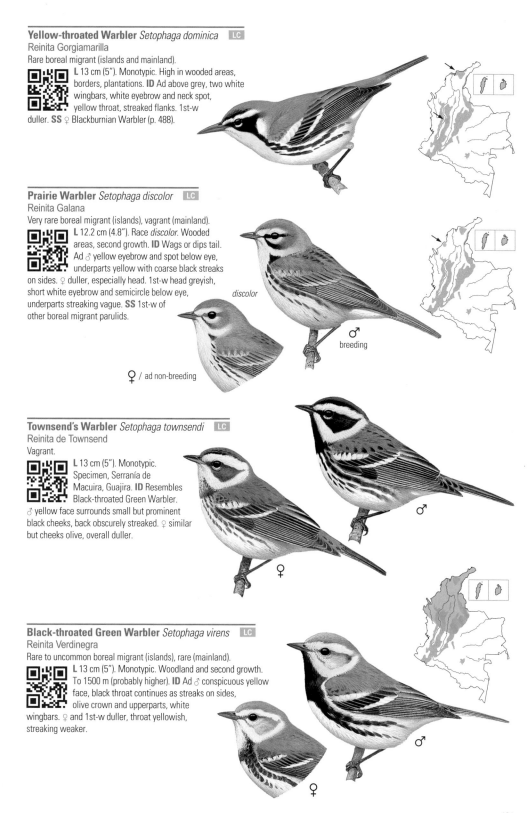

Yellow-throated Warbler *Setophaga dominica* `LC`
Reinita Gorgiamarilla
Rare boreal migrant (islands and mainland).
L 13 cm (5"). Monotypic. High in wooded areas, borders, plantations. **ID** Ad above grey, two white wingbars, white eyebrow and neck spot, yellow throat, streaked flanks. 1st-w duller. **SS** ♀ Blackburnian Warbler (p. 488).

Prairie Warbler *Setophaga discolor* `LC`
Reinita Galana
Very rare boreal migrant (islands), vagrant (mainland).
L 12.2 cm (4.8"). Race *discolor*. Wooded areas, second growth. **ID** Wags or dips tail. Ad ♂ yellow eyebrow and spot below eye, underparts yellow with coarse black streaks on sides. ♀ duller, especially head. 1st-w head greyish, short white eyebrow and semicircle below eye, underparts streaking vague. **SS** 1st-w of other boreal migrant parulids.

discolor

♂ breeding

♀ / ad non-breeding

Townsend's Warbler *Setophaga townsendi* `LC`
Reinita de Townsend
Vagrant.
L 13 cm (5"). Monotypic. Specimen, Serranía de Macuira, Guajira. **ID** Resembles Black-throated Green Warbler. ♂ yellow face surrounds small but prominent black cheeks, back obscurely streaked. ♀ similar but cheeks olive, overall duller.

♂

♀

Black-throated Green Warbler *Setophaga virens* `LC`
Reinita Verdinegra
Rare to uncommon boreal migrant (islands), rare (mainland).
L 13 cm (5"). Monotypic. Woodland and second growth. To 1500 m (probably higher). **ID** Ad ♂ conspicuous yellow face, black throat continues as streaks on sides, olive crown and upperparts, white wingbars. ♀ and 1st-w duller, throat yellowish, streaking weaker.

♂

♀

491

Genus *Myiothlypis* Formerly *Basileuterus*. Dull-plumaged resident species of montane forest or light woodland (Flavescent and Buff-rumped Warblers in lowlands), where active at low or mid-levels. Sexes alike. Songs more energetic than melodious.

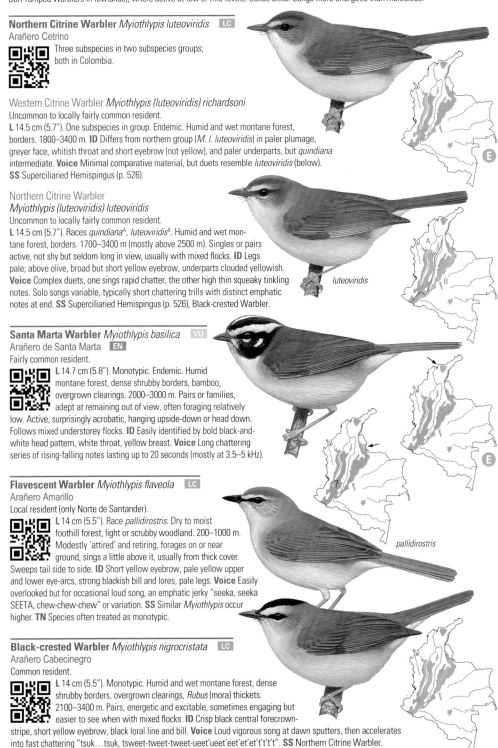

Northern Citrine Warbler *Myiothlypis luteoviridis* LC
Arañero Cetrino

Three subspecies in two subspecies groups; both in Colombia.

Western Citrine Warbler *Myiothlypis (luteoviridis) richardsoni*
Uncommon to locally fairly common resident.
L 14.5 cm (5.7"). One subspecies in group. Endemic. Humid and wet montane forest, borders. 1800–3400 m. **ID** Differs from northern group (*M. l. luteoviridis*) in paler plumage, greyer face, whitish throat and short eyebrow (not yellow), and paler underparts, but *quindiana* intermediate. **Voice** Minimal comparative material, but duets resemble *luteoviridis* (below). **SS** Superciliaried Hemispingus (p. 526).

Northern Citrine Warbler
Myiothlypis (luteoviridis) luteoviridis
Uncommon to locally fairly common resident.
L 14.5 cm (5.7"). Races *quindiana*[A], *luteoviridis*[B]. Humid and wet montane forest, borders. 1700–3400 m (mostly above 2500 m). Singles or pairs active, not shy but seldom long in view, usually with mixed flocks. **ID** Legs pale; above olive, broad but short yellow eyebrow, underparts clouded yellowish. **Voice** Complex duets, one sings rapid chatter, the other high thin squeaky tinkling notes. Solo songs variable, typically short chattering trills with distinct emphatic notes at end. **SS** Superciliaried Hemispingus (p. 526), Black-crested Warbler.

luteoviridis

Santa Marta Warbler *Myiothlypis basilica* VU
Arañero de Santa Marta EN
Fairly common resident.
L 14.7 cm (5.8"). Monotypic. Endemic. Humid montane forest, dense shrubby borders, bamboo, overgrown clearings. 2000–3000 m. Pairs or families, adept at remaining out of view, often foraging relatively low. Active, surprisingly acrobatic, hanging upside-down or head down. Follows mixed understorey flocks. **ID** Easily identified by bold black-and-white head pattern, white throat, yellow breast. **Voice** Long chattering series of rising-falling notes lasting up to 20 seconds (mostly at 3.5–5 kHz).

Flavescent Warbler *Myiothlypis flaveola* LC
Arañero Amarillo
Local resident (only Norte de Santander).
L 14 cm (5.5"). Race *pallidirostris*. Dry to moist foothill forest, light or scrubby woodland. 200–1000 m. Modestly 'attired' and retiring, forages on or near ground, sings a little above it, usually from thick cover. Sweeps tail side to side. **ID** Short yellow eyebrow, pale yellow upper and lower eye-arcs, strong blackish bill and lores, pale legs. **Voice** Easily overlooked but for occasional loud song, an emphatic jerky "seeka, seeka SEETA, chew-chew-chew" or variation. **SS** Similar *Myiothlypis* occur higher. **TN** Species often treated as monotypic.

pallidirostris

Black-crested Warbler *Myiothlypis nigrocristata* LC
Arañero Cabecinegro
Common resident.
L 14 cm (5.5"). Monotypic. Humid and wet montane forest, dense shrubby borders, overgrown clearings, *Rubus* (mora) thickets. 2100–3400 m. Pairs, energetic and excitable, sometimes engaging but easier to see when with mixed flocks. **ID** Crisp black central forecrown-stripe, short yellow eyebrow, black loral line and bill. **Voice** Loud vigorous song at dawn sputters, then accelerates into fast chattering "tsuk…tsuk, tsweet-tweet-tweet-ueet'ueet'eet'et'et't't't". **SS** Northern Citrine Warbler.

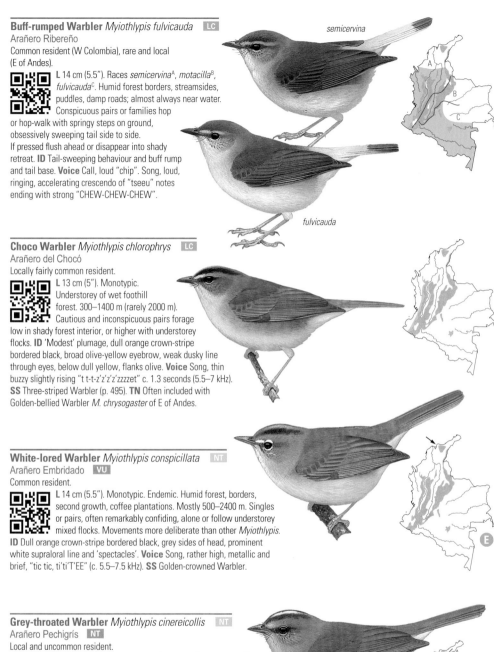

Buff-rumped Warbler *Myiothlypis fulvicauda* `LC`
Arañero Ribereño
Common resident (W Colombia), rare and local
(E of Andes).

L 14 cm (5.5"). Races *semicervina*[A], *motacilla*[B], *fulvicauda*[C]. Humid forest borders, streamsides, puddles, damp roads; almost always near water. Conspicuous pairs or families hop or hop-walk with springy steps on ground, obsessively sweeping tail side to side. If pressed flush ahead or disappear into shady retreat. **ID** Tail-sweeping behaviour and buff rump and tail base. **Voice** Call, loud "chip". Song, loud, ringing, accelerating crescendo of "tseeu" notes ending with strong "CHEW-CHEW-CHEW".

semicervina

fulvicauda

Choco Warbler *Myiothlypis chlorophrys* `LC`
Arañero del Chocó
Locally fairly common resident.

L 13 cm (5"). Monotypic. Understorey of wet foothill forest. 300–1400 m (rarely 2000 m). Cautious and inconspicuous pairs forage low in shady forest interior, or higher with understorey flocks. **ID** 'Modest' plumage, dull orange crown-stripe bordered black, broad olive-yellow eyebrow, weak dusky line through eyes, below dull yellow, flanks olive. **Voice** Song, thin buzzy slightly rising "t t-t-z'z'z'z'zzzzet" c. 1.3 seconds (5.5–7 kHz). **SS** Three-striped Warbler (p. 495). **TN** Often included with Golden-bellied Warbler *M. chrysogaster* of E of Andes.

White-lored Warbler *Myiothlypis conspicillata* `NT`
Arañero Embridado `VU`
Common resident.

L 14 cm (5.5"). Monotypic. Endemic. Humid forest, borders, second growth, coffee plantations. Mostly 500–2400 m. Singles or pairs, often remarkably confiding, alone or follow understorey mixed flocks. Movements more deliberate than other *Myiothlypis*. **ID** Dull orange crown-stripe bordered black, grey sides of head, prominent white supraloral line and 'spectacles'. **Voice** Song, rather high, metallic and brief, "tic tic, ti'ti'T'EE" (c. 5.5–7.5 kHz). **SS** Golden-crowned Warbler.

Grey-throated Warbler *Myiothlypis cinereicollis* `NT`
Arañero Pechigrís `NT`
Local and uncommon resident.

L 14 cm (5.5"). Races *pallidula*[A], *zuliensis*[B], *cinereicollis*[C]. Near-endemic (also W Venezuela). Vine-strewn undergrowth in humid premontane forest, overgrown landslides and treefalls. 800–2100 m. Pairs, retiring and inconspicuous, can be challenging to see. Not always with mixed flocks. **ID** Grey hood imparts dark-headed appearance, semi-concealed yellow crown-stripe, yellow belly. **Voice** Thin, wiry high-pitched song a weak, easily overlooked "sa see-see-sa-SEE!" or "we, we-E-E-a-WEEK!" (last note stronger, higher). **SS** Russet-crowned Warbler (higher elevations).

cinereicollis

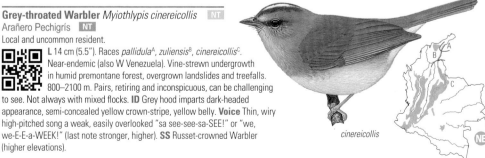

Russet-crowned Warbler *Myiothlypis coronata* `LC`
Arañero Coronado

Eight subspecies in two subspecies groups; one in Colombia.

regulus

Russet-crowned Warbler *Myiothlypis (coronata) coronata*
Fairly common resident.
L 14.5 cm (5.7"). Races *regulus*[A], *elata*[B], *orientalis*[C]. Humid and wet forest. 1500–3100 m. Quiet unassuming pairs forage low in dark understorey, sometimes with mixed flocks. **ID** Rather large dark warbler; head iron-grey, black stripe through eyes, orange-rufous crown-stripe bordered black. **Voice** Sings for short period at first hint of light, a few sputtering notes and smoothly rising glissando "teet, tut't't'u'u'treeeeeEE" or variation, alternately by ♂ and ♀, or in duet, one bird's song rising, the other dropping at end. **SS** Grey-throated Warbler.

Genus *Basileuterus* Mostly dull-plumaged (except Rufous-capped Warbler) resident species of forest or wooded understorey; regularly follow mixed flocks. All have a striped crown or an eyebrow, and a rounded tail; larger and more robust than boreal migrants.

Rufous-capped Warbler *Basileuterus rufifrons* `LC`
Arañero Cabecirrufo

Eight subspecies in two subspecies groups; one in Colombia.

mesochrysus

Chestnut-capped Warbler *Basileuterus (rufifrons) delattrii*
Common resident.
L 13 cm (5"). Race *mesochrysus*. Dry to moist woodland, shrubby borders, coffee plantations. To 1800 m (mostly below 1300 m). Singles or pairs, 'chipper' and spritely, with jaunty cocked tail, forage in thickets or hop on ground. Quite easy to see. **ID** Rufous cap and cheeks separated by white eyebrow. **Voice** Song, fast energetic "tis-tis weecha weecha beEEcher" or variation, ending emphatically.

Pirre Warbler *Basileuterus ignotus* `VU`
Arañero de Pirre `EN`
Local resident (Cerro Alto de Nique, Cerro Tacarcuna).

L 13 cm (5"). Monotypic. Near-endemic (also adjacent Panama). Understorey of humid montane and wet elfin forest. 1000–1800 m. Pairs or small groups, often with mixed flocks. **ID** Chestnut crown, long bold yellowish-white eyestripe, dark olive above, much duller and paler below. **Voice** Call, very high "tzeet" (7.5–8 kHz). Song unrecorded. **SS** Tacarcuna Warbler. **TN** Often regarded as a race of Black-cheeked Warbler *B. melanogenys* of Central America.

Golden-crowned Warbler *Basileuterus culicivorus* `LC`
Arañero Coronidorado

Fourteen subspecies in four subspecies groups; one in Colombia.

Cabanis's Warbler *Basileuterus (culicivorus) cabanisi*
Fairly common resident.
L 13 cm (5"). Races *indignus*[A], *cabanisi*[B], *occultus*[C], *austerus*[D]. Moist (semi-deciduous) to humid forest, light woodland, plantations, shady areas with thickets. 300–2100 m. Confiding pairs or families work through lower vegetation, flicking tail up; may follow mixed flocks. **ID** Grey upperparts contrast with striped crown, orange to yellow coronal stripe, bright yellow underparts. **Voice** Song, chattering "pits-seet-seet-seet-SEET-sit". **SS** Crisper cleaner upperparts than allies; Three-striped Warbler. **TN** All four subspecies groups sometimes treated as species. **AN** Yellow-crowned Warbler.

cabanisi

Three-striped Warbler *Basileuterus tristriatus* `LC`
Arañero Cabecirrayado

Ten subspecies in four to seven subspecies groups (taxonomy-dependent); two in Colombia.

Tacarcuna Warbler *Basileuterus (tristriatus) tacarcunae*
Arañero de Tacarcuna
Local and poorly known resident.
L 13 cm (5"). One subspecies in group. Near-endemic (also adjacent Panama). Undergrowth in humid montane forest. 600–2200 m (?). **ID** Very like Three-striped Warbler, differs in median crown-stripe pale orange (not buff), cheeks olive (not blackish), underparts more yellowish, upperparts paler olive-brown. **Voice** Only one recording known; high jumbled notes (6–8 kHz). **TN** Here treated as an isolated race of Three-striped Warbler. Based on molecular data, now elevated to species status on most checklists. Genetically closest to Three-banded Warbler *B. trifasciatus* of SW Ecuador to NW Peru.

Three-striped Warbler *Basileuterus (tristriatus) tristriatus*
Arañero Cabecirrayado
Common resident.
L 13 cm (5"). Races *sanlucasensis*[A], *daedalus*[B], *auricularis*[C], *baezae*[D] (or *auricularis*?). Humid montane forest, borders, old second growth. 500–2500 m. Pairs or lively, exuberant groups flick up tails as follow understorey flocks or wander alone. **ID** Strong face pattern (intensity varies with race), whitish area below eye, blackish cheeks, underparts more yellowish (*sanlucasensis*). **Voice** Incessant husky "che-weép" while foraging. Song, fast unmusical chipping, more chattering, jumbled at end, sometimes in excitable almost frenzied duets, or several add their voices. **TN** Both Central American races sometimes treated as separate species.

daedalus

Canada Warbler *Cardellina canadensis* `LC`
Reinita de Canadá
Fairly common boreal migrant (Oct–Apr).

L 13 cm (5"). Monotypic. In humid foothill and montane forest, patches of light woodland, coffee plantations. 500–2600 m (scarce in lowlands and Caribbean region where transient, rare E of Andes). Singles, active, sprightly but inconspicuous in understorey, sometimes with mixed flocks. **ID** Grey upperparts, yellow supraloral and eye-ring. ♂'s black 'necklace' fainter in ♀ and 1st-y.

♂

♀

Wilson's Warbler *Cardellina pusilla* `LC`
Rare boreal migrant.

L 13 cm (5"). Races *pileolata* or *chryseola* (latter more likely?), duller eastern *pusilla* (?). Low at humid forest borders, shrubby second growth. To 1800 m. Known from a few sight records and photos. **ID** ♂ small black cap (like yarmulke), yellow foreface and underparts. ♀ cap duller or lacking. Upperparts of western *pileolata* tinged olive. **TN** Eastern and western populations in North America genetically distinct, but identity of Colombian birds unknown.

♂

chryseola

♀

Genus *Myioborus* Widespread montane genus; conspicuous, arboreal and given to bouts of hyperactivity, habitually flashing white in fanned tail, hence often called 'whitestarts' although traditionally known as 'redstarts'. Several species replace one another geographically or elevationally.

Slate-throated Whitestart (Slate-throated Redstart)
Myioborus miniatus `LC`
Abanico Pechinegro

Twelve subspecies in five subspecies groups; one in Colombia.

Yellow-bellied Whitestart *Myioborus (miniatus) verticalis*
Common resident.
L 13.5 cm (5.3"). Races *ballux*[A], *sanctaemartae*[B]. Humid foothill and montane forest, borders. Mostly 1200–2400 m (records 500–2700 m). Fearless, endearing little 'fan-tailed' imp with 'flush-and-chase' foraging strategy, constantly spreading tail, drooping wings, pivoting or executing hyperactive aerobatics. In pairs, often with mixed flocks. **ID** Most widespread *Myioborus*. Dark throat unique. Generally at lower elevations than other *Myioborus*. **Voice** Lively but colourless little warbled "sit-see-see-see-seet" run together. **TN** Based on molecular data, here regarded as a subspecies group separate from Central American groups.

sanctaemartae

Yellow-crowned Whitestart (Yellow-crowned Redstart)
Myioborus flavivertex `LC`
Abanico Colombiano
Common resident.

L 14 cm (5.5"). Monotypic. Endemic. 1200–3100 m. Habits recall Slate-throated Whitestart and sometimes occurs with it, although is a little less animated. **ID** Easily separated by yellow crown, 'spectacles' and all-yellow underparts. **Voice** Song, energetic chippy series of rapid rising-falling notes lasting up to 20 seconds (moderately high, 4–7 kHz). **SS** Slate-throated Whitestart.

Golden-fronted Whitestart (Golden-fronted Redstart)
Myioborus chrysops `LC`
Abanico Cariblanco
Common resident.

L 14 cm (5.5"). Monotypic. Endemic. Humid upper montane forest, borders, cold treeline elfin woodland. 1800–3600 m. Plucky, impertinent pairs flit and sally low to high on periphery of shrubs and trees, sometimes incautiously close to observers, although less animated than Slate-throated Whitestart. Usually with mixed flocks. **ID** Small crest; forecrown, foreface and underparts bright yellow. **Voice** Song, long (up to 20 seconds) rapid energetic jumble of semi-musical rising-falling notes. **TN** May hybridize with Spectacled Whitestart (next page) in E Nariño and adjacent N Ecuador, where apparent intermediates have less yellow on face (so appear more 'spectacled') and varying amounts of rufous on crown. Usually treated as conspecific with *M. ornatus* under name Golden-fronted Redstart.

Yellow-fronted Whitestart (Yellow-fronted Redstart)
Myioborus ornatus `LC`
Abanico Cariblanco
Common resident.

L 14 cm (5.5"). Monotypic. Near-endemic (also adjacent Venezuela). Habitat, elevation, voice and plumage very like Golden-fronted Whitestart but no range overlap. **ID** Differs from Golden-fronted Whitestart mainly in sides of face and small ear-coverts spot white (not yellow). **TN** This and previous species often treated as races of same species.

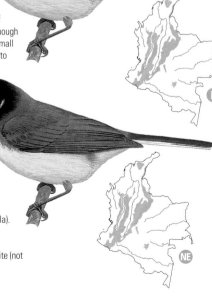

Spectacled Whitestart (Spectacled Redstart)
Myioborus melanocephalus `LC`
Abanico Sureño

 Five subspecies in two subspecies groups; one in Colombia.

ruficoronatus

Rufous-crowned Whitestart *Myioborus (melanocephalus) ruficoronatus*
Abanico Sureño
Uncommon and local resident.
L 13.5 cm (5.3"). Race *ruficoronatus*. Humid upper montane forest and borders, to treeline. 2100–3600 m. Active, conspicuous, sometimes fearless. Typically with mixed flocks. **ID** Supraloral line and eye-ring yellow ('spectacles'), crown patch rufous, underparts yellow. Possible *M. ornatus × M. melanocephalus* hybrids (E Nariño) may show yellow frontlet, larger yellow ocular area. **Voice** Rambling jumbled song similar to Golden-fronted Whitestart. **TN** Relationship to Golden-fronted Whitestart (previous page) unclear.

MITROSPINGIDAE
Aberrant Tanagers
4 extant species, 1 in region

Recently erected family consisting of four species in three genera. All were included with tanagers (Thraupidae) but now united by the results of DNA analysis. Three are dull-plumaged, the fourth black and white with a bright red bill. All are gregarious, opportunistically take fruit and insects, and range over large areas.

Dusky-faced Mitrospingus *Mitrospingus cassinii* `LC`
Maraquera Carisucia
Common resident.

cassinii

 L 18 cm (7"). Race *cassinii*. Thickets, second growth, dense vegetation at humid and wet forest borders and streamsides. To 1200 m. Wander around in small noisy mobs in damp understorey, usually on their own, but occasionally with Tawny-crested Tanagers; generally permit only uncharitably brief views. Nervous, jerky, wing-flicking behaviour distinctive. **ID** Dull and dark, crown and nape 'old gold', sides of head and throat black, eyes white. **Voice** Noisy; a harsh clattering "cheet" and "cheet-it" given incessantly. Apparent song similar but faster and thinner. **AN** Dusky-faced Tanager.

CARDINALIDAE
Cardinals
52 extant species, 26 in region + 1 vagrant

Distinctive family of predominantly Northern Hemisphere, nine-primaried oscines that now includes numerous genera formerly regarded as tanagers (Thraupidae). Two groups predominate, those with strong bills adapted for eating seeds and mixed diets, and those with less robust bills that take softer items including fruit, flowers, buds, and insects. Sexes generally differ, with males often dressed in bold colours. Many are gifted singers; and northern species are mostly migratory.

Genus *Pheucticus* Large and robust, with bold plumage, extremely thick bills, and large white wing spots. Montane and arboreal.

Golden Grosbeak *Pheucticus chrysogaster* `LC`
Picogordo Amarillo

 Two subspecies in two subspecies groups; both in Colombia.

Northern Golden Grosbeak *Pheucticus (chrysogaster) laubmanni*
Fairly common resident.
L 20 cm (8"). One subspecies in group. Humid forest borders, brushy clearings, scrub. 1500–2800 m. Alone or in pairs. Sluggish, often perch fairly high and in open for long periods. **ID** ♂ head and underparts golden-yellow, back black fringed yellow, bold white wingbars, white primary patch (conspicuous in flight), outer primaries edged white, inner flight feathers tipped white. ♀ like ♂ but duller, above streaky and brownish. **Voice** Rich mellow song recalls carolling of *Turdus* thrushes, but smoother, sweeter and slower. Call, high "eek" like other *Pheucticus*.

Southern Golden Grosbeak
Pheucticus (chrysogaster) chrysogaster
Fairly common resident.
L 20 cm (8"). One subspecies in group.
Drier semi-open woodland, woodlots,
patches of brushy second growth.
1700–2800 m. **ID** Much like *laubmanni*
(previous page) but back black (no yellow),
no white primary edges, minor white tips
to inner flight feathers. **Voice** Much like
northern *laubmanni* race of Golden Grosbeak.
SS Both sexes differ from *crissalis* race of
Black-backed Grosbeak (below) by golden-yellow
head; ♀ also by streaked back.

Black-backed Grosbeak *Pheucticus aureoventris* LC
Picogordo Pechinegro

Five subspecies in three subspecies groups;
two in Colombia.

Yellow-throated Grosbeak *Pheucticus (aureoventris) crissalis*
Uncommon and local resident.
L 22 cm (8.5"). One subspecies in group. Moist to arid montane woodland,
brushy semi-open highlands, hedgerows, woodlots. 1700–3200 m (infrequent
lower). Conspicuous and sluggish, sings from high in trees. Singles, pairs,
or several at fruiting trees, usually independent of mixed flocks.
ID ♂ head and upperparts black, bold white wing markings,
throat and chest yellow or flecked with black, rump mostly
yellow. ♀ upperparts tinged olive-brown, indistinct pale
eyebrow. **Voice** Rich mellow carolling much like other
Pheucticus. Call, high "eek". **SS** Southern Golden
Grosbeak (*chrysogaster*).

Yellow-rumped Grosbeak
Pheucticus (aureoventris) uropygialis
Uncommon and local resident.
L 22 cm (8.5"). Race *uropygialis*. Habitat
as *crissalis* (above) but also occurs in more
humid zones. 1700–3200 m. **ID** Similar to
Yellow-throated Grosbeak, but throat and chest
black, rump spotted yellow. **Voice** As above.
SS Northern Golden Grosbeak (*laubmanni*).

uropygialis

Rose-breasted Grosbeak *Pheucticus ludovicianus* LC
Picogordo Degollado
Fairly common boreal migrant (Oct–Apr).
L 19 cm (7.5"). Monotypic.
Dry to humid forest borders, older
second growth, coffee plantations
and parks. To 3400 m (mostly
foothills or higher). Singles or several at fruiting
trees. Gathers in varying-sized groups prior to
migration. **ID** Br ♂ black and white, rose-red bib,
white wing patch. Non-br ♂ tinged and flecked
brownish. ♀ like large brown 'sparrow', with thick bill,
whitish eyebrow and wingbars, streaky underparts.
Voice Sings a little prior to northbound migration,
a sweet syrupy carolling. Call, high "eek".

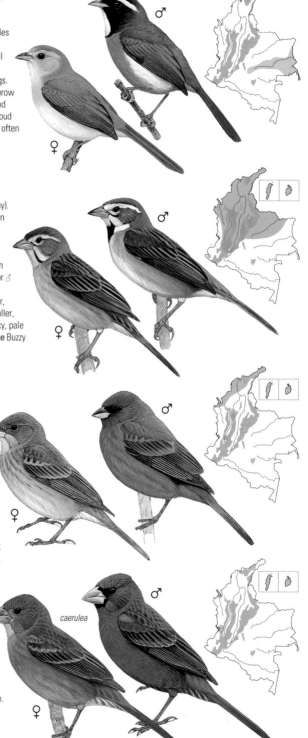

Rose-breasted Chat *Granatellus pelzelni*
Candelita Pechirroja

Uncommon resident (pairs local or widely spaced). **L** 14 cm (5.5"). Monotypic. High vine tangles in humid *várzea* and *terra firme* forest, borders, old treefalls. Distribution not well known. To 300 m. Inconspicuous pairs, mid-levels to canopy, regularly cock tail and droop wings. Often follows mixed flocks. **ID** Gaudy ♂ has white eyebrow and throat, lovely rose underparts. ♀ cinnamon head and chest, and pinkish-rose vent (best mark). **Voice** Song, loud whistled "wheet-wheet-wheet-…" to c. 8 notes. Most often detected by nasal "tank" or "tank-tank" call.

Dickcissel *Spiza americana*
Arrocero Norteño

Uncommon to abundant boreal migrant (Sept–early May). **L** 15 cm (6"). Monotypic. Brushy semi-open terrain, agricultural areas, rice fields. To c. 1600 m. Singles or small mobile groups, but gathers in immense numbers in rice fields, especially if nearby cover offers protection from aerial predators. Feeds on or near ground. **ID** Ad br ♂ sparrow-like; strong bill, greyish head, yellow eyebrow becomes white rearward, yellow malar, rufous shoulder, black V on yellow breast. ♂ non-br duller. Ad ♀ even duller, less yellow, black V faint or lacking. 1st-w above streaky, pale eyebrow, hint of yellow on finely streaked breast. **Voice** Buzzy "fit" in flight. **SS** Grassland Yellow-finch (p. 530).

Indigo Bunting *Passerina cyanea*
Azulillo Norteño

Common boreal migrant (islands), rare mainland (Oct–mid-Apr). **L** 14 cm (5.5"). Monotypic. Dry to humid wooded borders, brushy thickets. To 1800 m. Singles or small loose groups on islands; one or a few reported annually on mainland. **ID** Small. Ad ♂ rich cobalt-blue. Ad non-br ♂ brownish with flecks or patches of blue. Ad non-br ♀ brownish, two weak cinnamon wingbars, throat whitish, otherwise below dingy cinnamon-brown, vaguely streaked, bill bicoloured. Br ♀ like non-br but tail bluish. **Voice** Flight call, buzzy "jzzk". **SS** ♀ Blue Seedeater, Blue Grosbeak.

Blue Grosbeak *Passerina caerulea*
Azulón Norteño

Rare boreal migrant (islands), vagrant (mainland). **L** 16.5 cm (6.5"). Race *caerulea*? Dry to humid wooded areas. **ID** Ad ♂ deep blue, bold rufous wingbars, thick bill dark above. Ad ♀ pale grey-brown, wingbars buffy brown. 1st-w ♂ and ♀ like br ♀ but reddish brown. 1st-s ♂ mixed blue and brown, rufous wingbars. **SS** Indigo Bunting.

caerulea

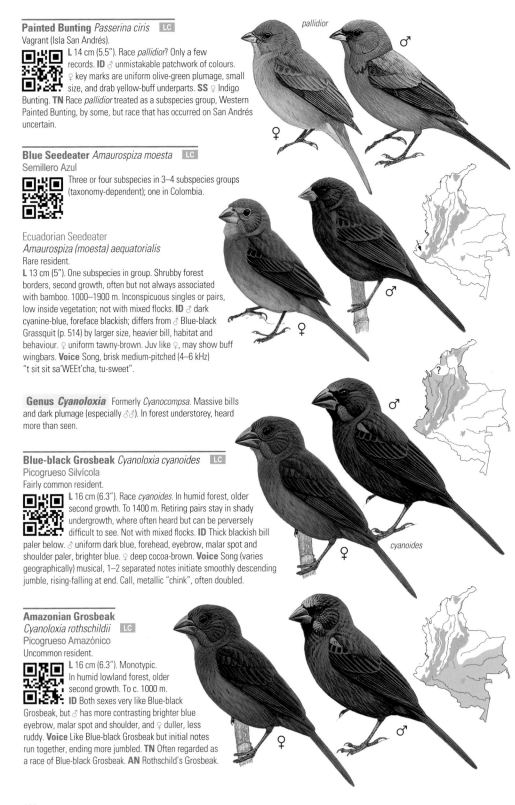

Painted Bunting *Passerina ciris* `LC`
Vagrant (Isla San Andrés).

L 14 cm (5.5"). Race *pallidior*? Only a few records. **ID** ♂ unmistakable patchwork of colours. ♀ key marks are uniform olive-green plumage, small size, and drab yellow-buff underparts. **SS** ♀ Indigo Bunting. **TN** Race *pallidior* treated as a subspecies group, Western Painted Bunting, by some, but race that has occurred on San Andrés uncertain.

pallidior

♂

♀

Blue Seedeater *Amaurospiza moesta* `LC`
Semillero Azul

Three or four subspecies in 3–4 subspecies groups (taxonomy-dependent); one in Colombia.

Ecuadorian Seedeater
Amaurospiza (moesta) aequatorialis
Rare resident.

L 13 cm (5"). One subspecies in group. Shrubby forest borders, second growth, often but not always associated with bamboo. 1000–1900 m. Inconspicuous singles or pairs, low inside vegetation; not with mixed flocks. **ID** ♂ dark cyanine-blue, foreface blackish; differs from ♂ Blue-black Grassquit (p. 514) by larger size, heavier bill, habitat and behaviour. ♀ uniform tawny-brown. Juv like ♀, may show buff wingbars. **Voice** Song, brisk medium-pitched (4–6 kHz) "t sit sit sa'WEEt'cha, tu-sweet".

♂

♀

Genus *Cyanoloxia* Formerly *Cyanocompsa*. Massive bills and dark plumage (especially ♂♂). In forest understorey, heard more than seen.

♂

Blue-black Grosbeak *Cyanoloxia cyanoides* `LC`
Picogrueso Silvícola
Fairly common resident.

L 16 cm (6.3"). Race *cyanoides*. In humid forest, older second growth. To 1400 m. Retiring pairs stay in shady undergrowth, where often heard but can be perversely difficult to see. Not with mixed flocks. **ID** Thick blackish bill paler below. ♂ uniform dark blue, forehead, eyebrow, malar spot and shoulder paler, brighter blue. ♀ deep cocoa-brown. **Voice** Song (varies geographically) musical, 1–2 separated notes initiate smoothly descending jumble, rising-falling at end. Call, metallic "chink", often doubled.

cyanoides

♀

Amazonian Grosbeak
Cyanoloxia rothschildii `LC`
Picogrueso Amazónico
Uncommon resident.

L 16 cm (6.3"). Monotypic. In humid lowland forest, older second growth. To c. 1000 m. **ID** Both sexes very like Blue-black Grosbeak, but ♂ has more contrasting brighter blue eyebrow, malar spot and shoulder, and ♀ duller, less ruddy. **Voice** Like Blue-black Grosbeak but initial notes run together, ending more jumbled. **TN** Often regarded as a race of Blue-black Grosbeak. **AN** Rothschild's Grosbeak.

♂

♀

Ultramarine Grosbeak *Cyanoloxia brissonii* `LC`
Picogrueso Ultramarino

Local resident (arid Dagua, Patía and upper Cauca Valleys). **L** 15 cm (6"). Race *caucae*. Dry to arid woodland, brushy ravines, scrub. 300–1600 m. Skulking like Blue-black Grosbeak but easier to see in dry vegetation. Singles or pairs stay low, not with other birds. **ID** ♂ and ♀ resemble Blue-black Grosbeak but habitat and range differ, bill shorter, swollen. ♂'s frontlet, eyebrow, malar spot and shoulder much brighter azure-blue. ♀ snuff-brown, decidedly paler than ♀ Blue-black, especially below. **Voice** Recalls Blue-black Grosbeak but higher and faster. Call, metallic "pik".

caucae

♂

♀

Genus *Habia* Robust with strong bills. In forest understorey, lowlands or foothills (one higher). Often noisy. Two groups, (1) four species, ♂♂ with red in plumage, crested or coloured crown-stripes, and simple musical songs; all wary, and follow army ant swarms to varying degrees; (2) four species, all formerly in *Chlorothraupis*, dull-plumaged, but less wary, mostly in foothills, and have complex dawn songs.

Red-throated Ant-tanager *Habia fuscicauda* `LC`
Habia Gorgirroja

Six subspecies in two subspecies groups; one in Colombia.

♂

Red-throated Ant-tanager *Habia (fuscicauda) fuscicauda*
Habia Gorgirroja

Very local, declining and range-restricted resident. **L** 19 cm (7.5"). Race *erythrolaema*. Dry to moist forest, older second growth. To 200 m. Pairs or small groups, low inside forest; may follow army ants. **ID** ♂ dull, dusky red, concealed scarlet coronal stripe, throat rose-red. ♀ above olive-brown, below olive-yellow, throat yellowish. **Voice** Main song musical, a few slow, halting, low whistles, often in repetitive 2–3-note patterns. Large repertoire of calls, mob with raspy "juu, juu…".

erythrolaema

♀

Sooty Ant-tanager *Habia gutturalis* `NT`
Habia Ceniza `NT`

Local resident. **L** 19 cm (7.5"). Monotypic. Endemic. Shady undergrowth in humid forest, dense second growth, bushy borders in lowlands and foothills. 100–1400 m. Pairs or families, wary but sometimes curious; invariably noted first by voice. Usually not with mixed flocks. **ID** Unmistakable ♂ slaty black with bright pinkish-red crest and throat. ♀ similar, crest shorter, red throat restricted. **Voice** Halting song of low-pitched musical 2–4-note whistled phrases, repetitive and hypnotic but interspersed by raspy chattering.

Crested Ant-tanager *Habia cristata* `LC`
Habia Copetona

Fairly common resident. **L** 19 cm (7.5"). Monotypic. Endemic. Shady undergrowth in humid and wet forest, steep ravines, dense streamside vegetation. 700–2100 m. Pairs, families or small groups, fast-moving, noisy, always wary and suspicious, sometimes with mixed flocks. Mixed fruit and insect diet. **ID** ♂ large crest and foreparts bright red, rear parts darker, dusky red, belly greyish. ♀ slightly duller, crest shorter. **Voice** Mobs with shrill "chi-veek!". Dawn song, 3–4 unmusical "che'ik" notes.

Red-crowned Ant-tanager *Habia rubica* `LC`
Habia Coronada

Seventeen subspecies in three subspecies groups; one in Colombia.

Scarlet-throated Ant-tanager *Habia (rubica) rubra*
Fairly common resident.
L 18 cm (7"). Races *perijana*[A], *coccinea*[B], *rhodinolaema*[C].
Understorey in humid forest, tall second growth.
To 800 m. Pairs or groups, wary, apt to move away
quickly but sometimes curious; may follow understorey
mixed flocks. **ID** ♂ brownish red, semi-concealed red crest
bordered black, throat red. ♀ above olive, semi-concealed
crown-stripe and throat brownish yellow. **Voice** Scold, rough
grating "chak". Sweet dawn, day and dusk songs vary geographically,
melancholy 2–4-syllable phrases repeated slowly, "tjee, dear, dear".

coccinea

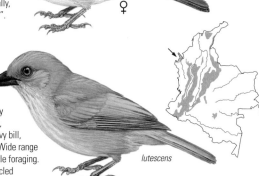

Carmiol's Tanager *Habia carmioli* `LC`
Guayabero de Carmiol
Local resident (Panama border).

L 18 cm (7"). Race *lutescens*. Humid and wet
foothill forest, tall second growth. 200–1400 m. Noisy
groups up to 15+ actively work through lower growth,
sometimes with other species. **ID** Robust shape, heavy bill,
dull ♀-like plumage. Olive-green, slightly yellowish below. **Voice** Wide range
of chatters, squeaks, churrs and other notes, given incessantly while foraging.
SS ♀ Red-crowned and Red-throated Ant-tanagers, Lemon-spectacled
Tanager. **TN** Formerly in *Chlorothraupis*.

lutescens

Yellow-lored Tanager *Habia frenata* `LC`
Guayabero Cejiamarillo
Uncommon resident.

L 18 cm (7"). Monotypic. Inside humid and wet foothill forest, dense
ravines. 500–1100 m. Small groups at low to mid-levels, active and
noisy, often with mixed flocks. **ID** Both sexes very like Carmiol's
Tanager (no overlap) but voices quite different. ♂ has lores and face
paler. ♀ lores, face and throat more yellowish. **Voice** Harsh raspy chattering.
Remarkable dawn song, for short periods, variable stream of loud non-stop phrases,
each repeated a few times, then changes. **TN** Formerly in *Chlorothraupis*. Usually
considered a race of Carmiol's Tanager.

Lemon-spectacled Tanager *Habia olivacea* `LC`
Guayabero Oliváceo
Uncommon resident.

L 18 cm (7"). Monotypic. Near-endemic (also extreme
SE Panama and NW Ecuador). Understorey to mid-levels
in wet lowland and foothill forest. To 1000 m (mostly below
600 m). Inconspicuous, pairs or small groups, often with
mixed flocks. **ID** Heavy dusky bill; dark olive with bright yellow 'spectacles',
yellowish throat. **Voice** Incessant chattering "chu, chu…cheat, cheat, turee,
turee…" while foraging. Long complex dawn song. **SS** Ochre-breasted Tanager
(foothills and higher). **TN** Formerly in *Chlorothraupis*.

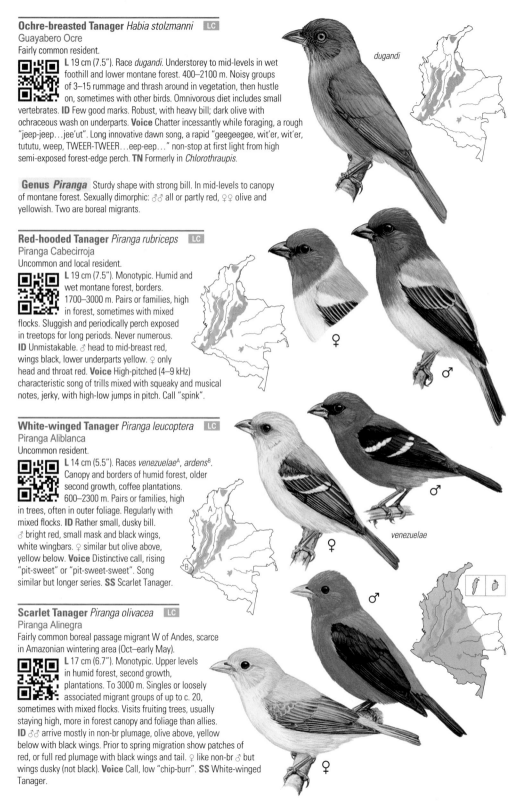

Ochre-breasted Tanager *Habia stolzmanni* `LC`
Guayabero Ocre
Fairly common resident.

L 19 cm (7.5"). Race *dugandi*. Understorey to mid-levels in wet foothill and lower montane forest. 400–2100 m. Noisy groups of 3–15 rummage and thrash around in vegetation, then hustle on, sometimes with other birds. Omnivorous diet includes small vertebrates. **ID** Few good marks. Robust, with heavy bill; dark olive with ochraceous wash on underparts. **Voice** Chatter incessantly while foraging, a rough "jeep-jeep…jee'ut". Long innovative dawn song, a rapid "geegeegee, wit'er, wit'er, tututu, weep, TWEER-TWEER…eep-eep…" non-stop at first light from high semi-exposed forest-edge perch. **TN** Formerly in *Chlorothraupis*.

dugandi

Genus *Piranga* Sturdy shape with strong bill. In mid-levels to canopy of montane forest. Sexually dimorphic: ♂♂ all or partly red, ♀♀ olive and yellowish. Two are boreal migrants.

Red-hooded Tanager *Piranga rubriceps* `LC`
Piranga Cabecirroja
Uncommon and local resident.

L 19 cm (7.5"). Monotypic. Humid and wet montane forest, borders. 1700–3000 m. Pairs or families, high in forest, sometimes with mixed flocks. Sluggish and periodically perch exposed in treetops for long periods. Never numerous. **ID** Unmistakable. ♂ head to mid-breast red, wings black, lower underparts yellow. ♀ only head and throat red. **Voice** High-pitched (4–9 kHz) characteristic song of trills mixed with squeaky and musical notes, jerky, with high-low jumps in pitch. Call "spink".

♀

♂

White-winged Tanager *Piranga leucoptera* `LC`
Piranga Aliblanca
Uncommon resident.

L 14 cm (5.5"). Races *venezuelae*[A], *ardens*[B]. Canopy and borders of humid forest, older second growth, coffee plantations. 600–2300 m. Pairs or families, high in trees, often in outer foliage. Regularly with mixed flocks. **ID** Rather small, dusky bill. ♂ bright red, small mask and black wings, white wingbars. ♀ similar but olive above, yellow below. **Voice** Distinctive call, rising "pit-sweet" or "pit-sweet-sweet". Song similar but longer series. **SS** Scarlet Tanager.

♀

♂

venezuelae

Scarlet Tanager *Piranga olivacea* `LC`
Piranga Alinegra
Fairly common boreal passage migrant W of Andes, scarce in Amazonian wintering area (Oct–early May).

L 17 cm (6.7"). Monotypic. Upper levels in humid forest, second growth, plantations. To 3000 m. Singles or loosely associated migrant groups of up to c. 20, sometimes with mixed flocks. Visits fruiting trees, usually staying high, more in forest canopy and foliage than allies. **ID** ♂♂ arrive mostly in non-br plumage, olive above, yellow below with black wings. Prior to spring migration show patches of red, or full red plumage with black wings and tail. ♀ like non-br ♂ but wings dusky (not black). **Voice** Call, low "chip-burr". **SS** White-winged Tanager.

♂

♀

Summer Tanager *Piranga rubra* `LC`
Piranga Abejera

Common boreal winter resident (Oct–early May). **L** 18 cm (7"). Race *rubra*. Generally high at humid forest borders, open second growth, plantations. To 3200 m. Singles or small post- and pre-migratory groups, often with mixed flocks. **ID** Stout pale yellowish bill, darker post-breeding. Ad ♂ bright rosy red. 1st-s ♂ variably blotched red, yellow and olive. ♀ above olive including wings (no wingbars), below yellowish to orange-yellow, faint broken whitish eye-ring. **Voice** Call, descending "pik'a-tuk". **SS** Hepatic Tanager, ♀ Scarlet Tanager.

Hepatic Tanager *Piranga hepatica* `LC`
Piranga Bermeja

Eleven subspecies in two subspecies groups; one in Colombia.

Highland Hepatic-tanager *Piranga (hepatica) lutea*
Fairly common resident.

L 18 cm (7"). Races *desidiosa*[A], *lutea*[B], *faceta*[C], *toddi*[D]. Open montane woodland, borders, clearings. 1500–2400 m. Singles or pairs, low to high (usually fairly high), follow flocks. **ID** Bill dusky above, paler below. ♂ dull geranium-red (brightness varies with race, *lutea* brightest), lores, wings and tail dusky red. ♀ above dusky olive, below yellowish. **Voice** Husky "chup", heavy staccato "chid'di'dit". Song, 5–10 slow musical notes, recalls *Turdus* thrush. **SS** Summer Tanager, ♀ Scarlet Tanager.

Vermilion Cardinal *Cardinalis phoeniceus* `LC`
Cardenal Guajiro `VU`

Fairly common resident.

L 20 cm (8"). Monotypic. Desert scrub, arid thickets, scrub woodland. To 400 m. ♂♂ perch up with erect posture and upstanding crest, atop *Acacia* to sing at dawn; otherwise pairs in thickets or on ground. Wary but sharp "chip" notes betray presence. **ID** Thick bill, unusually tall crest. ♂ unmistakable. ♀ more sombre, thick bill and crest diagnostic. **Voice** Not a persistent singer. Song, slow sweet whistled "cheer…o-weet…toweet, toweet, toweet" or "swit-sweet…chee-chEEo…swit-sweet…", halting and pattern variable. Sings more at onset of rains in May.

Yellow-green Grosbeak *Caryothraustes canadensis* `LC`
Picogordo de Antifaz

Uncommon to locally common resident.

L 16.5 cm (6.5"). Races *canadensis*[A], *simulans*[B] (Alto de Nique, Panama; Colombia?). Humid forest, borders. Commonest in white-sand forests (*canadensis*, to 400 m); humid foothills on Panama border (750–1200 m). Vocal pairs or groups troop around in mid-levels or higher, with mixed flocks or independently. **ID** Olive plumage, small black foreface, bicoloured bill. **Voice** Loud, often-repeated "teach-yerp" or buzzy "bzzit". Dawn song, monotonously repeated "chap-chap-cheeweep".

408 extant species, 179 in region + 1 vagrant

This huge, diverse family has recently undergone dramatic taxonomic revisions based on molecular data, and now includes many genera formerly placed in other families (e.g. *Emberizoides*, *Melanospiza*, *Asemospiza*, *Coryphospingus*, *Rhodospingus*, *Saltator*, *Tiaris*, *Sporophila*, *Geospizopsis*, *Spodiornis*, *Catamenia*, *Paroaria* etc.). Several long-established genera (e.g. *Tangara*) have been split into multiple genera, but relationships in others (e.g. *Tachyphonus*) remain unresolved. The family includes colourful canopy-dwelling nectarivores, frugivores, insectivores and omnivores, and now also many open-country seed-eating species. Several genera formerly regarded as tanagers, e.g. *Euphonia*, *Chlorothraupis*, *Chlorospingus*, *Mitrospingus* and *Piranga* have been transferred elsewhere. Further taxonomic revisions are likely, as well as English name changes.

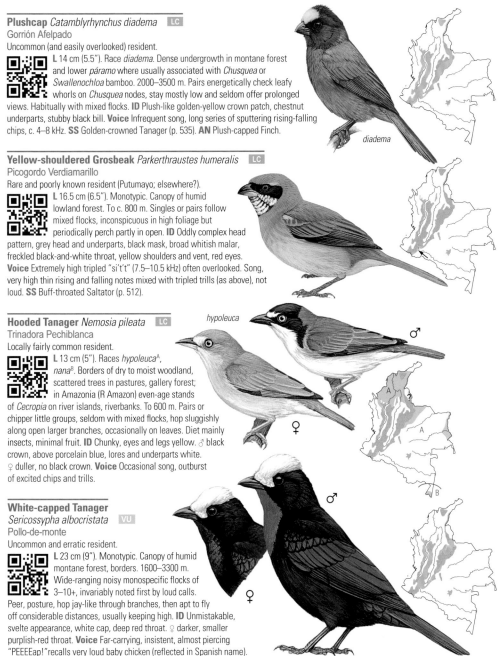

Plushcap *Catamblyrhynchus diadema* LC
Gorrión Afelpado
Uncommon (and easily overlooked) resident.
L 14 cm (5.5"). Race *diadema*. Dense undergrowth in montane forest and lower *páramo* where usually associated with *Chusquea* or *Swallenochloa* bamboo. 2000–3500 m. Pairs energetically check leafy whorls on *Chusquea* nodes, stay mostly low and seldom offer prolonged views. Habitually with mixed flocks. **ID** Plush-like golden-yellow crown patch, chestnut underparts, stubby black bill. **Voice** Infrequent song, long series of sputtering rising-falling chips, c. 4–8 kHz. **SS** Golden-crowned Tanager (p. 535). **AN** Plush-capped Finch.

diadema

Yellow-shouldered Grosbeak *Parkerthraustes humeralis* LC
Picogordo Verdiamarillo
Rare and poorly known resident (Putumayo; elsewhere?).
L 16.5 cm (6.5"). Monotypic. Canopy of humid lowland forest. To c. 800 m. Singles or pairs follow mixed flocks, inconspicuous in high foliage but periodically perch partly in open. **ID** Oddly complex head pattern, grey head and underparts, black mask, broad whitish malar, freckled black-and-white throat, yellow shoulders and vent, red eyes. **Voice** Extremely high tripled "si't't" (7.5–10.5 kHz) often overlooked. Song, very high thin rising and falling notes mixed with tripled trills (as above), not loud. **SS** Buff-throated Saltator (p. 512).

Hooded Tanager *Nemosia pileata* LC
hypoleuca
Trinadora Pechiblanca
Locally fairly common resident.
L 13 cm (5"). Races *hypoleuca*[A], *nana*[B]. Borders of dry to moist woodland, scattered trees in pastures, gallery forest; in Amazonia (R Amazon) even-age stands of *Cecropia* on river islands, riverbanks. To 600 m. Pairs or chipper little groups, seldom with mixed flocks, hop sluggishly along open larger branches, occasionally on leaves. Diet mainly insects, minimal fruit. **ID** Chunky, eyes and legs yellow. ♂ black crown, above porcelain blue, lores and underparts white. ♀ duller, no black crown. **Voice** Occasional song, outburst of excited chips and trills.

White-capped Tanager
Sericossypha albocristata VU
Pollo-de-monte
Uncommon and erratic resident.
L 23 cm (9"). Monotypic. Canopy of humid montane forest, borders. 1600–3300 m. Wide-ranging noisy monospecific flocks of 3–10+, invariably noted first by loud calls. Peer, posture, hop jay-like through branches, then apt to fly off considerable distances, usually keeping high. **ID** Unmistakable, svelte appearance, white cap, deep red throat. ♀ darker, smaller purplish-red throat. **Voice** Far-carrying, insistent, almost piercing "PEEEEap!" recalls very loud baby chicken (reflected in Spanish name).

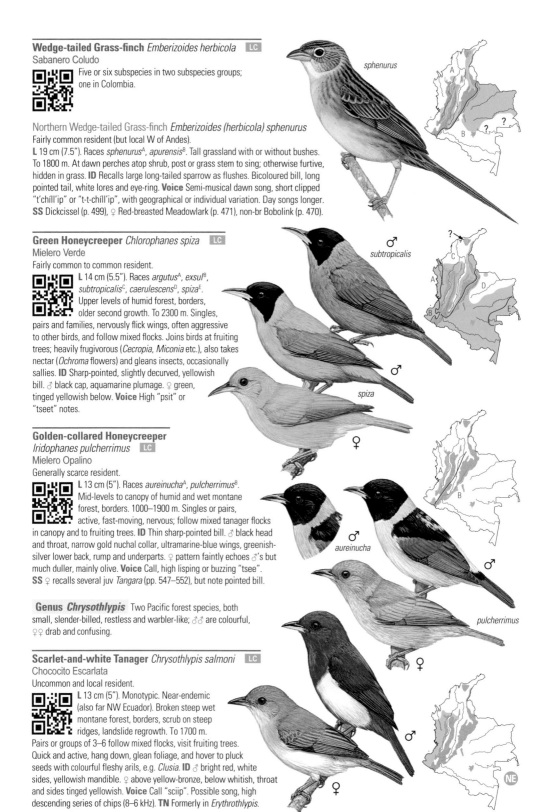

Wedge-tailed Grass-finch *Emberizoides herbicola* `LC`
Sabanero Coludo

Five or six subspecies in two subspecies groups; one in Colombia.

Northern Wedge-tailed Grass-finch *Emberizoides (herbicola) sphenurus*
Fairly common resident (but local W of Andes).
L 19 cm (7.5"). Races *sphenurus*[A], *apurensis*[B]. Tall grassland with or without bushes. To 1800 m. At dawn perches atop shrub, post or grass stem to sing; otherwise furtive, hidden in grass. **ID** Recalls large long-tailed sparrow as flushes. Bicoloured bill, long pointed tail, white lores and eye-ring. **Voice** Semi-musical dawn song, short clipped "t'chíll'ip" or "t-t-chíll'ip", with geographical or individual variation. Day songs longer. **SS** Dickcissel (p. 499), ♀ Red-breasted Meadowlark (p. 471), non-br Bobolink (p. 470).

Green Honeycreeper *Chlorophanes spiza* `LC`
Mielero Verde

Fairly common to common resident.

L 14 cm (5.5"). Races *argutus*[A], *exsul*[B], *subtropicalis*[C], *caerulescens*[D], *spiza*[E]. Upper levels of humid forest, borders, older second growth. To 2300 m. Singles, pairs and families, nervously flick wings, often aggressive to other birds, and follow mixed flocks. Joins birds at fruiting trees; heavily frugivorous (*Cecropia, Miconia* etc.), also takes nectar (*Ochroma* flowers) and gleans insects, occasionally sallies. **ID** Sharp-pointed, slightly decurved, yellowish bill. ♂ black cap, aquamarine plumage. ♀ green, tinged yellowish below. **Voice** High "psit" or "tseet" notes.

Golden-collared Honeycreeper
Iridophanes pulcherrimus `LC`
Mielero Opalino

Generally scarce resident.

L 13 cm (5"). Races *aureinucha*[A], *pulcherrimus*[B]. Mid-levels to canopy of humid and wet montane forest, borders. 1000–1900 m. Singles or pairs, active, fast-moving, nervous; follow mixed tanager flocks in canopy and to fruiting trees. **ID** Thin sharp-pointed bill. ♂ black head and throat, narrow gold nuchal collar, ultramarine-blue wings, greenish-silver lower back, rump and underparts. ♀ pattern faintly echoes ♂'s but much duller, mainly olive. **Voice** Call, high lisping or buzzing "tsee". **SS** ♀ recalls several juv *Tangara* (pp. 547–552), but note pointed bill.

Genus *Chrysothlypis* Two Pacific forest species, both small, slender-billed, restless and warbler-like; ♂♂ are colourful, ♀♀ drab and confusing.

Scarlet-and-white Tanager *Chrysothlypis salmoni* `LC`
Chococito Escarlata

Uncommon and local resident.

L 13 cm (5"). Monotypic. Near-endemic (also far NW Ecuador). Broken steep wet montane forest, borders, scrub on steep ridges, landslide regrowth. To 1700 m. Pairs or groups of 3–6 follow mixed flocks, visit fruiting trees. Quick and active, hang down, glean foliage, and hover to pluck seeds with colourful fleshy arils, e.g. *Clusia*. **ID** ♂ bright red, white sides, yellowish mandible. ♀ above yellow-bronze, below whitish, throat and sides tinged yellowish. **Voice** Call "sciip". Possible song, high descending series of chips (8–6 kHz). **TN** Formerly in *Erythrothlypis*.

sphenurus

subtropicalis

♂

spiza

♀

aureinucha

♂

♀

pulcherrimus

♀

♂

♀

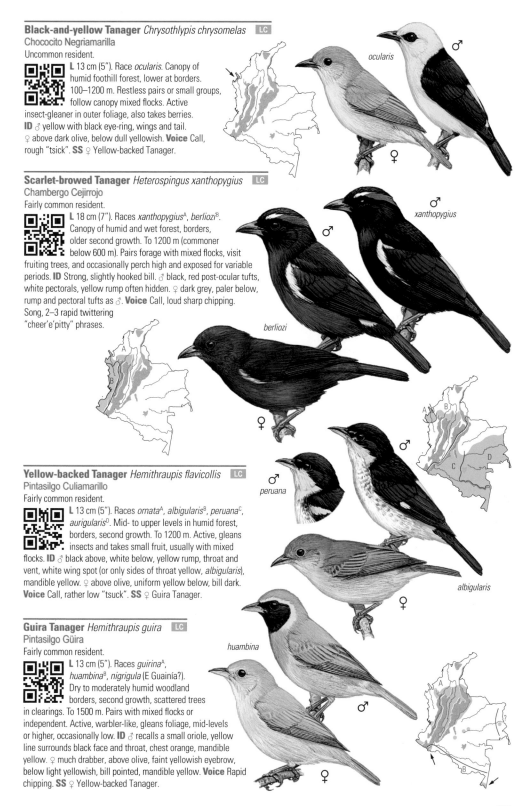

Black-and-yellow Tanager *Chrysothlypis chrysomelas* `LC`
Chococito Negriamarilla
Uncommon resident.

L 13 cm (5"). Race *ocularis*. Canopy of humid foothill forest, lower at borders. 100–1200 m. Restless pairs or small groups, follow canopy mixed flocks. Active insect-gleaner in outer foliage, also takes berries. **ID** ♂ yellow with black eye-ring, wings and tail. ♀ above dark olive, below dull yellowish. **Voice** Call, rough "tsick". **SS** ♀ Yellow-backed Tanager.

ocularis

Scarlet-browed Tanager *Heterospingus xanthopygius* `LC`
Chambergo Cejirrojo
Fairly common resident.

L 18 cm (7"). Races *xanthopygius*[A], *berliozi*[B]. Canopy of humid and wet forest, borders, older second growth. To 1200 m (commoner below 600 m). Pairs forage with mixed flocks, visit fruiting trees, and occasionally perch high and exposed for variable periods. **ID** Strong, slightly hooked bill. ♂ black, red post-ocular tufts, white pectorals, yellow rump often hidden. ♀ dark grey, paler below, rump and pectoral tufts as ♂. **Voice** Call, loud sharp chipping. Song, 2–3 rapid twittering "cheer'e'pitty" phrases.

xanthopygius

berliozi

Yellow-backed Tanager *Hemithraupis flavicollis* `LC`
Pintasilgo Culiamarillo
Fairly common resident.

L 13 cm (5"). Races *ornata*[A], *albigularis*[B], *peruana*[C], *aurigularis*[D]. Mid- to upper levels in humid forest, borders, second growth. To 1200 m. Active, gleans insects and takes small fruit, usually with mixed flocks. **ID** ♂ black above, white below, yellow rump, throat and vent, white wing spot (or only sides of throat yellow, *albigularis*), mandible yellow. ♀ above olive, uniform yellow below, bill dark. **Voice** Call, rather low "tsuck". **SS** ♀ Guira Tanager.

peruana

albigularis

Guira Tanager *Hemithraupis guira* `LC`
Pintasilgo Güira
Fairly common resident.

L 13 cm (5"). Races *guirina*[A], *huambina*[B], *nigrigula* (E Guainía?). Dry to moderately humid woodland borders, second growth, scattered trees in clearings. To 1500 m. Pairs with mixed flocks or independent. Active, warbler-like, gleans foliage, mid-levels or higher, occasionally low. **ID** ♂ recalls a small oriole, yellow line surrounds black face and throat, chest orange, mandible yellow. ♀ much drabber, above olive, faint yellowish eyebrow, below light yellowish, bill pointed, mandible yellow. **Voice** Rapid chipping. **SS** ♀ Yellow-backed Tanager.

huambina

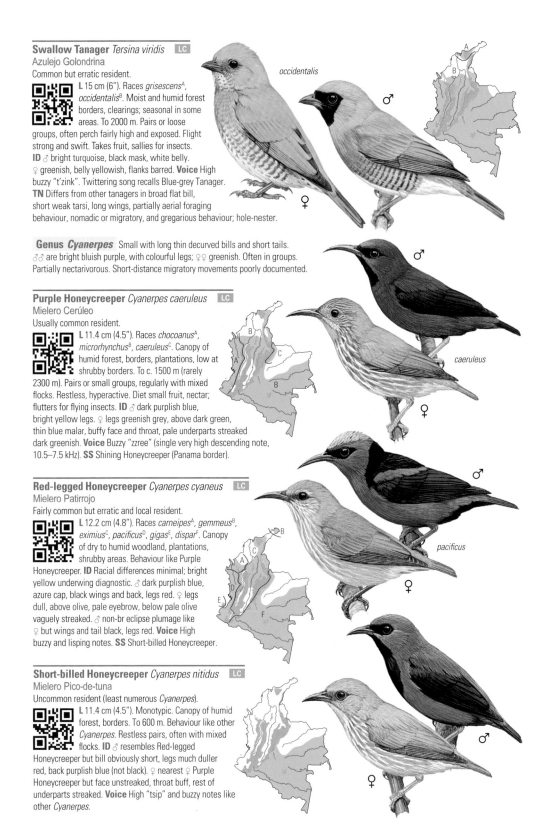

Swallow Tanager *Tersina viridis* `LC`
Azulejo Golondrina

Common but erratic resident.

L 15 cm (6"). Races *grisescens*[A], *occidentalis*[B]. Moist and humid forest borders, clearings; seasonal in some areas. To 2000 m. Pairs or loose groups, often perch fairly high and exposed. Flight strong and swift. Takes fruit, sallies for insects. **ID** ♂ bright turquoise, black mask, white belly. ♀ greenish, belly yellowish, flanks barred. **Voice** High buzzy "t'zink". Twittering song recalls Blue-grey Tanager. **TN** Differs from other tanagers in broad flat bill, short weak tarsi, long wings, partially aerial foraging behaviour, nomadic or migratory, and gregarious behaviour; hole-nester.

occidentalis

♂

♀

Genus *Cyanerpes* Small with long thin decurved bills and short tails. ♂♂ are bright bluish purple, with colourful legs; ♀♀ greenish. Often in groups. Partially nectarivorous. Short-distance migratory movements poorly documented.

Purple Honeycreeper *Cyanerpes caeruleus* `LC`
Mielero Cerúleo

Usually common resident.

L 11.4 cm (4.5"). Races *chocoanus*[A], *microrhynchus*[B], *caeruleus*[C]. Canopy of humid forest, borders, plantations, low at shrubby borders. To c. 1500 m (rarely 2300 m). Pairs or small groups, regularly with mixed flocks. Restless, hyperactive. Diet small fruit, nectar; flutters for flying insects. **ID** ♂ dark purplish blue, bright yellow legs. ♀ legs greenish grey, above dark green, thin blue malar, buffy face and throat, pale underparts streaked dark greenish. **Voice** Buzzy "zzree" (single very high descending note, 10.5–7.5 kHz). **SS** Shining Honeycreeper (Panama border).

♂

caeruleus

♀

Red-legged Honeycreeper *Cyanerpes cyaneus* `LC`
Mielero Patirrojo

Fairly common but erratic and local resident.

L 12.2 cm (4.8"). Races *carneipes*[A], *gemmeus*[B], *eximius*[C], *pacificus*[D], *gigas*[E], *dispar*[F]. Canopy of dry to humid woodland, plantations, shrubby areas. Behaviour like Purple Honeycreeper. **ID** Racial differences minimal; bright yellow underwing diagnostic. ♂ dark purplish blue, azure cap, black wings and back, legs red. ♀ legs dull, above olive, pale eyebrow, below pale olive vaguely streaked. ♂ non-br eclipse plumage like ♀ but wings and tail black, legs red. **Voice** High buzzy and lisping notes. **SS** Short-billed Honeycreeper.

♂

pacificus

♀

Short-billed Honeycreeper *Cyanerpes nitidus* `LC`
Mielero Pico-de-tuna

Uncommon resident (least numerous *Cyanerpes*).

L 11.4 cm (4.5"). Monotypic. Canopy of humid forest, borders. To 600 m. Behaviour like other *Cyanerpes*. Restless pairs, often with mixed flocks. **ID** ♂ resembles Red-legged Honeycreeper but bill obviously short, legs much duller red, back purplish blue (not black). ♀ nearest ♀ Purple Honeycreeper but face unstreaked, throat buff, rest of underparts streaked. **Voice** High "tsip" and buzzy notes like other *Cyanerpes*.

♂

♀

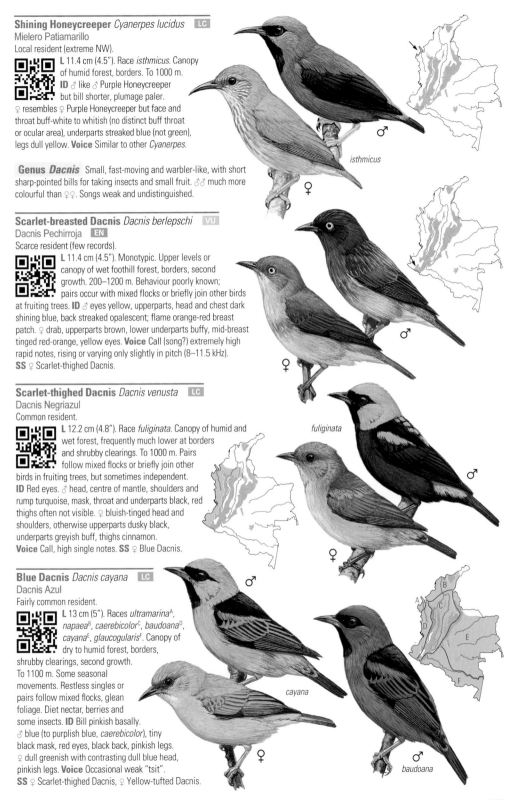

Shining Honeycreeper *Cyanerpes lucidus* `LC`
Mielero Patiamarillo
Local resident (extreme NW).
L 11.4 cm (4.5"). Race *isthmicus*. Canopy of humid forest, borders. To 1000 m. **ID** ♂ like ♂ Purple Honeycreeper but bill shorter, plumage paler.
♀ resembles ♀ Purple Honeycreeper but face and throat buff-white to whitish (no distinct buff throat or ocular area), underparts streaked blue (not green), legs dull yellow. **Voice** Similar to other *Cyanerpes*.

isthmicus

Genus *Dacnis* Small, fast-moving and warbler-like, with short sharp-pointed bills for taking insects and small fruit. ♂♂ much more colourful than ♀♀. Songs weak and undistinguished.

Scarlet-breasted Dacnis *Dacnis berlepschi* `VU`
Dacnis Pechirroja `EN`
Scarce resident (few records).
L 11.4 cm (4.5"). Monotypic. Upper levels or canopy of wet foothill forest, borders, second growth. 200–1200 m. Behaviour poorly known; pairs occur with mixed flocks or briefly join other birds at fruiting trees. **ID** ♂ eyes yellow, upperparts, head and chest dark shining blue, back streaked opalescent; flame orange-red breast patch. ♀ drab, upperparts brown, lower underparts buffy, mid-breast tinged red-orange, yellow eyes. **Voice** Call (song?) extremely high rapid notes, rising or varying only slightly in pitch (8–11.5 kHz).
SS ♀ Scarlet-thighed Dacnis.

Scarlet-thighed Dacnis *Dacnis venusta* `LC`
Dacnis Negriazul
Common resident.
L 12.2 cm (4.8"). Race *fuliginata*. Canopy of humid and wet forest, frequently much lower at borders and shrubby clearings. To 1000 m. Pairs follow mixed flocks or briefly join other birds in fruiting trees, but sometimes independent. **ID** Red eyes. ♂ head, centre of mantle, shoulders and rump turquoise, mask, throat and underparts black, red thighs often not visible. ♀ bluish-tinged head and shoulders, otherwise upperparts dusky black, underparts greyish buff, thighs cinnamon.
Voice Call, high single notes. **SS** ♀ Blue Dacnis.

fuliginata

Blue Dacnis *Dacnis cayana* `LC`
Dacnis Azul
Fairly common resident.
L 13 cm (5"). Races *ultramarina*[A], *napaea*[B], *caerebicolor*[C], *baudoana*[D], *cayana*[E], *glaucogularis*[F]. Canopy of dry to humid forest, borders, shrubby clearings, second growth. To 1100 m. Some seasonal movements. Restless singles or pairs follow mixed flocks, glean foliage. Diet nectar, berries and some insects. **ID** Bill pinkish basally.
♂ blue (to purplish blue, *caerebicolor*), tiny black mask, red eyes, black back, pinkish legs. ♀ dull greenish with contrasting dull blue head, pinkish legs. **Voice** Occasional weak "tsit".
SS ♀ Scarlet-thighed Dacnis, ♀ Yellow-tufted Dacnis.

cayana

baudoana

509

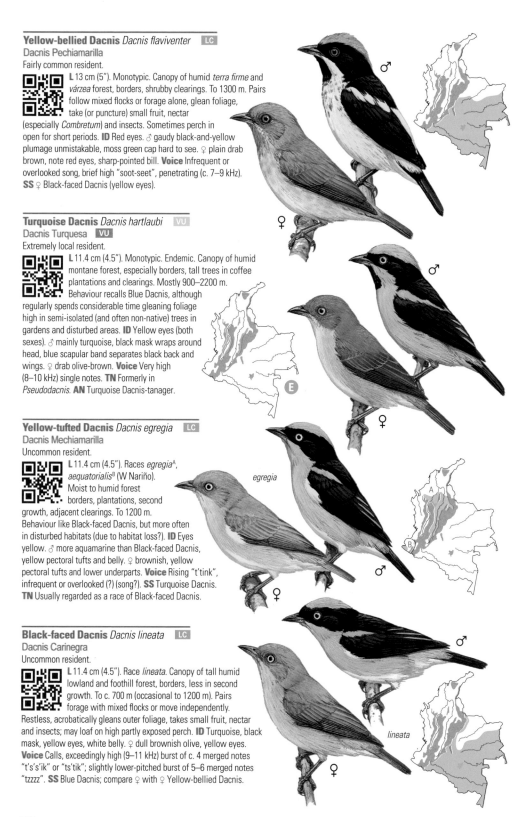

Yellow-bellied Dacnis *Dacnis flaviventer* LC
Dacnis Pechiamarilla
Fairly common resident.

L 13 cm (5"). Monotypic. Canopy of humid *terra firme* and *várzea* forest, borders, shrubby clearings. To 1300 m. Pairs follow mixed flocks or forage alone, glean foliage, take (or puncture) small fruit, nectar (especially *Combretum*) and insects. Sometimes perch in open for short periods. **ID** Red eyes. ♂ gaudy black-and-yellow plumage unmistakable, moss green cap hard to see. ♀ plain drab brown, note red eyes, sharp-pointed bill. **Voice** Infrequent or overlooked song, brief high "soot-seet", penetrating (c. 7–9 kHz). **SS** ♀ Black-faced Dacnis (yellow eyes).

Turquoise Dacnis *Dacnis hartlaubi* VU
Dacnis Turquesa VU
Extremely local resident.

L 11.4 cm (4.5"). Monotypic. Endemic. Canopy of humid montane forest, especially borders, tall trees in coffee plantations and clearings. Mostly 900–2200 m. Behaviour recalls Blue Dacnis, although regularly spends considerable time gleaning foliage high in semi-isolated (and often non-native) trees in gardens and disturbed areas. **ID** Yellow eyes (both sexes). ♂ mainly turquoise, black mask wraps around head, blue scapular band separates black back and wings. ♀ drab olive-brown. **Voice** Very high (8–10 kHz) single notes. **TN** Formerly in *Pseudodacnis*. **AN** Turquoise Dacnis-tanager.

Yellow-tufted Dacnis *Dacnis egregia* LC
Dacnis Mechiamarilla
Uncommon resident.

L 11.4 cm (4.5"). Races *egregia*[A], *aequatorialis*[B] (W Nariño). Moist to humid forest borders, plantations, second growth, adjacent clearings. To 1200 m. Behaviour like Black-faced Dacnis, but more often in disturbed habitats (due to habitat loss?). **ID** Eyes yellow. ♂ more aquamarine than Black-faced Dacnis, yellow pectoral tufts and belly. ♀ brownish, yellow pectoral tufts and lower underparts. **Voice** Rising "t'tink", infrequent or overlooked (?) (song?). **SS** Turquoise Dacnis. **TN** Usually regarded as a race of Black-faced Dacnis.

egregia

Black-faced Dacnis *Dacnis lineata* LC
Dacnis Carinegra
Uncommon resident.

L 11.4 cm (4.5"). Race *lineata*. Canopy of tall humid lowland and foothill forest, borders, less in second growth. To c. 700 m (occasional to 1200 m). Pairs forage with mixed flocks or move independently. Restless, acrobatically gleans outer foliage, takes small fruit, nectar and insects; may loaf on high partly exposed perch. **ID** Turquoise, black mask, yellow eyes, white belly. ♀ dull brownish olive, yellow eyes. **Voice** Calls, exceedingly high (9–11 kHz) burst of c. 4 merged notes "t's's'ik" or "ts'tik"; slightly lower-pitched burst of 5–6 merged notes "tzzzz". **SS** Blue Dacnis; compare ♀ with ♀ Yellow-bellied Dacnis.

lineata

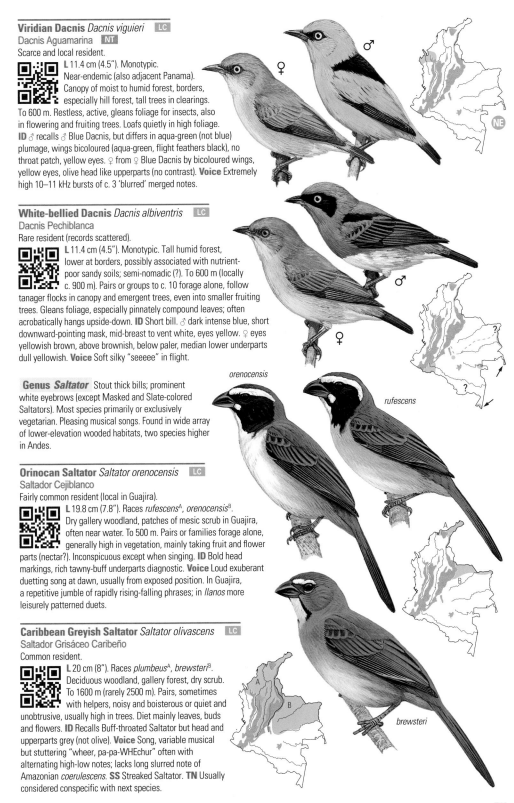

Viridian Dacnis *Dacnis viguieri* LC
Dacnis Aguamarina NT
Scarce and local resident.

L 11.4 cm (4.5"). Monotypic.
Near-endemic (also adjacent Panama).
Canopy of moist to humid forest, borders,
especially hill forest, tall trees in clearings.
To 600 m. Restless, active, gleans foliage for insects, also
in flowering and fruiting trees. Loafs quietly in high foliage.
ID ♂ recalls ♂ Blue Dacnis, but differs in aqua-green (not blue)
plumage, wings bicoloured (aqua-green, flight feathers black), no
throat patch, yellow eyes. ♀ from ♀ Blue Dacnis by bicoloured wings,
yellow eyes, olive head like upperparts (no contrast). **Voice** Extremely
high 10–11 kHz bursts of c. 3 'blurred' merged notes.

White-bellied Dacnis *Dacnis albiventris* LC
Dacnis Pechiblanca
Rare resident (records scattered).

L 11.4 cm (4.5"). Monotypic. Tall humid forest,
lower at borders, possibly associated with nutrient-
poor sandy soils; semi-nomadic (?). To 600 m (locally
c. 900 m). Pairs or groups to c. 10 forage alone, follow
tanager flocks in canopy and emergent trees, even into smaller fruiting
trees. Gleans foliage, especially pinnately compound leaves; often
acrobatically hangs upside-down. **ID** Short bill. ♂ dark intense blue, short
downward-pointing mask, mid-breast to vent white, eyes yellow. ♀ eyes
yellowish brown, above brownish, below paler, median lower underparts
dull yellowish. **Voice** Soft silky "seeeee" in flight.

Genus *Saltator* Stout thick bills; prominent
white eyebrows (except Masked and Slate-colored
Saltators). Most species primarily or exclusively
vegetarian. Pleasing musical songs. Found in wide array
of lower-elevation wooded habitats, two species higher
in Andes.

orenocensis

rufescens

Orinocan Saltator *Saltator orenocensis* LC
Saltador Cejiblanco
Fairly common resident (local in Guajira).

L 19.8 cm (7.8"). Races *rufescens*[A], *orenocensis*[B].
Dry gallery woodland, patches of mesic scrub in Guajira,
often near water. To 500 m. Pairs or families forage alone,
generally high in vegetation, mainly taking fruit and flower
parts (nectar?). Inconspicuous except when singing. **ID** Bold head
markings, rich tawny-buff underparts diagnostic. **Voice** Loud exuberant
duetting song at dawn, usually from exposed position. In Guajira,
a repetitive jumble of rapidly rising-falling phrases; in *llanos* more
leisurely patterned duets.

Caribbean Greyish Saltator *Saltator olivascens* LC
Saltador Grisáceo Caribeño
Common resident.

L 20 cm (8"). Races *plumbeus*[A], *brewsteri*[B].
Deciduous woodland, gallery forest, dry scrub.
To 1600 m (rarely 2500 m). Pairs, sometimes
with helpers, noisy and boisterous or quiet and
unobtrusive, usually high in trees. Diet mainly leaves, buds
and flowers. **ID** Recalls Buff-throated Saltator but head and
upperparts grey (not olive). **Voice** Song, variable musical
but stuttering "wheer, pa-pa-WHEchur" often with
alternating high-low notes; lacks long slurred note of
Amazonian *coerulescens*. **SS** Streaked Saltator. **TN** Usually
considered conspecific with next species.

brewsteri

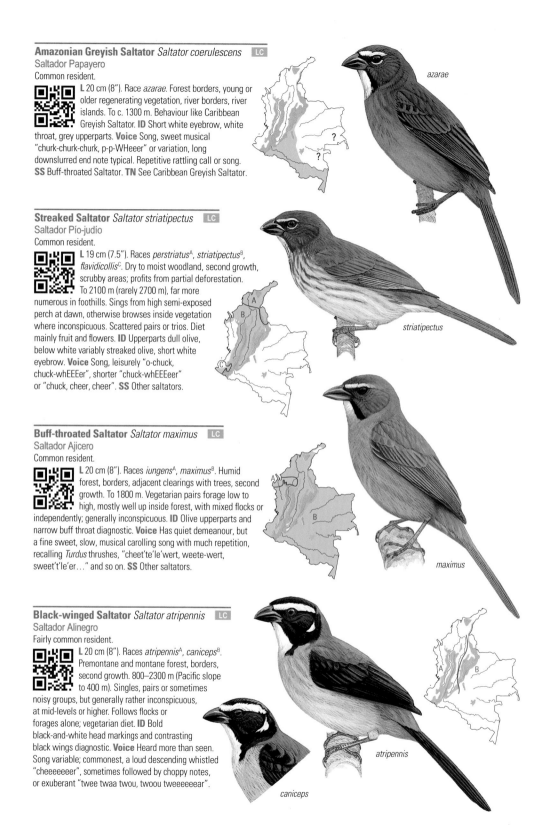

Amazonian Greyish Saltator *Saltator coerulescens* `LC`
Saltador Papayero
Common resident.

L 20 cm (8"). Race *azarae*. Forest borders, young or older regenerating vegetation, river borders, river islands. To c. 1300 m. Behaviour like Caribbean Greyish Saltator. **ID** Short white eyebrow, white throat, grey upperparts. **Voice** Song, sweet musical "churk-churk-churk, p-p-WHeeer" or variation, long downslurred end note typical. Repetitive rattling call or song. **SS** Buff-throated Saltator. **TN** See Caribbean Greyish Saltator.

azarae

Streaked Saltator *Saltator striatipectus* `LC`
Saltador Pío-judío
Common resident.

L 19 cm (7.5"). Races *perstriatus*[A], *striatipectus*[B], *flavidicollis*[C]. Dry to moist woodland, second growth, scrubby areas; profits from partial deforestation. To 2100 m (rarely 2700 m), far more numerous in foothills. Sings from high semi-exposed perch at dawn, otherwise browses inside vegetation where inconspicuous. Scattered pairs or trios. Diet mainly fruit and flowers. **ID** Upperparts dull olive, below white variably streaked olive, short white eyebrow. **Voice** Song, leisurely "o-chuck, chuck-whEEEer", shorter "chuck-whEEEeer" or "chuck, cheer, cheer". **SS** Other saltators.

striatipectus

Buff-throated Saltator *Saltator maximus* `LC`
Saltador Ajicero
Common resident.

L 20 cm (8"). Races *iungens*[A], *maximus*[B]. Humid forest, borders, adjacent clearings with trees, second growth. To 1800 m. Vegetarian pairs forage low to high, mostly well up inside forest, with mixed flocks or independently; generally inconspicuous. **ID** Olive upperparts and narrow buff throat diagnostic. **Voice** Has quiet demeanour, but a fine sweet, slow, musical carolling song with much repetition, recalling *Turdus* thrushes, "cheet'te'le'wert, weete-wert, sweet't'le'er…" and so on. **SS** Other saltators.

maximus

Black-winged Saltator *Saltator atripennis* `LC`
Saltador Alinegro
Fairly common resident.

L 20 cm (8"). Races *atripennis*[A], *caniceps*[B]. Premontane and montane forest, borders, second growth. 800–2300 m (Pacific slope to 400 m). Singles, pairs or sometimes noisy groups, but generally rather inconspicuous, at mid-levels or higher. Follows flocks or forages alone; vegetarian diet. **ID** Bold black-and-white head markings and contrasting black wings diagnostic. **Voice** Heard more than seen. Song variable; commonest, a loud descending whistled "cheeeeeeer", sometimes followed by choppy notes, or exuberant "twee twaa twou, twoou tweeeeeear".

caniceps

atripennis

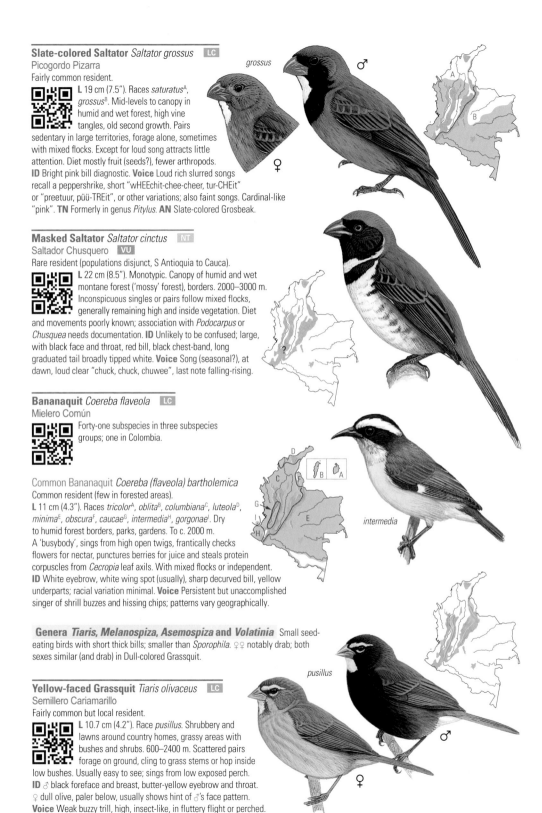

Slate-colored Saltator *Saltator grossus* `LC`
Picogordo Pizarra
Fairly common resident.

grossus

♂

L 19 cm (7.5"). Races *saturatus*[A], *grossus*[B]. Mid-levels to canopy in humid and wet forest, high vine tangles, old second growth. Pairs sedentary in large territories, forage alone, sometimes with mixed flocks. Except for loud song attracts little attention. Diet mostly fruit (seeds?), fewer arthropods. **ID** Bright pink bill diagnostic. **Voice** Loud rich slurred songs recall a peppershrike, short "wHEEchit-chee-cheer, tur-CHEit" or "preetuur, püü-TREit", or other variations; also faint songs. Cardinal-like "pink". **TN** Formerly in genus *Pitylus*. **AN** Slate-colored Grosbeak.

♀

Masked Saltator *Saltator cinctus* `NT`
Saltador Chusquero `VU`
Rare resident (populations disjunct, S Antioquia to Cauca).

L 22 cm (8.5"). Monotypic. Canopy of humid and wet montane forest ('mossy' forest), borders. 2000–3000 m. Inconspicuous singles or pairs follow mixed flocks, generally remaining high and inside vegetation. Diet and movements poorly known; association with *Podocarpus* or *Chusquea* needs documentation. **ID** Unlikely to be confused; large, with black face and throat, red bill, black chest-band, long graduated tail broadly tipped white. **Voice** Song (seasonal?), at dawn, loud clear "chuck, chuck, chuwee", last note falling-rising.

Bananaquit *Coereba flaveola* `LC`
Mielero Común

Forty-one subspecies in three subspecies groups; one in Colombia.

Common Bananaquit *Coereba (flaveola) bartholemica*
Common resident (few in forested areas).
L 11 cm (4.3"). Races *tricolor*[A], *oblita*[B], *columbiana*[C], *luteola*[D], *minima*[E], *obscura*[F], *caucae*[G], *intermedia*[H], *gorgonae*[I]. Dry to humid forest borders, parks, gardens. To c. 2000 m. A 'busybody', sings from high open twigs, frantically checks flowers for nectar, punctures berries for juice and steals protein corpuscles from *Cecropia* leaf axils. With mixed flocks or independent. **ID** White eyebrow, white wing spot (usually), sharp decurved bill, yellow underparts; racial variation minimal. **Voice** Persistent but unaccomplished singer of shrill buzzes and hissing chips; patterns vary geographically.

intermedia

Genera *Tiaris, Melanospiza, Asemospiza* and *Volatinia* Small seed-eating birds with short thick bills; smaller than *Sporophila*. ♀♀ notably drab; both sexes similar (and drab) in Dull-colored Grassquit.

pusillus

Yellow-faced Grassquit *Tiaris olivaceus* `LC`
Semillero Cariamarillo
Fairly common but local resident.

L 10.7 cm (4.2"). Race *pusillus*. Shrubbery and lawns around country homes, grassy areas with bushes and shrubs. 600–2400 m. Scattered pairs forage on ground, cling to grass stems or hop inside low bushes. Usually easy to see; sings from low exposed perch. **ID** ♂ black foreface and breast, butter-yellow eyebrow and throat. ♀ dull olive, paler below, usually shows hint of ♂'s face pattern. **Voice** Weak buzzy trill, high, insect-like, in fluttery flight or perched.

♀

♂

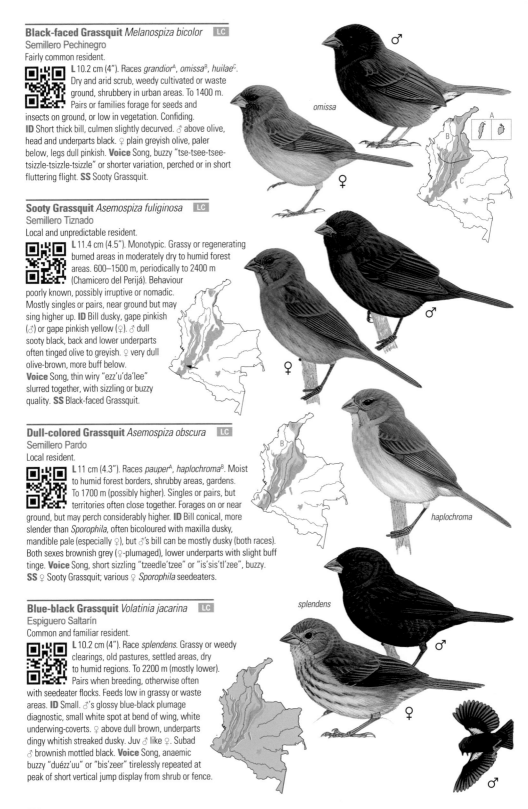

Black-faced Grassquit *Melanospiza bicolor* LC
Semillero Pechinegro
Fairly common resident.

L 10.2 cm (4"). Races *grandior*[A], *omissa*[B], *huilae*[C]. Dry and arid scrub, weedy cultivated or waste ground, shrubbery in urban areas. To 1400 m. Pairs or families forage for seeds and insects on ground, or low in vegetation. Confiding. **ID** Short thick bill, culmen slightly decurved. ♂ above olive, head and underparts black. ♀ plain greyish olive, paler below, legs dull pinkish. **Voice** Song, buzzy "tse-tsee-tsee-tsizzle-tsizzle-tsizzle" or shorter variation, perched or in short fluttering flight. **SS** Sooty Grassquit.

omissa

Sooty Grassquit *Asemospiza fuliginosa* LC
Semillero Tiznado
Local and unpredictable resident.

L 11.4 cm (4.5"). Monotypic. Grassy or regenerating burned areas in moderately dry to humid forest areas. 600–1500 m, periodically to 2400 m (Chamicero del Perijá). Behaviour poorly known, possibly irruptive or nomadic. Mostly singles or pairs, near ground but may sing higher up. **ID** Bill dusky, gape pinkish (♂) or gape pinkish yellow (♀). ♂ dull sooty black, back and lower underparts often tinged olive to greyish. ♀ very dull olive-brown, more buff below. **Voice** Song, thin wiry "ezz'u'da'lee" slurred together, with sizzling or buzzy quality. **SS** Black-faced Grassquit.

Dull-colored Grassquit *Asemospiza obscura* LC
Semillero Pardo
Local resident.

L 11 cm (4.3"). Races *pauper*[A], *haplochroma*[B]. Moist to humid forest borders, shrubby areas, gardens. To 1700 m (possibly higher). Singles or pairs, but territories often close together. Forages on or near ground, but may perch considerably higher. **ID** Bill conical, more slender than *Sporophila*, often bicoloured with maxilla dusky, mandible pale (especially ♀), but ♂'s bill can be mostly dusky (both races). Both sexes brownish grey (♀-plumaged), lower underparts with slight buff tinge. **Voice** Song, short sizzling "tzeedle'tzee" or "is'sis'tl'zee", buzzy. **SS** ♀ Sooty Grassquit; various ♀ *Sporophila* seedeaters.

haplochroma

splendens

Blue-black Grassquit *Volatinia jacarina* LC
Espiguero Saltarín
Common and familiar resident.

L 10.2 cm (4"). Race *splendens*. Grassy or weedy clearings, old pastures, settled areas, dry to humid regions. To 2200 m (mostly lower). Pairs when breeding, otherwise seen with seedeater flocks. Feeds low in grassy or waste areas. **ID** Small. ♂'s glossy blue-black plumage diagnostic, small white spot at bend of wing, white underwing-coverts. ♀ above dull brown, underparts dingy whitish streaked dusky. Juv ♂ like ♀. Subad ♂ brownish mottled black. **Voice** Song, anaemic buzzy "duézz'uu" or "bis'zeer" tirelessly repeated at peak of short vertical jump display from shrub or fence.

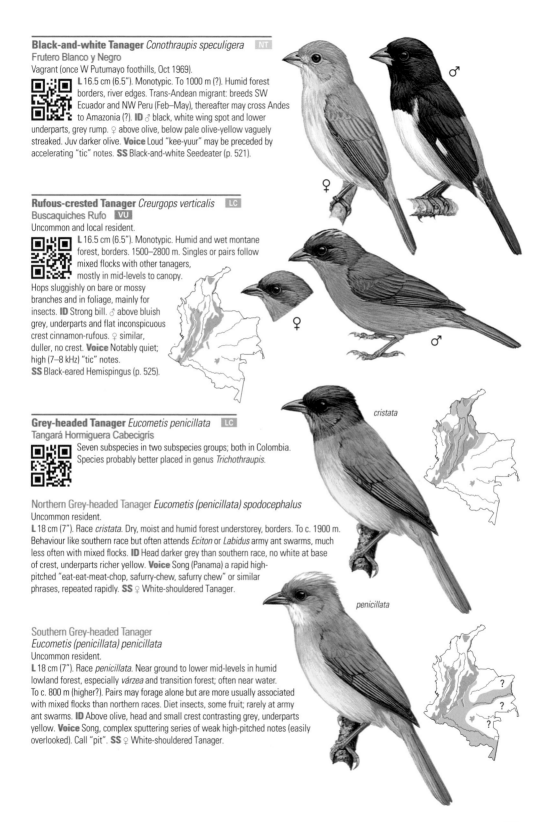

Black-and-white Tanager *Conothraupis speculigera* `NT`
Frutero Blanco y Negro
Vagrant (once W Putumayo foothills, Oct 1969).

L 16.5 cm (6.5"). Monotypic. To 1000 m (?). Humid forest borders, river edges. Trans-Andean migrant: breeds SW Ecuador and NW Peru (Feb–May), thereafter may cross Andes to Amazonia (?). **ID** ♂ black, white wing spot and lower underparts, grey rump. ♀ above olive, below pale olive-yellow vaguely streaked. Juv darker olive. **Voice** Loud "kee-yuur" may be preceded by accelerating "tic" notes. **SS** Black-and-white Seedeater (p. 521).

Rufous-crested Tanager *Creurgops verticalis* `LC`
Buscaquiches Rufo `VU`
Uncommon and local resident.

L 16.5 cm (6.5"). Monotypic. Humid and wet montane forest, borders. 1500–2800 m. Singles or pairs follow mixed flocks with other tanagers, mostly in mid-levels to canopy. Hops sluggishly on bare or mossy branches and in foliage, mainly for insects. **ID** Strong bill. ♂ above bluish grey, underparts and flat inconspicuous crest cinnamon-rufous. ♀ similar, duller, no crest. **Voice** Notably quiet; high (7–8 kHz) "tic" notes. **SS** Black-eared Hemispingus (p. 525).

Grey-headed Tanager *Eucometis penicillata* `LC`
Tangará Hormiguera Cabecigrís

Seven subspecies in two subspecies groups; both in Colombia. Species probably better placed in genus *Trichothraupis*.

cristata

Northern Grey-headed Tanager *Eucometis (penicillata) spodocephalus*
Uncommon resident.
L 18 cm (7"). Race *cristata*. Dry, moist and humid forest understorey, borders. To c. 1900 m. Behaviour like southern race but often attends *Eciton* or *Labidus* army ant swarms, much less often with mixed flocks. **ID** Head darker grey than southern race, no white at base of crest, underparts richer yellow. **Voice** Song (Panama) a rapid high-pitched "eat-eat-meat-chop, safurry-chew, safurry chew" or similar phrases, repeated rapidly. **SS** ♀ White-shouldered Tanager.

Southern Grey-headed Tanager
Eucometis (penicillata) penicillata
Uncommon resident.
L 18 cm (7"). Race *penicillata*. Near ground to lower mid-levels in humid lowland forest, especially *várzea* and transition forest; often near water. To c. 800 m (higher?). Pairs may forage alone but are more usually associated with mixed flocks than northern races. Diet insects, some fruit; rarely at army ant swarms. **ID** Above olive, head and small crest contrasting grey, underparts yellow. **Voice** Song, complex sputtering series of weak high-pitched notes (easily overlooked). Call "pit". **SS** ♀ White-shouldered Tanager.

penicillata

Genus *Loriotus* (name has priority over *Islerothraupis*) Species formerly placed in *Tachyphonus*, and separation based heavily on molecular evidence.

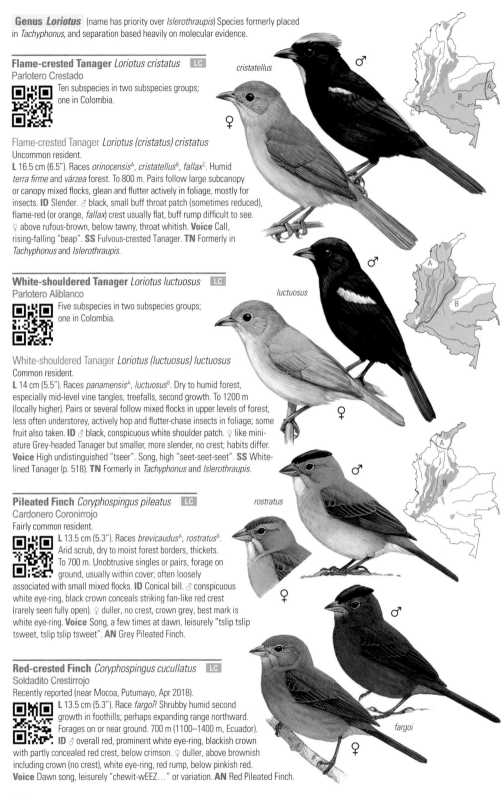

cristatellus

♂

♀

Flame-crested Tanager *Loriotus cristatus* `LC`
Parlotero Crestado

Ten subspecies in two subspecies groups; one in Colombia.

Flame-crested Tanager *Loriotus (cristatus) cristatus*
Uncommon resident.
L 16.5 cm (6.5"). Races *orinocensis*[A], *cristatellus*[B], *fallax*[C]. Humid *terra firme* and *várzea* forest. To 800 m. Pairs follow large subcanopy or canopy mixed flocks, glean and flutter actively in foliage, mostly for insects. **ID** Slender. ♂ black, small buff throat patch (sometimes reduced), flame-red (or orange, *fallax*) crest usually flat, buff rump difficult to see. ♀ above rufous-brown, below tawny, throat whitish. **Voice** Call, rising-falling "beap". **SS** Fulvous-crested Tanager. **TN** Formerly in *Tachyphonus* and *Islerothraupis*.

luctuosus

♂

♀

White-shouldered Tanager *Loriotus luctuosus* `LC`
Parlotero Aliblanco

Five subspecies in two subspecies groups; one in Colombia.

White-shouldered Tanager *Loriotus (luctuosus) luctuosus*
Common resident.
L 14 cm (5.5"). Races *panamensis*[A], *luctuosus*[B]. Dry to humid forest, especially mid-level vine tangles, treefalls, second growth. To 1200 m (locally higher). Pairs or several follow mixed flocks in upper levels of forest, less often understorey, actively hop and flutter-chase insects in foliage; some fruit also taken. **ID** ♂ black, conspicuous white shoulder patch. ♀ like miniature Grey-headed Tanager but smaller, more slender, no crest; habits differ. **Voice** High undistinguished "tseer". Song, high "seet-seet-seet". **SS** White-lined Tanager (p. 518). **TN** Formerly in *Tachyphonus* and *Islerothraupis*.

rostratus

♂

♀

Pileated Finch *Coryphospingus pileatus* `LC`
Cardonero Coronirrojo
Fairly common resident.

L 13.5 cm (5.3"). Races *brevicaudus*[A], *rostratus*[B]. Arid scrub, dry to moist forest borders, thickets. To 700 m. Unobtrusive singles or pairs, forage on ground, usually within cover; often loosely associated with small mixed flocks. **ID** Conical bill. ♂ conspicuous white eye-ring, black crown conceals striking fan-like red crest (rarely seen fully open). ♀ duller, no crest, crown grey, best mark is white eye-ring. **Voice** Song, a few times at dawn, leisurely "tslip tslip tsweet, tslip tslip tsweet". **AN** Grey Pileated Finch.

♂

♀

fargoi

Red-crested Finch *Coryphospingus cucullatus* `LC`
Soldadito Crestirrojo
Recently reported (near Mocoa, Putumayo, Apr 2018).

L 13.5 cm (5.3"). Race *fargoi*? Shrubby humid second growth in foothills; perhaps expanding range northward. Forages on or near ground. 700 m (1100–1400 m, Ecuador). **ID** ♂ overall red, prominent white eye-ring, blackish crown with partly concealed red crest, below crimson. ♀ duller, above brownish including crown (no crest), white eye-ring, red rump, below pinkish red. **Voice** Dawn song, leisurely "chewit-wEEZ…" or variation. **AN** Red Pileated Finch.

Crimson-breasted Finch *Rhodospingus cruentus*  LC
Pinzón Carmesí

Local resident (numerous records SW Nariño).

 L 11.4 cm (4.5"). Monotypic. Recent range expansion from Ecuador. Second growth, brushy wooded borders. To 200 m. May associate with seedeaters, also ascends well up in flowering and fruiting trees. **ID** ♂ above black, crown patch and underparts scarlet, paler on belly. ♀ plain and confusing, relatively slender bill (cf. seedeaters), above light brown, below pale yellowish buff, flanks brownish. **Voice** Song, brief buzzy "tizzz'seee".

Genera *Maschalethraupis*, *Chrysocorypha* and *Tachyphonus* In general ♂♂ black, ♀♀ brownish to rufous. Mostly forest borders or in shrubby semi-open habitats. Taxonomic relationships of several species unresolved.

Fulvous-crested Tanager
Maschalethraupis surinama  LC
Parlotero Culiamarillo

Fairly common resident.

 L 16.5 cm (6.5"). Race *brevipes*. Humid forest, especially borders and shrubby areas; commonest in white-sand regions. To 800 m. Nervous-acting pairs follow mixed flocks, mid-levels or lower, often low at borders; less often subcanopy. **ID** ♂ mostly black, best marks are tawny flanks (watch for wing flicks), all-black throat (no buff patch). ♀ plain, key marks are greyish head and distinct but ill-defined ochre-yellow ocular area. **Voice** High sharp notes (8–10 kHz), bursts of rapid doubled notes. **SS** Flame-crested Tanager (mainly canopy). **TN** Previously in *Tachyphonus*; genetic affinities unresolved.

Tawny-crested Tanager *Chrysocorypha delatrii* LC
Parlotero Crestado

Common resident.

 L 14 cm (5.5"). Monotypic. Humid and wet forest, borders, older second growth. To c. 800 m (locally to 1300 m). Noisy, fast-moving gangs of 3–20 swarm through understorey, typically offering only glimpses as search for fruit and insects; Dusky-faced Mitrospingus may accompany them, less often slower species. In pairs when nesting. **ID** ♂ black, with prominent close-cropped tawny-orange crest. ♀ by uniform dark brown plumage. **Voice** Call, smacking "chit" or "tswik" constantly as forage. **TN** Previously in *Tachyphonus*; genetic affinities unresolved.

Red-shouldered Tanager
Tachyphonus phoenicius LC
Parlotero Hombrirrojo

Fairly common but local resident.

 L 15 cm (6"). Monotypic. Bushy white-sand savanna, scrub woodland around rock outcrops. To 400 m. Restless and rather wary pairs or families forage alone, low, mostly independent of mixed flocks. **ID** ♂ glossy black, underwing-coverts white, tiny red spot at bend of wing (best noted, if at all, in flight). ♀ above greyish brown, head darker, mask dusky, throat contrastingly white. **Voice** Calls, high weak "cheup" and "sit". Dawn song "chi'lip, cheeu", over and over.

brevipes

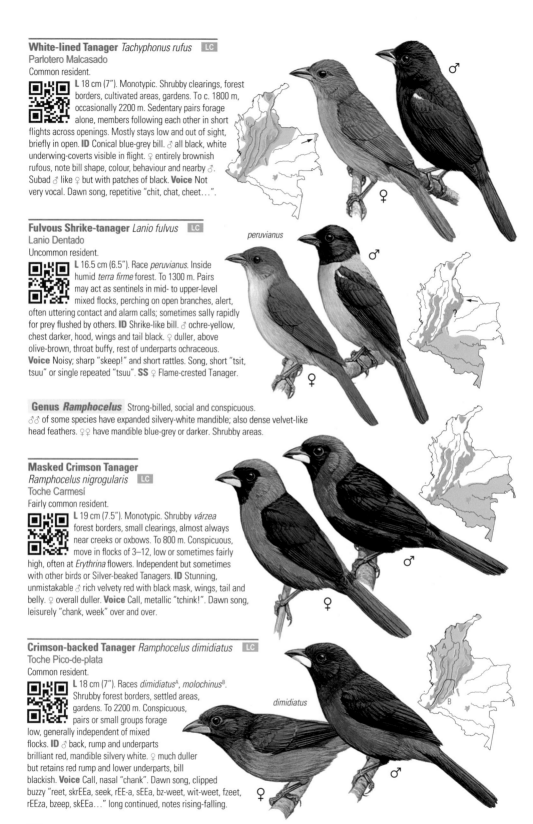

White-lined Tanager *Tachyphonus rufus* `LC`
Parlotero Malcasado
Common resident.

L 18 cm (7"). Monotypic. Shrubby clearings, forest borders, cultivated areas, gardens. To c. 1800 m, occasionally 2200 m. Sedentary pairs forage alone, members following each other in short flights across openings. Mostly stays low and out of sight, briefly in open. **ID** Conical blue-grey bill. ♂ all black, white underwing-coverts visible in flight. ♀ entirely brownish rufous, note bill shape, colour, behaviour and nearby ♂. Subad ♂ like ♀ but with patches of black. **Voice** Not very vocal. Dawn song, repetitive "chit, chat, cheet…".

Fulvous Shrike-tanager *Lanio fulvus* `LC`
Lanio Dentado
Uncommon resident.

peruvianus

L 16.5 cm (6.5"). Race *peruvianus*. Inside humid *terra firme* forest. To 1300 m. Pairs may act as sentinels in mid- to upper-level mixed flocks, perching on open branches, alert, often uttering contact and alarm calls; sometimes sally rapidly for prey flushed by others. **ID** Shrike-like bill. ♂ ochre-yellow, chest darker, hood, wings and tail black. ♀ duller, above olive-brown, throat buffy, rest of underparts ochraceous. **Voice** Noisy; sharp "skeep!" and short rattles. Song, short "tsit, tsuu" or single repeated "tsuu". **SS** ♀ Flame-crested Tanager.

Genus *Ramphocelus* Strong-billed, social and conspicuous. ♂♂ of some species have expanded silvery-white mandible; also dense velvet-like head feathers. ♀♀ have mandible blue-grey or darker. Shrubby areas.

Masked Crimson Tanager
Ramphocelus nigrogularis `LC`
Toche Carmesí
Fairly common resident.

L 19 cm (7.5"). Monotypic. Shrubby *várzea* forest borders, small clearings, almost always near creeks or oxbows. To 800 m. Conspicuous, move in flocks of 3–12, low or sometimes fairly high, often at *Erythrina* flowers. Independent but sometimes with other birds or Silver-beaked Tanagers. **ID** Stunning, unmistakable ♂ rich velvety red with black mask, wings, tail and belly. ♀ overall duller. **Voice** Call, metallic "tchink!". Dawn song, leisurely "chank, week" over and over.

Crimson-backed Tanager *Ramphocelus dimidiatus* `LC`
Toche Pico-de-plata
Common resident.

L 18 cm (7"). Races *dimidiatus*[A], *molochinus*[B]. Shrubby forest borders, settled areas, gardens. To 2200 m. Conspicuous, pairs or small groups forage low, generally independent of mixed flocks. **ID** ♂ back, rump and underparts brilliant red, mandible silvery white. ♀ much duller but retains red rump and lower underparts, bill blackish. **Voice** Call, nasal "chank". Dawn song, clipped buzzy "reet, skrEEa, seek, rEE-a, sEEa, bz-weet, wit-weet, fzeet, rEEza, bzeep, skEEa…" long continued, notes rising-falling.

dimidiatus

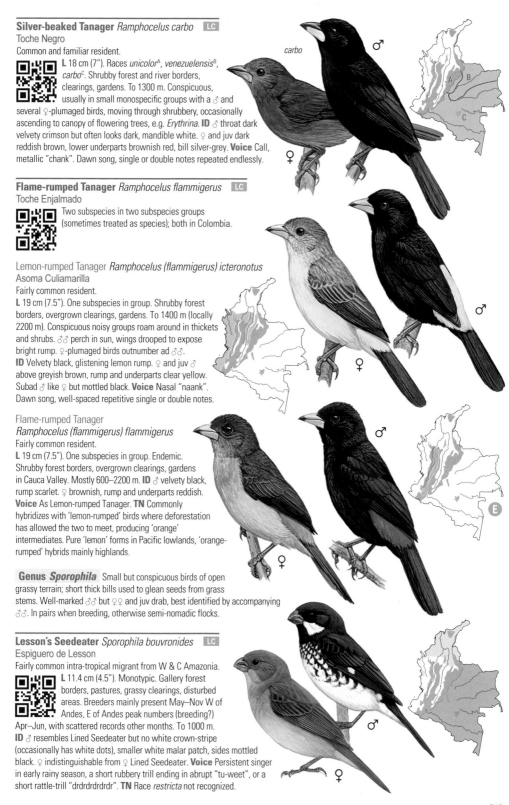

Silver-beaked Tanager *Ramphocelus carbo* `LC`
Toche Negro

Common and familiar resident.

L 18 cm (7"). Races *unicolor*[A], *venezuelensis*[B], *carbo*[C]. Shrubby forest and river borders, clearings, gardens. To 1300 m. Conspicuous, usually in small monospecific groups with a ♂ and several ♀-plumaged birds, moving through shrubbery, occasionally ascending to canopy of flowering trees, e.g. *Erythrina*. **ID** ♂ throat dark velvety crimson but often looks dark, mandible white. ♀ and juv dark reddish brown, lower underparts brownish red, bill silver-grey. **Voice** Call, metallic "chank". Dawn song, single or double notes repeated endlessly.

carbo

Flame-rumped Tanager *Ramphocelus flammigerus* `LC`
Toche Enjalmado

Two subspecies in two subspecies groups (sometimes treated as species); both in Colombia.

Lemon-rumped Tanager *Ramphocelus (flammigerus) icteronotus*
Asoma Culiamarilla

Fairly common resident.

L 19 cm (7.5"). One subspecies in group. Shrubby forest borders, overgrown clearings, gardens. To 1400 m (locally 2200 m). Conspicuous noisy groups roam around in thickets and shrubs. ♂♂ perch in sun, wings drooped to expose bright rump. ♀-plumaged birds outnumber ad ♂♂. **ID** Velvety black, glistening lemon rump. ♀ and juv ♂ above greyish brown, rump and underparts clear yellow. Subad ♂ like ♀ but mottled black. **Voice** Nasal "naank". Dawn song, well-spaced repetitive single or double notes.

Flame-rumped Tanager
Ramphocelus (flammigerus) flammigerus
Fairly common resident.

L 19 cm (7.5"). One subspecies in group. Endemic. Shrubby forest borders, overgrown clearings, gardens in Cauca Valley. Mostly 600–2200 m. **ID** ♂ velvety black, rump scarlet. ♀ brownish, rump and underparts reddish. **Voice** As Lemon-rumped Tanager. **TN** Commonly hybridizes with 'lemon-rumped' birds where deforestation has allowed the two to meet, producing 'orange' intermediates. Pure 'lemon' forms in Pacific lowlands, 'orange-rumped' hybrids mainly highlands.

Genus *Sporophila* Small but conspicuous birds of open grassy terrain; short thick bills used to glean seeds from grass stems. Well-marked ♂♂ but ♀♀ and juv drab, best identified by accompanying ♂♂. In pairs when breeding, otherwise semi-nomadic flocks.

Lesson's Seedeater *Sporophila bouvronides* `LC`
Espiguero de Lesson

Fairly common intra-tropical migrant from W & C Amazonia.

L 11.4 cm (4.5"). Monotypic. Gallery forest borders, pastures, grassy clearings, disturbed areas. Breeders mainly present May–Nov W of Andes, E of Andes peak numbers (breeding?) Apr–Jun, with scattered records other months. To 1000 m. **ID** ♂ resembles Lined Seedeater but no white crown-stripe (occasionally has white dots), smaller white malar patch, sides mottled black. ♀ indistinguishable from ♀ Lined Seedeater. **Voice** Persistent singer in early rainy season, a short rubbery trill ending in abrupt "tu-weet", or a short rattle-trill "drdrdrdrdrdr". **TN** Race *restricta* not recognized.

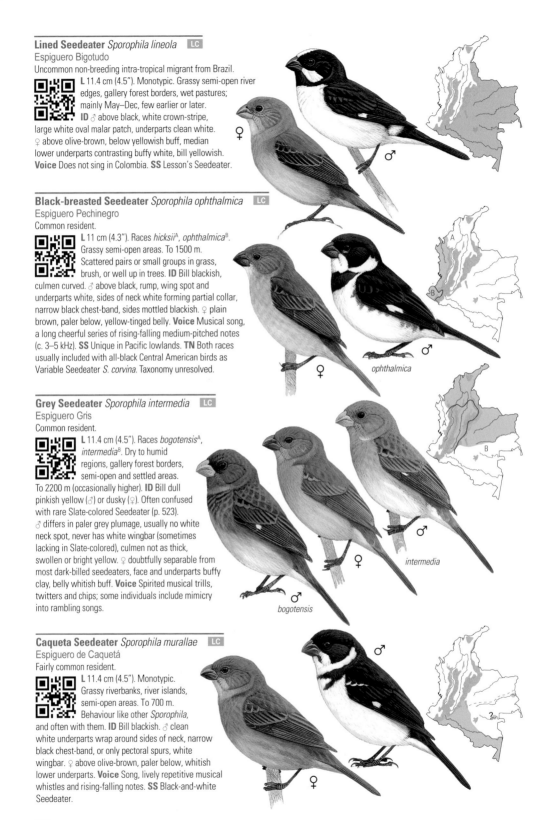

Lined Seedeater *Sporophila lineola* LC
Espiguero Bigotudo
Uncommon non-breeding intra-tropical migrant from Brazil.
L 11.4 cm (4.5"). Monotypic. Grassy semi-open river edges, gallery forest borders, wet pastures; mainly May–Dec, few earlier or later. **ID** ♂ above black, white crown-stripe, large white oval malar patch, underparts clean white. ♀ above olive-brown, below yellowish buff, median lower underparts contrasting buffy white, bill yellowish. **Voice** Does not sing in Colombia. **SS** Lesson's Seedeater.

Black-breasted Seedeater *Sporophila ophthalmica* LC
Espiguero Pechinegro
Common resident.
L 11 cm (4.3"). Races *hicksii*[A], *ophthalmica*[B]. Grassy semi-open areas. To 1500 m. Scattered pairs or small groups in grass, brush, or well up in trees. **ID** Bill blackish, culmen curved. ♂ above black, rump, wing spot and underparts white, sides of neck white forming partial collar, narrow black chest-band, sides mottled blackish. ♀ plain brown, paler below, yellow-tinged belly. **Voice** Musical song, a long cheerful series of rising-falling medium-pitched notes (c. 3–5 kHz). **SS** Unique in Pacific lowlands. **TN** Both races usually included with all-black Central American birds as Variable Seedeater *S. corvina*. Taxonomy unresolved.

ophthalmica

Grey Seedeater *Sporophila intermedia* LC
Espiguero Gris
Common resident.
L 11.4 cm (4.5"). Races *bogotensis*[A], *intermedia*[B]. Dry to humid regions, gallery forest borders, semi-open and settled areas. To 2200 m (occasionally higher). **ID** Bill dull pinkish yellow (♂) or dusky (♀). Often confused with rare Slate-colored Seedeater (p. 523). ♂ differs in paler grey plumage, usually no white neck spot, never has white wingbar (sometimes lacking in Slate-colored), culmen not as thick, swollen or bright yellow. ♀ doubtfully separable from most dark-billed seedeaters, face and underparts buffy clay, belly whitish buff. **Voice** Spirited musical trills, twitters and chips; some individuals include mimicry into rambling songs.

bogotensis

intermedia

Caqueta Seedeater *Sporophila murallae* LC
Espiguero de Caquetá
Fairly common resident.
L 11.4 cm (4.5"). Monotypic. Grassy riverbanks, river islands, semi-open areas. To 700 m. Behaviour like other *Sporophila*, and often with them. **ID** Bill blackish. ♂ clean white underparts wrap around sides of neck, narrow black chest-band, or only pectoral spurs, white wingbar. ♀ above olive-brown, paler below, whitish lower underparts. **Voice** Song, lively repetitive musical whistles and rising-falling notes. **SS** Black-and-white Seedeater.

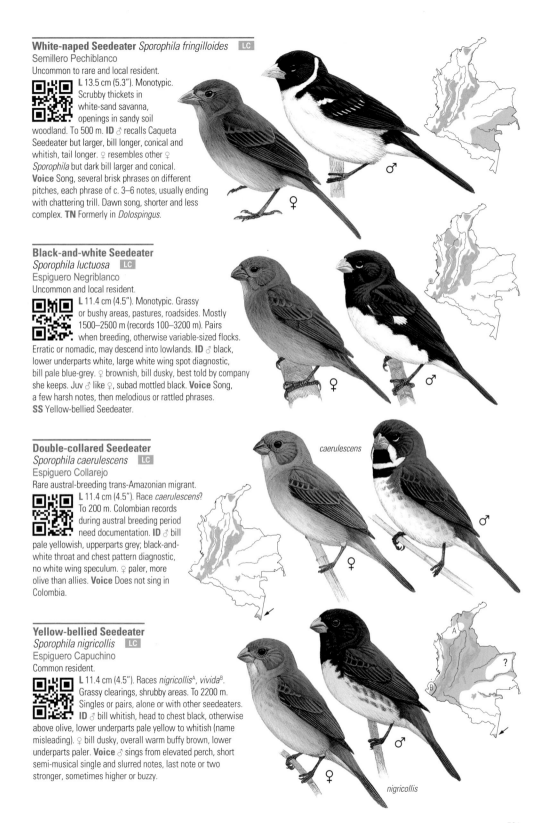

White-naped Seedeater *Sporophila fringilloides* `LC`
Semillero Pechiblanco
Uncommon to rare and local resident.
L 13.5 cm (5.3"). Monotypic. Scrubby thickets in white-sand savanna, openings in sandy soil woodland. To 500 m. **ID** ♂ recalls Caqueta Seedeater but larger, bill longer, conical and whitish, tail longer. ♀ resembles other ♀ *Sporophila* but dark bill larger and conical. **Voice** Song, several brisk phrases on different pitches, each phrase of c. 3–6 notes, usually ending with chattering trill. Dawn song, shorter and less complex. **TN** Formerly in *Dolospingus*.

Black-and-white Seedeater
Sporophila luctuosa `LC`
Espiguero Negriblanco
Uncommon and local resident.
L 11.4 cm (4.5"). Monotypic. Grassy or bushy areas, pastures, roadsides. Mostly 1500–2500 m (records 100–3200 m). Pairs when breeding, otherwise variable-sized flocks. Erratic or nomadic, may descend into lowlands. **ID** ♂ black, lower underparts white, large white wing spot diagnostic, bill pale blue-grey. ♀ brownish, bill dusky, best told by company she keeps. Juv ♂ like ♀, subad mottled black. **Voice** Song, a few harsh notes, then melodious or rattled phrases. **SS** Yellow-bellied Seedeater.

Double-collared Seedeater
Sporophila caerulescens `LC`
Espiguero Collarejo
Rare austral-breeding trans-Amazonian migrant.
L 11.4 cm (4.5"). Race *caerulescens*? To 200 m. Colombian records during austral breeding period need documentation. **ID** ♂ bill pale yellowish, upperparts grey; black-and-white throat and chest pattern diagnostic, no white wing speculum. ♀ paler, more olive than allies. **Voice** Does not sing in Colombia.

Yellow-bellied Seedeater
Sporophila nigricollis `LC`
Espiguero Capuchino
Common resident.
L 11.4 cm (4.5"). Races *nigricollis*[A], *vivida*[B]. Grassy clearings, shrubby areas. To 2200 m. Singles or pairs, alone or with other seedeaters. **ID** ♂ bill whitish, head to chest black, otherwise above olive, lower underparts pale yellow to whitish (name misleading). ♀ bill dusky, overall warm buffy brown, lower underparts paler. **Voice** ♂ sings from elevated perch, short semi-musical single and slurred notes, last note or two stronger, sometimes higher or buzzy.

caerulescens

nigricollis

Thick-billed Seed-finch *Sporophila funerea* `LC`
Arrocero Piquigrueso
Fairly common resident.

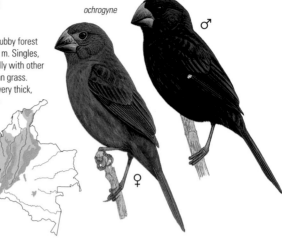

ochrogyne

♂

L 13 cm (5"). Races *ochrogyne*[A], *aethiops*[B]. Shrubby forest borders, grassy and shrubby clearings. To 1000 m. Singles, pairs, much less often small groups, occasionally with other seedeaters but favours shrubby areas more than grass. Largely sedentary (unlike many *Sporophila*). **ID** ♂ bill black, very thick, culmen slightly decurved; plumage black, underwing-coverts white, small white spot at base of primaries. ♀ bill black, plumage dark brown, paler below. **Voice** As Chestnut-bellied Seed-finch. **SS** Large-billed Seed-finch. **TN** Formerly included Chestnut-bellied Seed-finch (mainly E of Andes), the two united as Lesser Seed-finch *Oryzoborus angolensis*; they interbreed locally in Santa Marta area and Magdalena Valley.

♀

Chestnut-bellied Seed-finch *Sporophila angolensis* `LC`
Arrocero Buchicastaño
Fairly common resident (declining locally due to cagebird trapping).

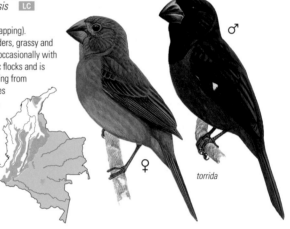

♂

L 13 cm (5"). Race *torrida*. Shrubby forest borders, grassy and shrubby fields. Usually alone or in pairs, only occasionally with other seedeaters. Does not form monospecific flocks and is largely sedentary (not nomadic). ♂♂ usually sing from relatively open, fairly high perches, but otherwise both sexes remain low and mostly out of sight. Feeds mostly on seeds. **ID** ♂ very like Thick-billed Seed-finch but lower underparts chestnut. ♀ similar to Thick-billed Seed-finch. **Voice** ♂'s delightful long-continued song of sweet whistled phrases and slurred notes. Unfortunately, because of its pleasing and persistent song, it is much persecuted in some areas by trappers. **SS** Thick-billed Seed-finch. **TN** See previous species.

♀

torrida

Large-billed Seed-finch *Sporophila crassirostris* `LC`
Arrocero Renegrido
Uncommon to rare, declining and local resident.

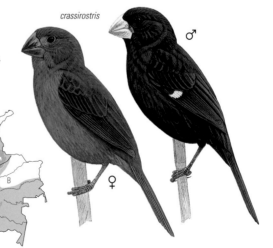

crassirostris

♂

L 14 cm (5.5"). Races *occidentalis*[A], *crassirostris*[B] (nearly identical). Shrubby and grassy areas, marshes, riparian thickets. To 1300 m. Pairs or small groups, usually alone. Persecuted for cagebird trade. Nomadic (follows seed crops?), movements poorly documented. **ID** ♂ bill chalky white, enormously thick and oversized; plumage black, small white wing spot. ♀ dark brown, paler buffy brown below, bill dusky, no white wing spot. **Voice** Song, melodious but somewhat brittle series of rising-falling notes that gradually accelerates. **SS** Thick-billed Seed-finch. **TN** Taxonomy unsettled.

♀

Slate-colored Seedeater *Sporophila schistacea* `LC`
Espiguero Pizarra
Rare and nomadic resident.

L 11.4 cm (4.5"). Races *schistacea*[A], *incerta*[B], *longipennis*[C]. Shrubby humid forest borders, brushy clearings. To 2000 m. Behaviour poorly understood, may depend on bamboo (or other?) seed crops. **ID** Often confused with Grey Seedeater (p. 520). ♂ peculiarly thick bright yellow bill (mandible much deeper than maxilla, tomia of maxilla downcurved), plumage dark grey, wings and tail slaty, narrow inconspicuous white crescents above and below eye, small white neck spot, usually one partial or complete white wingbar, small white speculum (both sexes), centre of lower underparts whitish. ♀ above pale olive-brown, below tawny buff, belly whitish, bill horn-grey. **Voice** Song (*schistacea*, varies?), short "ti'Tl'chuchu'titititit", second note very high, middle two low-pitched, ending in high trill (3.5–9.5 kHz).

longipennis

♂

♀

schistacea

♀

Plumbeous Seedeater *Sporophila plumbea* `LC`
Espiguero Plomizo
Local resident (distribution W of Andes poorly documented).

L 11 cm (4.3"). Races *colombiana*[A], *whiteleyana*[B]. Damp or low-lying grassland, semi-open areas with bushes and trees, gallery forest borders. To 1500 m. Pairs when breeding, singles or in small seedeater flocks at other times. Nomadic or seasonal. **ID** ♂ only 'grey' seedeater with dark bill, whitish malar area. ♀ duller, greyer (less buffy) than other ♀ seedeaters, bill somewhat bicoloured. **Voice** Song, especially Jun–Jul, warbled phrases with much repetition.

♀

♂

whiteleyana

Chestnut-throated Seedeater
Sporophila telasco `LC`
Espiguero Pechiblanco
Fairly common resident (SW Nariño).

L 10.2 cm (4"). Monotypic. Dry to humid grassy, shrubby and agricultural areas. To 200 m. Pairs breed in rainy season, forms small loose flocks at other times. **ID** ♂ above faintly streaked, rump, base of tail, wing spot and underparts whitish; chestnut throat patch often hard to see (or obscure). ♀ white wing spot, dusky streaking on crown and mantle diagnostic. **Voice** Song, variable brisk sputter of sharply rising-falling semi-musical notes. **TN** Includes former Tumaco Seedeater *S. insulata*.

♀

♂

Chestnut-bellied Seedeater
Sporophila castaneiventris `LC`
Espiguero Buchicastaño
Common resident.

L 10.2 cm (4"). Monotypic. Tall grass and shrubs on riverbanks, borders of oxbows, grassy pastures, agricultural areas. To 1200 m (occasionally higher). Breeds in pairs, joins loose monospecific or mixed seedeater flocks at other times. **ID** Small. ♂ bright blue-grey, diagnostic broad maroon-chestnut stripe on median underparts. ♀ plain, median underparts pale, washed ochraceous. **Voice** Song, lively series of rather repetitive musical phrases. **SS** Ruddy-breasted Seedeater.

♀

♂

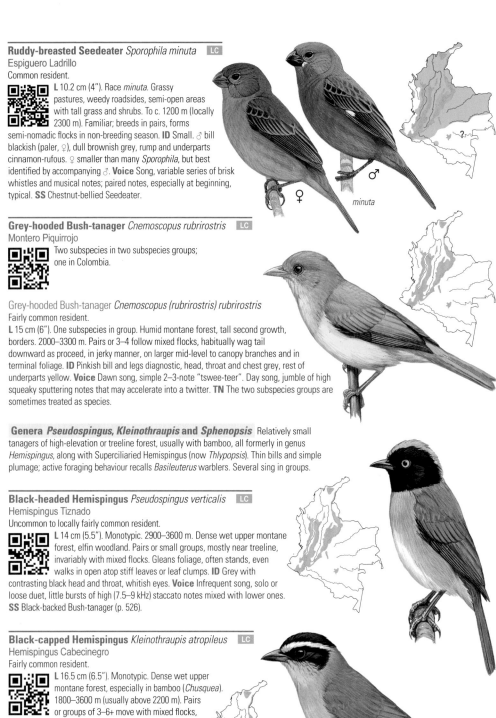

Ruddy-breasted Seedeater *Sporophila minuta* `LC`
Espiguero Ladrillo
Common resident.
L 10.2 cm (4"). Race *minuta*. Grassy pastures, weedy roadsides, semi-open areas with tall grass and shrubs. To c. 1200 m (locally 2300 m). Familiar; breeds in pairs, forms semi-nomadic flocks in non-breeding season. **ID** Small. ♂ bill blackish (paler, ♀), dull brownish grey, rump and underparts cinnamon-rufous. ♀ smaller than many *Sporophila*, but best identified by accompanying ♂. **Voice** Song, variable series of brisk whistles and musical notes; paired notes, especially at beginning, typical. **SS** Chestnut-bellied Seedeater.

♀   ♂   *minuta*

Grey-hooded Bush-tanager *Cnemoscopus rubrirostris* `LC`
Montero Piquirrojo
Two subspecies in two subspecies groups; one in Colombia.

Grey-hooded Bush-tanager *Cnemoscopus (rubrirostris) rubrirostris*
Fairly common resident.
L 15 cm (6"). One subspecies in group. Humid montane forest, tall second growth, borders. 2000–3300 m. Pairs or 3–4 follow mixed flocks, habitually wag tail downward as proceed, in jerky manner, on larger mid-level to canopy branches and in terminal foliage. **ID** Pinkish bill and legs diagnostic, head, throat and chest grey, rest of underparts yellow. **Voice** Dawn song, simple 2–3-note "tswee-teer". Day song, jumble of high squeaky sputtering notes that may accelerate into a twitter. **TN** The two subspecies groups are sometimes treated as species.

Genera *Pseudospingus*, *Kleinothraupis* and *Sphenopsis* Relatively small tanagers of high-elevation or treeline forest, usually with bamboo, all formerly in genus *Hemispingus*, along with Superciliaried Hemispingus (now *Thlypopsis*). Thin bills and simple plumage; active foraging behaviour recalls *Basileuterus* warblers. Several sing in groups.

Black-headed Hemispingus *Pseudospingus verticalis* `LC`
Hemispingus Tiznado
Uncommon to locally fairly common resident.
L 14 cm (5.5"). Monotypic. 2900–3600 m. Dense wet upper montane forest, elfin woodland. Pairs or small groups, mostly near treeline, invariably with mixed flocks. Gleans foliage, often stands, even walks in open atop stiff leaves or leaf clumps. **ID** Grey with contrasting black head and throat, whitish eyes. **Voice** Infrequent song, solo or loose duet, little bursts of high (7.5–9 kHz) staccato notes mixed with lower ones. **SS** Black-backed Bush-tanager (p. 526).

Black-capped Hemispingus *Kleinothraupis atropileus* `LC`
Hemispingus Cabecinegro
Fairly common resident.
L 16.5 cm (6.5"). Monotypic. Dense wet upper montane forest, especially in bamboo (*Chusquea*). 1800–3600 m (usually above 2200 m). Pairs or groups of 3–6+ move with mixed flocks, forage low, even near ground, to mid-levels; inspect foliage and leafy whorls of bamboo. **ID** Head black with long buffy-white eyestripe, below ochraceous, richest on throat. **Voice** Pairs or several simultaneously sing complex jumbled songs (duets, trios, quartets). **SS** Superciliaried Hemispingus (higher forest strata).

Oleaginous Hemispingus *Sphenopsis frontalis* `LC`
Hemispingus Verdoso
Fairly common resident.

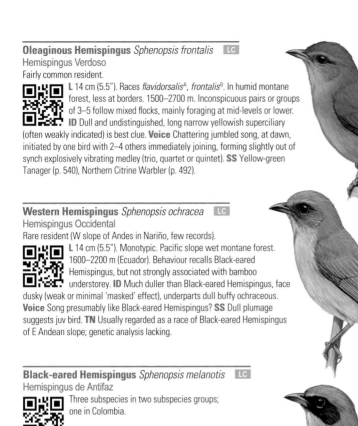
frontalis

L 14 cm (5.5"). Races *flavidorsalis*[A], *frontalis*[B]. In humid montane forest, less at borders. 1500–2700 m. Inconspicuous pairs or groups of 3–5 follow mixed flocks, mainly foraging at mid-levels or lower. **ID** Dull and undistinguished, long narrow yellowish superciliary (often weakly indicated) is best clue. **Voice** Chattering jumbled song, at dawn, initiated by one bird with 2–4 others immediately joining, forming slightly out of synch explosively vibrating medley (trio, quartet or quintet). **SS** Yellow-green Tanager (p. 540), Northern Citrine Warbler (p. 492).

Western Hemispingus *Sphenopsis ochracea* `LC`
Hemispingus Occidental
Rare resident (W slope of Andes in Nariño, few records).

L 14 cm (5.5"). Monotypic. Pacific slope wet montane forest. 1600–2200 m (Ecuador). Behaviour recalls Black-eared Hemispingus, but not strongly associated with bamboo understorey. **ID** Much duller than Black-eared Hemispingus, face dusky (weak or minimal 'masked' effect), underparts dull buffy ochraceous. **Voice** Song presumably like Black-eared Hemispingus? **SS** Dull plumage suggests juv bird. **TN** Usually regarded as a race of Black-eared Hemispingus of E Andean slope; genetic analysis lacking.

Black-eared Hemispingus *Sphenopsis melanotis* `LC`
Hemispingus de Antifaz

Three subspecies in two subspecies groups; one in Colombia.

Northern Black-eared Hemispingus *Sphenopsis (melanotis) melanotis*
Fairly common resident.
L 15 cm (6"). One subspecies in group. Lower growth to subcanopy of humid montane forest, borders, especially in bamboo. 1700–2900 m. Pairs or small groups habitually forage with mixed flocks, usually rather low and within cover. Actively inspects foliage. **ID** Plumage not strongly contrasting, grey crown, blackish mask, cinnamon-buff underparts. **Voice** Song, of explosive jumbled notes by pairs or groups, resembles that of Oleaginous Hemispingus. **SS** Rusty Flowerpiercer (p. 533), Rufous-crested Tanager (p. 515).

Genus *Thlypopsis* Small, restless, thin-billed and warbler-like, most species with contrasting orange to rufous head or foreparts, and preference for shrubby areas (except Superciliaried Hemispingus, which was recently moved to this genus based on DNA evidence).

Fulvous-headed Tanager *Thlypopsis fulviceps* `LC`
Zarcerito Encapuchado
Uncommon and local (?) resident.

intensa

obscuriceps

L 13 cm (5"). Races *obscuriceps*[A], *intensa*[B], race? (Santa Marta Mts). Canopy vines and shrubby second growth in moist to humid woodland. 1500–2400 m. Singles, pairs or families, regularly follow mixed flocks in forest canopy, lower at borders, actively glean foliage, checking curled hanging dead leaves; eat small fruit. **ID** Small and grey, paler below, head and throat reddish chestnut (*intensa*) or orange-rufous (*obscuriceps*); Santa Marta birds nearest *intensa*. **Voice** Infrequent song, high accelerating trill. Call, weak "tsit".

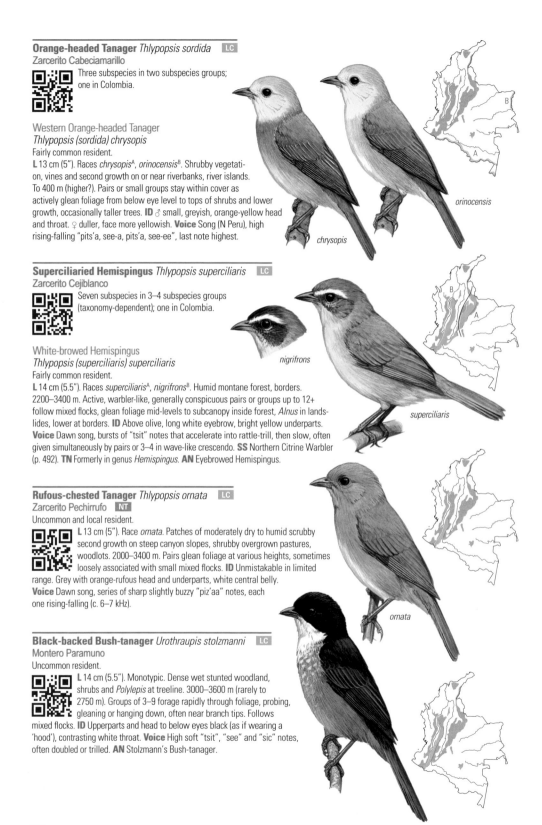

Orange-headed Tanager *Thlypopsis sordida* LC
Zarcerito Cabeciamarillo

Three subspecies in two subspecies groups; one in Colombia.

Western Orange-headed Tanager
Thlypopsis (sordida) chrysopis
Fairly common resident.
L 13 cm (5"). Races *chrysopis*[A], *orinocensis*[B]. Shrubby vegetation, vines and second growth on or near riverbanks, river islands. To 400 m (higher?). Pairs or small groups stay within cover as actively glean foliage from below eye level to tops of shrubs and lower growth, occasionally taller trees. **ID** ♂ small, greyish, orange-yellow head and throat. ♀ duller, face more yellowish. **Voice** Song (N Peru), high rising-falling "pits'a, see-a, pits'a, see-ee", last note highest.

orinocensis

chrysopis

Superciliaried Hemispingus *Thlypopsis superciliaris* LC
Zarcerito Cejiblanco

Seven subspecies in 3–4 subspecies groups (taxonomy-dependent); one in Colombia.

White-browed Hemispingus
Thlypopsis (superciliaris) superciliaris
Fairly common resident.
L 14 cm (5.5"). Races *superciliaris*[A], *nigrifrons*[B]. Humid montane forest, borders. 2200–3400 m. Active, warbler-like, generally conspicuous pairs or groups up to 12+ follow mixed flocks, glean foliage mid-levels to subcanopy inside forest, *Alnus* in landslides, lower at borders. **ID** Above olive, long white eyebrow, bright yellow underparts. **Voice** Dawn song, bursts of "tsit" notes that accelerate into rattle-trill, then slow, often given simultaneously by pairs or 3–4 in wave-like crescendo. **SS** Northern Citrine Warbler (p. 492). **TN** Formerly in genus *Hemispingus*. **AN** Eyebrowed Hemispingus.

nigrifrons

superciliaris

Rufous-chested Tanager *Thlypopsis ornata* LC
Zarcerito Pechirrufo NT
Uncommon and local resident.

L 13 cm (5"). Race *ornata*. Patches of moderately dry to humid scrubby second growth on steep canyon slopes, shrubby overgrown pastures, woodlots. 2000–3400 m. Pairs glean foliage at various heights, sometimes loosely associated with small mixed flocks. **ID** Unmistakable in limited range. Grey with orange-rufous head and underparts, white central belly. **Voice** Dawn song, series of sharp slightly buzzy "piz'aa" notes, each one rising-falling (c. 6–7 kHz).

ornata

Black-backed Bush-tanager *Urothraupis stolzmanni* LC
Montero Paramuno
Uncommon resident.

L 14 cm (5.5"). Monotypic. Dense wet stunted woodland, shrubs and *Polylepis* at treeline. 3000–3600 m (rarely to 2750 m). Groups of 3–9 forage rapidly through foliage, probing, gleaning or hanging down, often near branch tips. Follows mixed flocks. **ID** Upperparts and head to below eyes black (as if wearing a 'hood'), contrasting white throat. **Voice** High soft "tsit", "see" and "sic" notes, often doubled or trilled. **AN** Stolzmann's Bush-tanager.

Genus *Conirostrum* Small and warbler-like, with thin, sharp-pointed bills used to glean leaflets, leaf clusters and leaf axils. Lowland and high-elevation groups possibly represent different genera, although both are mostly blue or blue-grey above.

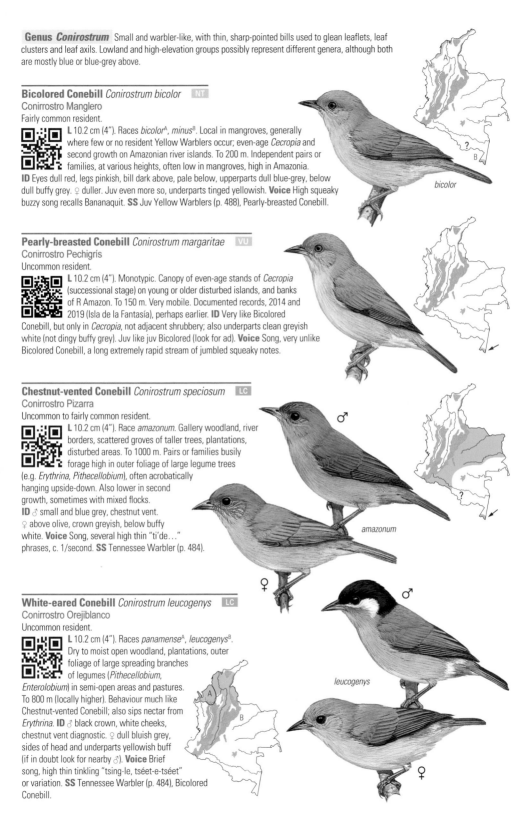

Bicolored Conebill *Conirostrum bicolor* NT
Conirrostro Manglero
Fairly common resident.

L 10.2 cm (4"). Races *bicolor*[A], *minus*[B]. Local in mangroves, generally where few or no resident Yellow Warblers occur; even-age *Cecropia* and second growth on Amazonian river islands. To 200 m. Independent pairs or families, at various heights, often low in mangroves, high in Amazonia. **ID** Eyes dull red, legs pinkish, bill dark above, pale below, upperparts dull blue-grey, below dull buffy grey. ♀ duller. Juv even more so, underparts tinged yellowish. **Voice** High squeaky buzzy song recalls Bananaquit. **SS** Juv Yellow Warblers (p. 488), Pearly-breasted Conebill.

bicolor

Pearly-breasted Conebill *Conirostrum margaritae* VU
Conirrostro Pechigrís
Uncommon resident.

L 10.2 cm (4"). Monotypic. Canopy of even-age stands of *Cecropia* (successional stage) on young or older disturbed islands, and banks of R Amazon. To 150 m. Very mobile. Documented records, 2014 and 2019 (Isla de la Fantasía), perhaps earlier. **ID** Very like Bicolored Conebill, but only in *Cecropia*, not adjacent shrubbery; also underparts clean greyish white (not dingy buffy grey). Juv like juv Bicolored (look for ad). **Voice** Song, very unlike Bicolored Conebill, a long extremely rapid stream of jumbled squeaky notes.

Chestnut-vented Conebill *Conirostrum speciosum* LC
Conirrostro Pizarra
Uncommon to fairly common resident.

L 10.2 cm (4"). Race *amazonum*. Gallery woodland, river borders, scattered groves of taller trees, plantations, disturbed areas. To 1000 m. Pairs or families busily forage high in outer foliage of large legume trees (e.g. *Erythrina*, *Pithecellobium*), often acrobatically hanging upside-down. Also lower in second growth, sometimes with mixed flocks. **ID** ♂ small and blue grey, chestnut vent. ♀ above olive, crown greyish, below buffy white. **Voice** Song, several high thin "ti'de…" phrases, c. 1/second. **SS** Tennessee Warbler (p. 484).

♂

amazonum

♀

White-eared Conebill *Conirostrum leucogenys* LC
Conirrostro Orejiblanco
Uncommon resident.

L 10.2 cm (4"). Races *panamense*[A], *leucogenys*[B]. Dry to moist open woodland, plantations, outer foliage of large spreading branches of legumes (*Pithecellobium*, *Enterolobium*) in semi-open areas and pastures. To 800 m (locally higher). Behaviour much like Chestnut-vented Conebill; also sips nectar from *Erythrina*. **ID** ♂ black crown, white cheeks, chestnut vent diagnostic. ♀ dull bluish grey, sides of head and underparts yellowish buff (if in doubt look for nearby ♂). **Voice** Brief song, high thin tinkling "tsing-le, tséet-e-tséet" or variation. **SS** Tennessee Warbler (p. 484), Bicolored Conebill.

♂

leucogenys

♀

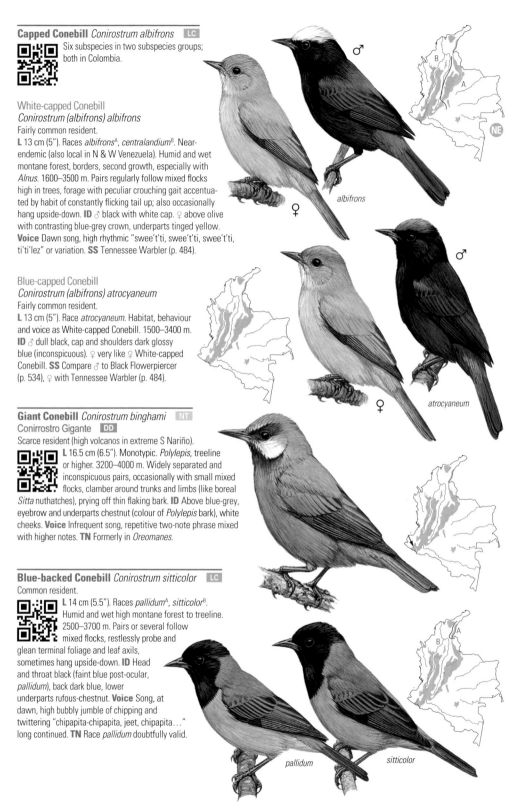

Capped Conebill *Conirostrum albifrons* LC

Six subspecies in two subspecies groups; both in Colombia.

White-capped Conebill
Conirostrum (albifrons) albifrons
Fairly common resident.
L 13 cm (5"). Races *albifrons*[A], *centralandium*[B]. Near-endemic (also local in N & W Venezuela). Humid and wet montane forest, borders, second growth, especially with *Alnus*. 1600–3500 m. Pairs regularly follow mixed flocks high in trees, forage with peculiar crouching gait accentuated by habit of constantly flicking tail up; also occasionally hang upside-down. **ID** ♂ black with white cap. ♀ above olive with contrasting blue-grey crown, underparts tinged yellow. **Voice** Dawn song, high rhythmic "swee't'ti, swee't'ti, swee't'ti, ti'ti'lez" or variation. **SS** Tennessee Warbler (p. 484).

Blue-capped Conebill
Conirostrum (albifrons) atrocyaneum
Fairly common resident.
L 13 cm (5"). Race *atrocyaneum*. Habitat, behaviour and voice as White-capped Conebill. 1500–3400 m. **ID** ♂ dull black, cap and shoulders dark glossy blue (inconspicuous). ♀ very like ♀ White-capped Conebill. **SS** Compare ♂ to Black Flowerpiercer (p. 534), ♀ with Tennessee Warbler (p. 484).

albifrons

♀

♂

atrocyaneum

♂

♀

Giant Conebill *Conirostrum binghami* NT
Conirrostro Gigante DD

Scarce resident (high volcanos in extreme S Nariño).
L 16.5 cm (6.5"). Monotypic. *Polylepis*, treeline or higher. 3200–4000 m. Widely separated and inconspicuous pairs, occasionally with small mixed flocks, clamber around trunks and limbs (like boreal *Sitta* nuthatches), prying off thin flaking bark. **ID** Above blue-grey, eyebrow and underparts chestnut (colour of *Polylepis* bark), white cheeks. **Voice** Infrequent song, repetitive two-note phrase mixed with higher notes. **TN** Formerly in *Oreomanes*.

Blue-backed Conebill *Conirostrum sitticolor* LC
Common resident.
L 14 cm (5.5"). Races *pallidum*[A], *sitticolor*[B]. Humid and wet high montane forest to treeline. 2500–3700 m. Pairs or several follow mixed flocks, restlessly probe and glean terminal foliage and leaf axils, sometimes hang upside-down. **ID** Head and throat black (faint blue post-ocular, *pallidum*), back dark blue, lower underparts rufous-chestnut. **Voice** Song, at dawn, high bubbly jumble of chipping and twittering "chipapita-chipapita, jeet, chipapita…" long continued. **TN** Race *pallidum* doubtfully valid.

pallidum

sitticolor

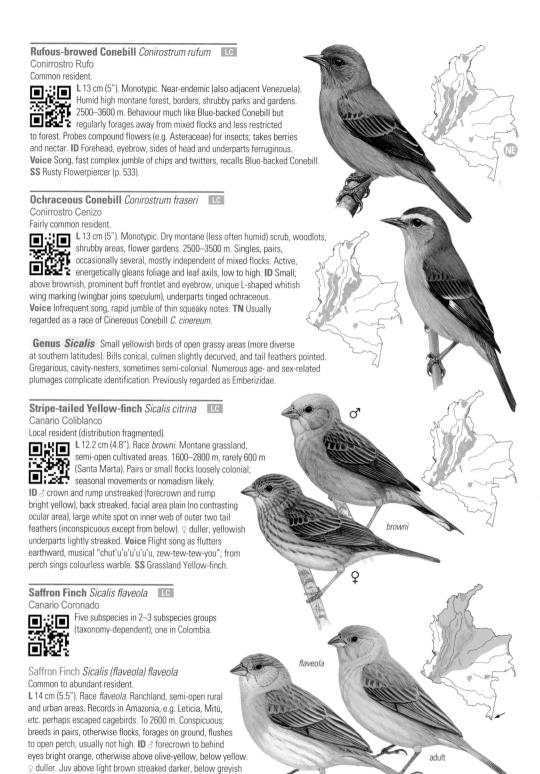

Rufous-browed Conebill *Conirostrum rufum* `LC`
Conirrostro Rufo
Common resident.

L 13 cm (5"). Monotypic. Near-endemic (also adjacent Venezuela). Humid high montane forest, borders, shrubby parks and gardens. 2500–3600 m. Behaviour much like Blue-backed Conebill but regularly forages away from mixed flocks and less restricted to forest. Probes compound flowers (e.g. Asteraceae) for insects; takes berries and nectar. **ID** Forehead, eyebrow, sides of head and underparts ferruginous. **Voice** Song, fast complex jumble of chips and twitters, recalls Blue-backed Conebill. **SS** Rusty Flowerpiercer (p. 533).

Ochraceous Conebill *Conirostrum fraseri* `LC`
Conirrostro Cenizo
Fairly common resident.

L 13 cm (5"). Monotypic. Dry montane (less often humid) scrub, woodlots, shrubby areas, flower gardens. 2500–3500 m. Singles, pairs, occasionally several, mostly independent of mixed flocks. Active, energetically gleans foliage and leaf axils, low to high. **ID** Small; above brownish, prominent buff frontlet and eyebrow, unique L-shaped whitish wing marking (wingbar joins speculum), underparts tinged ochraceous. **Voice** Infrequent song, rapid jumble of thin squeaky notes. **TN** Usually regarded as a race of Cinereous Conebill *C. cinereum*.

Genus *Sicalis* Small yellowish birds of open grassy areas (more diverse at southern latitudes). Bills conical, culmen slightly decurved, and tail feathers pointed. Gregarious, cavity-nesters, sometimes semi-colonial. Numerous age- and sex-related plumages complicate identification. Previously regarded as Emberizidae.

Stripe-tailed Yellow-finch *Sicalis citrina* `LC`
Canario Coliblanco
Local resident (distribution fragmented).

L 12.2 cm (4.8"). Race *browni*. Montane grassland, semi-open cultivated areas. 1600–2800 m, rarely 600 m (Santa Marta). Pairs or small flocks loosely colonial; seasonal movements or nomadism likely. **ID** ♂ crown and rump unstreaked (forecrown and rump bright yellow), back streaked, facial area plain (no contrasting ocular area), large white spot on inner web of outer two tail feathers (inconspicuous except from below). ♀ duller, yellowish underparts lightly streaked. **Voice** Flight song as flutters earthward, musical "chut'u'u'u'u'u'u, zew-tew-tew-you"; from perch sings colourless warble. **SS** Grassland Yellow-finch.

Saffron Finch *Sicalis flaveola* `LC`
Canario Coronado

Five subspecies in 2–3 subspecies groups (taxonomy-dependent); one in Colombia.

Saffron Finch *Sicalis (flaveola) flaveola*
Common to abundant resident.

L 14 cm (5.5"). Race *flaveola*. Ranchland, semi-open rural and urban areas. Records in Amazonia, e.g. Leticia, Mitú, etc. perhaps escaped cagebirds. To 2600 m. Conspicuous; breeds in pairs, otherwise flocks, forages on ground, flushes to open perch, usually not high. **ID** ♂ forecrown to behind eyes bright orange, otherwise above olive-yellow, below yellow. ♀ duller. Juv above light brown streaked darker, below greyish white, rump and vent yellowish. Imm like juv but broad diffuse yellow band on chest. **Voice** Song, dry rambling chatter. **SS** Orange-fronted Yellow-finch.

browni

♂

♀

flaveola

adult

immature

529

Orange-fronted Yellow-finch *Sicalis columbiana* LC
Canario Ribereño

Uncommon to common but local resident.

L 13 cm (5"). Race *columbiana*. Ranchland, especially wetter low *llanos*, streambanks, waterholes, ports (e.g. Puerto Inírida). To 350 m. Behaviour like commoner Saffron Finch, sometimes with latter, and they are often confused. **ID** ♂ from Saffron Finch by smaller size, overall greenish-olive (not yellowish) upperparts, duller yellowish-olive underparts, sharply defined orange band on forehead (not extending behind eyes), rest of head olive to yellowish olive (not yellow), dusky ocular area. ♀ from ♀ Saffron Finch by dull brownish-grey plumage, paler below, blackish area around eyes, yellowish-olive wings and tail. **Voice** Call, soft "chu're'reet". Song, chippy and unmusical.

columbiana

Grassland Yellow-finch *Sicalis luteola* LC
Canario Sabanero

Eight subspecies in four subspecies groups; two in Colombia.

Montane Yellow-finch *Sicalis (luteola) bogotensis*
Local resident.

L 13.2 cm (5.2"). Race *bogotensis*. Open areas of taller grass in mountains, especially wet or marshy areas. 2500–3400 m. Behaviour and voice as *luteola* (below). **ID** Similar to *luteola* but slightly larger, head and ocular area brighter yellow and less contrasting, upperparts slightly darker, more olive. **SS** Stripe-tailed Yellow-finch.

bogotensis

Grassland Yellow-finch *Sicalis (luteola) luteola*
Locally common resident (*llanos*).

L 13 cm (5"). Race *luteola*. Grassland, semi-open cultivated areas. To 2000 m. Abundance unpredictable; singles to variable-sized flocks, breeding probably semi-colonial. Restless, flushes erratically from grass. **ID** ♂ resembles Stripe-tailed Yellow-finch, but crown streaked, lores and ocular area yellowish, no white in tail. ♀ like ♀ Stripe-tailed Yellow-finch but underparts unstreaked. **Voice** Song, perched or in high flight display, rapid chips, buzzes and trills. Call "tease-zip".

luteola

Plumbeous Sierra-finch *Geospizopsis unicolor* LC
Gorrión Paramuno

Seven subspecies in three subspecies groups; one in Colombia.

Northern Plumbeous Sierra-finch
Geospizopsis (unicolor) geospizopsis
Common resident.

L 15 cm (6"). Races *nivaria*[A], *geospizopsis*[B]. Shrubby or grassy areas from treeline to snowline. 3000–4500 m. Pairs or small groups peck at seeds on ground or roadsides, often with other birds. Confiding, flushes to rocks or bushes. **ID** ♂ plump and grey, small conical bill, faint pale eye-ring, pinkish to greyish-pink legs (both sexes). ♀ above brownish, below dull whitish, heavily streaked throughout. **Voice** Infrequent song, short buzz increasing dramatically in volume. Sharp "spit" call. **SS** Juv Rufous-collared Sparrow (p. 470). **TN** Formerly in genus *Phrygilus*.

nivaria

Slaty Finch *Spodiornis rusticus* `LC`
Gorrión Pizarra

Scarce and unpredictable resident.

 L 13 cm (5"). Race *rusticus*. Shrubby humid forest borders, especially with bamboo. 1200–2800 m. Nomadic; seeks patches of dying bamboo (*Chusquea*) with heavy seed crops for breeding, when temporarily numerous, but otherwise scattered and infrequently seen. Usually on or near ground. **ID** Slender conical bill diagnostic. ♂ uniform slate-grey. ♀ above dark olive-brown, underparts buffy olive, somewhat streaked. **Voice** Song, long or short, typically thin rapid trills increasing in volume and complexity. **SS** *Catamenia* seedeaters, Plumbeous Sierra-finch.

Genus *Catamenia* Small seedeaters, in Colombia found only at high elevations, in semi-open areas or dense humid wooded borders. ♂♂ grey with chestnut vent and thick stubby pinkish to yellow bills. ♀♀ streaky brown with chestnut vent (except ♀ Band-tailed).

Band-tailed Seedeater *Catamenia analis* `LC`
Semillero Coliblanco

Fairly common but local resident.

 L 12.2 cm (4.8"). Races *alpica*[A], *schistaceifrons*[B]. Semi-open shrubby and grassy areas near or in *páramo*. 2500–3800 m. Singles or pairs, forage on or near ground. **ID** ♂ stubby deep yellow bill, plumage grey, chestnut vent, white tail-band most visible in flight. ♀ heavily streaked above and below, tail as in ♂. **Voice** Song, mostly in display flight, short buzzy trill, slower than Plumbeous Sierra-finch. **SS** Other *Catamenia* seedeaters.

Plain-colored Seedeater *Catamenia inornata* `LC`
Semillero Andino

Common resident.

 L 13 cm (5"). Race *minor*. Shrubby semi-open grassland near treeline and *páramo*. Mostly 2600–3800 m. Pairs when breeding, otherwise little flocks; partially nomadic. Often forages on ground, e.g. on *Espeletia* (Asteraceae) seeds. **ID** Bill orange-pink (much duller, ♀). ♂ plain grey, upperparts streaked, vent chestnut. ♀ brownish, above streaked, below paler and finely streaked, vent chestnut. Juv more heavily streaked than ♀. **Voice** Song, 2–3 notes, then 2–4 slow buzzes "chit-t-t, zreeee, bzzzz, breeee" (last three, inhale, exhale and inhale). **SS** ♀ Paramo Seedeater.

Paramo Seedeater *Catamenia homochroa* `LC`
Semillero de Páramo

 Three subspecies in three subspecies groups; two in Colombia. Taxonomy unresolved; needs DNA analysis.

Santa Marta Seedeater *Catamenia (homochroa) oreophila*
Uncommon and local resident.

L 12 cm (4.7"). One subspecies in group. Endemic. Shrubby humid forest borders, dense low shrubby second growth in clearings. 2200–3300 m. Behaviour, as far as known, like Andean race *homochroa* (next page). **ID** Similar to *homochroa* but bill shorter, tail longer, overall paler, more uniform in colour, breast tinged brownish. **Voice** As Andean *homochroa*. **TN** Has been regarded as a species.

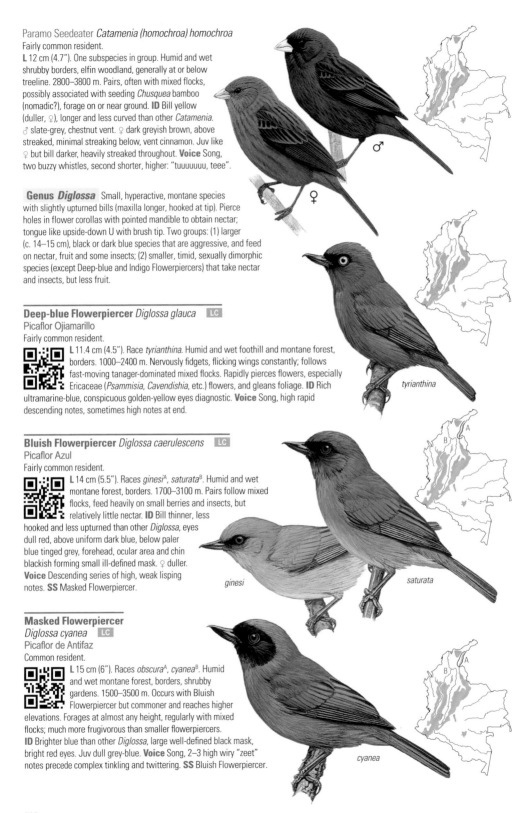

Paramo Seedeater *Catamenia (homochroa) homochroa*
Fairly common resident.
L 12 cm (4.7"). One subspecies in group. Humid and wet
shrubby borders, elfin woodland, generally at or below
treeline. 2800–3800 m. Pairs, often with mixed flocks,
possibly associated with seeding *Chusquea* bamboo
(nomadic?), forage on or near ground. **ID** Bill yellow
(duller, ♀), longer and less curved than other *Catamenia*.
♂ slate-grey, chestnut vent. ♀ dark greyish brown, above
streaked, minimal streaking below, vent cinnamon. Juv like
♀ but bill darker, heavily streaked throughout. **Voice** Song,
two buzzy whistles, second shorter, higher: "tuuuuuu, teee".

Genus *Diglossa* Small, hyperactive, montane species
with slightly upturned bills (maxilla longer, hooked at tip). Pierce
holes in flower corollas with pointed mandible to obtain nectar;
tongue like upside-down U with brush tip. Two groups: (1) larger
(c. 14–15 cm), black or dark blue species that are aggressive, and feed
on nectar, fruit and some insects; (2) smaller, timid, sexually dimorphic
species (except Deep-blue and Indigo Flowerpiercers) that take nectar
and insects, but less fruit.

Deep-blue Flowerpiercer *Diglossa glauca* LC
Picaflor Ojiamarillo
Fairly common resident.
L 11.4 cm (4.5"). Race *tyrianthina*. Humid and wet foothill and montane forest,
borders. 1000–2400 m. Nervously fidgets, flicking wings constantly; follows
fast-moving tanager-dominated mixed flocks. Rapidly pierces flowers, especially
Ericaceae (*Psammisia*, *Cavendishia*, etc.) flowers, and gleans foliage. **ID** Rich
ultramarine-blue, conspicuous golden-yellow eyes diagnostic. **Voice** Song, high rapid
descending notes, sometimes high notes at end.

tyrianthina

Bluish Flowerpiercer *Diglossa caerulescens* LC
Picaflor Azul
Fairly common resident.
L 14 cm (5.5"). Races *ginesi*[A], *saturata*[B]. Humid and wet
montane forest, borders. 1700–3100 m. Pairs follow mixed
flocks, feed heavily on small berries and insects, but
relatively little nectar. **ID** Bill thinner, less
hooked and less upturned than other *Diglossa*, eyes
dull red, above uniform dark blue, below paler
blue tinged grey, forehead, ocular area and chin
blackish forming small ill-defined mask. ♀ duller.
Voice Descending series of high, weak lisping
notes. **SS** Masked Flowerpiercer.

ginesi

saturata

Masked Flowerpiercer
Diglossa cyanea LC
Picaflor de Antifaz
Common resident.
L 15 cm (6"). Races *obscura*[A], *cyanea*[B]. Humid
and wet montane forest, borders, shrubby
gardens. 1500–3500 m. Occurs with Bluish
Flowerpiercer but commoner and reaches higher
elevations. Forages at almost any height, regularly with mixed
flocks; much more frugivorous than smaller flowerpiercers.
ID Brighter blue than other *Diglossa*, large well-defined black mask,
bright red eyes. Juv dull grey-blue. **Voice** Song, 2–3 high wiry "zeet"
notes precede complex tinkling and twittering. **SS** Bluish Flowerpiercer.

cyanea

Indigo Flowerpiercer *Diglossa indigotica* `LC`
Picaflor del Chocó
Local resident.

 L 11.4 cm (4.5"). Monotypic. Near-endemic (also W Ecuador). Wet mossy foothill and montane forest. 800–2200 m (mostly below 1800 m). Behaviour much like Deep-blue Flowerpiercer. **ID** Rich ultramarine-blue, bright red eyes. **Voice** Song, very high (c. 9–7 kHz) thin smoothly descending series of "ti" notes, c. 6–7/second for 3–8 seconds, sometimes preceded by softer warbling notes. **SS** Larger Masked Flowerpiercer.

Rusty Flowerpiercer *Diglossa sittoides* `LC`
Picaflor Canela
Uncommon to locally fairly common resident.

dorbignyi

 L 11.4 cm (4.5"). Races *hyperytha*[A], *coelestis*[B], *dorbignyi*[C]. Bushy wooded borders, coffee plantations, shrubby flower gardens; in drier more sunny areas than other *Diglossa*. Mostly 1400–3000 m. Singles or pairs, restless, fidgety. Incidental with mixed flocks; territorial. Primarily pierces flowers for nectar, but sallies for flying insects. Some seasonal movements. **ID** ♂ above dull blue, small black mask, below cinnamon (paler cinnamon, *hyperytha*). ♀ above brownish, below paler, lightly streaked. **Voice** Song, short variable-pitched chattering trill; also even-pitched or descending trill of variable speed.

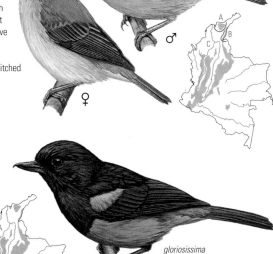

♂

♀

Chestnut-bellied Flowerpiercer
Diglossa gloriosissima `NT`
Picaflor Pechirrufo `VU`
Fairly common but local resident.

 L 14 cm (5.5"). Races *boylei*[A] (S to Tatamá National Park region), *gloriosissima*[B] (few records, S Valle, Cauca). Endemic. Stunted mossy forest to treeline, dense shrubbery on ridges, borders. 2400–3800 m. Singles or pairs, alone or with mixed flocks, pierce flowers (especially Ericaceae), eat fruit (e.g. *Miconia*). **ID** Unique in tiny range; black, mid-breast to vent rufous-chestnut, grey shoulder patch. **Voice** Song, mostly at dawn, long galloping series of bright chattering notes c. 4–6 kHz. Call, sharp "peek". **TN** Sometimes treated as monotypic.

gloriosissima

Glossy Flowerpiercer *Diglossa lafresnayii* `LC`
Picaflor Lustroso
Common resident (commonest near treeline).

 L 14.5 cm (5.7"). Monotypic. Humid montane forest, borders, shrubby areas; less in gardens and disturbed areas (vs. Black Flowerpiercer). 2500–3800 m (rarely lower). Territorial singles or pairs, alone or with mixed flocks, hide in cover, briefly appear, pierce a few flowers then quickly disappear. **ID** Easily confused with Black Flowerpiercer (especially E Andes) but larger, bill heavier, plumage glossier, shoulder patch more bluish than grey, more associated with forest. **Voice** Song (C Andes) from bush top, long-sustained, rambling two-syllabled semi-musical notes c. 5 kHz; in E Andes, similar two-syllable notes but 'choppier'.

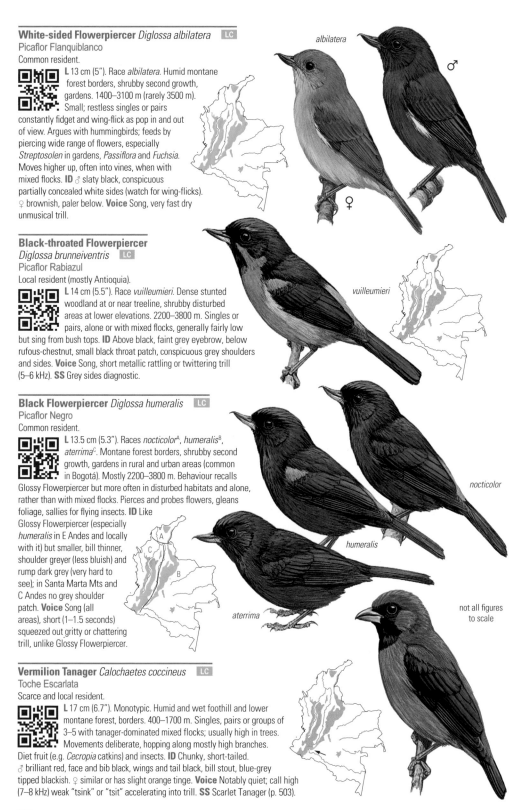

White-sided Flowerpiercer *Diglossa albilatera* `LC`
Picaflor Flanquiblanco
Common resident.

L 13 cm (5"). Race *albilatera*. Humid montane forest borders, shrubby second growth, gardens. 1400–3100 m (rarely 3500 m). Small; restless singles or pairs constantly fidget and wing-flick as pop in and out of view. Argues with hummingbirds; feeds by piercing wide range of flowers, especially *Streptosolen* in gardens, *Passiflora* and *Fuchsia*. Moves higher up, often into vines, when with mixed flocks. **ID** ♂ slaty black, conspicuous partially concealed white sides (watch for wing-flicks). ♀ brownish, paler below. **Voice** Song, very fast dry unmusical trill.

albilatera

♂

♀

Black-throated Flowerpiercer
Diglossa brunneiventris `LC`
Picaflor Rabiazul
Local resident (mostly Antioquia).

L 14 cm (5.5"). Race *vuilleumieri*. Dense stunted woodland at or near treeline, shrubby disturbed areas at lower elevations. 2200–3800 m. Singles or pairs, alone or with mixed flocks, generally fairly low but sing from bush tops. **ID** Above black, faint grey eyebrow, below rufous-chestnut, small black throat patch, conspicuous grey shoulders and sides. **Voice** Song, short metallic rattling or twittering trill (5–6 kHz). **SS** Grey sides diagnostic.

vuilleumieri

Black Flowerpiercer *Diglossa humeralis* `LC`
Picaflor Negro
Common resident.

L 13.5 cm (5.3"). Races *nocticolor*[A], *humeralis*[B], *aterrima*[C]. Montane forest borders, shrubby second growth, gardens in rural and urban areas (common in Bogotá). Mostly 2200–3800 m. Behaviour recalls Glossy Flowerpiercer but more often in disturbed habitats and alone, rather than with mixed flocks. Pierces and probes flowers, gleans foliage, sallies for flying insects. **ID** Like Glossy Flowerpiercer (especially *humeralis* in E Andes and locally with it) but smaller, bill thinner, shoulder greyer (less bluish) and rump dark grey (very hard to see); in Santa Marta Mts and C Andes no grey shoulder patch. **Voice** Song (all areas), short (1–1.5 seconds) squeezed out gritty or chattering trill, unlike Glossy Flowerpiercer.

nocticolor

humeralis

aterrima

not all figures to scale

Vermilion Tanager *Calochaetes coccineus* `LC`
Toche Escarlata
Scarce and local resident.

L 17 cm (6.7"). Monotypic. Humid and wet foothill and lower montane forest, borders. 400–1700 m. Singles, pairs or groups of 3–5 with tanager-dominated mixed flocks; usually high in trees. Movements deliberate, hopping along mostly high branches. Diet fruit (e.g. *Cecropia* catkins) and insects. **ID** Chunky, short-tailed. ♂ brilliant red, face and bib black, wings and tail black, bill stout, blue-grey tipped blackish. ♀ similar or has slight orange tinge. **Voice** Notably quiet; call high (7–8 kHz) weak "tsink" or "tsit" accelerating into trill. **SS** Scarlet Tanager (p. 503).

Genus _Iridosornis_ Richly attired dark blue tanagers with golden-yellow on head or throat, chestnut undertail-coverts, and short thick bills (blue-grey tipped dusky). Quiet and inconspicuous.

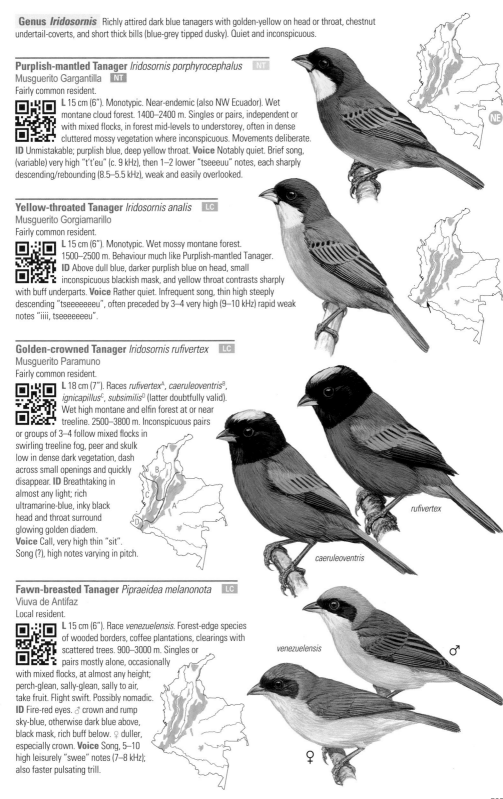

Purplish-mantled Tanager _Iridosornis porphyrocephalus_ NT
Musguerito Gargantilla **NT**
Fairly common resident.

L 15 cm (6"). Monotypic. Near-endemic (also NW Ecuador). Wet montane cloud forest. 1400–2400 m. Singles or pairs, independent or with mixed flocks, in forest mid-levels to understorey, often in dense cluttered mossy vegetation where inconspicuous. Movements deliberate. **ID** Unmistakable; purplish blue, deep yellow throat. **Voice** Notably quiet. Brief song, (variable) very high "t't'eu" (c. 9 kHz), then 1–2 lower "tseeeuu" notes, each sharply descending/rebounding (8.5–5.5 kHz), weak and easily overlooked.

NE

Yellow-throated Tanager _Iridosornis analis_ LC
Musguerito Gorgiamarillo
Fairly common resident.

L 15 cm (6"). Monotypic. Wet mossy montane forest. 1500–2500 m. Behaviour much like Purplish-mantled Tanager. **ID** Above dull blue, darker purplish blue on head, small inconspicuous blackish mask, and yellow throat contrasts sharply with buff underparts. **Voice** Rather quiet. Infrequent song, thin high steeply descending "tseeeeeeeu", often preceded by 3–4 very high (9–10 kHz) rapid weak notes "iiii, tseeeeeeeu".

Golden-crowned Tanager _Iridosornis rufivertex_ LC
Musguerito Paramuno
Fairly common resident.

L 18 cm (7"). Races _rufivertex_[A], _caeruleoventris_[B], _ignicapillus_[C], _subsimilis_[D] (latter doubtfully valid). Wet high montane and elfin forest at or near treeline. 2500–3800 m. Inconspicuous pairs or groups of 3–4 follow mixed flocks in swirling treeline fog, peer and skulk low in dense dark vegetation, dash across small openings and quickly disappear. **ID** Breathtaking in almost any light; rich ultramarine-blue, inky black head and throat surround glowing golden diadem. **Voice** Call, very high thin "sit". Song (?), high notes varying in pitch.

rufivertex

caeruleoventris

Fawn-breasted Tanager _Pipraeidea melanonota_ LC
Viuva de Antifaz
Local resident.

L 15 cm (6"). Race _venezuelensis_. Forest-edge species of wooded borders, coffee plantations, clearings with scattered trees. 900–3000 m. Singles or pairs mostly alone, occasionally with mixed flocks, at almost any height; perch-glean, sally-glean, sally to air, take fruit. Flight swift. Possibly nomadic. **ID** Fire-red eyes. ♂ crown and rump sky-blue, otherwise dark blue above, black mask, rich buff below. ♀ duller, especially crown. **Voice** Song, 5–10 high leisurely "swee" notes (7–8 kHz); also faster pulsating trill.

venezuelensis

♂

♀

Carriker's Mountain-tanager *Dubusia carrikeri* `EN`
Tangará Diadema de Carriker
Uncommon resident.

 L 19 cm (7.5"). Monotypic. Endemic. 2200–3300 m (higher?). **ID** Like *taeniata* (below) but eyebrow mostly blue (no frosty streaks), buff chest-band larger, reaches throat. **Voice** Much thinner, weaker, higher-pitched and pattern unlike *taeniata*, a 2–4-note "siiiiap, siiiiap, siiiiieeee", first notes descending (c. 5.5–4.5 kHz), last note much higher and also descending (c. 9–6 kHz). **TN** Usually treated as a race of Buff-breasted Mountain-tanager.

Buff-breasted Mountain-tanager
Dubusia taeniata `LC`
Tangará Diadema
Fairly common but unpredictable resident.

 L 19 cm (7.5"). Race *taeniata*. Humid and wet montane forest, borders, elfin woodland to treeline. 2400–3600 m. Singles or pairs with mixed tanager flocks or alone. Generally high in trees, may perch in open briefly, roams over large territories. **ID** Black head and throat, long frosty-streaked eyebrow diagnostic, buff chest not particularly obvious. **Voice** Distinctive two-note song, repeatedly given at dawn, loud "pheeeee-bay", first note higher, both gradually slurred lower (c. 5.5–3.5 kHz). **TN** See previous species.

taeniata

Hooded Mountain-tanager
Buthraupis montana `LC`
Azulejo Real
Fairly common but low-density resident.

 L 23 cm (9"). Races *gigas*[A], *cucullata*[B]. Humid and wet montane forest to treeline. 2200–3600 m. Conspicuous groups of 3–10 roam over large areas, often with jays and caciques or loosely associated with smaller species, hop along relatively open branches and lean down to inspect sides. Apt to fly off considerable distances. **ID** By large size, black head, blue-and-yellow plumage; up close red eyes. **Voice** Dawn song, long series of repetitive "see'ak" or "seek" notes. At other times 2–4-note calls and chattering. Rarely, flight display song.

cucullata

Blue-capped Tanager *Sporathraupis cyanocephala* `LC`
Azulejo Montanero

 Eight subspecies in two subspecies groups; one in Colombia.

Blue-capped Tanager *Sporathraupis (cyanocephala) cyanocephala*
Common resident.
L 19 cm (7.5"). Races *margaritae*[A], *auricrissa*[B], *annectens*[C], *cyanocephala*[D]. Non-forest species of wooded borders, patches of second growth, shrubby areas. 1500–3200 m. Pairs or several, alone or with mixed flocks. Conspicuous; remain high in trees, often at fruiting trees. **ID** Handsome but so common it garners little attention. Above bright yellow-olive, crown cobalt-blue, below blue-grey (or bluish, *annectens*), yellow underwings, vent and thighs. **Voice** Infrequent song, a twittering unmusical jumble of notes. **TN** Formerly in *Thraupis*.

cyanocephala

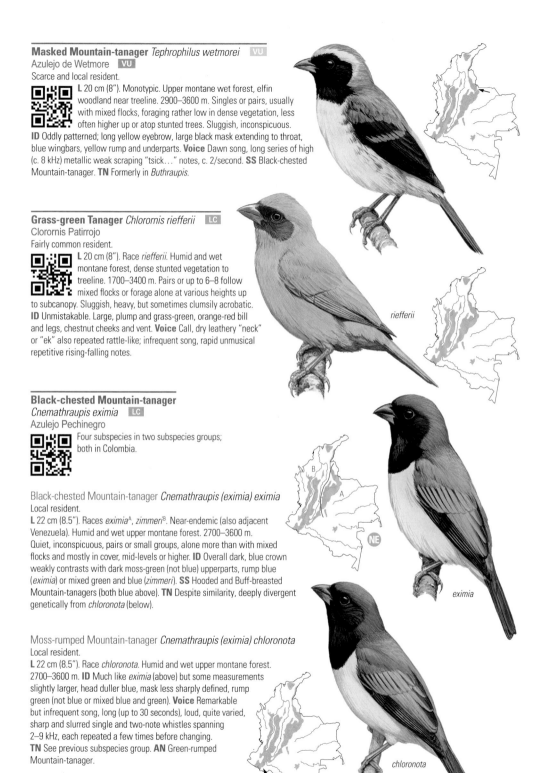

Masked Mountain-tanager *Tephrophilus wetmorei* VU
Azulejo de Wetmore VU
Scarce and local resident.

L 20 cm (8"). Monotypic. Upper montane wet forest, elfin woodland near treeline. 2900–3600 m. Singles or pairs, usually with mixed flocks, foraging rather low in dense vegetation, less often higher up or atop stunted trees. Sluggish, inconspicuous. **ID** Oddly patterned; long yellow eyebrow, large black mask extending to throat, blue wingbars, yellow rump and underparts. **Voice** Dawn song, long series of high (c. 8 kHz) metallic weak scraping "tsick…" notes, c. 2/second. **SS** Black-chested Mountain-tanager. **TN** Formerly in *Buthraupis*.

Grass-green Tanager *Chlorornis riefferii* LC
Clorornis Patirrojo
Fairly common resident.

L 20 cm (8"). Race *riefferii*. Humid and wet montane forest, dense stunted vegetation to treeline. 1700–3400 m. Pairs or up to 6–8 follow mixed flocks or forage alone at various heights up to subcanopy. Sluggish, heavy, but sometimes clumsily acrobatic. **ID** Unmistakable. Large, plump and grass-green, orange-red bill and legs, chestnut cheeks and vent. **Voice** Call, dry leathery "neck" or "ek" also repeated rattle-like; infrequent song, rapid unmusical repetitive rising-falling notes.

riefferii

Black-chested Mountain-tanager
Cnemathraupis eximia LC
Azulejo Pechinegro

Four subspecies in two subspecies groups; both in Colombia.

Black-chested Mountain-tanager *Cnemathraupis (eximia) eximia*
Local resident.
L 22 cm (8.5"). Races *eximia*[A], *zimmeri*[B]. Near-endemic (also adjacent Venezuela). Humid and wet upper montane forest. 2700–3600 m. Quiet, inconspicuous, pairs or small groups, alone more than with mixed flocks and mostly in cover, mid-levels or higher. **ID** Overall dark, blue crown weakly contrasts with dark moss-green (not blue) upperparts, rump blue (*eximia*) or mixed green and blue (*zimmeri*). **SS** Hooded and Buff-breasted Mountain-tanagers (both blue above). **TN** Despite similarity, deeply divergent genetically from *chloronota* (below).

NE

eximia

Moss-rumped Mountain-tanager *Cnemathraupis (eximia) chloronota*
Local resident.
L 22 cm (8.5"). Race *chloronota*. Humid and wet upper montane forest. 2700–3600 m. **ID** Much like *eximia* (above) but some measurements slightly larger, head duller blue, mask less sharply defined, rump green (not blue or mixed blue and green). **Voice** Remarkable but infrequent song, long (up to 30 seconds), loud, quite varied, sharp and slurred single and two-note whistles spanning 2–9 kHz, each repeated a few times before changing. **TN** See previous subspecies group. **AN** Green-rumped Mountain-tanager.

chloronota

Genus *Anisognathus* Colourful high-Andean tanagers with a mixed diet but highly frugivorous. More conspicuous and gregarious than *Iridosornis*, smaller and more agile than *Buthraupis*, *Tephrophilus* and *Cnemathraupis*, and none is remotely similar vocally to *Dubusia*.

Blue-winged Mountain-tanager *Anisognathus somptuosus* LC
Tangará Primavera
Fairly common to common resident.

 L 19 cm (7.5"). Races *antioquiae*[A], *victorini*[B], *cyanopterus*[C], *baezae*[D]. Humid and wet montane forest, borders, older second growth. 1300–2800 m. Conspicuous, active pairs or groups of 3–10 follow mixed flocks or forage alone, in lower growth to subcanopy, often in open along smaller leafy branches. **ID** Colourful, median crown-stripe yellow, back black (or moss-green, *victorini*, *baezae*), shoulders and flight feathers blue. **Voice** Rather quiet. Song, rapid high twittering, louder, faster, then fading. **SS** Black-chinned Mountain-tanager.

baezae

cyanopterus

Black-chinned Mountain-tanager *Anisognathus notabilis* LC
Tangará del Pacífico
Uncommon and local resident.

 L 19 cm (7.5"). Monotypic. Near-endemic (also NW Ecuador). Humid and wet mossy montane forest. Overlaps Blue-winged Mountain-tanager but centre of distribution lower. 900–2200 m. Behaviour recalls Blue-winged Mountain-tanager, but typically only pairs, less conspicuous, much less numerous, the two occasionally together. **ID** Best marks are yellow-olive back, longer more conical bill. **Voice** Song, repeated undistinguished high "tsit" notes. **SS** Blue-winged Mountain-tanager.

NE

Santa Marta Mountain-tanager (Black-cheeked Mountain-tanager)
Anisognathus melanogenys LC
Tangará Serrana
Fairly common to common resident.

 L 19 cm (7.5"). Monotypic. Endemic. Humid and wet montane forest, regenerating second growth, borders. 1900–3200 m (locally 1600 m). Pairs or small groups, regularly with mixed flocks or other birds at fruiting trees, lower growth to mossy subcanopy. **ID** Blue crown and nape, blackish sides of head, small yellow 'teardrop' below eye, yellow underparts. **Voice** Very high "tick" notes (c. 9 kHz).

E

Scarlet-bellied Mountain-tanager
Anisognathus lunulatus LC
Tangará Escarlata
Common resident.

 L 18.5 cm (7.3"). Races *lunulatus*[A], *erythrotus*[B]. Humid montane forest, stunted treeline woodland, trees in pastures, fence rows, shrubby agricultural areas. 2400–3600 m. One of the showiest mountain-tanagers in Colombia. Pairs or groups up to a dozen follow mixed flocks or more often forage independently. Tends to remain in cover, where inconspicuous, then flies some distance. **ID** Mostly black, sky-blue rump and shoulder patch, red triangle behind cheeks and red lower underparts. Juv duller. **Voice** Unusual mechanical-sounding song of repeated, tinkling rising-falling phrases. **TN** The three northern races (two in Colombia) usually included with southern *igniventris* as a single species *A. igniventris*.

erythrotus

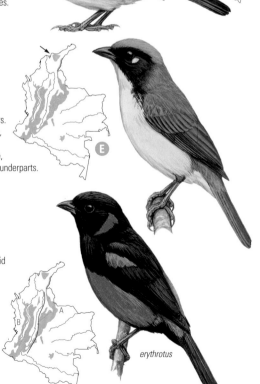

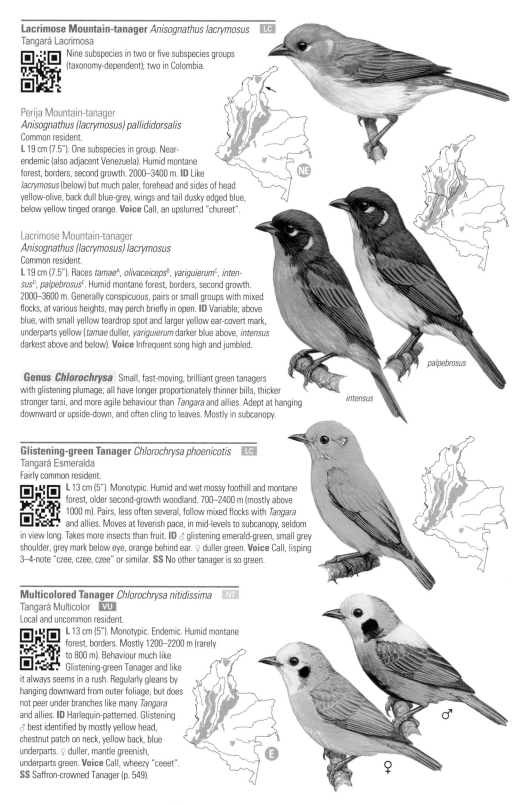

Lacrimose Mountain-tanager *Anisognathus lacrymosus* `LC`
Tangará Lacrimosa

Nine subspecies in two or five subspecies groups (taxonomy-dependent); two in Colombia.

Perija Mountain-tanager
Anisognathus (lacrymosus) pallididorsalis
Common resident.
L 19 cm (7.5"). One subspecies in group. Near-endemic (also adjacent Venezuela). Humid montane forest, borders, second growth. 2000–3400 m. **ID** Like *lacrymosus* (below) but much paler, forehead and sides of head yellow-olive, back dull blue-grey, wings and tail dusky edged blue, below yellow tinged orange. **Voice** Call, an upslurred "chureet".

Lacrimose Mountain-tanager
Anisognathus (lacrymosus) lacrymosus
Common resident.
L 19 cm (7.5"). Races *tamae*[A], *olivaceiceps*[B], *yariguierum*[C], *intensus*[D], *palpebrosus*[E]. Humid montane forest, borders, second growth. 2000–3600 m. Generally conspicuous, pairs or small groups with mixed flocks, at various heights, may perch briefly in open. **ID** Variable; above blue, with small yellow teardrop spot and larger yellow ear-covert mark, underparts yellow (*tamae* duller, *yariguierum* darker blue above, *intensus* darkest above and below). **Voice** Infrequent song high and jumbled.

Genus *Chlorochrysa* Small, fast-moving, brilliant green tanagers with glistening plumage; all have longer proportionately thinner bills, thicker stronger tarsi, and more agile behaviour than *Tangara* and allies. Adept at hanging downward or upside-down, and often cling to leaves. Mostly in subcanopy.

palpebrosus

intensus

Glistening-green Tanager *Chlorochrysa phoenicotis* `LC`
Tangará Esmeralda
Fairly common resident.

L 13 cm (5"). Monotypic. Humid and wet mossy foothill and montane forest, older second-growth woodland. 700–2400 m (mostly above 1000 m). Pairs, less often several, follow mixed flocks with *Tangara* and allies. Moves at feverish pace, in mid-levels to subcanopy, seldom in view long. Takes more insects than fruit. **ID** ♂ glistening emerald-green, small grey shoulder, grey mark below eye, orange behind ear. ♀ duller green. **Voice** Call, lisping 3–4-note "czee, czee, czee" or similar. **SS** No other tanager is so green.

Multicolored Tanager *Chlorochrysa nitidissima* `NT`
Tangará Multicolor `VU`
Local and uncommon resident.

L 13 cm (5"). Monotypic. Endemic. Humid montane forest, borders. Mostly 1200–2200 m (rarely to 800 m). Behaviour much like Glistening-green Tanager and like it always seems in a rush. Regularly gleans by hanging downward from outer foliage, but does not peer under branches like many *Tangara* and allies. **ID** Harlequin-patterned. Glistening ♂ best identified by mostly yellow head, chestnut patch on neck, yellow back, blue underparts. ♀ duller, mantle greenish, underparts green. **Voice** Call, wheezy "ceeet". **SS** Saffron-crowned Tanager (p. 549).

♂

♀

Orange-eared Tanager *Chlorochrysa calliparaea* `LC`
Tangará Orejinaranja
Uncommon resident.
L 13 cm (5"). Race *bourcieri*. Humid and wet foothill and lower montane forest, borders. 900–2000 m. Singles, pairs or trios, invariably with fast-moving, tanager-dominated mixed flocks in upper forest levels. Like other *Chlorochrysa*, energetic and nimble, rapidly gleans or hangs downward in foliage, mostly for insects, then quickly moves on. **ID** ♂ glistening emerald-green, orange rump (visible in flight), black throat joins orange-red patch on sides of neck, orange-red crown spot. ♀ duller, throat greyish. **Voice** Seldom heard song, high wispy repeated twittering.

bourcieri

Genus *Bangsia* Distinctive Chocó-Pacific genus. Plump, short-tailed, heavy-billed, and sluggish. Attractive plumage combinations of black, navy-blue, moss-green and yellow (except *B. flavovirens*). Subcanopy to lower mid-levels.

Yellow-green Tanager *Bangsia flavovirens* `VU`
Tangará Verdiamarillo `VU`
Rare and local resident.
L 15 cm (6"). Monotypic. Near-endemic (also NW Ecuador). Wet mossy lower montane forest, borders. 800–1250 m. Verifiable records mainly W Andean slope in Valle (R Anchicayá) and Nariño. Groups of 3–5, alone or with mixed flocks including *Chlorospingus*, but usually forage higher, mid-levels to canopy (median 12 m, regularly 22–30 m up), rarely low. Hustles along larger mossy limbs or in foliage. Mixed fruit (*Miconia*, *Cecropia*, mistletoe) and insect diet; often at flowers. **ID** Drab, easily confused; above dark olive, below olive-yellow, throat slightly paler, lores and ocular area smudged dusky, eyes brown. **Voice** Persistently vocal; husky rasping "chut". **SS** Various *Chlorospingus* (p. 462), Oleaginous Hemispingus (p. 525), juv *Tangara* (pp. 547–552). **TN** Formerly in *Chlorospingus* and called Yellow-green Chlorospingus.

`NE`

Blue-and-gold Tanager *Bangsia arcaei* `NT`
Tangará Azul-y-oro
Recently reported on Colombian side of Cerro Tacarcuna.
L 16 cm (6.3"). Race *arcaei*. Humid foothill and lower montane forest. c. 300–1200 m. Behaviour most like Black-and-gold Tanager. **ID** Head, throat and upperparts navy-blue, lower underparts deep yellow. **Voice** Short song, a few jerky chattering notes and rising-falling phrases, mostly at 5–7 kHz. Call, weak high downward inflected "tzee".

arcaei

Gold-ringed Tanager *Bangsia aureocincta* `EN`
Tangará de Tatama `VU`
Fairly common but local resident (narrow elevational zone).
L 16 cm (6.3"). Monotypic. Endemic. Wet mossy montane forest, borders and old landslides. 1500–2200 m. Singles or pairs with mixed flocks or independently, low mid-levels or higher. Primarily frugivorous. Regularly perches high in open. **ID** Dull moss-green, head and throat black, conspicuous gold ring encircles sides of head, yellow chest patch. **Voice** Song, chattering rattle-trill, rising-falling, louder in middle c. 4–5.5 kHz.

`E`

540

Moss-backed Tanager *Bangsia edwardsi* `LC`
Tangará Cariazul `NT`
Locally common resident.

 L 16 cm (6.3"). Monotypic. Near-endemic (also far NW Ecuador). Wet mossy foothill and lower montane forest, second growth, borders. 400–2100 m. Singles or pairs, sluggish, in lower levels to subcanopy, often quite unsuspicious; independent or less often with mixed flocks. Like Gold-ringed Tanager, regularly perches in open at borders for long periods. **ID** Head and throat black, sides of head cobalt-blue, chest patch yellow. **Voice** Song, buzzy rising-falling rattling trill: "tr'e'e'E'E'e'e'r'tr'e'e'E'E'e'e'r...".

Golden-chested Tanager *Bangsia rothschildi* `LC`
Tangará Pechidorada
Uncommon resident.

 L 16 cm (6.3"). Monotypic. Near-endemic (also far NW Ecuador). Wet mossy foothill forest, adjacent second growth. 200–1100 m. Lethargic, unobtrusive singles or pairs regularly forage with mixed flocks, in lower growth to mid-levels, less in subcanopy, peer and hop heavily, barbet-like. **ID** Unmistakable; navy-blue patch on chest and lower underparts yellow. **Voice** Calls, shrill high "jeek" and harsh metallic "wheek" notes. Rarely heard song (?) very high (9 kHz) insect-like buzz "tiz'ez'ez'e" (may be rapidly repeated).

Black-and-gold Tanager *Bangsia melanochlamys* `VU`
Tangará Aurinegra `VU`
Uncommon and local resident.

 L 16 cm (6.3"). Monotypic. Endemic. Wet mossy montane forest. 1200–2400 m. Sluggish behaviour recalls other *Bangsia* but seems to forage much higher, mainly subcanopy or canopy. Occasionally perches in open, follows mixed flocks, searching mossy epiphyte-covered limbs; heavily frugivorous. **ID** Head, throat, upperparts and flanks matt black, shoulders blue, chest and most of lower underparts yellow. **Voice** Song, high (c. 7.5 kHz) galloping twitter "piti'seea'piti'seea", several times, followed by a few high single notes.

leverianus

Magpie Tanager *Cissopis leverianus* `LC`
Tangará Urraca
Common resident.

L 25 cm (10"). Race *leverianus*. Humid forest borders, shrubby regenerating clearings with tall trees, second growth at river borders. To 1800 m. Conspicuous pairs or small groups, fly in open across clearings, may perch fairly high in open, hop up through shrubbery jay-like; infrequently join mixed flocks. **ID** Large; pied plumage, yellow eyes. Head and foreparts glossy black, feathers pointed (imparting shaggy appearance), long rounded tail black tipped white. **Voice** Noisy. Call, loud metallic "chink". Infrequent song, sputtering and chattering mix of sharp and softer notes with irregular pauses.

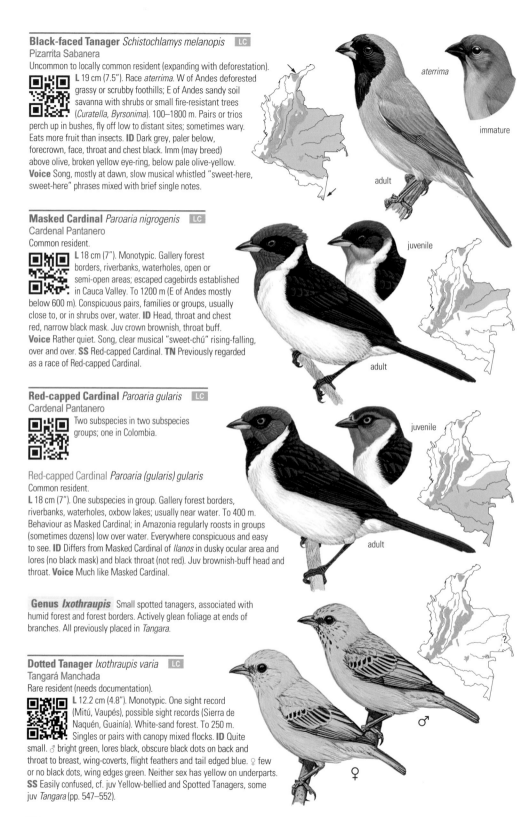

Black-faced Tanager *Schistochlamys melanopis* LC
Pizarrita Sabanera

Uncommon to locally common resident (expanding with deforestation). **L** 19 cm (7.5"). Race *aterrima*. W of Andes deforested grassy or scrubby foothills; E of Andes sandy soil savanna with shrubs or small fire-resistant trees (*Curatella, Byrsonima*). 100–1800 m. Pairs or trios perch up in bushes, fly off low to distant sites; sometimes wary. Eats more fruit than insects. **ID** Dark grey, paler below, forecrown, face, throat and chest black. Imm (may breed) above olive, broken yellow eye-ring, below pale olive-yellow. **Voice** Song, mostly at dawn, slow musical whistled "sweet-here, sweet-here" phrases mixed with brief single notes.

aterrima

immature

adult

Masked Cardinal *Paroaria nigrogenis* LC
Cardenal Pantanero

Common resident. **L** 18 cm (7"). Monotypic. Gallery forest borders, riverbanks, waterholes, open or semi-open areas; escaped cagebirds established in Cauca Valley. To 1200 m (E of Andes mostly below 600 m). Conspicuous pairs, families or groups, usually close to, or in shrubs over, water. **ID** Head, throat and chest red, narrow black mask. Juv crown brownish, throat buff. **Voice** Rather quiet. Song, clear musical "sweet-chú" rising-falling, over and over. **SS** Red-capped Cardinal. **TN** Previously regarded as a race of Red-capped Cardinal.

juvenile

adult

Red-capped Cardinal *Paroaria gularis* LC
Cardenal Pantanero

Two subspecies in two subspecies groups; one in Colombia.

Red-capped Cardinal *Paroaria (gularis) gularis*
Common resident.

L 18 cm (7"). One subspecies in group. Gallery forest borders, riverbanks, waterholes, oxbow lakes; usually near water. To 400 m. Behaviour as Masked Cardinal; in Amazonia regularly roosts in groups (sometimes dozens) low over water. Everywhere conspicuous and easy to see. **ID** Differs from Masked Cardinal of *llanos* in dusky ocular area and lores (no black mask) and black throat (not red). Juv brownish-buff head and throat. **Voice** Much like Masked Cardinal.

juvenile

adult

Genus *Ixothraupis* Small spotted tanagers, associated with humid forest and forest borders. Actively glean foliage at ends of branches. All previously placed in *Tangara*.

Dotted Tanager *Ixothraupis varia* LC
Tangará Manchada

Rare resident (needs documentation). **L** 12.2 cm (4.8"). Monotypic. One sight record (Mitú, Vaupés), possible sight records (Sierra de Naquén, Guainía). White-sand forest. To 250 m. Singles or pairs with canopy mixed flocks. **ID** Quite small. ♂ bright green, lores black, obscure black dots on back and throat to breast, wing-coverts, flight feathers and tail edged blue. ♀ few or no black dots, wing edges green. Neither sex has yellow on underparts. **SS** Easily confused, cf. juv Yellow-bellied and Spotted Tanagers, some juv *Tangara* (pp. 547–552).

♂

♀

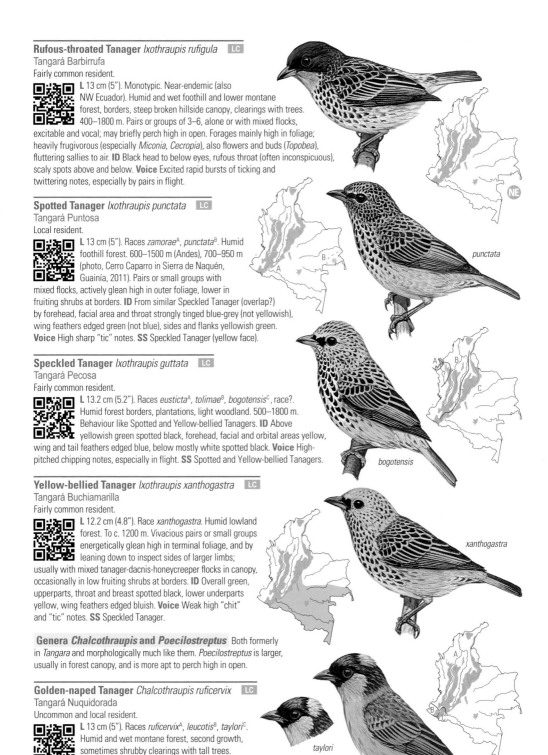

Rufous-throated Tanager *Ixothraupis rufigula* `LC`
Tangará Barbirrufa
Fairly common resident.

L 13 cm (5"). Monotypic. Near-endemic (also NW Ecuador). Humid and wet foothill and lower montane forest, borders, steep broken hillside canopy, clearings with trees. 400–1800 m. Pairs or groups of 3–6, alone or with mixed flocks, excitable and vocal; may briefly perch high in open. Forages mainly high in foliage; heavily frugivorous (especially *Miconia*, *Cecropia*), also flowers and buds (*Topobea*), fluttering sallies to air. **ID** Black head to below eyes, rufous throat (often inconspicuous), scaly spots above and below. **Voice** Excited rapid bursts of ticking and twittering notes, especially by pairs in flight.

Spotted Tanager *Ixothraupis punctata* `LC`
Tangará Puntosa
Local resident.

L 13 cm (5"). Races *zamorae*[A], *punctata*[B]. Humid foothill forest. 600–1500 m (Andes), 700–950 m (photo, Cerro Caparro in Sierra de Naquén, Guainía, 2011). Pairs or small groups with mixed flocks, actively glean high in outer foliage, lower in fruiting shrubs at borders. **ID** From similar Speckled Tanager (overlap?) by forehead, facial area and throat strongly tinged blue-grey (not yellowish), wing feathers edged green (not blue), sides and flanks yellowish green. **Voice** High sharp "tic" notes. **SS** Speckled Tanager (yellow face).

punctata

Speckled Tanager *Ixothraupis guttata* `LC`
Tangará Pecosa
Fairly common resident.

L 13.2 cm (5.2"). Races *eusticta*[A], *tolimae*[B], *bogotensis*[C], race?. Humid forest borders, plantations, light woodland. 500–1800 m. Behaviour like Spotted and Yellow-bellied Tanagers. **ID** Above yellowish green spotted black, forehead, facial and orbital areas yellow, wing and tail feathers edged blue, below mostly white spotted black. **Voice** High-pitched chipping notes, especially in flight. **SS** Spotted and Yellow-bellied Tanagers.

bogotensis

Yellow-bellied Tanager *Ixothraupis xanthogastra* `LC`
Tangará Buchiamarilla
Fairly common resident.

L 12.2 cm (4.8"). Race *xanthogastra*. Humid lowland forest. To c. 1200 m. Vivacious pairs or small groups energetically glean high in terminal foliage, and by leaning down to inspect sides of larger limbs; usually with mixed tanager-dacnis-honeycreeper flocks in canopy, occasionally in low fruiting shrubs at borders. **ID** Overall green, upperparts, throat and breast spotted black, lower underparts yellow, wing feathers edged bluish. **Voice** Weak high "chit" and "tic" notes. **SS** Speckled Tanager.

xanthogastra

Genera *Chalcothraupis* and *Poecilostreptus* Both formerly in *Tangara* and morphologically much like them. *Poecilostreptus* is larger, usually in forest canopy, and is more apt to perch high in open.

Golden-naped Tanager *Chalcothraupis ruficervix* `LC`
Tangará Nuquidorada
Uncommon and local resident.

L 13 cm (5"). Races *ruficervix*[A], *leucotis*[B], *taylori*[C]. Humid and wet montane forest, second growth, sometimes shrubby clearings with tall trees. 1500–2500 m. Pairs often follow mixed flocks, generally high inside forest, less at borders. Searches alternate sides of branches, peering head-down like Golden Tanager; occasionally hovers or sallies to foliage. **ID** Turquoise-blue with black cap, buff belly and vent, small golden band on rear crown (*taylori*) or golden-rufous (*leucotis*). **SS** Saffron-crowned Tanager (p. 549).

taylori

ruficervix

Grey-and-gold Tanager *Poecilostreptus palmeri* `LC`
Tangará Platinada
Uncommon and local resident.

 L 14.7 cm (5.8"). Monotypic. Near-endemic (also extreme E Panama and NW Ecuador). Wet foothill and lower montane forest, borders. Mostly 300–1100 m (sparingly in lowlands). Vocal and excitable, pairs or 3–8 briefly join mixed flocks but soon fly off to rest on high perch atop foliage; seldom low. Diet mainly fruit; sally-flutters to air for flying insects, infrequently searches branches or foliage. **ID** Large, plump; pale grey, small black mask, back, neck and chest sprinkled black, gold chest flecking inconspicuous. **Voice** Calls louder and lower-pitched than *Tangara* (and allies); rising "chup-sweeeet" or either note singly.

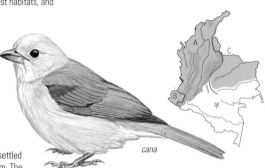

Genus *Thraupis* Genetically near *Tangara* and allies (and sometimes placed within *Tangara*). Differ in larger size, robust proportions, plainer and less colourful plumage, rapid squeaky songs, predominantly non-forest habitats, and more generalized (less stereotyped) foraging behaviour.

Blue-grey Tanager *Thraupis episcopus* `LC`
Azulejo Común

 Fourteen subspecies in two subspecies groups; both in Colombia.

Blue-grey Tanager *Thraupis (episcopus) cana*
Abundant resident.

L 17 cm (6.7"). Races *cana*[A], *quaesita*[B], *nesophila*[C]. Throughout settled areas, except at high elevations; scarce in arid Guajira. To 2700 m. The familiar 'azulejo' of gardens and parks in rural and urban areas, and ranchland in *llanos*, is one of Colombia's best-known birds. Omnivorous diet, sometimes damages cultivated fruit, e.g. papaya. **ID** Pale grey head, neck and underparts contrast with darker back, wings and tail, wing-coverts bluish or lavender-blue. Juv duller. **Voice** Calls, rising "seeee" and strained "tsuup". Squeaky twittering song. **SS** Glaucous Tanager.

cana

White-edged Tanager *Thraupis (episcopus) episcopus*
Common resident.

L 17 cm (6.7"). Races *leucoptera*[A], *mediana*[B], *coelestis*[C]. Settled areas, gallery forest, ranchland in *llanos*, and river edges and second growth in Amazonia. To c. 2200 m. **ID** Similar to previous group, but shoulders white, lesser wing-coverts edged white forming single wingbar (*coelestis*), or shoulders and wingbar bluish white (*leucoptera*), or shoulders cobalt-blue, wingbar white (*mediana*). **Voice** Like Blue-grey Tanager. **TN** Racial boundaries of *leucoptera* and *coelestis* unclear.

coelestis

Glaucous Tanager *Thraupis glaucocolpa* `LC`
Azulejo Glauco
Uncommon to locally fairly common resident.

 L 17 cm (6.7"). Monotypic. Dry and arid scrub, dry woodland, fewer in gardens and settled areas. To 500 m. Less confiding and less conspicuous than Blue-grey Tanager, stays high in trees. **ID** From Blue-grey Tanager by same colour as back, contrasting white belly, small black patch at base of outer flight feathers, aqua-green (not blue-grey) flight feathers. Overall dingy greyish appearance. **Voice** Song, pulsating high-pitched (7.5 kHz) "e-e-e-ee-ee-eee-eee-see-SEE-SEE-SEE" (swelling in volume). Call "sweEEeeee", descending at end. **SS** Juv Blue-grey Tanager.

Palm Tanager *Thraupis palmarum* LC
Azulejo Palmero

 Four subspecies in two subspecies groups; both in Colombia.

Olive Palm Tanager *Thraupis (palmarum) palmarum*
Common resident.
L 18 cm (7"). Races *atripennis*[A], *melanoptera*[B]. Forest canopy and borders, second growth, clearings, plantations. To 2600 m. More forest-based than Blue-grey Tanager, less at home in urban areas. Foraging behaviour versatile; clings to palm fronds, eats fruit and flower petals, gleans and sallies. **ID** Rear half of folded wing dusky black, otherwise generally smoky grey, forecrown variably tinged yellowish. **Voice** Song like Blue-grey Tanager but squeakier, less musical and lacks "tsuee" notes.

Violaceus Palm Tanager
Thraupis (palmarum) violilavata
Common resident.
L 18 cm (7"). One subspecies in group. Forest borders, second growth, clearings with trees. To c. 1500 m (?). **ID** Like *palmarum* races (above) but plumage tinged smoky violet-grey, otherwise appears undifferentiated. **TN** Doubtfully merits subspecies group separation.

Genus *Stilpnia* All formerly in *Tangara* and morphologically similar but mainly in forest borders, clearings, open woodland or scrub, primarily glean foliage (not branches) and diet predominantly small fruit. Several have distinctive ringing or buzzy songs. Juvs very dull.

Black-headed Tanager *Stilpnia cyanoptera* LC
Tangará Encapuchada
Locally fairly common resident.

 L 13 cm (5"). Monotypic. Moist to moderately humid foothill and lower montane forest borders, light woodland, shade-coffee plantations. 500–2000 m. Pairs, alone or loosely associated with mixed flocks, generally stay high.
ID ♂ opalescent to straw-coloured plumage (varies with light), black head, wings and tail. ♀ featureless and confusing, crown and back greyish blue, otherwise above pale greenish, below dingy whitish, sides and flanks yellowish. **Voice** High lisping notes.
SS ♀ Black-capped Tanager. **TN** Often includes tepui *whitelyi* (Black-hooded Tanager) as a race.

Black-capped Tanager *Stilpnia heinei* LC
Tangará Capirotada
Fairly common resident.

 L 13.2 cm (5.2"). Monotypic. Humid forest borders, shrubby clearings, second growth. Mostly 1500–2400 m. Singles, pairs or families wander alone, visit fruiting trees with other tanagers, less often with mixed flocks. Hops along branches, alternately peering down one side then the other for insects. **ID** ♂ black cap, faintly streaked aqua-green throat. ♀ pattern echoes ♂ but much duller, back and wings greenish, flanks greenish yellow. **Voice** Song, rapid oddly mechanical ringing "t'kling-t'kling…" (not loud). **SS** ♀ Black-headed Tanager.

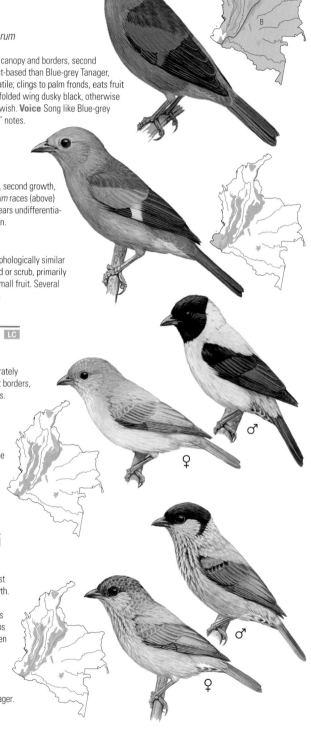

melanoptera

♂

♀

♂

♀

Golden-hooded Tanager *Stilpnia larvata* LC
Tangará Collareja
Common resident.

 L 13 cm (5"). Race *fanny*. Humid forest borders, clearings with scattered trees, bushy pastures. To 1200 m. Open-situation tanager, in pairs or families, mostly frugivorous, occasionally fluttering up for flying insects. Mid-levels or higher, loafing high in trees. **ID** Gold crown and neck surround pale blue forehead and face, and small black mask, back, chest and sides black, belly white. **Voice** Calls "cjek" and "tic". Song, a few "cjek" notes and a ticking trill, sometimes with buzzy notes added. **SS** Blue-necked Tanager. **TN** Formerly included Masked Tanager.

Blue-necked Tanager *Stilpnia cyanicollis* LC
Tangará Real
Common resident.

 L 13 cm (5"). Races *hannahiae*[A], *granadensis*[B], *caeruleocephala*[C], *cyanopygia*[D]. Humid forest borders, clearings with scattered trees, bushy pastures. 400–2400 m. Lively, open-situation tanager which profits from deforestation. Pairs or families, mostly at mid-levels, not regularly with mixed flocks. Frugivorous, also flower buds and occasionally flutters inelegantly after flying insects. **ID** Mostly black, head turquoise, shoulders gold (*caeruleocephala*, *hannahiae*) or tinged turquoise (*cyanopygia*). **Voice** Streams of rapid chittering notes when excited; various weak chipping notes.

granadensis

hannahiae

Masked Tanager *Stilpnia nigrocincta* LC
Tangará Enmascarada
Uncommon resident.

 L 13 cm (5"). Monotypic. Humid forest borders, old clearings or pastures with tall trees, top of canopy (horizontal edge) in *terra firme* forest. To 1400 m. Behaviour much like Golden-hooded Tanager, although sometimes peripherally with canopy mixed flocks, lower at edges. **ID** Faded version of Golden-hooded Tanager; small black mask surrounded by lavender-blue (not golden) hood, black back, broad chest-band and sides, white belly. ♀ resembles ♂ but overall duller, back and breast dusky. **Voice** Similar to Golden-hooded Tanager.

♀

♂

Scrub Tanager *Stilpnia vitriolina* LC
Tangará Rastrojera
Common resident.

 L 14 cm (5.5"). Monotypic. Near-endemic (also N Ecuador). Drier scrubby or cultivated areas, plantations, overgrown pastures, gardens. 300–2500 m. Singles or pairs forage for fruit and insects in shrubbery, mostly rather low and apart from mixed flocks. **ID** Muted colours, rufous crown, black cheeks, wings edged aqua-green, otherwise dingy silvery grey, paler below. **Voice** Song, a few hesitant bisyllabic notes accelerating into complex musical tinkling "chup'pik, chup'pik, chit'til'le-chit'til'le-…" (c. 4 seconds at 7–8 kHz). **SS** Burnished-buff Tanager.

NE

Burnished-buff Tanager *Stilpnia cayana* LC
Tangará Triguera
Common resident.

L 14 cm (5.5"). Races *fulvescens*[A], *cayana*[B]. Drier open habitats, ranchland, gallery forest borders, bushy savanna; expanding into E Andes with deforestation. To 1600 m. Singles, pairs or families, often seen whizzing by in flight to distant fruiting tree. Not with mixed flocks; insect-searching dilettante. **ID** Light angle affects colour. ♂ rich burnished- to opalescent-buff, wings and tail edged greenish blue, forecrown rufous, mask black, throat and chest greyish blue (variable). ♀ and juv duller smoky greenish buff. **Voice** Infrequent song, rapid pulsating buzzy "sizza'sizza'sizza…" (2–3 seconds). **SS** Scrub Tanager.

Genus *Tangara* Large genus that formerly also included *Chalcothraupis*, *Poecilostreptus*, *Stilpnia* and *Ixothraupis*; genetically close to *Thraupis*. Colourful, often idiosyncratic plumage patterns. Small, hyperactive forest species, habitually with mixed flocks and high in trees. Patronize fruiting trees with small berry-like fruits (e.g. *Ficus*, *Miconia*, *Trema*) or catkins (*Cecropia*). Typical of steep Andean slopes, landslides, gaps and lowland rainforest canopy, they tirelessly search branches, a few also foliage, for insects, almost always employing genus-specific stereotyped technique. Songs thin, high, weak and easily overlooked, some undescribed. ♀♀ like ♂♂ but duller; juvs nearly featureless.

Blue-and-black Tanager *Tangara vassorii* LC
Tangará Negriazul

Two subspecies in two subspecies groups; one in Colombia.

Blue-and-black Tanager *Tangara (vassorii) vassorii*
Fairly common resident.
L 13 cm (5"). One subspecies in group. Humid and wet (mossy) montane forest, borders, stunted forest to treeline. 2000–3400 m (no other *Tangara* occurs as high). Pairs or several follow mixed flocks, restlessly glean foliage, and occasionally peer head down at sides of branches briefly, before rushing off. **ID** Bill short. ♂ shining cobalt-blue, small black mask, wings black, greater coverts tipped blue forming single band. ♀ slightly duller. **Voice** Infrequent song, a rapid galloping complex of chittering notes.

Beryl-spangled Tanager *Tangara nigroviridis* LC
Tangará Berilina
Common resident.

L 13 cm (5"). Races *cyanescens*[A], *lozanoana*[B], *nigroviridis*[C]. Humid and wet (mossy) montane forest, borders, second growth. 1200–2800 m. Pairs, or more often groups of 3–15+, with mixed flocks, mostly high, occasionally low at borders. Feeds heavily on *Miconia* berries, alternately leans down to search sides and undersides of small branches and thin bare terminal twigs for insects. **ID** No other small *Tangara* in highlands is so dark and spotted. Small black mask, opalescent crown, otherwise black spotted opalescent blue, wings edged blue. **Voice** Infrequent song, high thin "see, sit, sit".

Green-naped Tanager *Tangara fucosa* NT
Tangará Nuquiverde VU
Uncommon resident.

L 13 cm (5"). Monotypic. Known from Alto de Nique and Cerro Tacarcuna on Panama border. Upper levels or canopy in humid montane forest. 700–1600 m. Pairs or small groups with mixed flocks. **ID** Patchy unkempt appearance, above mostly black, silvery-green spangling on hindcrown and neck, wings edged blue, rump silvery blue, breast spangled blue and black, lower underparts cinnamon. **Voice** Song unreported. Call "tsit", singly or in rapid series.

cayana

nigroviridis

Blue-browed Tanager *Tangara cyanotis* LC
Tangará Cejona
Uncommon or rare resident.

 L 12.2 cm (4.8"). Race *lutleyi*. Upper levels or canopy of humid montane forest. 1100–2200 m. **ID** Behaviour and plumage much like commoner and very similar Metallic-green Tanager but has broad turquoise-blue eyebrow (not entire forehead and eyebrow straw gold), black mantle (not silvery green), entire sides of head black; also note silvery turquoise-blue lesser wing-coverts and rump, buff belly. **Voice** Presumed song rapid chattering series of metallic scraping notes, abruptly accelerating, higher at end (6–7 kHz).

lutleyi

Metallic-green Tanager *Tangara labradorides* LC
Tangará Verdiplata
Locally fairly common resident.

 L 13 cm (5"). Race *labradorides*. Humid montane forest, borders. 1300–2600 m. Fast-moving pairs or families accompany other tanagers high in forest, acrobatically searching small branches, twigs and outer foliage, less often bending down to inspect sides of larger branches. Diet mainly *Miconia* berries and other small fruit. Occasionally quite low in fruiting shrubs at forest borders.
ID Confusing; colour varies with light, typically appears silvery green to bluish green, forehead and eyebrow opalescent, median crown and mask black, lores and narrow ocular ring black, entire central back and rump silvery green, belly and undertail-coverts cinnamon-buff. **Voice** High sharp "jit".
SS Blue-browed Tanager.

labradorides

Bay-headed Tanager *Tangara gyrola* LC
Tangará Cabecirrufa

 Nine subspecies in three subspecies groups; two in Colombia.

Bay-and-blue Tanager *Tangara (gyrola) albertinae*
Common resident.
L 14 cm (5.5"). Races *deleticia*[A], *nupera*[B], *catharinae*[C], *parva*[D]. Humid and wet foothill and montane forest, borders, clearings with trees, plantations. 400–2200 m (W of Andes) or to c. 1500 m (E of Andes). Singles, pairs or families, often with mixed flocks, heavily frugivorous (*Miconia*, *Trema*, *Ficus*, *Cecropia*), industriously searching live bare (not moss-covered) branches and twigs for insects, alternately peering head down on one side, then the other, moving outwards. **ID** Above green, head chestnut, underparts blue, or with golden nuchal collar (*catharinae*, *parva*). **Voice** Calls, buzzy falling-rising "sseeaawee", and coarse "shree" in flight. **SS** Rufous-winged Tanager.

Bay-and-green Tanager *Tangara (gyrola) viridissima*
Common resident.
L 14 cm (5.5"). Race *toddi*. Mostly 800–2200 m. Behaviour and voice as previous group. **ID** Similar to *albertinae* group (above) but under-parts green (not blue). **SS** Green Honeycreeper (p. 506).

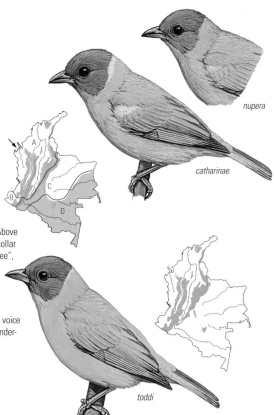

nupera

catharinae

toddi

Rufous-winged Tanager *Tangara lavinia* LC
Tangará Alirrufa
Uncommon and local resident.

L 13.2 cm (5.2"). Race *lavinia*. Humid and wet lowland and foothill forest, borders, older second growth. To c. 800 m (locally 1300 m). Behaviour recalls much commoner Bay-headed Tanager but more restless, fidgety, less diligently searches branches for insects, and often noisier, sometimes calling constantly. Regularly low in fruiting shrubs. **ID** Distinguished by combination of rufous-chestnut head and wings, extensive golden sheen to nape and back. ♀ much duller, plain green, head pale greenish brown, minimal rufous on wings. **Voice** Buzzy "breezeet". **SS** Bay-headed Tanager (higher elevations).

Golden-eared Tanager *Tangara chrysotis* LC
Tangará Pechirrufa
Uncommon resident.

L 14 cm (5.5"). Monotypic. Mid-levels to canopy in humid montane forest, adjacent woodland, borders. 1100–2400 m. Like most *Tangara* often with mixed flocks, singles or pairs methodically search branches, alternately inspecting one side then other as move steadily outward (but at less feverish pace than smaller allies). Mixed diet includes much fruit. **ID** Overall opalescent green, broad yellow forecrown and eyestripe surround deep coppery-gold ear-coverts, black median crown and streaks on mantle, cinnamon-rufous lower underparts. **Voice** Call, high forced "seeit", sharply downslurred. **SS** Metallic-green Tanager.

Saffron-crowned Tanager *Tangara xanthocephala* LC
Tangará Coronada
Common resident.

L 13.2 cm (5.2"). Race *venusta*. Mid-levels to canopy in humid montane forest, borders, tall second growth. 1200–2600 m. Energetic pairs or several follow mixed flocks, search smaller branches for insects with methodical stereotyped movements, methodically inspecting one side, then the other, progressing outward. More than half of diet small fruit. **ID** Colourful; head mostly yellow, body opalescent blue, small mask and central throat black, cinnamon lower underparts. ♀ duller. **Voice** High "tsit".

Flame-faced Tanager *Tangara parzudakii* LC

Three subspecies in two subspecies groups; both in Colombia.

Yellow-faced Tanager *Tangara (parzudakii) lunigera*
Tangará Rubicunda
Uncommon to fairly common resident.

L 13.2 cm (5.2"). One subspecies in group. Near-endemic (also NW Ecuador). Canopy and borders of premontane and montane wet forest, especially those where trunks and limbs are heavily covered with moss and epiphytes. 800–2300 m. Usually pairs, less often singles or several, regularly follow mixed flocks containing other *Tangara*, mostly at mid-levels or higher. Methodically searches branches for insects by leaning down to inspect one side, then the other, frequently also hangs head down, or upside-down, especially to reach small fruits. **ID** Like *parzudakii* (next page) but forecrown red-orange becoming paler orange-yellow (not red) on crown and face, breast slightly more golden green (less opalescent green). **TN** Sometimes treated as separate species.

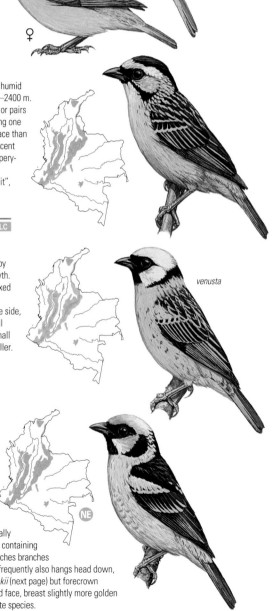

lavinia

♂

♀

venusta

NE

Flame-faced Tanager *Tangara (parzudakii) parzudakii* `LC`
Tangará Rubicunda
Uncommon to fairly common resident.
L 14.2 cm (5.6"). Race *parzudakii*. Mostly 1500–2500 m. Mid-levels
to canopy in humid montane forest, borders, adjacent open second
growth. Singles or pairs with mixed flocks or alone. Methodical
branch-searcher like many *Tangara* (see Golden-eared Tanager).
ID Large *Tangara*; forecrown and face deep flame-red, rear
crown yellow, back black, shoulders, rump and underparts opalescent. **Voice** High (c. 7–8 kHz) tinkling "tink" notes, often
in rapid fitful series. **SS** Saffron-crowned Tanager.

Blue-whiskered Tanager *Tangara johannae* `NT`
Tangará Bigotuda `NT`
Uncommon resident.
L 13 cm (5.2"). Monotypic. Near-endemic (also NW Ecuador).
In humid and wet (mossy) foothill forest, less at borders, local
in lowlands. To 1000 m (mostly below 700 m). Singles or pairs
follow mixed flocks, mid-levels to subcanopy, but sometimes low
inside forest. Like Golden Tanager a tireless branch-searcher for insects, but
diet seems to be mainly small fruit. **ID** Mainly apple-green, black face and throat
enclose large, but not particularly conspicuous, blue malar, blue wing fringes.
Voice High shrill buzzy "tzzeee". Song unreported. **SS** Emerald Tanager (foothills).

Green-and-gold Tanager *Tangara schrankii* `LC`
Tangará Carinegra
Fairly common resident.
L 13 cm (5.2"). Race *schrankii*.
Subcanopy, canopy and emergent
trees (e.g. *Ceiba*) in humid
lowland forest, lower at borders.
To 1200 m (higher?). Pairs or groups of up
to 6+ persistently forage with Paradise
Tanagers, regularly with canopy mixed
flocks, foraging rapidly, often moving well
ahead of flock. Diet fruit, also some insects by
bending down to briefly inspect alternate sides of high
branches. **ID** Emerald-green with black mask, yellow
crown, yellow median lower underparts. ♀ duller, little
or no yellow on crown. **Voice** Excited bursts of
chipping notes.

Golden Tanager *Tangara arthus* `LC`
Tangará Dorada
Nine subspecies in three
subspecies groups
(taxonomy-dependent);
all three in Colombia.

Western Golden Tanager
Tangara (arthus) aurulenta
Common resident.
L 13.5 cm (5.3"). Races *occidentalis*[A], *aurulenta*[B], *palmitae*[C],
goodsoni[D], *sclateri*[E]. Humid and wet montane forest, borders, older second
growth woodland. 900–2500 m. Pairs, families or several habitually follow mixed
flocks. Heavily frugivorous, but diligently searches for insects, mainly on mossy
branches, leaning down to inspect alternate sides of branch. **ID** All races have generally
golden-yellow plumage (shading differs), black ear-coverts patch and streaked back. Head
and underparts deep golden-yellow (*occidentalis*), lighter golden-yellow (*aurulenta*), bright
yellow (*goodsoni*), or head deep golden-yellow, underparts entirely cinnamon-rufous (*sclateri*).
Voice Call, a slightly buzzy "cheet". **TN** Race *palmitae* doubtfully distinct. Dark race *sclateri*
seems better aligned with *arthus* group (next page).

parzudakii

schrankii ♂

♀

aurulenta

sclateri

goodsoni

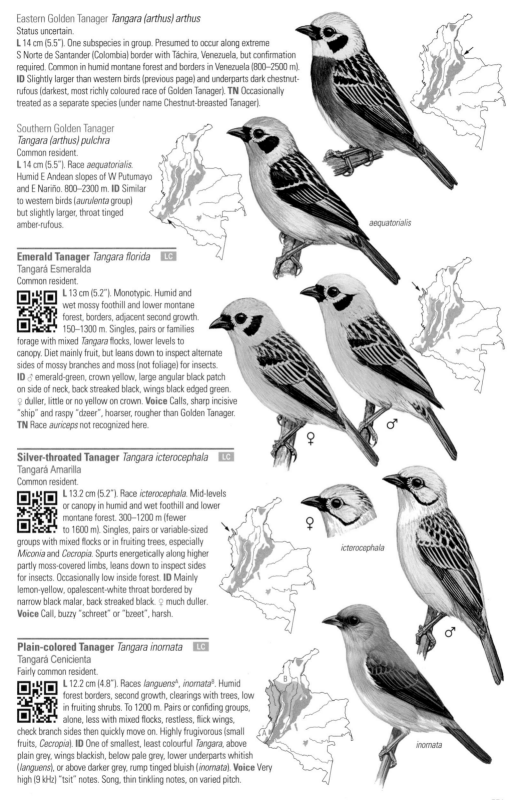

Eastern Golden Tanager *Tangara (arthus) arthus*
Status uncertain.
L 14 cm (5.5"). One subspecies in group. Presumed to occur along extreme
S Norte de Santander (Colombia) border with Táchira, Venezuela, but confirmation
required. Common in humid montane forest and borders in Venezuela (800–2500 m).
ID Slightly larger than western birds (previous page) and underparts dark chestnut-
rufous (darkest, most richly coloured race of Golden Tanager). **TN** Occasionally
treated as a separate species (under name Chestnut-breasted Tanager).

Southern Golden Tanager
Tangara (arthus) pulchra
Common resident.
L 14 cm (5.5"). Race *aequatorialis*.
Humid E Andean slopes of W Putumayo
and E Nariño. 800–2300 m. **ID** Similar
to western birds (*aurulenta* group)
but slightly larger, throat tinged
amber-rufous.

aequatorialis

Emerald Tanager *Tangara florida* LC
Tangará Esmeralda
Common resident.
L 13 cm (5.2"). Monotypic. Humid and
wet mossy foothill and lower montane
forest, borders, adjacent second growth.
150–1300 m. Singles, pairs or families
forage with mixed *Tangara* flocks, lower levels to
canopy. Diet mainly fruit, but leans down to inspect alternate
sides of mossy branches and moss (not foliage) for insects.
ID ♂ emerald-green, crown yellow, large angular black patch
on side of neck, back streaked black, wings black edged green.
♀ duller, little or no yellow on crown. **Voice** Calls, sharp incisive
"ship" and raspy "dzeer", hoarser, rougher than Golden Tanager.
TN Race *auriceps* not recognized here.

♀ ♂

Silver-throated Tanager *Tangara icterocephala* LC
Tangará Amarilla
Common resident.
L 13.2 cm (5.2"). Race *icterocephala*. Mid-levels
or canopy in humid and wet foothill and lower
montane forest. 300–1200 m (fewer
to 1600 m). Singles, pairs or variable-sized
groups with mixed flocks or in fruiting trees, especially
Miconia and *Cecropia*. Spurts energetically along higher
partly moss-covered limbs, leans down to inspect sides
for insects. Occasionally low inside forest. **ID** Mainly
lemon-yellow, opalescent-white throat bordered by
narrow black malar, back streaked black. ♀ much duller.
Voice Call, buzzy "schreet" or "bzeet", harsh.

♀
icterocephala
♂

Plain-colored Tanager *Tangara inornata* LC
Tangará Cenicienta
Fairly common resident.
L 12.2 cm (4.8"). Races *languens*[A], *inornata*[B]. Humid
forest borders, second growth, clearings with trees, low
in fruiting shrubs. To 1200 m. Pairs or confiding groups,
alone, less with mixed flocks, restless, flick wings,
check branch sides then quickly move on. Highly frugivorous (small
fruits, *Cecropia*). **ID** One of smallest, least colourful *Tangara*, above
plain grey, wings blackish, below pale grey, lower underparts whitish
(*languens*), or above darker grey, rump tinged bluish (*inornata*). **Voice** Very
high (9 kHz) "tsit" notes. Song, thin tinkling notes, on varied pitch.

inornata

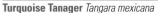

Turquoise Tanager *Tangara mexicana* `LC`
Tangará Turquesa
Locally common resident.

L 13 cm (5.2"). Races *media*[A], *boliviana*[B]. Humid forest borders, top of forest canopy (horizontal border), shrubby second growth, trees in clearings. To 1000 m. Foraging generalist; pairs or lively groups usually independent of mixed flocks, high to fairly low, sprint along branches, lean down in perfunctory manner to inspect bare branch sides, quickly lose interest and rush off. Gleans foliage, inspects flowers, and loafs high in trees. **ID** Resembles unfinished patchwork quilt; bright yellow lower underparts diagnostic, above mostly black, wings dark blue flecked black, shoulder turquoise (*boliviana*), or more blue in wings, flank spots larger, belly creamy yellow (*media*).

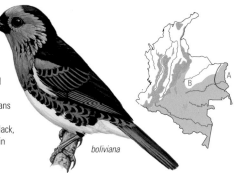
boliviana

Paradise Tanager *Tangara chilensis* `LC`
Tangará Sietecolores
Locally common resident.

L 14.2 cm (5.6"). Races *caelicolor*[A], *chilensis*[B]. Canopy and emergent trees in humid lowland and foothill forest, borders, older second growth. To 1400 m. Typically in vivacious, spirited groups, often faithfully accompanied by Green-and-gold Tanagers; also joins mixed flocks. Rushes from treetop to treetop, briefly pausing to inspect branch sides or eat small fruits. **ID** Unmistakable; apple-green head and blue underparts diagnostic, other colours require closer observation; rump red (*chilensis*) or red and yellow (*caelicolor*). **Voice** Noisy, streams of rapid chip notes.

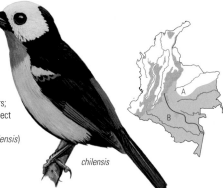
chilensis

Opal-crowned Tanager *Tangara callophrys* `LC`
Tangará Cejiopalina
Fairly common resident (Amazonia).

L 14.2 cm (5.6"). Monotypic. Canopy of humid lowland forest, borders; scarce (few records) in white-sand regions of Vaupés and Guainía. To 800 m. Behaviour much like Opal-rumped Tanager, searches for insects by peering under large branches. **ID** Easily confused with Opal-rumped Tanager (both have opal rump and often together in mixed flocks), but differs in opal forecrown and eyebrow, lower underparts dark blue (not chestnut). **Voice** Call, high single "tsit" or trilled triplets.

Opal-rumped Tanager *Tangara velia* `LC`
Tangará Culiopalina
Fairly common resident.

L 14.2 cm (5.6"). Race *iridina*. Humid lowland forest, borders. To 700 m. Pairs or families follow mixed flocks in canopy or fruiting trees, search for insects moving outward along high (often smaller) branches, lean down to inspect alternate sides but attention span brief. **ID** At any distance looks dark blue to blackish, rufous lower underparts diagnostic. **Voice** Call, high (9–10 kHz) paired "tsit" notes or bursts of 4–5 notes. **SS** Opal-crowned Tanager.

iridina

Band-tailed Antbird *Hypocnemoides maculicauda* LC
Hormiguero de Cola Bandeada
Presumably local resident.

L 12 cm (4.7"). Monotypic. First records (photos) Puerto Nariño, Feb 2019 (common, N Peru). *Várzea* and forested creek borders, lake edges; swampy areas. To 200 m. Behaviour like Black-chinned Antbird (p. 283). Confiding pairs forage alone, very low in vegetation adjacent to or overhanging water. **ID** Diagnostic broad white tips to short black, often dipped, tail. ♂ grey, black throat, three white-fringed wingbars. ♀ underparts whitish clouded grey. **Voice** Song, penetrating slightly rising (3.5–4 kHz) "w,we,we'we'wee'weep, gee, gee, geep, geep, juee, juee", slowing, harsh, burry at end; c. 4 seconds. **SS** See Black-chinned Antbird.

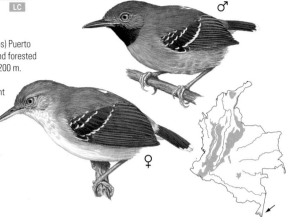

Black-tailed Antbird *Myrmoborus melanurus* VU
Hormiguero Colinegro
Presumably very local resident.

L 12.2 cm (4.8"). Monotypic. First records (photos) Puerto Nariño, Feb 2019 (very local, Peru; R Amazon and tributaries). Seasonally flooded (*várzea*) forest; along low-lying creeks. To 200 m. Territorial pairs, low in vines and dense undergrowth, but may ascend 10 m above ground. Not with mixed flocks. **ID** Eyes red, inter-scapular patch white (both sexes). ♂ entirely blackish, foreparts blacker, 2–3 white-fringed wingbars. ♀ head and upperparts soft brown, face greyish, wingbars like ♂, below white with buff-brown breast-band. **Voice** Loud clear "pip'pip'pipi'p'p'p'p'p'p'p'p", rising (c. 2.5–3 kHz) and increasing in volume, then descending, accelerating and fading, c. 25–30 notes in 2.5 seconds. **SS** ♂ resembles ♂ Black-headed Antbird (p. 288) but differs in smaller size, shorter tail, red (not light grey) eyes, and plain (not black) throat; also cf. ♂ Riparian Antbird (p. 277). ♀ nearest females of Black-faced (p. 286) and Ash-breasted Antbirds (p. 287), but note habitat differences and plain face (no black mask); also cf. ♀ Black-headed Antbird.

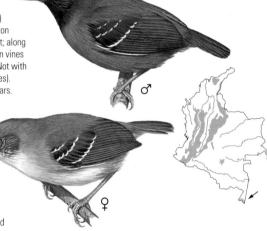

Álvarez, M., Umaña, A.M., Mejía, G.D., Cajiao, J., von Hilde-brandt, P. & Gast, F. (2003). Aves del Parque Nacional Natural Serranía de Chiribiquete, Amazonia-Provincia de la Guyana, Colombia. *Biota Colombiana* **4**: 49–63.

Angehr, G.R. & Dean, R. (2010). *The Birds of Panama: A Field Guide.* Cornell University Press, Ithaca, NY.

Ascanio, D., Rodríguez, G.A. & Restall, R. (2017). *Birds of Venezuela.* Christopher Helm, London.

Asociación Bogotana de Ornitología (ABO). (2000). *Aves de la Sabana de Bogotá: Guía del Campo.* Corporación Autónoma Regional de Cundinamarca, Bogotá.

Avendaño, J.E. (2012). La avifauna de las tierras bajas del Catatumbo, Colombia: inventario preliminar y ampliaciones de rango. *Bol. Soc. Antioqueña Orn.* **21**: 27–40.

Avendaño, J.E., Barker, F.K. & Cadena, C.D. (2016). The Yellow-green Bush-tanager is neither a bush-tanager nor a sparrow: molecular phylogenetics reveal that *Chlorospingus flavovirens* is a tanager (Aves: Passeriformes; Thraupidae). *Zootaxa* **4136**: 373–381.

Avendaño, J.E., Bohórquez, C.I., Rosselli, L., Arzuza-Buelvas, D., Estela, F.A., Cuervo, A.M., Stiles, F.G. & Renjifo, L.M. (2017). Lista de chequeo de las aves de Colombia: Una síntesis del estado del conocimiento desde Hilty & Brown (1986). *Orn. Colombiana* **16**: eA01. 83 pp.

Ayerbe-Quiñones, F. (2018). *Guía Ilustrada de la Avifauna Colombiana.* Second edn. Wildlife Conservation Society, Bogotá.

Ayerbe-Quiñones, F. (2019). *Birds of Colombia.* Wildlife Conservation Society, Bogotá.

Bayly, N.J., Cárdenas Ortiz, L., Rubio, M. & Gómez, C. (2014). Migration of raptors, swallows and other diurnal migratory birds through the Darien of Colombia. *Orn. Neotrop.* **25**: 63–71.

Beckers, J. & Florez, P. (2013). *Birdwatching in Colombia.* Privately published.

Burns, K.J., Shultz, A.J., Title, P.O., Mason, N.A., Barker, F.K., Klicka, J., Lanyon, S.M. & Lovette, I.J. (2014). Phylogenetics and diversification of tanagers (Passeriformes: Thraupidae), the largest radiation of Neotropical songbirds. *Mol. Phylogenet. Evol.* **75**: 41–77.

Burns, K.J., Unitt, P. & Mason, N.A. (2016). A genus-level classification of the family Thraupidae (Class Aves: Order Passeriformes). *Zootaxa* **4088**: 329–354.

Cadena-López, G. & Naranjo, L.G. (2010). Distribución, abundancia y reproducción de las aves marinas residentes en el Parque Nacional Natural Gorgona, Colombia. *Bol. Soc. Antioqueña Orn.* **20**: 22–32.

Cárdenas, G., Ramírez-Mosquera, D., Eusse-González, D., Fierro-Calderón, E., Vidal-Astudillo, V. & Estela, F.A. (2020). Aves del departamento del Valle del Cauca, Colombia. *Biota Colombiana* **21**: 72–108.

Chapman, F.M. (1917). The distribution of bird-life in Colombia; A contribution to a biological survey of South America. *Bull. Amer. Mus. Nat. Hist.* **36**: 1–169.

Chesser, R.T., Isler, M.L., Cuervo, A.M., Cadena, C.D., Galen, S.C., Bergner, L.M., Fleischer, R.C., Bravo, G.A., Lane, D.F. & Hosner, P.A. (2020). Conservative plumage masks extraordinary phylogenetic diversity in the *Grallaria rufula* (Rufous Antpitta) complex of the humid Andes. *Auk* **137**: 1–25.

Clements/eBird Checklist of Birds of the World. (2019). The Cornell Lab of Ornithology, Ithaca, NY. https://www.birds.cornell.edu/clementschecklist/overview-august-2019/.

Collar, N.J. & Salaman, P. (2013). The taxonomic and conservation status of the *Oxypogon* helmetcrests. *Conserv. Colombiana* **19**: 31–38.

Cooper, M. (2011). *Birds in Colombia.* Villegas Asociados, Bogotá.

Córdoba-Córdoba, S. (2009). Historia de la ornitología colombiana: sus colecciones científicas, investigadores y asociaciones. *Bol. Soc. Antioqueña Orn.* **19**: 1–26.

Cuervo, A.M., Stiles, F.G., Cadena, C.D., Toro, J.L. & Londoño, G.A. (2003). New and noteworthy bird records from the northern sector of the Western Andes of Colombia. *Bull. Brit. Orn. Club* **123**: 7–24.

Cuervo, A.M., Pulgarín, P.C. & Calderón, D. (2008a). New distributional bird data from the Cordillera Central of the Colombian Andes, with implications for the biogeography of northwestern South America. *Condor* **110**: 526–537.

Cuervo, A.M., Pulgarín, P.C., Calderón, D., Ochoa-Quintero, J.M., Delgado, C.A., Palacio, A., Botero, J.M. & Múnera, W.A. (2008b). Avifauna of the northern Cordillera Central of the Andes, Colombia. *Orn. Neotrop.* **19**: 495–515.

Cuervo, A.M., Stiles, F.G., Lentino, M., Brumfield, R.T. & Derryberry, E.P. (2014). Geographic variation and phylogenetic relationships of *Myiopagis olallai* (Aves: Passeriformes; Tyrannidae), with the description of two new taxa from the Northern Andes. *Zootaxa* **3873**: 1–24.

Digby, A., López, P., Ribeiro, I., Alarcón, J. & Gartner, A. (2015). Caribbean Colombia: pelagic bird observations in 2014 and 2015. *Conserv. Colombiana* **23**: 50–57.

Donegan, T.M. (2012). Range extensions and other notes on the birds and conservation of the Serranía de San Lucas, an isolated mountain range in northern Colombia. *Bull. Brit. Orn. Club* **132**: 140–161.

Donegan, T.M. & Huertas, B. (2018). Notes on some migratory birds rare, new or poorly known on Isla Providencia, Colombia. *Conserv. Colombiana* **25**: 56–63.

Donegan, T.M., Avendaño, J.E., Briceño, E.R., Luna, J.C., Roa, C., Parra, R., Turner, C., Sharp, M. & Huertas, B. (2010). Aves de la Serranía de los Yariguíes y tierras bajas circundantes, Santander, Colombia. *Cotinga* **32**: 72–89.

Donegan, T.M., Ellery, T., Pacheco, J.A., Verhelst, J.C. & Salaman, P. (2018). Revision of the status of bird species occurring or reported in Colombia 2018. *Conserv. Colombiana* **25**: 4–47.

Estela, F.A., López-Victoria, M., Castillo, L.F. & Naranjo, L.G. (2010). Estado del conocimiento sobre aves marinas en Colombia, después de 110 años de investigación. *Bol. Soc. Antioqueña Orn.* **20**: 2–21.

Florez, P. (2017). A mysterious antshrike from eastern Colombia. *Neotrop. Birding* **20**: 21–24.

Freeman, B.G., Hilty, S.L., Calderón, D., Ellery, T. & Urueña, L.E. (2012). New and noteworthy bird records from central and northern Colombia. *Cotinga* **34**: 5–16.

Friedel, T. (2020). Records of three new antbirds for Colombia. *Conserv. Colombiana* **26**: 19–20.

Gaviria Obregón, R. (2013). *Las Aves Más Hermosas de Colombia.* Ed. Guacharaca, Medellín.

Gaviria Obregón, R. (2019). *Aves Silvestres de Colombia*. Asociación Colombiana de Ornitología, Bogotá.

Gentry, A.H. (1993). *A Field Guide to the Families and Genera of
Woody Plants of Northwest South America (Colombia, Ecuador,
Peru) with Supplementary Notes on Herbaceous Taxa*.
Conservation International, Washington, D.C.

Gómez, D., Orozco, K., Cardona, F., Pineda, M., Beboya, M.L.
& Ocampo, D. (2020). Avifauna del Parque Nacional Natural
Selva de Florencia (Samaná, Caldas, Colombia): nuevos registros
y ampliaciones de distribución. *Biota Colombiana* 21: 40–71.

Haffer, J. (1975). Avifauna of northwestern Colombia, South
America. *Bonn. zool. Monogr.* 7: 1–182.

Harvey, M.G., Bravo, G.A., Claramunt, S., Cuervo, A.M.,
Derryberry, G.E., Battilana, J., Seeholzer, G.F., McKay,
J.S., O'Meara, B.C., Faircloth, B.C., Edwards, S.V., Pérez-
Emán, J., Moyle, R.G., Sheldon, F.H., Aleixo, A., Smith,
B.T., Chesser, R.T., Silveira, L.F., Cracraft, J., Brumfield,
R.T. & Derryberry, E.P. (2020). The evolution of a tropical
biodiversity hotspot. *Science* 370: 1343–1348.

Hilty, S.L. (1997). Seasonal distribution of birds at a cloud-forest
locality, the Anchicayá Valley, in western Colombia. Pp. 321–343
in: Remsen, J.V. (ed.) *Studies in Neotropical Ornithology honoring
Ted Parker*. Ornithological Monographs No. 48. American Ornithologists' Union, Washington, D.C.

Hilty, S.L. (2003). *Birds of Venezuela*. Princeton University Press,
Princeton, NJ.

Hilty, S.L. (2005). *Birds of Tropical America: A Watcher's
Introduction to Behavior, Breeding, and Diversity*. University
of Texas Press, Austin.

Hilty, S.L. & Brown, W.L. (1986). *A Guide to the Birds of Colombia*.
Princeton University Press, Princeton, NJ.

Hilty, S.L. &. Brown, W.L. (2001). *Guía de las Aves de Colombia*.
Princeton University Press, American Bird Conservancy,
Universidad del Valle & Sociedad Antioqueña de Ornitología,
Cali.

Holdridge, L.R. (1967). *Life Zone Ecology*. Tropical Science Center,
San José, Costa Rica.

del Hoyo, J. & Collar, N.J. (2014). *HBW and BirdLife International
Illustrated Checklist of the Birds of the World*. Vol. 1.
Non-passerines. Lynx Edicions, Barcelona.

del Hoyo, J. & Collar, N.J. (2016). *HBW and BirdLife International
Illustrated Checklist of the Birds of the World*. Vol. 2. Passerines.
Lynx Edicions, Barcelona.

del Hoyo, J., Elliott, A. & Sargatal, J. (eds.) (1992–2002).
Handbook of the Birds of the World. Vols. 1–7. Lynx Edicions,
Barcelona.

del Hoyo, J., Elliott, A. & Christie, D.A. (eds.) (2003–2011).
Handbook of the Birds of the World. Vols. 8–16. Lynx Edicions,
Barcelona.

Instituto de Investigación de Recursos Biológicos Alexander
von Humboldt. (2012). *Colección de Sonidos Animales*.
Instituto de Investigación de Recursos Biológicos Alexander von
Humboldt, Bogotá.

Isler, M.L., Chesser, R.T., Robbins, M.B., Cuervo, A.M., Cade-
na, C.D. & Hosner, P.A. (2020). Taxonomic evaluation of the
Grallaria rufula (Rufous Antpitta) complex (Aves: Passeriformes:
Grallariidae) distinguishes sixteen species. *Zootaxa* 4817: 1–74.

Johnson, O., Howard, J.T. & Brumfield, R.T. (2021). Systematics of a Neotropical clade of dead-leaf-foraging antwrens
(Aves: Thamnophilidae; *Epinecrophylla*). *Mol. Phylogenet. Evol.*
154: 106962.

Kirwan, G.M., Levesque, A., Oberle, M. & Sharpe, C.J. (2019).
Birds of the West Indies. Lynx and BirdLife International Field
Guides. Lynx Edicions, Barcelona.

Klicka, J., Barker, F.K., Burns, K.J., Lanyon, S.M., Lovette, I.J.,
Chaves, J.A. & Bryson, R.W. (2014). A comprehensive multi-
locus assessment of sparrow (Aves: Passerellidae) relationships.
Mol. Phylogenet. Evol. 77: 177–182.

Krabbe, N., Flórez, P., Suárez, G., Castaño, J., Arango, J.D.
& Duque, A. (2006). The birds of Páramo de Frontino, western
Andes of Colombia. *Orn. Colombiana* 4: 37–48.

Kricher, J. (2006). *Un Compañero Neotropical: Una Introducción
a los Animales, Plantas, y Ecosistemas del Trópico del Nuevo
Mundo*. Second edn. American Birding Association, Colorado
Springs, CO.

Laverde, O. & Gómez, F. (2016). *Las Aves de Santa María (Boyacá,
Colombia)*. Universidad Nacional de Colombia, Bogotá.

Laverde, O., Stiles, F.G. & Múnera, C. (2005). Nuevos registros e
inventario de la avifauna de la Serranía de las Quinchas, un área
importante para la conservación de las aves (AICA) en Colombia.
Caldasia 27: 247–265.

Linares-Romero, L.G., Stiles, F.G., Rosselli, L., Camargo, P.,
Candil, J., Galindo, R., Avellaneda, F.E. & Pulido, A.R.
(2017). *La Magia de las Aves de Chingaza*. La Imprenta Editores,
Bogotá.

López, J.P., Avendaño, J.E., Gutiérrez-Pinto, N. & Cuervo, A.M.
(2014). The birds of the Serranía de Perijá: The northernmost
avifauna of the Andes. *Orn. Colombiana* 14: 62–93.

López-Victoria, M. & Estela, F.A. (2007). Una lista anotada de
las aves de la Isla Malpelo. *Orn. Colombiana* 5: 40–53.

Mazariegos, L.A. (2000). *Hummingbirds of Colombia*.
The Hummingbird Conservancy, Colombia.

McCormack, J.E., Harvey, M.G., Faircloth, B.C., Crawford,
N.G., Glenn, T.C. & Brumfield, R.T. (2013). A phylogeny of
birds based on over 1,500 loci collected by target enrichment
and high-throughput sequencing. *PLoS ONE* 8(1): e54848.

McGuire, J.A., Witt, C.C., Remsen, J.V., Dudley, R. & Altshuler,
D.L. (2009). A higher-level taxonomy for hummingbirds.
J. Orn. 150: 155–165.

McMullan, M. & Donegan, T.M. (2014). *Field Guide to the Birds
of Colombia*. Fundación ProAves de Colombia, Bogotá.

McNish, T. (2007). *Las Aves de los Llanos de la Orinoquía*.
M&B Producciones y Servicios Limitada, Bogotá.

McNish, T. (2010). *La Fauna del Archipiélago de San Andrés,
Providencia y Santa Catalina, Colombia, Sudamérica*.
M&B Producciones y Servicios Limitada, Bogotá.

Meyer de Schauensee, R. (1948–1952). The birds of the Republic
of Colombia. *Caldasia* 22–26: 251–1212.

Meyer de Schauensee, R. (1964). *The Birds of Colombia and
Adjacent Areas of South and Central America*. Livingston
Publishing Company, Narbeth, PA.

Murillo-Pacheco, J.I., Bonilla Rojas, W.F. & de las Casas, J.C.
(2013). Listado y anotaciones sobre la historia natural de las
aves del litoral de San Andrés de Tumaco, Nariño (Colombia).
Biota Colombiana 14: 273–287.

Naranjo, L.G. (2016). La pájara vida: breve historia de la
observación de aves en Colombia. *Bol. Cult. Bibliogr.*
50(91): 21–31.

Olaciregui, C., Quevedo, A., González, F. & Barrera, L.F. (2016).
Range extensions and noteworthy records of birds from the
Serranía de Abibe, north-west Colombia. *Bull. Brit. Orn. Club*
136: 243–262.

Olivares, A. (1969). *Aves de Cundinamarca*. Universidad Nacional
de Colombia, Dirección de Divulgación Cultural Publicaciones,
Bogotá.

Olivares, A. (1974). *Aves de la Orinoquía Colombiana*. Centro
de Desarrollo Integrado "Las Gaviotas" Orinoquía Colombiana,
Imprenta Nacional, Bogotá.

Pacheco-Garzón, A. (2012). Estudio y conservación de las aves de la Isla de San Andrés. *Conserv. Colombiana* **16**: 1–56.

Prum, R.O., Berv, J.S., Dornburg, A., Field, D.J., Townsend, J.P., Lemmon, E.M. & Lemmon, A.R. (2015). A comprehensive phylogeny of birds (Aves) using targeted next-generation DNA sequencing. *Nature* **526**: 569–573

Remsen, J.V., Areta, J.I., Bonaccorso, E., Claramunt, S., Jaramillo, A., Lane, D.F., Pacheco, J.F., Robbins, M.B., Stiles, F.G. & Zimmer, K.J. (2021). A classification of the birds of South America. http://www.museum.lsu.edu/~Remsen/SACC Baseline.htm.

Renjifo, L.M., Franco-Maya, A.M., Amaya-Espinel, J.D., Kattan, G.H. & López-Lanús, B. (eds.). (2002). *Libro Rojo de Aves de Colombia*. Serie Libros Rojos de Especies Amenazadas de Colombia. Instituto de Investigación de Recursos Biológicos Alexander von Humboldt & Ministerio del Medio Ambiente, Bogotá.

Renjifo, L.M., Gómez, M.F., Velásquez-Tibatá, J., Amaya-Villarreal, A.M., Kattan, G.H., Amaya-Espinel, J.D. & Burbano-Girón, J. (2014). *Libro Rojo de Aves de Colombia*. Vol. 1. Editorial Pontificia Universidad Javeriana & Instituto Alexander von Humboldt, Bogotá.

Renjifo, L.M., Amaya-Villarreal, A.M., Burbano-Girón, J. & Velásquez-Tibatá, J. (2016). *Libro Rojo de Aves de Colombia*. Vol. 2. Editorial Pontificia Universidad Javeriana & Instituto Alexander von Humboldt, Bogotá.

Renjifo, L.M., Repizo, A., Ruiz-Ovalle, J.M., Ocampo, S. & Avendaño, J.E. (2017). New bird distributional data from Cerro Tacarcuna, with implications for conservation in the Darién highlands of Colombia. *Bull. Brit. Orn. Club* **137**: 46–66.

Restall, R., Rodner, C. & Lentino, M. (2006a). *Birds of Northern South America: An Identification Guide*. Vol. 1. Species Accounts. Christopher Helm, London.

Restall, R., Rodner, C. & Lentino, M. (2006b). *Birds of Northern South America: An Identification Guide*. Vol. 2. Plates and Maps. Christopher Helm, London.

Ridgely, R.S. & Greenfield, P.J. (2001a). *The Birds of Ecuador*. Vol. 1. Status, Distribution and Taxonomy. Cornell University Press, Ithaca, NY.

Ridgely, R.S. & Greenfield, P.J. (2001b). *The Birds of Ecuador*. Vol. 2. Field Guide. Cornell University Press, Ithaca, NY.

Ridgely, R.S. & Gwynne, J.A. (1993). *Guía de las Aves de Panamá*. Universidad de Princeton & Asociación Nacional para la Conservación de la Naturaleza (ANCON), Panamá.

Ridgely, R.S. & Tudor, G. (2009). *Field Guide to the Songbirds of South America: The Passerines*. University of Texas Press, Austin, TX.

Rodríguez-Mahecha, J.V. & Hernández-Camacho, J.I. (2002). *Loros de Colombia*. Conservation International, Bogotá.

Ruiz-Guerra, C., Johnston-González, R., Cifuentes-Sarmiento, Y., Estela, F.A., Castillo, L.F., Hernández, C.E. & Naranjo, L.G. (2007). Noteworthy bird records from the southern Chocó of Colombia. *Bull. Brit. Orn. Club* **127**: 283–293.

Salaman, P., Donegan, T.M. & Cuervo, A.M. (1999). Ornithological surveys in Serranía de los Churumbelos, southern Colombia. *Cotinga* **12**: 29–39.

Salaman, P., Donegan, T.M., González, C., Bustos, X. & Cuervo, A.M. (2001). The first biological assessment of Serranía de San Lucas. Colombian EBA Project Report Series No. 3: Serranía de San Lucas. Fundación ProAves, Colombia.

Salaman, P., Stiles, F.G., Bohórquez, C.I., Álvarez, M., Umaña, A.M., Donegan, T.M. & Cuervo, A.M. (2002). New and noteworthy bird records from the east slope of the Andes of Colombia. *Caldasia* **24**: 157–189.

Salaman, P., Donegan, T.M., Davison, D. & Ochoa, J.M. (2007). Birds of Serranía de los Churumbelos, their conservation and elevational distribution. *Conserv. Colombiana* **3**: 29–58.

Schulenberg, T.S., Stotz, D., Lane, D.F., O'Neill, J.P. & Parker, T.A. (2007). *Birds of Peru*. Princeton University Press, Princeton, NJ.

Stiles, F.G. (2010). La avifauna de la parte media del Río Apaporis, departamentos de Vaupés y Amazonas, Colombia. *Rev. Acad. Colombiana Cienc.* **34**: 381–396.

Stiles, F.G. & Avendaño, J.E. (2019). Distribution and status of *Turdus* thrushes in white-sand areas of eastern Colombia, with a new subspecies of *T. leucomelas*. *Zootaxa* **4567**: 161–175.

Stiles, F.G. & Beckers, J. (2016). Un inventario de las aves de la region de Inírida, Guainía, Colombia. *Orn. Colombiana* **15**: 21–52.

Stiles, F.G. & Naranjo, L.G. (2018). La avifauna del Parque Nacional Natural Chiribiquete: resultados de tres expediciones recientes a sectores previamente inexplorados. *Rev. Colombia Amazónica* **10**: 141–160.

Stiles, F.G. & Skutch, A.F. (1989). *A Guide to the Birds of Costa Rica*. Cornell University Press, Ithaca, NY.

Stiles, F.G., Remsen, J.V. & McGuire, J.A. (2017). The generic classification of the Trochilini (Aves: Trochilidae): reconciling taxonomy with phylogeny. *Zootaxa* **4353**: 401–424.

Todd, W.E.C. & Carriker, M.A. (1922). The birds of the Santa Marta region of Colombia: A study in altitudinal distribution. *Ann. Carnegie Mus.* **14**: 1–611.

Villarreal-Leal, H., Álvarez-Rebolledo, M., Higuera-Díaz, M., Aldana-Domínguez, J., Gregory, J.D., Villa-Navarro, F.A., von Hildebrandt, P., Prieto-Cruz, A., Maldonado-Ocampo, J.A., Umaña-Villaveces, A.M., Sierra, S. & Forero, F. (2009). *Caracterización de la Biodiversidad de la Selva de Mataven, Vichada, Colombia*. Instituto de Investigación de Recursos Biológicos Alexander von Humboldt & Asociación de Cabildos y Autoridades Tradicionales Indígenas de la Selva de Mataven (ACATISEMA), Bogotá.

567

FAMILY INDEX

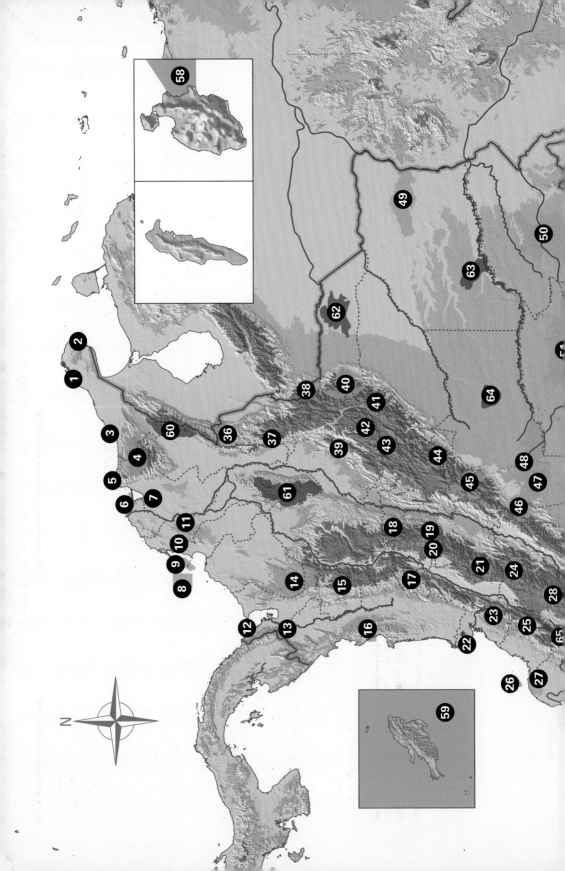